c.100 stern rudder, China
c.200 shafts for wagons, Europe
c.300 saddle and bit evolved, central Asia
compartmentalized hulls in junks, China
c.400 paddle-wheel propulsion, China
c.500 clinker-built ships, Scandinavia
c.850 lateen sail in Mediterranean; vessels with multiple sails and masts
800 horse collar appears in West
1119 mariner's compass, China
1300 Portolano maps, Mediterranean
c.1350 suspended-chassis vehicles
c.1420 Portuguese caravels
1492 Columbus reaches America
1519–22 Magellan's voyage around world
1574 ship's log invented
1594 Mercator's world *Atlas*
1620 Drebbel demonstrates submarine

c.60 Hero's automata, Greece
1–99 Hero's treatise *Mechanical syntax*
840 first use of crank in Europe
1100–1200 large chopping axe
soda replaces potash in glass-making
c.1250 pole lathe
c.1410 first representation of crank and connecting-rod system
1588 Ramelli, *Le diverse et artificiose machine*
1698 Papin's steam-engine, France
Savery's 'Miners' Friend' steam pump
1712 Newcomen designs practical steam-engine, Britain

40 Dioscorides, *De materia medica*
180 Galen, *Treatise on Medicine*
1010 Avicenna, *Canon of Medicine*
1543 Vesalius, *De humani corporis fabrica*
1628 Harvey discovers circulation of blood

c.350 plane astrolabe, Near East
600 mechanical clocks, China
c.1270 mechanical clocks, Europe
c.1286 spectacles (for far-sighted), Italy
spring-driven clocks, Italy
1502 spring-driven pocket watch, Germany
c.1535 nautical astrolabe, Portugal
1551 theodolite, Britain
1582 Gregorian calendar
1590 refracting telescope
c.1590 compound microscope, The Netherlands
1592 thermometer, Galileo, Italy
1602 Galileo discovers isochronism of pendulum, Italy
1644 Toricelli's mercury barometer, Italy
1645 vacuum pump
1657 Huygens' pendulum clock, The Netherlands
1668 reflecting telescope (Newton), Britain
1675 Greenwich Observatory founded, Britain
Huygens' balance-spring regulator
1726 Harrison's bimetallic pendulum, Britain
1731 quadrant, Philadelphia

c.750 Chinese bring paper-making to Samarkand
770 early wood-block printing, China
368 earliest printed work (*Diamond Sutra*)
1045 movable type, China
c.1190 paper mills in Europe
1446 intaglio printing, Germany
c.1450 Gutenberg prints from movable type

1672 machine for producing constant static electricity

200 abacus, China
1617 Napier's bones (calculator), Scotland
1642 mechanical calculator (Pascal), France

1750 to 1849

1784 Meikle's threshing machine, Britain
1793 Whitney's cotton gin, USA
1802 sugar beet introduced as field cr[…] Germany
1804 Appert's preserved foods factory, […]
c.1820 formation of US 'wheat belt' to spre[…] wheat growing
1826 Bell's harvester, UK
1831–4 McCormick develops his harvester, […]
1833–50 Hussey's harvesters, UK
1837 steel ploughshare in use, USA
1843 Rothamsted agricultural research station, UK

1760 Smeaton's Eddystone lighthouse completed, Britain
1779 world's first all-iron bridge, Coalbrookdale, Britain
1801 first modern suspension bridge, Britain
1824 Aspdin's Portland cement, Britain
1828 corrugated iron
1832 Gotha Canal, Germany

1816 miner's safety lamp, by Davy, UK
1849 safety-pin

1761 Shrapnel invents shrapnel shell, Britain
1812 cartridge loading for firearms, Austria
1835 Colt's revolver, USA
1837 Dreyse needle-gun: breech-loading, bolt action, Germany
1846 gun-cotton (nitro-cellulose) invented by Schönbein, Germany
1847 Sobrero discovers nitro-glycerine, Italy

1774 chlorine used for bleaching, Sweden
1774–9 Crompton's spinning mule, Britain
1784 Cort's puddling process for wrought iron, Britain
1787 Cartwright's weaving machine, Britain
1790 Leblanc's process for soda manufacture
1792 Cartwright's wool-carding machine
1799 bleaching powder, Britain
1801–6 Jacquard loom developed, France
1829 Neilson's pre-heater for blast-furnaces
1832 Muntz metal, Britain
1841 vulcanized rubber, USA
1843 Lawes' superphosphate fertilizer factory
electroplating
Howe's sewing-machine, Britain

1799 Lebon patents production of coal gas
1802 gas lighting demonstrated, UK
1845 safety matches, Sweden

1769 Cugnot's steam road-carriage, France
1776 Bushnall designs submarine, USA
1783 first manned flight (Montgolfier balloon)
steamboat *Pyroscaphe* on Seine, France
first parachute descent, France
1785 balloon crossing of English Channel
1787 Fitch launches first US steamboat
beginning of iron shipbuilding, Britain
1801 Trevithick's road steamer, UK
trials of Fulton's steamship *Nautilus*, USA
1804 Trevithick's steam railway locomotive
1812 *Comet* steamship on Clyde, UK
1816 paddle-steamer *Elise* crosses English Channel
1819 first steamship *Savannah* crosses Atlantic
McAdam's new system of road construction, UK
1825 Stockton–Darlington railway opened, UK
1826–30 Liverpool–Manchester railway built by G. Stephenson, UK
1831 Gurney's steam carriage, UK
1845 I.K. Brunel's *Great Britain* first iron steamship to cross Atlantic

1751 […]nvented by
[…]chine-tools
[…]ritain
[…], Britain
[…]ne, Britain
[…]ents, Britain
[…]ne, Britain
[…]engine,
[…]Wilkinson's boring engine, Britain
1781 compound steam-engine, Britain
1782 Carnot: *Essai sur les machines en général*
1785 steam used in textile industry, Britain
1787 Cartwright's power loom, Britain
1793 Bentham's wood-working machines
1795 hydraulic press (Bramah), Britain
1797 Maudslay's slide rest for lathes, Britain
1798 Maudslay's screw-cutting lathe, Britain
1800 Trevithick's high-pressure steam-engine
c.1800 products made with interchangeable parts (Whitney in the USA; M.I. Brunel in Britain)
1804 Evans's high pressure steam-engine, UK
1810 machine-tool factory set up by Maudslay and Field, UK
1814–47 machine-tools improved by Fox, UK
1816 Stirling engine patented, UK
1817 Roberts's metal-planing lathe, UK
1818 Brunel's tunnelling machine, UK
1827 Fourneyron's water turbine, France
1828 ring-spinning frame
1828–30 multi-tubular boilers (Seguin), France
1829 articulated chain by Galle
1830 lawn-mower, UK
1835 Whitworth's planing machine, UK
1840 automation of machine-tools begins, UK
1841–2 steam-driven forge hammer patented by Bourdon and Nasmyth, UK

1796 Jenner promotes vaccination, Britain
1815 stethoscope (Laennec), France
1844 laughing gas (nitrous oxide) used as anaesthetic, USA
1846 ether used as anaesthetic, USA
chloroform used as anaesthetic, UK

1755 achromatic microscope objectives (Dollond), Britain
1757 sextant
1761 Harrison's No. 4 chronometer, Britain
1775 bifocal spectacles, Philadelphia
1791–5 metric system introduced, France
1830 thermostat (bimetallic strip)

1751–72 Diderot and d'Alembert's 28-volume *Encyclopédie*, France
1783 mechanical printing of cloth with rollers developed by Bell, Britain
1794 Chappe semaphore system, France
1826 permanent photograph (Niépce)
1830 Braille writing for blind, France
c.1833 Gauss and Weber experiment with electromagnetic telegraphy
1837 Morse demonstrates his telegraph, USA
electric telegraph (Cooke and Wheatstone), UK
1839 daguerreotype photographic process
1840 Talbot's calotype process, UK
1844 Morse telegraph, Washington–Baltimore
1846 Hoe's rotary printing press, USA

1800 Volta's electric pile, Italy
1828 Faraday discovers electromagnetic induction, UK
1832 Pixii's dynamo, France

1834 Babbage's mechanical computer, UK

mechanical engineering | medicine | measurement and observation | communications | electrical engineering | computing | space

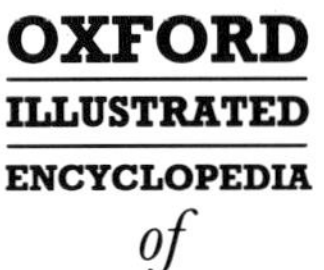

INVENTION AND TECHNOLOGY

OXFORD ILLUSTRATED ENCYCLOPEDIA *of* INVENTION AND TECHNOLOGY

Volume Editor
Sir Monty Finniston

Consultant Editor
Trevor Williams

Associate Editor
Christopher Bissell

BCA
LONDON · NEW YORK · SYDNEY · TORONTO

This edition published 1992 by BCA by arrangement with Oxford University Press

CN 5886

Text processed by Oxford University Press
Printed in Hong Kong

Foreword

The Foreword to this volume of the *Oxford Illustrated Encyclopedia* should have been written by Sir Monty Finniston, who was appointed Editor when work on it began in 1986. It was a singularly appropriate choice, for his knowledge and experience of modern technology, and its communication, was unrivalled. Sadly he died on 2 February 1991, only a few days before he would have been sent the first round of proofs for approval.

Today, technology may be regarded as the application of science to useful ends. While this is a fair generalization in respect of the modern world with its economy increasingly dominated by science-based industries, it was certainly not always so. Many modern technologies—agriculture and irrigation, the smelting and working of metals, the spinning and weaving of textiles, and the firing of clay—date from the dawn of history, long before the term 'science' was ever used. Others, such as those techniques used in biotechnology to produce penicillin and other antibiotics, were derived from fermentation processes that have been used for brewing and breadmaking for thousands of years. Science in the modern sense—whether as an intellectual discipline or having utilitarian goals—did not emerge until the Scientific Revolution of the mid-16th century. In the early 17th century Francis Bacon conceived 'a grand instauration of the sciences' which would systematically summarize the state of knowledge as it existed in his day, extend it by experiment, and use it for the benefit of humanity. In the foundation charter of 1662 of the Royal Society of London we witness a growing convergence of science and technology in its declared aim 'to promote by the authority of experiments the sciences of natural things and of useful arts'. Our own century sees technology as power: political, military, and economic. So powerful, indeed, that a leading modern technologist, Dennis Gabor, has said that 'the most important and urgent problems of technology of today are no longer the satisfaction of the primary needs or of archetypal wishes but the reparation of the evils and damages wrought by the technology of yesterday'.

In industrialized countries today, technology is fairly uniformly developed: electricity supply, radio and television, air and road transport, and information storage and retrieval follow much the same general pattern. But much modern technology is often unknown and irrelevant to many people in Third World countries. Much of the industrialized world's food is produced by intensive agriculture based on a high degree of mechanization and extensive use of artificial fertilizers and agrochemicals. This aspect is emphasized in the relevant entries in this volume, but there is also a recognition that hundreds of millions of people still practise subsistence agriculture, which has changed little over thousands of years. Although there are more than twenty million tractors in use in the world, there are still nearly ten times as many draught animals, pulling primitive equipment and vehicles.

Progress depends on creative innovation, and we include some 150 biographies of eminent technologists. They show very few women, because technology was traditionally not a field in which women could find opportunities, and their achievements were subsumed into those of their male colleagues. More recently the contribution made by women to technology is difficult to assess; women scientists have found greater acceptance and recognition.

In this volume we have sought to present a broad conspectus of modern technology, with an international outlook. We are reviewing a dynamic situation: the seeds of tomorrow's technologies are already sown. The tempo of change is great: some entries in such areas as communications, electronics, and materials science needed to be updated almost as the work went to press. One of the most rapidly developing areas is that of microelectronics and information technology, whose impact on the modern world has been enormous. This volume deals with the latest developments in computing, from the numerical control of machine-tools to artificial intelligence and neural networks. Space technology is another comparatively new arrival on the scene. While it is well represented, the selection of entries reflects the fact that it will be the subject of a separate volume in the series, appearing shortly. Genetic engineering has emerged as a new development in biotechnology. Change will become even more rapid as human ingenuity, fanned by the new climate of international co-operation and competition, creates more and faster technological innovations.

With characteristic thoughtfulness, Sir Monty's draft Foreword included a reminder to himself to acknowledge the friendly co-operation and professional advice of past and present members of the staff of the Oxford University Press. These would certainly have included Christopher Riches and Richard Beatty, his collaborators in the early stages, but more particularly Bridget Hadaway, Emma Morgan Williams, and Andrew Solway who were primarily responsible for compiling and shaping this volume throughout its later stages.

TREVOR I. WILLIAMS

CONTRIBUTORS

Dr Rosalind Armson
Dr David Barlex
Beryl E. Beadle
Richard C. Beatty
Dr E. J. Becklake
Sue Becklake
Dr Christopher C. Bissell
Timothy M. Boon
R. Brocklehurst
Malcolm Buchanan
James R. Campling
Lt. - Commander Kendall Carter
Dr Harold Catling
Dr J. A. Coiley
Paul Cornish
Susan Crossley
Dr P. D. Dennis
Dr M. J. Denton
Dr Brian Derby
James Doughty
Commander A. G. Dunne, RN
W. R. Durrant
Dr David Elliott
J. L. M. Fletcher
Dr N. F. Gray
Bridget Hadaway
Colin W. Harding
Ruth Hepworth
John S. Hughes
Dr Kevin G. Jones
Professor R. S. Jones
Lt. - Commander Peter Kemp
Gillian Kirkup
Dr Ghislaine M. Lawrence
Dr Irvine Loudon
David J. Lyon
Michael March
Dr James Mason
Dr Stephen McClelland
C. T. Massey
Peter Mellett
Dr Lionel R. Milgrom
A. W. L. Nayler
Laurie Newton
S. M. Nugent
Professor Hugh Oliver
Dr Ian Page
Dr Adrian Parnaby-Price
Andrew Patterson
Jane Powell
Dr Janet Ramage
Dr Jake Reynolds
Christopher Riches
Dr J. E. E. Sharpe
R. A. R. Smith
Andrew Solway
P. A. Solway
Paul M. Szuscikiewicz
Dr Glyn Taylor
Howard Timms
Dr J. M. Walker
Dr J. J. Wellington
Keith Wicks
Emma Morgan Williams
Trevor I. Williams
Stuart S. Wilson
P. Wiseman
Alan Woodley
Barry Woods

General Preface

The *Oxford Illustrated Encyclopedia* is designed to be useful and to give pleasure to readers throughout the world. Particular care has been taken to ensure that it is not limited to one country or to one civilization, and that its many thousands of entries can be understood by any interested person who has no previous detailed knowledge of the subject.

Each volume has a clearly defined theme made plain in its title, and is for that reason self-sufficient: there is no jargon, and references to other volumes are avoided. Nevertheless, taken together, the eight thematic volumes (and the Index and Ready Reference volume which completes the series) provide a complete and reliable survey of human knowledge and achievement.

Within each independent volume, the material is arranged in a large number of relatively brief articles in A–Z sequence, varying in length from fifty to one thousand words. This means that each volume is simple to consult, as valuable information is not buried in long and wide-ranging articles. Cross-references are provided whenever they will be helpful to the reader.

The team allocated to each volume is headed by a volume editor eminent in the field. Over four hundred scholars and teachers drawn from around the globe have contributed a total of 2.4 million words to the Encyclopedia. They have worked closely with a team of editors at Oxford whose job it was to ensure that the coverage and content of each entry form part of a coherent whole. Specially commissioned artwork, diagrams, maps, and photographs convey information to supplement the text and add a lively and colourful dimension to the subject portrayed.

Since publication of the first of its volumes in the mid-1980s, the *Oxford Illustrated Encyclopedia* has built up a reputation for usefulness throughout the world. The number of languages into which it has been translated continues to grow. In compiling the volumes, the editors have recognized the new internationalism of its readers who seek to understand the different cultural, political, technological, religious, and commercial factors which together shape the world-view of nations. Their aim has been to present a balanced picture of the forces that influence peoples in all corners of the globe.

I am grateful alike to the volume editors, contributors, consultants, editors, and illustrators whose common aim has been to provide, within the space available, an encyclopedia that will enrich the reader's understanding of today's world.

HARRY JUDGE

A User's Guide

This book is designed for easy use, but the following notes may be helpful to the reader.

ALPHABETICAL ARRANGEMENT The entries are arranged in a simple letter-by-letter alphabetical order of their headings (ignoring the spaces between words) up to the first comma (thus **electricity meter** comes before **electric lighting**). When two entry headings are the same up to the first comma, then the entries are placed in alphabetical order according to what follows after the comma (thus **computer, history of** comes before **computer architecture**).

ENTRY HEADINGS Entries are usually placed after the key word in the title (the surname, for instance, in a group of names, or the title, for example, **Pasteur, Louis; insulation, thermal**). The entry heading appears in the singular unless the plural form is the more common usage.

ALTERNATIVE NAMES Where there are alternative forms of names or abbreviations in common use, a cross-reference, indicated by an asterisk (*), directs the reader to the main headword: **pre-Columbian technology *meso-American technology; PWR *pressurized water reactor**. For Chinese names the pinyin transliteration system has been used.

CROSS-REFERENCES An asterisk (*) in front of a word denotes a cross-reference and indicates the entry heading to which attention is being drawn. Cross-references in the text appear only in places where reference is likely to amplify or increase understanding of the entry being read. They are not given automatically in all cases where a separate entry can be found, so if you come across a name or a term about which you would like to know more, it is worth looking for an entry in its alphabetical place even if no cross-reference is marked. The limited space available has meant that some inventors have no biographical entry, but they are often covered in entries on close associates. Thus, for example, Wilhelm Maybach is covered in the entry on **Daimler, Gottlieb (Wilhelm)**. In most cases cross-references are provided to indicate this. Again for reasons of space, many people could only be included in major entries (such as Geoffrey Dummer and Jack Killey under **integrated circuit**).

ILLUSTRATIONS Pictures and diagrams usually occur on the same page as the entries to which they relate, or on a facing page. The picture captions supplement the information given in the text and indicate in bold type the title of the relevant entry. The time-charts to be found on the endpapers provide easy-to-read information on major technological achievements from the earliest times to the present.

WEIGHTS AND MEASURES Both metric measures and their non-metric equivalents are used throughout. Metric units are always abbreviated: a full list of abbreviations is given in the table under *unit. The following prefixes are used to indicate multiples of standard units:

giga- (G) 10^9 ($\times$1,000,000,000)
mega- (M) 10^6 ($\times$1,000,000)
kilo- (k) 10^3 ($\times$1,000)

milli- (m) 10^{-3} (one thousandth)
micro- (μ) 10^{-6} (one millionth)
nano- (n) 10^{-9} (one thousand-millionth)

In some contexts exponential notation is used to indicate the magnitude of a unit or number (for example, the square of the speed of light, 9×10^{16} m^2/s^2). The non-metric equivalent of the tonne (the ton) is not given since the two units are approximately equal: measurements are given in metric tonnes even for those quantities (for example, displacement of warships) that are still measured in tons. The unit of pressure used throughout is the bar, 10^5 pascals, or roughly equivalent to the standard atmosphere. In entries on chemicals, at. no. is used as an abbreviation for atomic number, while r.a.m. denotes relative atomic mass.

RELATIONSHIP TO OTHER VOLUMES This volume on Invention and Technology is Volume 6 of a series, the *Oxford Illustrated Encyclopedia*, which will consist of eight thematic volumes (and an index). Each book is self-contained and is designed for use on its own. Further information is contained in the General Preface and Foreword to this volume, which offer a fuller explanation of the book's scope and organization.

The titles in the series are:

1 *The Physical World*
2 *The Natural World*
3 *World History: from earliest times to 1800*
4 *World History: from 1800 to the present day*
5 *The Arts*
6 *Invention and Technology*
7 *Peoples and Cultures*
8 *The Universe*
9 *Index and Ready Reference*

abacus, an ancient *calculating machine. The abacus probably originated in Mesopotamia around 3500 BC. It evolved from a simple grooved board with counters, to the wire frame carrying beads still used today in the Middle East, the Soviet Union, Japan, and China. Demonstrations have proved that an abacus, expertly used, is faster than many early 20th-century calculating machines. The modern abacus uses a decimal number system, designating each bead wire as a multiple of ten; some wires can be reserved for storage of intermediate results. Addition and subtraction are performed directly; multiplication and division are repeated additions and subtractions.

abattoir (slaughterhouse), a place in which animals are killed and prepared as carcasses of *meat for supply to retailers. In the past many small butcher's shops ran their own abattoirs, but legislation on hygiene and animal welfare led to the process becoming more centralized. In modern abattoirs, animals are stunned, using either a special gun or an anaesthetic gas, before slaughter. In large abattoirs chain-conveyor production lines may be used. Most commonly animals are killed by cutting a vein or artery in the neck. Carcasses are then generally skinned, eviscerated, and split before refrigeration. In some abattoirs specialized facilities are provided for slaughtering animals for specific religious groups.

Abbe, Ernst (1840–1904), German physicist who made major improvements in microscope design. While teaching at the University of Jena, he was recruited in 1866 by *Zeiss to be research director for his optical works. In 1868 Abbe invented the apochromatic *lens for microscopes, a lens that compensates for distortion due to faults in lens shape and for differential refraction (bending) of different colours of light. He also introduced other improvements, such as the addition of a condenser to provide a strong, even light. After Zeiss's death in 1888, Abbe took charge of the optical works, which he later turned into a co-operative.

abrasive, a material used to wear away the surfaces of other, softer materials. Abrasives are used in manufacturing industries to shape surfaces accurately and as a finishing treatment, for example in polishing. Highly brittle materials such as *ceramics, *glass, and *cermets (ceramic metals) can be machined to shape only through the use of abrasives. Abrasives must be hard, and natural materials such as *flint and sand (forms of silicon dioxide, SiO_2), pumice (hardened lava foam), *alumina and emery (forms of aluminium oxide, Al_2O_3), and *diamond meet this requirement. Flint is used in the manufacture of sandpaper, and sand in sand blasting; pumice is not so hard and finds application in metal polishes. Alumina and emery are used to some extent on abrasive papers and grinding wheels, but for most industrial purposes synthetic materials such as *silicon carbide (carborundum) and synthetic diamond are used. Materials for use as abrasives are first crushed to a powder, in which the particle size depends on the intended application; they are then mixed with a binding agent and pressed into wheels or blocks, or glued to the surface of paper or cloth. Abrasive powders are also added to most household cleaning agents, to supplement the action of the *soap or *detergent.

ABS plastic *polymer.

Académie des Sciences, French scientific society, one of the oldest and most prestigious in the world. Founded in 1666, four years after the *Royal Society of London, it developed out of informal gatherings of scientists, including René Descartes and *Pascal, who met in the house of the mathematician Marin Mersenne. The Académie was originally intended by Louis XIV (1638–1715) to embrace history and literature as well as science. Its members received a state pension, plus financial assistance with their research. The Académie served as a model for the *Academy of Sciences of the USSR.

Academy of Sciences of the USSR, the leading Soviet scientific society. It was founded in 1725 by Peter the Great, primarily to attract foreign scientists to imperial Russia. Originally it was like the *Royal Society, essentially an organization of individual scientists, but in 1915 it became involved in a wide range of industrial and military problems. After the Revolution of 1917 the Academy remained independent for a few years, but in the 1930s it became a rigid bureaucracy, responsible for a number of research institutes. Since 1986, and the advent of perestroika, a radical restructuring and decentralization has taken place.

Accademia Nationale dei Lincei (National Academy of the Lynx), Italy's premier scientific society. It derives its title from the short-lived Accademia dei Lincei, which was founded in 1603 by the botanist Federigo Cesi and had *Galileo as one of its members. This was revived in 1847 by Pope Pius IX and the Italian government established the Academy in its present form in 1875.

acceleration, increase of speed, defined as the rate of change of velocity per unit of time, measured in seconds. Hence the units of acceleration are m/s^2. An object falling freely under the gravitational attraction of the Earth has an acceleration of about 9.81 m/s^2, often referred to as *g*.

accelerometer, an instrument for measuring acceleration, especially in connection with the measurement of vibration. Older (linear or angular) accelerometers depend on a mass which is free to move in one direction against the constraint of a spring. In modern accelerometers used in *inertial navigation systems, the force produced by the acceleration is applied to a *piezo-electric crystal, which generates a voltage proportional to the acceleration.

accumulator, a secondary or storage *battery, in particular the rechargeable lead–acid battery. All batteries contain electrochemical cells that change chemical energy into electrical energy during discharge. In an accumulator, this process can be reversed. A current is passed through the cell in the direction opposite to the discharge flow, and the original chemicals are regenerated. Thus an accumulator can store electrical energy. The modern lead–acid accumulator is a direct development of Gaston Plante's 1859 invention. The negative electrode is spongy lead, the positive electrode is lead dioxide on a lead support, and the electrolyte is sulphuric acid. During discharge, the surface materials of both electrodes are converted to lead sulphate, and the electrolyte becomes more dilute. Accumulators provide the large cur-

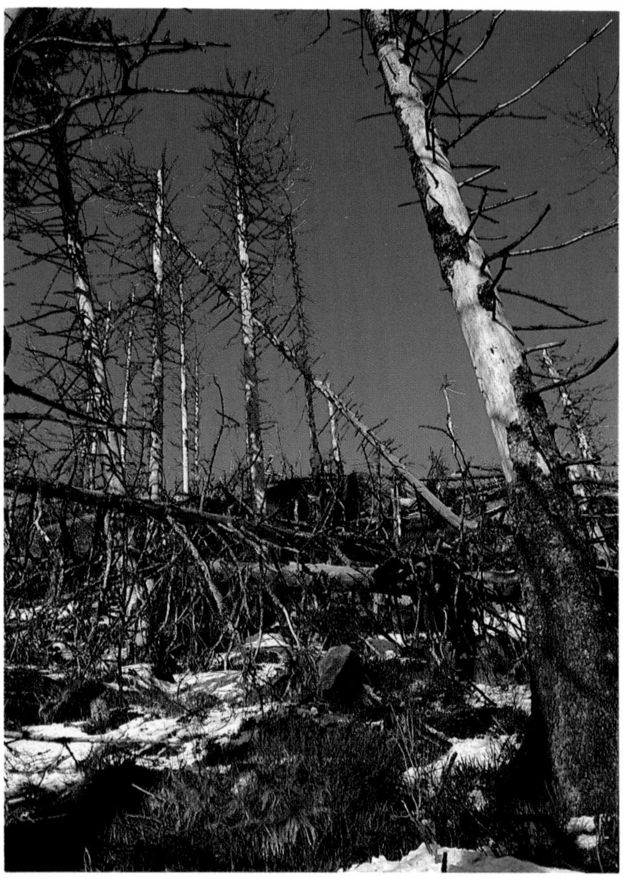

Severe damage to trees in the Black Forest, Germany, thought to be caused by long-term changes in forest soils brought about by **acid rain**.

rents required for traction motors and motor cars. Electrical *generators, powered by the engine, keep the accumulators charged.

ACE *computer, history of.

acetone *propanone.

acetylene *ethyne.

achromatic lens (achromat), a combination of *lenses, used in most optical instruments, that reduces image blurring due to chromatic aberration. This aberration occurs with simple lenses, which refract (bend) the different *colours in white light by different amounts, resulting in images with coloured fringes. The achromat was invented in about 1733. The simplest type combines a concave and a convex lens with different dispersions (dispersion measures the amount of colour separation). It reduces blurring by bringing together red and blue light. Image quality can be further improved using achromats with more lenses or combinations, in contact or separated.

acid rain, a type of *air pollution occurring when sulphur dioxide and nitrogen oxides from the burning of *fossil fuels combine with water vapour in the atmosphere. The resulting rain is an acidic solution that is lethal to water life and damages forests and the soil. It also corrodes buildings and is believed to be hazardous to human health. Reports of acid rain are widespread; from Sweden to Canada, and across the USA from New England to Texas. It is difficult to pinpoint the sources because the contaminants are carried long distances across international boundaries, making control difficult. Little can be done about the damage already caused, although attempts have been made to neutralize acid lakes in Europe. Acceptable burning of fossil fuels can be handled in two ways: by removal of the *sulphur and *nitrogen from the fuels before combustion, or by removal of the oxides formed after combustion by scrubbing out with alkali solution or trapping in molecular sieves. Both options are expensive. Reducing the amount of fossil fuel burnt by supplementing energy needs with less polluting forms seems the best long-term approach.

acids, bases, and salts. An acid is a substance that tends to donate protons (hydrogen ions, H^+): in aqueous solution acids dissociate into a negative ion and one or more protons. Bases tend to accept protons; the term includes *alkalis but has a wider application. A base in aqueous solution dissociates to form a positive ion and one or more hydroxyl ions, OH^-. Both acids and bases are often corrosive substances. Aqueous solutions of acids and bases, when mixed, neutralize each other to form water and a *salt: for example, *sodium hydroxide (NaOH) and *hydrochloric acid (HCl) mix to form sodium chloride (common salt, NaCl) and water. An indication of the acidity or alkalinity of an aqueous solution is given by its pH number, a measure of the hydrogen ion concentration in the solution. The lower the pH number, the more hydrogen ions in the solution. Acids have pH numbers lower than 7, while the pH numbers of alkalis are greater than 7. Acids, bases, and salts find widespread application in the chemical industry. Certain acids and bases are manufactured in large tonnages, for example *sulphuric, *nitric, and *phosphoric acids, *sodium hydroxide, and *ammonia. Ammonia is reacted with sulphuric and phosphoric acids to produce the salts ammonium sulphate and ammonium phosphate, which are widely used as *fertilizers. Sodium hydroxide and other alkali solutions are good degreasing agents, reacting with fats and breaking them down into water-soluble substances.

acoustics, architectural, methods of controlling the passage of noise through buildings, in particular ensuring optimum *sound conditions in concert halls, theatres, and broadcasting and recording studios. External traffic noise is reduced by making a wall heavy, by limiting the area of windows, and by using widely spaced double windows. In a high-rise building, concrete floors limit airborne sound, while resilience in the floor construction reduces impact sounds such as footsteps. In an auditorium, the dimensions and the reflectivity of the surfaces determine the reverberation time; walls can be lined with adjustable sound-absorption panels, allowing the acoustic properties of the auditorium to be adjusted. For sound recording, a studio requires isolation from noise from surrounding buildings. A double-skin construction (a box within a box), with minimum connection between the skins, helps to achieve this.

acrylic fibre, a synthetic fibre *polymer composed of macromolecules of recurring acrylonitrile ($CH_2{=}CH{\cdot}C{\equiv}N$) groups. The fibres have a wool-like feel and are used extensively as a substitute for *wool. The fibre is seldom used as continuous filament, but is cut into short lengths for *spinning into *yarn. Because acrylonitrile is highly flammable, various additions to the basic synthetic material are used to reduce flammability; such low fire-risk fibres are referred to as modacrylics. Acrylic fabrics wash and dry readily and are resistant to bleaches, dilute acids and alkalis, and to microbiological attack. *Carbon fibres are made by heat treatment of acrylic fibres.

active and semi-active radar homing *guided missile.

acupuncture, a form of medical treatment originating in ancient China, in which the skin or tissues of the body are pricked with needles. Small needles are placed into the skin at specific points in the body to produce a variety of effects, which include the loss of pain sensation (usually in one particular part of the body). The effects differ depending on the sites of the needles. Some techniques can induce feelings of well-being or relaxation or even induce *anaesthesia; others can help to relieve stress or overcome habits such as smoking. The needles are thought to produce their effects by stimulating certain nerves in the spinal cord that interfere with the normal sensory pathways.

ADA *computer language.

address (computing), the term used to refer to a location in a computer's *memory. Each location, usually capable of storing one *byte of information, has a unique address represented in *binary code. The process of accessing stored information is known as addressing. On some systems, disks and other *peripherals can also be addressed.

adhesive, a material, usually a liquid, used to join together solid materials. A thin layer of adhesive is applied to each of the components to be joined, which are then brought together either overlapping (lap-joint) or abutting (butt-joint). The adhesive solidifies by a combination of chemical reaction and evaporation of water to form a bond: it may bond chemically to the solid surfaces, or interlock mechanically with surface roughnesses. The principle is very similar to that used in *brazing and *soldering. Adhesives were first manufactured from natural sources using starch and animal protein (bones and hoofs). Today a wide range of adhesives is available (see table). Adhesives form stiff, light, economical joints, free from surface blemishes. They are used extensively in the manufacture of plastic and wooden articles, and are increasingly being used for joining metals. They are of particular importance in the aerospace industry, where they were first used extensively in the 1940s in the manufacture of the De Havilland Mosquito aeroplane from plywood, and today are used to join aluminium airframe components.

adit mining, a tunnel driven from the surface, sloping gently upwards, used to give access to a body of ore or to drain a mine of water. In cases where the mineral vein outcrops at the surface, the adit may follow the vein until it is worked out. Where circumstances permit, the adit has the advantage of offering easy access and dispensing with the need for hoisting machinery. However, a railway system of some kind will usually be needed to extract the spoil.

adobe *mud building.

advanced gas-cooled reactor (AGR), an improved version of the *Magnox reactor, developed in the UK in the 1960s. Like the Magnox, the AGR uses graphite as a moderator (see *fission, nuclear) and carbon dioxide as the coolant, but it operates at much higher temperatures, mak-

Properties and applications of a range of adhesives

Adhesive	Description	Application
Natural adhesives		
Animal glues	Glues prepared from animal skin, bone, or sinew, with high initial tack (stickiness)	Traditionally used in bookbinding, wood joining, and many other areas. Now largely replaced by synthetic glues
Casein glues	Glues prepared from casein, a protein present in milk	Added to paints and coatings to improve adherence
Blood albumen	Glue made from albumen (protein) component of blood	Large quantities used in plywood industry
Vegetable adhesives	Water-soluble adhesives from plant sources of many types, consisting mainly of starches and dextrins. Also natural gums	Used for corrugated board and wallpaper adhesives. Gums used mainly in water-remoisturizable products (e.g. 'sticky labels')
Synthetic adhesives		
Amino adhesives	Urea-formaldehyde resin adhesives in the form of water-based syrups or powdered solids for mixing with water	Commonly used in the woodworking industry for bonding, and for lamination of wood and wood-associated materials
Anaerobic adhesives	Based on acrylic polyester resins. Bond only in the presence of metals and in the total absence of oxygen	Used for joint-sealing and for retention of coaxial metal components, which may be threaded, splined, or smooth
Contact adhesives	Based on solvent solutions of the synthetic rubber neoprene. Both surfaces are coated with adhesive, and form a strong bond on contact	Widely used for strong bonds with high shear-resistance, for example in laminates
Cyanoacrylate adhesives	Low-viscosity liquids based on acrylic monomers. Extremely fast-setting, some giving strong joints within two or three seconds	Assembly of all kinds of small rubber, plastic, and metal parts, particularly weather seals
Emulsion adhesives	Milky-white dispersions often based on polyvinyl acetate	Used extensively in the woodworking and packaging industries; applications also with fabrics and fabric-based components, and in engineered products such as loudspeaker cones
Epoxy resin adhesives	Thermosetting resins which solidify by polymerization and, once set, will soften but not melt on heating. Two-part resin/hardener adhesives solidify on mixing, while one-part materials require heating	Strength and low-creep properties make them ideal for a wide range of low-load structural applications, although high viscosity limits their use on smaller components
Hot-melt adhesives	Thermoplastic material applied in molten form (in the 65–180 °C range), which solidifies on cooling to form strong bonds between a wide range of materials	Extremely rapid assembly of all types of lightly stressed components unlikely to be exposed to high temperatures or extreme environments

Aeroplane

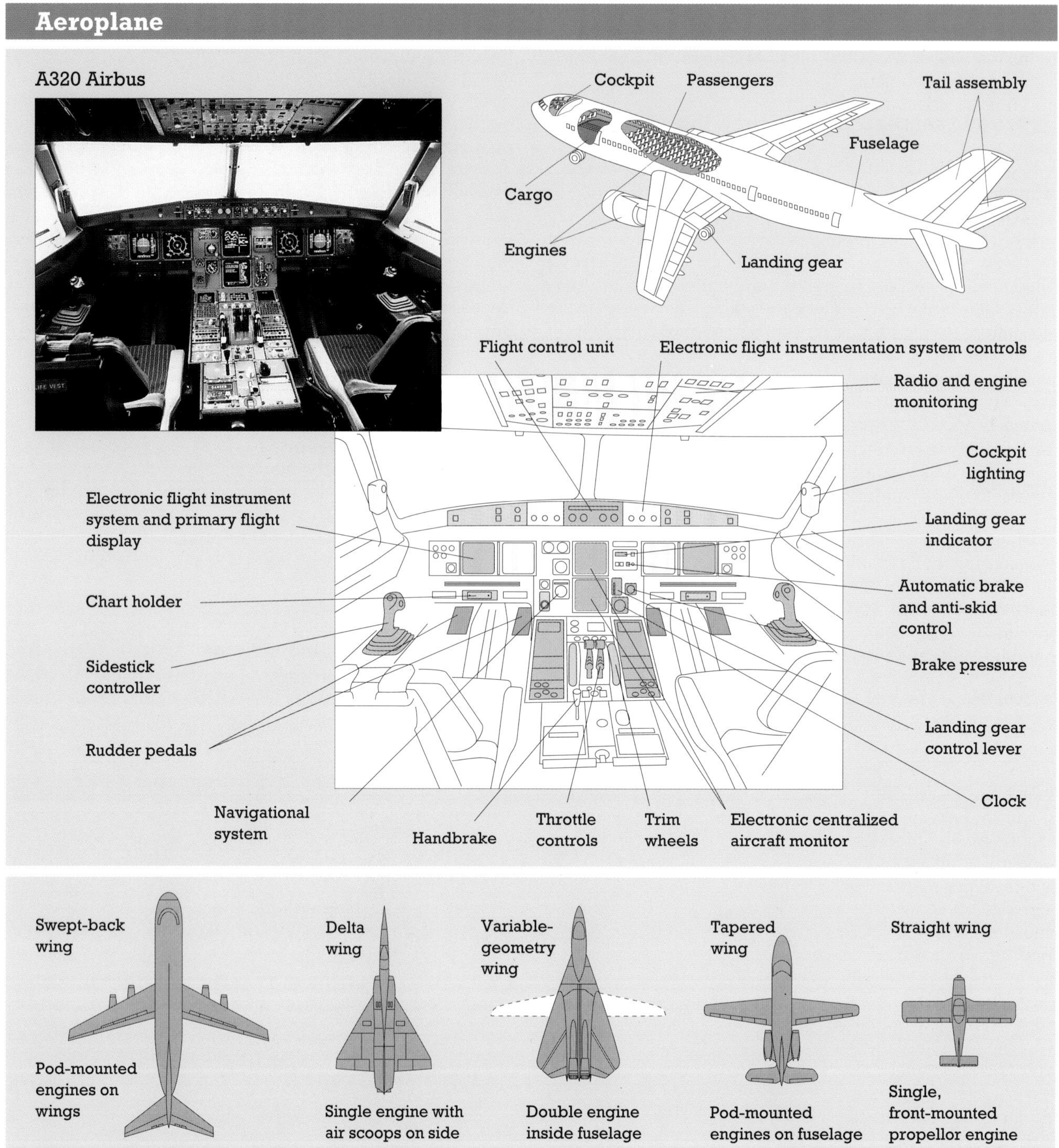

ing it more efficient. The fuel assemblies also differ, being small pellets of enriched uranium dioxide packed in stainless steel tubes, rather than uranium metal. The reactors are designed to allow fuel elements to be changed while the reactor is running. The high-temperature, gas-cooled reactor (HTGR) operates at even higher temperatures: it uses helium as a coolant instead of carbon dioxide. The AGR is claimed to be safer than the *pressurized-water reactor, because of its massive concrete pressure structure and its use of a gas coolant. (For illustration see *nuclear reactor.)

adze, a heavy hand tool in which the cutting edge of the head is set at right angles to a wooden handle. With the *axe it is one of the oldest of all woodworking tools, dating back to Neolithic times, when the head was of flint. Adze heads were later made in bronze, iron, and steel. The principal use of the adze is to square up timber before achieving a finer finish with a chisel or plane. Its basic design has changed little over the centuries, though it has been modified to suit coopers, shipwrights, and other skilled workers. (For illustration see *tools, history of.)

aerial *antenna.

aerodynamics, the study of the movement of air or other gaseous fluids relative to bodies immersed in them, and the forces produced. One of the major tools in aerodynamics is testing in a *wind tunnel. A knowledge of aerodynamics is essential for applications ranging from low-speed air-flow around buildings (industrial aerodynamics) through drag reduction on cars and ships' superstructures (*streamlining), to the prediction of the behaviour of aeroplanes, rockets, and missiles. (See also *flight, principles of; *fluid mechanics; *supersonic flight.)

aerofoil (US, airfoil), a structure whose cross-section is shaped so as to produce a desired aerodynamic reaction (such as lift) by its motion through air without at the same time producing excessive drag (see *flight, principles of). Aircraft examples include wings, control surfaces, tail fins, *propellers, turbine blades, and *helicopter rotor blades. Other examples include sails, some windmill blades, and racing-car aerofoils.

aeronautics *flight, principles of.

aeroplane (US, airplane), a power-driven, heavier-than-air aircraft with fixed wings. Aeroplanes vary enormously in size, performance, and function, from single-engined sport planes to large *airliners or supersonic *fighter aircraft. Before the 1930s aeroplanes had wooden, wire-braced airframes covered by fabric, but modern aircraft are constructed as a shell of thin metal sheeting strengthened by ribs and longitudinal members. The commonest aircraft structural materials are *aluminium alloys, which are cheap, strong, and fairly light. Alloys of *titanium, and *composite materials such as *fibre-reinforced plastics, are increasingly used for structural components because of their lightness.

The basic components of an aeroplane are the fuselage, wings, engines, tail assembly (empennage), and undercarriage. The fuselage carries the passengers, crew, and cargo. The shape of the fuselage relates to the aircraft's operating speed. Low-speed aircraft have little *streamlining, while the shapes of high-speed subsonic and *supersonic aircraft are shaped to minimize drag at normal operating speeds. Most modern aeroplanes are *monoplanes, with only one pair of wings. Wing shape varies with function (see figure). Most aeroplanes are powered by combinations of a piston engine and propellers, by turboprops, or by turbojet engines (see *jet engine). In single-engined aircraft the engine is mounted in the fuselage, while multiple engines may be mounted on the wings, fuselage, or tail. The tail unit consists of a horizontal stabilizer, usually projecting from the mid-line of the rear fuselage, and a vertical tail fin. In the T-tail configuration, the horizontal stabilizer is placed at the top of the fin: this configuration is often used when engines are part of the tail structure. Pneumatic-tyred undercarriages are fitted on virtually all modern aeroplanes. On older aircraft, and on some light aircraft today, the main wheels are located well forward, with a smaller wheel or skid on the tail, but most aeroplanes now use a 'tricycle' undercarriage, with the main wheels behind the centre of gravity and a smaller wheel at the nose. Undercarriages are often retractable, as this greatly improves flight performance. Aeroplane controls comprise a control column or wheel for operating ailerons and elevators, a rudder bar moved by the feet, and the engine ignition and throttle. In addition to this basic array there may be many other controls and instruments. Computers are often used to monitor aircraft functions, or actually to control the aeroplane. (See also *flight, principles of, *flying, history of, and individual aircraft types.)

aerosol, a dispersion of finely divided solid or liquid particles in a gas, for example fog or smoke (see *colloid). The term has come to apply also to a device for producing an aerosol spray—a metal canister (with a release valve) containing a liquid and a propellent gas under pressure. *Hydrocarbon gases such as propane, isobutane, and dimethyl ether are used as propellants. The addition of chloromethane to these gases reduces flammability. *Chloro-fluorocarbons (CFCs), at one time the most widespread aerosol propellants, have been banned in many countries, owing to their adverse environmental effects. Newer aerosols use carbon dioxide gas generated in the canister as a propellant. Aerosols are used in industry to spray paint and insecticides. Consumer aerosols include paints, polishes, perfumes, cleaners, deodorants, shaving cream, and whipped cream. Some medications for respiratory complaints are taken via dosage-controlled aerosols.

aggregate, a building material used to provide bulk, particularly in *concrete and *mortar. For most concrete work the aggregates used are gravels or crushed rock and sand. Lightweight aggregates are commonly used for their thermal resistance in cavity walls, or when a reduced load is required on a structure. Shielding against ionizing radiation requires high-density aggregates of barium sulphate or iron pellets.

Agricola, Georgius (Georg Bauer) (1494–1555), German pioneer of chemical and mining technology. He published several critiques of the methods used at the time to mine and extract metals, but his greatest work was *De Re Metallica* ('On Metals') (1556), a comprehensive treatise in Latin, profusely illustrated with fine woodcuts. Universally adopted as a working manual by mining engineers, it also appeared in German and Italian editions, and in 1912 was translated into English by US President Henry Hoover.

agricultural machinery, machines designed to facilitate crop and animal production. The widespread use of machines on farms is a relatively recent phenomenon. Mechanization began with the invention of machines such as the first *reaper (1826) and the reaper and binder (1886), which enabled the great wheat prairies of the USA and Canada to be opened up at the end of the 19th century. Today, machinery is a central element of agriculture, par-

A woodcut from **Agricola**'s *De Re Metallica*, showing a round oven used for assaying. In the 16th century small samples of metal or ore were assayed either to assess the profitability of working an ore seam, or to test the quality of coins or jewellery. The assayer holds a board with a slit in it, which protects his face and eyes when looking into the furnace.

Agricultural implements and machinery

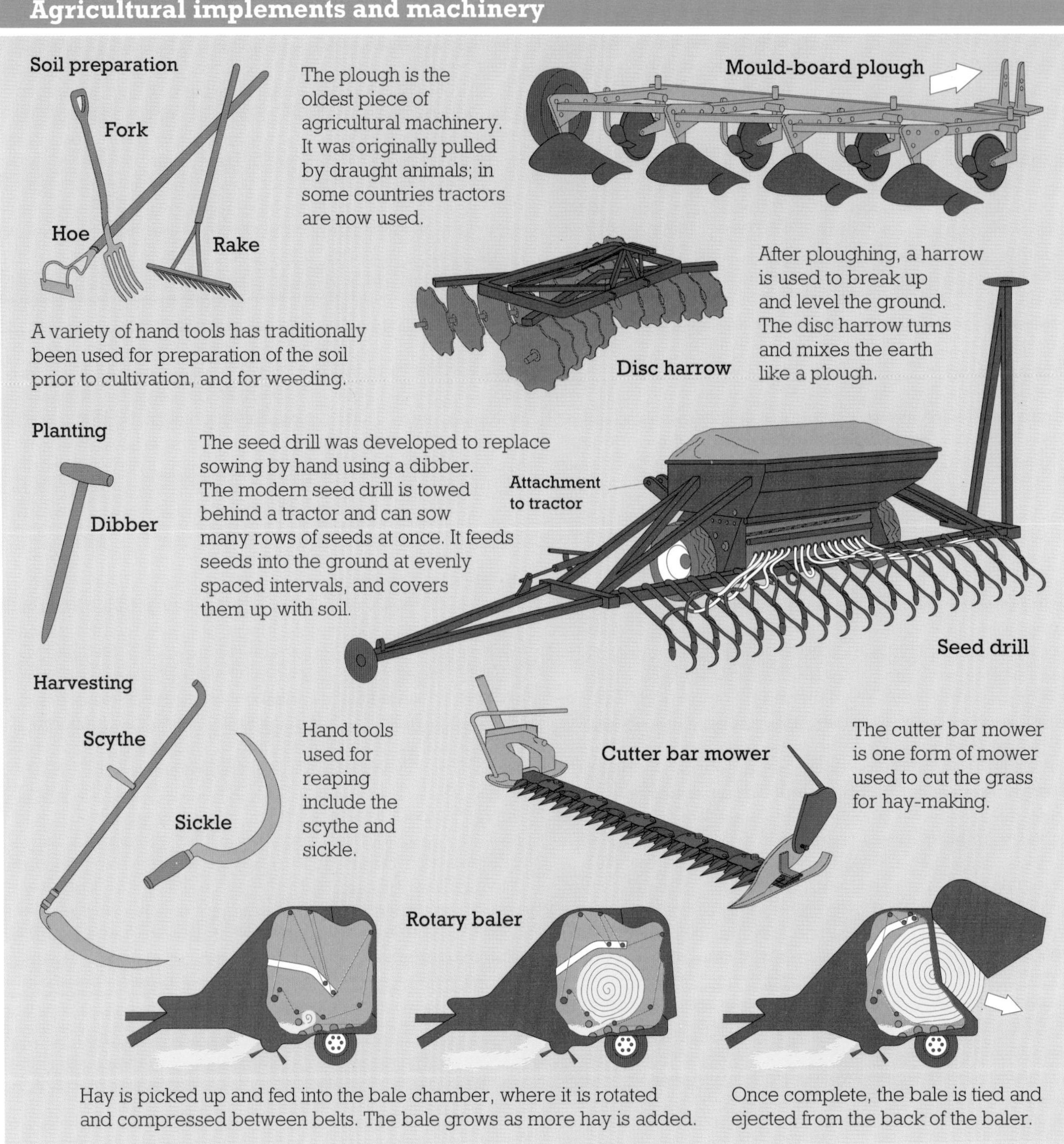

Soil preparation
Fork
Hoe
Rake
The plough is the oldest piece of agricultural machinery. It was originally pulled by draught animals; in some countries tractors are now used.
Mould-board plough
A variety of hand tools has traditionally been used for preparation of the soil prior to cultivation, and for weeding.
Disc harrow
After ploughing, a harrow is used to break up and level the ground. The disc harrow turns and mixes the earth like a plough.
Planting
Dibber
The seed drill was developed to replace sowing by hand using a dibber. The modern seed drill is towed behind a tractor and can sow many rows of seeds at once. It feeds seeds into the ground at evenly spaced intervals, and covers them up with soil.
Attachment to tractor
Seed drill
Harvesting
Scythe
Sickle
Hand tools used for reaping include the scythe and sickle.
Cutter bar mower
The cutter bar mower is one form of mower used to cut the grass for hay-making.
Rotary baler
Hay is picked up and fed into the bale chamber, where it is rotated and compressed between belts. The bale grows as more hay is added.
Once complete, the bale is tied and ejected from the back of the baler.

ticularly of crop production. The essential and ubiquitous farm machine is the *tractor. Other machinery can conveniently be divided into soil cultivation, planting, tending, and harvesting machinery (see figure). Cultivation, the creation of a proper soil tilth, has traditionally been achieved by the successive use of various types of *plough, *harrow, and *cultivator. Planting is accomplished by *seed drills or transplanters. Once established, plants are treated with a variety of agrochemicals applied using crop-spraying equipment and broadcasters. Machinery for harvesting is relatively specialized. The familiar *combine harvester may, with adjustments, harvest cereals, oil-seed rape, dried peas, or soya bean. Sugar beet and potatoes can be excavated by purpose-built machines. *Mowing-machines and *balers are necessary for harvesting hay. This list of machinery is far from exhaustive, yet still contrasts with the relatively little equipment employed for livestock husbandry. *Milking machines are important in dairying, and *shearing equipment for sheep farming. Some animal enterprises use machines for feedstuff preparation, manure slurry handling, and livestock weighing. All machinery represents a considerable capital investment for the farmer; machines are sometimes bought and operated on a co-operative basis or hired from a contractor.

agricultural research station, a government, university, or corporate establishment set up to research and develop improvements in agricultural production. It was not until the 19th century that formal husbandry experiments were undertaken. In 1840 *Lawes established one of the first agricultural research stations at Rothamsted, Herefordshire, UK. Early research was on fertilizers and soil nutrients. Today there are many highly specialized research stations, some run by the chemical and pharmaceutical industries.

agriculture, cultivation of the soil, including the allied pursuits of gathering crops and rearing livestock. The 'Neolithic revolution', the change from an economy based on hunting and gathering to one based on settled agriculture, is thought to have begun in many independent centres around the world, at very roughly the same time: changes in climate may have been a trigger for this process. Archaeological evidence suggests at least three independent centres of origin for agriculture based on grain crops (the Near East, the Far East, and meso-America), plus other sites (for example, Peru and Indonesia), where root vegetables formed the main crops. The most complete evidence has come from the Near East, where domesticated barley and emmer wheat strains have been found which date from about 8000 BC. Domesticated animals were reared in large numbers from at least 7000 BC, and there is evidence for the use of the ox-drawn wooden *plough from 5000 BC. In the early civilizations of Babylonia, Egypt, the Indus Valley, and China (from *c*.3000 BC), large-scale *irrigation systems were developed.

Agricultural practices spread gradually from the different centres to other parts of the world, and were adapted to local conditions. In Europe and the Mediterranean, practices, once established, remained basically unchanged for many years. Roman farmers used an ox-drawn, wheelless plough with iron shares or blades. They sowed seed by hand, harvested using a curved sickle, threshed grain with a hand flail, and winnowed it by throwing it into the air and letting the wind carry away the chaff. By the 4th century AD, high labour input, the transplanting of seedlings, and use of *fertilizers were producing cereal yields in China not matched elsewhere until the 19th century. In the Americas, maize was the main crop in some areas, the potato in others. The llama was domesticated as a beast of burden, while the alpaca was kept for its wool, and the guinea-pig for meat. In medieval Europe, slow improvements were made in agricultural practice, particularly in northern areas. From the 5th to the 12th centuries, agricultural land was created by forest clearance, or was reclaimed from marshland and the sea. From the late 13th to the early 15th centuries, much arable land fell into disuse due to the effects of floods, famine, plague, and wars. Recovery began slowly in the 15th century.

Tobacco plants, *Nicotinia tabacum*, being grown in a greenhouse at an **agricultural research station**.

In the 17th and 18th centuries several different developments led to improvements in crop yields and in livestock production. An important element in these changes was the Norfolk four-course system, in which grain and fodder or grazing crops were grown in a four-year rotation. The effects of this system were cumulative: grazing animals manured the land and increased its fertility, while the growing of winter fodder and summer grazing crops meant that animals were better fed, and more productive. In the 18th century selective breeding was introduced, and the Rotherham plough (the forerunner of the modern plough) was developed, along with a variety of simple machines for threshing, chopping animal feed, hoeing, and seed drilling. However, it was not until the mid-19th century that *agricultural machinery, for example the *reaper and the *traction-engine, began to be adopted by farmers.

The 19th century also saw the development of agricultural science, with the introduction of the earliest chemical and synthetic *fertilizers, and the opening of *agricultural research stations in several countries. During this period large areas of the USA, Canada, South America, and Australia were settled: huge sheep and cattle ranches were established, and large areas were given over to wheat farming. In colonial countries, *plantation farming of *beverage crops, rubber, and *sugar-cane expanded tremendously, although these developments had little effect on indigenous agricultural practices. Much of the cheap food generated by the opening up of these new areas was exported to Europe.

The 20th century has seen far-reaching changes in *farming practices. The internal-combustion engine has replaced steam-power for *agricultural machinery, and improved transport has led to the development of a world market for some agricultural products. The *green revolution saw increased crop production in Third World countries. *Agrochemicals were being used in huge quantities by the 1960s, but since that time the hazards of indiscriminate pesticide use have led to the development of other strategies such as the breeding of disease-resistant plant strains and the use of biological methods of pest control favoured by *organic farmers. Genetic development of plant strains and intensive *animal breeding have greatly increased the productivity of croplands and livestock in developed countries. However, surpluses of some commodities in developed countries have not helped Third World countries, in particular in Africa, where population growth has not been matched by increases in agricultural productivity. Western aid has too often failed to recognize the efficiency of local agricultural practices.

agrochemical, a chemical produced specifically for use in farming. Agrochemicals include *fertilizers to increase plant growth, and *pesticides and *herbicides to control agents that cause plant disease or damage crops during growth or storage. Agrochemicals are also used to control such physical processes as fermentation in the making of *silage. The term may also include veterinary products, hormones to improve animal or plant growth, and detergents used to keep equipment clean. There is public concern over the widespread use of agrochemicals because many are toxic to humans, they persist in the food chain, and they can cause build-up of high concentrations of phosphates, nitrates, and other potentially harmful substances in water supplies.

Aids (*a*cquired *i*mmune *d*eficiency *s*yndrome), an often fatal syndrome, marked by severe loss of resistance to disease, resulting from infection with HIV (*h*uman *i*mmune *d*eficiency) virus. The main target cells of the virus within the body are those of the immune system (see *immunology), notably T helper cells (which manufacture antibodies), and macrophages (which engulf bacteria and other foreign bodies). HIV is a retrovirus: its genetic material is RNA (see *DNA), from which it makes DNA within the host cell by means of the enzyme reverse transcriptase. This viral DNA is then incorporated into the host cell chromosomes, where it may lie dormant for many years before being activated to make new copies of the virus. Mortality from Aids is high, and a large research effort has been made world-wide to find a treatment. The most effective drug treatment to date is zidovudine (formerly known as AZT), which is an analogue of one of the nucleotides that form the building blocks of DNA. Zidovudine acts by blocking the production of DNA from the viral RNA. Trials in the USA suggest that it and a related drug, ddI, can delay death from Aids, although there are serious side-effects. Another promising agent for inhibiting HIV growth is a protein extracted from the leaves of a poisonous plant, the pokeweed.

aileron *flight, principles of.

air-brake, a mechanical brake applied by means of the pressure of compressed air; the term is also used for extendible flaps that provide a braking effect on *aeroplanes. Compressed-air brakes are common on *lorries and on some railway rolling stock. An engine-driven *compressor charges an air tank to provide a reservoir of high-pressure air that can be applied to the brake pistons or diaphragms when needed. When this air pressure is released there is a characteristic hiss. Another form of air-brake is a *parachute attached to the tail of an aircraft, which is opened on landing to slow the vehicle.

air conditioning, environmental control of the interior of a building (or other enclosed space such as a car) by the mechanical circulation of air at the desired temperature and relative humidity. An air conditioning plant includes a chiller, heater, humidifier and *dehumidifier, air filters, and circulation fans. The air is distributed through the building via ducts above ceilings or under raised floors; stale air is returned to the air-conditioning plant for recycling via a further duct system. The interior of the building is sealed against the external atmosphere (having no openable windows). In hot climates, solar heat-gain through windows and *curtain walls is considerable, and large amounts of energy are required to keep the internal environment comfortable. Recently, problems have arisen from bacterial contamination of air-conditioning, and it has been suggested that these systems are responsible for 'sick-building syndrome', a high incidence of illness in office workers, attributed to the immediate working environment.

aircraft *aeroplane, *airliner, *helicopter, *military aircraft.

aircraft carrier, a *warship designed to operate aircraft at sea. Carriers are usually fitted with a flight-deck for launching and landing, and have hangars below for stowage and servicing of aircraft. The first aircraft carriers, before World War I, were converted merchant ships or warships carrying seaplanes; later some *cruisers were converted, by the addition of a flight-deck over the foredeck. Towards the end of World War I, carriers were built with a flight-deck running the whole length of the ship, capable of handling the faster and heavier aircraft being developed. They were fitted with arrester wires (often spring-loaded) to enable the aircraft's momentum on landing to be absorbed within the length of the deck. With the introduction of *jet-engined aircraft an angled deck was developed, and a steam catapult permitted more efficient and faster handling of aircraft during operations. The most modern carriers have a displacement of around 90,000 tonnes and accommodate over 100 aircraft. The development of *vertical take-off and landing aircraft and the increasing use of *helicopters have now reduced the need for long flight-decks, so that the days of the giant carrier may be passing.

Air conditioning pipework on the exterior of the Pompidou centre, Beaubourg, Paris.

airgun, a weapon that shoots its *ammunition by means of compressed air or other gas. The earliest known practical airgun was made in Nuremberg, Germany, in 1530. In the modern weapon, pulling the trigger sets off a piston that compresses air, which in turn propels the projectile. There are also guns that use a pump to build up a charge of compressed air, which is released when the trigger is pulled. The pressure of the air-charge can be varied to increase or decrease the projectile's velocity. Other 'air' guns use a gas cylinder to provide propellant.

airliner, a large passenger-carrying *aeroplane, certified (licensed) to carry passengers on both scheduled and charter flights, and to carry mail and freight. Air transport services first began to proliferate after World War I. Early airliners were spartan, ex-military aircraft, but by the 1930s European and US airlines were operating comfortable, purpose-built aeroplanes on a network of routes. Long-distance services initially used *flying boats, but these were replaced after World War II by land-based aircraft. *Jet-engined airliners were generally adopted after 1958. More recent developments have been the introduction of *supersonic airliners and *wide-bodied aircraft. (See also *flying, history of.)

airlock, a two-door chamber separating spaces of differing air pressures. When someone enters from one pressure region, the door on that side is sealed and the pressure in the chamber is changed, allowing access to the other pressure region with minimal loss of air. Airlocks are used in buildings in which parts of the interior are kept slightly above atmospheric pressure in order to maintain extremely clean environments, for example when making electronic components. Some laboratories are kept slightly below atmospheric pressure to prevent the escape of dangerous organisms. Other important uses of airlocks are in *deep-sea diving and in *space exploration.

air pollution, pollution caused by the release into the atmosphere of gases, or finely dispersed solid or liquid particles, at rates too great to dissipate or to be incorporated into the land or water. Natural causes of air pollution include dust storms, forest or grass fires, and volcanic activity. Air pollution caused by humans comes from a variety of sources. Motor car fuel emission is responsible for major urban air pollution, in particular smog (smoke plus fog), and lead pollution arising from the addition of *lead tetraethyl to petrol. Another major source of air pollution is the burning of *fossil fuels in power-stations. Pesticides have been discovered in Antarctica, where they have never been used, indicating that the atmosphere can carry pollutants over large distances. Radioactive pollution is a continual threat, and a major catastrophe occurred in 1986, when the *Chernobyl nuclear plant released radioactive contaminants into the atmosphere.

Efforts are being made to reduce air pollution from some sources. Air pollution from volatile hydrocarbons may be reduced by the development of solvent-free *paints. Devices such as the *catalytic converter are used to reduce carbon monoxide and hydrocarbon levels in motor car exhaust emissions, and the use of lead-free petrol is mandatory in some countries and strongly encouraged in others. Low-pollution methods for burning fossil fuels plus the shift to less polluting forms of power generation—*wind and *solar power, for example—can be used to reduce air pollution significantly. (See also *greenhouse effect, *acid rain.)

airport, a defined area on land or water for the take-off and landing of aircraft, with facilities for their shelter, servicing, and repair, and for passengers and cargo. While some airports are quite small and serve the requirements of perhaps only one company (for example, at an oilfield), others operate to deal with the requirements of international airlines. Such large international airports cover vast areas: London's Heathrow Airport, for example, covers 1,141 ha (2,819 acres). The main runways are positioned to face the prevailing winds, with a cross-runway interconnecting them in many cases. The control tower, which supervises the landing and take-off of aircraft as well as the movement of aircraft and vehicles on the runways, taxi-ways, and aprons, is sited so as to overlook the majority of the airport (although *air traffic control relies heavily on *radar. Around the air-

Düsseldorf **airport** at night.

port are positioned servicing hangars, passenger terminals, and cargo facilities. These have to be easily accessible by road and rail. The passenger terminals have separate channels for arrival and departure, so that their luggage and check-in facilities (and, if international, the customs services) are kept separate. Most large airports have shops, restaurants, and banks in the terminal building, plus special lounges for departing passengers. Terminals and aprons are designed to minimize the turn-around time between flights: this is especially important for short-haul aircraft. Aircraft can be refuelled, serviced, and provided with in-flight catering while parked adjacent to the terminal building. The siting of an airport is crucial. It has to be accessible to those who work there and those who use it, but sufficiently isolated that the noise of aircraft taking off and landing should not disturb people living nearby.

air-raid shelter (US, bunker), a structure protecting its occupants from an aerial attack. Shelters for the civil population were widely used during World War II. In the UK the arch-shaped, corrugated steel 'Anderson' shelter (named after the Minister of Home Security in 1939) gave good protection against blast, but was ineffective against direct hits. Very effective deep shelters were provided in four of London's underground railway stations. In Hanoi during the Vietnam War (1964–75), shelters under the streets could withstand all but the most powerful direct hits. Shelters to protect occupants from nuclear attack are designed primarily to protect against *fall-out rather than blast. Thick walls are needed to absorb radiation, and ventilating air must be filtered to remove the fall-out.

airship, a power-driven, lighter-than-air aircraft developed from the *balloon. Practicable designs for steerable, cigar-shaped airships were first produced in 1784 by the French military engineer J.-B.-M.-C. Meusnier de la Place. *Giffard, another Frenchman, developed the first airship actually to fly (1852). In 1894 the French government financed a more successful, electric-powered airship, but it was not until the advent of the internal-combustion engine that airship developments really began. Early airships had non-rigid, gas-filled fabric envelopes. Later developments were the semi-rigid design, with a structural fore-and-aft keel; and rigid airships comprising an external skeleton covered by light fabric surrounding a series of internal gas-filled cells. Large, rigid airships with light-alloy frames were developed principally in Germany by von *Zeppelin. They were successfully used for military and passenger purposes between 1900 and 1930, but a series of disasters in the 1930s, attributable to the highly flammable nature of the hydrogen-filled envelope, led to their decline. Airships using non-flammable helium were used on the east coast of the USA for early warning until 1961, and have found applications since the 1970s in advertising and aerial photography. Since 1987 the US Coast Guard has operated sophisticated aerostat airships for coastal patrol. These aircraft carry nineteen personnel, and can stay at sea for up to thirty-one days. (See also *flying, history of.)

air traffic control, a system for controlling the safe, orderly, and speedy movement of aircraft at take-off and landing, during flight, and while on the ground at an *airport. Once an aircraft takes off, its flight is controlled by the local air traffic control centre. The pilot flies a pre-arranged course and height, which is monitored by *radar, and progress reports are made by the pilot at regular intervals. At some point *en route* the pilot will be handed on to the next air traffic control centre, and this process continues until the aircraft reaches its destination, where the pilot will receive detailed landing instructions. If during flight, or even before an aircraft takes off, one or more of the air traffic control centres on its route is fully occupied, the pilot may be asked to delay take-off or go into a *stacking system until it is possible to proceed.

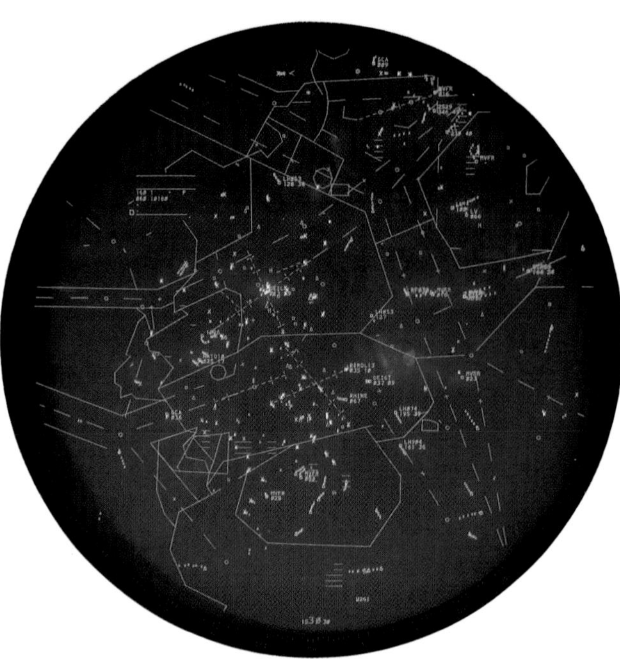

An **air traffic control** radar screen, showing positions of aircraft in the controlled airspace around Düsseldorf airport.

alchemy, a pseudo-science originating independently in China, Greece, and India in about the 3rd century BC, concerned with the transmutation of base metals such as lead into gold. The transmutation was variously an end in itself, a means by which to make an elixir of life, and a route to the creation of a panacea, or universal medicine. Early alchemy degenerated into superstition and mysticism, but the art flourished once again in the 8th century AD in Arab countries. Translations of Arabic alchemical texts led in the 12th century to a second revival of alchemy in Europe, notably in Prague. During the Renaissance it fell into disrepute, but the chemical experience accumulated by alchemists over many centuries became the basis upon which the modern science of chemistry was built.

alcohol, the term used to denote a group of *hydrocarbons containing a hydroxyl (−OH) group, but sometimes restricted to one specific alcohol, *ethanol. Ethanol is a colourless volatile liquid, the intoxicant present in wine, beer, and spirits. Alcohols are important *organic chemicals, with a variety of industrial applications both in the manufacture of other materials (such as detergents and plastics), and in their own right as fuels and *solvents.

alcoholic drink, a drink containing alcohol (*ethanol) produced by the *fermentation of sugars by yeast, a single-celled *fungus. In *wine-making the sugar is present in the grapes, while in *brewing, the sugar must be introduced. The alcoholic strength of a drink made by fermentation alone has an upper limit of around 15 per cent by volume, as the yeast dies when the alcohol levels rise higher than this. Two other processes—distilling and fortification—are used to increase alcohol content beyond 15 per cent. In distillation the fermented liquid is heated: the lower-boiling-point alcohol fraction vaporizes before the aqueous portion, and thus can be separated. Distillation is used to make spirits such as whisky, gin, rum, and vodka. Fortification involves the addition of spirits to wine to increase the alcohol content: examples are port, sherry, and vermouth. Alcoholic drinks are most commonly made from fermented grapes or grain cereals, but many other raw materials can be used.

alginate, a high-molecular-weight carbohydrate obtained from seaweeds and other algae. Alginates are surfactants, which, by lowering the *surface tension of water, cause emulsions to form and become stable. This is their main use in the food, pharmaceutical, cosmetic, and textile industries.

ALGOL *computer language.

algorithm, a term used in computing to describe a well-defined sequence of instructions designed to carry out a particular task. Algorithms are usually represented in some kind of formal notation such as a *flow chart and form the basis of all conventional computer *programs. The terms algorithm and program are very close in meaning: both refer to a precise set of operations to solve a problem. A program can be considered to be a set of algorithms translated into a particular *computer language or *machine code to perform a specific task.

alizarin *Perkin, William Henry.

alkali, any of a class of substances that form caustic or corrosive solutions in water and neutralize acids to form salts (see *acids, bases, and salts). For substances in aqueous solution the term is virtually synonymous with base. Alkali metals are any of the six chemically related metals lithium, sodium, potassium, rubidium, caesium, and francium: their hydroxides form alkaline solutions in water.

alloy, material that is formed by mixing *metals, sometimes with the addition of non-metals. This process causes significant changes to the crystal structure, and therefore the properties, of the metal. The result may be a harder, stronger, stiffer, more corrosion-resistant, or less dense material (see table). The first alloys, *bronze and *brass, were probably formed accidentally by the chance *smelting of mixed metal ores and have been known since about 3500 BC. Alloys of *iron began to be developed about 1000 BC. *Steel was made in small quantities in early times, but it was not until the mid-19th century that it was manufactured on a large scale in the *iron and steel industry. The commercial production of pure *aluminium in about 1890 heralded a new range of alloys (such as duralumin, an alloy of about 94 per cent aluminium, with small quantities of copper, manganese, magnesium, and silicon) that are both light and strong. *Nickel is frequently mixed with other metals for specialist purposes: 'silver' coinage in the UK is made from cupro-nickel (75 per cent copper, 25 per cent nickel), and constantan (60 per cent copper, 40 per cent nickel) is used for electrical resistance wire. Nickel silver (50–60 per cent copper, 20 per cent zinc, 20–30 per cent nickel) has the appearance of silver, but is more hard-wearing, and can serve as a cheaper substitute in jewellery and fine metalwork. Permalloy is a nickel–iron alloy that is magnetically soft (that is, the polarity of its magnetic field can be easily changed) and is used for *transformer cores. Monel metals contain about two parts nickel to one part copper, plus other elements. They are stronger than nickel and extremely

Principal commercial alloys

Name	Date of introduction	Constituent elements	Typical uses
Brasses	Known since *c.*3500 BC and used extensively since 17th century	Copper and zinc	Plumbing fittings, industrial tubing
Bronzes	Known since *c.*3500 BC and used extensively since 17th century	Copper, tin, and zinc	Coinage, ships' propellers
Cast iron	Known and used since 17th century	Iron plus 2–4 per cent carbon	Engine blocks, industrial machinery
Carbon steels	Used extensively since mid-19th century	Iron plus 0.1–0.8 per cent carbon	Car bodies, bridges
Nickel steel	Developed during late 19th century and used extensively since	Iron plus 0.6 per cent carbon and 3 per cent nickel	Armour-plating
High-speed steel	Developed early 20th century	Iron plus various amounts of tungsten, vanadium, and molybdenum	Lathe cutting tools
Stainless steel	Developed early 20th century	Iron plus 12 per cent chromium (minimum) and nickel	Cutlery, chemical engineering
Magnesium alloys	Used extensively since early 20th century	Magnesium, zinc, and zirconium	Gas-cooled nuclear power-stations
Aluminium alloys	Used extensively since mid-20th century	Aluminium plus lithium, magnesium, copper, silicon, or zinc	Lightweight castings for car engines, aerospace applications
Titanium alloys	Use has developed since World War II	Titanium plus aluminium, vanadium, molybdenum, and tin	Aerospace applications, fan blades of gas-turbines
Spheroidal graphitic cast iron	Developed in mid-20th century	Iron plus 2–4 per cent carbon and 0.04 per cent magnesium or cerium	Pressure pipes
Nimonics	Used extensively since mid-20th century	Nickel plus 20 per cent chromium and other metals	High-temperature, creep-resistant alloys for gas-turbine engines

corrosion-resistant, making them useful in handling *fluorine. Electrum is a natural or artificial alloy of gold containing 15–45 per cent silver. It was used in the ancient world for coinage. Bismuth frequently forms part of alloys with low melting-points. Today, with increased metallurgical understanding, alloys can be designed for particular applications.

alternating current (a.c.) *circuits, electrical and electronic, *electricity generation and supply.

alternative technology *appropriate technology.

alternator *generator, electrical.

altimeter, an instrument used in aircraft for measuring altitude above land or sea. The pressure altimeter utilizes the fact that atmospheric pressure decreases with altitude by measuring pressure using an evacuated metal bellows similar to that in a *barometer, and converting this pressure reading into a height measurement. Such an altimeter must be adjusted to compensate for variations in sea-level pressure and changes of pressure with temperature. Radio altimeters measure height by transmitting a vertical radio signal and comparing the phase of the transmitted signal with that reflected back from the ground: they measure distance above ground rather than height above sea-level.

alum (potassium aluminium sulphate, $KAl(SO_4)_2 \cdot 12H_2O$), a white crystalline compound used in the dyeing industry as a *mordant, in water purification, in dressing leather, sizing paper, in waterproofing fabrics, in fireproofing, and in medicine as a styptic and astringent. It is manufactured by treating bauxite with sulphuric acid and then potassium sulphate. The name alum also refers to a general type of double sulphate salt.

alumina (aluminium oxide, Al_2O_3), an inert, very hard, *ceramic material used mainly as an *abrasive and as an electrical insulator. It occurs naturally as the mineral corundum, or is obtained from bauxite ore by heating to 90 °C. Alumina ceramic fibres are used for high-temperature thermal insulation and as reinforcements in *composites. Many naturally occurring gemstones are composed of aluminium oxide crystals, coloured by impurities. Artificial gemstones can be manufactured from alumina for various applications: for example, sapphire crystals are used as insulating substrates in electronics, while artificial rubies have applications in *lasers. Alumina is also an important constituent of many pottery and porcelain compositions.

aluminium (US, aluminum: symbol Al, at. no. 13, r.a.m. 26.98), a soft metallic element, which in air has a thin, unreactive, and strongly adherent oxide coating that protects it from *corrosion. This protects the metal from further oxidation and accounts for its apparently low reactivity. Aluminium is an excellent conductor of heat. This property, together with its resistance to corrosion and its low density, explains why it is used for cooking utensils and, increasingly, in the canning industry. Aluminium powder is used in paints and in the thermite reaction (see *welding). *Alloys of aluminium, such as duralumin, have high tensile strengths and are of considerable industrial importance, particularly in the aerospace industry. The most important *ore is the hydrated oxide, bauxite (approximately $Al_2O_3 \cdot 2H_2O$). This is dissolved in hot sodium hydroxide, precipitated, and heated to form *alumina. Alumina is then reduced to aluminium by

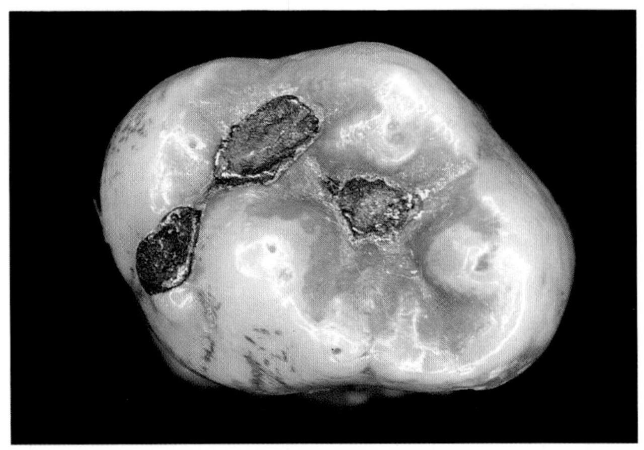

An extracted molar with **amalgam** fillings. The amalgam is mixed immediately before use and inserted into the tooth cavity with a small, gun-like instrument. The amalgam sets after about an hour, and is fully hard after about a day.

an electrolytic process developed by *Hall and *Héroult. It is also a good conductor of electricity and is widely used in overhead *cables. Articles made of aluminium can be coloured and given additional resistance to wear by *anodizing. Aluminium chloride is used as a catalyst in organic chemistry and for *cracking petroleum. Aluminium in the form of *alum is used in the purification of water as a *mordant for dyes.

aluminium–lithium alloys, extremely stiff, low-density alloys of aluminium and lithium. They were first manufactured in Germany in the 1920s, but significant development did not take place until the 1980s. The alloys have high strength and good fatigue-resistance due to the formation of small Al_3Li particles (precipitation hardening) within the alloy. Commercial alloys also contain small amounts of copper, magnesium, and zirconium. The weight of a large airliner is reduced by about 5 tonnes if aluminium–lithium alloys are used instead of conventional aluminium alloys.

AM (amplitude modulation) *modulation.

amalgam, a solution of a metal in mercury. Gold in particular is highly soluble in mercury: this property has been exploited to extract small metallic gold particles from the insoluble (non-metallic) ore. The mercury is later driven off by heat. Amalgams containing tin, silver, gold, or other metals are used to make dental fillings.

ambulance, a vehicle for conveying the sick or injured. Ambulances came into use during the Crimean War (1853–6): the original horse-drawn ambulance was little more than a means of carrying stretchers. Motorized vehicles have been in use since the beginning of this century, and in the 1960s the United States pioneered helicopter ambulances during its war in Vietnam. Today's ambulances carry sophisticated equipment, and their staff are trained to perform monitoring and emergency treatments to reduce the numbers of patient deaths in transit. Recently, some ambulances have been provided with defibrillators to treat cardiac arrests (see *cardiology).

American Association for the Advancement of Science (AAAS), a US scientific society. Derived from the

Association of American Geologists and Naturalists (1840), it was founded as the AAAS in 1848, and modelled on the *British Association for the Advancement of Science (1831). Like the latter, it aims to inform the public about the progress of science, mainly through a large annual meeting.

ammeter, an instrument used to measure electric current in a *circuit. Ideal ammeters have negligible internal resistance and thus do not take any power from the circuit. Ammeters are specified by their full-scale reading, or the maximum current they can measure; this may range from microamperes to many tens of amperes. The *galvanometer is a type of ammeter.

ammonia (nitrogen trihydride, NH_3), a colourless gas with a characteristic, irritating smell; it is readily soluble in water, giving an *alkaline solution. It is also toxic, causing blindness and respiratory problems, although small quantities are administered via smelling salts to revive people who have fainted. Ammonia is manufactured at high temperature and pressure from the elements nitrogen and hydrogen, using the *Haber–Bosch process. Solid salts of ammonia, such as ammonium sulphate, ammonium nitrate, and urea, are important *fertilizers. Ammonia is also used in the manufacture of *nitric acid.

ammunition *bullet, *shell, *shrapnel.

amniocentesis, a technique in *obstetrics and gynaecology involving the removal and testing of a sample of the amniotic fluid surrounding the foetus in the womb. The sample is usually taken between the twelfth and eighteenth weeks of pregnancy, using a hollow needle. It allows prenatal diagnosis of diseases caused by chromosomal abnormality, such as Down's syndrome, and developmental disorders such as spina bifida.

ampere (amp, A) *unit.

amphibious vehicle, a vehicle designed to be used on land or on water, for military, rescue, or agricultural purposes. In 1918 an amphibious car was manufactured in the USA, and between 1920 and 1925 an amphibious tank was developed in the UK. By World War II several amphibious vehicles were being used by the military, including the US DUKW or 'Duck', the British 'Terrapin', and the German Volkswagen Schwimmwagen. The USA has led in the post-war development of amphibious military vehicles. Today, *hovercraft and *low-ground-pressure vehicles are used in many amphibious applications.

amplifier, an electronic device or circuit that provides *gain, using an external energy source to produce a signal output larger than the input. Amplifiers are used extensively to magnify weak signals from *microphones, *transducers, and tuning circuits, in order to provide a large enough signal to drive a *loudspeaker, *cathode-ray tube, transmitter, or other device. If one amplifier unit alone provides insufficient amplification, several amplifiers may be joined together in stages. Excessive amplification, however, may cause malfunction or distortion. Although amplifiers were in the past made from *thermionic valves, the vast majority of modern amplifiers use *transistors or *integrated circuits. The transistors are the devices that actually amplify the elec-

Surgery in progress at St Stephen's Hospital, London. The anaesthetist (*right*) continually monitors the patient's condition, and administers **anaesthetic** when required.

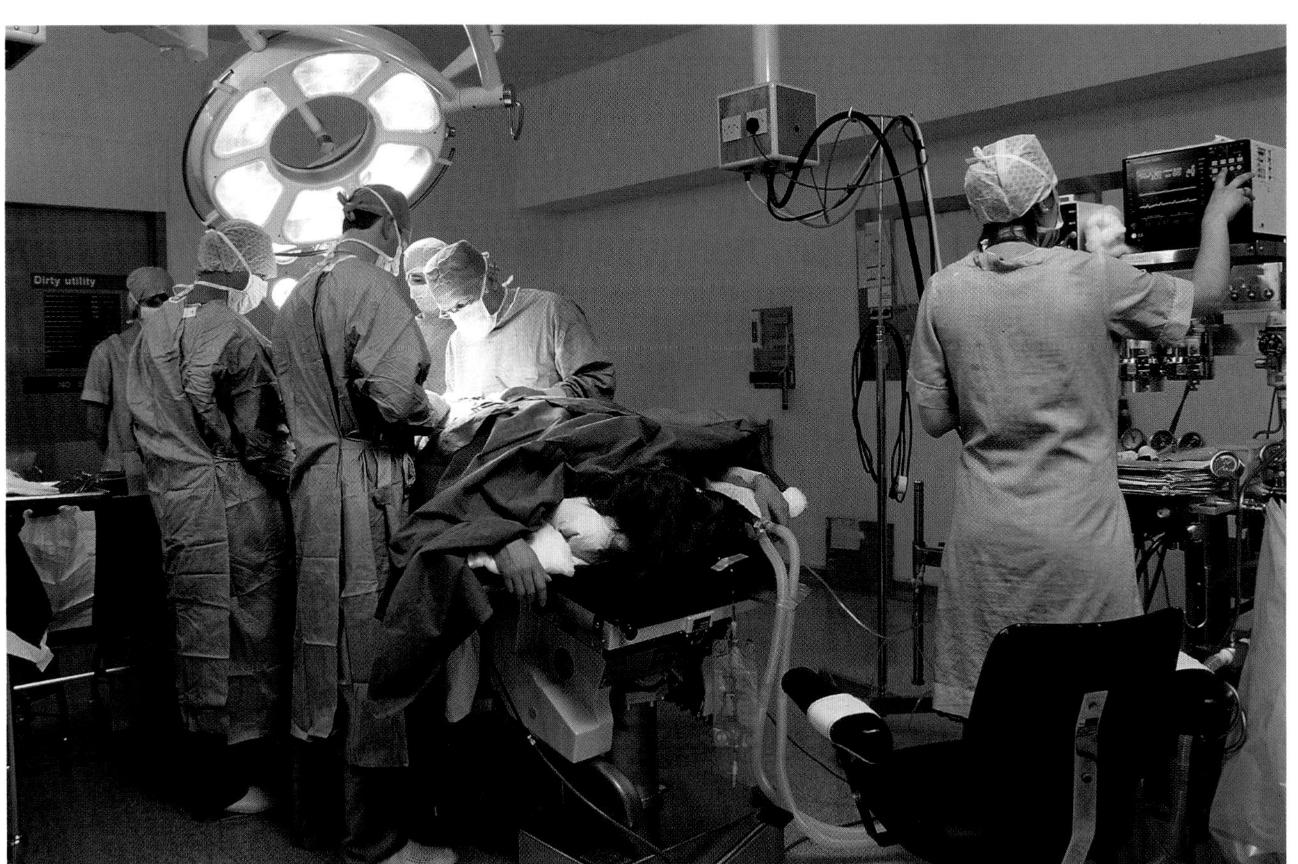

trical signal (see *semiconductor devices for illustration). Many types of amplifier exist, their design depending on whether they amplify electrical voltage or current, and their application. They include audio-frequency amplifiers used for *sound recording and reproduction, and radio-frequency amplifiers used to boost tuned radio and television receiver signals. Amplifiers may also be categorized as 'small signal' amplifiers, using relatively small input and output signals, or 'power' amplifiers, delivering enough signal to energize such devices as loudspeakers. Other variants include push-pull amplifiers and tuned amplifiers, both of which are used to provide high-efficiency, high-gain, but very low-distortion performance.

anabolic steroid *steroids and steroid treatment.

anaesthesia, loss of feeling in all or a part of the body. Anaesthesia of part of the body may occur through injury to or disease in a nerve, but the term is more usually applied to the reduction or abolishing of surgical pain using drugs, or other methods such as *acupuncture or hypnosis. In about AD 70, Aulus Cornelius Celsus recorded that the Romans used mandrake and poppy extracts for post-operational pain relief while the Chinese surgeon Hua Tuo (d. AD 208) is known to have used drugs for surgical anaesthesia. In the mid-19th century in the USA and Europe the anaesthetics ether, *chloroform, and nitrous oxide were first used for pain relief during operations. Anaesthetic drugs act on the fatty membranes of nerve cells, disrupting the transmission of electrical impulses. Anaesthesia may be general, regional, or local. Local anaesthesia blocks nerve transmission at the site where it is administered, so that pain and other sensory signals do not reach the central nervous system. Nerves carrying pain impulses, especially those associated with sharp pain, are the first to be affected by a local anaesthetic. In regional anaesthesia, the anaesthetic is applied to large nerves whose branches supply a wide area of the body, or to an area around the spinal cord. Regional anaesthetic techniques have made surgery available to many patients too frail to undergo general anaesthesia. General anaesthesia relies on drugs that readily dissolve in nerve cells throughout the central nervous system, thus disrupting its function and leading to unconsciousness. It produces a much more complete analgesia (pain relief) than both local and regional techniques, and when given in conjunction with neuromuscular blocking drugs such as *curare it produces complete muscular relaxation, which makes surgery easier. (See also *pharmacology.)

analgesic, a drug that reduces pain. *Narcotic analgesics act on the brain: opium derivatives such as morphine are powerful, but easily produce addiction and their supply is strictly controlled by law. Non-narcotic analgesics, of which aspirin and paracetamol (and, more recently, anti-inflammatories such as ibuprofen), are the most common, act peripherally by preventing the formation of pain-producing substances in injured or inflamed tissues. Although far less powerful than narcotic analgesics, they are effective for headaches and minor pains and usually have no serious side-effects. (See also *pharmacology.)

analog *digitization.

analog computer, a computer that uses continuously variable (analog) quantities to represent numbers. A voltage between 0 and 1 volts might represent numbers between 0.0 and 100.0, for example. Analog computers can perform complex arithmetical operations extremely quickly with very few components, but they are not very accurate. Digital computers have replaced them almost entirely except in *signal processing, where the basic analog computing elements are still used very widely. Recent work suggests that analog computing techniques might have a significant future in *neural network computers.

analog-to-digital converter *signal processing.

analytical engine *Babbage, *computer, history of.

anchor, a device for securing a ship to the sea-bed or river-bed. It is attached to the ship by a chain or cable, which hangs in a deep curve (catenary) in the water, thus improving the anchor's holding power. Originally, a heavy stone, or a basket of stones, was used, and stone anchors are still in use in some places. As ships grew larger, hooked anchors were introduced, later incorporating a stock or shaft at right angles to the hooks for improved holding power. When iron replaced wood as a shipbuilding material in the 19th century, ships' anchors increased considerably in size and weight. The anchor arms were developed into large flukes (blade-like projections), pivoted about the central shaft, and anchor chains replaced rope cables. In the 20th century several new anchor designs have been introduced, offering still greater holding power. Some designs fold up for ease of storage.

anemometer, an instrument for measuring air speed, particularly wind-speed, used in meteorology and in wind-tunnels, ventilation shafts, and so on. There are two main types of anemometer, mechanical and hot-wire. In the former, the moving air rotates either a vertical shaft fitted with fan-like vanes or cups, or a propeller mounted on a horizontal shaft. The rate of rotation gives a measure of air-speed. In hot-wire anemometers, wind-speed is measured in terms of its cooling effect on an electrically heated wire. Hot-wire anemometers are particularly useful for measuring rapid wind changes in turbulent conditions.

angling *fishing industry.

aniline (aminobenzene, $C_6H_5NH_2$), an oily, colourless liquid, turning brown on oxidation. It is the starting material for the production of a wide range of chemicals, the most important being *azo dyes. Aniline is related to *benzene: it is produced industrially by reacting nitrobenzene vapour with hydrogen gas over a copper *catalyst at a temperature of around 300 °C.

animal breeding, the deliberate selection of mating partners in domesticated animals to maximize the desirable characteristics of the species, for example meat, milk, or wool production, strength, stamina, or speed. Animal breeding has been practised for centuries, and a wide variety of animals have been bred for many different purposes, for example sheep, cattle, and pigs for food, dogs for hunting or herding, horses for racing or for pulling heavy loads, and mice and rats for scientific research. Since World War II, intensive breeding underpinned by the principles of genetics has greatly improved yields of milk, meat, and wool from farm animals in Western countries. Animals are selected for breeding on their physical characteristics, the character of their parents and siblings, and on the results of *progeny

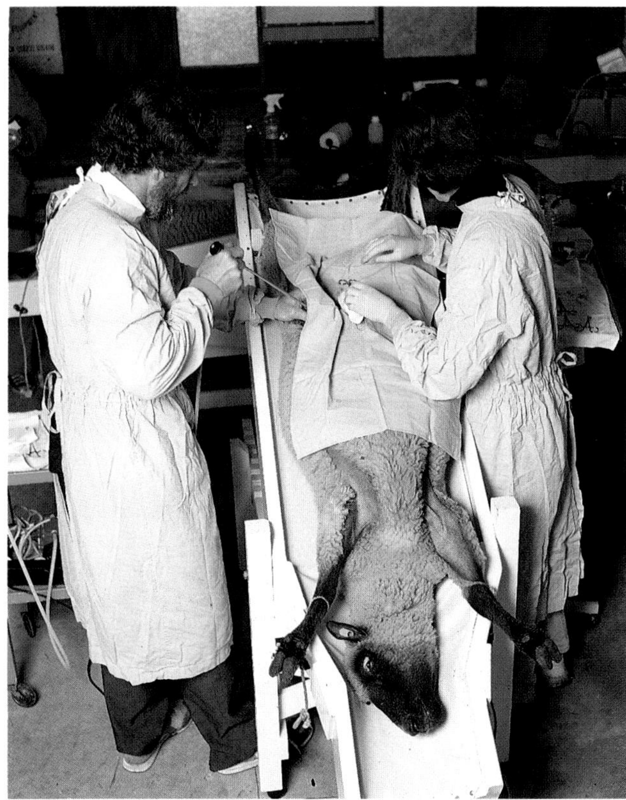

Implantation of an embryo into a ewe. Eggs from a female with the desired breeding characteristics undergo *in vitro* fertilization, and after a period of growth are transferred to surrogate mothers. The technique is widely used in **animal breeding**.

testing. Animals may be inbred (mated with closely related individuals) to maintain desirable characteristics, or cross-bred (mated with different breeds) or outbred (mated with unrelated individuals) to increase the genetic pool of a particular line or strain. *Artificial insemination is particularly important in dairy cattle, and is becoming more so in beef cattle, sheep, and pigs. This allows large numbers of offspring to be produced from a single sire which has desirable characteristics. The widespread adoption of a small number of breeds or even of lines within a breed, and the consequent disappearance of many other breeds, has led to concern about the reduction in *genetic resources that this implies.

animal husbandry *livestock farming.

animals, domestication of, the process by which wild animals are bred and reared under human control and adapted for such purposes as meat, milk, or wool production, and hunting. Domestication has only been achieved with a small number of the wild species available. In most cases the time and place of domestication remain obscure, but cattle, goats, sheep, pigs, and camels were certainly domesticated at least 7,000 years ago. The initial reason for domestication was invariably the provision of meat. However, livestock were readily adapted to provide more than one resource. Cattle also supplied milk and hides, sheep gave wool, and domestic birds provided eggs. Domestication of multi-purpose animals occurred world-wide. Llamas and reindeer provide region-specific examples. More recent domestications have been confined to specialized animals, like the silkworm.

annealing, a heat treatment in which a material at high temperature is cooled slowly. In metalworking this is done to reverse changes such as *work-hardening that have taken place during cold working, so that the metal once more becomes malleable and ductile (capable of being drawn out without cracking). Unlike *tempering, annealing is not a finishing process. Glass is annealed to avoid internal stresses, so that the cold glass does not shatter.

anode, the positive *electrode, usually made of metal, in a *thermionic valve, *cathode-ray tube, or *battery. The anode attracts negative charges or electron current, and is the electrode by which electrons leave a system. (See also *circuits, electrical and electronic.)

anodizing, a process in which a tough, thin, adherent film of metal oxide is built up by *electrolysis on the surface of a metal to protect it from *corrosion and physical damage. Anodized aluminium appears white, but can be coloured with dyes; anodized titanium can show a variety of colours depending on the thickness of the oxide film.

answering machine, a device that connects to a subscriber's *telephone receiver to record messages from callers while the subscriber is unavailable. Messages are recorded on magnetic tape. A request to leave a message is recorded on the first part of the tape, the callers' messages on the remainder. After each message the tape rewinds to the start. At the next call, the invitation is replayed and the tape then winds quickly forwards to the end of the previous message. The subscriber can play back messages over the telephone by using a sound signal to activate the machine.

antenna, a device, usually a simple conductor, for the transmission or reception of *electromagnetic radiation, also known as an aerial. If the transmitting antenna is vertical, the most effective reception antenna will also be vertical. The transmission effectiveness of an antenna system depends greatly on the signal *frequency used. Conventional ultra-high frequency (UHF) and very high frequency (VHF) transmissions for radio and television can normally only be received on a line-of-sight basis. Any conductor may act as an antenna, although at microwave frequencies a simple slot cut in a *waveguide will suffice. However, the commonest type of antenna is the simple *dipole, more usually represented in refined form as the *Yagi antenna used for UHF (ultra-high frequency) television reception.

anthracite *coal.

anti-ballistic missile (ABM), a *missile designed to destroy *ballistic missiles or *warheads in flight, either just before or after re-entering the atmosphere. Their numbers were limited as a result of the Strategic Arms Limitation Talks (SALT) (1969–79) and very few have been deployed. The Soviet Union has a screen of ABMs protecting Moscow, and the USA deployed Patriot ABMs during the Gulf War (1991). The problems involved in destroying the large numbers of warheads released by a *multiple independently targetable re-entry vehicle just before they fall on the target has resulted in other anti-ballistic defence systems being investigated, such as the *Strategic Defense Initiative ('Star Wars') in the USA.

antibiotic, any substance produced by a living organism, or made synthetically, that is capable of destroying or inhibiting the growth of micro-organisms. Antibiotics are widely used in the *chemotherapy of microbial infections. The first antibiotic, *penicillin, was discovered by Alexander *Fleming in 1928 and developed for clinical use by *Florey. Streptomycin was developed by *Waksman in 1944, and was later followed by tetracyclines, cephalosporins, and other compounds. Antibiotics differ from each other in their chemical structures and mode of action. Most are selective, in that they are effective against only a few types of organism. Recently, however, synthetic derivatives have been produced with a wider range of activity, the so-called broad-spectrum antibiotics. Like other chemotherapeutic agents, antibiotics may be harmful to the host as well as killing the target micro-organism; streptomycin, for instance, may occasionally damage the inner ear. In addition, some patients develop an allergy which, in the case of penicillin, may be dangerous. The most serious problem is that the organism may become resistant to the antibiotic, making treatment ineffective. Resistant bacterial strains can cause epidemics that cannot be treated by the usual antibiotics. Resistance is most likely to arise in patients who receive inadequate doses of a drug repeatedly or over long periods. For this reason antibiotics should be taken only under medical supervision. Despite their dangers and disadvantages, antibiotics remain powerful tools in human and veterinary medicine, and their use has contributed greatly to the dramatic fall in the death-rate from communicable diseases over the last fifty years.

antibody *immunology.

anticoagulant, a substance that prevents clotting, especially of the blood. Anticoagulants such as heparin are added to blood that is to be stored before use in *blood transfusion and to specimens taken for laboratory examination. They are given to patients in *cardiology and cardiac surgery to reduce the risk of thrombosis (blood-clot formation) after heart operations.

antidepressant *psychotropic drug.

antifreeze, now almost always an approximately equal mixture of ethylene glycol ($CH_2OH{\cdot}CH_2OH$) and deionized water to which rust inhibitors are added. Such formulations are used extensively to protect *cooling systems such as car radiators, which rely on circulating water. Antifreezes give freeze protection down to −40 °C and boil at about 116 °C.

antigen *immunology.

antimony (symbol Sb, at. no. 51, r.a.m. 121.75), a lustrous, silvery-white, brittle element, intermediate in properties between a non-metal and a metal. The principal *ore is stibnite, which occurs in China and South America. Antimony is obtained by heating the ore with iron, or by roasting it to form the oxide, followed by reduction (see *oxidation and reduction) with carbon. Antimony is used in semiconductors, alloys for bearings, storage-battery plates, and *type metal. Antimony trisulphide is used in safety matches.

anti-oxidant, a general term to describe compounds that prevent reaction of a substance with *oxygen from the air. Anti-oxidants are important *food preservatives, and are used in the formulation of paints and plastics and to prevent the formation of gum in the *petrol for car engines.

antisepsis, prevention of the spread of disease-carrying micro-organisms. The term was first used by the British physician John Pringle in 1752. Many surgeons of the 18th and 19th centuries noted that by observing strict cleanliness during operations they could significantly reduce the incidence of infection, though they were unable to explain why. Later, the work of *Pasteur and others identified the cause of these infections as bacteria. This led to the use, by *Lister and others, of carbolic acid to eradicate them. Since then, other methods of killing bacteria and viruses have been introduced, including heat treatment (autoclaving) and ultraviolet light. (See also *asepsis, *sterilization.)

anti-tank gun, an *artillery weapon firing ammunition designed to destroy *tanks. The problem of piercing a tank's armour was at first solved by using solid shot at high velocities, so that at impact the round broke through the armour. During World War II, tank armour became too thick to be penetrated in this way, and the hollow charge shell was developed. This shell had a hollow metal nose, behind which was an explosive charge that detonated on impact. The detonation wave passed forwards, melting the hollow nose of the shell and directing a high-speed jet of molten metal and explosive gas against the target. Most modern anti-tank missiles also use hollow charges.

anvil, in its modern form, a heavy block of iron, often with its surface hardened by *tempering or facing with steel, on which work is supported while *forging. Early anvils were flat stones, used only for the simplest *blacksmithing work. Modern anvils vary in design according to the work to be done: commonly there is a flat beak at one end, and at the other a rounded one for making forgings such as horseshoes. The anvil is as old as the working of metals, and was in use before the Iron Age.

aperture (photography), the opening through which light is allowed into a *camera. The size of the aperture is controlled by the iris diaphragm, a ring of overlapping plates within the lens system, with a central opening that can be varied in size. The aperture size controls the amount of light entering the camera: together with shutter speed, it determines the amount of exposure that a film receives. The diaphragm control ring has a scale of *f*-numbers; the squares of the *f*-numbers being inversely proportional to the amount of light admitted to the camera. For the same light conditions, similar film exposures can be achieved using a large aperture with a fast *shutter speed, or a smaller aperture with a slower shutter speed. However, the two exposure settings will give different results, because with a smaller aperture the depth of field (the depth of the image that is in focus at one time) will be greater than with a larger aperture. (See also *exposure meter, *automatic exposure.)

apiculture, the care and breeding of bees to obtain honey and, to a lesser degree, beeswax and 'royal jelly' (food prepared by the bees for young queens). Although evidence exists for the tending of bees since 2400 BC, apiculture on a commercial scale became possible only with the invention of the modern framed hive, patented by the US clergyman L. L. Langstruth in 1852. This permitted continuous collection of honey without disturbing the colony and made it possible to retain bees with desirable characteristics. Apiculture is

Edwin 'Buzz' Aldrin descending from the lunar module during the **Apollo** 11 mission in 1969, in which astronauts first landed on the moon.

also important for the pollination of seed and fruit crops. For example, to obtain good yields from high acreages of beans, farmers must supplement natural bee populations with hived insects. Great care must be exercised in the application of *insecticides to avoid killing the pollinators. Although wild bees provide a source of honey world-wide, their mixing with hived stock is generally undesirable, as interbreeding between wild and domestic bees can affect the latter's productivity and docility.

Apollo programme, the US space programme, announced by President John F. Kennedy in 1961, aimed at 'landing a man on the Moon and returning him safely to Earth'. After a number of ground tests (including one for the abandoned *Apollo 1* launching in which three astronauts were killed) and three unmanned flights, the first manned mission (*Apollo 7*) flew in 1968, powered by a *Saturn V* *launch vehicle. Three further *Apollo* flights tested the equipment and techniques to be used in the Moon landing. Then in 1969 *Apollo 11* was launched to make the first manned Moon landing. The three astronauts travelled in the command module, which was docked during flight to both the lunar module and the service module, the latter carrying fuel and supplies. On reaching the Moon, the command and service modules remained in orbit with Michael Collins on board, while Neil Armstrong and Edwin ('Buzz') Aldrin landed on the Moon's surface in the lunar module. There were five more successful missions to the Moon; for the last three the astronauts had a wheeled lunar roving vehicle to help them explore further. In all, *Apollo* astronauts took about fifty experiments to the Moon and brought over 380 kg (840 pounds) of rock back to Earth. Since the last Apollo mission in 1972, there have been no further manned flights to the Moon.

Apollo–Soyuz project, the only docking in space to date of Soviet and US spacecraft. The *Apollo* and *Soyuz* spacecraft could not be directly joined because they had different atmospheres, and so a docking module incorporating an airlock was built. In 1975 the two spacecraft were launched, *Apollo* carrying the docking module; they docked two days later. The two cosmonauts and three astronauts, who had trained together and learned each other's languages, each visited the other spacecraft and together they carried out joint experiments for two days. This co-operation demonstrated the feasibility of a space rescue by either country, should this prove necessary.

Appert, Nicolas François (1750–1841), French pioneer of food preservation by canning. The son of a hotelier, and resident chef in his father's hotel, he first experimented with the preservation of food by traditional methods such as pickling. He later discovered that food could be preserved indefinitely by prolonged heating and then sealing in the absence of air, anticipating *Pasteur's research on bacterial spoilage by fifty years. In 1812, he established a commercial plant at Massy, France, from which grew a vast international canning industry. At first he used glass containers, but in about 1814 metal cans were introduced.

applications program, a computer *program such as a *spreadsheet designed to perform the functions required by the end-user, rather than being part of the *operating system. An applications package is a suite of programs directed at some generic application (for example, *word processing or *computer graphics) that can be tailored to the needs of specific instances of that application.

applied mathematics, a branch of mathematics which deals with the manipulation of experimental data and other information relating to real physical systems. At its simplest, applied mathematics can be used to calculate the time taken for a steadily moving projectile to reach its destination. At its most complex, it can predict the existence of subatomic particles that have yet to be discovered. The origins of applied mathematics are documented in early Egyptian writings of 1700 BC, when arithmetical calculations were developed to meet the practical need for counting and dividing up goods and money, calculating land and building areas, and calculating volumes of various materials. There is also evidence of the use of mathematics in China from the Shang dynasty (16th–11th century BC) onwards. Applied mathematics deals with equations whose variables refer to real systems. It is used today throughout all aspects of the pure and applied sciences and technology. The solution of problems in *mechanical, *civil, *electrical, and *chemical engineering depends heavily on applied mathematics. Experimental data from real systems can be processed using calculations which lead to more generally applicable conclusions.

One of the most important research tools of applied mathematics is mathematical modelling, which is able to predict how an experimental system will behave without actually having to build it in reality. Computer *simulation using mathematical models can, for example, enable medical students to experiment with different courses of treatment without any risk to real patients. The reactions of trainee astronauts to equipment malfunction can be tested without exposing them to danger. Attempts by chemists and physicists to describe the structure and nature of matter have relied heavily on applied mathematics. The systems involved are made up of small atomic or subatomic particles that do not obey the classical or Newtonian equations of motion. Quantum mechanics is the applied mathematics of the subatomic world. At the other end of the scale, astronomers use Einstein's theories of relativity to describe the structure of the universe and to interpret processes that occur in vast expanses of space and time.

Manufacture of a low-cost Pelton wheel (a type of water turbine) in Lima, Peru, an example of the use of **appropriate technology**. The turbines are used in small-scale hydroelectricity generation.

appropriate technology (alternative technology, intermediate technology), an approach to the development and use of technology, dating from the late 1960s, reflecting a concern for minimizing environmental impact and increasing social equity. A pioneer in this field was the British economist E. F. Schumacher, whose book *Small is Beautiful* (1969) argued against large-scale, centralized technology based on profit considerations, and called for a more human-oriented approach. Attempts to apply this approach in the Third World have led to the development of an intermediate technology, using local skills and resources, as opposed to capital-intensive high technology, or indigenous low technology. Intermediate technology has made significant contributions to health care, agricultural practice and food production, manufacturing, and energy production. Examples include the development of small, locally made water turbines to drive grinding mills and to generate electricity; inexpensive, easily manufactured building materials for low-cost housing; the manufacture of cheap, efficient stoves able to utilize a range of fuels; and improved tools and equipment for agriculture and craft professions. The organization of collective or co-operative groups has given many poorer people access to otherwise unaffordable technology, for example pumps for irrigation or to ensure water supplies. Somewhat similar concepts applied in Western countries have given rise to the term 'alternative technology', implying an alternative to existing forms of technology. The initial emphasis of alternative technology was on rural self-sufficiency, often using *organic farming practices. Subsequently the Western alternative technology movement, along with the environmental movement, has emphasized renewable energy technology (for example, *solar, *wind, or *tidal energy); and conservation of energy and raw materials through such methods as improved building *insulation and *recycling. In the 1980s commercial wind farms were developed in California, USA, and Denmark, and research was undertaken world-wide into solar and *geothermal energy, *biofuel energy crops, and other renewable energy sources. Some developments have moved away from the 'small is beautiful' concept into large-scale high technology. However, given proper funding, renewable energy technology could play an important role in helping to solve many of our perceived energy and environmental problems.

aquaculture, the growing of aquatic plants and animals under controlled conditions for commercial, scientific, and recreational purposes. Aquaculture has existed since about 500 BC, but has gained widespread commercial importance only in the past 40 years. *Fish farming provides fish for food, and also supplies stock for sporting waters and for ornamental use. Invertebrates such as shrimp, crayfish, lobsters, prawns, food and pearl oysters, mussels, and scallops are also reared in *shellfish farming. Edible seaweed is a traditional part of Japanese diet and is grown by aquaculture in sheltered coastal regions. Aquaculture also provides *fish products for the pharmaceutical and chemical industries.

aqualung, a device invented in 1943 by the Frenchmen Jacques-Yves Cousteau and Emile Gagnon to enable a diver to operate independently under water. The diver carries compressed air in one or more cylinders on his or her back. Air passes from the tanks to the diver's mouth via a tube, the regulator, which equalizes the pressure difference between the water outside and the air inside the diver's lungs. The safe depth limit for diving with an aqualung is around 60 m (200 feet). (See also *deep-sea and diving technology.)

aqueduct, often a *bridge that carries a water channel, but also, more generally, the system of *canals, *siphons,

The Pont du Gard **aqueduct** near Nîmes, France. This Roman aqueduct was built in the 1st century AD, and still carries water at a height of over 55 m (180 feet) above the valley floor. Three tiers of arches were used to achieve the required height without loss of stability.

*tunnels, and bridges forming the main distribution channel for domestic or industrial water supply, for irrigation, or for *hydroelectric power generation. Water loss to the ground can be prevented by lining the canals with concrete or asphalt, while the risk of contamination to drinking-water supplies is reduced by covering over the channel. The aqueduct is built to a gradient of at least 1 in 6,000 so that water flows by gravity where the general slope of the terrain allows. In a pressure conduit the water may flow by gravity (as in an inverted siphon) or it may be pumped; it is confined within the closed conduit and exerts a bursting pressure upon its walls. To cope with this, conduits are commonly made from large-diameter welded steel or reinforced concrete, or are lined tunnels through solid rock. In hydroelectric schemes the water pressure in the penstocks (the pipes delivering water to the turbines) may be very high, on account of the fall between the reservoir and the turbines. Notable modern aqueducts include those serving Los Angeles and New York; the most extensive of the ancient systems are Roman aqueducts.

Arab technology. The science and technology of the Arab world found its full flowering with the advent of Islam in the 7th century. It derives from the Hellenistic tradition associated with the great centre of learning at Alexandria. The influence of Islam stretched from Baghdad to Cordoba. Arab scholars translated long-forgotten classical texts, enriching them with Arabic innovations and the wisdom of India and China. These texts were later discovered by Western scholars, and served to fuel the European intellectual movement of the Renaissance. From this stemmed the Scientific Revolution of the 16th and 17th centuries, Newtonian physics in the 17th, and the Industrial Revolution in the 18th. Arabic technology flourished in many fields, including water-raising devices and irrigation, *windmills, textiles, *paper, ceramics, glass, and metalworking.

arable farming, the cultivation of large areas of land, as opposed to smaller-scale, more intensive *horticultural cultivation. *Cereals are the major arable crops, accounting for over 50 per cent of all cultivated land world-wide; *root and *forage crops are also important. The first stage in crop production is to prepare the soil, which should have a structure of large pores for drainage and aeration, interspersed with smaller pores to retain moisture. Weeds must be cleared, and previous crop residues broken up. These objectives are achieved by tillage: initially the ground is *ploughed, and then broken up further by *harrows, land rollers, or *cultivators. Weeds may be killed with *herbicides. In *minimum-tillage farming this ground preparation is kept to a minimum, to preserve as much as possible the soil's natural structure. *Fertilizers and other soil conditioners may be added at this stage, then the seed is sown using a *seed drill. The developing crop is protected by *pesticides and other forms of pest management, and when ripe it is harvested by a *combine harvester or other appropriate *agricultural machinery. The types of crop grown on the same land year by year is known as the cropping system. Crops may be rotated, with a variety of crops being grown to maintain the nutrient balance of the soil, or the same crop may be grown each year (monoculture), with chemical fertilizers supplying nutrient deficiencies. Monoculture carries a potential threat of disease, and usually 'break' crops are grown at intervals to reduce this risk. Break crops may be animal *forage, pulses, temporary pasture, or cash-crops such as oil-seed rape, sugar beet, sunflowers, tobacco, or cotton.

A hand-cranked **Archimedean screw** being used in Egypt to raise water. Such devices are cheap, sturdy, reliable, and do not require a weed screen to filter out debris from the water.

aramid fibre *nylon, *liquid-crystal polymer.

arch *structural engineering.

Archimedean screw, a spiral screw rotating inside a close-fitting cylinder or semicircular conduit, used as a conveyor or lifting device for water or granular material. It is named after *Archimedes, who is reputed to have used such a device to empty a ship of water, but is probably earlier. It offers a very energy-efficient way of providing a hydraulic head at water and *sewage-treatment works.

Archimedes (*c.*287–212 BC), Greek mathematician and inventor. Although best known as a brilliant mathematician and the founder of the sciences of statics and hydrostatics, he was also an ingenious engineer who applied his talents to a wide range of practical problems. When the Romans besieged his native Syracuse in 213 BC, he invented a range of ballistic weapons that considerably delayed the capture of the city. Archimedes also developed in detail the principle of the lever and of the multiple pulley. However, inventions such as the *Archimedean screw may have been wrongly ascribed to him.

arc lamp, a lamp invented by *Davy in 1805 that emits a brilliant light by the production of an electric spark, or arc, between two closely spaced carbon electrodes in air. The arc lamp was used in the 19th century for street-lighting, but proved unpopular due to its unreliability. Arc lamps have been largely superseded by *incandescent lamps, but have been retained in applications that require an intense light, for example searchlights and lighthouse lamps.

Argand burner, an efficient type of oil lamp, patented in 1784 in Britain by Aimé Argand, a Swiss. Air is admitted via a metal tube to the inside of a cylindrical wick: a glass chimney further increases the air supply. The wick provides a large contact area between the flame and the fuel, while the air supply ensures complete combustion. The principle of the Argand lamp was later applied to *gas lighting.

argon (symbol Ar, at. no. 18, r.a.m. 39.9), an inert, gaseous element found in minute proportions in the Earth's atmosphere. It is obtained from the *fractional distillation of air. It is used in gas-discharge lamps, to provide an inert atmosphere in electric light bulbs, and create a non-oxidizing atmosphere in modern arc-welding equipment.

Ariane *launch vehicle.

arithmetic and logic unit *central processing unit.

Arkwright, Sir Richard (1732–92), British inventor of machinery for spinning cotton. After working as a barber and wig-maker in Lancashire, he turned his attention to local industry and to mechanizing the spinning of cotton. He took out his first patent in 1769 and eventually perfected a *spinning machine in which the cotton was drawn out by rollers. Originally Arkwright's frame was operated by a horse, but in 1771 he replaced horse-power by water-power and the machine became known as the water-frame. Later, he mechanized all the preparatory and spinning processes.

armature, the rotating assembly of coils and windings on a core (usually of soft iron or other similar magnetic material) that forms the rotor of an *electric motor or *generator. The term is also used to describe the component in an *electromagnet or *solenoid that moves in response to the electromagnetic field.

armillary sphere, the earliest known astronomical device, used from at least the 2nd century BC for observations of the heavens. It consisted of a skeletal celestial sphere with the Earth at the centre surrounded by a number of rotatable metal rings (usually nine) representing the Sun, Moon, and planets. It was widely used in the 14th and 15th centuries to teach navigators about the arrangement and motions of the heavenly bodies.

armour *body armour.

armoured vehicle, an armed, motorized military vehicle protected from enemy fire by armour plating. *Tanks are the principal type of armoured vehicle: other examples include armoured cars, armoured personnel carriers, *self-propelled guns, *amphibious vehicles, and specialized vehicles such as armoured bulldozers and bridge-layers. In the early part of World War I some automobile chassis were converted into armoured cars, and later the purpose-built armoured car (a wheeled vehicle with the main armament in a gun turret) was developed. Experiments were made with half-track vehicles, which have wheels at the front but tracks at the rear, but they proved inadequate for the terrain. World War II saw the development of two new vehicle types: the self-propelled gun, providing much greater mobility for *artillery; and the armoured personnel carrier, now probably the most important armoured vehicle after the battle tank. Originally, armoured personnel carriers were intended to carry troops into battle with more protection than in an unarmoured lorry, but since the 1960s they have been used for fighting as well as for transport. Purpose-built vehicles of this sort are known as MICVs (mechanized infantry combat vehicles). Generally, they carry a gun turret and perhaps a machine-gun or other weaponry, plus provision for its occupants to fire their own weapons from within.

Armstrong, Edwin Howard (1890–1954), US electrical engineer who made important contributions to *radio communication. In 1912, using the work of *De Forest and *Langmuir, he invented the regenerative circuit, which greatly increases the sensitivity of receivers and is the basis of all radio and television broadcasting. In the same year he and *Fessenden developed the heterodyne system, in which a weak received signal modulates a stronger, locally generated wave (see *radio receiver). In 1933 Armstrong pioneered a wide-band *frequency modulation (FM) system which greatly reduces interference from static, and in 1951 he devised the super regenerative circuit, which reduces noise from oscillations.

aromatic compounds *benzene, *hydrocarbon.

arrow *bow.

arsenic (symbol As, at. no. 33, r.a.m. 74.92), an element that occurs in three different forms, the commonest being a grey metallic substance. Arsenic is used in alloys as a hardening agent; in combination with *gallium it is widely used in *semiconductor devices. Many arsenic compounds are poisonous, and have been used as insecticides, wood preservatives, and weedkillers.

articulated locomotive, a railway engine with one or more pivoted driving units (power *bogies). Originally it was developed to provide greater power without loss of manœuvrability, or to spread the weight of a heavy locomotive over many axles for work on light track. The first articulated *steam locomotive was built in Switzerland in 1888. One of

A Beyer-Garratt **articulated locomotive**. Such locomotives were built for many countries, but were especially prevalent in south and east Africa.

the most successful articulated designs was the Beyer-Garratt locomotive, developed in the early 1900s. It carried the boiler and cab on a frame between two power units carrying fuel and water supplies. A number of such locomotives are still in use, for example in Zimbabwe. Almost all modern *diesel and *electric locomotives may be regarded as articulated, in that they are carried on pivoted power bogies.

artificial horizon, an instrument used in conjunction with a *sextant to measure the altitude (angle above the horizon) of a celestial body when the real horizon is obscured. Several types of artificial horizon are in use, but all provide a horizontal line or plane parallel to the plane of the true horizon, from which readings can be taken. This may be a spirit-level bubble or, more usually in aircraft, a horizontal reference provided by a spinning *gyroscope.

artificial insemination, the injection of semen into the female reproductive tract by other than natural means. Semen for insemination can be diluted, treated, and stored frozen for a considerable period. It is therefore possible to produce a large number of offspring from one sire. In animal breeding, *progeny testing is used to ensure the development of animals with desirable characteristics. Artificial insemination may also be used in humans if conception by natural means is not possible.

artificial intelligence (AI), a branch of computer science concerned with the theory and development of computer programs or systems which can perform tasks that are normally associated with human intelligence. Such tasks include decision-making and diagnosis, *pattern recognition, *speech recognition, computer vision, *machine translation of natural languages, and *robotics. At its most ambitious level AI has the goal of creating computers and robots capable of reproducing a broad range of human behaviour. There remain doubts about whether such systems are theoretically or practically possible.

Developing intelligent systems requires fundamentally different approaches from most conventional computing. To date, AI has been mainly a research activity in which much effort has been devoted to investigating the basic processes of thought, learning, decision-making, sensory processing, and language use. These aspects of AI are closely related to work in other fields, such as physiology, neurology, psychology, philosophy, linguistics, and mathematics. An important result to emerge from this research is the development of systems known as *neural networks, which can be 'taught' to solve problems. These show promise for a number of different AI applications, particularly those involving pattern recognition. The demands of AI have also stimulated the development of *computer languages, such as PROLOG and LISP, which are better suited to represent and process symbolic structures than more conventional languages.

Most approaches to AI require powerful computer *hardware, and it is only within the past decade that this has become sufficiently cost-effective to make practical applications possible. *Fifth-generation computers are being developed specifically for use in artificial intelligence. *Expert systems were amongst the first AI techniques to be used in practical applications.

artificial limb, a device replacing a limb, or part of a limb, for cosmetic or functional reasons. The earliest examples date back to the ancient Greeks. The French surgeon Ambroise Paré (1510–90) was the first to use artifical limbs in Europe. During the 20th century, new technologies have increased the usefulness and comfort of artificial limbs, notably in providing means to control movement in the replacement parts, in some cases by the detection of nerve impulses from neighbouring muscle groups. Uneven growth of limbs in children can be countered using prosthetic extensions. Customized prostheses to fit individual bones are made on computer-driven lathes. Today's carbon-fibre limbs are much stronger and lighter than artificial limbs of the past. Research is being conducted into computer-controlled and compressed-gas-powered limbs, intended to mimic closely the natural movements of the replaced limb.

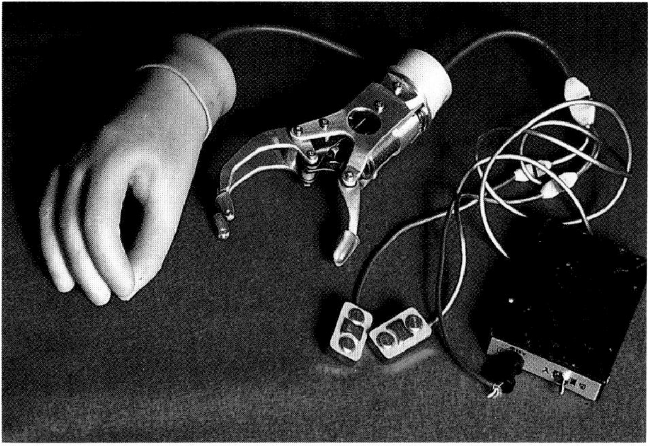

Photograph showing the development of the artificial hand. Technological achievements in the field of robotics have enabled more flexible and responsive **artificial limbs** to be manufactured.

artillery, war engines or *firearms too large to be managed by a single soldier. *Ballistas, onagers, and *catapults were early examples of artillery (see figure overleaf). Their use was largely restricted to siege warfare, and it was in such operations that *cannon came to replace them. Modern artillery functions in the same way as all firearms, but fires larger projectiles over longer distances. As with *rifles, the history of artillery has had two paths of development. Muzzle-loaders, common from the 15th to the 19th century, had their explosive charge and *ammunition loaded from the front of the barrel. Breech-loaders, used in the 15th and 16th centuries and reintroduced on a large scale in the mid-19th century, have the charge and shot loaded at the rear. Modern categories of artillery fire solid shot, *shrapnel, or explosive *shells. They include field guns, which fire with a flat trajectory, howitzers and *mortars, which have arching trajectories, *anti-tank guns, firing high-velocity shot, and *self-propelled guns. Since 1918 there has been a decline in the importance of heavy artillery as missiles, bomber aircraft, and armed helicopters have taken over many of their roles, while mortars have taken over many light artillery roles.

asbestos, a mineral fibre occurring in nature and obtained from silicate minerals containing SiO_4 groups linked into chains. The fibres are released from the rock by crushing followed by blowing. Only those fibres at least 1 cm (0.4 inches) in length are suitable for *spinning into yarn. Shorter fibres are used for such products as paper, millboard, and asbestos–cement building materials. Spun products usually contain 10–25 per cent of a rough-surfaced fibre such as cot-

Artillery

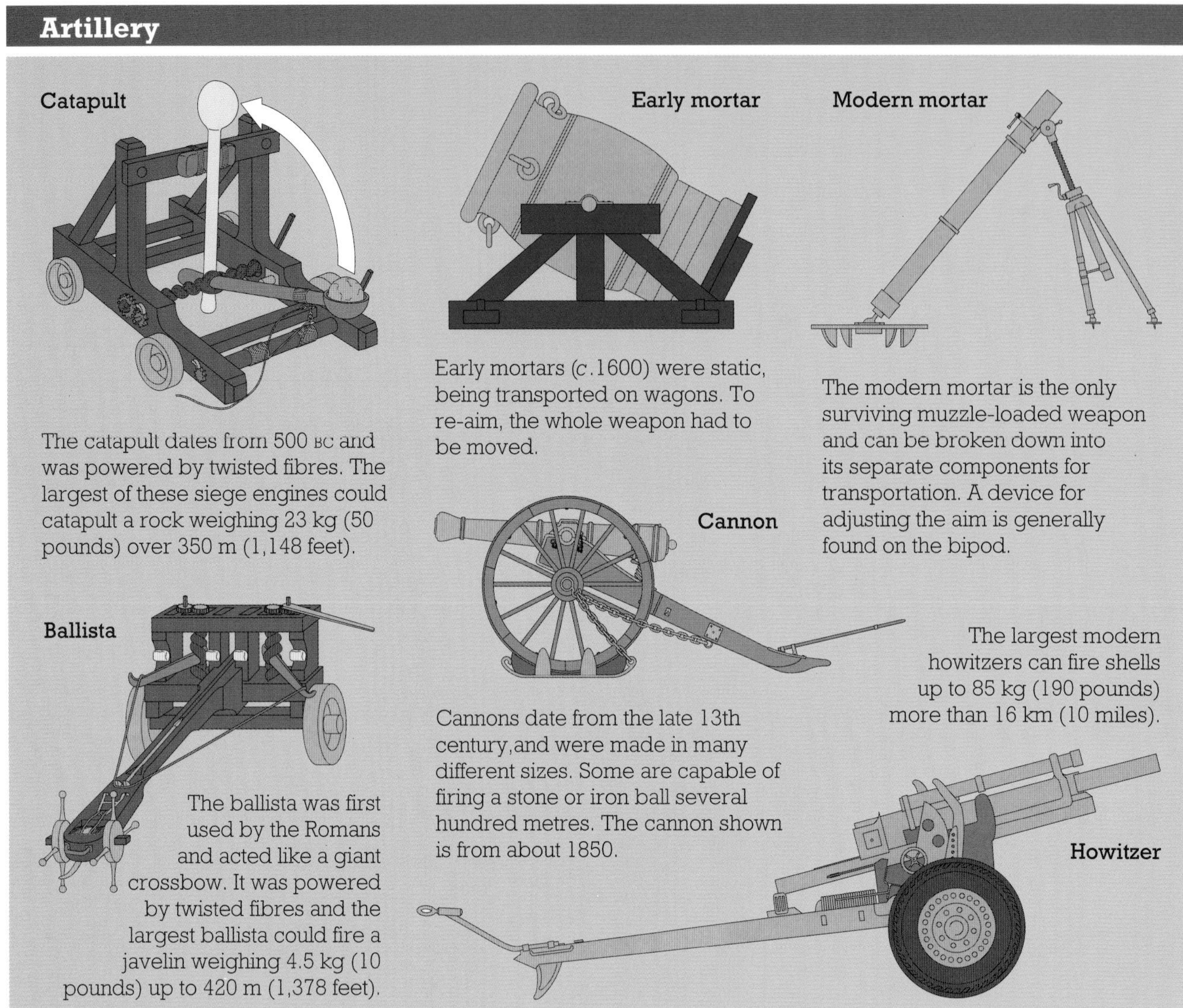

Catapult
Early mortar
Modern mortar
Early mortars (c.1600) were static, being transported on wagons. To re-aim, the whole weapon had to be moved.
The modern mortar is the only surviving muzzle-loaded weapon and can be broken down into its separate components for transportation. A device for adjusting the aim is generally found on the bipod.
The catapult dates from 500 BC and was powered by twisted fibres. The largest of these siege engines could catapult a rock weighing 23 kg (50 pounds) over 350 m (1,148 feet).
Cannon
Ballista
The largest modern howitzers can fire shells up to 85 kg (190 pounds) more than 16 km (10 miles).
Cannons date from the late 13th century,and were made in many different sizes. Some are capable of firing a stone or iron ball several hundred metres. The cannon shown is from about 1850.
The ballista was first used by the Romans and acted like a giant crossbow. It was powered by twisted fibres and the largest ballista could fire a javelin weighing 4.5 kg (10 pounds) up to 420 m (1,378 feet).
Howitzer

ton to facilitate the spinning of the smooth, brittle fibres. It is the non-flammable nature of asbestos fibre that gives it its industrial importance. Applications include brake linings, *building materials, electrical equipment, and thermal *insulation materials. Asbestos fabrics are used for *fire-fighting suits, safety apparel, and fire curtains. Since the early 1970s there has been growing concern about the effect of short asbestos fibres on human health. The short fibres are thought to cause asbestosis, a lung disorder leading to progressively greater breathing difficulties plus concomitant heart strain, and mesothelioma, a rapidly fatal form of lung cancer. This has led to a limitation in its use and to elaborate procedures for its safe removal from public buildings.

ASCC (computer) *computer, history of.

ASCII (American Standard Code for Information Interchange), the commonest way of representing text characters using *binary code in digital computer systems. The code covers the numbers 0 to 9, the alphabet, punctuation marks, and other special characters. Each number or letter is assigned a unique binary number: thus the character 'A' is 01000001 and '?' is 00111111. Each character is usually stored in one *byte. In computing terminology an ASCII file refers to a file that consists only of text or data without any special characters for controlling *peripherals. Another common data communication code is EBCDIC ('ebbseedik', Extended Binary Coded Decimal Interchange Code), which can code for 256 different characters, as opposed to the 128 codes available in ASCII. A new character set, called Unicode, represents characters with 16-bit rather than 8-bit 'words', and can therefore code for 27,000 different characters. This makes it possible to represent most letters, ideographs, and symbols of the world's main languages in Unicode.

ASDIC *sonar.

asepsis, the modern practice of rendering all equipment in contact with surgical or other wounds free from microbiological material which may lead to infection. Asepsis was combined with *antisepsis in the late 19th century, and largely replaced antisepsis in the 20th. Whereas antisepsis attempted chemically to disinfect instruments and especially wounds, aseptic techniques rely on heat or other physical methods for the *sterilization of equipment and so minimize the chances of wound contamination. Aseptic technique is now standard for any medical procedure, minor or major, where the skin is broken or where normally sterile internal cavities are opened.

Chrysler car bodies being welded on a robot **assembly line**, using spot-welding techniques under computer control.

aspect ratio *flight, principles of.

asphalt *bitumen.

aspirin *analgesic, *pharmacology (table).

assaying, the testing of metals or ores to determine their composition. Wet assaying methods involve the use of chemicals in solution and tend to be messy and slow. They have largely been displaced by dry physical methods, such as spectrometry and *mass spectroscopy, which require much more sophisticated apparatus, but give more accurate results quickly and easily. However, some simple assaying methods, such as the *touchstone, are still in use.

assembly language, a computer language that represents *machine code programs in a form people can read. Each machine code instruction is represented by a short mnemonic code. *Memory registers and storage *addresses may be referred to by symbolic names rather than numeric codes, and labels and comments can be used to improve legibility. Assembly language programs have to be translated into machine code by a special program called an assembler before they can be run on the computer. Because an assembly language represents machine code instructions directly, it is specific to a particular type of *central processing unit.

assembly line, a method of manufacturing a complicated product by means of a series of operations performed by people or machines, each operation adding one or more parts. The method has largely superseded traditional manufacturing methods in which one person built a complete unit from constituent parts. Frequently the assembly line is formed around a moving belt or a railed track along which the product is moved either continuously or intermittently. This method was pioneered for motor-car assembly by *Ford in 1913; it enabled him to use semi-skilled labour to produce cars cheaply and in quantity. An assembly line is appropriate for manual assembly of parts, but is equally applicable to *automation, where parts are made and assembled by machines. The assembly line is a major concern of production engineering; its success depends on careful planning and design, mechanical handling of parts, continuous supply of material, inspection, maintenance, and control. In some fields, linear assembly lines are being replaced by cellular assembly, in which small teams of workers are responsible for a particular stage of production, for example preparation and painting of a car's bodywork. (See also *mass production, *robotics.)

astrolabe, mariner's, an early instrument for *navigation. It was derived from the older astronomical astrolabe (a two-dimensional model of the heavens with sights for observations) by the Portuguese in the late 15th century. It was used by navigators to measure the altitude (angle above the horizon) of a celestial body, and comprised a metal disc graduated in degrees, with a rotating sight vane pivoted at the centre. The astrolabe was held or hung vertically, and the sight vane adjusted to align with the celestial body. A much cheaper instrument serving the same purpose was the *cross-staff.

atomic bomb *nuclear weapon.

atomic pile, the name given to the world's first *nuclear reactor, built under a squash court at Chicago University in 1942 by *Fermi. Rods of *uranium fuel were interspersed in a 'pile' of graphite blocks: the graphite acted as a moderator (see *fission, nuclear), slowing down neutrons to speeds at which they were effective in splitting further uranium atoms. Rods of cadmium were used to control the reactor. The pile was activated only long enough to achieve a self-sustaining *chain reaction: it was then shut down. The atomic pile demonstrated that controlled nuclear fission was feasible, and it provided the basis for early nuclear reactor designs.

atomic power *nuclear power.

atoms and molecules. Atoms are the smallest stable particles into which an element can be subdivided. Molecules are groups of two or more atoms chemically bonded together: a molecule is the smallest portion of a substance to retain that substance's chemical identity. The many complex materials around us can be separated into pure substances of two sorts: elements, which are composed of identical atoms and cannot be broken down into simpler substances; and compounds, which are composed of identical molecules. Substances exist in one of three states, solid, liquid, or gas (see figure overleaf). Changes of state can be brought about by changes in temperature or pressure.

The atoms of any one element are different from the atoms of all other elements: the unique nature of the atoms and molecules in a pure substance give it a unique set of physical and chemical properties. Atoms are composed of even smaller, 'subatomic' particles, which cannot exist in isolation. Most important of these are the electron, the proton, and the neutron. They were discovered through investigations into the nature of radioactivity. The relative atomic mass (r.a.m.) of an atom is concentrated in the protons and neutrons of the nucleus. The total positive charge on the nucleus is governed by the number of protons it contains and is called the atomic number (at. no.) of the element. (The number of electrons in an atom is also equal to the atomic number, since in an electrically neutral atom numbers of protons and electrons must be equal.) Each element has a different atomic number. The number of neutrons associated with the protons in the nucleus can vary, and therefore a range of atomic masses (*isotopes) is possible for a single element. Chemical reactions occur through interaction and redistribution of electrons in the outer layer (shell) of the atom. *Electricity and magnetism are also properties

Atoms and molecules

States of matter

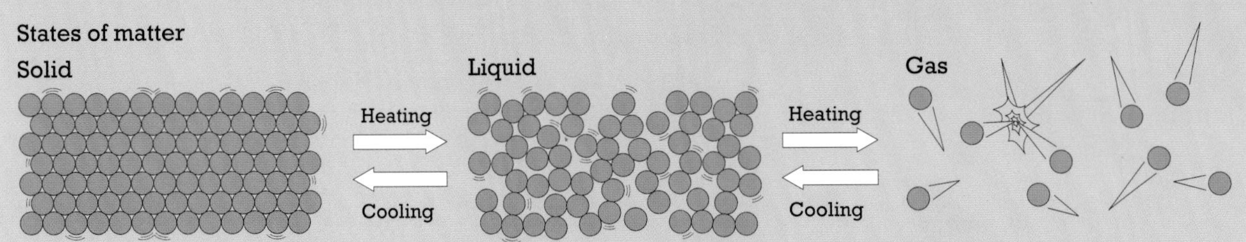

In solids the particles are closely packed in regular array, and vibrating about fixed positions.

In liquids the particles are closely packed but disordered, and move randomly.

In gases the particles are far apart, and travel rapidly in straight lines between collisions.

Atomic structures

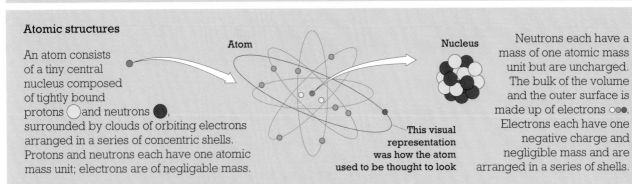

An atom consists of a tiny central nucleus composed of tightly bound protons ◯ and neutrons ●, surrounded by clouds of orbiting electrons arranged in a series of concentric shells. Protons and neutrons each have one atomic mass unit; electrons are of negligable mass.

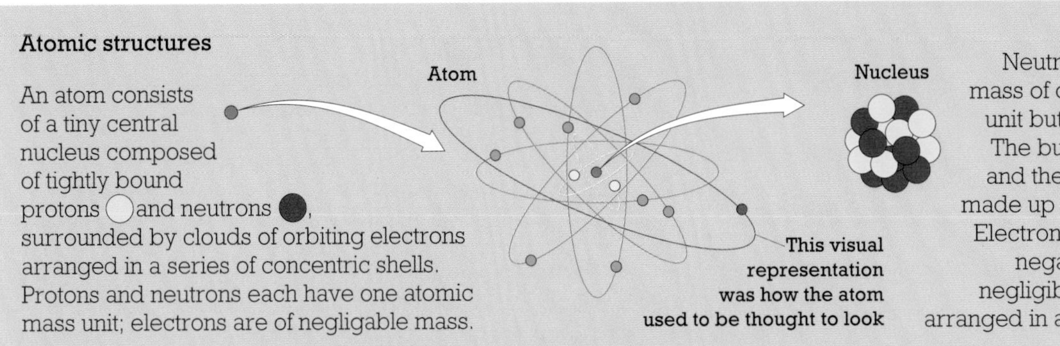

Neutrons each have a mass of one atomic mass unit but are uncharged. The bulk of the volume and the outer surface is made up of electrons. Electrons each have one negative charge and negligible mass and are arranged in a series of shells.

Forming compounds: Ionic bonding

When a sodium atom reacts with a chlorine atom an electron is transferred from the outer shell of the sodium atom to the outer shell of the chlorine atom. This leaves the sodium as a positive ion with an overall charge of plus one and the chlorine as a negative ion with an overall charge of minus one. Both ions now have full outer electron shells. Thus sodium chloride is made of positive sodium ions and negative chloride ions locked together in a lattice by electrostatic attraction.

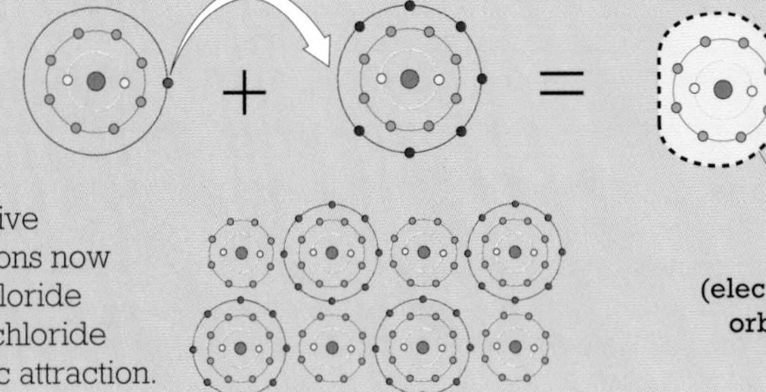

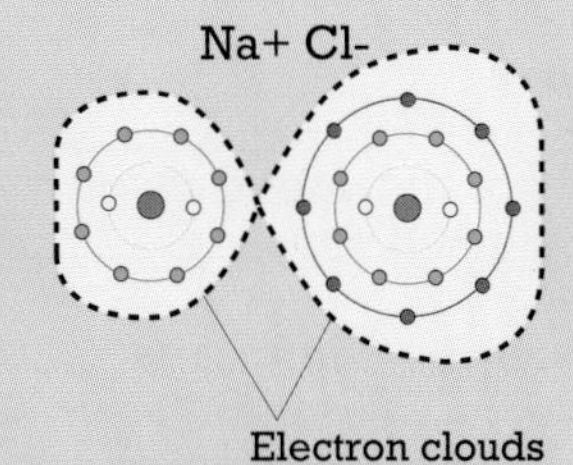

Electron clouds (electrons transferred; orbitals repulsed by each other)

Covalent bonding

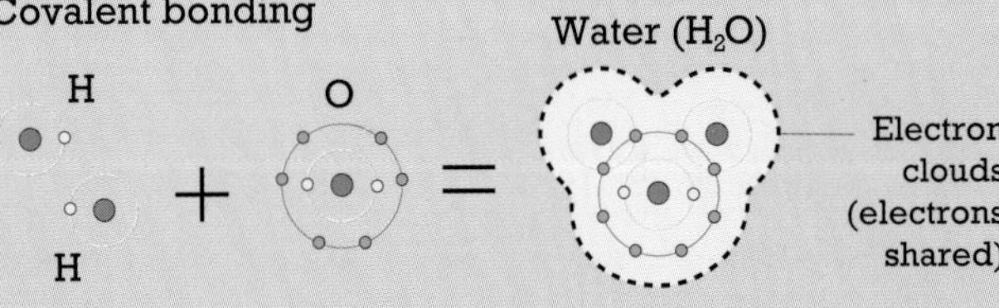

Electron clouds (electrons shared)

Water molecules are formed when hydrogen reacts with oxygen. In forming the water molecule hydrogen and oxygen atoms share electrons, to form strong, two-electron bonds. The forces of attraction between atoms within the molecule are much stronger than the forces of attraction between the separate molecules.

The Periodic Table of chemical elements

The elements are arranged in the periodic table in six horizontal rows (periods) in order of increasing atomic number. Elements in the same vertical column (group) have the same number of electrons in their outer shells. The number of electrons in the outer shell determines the chemical properties of that element, because chemical reactions depend on outer electron transactions.

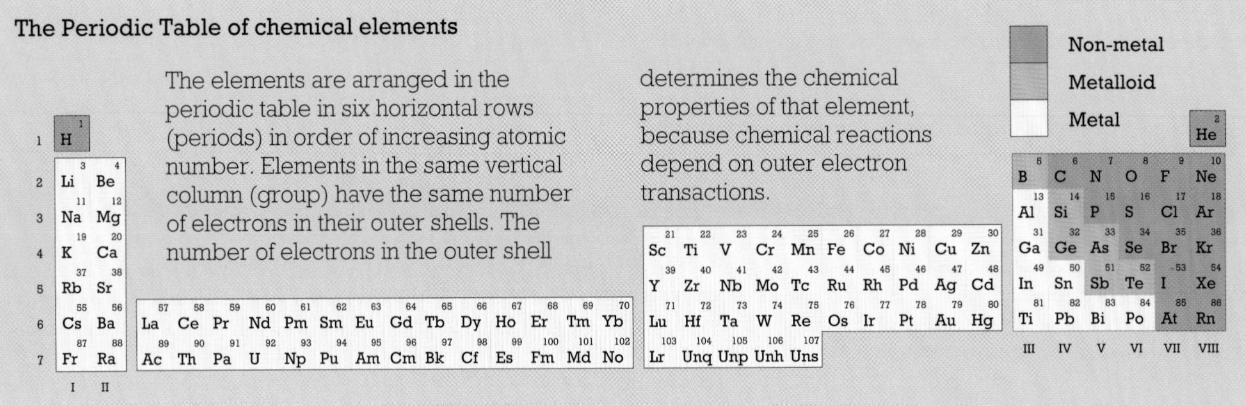

of the electrons of an atom. Atoms can react by losing electrons to form positively charged *ions (as most metals do), by gaining electrons to form negatively charged ions (as most non-metals do), or by sharing electrons to form covalent molecules (as most non-metals also do, particularly in *organic chemistry). *Nuclear energy is derived from the splitting (*fission) or *fusion of atomic nuclei.

If the elements are arranged in order of increasing atomic number, certain characteristic properties are seen to repeat at regular intervals. This is the basis of the periodic table, devised in 1868 by Dmitry Mendeleev (1834–1907), in which elements with similar properties are arranged in vertical groups. All elements in a particular group have the same number of electrons in their outer shells. Elements in group I, for example each have one electron in the outer shell. Using the patterns of properties within and across the groups of the periodic table, chemists have been able to predict the existence of previously unsuspected elements and the nature of their properties. Chemists can use this understanding of atomic structure to produce materials with desirable properties.

audiometer, a device used to measure acuteness of hearing. The most common type, the pure tone audiometer, comprises an adjustable-frequency *oscillator, an amplifier, and a precision volume control. Signals from the audiometer are played through headphones to subjects being tested, who indicate the lowest sound intensity that they can detect at a range of frequencies. The results are then compared with established standards of normal hearing.

Auer, Carl, Freiherr von Welsbach (1858–1929), Austrian chemist who invented the gas-mantle. At the University of Heidelberg, under the German chemist Robert *Bunsen, he pursued research on the group of closely related metals known as the *rare earths. There he discovered that an intense light is emitted when asbestos fibres impregnated with salts of cerium and thorium are strongly heated. This is the basis of the gas-mantle, which he patented in 1885. This discovery prolonged the life of gas lighting, then being increasingly threatened by *electricity. He also invented Auer metal (a cerium–iron alloy), the 'flint' of gas and cigarette lighters.

auger *drilling and boring tools.

autofocus, a mechanism on a camera for automatically moving the lens in order to focus an image on the film. This can be achieved by measuring the distance to the photographic subject. A pulse of infra-red rays or *ultrasound emitted by the camera bounces off the subject and returns to a detector in the camera. The time delay between sending and receiving the pulse is a measure of the distance between camera and subject. An electric motor moves the lens to the correct focal position on the basis of this measurement. Another type of autofocus adjusts the lens for maximum image contrast, which is achieved when the image is sharply focused.

autogyro (US, autogiro), an *aeroplane propelled by a conventionally mounted engine and propeller, which obtains most of its lift from an unpowered rotor similar to that of a *helicopter. The rotor spins in the airstream generated by the aircraft's forward motion, thus providing the required lift. First developed by the Spanish engineer Juan de la Cierva in 1923, the autogyro was popular during the early 1930s because of its short take-off and landing capabilities. Development ceased with the advent of the helicopter.

automata, animated models of, for example, human figures, animals, or birds, which contain their own motive power such as a wound spring. Their origins go back to the Greeks; in 400 BC Archytas of Tarentum is said to have made a wooden pigeon that could fly. In the Middle Ages, German and Swiss inventors constructed many ingenious automata, such as singing birds in a cage, and these became very popular in the 19th century. Between 1875 and 1880 the British magician J. N. Maskelyne exhibited automata that played cards and drew pictures. Fairground organs often included one or more moving figures playing instruments. Since the 1960s a great variety of self-acting toys has become available, usually electrically powered from a battery and sometimes radio-controlled. Automata theory is a branch of mathematics concerned with the study of abstract, rather than practical, machines. In particular, it underlies the theory of computation. The *Turing machine is an abstract machine of fundamental importance. (See also *robotics.)

automatic exposure, an electronic system in a *camera that automatically selects the correct *aperture and *shutter settings to give a correct film exposure in different lighting conditions. There are three main types of automatic exposure control. In aperture priority, the photographer chooses the aperture setting and the camera selects the appropriate shutter speed. With shutter priority, the photographer selects a suitable shutter speed, and the camera automatically sets the correct aperture. In programmed selection, both aperture and shutter speed are chosen automatically according to a pre-programmed system.

automatic landing (US, autoland), a method whereby, especially in conditions of poor visibility, an aeroplane fitted with appropriate equipment can approach an airport and receive high-precision signals from an instrument landing system. It is automatically guided down on to the runway, has its engines throttled back, and its brakes applied, all without the aid of the pilot. Now fitted to many *airliners, the system was first tried experimentally in 1964, and first used commercially in 1965.

automatic pilot (autopilot, autohelmsman), an electronic device in an *aeroplane, *spacecraft, or *ship which automatically steers and keeps the vehicle on a pre-set course and at a pre-set speed. The steering vane used by single-handed yachtsmen is perhaps the simplest type of automatic pilot: the vane is set to the wind, and keeps the vessel on a constant course as long as the wind stays constant. Complex automatic pilots note deviations on *gyroscopes within *gyro-compasses and *accelerometers and automatically stabilize a vehicle about its three axes of yaw, pitch, and roll (see *flight, principles of). They also restore it to the pre-set course and speed if there is any divergence, and can be programmed to alter the vehicle's direction and speed automatically. On many long-distance air journeys an automatic pilot is used to cut down crew workload. On *military aircraft the device can also receive signals from sensing and weapon-aiming systems to direct the aircraft towards a target. *Automatic landing devices for aircraft are a form of autopilot.

automatic train control, a system to ensure that the instructions from trackside railway signals are not ignored by the driver. Where there are very intensive services, such as on London's underground railway, the system automatically halts the train in the event of the driver over-running a stop signal. On main-line services a more flexible train control system, such as the UK's Automatic Warning System (AWS), is needed. A magnetic device between the tracks, some 200 m (650 feet) before the signal, sounds a horn in the driver's cab if the signal shows danger. If the driver does not acknowledge the horn, the train's brakes are applied automatically. A more recent development is fully automatic train operation (ATO). This not only provides for safe operation of trains but controls their speed throughout the route and stops the train in a controlled manner at each station.

automatic transmission, a replacement for the manually controlled *gearbox, which adjusts itself automatically to conditions of speed, acceleration, and gradient. There are three main types: the earliest, a semi-automatic fluid drive, used a hydraulic coupling with epicyclic *gears, and enabled gear changes to be made by simply pressing a pedal. Later a hydraulic torque converter was developed, for use with or without an epicyclic gearbox. The latest type is a continuously variable transmission (CVT), using a steel or rubber belt running between 'vee' pulleys (see *belt and chain drive) of variable spacing. All automatic transmissions aim to match the power and *torque available from the engine to the demands of the vehicle; when the gearbox has a finite number of gear ratios an ideal match cannot be obtained at all times, and there is a small jerk on changing gear. A torque converter gives stepless changes, but energy is lost in fluid function, increasing fuel consumption. The CVT is more efficient, and can give smooth operation with low fuel consumption, due to ideal matching of engine and gearbox under microprocessor control.

automation, the use of automatic machinery and systems, particularly those manufacturing or data-processing systems which require little or no human intervention in their normal operation. The term was used in 1946 to describe machinery being developed by the Ford Motor Company to move automobile components and workpieces automatically to and from other machines. The origins of the concept are much older, dating at least to the early *time and motion studies carried out by Frederick Taylor in Philadelphia, USA, during the 1880s in an attempt to improve the efficiency and productivity of workers and machines.

The most familiar example of a highly automated system is perhaps an assembly plant for automobiles or other complex products. Such a plant might involve the automatic machining, welding, transfer, and assembly of parts, using equipment and techniques such as *numerically controlled *machine-tools, automatically controlled *robot arms, and guided vehicles, automated warehousing, materials handling, stock control, and so on. Advances in automation have been the result of a combination of many factors, including modifications to the physical layout of production or processing facilities to ease handling; improvements in materials to facilitate manufacturing processes; increasing mechanization of individual processes (the carrying out of tasks by machine rather than human actions), which often necessitates changes to the processes themselves; changes in product design to aid mechanization and mass production; more advanced *instrumentation and *control systems for both individual machines and for plants as a whole; and the adoption of *information technology as an integral part of the production process, leading ultimately to the concept of *computer-integrated manufacturing. Over the last few decades automation has evolved from the comparatively straightforward mechanization of tasks traditionally carried out by hand, through the introduction of complex automatic control systems, to the widespread automation of information collection and processing. Whereas in the past automation has involved a high degree of standardization and uniformity in production, the increasing use of information technology has now made it possible to develop more *flexible manufacturing systems.

automobile *motor car, *motor car, history of.

aviation *flight, principles of, *flying, history of.

aviation fuel, a petroleum derivative (see *petroleum refining) used to power aeroplanes. Aviation spirit is a very high-octane petrol designed for use in piston-type aircraft engines. Jet engines use a fuel derived from paraffin (US, kerosene): military aircraft use fuels including both petrol and kerosene. Aviation fuels must burn very cleanly, and must have a low freezing-point to avoid solidification at high altitudes.

avionics, usually, electronics as applied to aircraft, spacecraft, or missiles, although ground-based equipment may sometimes be included. Electronic instrumentation onboard aircraft has reached a high level of sophistication. For example, after take-off a *military aircraft such as a *fighter plane can be flown automatically to the target area by computer control of the *automatic pilot. *Radar systems can then search for and locate a target, guide the aircraft towards it, and fire weapons at the optimum moment, all without pilot aid. Modern navigational systems offer a high degree of accuracy, and head-up displays avoid the pilot having to glance down at critical moments by projecting vital information directly on to the aircraft windscreen. (See also *fly-by-wire systems.)

AWACS (Airborne Warning And Control System), a term used to describe an aeroplane carrying a large *radar capable of detecting distant enemy aircraft, missiles, and occasionally ships. By flying the radar at altitude, its range and early-warning capability are greatly increased compared to ground-based radar. The AWACS can transmit information to a ground- or ship-based control centre, or deal with

A Boeing E-3A Sentry aircraft carrying **AWACS** equipment. The rotodome mounted on top of the fuselage carries the rotating antenna of a very powerful search radar.

the threat itself by calling up fighter aircraft, missiles, or ships. The first aircraft designated AWACS was the Lockheed RC-121C in 1954, part of the US Early Warning and Control Squadron.

awl *drilling and boring tools.

axe, a hand tool with the blade running parallel to the handle, generally used for splitting timber. It is one of the most important of all hand tools, dating from Neolithic times. Although primarily a woodworking tool, the axe has found other uses, for instance as the double-headed battle axe. Occasionally an axe and an *adze blade were combined in a double head. Generally a heavy, two-handed tool, the axe exists in a smaller version, often with a hammer-head as well as a cutting edge, commonly known as a hatchet. The earliest axes were made of reindeer antlers, with the tine (point) sharpened to a cutting edge. Later, the stump end was hollowed out to hold a sharp flint, and later still, the heavy flint head was lashed to a wooden handle. When casting in bronze, and later iron, was introduced, it became possible to make a socket into which the handle could be inserted. (For illustration see *tools, history of.)

axle, a fixed or rotating rod to which a wheel or group of wheels is attached: in most cases the axle is fixed, while the wheel turns. There is usually some kind of lubrication between the axle and the wheel, and often the wheel turns on *bearings. The axle itself often bears the load of the vehicle to which it is attached, for example in carriages and bicycles. However, in the motor car and the lorry the axle is mounted within a tube or secondary axle, which is the load-bearing component.

azo dye, any member of a group of *dyes produced from a diazonium salt (formed by the reaction of *aniline, or a derivative, and nitrous acid at low temperature) and a *phenol or amine. The linking group between the atoms of the salt and the coupling agent is called an 'azo' group (−N=N−). Varying the nature of the aniline derivative and the reacting phenol or amine produces different colours. Azo dyes are used to dye cloth, and also as food colouring (see *food additives). The first azo dye (aniline yellow) was made in the 19th century by *Griess. Materials can be dyed by soaking in a solution of the phenol or amine, drying, and subsequently reacting with a diazonium salt solution; by this method the dye is formed within the fibres.

B

Babbage, Charles (1792–1871), British pioneer of mechanical computing. While Professor of Mathematics at Cambridge University (1828–39), he sought to eliminate errors in mathematical and astronomical tables through machines that would both perform the calculations and print the results. In 1822 he demonstrated a 'difference engine', to compile tables of logarithms, to the Royal Astronomical Society, but the machine was never finished. From 1832 he began to work instead on an 'analytical engine', designed to perform a variety of arithmetical operations and programmed by punched cards adopted from the *Jacquard loom. Although never completed, the analytical engine embodied all the essential elements of a modern digital computer—control, memory, arithmetic unit, input, and output. It also incorporated conditional branching—the ability to modify the course of calculation according to results already achieved. Babbage was actively assisted by *Lovelace. The *Science Museum is currently raising money to build a working version of the analytical engine. (see also *computer, history of.)

back-staff *quadrant.

bacterium, a single-celled micro-organism lacking a nucleus and enclosed in a complex cell wall (for illustration see *cell biology). Bacteria display little variety of shape, but are chemically extremely diverse. They grow very fast by simple cell division (*cloning) to form colonies. Bacteria are essential in the decomposition of organic matter, and in soil formation. They are also necessary for the breakdown of sewage, and are used in the production of certain fermented foods, for example cheese and other *dairy products, and pickles. They may also be used in the future to break up oil slicks in a technique known as bioremediation: hydrocarbons in the oil are turned into carbon dioxide, and fatty tissues into food for sea life. In *biotechnological applications, bacteria are cultured on a large scale to produce chemical products such as vitamins and enzymes in industrial quantities. A minority of bacteria cause disease, often through the manufacture of toxins. The control of such bacteria is important in *food preservation, and in many medical situations. Other bacterial species are the source of antibiotics, both against other bacteria, and against fungi. Bacteria are used as tools in *genetic engineering; for example, bacteria can be used to insert genes for disease or herbicide resistance into plants; they are also used in *biological pest control.

Baekeland, Leo Hendrik (1863–1944), Belgian-born US chemist who invented bakelite, the first industrially important plastic. He graduated from the University of Ghent, Belgium, in 1882, emigrating to the USA in 1889. There he made a fortune from his development of Velox photographic paper, an invention which he sold to *Eastman (pioneer of the Kodak camera) in 1899. In 1905, he began exploring the thermosetting plastic product resulting from the reaction between phenol and formaldehyde, and in 1909 he patented bakelite (a *phenol-formaldehyde resin), which he began to manufacture in 1911. It was used for hard-wearing items such as handles and electrical fittings.

John Logie **Baird** demonstrating an early television system in London, 1925. The picture on the tiny screen was made up of just thirty lines, and only five pictures were transmitted per second.

Bailey bridge *bridge.

Baird, John Logie (1888–1946), British pioneer of *television. Baird was educated in Glasgow, and embarked on various unsuccessful business ventures before his health failed. He then devoted much of his time to developing a primitive television system, with which he gave many public demonstrations from 1925 onwards. From 1929 Baird's equipment was used for UK public television broadcasts, taken over by the BBC from 1932. However, in 1935 Baird's photo-mechanical system was displaced by an electronic system developed by *Blumlein for EMI in 1935. In 1944 Baird developed the Telechrome tube, the forerunner of modern electronic colour television.

bakelite *Baekeland, *phenol-formaldehyde resin.

bakery, a place in which *bread and cakes are made, and sometimes also sold. In all bakeries, the processes involved in bread-making are essentially similar, but large modern bakeries are usually highly mechanized (see figure). Often a sponge dough process is used for leavened bread, in which all the yeast and some of the flour are mixed and left to ferment, then the rest of the flour is added to form the final dough. After the second mixing the dough is divided up and rounded by machine, then left to 'proof' or rise: this intermediate proofing restores elasticity, pliability, and volume to the dough. A moulder then flattens the dough and rolls it into cylinders before it is put into loaf tins and left to proof a second time. Bread ovens may be of various types, but the most common for large-scale production is the tunnel oven, in which the loaves travel on a metal belt through a connected series of baking chambers. After baking, the bread may be sliced and packaged before distribution to retail outlets.

Bakewell, Robert (1725–95), British animal breeder who did much to improve existing breeds of horses, sheep, and cattle, especially for meat. As such improvements were then not eligible for protection by patent, he did not disclose his methods. It appears, however, that he developed desirable traits by outbreeding and then stabilized them by inbreeding (see *animal breeding). He rarely sold his beasts, making his money by renting out stallions, bulls, and rams by the season.

balance *weighing machine.

baler, a machine used on high-volume crops such as hay to make tightly packed bundles, convenient for transport and storage. The crop is forced into a chamber by a ram, and then tied. Stationary balers, developed in the 19th century, used wire to tie bales. Early tractor-pulled balers used their own engines to power the compression rams and the pick-up mechanism that collected the crop from the ground. Modern rotary balers use plastic twine or tape for tying, and roll the crop into high-density bales weighing around half a tonne. (See *agricultural machinery for illustration.)

ball-bearing *rolling bearing.

Bakery

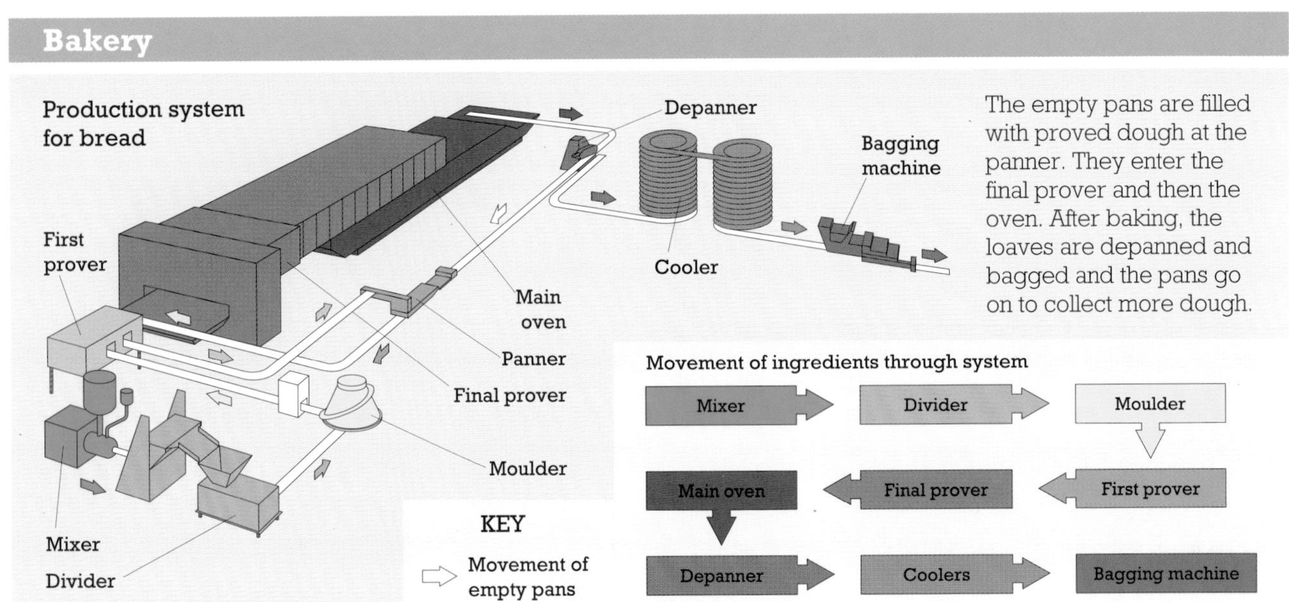

The German V2 rocket, the first successful **ballistic missile**. The V2 had a range of around 350 km and carried a 1-tonne conventional warhead at a speed of over 5,000 km/h (3,500 m.p.h.).

ballista, an early form of mechanical *artillery. The earliest Greek version, dating from the first half of the 4th century BC, used a large *bow laid across one end of a grooved batten. A refined model, developed by the Romans, replaced the bow with two vertical springs made from bundles of animal sinews, each with an arm passing through it. The arms were connected by a bowstring. The bowstring was pulled back by a windlass, secured at the end of the batten, then released, propelling a bolt or stone. (See artillery for illustration.)

ballistic missile, a *missile which, after launching, follows a trajectory determined by speed and gravity only. Strictly speaking, spears and shells are ballistic missiles, but today the term refers chiefly to long-range nuclear missiles, which make most of their flight outside the Earth's atmosphere. The first long-range ballistic missile was the V2 rocket, developed in Germany from 1936 under the technical direction of von *Braun. During World War II, more than 2,000 V2s were launched against Belgium and the UK. Modern ballistic missiles are accelerated to high velocities by *rocket motors for approximately 3–5 minutes, but after burn-out they follow an unpowered, ballistic trajectory. During powered flight they use *inertial navigation systems to attain the correct speed and direction, and homing devices (see *guided missile) to divert them from their natural trajectory towards their intended target at the end of the flight. The largest ballistic missiles are the inter-continental ballistic missiles (ICBMs), which, with a range of over 10,000 km (6,000 miles), have revolutionized the practice of warfare. The first ICBM was the Soviet SS-6, which was introduced in 1957. The latest types can launch a *multiple independently targetable re-entry vehicle, striking separate targets over a wide area. (See also *anti-ballistic missile, *Strategic Defense Initiative.)

balloon, a lighter-than-air aircraft with no propulsive power. It usually consists of a large, rounded bag (the envelope) inflated with hot air or a light gas such as helium or hydrogen. It may have instruments or a passenger basket suspended beneath it. A small hot-air balloon was demonstrated in Lisbon in 1709, but attracted little attention. The first free flight by humans was made in a hot-air balloon, built by the *Montgolfier brothers, in 1783. Balloons developed quickly in the 19th century, but with the advent of *airships and *aeroplanes, interest died for a time. However, balloons became an important tool in upper atmospheric research in the 1930s, and during World War II balloon barrages were used extensively in the UK to protect cities, ports, and important installations from low-flying aircraft. Ballooning as a sport remains popular today. (See also *flight, principles of, *flying, history of.)

bandwidth, a range of *frequencies needed to transmit a signal. A telephone signal requires a bandwidth of 4 kHz, whereas a television picture is much more complex, requiring over 5 MHz. In computing, bandwidth refers to the number of *bits per second transmitted between two digital devices. The bandwidth between a microcomputer and its hard disk is around 10 Mbit (10 million bits) per second; between a supercomputer and its memory the bandwidth could be around 100,000 Mbit.

Banting, Sir Frederick Grant (1891–1941), Canadian physician who led the team that developed the successful treatment of diabetes with insulin. After serving in World War I, he set up in practice as a surgeon in London, Ontario. In 1920, inspired by an article linking the malfunction of certain pancreatic cells to diabetes, he conceived the idea of extracting an anti-diabetic hormone from these cells. By 1922, in association with C. H. Best (a student), J. J. R. Macleod (a medical colleague), and J. B. Collip (a chemist), he had demonstrated that diabetes could be controlled with an extract from the pancreas that they named insulin. For their discovery, Banting and Macleod were awarded the Nobel Prize for Physiology and Medicine in 1923.

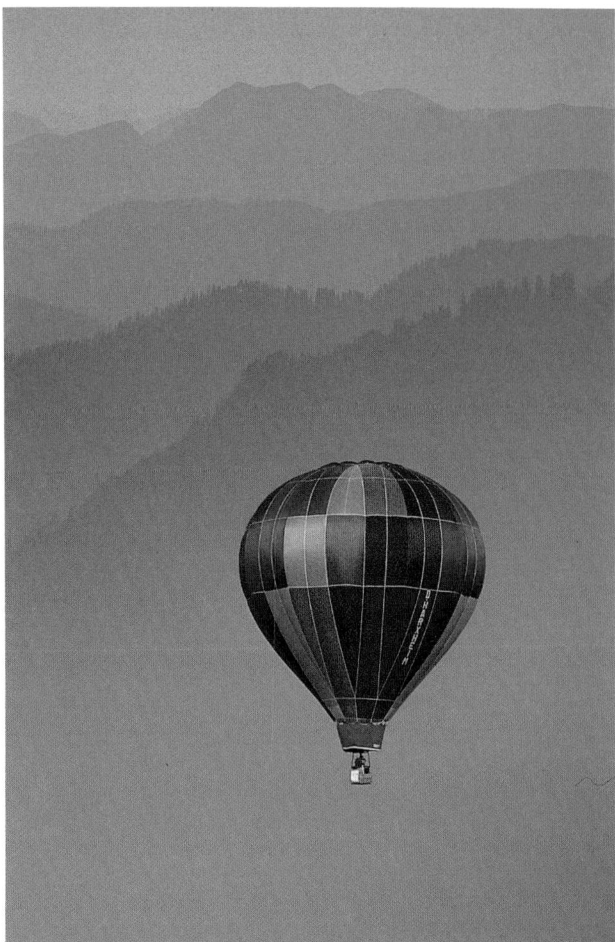

A hot-air **balloon** of the type widely used for sport and leisure since the 1960s, when the compact propane burner and lightweight synthetic materials were introduced.

Barbegal water-mill *water power.

barbiturate, any member of a group of drugs derived from barbituric acid, that are used for their action on the brain. Barbiturates can be injected intravenously before an operation to induce *anaesthesia. At one time they were taken orally for sleeplessness or anxiety, but since they produce dependence they have now been largely superseded by *tranquillizers. They are still used in the treatment of epilepsy. (See also *pharmacology.)

bar code, an identification system that can be read by a computer. Though there are several variations, they all consist of printed patterns of lines and spaces which record information such as price and batch number as a *binary code. A computer-based *cash register or *point-of-sale system can read bar codes optically.

Bardeen, John *Shockley, William Bradford.

barge, a term used for several types of vessel, but most commonly for a flat-bottomed freight vessel used chiefly on inland waterways and in shallow coastal waters. Early barges were sailing vessels, but with the construction of *canals, animal and later mechanical haulage became common (see *canal barge). In the late 19th and early 20th centuries steam-powered, and later diesel-engined barges were introduced. As competition from rail and road haulage became more fierce in the 20th century, larger-capacity barges were introduced. On suitable river navigations such as the Mississippi and Ohio rivers (USA) and the Rhine and Mosel (Europe), powered barges are now used to tow assemblies of up to forty unpowered (dumb) barges. Dumb barges or 'lighters' are also used for unloading ships, and for general port and river use.

barium (symbol Ba, at. no. 36, r.a.m. 137.33), a soft, silvery-white metal. It is a reactive element, which ignites spontaneously in moist air. Barium is obtained by the *electrolysis of fused barium chloride or by reduction of the metal oxide with aluminium in a vacuum furnace. It is used in alloys, and in fireworks to give a green flame. Barium compounds are generally toxic, but barium sulphate can be ingested, and is widely used in medicine as a contrast medium for *radiology of the gut.

Barnard, Christiaan Neethling (1922–), South African pioneer of heart *transplant surgery. After various clinical appointments he became a specialist cardio-thoracic surgeon at the University of Cape Town in 1958. He became interested in the possibility of replacing fatally diseased hearts by healthy ones from accident victims. He performed the world's first human heart transplantation operation in 1967. He also initiated the replacement of diseased heart valves by artificial ones.

barometer, a device for measuring atmospheric pressure, one of the most important of all meteorological instruments. In the traditional instrument, devised by Evangelista Torricelli in 1644, the pressure of the atmosphere is balanced against that of a column of mercury: the height of the column is a measure of the pressure. Standard atmospheric pressure is defined as 760 mm (30 inches) of mercury (Hg) at mean sea-level, but modern meteorologists use the bar: 1 bar = 750.07 mm Hg. The aneroid barometer depends on the very tiny movement of the surface of an evacuated metal capsule in response to pressure changes. The movement is mechanically transmitted to a pointer pivoted at the centre of a circular dial. Because it is portable, compact, and cheap, this arrangement is widely used for domestic barometers. The same principle is used in barometric *altimeters, to measure height above sea-level. In barographs a continuous record of pressure changes is made on a rotating drum.

barque (US, bark), a term commonly used to describe a small sailing ship. From the mid-18th century it denoted a type of ship's hull, flat-bottomed and designed for carrying cargo. Around the beginning of the 19th century, the term referred to a way of rigging a three-masted ship, with a *square-rig on the fore and main masts, and *fore-and-aft rigging on the mizen or rear mast (see *sailing ships and boats for illustration). A variation was the barquentine, square-rigged only on the foremast. In the late 19th century, large, multi-masted bulk carriers that shipped grain and other cargoes to South America and Australia were barque-rigged because this required fewer crew.

bascule bridge, a bridge with a pivoted, counterbalanced floor (deck) which can be raised at one end. This or a *swing bridge is used to span waterways with a low clearance height between the deck and the water, while still allowing the passage of occasional tall shipping below. The counterweight

Basket-work in Rajasthan, India. No satisfactory basket-making machine has yet been devised, and there is therefore still a substantial demand for hand-made baskets, particularly in Third World countries.

reduces the effort needed to raise the deck. Amsterdam has many wooden bridges with overhead counterbalance beams and counterweights. Larger steel bridges use tanks, which can be filled with water or emptied, to assist the raising and lowering of the deck. London's Tower Bridge over the River Thames, built in 1886–94, uses two bascules to span 61 m (200 feet).

base (chemistry) *acids, bases, and salts.

BASIC *computer language.

basic oxygen process (steel-making) *iron and steel industry.

basket-work, articles made from the plaiting or interweaving of such materials as osiers (willow shoots), reeds, cane, and split bamboo. Since antiquity, people have used basket-work to make dwellings, furniture, screens, boats, and containers. The raw material is first softened and then manipulated to form the complete article. Because the *tools required are few and elementary, basket-making represents an ideal home industry. Until the advent of machine-made containers, basket-work was generally the most economic method of making containers for industry.

bathysphere, a spherical steel vessel, forerunner of the modern *submersible designed by the US zoologist *Beebe for deep-sea exploration. It had a diameter of 1.45 m (4.75 feet), weighed 2,450 kg (5,400 pounds), and was fitted with Perspex windows. In 1934 Beebe and Otis Barton were lowered in it to a depth of 923 m (3,028 feet), then a record for deep-sea diving. Lateral movement was provided by a support ship on the surface, from which the bathysphere was slung. A development from the bathysphere was the bathyscaphe, an electrically powered deep-sea observation vessel that descended in 1960 to a depth of 11,000 m (36,000 feet).

battering ram *siege warfare.

battery, a term commonly used to denote a single voltaic cell; more correctly, it is two or more such cells connected together. A voltaic cell is a device that changes chemical

Battery

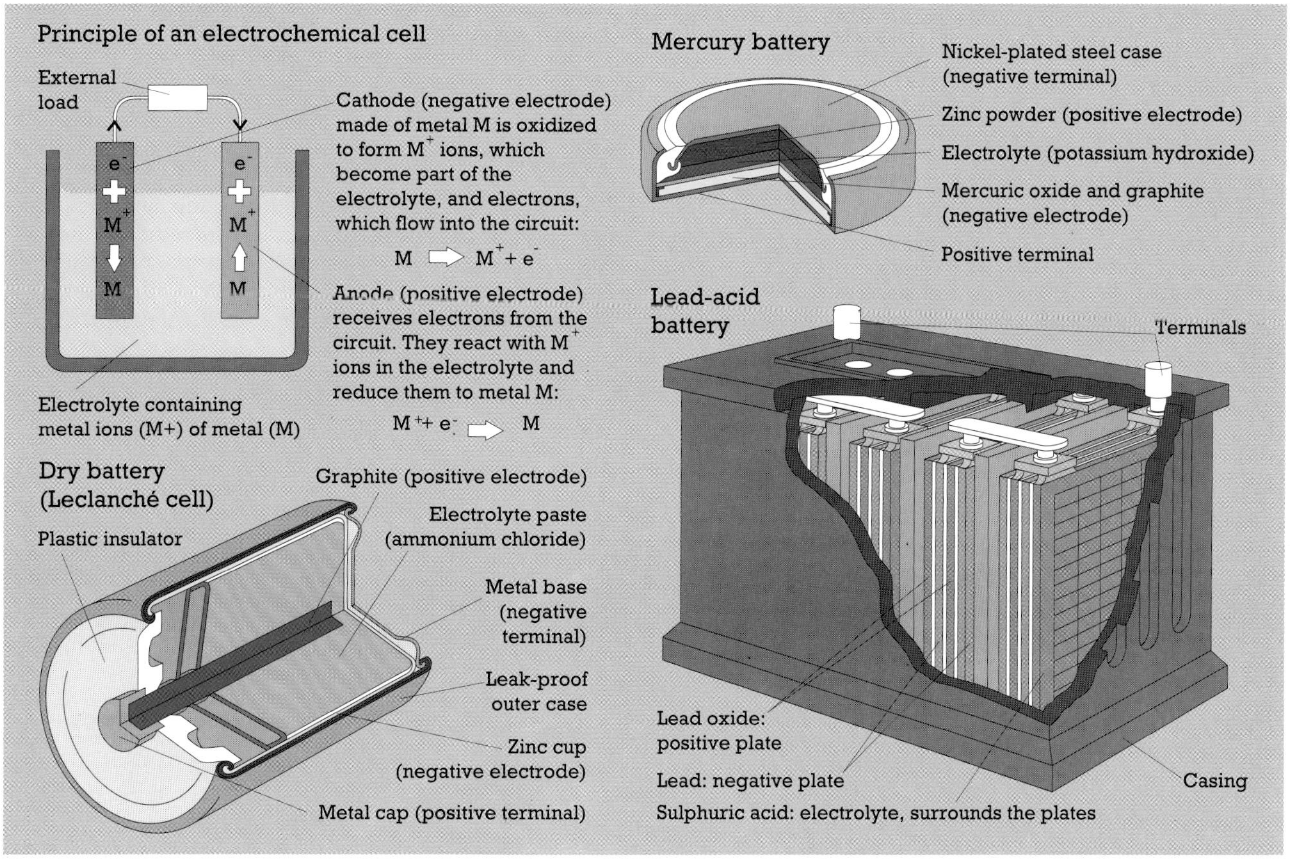

Principle of an electrochemical cell

External load

Cathode (negative electrode) made of metal M is oxidized to form M^+ ions, which become part of the electrolyte, and electrons, which flow into the circuit:

$$M \Rightarrow M^+ + e^-$$

Anode (positive electrode) receives electrons from the circuit. They react with M^+ ions in the electrolyte and reduce them to metal M:

$$M^+ + e^- \Rightarrow M$$

Electrolyte containing metal ions (M+) of metal (M)

Dry battery (Leclanché cell)

Plastic insulator

Graphite (positive electrode)

Electrolyte paste (ammonium chloride)

Metal base (negative terminal)

Leak-proof outer case

Zinc cup (negative electrode)

Metal cap (positive terminal)

Mercury battery

Nickel-plated steel case (negative terminal)

Zinc powder (positive electrode)

Electrolyte (potassium hydroxide)

Mercuric oxide and graphite (negative electrode)

Positive terminal

Lead-acid battery

Terminals

Lead oxide: positive plate

Lead: negative plate

Casing

Sulphuric acid: electrolyte, surrounds the plates

energy directly into electrical energy (see figure on the previous page). The first battery was constructed by *Volta in 1800. Similar principles but differing constructions were used for the *Daniell cell (1836) and the *Leclanché cell (1868), which developed into the universal dry battery. Such primary cells can be used once only and are used as portable sources of electrical energy in torches and communications equipment. Secondary cells (*accumulators), for example nickel–cadmium and lead–acid batteries, can be discharged and recharged and are used for heavy duty: car and lorry starter motors and emergency lighting systems, and for propulsion motors in submarines and specialist vehicles.

All voltaic cells contain two *electrodes, which are of different materials and are separated by, but are in contact with, an electrolyte. An electrolyte is a compound, or its solution in water, which conducts electricity through ionization (see *ion). When the connections are joined by an external wire, a current flows through the wire. A direct electric current leaves the cell from the positive electrode and re-enters by the negative electrode. The larger the surface area of the electrodes, the larger the current that the cell can provide. The electromotive force (e.m.f.) of a single electric cell is the maximum voltage that it can generate, that is the voltage across the cell when it is supplying no current. The value of the e.m.f. depends on the chemicals from which the electrodes are constructed. It is rarely greater than 2 volts, but cells can be connected in a series to make batteries that have higher voltages.

The electrolyte contains mobile ions and may be a solution, a paste, a molten salt, or a solid. It frequently contains a depolarizer which inhibits the formation of insulating gas bubbles on the electrodes. Wet cells, for example the lead–acid *accumulator, contain a mobile liquid electrolyte. Dry cells such as the zinc–carbon cell have a liquid electrolyte that has been immobilized by converting it into a gel or paste. The sodium–sulphur cell—still under development—is one of the few examples of a true dry cell. Operating at a temperature of 250 °C, it has an electrolyte of solid aluminium oxide. (See also *energy storage, *fuel cell.) .

battery farming *factory farming.

battleship, a class of warship carrying the heaviest armour and the largest guns. The name was first used after the *Industrial Revolution, when wood gave way to steel, and sail to steam. Perhaps the first true battleship (though not so called) was the British 9,210-tonne *Warrior*, launched in 1860. With the development of efficient breech-loading guns mounted in turrets and the introduction of a reliable steam-engine, the battleship achieved its fully developed form. In the early 1900s both the UK and the USA designed a new type of battleship, with a main armament of at least eight large-calibre guns, and powered by *steam-turbines. The ships were called dreadnoughts after the first vessel to be commissioned, HMS *Dreadnought*. Their appearance stimulated other navies to copy the design, but by the end of World War I dreadnoughts were in decline. Battleships continued to be important until the end of World War II, after which there was a decline in their use. By the early 1990s very few were in service.

baud rate, the unit which measures the rate of data transmission in computer communication systems, named after J.-M.-E. Baudot (1845–1903), a French telegraph engineer. Usually 1 baud is defined as a rate of 1 *bit of information per second.

Bazalgette, Sir Joseph William (1819–91), British civil engineer who rebuilt London's drainage system. Two major outbreaks of cholera in 1849 and 1853–4 made it clear that London's drainage system was totally inadequate for a city with a population of 7.5 million. In 1855 Bazalgette was appointed chief engineer to the Metropolitan Board of Works and within 20 years he had created a radically new drainage system. This involved construction of 160 km (100 miles) of large-diameter sewers and was the first large-scale use of concrete made with Portland cement, 70,000 tonnes of which were used.

beam *structural engineering.

beam-engine (lever engine), the earliest form of *steam-engine, invented by *Newcomen in 1712 for pumping water from mines. Chains were attached to either end of a rocking beam: one chain led to a piston enclosed in a cylinder, the other to the pump-rod down the mine-shaft. Steam from a *boiler entered the cylinder and pushed up the piston; the steam was then condensed by a spray of cold water, causing the piston to depress again, raising the pump-rod and delivering water. In 1765 *Watt greatly improved the *efficiency of the engine by using a separate condenser, and in 1782 he produced a double-acting engine in which the chains were replaced by rods to provide a push–pull action. Beam-engines are still used in a few water-pumping stations.

bearing, a support used in almost all machines to reduce friction and wear between moving surfaces, and to dissipate heat (see figure). The commonest use of bearings is to support a rotating shaft. In a journal bearing, the shaft fits closely within a smooth cylindrical sleeve made of a low-friction material such as brass, tin-based alloy, or a plastic. Lubrication is achieved by pumping *lubricating oil into the interface between shaft and sleeve. Some bearings are self-lubricating, being coated with a layer of powdered copper or bronze impregnated with oil or graphite. In *rolling bearings, polished chromium steel balls or cylinders are used between the moving surfaces, replacing the sliding action with a rolling one. Tilting-pad thrust bearings, used in ships, have pads between the moving surfaces, and oil is forced between pad and surface by a wedging action. Dental drills and centrifuges have air bearings, in which the moving surfaces are separated by a film of air.

A **beam-engine** made in 1788 by the British firm Boulton and Watt.

Bearing

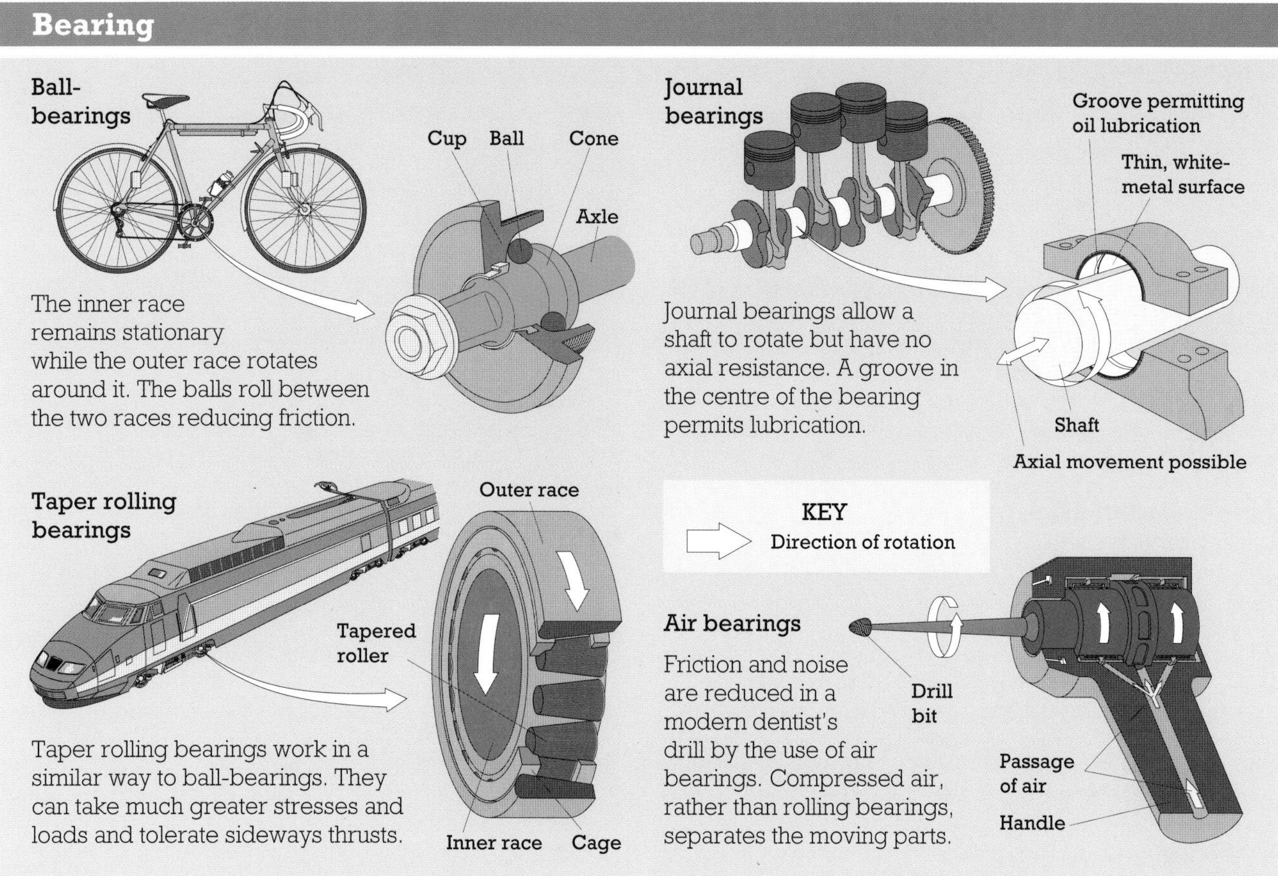
Ball-bearings
Cup Ball Cone
Axle
The inner race remains stationary while the outer race rotates around it. The balls roll between the two races reducing friction.
Journal bearings
Groove permitting oil lubrication
Thin, white-metal surface
Journal bearings allow a shaft to rotate but have no axial resistance. A groove in the centre of the bearing permits lubrication.
Shaft
Axial movement possible
Taper rolling bearings
Outer race
KEY
Direction of rotation
Tapered roller
Taper rolling bearings work in a similar way to ball-bearings. They can take much greater stresses and loads and tolerate sideways thrusts.
Inner race Cage
Air bearings
Friction and noise are reduced in a modern dentist's drill by the use of air bearings. Compressed air, rather than rolling bearings, separates the moving parts.
Drill bit
Passage of air
Handle

Beebe, Charles William (1877–1962), US pioneer of underwater exploration. Beebe was director of tropical research for the New York Zoological Society from 1919, and led numerous scientific expeditions. In 1930 he invented and constructed the *bathysphere, for use in underwater observations. In 1934, he and Otis Barton reached a depth of 923 m (3,028 feet) near Bermuda, and later dives reached depths of around 1.5 km (nearly 1 mile).

bee-keeping *apiculture.

beeswax, a type of *wax secreted from glands under the abdomen of a worker bee, from which it constructs honeycomb. Beeswax is commercially extracted by melting the honeycomb after the removal of the honey, then straining and pressing the wax to rid it of impurities. It is soft to brittle in texture and consists mainly of fatty acids and esters, which are insoluble in water but dissolve in organic *solvents. It melts at about 70 °C, and is used to make *candles, polishes, inks, cosmetics, and ointments.

Bell, Alexander Graham (1847–1922), UK-born US inventor of the *telephone and pioneer of sound recording. Bell's father was an authority on speech correction and elocution, and from 1868 Bell worked with him, teaching deaf children to speak. In 1873, he was appointed Professor of Vocal Physiology at the University of Boston. Working in his spare time, he and a mechanic, Thomas Watson, developed his ideas for transmitting speech electrically, and in 1876 he was granted a patent for 'transmitting vocal or other sounds telegraphically'. He gave the first public demonstration of the telephone in Philadelphia later that year, and commercial development soon followed. The immensely successful Bell Telephone Company was founded in 1877. Bell continued to experiment in electrical communication. He developed a photophone, which transmitted sound on a light beam; he also made several improvements to *Edison's gramophone, and developed a graphophone, a sound-recording device employing a stylus, wax cylinders, and discs. In his later years Bell extended his investigations into many other areas, including giant kites for carrying people, hydrofoil speedboats, a new strain of sheep, and a prototype iron lung.

Bell, Patrick *reaper.

bell founding, the process by which bells are made. The mould consists of an inner 'core' and an outer 'cope', with a void between them of the exact shape and form desired for the bell. The sides of the mould are insulated with loam or sand to prevent rapid cooling. Molten metal, usually *bronze, is poured into the mould, which is tamped as the metal is poured to release any gases formed and to ensure that the void is completely filled. Cooling is carefully regulated to prevent the outer surface from cooling faster than the inner, which would result in the formation of cracks. Large bells take up to two weeks to cool. After removal of the mould, the rough casting is sand-blasted and polished. If a certain pitch is required, small amounts of metal may be machined from the bell's inner surface.

belt drive and chain drive, forms of power transmission for connecting two shafts, either by an endless belt running over a *pulley on each shaft, or by a chain running over sprockets. Pulleys or sprockets are often of differing diameters in order to obtain a change in shaft speed. For flat belts, one of the pulleys is 'crowned' or slightly barrel-shaped, to prevent the belt from moving sideways. Vee and polyvee belts carry one or more raised, V-shaped ridges on the inside of the belt, which fit into grooves on the pulleys. These belt types are more compact and give greater power than flat belts; they are commonly used in car engines to drive the fan, alternator, and water pump. A recent development is the toothed belt running on flat, toothed pulleys. Chain drives are used for similar purposes to belts, but can also handle very large powers. The definitive chain design is the bush roller chain, developed in 1880 by Hans Renold for textile machines, which has been widely adopted for bicycles, motor cycles, and many other uses. Chain and toothed belt drives are more efficient than flat or vee belt drives, since there is no slip or 'creep' due to alternate stretching and contraction. However, chain drives are noisier than belts and need lubrication.

Benz, Carl Friedrich (1844–1929), German pioneer of the *petrol engine and the motor car. After factory experience in engineering, he turned his attention to the internal-combustion engine. As four-stroke engines were then precluded by the patent granted to *Otto in 1876, he concentrated on developing a two-stroke engine. When Otto's patent was revoked in 1886, he designed a four-stroke engine specifically for road vehicles. His three-wheel car attracted little attention at the Paris Universal Exhibition of 1889, but by the end of the century some 2,000 improved four-wheel models had been sold.

benzene (C_6H_6), a clear, colourless, volatile liquid, highly toxic whether inhaled or absorbed through the skin. The benzene molecule consists of a hexagonal ring of six carbon atoms, with a hydrogen atom attached to each carbon. Benzene was discovered by *Faraday in 1825, and is the simplest of the aromatic hydrocarbons, all of which are characterized by a benzene ring. It was originally produced by the fractional distillation of coal-tar, but is now obtained from certain petroleum fractions by catalytic *reforming. Benzene and its derivatives are widely used in the manufacture of dyes, pharmaceuticals, explosives, and plastics.

Berger, Hans (1873–1941), German psychiatrist who invented *electroencephalography as a means of diagnosing brain disorders. After qualifying in medicine, having earlier studied physics and mathematics, he joined a psychiatric clinic at Jena, where in 1919 he was appointed Professor of Psychiatry. In 1924, inspired by the research of *Einthoven on electrocardiography, he began to record electric currents in the brain, first in animals and then in humans.

beryllium (symbol Be, at. no. 4, r.a.m. 9.01), a light, highly toxic, silvery-white metallic element, usually obtained by the *electrolysis of fused beryllium chloride. It is used for making special alloys, which are vibration-resistant, have high thermal and electrical conductivity, and do not spark when struck. It is also used in the windows of X-ray tubes.

Bessemer, Sir Henry (1813–98), British engineer who invented a process for the large-scale manufacture of cheap *steel. Until the middle of the 19th century, steel was scarce and expensive in Europe. Bessemer's process removed carbon from *iron—necessary for its conversion to steel—by blowing air through the molten metal. His tilting converter, into which molten pig-iron was poured before the air was blown in, was introduced in Sheffield in 1860 and was soon widely used in Europe. In the USA, steel was made by a similar process patented by *Kelly.

Tea-picking at the Longjing tea plantation in Zhejiang, China. For this **beverage crop**, only the shoots (bud plus two leaves) of the plant are picked: over 2,000 shoots are required for 500 g (1 pound) of tea.

Best, Charles Herbert *Banting, Frederick Grant.

beta-blocker, a drug that acts on the sympathetic nervous system (a subdivision of the autonomic nervous system that controls the body's involuntary muscles). Beta-blockers block sympathetic (beta) receptors, which accelerate the heartbeat and dilate the bronchi in the lungs. Thus, blockers acting specifically on receptors in the heart slow its rate, and may be used in *cardiology to treat disordered cardiac rhythm. They also reduce the force of cardiac contraction and are therefore sometimes used to treat high blood pressure. Since their actions reduce the amount of work required of the heart, beta-blockers are also used to treat angina. (See also *pharmacology table.)

betatron *particle accelerator.

Bevan, Edward John *Cross, Charles Frederick.

beverage crop, a crop grown specifically to supply ingredients for drinks. The most important beverage crops are tea, coffee, and cacao. Tea is grown in China, India, Japan, Java, Kenya, Malawi, the Soviet Union, Sri Lanka, Iran, South Africa, and Turkey. It is an evergreen shrub, the youngest leaves of which are periodically harvested by hand throughout the growing season. Coffee is grown in similar areas to tea, plus Central and South America. It is a small shrub, the berries of which contain coffee beans. Both tea and coffee are grown commercially using methods of *plantation farming. The cacao plant is a tropical evergreen tree, from the beans of which are produced cocoa and *chocolate. Most cacao plants, however, are grown on small peasant holdings.

Bhopal, a city in Madhya Pradesh, India, the site of probably the largest industrial accident in history, when in 1984 large quantities of methyl isocyanate gas from a plant manufacturing insecticide were released over a densely populated area. In the mass panic as the inhabitants tried to escape, over 2,500 people were killed and 50,000 were injured. In the longer term, the gas caused chronic respiratory problems, eye irritation, and blindness in many thousands of people. Litigation for liability lasted for almost three years, with the owners of the US plant (Union Carbide) claiming that industrial sabotage was responsible for the disaster. The inquiry into the disaster found that poor operating and safety procedures plus inadequate staffing levels were the major causes.

bias, the voltage that must be applied to the input of a transistor, thermionic valve, or amplifier circuit to ensure correct functioning of the circuit. For an amplifier, bias is usually a direct current that enables the circuit to provide a faithful, amplified, output signal for each input signal, without introducing distortion.

bicycle, a human-powered vehicle comprising two *wheels, one behind the other, connected by a frame (see figure). A precursor of the pedal-powered cycle was the hobby-horse, which was pushed along with the feet. The first pedal-operated bicycle was invented in 1839 by Kirkpatrick Macmillan, a British blacksmith, but he built only one or two of his foot-treadle-operated machines. In 1863 the brothers Pierre and Ernest Michaux invented the 'velocipede', essentially a hobby-horse with pedals attached directly to the front wheel. The Michaux concept was widely copied and improved, and the 'bone-shaker' cycle became a popular plaything for the rich. During the 1870s the bicycle's front wheel was gradually enlarged, enabling the cyclist to go further for each revolution of the pedals. This trend culminated around 1880 in the 'Ordinary' or 'Penny-farthing' cycle, invented by the British engineer James Starley, with a front-wheel diameter of up to 127 cm (50 inches). The first chain-driven cycle was designed by H. J. Lawson in 1879, but the first successful design was the Rover safety cycle. This was the forerunner of the modern bicycle, built in 1885 by John Starley, nephew of James. In 1889 pneumatic *tyres were introduced. By the beginning of the 20th century the bicycle had become a cheap form of personal transport for work and leisure. From the 1920s the rise of the *motor car diminished the importance of the bicycle in the West, but since the 1960s there has been a resurgence of interest. Lightweight racing and touring models and more recently BMX (Bicycle Moto-Cross) and mountain bicycles (see figure), have become popular for commuting, sport, and leisure. In many countries, bicycles and *tricycles are used extensively for commercial purposes, such as delivery vehicles and as taxis (see *rickshaw).

bicycle gear, a mechanism designed to enable the cyclist to develop power most efficiently at a pedalling rate of between 60 and 120 revolutions per minute, whatever the speed over the road. Originally the pedals drove the front wheel directly, but to obtain adequate road speed the wheels had to be of uncomfortably large diameter. The chain-and-sprocket drive to the rear wheel provided the solution to this

Bicycle

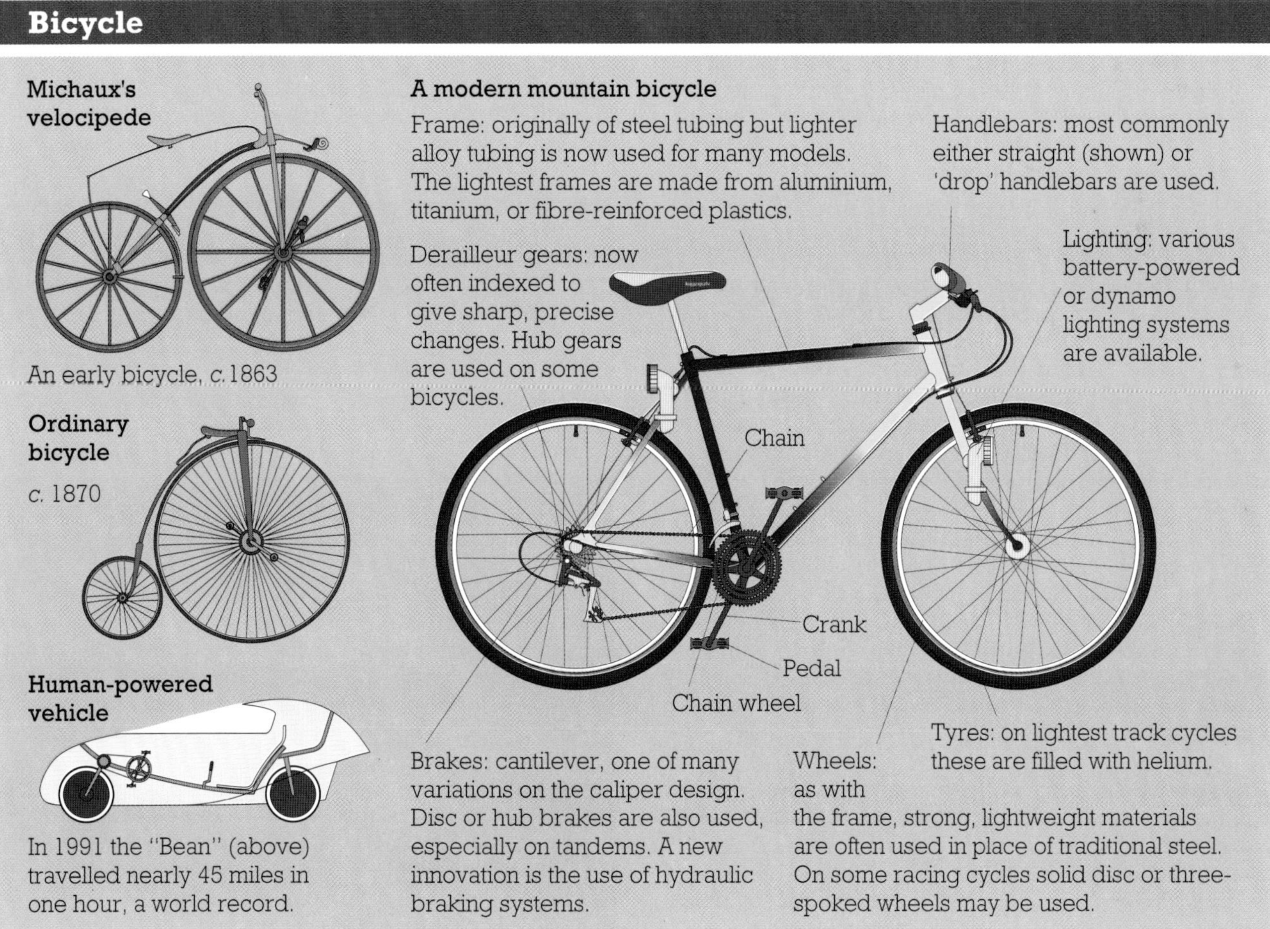

Michaux's velocipede
An early bicycle, c.1863
Ordinary bicycle
c. 1870
Human-powered vehicle
In 1991 the "Bean" (above) travelled nearly 45 miles in one hour, a world record.
A modern mountain bicycle
Frame: originally of steel tubing but lighter alloy tubing is now used for many models. The lightest frames are made from aluminium, titanium, or fibre-reinforced plastics.
Handlebars: most commonly either straight (shown) or 'drop' handlebars are used.
Lighting: various battery-powered or dynamo lighting systems are available.
Derailleur gears: now often indexed to give sharp, precise changes. Hub gears are used on some bicycles.
Chain
Crank
Pedal
Chain wheel
Tyres: on lightest track cycles these are filled with helium.
Brakes: cantilever, one of many variations on the caliper design. Disc or hub brakes are also used, especially on tandems. A new innovation is the use of hydraulic braking systems.
Wheels: as with the frame, strong, lightweight materials are often used in place of traditional steel. On some racing cycles solid disc or three-spoked wheels may be used.

problem. To enable the rider to tackle a variety of gradients or wind conditions, a choice of gear is desirable. The simplest type of multiple gear is the derailleur system, in which one of up to three chain-wheels, connected to the pedals, drives one of a selection of gear sprockets on the rear wheel. Movement of the chain from one gear sprocket to another is achieved by a mechanism that pushes the chain sideways while pedalling. An alternative is the hub gear, which works by means of epicyclic *gears. The hub gear requires less maintenance but gives a more limited gear range, and pedalling must stop while changing gear.

Biffen, Sir Rowland Henry (1874–1949), British botanist who made important contributions to the improvement of crop plants, notably cereals. In 1912 he was appointed the first director of the newly created Plant Breeding Institute in Cambridge, where he established agricultural botany as a subject in its own right. Using the rudimentary principles of genetics discovered by the Austrian botanist Gregor Mendel (1822–84), he improved cultivated plants by hybridization. His first major success was to demonstrate that susceptibility to yellow rust in wheat results from a single, dominant factor. He was responsible for producing two important new wheat varieties.

bifocal lens *spectacles.

bimetallic strip, a strip formed of two different metals welded together. By using metals of very different coefficients of thermal expansion, such as steel and brass, the strip will curve when heated. A bimetallic strip in the form of a spiral can be used as a thermometer: a pointer is fixed to the centre of the spiral, and moves across a calibrated scale in response to movements of the strip. Some *thermostats also employ bimetallic strips. A further use of bimetallic strips is for the protection of electric motors from thermal overload. In this context the circuit-breaker may be a bimetallic domed disc, which suddenly changes shape from concave to convex when a critical temperature is reached.

binary code, the base-two number system that is the foundation for modern digital *computing. Binary code is especially suitable for use by computers as it uses just two numbers—0 and 1—represented in the computer as the absence or presence of an electrical signal (see *machine code). Values greater than 1 can be represented as a sequence of binary digits, known as *bits. Each bit in the sequence represents a value twice the previous one. Thus the number 6, for example, is represented in binary code as 110—no ones, one two, and one four. Most computer systems use fixed-length 'words' which are multiples of 8 bits (a *byte). Thus a small word-length of 8 bits can code for only 256 different numbers or characters: a 16-bit word can code for over 65,000 characters, and larger words can code for an extremely large number of characters. Frequently, slightly modified versions of basic binary code are used to allow the representation of negative numbers or decimal fractions.

binnacle *magnetic compass.

binoculars, a pair of refracting *telescopes, joined together for use with both eyes, giving stereoscopic viewing. (In some binoculars the two objective lenses are further apart than the eyes, which enhances the stereoscopic effect.) Binoculars differ from simple telescopes in the inclusion of a pair of prisms between the objective and eyepiece *lenses in each telescope. These prisms invert and reverse the image from the objective lens so that the final image corresponds with the original object. They also increase the internal light path, increasing the magnification obtainable in a short tube, although some compact modern binoculars have a straight-through prism. Binoculars usually have a wider field of view than a telescope. Each eyepiece can be focused separately, or both can be moved together by a screw adjustment, to focus for different distances. Magnification and light-gathering power are given numerically—6×30 denotes a magnification factor of six and an objective lens aperture 30 mm (1.17 inches) in diameter.

bioengineering, the application of engineering techniques to biological processes. It describes the design, manufacture, and fitting of devices such as artificial limbs, heart valves and *pacemakers, or *hearing-aids. Such devices, known as prostheses, are required to replace or aid body parts that have been removed or are defective. Bioengineering is also the design, manufacture, and use of medical monitoring or treatment devices such as *haemodialysis machines (used to remove toxic wastes from the blood), electrocardiographs, and heart–lung machines.

biofuel, a source of energy based on biomass, the natural material of living organisms, including vegetable matter (from algae to trees), animal tissue, and manure. Biomass can be burned directly, or chemically or biologically processed into more convenient solid, liquid, or gaseous fuels. Forestry has provided wood as a biofuel over many centuries. Wood, other plant materials, and dried dung are still used in non-industrialized areas of the world for heating water and for cooking. However, the uncontrolled cutting of wood leads to deforestation and soil erosion, and manure is more usefully employed as a soil fertilizer. Waste materials from agriculture and forestry can serve as biofuels for furnaces and boilers. In the USA, the entire cotton harvest is dried by heat from burning *cotton-gin waste. Sawmills frequently use bark and other offcuts as fuel in drying kilns to accelerate the seasoning of cut planks. Heating wood or other vegetable matter in the absence of air produces a gas with a high proportion of *methane, together with an oily tar and a solid carbon or charcoal residue. All three products can be used as biofuels, although the tar requires further

An anaerobic fermentation plant for making biogas, a type of **biofuel** made from human and animal waste. Over 100,000 such plants are in operation in India.

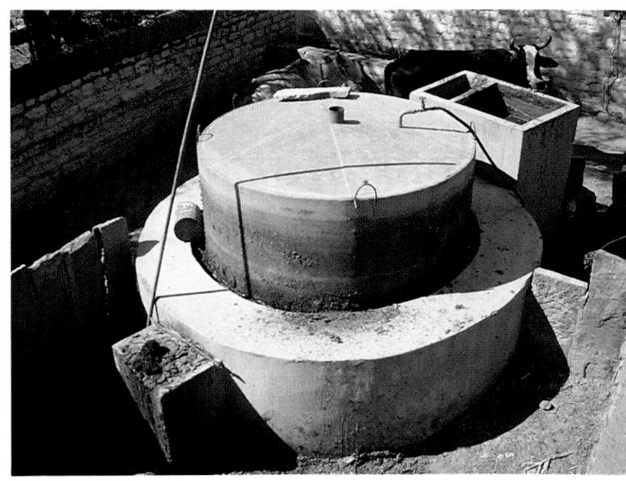

processing. Methane gas is also produced as a biofuel—biogas—by the bacterial fermentation of wastes with a high water content, such as human waste, animal manure, and crop residues. This process, which is used in China and India among other countries, also converts the wastes into nitrogen-rich fertilizer. Sewage works in the UK generate most of the heat and power they require by burning the methane gas produced from sewage *fermentation. Fermentation of sugars by yeast, followed by distillation, gives pure *ethanol. In Brazil ethanol is made from sugar-cane and cassava and mixed with petrol to produce 'gasohol', thereby reducing the dependence on imports of crude oil.

biological pest control, the use of living organisms to control agricultural or other pests, for example, to encourage the natural predators of a pest. In Indonesia, for example, measures designed to encourage predators of the brown planthopper, a notorious rice pest, improved rice yields and greatly reduced *pesticide use within three years. A second strategy is to spray a biological pesticide, a living organism (usually a *bacterium or a *fungus) that is toxic to a particular pest species. A third form of control is to introduce an organism from another country (an exotic species). In Australia in the 1920s, the Argentinian moth *Cactoblastis cactorum* was used to control the widespread growth of the prickly pear, a cactus of the genus *Opuntia*. Biological pest control can be highly species-specific and has few adverse environmental effects. However, careful research is needed, especially before the introduction of an exotic species, to investigate the ecological impact of the proposed measure.

biopsy, the removal of a small amount of a patient's tissue for diagnostic purposes. Sections of tissue are stained and examined under a microscope for abnormal cells, which may indicate the presence of disease. Biopsies are obtained through the skin, using hollow needles and syringes (as in renal or liver biopsy), in exploratory operations, by *endoscopy, or by scraping off surface cells. Specialized techniques include the use of vacuum capsules to examine the intestinal lining. Biopsy is especially useful in the diagnosis of *cancer.

bioreactor, a vessel, usually of stainless steel, in which *fermentation is carried out. Bioreactors are central to *biotechnology; they provide all the conditions for optimum production of the desired product by cells—a supply of nutrients and oxygen, constant temperature and acidity, and freedom from contamination by unwanted micro-organisms. The reaction mixture must be kept homogenous by agitating it with rotating paddles or by means of air bubbles. Bioreactors may be operated on continuous flow principles, but most success has been achieved by batch processing. Common bioreactor uses are for beer fermentation, penicillin production, and methane gas formation from waste organic material (see *biofuel).

biosensor, a miniature device incorporating a biochemical substance and electronic circuitry, which can monitor biochemical reactions in the laboratory or substances in body fluids. Biosensors recognize specific molecules in solutions or mixtures and produce electrical signals which indicate their concentration. Results are obtained far more quickly using biosensors than by traditional chemical analysis. At present, applications of biosensors, mainly in *biotechnology and *food technology, are still at the research or development stage.

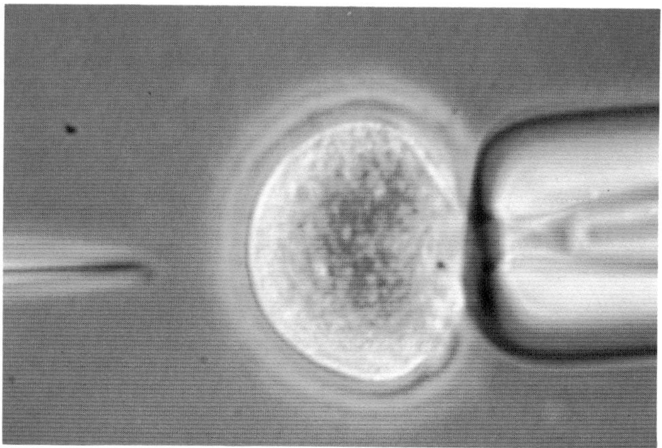

Microinjection of extra genetic material into a cell, a technique used in **biotechnology**. The photograph shows a suction tube holding the cell (*right*), while a probe (*left*) is used to insert the genetic material.

biotechnology, in its widest sense, any application of machines to living organisms, especially humans, or the study of the interactions of organisms and technological devices. The roots of biotechnology go back to at least 6000 BC. *Wine-making, *brewing, and leavening of bread, all processes involving *fermentation, were practised by the ancient Mesopotamians and Egyptians. It was not realized, however, that living organisms were responsible for these processes until the discovery of yeast in the 17th century, and of *bacteria (by *Pasteur) in the 19th century. By the end of the 19th century products such as *ethanol and acetic acid were being produced by deliberate use of microbial (micro-organism) fermentation. However, this was non-sterile biotechnology, in which a variety of organisms competed for the substrate and made a mixture of end-products. In the 1940s, demand for large quantities of the newly discovered *antibiotics led to the introduction of sterile fermentation procedures. In these the desired organism alone was encouraged, through the application of complicated engineering techniques, to produce the desired product in relatively high yield. Since the late 1960s developments in molecular biology and process control have resulted in the beginning of a biotechnological revolution. Using *genetic engineering techniques it is possible to 'up-regulate' genes coding for desired products, or even to insert genes for desired products (for example, human antibodies) into an organism. (See also *immobilized cell technology, *monoclonal antibody.)

The term biotechnology is generally used today to refer to industrial production using living organisms, especially micro-organisms, processes sometimes described as biochemical engineering. Biotechnology in this sense involves the production of either whole cells (biomass), as in *single-cell protein production, or of a particular end-product, such as an *enzyme, antibiotic, or organic acid. The process of obtaining a desired product involves three major steps. First, a suitable organism must be obtained, either by selective breeding or by genetic engineering. Next, the organism undergoes fermentation under suitable conditions in a *bioreactor. Finally, further processing, often the most expensive step, is required to separate the desired product from other material. Alternatively, microbial action may be used to decompose pollutants, as in *sewage treatment or the treatment of oil-slicks. Microbial action can also be used to recover metal from low-grade ores. Biotechnology results from the integration of many branches of biology (microbio-

Two Tiger Moth **biplanes** in flight. The Tiger Moth was originally built by Geoffrey de Havilland as a training aircraft, but it is popular today as a sport plane.

logy, biochemistry, genetics, and molecular biology) with chemical and *systems engineering. It has the potential to manufacture products more economically, in a less energy-demanding manner, and more safely than traditional industry, and to solve new problems of medicine, production, pollution control, and energy sources. This potential has by no means yet been fully realized.

biplane, an *aeroplane or *glider with two sets of wings, one above the other. The first powered flight was made by the *Wright brothers in a biplane, and during World War I the biplane configuration was generally adopted for most aircraft (although some triplane designs were successful). The performance advantages of the biplane arose from its greater lift and lower stalling speeds. In the 1930s increased engine power and better aircraft design led to higher airspeeds; maximizing lift became less important, and the reduced drag and lighter weight of the monoplane predominated. Biplanes still find applications in aerobatics and crop-spraying, where their greater manœuvrability and low flying speeds are advantageous.

Birdseye, Clarence (1886–1956), US pioneer of the modern deep-freeze industry. In 1916 he became interested in *food preservation by freezing. Large-scale refrigeration of meat and other foods was by then already established, but the quality of the thawed product was very variable, as the slow freezing process used at the time led to the formation of destructively large ice crystals. Birdseye discovered that the quality of such foods as fish, legumes, and bread is much improved by rapid freezing.

Birkeland, Kristian Olaf Bernhard (1867–1917), Norwegian physicist who, with fellow Norwegian Samuel Eyde, devised the first commercially successful process for the fixation of atmospheric *nitrogen. The process involved passing nitrogen and oxygen through an electric arc fanned out by electromagnets, and its economic viability depended on cheap electricity, available to Birkeland from *hydroelectric installations. The process was used in Norway from 1905 until the early 1920s, but was later displaced by the more efficient *Haber–Bosch process.

bismuth (symbol Bi, at. no. 83, r.a.m. 208.98), a lustrous, hard, brittle metal with a reddish tint. It is obtained mostly as a by-product of smelting lead and copper ores. Bismuth is used to make alloys that melt at low temperatures. These alloys are used for electrical fuses, and for safety plugs in boilers and automatic sprinkler systems.

bit (*bi*nary digi*t*), the smallest item of information that can be stored in a digital *computer. A single bit exists in one of two states, labelled 0 or 1, and is usually represented in the computer as an electrical signal that is either absent or present. Groups of bits form a *binary code to represent numerical and other data.

bitumen, the generic name for thick, dark, liquid or solid flammable water-resistant mineral substances composed of hydrocarbons. An example is asphalt, which occurs in natural deposits or can be obtained as a by-product of *petroleum refining. Bitumen-impregnated felt is widely used for roof coverings and for *damp-proof courses. Bituminous paint provides an inexpensive protection for ferrous products which may corrode. Bitumen is also used as an adhesive. When mixed with *aggregate it is used as a road surface. In ancient times it was used as a cement in building.

black box (aviation) *flight recorder.

blacksmithing, the fabrication of objects from iron by hot and cold *forging, using a variety of tools. Two central features of a blacksmith's workshop are the *anvil and the forge. The *anvil is a massive steel block, on which hot and cold iron is beaten into shape. Traditionally the forge was charcoal-fired and linked to hand-operated bellows which pumped air into the fire to control the temperature; temperature control is critical for ironworking. Modern forges burn gas, are equipped with a compressor for supplying draughts, and are packed with ceramic chips, which do not burn. Although the modern forge is more convenient to use, considerable skill is still needed to control the temperature.

blast-furnace, a chamber in which *iron is extracted from iron ore, an essential process in the *iron and steel industry. The furnace is filled from the top with a charge of iron ore, *coke, and limestone; the major ore used is haematite (Fe_2O_3). Blasts of hot air introduced near the base of the furnace burn the coke and melt the iron oxide in the material around the lower edges of the furnace (see figure). The burning of the coke gives off carbon monoxide, which is the main reducing agent for converting the iron oxide to

A **blacksmith** at work in Missouri, USA. The furnace, the anvil, and the quenching bin for rapidly cooling hot metal are shown here.

Blast-furnace

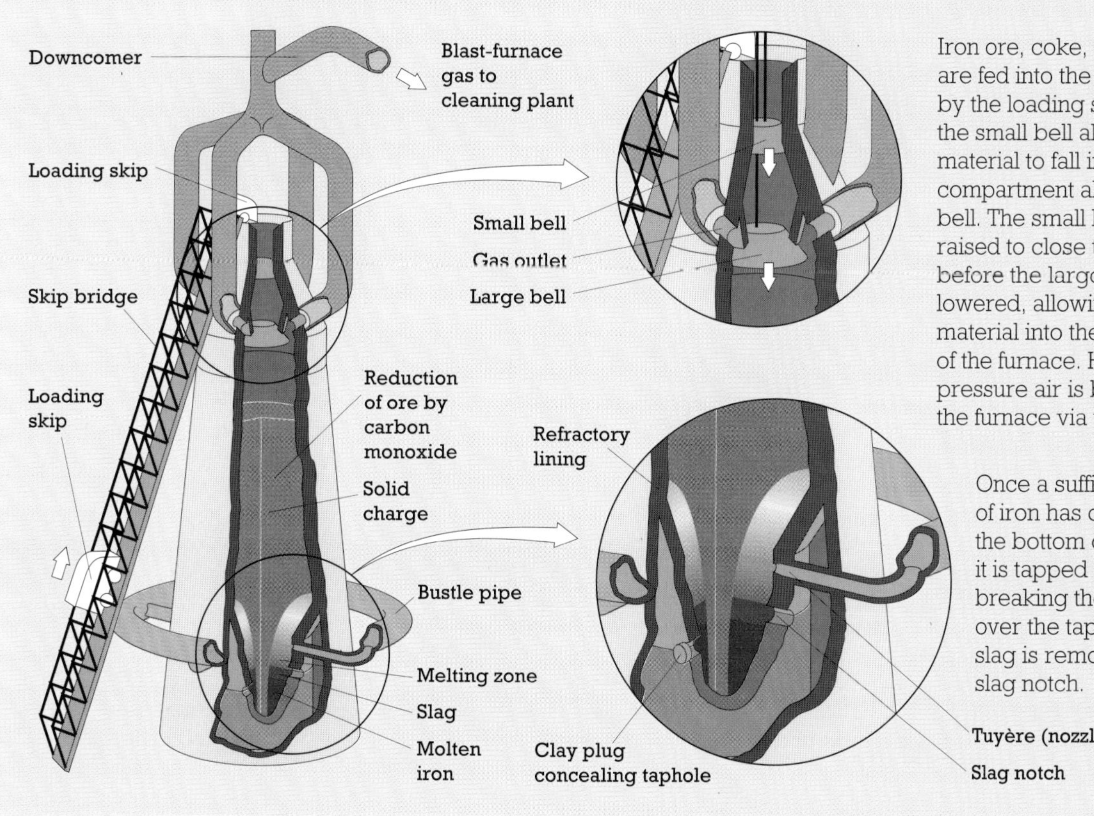
Downcomer
Blast-furnace gas to cleaning plant
Loading skip
Small bell
Gas outlet
Large bell
Skip bridge
Loading skip
Reduction of ore by carbon monoxide
Solid charge
Refractory lining
Bustle pipe
Melting zone
Slag
Molten iron
Clay plug concealing taphole
Tuyère (nozzle)
Slag notch
Iron ore, coke, and limestone are fed into the blast-furnace by the loading skip. Lowering the small bell allows this material to fall into the compartment above the large bell. The small bell is then raised to close the furnace before the large bell is lowered, allowing the material into the main body of the furnace. Hot, high-pressure air is blown into the furnace via the tuyères.
Once a sufficient amount of iron has collected at the bottom of the furnace, it is tapped off by breaking the clay plug over the taphole. The slag is removed via the slag notch.

iron. As it is formed, the iron melts and runs down to collect in a pool at the bottom of the furnace, while the molten slag floats on the surface. The iron and slag can then be tapped off. The furnace is built of steel and lined with heat-resistant bricks. Once started, it runs continuously for two or more years, until the lining begins to fail.

bleach, a chemical used to whiten coloured materials. The active ingredient (usually *chlorine) reacts with coloured material to form colourless substances. Bleaches are used extensively to treat wood-pulp for paper manufacture, in the textile industry to treat cotton and linen, and domestically for cleaning stained surfaces. Originally, textiles were bleached by exposure to sunlight in 'bleach fields'. Later industrial bleaching used bleaching powder, a mixture of chlorine with calcium hydroxide first manufactured by *Tennant in 1799. The powder was easier to store and transport than chlorine itself. However, as new techniques for handling chlorine have been developed, bleaching powder has been largely replaced by liquid chlorine. Bleaching powder is still used for domestic cleaning, although liquid bleaches are now more common. Some of these contain sodium hypochlorite solution as the active ingredient. Some *washing powders also contain mild bleaches. Sulphur dioxide gas is used to bleach materials such as straw, which would be damaged by the action of chlorine. Worries about the adverse environmental impact of chlorine or sulphur dioxide bleaches has led to the increased use of 'environmentally friendly' bleaches based on *hydrogen peroxide.

Blériot, Louis (1872–1936), French pioneer aviator. Originally a motor-car manufacturer, he later turned his attention to aircraft construction, experimenting first with gliders and then with lightweight engines. After a successful flight over the mouth of the Seine he piloted a powered aircraft across the English Channel on 25 July 1909. This was the first flight across the sea in a heavier-than-air aircraft. His aircraft was a *monoplane with cantilever wings for extra strength and a tractor (pulling) propeller, features that later became standard on nearly all *aeroplanes.

block and tackle *pulley.

blood disorders and treatment *haematology.

blood gas analysis, a means of determining the proportions of gases, particularly oxygen and carbon dioxide, present in blood. Physiologists became interested in the subject in the mid-19th century, after it was discovered that respiratory gases are transported in blood. Early approaches were based on chemical techniques to analyse the proportions of different gases extracted from blood samples by means of vacuum pumps. Spectrophotometry (see *spectroscopy) was used experimentally to analyse the blood's oxygen capacity from the late 19th century. Clinical blood gas analysers date from the 1950s; they employ electrochemical electrodes with plastic membranes permeable to oxygen or carbon dioxide (but not to other blood constituents). These can quickly provide useful information for the assessment of a patient's respiratory function.

blood transfusion, the injection of blood previously taken from a healthy person into the veins of a patient. In early transfusions serious mishaps occurred due to blood incompatibility: blood from the donor agglutinated (clotted) on being transfused, due to the presence of antigens in the donor blood that caused an immune response in the patient (see *immunology). In 1900 *Landsteiner devised the ABO blood group system, in which a person's blood was classified according to which other bloods it agglutinated. It was only after identification of blood groups and the adoption of methods to prevent clotting that transfusion became a useful technique. These developments allowed blood to be stored and made possible the practice of 'indirect' transfusion (without the presence of the donor). In 1935 a process for freezing and drying blood plasma for later use was developed. During World War II, blood banks were established for the storage and management of blood and plasma. At the same time, the blood components albumin and gamma globulin became available for therapeutic purposes. Since then, the expansion in blood transfusion services and their universal acceptance have resulted in a great proliferation of blood products, such as Factor IX (for treatment of haemophilia-B patients) and gamma globulin concentrates.

blowlamp, a hand-held burner giving an intensely hot flame, used for paint-stripping, welding, and similar purposes. Blowlamps originally burned vaporized paraffin, but are now increasingly fuelled with liquid gas.

Blumlein, Alan (1903–42), British inventor. He studied electrical engineering, and in 1929 joined Columbia Gramophone (later EMI). In 1931 he conceived the idea of stereo recording, and by 1933 he had begun to make test recordings, though stereo systems were not commercially adopted until 1958. In 1935–6 he developed a 405-line electronic *television system, which replaced *Baird's photomechanical system in the early BBC television transmissions. During World War II, he adapted his stereo-sound system to radar, which greatly improved accuracy in the pin-pointing of targets. He died in a plane crash during airborne testing of his equipment.

boat *canoe, *coracle, *dinghy, *sailing ships and boats, *ship's boat.

body armour, clothing or equipment designed to protect the wearer during fighting. The earliest form of armour was probably the shield, made of wood, leather, or wicker, then later of metal, and recently of toughened glass or Perspex. Protective shirts made of copper, bronze, or hide scales were worn by the Egyptians as early as the 3rd millennium BC. Rhinoceros-hide armour was used in the 11th century BC in China. Armour made of fabric dates back to earliest times; 19th-century examples from India are often quilted, and sometimes also studded with small nails. Rigid armour was constructed in various ways. Small overlapping plates of material could be inserted between layers of leather or other material (brigandine armour). Another construction pattern was lamellar, in which small overlapping plates were held together by laces. This type of armour found its most elaborate expression in Japanese armour of the 8th to 12th centuries AD. Metal *chain-mail armour had its origins in Roman times and was the dominant form of body armour in Europe between the 8th and 14th centuries. Scale armour consisted of small 'scales', usually with a curved or pointed lower edge, arranged in overlapping rows: it existed in primitive form in ancient Egypt and was used in all parts of Europe, particularly in the 10th to 12th centuries, and in India and China until the 19th century. Plate armour, as its name suggests, was made up of large plates, usually of metal, linked by loose rivets or chain-mail. This type was most fully

A complete suit of Japanese Samurai **body armour** from the late 19th century. The main torso armour consists of small, overlapping lacquered metal plates, laced together. A socket in the back of the armour supports the warrior's personal banner.

developed in Europe during the 15th and early 16th centuries (see illustration in *military technology). Armour was almost entirely discarded in Europe by the middle of the 18th century because it was ineffectual against guns. During World War I metal helmets were reintroduced to protect the head from *shrapnel, and body armour was worn by assault engineers and others required to take up exposed positions. In World War II flak jackets comprising plates of manganese steel or fibreglass in a jacket of brigandine construction were developed to protect the body. Modern flak jackets and bullet-proof vests have plates of dual-hardness steel or, for lightweight protection, ceramic–plastic *composites.

body scanner *computerized axial tomography (CAT), *radiology, *tomography.

bogie, a sub-frame of a locomotive, carriage, or freight wagon that carries a set of wheels (usually on two axles) and which is pivoted with respect to the main frame of the vehicle to facilitate the negotiation of sharp curves. On most four-wheel bogies springing or suspension improves the smoothness of the ride. The bogie may also carry brake-gear; power bogies, fitted to most diesel-electric or electric locomotives, carry the vehicle drive units.

boiler, a device for producing steam from water, though the term is also applied to water heaters for domestic and other *heating systems. The major use of large-scale boilers is to provide steam for electricity generation (see *power-station). Early boilers, developed for *steam-engines, comprised a crude vessel for water over a coal-fired furnace. *Trevithick improved on this with a tubular furnace surrounded by a cylindrical drum containing water. In the Lancashire boiler, several furnace tubes gave a larger surface for heat transfer, while the locomotive boiler (see *steam locomotive) had many small fire tubes. Fire-tube boilers are still in use for many small-scale applications. Large-scale boilers use a water-tube design developed in the USA: water is passed through small-diameter tubes, over which the hot furnace gases are passed. A very high rate of heat transfer is achieved. As the hot furnace gases cool, they are used to pre-heat the cool feed-water entering the water tubes, and to pre-heat the air entering the furnace. By such means boilers are able to achieve efficiencies of over 95 per cent. The major fuels for boilers are coal, petroleum, gas, and nuclear power: coal is the most widely used, although its combustion releases sulphur oxides and other atmospheric pollutants, and leaves large amounts of inert ash. In large-scale water-tube boilers the fuel is usually pulverized or atomized and blown into the furnace in a current of air. Coal-fired *fluidized-bed boilers use larger fragments.

boiling-water reactor *pressurized-water reactor.

bolas, a throwing weapon from South America. It consists of two or more balls or stones connected together by strong cord, which are swung round the head before being thrown. Once thrown, the cord wraps itself around the quarry.

bolometer *radiometer.

bolt *nuts and bolts.

bomb, an *explosive or incendiary device which is thrown, dropped from an aircraft, or placed in position. Most com-

The **bolas** being used to hunt the rhea, a large, flightless, South American bird. (From *Le Journal de la jeunesse*, 1889.)

monly bombs are dropped from aircraft, and a variety of such bombs have been developed. Demolition bombs are designed with very thin cases and rely on their explosive power to destroy targets. Armour-piercing bombs have a much thicker casing and use kinetic impact to break through armour plate or concrete and explode in the vital areas being protected. General-purpose bombs have a casing of intermediate thickness. In incendiary bombs, flammable substances are mixed with explosive to start fires. Bombs are usually of a tear-drop or cylindrical shape, with stabilizing fins at the rear. On some types, a propeller on the nose provides added stability. The most powerful bombs are atomic and hydrogen bombs (see *nuclear weapons), which utilize the explosive energy of a nuclear chain reaction.

bomb disposal, the disarming of *bombs. The technology developed out of the need to defuse bombs and land *mines during World War II. At first, bomb disposal was a dangerous job that had to be done by hand. In 1972, however, the British Army introduced a remote-controlled robot to defuse bombs. It includes a battery-operated motor to provide the propulsive force and a selection of mechanical arms fitted to a boom that rises above the chassis. A television camera sends a picture to the operator's monitor. Various devices help the robot get in and out of doors and windows, and it carries a kind of *water cannon for flushing out explosives. The main task in bomb disposal is to disengage the *detonator from the explosives so that the explosives can be removed and blown up harmlessly under controlled conditions. (See also *minesweeper.)

bomber, a *military aircraft primarily designed and equipped to carry *bombs against enemy targets. Bombs are usually carried in an internal bomb bay and released through a bomb door, but they can also be carried on special external wing racks. In the earliest use of bombs from aircraft they were simply dropped over the side, but by 1910 research into purpose-built aeroplanes was being carried out. An early light bomber was the De Havilland DH9A, which could carry a 200-kg (450-pound) load under its wings. By World War II bombers were carrying much greater loads; Lancaster bombers could carry a 10,000-kg (22,000-pound) load of bombs by the end of the War. Dive-bombers were designed to drop their bomb loads at the bottom of a steep dive in order to obtain pin-point accuracy. They played an important role in World War II. Land- and submarine-based intercontinental *ballistic missiles have lessened the importance of long-range strategic bombers, although both the USA and the Soviet Union have continued to develop such aircraft (for example, the US Rockwell B-1B and the Soviet Tupolev Blackjack). (See also *fighter-bomber.)

bookbinding, the process of making a book by joining together written or printed sheets inside a cover that identifies and protects them. Since leaves of manuscript were bound inside covers well before the 15th century, bookbinding pre-dates printing. Binding single leaves was achieved originally by side-sewing, but such books could not open flat. Later, pages were produced in pairs on each side of a sheet that folded to form a four-page folio. Inserting folios one into another made a section that could be sewn together by looping threads through the spine. Several sections could then be joined by passing threads from one section to the next. This method of sewing produced a more flexible book-block (the book prior to adding a cover). Sewing of sections (saddle-stitching) is now mechanized, and is complemented by cutting, folding, and gathering machines, which convert printed sheets into sections (usually of sixteen or thirty-two pages) and collate them into order. However, unsewn methods of binding can now continuously convert bundles of loose sections directly into book-blocks, usually by cutting off the folded spines and gluing the cut edges together with plasticized adhesive (perfect binding). Most cheaper editions are produced this way. Book covers were originally two pieces of leather-covered wood attached by thongs round the spine. Following the introduction of printing to Europe (*c.*1450), many more book covers were required. While individual leather-bound covers were still produced, many covers (cases) were made from substitute materials. Today cases are made from heavy cardboard covered with cloth or paper. Case-making runs parallel with book-block manufacture, as does the printing of paperback covers. Combining book-blocks and covers is now done automatically on lines of casing-in or bookbinding machines. Modern adhesives have helped speed up production times from a few hundred per hour to between 1,500 and 6,000 per hour for hard-cased books, and 2,500 to 10,000 or more per hour for paperbacks.

boomerang, a flat, curved wooden projectile that spins in flight, used for hunting and warfare. It is commonly associated with the Australian Aborigines, but boomerang-type weapons have also long been used by peoples of North America, India, and Africa. Boomerangs that return to the thrower are toys rather than weapons. War boomerangs have sharp edges and are slightly convex on one side, and can be designed to swerve to the left or right.

bootstrap, the sequence of start-up instructions executed by a *computer when it is initially switched on. It may include loading all the relevant systems programs into computer memory (called 'booting' the computer), or simply loading a program to make sure that all the parts of the *central processing unit are put into a specific state (initialized), ready for the main *operating system and other programs to function correctly. In a *microcomputer, a bootstrapping program is usually stored in read-only *memory and cannot normally be altered by the user.

borax (sodium borate, $Na_2[B_4O_5(OH)_4]\cdot 8H_2O$), a white crystalline solid, the chief mineral source of *boron. Deposits of borax occur naturally in dry lake beds, especially in Death Valley, California, USA. Since the Middle Ages, borax has been used as a flux to remove oxides from metal surfaces in soldering and brazing. Modern uses include the manufacture of specialist glass and enamel, and in the sizing of paper.

bord-and-pillar mining, a *mining technique whereby chambers of ore are excavated, leaving pillars of material in place to support the roof. This method of excavation, known as partial extraction, is favoured when mining beneath surface buildings or under seas and lakes. The pillars are left in position to minimize movement of the ground at the surface. If conditions permit, the pillars are later excavated working back towards the mine entrance, causing the roof to collapse. The technique is not normally used at great depths because of the danger of roof collapse. When highly mechanized, this system can produce up to 5,000 tonnes of material per day.

boring machine, a type of *lathe designed to produce smooth, accurate, large-diameter holes by enlarging rough

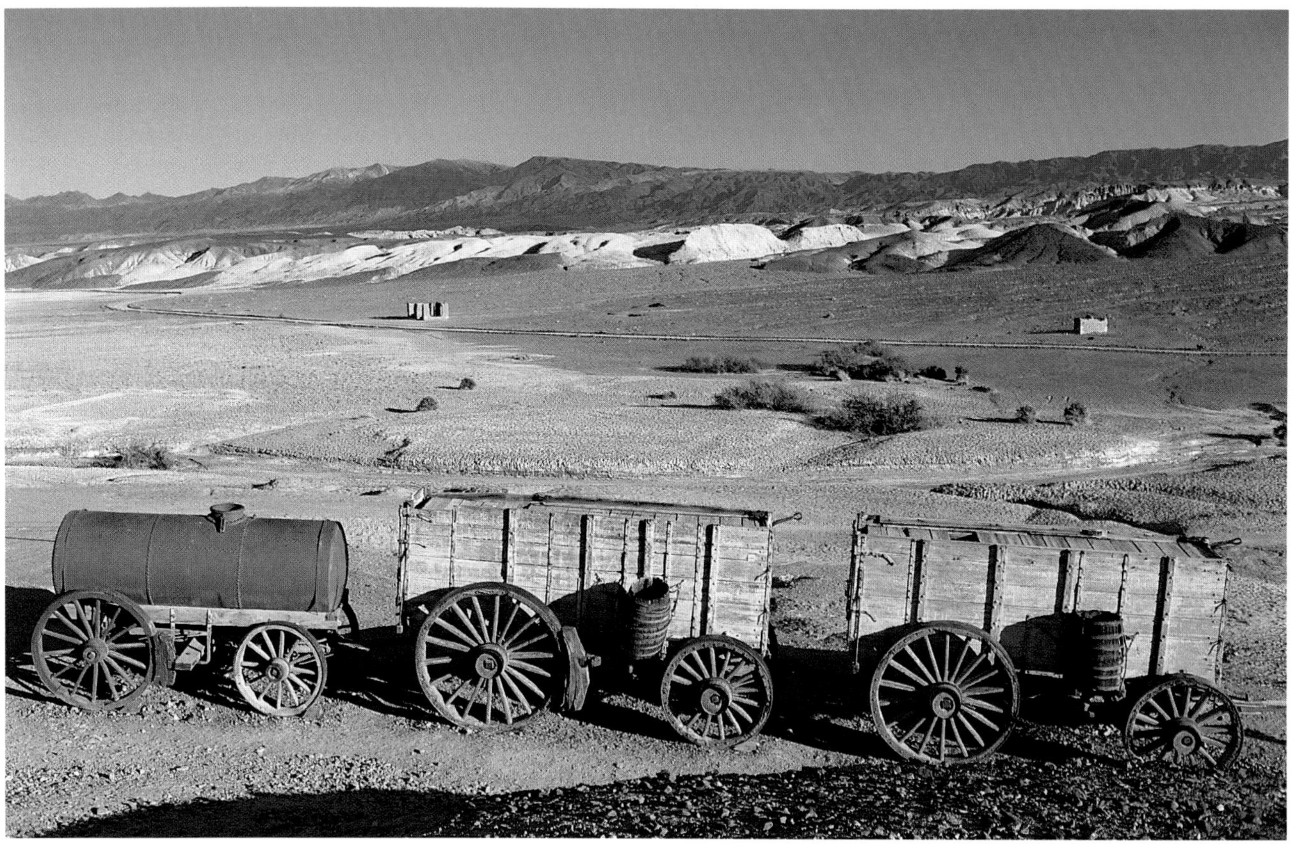

Death Valley, California, USA, the site of many naturally occurring **borax** deposits. In the foreground are abandoned railway vehicles from earlier mining activities.

holes in metal castings. It was originally developed to bore cylinders for early *steam-engines. Boring operations carried out on a conventional lathe proved inadequate for making large steam-engine cylinders. A boring machine was developed by the British ironmaster John Wilkinson (1728–1808) to solve this problem. In it, the casting was firmly fixed, while a cutter on a rotating boring bar, supported at either end, was fed through the workpiece. More recent boring machines rotate the workpiece rather than the cutter. Cylinders up to 3.7 m (12 feet) in diameter can be bored. (See also *shield excavators.)

boron (symbol B, at. no. 5, r.a.m. 10.81), a yellow-brown, non-metallic element. It occurs as the ore orthoboric acid $B(OH)_3$ and as borates such as *borax. Pure boron is produced from the oxide B_2O_3 by reaction with magnesium followed by chlorination and reduction with hydrogen. Crystalline boron is transparent, brittle, a non-conductor, and nearly as hard as diamond. Treating the surface of *steel with boron makes it very hard. *Alloys of boron and steel are used in the control rods of nuclear reactors because of the fact that boron is a strong neutron absorber. Boron oxide is used in making glasses, enamels, and glazes, and also as a mild antiseptic.

Bosch, Carl (1874–1940), German industrial chemist who transformed *Haber's ammonia synthesis into a workable large-scale process (see *Haber–Bosch process). After reading chemistry at Leipzig, Bosch joined the Badische Anilin- und Soda-Fabrik (BASF) in 1899. In 1908 Haber told BASF about his ammonia synthesis, and Bosch was made responsible for its industrial development. After World War I Bosch co-operated with *Bergius in making petroleum from coal, and in 1931 shared the Nobel Prize for Chemistry with him.

Böttger, Johann Friedrich (1682–1719), German alchemist to the Elector of Saxony and the first potter in Europe to make true hard-paste *porcelain, previously imported from China. In 1708 he made a hard red stoneware by mixing the normally infusible local clay with alabaster, and shortly afterwards perfected a white porcelain using kaolin (a type of clay) from Aue, Germany. On the basis of these technological advances he founded the Meissen porcelain works with the mathematician E. W. von Tschirnhausen.

Boulton, Matthew (1728–1809), British manufacturing engineer who promoted the *steam-engine in partnership with *Watt. He had little formal education, but in 1762 he opened his great Soho factory in Birmingham, which became world-famous not only for steam-engines but also for a variety of metal products—silverware, coins, and ormolu ornaments. In 1776 he was a founder of the Lunar Society of Birmingham, which bridged the gap between science and industry.

Boussingault, Jean-Baptiste Joseph Dieudonné (1802–87), French chemist who was one of the first to apply chemical principles to *agriculture. He recognized that *nitrogen was necessary for the growth of plants and that soil was able to fix atmospheric nitrogen; he suggested that this was due to the presence of micro-organisms. He developed a process for making *oxygen from barium oxide, and with his compatriot J.-B.-A. Dumas determined the relative proportions of gases in the atmosphere.

bow, a device for shooting arrows, consisting in its simplest form (the longbow) of a single piece of flexible wood with a piece of string under tension fastened to its two ends. The arrow is propelled by the energy stored in the bow when the string is drawn back. The arrow is a piece of wood with a point, sometimes made of metal, at one end and a notch cut at the other. The string fits in the notch when the arrow is to be fired. Arrows usually have two or three feathers glued to the end of the shaft; these act as a tailplane, making the arrow fly straighter. More powerful bows are made from several pieces of wood (the built bow), wood, horn, and sinew (the composite bow), or, for modern target-shooting bows, fibreglass. The *crossbow is a mechanical weapon.

box-frame *frame (building).

box-girder, a thin-walled hollow girder of steel, timber, or concrete. It has a rectangular or trapezoidal cross-section, which, compared with the more traditional 'I' section, gives increased stiffness and resistance to torsion (twisting). Internal transverse diaphragms prevent buckling of the box-girder walls. *Prefabrication of long girders is common in bridges, where steel or pre-cast concrete box-sections can be progressively added by forming a cantilever from an abutment or a pier. Steel box-girders of aerofoil cross-section have superseded trussed girders in the floors of long-span suspension bridges. Spans of about 15 m (50 feet) are possible with timber girders, in which plywood vertical membranes are bonded to each side of solid wood top and bottom flanges.

braille, a type of printing consisting of raised dots on the paper which can be read by the blind. The method was devised by the French teacher Louis Braille (1809–52), who was himself blind from the age of 3 and was a teacher of the blind. Each letter of the alphabet is represented by a different pattern of six dots in a domino 3×2 matrix, the size of which is suitable for the fingertips. Special patterns are used for common words and 'contractions' (commonly occurring groups of letters).

A **box-girder** bridge in construction over the river Mosel, Germany. The box-section of the central girder can be clearly seen.

brain scanner *computerized axial tomography (CAT), *magnetic resonance imaging, *radiology.

brake-van (US, caboose), a vehicle at the end of a freight train that provides braking, as well as accommodation for the train guard. Continuous *braking systems on all vehicles of a train were introduced in the mid-19th century. Before this, brake-vans provided the only braking other than that on the locomotive. In trains which had simple chain-link *couplings, the brake was used by the guard (or brakeman) in order to minimize the longitudinal motion of the train on starting and stopping.

braking system, a device used to retard or stop the motion of a vehicle or machine. Carts use simple brake-blocks pressed against the wheel-rim; *bicycles also most commonly use rim brakes with callipers to press rubber or leather blocks against both sides of the rim. Early motor cars used band brakes, in which a metal band lined with friction material was wrapped around a brake wheel. These had a tendency to 'lock' (seize solidly) and were supplanted by drum brakes (see figure), in which, when the brake pedal is depressed, two pivoted brake shoes are forced apart at their free ends to press against the inside of a brake drum. Operation was originally mechanical, by a *cam or cone, but *hydraulic brakes are now universal, although the hand-brake is still operated mechanically. Much heat is dissipated in braking and may cause 'brake fade' through reduced friction between brake drum and shoe at higher temperatures. For this reason most cars and some *motor cycles use disc brakes, at least on the front wheels. Brake pads are applied to both sides of a cast-iron disc by means of hydraulic cylinders held in a calliper. The disc is open to the atmosphere except where it passes through the calliper, so cooling is very effective. With disc brakes a larger brake force is needed, and the pedal action is therefore usually augmented by a *servo-mechanism. Pressure hydraulic brakes, which use a hydraulic system with a pump and microprocessor anti-lock control, are becoming common in cars. They are known as ABS (anti-lock braking systems).

Early trains used friction brakes on the locomotive and *brake van until continuous braking systems such as *Westinghouse's *air-brake (1868) were developed. Continuous braking systems use either a vacuum or compressed air to transfer braking force generated in the locomotive to every vehicle in the train. Friction brakes using cast iron brake-blocks gave way in the 1970s to disc brakes. Modern electric and diesel-electric locomotives use regenerative braking, in which the traction motor acts as a brake by running in reverse: kinetic energy is converted to electrical energy, which is fed back to the supply system (regenerative braking) or dissipated as heat in resistors. Heavy goods vehicles use compressed *air-brakes. *Aeroplanes use drum brakes inside the wheel hubs, assisted by the action of flaps and spoilers on the wings. *Machine-tools also need powerful brakes to stop the workpiece safely; these are commonly a form of disc brake, similar to a multi-plate friction *clutch. For most forms of brake the material used for the friction pads is either a compound of asbestos or other fibrous material rein-

Braking system

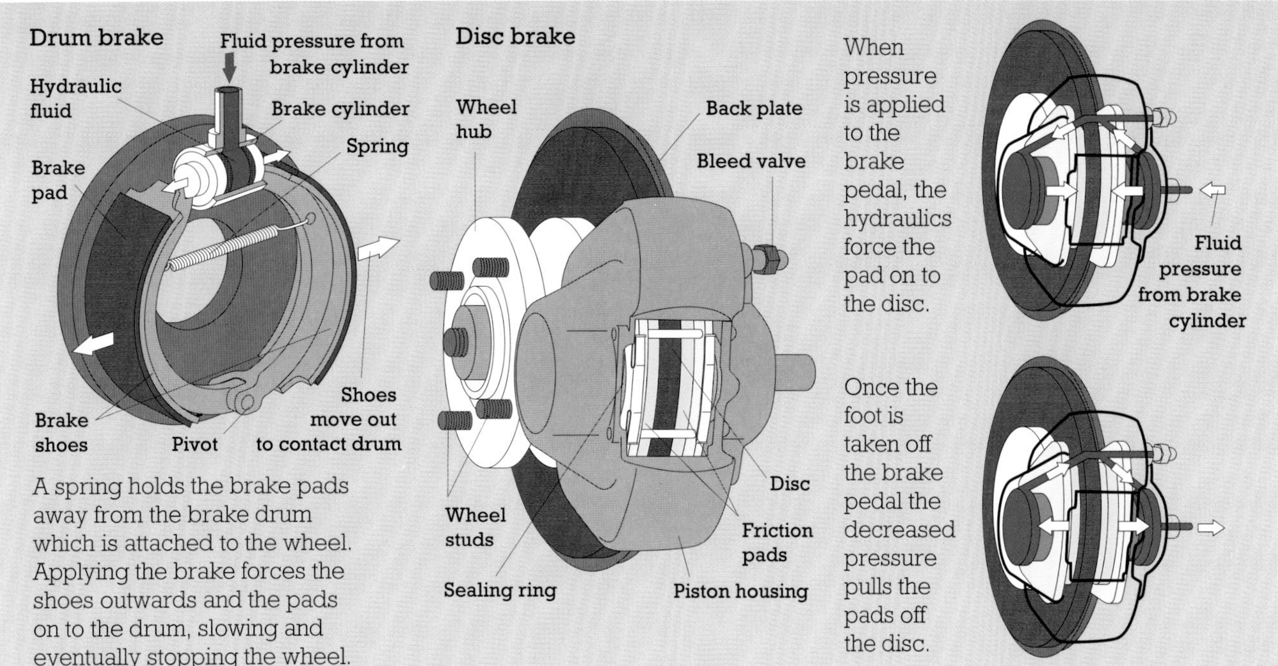
Drum brake
Fluid pressure from brake cylinder
Hydraulic fluid
Brake cylinder
Spring
Brake pad
Shoes move out to contact drum
Brake shoes
Pivot
A spring holds the brake pads away from the brake drum which is attached to the wheel. Applying the brake forces the shoes outwards and the pads on to the drum, slowing and eventually stopping the wheel.
Disc brake
Wheel hub
Back plate
Bleed valve
Disc
Wheel studs
Friction pads
Sealing ring
Piston housing
When pressure is applied to the brake pedal, the hydraulics force the pad on to the disc.
Fluid pressure from brake cylinder
Once the foot is taken off the brake pedal the decreased pressure pulls the pads off the disc.

forced with metal fibres, or a ceramic compound. Braking systems are also used in the absorption *dynamometer.

Bramah, Joseph (1748–1814), British engineer and inventor, whose lock-manufacturing shop was a cradle of the machine-tool industry. His greatest invention was a hydraulic press capable of exerting a force of several thousand tonnes, which he developed with *Nasmyth (1795). His other inventions included a machine for sequentially numbering banknotes and a planing machine. Bramah hired *Maudslay to develop *machine-tools to make a pick-proof lock (1784), which remained unpicked for sixty-seven years.

brass, originally an *alloy of copper and zinc. Brass was first made in the 1st millennium BC. It is suitable for *casting, resists corrosion, and is stronger, harder, and tougher than copper alone. There are two main types of brass: one with more than 64 per cent copper, which can be worked cold (such as pinchbeck, or gilding metal, containing 7–11 per cent zinc and used for decorative metalwork); the other with less copper, which must be worked hot. Other metals can be added to give desirable properties: the addition of manganese increases strength, and adding nickel gives high-tensile brass. Brass has been widely used for both decorative and functional items such as buttons, buckles, tubes, and boilers, but is less widespread now due to replacement by plastics and more recently developed alloys.

Brattain, Walter Hauser *Shockley, William Bradford.

Braun, Karl Ferdinand (1850–1918), versatile German physicist who is best remembered for his inventions in *radio wireless telegraphy. Braun's discovery in 1874 that crystals of galeria (an ore of lead sulphide) can act as rectifiers later led to the development of the crystal *radio receiver. To overcome the limited range of *Hertz's spark transmitter, in 1909 Braun invented a sparkless antenna circuit coupled magnetically to the transmitter; his system was soon widely adopted. He also developed a directional antenna. In 1897 he built the first *cathode-ray tube oscillograph, forerunner of the modern *television receiver. In 1909 he shared the Nobel Prize for Physics with *Marconi.

Braun, Wernher Magnus Maximilian von (1912–77), German-born US pioneer of rocket propulsion (see *rocketry, history of) and space exploration. An engineering graduate, he was inspired by the work of the Romanian-born physicist Hermann Oberth to devote himself to problems of rocket propulsion. He worked with Oberth and others to develop the supersonic V2 *ballistic missile, more than 1,000 of which were launched against southern England towards the end of World War II. After the War, von Braun and others were immediately employed by the USA to develop long-range military rockets and, later, rockets for space exploration. He was associated with the early US programmes to launch artificial satellites and unmanned space probes; and participated in the **Apollo* programme, which in 1969 successfully landed people on the Moon.

brazing, the joining of two metals by heating, using *brass as a filler. The surfaces of the two metals to be joined are placed next to each other and cleaned by heating with a *flux. When both pieces are at red heat the brass (sometimes called spelter) is introduced. It melts and flows between the two surfaces. On cooling, the brass solidifies and the two pieces are held firmly together. Only those metals with a melting-point significantly above that of brass can be joined in this way, and the joint is not as strong as one made by *welding.

bread, a staple food made by baking a dough composed principally of meal or flour mixed with water. Leavened bread is made with yeast, which causes the dough to rise, while unleavened bread uses no yeast and produces a flat bread. Types of unleavened bread include Mexican tortillas, made from a special type of corn flour, and Indian chapatis and Greek pitta bread, both made from wheat flour. Leavened bread is nearly always made with wheat, as it is unique in forming an elastic, springy dough when kneaded with water. This elastic texture is due to a protein, gluten, present in the wheat. For bread-making, flour that is high in protein is generally used, derived from bread wheat (*Triticum aestivum*). The milled grain (see *milling) is mixed to a dough with water and yeast. Bakers' yeast, *Saccharomyces cerevisiae*, is used commercially. The dough is left for a period to rise: during this time the yeast reacts with sugars in the dough to form carbon dioxide gas, the raising agent, and *ethanol, which is vaporized during baking and contributes to the smell of the freshly baked bread. Other fermentation products add to the texture or flavour of the final bread. Although the simplest breads (such as the French baguette or Italian-style bread) use only white flour, salt, and yeast, other breads have added ingredients. Different flours, such as wholewheat (milled from whole grains), rye, and potato flour, produce breads with different colours, flavours, and textures. Small amounts of shortening (fat or oil) can be added to soften the bread, and sugar may sometimes be added for sweetening and in order to increase the amount of material available for fermentation. In soda bread, baking powder is used to leaven the bread instead of yeast, while in sour-dough bread, bacteria which produce lactic acid are present in addition to yeasts, and add other flavours to the bread. (See *bakery for an illustration of modern baking processes.)

breakwater *ports and harbours.

Brearley, Harold (1871–1948), British metallurgist responsible for the commercial development of *stainless steel. The latter part of the 19th century saw intense interest in the development of alloy *steels for use with *machine-tools, and for manufacturing the teeth of power shovels and other equipment subject to severe abrasion. In 1912, while investigating the use of high-chromium steel for rifle barrels, Brearley noted its exceptional resistance to *corrosion and suggested its use in cutlery. The first stainless steel knives were made for him in Sheffield, UK, in 1914.

breathalyser, a simple, portable apparatus that estimates the concentration of alcohol in the blood by testing alcohol levels in the breath, usually by noting the colour change in crystals of potassium dichromate. It is commonly used to test whether drivers have exceeded permitted levels of alcohol intake: in the UK this limit is 35 μg of alcohol per 100 ml of breath. A positive breathalyser test will usually be followed up by a more accurate breath test, and tests of blood or urine alcohol levels.

brewing, the process by which beers, ales, and lagers are made. In the West the basic ingredient of beer is barley, while in Africa millet or maize may be used, and rice beer is made in Japan. In beer-making (see figure) the barley or other grain is germinated, and the young seedlings are then dried to produce malt. The malt is ground, and placed in a mash tub with water and cereal, where enzymes in the malt convert the starch into fermentable sugars. The resulting liquid, called wort, is transferred to a brewing kettle, where flavourings, particularly hops, are added, and the mixture is boiled. The mixture is then filtered, and *fermentation is stimulated by the introduction of yeast. Traditionally, the liquid at this stage is filtered again and placed in wooden barrels, where fermentation continues. Ales and stouts are usually fermented at 15–20 °C, while lagers are fermented at 6–8 °C for longer periods. In modern keg beers and lagers, fermentation is stopped after only a short period by placing the liquid in sealed metal barrels and introducing carbon dioxide. *Food additives may be introduced into the beer to alter its flavour or appearance, or to improve its keeping qualities. A recent development is the brewing of non-alcoholic beers or lagers. These are made either by adding carbon dioxide directly to the wort, or by removing the alcohol from fully fermented beer.

brick, a rectangular manufactured block of dried or fired clay, small enough to be lifted and placed with one hand, used in building. Bricks are *ceramics, and were first made by drying mixtures of mud and straw (adobe), and such bricks are still used in hot, dry climates. *Kiln-fired bricks were first made in Mesopotamia in about 3200–2800 BC. Firing made the bricks harder and resistant to rain erosion.

Brewing

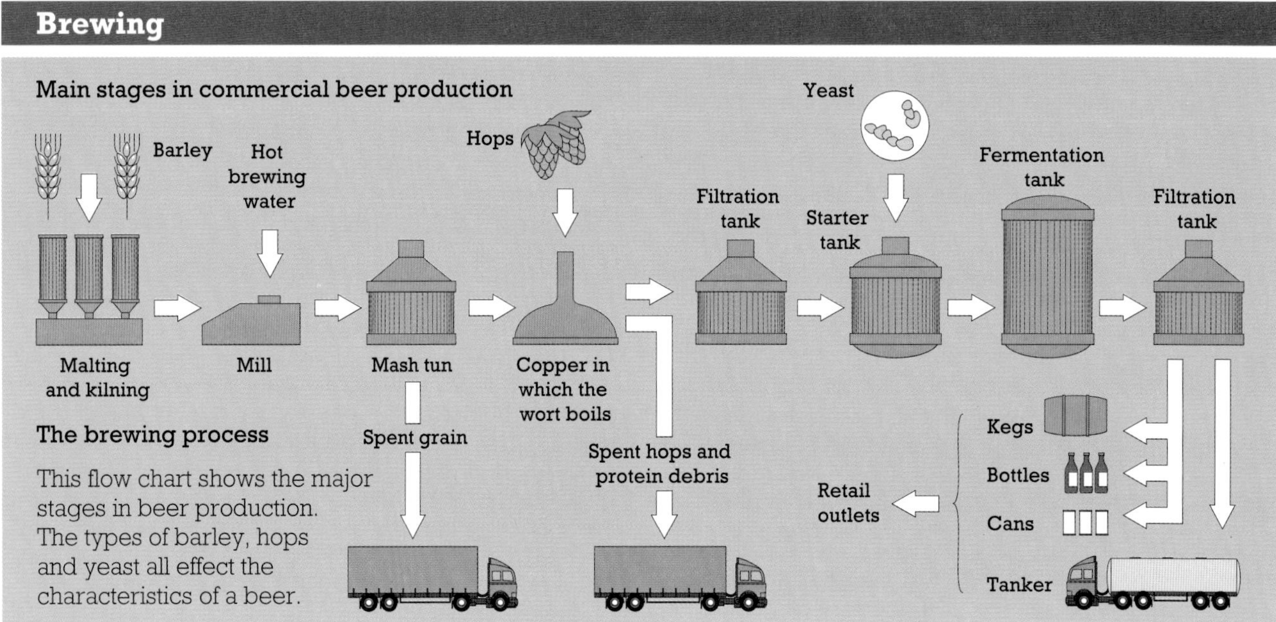

The brewing process

This flow chart shows the major stages in beer production. The types of barley, hops and yeast all effect the characteristics of a beer.

Brick-making remains essentially the same today: clay or shale is blended to a plastic consistency with water, then moulded to shape. In large-scale production the clay is either *extruded and then cut to size by wires, or *moulded under high pressure in steel moulds. The bricks are then fired in kilns. *Refractory bricks are made from special clays with high concentrations of silica or *alumina.

bricklaying, the process of arranging *bricks in a wall. Bonding (overlapping the bricks in successive courses) ensures strength and stability. Different bonding patterns result from different arrangements of stretchers (bricks with the long axis parallel to the wall) and headers (bricks with the long axis at right angles to the wall). In *cavity walls, the two walls (leaves) are laid in stretcher bond and linked with metal ties across the cavity. For solid walls, various bonds are used, with the headers tying the wall across its width. The bricks are laid in *mortar; where the brickwork is visible in the finished building, clean and regular jointing between the bricks is important. In building a wall, the quoins (corners) are normally built first, to ensure the wall is vertical and course depths are regular. The bricklayer then lays the bricks in the main part of the wall against a string line stretched between the quoins. Full-size templates are used as guides for curved walls and for those with a battered (sloping) face.

bridge, a structure, usually built over a river, road, or railway, enabling road or rail vehicles or pedestrians to cross. One type of primitive bridge is the clapper bridge, in which large stone slabs are supported on stone piers (see figure overleaf). Examples are still to be found in Devon, UK, and at Fujian in China, where 200-tonne granite slabs 21 m (70 feet) long were used. The Romans were the first to use the masonry arch in bridge-building. An example is the Alcántara road bridge (AD *c*.100) over the River Tagus in Spain. The Romans also used timber to build bridges: Trajan's column in Rome depicts such a bridge, built over the River Danube AD *c*.100. Roman arches were invariably semicircular, but in China flatter, segmental-arch bridges were built, which could span greater distances than the semicircular arch. The earliest example is the Anji Bridge at Zhao Xian, built in AD 610 and still in use. Arched bridges of this type were first built in Europe in the 14th century. An example is the Ponte Vecchio in Florence, Italy (completed in 1345).

In 1779 the Coalbrookdale *Iron Bridge heralded a new era of iron and steel arch bridges. Cast iron was soon replaced by wrought iron because of its greater strength under bending loads. The use of wrought iron reached its peak in 1885 with the completion of the Luiz I bridge at Oporto in Portugal, which spanned 173 m (566 feet). Since then, several steel arch bridges have been built with spans of over 500 m (1,650 feet). Examples are the Sydney Harbour Bridge, Australia (1932) and the Bayonne Bridge in New York (1930). The Forth Bridge, in Scotland, UK, built between 1882 and 1889, was the first long-span *cantilever bridge and has two spans, each of 520 m (1,710 feet). The concrete arch of the Gladesville Bridge in Sydney, built in 1964, spans 305 m (1,000 feet). The earliest *suspension bridges, which were widespread geographically, had three ropes which hung from anchorages on each side and formed a V-shaped walkway with handrails. The Lan Jin Bridge, built in AD 65 at Yunnan in China, used iron chains to support a wooden deck. In the *Industrial Revolution chains were first used in Europe, as in *Telford's bridge over the Menai Straits, Anglesey, UK, which was completed in 1826.

Many types of bridge have been designed for specialized use. These include the *bascule bridge, the *swing bridge, and the *transporter bridge, all designed for crossing waterways while allowing tall shipping to pass beneath. The Bailey bridge, originally designed for military use in World War II, and the pontoon bridge, are usually temporary structures. The Bailey bridge (named after its designer, Donald Bailey, 1901–85) is a prefabricated steel bridge, for temporary use such as to cross a river or road. In a pontoon bridge, relatively short spans are supported on floating pontoons, held in position by anchors. (See also *drawbridge, *viaduct.)

brig, a small two-masted sailing vessel *square-rigged on both masts, widely used in the days of sail on short sea routes and for coastal trading (see *sailing ships and boats for illustration). A brigantine is similar but is *fore-and-aft rigged on the mainmast. A hermaphrodite brig has the usual square-rigged foremast combined with the mainmast of a *schooner, a rig designed to increase speed with the wind abeam (from the side). Brigs were also used in some navies as training ships for boys selected to become seamen. The marine steam-engine made brigs obsolete, although some are still used by navies for sail training.

brightening agent, a fluorescent substance added to soapless detergents (for example *washing powders) which absorbs ultraviolet light and emits blue light, thereby counteracting the yellowing of white fabrics caused by repeated washings. Brightening agents provide no extra cleaning effect. They are also used to enhance the appearance of new fabrics.

Brindley, James (1716–72), pioneer British *canal builder. Brindley had virtually no education, but he had a thorough grasp of civil engineering problems. In association with the Duke of Bridgewater, he built the Bridgewater Canal in Lancashire. It had no locks and was only 16 km (10 miles) long, but included a masonry arched *aqueduct crossing the River Irwell at a height of 12m (40 feet). Brindley subsequently built the 150-km (93-mile) Grand Trunk Canal linking the rivers Mersey and Trent, completed in 1777.

briquetting, a process in which fine coal is compressed into a briquette or block, sometimes with the use of a binder. Coal briquettes were first made in the 1840s and 1850s in Germany. Coal was mixed with a medium-soft tar or asphaltic pitch, heated with steam, and then compressed. Substances now used as binders include inorganic materials such as Portland cement, silica, soda, limestone, and clay; and organic materials such as resins, pitch, molasses, and starch. Binderless briquettes are also produced by carbonizing the coal (see *coke) at about 450 °C and then briquetting the resulting char.

British Association for the Advancement of Science, a society founded in 1831 to offer an alternative to the *Royal Society. Its aims are to provide a forum where scientists can discuss topics of common interest, and to inform the public. It is peripatetic, meeting annually in a UK city, and very occasionally in the Commonwealth. More recently it has taken a particular interest in the social impact of science.

broadcasting, the transmission of *radio and *television programmes for public reception. The first radio broadcast

Bridge

Clapper bridge

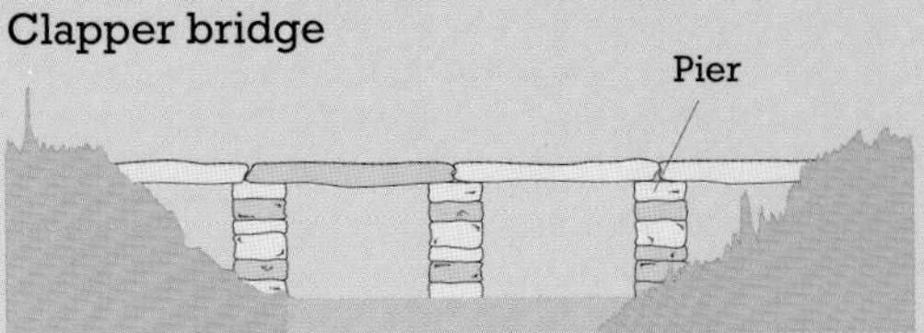

Each stone spanning a gap acts as a beam. Both the weight of the stones themselves and any load they have to carry is transmitted to the piers.

Truss bridge

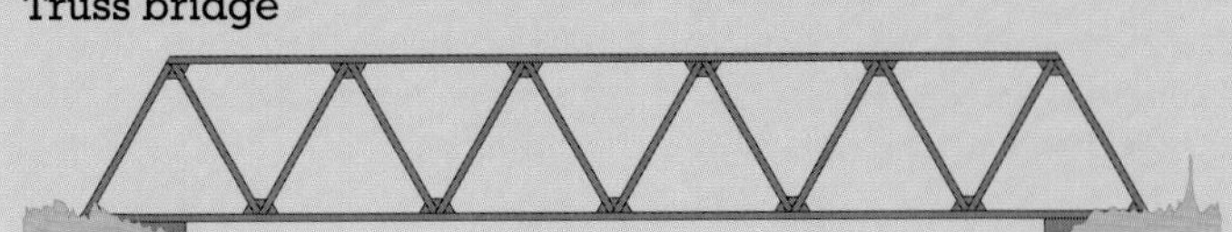

The truss acts like a deep beam, transmitting the load to the abutments (supports). The depth provided by the open framework gives a much stiffer structure when compared with a completely solid beam made from an equivalent amount of the same material.

Bowstring arch bridge

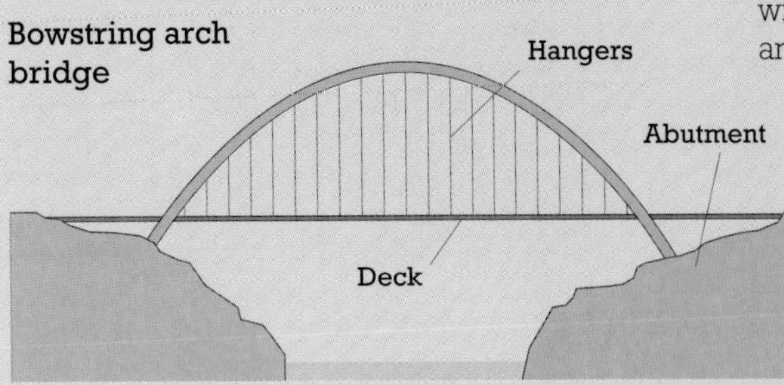

The deck is supported by hangers; the overall load is transmitted via the arch as thrusts against the abutments.

Masonry bridge

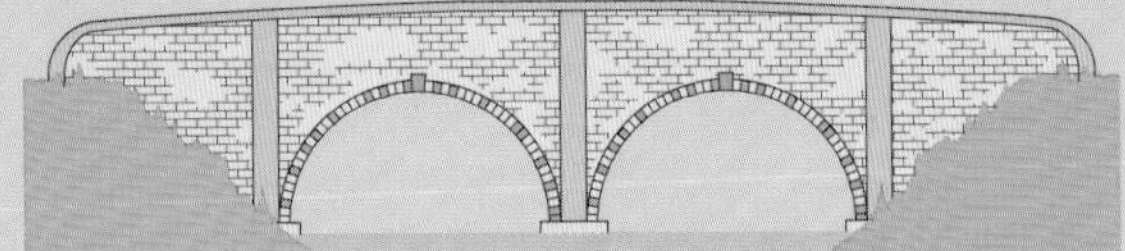

The arch transmits the downward load as diagonal thrusts against the banks. Where two arches meet the lateral thrusts counteract each other.

Suspension bridge

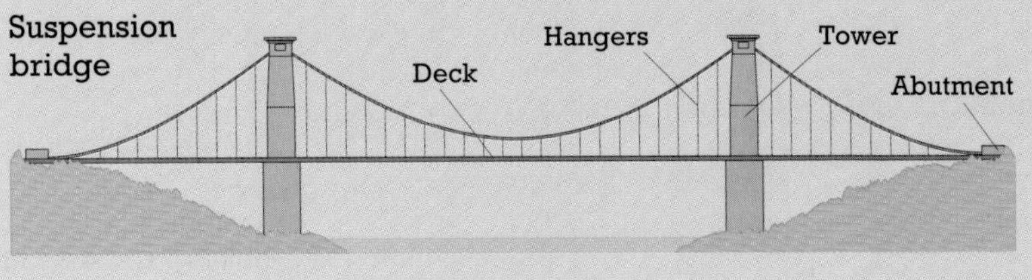

The deck and any load on it are supported by hangers. This creates tension in the cables which is resisted by the anchorage in the abutments. It also puts the towers supporting the cables under large compressive forces.

Cable-stayed bridge

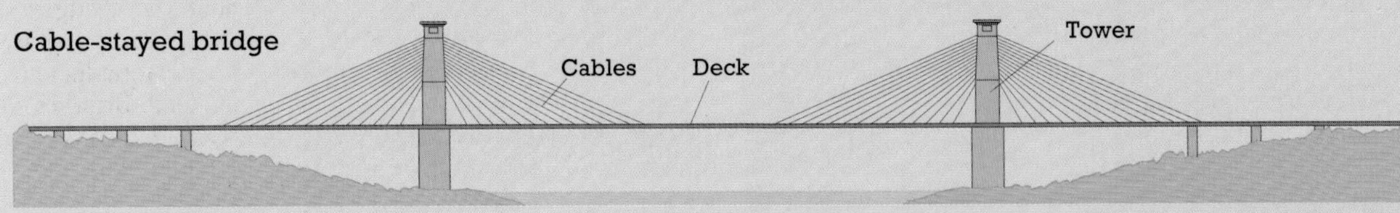

The cables support the deck and transmit the load to the towers, putting them under large compressive forces. Unlike the suspension bridge, the load is not transmitted to the abutments.

Cantilever bridge

The cantilever frameworks are balanced on either side of each main support and a short truss (the central span) connects the two cantilevers.

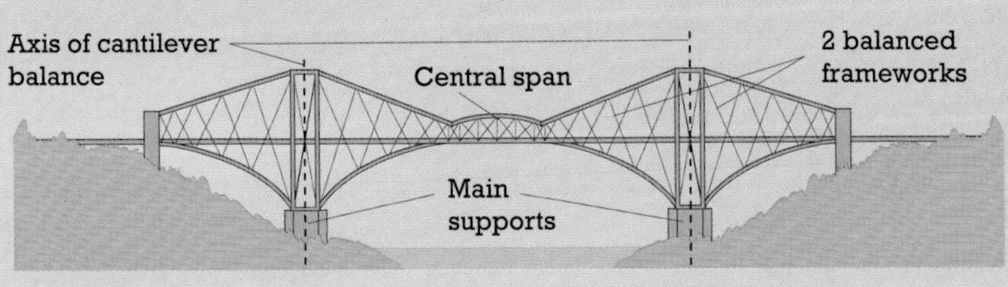

was made in 1906, when a broadcast in the USA by *Fessenden was received by numerous ships' wireless operators. The first commercial radio station began broadcasting from Pittsburgh, USA, in 1920. By 1931 television broadcasting was technically feasible, and a complete high-definition broadcasting system was first used for public broadcasts by the BBC in 1935. Television broadcasting in the USA followed in 1939, but other countries did not begin wide-scale broadcasts until the 1950s. By the early 1960s *communications satellites made it possible to link the television networks of Europe and the USA, and by the early 1970s satellite links could be made to nearly all parts of the world. Recent advances in broadcasting include digital and stereophonic transmissions, and video broadcasts linked to stereo sound transmissions. (See also *telecommunications.)

bromine (symbol Br, at. no. 35, r.a.m. 79.90), a dense, deep reddish-brown liquid that readily vaporizes. It occurs as bromide in sea-water, from which it is extracted commercially, and in salt deposits. Its main application has been as 1,2-dibromoethane, an additive to leaded petrol, but since the introduction of lead-free petrol this application has declined. It is also used in the manufacture of silver bromide for photographic emulsions, in fire-extinguishing and flame-retardant agents, in fumigants, and in chemical synthesis.

bronze, originally an *alloy of copper and tin, known since *c*.3500 BC. It is harder than copper and has a lower melting-point, making it suitable for *casting. Varying the ratio of copper to tin gives alloys with different properties. Bell metal contains 20–25 per cent tin and is remarkable for its sonorous quality, whereas statuary bronze has only 10 per cent tin, plus a little zinc to increase hardness. Adding phosphorus (around 0.5 per cent) greatly increases the strength, and phosphor bronzes are used for pump plungers and valves. Most 'copper' coins are made from bronze with added zinc to prevent wear. The term bronze is sometimes used for other copper alloys, containing no tin. Aluminium bronzes contain copper with up to 10 per cent aluminium and occasionally silicon, manganese, iron, nickel, and zinc. They are lightweight, very strong, and resistant to corrosion, so are used in engines for crankcases and connecting-rods.

Brunel, Sir Marc Isambard (1769–1849) and **Isambard Kingdom** (1806–59), outstanding mechanical and civil engineers. Marc was born in France, and achieved renown as an engineer and architect in the USA, before moving to the UK in 1799. Here, he secured a contract to produce 100,000 pulley-blocks per year for the Royal Navy. Using steam-driven machinery of his own design, he developed production techniques which reduced the labour force from 110 skilled workers to 10 unskilled. Thus Brunel, along with *Witney in the USA, was the first to develop machines that could produce parts accurately enough to be interchangeable, a key innovation in the development of *mass production. Brunel next directed his attention to a number of inventions, including *stereotype plates for printing and a *knitting machine. Then in 1825 he was commissioned to construct a pedestrian *tunnel under the River Thames in London (completed 1843), for which purpose he designed a three-tier *shield excavator. The British-born Isambard, Marc's son, also worked on the Thames tunnel. In 1828 he was injured in the course of this work, and while recovering worked on a design for the Clifton suspension bridge over the River Avon, in Bristol (the bridge was eventually built to this design but was not completed until after his death). Other important civil engineering projects included the Monkwearmouth docks (1831) and similar work at other ports; and many other bridges, the most notable being that across the River Wye at Chepstow (1849–52); over 1,500 km (1,000 miles) of railway, most of it on the broad-gauge Great Western Railway, for which he was chief engineer. Brunel also designed three ships, each the largest and most advanced of its time when constructed. The *Great Western* (1837), a wooden paddle-steamer, became the first regular transatlantic vessel of its kind. This was followed by the iron-hulled **Great Britain* (1843), and in 1858 by the *Great Eastern*. This included a revolutionary double iron hull and was driven by both paddles and screw propeller, but the design proved unsuccessful as a passenger vessel. Brunel also produced a floating armoured barge and a prefabricated military hospital, both used to great effect in the Crimean War (1853–6).

Isambard Kingdom **Brunel**'s steamship the *Great Eastern*, ready for launch in 1857. The man in the top hat is John Scott Russell, who built the ship to Brunel's design.

bubble chamber *particle detector.

buffer, a device, usually one of a pair, on the front and rear of a railway vehicle, used to constrain buffing—the compressive movement between vehicles of a train. Originally buffers were solid wooden blocks, but were soon replaced by padded leather blocks and later by sprung metal buffer designs using coils or, more recently, hydraulic springs. Although buffers are still used on most European railways, elsewhere their role has been combined with that of automatic centre *couplings. Buffers are also provided to stop a train at the end of a track.

building material, a material used in construction. Timber, concrete, stone, brick, and steel are common structural materials. When choosing a material, such properties as strength in tension and compression, stiffness, density, and dimensional changes with changes in temperature or humidity need to be considered. Other constructional materials are chosen for different properties. Insulating materials such as plastic foams and mineral fibre have low thermal conductivity; materials used in *damp-proof courses are chosen for their water resistance. *Fire-resistance is another important consideration in most buildings. The durability of materials in the local climate is important for external materials. Other properties may be important in specific applications, for example sound absorption, or the ability to resist aggressive chemicals. A major consideration in the choice of all building materials is cost. A material such as concrete is inexpensive to make, and building techniques developed for use with concrete offer savings in terms of time and labour over traditional methods.

building techniques. Archaeological evidence suggests that building as a specialized activity probably began in Mesopotamia (*c*.7000 BC), where there is little building stone. *Mud buildings were generally roofed either with wooden beams supporting clay-daubed matting or with a *vault (a three-dimensional arched structure). True arches were used

Building techniques

Reed dwellings
*c.*3000 BC

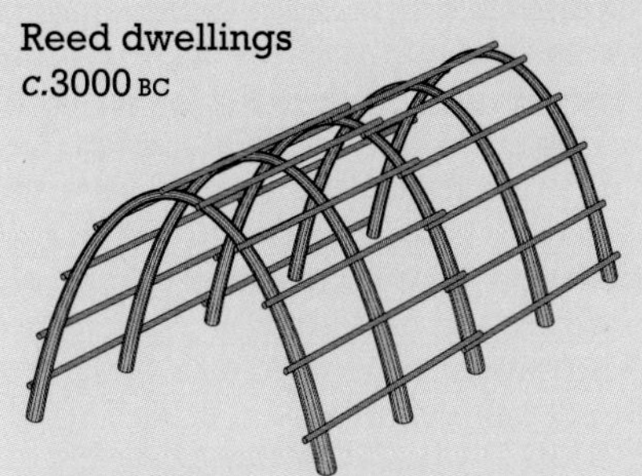

Simple, single-room dwellings have been built with easily available material since prehistoric times, as in this Egyptian reed hut (framework only shown).

Egyptian pillar and lintel in stone
*c.*2000 BC

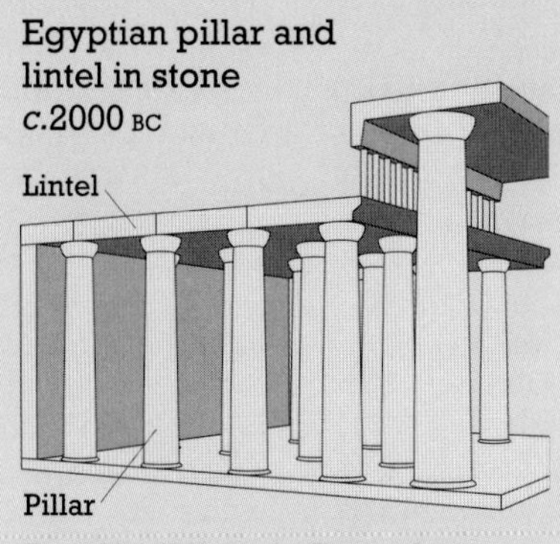

Royal buildings in Egypt from around 2700 BC were largely of stone. They were generally of pillar and lintel construction, although the arch was known in Egypt at this time.

Parthenon *c.*450 BC

Timber beams, which could span wider gaps than stone beams, were used in Greek temples such as the Parthenon in Athens.

St Paul's Cathedral, London 1685–1710

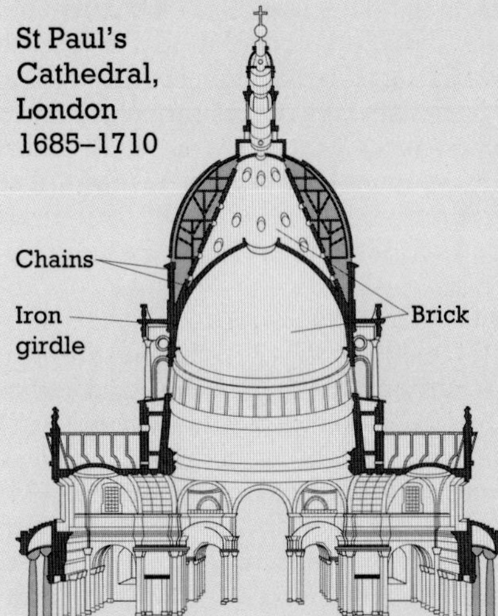

The dome of St Paul's was a major achievement of 17th century English building. Iron chains on an iron 'girdle' held the outward thrust of the dome.

Salisbury Cathedral, UK 1237–58

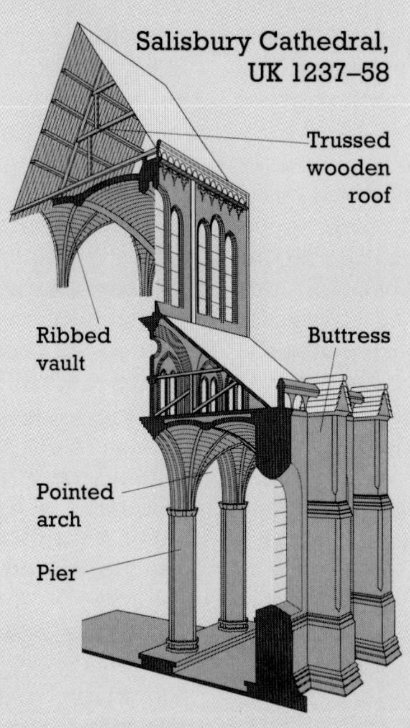

Medieval Gothic cathedrals supported a stone vault, ribbed for lightness and covered by a wooden roof, on slender piers augmented by buttresses. This construction allowed a very large window area.

Chinese and Japanese building

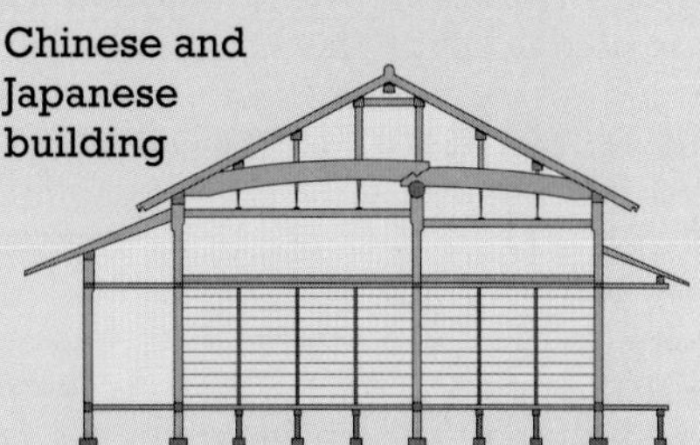

Elegant timber-frame construction with screen walls still survives in Japan today.

Saulnier's chocolate factory 1871–2

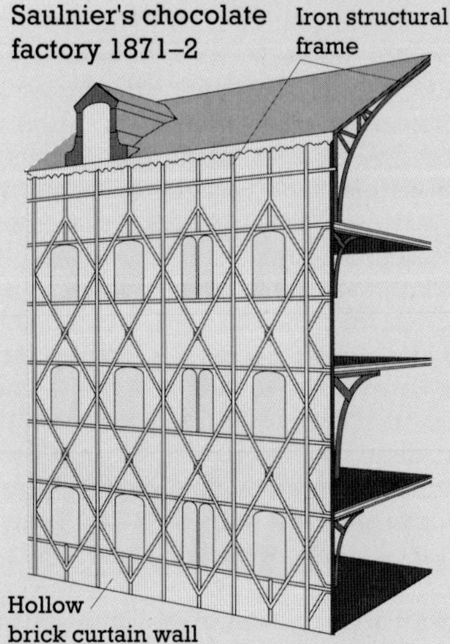

The use of iron as the major structural component in a building began towards the end of the 19th century.

Olympic stadium, Munich, late 20th century

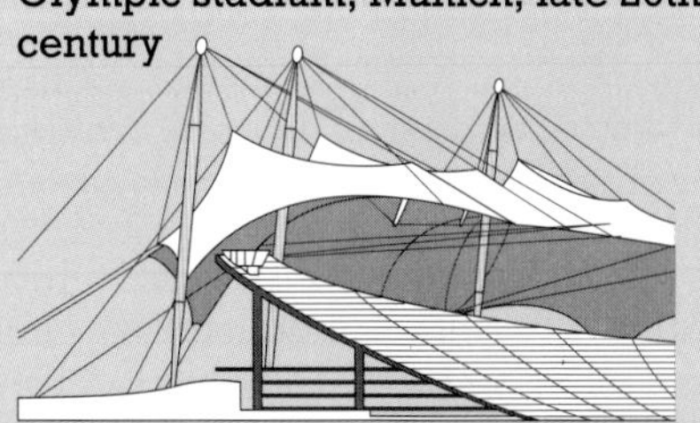

The availability of computer programs to analyse stress flow in composite materials has allowed the development of large tension structures in the second half of the 20th century.

Skyscraper late 20th century

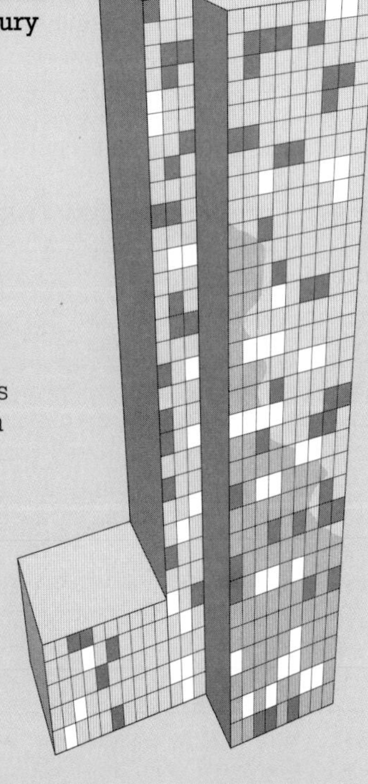

Modern skyscrapers are built from a central core of reinforced concrete. Concrete and steel floors are hung on this, reaching out to a steel perimeter structure which is covered by a light-weight curtain wall.

for openings, and methods of building vaults without centring (using a wooden framework to support the vault while building) were also known. The Ur-Nammu ziggurat at Ur, Mesopotamia (*c.*2100 BC), had an adobe core that was faced with fired bricks bedded in bitumen and reinforced with reed mats. Building with stone seems to have begun in the Nile valley, with the construction of important religious buildings. Although the arch was known to the Egyptians, they preferred massive columns supporting short lintels for their temples (see figure). The Great Pyramid (*c.*2500 BC) was built with stones up to 200 tonnes each, faced with finely jointed limestone bedded in *lime. Before stone-quarrying began, Egyptian buildings were made from reed bundles covered with reed matting, a technique still in use in southern Iraq. Buildings were often built from wood where it was plentiful. Early buildings used wooden posts, planking, or entire logs to form walls and roof; later, timber *frame construction was introduced to save on wood. *Roofs were covered with thatching (vegetable material such as reeds or brushwood laid over the rafters) or *tiles. In Greece, this frame construction, translated into marble, is evident in such temples as the Parthenon, Athens (*c.*450 BC). The Romans developed a strong, durable form of *concrete by adding silica-rich crushed brick or pozzolana (volcanic ash) to lime. Large public buildings were roofed by concrete and masonry semicircular *vaults or domes. The Pantheon dome in Rome (built in 27 BC) spans 43 m (141 feet)—a span unequalled until the 19th century.

Meanwhile, in China, there was a tradition of timber construction very different from that in the West. This type of design spread to Korea and Japan and lasted until modern times. In Europe, the medieval mason extended Roman methods to develop slender Gothic churches with large tracery windows. Timber trussed roofs protected the *masonry from the weather. Humbler buildings were still of timber, with the upper floors and roof supported by walls of closely spaced posts. During the Renaissance, masonry remained the material for large structures, with arches being used to span openings. The domes of St Peter's, Rome (1546–64), and of St Paul's, London (1685–1710), were not buttressed externally but were encircled by iron chains to contain the outward thrust on the supporting walls below. Increasingly, metal reinforcements were used to strengthen masonry. In France in the 1670s, Claude Perrault designed lintels for a colonnade at the Louvre, which were made from small stone blocks reinforced with an iron cage—a precursor of reinforced concrete.

By the late 1700s in Britain a number of disastrous fires in mill buildings prompted the replacement of wood with *cast-iron columns and beams as the internal support for floors (external walls were still of masonry) and the development of iron windows and brick and iron vaulted floors. In a series of large botanical glasshouses, sheet *glass (which could now be manufactured in large sizes) enclosed an iron framework; masonry walls were not used at all. This technique culminated in the Crystal Palace, London (1851)— the first large building to be assembled from prefabricated components—and in the roofs of many large train stations and sheds. The first fully framed building was probably the four-storey Menier chocolate factory built over the River Marne (to utilize water power) at Noisel, France (1871). In Chicago, development of a safe passenger *lift led to the construction of *skyscrapers. The Forth Bridge (1882–9) was the first major steel structure to be built in the UK.

Meanwhile, concrete had undergone significant development. In the 1760s, *Smeaton had discovered that mixtures of clay and limestone produced a hydraulic *cement which hardened under water—essential for his work in rebuilding the Eddystone Lighthouse off Plymouth, UK. Subsequently, the compressive strength and reliability of these cements improved, but the concrete made with them lacked tensile strength, essential to resist the stresses in a floor or beam. In the UK and France reinforcement techniques were developed for concrete. In the UK in 1854, A. B. Wilkinson patented beams reinforced with wire ropes and iron bars and built a *reinforced concrete house (1865). In France, Joseph Monier made reinforced concrete tubs for orange trees (1849), and in 1892 a reinforced concrete building frame was patented which had many features still in use today.

Modern *skyscrapers have hull-and-core structures, with a light-weight *curtain wall enclosing the building. The central core is a reinforced concrete tower. While reinforced concrete is also often used as the skeleton frame for blocks of flats and similar buildings, a load-bearing wall structure is usually more appropriate. The main walls run across the building to support the floors and are buttressed by internal longitudinal walls (cross-wall construction) as in the Unités d'Habitation (1947–52) by the Swiss-born French architect Le Corbusier. For large-area single-storey buildings, both thin concrete *shells and steel *space frames are widely used, and by the 1980s the availability of durable polymer fabrics made possible the construction of tent-like *tension structures typified by the Hajj terminal in Saudi Arabia. A major force for the development of building techniques has been the improvement in materials manufacture and in fabrication and jointing techniques. Another has been the better understanding of structural behaviour and the evolution of mathematical techniques of structural analysis since the 16th century.

bulk carrier, a generic name for any *merchant ship designed to carry cargoes in bulk, either dry (for example, grain, mineral ores, and coal), or liquid (such as oil, liquefied gas, and wine). Those fitted to carry liquid cargoes are more generally described as *tankers, but are still part of the family of bulk carriers. The earliest specialist bulk carriers appeared in the last quarter of the 19th century. Ships designed to carry dry cargoes are fitted with extra-large holds: these are loaded and unloaded automatically using mechanical chutes. The majority have their engines aft. The largest dry carriers hold up to 120,000 tonnes.

bulkhead, a vertical partition dividing the hull of a ship into watertight compartments, first seen in the Chinese *junk. Main bulkheads, across the whole hull, are normally made watertight to limit flooding, should the hull be holed. A collision bulkhead is a watertight bulkhead near the bows of a ship, which is intended to prevent extensive flooding after a collision.

bulldozer, an earth-moving *tractor with a wide steel blade at the front used to spread and compact soil and broken rock by pushing or dragging with the blade. Steam-powered crawler tractors were first fitted with a blade attachment in 1923, by La Plante Choate Co., USA. Modern bulldozers may have either *caterpillar tracks or wheels. A movable arm with one or more steel teeth can be fitted to the back to break up soft rock or concrete so that it can be spread more easily. A bulldozer can also be used to pull a *scraper for levelling rough ground or clearing waste material from mining.

bullet, a small round or cylindrical projectile fired from a hand-held *firearm. Originally bullets were lead balls slightly smaller in diameter than the firearm barrel. When shot, they bounced from side to side up the barrel, with consequent loss of accuracy. The *rifling of firearm barrels improved accuracy by imparting spin to the bullet, but for this to work the bullet had to fit the barrel more snugly, which slowed the loading process. To rectify this, in 1849 a French captain, Claude-Etienne Minié, designed a soft metal bullet that expanded into the rifling grooves after the propellant had exploded. Because the bullet tip was no longer involved in the firing action, it could be given a cone shape to improve flight accuracy. A *cartridge containing a *detonator and the propellant charge was also joined to the bullet. Tracer bullets incorporate a chemical compound that burns in flight, allowing the direction of flight to be observed and aim corrected accordingly. Recent developments include the *plastic bullet.

Bunsen burner, a type of gas burner, named after the German chemist Robert Bunsen, for heating *laboratory equipment and chemicals. It was probably devised and sold by Bunsen's assistant, Peter Desdega, based on a design by *Faraday. It quickly became a standard piece of laboratory equipment. An adjustable collar allows air to be drawn into the barrel via a small hole. The gas–air mixture burns at the top of the barrel. By varying the amount of air entering the barrel, a wide range of heat intensity can be achieved. At its hottest, the flame has a pale blue cone at the centre, and can reach temperatures of 1,400–1,500 °C. The Bunsen burner has now been largely superseded by electric heating mantles and *spectrometers.

buoy, a fixed, floating mark, anchored to the sea-bed, to assist navigation by marking fairways and indicating underwater dangers such as sandbanks. A buoy can also be a float, often steel or plastic, moored to the sea-bed and having an upper point of attachment allowing vessels to moor. Buoys are known to have been in use from the Middle Ages, but are probably much older. Through the centuries national buoyage systems developed into two types: 'lateral' buoys, marking the sides of shipping lanes, and 'cardinal' buoys, indicating the direction of hazards. In 1987 agreement was reached on an international system of both lateral and cardinal buoys. Buoys usually carry lights to allow recognition at night. Different types are recognized by differences in shape, colour, and top marking.

A lifebuoy or lifebelt is a buoy (usually a ring) designed to support the human body in the water.

burette, a thin, cylindrical, graduated glass tube commonly of 50 ml capacity, open at one end and with a glass or Teflon stopcock at the other, which allows measured amounts of liquid to be run out. It is a standard piece of laboratory equipment used for routine anlysis.

bus (computing), the channel that carries signals within a *computer and sometimes also from the computer to *peripherals. Conventional computers use two main kinds of bus: the address bus and the data bus. The address bus locates in *memory the data that the *central processing unit needs to access; the data bus is the pathway by which this data is entered or extracted. The width of the bus is measured as the number of *bits which can be transmitted simultaneously, usually 8, 16, 32, or 64 bits. A wide bus can greatly increase the performance of a computer.

buses and coaches. A bus is a public-service road vehicle for the use of fare-paying passengers, usually operating along fixed routes and often running to a timetable. Motor coaches tend to be used for longer-distance routes. The term bus was probably first used of horse-drawn vehicles in Paris around 1827. The first self-propelled buses were *steam-powered vehicles. The first internal-combustion-engined bus, designed by *Benz, came into service in Germany in 1895. By the early years of this century, buses were much improved. Before 1920 buses were built on *lorry chassis, but later buses were designed as specialist vehicles, with improved comfort. *Diesel-engined buses were introduced in 1938; the diesel engine gave greater reliability and longevity. The modern long-distance inter-city or international touring coach has evolved separately from the urban bus and can now give the passenger a range of facilities such as air-conditioning and on-board toilets.

butane, a gaseous *hydrocarbon (C_4H_{10}), obtained either from natural gas or from *petrol refining. It exists both as a straight chain and as a branched structure (isobutane), which differ in their boiling-point: −0.5 °C for the straight chain and −11.7 °C for the branched. Butane is readily liquefied by the application of pressure. In pressurized containers it is widely used for domestic and industrial purposes, and in cigarette lighters.

butter manufacture. Butter is a *dairy product made by removing water from cream by mechanical means. Cream will rise to the surface of milk left to stand, and the cream can then be skimmed off with a ladle. A centrifugal cream separator, developed by *Laval in the 19th century, speeded up this process, extracting the cream more efficiently and hygienically. The cream is composed of 35 per cent fat globules in 65 per cent water: when agitated in a churn, the fat globules combine to form butter, which is 15 per cent water suspended in 85 per cent fat. The excess water is squeezed out of the butter as it is formed into pats or slabs. *Margarine is a synthetic butter-like spread.

button, a disc used to fasten clothing and other textile articles, or purely for decoration on a piece of clothing. Buttons are secured flexibly to one edge of the piece of clothing; to fasten, they are inserted though a slot, hole, or loop on the other edge. Horn, bone, leather, and wood have long been used to make buttons, but moulded plastics, often imitating the traditional materials, are now almost universal. The *zip-fastener has replaced the button in some applications, but buttons are still widely used in the textile industry.

buttress *structural engineering.

byte, a group of eight *bits. *Computer information is usually transferred or stored as *binary code in byte-sized groups. One byte can represent the integer numbers between 0 and 255, two bytes together represent 0 to over 64,000, and so on. One-byte groups can represent numbers, letters, punctuation characters, or other specified data. A group of eight bits is also known as an octet, particularly in telecommunications.

C *computer language.

cable, a thick strong rope of hemp, wire, or other material; an anchor chain; or a nautical measure of length: one-tenth of a nautical mile, 185 m (607 feet). Apart from nautical uses, cables are much used for engineering purposes: modern suspension bridges use cables made from many parallel strands of strong steel wire bound tightly together. Cables are also used for *cable-cars, for haulage of passenger trains and of mining cars underground, and for passenger lifts and mining hoists.

An electrical cable is an insulated, wire-based conductor or bundle of metallic conductors made of copper or aluminium. An *insulator normally sheathes the conductor completely. Cables may be used to carry electrical signals or power. Most cable conductors are built up from individual fine strands of conductor braided together. The braiding provides increased mechanical strength, flexibility, and superior current-carrying capacity. The earliest underground cables were insulated with rubber or jute. Later developments included vulcanized bitumen insulators in the UK, and in the USA paper insulation and concentric cables: in the latter, two conductors, one forming an outer sheath to the other, are separated by an insulating layer. As underground cables were required to carry ever-increasing amounts of power, greater insulation and methods for dissipating heat in the cables became necessary. In oil cables, an oil filling is used to dissipate heat, while cables using superconductors (see *superconductivity) can transmit large amounts of power because of their extremely low resistance. Overhead cables are made of aluminium for lightness, with an iron core for strength. *Coaxial cables possess an additional outer, earthed, braiding. *Optical-fibre cables are made up of fine glass fibres rather than copper strands. Cables are specified by maximum current capacity (determined by total conductor cross-sectional area), capacitance (tendency of the cable to store charge), and resistance. (See also *electricity generation and supply.)

cable-car, a method of transporting passengers and goods across terrain where it would be difficult and expensive to build a railway. Passenger-carrying cars or goods hoppers are suspended from a steel *cable and hauled by another cable. Various suspension and haulage systems are used: the cables may be continuous, passing around large pulleys; or a balanced pair of cars may operate on two separate suspension ropes joined by a haulage cable, as in a *funicular. Aerial ropeways for transporting minerals from mining sites may run for as much as 10 km (6 miles), carrying 500 tonnes per hour, while cableways may operate at heights of over 1 km (0.6 mile) with up to 100 passengers on board.

cable-ship, a vessel specially fitted for laying or repairing underwater telegraph or telephone *cables. A cable-ship has a large hold to carry the coils of cable and to allow the cable to run freely when it is being laid; and a large roller built out over the bow (and sometimes also over the stern) to pay out the cable evenly when laying. The roller also serves for taking in an existing cable when lifting it for repairs. An early cable-ship was I. K. *Brunel's *Great Eastern*, then the largest ship in the world, chartered in 1866 by Daniel Gooch to lay the first Atlantic cable. In this case the ship was converted for the purpose but most cable-ships have been purpose-built. Although satellite communication seemed at one stage likely to render cables obsolete, cables for *optical fibres are now proving cheap and reliable.

cable-stayed bridge *suspension bridge.

cable television, a system whereby television signals are transmitted to receivers via cables rather than through radio-frequency broadcasting. It was first used in rural areas in the USA, where a hilltop receiving station would pick up and amplify weak broadcast signals, which were then cabled to houses in the area. A similar system was developed for hotels and apartment buildings, where one antenna could serve all the receivers in the building. Cable networks in the USA and elsewhere now connect subscribers directly to transmitting stations. Up to forty different television channels can be carried by one cable.

cadmium (symbol Cd, at. no. 48, r.a.m. 112.41), an unreactive silvery metal occurring in the rare mineral greenockite, but extracted as a by-product of *zinc production. It is used in alloys of low melting-point, in metals for *bearings, in nuclear reactor control rods, nickel–cadmium *batteries, and in *electroplating to protect and embellish more reactive metals. Cadmium sulphide is a yellow paint pigment. Many cadmium compounds are toxic.

caisson, a bottomless, *reinforced concrete box or cylindrical structure used for building *foundations in unstable and waterlogged ground. It is built upwards from ground level, and when it reaches the required height, soil is removed from inside and the caisson sinks under its own weight until foundation level is reached. For foundation works under water, a caisson that is taller than the water depth is floated out and sunk. Water is then pumped out, allowing the foundation to be built. A pneumatic caisson is sealed at the top and water is excluded by compressed air. Caissons are also used in *dry docks.

calcium (symbol Ca, at. no. 20, r.a.m. 40.08), a silvery white metal, the fifth most abundant element in the Earth's crust, occurring in *limestone and many other forms of calcium carbonate (including chalk, marble, marine shells, and pearls). It also occurs as *gypsum, and as a component of *lime. Calcium is obtained by the *electrolysis of molten calcium chloride (produced in the manufacture of *sodium carbonate), followed by distillation under high vacuum or in *argon to obtain the pure metal. Calcium is used as a dehydrating agent for organic solvents and to remove gases from molten metals prior to casting. It is also used as a hardening agent in lead for cable covering, for making storage battery grids and bearings, and, alloyed with silicon, in steel.

calculator, a device that performs arithmetical calculations. An early aid to calculation was the *abacus, a bead frame still used in the Arab world, the Soviet Union, and South-East Asia and China. In the early 17th century, the British mathematician John Napier invented logarithmic tables. Soon afterwards, in 1624, the German mathematician Wilhelm Schickard built a calculating machine for the creation of astronomical tables, probably the first use of gears in a calculator. In 1642 *Pascal devised the first automatic adding machine, used for accountancy calculations. This had gears which were turned and engaged during the adding process. The German philosopher and mathematician Gottfried Leibniz improved on Pascal's design, producing in 1671 a stepped-wheel machine to perform multiplication, the principles of which have been used in almost every subsequent mechanical calculator. Calculating machines remained isolated curiosities until the mid-19th century, when improved reliability led to their more general use.

The first half of the 20th century saw a great demand for adding machines, typically desk-top mechanical devices, hand-operated by a lever. Their calculations were based on addition, with multiplication, for example, being performed by repeated addition. Information was stored and sorted using punched cards. For more specialized work, engineers began to explore methods of programming desk calculators, research which ultimately led to the modern digital computer (see *computer, history of). The calculating machine itself evolved into the present-day hand-held electronic calculator, in which a small number of *integrated circuits replace the gears of the mechanical calculator. Data and commands are entered through a simple key-pad and are usually read from a *seven-segment display. Numbers processed by electronic calculators usually have a 'floating point', that is, the position of the decimal point is automatically adjusted during each calculation. This means that a very wide range of numerical values can be processed. Frequently, a *memory is used to store partial or temporary results. A programmable calculator resembles a simple computer system in that a complex *program involving many calculation steps may be entered into memory and executed on different data each time the program is run.

Calder Hall reactor, the world's first commercially operating nuclear power-station, which opened in the UK in 1956. It was the first of a series of eighteen *Magnox reactors built over the next fifteen years, which gave the UK an early lead in electricity generation using *nuclear power.

calendar, any system for fixing the beginning, length, order, and subdivision of years. Calendrical systems have been used by societies since the earliest times, nearly all of them based on one of two astronomical cycles: the cycle of the phases of the Moon, often of major ritualistic and religious significance, and the cycle of the seasons (the period of the Earth's orbit around the Sun), of importance in agriculture. The two cycles are incompatible, in that the lunar month has a period of about 29.5 days, giving a lunar 'year' (12 months) of just over 354 days, while the mean solar year is over 11 days longer at 365.2422 days. In most societies the lunar calendar was the first to be used, and different systems were developed to reconcile this cycle with that of the seasons. The early Egyptians had two completely separate calendars running concurrently, one for religious purposes and one for agricultural use. The Mayan civilization of Central America also had two calendars, but the ritual calendar was based on a 260-day cycle of thirteen 20-day periods, rather than on a lunar cycle. The Babylonians used a 12-month lunar year, but intercalated (added) months as necessary, to maintain the correspondence with the seasons. At first this intercalation was made as needed, but by the 4th century BC definite rules had been established, based on a cycle of 19 years. The Gregorian calendar, first introduced in 1582 and in almost universal civil use today, was developed from a lunar calendar, as is evident from its division into 12 months.

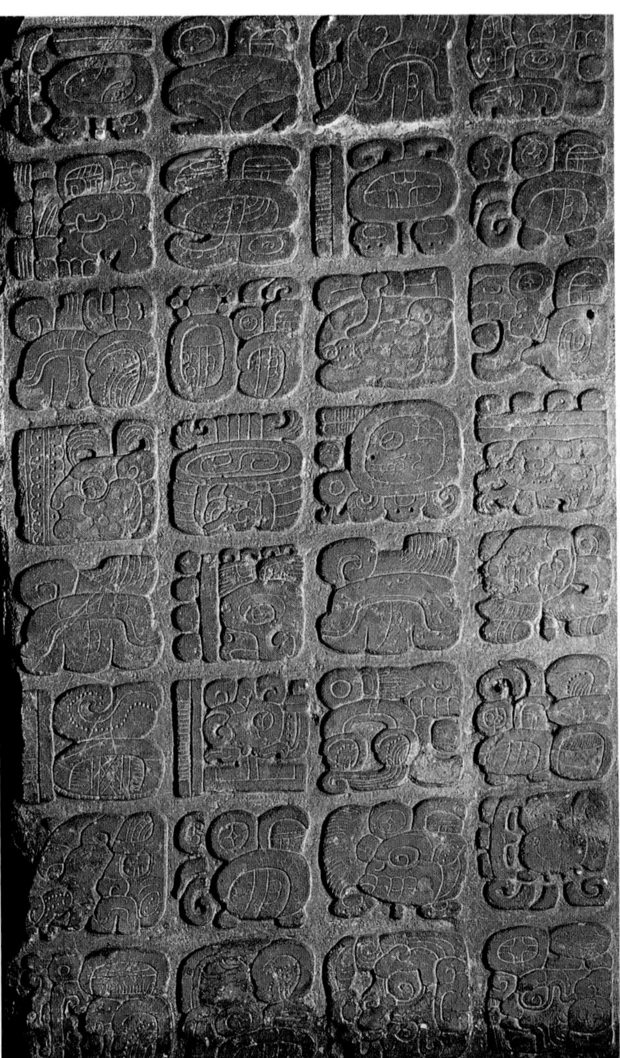

The lintel of an 8th-century Mayan building in Yaxchilan, Guatemala. The inscribed symbols or glyphs refer to the Mayan ritual **calendar**. This was a 260-day cycle that coincided with the 365-day seasonal calendar every 52 years (the 'Calendar Round').

However, the months no longer correspond to lunations, as days have been added to give a total year length of 365 days. Almost exact correspondence with the mean solar year of 365.2422 days is maintained by the intercalation of an extra day (a 'leap year') in 99 out of every 400 years. Other calendrical systems continue to be used, particularly for religious purposes, alongside the Gregorian system. The Islamic calendar, for example, is wholly lunar, the year always containing 12 months of 29 or 30 days each. The twelfth month (*Dulheggia*) has an intercalatory day in 11 out of every 30 years, making the Islamic calendar as accurate in its correspondence with the lunar cycle as the Gregorian calendar is with the solar cycle.

calendering *paper manufacture.

calorimeter, an instrument for measuring the *heat energy changes taking place in a chemical reaction, or the heat required to melt a solid, or the heat capacity of a substance. It consists of a closed vessel in which the reaction takes place. The vessel is either heavily insulated, in which case the temperature change during the reaction is measured; or the heat is transferred to a known amount of water, and the temperature rise in the water is measured. For liquids, a continuous-flow type of calorimeter can be used. Measurements on combustion reactions are carried out in bomb calorimeters, sealed vessels containing oxygen under pressure.

calotype *photography.

cam, a projecting part of a wheel or rotating shaft designed to impart an alternating or variable motion to another mechanism such as a *valve or oscillating shaft. In an automotive *petrol engine the valves are operated in sequence by a series of cams on the camshaft, which rotates at half engine speed. Each cam is circular for about three-quarters of its periphery, the rest forming a curved nose which lifts the valve at a specific point in the rotation of the camshaft (see *petrol engine for illustration). A four- or six-sided cam is used to operate the contact-breaker in some car *ignition systems, although electronic switches are often now used.

camcorder *video camera.

camera, an instrument for producing a photographic image. All cameras, including *cine-cameras used in *cinematography, share the same basic design: a light-tight compartment with a *lens at one end, through which light can pass to form an image on a light-sensitive *film surface at the other. The amount of light entering the camera is controlled by the *shutter and an *aperture, so that only enough light is admitted to produce a satisfactory exposure. A focusing mechanism adjusts the position of the lens so that a sharp image can be recorded of a subject at any distance from the lens. A viewfinder enables the user to aim the camera accurately at the subject. Modern cameras for amateur use have evolved into a number of basic types. Direct-viewfinder cameras are designed for general snapshot photography. The subject is observed through a viewfinder lens, separate from the lens system used to expose the film. 'Compact' cameras taking 35-mm film fall into this category. These are produced in a wide range of models, the most sophisticated versions incorporating the latest electronic technology—*autofocus, *automatic exposure, *DX coding, and a built-in electronic *flash. Single-lens reflex (SLR) cameras (see figure) use the same lens for the view-finder as for film exposure, so the photographer sees the subject framed exactly as it will be on the photograph. A variety of interchangeable lenses and accessories is available for SLR cameras, enabling them to perform the widest possible range of photography. Twin-lens reflex (TLR) cameras use two lenses of the same focal length, mounted one above the other and sharing a common focusing mechanism. The top lens acts as a viewing lens, forming an image reflected by a mirror on to a viewing screen on the top of the camera, while the bottom lens is used for exposing the film, and is fitted with a shutter and diaphragm.

camera obscura, a darkened room or box with a lens or small hole in one side, through which light can enter and form an inverted image on a screen of the scene outside. The Islamic scholar Alhazen (*c*.965–1039) first proposed the use of the camera obscura for the observation of solar eclipses. For over five centuries its form remained unchanged, but in

Camera

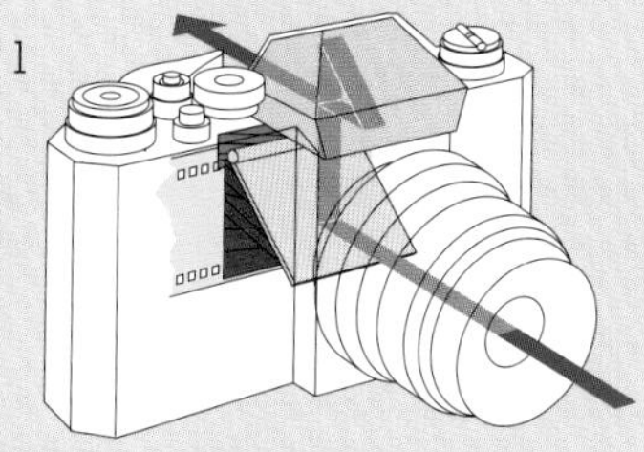

Before a picture is taken, blind 1 is in front of the film. The mirror is down, enabling light from the object to be reflected through the pentaprism and into the viewer's eye.

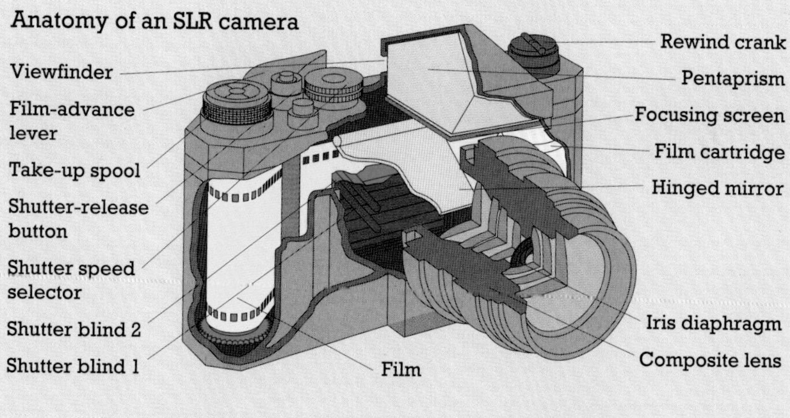

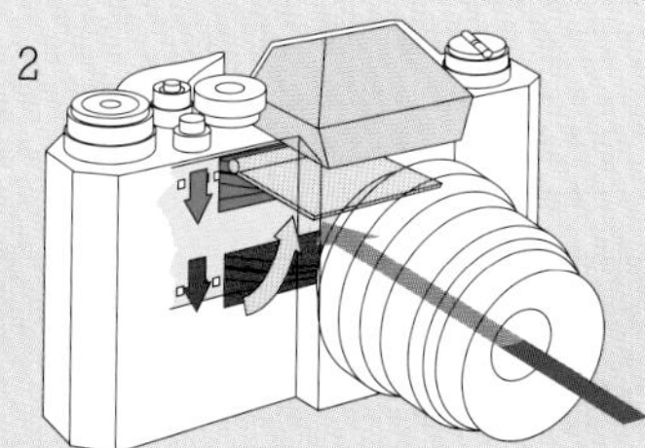

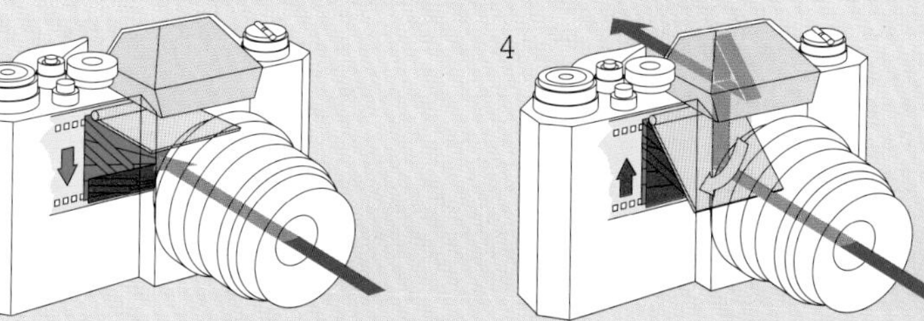

When the shutter-release button is pressed, the mirror flips into the up position, so light can reach the film. Blind 1 moves from in front of the film and is replaced by blind 2: the time it takes for blind 2 to replace blind 1 determines the amount of light reaching the film.

After the shutter has closed, the mirror flips down again into its original position, so that the image can once more be seen in the view-finder. When the film is advanced by one frame, the camera is ready to take another picture.

the 16th century the introduction of a lens and a diaphragm improved the image obtained, and a concave mirror was used to correct the reversal of the image. The camera obscura became a photographic camera when light-sensitive material was used to make a permanent record of the image.

camouflage, the disguising of military equipment, vehicles and personnel by making them blend with their surroundings. Camouflage has been used by armies from very early times, but the term camouflage only came into general use during World War I, when ground troops used camouflage as a protection from aerial reconnaissance and it provided effective cover for snipers. Much greater use of camouflage was made in World War II; troops, vehicles, and installations were disguised to avoid air bombardment, and elaborate dummy harbours, manufacturing plants, and even cities were constructed to protect vital sites. Certain methods of *electronic warfare such as false radar signals and jamming transmitters can be seen as extensions of camouflage techniques.

canal, an artificial waterway built for navigational purposes, for *water supply, or for *land drainage. Ship canals such as the *Panama Canal and the *Suez Canal are made for sea-going vessels. Canals built for inland navigation are much smaller and generally used by *canal barges. Obstacles such as hills are negotiated by building the canal along the contours of the land wherever possible. However, it is occasionally necessary to tunnel beneath hills, or to climb over broad, high hills using *locks. Where the slope is steep, a flight of locks is used, in which one lock's upper gate acts as the next lock's lower gate. This series of small rises reduces the water pressure on the gates. Very steep slopes require a canal lift: a wheeled container, large enough to carry a barge, that is winched up or down an incline. Water is fed into the summit of a canal either from reservoirs or by diverting river water.

Irrigation canals have been built since at least 3000 BC, and most of the ancient civilizations built extensive irrigation and canal networks. The most impressive of these early canals is the Nahrwan Canal between the Tigris and Euphrates rivers (*c.*2400–2200 BC), which is 300 km (185 miles) long and 122 m (400 feet) wide. The Egyptian pharaohs built a canal linking the Mediterranean with the Red Sea, and this was used by Roman shipping, having been restored in 539 BC and again in 285 BC. In China, the first section of the *Grand Canal was completed in AD 610. Canals in Europe were not of importance until the late Middle Ages. The first developments were in the Netherlands, where in the 13th and 14th centuries drainage canals were adapted to carry boat traffic. In the 17th century several important canals were constructed in France, the greatest of which was the 240-km (150-mile) Languedoc Canal (Canal du Midi), built from 1661 by the engineer *Riquet. In the UK, canal building started in about 1750, with *Brindley's Bridgewater Canal in Lancashire. At its height, canal-building employed thousands of labourers known as navigators (navvies), but with the advent of the railways during the first half of the 19th century, canal-building virtually ceased.

The railway bridge over the impressive Corinth Canal in Greece. The 6.5-km (4-mile) **canal** crosses the Isthmus of Corinth, joining the Gulf of Corinth with the Saronic Gulf.

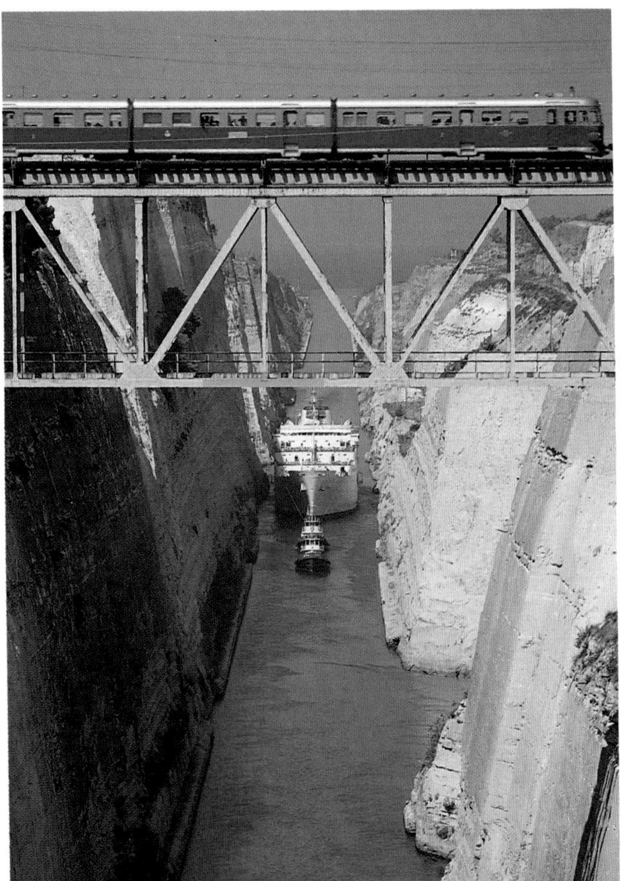

canal barge, a long, shallow, square-sectioned vessel specifically developed for use on canals, where the width of the smallest lock-gate dictates the boat's beam (width). The narrowest barges of this type are the British narrow boats. Early canal boats were towed by a horse moving along the canal towpath, but later they were steam- or diesel-powered. The development of the railways and later road transport has made commercial canal barges largely obsolete in many countries; they are now widely used for leisure purposes.

cancer and cancer therapy. Cancer is a disease caused by a malignant growth or tumour resulting from an abnormal and uncontrolled division of body cells. Tumours may be benign, in which case they displace and compress but do not invade ordinary tissue. Malignant tumours, known as cancers, invade and destroy normal structures, and often travel in the blood or lymphatic system to other tissues or organs. Normally, cell growth is limited by some factor produced in the tissues. In cancer, either the production of this factor or the cell's ability to respond to it is defective. The causes of cancer may be environmental (for example, certain types of radiation, and some chemicals and *viruses) or, less commonly, genetic, but the molecular mechanism by which these factors result in cancer is not yet understood. Cancers may cause death, partly because of their tendency to invade other tissues and interfere with their normal function, but also because they alter the body's metabolism in some way to produce very profound weight loss (cachexia): even a high-protein diet cannot reverse this process. Therapy is directed at reducing the primary tumour, for example by surgical excision where this is practicable; this may be supplemented by treatment to limit the growth of metastatic tumours, and to destroy any stray cells left behind after the surgery. Cancer chemotherapy aims to destroy malignant cells without harming normal tissues. This was originally achieved by means of cytotoxic drugs, which were toxic to all cells, but particularly affected rapidly growing cells such as cancer cells. Since rapidly growing normal cells (for example, in the bone marrow) were often also affected, these drugs produced many unpleasant side-effects. The development of *monoclonal antibodies specific to cancer cells has more recently permitted more selective cytotoxic therapy. Antibodies are raised to a specific tumour, and then attached to a cytotoxic drug: the combination is then injected into the patient, and the antibody causes the cytotoxic chemical to be concentrated in the tumour mass, thus killing the cancer with minimal effect on other tissues. The problems so far have been that it is difficult and expensive to develop specific antibodies, but the technology is still improving. *Radiotherapy uses radiation to destroy localized tumours; it is often used as an adjunct to surgical and chemical cancer therapy. Techniques such as *cervical screening aim to detect pre-cancerous changes in the body. A new, non-invasive technique currently under development uses focused *ultrasound to selectively destroy tumours without harming other tissues.

candle, a light source consisting of a fibrous wick surrounded by a cylinder of *fat or *wax. The development of the candle started in Ancient Egypt with bundles of twisted fibres soaked in fat. The present candle design was arrived at in Roman times. Cheaper, moulded candles were introduced in the 17th century. Fats were replaced in the 1820s by stearine, a mixture of purified fatty acids that is harder and gives a brighter flame than fat. The emerging petroleum industry replaced stearine with *paraffin wax in the 1860s. The introduction of plaited wicks for candles by the Frenchman Jean-Jacques Cambaracérès in 1824 ensured an even, smokeless flame without the need for trimming.

CANDU reactor (*Can*adian *Deu*terium), a type of thermal *nuclear reactor that uses *heavy water as both a coolant and a moderator (see *fission, nuclear), and natural *uranium as a fuel. Such reactors were first developed in Canada between 1945 and 1947, with the help of French and UK scientists. Heavy-water reactors find military application in the production of tritium, a radioactive form of hydrogen used in the manufacture of *nuclear weapons. CANDU reactors have also been developed for the commercial generation of electricity, in which they have an excellent safety and reliability record. Heavy water is a very good moderator, but is expensive to produce, and to date only Canada has developed facilities for producing it in large quantities. (For illustration see *nuclear reactor.)

canning, a *food preservation process in which the food is sealed into airtight metal containers and then sterilized using heat. A similar process is heat sterilization combined with aseptic packaging, in which the food is sterilized before being sealed in the can. For large containers it may be necessary to agitate the cans during sterilization to ensure even heating of the contents. Cans can also be filled with precooked foods in aseptic conditions. Hygenic conditions reduce the risk of food poisoning caused by the bacteria of the genus *Salmonella*, or by *Clostridium botulinum*. Canning is of particular value for soups and stews, which can be pumped easily through tubes. The can is usually made of *tin plate or, increasingly, of aluminium, with a coating of inert enamel on the inside to prevent reaction between food and container. *Appert was the first to heat-sterilize foods in the 1790s, using glass jars, while *Donkin was the first to use metal cans on a large scale.

cannon, a large, heavy gun installed on a carriage or mounting, the earliest class of gunpowder *artillery. The earliest cannon were developed in Europe during the first half of the 14th century, soon after the introduction of *gunpowder. They consisted simply of a tube, closed at one end and pierced there with a touch-hole. Gunpowder was packed at the base of the tube, a projectile inserted, and a lighted match applied to the touch-hole to ignite the gunpowder and fire the projectile. Cannon were mounted on two-wheeled carriages, with a balancing trail projecting behind the axle. Cylindrical projections (trunnions) on either side of the barrel provided pivot points by which the cannon could be mounted on the carriage, allowing the barrel to be raised or lowered for aiming. Naval cannon at first had the same appearance as land cannon. However, during the 1530s the four-wheeled truck carriage was developed by the English and later became standard in other navies, remaining so until turret mountings were introduced in the late 19th century. Cannon is also used as a term for a heavy *machine-gun, of a calibre greater than 20 mm (0.78 inches). (See also *water cannon.)

canoe, a light, narrow craft with pointed or square ends, powered by paddles or sails. The dug-out, a type of canoe made by hollowing out a tree trunk, was one of the earliest types of boat. In Sri Lanka, dug-outs are widened by heating the wood to soften it, and in some designs strakes (lines of planking) are added to the sides, to increase the loading capacity. Modern dug-outs are often powered by outboard motors. Other types of canoe include the outrigger canoe (with a log fixed parallel to the canoe to stabilize it), used particularly in the Pacific islands; light, portable canoes made of birch bark stitched to a bent-ash frame, developed in Canada; and the Arctic kayak, which was originally made of skins and had a watertight cover to improve its chances of righting after a capsize. Canadian canoes and kayaks have been developed into modern sport canoes, usually made of glass-*fibre-reinforced plastic and used for sport and leisure in many parts of the world.

cantilever *structural engineering.

cantilever bridge, a bridge in which a central span is supported by outer spans, each of which forms a cantilever (see *structural engineering). The outer spans are usually anchored at the abutments and project over piers into the central space. The first long-span cantilever bridge was the Forth Bridge, in the UK. Built between 1882 and 1889, it has two steel truss cantilever spans, each measuring 520 m (1,710 feet). The Quebec Bridge (Canada), completed in 1917, has a central span of 549 m (1,801 feet) supported by side spans of 157 m (510 feet). (For illustration see *bridge.)

canvas, a strong cloth, usually of plain *weave, originally made from hemp. Later, flax replaced hemp, and canvas became widely used for making *sails. Today, there is no standard specification: canvas may be made from flax, cotton, or *synthetic-fibre yarns and is used as a general-purpose strong cloth.

capacitor, an electronic component used to store electrical charge. A typical capacitor consists of two parallel metal plates or electrodes separated by an *insulator or dielectric.

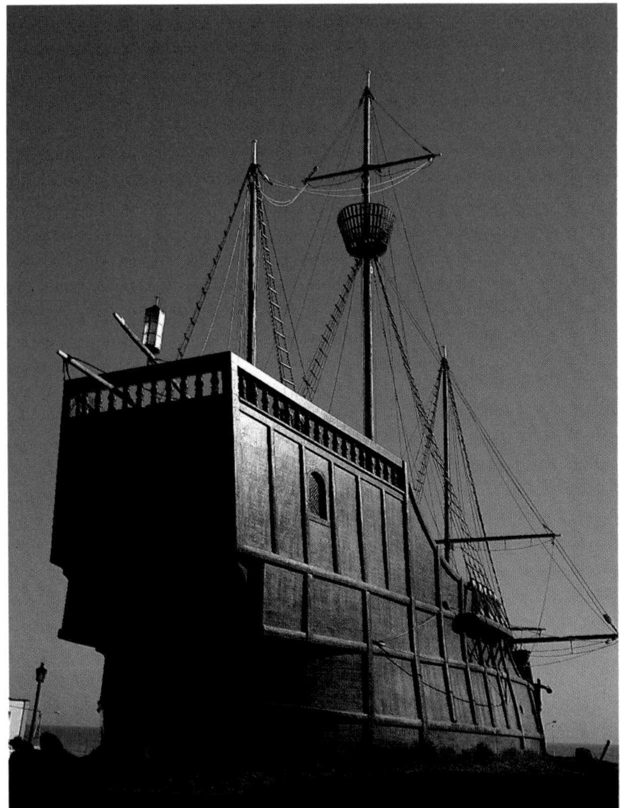

A replica of the *Santa María*, a Portuguese ship described as a **caravel**, which was chartered by Christopher Columbus for his voyage to America in 1492.

The ability of a capacitor to store electrical charge is termed its capacitance, and is measured in farads (F). A capacitor presents an extremely high resistance to a direct current (d.c.): no current will flow in a d.c. circuit containing a capacitor. However, alternating current (a.c.) is allowed to pass much more easily, and the higher the *frequency of the a.c. signal, the less opposition the capacitor presents. Because of this ability to separate a.c. and d.c. signals, capacitors are frequently employed in both filters and power supplies. Several types of capacitor exist. Ceramic capacitors are used in radio-frequency circuits, while capacitors made from polyester and polycarbonate plastics have general application. Small electrolytic capacitors, with large values of capacitance, are used to eliminate mains 'hum' from power supplies.

capillarity *surface tension.

capstan, a cylindrical barrel, vertically mounted on the decks of larger ships, for heavy lifting when working *anchors and *cables. A *ratchet-and-pawl mechanism below the barrel prevents backslipping when lifting heavy loads. Smaller ships use a windlass, which is similar to a capstan but is mounted horizontally.

car *motor car, *motor car, history of.

caravan (US, trailer), a vehicle equipped for living in, usually towed by a horse or motor vehicle. Mobile homes are portable by lorry, but are not built to be towed. The modern caravan or mobile home owes its origins to the gipsy caravan (*varda*). The first motor caravans were designed in the 1920s, since when the caravan has evolved into a miniature portable house, constructed principally of aluminium and glass-reinforced plastics.

caravel, a small Mediterranean trading ship, used in the 14th–17th centuries. It was *lateen-rigged on two or sometimes three masts. Late in the 15th century, Spain and Portugal adapted the three-masted caravel for exploration and trade, *square-rigged on the two forward masts and lateen-rigged on the mizen. In ships of this type the explorer Bartholomew Diaz de Noraes rounded the Cape of Good Hope in 1488 and Christopher Columbus reached the West Indies in 1492. The ships used by the Portuguese navigators Vasco da Gama (who reached India in 1498) and Ferdinand Magellan (whose ship in 1522 completed the first circumnavigation of the world) also included caravels.

carbine *firearm.

carbolic acid *phenol.

carbon and carbon compounds (symbol C, at. no. 6, r.a.m. 12.01). Carbon is a non-metallic element, occurring in nature as *graphite and *diamond. *Coke, produced by the destructive distillation of coal, is almost pure carbon, and *charcoal is a form of carbon made from wood. *Carbon fibres are long chains of pure carbon formed by heat treatment of acrylic fibres. The vast majority of carbon compounds such as *hydrocarbons are *organic chemicals. There are two oxides, carbon dioxide and carbon monoxide. Carbon dioxide is a colourless gas that is heavier than air and does not support combustion. It can be made easily by the reaction of dilute *acids with carbonates: this reaction forms the basis of small foam *fire-extinguishers. Carbon monoxide is a poisonous, lighter-than-air gas that burns with a pale blue flame to form carbon dioxide. It is formed whenever carbon-containing compounds are burned in a limited quantity of air: hence the dangers of car exhaust fumes, and the need for adequate ventilation with paraffin stoves and similar heating devices.

carbon-black, a fine black powder obtained by burning *natural gas or liquid *hydrocarbons in a limited supply of air. It is insoluble and chemically inactive, and so it is used to make permanent *inks, *carbon-paper, and printer ribbons. It is also added to *rubber to make it tougher and more resistant to sunlight.

carbon dating *radio-carbon dating.

carbon fibre, a filament of pure carbon. Carbon fibres achieve extremely high strength and stiffness because the strong axis of the crystalline structure is aligned along the fibre axis. However, they lack tensile strength, which has limited their engineering applications. They were first manufactured at the Royal Aircraft Establishment, Farnborough, UK, in the 1960s, from acrylic fibres. These fibres were stretched to align their carbon chains and then converted to graphite at very high temperatures. Currently, carbon fibres are made from a number of different textile fibres and also from pitch, a by-product of petroleum refining. Carbon fibres are the stiffest engineering materials in common use, being over twice as stiff as steel. They are used in *fibre-reinforced plastics to make strong, low-density materials, which find application in aircraft wing and fuselage sections, and for a wide range of sports and specialist engineering equipment.

carbonless transfer paper, a special-purpose paper for multi-part business forms, in which an image from a pen, typewriter, printer, or other device may be transferred through a number of sheets by impact upon the top sheet, without the need for interleaved sheets of *carbon-paper. The papers are coated with colourless chemicals that will react upon impact to produce a coloured image. Carbonless papers were first made by the NCR (National Cash Register) Corporation in the USA, but there are now several variations and alternative chemistries.

carbon-paper, a thin paper or plastic sheet coated on one side with a mixture of mineral colour (usually *carbon-black) and a waxy substance, used for making copies. Typing or writing on a top sheet of paper is copied (through pressure transfer) by the carbon-paper on to an underlying sheet of paper. The widespread availability of *photocopiers and the development of *carbonless transfer papers have greatly reduced the use of carbon-paper.

carborundum *abrasive, *silicon carbide.

carburettor, a device used in an *internal-combustion engine to charge air with a spray of liquid fuel. At the heart of the carburettor is the *venturi, a constriction in the air passage through the carburettor. This constriction creates an area of faster-moving, low-pressure air, and the lowered pressure draws petrol into the air-stream from a jet nozzle on the side of the venturi (see figure). Petrol is supplied to the jet from a small reservoir in the carburettor, the float tank. The flow of the petrol–air mixture from the carburettor into the engine cylinders is controlled by the throttle butterfly *valve, which allows more or less mixture into the cylinder depending on the power needed. This basic carburettor mechanism provides an almost constant ratio of petrol–air mixture at different rates of air-flow. However, this ratio is not suitable for all driving conditions, and various methods are used to increase or reduce the amount of petrol in the mixture under different circumstances. The *choke controls the petrol–air mixture by increasing or decreasing the air supply, while in the variable-jet carburettor, the petrol supply is adjusted. In some engines there is no carburettor, and a fuel injection system is used. In this, a throttle butterfly regulates the amount of air passing into the cylinder, while the petrol is injected under pressure directly into the cylinder, the timing and amount of petrol injected being controlled electronically.

cardboard, a general term applied to any thick and stiff paper or paper-like substance especially for making cards or boxes. Originally, it was used to describe pasteboard, that is,

Carburettor (variable-jet)

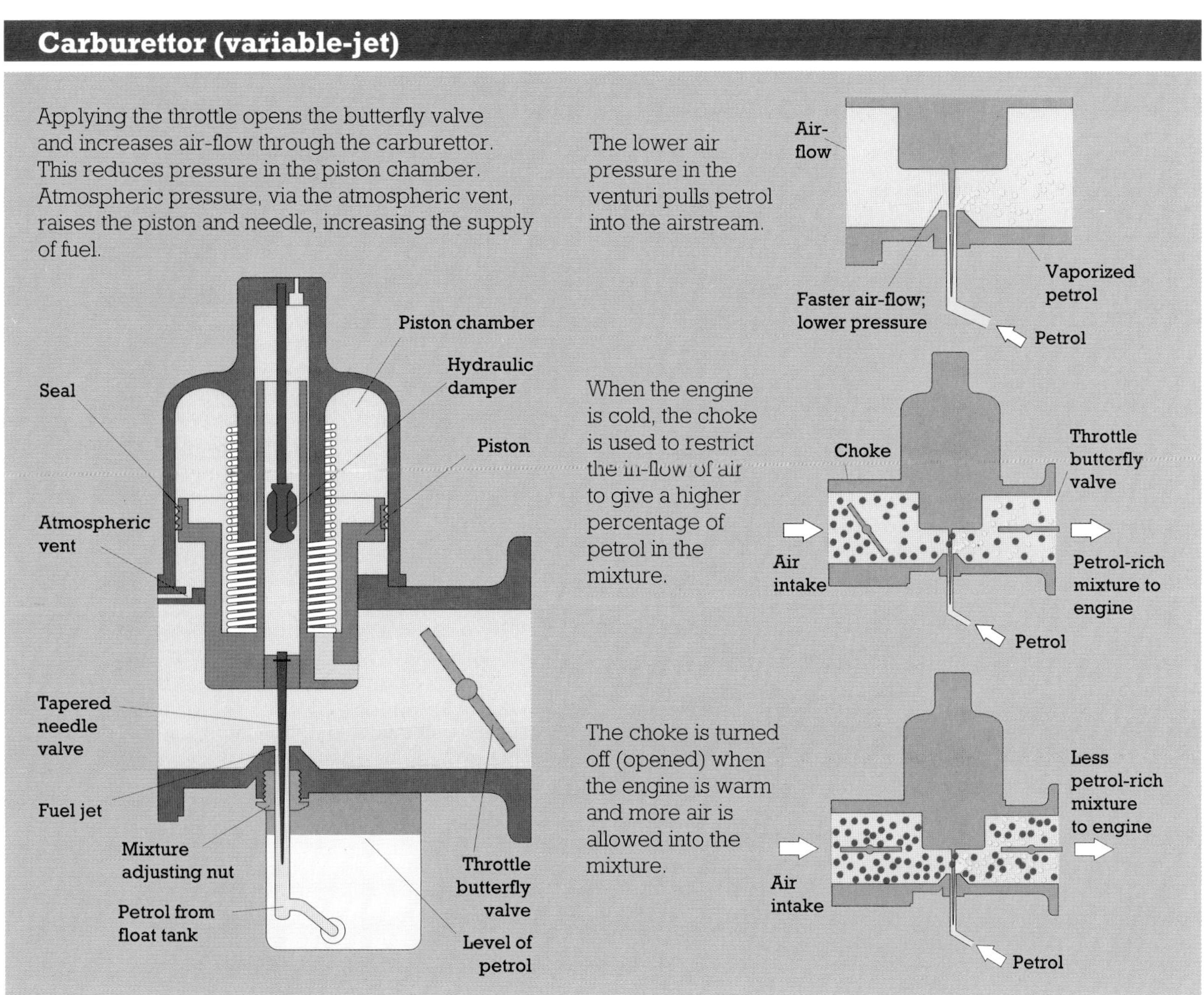
Applying the throttle opens the butterfly valve and increases air-flow through the carburettor. This reduces pressure in the piston chamber. Atmospheric pressure, via the atmospheric vent, raises the piston and needle, increasing the supply of fuel.
Piston chamber
Hydraulic damper
Seal
Piston
Atmospheric vent
Tapered needle valve
Fuel jet
Mixture adjusting nut
Petrol from float tank
Throttle butterfly valve
Level of petrol
The lower air pressure in the venturi pulls petrol into the airstream.
Air-flow
Faster air-flow; lower pressure
Vaporized petrol
Petrol
When the engine is cold, the choke is used to restrict the in-flow of air to give a higher percentage of petrol in the mixture.
Choke
Throttle butterfly valve
Air intake
Petrol-rich mixture to engine
Petrol
The choke is turned off (opened) when the engine is warm and more air is allowed into the mixture.
Less petrol-rich mixture to engine
Air intake
Petrol

a form of board made from a straw or other coarse base material on to which paper had been pasted to imitate thick, smooth card.

carding machine, a device for disentangling and aligning textile fibres preparatory to *spinning. Carding is applied to almost all natural fibres and to many manufactured ones. Layers of fibre are passed between moving, parallel surfaces densely covered with fine sharp spikes. Originally, this was done manually in small batches. Modern rotary carding machines accept a continuous layer of randomly oriented fibres and automatically deliver parallel fibres as a soft rope or 'sliver' 1–2 cm (0.4–0.8 inches) in diameter.

cardiology and cardiac surgery. Cardiology is the study of the heart and the vascular (blood) system, and of diseases affecting them. Heart (cardiac) failure is a failure of the heart to pump an adequate flow of blood round the body. This may result from a decreased contractile force in the muscle fibres, which can be treated with digitalis, an extract from the leaves of foxgloves, containing substances such as digoxin, which slows the heart rate and strengthens its contraction. Cardiac failure can also result from a failure of co-ordination between the individual heart-muscle fibres (fibrillation). These two conditions usually result from narrowing of the coronary arteries, from leaking or narrowed valves within the heart, or from an overgrowth (hypertrophy) of the heart muscle itself, usually in response to high blood pressure (hypertension). Echocardiography uses *ultrasound to provide a real-time picture of the heart, aiding the diagnosis of valvular and muscular abnormalities. Narrowing ('hardening') of the arteries (atherosclerosis) is common in affluent societies. It may affect any arteries: coronary atherosclerosis produces angina pectoris (pain in the chest resulting from a fall in oxygen supply to the heart), heart attack (sudden, and usually complete loss of cardiac function due to failure of the blood supply to part of the heart muscle), or cardiac failure (a chronic heart condition with symptoms of breathlessness, weakness, and lethargy).

Atherosclerosis may be treated by a surgical procedure in which a vein (usually taken from the leg) is grafted around the obstruction. A new technique that avoids open surgery involves the passing of a balloon-ended catheter into the narrowed artery: the balloon is then inflated for a few seconds, breaking the calcified tissue and effectively removing the obstruction. Blood clots can be treated with the drug streptokinase, an enzyme isolated from bacteria that softens the clot. (See also *electrocardiograph.)

car ferry, a ship designed to carry vehicles and passengers, usually on short-haul crossings. Early vehicle ferries were passenger ships with a specially adapted hold: vehicles were hoisted in and out by derricks and carried secured to the deck. Roll-on roll-off (ro-ro) ferries for trains appeared in the mid-19th century; ro-ro car ferries appeared in the 1920s. With these, vehicles can drive on one end of the ferry and drive off the other without turning. Wide, hydraulically operated ramps or doors, usually at bow and stern, can be manœuvred against purpose-built matching ramps at the shore-side sites being served. The larger car ferries now have two covered vehicle decks, with further decks above to accommodate passengers on the journey. They are usually fitted with bow and stern thruster *propellers to help them berth safely, and powerful *stabilizers to prevent movement of unsecured cargo. The large vehicle decks with no bulkheads make car ferries prone to rapid capsizing if holed. Regulations introduced by the International Maritime Organization in 1990 require increased clearance between the cargo doors and the water-line.

cargo ship *merchant ship.

Carlson, Chester Floyd (1906–68), US physicist and developer of the process of xerography (see *photocopier). A graduate of the California Institute of Technology, he worked briefly for the Bell Telephone Company before joining a New York electronics firm. There he developed between 1934 and 1938 a practical xerographic copying process, though it was not until 1944 that he was able to obtain funding for further development. In 1947 he sold the commercial rights for his invention to the Haloid Company (later the Xerox Corporation).

Carothers, Wallace Hume (1896–1937), US industrial chemist who invented *nylon. He joined the Du Pont Company, USA, in 1928, where he developed a special interest in organic compounds of high molecular weight. His research led to the discovery of neoprene, the first successful *synthetic rubber. He also discovered the fibre-forming properties of a whole class of synthetic organic polymers (the polyamides), the most important being nylon. Nylon was first marketed in 1939 for stockings.

carpentry and joinery, the craft concerned with the cutting, working, and joining of timber. The major work of a carpenter or joiner is in building construction: a carpenter fabricates structural members, while a joiner is concerned with fixings such as windows, door frames, and skirtings. In the past, most buildings were constructed with a timber *frame, and carpenters were among the principal building workers. With the widespread introduction of other constructional materials, such as steel and concrete, timber framing has become confined to houses and small buildings. However, carpenters are now required for the manufacture of *formwork for building in concrete. Many wooden components are now mass-produced; this means that the general bench joiner tends to work only on items in small batch quantities, especially high-quality items. Machinery is now used for much sawing, planing, and joining work (see *woodworking joints)—this machinery is often operated by a specialist woodworking machinist.

carpet manufacture. Most carpets consist of a base fabric supporting a more-or-less upright pile. The pile may be inserted into an already existing base fabric, or pile and fabric may be formed integrally during weaving. The earliest method of carpet manufacture involved firmly knotting tufts of textile fibre into a woven fabric base by hand; it is still practised as a craft industry. In modern tufted carpets, the insertion of pile into the base fabric occurs at high speed using a battery of hollow needles, the pile then being held in place by the application of latex or similar *adhesive. Such carpets predominate in world markets. Woven carpets, in which the pile and base fabric are formed integrally, are of two main types. In Wilton carpets, the pile yarns are raised above the backing or base fabric during weaving by means of wires or hooks, or by being extended between two, face-to-face, simultaneously woven backings. After weaving, pile may be cut by a bladed wire or by the cutting apart of the two facing structures. Brussels carpet, the earliest type to be woven mechanically, is of the Wilton type but with an uncut

Carriages and coaches

Stage-coach 1650 onwards

This was a large covered coach that could carry passengers and luggage both inside and outside. It was pulled by a team of four horses which were changed at 'stages' along the route.

Tumbrel (Scotch cart) *c.*1780

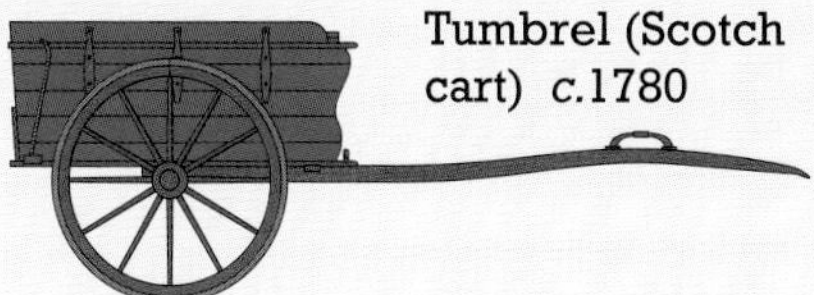

This was an unsprung, two-wheeled farm cart that was pulled by either one or two horses. It superseded the earlier English farm carts by virtue of its ability to tip and thus release a load.

Square landau *c.*1780

The landau could be either an open or closed carriage and seated four people. It was pulled by one or two horses and was driven by a coachman seated on a box at the front.

Hansom cab 1834

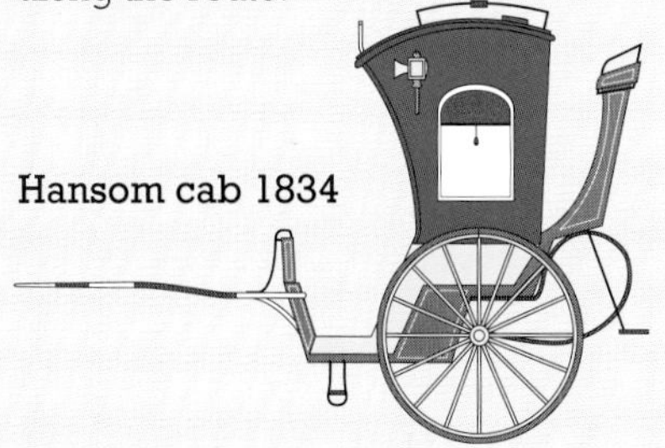

Designed by J. A. Hansom in 1834 to seat two passengers, this cab was used extensively for private hire in London. It was also very popular as a gentleman's private carriage.

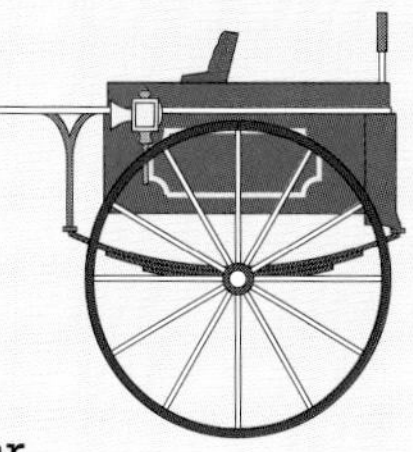

Irish jaunting car

This cart carried passengers on both sides facing outwards.

Phaeton *c.*1860

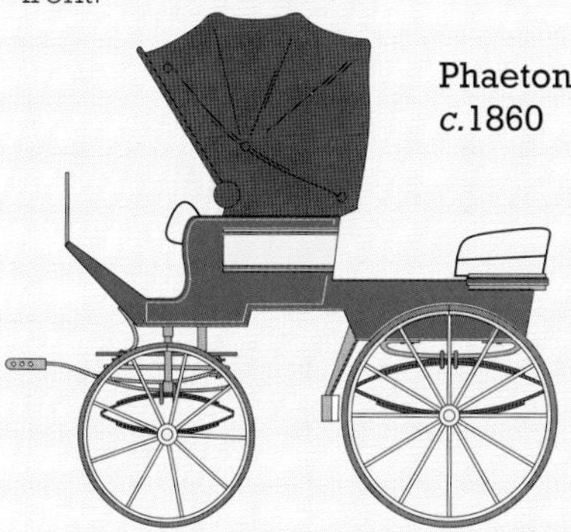

Phaeton has become a general term for an open, four-wheeled car that is driven by the owner rather than a hired coachman. It could seat two or four and could be fitted with a hood.

Sporting gig *c.*1830

The term gig is used to describe a two-wheeled vehicle that carried a maximum of two people and was drawn by a single horse.

Brougham 1839

Named after Lord Brougham, this type of low-slung, one-horse carriage was produced in large numbers for town use.

Governess car *c.*1900

This cart or 'tub trap' dates from about 1900 when it was widely used as safe transportation for children. The seats face inwards and it has a cranked axle to allow easy entry.

Victoria 1860

The Victoria seated two passengers facing forward and was driven by a coachman. It was pulled by either one or two horses.

(loop) pile. In Axminster carpet, the rows of pile are fed to the structure by devices which grip the pile (spools or grippers). In spool Axminster, tufts are cut at the weaving point; in gripper Axminster, tufts are cut from the yarn supply before being inserted into the fabric by the grippers. A wide range of colours and patterns may be used. Patterning is controlled by *Jacquard mechanisms. Other types of textile floor-covering include felted, needled, melt-bonded, and other *nonwoven structures. *Wool is the traditional fibre for the pile of woven carpets, but it is now usually blended with *nylon, *acrylic, or *polypropylene fibres. Most tufted carpets are made from bulked continuous filament (BCF) yarns of nylon or, increasingly, polypropylene.

carpet sweeper, a hand-operated sweeping machine. The first practical sweeper was patented in 1876 by Melville Bissell in the USA, and its overall design has changed little since then. The body is a flat box attached to a broom handle and mounted on four rubber-tyred wheels. These wheels drive a central cylindrical brush which sweeps debris into an internal compartment. The carpet sweeper has largely been superseded by the *vacuum cleaner.

carrack *sailing ships and boats.

carriages and coaches, horse-drawn vehicles designed to carry passengers. Four-wheeled vehicles carried fare-paying passengers in Roman times. In medieval Europe, passenger-carrying wagons fell out of use because of the poor state of the *roads, and land travel was mainly on horseback or on foot. In Hungary in the 15th century, light, covered, four-wheeled vehicles began to be built, which were suspended between the axles rather than resting on them. These early coaches spread throughout Europe during the 16th century. Initially such coaches were available only for the very rich, but in the 17th century various two- and four-wheeled designs arose—from large coaches carrying up to six people inside, to light, two-wheeled gigs for two people. Hackney coaches for hire were introduced in London in 1625, and stage-coaches for longer-distance travel in 1640. During the 18th and 19th centuries, carriage types proliferated, with many variations according to purpose, locality, and available materials (see figure for an illustration of several carriage types). Small carriages were generally owner-driven: larger vehicles could either be driven by a coachman, or by a rider (postilion) on the horses. (See also *road transport.)

carrier wave *modulation.

cartridge, a container for the propellant charge used in *firearms. First developed at the end of the 16th century, cartridges became standard military equipment in the early 19th century. Previously, the powder charge had been haphazardly measured by the soldier doing the loading. Early cartridge cases were of paper or cloth, and the percussion cap was often separate from the cartridge. The development of breech-loading firearms enabled the cartridge and *bullet to be combined, as they are in modern weapons. The breech-loader's firing pin strikes a percussion cap at the centre of the cartridge base. The percussion cap contains a *detonator, which ignites the propellant charge within the cartridge.

carts and wagons. A cart is a small, sturdy two- or four-wheeled horse-drawn vehicle; a wagon is a four-wheeled vehicle capable of hauling heavy or bulky loads. Wagons and carts were the earliest wheeled vehicles, developed over 5,000 years ago by the Sumerians. An important improvement to the wagon was the pivoted front axle, which allowed it to be steered. It is thought to have been developed in Scandinavia in about the 1st century BC. Many different kinds of cart and wagon have been evolved for different purposes. One of the most common types is the 'Scotch' cart or tumbrel (see *carriages and coaches for illustration). Later, lightweight 'spring' carts and traps were introduced; in the 20th century these have been replaced in many Western countries by the motor van. Wagons for heavy haulage have been superseded in many countries by motor *lorries. (See also *road transport.)

Cartwright, Edmund (1743–1823), British clergyman and inventor of the first power-*loom and the first wool-combing machine. Cartwright saw *Arkwright's spinning machine on a visit to Matlock, Derbyshire, in 1779, and later (1784) met Arkwright. In 1785 he took out his first patent on a crude power-loom, and the following year established a factory at Doncaster. He turned his attention also to other textile processes and patented a *wool comber in 1789–90. His other inventions included machines to make bricks, bread, and ropes, and a mechanical *reaper.

carvel construction *shipbuilding.

cash register, an electromechanical or electronic device for recording retail financial transactions. Cash registers evolved directly from mechanical *calculators and were pioneered and largely developed by US companies such as the NCR (National Cash Register) Corporation. They proved to be a major business innovation, with some 4 million being sold before 1950. The modern cash register is known as a *point-of-sale terminal.

cassette tape *magnetic tape.

casting, a process for making metal objects in a foundry, whereby molten metal is poured into a heat-resistant mould. As it cools, the metal solidifies into the shape and form of the cavity, after which it can be removed from the mould. Many cast items are produced from sand moulds. The mould is created by making a wooden pattern and assembling the mould in two halves around the pattern. The pattern is then removed and the mould reassembled. Pattern-making and mould assembly are extremely skilled occupations. Removal of the casting from a sand mould destroys the mould and it has to be reassembled for each casting. The casting always has a rough surface and often requires grinding or other surface treatments before use. Smaller items can be cast by *investment casting or, for a high-quality finish, by *die casting. *Plastics can be cast at lower temperatures by injection moulding. A huge variety of items is produced by casting, from ornaments to statues and ships' propellers.

Castner–Kellner cell, an apparatus for producing pure *sodium hydroxide. A direct electric current is passed through brine (salt solution), using a mercury cathode (negative electrode) and a graphite anode (positive electrode). *Chlorine is released at the anode, while *sodium is released at the cathode and combines with the mercury to form an amalgam. This amalgam is treated with water to produce sodium hydroxide solution. The by-products of the process (chlorine and hydrogen) are valuable, and make the expensive electrolytic process economically viable.

catalyst, a material that changes the rate at which a chemical reaction occurs without itself being consumed in that reaction. Catalysts are widely used in industry, either to increase the rate of a reaction, or to allow the reaction to take place without resorting to high temperatures and pressures. Many industrial reactions rely on the presence of catalysts, for example the *Haber–Bosch process. In this reaction, the reactant gases are passed over and through beds containing a catalyst supported on inert material; this is known as heterogeneous catalysis because the catalyst and reactants are in different phases (solid and gas). In homogeneous catalysis, catalyst and reactants are in the same phase: an example is the *oxidation of sulphur dioxide by oxygen (part of the *lead chamber process, used to make sulphuric acid), which is catalysed by oxides of nitrogen. *Enzymes are biological catalysts.

catalytic converter, a device used to promote combustion of unburned hydrocarbons in a motor-car exhaust, and thus reduce *air pollution. It is one of a range of exhaust emission control devices introduced since the 1960s. The converter comprises an insulated chamber containing a bed

A battery of **Castner–Kellner cells**, used for the production of sodium hydroxide, chlorine, and hydrogen by the electrolysis of brine.

of metal oxide *catalyst pellets. Hot exhaust gases are passed through the chamber, and carbon monoxide and hydrocarbon residues in the exhaust are further oxidized. Catalytic converters are required by law in the USA and Japan, and, since 1992, in the European Community.

catamaran, most commonly, a twin-hulled craft, first developed by the Polynesians but now also a type of *yacht. Sailing upright and requiring little wetted surface for support, it can, if kept light, go faster than a craft with a conventional hull, though it will not point as well to windward (into the wind). The term catamaran also describes a raft of two or more logs lashed together, used as a fishing craft in South India, as well as the rectangular float used in dockyards to hold a ship clear of quayside obstructions. In 1990 a Tasmanian-made catamaran began service as a *car ferry across the English Channel.

catapult, a forked stick (or piece of metal) with elastic for shooting small stones, or a large military machine worked by levers and ropes, for firing bolts, spears, stones, or gunpowder projectiles. The first examples of the medieval catapult were developed in Germany in the early 13th century, and were used in sieges of towns and castles. They consisted of a *sling attached to an arm that turned on a raised triangular pivot. A counterweight was placed on the arm at the opposite end to the sling. The arm was winched back by a pair of windlasses, and when released, the counterweight tilted the arm, hurling the projectile towards the target. Catapult-type devices were used as grenade launchers in World War I. Devices known as catapults are used to assist the launch of aircraft from *aircraft carriers, using hydraulic pressure, tension, or other force.

caterpillar track, a flexible belt of steel plates running around the wheels of a vehicle, used to give increased traction and to spread the weight of the vehicle over a larger area. Caterpillar tracks were originally evolved for the heavy agricultural tractor, but are now used principally for heavy earth-moving equipment, bulldozers, and tanks. The 'Marion' crawler used to transport the *Saturn V* *launch vehicle to its launch pad—the largest wheeled vehicle ever built—runs on caterpillar tracks.

catheter, a tube of small cross-section that is temporarily or permanently inserted into a body cavity or vessel to introduce or remove fluid. Catheters to drain the bladder, introduced into the urethra, have been known since ancient times. Originally made of metal, especially silver, the rigid catheter was largely replaced during this century by flexible rubber designs and, more recently, by plastic catheters. New materials have greatly expanded the use of catheters, allowing fine-bore tubes to be threaded into the vascular system for diagnostic or therapeutic purposes. Since the 1970s *optical-fibre instruments have facilitated such processes as cardiac catheterization, in which catheters inserted into the arms or legs are manipulated into the heart chambers.

cathode, the negative electrode of a *thermionic valve, *cathode-ray tube, *battery, or electrolytic cell. The cathode is the electrode by which electrons enter a system: they are emitted by, or flow from, the cathode. (See also *circuits, electrical and electronic.)

cathode-ray tube (CRT), a funnel-shaped *electron tube that converts electrical signals into a visible form that can be displayed. CRTs are used widely in *television receivers, visual display units for computers, and in displays for oscilloscopes. They consist primarily of an electron beam traversing the length of the tube, the intensity of which varies according to an input signal containing the visual information to be displayed. Acting on this electron beam are several sets of electrodes and magnetic coils, which together confine and direct the beam and enable it to be moved back and forth across a *phosphor coat on the back of the screen inside the tube. When the electron beam strikes the phosphor, a light spot is produced, the intensity of which is proportional to the intensity of the beam. As the beam scans up and down the screen, a full screen display is formed. (See *television receiver for illustration.)

CAT scan *computerized axial tomography.

Cat's-eye, a stud embedded in the road that acts as a guide to drivers in bad light by reflecting back the vehicle's headlights. Glass prisms are set in a rubber moulding mounted in a box which projects slightly above the road surface, usually in the centre of the road. When a vehicle drives over a Cat's-eye, the prisms are pressed down into the rubber moulding, thus wiping off any dirt. Cat's-eyes were developed by the British inventor Percy Shaw, and were first laid near Bradford, Yorkshire, UK, in 1934.

cattle farming, the rearing of cattle for milk or beef, or as *draught animals. Most modern cattle breeds are specialized for beef or *dairy farming, although there are some dual- or general-purpose breeds. Cattle are ruminants, and as such are able to utilize roughage and low-quality protein foods and convert them to high-quality foodstuffs. Most breeds of domestic cattle are derived from those domesticated in the Near East around 8000 BC (see *agriculture), but the water-buffalo is kept for draught purposes, for milk, and for beef in warmer areas of Asia and the Middle East, and in parts of Europe. The yak is farmed in parts of Asia. (See also *livestock farming.)

caulking, an operation to waterproof a wooden boat and strengthen its structure by driving materials into the seams of its planking using a caulking iron (a tool like a steel chisel). Suitable caulking materials include oakum (fibre from old ropes), cotton, and moss. After the caulking has been driven in, it is covered with hot pitch to protect it.

caustic soda *sodium hydroxide.

cavitation, the formation of cavities (bubbles) in moving liquids caused by rapid pressure changes. When the bubbles collapse, shock waves are produced in the liquid. In ships and boats, cavitation occurs around the *propeller when it is rotating at too high a speed, or when a vessel is travelling very quickly through the water. It causes vibration in the vessel, and heavy erosion of the propeller blades. Poor hull design, or a small propeller, can contribute to the occurrence of cavitation.

cavity wall, a wall built as two leaves, each about 100 mm (4 inches) thick, with a continuous void, typically 50 mm (2 inches) wide, between the leaves. Cavity walls were developed to keep out rain more effectively than a solid wall. Water penetrating the outer leaf drains down its inner face, whilst the inner leaf remains dry. The void is often filled with *insulation to reduce heat loss.

Cayley, Sir George (1773–1857), British founder of the science of *aerodynamics, and aerial navigation pioneer (see *flying, history of). He studied the principles of flight, and understood the essential features of flying machines: cambered wings to give lift, propeller propulsion, a rudder for steering, and rear elevators. However, at that time there was no power unit with a high enough power-to-weight ratio to translate these principles into practice. He did, however, demonstrate successful flight with small gliders, and in 1853 a larger one carried his coachman some 500 m (1,650 feet). He also invented the *caterpillar tractor.

CB radio (citizens' band radio), a system of local communication between individuals on special bands of radio frequencies. Following a decision in 1945 by the US government that its citizens should have this right, the US Federal Communication Commission allocated a *frequency of 467 mHz FM for the General Mobile Radio Service, now known as CB. In 1958 extra, lower-frequency channels were introduced on AM to encourage use. But it was not until the 1970s, when technology had advanced to reduce costs, that the CB market prospered, US truckers being at the head of the boom.

cell, electrical *battery.

cell structure. Since almost all living things are composed of cells, their study is fundamental to an understanding of biology. Current knowledge of cells owes much to the *microscope. The light microscope first revealed the existence of cells and their variety, while the *electron microscope has vastly enhanced knowledge of their inner structure (see figure). Coloured stains are used to show up cell components under the microscope: modern cell staining techniques can identify individual protein molecules, using fluorescent antibodies which glow under ultraviolet light. The high-speed *centrifuge has enabled subcellular components to be separated and studied and is extremely important in cell biochemistry. The culturing of cells is central to *biotechnology.

Cellophane, a tough, thin-film *plastic used for wrapping goods and for *dialysis, developed in 1910 by the Swiss inventor Edwin Brandenberger. Cellophane is made from regenerated cellulose. It is not as flexible as thin-film *polythene, but it is *biodegradable.

cellular telephone, a mobile *radio telephone communications system. The concept originated at the Bell Telephone Laboratories, USA, during 1947. It was first demonstrated in Chicago during 1977, and initiated in the UK in 1985. The basic system involves dividing the country into areas or cells, 2–13 km (1.25–8 miles) in radius, and employing different frequency bands in neighbouring cells to avoid interference. A mobile caller connects into the national *telephone network via *radio communication with the *telephone exchange in his cell. The mobile units must be able to retune to a new frequency as they pass from one cell to another, a process that demands a highly sophisticated electronic switching system.

Cell structure

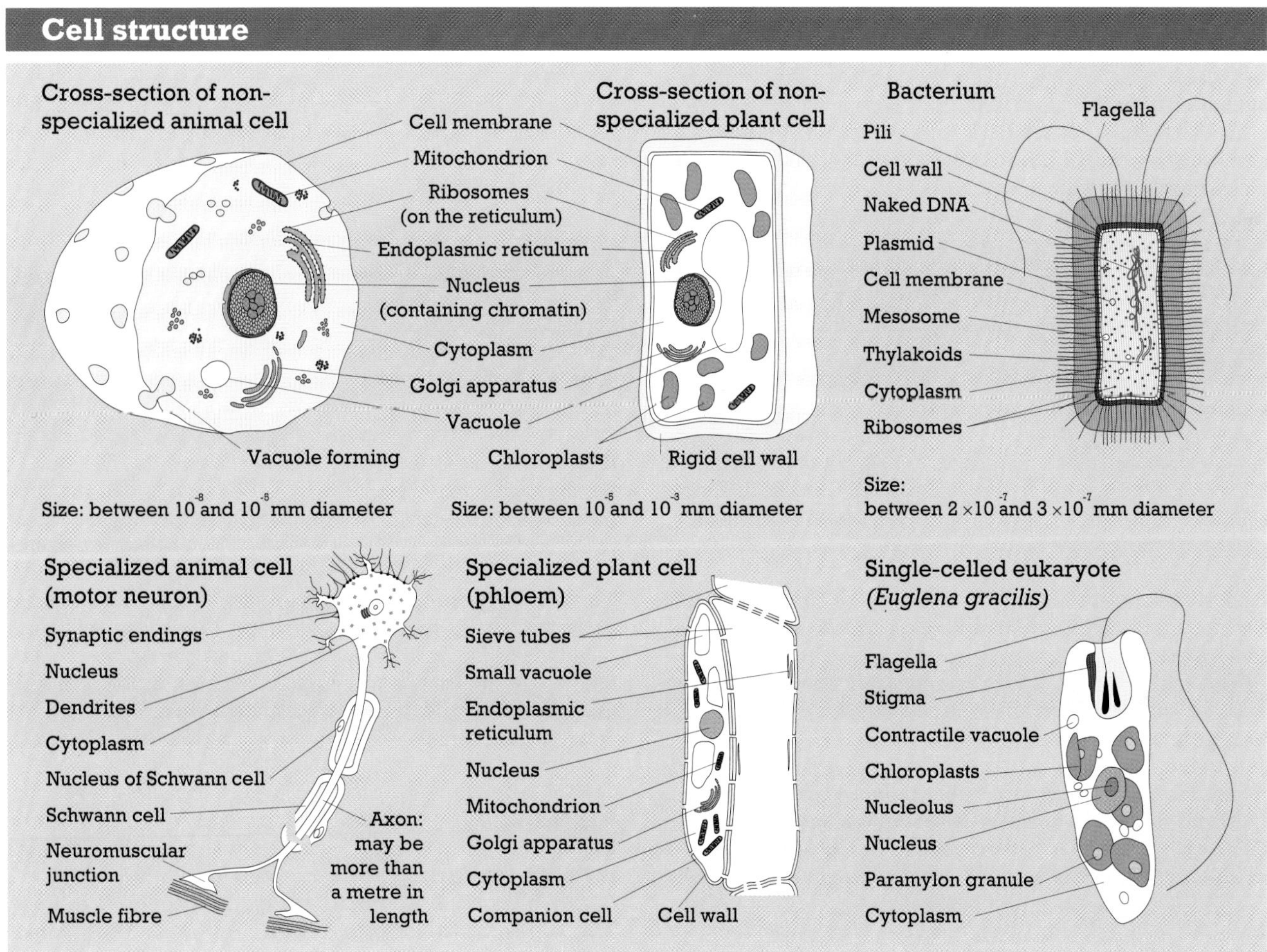

Central heating

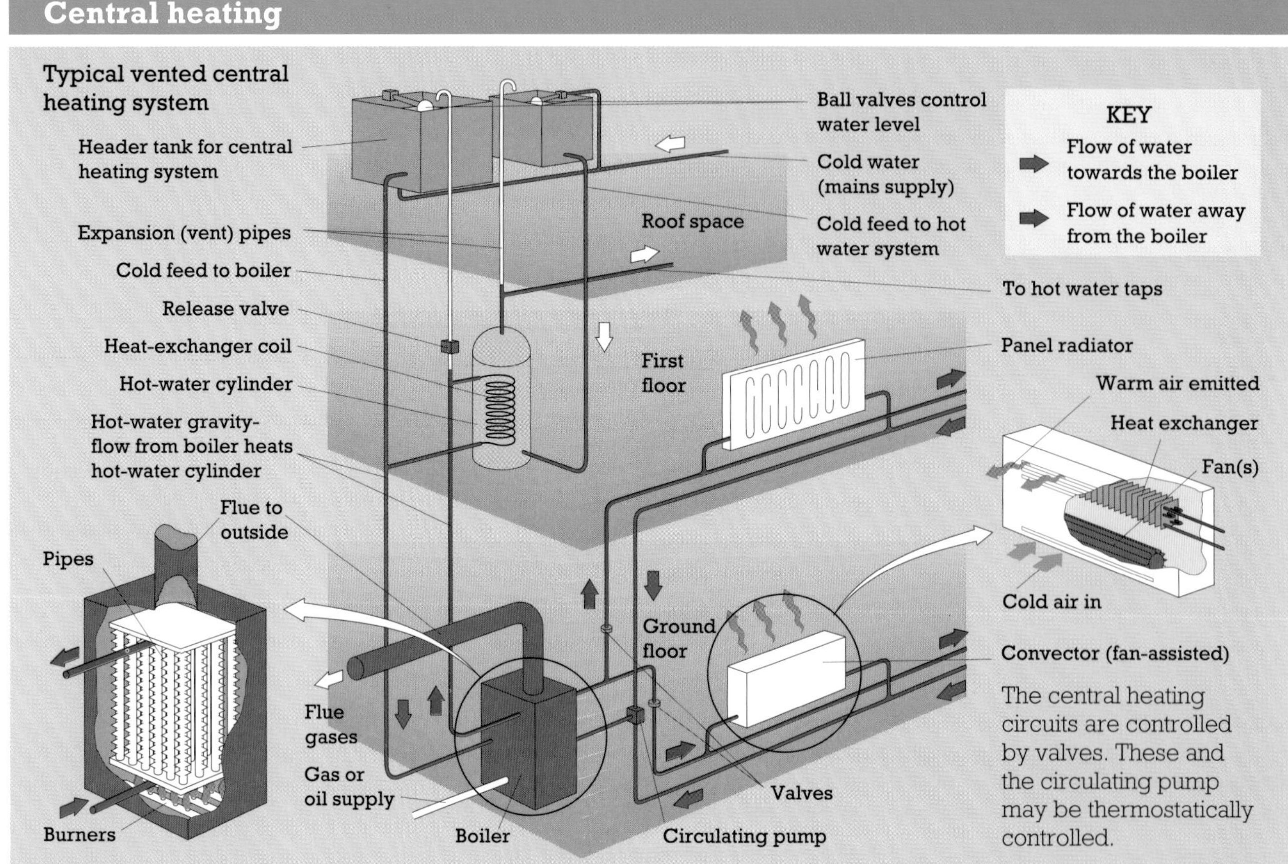

celluloid, a transparent, flammable plastic made by the action on *nitro-cellulose of a solution of camphor in ethanol. Celluloid was patented in 1870 by *Hyatt, who created the material while seeking a substitute for ivory in the manufacture of billiard balls. It was soon used in the USA for a range of household goods, and it was later used in sheet form for making photographic *film. In most applications it has now been replaced by less flammable materials.

cellulose $(C_6H_{10}O_5)_n$, a structural carbohydrate found in the cell walls of all plants: chemically it is a *polymer of the sugar glucose. For commercial use, cellulose is obtained mainly from wood pulp and cotton linters (cotton fibres too short for use in spinning). It is the principal raw material for *paper manufacture, and both *nitro-cellulose (cellulose nitrate) and *cellulose acetate are derived from it. Ethers of cellulose with methyl, ethyl, and benzyl alcohol are also of great industrial importance.

cellulose acetate, any of a family of non-flammable thermoplastics (see *plastic). Cellulose acetate is obtained by the action of acetic acid or acetic anhydride on purified cellulose (usually from short, waste-cotton fibres). Cellulose acetate was first manufactured by *Cross and Bevan using a process patented in 1894. Cellulose acetate photographic *film was first made in 1910, although it did not widely replace *celluloid until a stronger product was made in 1954. During World War I cellulose acetate was used as 'dope' to stretch the fabric skin of aircraft wings. In 1921 cellulose acetate fibres were first used in the manufacture of acetate *rayon; in the same year a prototype injection *moulding machine was designed, and cellulose acetate became the principal moulded thermoplastic. It was largely superseded after World War II by *polythene and *polystyrene, but it is still used for toys, spectacle frames, and packaging materials because of its impact resistance and ability to take colours.

cellulose nitrate *nitro-cellulose.

cement, a powdered mixture of calcium silicates and aluminates, applied in a soft state to the surfaces of solid bodies to make them cohere firmly. The commonest cement is *Portland cement. Hydraulic cements, first discovered by the Romans and reintroduced by *Smeaton in the 1760s, set hard even under water. Cement forms *concrete when mixed with *aggregate and water, and with sand and water it forms *mortar for masonry work or plastering. Other types of cement include rapid-hardening and sulphate-resisting cements. The latter are used for *foundations in some clay soils in place of ordinary Portland cement, which deteriorates when soluble sulphates are present. High-alumina cement, made from limestone and bauxite, is highly resistant to sulphates and to high temperatures, and strengthens rapidly after placement. However, structural members made from it sometimes fail in conditions of combined high humidity and high temperature. Mastic is a flexible cement used for sealing joints, for example between a window frame and the surrounding brickwork. The word cement is also used for certain *adhesives.

cementation, the process of introducing a *cement into a loose mass of particles. Cementation increases the soil strength and reduces its compressibility, and may be carried out to hold back water in the ground when excavating. Tubes are inserted into the ground, and a mixture of cement and water (grout) is pumped through them. The mixture sets in the spaces between the soil particles. In finer soils, low-viscosity silicates and resins are used. Cementation is also a process in which iron packed with charcoal is heated to make *steel.

central heating, a space-heating system in which fuel is converted at a single location into useful heat; the heat is then distributed to emitters throughout the building by a medium such as water, steam, or air. The earliest central heating system was probably the Roman *hypocaust. Where water or steam is the transfer medium, the fuel (coal, oil, gas, wood, or straw) is burnt in the fire chamber of a boiler to heat water contained in a separate internal vessel. The water circulates by gravity or, more commonly, by pumping through pipes around the building. In a gravity system, the water cools as it gives out its heat and becomes denser; the cooled water displaces the less dense, heated water from the boiler (see figure). Forced circulation by pumping allows smaller pipes to be used. Emitters (radiators or convectors) are sized to balance heat losses through the building fabric and from air circulation (draughts). Valves regulate the flow through an emitter and are often thermostatically controlled. Where air is the transfer medium, it is forced through a suitable heat exchanger by a fan and then passes through ducts directly into the spaces to be heated. A timer and *thermostat control a heating system to ensure fuel economy.

central processing unit (CPU, processor), the main operating unit of a digital *computer. The CPU is the part of the hardware of a computer that performs instructions and controls the flow of data according to instructions provided by the computer *software. The CPU of a conventional computer consists of two main components: a control unit and an arithmetic and logic unit (ALU), together with a limited number of local *memory locations, known as registers, which are used to store temporarily instructions, data, and results during the execution of a *program. The control unit interprets each *machine-code instruction sequentially and executes the appropriate operation, such as transferring data between the main memory and a register, or instructing the ALU to carry out a logical or arithmetical process. The complete *computing operation of fetching an instruction, decoding, and executing it is known as a fetch–execute cycle or sequence. In older and larger computers the CPU consisted of many individual components, but now an entire CPU can be contained on a single silicon chip (see *microprocessor). Computers designed for *parallel processing have multiple processors rather than a single CPU.

centreboard, an adjustable keel in dinghies and some racing yachts, raised or lowered through a slot to provide lateral resistance when sailing. It pivots at its forward end, and is adjusted by means of a wire at its after end. Other types of adjustable keel are lee-boards, used on either side of a flat-bottomed boat, and daggerboards, narrow keels that slide into the water rather than pivot.

Centre National de la Recherche Scientifique (CNRS), a French government institution established to co-ordinate and promote research in the sciences and humanities; to give grants to university laboratories and research institutes; and to maintain its own laboratories. Policy is formulated by the Comité National de la Recherche Scientifique, which is organized into some forty sections, each with twenty-six members. Affiliated laboratories include the Institut National d'Astronomie et de Géophysique and the Institut National de Physique Nucléaire et de Physique des Particules.

centrifuge, a machine for separating solids from liquids, or separating immiscible liquids, using the centripetal force generated by rapid rotation. Centrifuging greatly accelerates processes that might eventually take place under the influence of gravity alone, for example the settling of suspended solids in liquids. A typical laboratory centrifuge creates a centripetal force about 1,000 times greater than that of gravity. Ultra-centrifuges can create forces up to 750,000 times that of gravity, and are used to precipitate large biological molecules from solution. The conventional centrifuge is of the 'swinging bucket' type. In this, the liquid to be centrifuged is placed in carefully balanced open containers suspended on the arms of a rotor. As the rotor accelerates, the containers assume a horizontal position. With this type of centrifuge, material can be spun only in batches. Continuous separation is possible by feeding the liquid into a rotating cone fitted with a series of conical separating liners. Gases can also be separated centrifugally. For example, uranium can be separated into its two isotopes, U-238 and U-235, by centrifuging the gaseous compound uranium hexafluoride (see *nuclear fuels).

ceramic, a material made from inorganic, non-metallic chemicals, processed at high temperatures. Ceramics are one of the three main classes of engineering materials, the others being *metal and *plastic. In addition to traditional clay-based *pottery, ceramics include *bricks, *cement, and *concrete, *glass, *tiles, and modern engineering ceramics such as *alumina and *silicon carbide. Common features of ceramics are their hardness, brittleness and resistance to heat. Many are electrical insulators or have other electrical properties (see *electroceramics). Ceramics are made from raw materials with very high melting-points and are usually manufactured in the solid state from fine powders. Pottery is made from clay, a naturally occurring suspension of fine ceramic powder in water produced by the weathering of rock. Clays can be moulded to shape or mixed with water to form emulsified suspensions (slips). These slips can be cast in plaster moulds to form complicated shapes: the water from

Engineering **ceramics** being produced by the Toshiba Company in Japan. Such materials are durable, extremely heat-resistant, and unaffected by most chemicals.

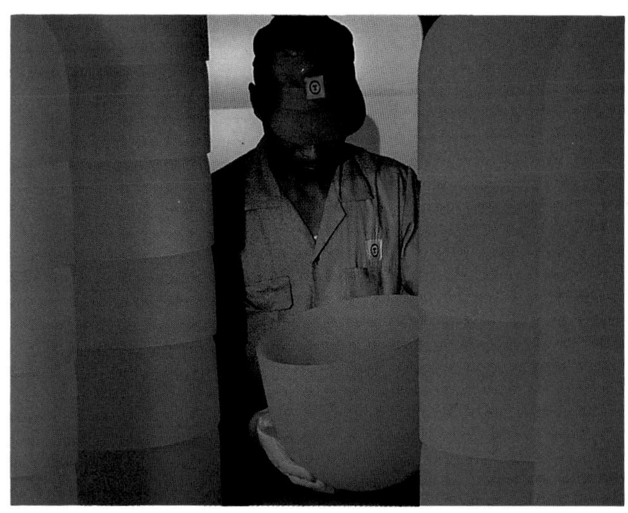

the slip is absorbed into the plaster. Once formed, the clay holds its shape before being fired in a kiln or furnace to harden it. The processing of engineering ceramics is carried out from source materials prepared in a similar way to clay-based minerals, and using similar processing before firing.

During firing, clays and other ceramic raw materials sinter (fuse without melting) to form a hard solid. Sintering is aided by small quantities of low-melting-point components, which melt during firing and help bind the other material together. In pottery, this low-melting-point phase comprises small amounts of silica glass. Much of the development of pottery has been shaped by the availability of clays that can be fired easily at low temperatures. China and *porcelain clays have a low glass content and therefore need much higher firing temperatures. This results in a much finer, almost translucent material.

Engineering ceramics are also sintered, but they require very high firing temperatures and are thus very expensive. Sometimes the starting material contains no low-melting-point phase. In such cases techniques such as hot isostatic pressing (HIP) must be used, in which high temperatures are combined with a large isostatic (uniform) pressure to form solid materials from a powder. It is very difficult to manufacture large components from ceramics and this is currently a limitation on their applications. Because of their extreme hardness, ceramics must be shaped by *abrasive techniques using diamond. Ceramics are used in high-temperature environments (for example, jet and diesel engines) and in articles which undergo high wear and require a long life (for example, artificial hip joints and teeth). The major limitation to their further use is their brittleness and the reduction in strength which occurs if small cracks are present. Newer developments include tougher ceramics, such as *zirconia and ceramic-matrix *composites.

cereal crop, any member of the grass family grown for its edible seed. Cereals were probably the earliest cultivated crops (see *agriculture), and now account for over 50 per cent of all *arable farming. Wheat, rice, maize, barley, oats, rye, millet, and sorghum are common cereals (see table). Cereals are the staple food in many parts of the world, since they have a high carbohydrate content and can be grown and stored in bulk. After harvesting, most cereals are threshed to separate the grain from the seed head. The grain may then be dried and stored, and is then *milled or polished to produce whole grains, meal, flakes, or flour. *Fermentation of cereals is important in *brewing and for the production of leavened *bread.

cermet (ceramic metal), a *composite material in which small particles of hard ceramics such as tungsten carbide or *silicon carbide are combined with small amounts of a ductile metal such as cobalt. This produces a material with the hardness and wear-resistance of a ceramic but which is easier to fabricate because of the presence of the metal. Cermets are very important for the manufacture of metal-cutting tools such as drill bits and lathe tools.

CERN *European Laboratory for Particle Physics.

cervical screening, a technique in *obstetrics and gynaecology involving the examination of cells from a woman's cervix (the neck of the womb) to detect early changes that may progress to *cancer. Such changes are treatable by a minor operation, whereas operations for more advanced cervical cancer are less successful. Since the 1950s, cervical screening has been widely employed as a routine preventive for healthy women. It consists of examining the cervix using a vaginal *speculum. A few cells from the cervical opening are scraped off with a wooden spatula for microscopical examination. It is commonly called a 'pap' smear after its inventor, George Papanicolaou (1883–1962).

cesspit (cesspool) *septic tank.

Major cereal crops of the world

Crop	Area grown	Uses
Barley	All parts of world, but especially cool highland regions in tropics	Animal feed, producing brewing malt, human consumption
Maize	Warm, dry climates; all parts of world	Human consumption, livestock feed
Millet		
African	East and Central Africa, Asia, Soviet Union	Ground to flour and eaten as porridge, or used to produce a malt for brewing. Stores for very long periods
Bullrush	Arid and semi-arid regions of Africa and India	Ground into flour and eaten as porridge, or boiled and eaten like rice. Fed green to livestock
Oats	Temperate regions, particularly moist climates	Crushed and eaten as porridge or hard, flat, dry cake. Rolled and fed to stock
Rice	Tropical and sub-tropical regions	Boiled and eaten whole. Can be ground into a flour, and also used to make the alcoholic drink saki
Rye	Temperate regions	Used as a forage crop for livestock. Rye bread—particularly in Germany and the former Eastern bloc—and hard, flat, dry rye crispbreads, particularly in Scandinavia. Rye whisky from USA and Canada
Sorghum	Semi-arid regions, USA	Human consumption in India, and in Africa where it is also used to make malt for brewing. Straw is used as a cooking fuel. In North and South America, Japan, and Europe it is used as Livestock feed
Wheat	All over the world, at higher altitudes in tropics	Ground into flour and consumed in a variety of forms ranging from bread and cakes to pasta and noodles

cetane number *diesel oil.

CFC *chloro-fluorocarbon.

chain drive *belt drive and chain drive.

chain-mail, *body armour made of interlinked rings of metal (usually iron or steel). The most widely used metallic armour, it may have originated among the Celtic tribes of Europe some time in the 4th century BC. Because iron rings are not individually flexible, mail is vulnerable to puncture by a small sharp point, such as an arrow. Chain-mail is, however, capable of blocking a long, slashing cut. It is also cheaper, and covers a far larger body area than armour made from individual plates. It also requires less skilled workmanship.

chain reaction (nuclear), a self-sustaining nuclear reaction, for example nuclear *fission, in which products of the reaction go on to induce the same nuclear reaction in other atoms. In a fission chain reaction a *uranium-235 atom is split by a bombarding neutron. This splits the nucleus into two fragments, and also releases two, sometimes three, neutrons. Under the right conditions these neutrons will go on to split other nuclei, with the release of more neutrons, and so on. In a nuclear reactor, this chain reaction proceeds in a controlled manner; in a *nuclear weapon such as an atomic bomb the chain reaction is allowed to continue unchecked, with a resultant explosive release of enormous amounts of energy.

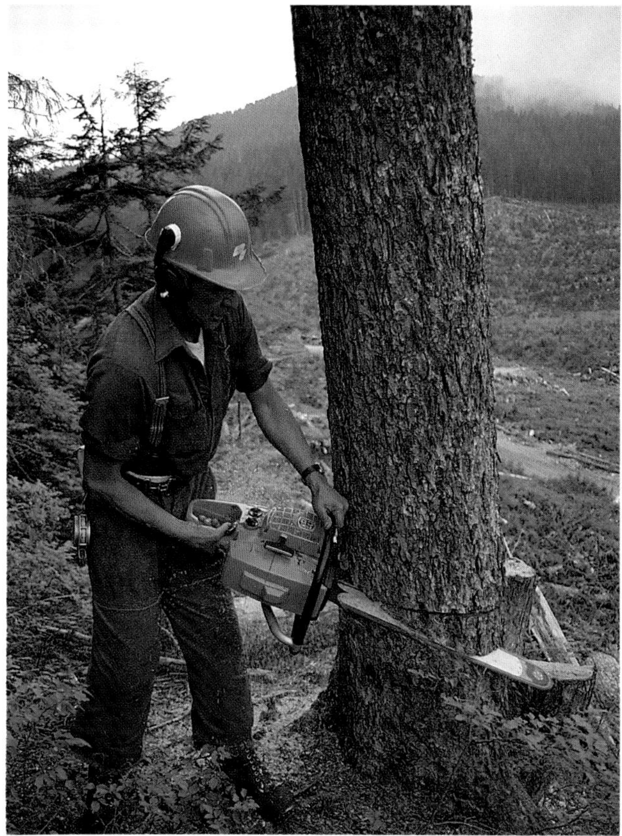

Tree-felling using a **chain-saw**. A wedge-shaped undercut is first made in the direction chosen for the tree to fall; a back-cut is then made on the opposite side of the trunk.

chain-saw, a power-driven saw in which the cutting action is achieved by means of a series of teeth attached to the links of an endless chain. The power is usually supplied by a compact petrol engine, or on some smaller models by an electric motor. In forestry, the chain-saw has largely replaced the *axe.

Chain, Sir Ernst Boris (1906–79), German-born British biochemist who, with *Florey, developed *penicillin as a uniquely valuable antibiotic. Chain came to the UK as a Jewish refugee from Nazi persecution in 1933, and after working briefly with *Hopkins at Cambridge University, was invited by Florey to join him in Oxford. There, in 1939, they initiated the research programme which, with the aid of the US chemical industry, led to the large-scale manufacture of penicillin. With E. P. Abraham, he established the initially controversial β-lactam formula for penicillin. He shared the Nobel Prize for Physiology and Medicine in 1945 with Florey and *Fleming. With scientists of the Beecham Group, he subsequently developed a range of semi-synthetic penicillins.

Chang Heng *Zhang Heng.

channel, a line of communication between a transmitter and a receiver. The channel may be a wire, a selected *radio frequency, or an optical wave (as in *optical fibre communications). A channel can carry several messages simultaneously by *multiplexing.

Channel Tunnel, a *tunnel beneath the English Channel providing a fixed link between the UK and France. Several schemes have been proposed since the early 19th century. Work actually started twice, in 1882 and 1974, though it was soon abandoned. The present tunnel was begun in 1986 and is due for completion in 1993. It comprises two tunnels, each 7.6 m (25 feet) in diameter and 49.4 km (30.7 miles) long, 37.5 km (23.3 miles) of which is under water, and a service tunnel. The tunnels are, on average, 40 m (130 feet) below the sea-bed. They are designed to carry high-speed shuttle trains with vehicles and passengers on board between the UK and France. It is estimated that the journey time will be about 30 minutes.

Chappe, Claude (1763–1805), French inventor who devised the visual *semaphore telegraph system. Destined for the Church, Chappe had his career plans upset by the French Revolution of 1789, after which he turned his attention to developing signalling systems (see *telegraphy). He finally settled on one in which movable wooden arms were pivoted on tall towers to represent letters of the alphabet and other symbols. In 1793 the government commissioned a telegraph line from Paris to Lille that involved fifteen relay stations. He completed the line in a year, and a second was commissioned, but he died before it was finished.

charcoal, black, brittle *carbon that results from the burning of organic material below 500 °C in a limited supply of air. It comprises almost pure amorphous carbon, and burns with great heat and no flame. One tonne of wood yields 200–350 kg (450–750 pounds) of charcoal, together with turpentine, creosote, methanol, pitch, and flammable gases. Charcoal is a constituent of *gunpowder, and before the introduction of coke, it was used for *smelting ores and *forging metals. Because of its reactivity and highly porous structure it finds modern applications in *respirators and in removing impurities from liquids and gases. It is also used as a drawing material.

charge-coupled device (CCD), a specialized form of *integrated circuit, constructed from MOS (metal-oxide semiconductor) *transistors. These are linked to form a chequerboard of miniature squares surrounded by metal tracks, which provide voltages. Application of appropriate voltages can induce individual tiny squares to capture and store electrons. Hence, a CCD is a single-chip, memory-like array which can store different patterns of electric charge. Electrical signals can be sequentially written into and read out from the CCD, a process known as 'clocking'. CCDs are used in computers as large-capacity analog and digital serial memories, and have a number of other applications. They are used in telecommunications to store and delay signals for short and specific time-lengths. The CCD elements can be made sensitive to light, with each square corresponding to one picture element (pixel). Such CCDs can be used to record visual images, for example in still *video cameras. They have several advantages over conventional photography, in that they are much more sensitive to light, and can record a very wide range of light intensities. Furthermore, unlike a film, a CCD can be used repeatedly, each successive image being rapidly read out on to a magnetic disk or other storage device. To date, the major use of CCDs as image detectors has been in astronomical *telescopes. CCDs are also used as *particle detectors and as detectors in spectroscopy, and X-ray diffraction.

chariot, a horse-drawn vehicle used in the past for warfare and racing. The first horse-drawn chariots were introduced around 2500 BC. Early chariots had four wheels, but two eventually became the standard pattern in China, India, Europe, and the Near East. Two- or four-horse teams pulled the chariots. Their crews consisted of two or three people, who were generally armed with *bows or javelins. In northern Europe, however, the chariot was used to carry into battle soldiers who fought on foot. A popular tactic was to equip chariot wheels with scythe blades to hack at the legs of enemy soldiers.

chart *maps and charts.

cheese manufacture, the production of the *dairy product cheese by separating milk into curd (mostly fat and the protein casein) and whey (sugars, some protein, water, and salts), pressing the curds to further remove moisture, and then ripening. This separation may be achieved by the addition to the milk of the *enzyme rennet; by the addition of a bacterial culture which acidifies the milk through fermentation; or by direct addition of acid. The milk is kept warm as it curdles; the curd is then cut and mildly heated to release the whey. The separated curd is pressed into moulds or hoops; most cheeses are then allowed to ripen, but some, like cottage cheese, may be sold fresh. In the ripening process, micro-organisms, most commonly lactic-acid-producing bacteria, act on the cheese to produce the desired body and flavour. Control of temperature and moisture during ripening is critical in obtaining the desired cheese.

A relief carving dated 883–859 BC ,from the Assyrian city of Nimrud in Northern Iraq, showing a **chariot** being used for a royal lion hunt.

chemical engineering, the practice of designing, building, operating, and maintaining chemical manufacturing plant. It embraces a wide range of disciplines: structural, electrical, and mechanical engineering, industrial and environmental chemistry, control and advanced manufacturing technologies, as well as financial and economic acumen. It is concerned primarily with the flow of materials and of energy throughout the plant and with maintaining safe operating conditions. Chemical engineering can be small scale (as in the production of some pharmaceuticals) or on a massive scale (as in the *chemical industry).

chemical industry. The major products of the chemical industry, called 'heavy' chemicals, are produced in quantities of millions of tonnes per year world-wide. Examples include hydrochloric acid, sodium carbonate, chlorine, hydrogen, ammonia, and organic chemicals such as benzene and ethene. Usually they are not consumed by individuals as chemical products but are used in the manufacture of a wide variety of other products. The production of a heavy chemical depends upon the availability of the raw materials and their economic conversion into a product of consistent quality. Short-term fluctuations in the demand of any particular retail product that depends on a heavy chemical for its production will have little, if any, effect on the overall production of that heavy chemical. The origins of the heavy chemical industry are to be found in the late 18th and early 19th centuries in the production of *sodium carbonate, a chemical needed for the manufacture of *soap and *glass. The *Leblanc process, in which *sulphuric acid is reacted with sodium chloride (*salt) and then with *limestone to produce sodium carbonate, was introduced to France in 1791 and to the UK in 1823. Sodium chloride was obtained by mining, but the sulphuric acid had to be manufactured, and the *lead chamber process for its production was another important early heavy chemical process. Typically, as chemical understanding has grown, both the Leblanc and lead chamber processes have been superseded. In the 1860s the *Solvay process, in which sodium chloride solution is treated to produce sodium carbonate, was introduced to Belgium. The adoption of this process throughout Europe (in preference to the Leblanc process) would have led to a drop in demand for sulphuric acid, had the emerging *dyeing industry not required it. However, the sulphuric acid required was of a higher concentration than could be produced by the lead chamber process, and therefore the *contact process (which had been known since 1831) was developed, and is still the major method of sulphuric acid production. At the same time, the development of electrical power generation in the late 19th century made electrolysis available to the chemical industry. The electrolysis of brine was used to pro-

A petrochemical plant in Lanzhou, China. Petroleum products are essential raw materials for the **chemical industry**.

duce *sodium hydroxide solution (using a *Castner–Kellner cell) and *sodium metal: this led to the decline of the less economic Solvay process.

The simultaneous production of chlorine and sodium hydroxide has led to this part of the chemical industry being known as the chlor–alkali sector. Large quantities of chlorine are used for bleaching and for purifying public water supplies. The main use of chlorine, however, is in making chemical compounds, including a wide range of metal chlorides and a variety of chlorinated organic compounds, such as vinyl chloride, used to make *PVC. The other halogens, *bromine and *fluorine, are produced to a much lesser extent, but fluorine is significant. It is produced electrolytically, and its extreme reactivity requires the use of fluorine-resistant materials in constructing the manufacturing plant.

The production of *fertilizers is dependent on several heavy chemicals—sulphuric acid, nitric acid, and ammonia—as well as such raw materials as phosphates, fossil fuels, and potassium salts. The phosphoric acid used in manufacturing fertilizers is obtained by treating phosphate rock with sulphuric acid. The ammonia is manufactured by the *Haber–Bosch process. Some of this ammonia is used to produce ammonium salts or urea for fertilizers, but the bulk is used to manufacture *nitric acid.

Until 1960 the term heavy chemical industry was employed to describe industrial chemistry based on inorganic chemicals. Since then, however, the production of such materials as *benzene, *ethene, and vinyl chloride has reached such proportions and has become of such significance in the production of other materials that they too have become known as heavy chemicals. From the early 19th century coal was destructively distilled to manufacture *coal-gas and *benzene, with other aromatic hydrocarbons (hydrocarbons containing a benzene ring) being obtained as by-products. The use of coal-gas has declined with the introduction of natural gas. The carbonization of coal to obtain coke for reducing metal ores did not produce enough benzene to meet requirements, and the chemical industry responded by developing methods to obtain benzene and related materials from *petroleum refining. Most of the hydrocarbons obtained from petroleum are simpler materials than benzene or other aromatics, but in addition to being used for fuels they can be 'cracked' to produce unsaturated hydrocarbons such as ethene, ethyne, propene, and butadiene, which, because of their reactivity, can be used as building blocks for a wide range of *petrochemicals.

chemical warfare, the use of manufactured poisonous substances to kill or injure an enemy. The first effective use of chemical weapons (devised by *Haber) occurred in 1915, during World War I, when the German forces released into the air a cloud of chlorine gas that was blown by the wind into trenches occupied by French and Canadian troops. The chemicals commonly used in warfare—chlorine, *phosgene, *mustard gas, and the various *nerve gases—are contained either in shells fired from artillery or in aerosol-spray canisters that are fitted to aircraft and flown over the target area. To be effective, the chemicals must be inhaled or come into contact with skin. The main defence against them is protective clothing—gas masks and special suits made of rubber or treated synthetic cloth—although some medical antidotes can be taken before entering a battlefield where chemical weapons have been used. Chemical warfare is prohibited by the Geneva Convention, but many signatories possess large arsenals of chemical weapons and *nerve gases.

chemotherapy, the treatment of infections or cancer with drugs. Early examples are arsenic for syphilis and quinine for malaria, both of which have been in use in Europe since the 17th century. Modern chemotherapy was founded by *Ehrlich. Some chemotherapeutic agents are extracted from moulds or fungi and are called *antibiotics, for example *penicillin and tetracyclines. Chemotherapy is also used to treat *cancer. (See also *pharmacology.)

Chernobyl, a nuclear power-station near Kiev in the Soviet Union, the site in 1986 of the worst nuclear accident in the world to date. Thirty-one people died trying to fight subsequent fires, and many more received radiation burns or suffered from associated diseases. The reactor was one of a group of four at the site that used a light-water coolant and a graphite moderator. The accident was the result of unauthorized experiments by the operators, in which safety systems were deliberately circumvented in order to learn more about the plant's operation. As a result the reactor rapidly overheated, and the water coolant 'flashed' into steam. Hydrogen then formed by reaction of the steam with the graphite moderator, causing two major explosions and fire. *Fall-out from the explosions, containing the *radioactive isotope caesium-137, affected large areas of Europe. In particular, livestock in high-rainfall areas received unacceptable doses of radiation.

Chinese Academy of Sciences, China's premier national scientific institution, founded in 1949. It was suppressed during the Cultural Revolution (1966–76), but has subsequently flourished. It conducts scientific research in both the pure and applied fields. Across its 120 research institutions, it employs some 60,000 scientists and technologists, of whom about 400 are accorded the formal status of Academician. It is also a publishing body. It is affiliated to the Chinese University of Science and Technology.

Chinese technology. China has the longest unbroken history of progress in science and technology (over 4,000 years) of any nation in the world. Four inventions that had a major impact on Western culture were *paper, *printing from movable type, *gunpowder, and the *magnetic compass. Paper-making began in China around 50 BC and by the 7th century AD had spread to Korea, Japan, and the Arab world. *Wood-block printing was well established in China by AD 1000, while movable type came about a century later. Gunpowder was first used in China early in the 12th century. It reached Europe less than a century later, where it almost overnight transformed the art of warfare. A form of magnetic compass was probably used in China as early as the 5th century BC, but it was not used for navigation until the 12th century, almost the same time as in Europe. An enormous number of other inventions have their origins in China. Examples include the stern rudder and compartmentalized hulls for ships (see *junk), the horse-collar *harness, *paddle-wheel propulsion, and the *seismograph. The *Great Wall of China and the *Grand Canal are outstanding Chinese civil engineering projects.

chipboard *manufactured board.

chiropractic, a system of alternative medicine, based on the belief that organic disease can be treated by manipulation of the spine and joints. Conventional medicine takes the view that manipulation is one possible form of manual therapy, useful only in diseases originating in vertebral disorders or misalignment.

chisels and gouges, hand tools with straight and curved cutting edges respectively, normally used in woodworking. They are fitted with wooden or plastic handles and may be applied direct to the work or tapped, usually along the grain of the wood, with a light mallet. They date back to antiquity and were made first of flint, then bronze, and later iron and steel. Their size and design varies with the intended purpose. Those in a carpenter's tool-box would normally range from 5 to 50 mm (0.2 to 2 inches) in width. Cold chisels are heavier tools with a hard cutting edge, used mainly for cutting metal, especially iron. They have no wooden handle and are struck with a hammer rather than a mallet. Cold chisels with a relatively long cutting edge are used by masons for cutting bricks and trimming stone. (For illustration see *tools, history of.)

chlorine (symbol Cl, at. no. 17, r.a.m. 35.45), a greenish-yellow, poisonous gas, a member of the halogen family of elements which also includes *bromine, *fluorine, and *iodine. As sodium chloride (*salt) it occurs in large quantities in sea-water and in salt deposits. It is produced by the electrolysis of sodium chloride solution in a *Castner–Kellner cell. Most community *water supplies and swimming pools are disinfected with small amounts of chlorine to kill bacteria. Large amounts are used in *bleaches for wood-pulp in *paper and *textile manufacture. In reactions with *hydrocarbons, chlorine is used to manufacture *PVC, *hydrochloric acid, and a wide variety of other chemicals.

chloro-fluorocarbon (CFC), any of a family of non-flammable, non-toxic, non-corrosive, colourless, and nearly odourless gases or liquids, widely used as refrigerant liquids in domestic refrigerators since the 1930s and, more recently, as a propellant for aerosol sprays. They are produced by the fluorination of chlorocarbons followed by *fractional distillation. Recently, there has been considerable concern over their effect on the environment. Exposure of CFCs to ultraviolet light in the upper atmosphere causes *ozone depletion. Two new families of chemicals, the hydrochloro-fluorocarbons (HCFCs) and the hydro-fluorocarbons (HFCs), were developed to replace CFCs. However, HCFC-123 appears to cause tumours in rats, and there are doubts as to whether these will be used as full substitutes for CFCs.

chloroform ($CHCl_3$), a volatile, colourless, and non-flammable liquid that induces *anaesthesia. Discovered by the German chemist Justus von Liebig in 1831, it was first used as ananaesthetic by *Simpson in 1847 and enjoyed considerable popularity before being eventually abandoned in the 1950s because of its toxicity and potentially fatal effect on heart rhythm.

chocolate, a food produced by grinding the shelled beans of the *beverage crop cacao. This produces a liquid known as chocolate liquor, containing fat-rich cocoa butter. Chocolate for *confectionery uses the full-fat liquor, mixed with *dairy products and vegetable fats. The fat content may be reduced for drinking chocolates by applying pressure to the butter. The resulting press cake is then ground to produce cocoa powder. Cocoa butter is used in *cosmetics. Chocolate as a beverage was drunk by the Aztecs; the drink was introduced to the Spanish court in the 16th century. Chocolate confectionery was first manufactured by the UK firm J. S. Fry & Son in the 19th century.

choke. In a motor car, a choke is a butterfly-valve in the air-intake passage of the *carburettor, used to control the volume of air drawn in to mix with the petrol. For cold starts the mixture is kept rich, while for normal running it is leaner (contains less petrol). The choke may be controlled manually or automatically.

chromatic aberration *achromatic lens.

chromatography, a technique for analysing or separating mixtures of compounds in which a mobile phase (liquid or gas) containing a mixture of substances flows over a stationary phase (solid or liquid). Each component in the mobile phase has its own 'stickiness' with regard to the stationary phase; as the mixture moves over the stationary phase, the components of the mixture are separated into a series of single-substance 'bands' according to their retention on the stationary phase. On reaching the end of the stationary phase, the materials emerge as a series of pure substances. Separation is improved in some mixtures by the application of an electrical voltage across the stationary phase (electrophoresis). Chromatography is used extensively in chemical, pharmaceutical, and biochemical research throughout the world.

An agar gel (a type of gel made from seaweed) being prepared for electrophoresis (a kind of **chromatography**) of DNA samples.

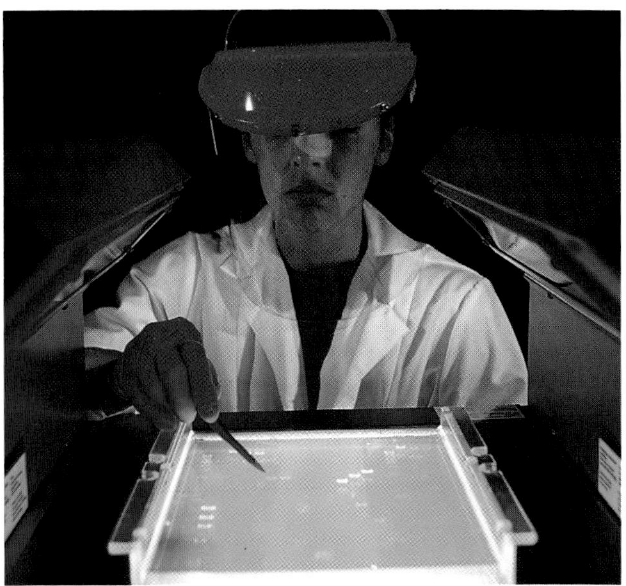

chromium (symbol Cr, at. no. 24, r.a.m. 52.00), a silvery-white metallic element. It resists corrosion and this, along with its metallic lustre, is the reason for its use in the *electroplating of iron and copper objects such as automobile trim and plumbing fixtures. The main ore is chromite ($FeCr_2O_4$), and reduction by carbon in an *electric-arc furnace yields an *alloy of iron and chrome which is used in making chromium and stainless *steel. Chromium steels are very hard and strong and are used for armour plating, bank vaults, safes, cutting tools, and automobile parts. Compounds of chromium are used for paint pigments, dye *mordants, in *breathalysers, and for *tanning leather.

chronometer, mariner's, a robust, accurate *clock or watch used for measuring longitude at sea. This method of measuring longitude was first suggested in the 16th century, but until the 18th century there was no timepiece accurate and reliable enough to maintain the reference time over a voyage that could last many months. Several countries offered prizes for a sufficiently reliable chronometer: in Britain, the prize offered was won in 1762 by *Harrison (although he did not receive the money until 1773). By the mid-19th century chronometers were cheap enough to be carried by most ocean-going vessels. Since the 1930s, with the advent of radio time-signals and the development of *radio aids to navigation and later *navigation satellites, chronometers have become less important navigational aids. Modern chronometers are quartz rather than mechanical devices.

cigarette lighter, a portable device providing a more convenient flame source than matches. Late 19th-century designs, still in use in some lighters, struck sparks by rotating a serrated steel wheel against a flint; the sparks ignited a petroleum spirit fuel, which burned at a wick. Modern lighters use *piezo-electric spark-ignition and liquefied *butane gas as a fuel.

cine-camera, a camera that takes motion pictures. Its basic elements are similar to those of a still *camera: a light-tight compartment for the film, a lens, and a shutter. A cine-camera, however, has to be able to take a series of photographs in rapid succession at a steady speed. This is achieved by a film-transport mechanism, which moves the film intermittently, one frame at a time, past an opening or 'gate' through which the film is exposed. This intermittent motion is produced by a claw device that engages with perforations on the edge of the film and moves it on one frame. The film is then stationary for a brief interval as the claw engages further along the film: it is in this stationary interval that the film is exposed. The cine-camera's shutter is a rotating, partially cut-away disc that is geared to the intermittent mechanism. The opaque section of the disc prevents any light from reaching the film while it is moving.

cinematography, history and principles of. Cinematography is the technique of making motion-picture films. It is based on the phenomenon of persistence of vision, in which the eye retains the image of an object for a fraction of a second after the object has been removed. This phenomenon was first studied in detail in 1824, when the British physician P. M. Roget carried out the first experiments into the persistence of vision. A number of 'optical toys' based on the effect soon appeared. These devices, such as the thaumotrope, phenakinetoscope, and zoetrope, used a series of drawings which, when viewed in rapid succession, gave the illusion of movement. Attempts were made to adapt these devices for projection by a magic lantern (a simple form of image-projector using slides), but the results were disappointing, as only dim, blurred images were produced.

An important development came in the 1880s with the discovery of the principle of intermittent movement. In a device called a choreutoscope, a magic lantern projected a series of images in quick succession, while a moving shutter prevented light from reaching the images when they were being changed. This is the basic principle upon which all *cine-cameras and *projectors operate. Photography had developed in the 1830s, but it was only in the 1850s that exposure times were short enough to capture movement. Chronophotography, the use of photographs taken at regular intervals to analyse motion, began during the 1870s. The British photographer Eadweard Muybridge (1830–1904) and the French physiologist Etienne-Jules Marey (1830–1904), among others, developed apparatus to produce photographic studies of people and animals in motion. During the 1880s, a number of inventors worked to combine the two principal components of cinematography: the photographic recording of movement, and the creation of the illusion of movement through the projection of individual images. In

Circuits, electrical and electronic

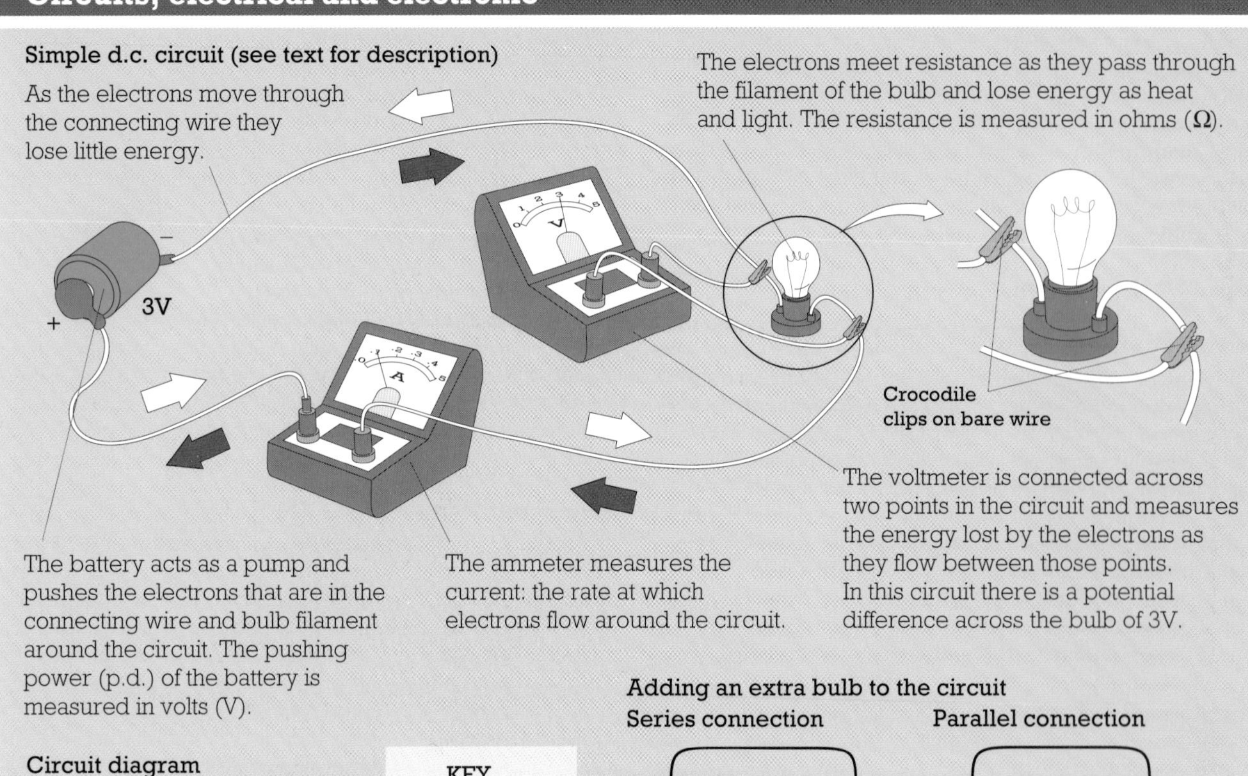

Simple d.c. circuit (see text for description)
As the electrons move through the connecting wire they lose little energy.
The electrons meet resistance as they pass through the filament of the bulb and lose energy as heat and light. The resistance is measured in ohms (Ω).
3V
+
–
Crocodile clips on bare wire
The voltmeter is connected across two points in the circuit and measures the energy lost by the electrons as they flow between those points. In this circuit there is a potential difference across the bulb of 3V.
The battery acts as a pump and pushes the electrons that are in the connecting wire and bulb filament around the circuit. The pushing power (p.d.) of the battery is measured in volts (V).
The ammeter measures the current: the rate at which electrons flow around the circuit.

Adding an extra bulb to the circuit

Circuit diagram

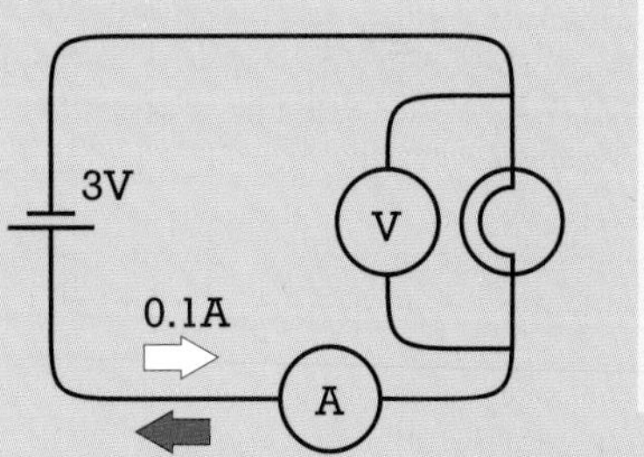

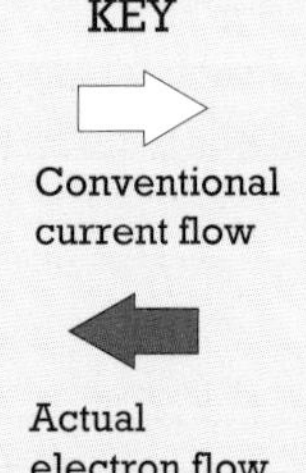

Series connection

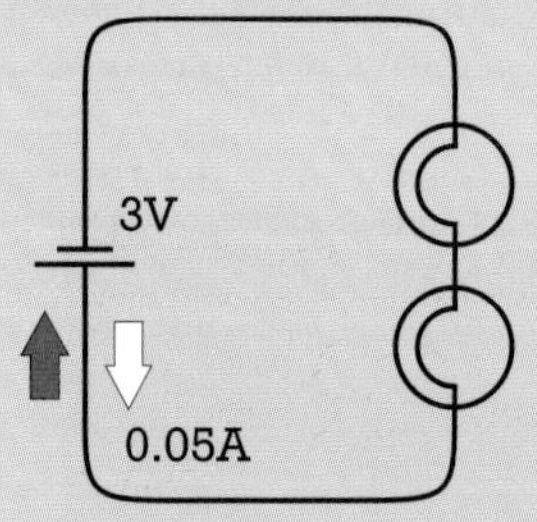

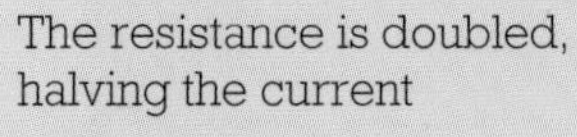

Parallel connection

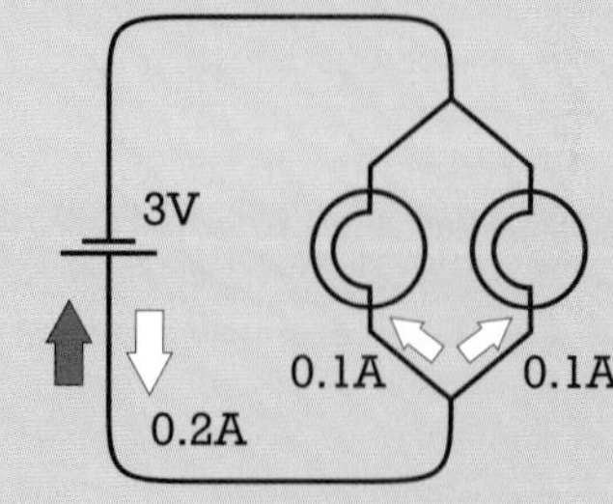

The current is doubled, causing the battery to run down more quickly.

Half-wave rectification

As diodes conduct electricity in one direction only they can be used to turn alternating current (a.c.) into direct current (d.c.). This is called rectification. Half-wave rectification uses only a single diode; only half the power of the input signal is obtained. To utilize all the a.c. input, four diodes are required. This is full-wave rectification (not shown).

Circuit diagram

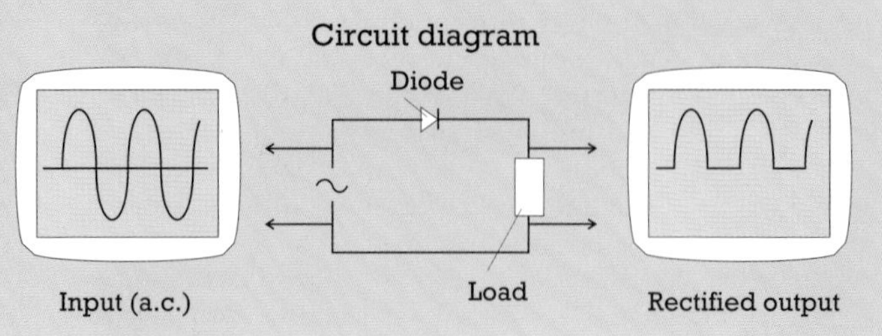

1889 *Edison developed a working cine-camera, which he called a kinetagraph. This used flexible, transparent, roll film, which had recently been developed for the first Kodak cameras. Edison's films were viewed in kinetoscopes, rather like peep-show machines. The first public projection of a moving film was made by the Lumière brothers in France in 1895, using a combined camera and projector. Simultaneously but independently, several other inventors in Europe and the USA produced their own devices.

Since the 1890s the basic principles of cine-camera and projector design have changed remarkably little. The major technological advances this century have been in the development of sound and colour for cinematography. The first commercial sound films were produced in 1926, using the Vitaphone sound-on-disc system, in which the sound was on a separate record. A number of alternative sound-on-film recording systems appeared in the 1930s. An example was the Movietone system, in which light was shone through a sound-track of variable density on to a photocell, producing an electrical signal corresponding to the sound, which drives a loudspeaker. The sound-track was recorded on to the edge of the film to synchronize with the pictures. Such systems were superseded by magnetic recording techniques developed during and immediately after World War II. Some of the earliest moving films were in colour—hand-painted, frame by frame. Kinemacolor, introduced in 1911, was an additive *colour cine-process using projection through a rotating red and green filter. Other two- and three-colour additive processes appeared in the 1920s. Modern colour films are based on subtractive processes, in which colour images are formed directly on the film. The Technicolor process, introduced in the 1930s, used three separate films, exposed simultaneously in a special camera.

circuit-breaker, a simple automatic safety switch used in electrical *circuits that cuts off the current flow if it becomes too large and potentially damaging. The switch is usually magnetically operated, and, unlike a *fuse, it may be reset without replacement when the fault condition has been repaired. Circuit-breakers have replaced fuses in mains *wiring for most domestic and industrial purposes.

circuits, electrical and electronic, the connection of electrical components in specific arrangements to perform useful work. In an electric circuit, the positive and negative terminals (the *anode and *cathode) of a *battery or other source of electrical power are connected by a conducting path. The rate of flow of charge through the circuit is the current (I), usually measured in amperes (A), while the difference in potential energy between the positive and negative terminals of the power source is the potential difference (p.d.) or voltage (V), measured in volts (V). Resistance (R) is the opposition that a material presents to current flow: it is measured in units of ohms (Ω). The physical basis of current flow is the movement of negatively charged electrons around the circuit from negative to positive potential. However, current in a circuit is conventionally shown as moving in a positive to negative direction, since the convention was set before the discovery of the electron. A circuit may contain many different components: some examples are shown in the table.

The current flowing through a circuit may be direct current (d.c.—the current flows in one direction), or alternating current (a.c.—the direction of current flow changes regularly). In a d.c. circuit, the values of current, voltage, and resistance are related by Ohm's Law: $V = I \times R$. Any one of

Symbols for selected electrical components

Component	Symbol
Conducting path	
Alternating current	
Positive polarity	+
Negative polarity	−
Single electric cell	+ −
Battery (several cells)	+ −
Fixed-value resistor	
Variable resistor	
Incandescent lamp	
Neon lamp	
Crossing conductors (no electrical contact)	
Junction of conductors	
Earth	
Fixed-value capacitor	
Fixed-value inductor (coil)	
Transformer (magnetic core)	
Measuring instruments (type indicated by letter in circle)	A Ammeter, V Voltmeter, W Wattmeter
Rectifier (junction) diode	or
Light-emitting diode (LED)	
Transistors	C B E n-p-n; C B E p-n-p
Amplifier (single-ended)	
Fuse	
Circuit-breaker	
Single-pole, single-throw switch	
Anodes	Main, Intermediate
Cathodes	Directly heated, Indirectly heated

Symbols shown are those approved by the International Electrotechnical Commission.

the three quantities *V*, *I*, or *R* can be calculated if the other two are known. For example, the simple d.c. circuit illustrated (see figure on page 74) uses a 3V cell to power a small light bulb. The light bulb has a resistance of 30 Ω, and therefore a current of 3/30 or 0.1 A flows in the circuit ($V=IR$, so, by rearrangement, $I=V/R$). In an a.c. circuit the current does not flow one way, but changes direction with a regular *frequency. Alternating-current circuits do not always obey the simple form of Ohm's law shown above, due to a property known as *reactance, a component of the total impedance of an a.c. circuit that varies with frequency. The reactance of an a.c. circuit plus its resistance constitute the *impedance, a measure of the response of a circuit to an alternating current.

Circuits can be made with either series or parallel connections. Lamps are usually connected in parallel, because then the failure of one bulb does not break the circuit and stop the current to the others. The circuits used in most electrical devices are more complex than the simple ones discussed. In most applications, *integrated circuits which combine many components on one silicon chip have replaced individual components connected by wires. (See also *electricity and magnetism).

'cire perdue' process *investment casting.

citrus crop, a crop derived from the evergreen trees of the citrus family, which are grown for their fruit. Citrus crops grow in tropical and subtropical climates, mostly in the Mediterranean region, Japan, and Central and North America. *Plant breeding has concentrated on increasing fruit size, controlling acidity, and reducing the number of seeds. Oranges make up 75 per cent of citrus production, lemons and grapefruit each about 10 per cent. Other crops include limes, tangerines, mandarins, and pomelos (a type of grapefruit).

civil engineering, the design and construction of engineering structures. It includes environmental, municipal, structural, and transportation engineering, and covers the design and construction of *dams, *bridges, *tunnels, large-scale earthworks, embankments, and cuttings; *flood control and *coastal defences; *ports and harbours, and off-shore structures; *roads; *railways; *canals; the structure and *foundations of large *buildings; and *land drainage, *water supply, and *sewage treatment. Named to distinguish it from military engineering, civil engineering first became identified as a separate discipline in the late 18th century. The Institution of Civil Engineers was founded in London in 1818.

cladding, a layer applied to an external or internal building surface to provide weather or fire-resistance or to improve appearance. For masonry or timber-frame walls, traditional claddings are weatherboarding and *tiles or slates. Nowadays, in framed buildings, cladding describes a non-load-bearing external wall, usually thin-gauge metal sheeting, ribbed to improve stiffness, and supported on light 'rails' that span between main columns or beams. *Pre-cast concrete cladding panels, with a range of decorative finishes, are commonly supported on edge beams and tied back to the structure.

clamp, a hand tool used to hold material in place while it is shaped, glued, or otherwise worked on. Clamps come in various sizes and designs according to the function required, some being held in the hand, others fixed to a workbench. One of the commonest is the G-clamp, in which the work is secured by tightening a screw (for illustration see *tools, history of). Special designs enable work to be fixed at particular angles, for example corner clamps, used for gluing picture frames. Other clamps are designed to give a long reach.

Claude, Georges (1870–1960), French chemist and inventor. A graduate in chemistry, he devoted himself to developing new technological processes involving gases. In 1897 he discovered that acetylene could be safely handled and transported by dissolving it in acetone. Five years later he perfected a process for liquefying air by compressing it and allowing it to expand through a valve, which could be used to make oxygen and nitrogen industrially. He also developed neon *gas-discharge lighting and invented a synthetic ammonia process, similar to *Haber's but operated at much higher pressures.

clinker construction (US, lapstrake construction) *shipbuilding.

clipper, a loose generic term for certain types of very fast 19th-century sailing ship, long and low with a raked bow and overhanging stern. Fast, two-masted *schooners and *brigs, known as Baltimore clippers, were built in the USA in the early 19th century. In the mid-19th century three-masted, square-rig versions of these ships (the 'true' clippers) were built in both the USA and the UK. They were used for fast passages between Europe and California or Australia, carrying gold, or for carrying tea from China to London, where the year's first tea consignment fetched very high prices. Probably the best known of the tea clippers is the *Cutty Sark*, now preserved on the dockside at Greenwich in London. The opening of the *Suez Canal in 1869 removed the need for fast ships that could travel round the Cape of Good Hope, and heralded the end of the clipper era.

clock (computer), the *oscillator that determines the timing of operations within a computer's *central processing unit. The clock usually provides a sequence of square-wave electrical pulses, the edges of which trigger machine operation. Clock frequencies are necessarily high; *microprocessor clocks often operate at more than 10 MHz (10 million oscillations per second).

clocks and time measurement. Among the earliest time-measuring devices was the shadow clock, known from around 1500 BC. This was later developed into the sundial. Other early clocks were the clepsydra or water clock (see *Ctesibius), and the sand glass (still familiar as the egg-timer). Mechanical clocks were first made in China, where the escapement, a system of gears basic to all mechanical clocks, was developed in the 8th century AD by Yi Xing and Liang Lingzan. By the 11th century, the Chinese astronomer *Su Sung was building elaborate astronomical clocks. Early European mechanical clocks from the 14th century were driven by the controlled fall of a weight, but they were only accurate to within about an hour per day, so had no minute hand. Spring-driven mechanisms appeared in the mid-15th century, and were used to manufacture *watches as well as clocks. However, it was not until the 17th century, when the Dutch scientist Christiaan Huygens adopted the *pendulum and the balance spring, that more accurate timekeeping became possible. In the mid-18th century accurate

A replica of a weight-driven **clock** built in the 14th century by Giovanni de' Dondi of Padua, Italy. In addition to a dial showing the hour of the day, the clock shows the motion of the sun, the moon, and five other planets.

*chronometers, driven by balance springs, began to be used at sea for finding longitude. Electrically driven clocks appeared in the 19th century. By the early 20th century pendulum clocks accurate to 0.01 s per day could be built, but in 1929 the quartz crystal clock was developed, capable of an accuracy of 0.0001 s per day. In a quartz clock, a crystal of quartz is stimulated by a small electric signal to vibrate at high frequency. The quartz crystal is *piezo-electric, and so this vibration induces a very precise, constant, high-frequency electrical signal. This signal is fed to an *integrated circuit, which reduces the signal frequency to one pulse per second. This pulse is then used to drive the clock mechanism. In 1955 the first atomic clock was installed at the National Physical Laboratory in the UK, regulated by the extremely rapid, fixed oscillation rate of a specified energy transition in the nucleus of a caesium atom. Such atomic clocks vary by as little as one second every 3 million years. They are now internationally used as time standards (see *time-scales).

cloning, usually the production of two or more genetically identical organisms; in *genetic engineering cloning refers to the copying of *DNA molecules. Clones occur naturally wherever asexual reproduction (reproduction not involving the combination of male and female genetic material) takes place, as in the growth of a bacterial colony or in the production of runners by a strawberry plant. In agriculture, plant cloning can be used to advantage, in that individuals with desirable properties, such as pest-resistance or high growth rates, can be replicated exactly without the unpredictable results associated with sexual reproduction. Artificial cloning of animals and cells can be achieved by teasing apart the cells of the early embryo. Similarly, cells capable of growing into mature plants can be obtained from plant growth-regions (meristems).

closed-circuit television (CCTV), a system in which television signals are transmitted to specific pre-selected television receivers. Transmission can be through cables over short distances, or by microwaves over longer distances: international transmission may be via *satellite communications. *Optical fibres offer another alternative for long-distance transmission. CCTV has several applications. As part of a security system it can provide general surveillance of a building. Scientifically it can be used to monitor hazardous situations. In conjunction with *eidophors, sporting events can be relayed to large audiences. It can also be used for long-distance conferencing.

clothing manufacture. The first stage in the factory manufacture of clothing is to produce a set of garment panels from a previously designed and approved garment model of average size. Panels of other sizes or fittings may then be 'graded'. To prepare for cutting of fabric panels, templates are arranged side by side in a procedure known as lay-planning. Great care is exercised to ensure the most economical use of *fabric, taking account of the fabric's pattern. In the modern industry, some of these preliminary stages are computerized. Cloth is laid on cutting tables in many layers, the number depending on fabric type, thickness, and other production factors. The lay pattern is then placed on top and the fabrics are cut by a vertical band-knife or oscillating blade. Bundles of cut panels are distributed to sewing stations; computer-controlled overhead conveyors are used in modern factories. Much of the garment assembly is done by operators at individual *sewing-machines using *stitches appropriate to the fabric and seam in the garment. Linings and *zips are incorporated where required. Sewing aids or guides are often used. Increasingly, automatic sewing stations are employed for the most straightforward seams, with template sewing of such components as collars, cuffs, and pockets, in which the template automatically folds the fabric and guides it through the sewing sequence. Finally, buttonholes are formed and *buttons and other trimmings added. Garments are usually pressed on semi-automatic steam presses before final inspection and packaging. In the case of knitted garments, panels are often knitted to shape and assembled by linking.

cloud chamber *particle detector.

clutch, a device for connecting or disconnecting the drive between two rotating shafts. The simplest type is a dog or claw clutch, in which one shaft carries a castellated collar which can be slid into contact with a matching collar on the other shaft. With the dog clutch, gear changes are sudden; despite this, it is used in *motor-cycle gearboxes to engage gears when on the move. For most purposes, especially vehicles, a friction clutch is used, which prevents jerking by allowing some slip at engagement. Possible forms are cone (used for the synchromesh on a car *gearbox), multi-plate,

Clutch

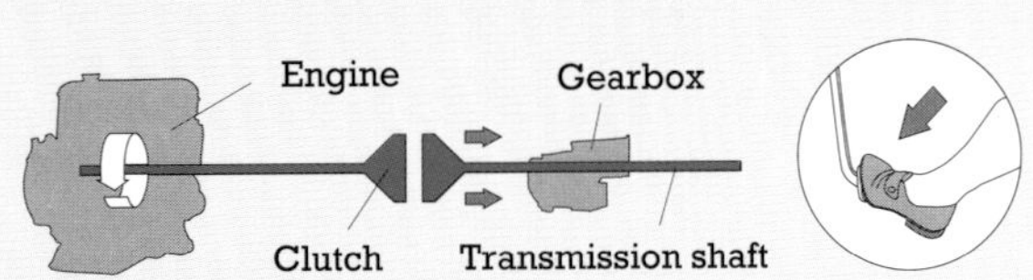

Clutch pedal fully depressed (disengaged): the engine is not linked to the wheels.

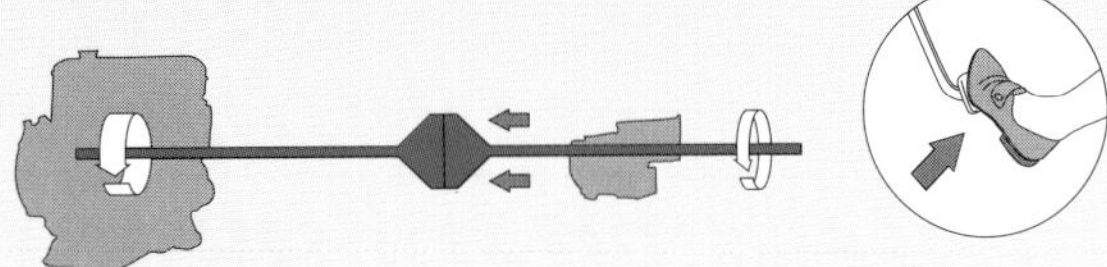

The biting point: the engine is linked to wheels, with slippage allowed.

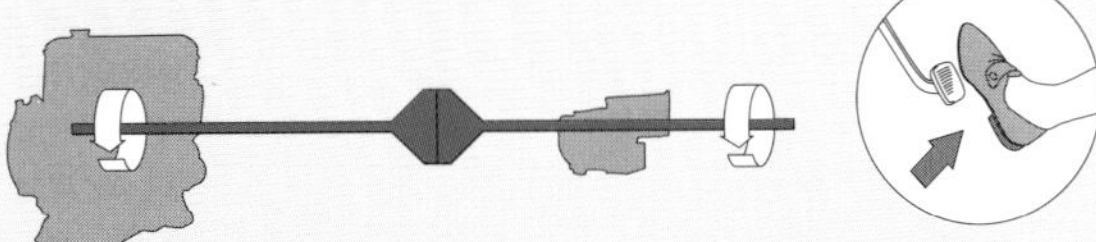

Pedal fully released (engaged): engine fully linked to wheels.

KEY

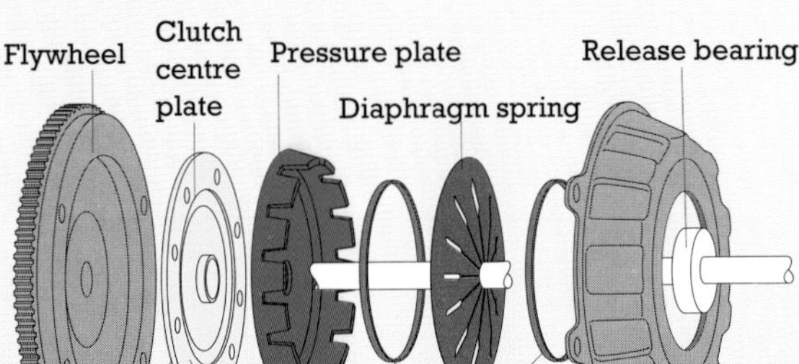

A typical modern clutch with diaphragm spring. In normal driving the spring acts via the pressure plate to clamp the clutch centre plate against the flywheel (which is powered by the engine). The friction lining allows power to be taken up gradually, without a sudden jerk.

Engaged

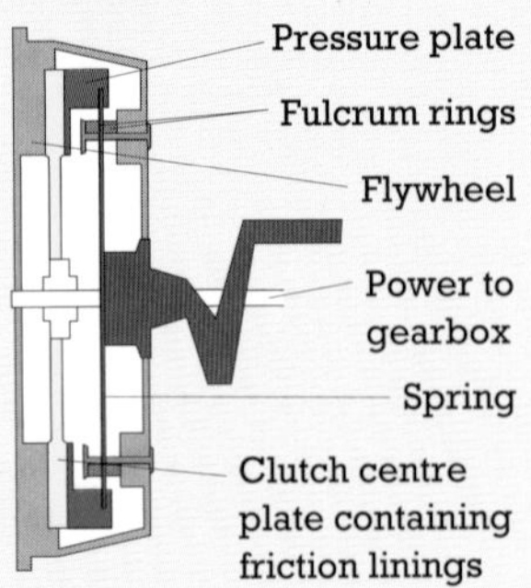

The diaphragm spring holds the friction lining against the flywheel.

Disengaged

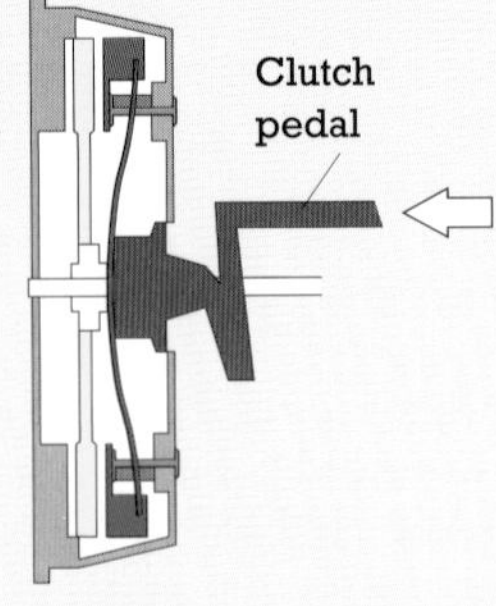

When the pedal is depressed, the spring is lifted off the pressure plate.

and single-plate clutches; the last is almost universal on modern manual gearbox cars (see figure). Other types of clutch are used in some machine-tools and in *automatic transmissions.

coach *buses and coaches, *carriages and coaches, *railway carriage.

coal, a hard, solid, opaque, black or blackish carbonaceous mineral: an important *fossil fuel. Coal is formed by the effect of pressure, temperature, and chemical processes on vegetable matter deposited millions of years ago. Coals are ranked according to their degree of carbonization; this relates to the amount of heat obtained when they are burnt. Anthracite is the highest grade coal, with a carbon content of over 90 per cent and a high-temperature, smokeless flame. However, its relative scarcity limits it to mainly domestic use. Bituminous coal, containing 80–90 per cent carbon, is the most common type, used in a variety of applications. The lowest grade is lignite, a soft, brown coal containing about 65 per cent carbon, which burns with a smoky flame. Lignite is used for power generation in some countries, and is often *briquetted for transport. Coal occurs in layers or seams typically 1–3 m (3–10 feet) thick, but they can be up to 20 m (66 feet) thick. The seams are separated by wider bands of rock, and may occur thousands of metres below ground. Such deposits often cover areas of thousands of square kilometres. However, seams may also occur near the surface, and are recovered by *open-cast mining. Coalfields are found in many parts of the world, but for economic or technological reasons there is little or no *coal-mining in most countries. Current estimates of world coal reserves vary, but typically suggest that known reserves will last 200 to 300 years. Coal was first used in China, Greece, and Italy over 2,000 years ago. It has been used for domestic heating and where high temperatures were required—for instance, by lime-burners, blacksmiths, and brickmakers. From the *Industrial Revolution onwards, however, coal overtook wood as the principal domestic and industrial fuel. It was used in the manufacture of iron (instead of charcoal); for the generation of steam for engines; in the production of *coal-gas; and later as a source of chemicals. Throughout this period, the UK was the largest producer of coal, but by 1900 it had been overtaken by the USA (total world production was then over 700 million tonnes per year). With strong competition from oil and nuclear energy, coal now provides only a quarter of the world's energy, but production in 1988 was still over 4,500 million tonnes, with the major producers being China, the Soviet Union, and the USA. Coal has generally been replaced by gas, oil, and electricity in the home; presently its main use is as fuel for *power-stations. Particular ranks of bituminous coal, known as metallurgical or coking coal, are used to produce *coke, primarily for the steel-making industry. Other uses of coal are as a feedstock for *smokeless fuel, *synthetic fuels, and coal-gas production. The burning of coal has adverse environmental effects: sulphur and nitrogen oxides produced can lead to *acid rain, and the carbon dioxide emissions account for approximately 15 per cent of the *greenhouse effect. However, coal technology is being improved, both to limit its environmental effects and to extend its range of uses, thus conserving less-plentiful reserves of *petroleum and *natural gas. *Fluidized-bed furnaces are more efficient than conventional furnaces, and when combined with flue-gas desulphurization can largely eliminate emissions of sulphates and nitrates. Such furnaces can also be used to produce fuel-gas from coal, and for *combined-cycle electricity generation. Another coal gasification process is used to produce synthesis gas (mostly carbon monoxide and hydrogen), from which a large range of products can be made, such as gaseous and liquid fuels, chemicals, fertilizers, and plastics.

Coalbrookdale Iron Bridge *Iron Bridge.

coal-cutter, mechanized equipment for cutting coal from the seams. Jib coal-cutters were developed for underground *coal-mining in the late 19th and early 20th centuries. The jib was a projecting horizontal arm carrying an endless chain to which cutter picks were fixed. In *long-wall mining, the introduction of armoured flexible conveyors—a line of steel trays (pans) containing a continuous scraper chain—led to the evolution of machines able to cut the coal and then load it on to a conveyor. Other coal-cutters include the plough, a blade attached to an endless chain that cuts slices of coal up to 10 cm (4 inches) thick, and the shearer-loader, which has one or more horizontally pivoted rotating drums lined with cutting picks, and can extract a channel of coal up to 2 m (6.7 feet) high and 1 m (3.3 feet) deep.

coal-gas, a valuable product of the manufacture of coke from *coal, containing largely hydrogen and methane, plus carbon oxides, ethene, and other gases. Coal-gas was used for *gas lighting and for heating in Europe for over 150 years. It was replaced in the 1970s by natural gas from the North Sea or from petroleum feedstocks.

coal-mining, the excavation of *coal from the ground. The use and *mining of coal dates back to Roman times in Britain and to at least 200 BC in China. Until the 18th century, all coal was mined near surface outcrops by surface excavation, *adit mining, or bell pits. A bell pit is essentially a well sunk to shallow seams. The seam is excavated until the workings begin to collapse; another bell pit is then sunk nearby. During the *Industrial Revolution, technology was introduced which eventually permitted shafts to be sunk as deep as 1,500 m (4,900 feet). New equipment was developed for pumping, ventilation, and the transport and cutting of coal. Today, the two main methods of mining coal underground are *bord-and-pillar and *long-wall mining. Both methods are now highly mechanized, using *coal-cutters and hydraulic *pit-props. Automation of coal production represents the next stage of technological advance. In the UK in the 1960s, attempts were made to automate coal production, but they failed because the equipment was not robust enough to withstand the underground environment. Presently, techniques are being introduced world-wide which allow remote control and automation of many mining operations and which should eventually lead to the full automation of underground coal production. Surface mining (strip or *open-cast mining) is undertaken where coal seams lie within about 200 m (650 feet) of the surface. The development of large earth-moving equipment in the last fifty years has resulted in surface mining replacing underground mining as the major source of coal world-wide. Since the 1950s other methods of mining coal have been tried. One of these is *hydraulic mining; another is underground coal gasification, in which an air or oxygen–steam mixture is injected at high pressure as a gasifying agent down a borehole; the resultant fuel-gas is forced to another borehole, from where it flows to the surface. To date, neither of these methods has presented a serious challenge to conventional coal-mining methods.

coal-tar, a thick, black, oily liquid by-product of the manufacture of gas and *coke from coal. It is a mixture of many different substances (mostly *hydrocarbons), which are used to produce paraffin, naphtha, benzene, creosote, anthracene oil, and pitch by *fractional distillation. Tar was used from about 1781 to waterproof the hulls of wooden ships and in road construction, but it has largely been replaced by petroleum-based *bitumen. In the latter half of the 19th century, the refining of tars and benzol products formed a large part of the world's organic chemical industry, notably in making the first synthetic aniline *dyes. In the early 1900s over 3 million tonnes of coal-tar were produced annually in the UK alone, and several industries were entirely dedicated to making coal-tar products such as resins and plastics, explosives, solvents, wood preservatives, and disinfectants. However, the market for organic chemicals is now dominated by cheap petroleum feedstocks, and coal-tar production is much reduced.

coastal defences, structures designed to resist the erosion of land by the sea. Banks and breakwaters (groynes) prevent the drifting of material along the shore by the daily tides. Earth embankments (dikes) protect low-lying coasts, and on the seaward side may need loose rocks (riprap) as additional protection against storm erosion. Where the shore is developed, sea-walls are built, usually of concrete. These often have curved profiles to deflect storm waves, and stepped bases to dissipate wave energy and prevent erosion of the ground under the seaward edge. Recent *land reclamations on the south-east and south-west coasts of Singapore are protected by sea-walls, breakwaters, and dikes. The Thames Barrier (UK) has submerged sluice gates, which can be raised to prevent storm surges passing upstream to London.

coaxial cable, a special type of *cable used for carrying high-frequency or weak electrical signals. Coaxial cables consist of a central group of insulated conductors carrying the signal, surrounded by a sheath of braided conductor which is earthed. The whole cable is further insulated. The presence of the earthed braid substantially shields the signal from *interference, which could cause errors or distortion. Coaxial cable is widely used in electronics, and is commonly used for the *antenna cable of domestic television receivers.

cob, a traditional walling material used in localities where chalk and clay occur naturally. The chalk and clay are mixed with water and straw, and the mixture is placed on the wall in layers and left to dry. Subsequently, the faces are smoothed by paring them down. External plastering and a large roof overhang are needed to protect the material against rain.

cobalt (symbol Co, at. no. 27, r.a.m. 58.93), a hard, silvery, magnetic metal with a pink tinge. Cobalt oxide is obtained mainly as a by-product in the extraction of nickel, copper, and iron ores. It is reduced to the metal with aluminium or hydrogen and then purified by *electrolysis. Cobalt is used in making special steels and magnetic materials, as a blue colouring for glass, and as an industrial *catalyst.

COBOL *computer language.

Cockerell, Sir Christopher (1910–), British engineer who invented the *hovercraft. From 1935 to 1950, he worked on the development of airborne and navigational equipment for Marconi Ltd., but then became a boat-builder. He conceived the idea of a vessel which, by riding on a cushion of air, reduced the frictional resistance of the land or water over which it travelled. He took out a patent in 1955, and four years later launched his first experimental craft, which attained speeds of 100 km/h (62 m.p.h.). The first hovercraft crossing of the English Channel was made in 1959.

cog (ship) *sailing ships and boats.

coil (electrical), an electrical component consisting of a coil of wire. Coils may function as *solenoids, *inductors, *transformers, and as parts of *microphones, *relays, *electric motors, and *generators. A coil is also an important part of the *ignition system of a motor car.

coir *fibre, textile (table).

coke, the solid residue left when coal is heated in the absence of air, or in a limited supply (carbonization). There is a limited domestic and industrial market for coke, and it is used primarily as a fuel or as a reducing agent in the iron and steel industry, most of it in *blast-furnaces. By-products of the coking process include *coal-gas and *coal-tar. *Darby was the first to use coke successfully for iron smelting early in the 18th century, an innovation which paved the way for the *Industrial Revolution. Next to combustion, carbonization is the largest application of coal. A small amount of coke is also made from other feedstocks. Petroleum refinery residues, for example, yield a coke used to make arc-steel electrodes and anodes for *aluminium smelting.

coke-oven, a vessel in which *coal is carbonized to produce *coke. The equipment consists of a battery of between 10 and 100 slot ovens which are ranged side by side and indirectly heated through the walls by the hot gases produced during carbonization. Each oven is generally about 14 m (50 feet) long, up to 6.5 m (20 feet) high, and 0.4–0.6 m (1.3–2.0 feet) wide. The ovens are each charged with over 20 tonnes of coal through holes in the oven top. Removable doors at each end are sealed to prevent air entering and gas leaking out. Coking is completed in 12–30 hours, depending on the coke type required, and the charge is then pushed by a ram into a quenching car.

Coke, Thomas William, Earl of Leicester (1752–1842), British landowner who made many innovations in agricultural practice. In 1776 he inherited Holkham Hall in Norfolk and devoted himself to the improvement of its estates. Following *Townshend, he introduced turnips as winter fodder; replaced rye with wheat; improved breeds of cattle, sheep, and pigs; and improved land by spreading clay (marling). He also introduced far-reaching changes in land tenure, granting long leases at fair rents to tenants, and encouraging them to discard old farming methods.

Collip, James Bertram *Banting, Sir Frederick Grant.

colloid, a mixture in which fine particles (between 10^{-9} and 10^{-6} m in diameter) of one substance (the disperse phase) are spread throughout another substance (the continuous phase). The phases can be solid, liquid, or gas. Examples include emulsions (liquid dispersed in liquid) such as cosmetic creams; *aerosols (liquid or solid dispersed in gas) such as mist; and sols (solid dispersed in liquid) such as *emulsion paint. The properties of colloidal systems are unique and are not simply the sum of the properties of the two component substances. This is due to the large total surface area of the particles and the specific electrical interactions between them. Modern developments of colloid systems include surfactants (see *surface tension), colloidal graphite (used as a high-temperature lubricant), and colloidal solid fuels, used in *fluidized-bed furnaces.

collotype printing, a method used to make high-quality colour prints by *lithography. Using a printing surface of sensitized gelatine on a glass plate, it is capable of producing delicate tonal effects without the need for *half-tone screening methods. This process is now used mostly for printing limited numbers of fine-art reproductions.

colorimetry *spectroscopy.

Colour

Additive colour mixing

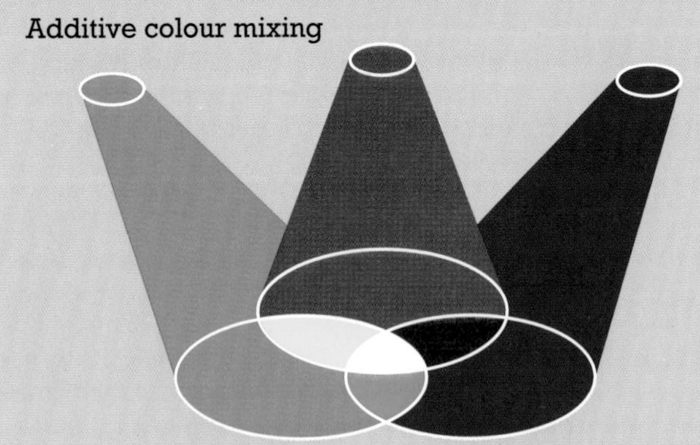

Coloured lights can be added to make other colours, for example red ● and green ● make yellow ●. The three primary colours, red ●, blue ●, and green ●, together make white light. Pairs of complementary colours that make approximate white light are blue ● and yellow ● red ● and cyan ●, or green ● and magenta ●

Subtractive colour mixing

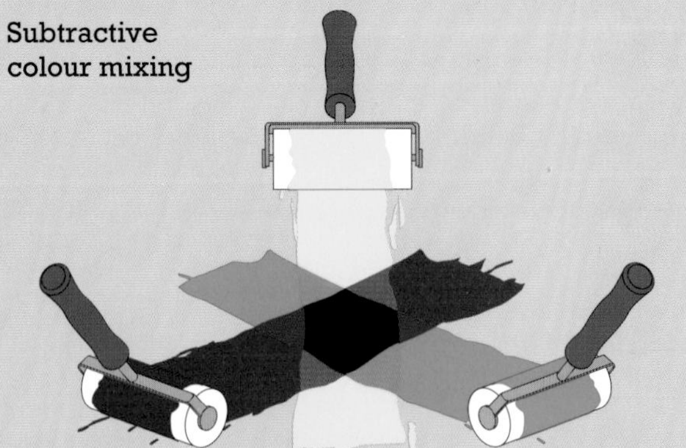

Mixed particles of different coloured pigments reflect some colours of light but absorb (subtract) others. The colour of a paint is that colour not absorbed by any of the pigments in the paint. A mixture of three primary colours makes approximately black, because together these pigments absorb all wavelengths of light.

Colossus *computer, history of.

colour, the different wavelengths of light as perceived and interpreted by the eye and brain. Visible light is *electromagnetic radiation of wavelengths between about 400 and 750 nm (10^{-9}m). It can be split into a spectrum of colours (red, orange, yellow, green, blue, indigo, and violet), red having the longest wavelength and violet the shortest. White light, as emitted by the Sun, contains all these wavelengths. The colour of an opaque object corresponds to the wavelengths it reflects (it absorbs all other wavelengths). Its apparent colour also depends on the colour of the incident light—a blue object in red light will look black because there is no blue light to reflect. Coloured lights can be mixed to produce other colours. Red, blue, and green lights together produce white light; they are called primary colours (see figure). Such white light does not contain the full range of wavelengths present in sunlight, but it is perceived as white by the human eye. Different combinations and intensities of red, blue, and green light can produce almost any colour sensation in the eye: this principle is exploited in the colour *television receiver, which produces a full range of colours using only red, blue, and green phosphors. The mixing of coloured lights is additive mixing, because the range of wavelengths reaching the eye is increased when colours are mixed. The situation with mixtures of coloured paints or dyes is, however, different. This is because the colour of a paint or dye pigment is determined by the wavelengths of light it reflects, all other wavelengths being absorbed: this is called subtractive mixing. Magenta, yellow, and cyan (green-blue) are often used as primary colours in *printing and *photography, where three superimposed layers, one in each of the primary colours, together with black, produce a full range of colours.

Colt, Samuel (1814–62), US inventor best known for his six-shot *pistol. Colt allegedly conceived his idea of a revolving-breech firearm while watching the turning of the ship's wheel as he sailed to India as a deck-hand. He patented his invention in 1836, but in 1842 his first company failed. In the following year he developed the first naval mine to be detonated by remote control. On the outbreak of the Mexican War in 1846 he received a large government order for firearms, and resumed firearms manufacture. He started a new firm in 1848, and became one of the wealthiest men of his time.

combined-cycle technology, a system of *electricity generation combining a *gas-turbine and a *steam-turbine. The gas-turbine is powered by hot, high-pressure gas, obtained either by burning fuel-gas or from a *fluidized-bed furnace. The turbine in turn drives an electric generator, while the exhaust gases are used to heat water in a boiler to raise steam. The steam powers a steam-turbine to generate additional electricity. There are several advantages to this arrangement, despite it being considerably more expensive than traditional electricity-generation plant. They are its efficiency, which may be as much as 44 per cent (traditional methods rarely exceed 38 per cent), and its consequent lower cooling-water requirement. In addition, it has a fast start-up, is less polluting, runs efficiently at part load and can use heavy fuel-oils, which are partially burnt to convert them to a suitable input fuel-gas. Combined-cycle technology continues to develop in Europe and North America and promises a major improvement in electricity-generation efficiency.

combined heat and power generation (CHP generation; US, cogeneration), the simultaneous production of *heat and *electricity. Heat production is inevitable when chemical or nuclear fuels are used to produce electricity. In conventional, electricity-only power-stations, achieving maximum generation efficiency means that the temperature of the heat produced is too low for it to be useful. CHP plants are designed to produce heat at a usefully high temperature. This usually involves a reduction in potential electricity output, but the overall conversion of fuel to useful energy output is much higher. The heat output can be in the form of hot water or steam for local industrial use or for *district heating.

combine harvester, a mobile machine that combines harvest operations with the threshing and cleaning of grain. In 1838, only seven years after the appearance of *McCormick's mechanical *reaper, a combine harvester built by the US inventor Hyram Moore was successfully operated in Michigan, USA. The combine had a cutting blade similar to that used on the reaper. Modern combine harvesters (see figure overleaf) are used for cereals, legumes, and oil-seed crops. They can cut around 5.5 m (18 feet) at one pass, harvesting over 12 ha (30 acres) in a day's work. Electronics and hydraulics allow the driver to exercise fine control over the various operations, minimizing grain loss in the harvesting process.

command module **Apollo* programme.

communications satellite, an artificial *satellite for world-wide telephone, television, and data communication, using microwaves (see *electromagnetic radiation). Microwaves can carry vast amounts of information because of their large *bandwidth and suitability for multiplexing. They are, however, easily absorbed by solid objects, so transmitter and receiver need to be in line of sight. Satellites provide a method of achieving line-of-sight communication over long distances: world-wide coverage can be achieved using as few as three satellites. The USA's *Echo 1* (1960) was the first satellite designed for radio communication experiments. Because *Echo 1* was merely a reflector, its signals were very weak. In 1962 the Bell Telephone Company launched *Telstar*, an active satellite carrying its own solar power source for signal amplification, which enabled the first live television *broadcast from the USA to Europe to be made. Because the *ground station's antennae could only 'see' the satellite for about 20 minutes on each orbit, that was the length of the broadcast. By 1963 rockets sufficiently powerful to place a satellite in geostationary orbit were available. *Syncom 1*, a US satellite for telephone and *telex use, was the first geostationary satellite. The first commercial geostationary satellite was *Early Bird* or *Intelsat 1*, launched in 1965 by the International Telecommunications Satellite Organization (see satellite for illustration). Intelsat soon had three satellites over the Atlantic, Pacific, and Indian Oceans for world-wide coverage, and today numerous communications satellites orbit the Earth. Modern communications satellites can handle tens of thousands of telephone calls, plus radio and television broadcasts.

commutator *generator, electrical.

compact disc (CD), a small disc on which audio signals, video signals, or other data can be recorded in digital form (see *digitization). The disc comprises a clear plastic layer

Combine harvester

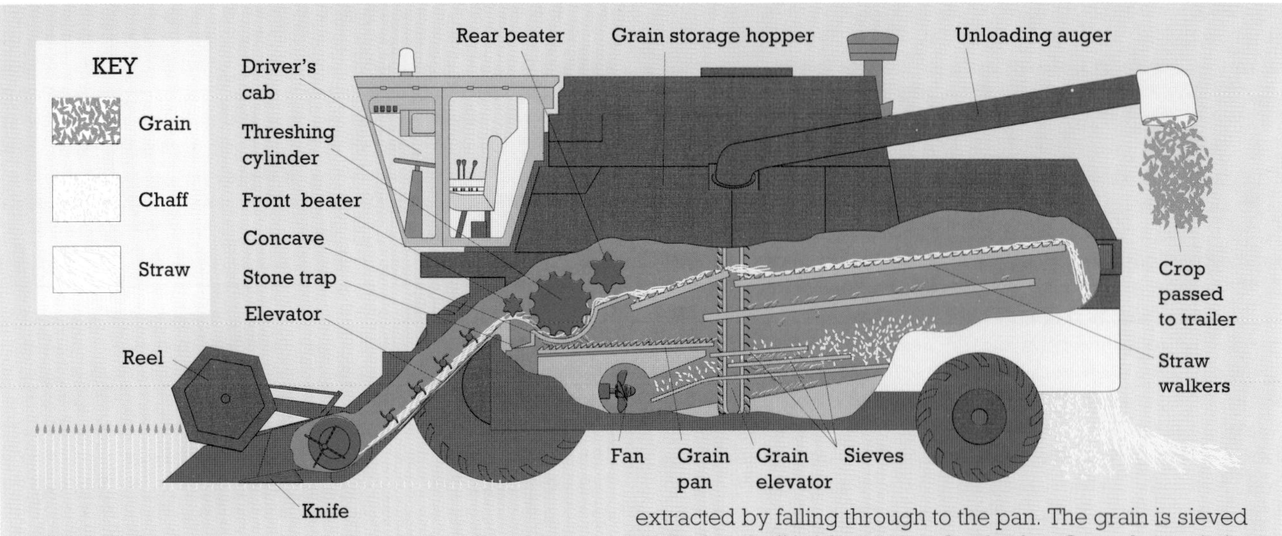

After being cut, the crop is transported up the elevator to the threshing apparatus. Once threshing has taken place the straw, with remnants of grain and chaff, is carried on to the straw walkers. Here more grain is extracted by falling through to the pan. The grain is sieved while the chaff is blown away by the fan. Once the grain is free of impurities it is lifted up through the grain elevator out of the unloading auger and into an adjacent trailer. Waste passes out through the back of the machine.

over a reflective aluminium surface. Data is stored on the disc in *binary code, the 'ones' of the code being dents in the plastic surface, the 'zeros' being the smooth plastic. When playing the disc, a *laser scans the disc surface: the beam is reflected back only by the 'zero' areas of the disc. The reflected pulses are picked up by a photodetector, which converts them into a digital electrical signal. The compact disc was first developed by Philips and Sony in the early 1980s. By the early 1990s it was the established medium for audio recordings. CD video applies the same technology to videos: discs can be replicated more quickly than videotape and it is easier to access a particular part of the recording. CDs are also used to store large amounts of computer information. CD-ROM (compact disc with read-only memory) is the most common format, but other forms of disc are available that allow data to be written on to the disc as well as read. Recent developments are the photo-CD, which records still images on a compact disc for viewing on a television screen or as hard copy, and the multimedia CD, which holds pictures, sound, and text on one CD and plays them back through a television receiver and hi-fi equipment.

compass *gyro-compass, *inductor compass, *magnetic compass.

compiler, a *computer program that translates high-level *computer languages, such as FORTRAN, ALGOL, and C, into *machine code that can be executed directly on the computer. Unlike an *interpreter, a compiler converts the whole program into machine code before running it, which is frequently more efficient.

composite, a material which consists of two or more physically different solid constituents, each of which largely retains its original structure and identity. Composites are distinct from alloys in that their structure is engineered by mixing two materials in an intimate solid mixture, with one component being embedded in the other. A common feature of composite materials is the use of small quantities of a relatively expensive, strong, often fibrous material to reinforce the bulk of a cheap matrix material. The properties of the resulting composite are usually intermediate to those of the components from which it is made. However, certain properties, notably toughness or resistance to fracture, are much better than those of either of the components, giving composites with unique properties. The earliest composites were probably the sun-dried adobe bricks used in the ancient civilizations of Egypt and Mesopotamia; these used straw to reinforce the brittle mud. *Reinforced concrete is a somewhat analogous modern material, in which steel reinforcing rods are used to give concrete strength in tension. Cement can also be reinforced by thin fibres, traditionally *asbestos, but now more often glass, polymers or natural fibres. *Laminates are also composite materials.

Since the 1960s the most important class of composite materials has been the *fibre-reinforced plastics: glass, carbon, or aramid (see *nylon) fibres in a plastic matrix. These composites can be used to make very light structures with good strength and stiffness. In the 1980s much interest has been shown in using metals to make metal-matrix composites (MMC). These use fibres of ceramics such as *alumina and *silicon carbide to reinforce light metal alloys based on *aluminium and *titanium. These materials are stiffer and lighter than their parent alloys and have high resistance to wear. They are, however, expensive to manufacture, a common feature of many fibre-reinforced composites. *Cermets are a second type of metal–ceramic composite. Composites with a ceramic matrix are another recent development, but new inert ceramic fibres usable at high temperatures are needed before the full potential of these materials can be realized.

compost, strictly, a friable (easily crumbled) material derived from the breakdown of vegetable matter, and added to soil to improve its physical properties and to provide a limited supply of nutrients. However, the term is often used to describe mixtures of rotted plant and animal waste or as a euphemism for manure. Compost is produced via the action of micro-organisms, which slowly degrade organic matter. Successful decomposition is dependent upon maintaining adequate aeration and controlling temperature. Potting composts used in *horticulture are mixtures of composted plant material, loam, sand, and *fertilizer.

compound-engine *steam-engine.

compression-ignition engine *diesel engine.

compression ratio, the ratio between the maximum and minimum volumes of a cylinder fitted with a moving piston. It is of greatest importance in *internal-combustion engines. For spark-ignition engines the highest compression ratio which can be used with a particular fuel before the onset of *knock depends on many factors, including the bore (diameter) of the cylinder and the design of the cylinder head. As a general rule, high-performance, high-compression-ratio *petrol engines require petrol of high *octane number, while low-compression-ratio engines can use lower-grade petrol. For compression-ignition (*diesel) engines, the need to reach a high enough temperature to give rapid ignition of the fuel means that a minimum compression ratio of 14:1 is required.

compressor, a *pneumatic device for compressing air or other gases. Compressed air is widely used in industry and in mining as a safe source of power, for drilling and for operating rams. Gas compression, often to a very high pressure, is at the heart of many large-scale chemical processes, and compressors are essential to *gas-turbine engines. The simplest type of compressor is the reciprocating piston and cylinder, often used in successive stages, each giving pressure ratios of up to 7:1. Gas is greatly increased in temperature during compression, so cooling is necessary. A more compact compressor is the rotary type, of which there are many forms. Cooling is often achieved by spraying oil droplets into the air during compression and subsequently separating the oil. For the largest flows a high-speed turbo-compressor is used, either centrifugal or axial; no cooling is possible.

computer, a device for storing and processing data, according to a program of instructions stored within the computer itself. The term computer normally refers to electronic digital computers, but *analog computers also exist for use in specialist applications. Computers are 'universal' information-processing machines: any information-processing task that can be specified by an algorithm (a well-defined sequence of instructions) can, in principle, be performed by a computer. Unlike most other machines, it is not necessary to build a new computer for each new task. Computers can therefore perform a very large number of useful tasks, although limits do exist: it can be proved that some problems are incomputable. The mathematical study of what tasks are capable of being computed is known as compatibility, and complexity is the study of how hard it is to compute a task. Numerical analysis concerns the fastest and most accurate way to solve numerical problems.

The digital computer is one of the most significant innovations of the 20th century (see *computer, history of). In the four decades since its introduction it has had an impact on almost all areas of human activity (see *information technology). Computers are very widely used commercially for *data processing and for *information storage and retrieval. Manufacturing industry has been affected by developments such as *computer-integrated manufacture, and *robotics. Much scientific research has been transformed by the ability to analyse large quantities of numerical data and by the use of *simulation techniques to model complex systems such as nuclear reactors and the weather. Many technical advances, such as space travel and advanced aircraft design, would have been impossible without the processing ability of computers. Digital computers are available in a very wide range of powers, sizes, and costs, suitable for different applications. Advances in technology have led to rapid improvements in the performance of all types of computer systems: many personal computers are now more powerful than much larger, mainframe computers of the 1960s.

A computer system can be regarded as being organized in a number of layers. The lowest layer is the *hardware (the physical components of the system, as opposed to the *software, the programs and other operating information used by the computer). Both the information which is being processed (the *data) and the processing instructions (the *program) are stored in the form of *bits of information in a *memory. The memory unit is connected by a *bus to the *central processing unit (CPU), which is the other essential hardware component. The CPU takes one instruction at a time from the memory, decodes it, and then performs the action specified by the instruction (see figure). Each instruction specifies a very simple operation, for example, multiplying together two numbers or checking that two pieces of information are identical. Other hardware items are *peripheral devices, which include permanent data storage devices such as hard and floppy disks, input devices for feeding information into the system, and output devices through which results are fed out. A small layer of software above the hardware, called the microcode, allows the computer to

Computer

The central processing unit (CPU) is connected to all other parts of the computer. It controls the flow of information to and from the INPUT and OUTPUT ports. In its turn the CPU is given instructions by the program stored in its memory.

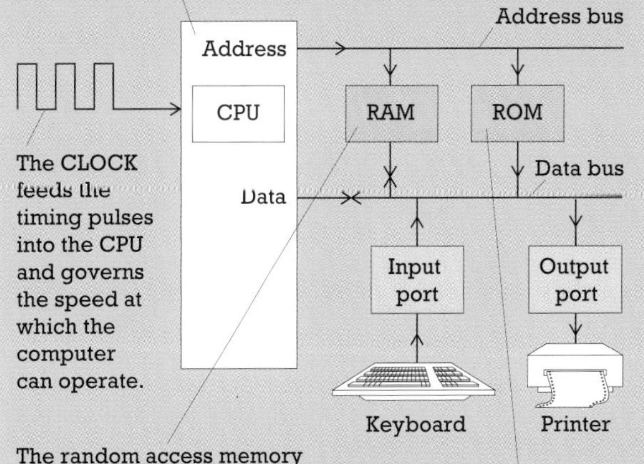
Address bus
Address
CPU
RAM
ROM
Data bus
Data
The CLOCK feeds the timing pulses into the CPU and governs the speed at which the computer can operate.
Input port
Output port
Keyboard
Printer
The random access memory (RAM) can have information and instructions written into it. These can be supplied by the software or via the keyboard. They are lost once power is disconnected.
The read only memory (ROM) contains information and instructions permanently stored in the computer and is not lost when the power supply is disconnected.

When a program is run, the CPU uses the information and instructions in both the ROM and RAM to run the program. The program can send information to the printer or other peripherals.

Timechart of computing since 1950

1950–1	J. Lyons and Co. install LEO, first commercial data handling computer, based on EDSAC computer designed at Cambridge University, UK UNIVAC I, the first commercial stored-program computer, marketed in USA
1954	IBM mass-produced the 701, their first commercial computer
1956	First compiler developed for FORTRAN I
1959	First monolithic integrated circuits made, by Texas Instruments, USA
1963	The Atlas, the first modern mainframe computer, marketed commercially
1971	First microprocessor, the Intel 4004, marketed by the Intel Corporation, USA Introduction by Bell Laboratories of UNIX, the first widely adopted operating system
1975	The Altair, the first personal computer, marketed by MITS, USA
1976	Launch of the Cray-1, the first supercomputer
1977	Reports from Sweden, Italy, and Canada of eye strain and other health problems connected with use of VDU screens
1978	Development by UK company INMOS of the transputer, a high-performance microcomputer in which both the processor and some memory are on the same chip
Early 1980s	Reduced Instruction Set (RISC) microchip introduced. Enables computers to work ten times faster than previously possible
1981	IBM personal computer introduced: lead to widespread use of personal computers in business
1984	Apple Mackintosh marketed: uses a mouse and menus for standard procedures, rather than keyboard
1988	Bill passed in USA to regulate time spent at VDU screens, requiring operators to take regular rest breaks
1989	Science Museum UK, begins campaign to raise £250,000 to construct Babbage's difference engine

execute a larger set of instructions than could be easily provided in hardware alone. The hardware and the microcode together execute *machine code.

The next layer in the computer's organization is a much larger body of software, the *operating system. It interprets additional, very complex instructions which allow reading from and writing to *files, input devices, and output devices. The layer above this is provided by the *compiler or *interpreter, which allows a programmer to write programs in a problem-orientated *computer language, rather than in machine code or *assembly language. The programmer working with such a language needs to know nothing of the layers below, so that a *FORTRAN programmer can regard any computer with a FORTRAN compiler as if it were with a FORTRAN machine.

The final layer of software comprises the computer's *applications programs. Computing is about the correct design and implementation of useful applications programs from a given specification. Techniques of software engineering are being developed which make specification, design, and implementation a less error-prone process. Mathematics and formal reasoning are used to prove logically that the implementation of computer systems correspond to their specifications. Improving the *reliability of programs is increasingly important as their use in safety-critical situations grows. Some large computer programs have many millions of instructions, each instruction being a separate 'working part' that must function correctly. On this basis, computer programs are the most complex artefacts built by humans. The major challenges of computing in the future are the development of software engineering techniques, very high-level computer languages, and *parallel processing.

computer, history of. Although the development of the computer has been largely played out during the 20th century, there is a long history of automatic calculation. *Hero wrote in the 1st century AD of representing numbers using a train of gears, but little real progress seems to have been made until the early 17th century, when the first *calculators were built, and the German mathematician Gottfried Leibniz speculated (1679) on the possibility of building a calculator using moving balls to represent numbers in *binary code. The notion of storing a sequence of instructions mechanically is also very old and was incorporated into self-playing musical instruments and other *automata even in ancient times. In 1725 Basile Bouchon invented a method of producing intricate woven patterns on a draw loom from instructions on a perforated paper tape. By 1800 this method had been refined by *Jacquard into a highly successful automatic loom controlled by punched cards. The idea of punched-card instructions was adapted by *Hollerith to record and analyse the results of the 1890 US census in the earliest example of large-scale *data processing.

In 1835 *Babbage conceived of the basic idea of an analytical engine in which can be found most of the elements of a truly general-purpose computer. He drew together the ideas of mechanical calculation and a set of instructions recorded on perforated paper tape. The development costs of the machine were very high: the British government eventually withdrew funding, and this pioneering machine was never completed. Babbage's ideas were subsequently lost until the 1930s, when work on electromechanical computers was started independently in Germany and the USA. In 1941 Konrad Zuse in Germany built the world's first working stored-program computer. His Z3 machine was based on electromechanical relays, and was used for military aircraft design. In the USA, the mathematician Howard Aiken, in association with IBM (International Business Machines), was working independently on a large electromechanical calculator that could be programmed using paper tape. The Automatic Sequence Controlled Calculator (ASCC), or Harvard Mark I, was completed in 1943; it was very similar in concept (although not in engineering realization), to Babbage's analytical machine.

Computers based on the electronic *thermionic valve were a major development, since they were much faster and more reliable than electromechanical computers. Among the earliest electronic computers were the Colossus series of special-purpose computers, developed secretly in the UK from 1943. They deciphered coded German messages produced on sophisticated mechanical systems called Enigma machines. An important member of the Colossus team was *Turing, who in 1936 had published a paper that defined in abstract terms the generalized concept of a universal computer. The concept of the stored-program computer (an idea attributed to von *Neumann), in which instructions for processing data are stored along with the data in the computer's own memory, proved to be very important, since it hugely enhanced the flexibility and potential of the computer. The earliest electronic stored-program computer was an experimental machine built under the leadership of Frederick Williams at Manchester University, UK, in 1948. This was followed by the Manchester Mark 1 computer in 1949 which, as the Ferranti Mark 1, was the first commercially available computer to be delivered. Other notable early computers in the UK were EDSAC at Cambridge, later marketed as LEO, and Turing's ACE at the National Physical Laboratory.

*Mauchly and Eckert at the University of Pennsylvania (USA) developed the ENIAC and EDVAC computers based on the highly influential ideas of von Neumann; they later developed the successful UNIVAC computer, which became commercially available in 1951. The development of the *transistor led to much cheaper, faster, and more reliable computers. The first transistorized computer was working at Manchester University in 1953, although the USA had a number of much larger computers operating within a few years. The first *compiler was developed at Manchester in 1952, and in 1954 John Backus of IBM in the USA developed FORTRAN, the first internationally used *computer language. A significant high point in this era was the joint development of the Atlas computer by Ferranti Ltd. and Manchester University. This was the world's first *supercomputer, and pioneered many aspects of *computer architecture that are common today. After this, most major developments took place in the USA. Particularly crucial was the development of the *integrated circuit (IC) in 1958 which allowed complete circuits to be manufactured on a tiny piece of silicon. In 1972 the Intel Corporation developed the world's first *microprocessor, the Intel 4004, which was very limited but was an immediate commercial success and led directly to the development of today's cheap, fast, and reliable *microcomputer as well as much more powerful *mainframe computers. (See also *information technology.)

computer-aided design (CAD), the use of computer systems in engineering and *desk-top publishing, for example to support the design of products. CAD complements the traditional design process, making it faster and more flexible, by providing an electronic drawing board for a design incorporating the required specifications. It usually employs a *visual display unit and *input devices such as enhanced keyboards and graphics pads. CAD systems typically use software libraries of previous designs and commonly used components, which can be included by the designer in the new specification. Sometimes *simulation can be used to test the feasibility of several alternative designs without requiring them to be manufactured. The final design can then be plotted out as an engineering drawing or used in software to provide *numerical control for machine-tools. (See also *computer-aided manufacture.)

computer-aided manufacture (CAM), the use of computer-based systems to control the machinery in manufacturing processes. CAM is an extension of *computer-aided design (CAD); CAM systems usually make use of detailed *databases produced by CAD systems. The databases (obtained either directly via a computer link, or from engineering drawings) are used to control *machine-tool operation. Most engineered components require many machining operations to be carried out sequentially; CAD data must therefore be adapted to control each machine-tool. Complexes of *numerically controlled machine-tools and handling equipment such as *transfer machines form *flexible manufacturing systems. CAM is advantageous particularly where a range of slightly different products is required, since changes can be implemented simply by modifying the *software. *Robotics represents an extension of CAM, where a general-purpose machine can be programmed for a variety of different tasks. A further development has been *computer-integrated manufacture, the integration of design and production with other disciplines such as planning, purchasing, and financial control.

computer architecture, the design and structure of the *hardware components of *computer systems. The term embraces general considerations, such as whether a system is based on *serial, *parallel, or distributed computing, in which several computers are linked together. It also covers more detailed aspects, such as a description of the internal structure of a *central processing unit (CPU). A *microcomputer is often described as having an 8-bit, 16-bit, or 32-bit architecture according to the length of *data word that can be processed by the CPU and the width of the data *bus.

computer-integrated manufacture (CIM), the integration of design and production aspects of manufacturing with traditionally separate areas such as planning, purchasing, *data processing, financial control, and management support. CIM has evolved out of earlier techniques such as *computer-aided design (CAD), *computer-aided manufacture (CAM), *numerical control of machine-tools, *robotics, *flexible manufacturing systems (FMS), and automated materials handling, all of which have been made possible by the use of *information technology and computer-based systems. As a result of the programmability and flexibility of the constituent processes, a CIM system can more easily be directed towards optimizing the effectiveness of the manufacturing operation as a whole, whereas earlier approaches to manufacturing often had to concentrate on maintaining or improving the efficiency of individual aspects only.

computer crime, any technique aimed at fraudulently manipulating information within a computer system for the purposes of personal gain. Computer crime is growing because valuable data are stored on computers and it is impossible to maintain absolute security around a computer system, particularly a large one with many users. Electronic banking systems are the commonest target, and industrial espionage involving computers is also becoming a serious threat. 'Computer viruses' are programs which are designed to replicate themselves and deliberately damage computer systems.

computerized axial tomography (CAT), a technique of producing images of 'slices' of the body using a specialized X-ray machine. The procedure was developed commercially by the British scientist Godfrey Hounsfield, who built the first scanner in the early 1970s. The patient lies between an X-ray tube and an array of detectors, which receive different amounts of radiation according to the density of the tissue scanned by the X-ray beam. As the tube and detectors move round the patient, a series of axial readings is converted into numbers, and a computer calculates an image from these data. The technique has been particularly useful in imaging soft tissues, notably those of the brain. (For illustration see *tomography.)

computer language, a specialized, formal language used to write computer *programs. Computer languages were developed to relieve programmers of the arduous task of writing programs directly in *machine code (some examples are given in the table). There are two broad classes of conventional programming languages: low-level languages, such as *assembly language, in which each instruction represents a single machine code operation, and high-level languages, in which each instruction may represent an operation involving many machine code instructions. In both cases a special program, either an assembler, a *compiler, or an *interpreter, must be used to translate the source code to machine code before the program can be run on a computer. A job-control language, or command language, is the usual interface between a computer and the *operating system. It allows the user to describe what tasks, or jobs, are to be processed by the computer. The system interprets the user's commands and runs the required *application programs.

The Swiss engineer Konrad Zuse is credited with the invention of the first programming language shortly after World War II. AUTOCODE, the first high-level language complete with translation program, was developed at Manchester University, UK, in the early 1950s. Since then hundreds of different programming languages have been designed, but only a few are in widespread use. The first two languages to be widely used (FORTRAN and COBOL) were released around 1957. Both languages dominated their respective fields for the next two decades and are still in widespread use. In 1958 ALGOL was developed by an international committee. Although ALGOL evolved over the next decade it had greater theoretical than practical significance. However, it did spawn PASCAL, one of today's most commonly used languages. BASIC, which was developed in the mid-1960s at Dartmouth College, USA, is the best-known language for programming *microcomputers. Nowadays, the preferred language for much professional program development is C, designed at Bell Laboratories, USA, in 1971 to implement the UNIX *operating system. Most *artificial intelligence applications use symbolic or logical languages, such as LISP and PROLOG, rather than conventional programming languages.

Important high-level computer languages

Language	Description
ADA	Specifically developed for the US Department of Defense to standardize programming operations. Increasingly used on large computer systems, especially those in military applications
ALGOL, ALGOL-68	ALGOrithmic Language, designed by IBM and favoured by professional programmers for its formality and structure. ALGOL languages have never attracted widespread popularity, but are still occasionally used for specific applications
BASIC	Beginner's All-purpose Symbolic Instruction Code. Designed to be easily learnt and useful for general programming applications. Very popular despite its limitations
C	An efficient language created by Bell Laboratories. Because, in some applications, it compares favourably in speed of execution with lower level languages like assembly language, C is now widely used by professional programmers, especially in system programs and personal computers
COBOL	COmmon Business-Oriented Language. Widely used on mainframe systems in business applications, where its English-like syntax makes it easy to understand
FORTRAN	FORmula TRANslator. Developed for programming of scientific, mathematical, and engineering calculations. Released commercially in 1957, it is widely used, especially on mainframe and minicomputer systems
LISP	LISt Processing language, produced in 1959 to simplify the processing of lists of separate but related items. Also used in artificial intelligence applications, including fifth-generation computer design
Pascal	A descendent of ALGOL, specifically designed to encourage good programming practice. Has become popular in professional computing communities
PROLOG	Developed by the University of Marseilles, France, for artificial intelligence applications. Now used in fifth-generation computer design

computer numerical control *numerical control.

Concorde *supersonic flight.

concrete, a mixture of a binder (usually *cement), *aggregate, and water that hardens to form a rock-like material. The Romans first used concrete on a large scale after discovering how to make *lime binder behave as a hydraulic *cement by adding silica-rich volcanic earths (pozzolanas), found at Pozzuoli, Italy. In the following centuries, simple lime concretes were used only as fillings for walls because of their low strength and solubility in water. However, in the late 1700s, *Smeaton investigated hydraulic cements, and this ultimately led to the development of *Portland cement in 1824. Since then, the reliability of these cements and of the concrete made with them has improved. While resistance to compression is high, concrete has insufficient tensile strength to be used alone in structural members such as floors and beams, where bending occurs. In the mid-1800s patents were granted for *reinforced concrete, in which ferrous bars or cables are placed in the tension zone of a member. The development of *pre-stressed concrete in 1929 led to much wider use of concrete in bridges and other structures, since it was stronger in tension than reinforced concrete and virtually maintenance-free. Pipes, covering panels, and other components are increasingly made from polymer and *glass-fibre-reinforced concretes. Concrete behaves as a fluid when fresh, then sets, and subsequently hardens. All three stages can be modified by adding other substances (admixtures). Hardening can be retarded in hot weather to allow time for placing before setting, or accelerated in cold conditions to reduce the risk of the wet concrete freezing. A concrete can also be given specific properties by using special cements.

concrete mixer, a machine in which water, *cement, and *aggregate are mixed together in a drum to form a homogeneous *concrete. In small mixers, the concrete is poured through a single opening by tilting the drum. Medium-capacity mixers have a drum that does not tilt but rotates in one direction for mixing; on reversing, fixed blades in the drum force the concrete through an opening. Large mixers have a fixed drum with rotating blades; materials are loaded from hoppers above, and the concrete is discharged through a flap to a vehicle below.

condenser (electrical) *capacitor.

condom *contraception.

confectionery, delicacies made with sweet ingredients. Confectioneries sweetened with honey were made in Egypt at least 3,000 years ago. In the Middle Ages the Persians developed confectionery made with refined cane sugar, and during the 18th century in Europe, machinery for confectionery manufacture was first developed. Boiled or hard sweets such as fruit drops and clear mints are made by boiling a flavoured solution of sugar and corn syrup until the sugar concentration reaches a high level. On cooling, a hard, glassy product is formed. Caramels and toffees are manufactured in a similar way, but the mixture includes condensed or evaporated milk. Fondant, the basis for the 'soft centres' of many *chocolates, is made by rapidly beating a hot, concentrated sugar mixture so that minute crystals are formed: fudge can be made by similarly beating hot caramel. Agar, pectin, or gelatine is added to sugar syrup to form jellies and Turkish delight, while gums and pastilles are made by dissolving gum arabic in sugar syrup.

Conservatoire National des Arts et Métiers, Paris, a French technical school and industrial museum, founded in Paris in 1775 by the engineer J. de Vaucanson. Today it offers technical and professional courses to over 90,000 students and carries out some research and development work through its many attached institutes, for example the Institut de la Construction et de l'Habitation, and the Institut de Transport Internationaux et des Ports.

contact lens, a small plastic lens placed on the surface of the eye to correct faulty vision, used as an alternative to *spectacles. Each lens is shaped to fit the eye, and variations in thickness correct the focusing deficiencies that cause long or short sight. Contact lenses may be either hard or soft. Hard lenses cover the pupil and part of the cornea; early designs were impermeable to gases and with prolonged use could starve the covered eye tissues of oxygen. More recently, gas-permeable hard lenses have been introduced. Soft lenses are manufactured dry, then hydrated in saline solution. They cover the whole cornea and part of the sclera (white), and are more comfortable than hard lenses. However, they deteriorate more rapidly and are associated with a higher incidence of eye infection.

contact process, the most important industrial process for the production of *sulphuric acid. Sulphur dioxide (formed by burning sulphur) is first reacted with oxygen from the air to form sulphur trioxide; the reaction requires the presence of a vanadium *catalyst (usually vanadium oxide) and a temperature in excess of 400 °C. The sulphur trioxide is dissolved in highly concentrated sulphuric acid to produce oleum (fuming sulphuric acid), which is subsequently diluted with water to produce 96 per cent sulphuric acid. The sulphur trioxide cannot be dissolved directly in water because the reaction produces so much heat that it turns the sulphuric acid into a fine mist.

container ship, a *merchant ship specially designed and built for the carriage of cargo pre-packed in containers. The containers are of internationally standardized dimensions and holds and deck spaces are purpose-built to fit them, leading to greater ease and efficiency in stowage and minimization of the risk of the cargo shifting dangerously during heavy weather at sea. The idea of container shipments originated during World War II and developed slowly until 1965, when there was a world-wide upsurge in container shipping. (See also *ports and harbours.)

continuously variable transmission (CVT) *automatic transmission.

contraception, the prevention of unwanted pregnancy, by a variety of mechanical or chemical means. The oldest barrier contraceptive is the condom, or sheath. Originally of animal gut, it was used in earlier times chiefly to protect against disease. Modern condoms are made of thin rubber, and protect against sexually transmitted diseases such as AIDS and hepatitis, as well as providing contraception. Condoms for women are currently being tested. Other barrier methods include rubber diaphragms and cervical caps, which, when worn in the vagina, prevent sperm from entering the cervix. Intra-uterine devices (IUDs), such as the coil, act by preventing the fertilized ovum from implanting in the uterus. Chemical spermicide pessaries or creams kill sperm before fertilization occurs, but are more effective when used in conjunction with barrier methods. The contraceptive pill, introduced in the 1960s, contains synthetic sex hormones (oestrogen and progesterone), which prevent ovulation. There has been some evidence that the contraceptive pill influences other bodily functions, in particular that it increases the risk of venous thrombosis (blood clotting), and thus carries the risk of strokes or heart attacks. To reduce this risk, a 'mini-pill' was devised, which contains progesterone but no oestrogen, and seems to have fewer associated side-effects. Some synthetic hormone preparations work over a longer period than the contraceptive pill. Depot provera, for example, is a synthetic progesterone preparation injected at three-monthly intervals, while Norplant and Norplant-2 are subdermal capsules implanted under the skin of the upper arm, which last five and two years, respectively. The current line of contraceptive research is aimed at developing a contraceptive vaccine. Sterilization, by vasectomy or ligature of the Fallopian tubes, is the most effective method of contraception.

control system, a system designed to cause a process or mechanism to conform to some specified behaviour under a set of given constraints. Control engineers often distinguish between regulators, designed to maintain a controlled variable at a constant set point (such as engine governors or central heating thermostats), and *servo-mechanisms, designed to force the controlled variable to change with time in some specified way (such as robot arm or machine-tool control systems). Computer-based control systems for large industrial plants can involve the control of hundreds or even thousands of individual variables, together with extensive alarm handling and safety sub-systems.

At the heart of a control system is a controller, which applies control action to the process in response to information about desired behaviour, actual behaviour, and/or external disturbances to the system. The figure illustrates this for three basic types of control system. Controllers can be mechanical, electrical, pneumatic, or electronic devices, or *computer programs. Control-system design normally involves the *dynamic modelling of the process to be controlled, followed by the development of a mathematical model of the controller by application of a mixture of control theory and heuristic rules (rules derived from practical testing); and finally, the implementation and testing of the proposed design. The simplest controller is the proportional controller, which generates a control action directly proportional to the error; other common types also take into account how the error changes with time (that is, as a function of time). Recent developments in control engineering include self-tuning and adaptive control systems, in which the controller settings are modified automatically in response to changing process and/or disturbance condi-

Control system

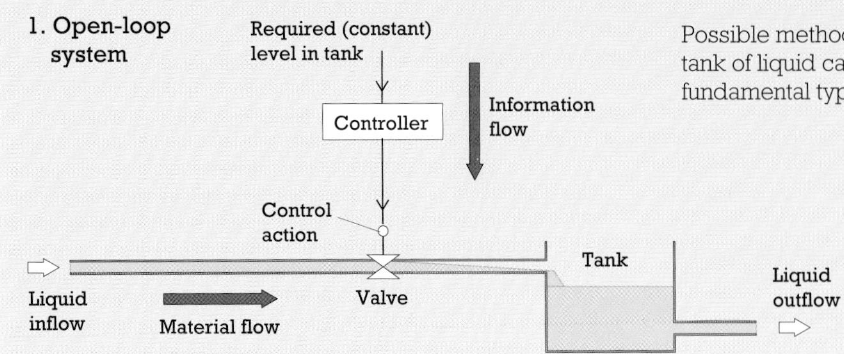

Possible methods for maintaining a constant level in a tank of liquid can be used to illustrate three fundamental types of control system.

The control action is achieved by turning the valve to a set position so that flow into and out of the tank maintains a constant liquid level. However, any variation of pressure in the supply pipe or rate of outflow (disturbances) will result in a change in level.

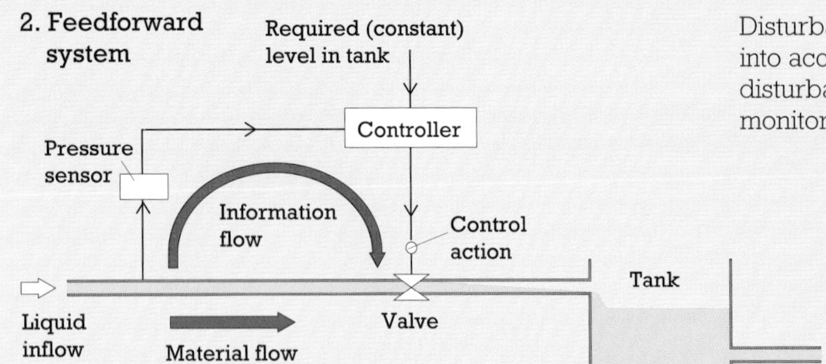

Disturbances to the system are monitored and taken into account when computing control action. Here, disturbances to the pressure in the supply pipe are monitored by a pressure sensor, which feeds the information to a controller. This opens or closes the valve in response to changes in pressure. In this way a constant flow rate into the tank is achieved. However, variations in outflow rate will change the liquid level.

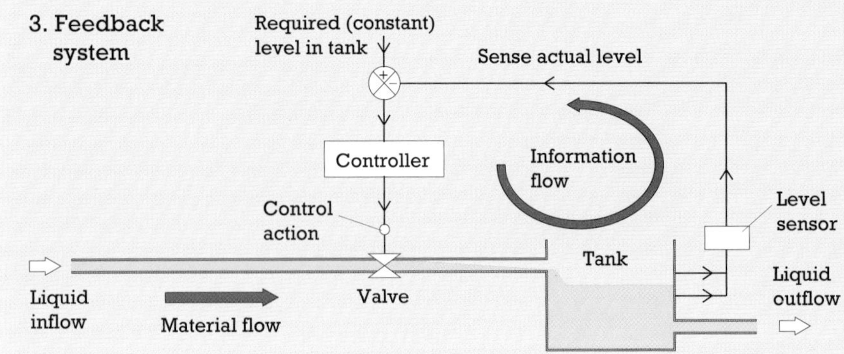

The level of the liquid in the tank is monitored by a level sensor, which feeds this information to a controller. The controller opens or closes the valve in response to the error between actual and required levels. In this way the flow rate is adjusted continuously to maintain the desired level in the presence of disturbances to either inflow or outflow.

tions; and the application of *neural networks and *artificial intelligence techniques, which mimic the actions of skilled human operators.

conveyor, a mechanism for the continuous transfer of goods or materials during extraction, manufacture, or dispatch, especially in a factory. There are many forms: roller conveyors, a series of closely spaced rollers running freely or driven, are widely used for boxes and crates. Belt conveyors consist of an endless band of rubberized fabric passing over a driven roller at one end, across a series of idler rollers, then round another drum at the far end and back underneath. Belt conveyors are used to convey minerals over many miles: the supporting rollers are in groups of three, the outer ones angled to form a shallow trough in the belt and so to retain the load. Other forms are bucket conveyors, used on *dredgers, and vibrating conveyors for powders, in which vibration causes the grains to progress by jumping. Pneumatic conveyors are much used for flour and cement. In these conveyors, the powders are blown along a pipe by a current of air.

Cooke, Sir William Fothergill (1806–79), British inventor who pioneered the electric *telegraph. In Heidelberg, Germany, he saw a demonstration of a prototype electric telegraph developed by Baron Schilling, attaché to the Russian embassy in Germany. Cooke entered into partnership with *Wheatstone in London. They were authorized by the railway companies to conduct telegraph experiments along railway tracks, as a result of which, in 1839, the first electric telegraph line was opened between Paddington and West Drayton, UK. However, the line was uneconomical because the transmitter–receiver was too complex. Commercial success came only when Cooke and Wheatstone developed the simpler twin- and single-needle transmitting instruments.

cookers and stoves, domestic appliances in which *heat is produced for cooking or for warming rooms. A cooker is designed specifically to cook food, while a stove can be used both for cooking and for space heating. In stoves, heat is generated inside an enclosed space and is radiated into the room from the walls of the stove and the flue pipe. This

A Sri Lankan woman using a ceramic liner stove, and improved, fuel-efficient version of traditional Sri Lankan **cookers**. The new stove can be made by local potters, and is 50 per cent more efficient than the traditional design.

results in better heat transfer from the fuel and food is cooked more steadily than on an open fire. From Roman times bread has been baked in brick ovens, but other food was cooked over an open fire. The first record of a stove was in the 1490s in Alsace, France. It was made of brick and tiles, and burnt wood. The first rudimentary cast-iron stove, which further improved heat transfer from the fuel, was made in 1642. *Franklin laid the foundations of modern stove design in his 'Pennsylvania Fireplace' of about 1744, which incorporated a grate and adjustable ventilation. In the 19th century, the cast-iron enclosed kitchen range (patented in the UK by George Bodley in 1802) replaced the open fire for cooking purposes. This had a central fire-grate burning coal, coke, peat, or wood, which heated hot-plates, a side oven, and often a hot-water tank. In 1924 the solid-fuel burning Aga cooker, notable for its fuel efficiency, was introduced by Gustav Dalen of Sweden. Today, Agas can run on solid fuel, gas, or oil.

Cooking by gas first became popular in the UK in the 1880s. Ovens powered by *electricity appeared in 1889, but did not begin to compete seriously with gas until the 1930s; today more than 40 per cent of UK households use electricity for cooking. Modern electric cookers heat by conduction and convection or by microwaves (in *microwave ovens). Gas and electricity are easily controlled heat sources, and led to the development of cookers separate from stoves for domestic *heating. In 1915 temperature regulation of ovens became possible by the use of *thermostats. Easy-to-clean enamelled cookers appeared in the 1930s, and in the 1970s *ceramic and cool-top hobs were made available, with self-cleaning surfaces within ovens.

Coolidge, William David (1873–1975), US innovator in the electrical industry. A versatile student, qualifying in electrical engineering, physics, and chemistry, he joined the General Electric Research Laboratory, USA, in 1905. There he devised (1908) a process for drawing the very refractory metal tungsten into wires fine enough for use as filaments in electric light bulbs, thereby greatly increasing the bulb's efficiency. Another of his inventions was an improved X-ray tube, which he patented in 1916.

cooling system (motor vehicles), the means of achieving the necessary cooling of a vehicle engine. Air cooling, widely used on small engines, motor cycles, and on such cars as the original Volkswagen, relies on air being blown across thin, closely spaced fins around the engine cylinders and cylinder heads. However, the majority of cars and commercial vehicles use water cooling. The cylinder and its head are double-walled; water is pumped through these spaces and passed to a heat exchanger, the radiator, consisting of parallel passages surrounded by many thin fins. Air passing through the radiator cools the water by forced convection (not by radiation, as the name implies). The air-flow may be solely due to the vehicle motion, but when this is insufficient, a mechanically or electrically driven fan is used to blow air through the radiator. The cooling system is usually designed to work at a pressure above atmospheric, in order to avoid boiling of the water. Up to 50 per cent *antifreeze is added to the radiator water to prevent it freezing in winter.

copper (symbol Cu, at. no. 29, r.a.m. 63.55), a reddish-yellow metallic element. It is ductile (capable of being drawn into a wire) and malleable (able to be hammered or pressed without breaking) and is a very good conductor of electricity when pure. Copper is chiefly used for electrical wiring, but also for tubes and pipes, cooking utensils, fermentation tanks, and sometimes as a roofing material. It can be combined with other metals to form alloys such as *brass, *bronze, and coinage metals. Copper salts are used in dyeing as *mordants in dyeing; as *fungicides, *insecticides, and algicides; and in the production of pigments and plastics. The chief copper *ore is chalcopyrites ($CuFeS_2$), but other ores are also important, and the free element is found naturally. Low-grade sulphide ores are concentrated by *ore flotation and then roasted with limestone to give a mixture of copper and iron sulphides called matte. Air is blown through the molten matte in a converter, oxidizing the iron to form a slag; sulphur is removed as SO_2 gas, leaving metallic copper. Traces of copper oxide formed by the air blast are removed by stirring the molten metal with poles of green wood, which provide reducing gases. The resulting copper requires purification by *electrolysis.

copper sulphate ($CuSO_4$), in its hydrated form ($CuSO_4 \cdot 5H_2O$), a blue crystalline solid; on heating it loses water and turns white (becomes anhydrous). It is used in the electrolytic refining of copper, in *electroplating, in the manufacture of pigments, as a *mordant for textiles, and to prevent growth of algae in swimming pools and reservoirs. Anhydrous copper sulphate is used to test for the presence of water.

coracle, a small and easily portable boat, occasionally circular but more often rectangular with rounded corners, constructed of wickerwork and made watertight. Coracles were originally made of hides but more recently of canvas covered in pitch. Coracles were used by the ancient Britons for river and coastal transport; today they are used by fishermen, mainly for salmon-fishing, on the rivers and lakes of Wales and Ireland. The bull-boat, similar in design and made of buffalo hides, was used by American Indians.

A shanty town in Haiti, West Indies. **Corrugated iron** is widely used as a building material despite its poor corrosion-resistance, because it is cheap and widely available.

cordite *nitro-cellulose.

cordless telephone *radio-telephone.

corrosion, the wearing away of materials, particularly of metals, by chemical action. Corrosion usually involves the combined action of oxygen and water on a metal. The presence of such substances as salt, acids, or bases, or air pollutants like sulphur dioxide, can speed up the corrosion process. The most common corrosion product is metal oxide (for example rust, which is iron oxide). In metals such as aluminium or copper, this oxide forms a tough surface layer, providing protection from further corrosion. Corrosion takes place at the metal surface: it can cause uniform tarnishing, pitting, or severe weakening of the metal structure. Many strategies are used to prevent or reduce corrosion. Most commonly, a surface coating of a non-corrosive metal (as in *galvanizing or *chromium plating) is applied, or a coating of paint, bitumen, plastic, or (for moving parts) grease. In aqueous environments, corrosion of steel structures is often prevented by cathodic protection. This involves electrically connecting 'sacrificial' anodes of aluminium or magnesium to the steel: the anodes are preferentially corroded, leaving the steel intact. Corrosion can also be reduced by controlling the surrounding environment. For example, oxygenating and neutralizing (see *acids and alkalis) the feed water in *boilers can significantly reduce corrosion of boiler tubes.

corrugated iron, thin, mild-steel sheeting (often *galvanized), folded so that it becomes stiffer and capable of supporting its own weight without significant deflection. It is structurally weak, but is used extensively for industrial roofing and cladding. Corrugated iron is now being superseded by polymer-based replacements which do not corrode so easily.

Cort, Henry (1740–1800), British ironmaster who invented the puddling process for converting pig-iron into wrought iron. Initially a supplier of wrought *iron for naval and ordnance use, Cort later set up his own forge near Fareham, Hampshire, and, in 1783, patented a process for passing iron through grooved rollers to avoid the laborious business of hammering. A year later, he patented the *puddling process for refining molten pig-iron by constant stirring. These innovations gave Britain a world-wide lead in ironworking in the 19th century.

corticosteroid *steroid and steroid treatment.

corvette, originally, a small sailing warship introduced in the 17th century. British copies of 18th-century French corvettes were known as *sloops. In the mid-19th century flush-decked steam corvettes with a single tier of guns were widely used in the UK. The name was revived briefly in the British Royal Navy at the start of World War II for a class of small anti-submarine convoy escorts. Smaller than *frigates, they were armed with one or two light guns, and *depth-charges. Since then, the name has been used occasionally to describe some small escorts or small ships built for Third World countries.

cosmetic, any substance used to beautify, preserve, or alter the appearance of a person. There is evidence of the use of body paints in south-western Europe from the Upper Paleolithic period; cosmetics have continued to be used in different cultures into modern times, and are now a major industry in the West. The simplest cosmetics are powders dusted on to the skin: traditional Chinese and Japanese make-up uses a heavy application of rice powder to whiten the face, while *batikha*, an Arabic cosmetic powder, contains ground shells, borax, rice, lemon, and eggs. Many other cosmetics are pastes or creams: Western cosmetics use paraffin wax, carnuba wax, lanolin, and other fats or waxes as a base, to which are added pigments and (for lipstick) flavourings. Elsewhere coloured clays, ochres, charcoal, and various oils or greases are common ingredients of face or body paints. The Paraguayan Caduveo people use a face and body paint made from plant juices which is colourless on initial application, but oxidizes after application to a blue-black pigment. Eye make-up can be composed of many different ingredients. Arabic kohl is a mixture of soot, lead ore, burnt copper, rose water, and sandalwood. Mascara also uses soot, but mixed with paraffin and caruba waxes to form a solid block. The ancient Egyptians used black galena (lead ore), which was both decorative and provided protection from the sun. Among hair preparations are shampoos, based on *detergents; conditioners; permanent-wave solutions to shape the hair; and dyes. (See also *perfume.)

cotton, a natural *textile fibre, accounting for almost 50 per cent (by weight) of world fibre production. The fibres grow as tubular hairs on the seeds of the cotton plant and, after picking, become convoluted collapsed tubes. Cotton is a staple (short) fibre, with an average fibre length between 1 and 4 cm (0.4–1.6 inches). The longer-fibre types are more difficult to grow, more expensive to buy, and are used only for the finest yarns. Typically, a cross-section of medium-weight *yarn contains about 500 fibres. Cotton is readily bleached and dyed; when blended with polyester fibre, it makes durable, easy-care fabrics.

cotton gin, a device for removing *cotton fibres from cotton seed, invented by *Whitney in 1793. There are two types: roller gins and saw gins. In roller gins (which are cheaper but less productive), the fibres, with seeds attached, are gripped by rollers and drawn through a gap small enough to hold back the seeds, and strip them off the fibres. In the saw gin, high-speed circular saws carry the fibres through slits too narrow for the seeds.

coulomb *unit.

coupling, railway, a mechanism used to connect the vehicles of a train. On early trains a short chain transferred the pull from one vehicle to the next. *Buffers enabled vehicles to be pushed against one another without damage. Chains were later replaced by screw couplings, which kept the vehicles in close contact, so minimizing 'snatch' and heavy contact when starting and stopping. Most vehicles throughout the world now use buckeye couplings (see figure), which may be connected or disconnected automatically. In modern designs the pipes and cables between vehicles may be integrated with the coupling.

CPU *central processing unit.

cracking, a chemical process in which long-chain *hydrocarbon molecules, particularly those derived from *petroleum refining, are broken down into smaller, economically important molecules such as *petrol. Taken to its extreme, the process would produce simply carbon and hydrogen. Both elements are common by-products of cracking, but the process is used particularly to increase the proportion of petrol produced from petroleum to as high as 80 per cent. Cracking is also used to produce raw materials for the chemical industry. Thermal cracking, the earliest system developed, was first used commercially in 1913. It involved distilling batches of fairly heavy gas oil at about 500 °C, and pressures up to 25 bar. Catalytic cracking, used since the 1930s, produces more precise results than thermal cracking, and eliminates the need for high pressures. The Houdry process, one of the first developed, uses granules of clay as a *catalyst, which promote the cracking reaction without themselves being changed. World War II brought a huge increase in demand for aviation fuel, and this led to the rapid development of fluid catalytic cracking. The process involves circulating the catalyst (since the 1960s, usually zeolite silicates) as a fine powder suspended in the oil. In the chemical industry, thermal cracking of ethane, *propane, naphtha, and *gas oil is used to manufacture *ethene and a variety of other compounds. Hydrocracking, originally developed in Germany for producing oil from lignite coal, is now used to produce further high-grade petrol from petroleum. Hydrocracking is basically catalytic cracking in a container pressurized by pumping in hydrogen gas. Valuable products are obtained without simultaneous formation of coke and gas, and the process is flexible enough to be applicable to many different oil fractions.

crane, a device for raising and moving heavy weights. Early cranes were manually operated, sometimes using several men in a treadmill. Steam cranes became common in the 19th century and much use was made by dock-side

Coupling, railway

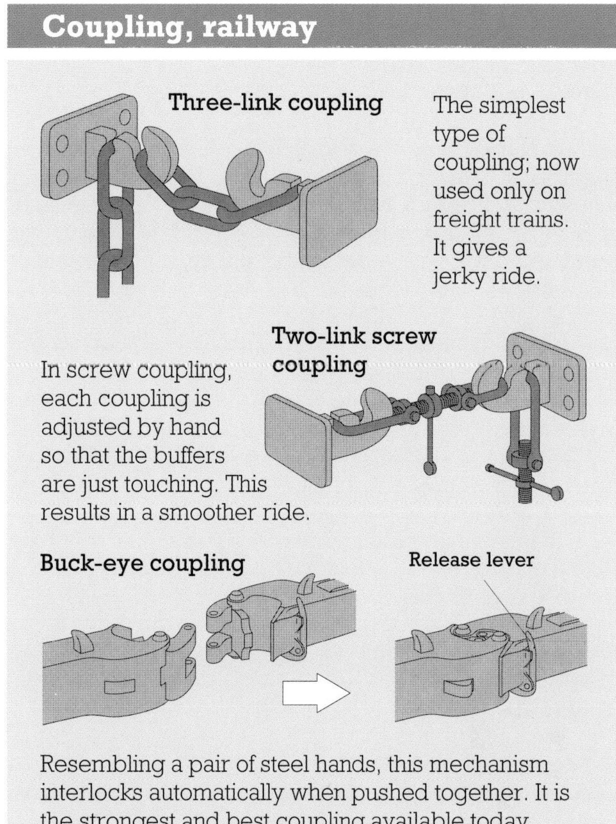

Three-link coupling
The simplest type of coupling; now used only on freight trains. It gives a jerky ride.
Two-link screw coupling
In screw coupling, each coupling is adjusted by hand so that the buffers are just touching. This results in a smoother ride.
Buck-eye coupling
Release lever

Resembling a pair of steel hands, this mechanism interlocks automatically when pushed together. It is the strongest and best coupling available today. Vehicles can be released by use of a lever located at the side of the coupling.

cranes of *hydraulic power, using rams supplied with high-pressure water from a system of pipes. Most cranes are now electrically operated, either from mains supply or from a diesel generator carried on the crane. There are two main types of crane: those with a revolving jib which can be rotated about a vertical post, and those which can traverse in two directions, so as to cover a rectangular area. The first type is typified by the derrick, in which the jib is pivoted at its base and supported by wire ropes from the top of a post. It can be raised or lowered and rotated to cover a circular area. Traversing cranes are typified by the overhead travelling crane and the gantry crane. Dockside cranes straddle the quayside road or railway and enable cargoes to be landed on the quayside or loaded into barges outboard of the ship. Heavy loads can be lifted by hammerhead cranes, in which the load is largely counterbalanced by the weight of the crane machinery, though sometimes weights are added. The hammerhead has evolved into the ubiquitous tower (cantilever) crane, to be seen on most building sites.

crankshaft, a common machine element used to convert reciprocating into rotary motion, or vice versa. A shaft carries a crank-arm which in turn carries a crankpin, a short length of shaft parallel to the main shaft and offset from it by a distance known as the throw. The reciprocating mechanism, such as a piston sliding in a cylinder, is linked to the crankpin by a connecting-rod so that each revolution of the crankshaft causes the piston to reciprocate through a distance, the stroke, of twice the throw. Multi-cylinder engines require a multi-throw crankshaft, with a series of crank-arms and crankpins (see illustration in *petrol engine). The use of simple crank handles is known from the Han dynasty (202 BC to AD 220) in China, and was described by *Hero in the 1st century AD. However, the crankshaft and connecting-rod appeared much later, in 15th-century Europe.

crease-resistant fabric *textile finishing.

credit card, a card issued to an individual, authorizing the purchase of goods or services on credit. The first credit cards were introduced by US oil companies in the 1920s, for the sale of petrol. 'Universal' credit cards, valid for a variety of goods and services, appeared in about 1950. The arrival of the business computer in the mid-1950s (see *information technology) signalled the beginning of a rapid expansion in the use and availability of credit cards, which continues to this day. A magnetic strip on the back of the credit card carries identifying information. Many retailers have machines from the credit company that immediately check the credit card's validity and automatically transfer payment from the customer's account. Recent increases in credit card fraud have led to the use of *holograms on cards, so as to make them difficult to reproduce, and of *cryptographic encoding of information carried within the computer systems of banks and credit companies.

creep (metallurgy) *metals and metalworking.

creosote *coal-tar.

Crompton, Samuel (1753–1827), British mechanic who invented the spinning mule. As a boy he worked in a Lancashire cotton mill and observed that with *Hargreaves's spinning-jenny, the yarn broke frequently. This led to his invention of the 'mule' (1779), so called because it was a cross between the jenny and *Arkwright's spinning frame. It was a versatile and effective *spinning machine, the speed of operation of which encouraged the development of power-looms to keep pace with the spinning process. Crompton did not patent his invention and so did not profit greatly from it.

crop rotation *rotation of crops.

crop-spraying, the process by which *agrochemicals are applied to a crop for its protection or to influence its growth. Most crop-spraying equipment comprises three components: a storage tank, a pump, and a boom to which spray nozzles are attached. The crop-sprayer may be carried on, or towed by, a tractor, or mounted on an aircraft. Numerous variations exist on the basic design to accommodate spraying in specialized areas such as orchards. Crops are frequently sown leaving gaps ('tramlines') to allow access for spraying equipment. For all chemical applications calm weather is needed to avoid spray drift.

Cross, Charles Frederick (1855–1935), British chemist who, with fellow-chemist E. J. Bevan, developed the viscose process for manufacturing *rayon. Cross and Bevan formed a partnership as consulting and analytical chemists in 1885. In 1892 they patented a process whereby cheap forms of cellulose, such as wood-pulp, were dissolved and then squirted through the fine holes of a spinneret (see *spinning) into a coagulating bath to produce fibres, a process that became the basis of the rayon industry. In 1894 they patented a process for making *cellulose acetate.

crossbow, a *bow that is attached horizontally across a stock and employs a mechanical firing action. In China, the oldest surviving example dates from around 220 BC, but crossbows were in use during the Zhou dynasty (*c.*1000–249 BC). In most cross-bows, the bowstring is gripped by a claw-like catch which is pulled back using a hand-winch. The arrow (called a bolt or quarrel) is fitted to the string, then fired by a trigger mechanism. The bowstring tension can be extremely high, allowing a heavier quarrel to be fired a greater distance than with a conventional bow.

cross-staff, an instrument that came into general use for marine navigation during the 16th century, used for measuring the altitude (angle above the horizon) of a celestial body at sea; this measurement could be used to determine the latitude of a ship (see *navigation). The cross-staff comprised a long wooden shaft with a movable cross-piece. The navigator sighted along the shaft, and moved the cross-piece until one end appeared to touch the horizon, the other the celestial body. The altitude could then be read from a scale on the shaft. The cross-staff could also be used for finding heights and distances in surveying.

crow-bar, an iron or steel rod, commonly 1.5–2 m (5–6.5 feet) in length, used as a lever or pry. It is usually forked at one end, resembling a crow's foot. A closely allied tool is the case-opener, or wrecking bar. This is shaped like an elongated S, with a fork at one end and wedge-shape at the other.

crucible steel *iron and steel industry, *Huntsman.

cruise control, a device designed to enable a motor vehicle to maintain a constant road speed irrespective of the road gradient or surface. The most obvious use of such a facility is in long-distance driving on a motorway. With the cruise control in operation a constant speed can be maintained without using the accelerator pedal. Cruise control is instantly overridable in the event of an emergency situation in which braking or other avoiding action has to be taken. 'Intelligent' cruise control, where the car's speed is adjusted in relation to the distance between it and the car in front, began development in the early 1990s.

cruise missile, generally a medium-range *guided missile, carrying a nuclear or conventional *warhead, that uses aerodynamic lift like an aeroplane. Cruise missiles are powered throughout their flight by conventional *ram-jet or *jet engines (unlike *ballistic missiles, which employ rocket motors for a short time only). The first cruise missile was the ground-launched V1 rocket used by Germany in World War II. It was powered by a single pulse jet, could carry a 1-tonne warhead a distance of 240 km (150 miles) at a speed of nearly 650 km/h (400 m.p.h.). About 8,000 V1s were fired from northern France against the UK between 1944 and 1945, and a comparable number were launched against Belgium. However, the V1's relatively slow speed exposed it to anti-aircraft fire and attack by high-performance aeroplanes. Modern cruise missiles are guided by *inertial navigation systems, which are checked using astronomical readings or *navigation satellites, or are updated during flight by means of terrain-comparison programs and data stored in on-board computers. They are very versatile, because they can be launched from land, sea, or air. Compared with a ballistic missile, a cruise missile can carry a much heavier payload relative to its size, delivering a warhead as heavy as 15 per cent of its own weight, whereas the equivalent figure for a ballistic missile is typically less than 1 per cent. It is also much harder to detect by radar, since it is smaller and flies at a low altitude, though its subsonic speed may make it vulnerable to counter-attack if it is identified.

cruiser, a large, fast *warship with medium armament. In the 18th century all warships on detached service (not operating as part of a fleet) were called cruisers. During the last quarter of the 19th century the term began to mean a specific warship type, and was used to replace 'frigate' and 'corvette' as a description for vessels next in power to the battleship. The biggest cruisers were often bigger than contemporary battleships, and faster, though not as well protected or as heavily armed. Cruisers varied in size more than any other type of ship, the smallest being merely enlarged *sloops. Their role was to act as scouting vessels for battleships and to maintain command of a sea area after it had been taken by the fleet; they also raided commercial shipping. In the 1900s light cruisers for scouting appeared; after 1918 the larger cruisers were known as heavy cruisers. After World War II, the cruiser (mostly still gun-armed) was for a time the largest conventional warship. The term is still sometimes used to refer to the largest guided-missile vessels. A cruiser—usually in the form 'cabin cruiser'—is also a small yacht intended for cruising rather than racing.

cryolite *Hall, Charles Martin.

cryptography, writing or solving ciphers. A code is an unvarying rule for representing one information symbol by another: the *Morse code is an example. Ciphers also replace or reorganize information symbols, but the rules governing the replacement (the key) are a secret known only to the transmitter and the legitimate receiver. As an illustration of the difference, *telephonic speech is always coded before transmission, the sound information being *digitized into a code of binary signals. However, on lines carrying sensitive information, the speech is also enciphered, and only someone with the cipher key will be able to receive the original message. An example of the use of cryptography is its use on cash cards, which have the account holder's personal identification number (PIN) encrypted on them. This can be read by the cash machine to check that the user has entered the correct PIN, but it is not accessible to non-authorized users. Other uses include securing data being transferred between computers, and protecting data-flow between *communications satellites and ground stations. As more and more confidential information about individuals is stored in computer databases, so cryptographic protection is vital for safeguarding individual rights.

crystal set *radio receiver.

CS gas *tear-gas.

Ctesibius (*fl.* 250 BC), Alexandrian Greek inventor of a number of ingenious mechanical devices. Little is known of his life, and his writings are lost, but he is credited with the invention of the force *pump and a hydraulic organ, and with making improvements to the clepsydra (see *clocks). The clepsydra measures time by recording the rate at which water escapes through a hole in the bottom of a cistern. To allow for the fact that the rate of flow reduces as the cistern empties, Ctesibius devised a means of continuously replenishing the cistern to keep the head of water constant. He also invented compressed-air weapons and a military catapult.

Cugnot, Nicolas-Joseph (1725–1804), French pioneer of steam traction. He served as an engineer in the Austro-Hungarian and French armies. In 1769 he was encouraged by the French Minister of War to develop a steam-propelled gun-carriage, the first ever steam-powered road vehicle. The following year he built a steam tricycle capable of carrying four passengers at walking pace. Lack of patronage prevented testing of a larger, two-cylinder machine, with direct drive by piston rods to the front wheel, but in 1801 this invention found its way into the *Conservatoire National des Arts et Métiers in Paris.

cultivar, a plant variety bred from a wild species that differs from the wild species as a result of that breeding. The difference is maintained by inbreeding within the new variety, and by selection of offspring that most closely resemble the parent. Breeding aims to exaggerate properties of the wild plant that are desirable in the cultivated crop.

cultivator, a general term applied to agricultural machinery used to convert the surface of a field carrying plant remains into an environment tailored to the sowing of the next crop. The term thus encompasses *ploughs, rotary cultivators, cultivators with spring tines or teeth, *harrows, and land rollers. Cultivators have a frame, often wheeled, to which are attached the units which work on the ground—hoe-type blades, or sprung metal prongs—the repeated action of which breaks up soil particles. Many machines are also fitted with rollers and harrow blades.

cupellation, an ancient method of extracting *silver from its ores. The silver is alloyed with lead and then heated in a porous ceramic dish called a cupel. The lead is oxidized and most of the oxide is swept away in an air blast. Any residual oxide is absorbed by the cupel, leaving behind pure silver.

cupro-nickel *alloy.

curare, a substance extracted from certain plants growing in tropical South America, and used as an arrow poison. The active ingredient, D-tubocurarine, prevents nerve impulses from reaching the muscles, thus causing paralysis, but it does not affect sensation. In controlled doses it can be used during *anaesthesia to obtain muscular relaxation.

current, electric *circuits, electrical and electronic, *electricity and magnetism.

curtain wall, a lightweight, non-load-bearing wall in which a metal or timber framework is supported in front of the building frame on brackets at the floor edges. The spaces within the framework are filled either with glass or with other thin sheet material, backed with thermal insulation.

cutter, a type of mercantile sailing ship, adopted as a small warship in the mid-18th century. It was single-masted with a gaff (*fore-and-aft) mainsail, a square topsail, and two foresails, armed with up to twenty light guns. From the 18th century, a cutter was also a *ship's boat, with one or two masts and carrying eight to fourteen oars. The term is now usually used for a sailing *yacht with a mainsail and two foresails, or for a motor vessel used in the USA for coastguard, ice, and weather patrol duties.

CVD *vapour deposition.

cybernetics (from the Greek, *kubernētēs*, steersman), the study of communication and control systems in machines, animals, and organizations. The discipline developed immediately after World War II, when *control-systems and *systems-engineering techniques were applied successfully to certain neurological problems. The term cybernetics was first applied in English by *Wiener. Cybernetics is characterized by a concentration on the flow of information (rather than energy or material) within a system, and on the use of *feedback or 'goal-directed activity' in both technological artefacts and living organisms. Major areas of cybernetic study have been biological control systems, *automation, animal communication, and *artificial intelligence (AI). The recent rapid expansion of AI as a subject area, together with the development of knowledge-based systems and *neural networks, have renewed interest in the general cybernetic approach, although the term 'cybernetics' itself is now rarely used.

cyclotron *particle accelerator.

cytotoxic drug *cancer and cancer therapy.

Daguerre, Louis Jacques Mandé (1789–1851), French painter who invented the daguerreotype, the first practicable photographic process (see *photography). As a young man Daguerre was a scenery painter in Paris; he used the *camera obscura for creating his designs and sought to fix its images chemically. This led him to the discovery that a silver-iodide image could be developed with mercury vapour: by 1837 the process was producing good images. However, this process gave only a single positive picture and was superseded by *Talbot's process, which created a negative from which unlimited positive prints could be made.

Daimler, Gottlieb Wilhelm (1834–1900), German pioneer of automobile engineering. In 1872 he began working with *Otto to perfect the latter's oil engine. Ten years later, he went into partnership with Wilhelm Maybach in Stuttgart. They developed one of the first high-speed *internal-combustion engines suitable for road vehicles (1885) and perfected a *carburettor that was petrol-fuelled. They used their first petrol engine to power a bicycle (possibly, the first motor cycle). In 1888 they exhibited a two-cylinder motor car in Paris, with an engine provided by the French automotive engineers René Panhard and Emile Levassor. In 1899 Daimler produced the first Mercedes, named after his daughter.

dairy farming, the husbandry of animals for the supply of milk and *dairy products. In the West, milk comes predominantly from dairy cows, but elsewhere the milk of sheep, goats, and water-buffalo is also consumed. The primary requirement for certain dairying is high-quality grassland. In New Zealand and some other countries, pastures support cows throughout the year. Elsewhere, where grass growth is seasonal, dairy cattle herds are housed over winter and fed on stored *silage, hay, or processed foods. The availability of concentrated cattle feeds, allowing herds to be enlarged without pressurizing land resources, and the use of *milking machines have greatly increased dairy farm productivity in the West. By contrast, dairy farming is almost completely absent from tropical regions, due to the lack of native breeds that produce sufficient milk.

dairy product, any food derived from milk. Milk is a suspension of fat globules in an aqueous solution containing protein, sugar, and minerals (notably calcium). Commercial production processes have generally been applied to cow's milk only. Almost half the milk consumed is drunk as fresh or skimmed milk; in the West this milk is *pasteurized to reduce bacterial levels and improve keeping qualities. Sweetened, condensed milk is popular in many tropical countries, as it has excellent keeping qualities, even without refrigeration. Sterilized and UHT (ultra heat treated) milk are other long-life forms of milk. *Butter and *cheese are the most common products made from milk: originally, they were made as a way of preserving the milk. In hot countries, yoghurt, a semi-fluid, fermented milk food with a slightly sour taste due to the presence of lactic acid, is also made to preserve milk. Yoghurt is an important food in many Islamic countries, and can also be made with many types of sweetening or flavouring, and fresh fruits or vegetables may be added to it. Ice-cream is a dairy product that has become popular since the late 19th century, when mechanical *refrigeration was first developed. Freezing is also used as a way of preserving cream and concentrated milk for use in the food industry. Many dairy products such as skimmed and full-cream milk are dried to prolong life and to save weight and storage space. These dried products are used in the commercial manufacture of many foods. Milk whey (essentially the aqueous portion of the milk) and the milk protein casein are dairy industry by-products with high nutritive value. They are used in both human and animal foods, and casein is also used in the manufacture of plastics and *adhesives.

dam, a barrier to hold back water, often forming a lake or reservoir behind. Dams may be used to store water for irrigation, to aid flood control, for *hydroelectric power, or for a combination of these purposes. The coffer-dam is normally a temporary dam used in building or excavation works. Many dams, however, are massive engineering structures, often built across valleys, with overflow channels (spillways) to prevent the impounded water from escaping over the top of the dam. Water is prevented from seeping under the dam by a cut-off, a deep trench dug beneath and filled with impermeable material such as clay or concrete to form a watertight barrier.

The gravity dam is designed so that its mass exerts sufficient downward force to resist overturning caused by the horizontal pressure of the impounded water. There must also be sufficient resistance to prevent the dam from sliding forwards. The arch dam is curved in plan so that the load from the water is transmitted to supports (abutments) at either side. The abutments must withstand outward thrusts, achieved by selecting a site in a steep valley with sides of sound rock. Generally, the arch dam is practical where the height is about five times the width. On wider sites, multiple-arch dams can be used. In a buttress dam, the water is retained by an inclined surface of slabs (deck) supported on a series of buttresses. The water pressure on the inclined deck creates a greater vertical load on the ground, but the dam has more stability against overturning. Each section can be made structurally independent so that different rates of *settlement can be more easily accommodated than in the multiple-arch dam.

Masonry dams are usually of the gravity type, though a masonry arch dam is recorded in the reign of the Byzantine emperor Justinian I (*c.*482–565). The Tibi Dam at Alicante in Spain was built in 1594 and still provides irrigation water. *Reinforced concrete is now widely used for all types of dam. Earth and rock-fill (embankment) dams are always of the gravity type and generally built in open valleys. Since these materials are usually not watertight, an impermeable core is used. Alternatively, the upstream face can be sealed with a concrete facing or with asphalt. (See also table.)

Construction of the 189-m (620-foot) Itaipù **dam**, on the River Paraná at the border between Brazil and Paraguay. It is the largest hydroelectric scheme in the world, with the capacity to generate 12,600 MW of electricity.

A selection of the world's highest dams

Name	Location	Type	Completion date	Height m (feet)
Hoover	Colorado River, Nevada, USA	Concrete arch	1936	221 (726)
Mauvoisin	Valais, Switzerland	Concrete arch	1957	237 (778)
Vajont	Veneto, Italy	Concrete arch	1961	262 (858)
Grande Dixence	Valais, Switzerland	Concrete gravity	1962	285 (935)
Mica	British Columbia, Canada	Earth fill	1973	244 (800)
Chivor	Bata River, Colombia	Rock fill with clay core	1975	237 (778)
Chirkey	Sulak River, Daghestan, Soviet Union	Double curvature arch	1978	236 (774)
Inguri	Inguri River, Georgia, Soviet Union	Concrete arch	1980	272 (892)
Sayany	Yenisei River, Siberia, Soviet Union	Composite arch and gravity	1980	245 (804)
Nourek	Vakhsh River, Tadzhikistan, Soviet Union	Earth fill with clay core	1980	317 (1040)
Rogun	Vakhsh River, Tadzhikistan, Soviet Union	Earth fill	1987	335 (1099)

damp-proof course, an impervious layer built into a wall to stop moisture movement in the pores of the wall. Without a damp-proof course, deterioration of moisture-sensitive materials such as *plaster and wood is likely. The damp-proof course usually comprises a thin strip of *bitumen, felt, slate, or plastic built into the wall just above ground level.

Daniell cell, an obsolete primary cell with zinc and copper electrodes, named after the British chemist John Frederic Daniell (1790–1845), which converts chemical energy into an electric current. It consists of a zinc rod (the *cathode) standing in a porous earthenware pot filled with zinc sulphate solution. This pot is itself immersed in a copper sulphate solution, which is contained in a copper pot (the *anode).

Darby, Abraham (1678–1717), English ironmaster, the first to smelt *iron with coke. In the 17th century the growing demand for iron was frustrated because the timber for making charcoal (the fuel used for *blast-furnaces) was scarce and expensive, and large furnaces were not feasible because charcoal was too soft to support a heavy charge of ore. Raw coal was an obvious alternative, but the presence of *sulphur in it spoilt the quality of the iron. At his Coalbrookdale works in 1709 Darby solved this problem by using coke, which burnt cleanly. Smelting iron with coke was a key process in the development of the *Industrial Revolution.

data (computing), information that has been prepared, often in a particular format, for a specific purpose. In computing, the term data is used for material distinct from instructions: for example, if a computer multiplies two numbers together, the numbers themselves are the data, operated on by an instruction (to multiply them together). In a more restricted sense, data may be the information input for a particular program, as opposed to the results or output. A third meaning uses data as a term for information not in the form of words, sounds, or images: such data is usually information that is stored in a highly organized and compact form suitable for *data processing.

database, a logically organized collection of related *data, generally accessed by a set of programs known as a database management system (DBMS), which oversees the creation and use of the database and controls access to the data. The organization of a database obviates the need to duplicate information to meet the various requirements of different groups of users, and ensures that the data always remains consistent. A large database requires extensive storage facilities. In some organizations and services databases can be accessed over *networks from *microcomputers or as *videotex. 'Relational' databases and *hypertext techniques include extensive and complex cross-reference facilities so that information on related items may be retrieved. Many database programs have been designed to run on microcomputers. Some of these contain computer languages that enable users to change the operation of the database to suit their requirements. For example, a mailing list on a microcomputer constitutes a simple database in which—if the information were available in a structured format—the DBMS could be instructed to print out the addresses of all the people called Smith, or of everyone on the mailing list living in Melbourne, Australia.

data processing, the use of a *computer to manipulate *data, particularly the routine tasks undertaken in large organizations. For example, the maintenance, retrieval, and analysis of financial records is faster and easier with the aid of computers. The amount of data which needs to be processed is frequently considerable. Therefore, the data is often organized in the form of a single *database. The database is stored on *hard disks, magnetic drums, or magnetic tapes attached to computers of substantial power. Large data-processing facilities are often distributed over *networks in which a user anywhere on the network can access data anywhere else on the network.

dating systems. Scientific evidence about the prehistory of the human race and of the Earth rests heavily on the accurate dating of recovered artefacts and rocks. Traditional methods of dating depend on factors such as depth of burial of an artefact, and comparison with material from other sites. These methods are now reinforced by several much more precise scientific techniques. Dendrochronology, developed in the 1930s, is based on measurement of growth rings in timber. *Radio-carbon dating uses the decay of the radioisotope carbon-14 to date organic material. A similar technique uses the decay of potassium-40 to argon-40 for dating volcanic rocks, and the decay of rubidium-87 to strontium-87 for dating other rocks. Both radio-carbon dating and dendrochronology are absolute dating systems; other methods must be calibrated first. Pottery and burnt flint are dated using thermoluminescence, which measures the light emitted when an object is heated. *Electron spin resonance is used to date shells, corals, and tooth enamel. In optical dating, a *laser is used to date silt and sediment samples.

Davy, Sir Humphry (1778–1829), British chemist, and pioneer of electrochemistry and agricultural science. At the Pneumatic Institution in Bristol, UK, he investigated the therapeutic effect of gases (including laughing gas, the first satisfactory *anaesthetic). He was invited by the British physicist Benjamin Thompson to the Royal Institution, London, where he discovered the elements *potassium, *sodium, *magnesium, *calcium, *strontium, and *barium. In 1813 he published his book *Elements of Agricultural Chemistry*, and two years later perfected the safety lamp to prevent firedamp (marsh-gas) explosions in mines.

DDT (dichloro-diphenyl-trichloro-ethane), a chlorinated hydrocarbon contact *insecticide. It was first synthesized in 1873, and its insecticidal properties were discovered by the Swiss scientist Paul Müller in 1942. DDT was more powerful than previously known insecticides, and was effective against a wide range of insects. Its most spectacular use was in the eradication of malarial mosquitoes. However, in the 1950s doses of DDT and other insecticides had to be doubled or trebled as resistant insect strains developed, and evidence began to grow that the chemical was concentrated in the food chain. Questions were raised about the chemical's safety, and in over twenty countries (for example, Norway in 1970 and the UK in 1984) DDT was banned. However, it is still widely used for malaria and pest control in Third World countries.

Deacon, Henry (1822–76), British industrial chemist and innovator in the alkali industry. After apprenticeship to an engineering firm, he joined Pilkington's Glassworks in 1848 and so became familiar with the alkali industry. At that time *sodium carbonate was made by the *Leblanc process, involving treatment of common salt with sulphuric acid and releasing hydrochloric acid. This was not only wasteful but also a cause for litigation with neighbouring landowners. Deacon devised a process whereby the gaseous hydrochloric acid could be converted to bleaching powder, a substance in great demand in the textile industry.

dead reckoning *navigation.

Decca Navigator, a short- to medium-range *radio aid to navigation, operational in many parts of the world, which allows ships' navigators to find their vessel's position with a high degree of accuracy. It was developed in 1944 by the Decca Radio and Television Company, London, to aid the Normandy troop landings. Decca is a phase-difference hyperbolic navigation system consisting of a master transmitter and two or three secondary transmitters spread within a radius of 110–220 km (60–120 nautical miles; see *knot) of the master station. The system gives navigational cover up to 550 km (300 nautical miles) from the master station by day, and is accurate to around 50 m (160 feet) up to 185 km (100 nautical miles) from the master station.

decibel (dB), a unit for measuring the relative intensity of sounds, or, in electronics, the relative power of electrical signals. The intensity of a sound in decibels is expressed relative to some standard intensity, commonly the minimum audible to the human ear. The decibel (one-tenth of a bel) derives its name from *Bell, the inventor of the telephone. It is a logarithmic scale, which means that a sound with an intensity of 3 bel (30 dB) is ten times louder than a sound of 2 bel (20 dB), and one hundred times louder than one of 1 bel (10 dB). Thus, the sound of a jet aircraft taking off (which may reach an intensity of 120 dB or more) is a million times louder than normal conversation (around 60 dB).

decompression chamber *deep-sea and diving technology.

deep-freeze, an appliance for the long-term storage of food at low temperatures, introduced by *Birdseye in 1929. A domestic deep-freeze uses a mechanical *heat-pump similar to that of a refrigerator but maintains its internal temperature below −7 °C. This form of *refrigeration depends on all the water contained in the food freezing to solid ice, thereby rendering spoilage organisms inactive. Some foodstuffs undergo permanent change on freezing and thawing: the expansion of water as it freezes ruptures cell walls, causing, for example, soft fruits such as strawberries to become flabby.

deep-sea and diving technology. Since antiquity, skin divers have undertaken various underwater tasks, from collecting pearls to building harbours using no diving equipment. However, the limitations of human physiology restrict such diving to depths of about 20 m (65 feet) and durations of well under 5 minutes. Attempts to overcome these limitations began in the 17th century, or perhaps earlier, when *diving-bells were first used for salvage work. The diving suit, specialized clothing that allows a diver to work under water, also first appeared in the 17th century. John Lethbridge's diving machine of 1715 was one of the most successful of the numerous early suits. Like the diving-bell, Lethbridge's suit was supplied with compressed air from the surface, using bellows. In the 1820s the brothers John and Charles Dean of Whitstable, UK, developed the first really successful diving suit. The design was bought from them and

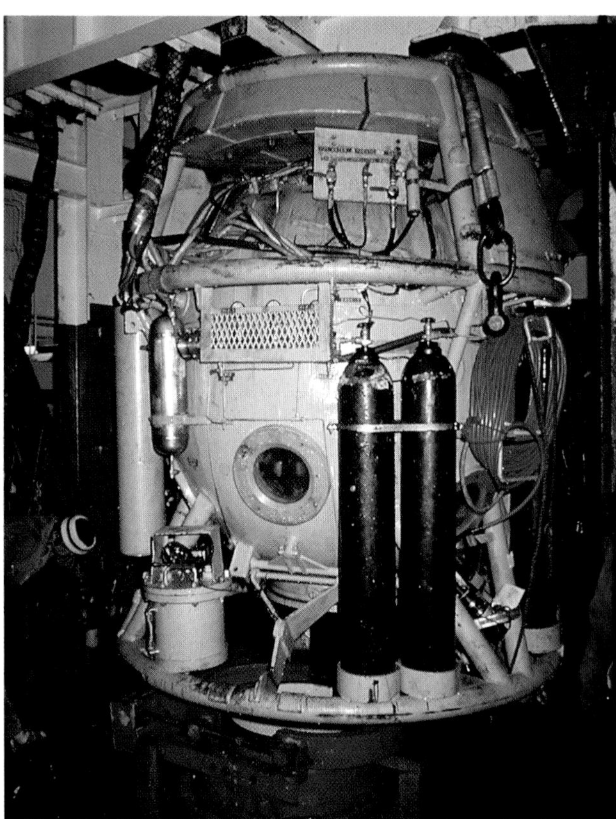

A diving bell used for **deep-sea diving** operations in the North Sea. Extra emergency breathing tanks are visible on the front of the bell.

improved by the German inventor Augustus Siebe (1788–1872): Siebe's design remained virtually unchanged from the 1830s until recent times. Self-contained diving suits were first produced in the late 19th century. These incorporated a 'demand valve', which adjusted the pressure of the air supply (contained in metal tanks strapped to the back) to the pressure at the diving depth. However, the idea was not developed, and was reinvented during World War II as the *aqualung. Between World Wars I and II an 'atmospheric' suit, in which the diver remains at surface pressure, was introduced for deep operations. The suit was armoured to withstand the high pressures of deep water. For still deeper operations armoured spheres were developed: the first of these was the *bathysphere, later followed by the bathyscaphe and the *submersible.

Since the late 1960s there have been dramatic advances in diving technology, many arising from the desire of the oil industry to exploit petroleum supplies beneath the sea. For divers working below about 10 m (32 feet) an inflatable dry suit (in which no water penetrates to the skin) is now used, along with a light, plastic helmet containing a gas regulator and communications equipment. For depths below 60 m (200 feet), and in cold northern waters, electrically heated undergarments and heating of the gas supply are necessary. For divers working at such depths, a major problem arises from breathing air at the high pressures encountered there. Nitrogen from the air is absorbed into the bloodstream and if pressure is reduced too rapidly during ascent after a dive, the absorbed nitrogen forms gas bubbles in the blood, causing the condition known as the 'bends' (caisson or decompression disease). The bends can be avoided by stopping for prescribed decompression periods during ascent from a dive. The decompression time required increases with increasing depth. An additional problem at depths greater than 40 m (130 feet) is 'nitrogen narcosis', in which the nitrogen absorbed into the body has adverse effects on the nervous system. Problems of decompression disease and nitrogen narcosis have been largely overcome by using mixtures of oxygen and another, more inert, gas (usually helium) in place of nitrogen. Divers operating with such mixtures can work at depths of 90 m (300 feet) or more, where decompression times are of the order of days. Under such conditions a technique known as 'saturation diving' is necessary to achieve effective work. Divers travel to the underwater work-site in a type of diving-bell known as a submersible decompression chamber (SDC). After working, they return to the ship in the SDC, still at diving pressure. Once on board they transfer to a deck decompression chamber (DDC), a comfortably equipped chamber maintained at the same pressure as the SDC, in which they live for periods of up to 15 days, diving each day in the SDC to the work-site. The SDC and the DDC both have *airlocks to maintain the required pressures. Because the divers remain at the pressure of the working depth, no decompression is required in returning from depth. At the end of the 15-day period the diving team undergoes decompression, and another team takes over the work. Another solution to the problems of decompression is the 'atmospheric' suit described earlier.

Because of the many problems involved in diving to great depths, piloted submersibles equipped with remotely controlled robot arms, or submersibles controlled from the surface (remotely piloted vehicles) are used whenever possible.

defoliant, a chemical agent that causes leaves to fall off trees and bushes, thereby denying cover to the enemy. Some defoliants were under development at the end of World War I, but were never used. At the beginning of US intervention in the civil war in Vietnam, the US Air Force sprayed some jungle areas near Saigon with four pesticides. The most common, Agent Orange, was a defoliant made up of the weed killers 2,4-D and 2,4,5-T. The use of 2,4,5-T produced a dangerous by-product, *dioxin, a synthetic toxic chemical that attacks the nervous system.

De Forest, Lee (1873–1961), US pioneer of electronics, especially the *thermionic valve. In 1896 he graduated in mechanical engineering at Yale University, but then turned his attention to *radio communication. In 1906 he improved J. A. *Fleming's diode by introducing a third electrode, creating the triode. Originally, the triode served only as an improved device for detecting radio waves, but later its ability to act as a high-frequency oscillator and amplifier made it a key component in the development of radio and other telecommunications.

C-123 Provider aircraft spraying **defoliants** on forest during US involvement in the Vietnam War (1964–75).

De Havilland, Sir Geoffrey (1882–1965), British aircraft designer and manufacturer. Inspired by the *Wright brothers, he built his own aeroplane in 1908–9, and was employed as an aircraft designer at the Royal Aircraft Factory, Farnborough, UK. During World War I he both designed and flew British military aircraft. He founded his own De Havilland Aircraft Company in 1920 and had great success with the lightweight Moth and the Tiger Moth trainer aircraft. In the 1930s he turned his attention to airliners. In World War II his outstanding design was the Mosquito, the most versatile aeroplane of its time. Later, he built the Comet (1952), the first jet-propelled airliner, and the Trident (1962).

dehumidifier, a device for reducing the moisture content of the air in living spaces. A fan draws damp air through the dehumidifier, passing it over a surface cooled by water or a refrigerant. This causes the water vapour in the air to condense. Dehumidifiers are frequently incorporated into *air-conditioning units.

delta-wing, term describing a triangular, swept-back aeroplane wing shape. Delta-wings have a low aspect ratio (see *flight, principles of), and are used on aircraft designed for supersonic flight. Examples include the Saab Viggen fighter-bomber (1967), and the Concorde airliner (1976).

demodulator circuit (detector), a circuit used in radio reception which extracts a low-frequency audio signal (speech or music) from the higher carrier signal upon which the audio signal has been modulated (see *radio). A basic demodulator for amplitude modulation employs a *diode, a *capacitor, and a *resistor.

demolition, the dismantling of a structure. In modern constructions, high stresses occur in some structural members, and the careless demolition of *pre-stressed concrete floors can lead to a sudden, explosive release of stress. Individual *pre-cast concrete components often need support by a crane while connections are cut prior to lowering. For isolated structures, rapid collapse is acceptable, and explosives can be positioned to break key connections between structural members. *Masonry can be demolished by hand (using mattocks, picks, or sledge-hammers) or, where possible, by crane and demolition ball. Demolishing some types of building, such as petrol storage tanks, involves special techniques. Furthermore, safe and effective methods for dealing with structures and materials contaminated with radioactivity are needed in decommissioning *nuclear reactors.

dental drill, an instrument used to remove areas of tooth erosion. The drilled hole is filled using gold, dental *amalgam (a mercury alloy), or a modern plastic. Early drills were clockwork, but in 1875 George Green invented an electric drill in the USA. Modern drills, which came into general use in the 1970s, are mostly powered by compressed-air turbines and have air bearings. They rotate at about 800,000 revolutions per minute. Currently, laser drills are being developed.

dentistry, the prevention, diagnosis, and treatment of diseases and conditions that affect any of the tissues of the mouth. The term especially denotes the repair and extraction of teeth, and the insertion of dentures, usually removable artificial replacements for teeth lost through decay, disease, or accident. Etruscan documents dating from around the 4th century BC show attempts to replace lost teeth by wiring human teeth to those remaining in the mouth; toothbrushes and dry, abrasive tooth powders in many forms have been familiar since early times. Frayed twigs were used as toothbrushes in Ancient China; the Greek physician Hippocrates recommended using a small ball of wool and honey (*c.*355 BC). Some of the first small brushes for cleaning the teeth appeared in Paris in about 1649. Until the late 19th century, however, dentistry consisted almost solely of painful extractions and occasional attempts to replace missing teeth with ill-fitting, carved dentures. The discovery of *anaesthesia, and the development of methods for taking impressions of the mouth facilitated treatment, while the invention of the *dental drill made it possible to remove areas of decay from teeth and then fill the cavity.

Modern dentistry emphasizes the need to help prevent tooth and gum diseases by good diet and oral hygiene. Fluoridated toothpastes and fluoride added to drinking water have contributed to a marked reduction in dental decay (caries) among nations in the West since the early 1980s. New technologies and materials have also led to improved treatments. Tooth-coloured plastics, which can be glued in place in the mouth, require less tooth to be drilled than do older kinds of filling. Missing teeth can be replaced in several ways. Removable dentures have a plastic or metal base carrying artificial teeth; the dentures are supported on the gums or on the remaining teeth. A fixed bridge is a permanent fitting in which some or all of the teeth are first ground to shape, then crowns are made to fit over them. Alternatively, metal implants to support dentures can be surgically placed into the jawbone where teeth are missing.

Orthodontics is the branch of dentistry involved with changing the position or angle of the teeth to improve their function or appearance. Tooth movements are achieved very slowly, over a period of months, either by the use of removable 'braces' made of wire and plastic, or more reliably and accurately by tiny brackets, glued to individual teeth. *Surgery plays a part in many aspects of dentistry, including extraction of teeth and roots, alteration of bone or gum to aid denture comfort or reduce gum disease, drainage of abscesses, removal of growths and tumours, and placement of implants. The pain and fear long associated with dental treatment have been reduced with the use of modern anaesthetic techniques. Important new developments in dental research include the use of *lasers to remove decay painlessly without an anaesthetic, and the possibility of substituting electric currents for local anaesthetics.

deoxyribonucleic acid *DNA.

depth-charge, a bomb capable of exploding under water, especially for use against submerged *submarines. It was designed during World War I, consisting of a canister filled with explosive and fitted with a pressure-sensitive device designed to detonate the charge at a pre-selected depth. The depth-charge was dropped over the stern of an anti-submarine escort or fired a short distance abeam (to one side) by a *mortar. During World War II, a forward-firing mortar was developed so that a submarine could be held in a *sonar beam throughout the attack. Later, depth-charges were adapted so that they could be dropped from aircraft. Modern depth-charges include devices carrying a nuclear explosive.

derailleur gear *bicycle gear.

desalination, the removal of salt, usually from sea-water or brackish water. Desalination is expensive, and is usually adopted only where other sources of drinkable water are inadequate, for example in some countries in the Middle East. Multi-stage flash distillation (MSF) is commonly used for desalting sea-water (about 3.5 per cent salt). The water is heated under pressure and fed into a container. The pressure is then reduced, causing the water to boil, and the resulting steam is condensed. Brackish waters (up to 0.5 per cent salt) can be treated by reverse osmosis, in which the water, after filtering, is forced through a semi-permeable membrane that does not allow the passage of salt. In electrodialysis, salts in brackish water are separated by attracting them through membranes to electrodes.

desk-top publishing (DTP), the production of printed matter with a desk-top computer and printer. The term desk-top publishing is a comparatively new development in printing and publishing and owes its origins to *word processing and the microcomputer. The purpose of a desk-top system is to originate, create, manipulate, and publish documents (for example, reports, newsletters, journals, and books). As the name implies, it is designed to produce the work on the desk-top, or environment with limited space. The basic items of equipment in a desk-top system are a *microcomputer with disk drive, a 'monitor' or *visual display unit (VDU), a keyboard with appropriate instructions for operator control of the system, and a print-out device, usually a *laser printer. In addition to these, there are a number of ancillary or 'peripheral' items of equipment available to expand the basic system. A DTP system depends on *software packages first marketed in the mid-1980s, and it can combine text in a variety of typefaces and formats with line artwork, continuous tone illustrations, and photographs, and display it all on the monitor as it will appear when printed. Layouts can be changed on screen, and artwork sized and manipulated as required. Colour reproduction is possible with the appropriate equipment.

destroyer, a light, fast *warship, smaller than a cruiser, the first being built in the UK in 1893. Destroyers were initially developed to counter the threat of the new *torpedo-boats. Their success was immediate, and the role of the torpedo-boat was taken over by the destroyer. During World War I destroyers were armed with *depth-charges and used as anti-submarine vessels, to protect convoys of merchant shipping, and as *mine-layers. The introduction of *sonar in the 1920s improved the destroyer's anti-submarine capability. In World War II, anti-aircraft weaponry became an important part of the destroyer's armament; smaller, slower *sloops, *corvettes, and destroyer escorts took over many of the destroyer's convoy escort duties. Modern destroyers are much larger than their predecessors (up to 8,000 tonnes), with sophisticated electronic equipment to detect and identify targets, and to compute firing data. Their weaponry consists mainly of *missiles, and many vessels carry helicopters. Modern destroyers are usually optimized for anti-aircraft work, *frigates taking over their anti-submarine role.

detergent, the active cleaning ingredient in *washing powders, *soaps, and some other cleaning materials. One end of the detergent molecule is hydrophilic (water-soluble), the other is hydrophobic (soluble in organic solvents). Grease, which is insoluble in water, is rendered soluble by the deter-

Detergent

Structure of detergent molecule

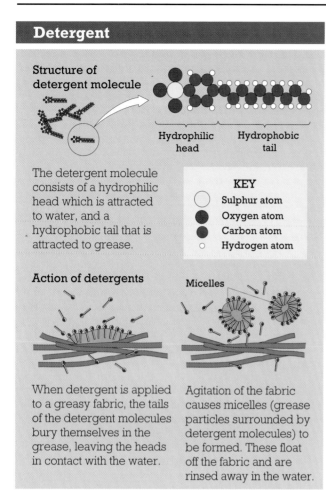

Hydrophilic head

Hydrophobic tail

The detergent molecule consists of a hydrophilic head which is attracted to water, and a hydrophobic tail that is attracted to grease.

KEY

- Sulphur atom
- Oxygen atom
- Carbon atom
- Hydrogen atom

Action of detergents

Micelles

When detergent is applied to a greasy fabric, the tails of the detergent molecules bury themselves in the grease, leaving the heads in contact with the water.

Agitation of the fabric causes micelles (grease particles surrounded by detergent molecules) to be formed. These float off the fabric and are rinsed away in the water.

gent because the hydrophobic parts of detergent molecules bury themselves in the grease particle and thereby cover its surface with hydrophilic groups (see figure), which are soluble in water. Provided the grease particle is not too large, it will be held in solution as if dissolved. Agitating the washing water breaks down the grease particles to a size that can be held in solution. There are two common types of detergent: *soaps, which are manufactured from animal fats or vegetable oils; and soapless (synthetic) detergents, which are *petrochemicals. The production of synthetic detergent involves several stages, each requiring a catalyst. Many synthetic detergents are sodium salts of sulphonic acids, and the principal advantage that they have over soaps is that their cleaning power is not affected by hard water. The first synthetic detergents were not biodegradable; this caused rivers and water-treatment plants to become covered and clogged with an unsightly foam that starved the water of oxygen. Modifications to the hydrophobic part of the molecule have resulted in materials that are biodegradable.

detonator, a small explosive charge that triggers a larger explosion or ignites the propellant charge in a *firearm; or an electric *fuse that creates a detonation. The use of mercury fulminate as a detonator was pioneered by *Nobel and patented by him in 1864. It was mixed with potassium chlorate and antimony sulphate, a combination producing very hot gases that cause inert explosives to detonate. Lead azide has now largely replaced mercury fulminate. Electric fuses are attached by wire to a small hand-operated generator. The generator makes the current overload the capacity of the fuse, which melts to ignite the explosives.

Developing and printing

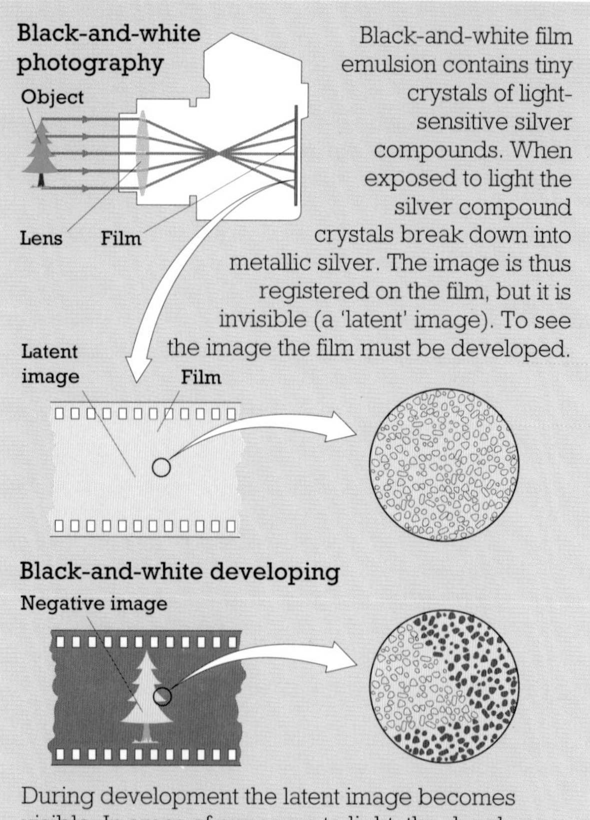

Black-and-white film emulsion contains tiny crystals of light-sensitive silver compounds. When exposed to light the silver compound crystals break down into metallic silver. The image is thus registered on the film, but it is invisible (a 'latent' image). To see the image the film must be developed.

During development the latent image becomes visible. In areas of exposure to light, the developer completes the silver compound breakdown to silver, which appears black on the film.

Fixing

Once rinsed in water, the film, now known as a negative, is placed in fixer to dissolve away unexposed areas of silver compound.

Black-and-white printing

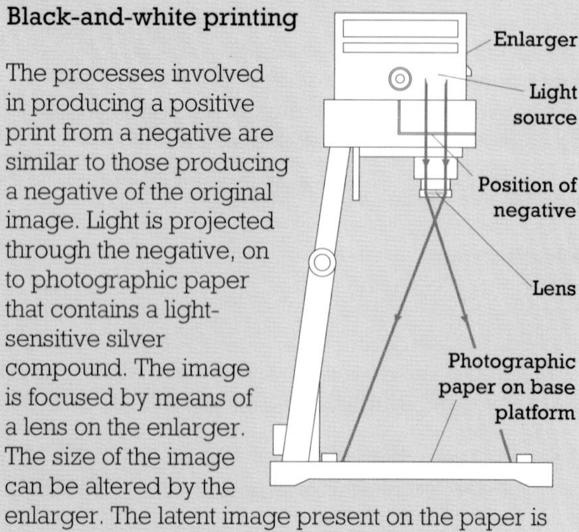

The processes involved in producing a positive print from a negative are similar to those producing a negative of the original image. Light is projected through the negative, on to photographic paper that contains a light-sensitive silver compound. The image is focused by means of a lens on the enlarger. The size of the image can be altered by the enlarger. The latent image present on the paper is then made visible by developing, and excess silver compound is removed by washing and fixing.

deuterium *heavy water.

developing and printing (photography), the processes of converting a latent (invisible) image on photographic *film or paper into a visible form and then producing a photographic image. When light falls on to photographic film, atoms of silver are formed in some of the silver halide crystals present in the emulsion. These chemical changes cannot be seen by the naked eye: a latent image is formed on the film. During developing, a chemical agent (the developer) converts the silver halide crystals that have been exposed to light into metallic silver (see figure). Unexposed silver salts are then washed away in the fixing and washing stages following developing, leaving visible grains of metallic silver where light fell on the film. The silver grains appear black, and thus form a negative image on the film. If light is then shone through the negative on to photographic paper, a 'negative' latent image is formed on the paper, which, when developed, gives a positive photographic print. Exposure to light can be made either with the negative in physical contact with the paper (contact printing), or by projecting an image of the negative on to the paper to produce an enlarged image (projection printing). The projection is carried out using an apparatus known as an enlarger. With an enlarger, the negative is illuminated by a light source and its image is focused by a lens on to a baseboard on which the photographic paper is placed. The exact degree of enlargement is determined by adjusting the distance between the lens and the paper—the greater the distance, the larger the image. Colour photographic materials are composed of three separate emulsion layers, sensitive to red, green, and blue light respectively. During developing, coloured dyes are formed, as well as metallic silver, wherever exposure has occurred. The blue-sensitive layer becomes yellow, the green-sensitive layer becomes magenta, and the red becomes cyan. After developing, the silver is chemically removed, leaving a coloured image formed by the mixing of the coloured dyes. When a colour negative is printed on colour photographic paper, the sequence is repeated, and dyes are formed in the emulsion layers of the paper. However, the colours are now the complements of those on the negative, and so the result is a positive photograph. With colour-reversal film, designed to give positive transparencies, there is no intermediate negative stage: the film undergoes an additional processing stage to produce a direct positive image.

dhow, a trading vessel of the Indian Ocean, Red Sea, and the Gulf, often used to carry merchandise between East Africa and the Arabian countries. There are many different types of dhow. Originally they were *lateen rigged, with up to three masts, and required a large crew to handle the yards. Modern dhows are often powered by diesel engines, though the wooden hulls still retain the traditional shape and character, being up to 200 tonnes in displacement, with a high stern and a beaked bow.

dialysis, the process in which a semi-permeable membrane (made of *Cellophane, for example) is used to separate particles of *colloidal size (10^{-9} to 10^{-6} m) from a solvent and from smaller molecules and ions dissolved in the solvent. The tiny holes in the membrane are too small to allow passage of the colloidal particles. In *haemodialysis, dialysis membranes are used to remove impurities from the bloodstream of patients suffering from kidney failure, while retaining proteins and blood cells.

diamond, a transparent gemstone, made of pure, crystalline carbon, the hardest natural substance. Diamonds are mined in South Africa, India, Brazil, and Australia. Only about 25 per cent of diamonds are suitable for gemstones: the rest are used as abrasives and drilling bits in industrial applications. Diamonds of industrial quality can also be made synthetically, by subjecting graphite to extremely high temperatures and pressures. In the late 1970s, B. V. Deryaguin and co-workers in the Soviet Union pioneered the growth of thin sheets of polycrystalline diamond using *vapour deposition techniques. Such films have applications as *semiconductors and as very hard coatings.

diaphragm (photography) *aperture.

diathermy, the technique of heating parts of the body using high-frequency alternating electric current applied by electrodes. Therapeutic diathermy is used in the treatment of rheumatism and arthritis. In surgical diathermy, one electrode takes the form of a conducting knife or snare, while the current has a coagulating effect and prevents bleeding from small blood vessels.

diazo printing (dye-line printing), a form of *photocopying developed in the 1920s, in which an image is reproduced on a positive printing paper (producing a positive rather than a negative image) impregnated with light-sensitive diazo dye, which dyes the paper fibres. For the process to

A **dhow** under construction in Bahrain, in the Gulf.

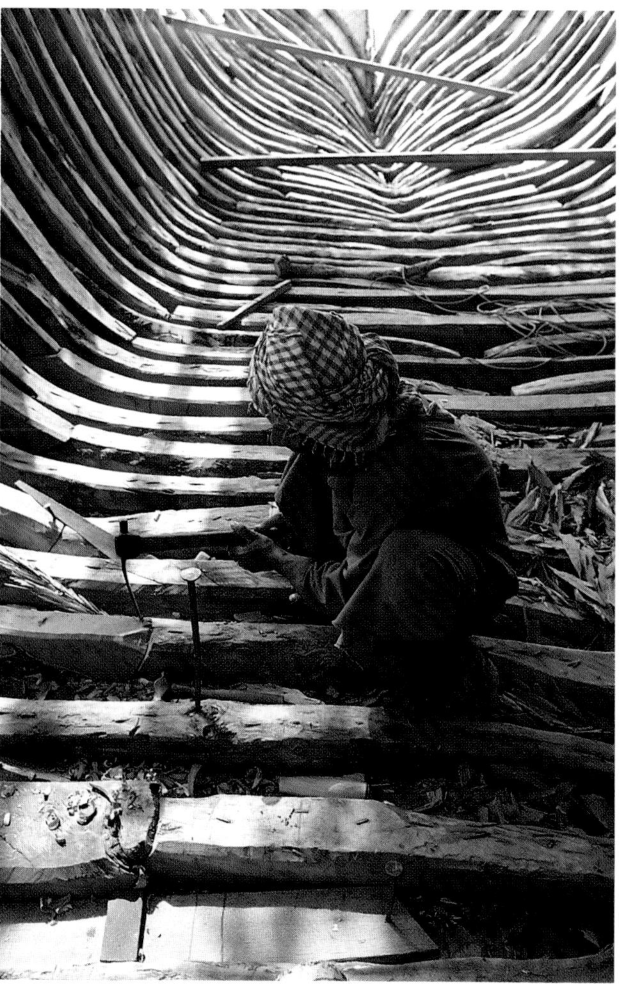

work, the image must be printed on a transparent or translucent base. Light (often ultraviolet) is shone through the original on to the printing paper. In those areas where there is no image the light passes through the translucent base, and the dye salts are broken down, leaving dye only in the image areas. The paper is then passed through an ammonia solution, which develops the dye in the image areas. A major use of diazo printing is for copying architectural drawings and blueprints.

Diderot, Denis (1713–84), French encylopedist and philosopher. He worked initially as a teacher and writer, but his criticisms of the French political and administrative systems led to a short prison sentence (1749). In 1745 Diderot began work, in association with the scientist Jean Le Rond d'Alembert, on what was originally conceived of as a translation of Ephraim Chambers's *Cyclopaedia* (1728). The project grew, however, into the great *Encyclopédie, ou Dictionnaire raisonné des sciences, des arts et des métiers* (1751–72), a lavishly illustrated review, in the broadest sense, of the science and technology of that period.

die *wire-drawing, *extrusion, *die casting, *forging.

die casting, a precision process in which metal objects are formed by injecting molten metal under pressure into a metal mould (die). Products range from tiny parts for sewing-machines to aluminium engine-block castings. Unlike *investment casting, the metal mould is designed to be reused many thousands of times. It can be split open, the casting removed, and then reassembled. Injection *moulding is a similar process for producing plastic components.

dielectric *capacitor.

Diesel, Rudolf (Christian Karl) (1858–1913), German pioneer of the high-compression *diesel engine, named after him. After studying thermodynamics in Munich, he went to Paris in 1880 to manage von *Linde's refrigeration plant. Here he began to explore the possibility of using *ammonia as the fluid medium in an expansion engine, but when this proved unsuccessful he turned his attention to the development of a new type of oil-fuelled internal-combustion engine, in which ignition was produced not by a spark but by the heat generated by compression of the fuel in the cylinder. Diesel applied for a patent in 1892 and over the next six years he developed his engine. When the prototype was exhibited in 1897, it attracted world-wide interest, and a new factory to manufacture the engine was established in Augsburg. The relatively low power-to-weight ratio of the engine at first limited its use to applications where weight was not an overriding consideration, as in submarines and ships.

An illustration from the *Encyclopédie* (1751–80), edited by Denis **Diderot**, showing stages in the manufacture of glass.

diesel engine, a type of *internal-combustion engine in which ignition of the mixture of fuel and air is achieved by compressing the air to a high temperature before adding the fuel. Hence the term 'compression ignition' is used to distinguish it from the spark-ignition engine. Diesel engines run on lower grade *diesel oil rather than petrol, and have the highest thermal *efficiency of any form of heat-engine. For this reason they are almost universally used in marine applications, railway locomotives, many stationary purposes, commercial road vehicles, taxis and, increasingly, for private motor cars. Although patented by *Diesel in 1892, engines working on essentially the same principle were produced by the Priestman brothers in the UK in 1885 and improved by the British engineer Herbert Ackroyd Stuart. A distinction is made between direct-injection engines, in which fuel-oil is sprayed directly into the cylinder, and indirect-injection engines, in which the fuel is injected into a separate combustion chamber, connected to the cylinder by a passage. The former type is gaining ground due to its lower heat loss and hence greater efficiency, despite its greater liability to *knock. Because diesel engines use higher pressures than petrol engines they must be made stronger and therefore heavier. To overcome this disadvantage many diesel engines are fitted with a turbo-charger, a form of *supercharger.

diesel locomotive, a locomotive powered by a *diesel engine. Attempts were made to use internal-combustion engines for locomotives in the 1920s and 1930s, but it proved difficult to find a transmission system that would enable the locomotive to start a heavy train. To overcome this problem many ingenious ideas were tried, including the combination of steam and diesel engines. During and after World War II hydraulic and electrical transmissions were developed that overcame the starting problem. In the diesel–electric locomotive, the engine drives a direct-current generator, which supplies traction motors to drive the wheels through a gear train. These traction motors can produce a very high torque (rotary power) output for starting, then speed up for normal running. More recently the somewhat troublesome generator has been replaced by the more reliable alternator, coupled with a solid-state rectifier. Before these alternator developments, diesel–hydraulic locomotives using a hydrodynamic transmission were an attractive alternative to the heavier diesel–electric locomotives. The engine and alternator of a diesel–electric locomotive are mounted on a main frame, along with the driving cabs and other auxiliary equipment. The traction motors are usually mounted in power *bogies, which carry the main frame. In addition to traction current, the locomotive also supplies considerable electrical power to the train for heating, air-conditioning, and so on. Diesel–electric locomotives are used widely for freight and passenger services. Locomotives with a mechanical hydraulic transmission are used for light rail-bus and shunting operations.

diesel oil, a fairly heavy *petroleum fraction, used as a fuel in *diesel engines. Diesel oil is predominantly a mixture of straight-chain *hydrocarbons containing between twelve and sixteen carbon atoms, characterized by its tendency to ignite spontaneously under pressure. It boils at temperatures between 200 and 360 °C. Grades of diesel oil are rated by their cetane number, a measure which compares their readiness to ignite with that of cetane (hexadecane), a sixteen-carbon alkane. For use in cars and lorries, diesel oil has a cetane rating of 40–50 per cent cetane.

differential gear, the mechanism which allows the driven wheels on either side of a vehicle to rotate at different speeds when cornering. The differential is housed within the final drive, which achieves the final transmission of power from engine to road wheels. The form of the differential is shown in the figure. In straight-line driving the small bevels do not rotate on their shaft, but drive both road wheels equally. When cornering, the outer wheel and its bevel rotate more quickly than the inner ones, so the small bevels rotate on their shaft, but each road wheel is still driven with an equal *torque. In slippery conditions, if one wheel skids the driving torque to both wheels is lost; some vehicles use a limited-slip differential to combat this. *Tractors use a differential lock or an independent brake on each wheel for the same purpose.

diffraction grating, a plate with a large number of closely spaced parallel slits or grooves used to produce and analyse spectra. Gratings are used in *spectroscopy, and can be made for use with ultraviolet and infra-red radiation as well as visible light. A typical grating has about 600 lines per mm (15,400 lines per inch).

digging tools, tools such as the pick, shovel, spade, and fork, used to break up soil or excavate a hole. Digging tools are used to cultivate the soil; to level ground for building; to construct irrigation and drainage canals; to build earthworks; and so on. Before mechanical excavators were introduced, the two main digging tools were the pick and shovel, the soil being carried away in baskets or wheelbarrows. In many parts of the world this is still current practice. The earliest picks were made from antler horns, but, as with other tools, bronze, iron, and steel were adopted as each became available. The modern pick is normally double-headed, one head being pointed and the other chisel-shaped. The spade differs from the shovel in having a cutting edge, so that it can be forced into the ground with pressure from the foot. It is sometimes straight-shafted and normally has a handle so that it can be grasped firmly. There is a large variety in the shape of the blade, according to the tool's intended use and, to some extent, regional custom. To break up the ground before planting, a fork with three or four prongs may be used. (See *agricultural machinery for illustration.)

digital audio tape (DAT), a sound recording system, developed in Japan, in which audio signals are recorded digitally (see *digitization) on to a small cassette tape to give recordings of comparable quality to those of a *compact disc. DAT recorders have a rapidly rotating recording head similar to that in a *video recorder, which records the audio signal in narrow oblique bands across the tape. DATs were first marketed in Western countries in 1990. Several other digital cassette systems are being developed in competition with DAT.

digital computer *computer.

Differential

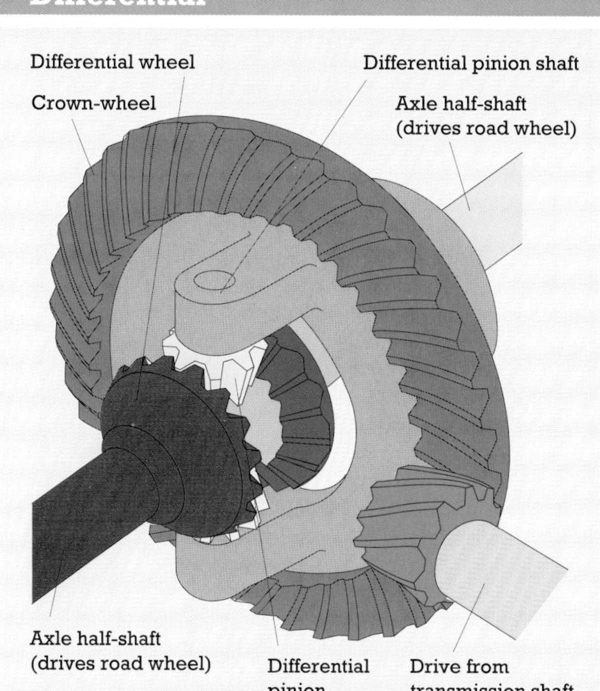

When driving straight ahead, the crown-wheel rotates, driven by the transmission shaft, and the differential pinion shafts go around with it. However, the differential pinions do not rotate on their own axes because all the wheels are travelling at the same speed.

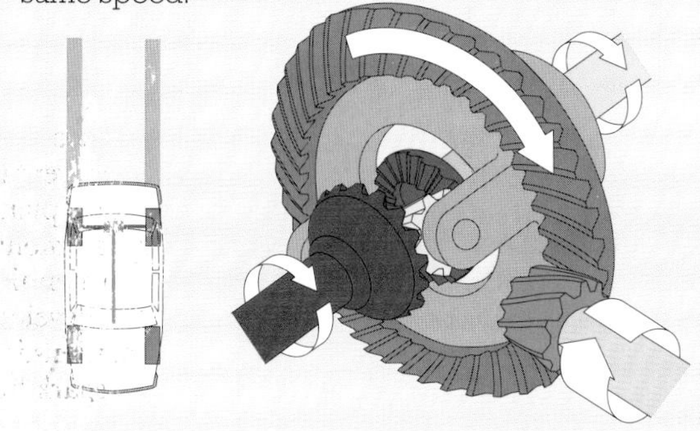

When the car corners, the outer wheels travel further than the inner wheels and must therefore rotate faster. The differential pinions rotate in order to allow this.

KEY

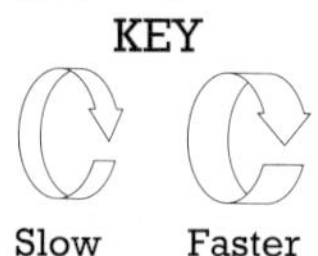

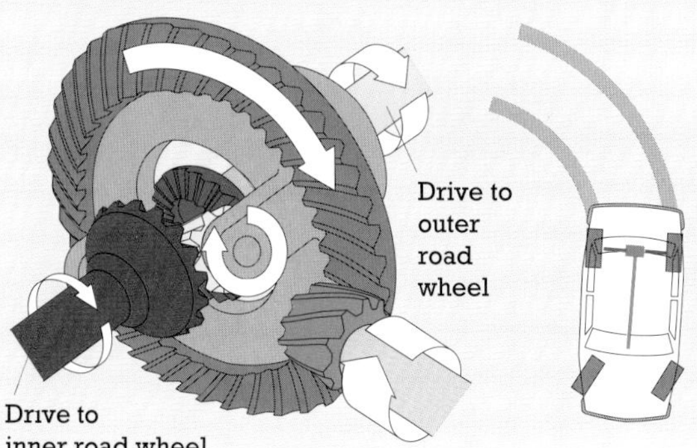

digital proofing, the technique of producing a preview 'soft proof' of a printed image by means of computer-controlled technology combined with a *digitized imaging system. In video imaging, the various elements (text, line illustrations, and photographs) are digitally analysed and displayed on a monitor. Control devices may be included to adjust variables such as colour balance, proportions, size, and definition. These soft proofs are useful for composition and any initial decision-making, but need to be translated into 'hard' proofs. To achieve this, the digitized information stored by the computer is used to produce a coloured facsimile image of the work. (See also *graphic image manipulation.)

digital-to-analog converter *signal processing.

digitization, the production of information recorded as a succession of discrete units, rather than as continuously varying (analog) parameters. Digital systems most often record information in binary code, using only two states: one and zero. Information such as a message or numerical data can be transmitted from a keyboard by coding the alphabet and other symbols digitally. A sound may also be recorded (*magnetic tape or *compact disc) or transmitted in digital form. The electrical signal, into which the sound is converted by a *microphone, is analog in form since the voltage is changing continuously with time, but if the signal is sampled at intervals, then each sample voltage can be coded as a binary number. For example, a 6-V signal would become 0110, or zero, pulse, pulse, zero. By frequent sampling the whole analog signal can be represented in a digital form. (See also *telephony.)

dike *coastal defences.

dinghy, a small open rowing-boat pulled by one pair of oars, used as a general work-boat; or a small rowing boat, sailing boat, or motor boat carried by larger ships such as *yachts. Some dinghies are of inflatable rubber. As pleasure-boating spread after World War I, racing dinghies multiplied and in the UK alone there are now more than 300 active classes of dinghy.

diode, a two-terminal electronic device that provides simple rectification: it conducts electricity in one direction but not the other. Diodes can be made either as *thermionic valves or, more commonly, as solid-state *semiconductor devices. They are used in rectifier circuits to generate direct-current signals from alternating current, and to protect circuits from power-supply overload or other misconnection. *Light-emitting diodies have several applications. Diodes also form an important part of the *demodulator circuits of radio and television receivers. (See *semiconductor devices for illustration.)

dioxin (2,3,7,8-tetrachlorodibenzo-*p*-dioxin), a poisonous compound produced as a by-product of the manufacture of certain insecticides and *defoliants. It was the active pollutant at *Seveso. Dioxin resists washing out by water or organic solvents but is taken up by fatty tissue in the body. It is known to cause chronic skin diseases, muscular dysfunction, cancers, birth defects, genetic mutations, and disorders of the nervous system. Small quantities of dioxin found in *bleached paper products have caused public concern, and there has been a move towards the use of paper products made using non-chlorine bleaches.

dip-circle, an instrument used in physics and for *navigation to measure the inclination of the Earth's magnetic field to the Earth's surface. It consists of a magnetic needle pivoted on a horizontal axis and moving over a graduated scale. It can be used to obtain accurate measurements of magnetic dip and thus complements the magnetic *compass, which measures the direction of the horizontal component of the field.

dipole, a pair of equal and opposite electrical charges or magnetic poles existing very close together. Some molecules exhibit dipole action. The water molecule (H_2O) is dipolar, with a slight positive charge on the hydrogens, and a slight negative charge on the oxygen. A dipole is also a simple, non-directional type of *antenna that is split into two equal halves, each half being the same length as one-quarter of a wavelength of the radiation being used.

direct current (d.c.) *circuits, electrical and electronic.

dishwasher, a domestic appliance for the automatic cleaning of crockery and cooking utensils. Simple dishwashers of the late 1920s consisted of racks or baskets which were filled with dirty dishes and utensils, and then immersed in a strong flow of hot water in a specially adapted sink. A modern electric dishwasher has a watertight front-loading door and contains plastic-coated wire racks to hold the crockery. A motor-driven pump sprays jets of hot water containing a caustic detergent to loosen and dissolve the grease. The appliance then rinses the crockery and dries it. The cycle is operated automatically under the control of an *electromechanical timer or a *microprocessor.

disinfectant *antisepsis.

disk (computing) *floppy disk, *hard disk.

distaff *spinning.

distillation, a purification or separation process of great antiquity, in which a liquid is boiled in a vessel that is connected to a cooled tube. The drop in temperature in the tube causes the liquid vapour to condense into a receptacle at the end of the tube. This is a useful way of purifying a liquid, because solids dissolved in it do not evaporate and are not present in the distillate. Mixtures of liquids of different boiling-points can be separated from each other by *fractional distillation. The process can be carried out in the laboratory or on an industrial scale. Other forms of distillation include *steam distillation and *vacuum distillation.

distributor *ignition system.

district heating, a system in which space and water heating are supplied to a number of buildings from a single fuel-burning plant. Often the plant has some other primary function, such as electricity generation or municipal refuse incineration. Heat that would otherwise be wasted is transferred to the points of use by water circulating in well-insulated pipes. At the user end, a *central heating system distributes the heat within the building. In Iceland and New Zealand, *geothermal energy sources (from the earth) are utilized in such systems.

diuretic, a drug that increases the flow of urine by promoting loss of sodium and water from the kidneys. In heart failure, oedema (the accumulation of fluid under the skin) may occur; diuretics such as frusemide reduce fluid retention so that the oedema disappears. Diuretics can occasionally cause excessive potassium loss and so potassium is often given in conjunction with them.

diving-bell, a container, open at the bottom, used to carry divers and their tools to their work on the bottom of the sea or river. Early bells relied on the air they contained at submersion; later ones were supplied with air pumped into the bell from the surface. The idea of a diving-bell is mentioned by the Greek philosopher Aristotle in the 4th century BC. Primitive bells were used with great success from the 17th century. The addition of a compressed-air pump by *Smeaton greatly improved the design, and it has been widely used since then for underwater construction and maintenance. A drawback of the diving-bell is the limited working area that it provides. (See also *deep-sea and diving technology.)

diving suit *deep-sea and diving technology.

DNA (deoxyribonucleic acid), the genetic material of most organisms, reproducing exact copies of itself and passing them from parent to offspring. DNA directs and regulates protein synthesis and thus provides a blueprint for the development of the whole organism. Since the discovery of the structure of DNA by James Watson and Francis Crick in 1953 in Cambridge, UK, the study of genetics has largely concerned itself with DNA behaviour. DNA is a double-stranded, ladder-like molecule twisted into a double helix. It is a giant *polymer, consisting of tens of thousands of sub-units, and measuring up to several millimetres in length. In most organisms, DNA is organized into chromosomes. Chromosome number, size, and DNA composition varies between species. The modern concept of the gene is as a length of DNA that codes for a *protein molecule such as an *enzyme. Sets of the three nucleotides (the base-sugar-phosphate units from which DNA is made) act as codons, each codon corresponding to an amino acid. In the biosynthesis of proteins the DNA 'message' is first 'transcribed' into a molecule of messenger ribonucleic acid (mRNA), which has a similar structure to DNA but is smaller and single-stranded. The mRNA then travels out of the nucleus to the ribosomes, the site of protein synthesis, where it is used as a template on which to build the precise amino-acid sequence of a particular protein. RNA is the genetic material of some viruses.

DNA fingerprinting (genetic fingerprinting), the analysis of genetic information from a blood sample or other small piece of human material as an aid to the identification of a person. The method was first proposed in 1984 by Alec Jeffreys of Leicester University, UK. Each individual has a unique complement of DNA: only identical twins have the same DNA. Jeffreys found that a particular section of *DNA is highly repetitive and varies greatly between unrelated individuals. In DNA fingerprinting, DNA is extracted from a sample of body fluid or tissue, and broken into fragments by *enzymes known as restriction endonucleases, which cut the DNA strand at specific points. The length, number, and variety of fragments formed are unique to each individual. To this mixture of DNA fragments is added a gene probe, a radioactive 'marker' molecule that attaches to a specific gene. The fragments then undergo electrophoresis (see *chromotography) which separates them into bands of different molecular weight, and the resulting band pattern is exposed to X-ray film. Any fragment carrying the gene probe appears as a dark band on the film. Humans usually have two copies of each gene, so if the gene is present, two bands appear. The process is generally repeated four times, using four different gene probes, to generate a multilocus genotype carrying eight bands. The chances of two unrelated individuals having the same multilocus genotype range from hundreds of thousands to several million to one. In paternity cases, prints from the putative father and the child are compared. Closely related individuals will have similar patterns, while those of unrelated individuals will differ greatly. The technique is also widely used in immigration disputes to establish the relationship between two people. It has been used forensically to identify people from a blood or semen sample, although there are doubts about the reliability of forensic evidence based solely on the technique.

dock, the area of water fully enclosed by piers and wharves in *ports and habours. In the USA the word refers only to the wharves and piers and not to the water enclosed. *Dry docks and floating docks are enclosed areas from which the water can be removed for shipbuilding and repair work.

Dolby system, an electronic circuit that reduces the background hissing noise present during replay of *magnetic tapes, developed by Ray Dolby in 1966. The noise arises because of the granular nature of the magnetic coating and is worse at slow tape speeds and with narrow tapes, typical of cassettes. The original recording must have been made with Dolby for the system to be effective in play-back.

Domagk, Gerhard (1895–1964), German pioneer of *chemotherapy and discoverer of the *sulphonamide drugs. Until the 1920s, the possibility of treating diseases caused by micro-organisms seemed remote. In 1927, while he was working for I. G. Farbenindustrie, Domagk was charged with seeking out, from among the hundreds of different chemicals available within the great industrial complex, substances capable of overcoming serious bacterial infections. In 1932 he discovered that Prontosil Red, used to dye leather, controlled streptococcal infections in mice. (Subsequently, J. Trefousel in Paris demonstrated that only part of the molecule, a sulphonamide, was biologically active.) His discovery, unrivalled until the advent of *penicillin in the 1940s, made it possible to treat a wide range of dangerous infections. Domagk was awarded the Nobel Prize for Physiology and Medicine in 1939.

Donkin, Bryan (1768–1855), versatile British mechanic remembered particularly for his contributions to *paper manufacture, *printing, and *food preservation. Between the years 1803–51 he built nearly 200 paper-making machines of steadily improved design, based on the patent of the brothers Henry and Sealy Fourdrinier. In 1813 he turned to printing, building a rotary press with inking rollers, which were soon widely adopted. He set up a factory for preserved foods in 1812 using a heat-sterilization process invented by *Appert.

doping *semiconductor device.

Doppler effect, the effect on sound *waves and *electromagnetic radiation of relative motion between the observer and the source of the waves. The Doppler shift is the change in the frequency of the waves resulting from the Doppler effect. If the source and receiver are approaching each other, the wave frequency measured by the receiver will be greater (and the wavelength less) than if they are stationary in relation to each other. If they are moving apart, the frequency measured will be lower. Thus, the whistle of a train sounds lower as it recedes. Doppler *radar and *sonar are used to differentiate between fixed and moving targets by observing the Doppler shift. Measuring this frequency shift accurately determines the velocity of moving targets. Other applications of this effect include use in astronomy and in *radio aids to navigation.

dosimeter, a device used to measure nuclear radiation for safety purposes. The dosimeter usually consists of a small piece of photographic film worn as a sealed badge. Any nuclear radiation present exposes the film through the sealing, with the amount of exposure being related to the radiation dose. This can be revealed by later photographic development.

double-glazing, a system in which two panes of glass separated by an air gap are fixed into a window or door. Single panes of glass have a low surface temperature owing to their heat transmittance; thus in winter, condensation on the inside is very common. Two panes provide improved thermal insulation and a higher surface temperature internally, reducing the likelihood of condensation and conserving energy. The space between the panes is usually sealed at the edges to prevent the entry and condensation of warm moist air. There is also some reduction in sound transmission.

drag-line, a machine used for large-scale excavation in *open-cast mining. A large bucket is positioned by means of a long boom and then dragged across the surface, scooping up earth as it moves. Once the bucket is full, it is raised and the boom traverses to deposit the load at the desired point. The first drag-lines were steam-powered, and were introduced in 1835. Today they are powered by large diesel engines. The largest drag-line *excavators weigh around 3,000 tonnes, with a bucket capacity of about 100 tonnes carried on a boom up to 80 m (260 feet) long.

drain, a pipe, usually underground, used to convey effluent and water from a building or paved area. The flow in the pipeline is preferably by gravity, but sometimes a pump may be used to raise the effluent. The pipeline should be watertight to prevent contamination by escaping effluent and to avoid influx of water from waterlogged ground. Fired clay and pre-cast concrete pipes are cheap and durable, but recently *PVC pipes have been widely adopted because of easy installation. Where high strengths are required—for example, where a pipeline passes under a building—cast-iron or spun-iron pipes may be used.

drainage *land drainage, *land reclamation, *sewage treatment and sewage, *storm-water drainage.

draught and pack animals, domesticated animals used to pull or carry heavy loads. Cattle and equine species are the commonest draught animals, but other animals such as camels, dogs, elephants, and reindeer are also used. Cattle are commonly *harnessed with a yoke, while a padded collar is used for horses. Draught animals were first used in the Near East (see *agriculture) in about 5000 BC. They are widely used for *road transport and in agriculture, although in Western countries motor vehicles have largely taken over these functions. Draught animals have also been used for pumping water, threshing grain, and pulling *canal barges. The most popular draught animal today is the water-buffalo, of which there are nearly 80 million in use world-wide. Draught animals offer advantages to small farmers in that they are for the most part cheap to feed, require little maintenance, reproduce, provide manure, and when they die can provide foodstuffs for other animals.

drawbridge, a bridge that can slide back along a track behind one of the abutments or has a pivoted surface that can be raised at one end. It is usually of low clearance height over a waterway and is moved to allow the passage of a boat. Drawbridges were used over the moat in ancient fortifications to bar entry when raised.

dreadnought *battleship.

dredger, a vessel used for deepening harbours and navigable rivers by removing part of the sea-bed or bottom of the river. An early steam-driven dredger was designed by *Trevithick in 1806 to clear the East India Dock in London. The commonest form is the bucket dredger, in which a continuous chain of buckets operating through a central well is emptied into barges secured alongside. Where the bottom to be dredged consists of soft mud or silt, a suction dredger is often used; this draws up the dredged material through a suction pipe. Occasionally cutters are needed to scrape the bottom. Small dredgers of up to 150 tonnes, which work on the *hovercraft principle, have been developed recently for use in shallow waters and in rivers and estuaries.

drift-mining, a *mining technique in which ore deposits are worked by means of downward-sloping tunnels driven from the surface. As drift-mining requires no vertical shafts,

A bucket **dredger** at work on the River Clyde near Glasgow, Scotland, UK. Alongside the dredger is a hopper vessel (*right*), into which dredged material is deposited.

Drilling and boring tools

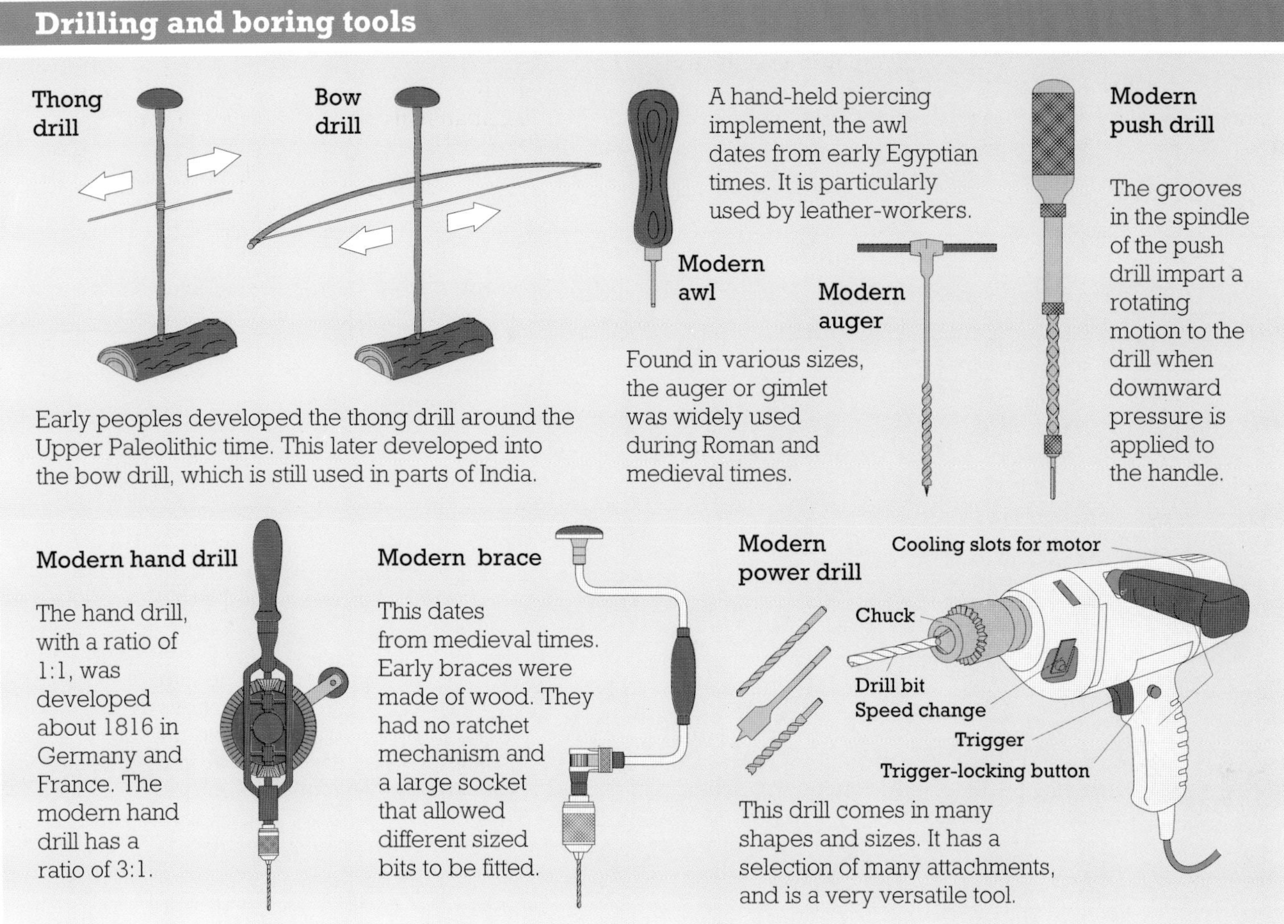

Thong drill
Bow drill
Early peoples developed the thong drill around the Upper Paleolithic time. This later developed into the bow drill, which is still used in parts of India.
A hand-held piercing implement, the awl dates from early Egyptian times. It is particularly used by leather-workers.
Modern awl
Modern auger
Found in various sizes, the auger or gimlet was widely used during Roman and medieval times.
Modern push drill
The grooves in the spindle of the push drill impart a rotating motion to the drill when downward pressure is applied to the handle.
Modern hand drill
The hand drill, with a ratio of 1:1, was developed about 1816 in Germany and France. The modern hand drill has a ratio of 3:1.
Modern brace
This dates from medieval times. Early braces were made of wood. They had no ratchet mechanism and a large socket that allowed different sized bits to be fitted.
Modern power drill
Cooling slots for motor
Chuck
Drill bit
Speed change
Trigger
Trigger-locking button
This drill comes in many shapes and sizes. It has a selection of many attachments, and is a very versatile tool.

it is much cheaper than deep mining. Drift-mining relies on an ore deposit running perpendicular to a vertical rock-face, which is worked by tunnelling directly into the deposit, shoring up the roof as necessary. This method was practised by miners in ancient times using hand tools, but in modern mines both the removal of material and the shoring up have been mechanized to the point where the machinery for the whole operation can be controlled by a single miner.

drilling and boring tools, hand tools used for making holes in materials such as wood, leather, and metal. The ability to pierce holes is a basic requirement when working materials. From earliest times, many tools have been devised for making holes. These include the hand-held awl (a piercing tool used particularly by leather-workers to make holes for sewing thread), and the auger, today known as the gimlet, which has a spoon-shaped cutter or cutting edges spirally arranged on an iron cylinder. Much more important than these, however, is the drill (see figure). This differs from the awl and auger in that it depends not on a direct piercing action but on continuous or intermittent rotation of a sharp drill bit. A drill consists of two parts: the stock, which provides the rotation, and the bit, which cuts the hole. The bit may be discarded when it becomes blunt, or sharpened for reuse. Various devices have been produced to achieve the necessary rotary action. One of the earliest, depicted in ancient Egyptian frescos (*c.*3100–2700 BC), was the bow-drill, in which the cord of a bow was wrapped round the circular stock of a drill, causing it to rotate as the bow was moved to and fro. In the pump-action drill, rotation was effected either by twisted cords or, in the Archimedean drill, by pushing a pierced guide up a spiral fluted stem. Both these devices provide rotation alternating in direction, and for maximum efficiency the bit must cut on both strokes. The cranked carpenter's brace of the Middle Ages achieved continuous rotary action in one direction. The familiar modern form of this drill, in which rotation is achieved by a crank handle driving two bevel wheels, dates from the early 18th century. The advent of reliable small electric motors has led, especially since World War II, to the widespread use of power-driven drills (see *power tools). Those with rechargeable batteries can be used at sites remote from mains supply.

drilling rig, an apparatus for well-sinking, used in particular in *petroleum exploration and recovery for drilling down into the earth or into the sea-bed in search of oil. A modern rig can drill through rock to a depth of up to 8,000 m (26,000 feet). A tower (the derrick) supports hoisting equipment used to raise and lower drill bits and pipes. Most rigs use rotary drilling, in which a rotating drill bit on the end of sections of pipe bears down on the material of the well bottom, thus gouging and chipping its way downward. The waste material from the drilling is carried up to the surface by a weighted fluid known as drilling mud. At the surface, the mud is filtered, then pumped down the pipe once again. Valves to prevent blow-outs at the surface shut down if high oil pressure is encountered, preventing damage to the rig and waste of oil. A wedge, known as a whipstock, can be used to turn the path of drilling away from the vertical. By this means, a number of differently angled holes may be drilled bending away from one vertical primary hole. Both land-based and offshore rigs use the same basic technology, although

PHB

because of high relocation costs, offshore drilling tends to use much more directional drilling. Offshore rigs are distinguished by the method of supporting the derrick and drilling equipment. Jack-up rigs actually stand on the sea-bed, whereas semi-submersibles float, and are anchored to the sea-bed by cables.

drug, an organic or inorganic medicinal substance that acts on living tissues to modify their function. Originally drugs were extracted from plants, but now most are synthesized. The manufacture, preparation, and dispensing of them is called *pharmaceutics. Official instructions about their preparation and the standard of purity required are published in a pharmacopoeia. The study of drugs is *pharmacology, which forms an important part of medical training, and includes the study of *hormones, which may be used in medicines.

dry-cleaning, a process introduced in Paris in the 1850s in which non-aqueous *solvents are used to remove greasy stains from clothing. These solvents dissolve the grease and, because they boil at low temperatures, they can then be easily reclaimed by evaporation followed by condensation. The solvent most commonly used is perchlorethene, but as this is toxic, it is being replaced by a *chloro-fluorocarbon (CFC). However, there is now some concern about this as CFCs are known to cause *ozone depletion.

dry dock, a watertight basin with one end open to the sea, used for shipbuilding and for the examination, repair, and cleaning of ships' hulls. The open end of the dock can be closed with a gate or caisson. With the caisson open the dock is flooded, and a ship can enter. The caisson is then closed, and the water in the dock is pumped out, exposing the hull for service or repair. Smaller vessels can be hauled up into the dock by means of slips or 'marine railways'.

A mobile variant of the dry dock is the floating dock. This is open at each end and floats on watertight tanks that can be flooded or pumped out as required. When the tanks are flooded the base of the dock is below water, and a ship can enter. The tanks are then pumped out, raising the dock until the ship's hull is exposed.

dry farming, the tillage system adopted in arid (less than 250 mm, 9.8 inches, of rain per year) and semi-arid (between 250 and 600 mm, 9.8–23.4 inches, of rain per year) conditions to allow crop cultivation without the use of irrigation. Vegetative cover loses water by transpiration, therefore no growth is allowed for one season in order to accumulate sufficient water for the subsequent season's crop. The bare soil, left uncultivated, dries out, but moisture below the surface is unable to reach the air, and is retained. To reduce water loss during ground preparation for the crop, tillage is kept to a minimum.

drying oil, an oil that, when spread into a thin film in the presence of air, dries to form a dry, tough, durable, elastic skin. Naturally occurring drying oils are hempseed oil and linseed oil (from flax), used to preserve wood and to coat canvas to make oilcloth, and to make *putty and *linoleum. These and similar synthetic oils are used in *paints, *varnishes, and printing *inks.

ductility *metals and metalworking.

A petroleum **drilling rig** on a platform in the North Sea.

Dufay, Louis (*fl.* 1900–10), French pioneer of colour *photography. He and the *Lumière brothers almost simultaneously introduced additive colour-photographic processes—so called because three differently coloured images were added to each other. In Dufay's Dioptichrome screen plate (1908), a film containing a large number of tiny red, green, and blue filter elements underlaid the photographic emulsion. The film was processed by dissolving the first silver image and then redeveloping after exposure to white light, to give a colour transparency.

dug-out *canoe.

dumper truck *lorry.

Dunlop, John Boyd (1840–1921), British veterinary surgeon, of Scottish extraction, who is remembered as the inventor of the pneumatic *tyre. In fact it was a reinvention, since a pneumatic tyre (the 'Aerial wheel') had been patented in 1845 by the British engineer R. W. Thomson but had failed to achieve commercial success. In 1867, Dunlop fitted primitive pneumatic tyres to his young son's tricycle. A year later he began to manufacture tricycles with pneumatic tyres, and subsequently bicycles.

duplicating machine, a small printing device for office use. There are two main kinds of duplicating machine. In spirit duplicating, the image is typed or drawn on a paper master which has a backing sheet containing a dye that adheres to the image area. The master is wrapped round a drum and rolled against paper damped with alcohol solution, transferring a dyed image at each rotation. Around 300 copies are possible from one master. In stencil duplicating, a strong wax or plastic-covered sheet serves as the master, and the image is cut through the surface by a typewriter or stylus. The master is then wrapped round the padded surface of an ink-filled drum from which ink is squeezed through the image by the pressure of the paper rolling against the master. Some 5,000 copies are possible from each master. Both types of duplicating machine have been largely superseded by the *photocopier.

Duralumin *alloy.

DX coding, a system for automatically setting the film speed on a camera. A series of electrically conducting patches on the film cartridge are 'read' by an interface unit in the camera to provide a digital electrical input. This signal is analysed by the camera's microprocessor to select the correct film-speed setting.

dyes and dyeing. Dyes are substances used to *colour textiles, paper, hair, or food. Unlike *paints, which remain on the surface, dyes are dispersed into, or chemically bonded to, the material they colour. Dye *pigments contain special chemical groups, known as chromophores, that confer colour on the material. The chromophore molecules themselves give only weak colour: in natural dyes, long conjugated chains (systems of alternating single and double bonds) enhance the colour of the chromophore, while in synthetic dyes, chemical groups called auxochromes fulfil the same function. Dyes have been known for many thousands of years. Until recently they were all obtained from natural sources (see table). The first synthetic dye, mauveine, was discovered in 1856 by *Perkin. Many thousands of synthetic dyes have since been made, and the active ingredients

A selection of dyes and their properties

Dye type	Characteristics
Natural dyes	
Cochineal, lac	Red dyes made from species of female scale insect (family Coccidae). Used since Neolithic times. Cochineal now used as a food colouring
Woad, indigo	Blue or purple dye from such plants as *Isatia tinctoria* (woad) and *Indigofera tinctoria* (indigo). Active ingredient is indigotin: since 1897 this has been manufactured synthetically
Madder	Red dye, mainly from plant *Rubia tinctorum*, cultivated for at least 2,000 years. Important until 1869, when the German Karl Graebe first synthesized the active ingredient, alizarin
Saffron, safflower, annatto	Yellow dyes from plants *Crocus sativa* (saffron), *Carthamus tinctorius* (safflower), and *Bixa orellana* (annatto). All three dyes of ancient origin. Annatto now used as food colouring
Logwood	Black dye from wood of tree *Haematoxylon campeachianum*, native to Central America and the Caribbean. Used in Europe from mid-16th century
Tyrian purple	Purple dye made from *Murex branderis* or other molluscs since 1500 BC. Very expensive: used by Romans only for emperors' togas
Synthetic dyes	
Basic (cationic) dyes Example: mauveine	Dissociate in water to give a cationic (positively charged) dye. Low colour fastness on most materials, but dye acrylics well
Acid dyes Example: Napthol Green	Anionic (negatively charged) in water, most commonly sodium salts of sulphonic acid ($-SO_3Na$). Used to dye protein fibres such as wool and silk
Direct dyes Examples: Congo Red, Cuprofix (navy blue)	First discovered in 1884 and still popular because cheap and easy to use. Molecules contain charged atoms that are attracted to charged sites on the fibres. Moderately fast
Dispersed dyes Example: 1-amino-4-hydroxyanthraquinone (red-violet/pink)	First produced in 1950s. Water-insoluble, but dissolve in synthetic fibres that are difficult to dye with direct dyes. Dyeing best carried out at high temperatures in pressure vessels
Developed dyes Example: azo dyes	Cheap and very fast to washing. Incorporated directly into the material fibres by chemical reactions between soluble materials in which the fibres have been soaked. Particularly useful for printed fabrics
Fibre-reactive dyes Examples: ICI Procion and CIBA Cibacron dyes	Available since 1956. Very fast to washing and usually to light. Medium-priced, easy to use, wide range of colours

of many natural dyes have been chemically synthesized. An important quality in a dye is its fastness or resistance to repeated washing and to fading. Different dyes require different strategies to make them fast. Nearly all natural dyes have no affinity for cellulose, and can be made fast on cotton only by the use of *mordants, which precipitate the colour within the fibres. In vat dyeing, used for over 4,000 years, an insoluble dye is made soluble by treatment with an alkaline reducing agent. The textile is immersed in the solution and left to dry in the air. The dye is then oxidized back to its insoluble, coloured, form. Synthetic dyes often bond to the material they are colouring, thus achieving fastness. Increasingly, dyeing is carried out in closed vessels.

dynamic modelling, the derivation of a mathematical model which describes how a system or device behaves with time, particularly in response to external circumstances acting upon it. Such a model may be derived either by applying the principles of physics (such as Newton's laws of motion) to the individual system components, or by system identification, a technique in which the model is obtained by experiment rather than analysis. Dynamic modelling always involves the simplification of the system being analysed by concentrating on the most salient features and ignoring those deemed to be unimportant for the particular application. After *simulation, such modelling assumptions may need to be revised in the light of the adequacy or otherwise of the model for the purpose for which it was designed.

dynamite, an *explosive used extensively for blasting operations in mines and quarries. It was developed in 1867 by *Nobel, who discovered that certain earths (metallic oxides) such as kieselguhr will absorb up to three times their weight of *nitro-glycerine and still remain dry. The absorbed nitro-glycerine in this solid form still retains its explosive properties but is much less sensitive. Commercial dynamite is usually moulded into sticks and encased in waxed-paper wrappers. It can be handled and shipped with comparative safety and is exploded with a percussion cap containing a *detonator.

dynamo *generator, electrical.

dynamometer, a device used in *mechanical engineering to measure the power, or more commonly the *torque (turning force), of a rotating shaft. Transmission dynamometers measure the amount of twist imparted to the shaft by rotation, or consist of a special torque meter inserted between sections of the shaft. Absorption dynamometers operate by creating a constant braking force on the shaft: this force may be produced by mechanical friction, fluid friction, or by *electromagnetic induction. The braking mechanism is freely cradled so that it has a tendency to rotate: it is prevented from doing so by a force applied to an arm extending a known distance from the axis of rotation. The value of this restraining force is a measurement of the torque.

Dyes on sale at the market in Pokhara, Nepal.

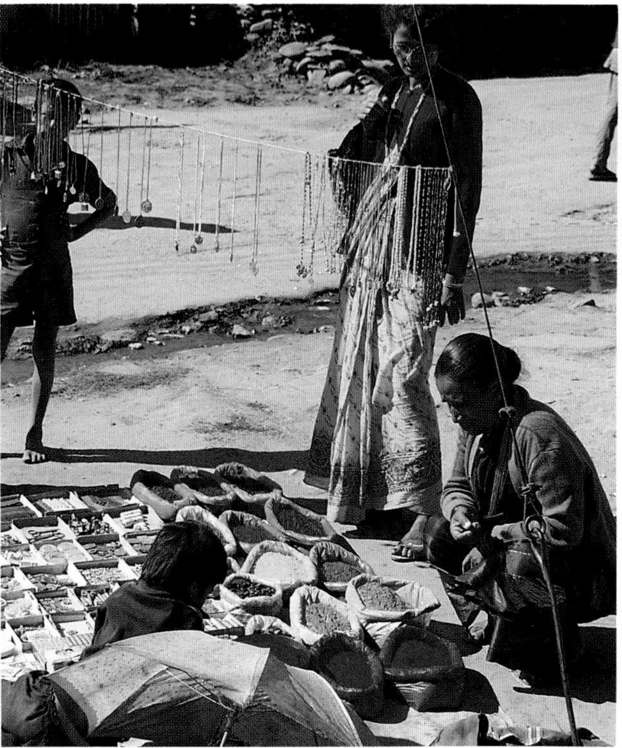

Eads, James Buchanan (1820–87), US engineer, remembered particularly as a *bridge builder. As a young man he built up a prosperous business salvaging wrecked steamers on the Mississippi, devising a *diving-bell for the purpose. During the American Civil War (1861–5) he built *ironclads for use on the western rivers. In 1867 he won a contract to build a railway bridge over the Mississippi at St Louis (completed 1874). The St Louis bridge was the first steel bridge to be built (although it had masonry pillars), and the largest in the world at that time.

ear, nose, and throat surgery *otorhinolaryngology.

early-warning system, a surveillance system that provides early warning of an approaching *ballistic missile or high-speed aircraft. Modern systems employ a combination of early warning satellites and powerful radars. The satellites detect the exhaust heat of ballistic missiles a few seconds after launch, and then radar systems comprising massive arrays of *antennae track the missiles as they rise above the horizon, using initial trajectory data produced by the satellites. The NATO early-warning stations are at Thule, Greenland; Clear, Alaska; and Fylingdale, UK. The advanced US Air Force Pave Paws radar is specifically designed to track launches from submarines. Early-warning systems can provide up to 30 minutes' warning of an approaching intercontinental *ballistic missile and 10 minutes' warning of a submarine-launched missile attack.

earthing (US, grounding), the connection of an electrical circuit to earth, which is considered to be at a constant electrical potential, arbitrarily designated as zero volts. The earthing of electrical appliances operating at mains voltage is often adopted for safety reasons. In the event of an accidental short circuit in the appliance, current will flow preferentially through the earth wire, rather than causing electrocution. Because the earth is assumed to be at zero potential without change, earthing is also used to shield electronic circuits, particularly *coaxial cables, to prevent external *interference.

Earth resources satellite, an artificial satellite supplying information about land use and about the distribution of natural resources such as water and minerals. Such satellites chiefly measure visible and infra-red radiation from the land and sea surface, using optical instruments and *radiometers. Earth resources satellites travel in a polar orbit, a north–south orbit that allows information to be collected from almost the whole of the Earth's surface. Information is transmitted to *ground stations for processing into visible images. Satellites such as the *Landsat* series (USA) and *Spot* (France) can distinguish details as small as individual buildings (a resolution of 10–30 m, 35–100 feet). The European *ERS-1* and Soviet *Almaz* satellites carry radar imaging equipment that allows the Earth's surface to be mapped through cloud or smoke cover. Information from such satellites can be used for many purposes. Remote areas can be mapped; crop types, yields, pests, and diseases can be identified; and areas likely to contain fossil fuels, minerals, or underground water can be pin-pointed. In addition, the paths of ocean currents can be tracked, good fishing areas identified, the extent of coastal erosion and silting revealed, and air and sea pollution monitored. (See *satellite, artificial for illustration.)

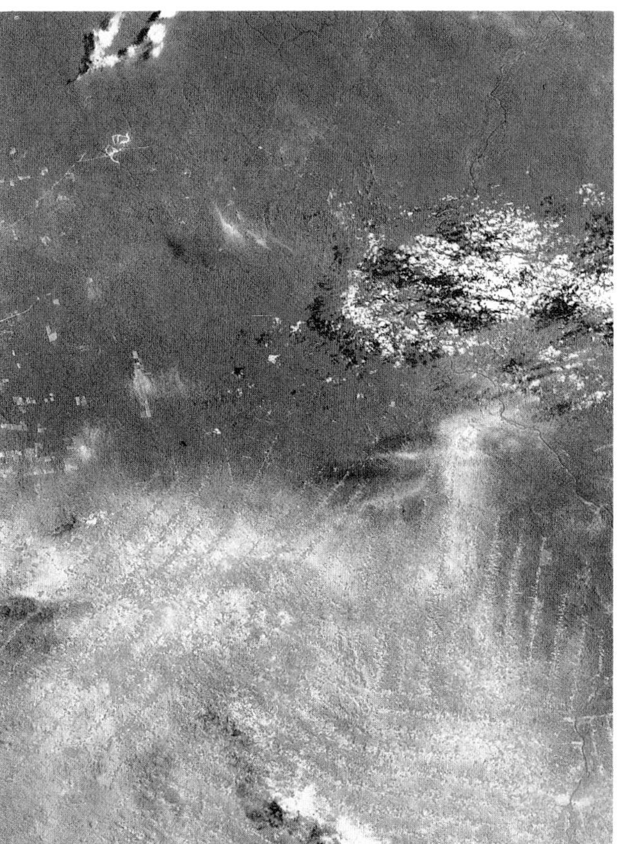

An infra-red photographic image of the Brazilian rain forest relayed from a *Landsat* **Earth resources satellite**. The blue and white areas show extensive deforestation caused by the practice of 'slash and burn' agriculture.

Eastman, George (1854–1932), US inventor and philanthropist. In the 1870s he recognized the commercial potential of *photography and devised a machine to coat glass plates with photographic emulsion. From this, he proceeded to the manufacture of the simple Kodak camera (1888), and roll film (invented by H. M. Reichenbach and patented in 1889). These developments transformed photography from an occupation for the professional to a hobby for everyone.

EBCDIC *ASCII.

echo-sounding, a type of *sonar used to determine the depth of a body of water. In echo-sounding a pulse of sound is transmitted vertically down towards the sea-bed, and the time elapsed before the return of the reflected echo is accurately measured. Knowing the speed of sound in sea-water (about 1,500 m/s, 5,000 feet per second), this time-value can be converted into a depth measurement. Echo sounding was first developed by *Fessenden in 1911, and first worked practically in 1914. Echo-sounders came into general use in about 1935. The echo-sounder is a tremendous improvement on the *lead-line for depth measurement, since it allows continuous depth monitoring. It can also be used to detect wrecks on the sea-bed and to locate shoals of fish.

The US inventor Thomas **Edison** in his laboratory.

Eckert, J. Presper *Mauchly, John William.

Edison, Thomas Alva (1847–1931), the most famous and versatile US inventor. After receiving a rudimentary education, he became an electric *telegraph operator during the American Civil War (1861–5). The technical knowledge of the system he acquired inspired him to invent the ticker-tape machine for transmitting stock exchange prices. His other inventions included quadruplex telegraphy (1874), a type of *multiplexing allowing four messages to travel simultaneously along the same telegraph wire; the carbon-particle microphone for the *telephone receiver and, perhaps the most original, the phonograph or *gramophone (1877). He also developed the *incandescent lamp, initially in rivalry with *Swan in the UK and Hiram Maxim in the USA. In 1881 he built the world's first central electric power-station at Pearl Street, New York. Though generally successful, Edison did have some failures. He failed to develop an early interest in cinematography, and his discovery of the 'Edison effect' was later exploited by *Fleming as the *thermionic valve.

EDSAC *computer, history of.

EDVAC *computer, history of.

efficiency (machine), a measure of the effectiveness of a machine's operation, defined as the ratio of effective output to effective input. Thus the thermal efficiency of, say, an engine, is its output in joules (see *energy) divided by the *heat energy at input. The efficiency of turbo-machines is defined differently, as the ratio of the actual work output to the ideal output, assuming no energy losses. Practical efficiencies of machines vary widely. Among the most efficient are electrical generators and transformers, which optimally have efficiencies of over 99 per cent. Boilers can be 90 per cent efficient, and an electric motor around 80 per cent. The efficiency of machines using heat-*engines is much lower, because even an ideal heat-engine can achieve only 60 per cent efficiency. A steam-turbine is optimally 45 per cent efficient, a diesel engine around 35 per cent efficient, but a petrol engine can achieve only around 25 per cent efficiency.

Egyptian and Mesopotamian technology, technology of the early civilizations in Egypt and in Mesopotamia, both of which arose in about 3000 BC. The early civilizations of Mesopotamia included the Sumerian, Assyrian, and Babylonian empires. These two areas provide the earliest known examples of many basic technologies—*pottery and *glass-making, the extraction and working of metals, textiles, woodworking, and building techniques—which were firmly established long before the Christian era. Both had highly developed *agricultural systems in which strictly controlled *irrigation played a critical role. They were skilled at astronomical observation and computation and devised intricate *calendars, important for observing the annual cycle of sowing, growth, and harvesting. Systems of pictographic writing were developed in both areas, and standardized weights and measures (see *unit) were introduced. Both civilizations had highly organized urban communities and established trading relationships with distant countries, facilitated by the development of *shipbuilding and of *road systems.

Ehrlich, Paul (1854–1915), German physician who founded *chemotherapy and made important contributions to bacteriology, *haematology, and *immunology. As a student, he became interested in *aniline dyes, using them for the first time to stain *bacteria. He also employed a similar technique to identify the different types of white blood corpuscles and the corresponding leukaemias. From 1889, he investigated the principles of immunization and two years later devised a means of standardizing diphtheria toxin. In 1911 he introduced the arsenical drug arsphenamine as a treatment for syphilis. He shared the 1908 Nobel Prize for Physiology and Medicine with Elie Metchnikoff.

eidophor, an apparatus that projects *television pictures to a size of up to 10 m (33 feet) square. Three valves, one for each primary colour (red, blue, and green), control the intensity and scanning of a xenon light beam, which forms the picture. Eidophors are used at rock concerts, sports events, and other similar events.

Eiffel, Alexandre Gustave (1832–1923), French constructional engineer with many major works to his credit, the best known being the 300-m (985-foot) Eiffel Tower in Paris, completed in 1889 to commemorate the centenary of the French Revolution. The Eiffel Tower was the last major structure to be built of wrought iron, steel being used thereafter. Eiffel also designed iron bridges built over the River Garonne at Bordeaux (1858) and over the River Douro at Oporto, Portugal (1876), as well as the framework of the Statue of Liberty in the USA. He was one of the first engineers to employ compressed-air *caissons in bridge-building.

Einthoven, Willem (1860–1927), Dutch inventor of *electrocardiography. A qualified physician, he also had some training in physics, which led him to apply the methods of

An **eidophor** being used to broadcast a televised opera performance to a large audience.

physics to medicine. In 1903 he devised a *galvanometer to record the electrical activity of the contracting heart. This type of galvanometer became a basic tool in the diagnosis of heart disease, although it was not Einthoven but Thomas Lewis in the UK and F. N. Wilson in the USA who pioneered its diagnostic use. Einthoven was awarded the Nobel Prize for Physiology and Medicine in 1924.

ejection seat, a seat fitted with a *parachute, capable of being ejected from an aeroplane in an emergency. It is fired from the aircraft by an explosive charge or rocket, and automatically deploys an auxiliary braking (drogue) parachute. If operated above about 3,000 m (9,800 feet), the main parachute will not automatically deploy until that height is reached. It can be operated at very low altitudes and has saved many lives. The first live test was made in the UK in 1946, from a Gloster Meteor aircraft.

elastic, a textile fabric, particularly a tape or webbing, which recovers its original shape after stretching. Elastic has long been made by wrapping *cotton or other *textile *yarns around *rubber cords. However, there are now synthetic fibres with recovery properties similar to those of rubber-cored elastics. These fibres are known as *elastomers; the best of them are stronger than rubber and behave elastically over a comparable range of extension.

elastomer, a plastic material which at room temperature can be stretched under low stress to at least twice its length, but snaps back to its original length on release of stress. This property depends on the fact that the contorted molecular chains making up the *polymer can be uncoiled by a tensile stress, but return to their original position due to the presence of a small degree of cross-linking between the chains. Natural and synthetic *rubbers are the commonest elastomers.

electrical engineering, the practical study and exploitation of *electricity and magnetism. This applies particularly to the development of electrical machines, such as *electric motors and *generators, and to power generation, storage, and distribution facilities; also to the conversion of electrical energy to useful work as in lighting, heating, and electric traction. Electrical engineering involves the study of high-current and high-power devices. The study of devices that operate at small current or power levels, or use active elements like *semiconductor devices or *thermionic valves, is usually termed *electronics.

electric-arc furnace, a chamber in which a high temperature is produced by a high-voltage electric arc passing between graphite electrodes. It is used in the *iron and steel industry to produce special steels, such as stainless steel, constructional alloys, and tool steels, from a mixture of scrap steel, pig-iron, and alloying additions.

electric car *electric vehicle.

electric cell *battery.

electric fire *heating, domestic.

electricity and magnetism, the fundamental phenomena on which electronics and electrical engineering are based. Electrostatics is the study of electric charges at rest, and is concerned with charged objects and the forces between them. Electrostatic properties can be simply demonstrated by experiment. For example, polythene and Perspex are materials that become charged with 'static electricity' if rubbed with a dry woollen or silk cloth. A charged polythene rod will exert an attractive force on a charged Perspex rod, but if two charged polythene rods are brought together they will repel each other. This experiment and others have been used to demonstrate that there are two types of electrostatic charge, one positive, the other negative. Like charges attract, while unlike charges repel, and the closer together the charges, the greater the force between them. Electrostatic forces are fundamental to matter. All materials are made up of *atoms, in which a nucleus containing positively charged protons is surrounded by a diffuse cloud of small, negatively charged electrons, attracted to the nucleus by electrostatic forces. Thus, many of the physical properties of materials, and all of their chemical interactions, are dependent on the simple laws of electrostatics.

If a charged body is connected by a metal wire to one that is neutral, or carries an opposite charge, a charge will be transferred between the two. This flow of charge is known as electrical current, and usually consists of a flow of electrons from the more negatively charged body to the more positively charged one. Metals and other materials that allow the flow of electrical charge through them are known as conductors. Materials that resist the passage of an electric current are known as insulators. The difference in electrical charge between two bodies that allows a current to flow when they are connected represents a difference in electrical potential, and is known as a potential difference (p.d.) In a battery or *generator, chemical or mechanical work is done to create a p.d. between one pole of the device and the other. When these poles are connected by a conducting path an electrical *circuit is formed, through which current flows.

This electrical current provides *energy to carry out useful work, such as driving an electric motor, or powering a light bulb.

Magnetic phenomena are closely related to electrical ones. *Magnets have positive and negative poles, and as with electric charges, like poles repel while unlike poles attract. A pair of magnetic poles creates a field, a region around the pole in which magnetic forces act. A charged body creates a similar electrical field. More importantly, an electric current flowing through a conductor generates a weak magnetic field around it: if the conductor is wrapped into a coil, and a core of iron or similar ferromagnetic material is placed in the centre, the magnetic field is greatly increased, and the coil becomes an *electromagnet. The interaction between electric and magnetic forces is crucial to many of the electrical devices commonly in use. The two most important interactions are *electromagnetic induction, in which an electric current is produced in a conductor if it is moved through a magnetic field (or held in a constantly changing magnetic field), and the related effect whereby a current-carrying conductor placed in a magnetic field experiences a force on it. These phenomena are the basis on which such devices as *electric motors, *generators, *relays, *solenoids, *microphones, and *loudspeakers operate.

electricity generation and supply. The principles of *electromagnetic induction, on which electricity generation and supply are based, were first formulated in the 1820s and 1830s. The potential of electricity as a source of power and illumination began to be recognized in the mid-19th century, when the earliest, small-scale electric *generators appeared, but the concept of a publicly accessible electricity utility did not appear until some twenty years later. The development of the *incandescent lamp led to a demand for electric lighting, and in 1878 both St George Lane-Fox in the UK and *Edison in the USA proposed systems to supply electrical energy for lighting to customers. In 1882 *power-stations began operation in both London and New York, supplying sufficient low-voltage, direct-current (d.c.) electricity for around 4,000 lamps. The first permanent electricity supply was installed at Brighton, UK, in 1881–2. The first public power-station to use *steam-turbines was opened at Forth Banks, Newcastle, in 1888. By 1900 there were some 250 electricity suppliers in the UK, many of them privately owned, while the USA had around 3,000, and Germany had also developed substantial generating capacity. However, the proliferation of producers resulted in technical incompatibilities between generating systems. In the late 19th century, de *Ferranti advocated consolidation and economies of scale. He designed a huge power-station at Deptford which by 1899 was supplying electricity to London at 10,000 V along 28 miles of underground cable. The various providers also faced a key technical question: whether to use d.c. or alternating-current (a.c.) transmission. Low-voltage d.c. systems proved inefficient, since substantial amounts of power were lost in the cabling. Alternating current, by contrast, could be easily transformed (see *transformer) to high voltages, involving far less power loss. This a.c. system was advocated by de Ferranti. The first practical a.c. transmission system was designed by the German engineer Oskar von Miller to supply power to Frankfurt-am-Main; it began operation in 1891. Economies of scale and high-voltage a.c. transmission led to low-price electricity supplies in most industrialized countries by the mid-20th century. Electricity supplies were standardized nationally: in the UK the Central Electricity Board was created in 1925, and in 1927 work was begun on the co-operative national grid network that adapts electricity supply to suit demand. It consists of a common network of cables connecting all producers and consumers, allowing peak loads in one area to be met by electricity generated in another. All the *power-stations share the load, so that if a generator fails, consumers still receive enough power.

Methods of electricity generation vary according to economic resources, but patterns of generation are similar internationally (see *energy resources). Modern electric *generators typically give an a.c. output of around 20,000 V at a *frequency of either 50 or 60 Hz. A three-phase a.c. transmission system is usually used, in which three conductors carry alternating currents that are out of step by one-third of a cycle: this gives a constant flow of power, and hence much smoother and more efficient operation than with a single-phase system. For long-distance transmission, the generated voltage is stepped up using *transformers to around 270,000 V, or up to 500,000 V on certain long-distance sections. Very high voltages are used because this substantially cuts power losses in the *cables. The voltage is then stepped down for domestic supply at local substations, to values of between 110 and 240 V, depending on the supply standards of the country. All common electricity grids are a.c. systems, but recent developments in technology and the development of *superconducting cables have led to renewed interest in d.c. distribution systems. Direct-current transmission is competitive over long distances because a cable can carry between two and ten times as much d.c. power as a.c. Long-distance power transmission in most countries is via overhead pylons, while urban distribution is usually by underground cable.

electricity meter, a device for measuring the total electric power consumption of households and other premises, for billing purposes. The meter is fitted into the electrical *wiring circuit so that any appliance consumption actuates a small *electric motor. The cumulative movement of this motor is registered on a series of dials or a digital read-out, which record that the total *energy consumption in kilowatt-hours (kWh) is the amount of energy used by a device running at a power of 1 kilowatt for 1 hour (the equivalent of 3.6 MJ). Ongoing power consumption is also indicated by the speed of a revolving disc indicator in the meter.

electric lighting *incandescent lamp, *fluorescent lamp, *arc lamp, *gas-discharge lamp, *lighting, history of.

electric locomotive, a locomotive powered by electricity. The first successful electric locomotive was demonstrated by E. W. von *Siemens in Berlin in 1879, operating with direct current (d.c.) at 150 V from a central third rail. A number of passenger railways and tramways followed, including *underground railways, using d.c. collected variously from channels below ground or from overhead wires. In 1884, the US electrical engineer Frank Sprague applied electric traction to the New York and Chicago elevated railways, coupling powered carriages together under the control of the driver in the leading vehicle. By the early 1900s routes through the Alps were being electrified, using low-cost *hydroelectric power. Precise control of the current to the electric motors helped the haulage of heavy loads on steep gradients. Systems with different power supplies developed until the 1930s, when the importance of through-running between different countries in Europe led to the standardization of overhead d.c. systems at 1,500 V. In the

UK, the major electrification projects were for the intense commuter services around London and some other cities. With the development of electrical technology since the 1940s, most modern electric railways operate using alternating current (a.c.) at high voltages: 15,000–25,000 V. Since, however, the electric traction motors driving the wheels still operate with d.c., a *rectifier is necessary on the locomotive. Modern locomotives often use regenerative *braking systems, in which the traction motors slow the train by operating as generators.

electric mixer *food processors and mixers.

electric motor, a device for converting electrical energy into rotary motion (but see also *linear motor). It is the complementary device to the electrical *generator, which converts rotary motion into electric current: most generators can be converted into motors, and vice versa. The key components of an electric motor are a coil mounted on a freely rotating shaft (the rotor or *armature); and a permanent magnet or an electromagnet (the stator) surrounding the rotor. The rotary motion produced by interaction between the rotor and stator relies on electromagnetic principles first formulated by André-Marie Ampère (1775–1836) and *Faraday (see *electromagnetic induction).

There are many different types of electric motor. If the motor uses direct-current (d.c.) electricity, then the stator has a fixed magnetic field, and the current passes through the rotor (see figure). Similar motors can operate from an alternating current (a.c.): universal motors, that can use either d.c. or a.c., are of this design and are used in vacuum cleaners, small power tools, and other domestic applications. More important in industrial contexts are induction and synchronous motors. In an induction motor, two or more coils on the stator produce a rotating magnetic field, which induces a current in the rotor. This in turn creates a turning force on the rotor, which continues to act until the rotor is moving at the same speed as the magnetic field. Induction motors are rugged, reliable, and can develop high starting *torques. They are suitable for use in haulage or traction. Synchronous motors operate on similar principles, but when full speed is reached, a current is applied to the rotor, which acts to 'lock' it at the same speed as the moving magnetic field. Synchronous motors are used in clocks, gramophones, navigational equipment, and other applications where accurate maintenance of speed is important.

electric vehicle, a vehicle propelled by electric power. An electric vehicle first became technologically feasible with the development of a suitable storage *battery in 1881, and the first electric vehicle, a tricycle, ran in the same year. By the end of the 19th century the electric vehicle was competing with steam-powered and internal-combustion vehicles. In 1899 an electric sprint car designed by a Belgian, Camille Jenatzy, took the world land speed record, travelling at 105 km/h (62 m.p.h.). As with *steam-powered vehicles, electric cars lost ground after the invention of the electric *starter motor in 1912, but they have continued to be used for short-distance work, for example in milk floats and fork-lift trucks. However, the new types of battery currently under development, and recent improvements in *fuel cells, may lead to a resurgence of electric vehicles. Solar-powered vehicles, still highly experimental, use *solar cells to drive an electric vehicle.

Electric motor

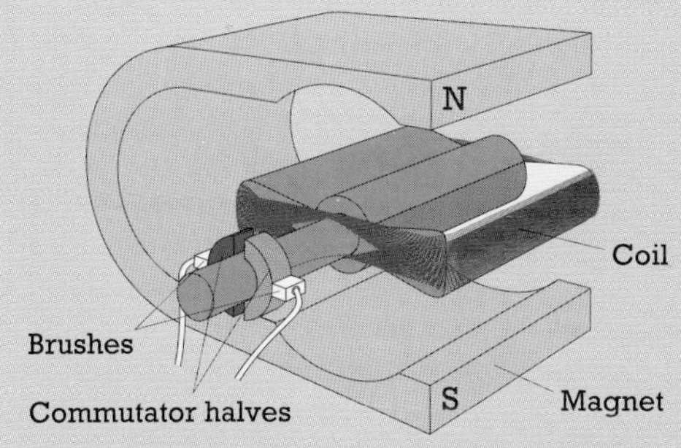

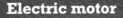

1 Before power is applied to the coil only one, permanent, magnetic field is present.

2 When current flows through the coil, a second magnetic field is generated, with a north pole above the coil and a south pole below it. The like poles of the permanent and secondary fields repel each other, causing the coil to rotate in a clockwise direction.

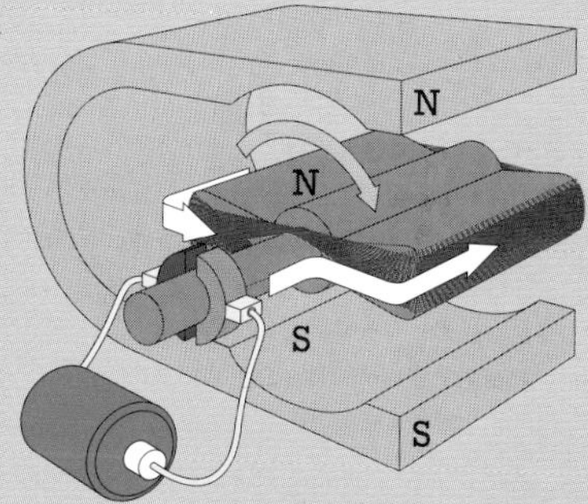

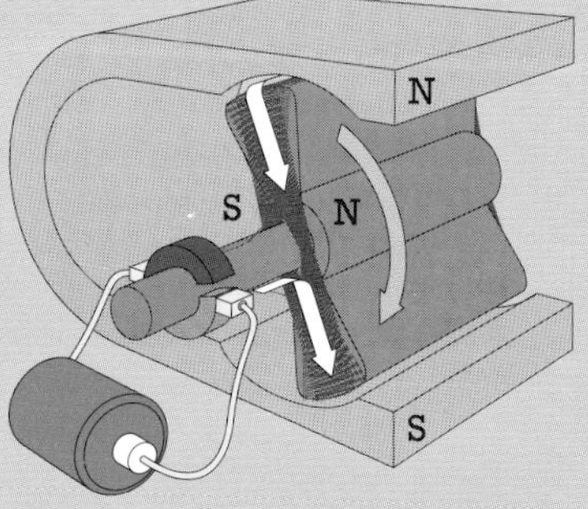

3 As the coil rotates to meet its attracting poles the two halves of the commutator change contact with the two brushes, reversing the direction of the current in the coil.

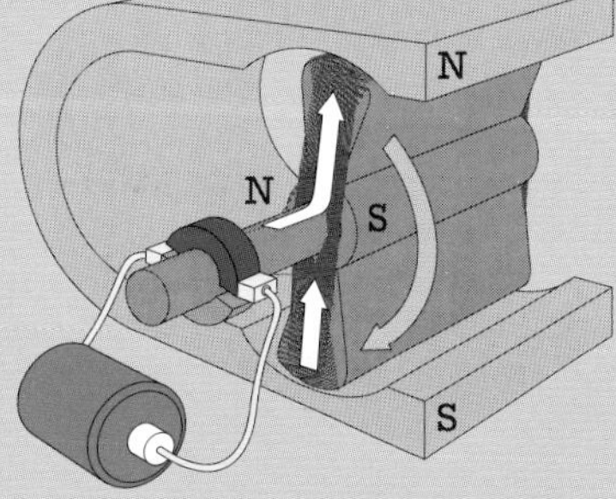

4 This produces a reversal in the polarity of the magnetic field generated by the coil. Repulsion between the two magnetic fields is thus maintained and the armature continues to spin.

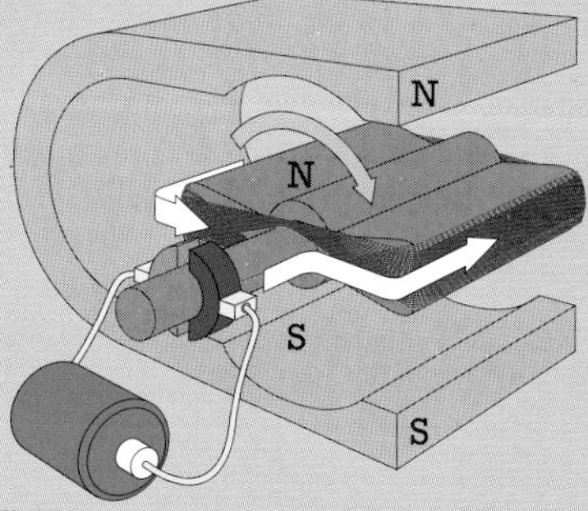

5 The process now repeats itself.

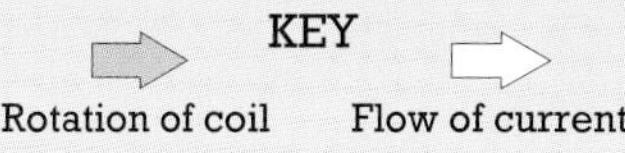

The Impact, a prototype **electric vehicle** launched by General Motors in 1990. Its performance matches that of many conventional vehicles, with a top speed of 160 km/h (100 m.p.h.), and a maximum distance between rechargings of about 200 km (125 miles). The car needs only one gear, and is extremely light and aerodynamically efficient.

electrocardiograph (ECG), a device used to display the electrical activity of the heart, producing a record called an electrocardiogram. Several recordings are taken using different pairs of electrodes placed on the chest and limbs (and in some cases in the oesophagus or in the heart itself by means of a *catheter). By testing a patient during exercise, electrocardiography can diagnose acute events, such as myocardial infarction (heart attack), or chronic impairment of function due, for example, to inadequate blood supply. Continuous ECG monitoring is a feature of *intensive-care units and in resuscitation, particularly to diagnose potentially fatal abnormal heart rhythms. Early clinical electrocardiographs used *Einthoven's string galvanometer to convert electrical signals into recordable movements; more recent machines use electronic amplification and oscilloscopes. Computers using *expert systems can now analyse ECG traces and suggest diagnoses.

electroceramics, *ceramics developed for their electrical properties. Many ceramics have such properties as *piezoelectricity and pyro-electricity (the development of an electric charge on heating), or are electrets (materials that hold a permanent electric dipole, analogous to the magnetic dipole of a magnet). A considerable number of ceramic magnets are also known. Many ceramics are also excellent electrical insulators, and have a very high dielectric constant (a measure of a material's ability to resist the flow of electric charge). The latter is a useful property in *capacitors. Conducting and semiconducting ceramics are also known. In terms of amounts produced, the most important electroceramic is barium titanate ($BaTiO_3$), which has a large dielectric constant, and can be made into an electret. In the mid-1980s scientists working for IBM in Switzerland synthesized a ceramic which became a *superconductor at −246 °C. Further superconducting oxide ceramics have since been discovered, some with relatively high superconducting temperatures.

electroconvulsive therapy (ECT), a form of treatment for severe depression or, occasionally, schizophrenia, in which electrodes are placed on the skull and an electrical current is passed through the brain. Introduced in 1938 by the Italians Ugo Cerletti and Lucio Bini, the technique has been modified, notably since 1940, by the use of accompanying muscle relaxants to prevent injury from the convulsions induced. How ECT works is not properly understood, and the technique has been criticized on the grounds that it might cause permanent brain damage. The use of ECT declined during the 1970s, but it is still employed in certain types of severe depression.

electrode, a conductive terminal which can be used to apply or extract electrical energy from a circuit or system. Usually made from metals such as copper, silver, or gold, electrodes are found in *thermionic valves, *semiconductor devices, electrolytic cells (see *battery), and many other devices, where they frequently function as *anodes and *cathodes.

electroencephalograph (EEG), a machine that detects and records electrical activity in the brain by registering potential differences between electrodes placed on the scalp, arising as a result of 'feeble currents' in the brain. It was first used by *Berger in 1924. Modern EEG machines register as many as sixteen 'channels' of brain activity on a multi-pen recorder (a polygraph). EEG signals are distinguished by their *frequency and by the region in which they arise. For example, alpha waves (8–13 Hz) arise in the occipital region and are associated with states of relaxation; beta waves (15–30 Hz) arise in the frontal region. The technique can be used in *neurology to diagnose disordered activity of the brain caused by epilepsy, and sometimes local disorders, such as a tumour. Until recently, EEGs required interpretation by a skilled clinician, but in the last decade tentative diagnoses for doctors have been provided by computers using *expert systems.

electrolysis, the breakdown of ionic compounds (compounds composed of positive and negative *ions), either molten or in solution, by the passage of a direct electric current. Metal elements or hydrogen are released at the negative *electrode (the cathode), and non-metal elements at the positive electrode (the anode). During the 19th century, application of this technique on a small scale led to the isolation and identification of many reactive metal elements that could not be obtained from their compounds by reduction with carbon or hydrogen (see *oxidation and reduction). Since then, the process has been developed for large-scale operations and has come to be used extensively in the industrial production and refining of metals such as aluminium, copper, sodium, magnesium, and nickel, and in the manufacture of non-metals such as fluorine, chlorine, bromine, and hydrogen. Electrolysis is also the basis of *electroplating and *anodizing.

electrolyte *battery.

electromagnet, a *magnet consisting of a coil, carrying electrical current, wound on a core of soft (easily magnetized) iron. When an electrical current is passed through the winding, the electromagnet produces a strong magnetic field. Unlike a permanent magnet, the magnetic field of an electromagnet may be switched on and off. This is because the magnetically 'soft' iron core does not retain its magnetism when not in a magnetic field: thus, when the current to the coil is switched off, the magnetic field collapses with no residual magnetism. The electromagnet is the basis of many electromechanical devices, such as *relays, *solenoids, *electric motors, and induction heaters.

Electromagnetic radiation

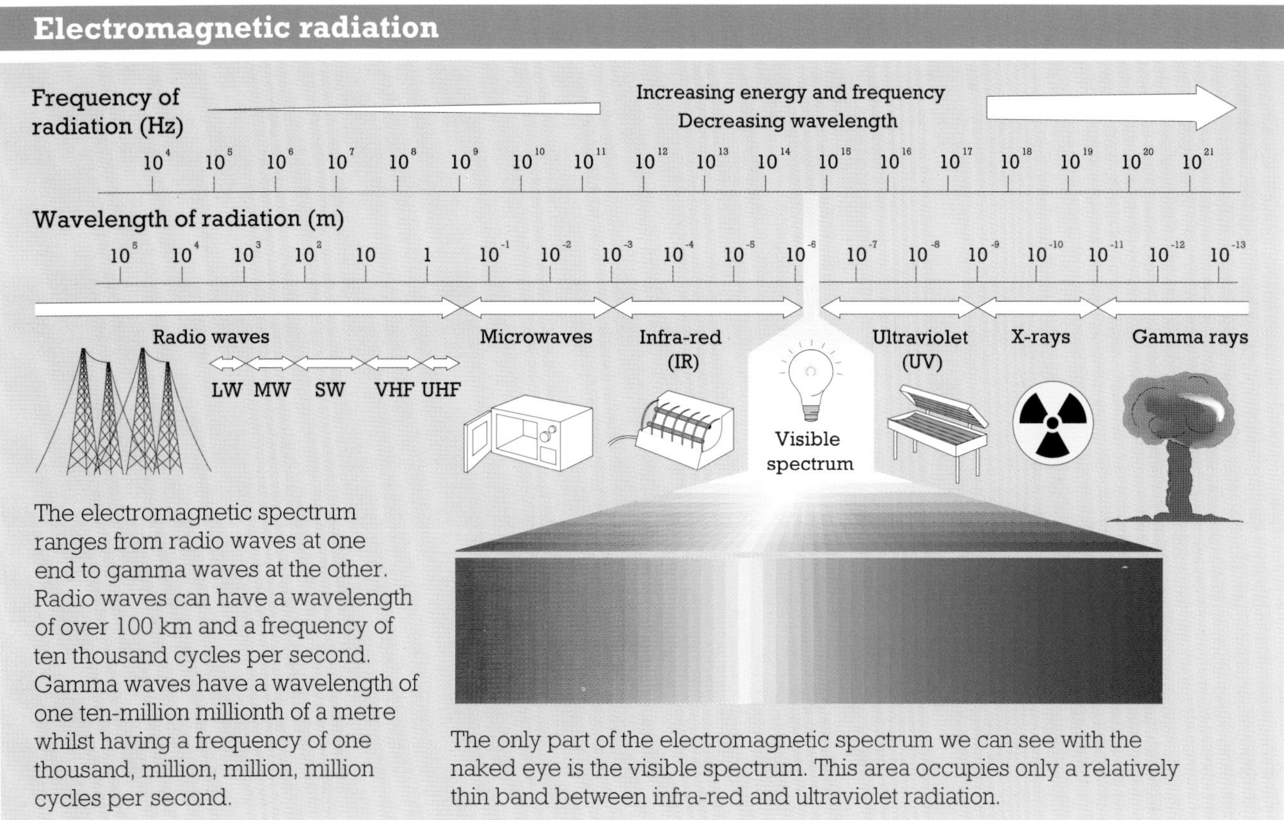

The electromagnetic spectrum ranges from radio waves at one end to gamma waves at the other. Radio waves can have a wavelength of over 100 km and a frequency of ten thousand cycles per second. Gamma waves have a wavelength of one ten-million millionth of a metre whilst having a frequency of one thousand, million, million, million cycles per second.

The only part of the electromagnetic spectrum we can see with the naked eye is the visible spectrum. This area occupies only a relatively thin band between infra-red and ultraviolet radiation.

The ALEPH experiment, one of four major experiments to examine the structure of matter at the large particle collider at the European Laboratory for Particle Physics (CERN). The instruments are contained within a large superconducting **electromagnet**, with a magnetic flux density of 1.5 tesla.

electromagnetic induction, the production of an electrical potential difference (p.d.) or voltage across a conductor situated in a changing magnetic field. *Faraday was able to describe this behaviour mathematically: he found that the size of the p.d. produced is proportional to the rate of change of the magnetic flux. This applies whether the flux itself changes in strength or the conductor is moved through it. Electromagnetic induction fundamentally underlies the operation of *generators, *electric motors, and most other electrical machines, along with the complementary law ascribed to André-Marie Ampère, who in 1820 demonstrated that if a conductor carrying an electrical current is placed in a magnetic field at right angles to current flow, the conductor will experience a force on it at right angles to both field and current.

electromagnetic radiation, the general term for combined electric and magnetic fields propagated across space. This radiation may be considered as a type of *wave, with a wide spectrum of frequencies and wavelengths (see figure). As the wavelength of radiation decreases (equivalent to its frequency increasing), the energy associated with it increases. The most important band of electromagnetic radiation is the very narrow region of the visible light spectrum, which has a wavelength of several hundred nanometres (10^{-9} m). This is subdivided into the various perceived colours, each of slightly differing frequency. Just beyond the perception of the human eye are the regions of ultraviolet (UV) and infra-red (IR) radiation. IR is radiated by hot bodies, and is used in communications and photographic applications. In technological terms, the most important area of the spectrum is the radio-wave region, responsible for broadcast communications (see *waveband). Microwaves are a high-frequency radiation used for communications, for *radar, and in *microwave ovens. The extremely high energies of *X-rays and gamma rays find applications in medicine and industrial inspection because of their ability to penetrate solids.

electromechanical device, a device that converts mechanical movement into an electrical signal, or vice versa. Electromechanical devices thus contain moving parts, and so are distinct from *semiconductor devices, which possess no moving parts. Common electromechanical devices include simple hand-operated *switches and *switch gear, *electric motors, *loudspeakers, and older types of telephone exchange.

electrometer, an instrument that uses the mechanical forces existing between electrostatically charged bodies to measure extremely low voltages and currents. Vacuum-tube electrometers (or the more recent semiconductor equivalents that use a pair of field-effect *transistors) can measure currents as small as 10^{-13} A (about 10,000 electrons per second). Electrometers are an integral part of *pH meters.

electromotive force (e.m.f.) *battery.

electron, a fundamental, stable, negatively charged particle, the natural unit of electric charge. Electrons, along with protons and neutrons, are one of the three primary constituents of *atoms, and were discovered by the British physicist Joseph Thomson in 1897. Understanding the behaviour of electrons has been crucial to the development of *electrical engineering and *electronics, since electric currents arise through the movement of free electrons in materials, and of chemistry, since chemical interactions take place between the outer electrons of an atom. (See also *electricity and magnetism.)

electron beam *electron tube.

electron gun *electron tube.

electronic funds transfer (EFT), the use of computer systems to make financial transactions. Business-to-business EFT is extremely important, but the most visible type of EFT is the automatic teller machine (ATM) serving the general public. ATMs are installed outside banks and other financial institutions to dispense or accept cash when activated with a suitably encoded plastic card. A related development is electronic funds transfer at point of sale (EFTPOS), which enables a purchase transaction to be made electronically with card verification and simultaneous debiting of the purchaser's bank account.

electronic mail (email), a term used to describe the sending of messages via computer systems. Many computer systems are now connected to local or wide-area *networks and users can communicate with other users anywhere on the network. Some services offer mail-box facilities that allow users not connected to a private network to send and receive messages via a *microcomputer, a telephone, and a *modem.

electronic page make-up, the make-up of pages for books, newspapers, and other documents by electronic means. Physical preparation of pages for printing by traditional means such as assembling metal type and picture blocks, or cutting and pasting pieces of paper on to a master sheet, is time-consuming and therefore expensive. The modern approach is to feed the information into a computer-controlled system, where it can be stored and retrieved as required. The information may then be called up for display on a video monitor and any modifications made before the image is released for feeding into the printing process. For simple monochrome work this procedure may be achieved by means of a *desk-top publishing system, but for multi-colour, multi-purpose, and multi-page work, a complete studio is needed. (See also *graphic image manipulation.)

electronics, the study, design, and application of devices that rely on the conduction of electricity through a vacuum, a gas, or a semiconductor. The electronics industry has developed only in the 20th century, although its foundations were laid in the 19th century. During his development of the *incandescent lamp, *Edison observed an unexplained bluish glow, and a reverse flow of current between the filaments of the lamp. This phenomenon was explained by the British physicist Joseph Thomson in 1897 as being due to the passage of electrons through a vacuum from the negative to the positive terminal of the filament. This effect was utilized by J. A. *Fleming in his diode for receiving *radio waves. The diode and other *thermionic valves were responsible for an enormous development of radio and other communications media. The *iconoscope, an early device for the production of electronic images, led to the development of *television, and by the 1930s television broadcasting had begun. After the War, communications technology continued to develop, but electronics also found applications in a wide range of other industries. A major impetus was the development in 1948 of the first *semiconductor device, the *transistor, by *Shockley and co-workers. The *integrated circuit was developed in 1959. The rapid improvement of integrated circuits, and their application in particular to *computers and *information technology, has led to an enormous expansion of the electronics industry.

electronic scanning, the use of a computer-controlled beam or detector to systematically scan a piece of artwork or other image, and *digitize that image on computer disk for later use in *printing procedures. The most common scanning device is a controllable light source such as a laser, which traverses the copy and analyses its content in terms of image shape, size, colour, and density. This information is then used to convert the original copy into dot patterns for *half-tone printing or colour separations for multicolour work.

electronic warfare, the military use of radio technology to intercept or disrupt enemy *radar and communications. The development of electronic communications systems at the end of the 19th century soon led to their military and naval deployment. In the 1920s wireless telegraphy was widely adopted by the military. During World War II, electronic devices for eavesdropping and for disrupting communications were used by both sides, as were electronic systems designed to guide bombers on to their targets. After the War many armies created special electronic warfare units. For signal interception, direction-finding receivers have been developed to locate enemy transmissions, which are usually encrypted and must be decoded (see *cryptography). To jam enemy transmissions, electronic noise signals are broadcast. Jamming equipment is normally mounted on tracked vehicles or lorries, and remotely piloted vehicles are also often used. A jamming system used by the US Army, EXJAM (*ex*pendable *jam*mer), is deployed from a

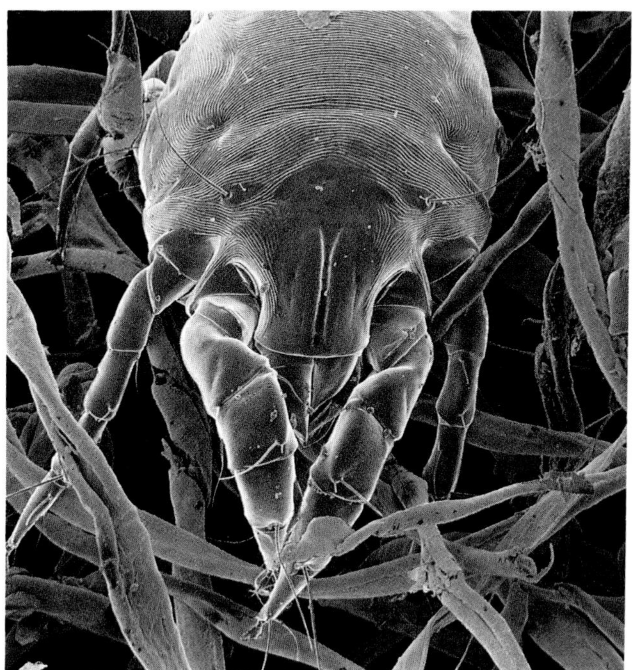

A false-colour photograph of a dust-mite taken through a scanning **electron microscope** (SEM). Unlike the transmission electron microscope (TEM), the SEM can be used for bulky specimens. It can operate at magnifications from about ×500 (as here) to about ×500,000.

shell. Shells carrying packages of transmitters are dropped at pre-set intervals; the shells embed in the ground, an antenna is raised electronically, and transmissions begin.

electron microscope, an instrument that uses an *electron beam to obtain very high magnification of biological and physical samples where optical *microscopes are inadequate. In operation, a stream of *electrons is focused into a very narrow beam and directed on to a specimen. The structure of the specimen causes specific diffraction, or scattering of the beam. The pattern of diffracted electrons is collected and displayed on a *cathode-ray tube screen or on a photographic plate. The image is representative to some degree of the microstructure of the specimen. Two main types of electron microscope exist: the transmission electron microscope (TEM) and the scanning electron microscope (SEM). In the TEM, the electron beam passes through the specimen, which must be very thin to permit this. The TEM gives a very high magnification, and can examine features typically 2 nm (2×10^{-9} m) wide, but it gives a 'flat' image, devoid of depth. In the SEM, the beam is scattered principally off the surface features of the specimen, and gives information apparently as a 'solid' image. The SEM is therefore used to examine surfaces, although it has lower resolution (ability to distinguish detail) than the TEM.

electron spin resonance, a technique used to investigate materials containing unpaired electrons. Electrons have a property called spin, which can be in one of two states. Most electrons in an atom or molecule are paired, the electrons in these pairs having opposed spin states. If a material containing single unpaired electrons is placed in a magnetic field, the spin of the unpaired electron will line up with the magnetic field. The energy required to cause a single unpaired electron to change from this spin state to one in which it is opposed to the magnetic field is dependent upon the environment of the unpaired electron. Measuring the magnitude of this energy change gives valuable information about the structure of the material.

electron tube, the generic term for an electronic device that generates a beam of *electrons for useful work. Electron tubes are usually sealed and contain a vacuum or traces of a gas. Common examples of devices utilizing electron tubes are *cathode-ray tubes, *thermionic valves, *visual display units, and *electron microscopes. The *thermionic valve is a very simple form of electron tube. A typical electron tube consists of an electron gun, or source of electrons, a positively charged *anode plate, and various mechanisms for focusing and controlling the electron beam, all in a near-vacuum inside a sealed glass or metal container. The electron source is a *cathode, usually heated to excite the electrons sufficiently to enable them to escape from the cathode surface. The released electrons are attracted and accelerated towards the anode plate. As the stream of electrons is negatively charged, it can be directed and focused during its passage, either by charged capacitor plates, which attract or repel the beam, or by magnets, which achieve similar effects by acting on the magnetic field generated by the beam. In many applications electron tubes have been superseded by *semiconductor devices, which perform many of the same functions more efficiently in both cost and reliability. However, in some applications, notably in picture generation, broadcasting, and high-frequency, high-power generation of signals for radar and similar purposes, they are still widely used.

electrophoresis *chromatography.

electroplating, a process in which a thin layer of metal is deposited from solution on to an article by *electrolysis. The article to be plated is connected to the negative terminal of

Electroplating being used to make the copper connecting tracks for flexible circuit boards. These are specialized electronic components for applications such as missile nose-cones, where rigid circuit boards could not be used.

a direct-current power supply and immersed in a solution containing *ions of the plating metal. The positive terminal is usually connected to an inert conductor. As the current flows through the solution the positive metal ions are attracted to the negative terminal, where they accept electrons to become uncharged metal atoms, which accumulate as a thin layer. Many metals can be applied by electroplating, including chromium, nickel, zinc, cadmium, tin, gold, silver, and platinum.

electrorheological fluid (ER, 'smart' fluid), a liquid suspension that reversibly solidifies to a jelly-like solid when a high-voltage electric field is applied across it. Most modern ER fluids are zeolites (silicates which absorb other molecules on to their surface) or metals coated with oxides or polymers. Possible applications currently in the research stage include an electrically operated *clutch, and a vibration damper whose properties could be varied electrically.

electroscope, an electrostatic instrument used to demonstrate the presence of small potential differences and electric charges. The gold-leaf electroscope contains a pair of gold leaves attached to a conductive support inside an electrically insulated chamber. When the support is charged, the charge passes down into the leaves, which visibly separate due to their mutual repulsion.

electrostatic precipitator, a device for removing particulate impurities from air or other gases. The principle was established early in the 19th century, but it was not until 1906 that F. G. Cottrell of the University of California, USA, developed a commercial process. An electrical discharge is fed into the gas, ionizing the impurity particles (giving them a negative charge). Positively charged electrode plates attract these particles and they are then removed. These devices are now widely used in the chimneys of coal-burning power-stations to remove the fine, pulverized fuel ash.

electrostatics *electricity and magnetism.

electrum *alloy.

element, chemical *atoms and molecules.

Elkington, George Richards (1801–65), British pioneer of *electroplating. With his cousin Henry, he developed an electrochemical process in which the article to be plated served as the *cathode in a bath containing silver cyanide. Electroplating made it possible to apply a very thin, even coat of silver to the article, and superseded other plating methods such as *Sheffield plate.

emulsifier *food additive.

emulsion, a term used to describe a mixture of two immiscible liquids in which one liquid (the disperse phase) is dispersed in the other liquid (the continuous phase) as fine droplets (10^{-9} to 10^{-7} m in diameter). Many synthetic food products are emulsions: for example, French dressing is an emulsion of vegetable oil in vinegar. Emulsifying agents are used to help form the emulsion, and stabilizing agents are used to help maintain it. Many *cosmetics are also emulsions: some are oil-in-water emulsions (foundation creams); others are water-in-oil emulsions (cold creams). Emulsions can be broken up by heat or mechanical agitation: butter is formed by de-emulsifying milk.

emulsion paint, a *paint in which particles of solid *pigment are dispersed in an aqueous liquid (strictly this is known as a sol rather than an emulsion: see *colloid). The liquid forms a skin on exposure to air, trapping a solid coat on the painted material. Emulsifiers and stabilizers are added to the paint to keep the pigment evenly dispersed, but stirring is usually required before use to ensure consistency. Non-drip emulsion paint is a combination of a foam (a gas dispersed in a liquid) and a sol. Stirring destroys the foam and removes the paint's non-drip properties.

enamel, readily fusible powdered glass that is used to coat metal for protection (as in kitchen utensils) or for decoration (for example, *cloisonné* ornaments). The item to be enamelled is coated with enamel powder and heated until the enamel melts. On cooling, the item has a solid glassy film on its surface. Opaque enamels contain opacifiers such as *titanium dioxide. A wide range of colours can be obtained by including metal compounds in the glass—for example, cobalt oxide produces blue enamel and manganese dioxide produces violet. Enamel is also used in a particular form of oil-bound *paint, giving a hard, glossy finish.

endoscopy, the visual examination of an internal part of a patient's body. Early forms of endoscope, such as the *opthalmoscope and laryngoscope (for examining the eyes and vocal cords, respectively), were developed during the 19th century, when localization of disease within the body became a prime concern. These instruments used light from the sun, or from a lamp, reflected into the organ under examination by means of mirrors or sometimes lenses. The introduction of the electric light made it possible to examine less accessible parts of the body, such as the stomach (using the gastroscope). When miniaturized light bulbs were developed, the light source could be mounted at the end of rigid or semi-rigid tubes containing telescopic lens systems and passed right into the organ concerned. Since the 1960s, the use of *optical-fibre systems, which permit the 'bending' of light rays, has revolutionized endoscope design, resulting in smaller instruments which can be introduced through bodily orifices or, more recently, through tiny incisions. The latter technique is used, for example, to examine joints (arthroscopy), the abdominal cavity (laparoscopy), or the foetus in the womb (foetoscopy). Most endoscopy is for diagnostic purposes (such as to reveal peptic ulcers or stomach cancer), but modern endoscopes can also take a *biopsy (tissue sample). Therapeutic procedures, such as cutting away an enlarged prostate gland, can also be performed through an endoscope. The term is also applied to analogous industrial techniques to examine sites not readily accessible.

energy, the capacity of objects or systems to do work. The concept of energy emerged during the mid-19th century, when it was realized that moving bodies could be made to move against resisting forces, thus doing work. This ability came to be known as kinetic energy. Raised bodies exhibit a potential for doing work when they fall, a property known as gravitational potential energy. It was realized that energy could take many forms, with the important characteristic that the total energy of a system remains constant. Other energy forms include chemical energy, thermal energy (*heat), electrical energy, and *nuclear energy. The standard *unit for all forms of energy is the joule (J). It is the energy required to move a distance of 1 metre against a force of 1 newton (N). Power, the rate at which energy is delivered or converted, is measured in J/s, or watts (W). Energy can be

Energy resources

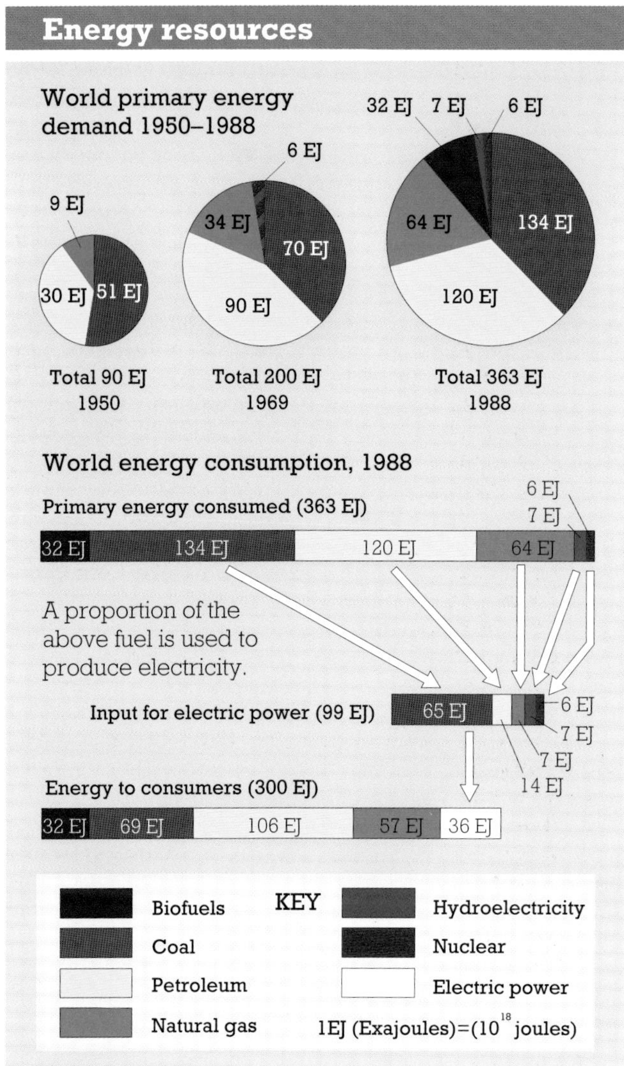

transferred from one body to another by work processes (involving movement), by heating (using their temperature differences), by *electromagnetic radiation (such as light and microwaves) and by *electricity (flow of electrical energy). Energy can also be converted from one form to another. For example, the potential energy of water in a highland reservoir is converted into kinetic energy as the water flows down the inlet tube to a *turbine, where it is converted into electrical energy. Energy conversion processes generally involve 'losses': energy is converted into an unwanted form, usually heat. This is especially so when thermal energy is converted into another form, as in internal-combustion engines or power-stations, where the maximum possible conversion *efficiency is limited by the temperatures involved.

energy resource, any available natural source of useful *energy, or more commonly any source that can be economically utilized with present technologies. In this latter sense, the world's main energy resources for more than a century have been the *fossil fuels. *Hydroelectricity and *nuclear power contribute a few per cent to present world annual energy consumption, and the *biofuels, in the form of firewood or other combustible plant or animal materials, are thought to provide about a tenth of the total (see figure). History has seen two major changes in the relative importance of different energy resources. Before the *Industrial Revolution, fuels provided heat but only rarely mechanical power. The mechanical power of machines came from flowing water or the wind. The invention of the *steam-engine brought the new possibility of converting the heat from burning fuels into mechanical energy. From the 18th until the early 20th century, as steam-power became progressively more widespread, world coal production doubled every 20 years or so. The development of the *internal-combustion engine was followed by a similar growth in *petroleum (oil) consumption. The relative cheapness and convenience of oil and *natural gas meant that by the 1960s they were also the preferred fuels for domestic and industrial heating, further increasing their consumption. The finite nature of the world's energy resources has caused concern for well over a hundred years. In the late 19th century there were predictions that coal supplies would be exhausted within decades, and warnings that the world might run out of oil had appeared before World War I. Consumption has indeed continued to rise, but exploration and new methods of extraction have meant that the known reserves of coal, oil, and gas have tended to keep pace. Nevertheless, serious consideration is being given to alternatives to these fossil fuels. The most fully developed alternatives to these fuels are nuclear power and hydroelectricity. Hydrolectric power offers potential for short-term expansion, but could not satisfy total world demand in the long term, while nuclear power is controversial because of fears concerning safety and undesirable environmental consequences. Other renewable resources that could in principle meet almost all the world's needs, such as *biofuels, *solar power, *wind power, and *wave power, are not yet technologically proven on a world scale, and their economic viability remains to be established. None of these alternatives solve the problem of finding a substitute for oil as a mobile source of energy for cars, ships, aeroplanes, and other vehicles. Newer energy technologies aim to use existing resources more efficiently. Examples include *combined heat and power generation and *fluidized-bed furnaces.

energy storage, a system or process for taking up *energy and retaining it for use at a later time. The storage of electrical energy and of heat are particularly important for the development of renewable energy resources such as *solar or *wind power, which are intermittent and variable. Useful amounts of electrical energy can be stored economically only by conversion into another form. It can be converted into chemical energy, either in rechargeable *batteries or by the electrolysis of water to produce hydrogen and oxygen. In *pumped storage systems electricity is converted into gravitational potential energy, and in night storage heaters to heat energy. Other systems use motors to convert electrical energy into the kinetic energy of a spinning *flywheel or the mechanical energy of a compressed gas. In terms of the volume of material needed, the capacities of all man-made systems are very low compared with natural *energy resources: to store the energy content of one gallon of oil would require eighty fully charged car batteries, twenty night storage heaters, or 60 tonnes of water raised through 300 m (1,000 feet). At present, the pumped storage of large volumes of water is the only practicable method for storing large amounts of electrical energy.

engine, generally, any mechanical contrivance of parts working together, including machines of war, but more usually a machine producing power from a source of heat (a heat-engine). The word motor is sometimes used for engine, but is more correctly applied to sources of power not directly deriving from heat, such as electricity or hydraulic power. The term engine is also applied to railway locomotives. Examples of engines include *steam-engines, air-engines (such as the *Stirling engine), *internal-combustion engines, and *gas-turbines. In all these engines a working fluid, such as water or air, is heated and expands, then cools and contracts. The expansion phase of this cycle can be harnessed to do useful work. Only a percentage of the heat energy of an engine can be converted to useful work: this percentage is the thermal *efficiency of the engine, which is maximally around 40 per cent for a modern engine. The maximum efficiency of any heat-engine has a theoretical limit, determined by the temperatures of the hot and cold sources. Heat-engines may be divided into external- and internal-combustion engines. The former are exemplified by steam-engines, where the fuel is burnt in a *boiler, which supplies steam to the engine. *Gas-engines and *petrol and *diesel engines use internal combustion, as do most gas-turbines. One major difference between external- and internal-combustion engines is that the former can use almost any fuel, but the latter are restricted to clean fuels of very rigid specifications.

engineering, the application of science to the design, building, and use of machines, constructions, and so on. Traditionally, engineering was divided into two main categories: *mechanical engineering, which dealt with the construction and operation of machinery; and *civil engineering, which dealt with large non-mechanical structures such as roads and bridges. Latterly, however, many new categories have had to be defined to take account of increasing specialization. These include *electrical, *environmental, *mining, *chemical, hydraulic, aeronautical, and *systems engineering. Since the late 1960s engineering has acquired a new connotation, in the phrase *genetic engineering. This is engineering at the sub-microscopic level to restructure the DNA that governs the biochemical functions of the cell.

engineering drawing, the graphical description of a solid object. *Leonardo da Vinci developed the skill of engineering drawing, and the French mathematician Gaspard Monge (1746–1818) introduced the orthographic method, which produces dimensionally true drawings to an appropriate scale and from which an engineer or builder can discern measurements. Isometric drawings or perspective views—often used when producing designs—may give a clearer and still accurate representation, but they cannot be dimensionally true to a flat scale.

engraving, an *intaglio process in which a design or image is cut into a smooth metal surface with a sharp tool for printing. A print may be taken from the engraving by rubbing printing ink into the grooves of the plate and then bringing the paper against the plate under high pressure. Engraving gives extremely sharp, clean lines, and has been used by many artists to provide a fine original for *printing. An engraving is also a print made from an engraved plate. (See also *laser engraving, *etching.)

ENIAC *computer, history of.

Enigma *computer, history of.

enlarger *developing and printing.

environmental engineering, engineering concerned with controlling damage to the environment caused by pollution and other hazards. In the 1960s and 1970s the term was applied to engineering relating to the environment within a building, for example *heating systems, water and gas supplies, *lighting, *air-conditioning and so on. Since the 1980s it has more commonly referred to all forms of engineering which have an environmental impact, particularly *sewage systems, waste disposal, and *water resources management.

enzyme, a biological *catalyst that accelerates and controls the reactions of metabolism. Enzymes are proteins, and most are highly specific in their action, working on just one or a narrow range of substrates and converting them to particular products. Glucose-6-phosphatase, for example, will remove phosphate only from one form of glucose-6-phosphate. Techniques to either enhance the activity of one enzyme in a bacterial cell or to isolate the enzyme in cell-free preparations have found wide applications. Amylases, enzymes that act on starch to produce glucose and other sugars, are used in textile manufacture, in some biological detergents, and in baking, to produce lighter loaves. Proteinases, which break down proteins, are used in the baking and brewing industries, as meat tenderizers, in *cheese manufacture, and medically to clean wounds. Other enzymes are used to clarify wines and fruit juices, and as aids to digestion. Immobilized enzymes (enzymes physically entrapped or chemically bonded to an insoluble material such as glass beads) have a greatly prolonged catalytic life, and are increasingly used in industry. In the USA, for example, immobilized glucose isomerase, which converts glucose to fructose, is used to produce high-fructose corn syrup.

epicyclic gear *gear.

epoxy resin, a thermoset *plastic containing epoxy ($\overset{O}{C{-}C}$) groups. Epoxy resins have outstanding adhesion, toughness, and resistance to attack from chemicals. They form strong bonds and have excellent electrical insulation properties. Large, complex, void-free *castings can be made from them. They are also used as *adhesives, and in *composites.

Epsom salts (hydrated magnesium sulphate, $MgSO_4{\cdot}7H_2O$), a white crystalline solid. It was first obtained by Nehemiah Grew in 1695 from a mineral spring at Epsom in Surrey, UK. It has been used as a purgative, as a dressing for cotton goods, as a fungicide, and as a treatment for *magnesium deficiency in plants.

ergonomics (human-factors engineering), the study of the efficient interaction between human beings, their environment, and technological devices and systems. At its simplest, ergonomics might deal with a single operator at a set of controls, or a cook in a kitchen; ergonomic study of the interaction between the human and the equipment is directed towards safety, efficiency, and ease of operation. This is achieved by applying psychological and physiological principles to such matters as the nature and layout of equipment, controls, and displays; the design of seating or other furniture; provision of heating or air-conditioning; and so on. With the increasing use of *information technology the design of the human–computer interface has become an important part of many ergonomic projects; other aspects include ease of maintenance of the equipment, and user-training considerations.

Ericsson, John (1803–89), Swedish-born US engineer, a pioneer of screw propulsion (see *propeller). In 1826 he came to London to exploit a new kind of heat-engine, but his efforts were unsuccessful. At that time there were great developments taking place in *steamship design, but the *paddle-wheels in vogue had the disadvantage of lifting out of the water in rough seas. Ericsson successfully combated this problem in 1838 by employing a screw propeller (patented in 1836) on a small ship, the *Archimedes*. I. K. Brunel promptly redesigned his ship the **Great Britain* for screw propulsion. Settling in the USA in 1839, Ericsson built a screw-driven frigate for the US Navy and, in 1862, built the *ironclad *Monitor*, the first ship to employ a revolving, armoured gun turret.

escalator, a continuously moving stairway. It carries more passengers than a lift but occupies a greater space. Like the travelator (a continuously moving walkway or ramp), it is designed to speed the movement of people in crowded areas and is often used in places such as shops, underground stations, and airports. Each step is carried by four wheels on concealed tracks, and is part of a continuous, circular chain. At the top and bottom, the steps level out to form a flat entry or exit section.

essential oil, a volatile, naturally occurring oil, often with a characteristic smell, containing as one of its main ingredients a substance belonging to a group of compounds known as terpenes. Essential oils are mostly extracted from plants, and are used mainly as *perfumes or as flavourings (see *food additive). They are also used extensively in certain alternative medical therapies. Examples of essential oils include bergamot, eucalyptus, ginger, pine, spearmint and wintergreen oils. Many essential oils are extracted by distillation, but other important extraction methods include enfleurage (extraction using fat) and mechanical pressing. Some oils can now be made synthetically.

etching, the reproduction of a line drawing or other black-and-white image on a metal printing plate (see *platemaking) using an acid or other corrosive agent to remove the metal. There are two basic etching methods. For relief or *letterpress printing, the image area of the metal is protected from the acid, and the non-image areas are etched away to leave the printing area standing in relief. For *intaglio or *gravure printing the image areas are etched into the plate.

ethanol (alcohol, CH_3CH_2OH), a clear, colourless, low-boiling-point (78.5 °C) liquid, the intoxicant in alcoholic drinks. For human consumption it is always produced by *fermentation, as in *brewing or *wine-making. For industrial use, it is sometimes produced by fermentation of cheap vegetable matter such as molasses—as in the production of ethanol for use as a *biofuel. Most commonly, however, ethanol is made by reacting *ethene with water in the presence of a catalyst (usually sulphuric acid or phosphoric acid). Industrial alcohol is treated with additives that are difficult to remove, which make it unpleasant to taste but do not interfere with its chemical properties. Ethanol is used to produce ethanal (acetaldehyde, CH_3CHO), used in the manufacture of vinyl and acrylic plastics. It is also used in the manufacture of vinegar, in the preparation of dyes and perfumes, and as a solvent for lacquers.

ethene (ethylene, $CH_2{=}CH_2$), a colourless, sweet-smelling, flammable gas, which burns readily in air. It occurs in natural gas, and is made by the *cracking of petroleum. Ethene is the simplest hydrocarbon to contain the reactive carbon–carbon double bond, and is a very important starting material in the *petrochemicals industry. It can be polymerized to form *polythene. It reacts with steam to form *ethanol, and with oxygen to form epoxyethane, which is used to make antifreeze, synthetic rubber, solvents, herbicides, detergents, and cosmetics. It reacts with chlorine to produce vinyl chloride and with benzene to produce styrene, both of which are precursors of important plastics (*PVC and *polystyrene, respectively).

ether *anaesthesia.

ethylene glycol *antifreeze.

ethyne (acetylene, $CH{\equiv}CH$), a colourless gas, the simplest *hydrocarbon to contain the very reactive carbon–carbon triple bond. It is formed from calcium carbide and water, or by oxidation of methane. Ethyne is an important industrial starting material for chemical synthesis and is used to produce ethanal (acetaldehyde, CH_3CHO) and halogenated hydrocarbons, such as the *chloro-fluorocarbons. It is also widely used for welding and cutting: the oxy-acetylene flame reaches temperatures of 2,800 °C. Ethyne is explosive when pressurized, so for welding it is dissolved under a pressure of 14 bar in acetone (*propanone) and contained in cylinders packed with absorbent inert material. Ethyne is also used to make many industrially important materials, such as vinyl chloride, vinyl acetate, and neoprene.

Euratom (European Atomic Energy Community), an agency set up in 1957 to promote within the European Community the industrial and technical conditions required to utilize discoveries in atomic physics, and particularly the large-scale production of *nuclear power. Membership was extended to Denmark, Ireland, and the UK in 1973, and to Greece in 1981.

European Laboratory for Particle Physics (CERN), a research institution founded in 1954 as the Conseil Européen pour la Recherche Nucléaire. In the post-war years the increasing cost of experimental research in nuclear physics—particularly that of machines for creating high-energy particles—became an impossible charge on the resources of all but the superpowers. As a response, CERN was established in Geneva as a joint initiative by twelve European countries. It maintains a small permanent staff, but is primarily a centre for providing visiting physicists with exceptional research facilities.

Evans, Oliver (1755–1819), US pioneer of high-pressure *steam-engines. After apprenticeship to a wagon-maker and some general engineering experience, Evans invented an improved *carding machine and built a fully automated milling plant (1784) before turning to steam-engines. Following work with conventional *Watt engines, he experimented with high-pressure steam, which reduced the size of the engine needed for a given power output. By 1804 he had built a successful engine working at a pressure of about 3.5 bar. Concurrently, *Trevithick was also building high-pressure engines in the UK. Evans constructed some fifty engines, most of them used for pumping.

excavator, a machine that digs soil and soft or loose rock. A back-acter or backhoe is an excavator that has a steel bucket on an articulated arm. The soil is dug by drawing the bucket towards the machine, then deposited clear of the excavated site. A face shovel excavates upwards and away from the machine, but digs only to a limited depth. The *drag-line scrapes up the soil by pulling in a single heavy bucket on a cable. Trenches can be dug with an excavator that pulls a chain of buckets.

exhaust system (motor car), the means whereby exhaust gases from a car *engine are discharged to the atmosphere. The exhaust gases from each cylinder are led through short pipes to a common exhaust pipe leading to the rear of the vehicle. Often there is an enlargement forming an expansion chamber, whose function is to smooth the pulsating gas flow before passing to the *silencer. Anti-pollution laws increasingly require a *catalytic converter in the exhaust system to limit the emission of pollutant gases.

expansion joint, a gap that divides a building, pipeline, bridge, road surface, or other structure into sections to allow for the differential expansion or contraction of members as temperatures vary. (Metals and glass, for example, expand more when heated than do brick and concrete.) The joint provides space into which the sections on either side of the gap can expand without constraint, while maintaining the alignment of their surfaces. Where necessary, a seal to protect the joint from moisture, rain, or wind can be provided by flexible mastic (*cement) sealants.

expert system, a computer program that attempts to replicate the expertise and decision-making abilities of a human expert. Expert systems are the most widely developed area of *artificial intelligence, with a variety of applications ranging from medical diagnosis through to financial decision-making and geological prospecting. They often use a heuristic or self-learning approach to the solution of a problem, in which feedback of the results of a particular course of action influences subsequent decisions. They usually have two principal parts: a knowledge base (a special *database, which contains facts and other information representing the rules and experience of an expert practitioner in a particular field); and an inference engine, which interprets the knowledge base in relation to the particular problem being presented. Knowledge engineering is the discipline concerned with building expert systems.

explosive, a chemical which, when detonated, produces a highly exothermic (heat-producing) chemical reaction with evolution of large volumes of gas (an explosion). There are two main types of explosive: deflagrating, or low explosives, and detonating, or high explosives. Low explosives are used as propellants for bullets and shells and for low-power blasting operations in quarries and mines. Such explosives consist either of intimate mixtures of substances which react with one another to release a considerable amount of energy (such as *gunpowder) or of chemical compounds that release energy on decomposition (such as *nitro-cellulose). In both cases, the explosive reaction has to be started by ignition, but once started, the energy released creates a chain reaction that spreads through the whole quantity of explosive in a small fraction of a second. High explosives decompose more rapidly than low explosives, and generate much higher pressures, resulting in much greater shattering power (brisance). They are used for tunnel-blasting and as military explosives. Some high explosives (for example, *dynamite) require detonation rather than ignition before they will explode; this makes them safer to handle. *Nobel patented the use of mercury fulminate as a *detonator for high explosives in 1864. Electrical firing was introduced in the late 19th century. Probably the most powerful high explosive is *TNT, first prepared in 1863, but not made in quantity until 1900. It is used for military purposes, and in combination with another explosive, RDX, it is used in torpedo warheads. In 1955, two major new explosives were developed in the USA—ANFOs (ammonium nitrate and fuel-oil mixtures) and slurry explosives (water gels based on ammonium nitrate). Together these now account for 70 per cent of the high explosives used for civilian purposes in the USA, although they are not widely used elsewhere. The major civilian areas of explosive use are in mining, construction work, seismic prospecting, agriculture, welding, metal hardening, and *riveting. Military uses include bombs, firearms, and warheads, and the use of *plastic explosives for demolition.

exposure (photography) *aperture, *shutter.

exposure meter (light meter), a device using a light-sensitive cell to measure the light reflected from a scene, or the light falling on it, in order to determine the correct exposure for photographic film. The meter may be a separate item, or it may be built into a *camera, perhaps linked to the *shutter or *aperture or to an *automatic exposure control. Some meters measure average light from the whole scene, whereas spot meters monitor a small area. Many hand-held meters use selenium cells, which need no batteries. Cadmium sulphide cells are more sensitive and can be used in dim light, but require battery power.

extrusion, a manufacturing technique for the production of long pieces of material with a common cross-section. The material is forced through a shaped hole, the die, so that it emerges as a continuous length (for illustration see *plastic). Extrusion is important in the manufacture of components from metals, ceramics, and plastics. Highly ductile metals such as aluminium are extruded cold (at room temperature) to form hollow bars and tubes for low-strength applications such as window frames. Other metals such as copper and brass are extruded hot to form water pipes and pipe fittings. In the ceramics industry, extrusion is used to form square-section bars which are cut into *bricks, while viscous *alumina slips are extruded into complex, thin-walled honeycombs, used as support media for catalysts. Thermoplastics become viscous on heating and can be extruded in many forms. Metals are usually extruded from single ingots and billets, while ceramic slips and plastics can be extruded from pellets, thus allowing continuous operation and very long extruded lengths. Extrusion techniques are also used in the manufacture of some foods (see *food technology).

Eyde, Samuel *Birkeland, Kristian Olaf Bernhard.

fabrics, types of, woven, knitted, lace, net, felted, and *nonwoven materials. Weaving (see *loom) produces fabrics of high dimensional stability because two sets of yarn—the *warp and the *weft—cross each other at right angles. Wovens are the most versatile of fabrics, ranging from diaphanous muslins to multiple-layer heavy webbings used in industry. Between these extremes of fabric density are woven pile fabrics such as velvet and corduroy, and heavier pile fabrics such as rugs and *carpets. Knitted fabrics (see *knitting) are more flexible and are readily distorted in the plane of the fabric, because they are formed by the interlocking of small loops of yarn. For applications which demand dimensional stability, straight yarns can be incorporated into the structure, usually along the length of the fabric. In *clothing manufacture, whereas wovens must be cut to shape, knitteds can be produced exactly to shape, thereby avoiding wastage of yarn and cloth. Lace, used mainly for decoration, has not only mutually perpendicular yarns (as have wovens) but also diagonally oriented yarns, providing high dimensional stability. *Lace-making machines are complex and expensive. Nets are woven structures, but, because the yarns are knotted at each crossing, they are not included in the general category of wovens. *Felts are fabrics made wholly from fibre; no yarn is involved. *Nonwoven fabrics are a diverse group of materials made directly from fibres, rather than from yarn. (See also *textiles.)

facsimile transmission *fax.

factory farming, highly intensive animal production. Scientific research into the environmental and nutritional requirements of animals have been applied to all livestock, but particularly to pigs and poultry. Specialist buildings are constructed to minimize heat losses: at optimum stocking rates and with controlled ventilation, animals provide their own heating. Carefully formulated diets fed automatically at regular intervals improve the utilization of animal *feedstuffs. These measures dramatically reduce the costs of raising each animal. *Animal breeding has helped to increase the yield obtainable from factory farming. In battery farming of poultry, chickens are kept in small groups in cages or 'batteries'. The cages are stacked in buildings in which temperature, humidity, and daylight length are controlled to stimulate maximum production. Battery farming in particular has been criticized for its neglect of the animals' welfare, and for its deleterious effects on meat and egg quality. There is now a growing demand for free-range poultry produce.

fall-out, *radioactive isotopes produced during a nuclear explosion, which fall to earth or enter the atmosphere. Nuclear *fission produces radioactivity, and the neutrons released also interact with adjacent matter, creating more radioactive waste. Low-altitude atomic bomb explosions (see *nuclear weapons) throw dust and radioactive material into the lower atmosphere, where most radioactive particles condense on the dust and fall quickly back to earth. High-altitude hydrogen bomb detonations eject radioactive material into the upper atmosphere, where it remains circling the earth for several years. Long-lived fall-out products such as *strontium-90 and caesium-137 enter the food chain. Early effects of radiation on humans include vomiting, secondary infections, and skin irritation; exposure to high-level radiation leads to death. Long-term effects include greatly increased incidences of potentially fatal cancers, and higher occurrences of birth defects.

Faraday, Michael (1791–1867), British chemist and physicist, a pioneer of electromagnetism. In 1813 *Davy employed Faraday as his assistant at the Royal Institution, where he eventually became its director. Working as an analytical chemist, he discovered *benzene in 1825 and prepared the first known compounds of *carbon and *chlorine. He also investigated the composition of alloy *steels and *optical glasses. But his greatest achievements were in electromagnetism. Following the Danish physicist Hans Oersted's discovery (1820) that an electric current produced a magnetic field, Faraday showed that the converse was also true—that a magnetic field can induce an electric current. In 1831 he published his laws of *electromagnetic induction and put them to practical use in the dynamo (see *generator, electrical) and the *transformer, two inventions that are fundamental to large-scale *electricity generation and supply.

farming, the combined range of activities carried out in the practice of *agriculture. Nearly half of the world's economically active population engage in farming, either as a means of subsistence or as a profit-making enterprise. The diversity of farming has primarily been moulded by climate and land quality, although economic and political considerations have also influenced farming practices. In the West farming has attained the status of an industry, in which a small proportion of the population provides the raw materials for food production on a national level. Here, farming involves a high degree of control over the biological processes that underlie agricultural production, for instance in the use of sophisticated methods of tillage, *rotation of crops, synthetic *pesticides, *herbicides, and *fertilizers, and *animal-breeding projects. With the help of outside experts, farmers can optimize soil fertility, water availability, *genetic resources and crop and livestock health. The transport and marketing of farm produce is equally organized. Advances in farming technology coupled with regular subsidies have encouraged specialization and removed the need for careful diversification in *arable and *livestock farming.

A watercolour painted by the artist Harriet Moore in 1852, showing Michael **Faraday** in his laboratory at the Royal Institution, London.

Some fats and oils of major importance

Name	Source	Use/importance	
Saturated fatty acids			
Palmitic acid	Palm oil	Manufacture of soaps and detergents	
Stearic acid	Animal fat		
Unsaturated fatty acids			
Oleic acid	Olive oil	Cooking, medicine	
†Linoleic, Linolenic acids	Linseed oil	Paints, linoleum	Important in animal cell membranes
†Arachidonic acid	Peanut (ground nut) oil	Cooking	
Mixed unsaturated oils	Sunflower and other vegetable oils	Sources of EFAs, margarine manufacture	
Other lipids			
Phosphatidyl choline (lecithin)	Variety of foods, e.g. eggs	Essential component of cell membranes	
Cholesterol	Fatty foods	Contributory factor in heart disease, gall stones	
Steroids	Synthesized in body	Sex and other hormones	
Fatty acid esters of cetyl alcohol	Sperm whale	Spermaceti (used in cosmetics and ointments)	
Myricyl palmitate	Beeswax	Furniture polish	
Terpenes	Various, mainly plant, sources	Turpentine, camphor, vitamin A	

†Essential fatty acids (EFAs).

Although highly productive, these 'advanced' farming systems require large capital investment to maintain and are vulnerable to changes in consumer demand. Such farming is increasingly having to respond to concerns regarding overproduction, energy usage, environmental damage, and animal welfare. Mixed farming, in which both crop and animal husbandry are practised as complementary enterprises, brings the farm unit closer to self-sufficiency for the needs of production. Much *organic farming is mixed. Most *tropical agriculture takes place in Third World countries, where the scarcity of employment, among other factors, keeps farming labour-intensive. (See also *factory farming.)

fast breeder reactor, a type of *nuclear reactor that uses no moderator to slow the neutrons produced during nuclear *fission, and breeds its own fuel in the form of *plutonium. Fission of *uranium-235 is most easily achieved by slow neutrons: fast neutrons are less effective in splitting the nucleus, and are also more easily absorbed by uranium-238, the more abundant *isotope in natural uranium. However, if the *nuclear fuel used in the reactor is enriched in fissionable material (such as U-235), a *chain reaction can be sustained using fast neutrons. The advantage of fast breeder reactors is that many neutrons emitted during the fission are absorbed by a 'blanket' of U-238 around the core, leading to the formation of a new type of fissionable material not normally found in nature—plutonium-239. The amount of plutonium generated in a fast breeder is greater than the amount of U-235 fuel consumed. If this plutonium is then used as nuclear fuel, an enormous improvement in reactor efficiency is achieved, from use of only around 1 per cent of the fuel in conventional reactors to up to 60 per cent in a fast breeder. However, the compact design of the reactor core is considered by some experts to be more vulnerable to catastrophic meltdown than a conventional reactor, and to date fast breeders have not been used commercially. (For illustration see nuclear reactor.)

fats and oils (animal and vegetable), major representatives of the lipid fraction of living organisms. Any organic substance which is insoluble in water but dissolves in organic solvents such as ether is classed as a lipid. The molecules of this heterogeneous group of compounds have in common only the fact that they are rich in hydrogen and poor in oxygen, nitrogen, and other groups that would make them water-soluble (see table). Fats and oils are compounds of fatty acids and glycerol. Fatty acids possess long hydrocarbon chains terminating in an acidic group. In fats and oils the fatty acids usually have from twelve to twenty-four carbon atoms and may be saturated (each carbon carrying as many hydrogen atoms as possible) or unsaturated (some hydrogens replaced by carbon–carbon double bonds). In general, animals yield saturated fats, which are solid at room temperature, while plants yield unsaturated oils, which are liquid. However, seafood also provides important unsaturated oils. The so-called essential fatty acids (EFAs) are polyunsaturated (rich in double bonds): they are essential because they cannot be manufactured in the human body, and small quantities are therefore essential in the diet. Diets in which EFAs form a high proportion of the total fat intake result in lower blood levels of cholesterol.

faucet *tap.

fax (facsimile transmission), a system whereby print and photographs can be transmitted by telephone and reproduced at the receiver. The original design (1843) involved electrical pulses being transmitted from a pendulum scanning embossed lettering; today's machines use an array of light-sensitive *diodes to detect light reflected from the subject. Transmission of photographs was first demonstrated in 1902 by the German physicist Arthur Korn; his transatlantic radio transmission in 1922 led to a commercial service in 1926. Fax is used today by, for example, newspapers, weather forecasting organizations, and businesses.

feedback, the process whereby information about the output of a system is fed back to the input in order to influence the behaviour of the system. Distinction is often made between negative feedback, in which the feedback tends to reduce a system input, and positive feedback, which tends to reinforce it. Negative feedback thus often has a stabilizing effect, while positive feedback can cause system output to grow or oscillate indefinitely. Under dynamic conditions, however (that is, when system input, output and feedback signal are changing with time), the distinction between positive and negative feedback can become less clear. Hence, for example, negative feedback systems can become unstable under certain conditions. Accurate predictions of behaviour require appropriate *dynamic modelling of the feedback system as a whole. Feedback occurs widely in biological systems and finds many technological applications, notably in closed-loop *control systems, operational *amplifiers, and *oscillators. (See control systems for illustration.)

feedstuff, animal, a food product developed to achieve high yields from domestic animals. Most livestock require a similar diet to humans—a balance of carbohydrate, fat, and protein—but ruminants such as cattle and sheep can utilize plant material high in cellulose, and low-quality sources of protein. During the growing season, most livestock are fed on pasture grasses and legumes; outside the growing season, livestock are fed a source of roughage (such as hay, *silage, or *root-crops) supplemented by a high-protein concentrate. Oilcake is a concentrate made from vegetable seeds such as soya beans or sunflower seeds after they have been processed to remove the oil. Cereal grains such as barley and sorghum may be mixed with oilcake to form a complete feed for pigs and poultry, or a supplement for ruminants and horses. Protein concentrates from animal products include fish, meat, blood, and bone-meal: fish-meal is particularly rich in protein, while bone-meal is high in the minerals calcium and phosphorus. Since the diagnosis of BSE (bovine spongiform encephalopathy) in 1986, tighter controls have been introduced, particularly in the UK, concerning the use of offal as a feedstuff supplement. Other feeds are by-products of other food processing industries, for example sugar-beet pulp, brewers' grains, pineapple bran, and products derived from the milling of wheat.

felt, a type of *nonwoven fabric, made by rolling and pressing, and shrinking *wool or other textile *fibres. It derives its strength and dimensional stability from mutual entanglement of its fibres. It is used in clothing, upholstery, and draperies, as well as in many industrial processes. Wool fibres, being naturally highly crimped, form strong entanglements and are easily felted. They are also used to assist in the binding of other fibres to form felts. A recent development is the making of felts from some *synthetic fibres, and these new felts are beginning to be used in large quantities.

fermentation, the breakdown of sugars to either *ethanol (alcohol) or lactic acid by micro-organisms such as yeasts and *bacteria in the absence of oxygen. Alcoholic fermentation occurs in the presence of yeasts, and is an important part of *bread-making and the manufacture of *alcoholic drink such as *wine. Lactic acid is produced in *bacterial fermentation, and is integral to *cheese and yoghurt production. Fermentation is also important in such agricultural processes as *silage-making and *grain storage.

Fermi, Enrico (1901–54), Italian-born US physicist, a major figure in the development of *nuclear energy and constructor of the first nuclear reactor (see *atomic pile). After a distinguished early career in theoretical physics, he turned to experimental work in the early 1930s. He was the first to bombard uranium with neutrons, causing nuclear *fission, although it was *Meitner and her colleagues in Germany who interpreted his results. Fermi received the Nobel Prize for Physics in 1938, and after the ceremony fled to the USA to escape the Fascist regime of the Italian dictator Benito Mussolini. In 1939, after the outbreak of World War II in Europe, he and a group of other leading physicists wrote to the US president Franklin Roosevelt, warning of the dangers if Germany developed nuclear weapons. In 1942, after the USA had entered the War, the letter led to the establishment of the *Manhattan Project to develop an atomic bomb. As part of the project, Fermi designed the atomic pile, which in December 1942 achieved the first controlled, self-sustaining nuclear reaction.

Ferranti, Sebastian Ziani de (1864–1930), British pioneer of high-voltage electricity generation and distribution. After some experimenting with electrical furnaces and inventing a new and more powerful dynamo, de Ferranti proposed a scheme for supplying electricity to the whole of North London using a single station (at Deptford) that generated alternating current (see *electricity generation and supply). To implement the scheme, the London Electric Supply Corporation was established in 1887, with de Ferranti as chief engineer. His conception of large-scale, high-voltage alternating-current power-stations serving a large area formed the model for modern electricity generation.

ferrite, any member of a family of *electroceramics based on iron oxides, particularly magnetite (Fe_3O_4). Ferrites are capable of holding a permanent magnetic dipole. They are usually very soft magnets (easily magnetized and demagnetized) and are of great importance as transformer cores, especially for high-frequency applications. They are electrical insulators and hence do not undergo losses from eddy currents within a transformer core.

ferry, a vessel designed to transport people, animals, and vehicles over a predetermined (usually short) route in protected waters. Ferries have been in existence for thousands of years, the earliest powered by a pole or oars, or towed back and forth across a stream by ropes or chains. On many inland waterways ferries have been made obsolete by the construction of *bridges. Since World War II, the term has also been applied to large ships, such as the roll-on, roll-off *car ferries formerly known as 'packets'.

fertility drug, a substance used to treat women who experience difficulty in becoming pregnant. One cause of infertility is an inadequate supply of gonadotrophins, *hormones that control ovulation (the release of an egg from the ovary). Natural gonadotrophins, or drugs such as clomiphene which stimulate gonadotrophin production, can bring about ovulation, but often more than one egg is released, resulting in a multiple birth. Another cause of infertility is endometriosis (degeneration of the uterus lining), which can be treated by oral *contraceptives. A third type of fertility drug is bromocriptine, used to regularize abnormalities in ovulation and the menstrual cycle.

fertilizer, a natural or artificial *agrochemical containing nutrients that is added to soil to improve the growth and productivity of plants. Fertilizers are primarily used to provide the three major elements required for plant growth—nitrogen, phosphorus, and potassium—along with other minor and trace elements. Lime, widely applied to combat soil acidity and provide calcium, is also considered a fertilizer. Organic fertilizers, such as manure and composts, have been in use since almost the beginning of agriculture. Such fertilizers contain complex nutrients which must be broken

Classification of textile fibres

Type of fibre	Source
Natural fibres	
Animal fibres	
Silk	Cocoon of the silkworm, *Bombyx mori*
Wool	Outer hair of sheep of many different breeds
Hair	Alpaca, camel, cattle, goat (mohair, cashmere), horse, rabbit, vicuña
Vegetable fibres	
Bast (fibres from stems of plants)	Flax (linen), hemp, jute, ramie
Leaf fibres	Abaca (manila), henequen, sisal
Seed fibres	Cotton, kapok, coir
Natural mineral fibres	
Asbestos (naturally occurring fibrous, hydrated silicates)	Actinolite, amosite, anthophyllite, chrysotile, (white asbestos), crocidolite (blue asbestos), tremolite
Manufactured fibres	
Manufactured mineral fibres	Fibres made from minerals that do not occur naturally in fibrous form, e.g. carbon, ceramic fibres, textile glass, metal fibres
Regenerated-polymer fibres	Fibres produced from naturally occurring fibre-forming polymers such as wood cellulose and casein. Examples include alginates, elastodiene (a type of rubber), regenerated protein fibres, regenerated cellulose fibres (rayon, viscose, modal), and cellulose esters (cellulose acetate and triacetate)
Synthetic-polymer	Fibres produced from a polymer synthesized from simpler chemical elements, commonly derived from petroleum. Examples are polycarbamides, polyolefins (polythene, polypropylene), polyvinyl derivatives (acrylic fibres, PTFE), polyurethanes, polyamides (nylon), aramid fibres, and polyesters

down by bacterial action before they can be used by plants. Traditionally, manure was mixed with straw or sawdust and fermented before use. Now, livestock are often housed on slatted floors, and their manure is collected and applied as a semi-liquid slurry. Sodium nitrate and guano (sea-bird excrement from South America containing phosphates and nitrates) were first used in the UK in the 1830s. Modern chemical fertilizers were first used in the 1840s: one of the earliest was 'superphosphate' (invented by *Lawes), made by dissolving bones (later mineral phosphates) in acid. A modification of this process forms the basis of today's phosphate fertilizer industry. Nitrogen fertilizers are almost universally derived from synthetic ammonia, produced from atmospheric nitrogen by the *Haber–Bosch process. Industry has coupled ammonia to a range of other compounds to yield ammonium salt and urea fertilizers. Potassium fertilizers are obtained as various mined salts. Most fertilizers are applied as solids, either powders or granules, but liquid fertilizers are popular in the USA, and ammonia gas can be liquefied under pressure and injected deep into soil. The exact fertilizer used depends on the climate, soil type, the crop, and economic factors. Synthetic fertilizers are essential to sustain today's intensive agricultural systems world-wide (for example, in the *green revolution). Nevertheless, their widespread use has been criticized because of the energy required to synthesize them, and *nitrate fertilizers have given cause for concern because they enter water supplies, with possible harmful consequences.

Fessenden, Reginald Aubrey (1866–1932), Canadian pioneer of radio engineering. Fessenden was the first to discover that, by using a microphone to *modulate the radio wave, sound (rather than a simple signal) could be transmitted. In 1906 his company successfully transmitted voice signals over long distances. His other inventions included *echo-sounding equipment, an electrolytic radio detector, a generator of high-frequency oscillations, and the heterodyne *radio receiver, forerunner of the superheterodyne system used today.

fibre, textile, the raw, fibrous material from which *fabrics and other *textiles are made. Textile fibres may be subdivided into two main groups: those occurring naturally, which may be of animal, vegetable, or mineral origin, and those which are manufactured, mainly from regenerated or synthetic polymers. Fibres are made into *yarn by *spinning. Spinning processes differ, depending on whether the fibres being spun are long, as in silk, or short, as for example in cotton and wool. Of the natural fibres, *cotton is by far the most important, comprising nearly 50 per cent by weight of the world's annual fibre supply. Other fibre-producing crops, such as flax, hemp, jute, and sisal, are of minor importance. Animal fibres provide about 6 per cent of the annual world-wide fibre supply. *Wool is the most important of these fibres. Others include the hair of varieties of goat, which provide *mohair and cashmere, and the *silk thread spun by the silkworm. Asbestos is the only significant naturally occurring mineral fibre. With the exception of silk, natural fibres are relatively short (on average, 2–50 cm, 1–20 inches). Such short fibres are generally known as 'staple' fibres.

The remainder of the world's fibre supply is manufactured. Some manufactured fibres are derived from naturally occurring fibre-forming polymers (for example, *rayons, made from natural cellulose). However, the majority are *synthetic fibres, produced from long-chain polymers, usually derived from oil. Manufactured fibres are extruded or 'spun' by pumping the fibre material in solution or in molten form through the fine holes of a spinneret (see spinning). More than 50 per cent of synthetic filament manufactured is cut or broken to form staple fibre. Most is then used, either alone or in blends with natural fibres, for the manufacture of spun *yarns.

fibreglass *glass fibre.

fibre optics *optical fibre.

fibre-producing crop *fibre, textile (table).

fibre-reinforced plastic, any of a range of *composite materials comprising comparatively cheap thermosetting or thermoplastic materials reinforced with strong, stiff fibres. Common matrix media are *epoxy resins and the thermoplastic polyether etherketone (PEEK). Glass-fibre-reinforced plastics (GFRP) are very important in modern engineering. Mats of glass fibres in thermosetting polyester and epoxy resins are used extensively in the construction of boats, ranging from small yachts and canoes to military ships of about 500 tonnes. GFRP is also important for sports goods, where continuous glass fibres are wound round formers to make hollow, light, stiff shafts for racquets, fishing rods, and golf clubs. It is now being used increasingly in the automobile industry in place of steel body panels: material reinforced with short glass fibres is used, because it can be injection moulded. GFRP is also important as a material for circuit boards. Carbon fibre-reinforced plastics (CFRP) are used extensively in the aerospace industry because of their high elastic stiffness and low weight. They are also used for sports goods and racing-car bodywork. The lightest composites are reinforced with ultra-high-strength polymer fibres such as aramids (see *nylon).

fifth-generation computer, a term applied to *computer systems currently being developed specifically to support *artificial intelligence. In the early 1980s Japan set up a major research project intended to develop the computer *hardware and *software necessary to perform complex tasks such as *machine translation of natural languages, *speech recognition, and vision in *robotics. Similar projects were also started in the USA and Europe. The use of artificial intelligence to solve practical problems requires very powerful computers and fifth-generation computers are likely to use more complex *computer architectures than conventional computers, involving *parallel processing. In 1991 Japan began a new ten-year research initiative, replacing the fifth-generation programme, to investigate *neural networks.

fighter aircraft, *military aircraft designed primarily to intercept and destroy other aircraft. Early fighters developed from reconnaissance aircraft; an example is the Vickers F.B.5. A major innovation of World War I was the German Fokker Eindecker, which incorporated an interrupter gear that allowed a machine-gun to be fired through the propeller. By the start of World War II most biplanes had been replaced by all-metal monoplanes like the Supermarine Spitfire, with wing-mounted machine-guns and, later, heavy-calibre cannon and rockets. Other developments included the rise of the *fighter-bomber, and the appearance of the jet-powered Gloster Meteor and Messerschmitt Me 262 in 1944. After the War (1948) an American F-100 Super Sabre fighter was the first jet aircraft to fly supersonically. Fighters of the late 1950s reached speeds greater than *Mach 2; many of these aircraft continued in front-line service into the 1980s, updated with advanced *avionics and weaponry. Post-war fighters, armed with air-to-air and air-to-ground guided *missiles, have changed roles. In the cold war of the 1950s the emphasis was on the interception of nuclear bombers, but with the development of agile, low-flying strike aircraft, air-to-air combat and close support of ground forces have become major roles. Avionics are as important to modern fighters as propulsion and weaponry. Recent fighters are inherently unstable in design, which makes them extremely agile. They rely on computer-aided, *fly-by-wire control to maintain flight stability. Another recent development is the US F-117 'stealth' fighter, designed to be extremely difficult to detect using *radar.

fighter-bomber, a *fighter aircraft able to carry bombs and other air-to-surface weapons for ground attack. The usefulness of agile, fast fighter aircraft to carry bombs was first proved by the Hawker Typhoon and Tempest in World War II. Modern strike or attack aircraft such as the Soviet Sukhoi Su-24 Fencer, the US F-111, or the European Panavia Tornado fulfil a similar role.

file (computing), a set of information stored in a *computer system, usually on a *hard or *floppy disk, or on magnetic tape. Files may contain *programs, *data, text, or other suitably coded information. Each file is identified by a name and is normally used to contain logically related information.

files and rasps, tools used to shape surfaces by abrasion. The file has a series of small raised cutting edges (whose size depends on the fineness of the work to be done), arranged so as to produce abrasion on the forward thrust. Early files (*c.*1000 BC) were made of iron and easily became blunt, but with the invention of alloy steels in the 19th century, much longer life was achieved. Files come in a wide range of shapes and sizes, depending on the nature of the work to be done. The most common shapes are flat, triangular, or round. The blade ends in a tang (pointed end), inserted into a wooden handle. The rasp is similar to the file, except that the abrasion is effected by rounded teeth rather than cutting edges. (For illustration, see *tools, history of.)

film (photography), light-sensitive material used for recording images in a *camera or *cine-camera. Films for different applications have a variety of formats (see table). Black-and-white film consists of a tough, flexible *cellulose acetate base carrying a thin layer of a light-sensitive emulsion (silver

Photographic film formats

Name	Image size on film	Description
35 mm	36 × 24 mm (1.4 × 0.9 inches)	Most popular film type. Wound on light-tight single spools, or can be bought in bulk
120	Usually 60 × 63 mm (2.3 × 2.5 inches)	Wide format, more detailed negative. Wound on single open spool. Film is paper-backed to exclude light when not in camera
Sheet	Commonly up to 250 × 200 mm (10 × 8 inches)	Single sheets of large-format film, or cassettes of several sheets in a holder. Used for high-quality, high resolution work
110/126	13 × 17 mm or 25 × 25 mm (0.5 × 0.7 inches or 1.1 × 1.1 inches)	Rolls of film in two-spool cartridges that fit easily into camera. Used mainly for snapshot cameras
Disc	As 110/126 film	Film mounted round edge of a disc
Polaroid	Various	Film cartridges or packs including own developing chemicals

Firearm

Hand cannon
This dates from about 1400 and is one of the original forms of small arms. Recoil was absorbed by positioning the hook over a wall.
Harquebus
The harquebus was a development from the hand cannon in about 1470.
Flintlock pistol
This dates from the mid-17th century. Being one-handed, it was a popular weapon for use on horseback.
Musket
Used between the 16th and 18th centuries, the musket was limited to one shot every 20 seconds and its aim was inaccurate for targets over 80 m (260 feet) away. However, this did not matter when the target was a densely packed unit of men.
The revolver dates from the mid-19th century and has changed little in format since then.
Colt revolver
Rifle
Firing pin
Cartridge
Bullet being fired
Hammer
Magazine
A rifle's barrel has spiral grooves cut into its inner surface (rifling), which imparts a spinning motion to the bullet, increasing its stability in flight. Modern automatic rifles can theoretically fire several hundred rounds per minute.
Sub-machine-gun
This is a fully automatic weapon, firing several hundred rounds per minute. It is used mainly for close combat.
Bazooka
Rocket
This weapon is operated by two people, firing a rocket up to 1200 m (4000 feet). It is used primarily against tanks with an effective range of about 100 m (330 feet).

halide crystals suspended in gelatine) and a protective coating. When a film is exposed, light falling on it causes changes in the structure of the silver halide crystals, recording a latent image of the scene being photographed on the film. In *developing, this latent image is converted to a permanent, negative image of light and dark areas. Film for colour *photography has not one but three emulsion layers, each sensitive to one of the three primary colours (see *developing and printing). Films of different speeds have different sensitivities to light: a fast film is very sensitive and so can work down to lower light levels, but it gives a coarser (grainier) picture quality.

filter circuit, an electrical circuit used to screen electrical *signals, usually on the basis of frequency, allowing only certain frequencies to pass. Filters can be low-pass (high frequencies eliminated), high-pass (low frequencies eliminated), or band-pass (one range of frequencies passed only). Band-stop filters pass all frequencies except for a specific range. Filters are widely used in *electronics and *broadcasting to 'clean' signals up, that is to eliminate distortion or unwanted signals. They must, however, be carefully designed otherwise they introduce their own distortion into the signal.

filtration, the separation of suspended solids from their suspending liquid by passing the suspension through a porous medium. Filtration is a widely used separation and purification procedure in the laboratory and industry: it is used in the manufacture of chemicals and biological substances, in food processing, in *paper manufacture, and in *water and *sewage treatment. Paper, cloth, and fine wire mesh are simple filtration media. Until recently asbestos was used in most types of filter, but its health hazards have led to the development of alternative materials. Filtration apparatus can vary from a simple paper filter in a funnel, to filter beds many square metres in area, or mechanized filtration drums or belts. The suspension or slurry may be forced through the filter under pressure, or a vacuum may be used to draw material through the filter.

Ultrafiltration is the separation of large molecules or particles of *colloidal size from a liquid medium, using a thin, semi-permeable cellulose acetate or other filtration membrane supported on a porous substructure. Flow rates are much higher than in conventional filtration, and a cake of solid residue is not formed on the filter surface. Ultrafiltration is widely used to separate proteins from solution: the process can be used in cream-cheese making.

firearm, generally, a hand-weapon from which projectiles are propelled by the combustion of gunpowder or other explosives. The first firearms were smaller versions of *cannon, developed in the 14th century (see figure). From around 1425 the firing of such weapons was improved by the invention of the matchlock, a mechanism by which a slow-burning match was brought into precise contact with a small pan of priming powder: burning of the priming powder then ignited the main charge. The harquebus was an early matchlock weapon; heavier harquebuses, known as muskets, were introduced in the 16th century (musket subsequently became the generic term for the infantryman's firearm). Lighter, shorter weapons (carbines) were developed for cavalrymen. In about 1515 a new ignition system, the wheel-lock, was developed in Germany. It generated a series of sparks in the priming pan by the movement of a spring-wound serrated wheel against a piece of iron pyrites (like the flint in some cigarette lighters). Wheel-locks were never widely adopted by infantry, but wheel-lock *pistols were often used by cavalry. A simpler ignition method, the flint-lock, used a flint held in a sprung lever, which was struck against a piece of steel to produce sparks. Flintlocks began to be adopted on a large scale in the late 17th century. In the mid-16th century, rifling of the barrels of small weapons was first introduced. This involved the cutting of grooves inside the gun barrel to make the bullets spin and improve their accuracy. *Rifled firearms proved impractical for military use because they could not be loaded quickly. It was not until the development (1849) of the Minié *bullet that these difficulties were overcome.

Early in the 19th century the first percussion-ignition systems appeared, using a *detonator activated by a sharp blow. *Cartridges containing a fixed explosive charge also began to be widely used at about this time. Another major 19th-century advance was the general adoption of breech-loading weapons, as opposed to muzzle-loaders in which charge and shot had to be inserted down the barrel. Centre-fire metal cartridges of the type that is familiar today were introduced in about 1870. Such weapons greatly improved the effectiveness of infantry fire. In the last quarter of the 19th century, the *machine-gun was developed.

In the 20th century firearm design changed little until World War II, when the pistol was superseded by the *sub-machine-gun, and semi-automatic rifles were introduced. Since World War II there have been many design innovations. Most modern rifles are fully automatic (that is, they continue to fire as long as the trigger is held back) and double as light machine-guns, while sub-machine-guns are now extremely light and compact. The development of higher velocity ammunition has improved accuracy, and new caseless ammunition (in which there is no cartridge, the bullet being embedded in propellant) has made high accuracy possible at extremely rapid fire rates. There are also many new heavy firearms, including high-powered rifles with laser sighting, hand-held grenade-launchers, and shoulder-fired *anti-tank or anti-aircraft weapons firing small, laser-guided missiles.

fire-extinguisher, a hand-held appliance for putting out fires. Different types of extinguisher are available for different kinds of fire. Each extinguisher operates on one or more of three basic principles: the burning material is extinguished by cooling; the fire is blanketed by an inert gas that excludes air; or the air supply is cut off by some solid material such as sand or a fireproof blanket. Water is the most widely used fire-quenching agent. It is applied as a fine spray or fog using carbon dioxide gas, generated within the appliance. It has a cooling effect and the steam produced helps blanket the fire. Water cannot be used, however, on electrical fires or those involving magnesium alloys, which it aggravates, nor in freezing conditions, unless some antifreeze agent is included. In such cases, a dry chemical extinguisher is needed. This normally contains powdered sodium bicarbonate, which both blankets the fire and generates carbon dioxide, to exclude air. Fire-extinguishers using *chloro-fluorocarbons (CFCs) are used for specific risks, such as computer suites. Replacement extinguishing media are being sought, mainly as a result of the environmental effects of CFCs.

fire-fighting, the techniques used to extinguish or control fires. Fire-fighting involves two principal approaches. One is the use of permanently installed equipment, notably *sprinkler systems, set to function automatically in response to *smoke detectors or thermal sensors. The other is based on the mobile fire-engine and ancillary equipment (see figure). For a blazing building the fire-engine must provide an extendable, manœuvrable ladder, and a variety of emergency apparatus. This will include hand-held fire hoses supplied from *hydrants, and *fire-extinguishers; axes, saws,

Fire-fighting

The most important mobile fire-fighting unit is the fire-engine. There are many types of fire-engine, each with varying degrees of fire-fighting and rescue capabilities. Most fire-fighting appliances carry a limited supply of water; a pump for delivering water and foam on to the fire; and a ladder for access and rescue. Some specialist vehicles carry ladders and powerful cutting equipment only.

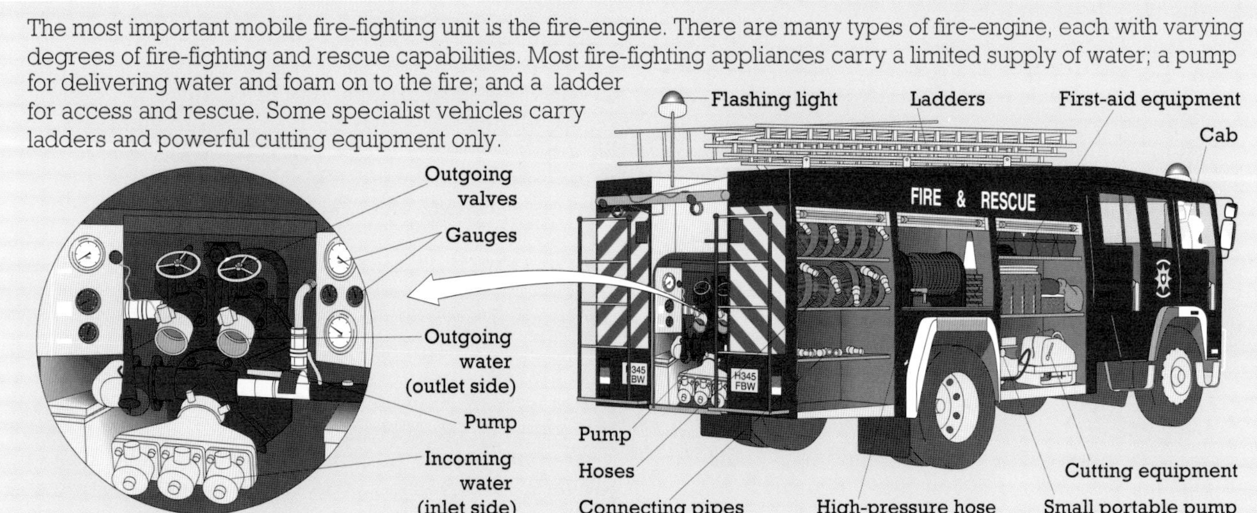

and other tools for effecting forced entry if necessary; and breathing apparatus to make it possible to enter areas full of smoke or noxious fumes. Structural fires are commonly fought by an over-and-under method, that is, ventilating the fire from below to prevent smoke and heat build-up, while aiming hoses at a level above the fire to prevent its spreading. Incidents such as those that result from road, rail, or aircraft accidents may require the use of heavy lifting equipment, metal cutters, and oxy-acetylene torches to free people trapped in wreckage. Fires, or potential fires, involving large quantities of highly flammable fuel, solvents, or paint—as with accidents to tankers or aircraft—will often need to be sprayed with a blanket of foam to exclude air. Large forest fires cannot usually be extinguished by direct means. Rather, they are contained within a limited area until they burn out, by cutting fire breaks and starting backfires to remove combustible fuel from the path of the fire; by using large teams of volunteers to beat out subsidiary fires; and by dropping water slurries from aircraft on to surrounding vegetation. A fire at an oil or gas well must be 'capped' to exclude oxygen, a job usually requiring a specialist trouble-shooting team. Fire prevention measures can help to reduce the incidence of fires. In many countries fire precautions are governed by law. They include such things as the provision of fire doors to prevent fire spreading along corridors or other natural ducts and to ensure a safe escape for the occupants of the building; restrictions on the use of certain types of lacquers and furniture upholstering; and *fireproofing of combustible materials.

fireless locomotive, a steam locomotive that operates without a live fire. Locomotives of this type were initially tried on the first *underground railway, where smoke was a major problem. They used a fire-box filled with pre-heated cast-iron blocks, but the method was not successful. Later locomotives operated with the boiler filled with high-pressure steam from a stationary source and were propelled using conventional cylinders and valve gear. These locomotives were employed on industrial railways, mainly for short-distance shunting duties at sites with a high fire risk from sparks: for example, munitions factories and paper mills.

fire-making device, a device for igniting combustible materials or fuels. Archaeological evidence suggests that humans used fire 500,000 years ago, taking advantage of blazes started by lightning or spontaneous combustion. More reliable fire-making techniques based on frictional heating were developed in about 7000 BC: an example is the fire-drill, a pointed wooden stick rapidly rotated in a tinder-filled hollow in a wooden plank. Primitive fire-making techniques also used sparks produced by striking flint against iron pyrites (a mineral sulphide of iron). Tinder-boxes employed this principle and were used until the 19th century; some modern *cigarette lighters and gas lighters also use this mechanism. The Incas made fire in the 15th century by concentrating the rays of the Sun with a concave mirror. The fire-piston of South-East Asia, later (around 1820) seen in Europe, used a piston forced rapidly into a cylinder to compress and heat air. This ignited flammable material inside the cylinder. Matches were developed from sulphur-tipped wooden splints used with tinder-boxes to assist in developing a flame. Early experiments with matches of various types were made in Paris from around 1805; by the late 1820s matches were being manufactured industrially in several countries. In 1831 white phosphorus was first incorporated into matches, which greatly improved their ignition properties. In 1845 the Austrian chemist Anton von Schrötter discovered red phosphorus, a non-toxic form of phosphorus which is still used in match manufacture. In modern safety matches the match-head contains combustible materials and oxidizing agents, which are ignited by friction with red phosphorus contained in the striking surface.

fireproofing, the treatment of flammable materials to reduce the risk of fire. Although many materials are combustible, fireproofing is most commonly identified with wood, plastics, and textiles. Wood in thick sections is surprisingly fire-resistant because it is a poor conductor of heat (see *fire-resistance); however, resistance can be much improved by impregnation with certain chemicals such as ammonium phosphate or borax. A great hazard is posed by surface coatings of paint or lacquer, which can burn fiercely and quickly. The lessons of past disasters have led to the introduction of legislation restricting the use of dangerous coatings. For fireproofing plastics and textiles, organic phosphorus compounds are widely used, but they are subject to certain constraints. They must, for example, be resistant to laundering and, in the case of clothing, be non-irritant. In these regards too, many countries have tightened safety regulations to protect the consumer.

fire-resistance (building), the ability of a building (or part of it) to withstand fire for a specified period of time, typically from 1–4 hours. Fire-resistant materials allow the safe evacuation of a building and prevent fire spreading to adjacent buildings as a result of premature collapse. When exposed to fire, steel quickly loses strength and must often be protected by facing with concrete or other insulating material. Timber, however, chars on the surface, and the charred layer protects the interior. Brickwork is highly fire-resistant. (See also *fireproofing.)

firework, a device that produces coloured flames and explosions in a variety of ways, often used to create a spectacular display against a night sky, but also as distress rockets or flares, or to locate targets in military operations. Fireworks are of ancient Chinese origin, and developed out of the use of *gunpowder for military rockets and missiles. Fireworks are ignited by lighting a fuse, the heat from which initiates a chemical reaction between components packed in a paper or cardboard tube. Fireworks always contain a fuel and an oxidizing agent so that the contents can burn. The colour of the flame can be varied by including metal salts—for example, strontium produces brick red, and barium gives green. The addition of metal powders produces sparks, and the inclusion of small quantities of explosives results in loud bangs. Components that burn with a sustained and rapid evolution of gas are used in rockets. Generally, the manufacture of fireworks requires a government licence as it involves using explosive and flammable materials.

fish curing, processing designed to preserve raw fish from spoilage. The three main fish curing methods are drying, salt curing, and smoking, all of which lower the food's water content and thus greatly inhibit the activity of spoilage bacteria and enzymes. In suitable climates, gutted fish will dry in the open air in about six weeks. In salt curing, the fish are placed in dry salt after removal of the head and backbone. This draws out the moisture and produces brine. The fish are then either pickled by storing in brine or are removed and dried. The first stage in smoking is to cut up the fish and soak them in brine. They are then dried by hanging in the

Feeding at a **fish-farm** in Indonesia.

flues of ovens fuelled by smouldering hardwood chips. Fish may artificially be given the appearance and flavour of being smoked by pickling in solutions containing dyes and other chemicals.

fish-farming, a branch of *aquaculture involving the rearing of fish under controlled conditions. Ideally, the environment is controlled so that natural predators are eliminated, optimum nutrition is provided, and the fish flourish. Until recently, the main commercial interest was in freshwater fish-farming of carp, catfish, gourami, milk-fish, salmon, tilapia, and trout. Marine farming, especially of salmon, is now increasing, and crustaceans and molluscs are also farmed in specialist *shellfish farming. Fish-farming accounts for about 7 per cent—5 million tonnes—of the world's annual fish harvest, half of which is from China. Simple fish-farms consist of ponds or flooded fields containing a naturally breeding population. Natural food is supplemented and fish are removed when mature. Increasing water pollution is curtailing the activities of such farms. Industrial freshwater fish-farms are based on concrete pools and hatcheries, where the environment is totally controlled. Spawning is triggered by injection of hormones into adult fish. Salt-water fish-farms consist of barricaded coastal waters, or cages suspended in the open sea.

fishing industry, a commercial enterprise concerned with the catching and removal from their natural habitats of aquatic life-forms. Fishing is distinct from angling, in which fish are caught mainly for sport. The main concern in fishing is with the catching, processing, marketing, and conservation of fish and shellfish. The major fish types caught are demersal fish, living on or near the sea-bed (see table), and pelagic fish, which live in the open sea near the surface. Specialized aspects of the fishing industry deal with molluscs (squid, cuttlefish, octopus, bivalves, and gastropods), crustaceans (crab, lobster, crayfish, shrimp, and prawn), mammals (whale, dolphin, seal, and walrus), amphibians, worms, coelenterates, sponges, and plants. Products are sold fresh, frozen, or *canned, or are cured by drying, salting, or smoking (see *fish curing). One-third of the global catch (around 95 million tonnes per year) is used to produce animal feed and other *fish products. The main source of fish is the oceans; less than 14 per cent of fish came from *freshwater sources in 1988. *Aquaculture, *fish-farming, and *shellfish farming also make a significant contribution. The majority of the ocean harvest comes from the shallow waters over continental shelves. Japan is the leading fishing country, followed by the Soviet Union, China, Peru, the USA, and Chile.

Prehistoric remains show that molluscs formed a large part of the diet of early humans living near lakes and the seashore. The development of *traps and *nets facilitated the catching of free-swimming fish. Individual fishing was later replaced by groups working together with improved equipment, going out to sea in ever-larger boats. By the Middle Ages, large fisheries had been established around the coasts of Europe, the most common catch being herring. Cod fishing started on the Grand Banks off the Newfoundland coast at the end of the 15th century. *Whaling was established in both the Atlantic and the South Pacific during the 17th century. Until the end of the 19th century, all fishing boats were propelled by sails, the tackle was worked by hand, and the fish located by experience. In the 20th century steam- and diesel engines gradually replaced sail, and the invention of the power winch allowed a great increase in the size of the tackle.

There are many types of fishing vessel, each suited to the type of fish sought, their location, and the duration of fishing voyages. Coastal vessels are between 8 and 40 m (25–130 feet) long with a crew of up to twenty-five. The catch is stored in refrigerated holds and processed on land. Small *trawlers fish in shallow waters such as the North Sea and the English Channel. Long-range fishing fleets stay at sea for months and travel great distances. These factory fleets include processor–catcher vessels with crews of 50–100 people, which can process thousands of tonnes of catch per day. They are supported by refrigerated transporters and supply ships. Fishing gear is suited to the type of fish sought, for example, seine, trawl, and gill nets, *longlines, traps, and *harpoons. Other fishing methods include fishing with trained animals (for example, otters and cormorants in China); stunning, spearing, or poisoning fish; and the use of harvesting machines such as mechanized dredgers, or gear that separates the catch from the water using pumps. As fish surface, they can be located by direct observation from a vessel or aircraft. Satellite surveys chart ocean currents associated with fish movements. *Sonar and other listening apparatus can locate fish, and microprocessors can be used to control the course of the vessel and the attitude of the tackle. All these activities lead to overfishing and the depletion of fish stocks. International laws and agreements for *marine resource management have been made to try to control overfishing, but fish stocks continue to be eroded.

fish product, a manufactured product that uses fish as a raw material. Industrial products include fish-oil and fishmeal, which are made from such species as anchovies, herring, and sardines. The fish are first cooked in steam and then pressed to extract oil and water. The residue is ground to make meal, which is used as fertilizer or added to livestock feed and pet-food. Fish-oil is used in the manufacture of some glues, fabrics, pharmaceuticals, and paints. Vitamin D is extracted from cod or shark liver. Isinglass (a kind of gelatine) from swim-bladders is used in the brewing industry. Food products include delicacies such as salmon, whitefish, and sturgeon roe (caviar). Fish fingers are manufactured from a compressed cod fillet and mince block, and sell successfully in the USA and UK. Shellfish by-products include animal feed and pearls.

fission, nuclear, the splitting of a heavy atomic nucleus into two approximately equal parts, with the emission of neutrons and large amounts of heat and nuclear *radiation. Fission can occur spontaneously, or may be induced by the impact of a neutron, an energetic charged particle, or a photon. The only naturally occurring fissionable material is an isotope of *uranium, U-235. U-235 is most easily split by slow, low-energy neutrons. Only about one uranium atom in 140 is U-235; the major isotope is U-238, which is non-fissionable. Natural uranium does not sustain a *chain reaction, in which the splitting of one atom provides at least one neutron for splitting another, because U-238 tends to absorb neutrons released by fission before they can split another atom. Two methods are currently used to sustain a chain reaction in uranium fuel. In the first, the neutrons released by fission of U-235 can be slowed down by a moderator, a material composed of light atoms which do not absorb neutrons but take energy from them. Slow neutrons more easily produce fission, and are less easily absorbed by U-238. Most *nuclear reactors used for power generation use this method. Alternatively, the uranium can be enriched (the proportion of fissionable material increased). Enriched fuel can sustain a chain reaction without moderation: this is the basis on which *fast breeder reactors work. Both fission and *fusion are used in *nuclear weapons.

flail tank, a *tank for clearing minefields. Two arms projecting from the sides of the tank have drums at their ends to which chains are attached. When the arms rotate, the chains strike the ground and detonate mines.

flame-thrower, a weapon that shoots a stream of burning oil, gasoline, or *napalm. It was first used by the German Army in 1915. The typical layout incorporates one or more tanks of fuel, a cylinder of compressed gas, a flexible hose, and a trigger nozzle. The gas forces the fuel out of the hose, and the nozzle ignites it. Small flame-throwers can be carried on a soldier's back, while larger ones are mounted on tanks or armoured cars. They are most often used against an enemy in fortified positions.

flash (photography), an artificial light source giving a brief, very bright illumination, used for photography at night, or indoors, when natural light is insufficient. There are at present two main types of flash: electronic and bulb. A flash-bulb consists of a glass bulb filled with flammable wire and oxygen, which burns to give a brilliant light of very short duration when ignited by a low-voltage current. Flash-bulbs have to be replaced after a single firing. An electronic flash is produced by a high-voltage discharge between two electrodes, which are enclosed in a glass tube filled with an inert gas. A current charges a capacitor to the required voltage needed to trigger the flash. Electronic flash units are rechargeable and can be used repeatedly. Flash synchronization ensures that the duration of the flash coincides with the maximum opening of the camera shutter: when the shutter is fully open an electrical circuit is completed, and the flash is immediately fired.

flavouring *food additive.

flax *linen.

Fleming, Sir Alexander (1881–1955), British bacteriologist of Scottish extraction, who discovered *penicillin. After qualifying in medicine (1906), he became assistant to the distinguished bacteriologist Almroth Wright at St Mary's Hospital, London. In 1922 he discovered lysozyme, an enzyme capable of lysing (breaking open) certain bacteria. Six years later he found that the mould *Penicillium notatum* produced a substance that was active against a wide range of pathogenic *bacteria; he called this substance penicillin. He used it to isolate pure strains of certain bacteria, but failed to realize its chemotherapeutic potential, and soon lost interest. In 1939 *Florey and *Chain began an independent investigation of penicillin, and developed it as a uniquely valuable chemotherapeutic agent. Fleming shared the Nobel Prize for Physiology and Medicine with Florey and Chain in 1945.

Fleming, Sir John Ambrose (1849–1945), British electrical engineer remembered particularly for his invention of the *thermionic valve. In 1900, utilizing an effect observed by *Edison in his development of the *incandescent lamp, he invented a thermionic valve (a *diode), which permitted electric current to flow in one direction only. Later, this device was improved by *De Forest, who incorporated a third electrode, to create the triode. For half a century, until challenged by the *transistor, thermionic valves were an essential part of virtually all radio transmitters, radio receivers, and other electronic devices.

flexible manufacturing system (FMS), an integrated, computer-controlled complex of automated material-handling equipment and programmable processing machines such as *numerically controlled *machine-tools. FMS operate as unattended stations (or cells of more than one station), and offer flexibility of product design, of the manufacturing process, and of rate of production. Because an FMS can carry out a variety of machining and assembly operations, high productivity is possible even where there is a comparatively short product life-span or a large number of product variants. (See also *automation, *computer-integrated manufacturing, *mass production.)

flexography, a relief printing process, similar in some respects to rotary *letterpress. However, in flexography the printing image is invariably on a resilient rubber, plastic, or *photopolymer material, not metal, and the ink is a free-flowing liquid rather than a viscous paste. The ink is applied to the plate from a supply trough, using a finely engraved applicator roller, the anilox. This contains a pattern of minute cells which ensure that a specific ink film thickness covers the whole printing surface, without the need for a multi-roller inking system as employed in letterpress and *offset lithography. The process was originally developed in the early part of this century for printing cheap paper bags and wrappers, but because of its simplicity and low cost it is now also used for business forms, newspapers, and magazine work.

flight, principles of. For a heavier-than-air aircraft to fly, it must generate a lifting force equal to or greater than its weight, and (for powered flights) sufficient power to overcome its drag. The aircraft must also be stable in flight, and for most purposes it must be possible to control direction and attitude of flight. *Balloons and *airships (lighter-than-air aircraft) exploit Archimedes' principle, whereby a body immersed in a fluid experiences a lifting force equal to the weight of fluid it displaces. The envelope of a balloon or airship displaces a large amount of air, but it is filled with a gas lighter than the surrounding air, so it experiences an appreciable lifting force. A heavier-than-air *aeroplane obtains its lift from its wings. An aircraft wing is essentially a plate presented edgewise to a moving air-stream (produced by the aeroplane's forward motion), with the leading edge slightly higher than the trailing edge. A component of the air pressure on this inclined plate creates lift; the rest causes drag. The lift generated by such an inclined plate can be experienced by holding your hand out of the window of a moving vehicle. The upward force on the hand is intermittent and slight because the hand's poor aerodynamic shape causes air turbulence and large amounts of drag, but the air-flow around the *streamlined, *aerofoil cross-section of an aircraft wing is much smoother, drag is minimized, and lift maximized (see figure). The lift-to-drag ratio is a measure of *aerodynamic efficiency. The overall shape of an aircraft wing also affects its lifting capabilities. A convenient measure of a wing's shape is its aspect ratio, defined as the square of the wing span divided by wing area. Wings with a high aspect ratio (long and thin) produce more lift: they are used for long-range, high-altitude, relatively slow aircraft, and for sailplanes. Low aspect-ratio wings (short and broad) tend to be used in fast, highly manœuvrable aircraft. The types of aerofoil used in aircraft wings are inherently unstable, in that the lifting force is produced behind the wing's centre of gravity. A turning effect is thus produced that tends to force the nose of the aircraft downwards. In most aircraft designs a small tail fin situated well back from the wing produces a negative lift to counteract this turning force. An alternative,

Flight, principles of

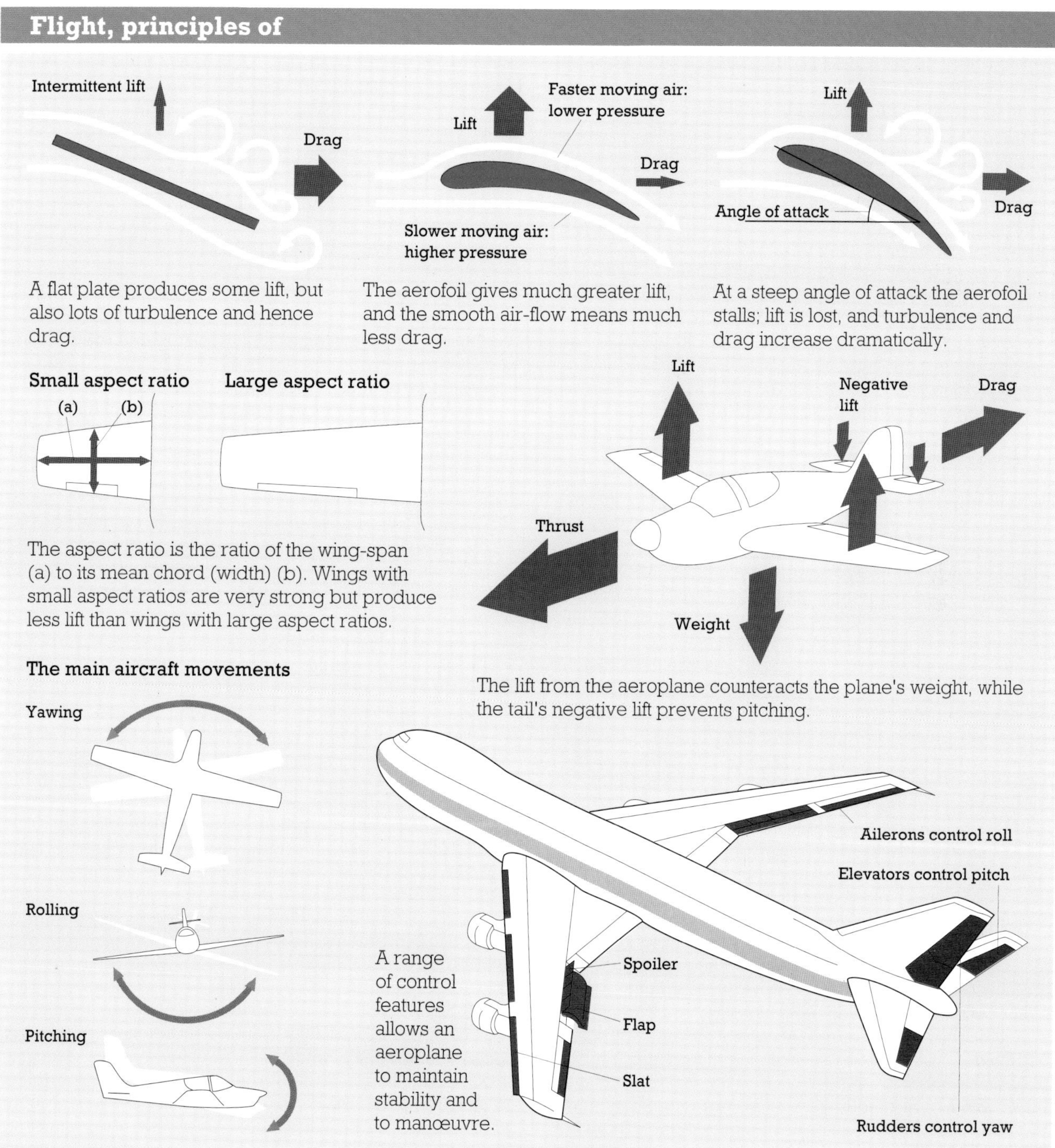
Intermittent lift
Drag
Lift
Faster moving air: lower pressure
Drag
Slower moving air: higher pressure
Lift
Angle of attack
Drag
A flat plate produces some lift, but also lots of turbulence and hence drag.
The aerofoil gives much greater lift, and the smooth air-flow means much less drag.
At a steep angle of attack the aerofoil stalls; lift is lost, and turbulence and drag increase dramatically.
Small aspect ratio
Large aspect ratio
(a)
(b)
The aspect ratio is the ratio of the wing-span (a) to its mean chord (width) (b). Wings with small aspect ratios are very strong but produce less lift than wings with large aspect ratios.
Lift
Negative lift
Drag
Thrust
Weight
The lift from the aeroplane counteracts the plane's weight, while the tail's negative lift prevents pitching.
The main aircraft movements
Yawing
Rolling
Pitching
A range of control features allows an aeroplane to maintain stability and to manœuvre.
Spoiler
Flap
Slat
Ailerons control roll
Elevators control pitch
Rudders control yaw

recently used on some *military aircraft, is a lifting surface (canard) forward of the wings. Aircraft with a canard are inherently unstable, and require advanced electronic control systems to confer artificial stability.

In order to manœuvre an aircraft and to maintain its stability in level flight it is necessary to be able to control pitch, yaw, and roll. Pitch is usually controlled by flaps (elevators) on the rear of the horizontal tail. Yaw is controlled by the rudder, a flap on the vertical tail fin. Roll is controlled by ailerons on the outer trailing edges of the wings—to produce or correct roll, one aileron is lowered while the other is lifted. The rudder and ailerons are used together when banking (turning). Spoilers, retractable flaps that 'spoil' the lift of the wing, may be used in combination with or instead of ailerons to control roll; they also increase drag. The amount of lift generated by an aircraft is proportional to the square of airspeed, which means that at high speeds, wings generate much more lift than at the low speeds of take-off and landing. Extra lift can be generated by increasing the angle of incidence of the wing to the air-flow (by lifting the nose), but beyond a certain point the smooth flow of air across the wing breaks down, lift is lost and drag is increased, a phenomenon known as wing stall. The design of modern high-speed aircraft is such that they cannot be flown slowly. Various devices are needed to enable such aircraft to take off and land at speeds that do not require excessively long runways. Slats on the leading edge of the wing and various flaps on the trailing edge provide an optimized arrangement by which the lift of the wing is maximized without unacceptable increases in drag.

A propulsive system is needed to produce forward motion in an aeroplane; this may be an engine- or turbine-driven *propeller, or a *jet engine. At take-off, the engine's thrust generates forward motion, and the resulting air-flow over the wings generates lift in excess of the total weight of the machine. (See also *flying, history of.)

flight recorder, an electronic device carried in an aircraft for automatically recording information on its operation. All main instrument readings available to the pilot (such as air speed, altitude, and engine speeds), the position of the control surfaces, and flight-crew speech, are recorded at one-second intervals on a multi-track steel or magnetic tape. The tape is recycled every twenty-five hours. The recorder, although often called a 'black box', is usually painted bright orange; it is designed to withstand severe crushing, impact loadings, and fire. Flight recorders are mandatory by international law on any aircraft certificated after 1969.

flight simulator, a piece of electronic equipment that can simulate all the flying characteristics of aircraft. It was originally designed as a completely equipped cockpit in which to train pilots to fly by use of their instruments alone. By mounting the flight simulator on digitally controlled hydraulic support jacks the modern version can give a very real impression of movement. Projections or computer graphics that reproduce the effects experienced visually during take-off, flight, and landing, together with simulated systems, air-flow, and engine noise, can make a simulated flight appear very real, especially with the latest wide-angle displays. The instructor controls all these effects as well as the instruments displayed to the pilot. Simulators are used for initial pilot training, upgrading, training for emergencies, and for simulation of military combat missions. They avoid the risks and considerable cost of using actual aircraft for such purposes.

flint, a hard rock composed of almost pure silicon dioxide (SiO_2). Flint stones are not single crystals but amorphous rock, and so do not cleave under impact, but instead spall, that is, small thin flakes break off. Flint tools were among the earliest examples of *prehistoric technology: arrowheads could be made from thin flint flakes, while larger stones were shaped into primitive scrapers and choppers. Other amorphous or finely crystalline rock such as basalt and obsidian was also used by early peoples. Flint mining was probably the first industrial activity in Britain; a mine at Grimes Graves, Norfolk, dates back to at least 2000 BC.

flintlock *firearm.

flip-flop circuit, a fundamental computer component, usually made as an *integrated circuit. The flip-flop, or bistable, is normally stable in either of two electrical states. On receipt of a suitable signal, it changes state. It is thus usable as a *memory device. Computers typically contain hundreds of thousands of flip-flops.

float glass, *plate glass produced by a continuous casting process that does not need grinding and polishing to achieve a good surface finish. Float glass can be produced in a wide variety of sizes much more cheaply than conventional plate glass. A ribbon of glass is poured from a furnace so that it floats on the surface of molten tin at a carefully controlled temperature. The furnace atmosphere is regulated to prevent oxidation of the tin. Heat applied from above melts the glass sufficiently so that it conforms to the flat surface of the molten tin. After cooling, the plate can be fed on to rollers and slowly cooled (annealed) without affecting the surface finish (see figure). The process, developed in the UK by Alistair Pilkington, became commercially successful in 1959.

floating dock *dry dock.

float switch, a simple electrical switch operated by a float in a sump, well, or tank. Float switches are used in *sewage treatment to control hydraulic loading rates and to prevent pumps running dry. The switch is activated when the depth of the liquid or sludge reaches a certain level, and a pump then begins emptying the tank. When the float falls to a preset level, the switch is turned off.

flood control, measures adopted to avoid flooding. The water-carrying capacity of a river depends upon the cross-sectional area of the water and its velocity, either of which can be increased to cope with floods. Greater capacity can be achieved with earth embankments (levées), which increase channel depth, and, if set back from the normal banks, width also. In urban areas, flood walls are used instead of levées, as they require less ground. Water velocity is determined by the channel gradient and its smoothness. Clearing aquatic vegetation often improves smoothness, and gradient can be increased by straightening the channel, particularly at meanders. The gradient must be optimized to avoid scouring of the banks and beds, which occurs at high velocities, or channel silting, which occurs at low velocities. Rural flood-plains (water meadows) can form temporary reservoirs at times of high rainfall, protecting downstream urban areas from flooding. Flood capacity can further be increased by bypass channels off the main river, controlled by side weirs. Barriers, for example across the River Thames in London, can be constructed to reduce the danger of flooding. (See also *water resources management.)

Float glass

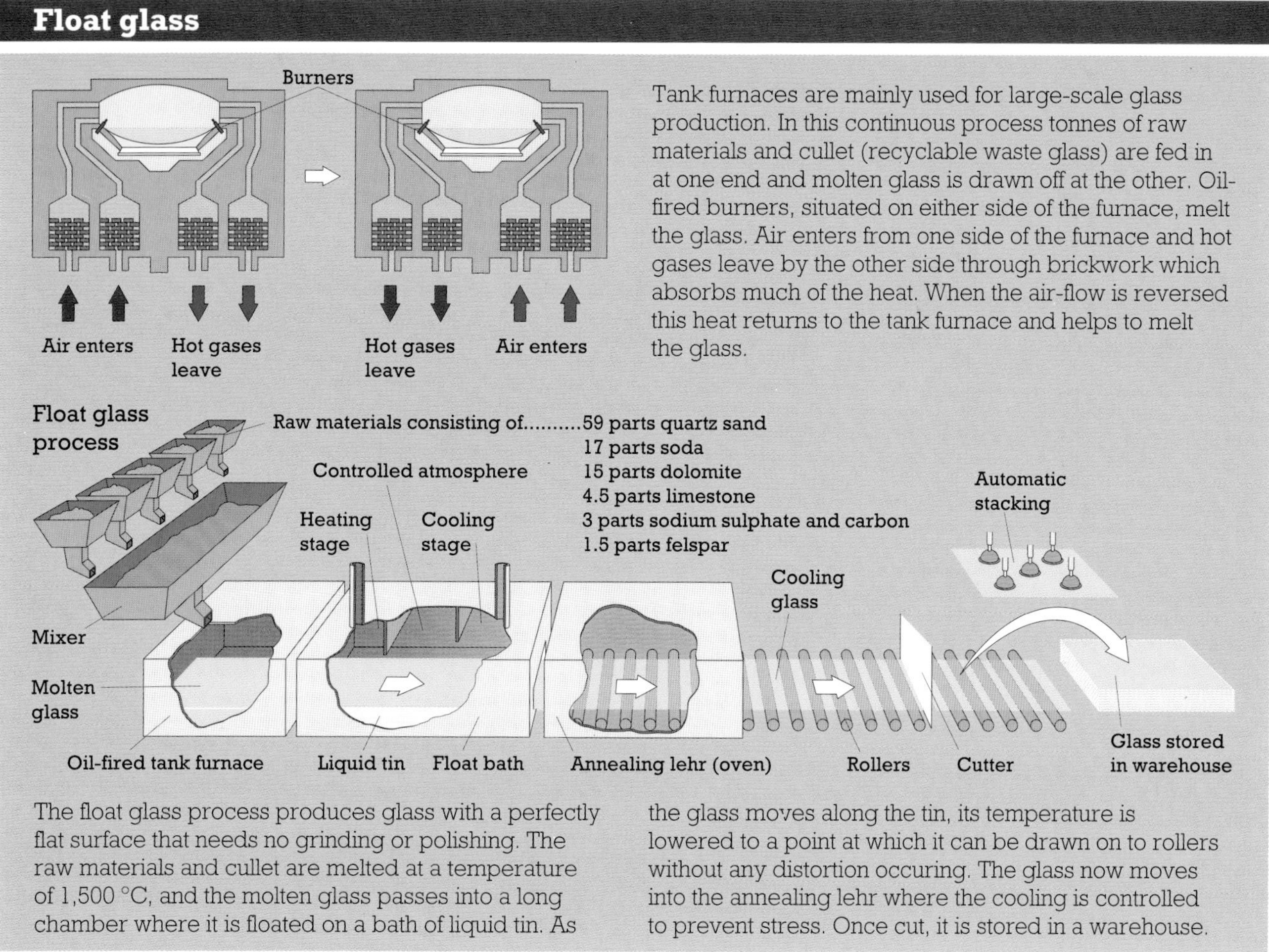

Tank furnaces are mainly used for large-scale glass production. In this continuous process tonnes of raw materials and cullet (recyclable waste glass) are fed in at one end and molten glass is drawn off at the other. Oil-fired burners, situated on either side of the furnace, melt the glass. Air enters from one side of the furnace and hot gases leave by the other side through brickwork which absorbs much of the heat. When the air-flow is reversed this heat returns to the tank furnace and helps to melt the glass.

The float glass process produces glass with a perfectly flat surface that needs no grinding or polishing. The raw materials and cullet are melted at a temperature of 1,500 °C, and the molten glass passes into a long chamber where it is floated on a bath of liquid tin. As the glass moves along the tin, its temperature is lowered to a point at which it can be drawn on to rollers without any distortion occuring. The glass now moves into the annealing lehr where the cooling is controlled to prevent stress. Once cut, it is stored in a warehouse.

floppy disk, a magnetic disk that may be inserted or withdrawn from a computer by the user. It is used for storing *data or *software and is distinguished from a *hard disk by being flexible, removable, and unsealed. Floppy disks are slower in operation, store less information, and are less reliable than hard disks. They are constructed from a plastic material, usually coated on both sides by a magnetic layer, and partially protected from dust by a plastic cover. The surfaces of the disk are divided (formatted) into areas on which information can be stored and the disk is held in a disk drive which rotates it inside its cover. The computer stores information on the disk, or retrieves information from the disk (known as 'writing' and 'reading' operations respectively) by a fixed magnetic head within the disk drive.

Florey, Howard Walter, Baron (1898–1968), Australian physician who, with *Chain and others, demonstrated the unique chemotherapeutic properties of *penicillin. After qualifying in medicine at Adelaide, he came to the UK in 1924 to do research. In 1939, with Chain, he began a systematic investigation of penicillin (discovered in 1928 by Alexander *Fleming) and the following year demonstrated its remarkable anti-bacterial potential. Florey toured the eastern USA to gain the support of the pharmaceutical industry, and as a result, sufficient penicillin was made to treat all World War II military casualties from D-Day (1944) onwards. After the War, penicillin soon became cheaply and widely available for civilian use. Florey, Chain, and Fleming shared the Nobel Prize for Physiology and Medicine in 1945.

flow chart, a design technique depicting the order of logical steps (*algorithm) required to solve a problem prior to writing a *computer software *program, or designing a computer system using *systems analysis techniques. Flow charts use specific symbols to represent particular operations, so that the logic of the chart is immediately apparent (for illustration see *program). Each symbol is equivalent to a statement or group of statements in the program, which facilitates the eventual writing and testing of the program, and the correction of errors. However, with the advent of software engineering (see computer), flow charting is in decline.

fluid drive *automatic transmission.

fluidics, the technique of using the flow of jets of gas or liquid as control elements in place of mechanical or electronic controls. Fluidic devices can be used to construct complex circuits to perform a variety of *control operations using the interaction of streams of fluids rather than moving parts. Typically, a fluidic element consists of a small block containing shaped passages which function as a supply jet, control jets, interaction region, and one or more output ports. The main advantage of fluidic controls are safety, reliability, ability to work in adverse conditions (for example, extreme heat or cold, vibration, nuclear radiation), and ease of integration with pneumatic or hydraulic systems. They have found uses in industry for machine-tools, process and assembly-line control, in missile and aircraft control, and in nuclear power plants.

fluidized bed furnace, a furnace in which coal is burnt in a hot, turbulent bed of sand or ash, through which air is passed. The bed behaves like a fluid, and the coal is burned very efficiently at lower temperatures, reducing emissions of polluting nitrogen oxides. If limestone is added to the bed along with the coal, then the emission of sulphur dioxide to the atmosphere is also greatly reduced. Fluidized beds that operate at atmospheric pressure have found applications throughout the world in air heaters, boilers, and furnaces. Used at higher pressures, fluidized beds represent an alternative technology to pulverized-fuel firing for raising steam in large-scale electricity generation. The hot, high-pressure combustion gas from the fluidized bed is used to drive a gas-turbine; the steam raised in tubes immersed in the hot bed is used to drive a steam-turbine. This so-called *combined cycle has a greater efficiency and is cleaner than the conventional system which uses a steam-turbine only. Fluidized beds are also used for the production of industrial fuel gas from coal (gasification).

fluid mechanics, the study of systems involving liquids or gases and the forces that act on them. Liquids and gases are considered together as fluids because they behave similarly when flowing. Fluid mechanics attempts to find mathematical equations to explain and account for the behaviour of fluids. It can be broken into two subdivisions: statics (fluids at rest) and dynamics (fluids in motion). Statics describes the pressures within stationary volumes of gas or liquid. This is important when designing a dam wall or the skin of a weather balloon. Hydrodynamics and *aerodynamics are of far greater importance to modern *engineering, and investigate liquid and gas flow, respectively, around solid and liquid surfaces. There are two main types of flow in fluids: laminar or viscous flow, in which the fluid flows smoothly with low energy losses, and turbulent flow, an irregular and disturbed flow with increased energy losses. The two most important properties in determining flow patterns in a fluid are its density and its viscosity (the amount of internal *friction within a fluid between adjacent moving layers). Hydrodynamics is concerned in the design of ships and submarines; it also describes the flow of fluids in pipes ranging in size from oil and petroleum pipelines to blood capillaries. Fluid mechanics finds further applications in convection (gravity-driven flow resulting from temperature differences within a fluid), *fluidics, *hydraulics, and turbo-machinery, which includes fans, pumps, compressors, and turbines.

fluorescent lamp, a lamp that generates light by fluorescence. Such lamps consist of a glass tube containing a vapour (usually mercury), maintained under low pressure. The inside of the tube is coated with a *phosphor layer. A current is passed through the gas, which is excited into producing ultraviolet rays. These then bombard the inner walls of the tube, causing the phosphor to fluoresce, and visible

Timechart of some important events in flying history

c. 1325	First known illustration of a (string-pull) helicopter model in a Flemish manuscript
1783	First manned flight by de Rozier and d'Arlandes in a hot-air balloon designed by the brothers Joseph-Michel and Jacques-Étienne Montgolfier, Paris. First hydrogen balloon flight by Frenchman J. A. C. Charles in Paris (in a balloon he designed and built)
1785	First (balloon) flight across English Channel by Jean-Pierre Blanchard of France and John Jefferies of the USA
1797	First successful parachute jump by Jacques Garnerin, from a balloon
1799	George Cayley proposed design for a human-carrying glider
1852	Henri Giffard made first flight by human-carrying airship
1853	George Cayley's coachman made first ever glider flight in Brompton Dale, Yorkshire
1891	Otto Lilienthal made first of over 1,000 successful glider flights in Germany
1900	First Zeppelin rigid airship flew in Germany
1903	First powered, sustained and controlled aeroplane flights made by the brothers Orville and Wilbur Wright near Kitty Hawk, N. Carolina, USA
1909	First aeroplane to cross English Channel, Calais to Dover, by Louis Blériot in his Blériot No. XI
1910	Zeppelin airships started first passenger service. First air-to-ground and ground-to-air radio transmission, by McCurdy in a Curtiss in USA
1911	Curtiss floatplane is first practical seaplane to fly. Aeroplane first used for military reconnaissance, against Turks by Italians in a Blériot
1915	Fokker EI fighters fitted with first practical interrupter gear to fire machine-guns through their propellers
1919	First direct non-stop transatlantic flight, in a Vickers Vimy by British pilots John Alcock and Arthur Brown
1923	Cierva C3 autogyro made first flight
1924	First round-the-world flight by US pilots Smith, Nelson and crew
1927	First solo crossing of Atlantic, by Charles Lindbergh in a Ryan monoplane
1928	First flight across the Pacific (USA to Australia) by Charles Smith and C.T.P. Ulm
1936	Douglas DC-3 airliner entered service. First practical helicopter flew, the twin-rotor Focke-Achgelis Fw-61
1939	First turbojet aeroplane, the German Heinkel He 178, flown by Erich Warsitz
1943	First jet fighter flew, the German Messerschmitt Me. 262
1949	First aeroplane exceeded speed of sound, the Bell X-1 piloted by Charles Yeager of the USAF. First turbojet airliner flew, the De Havilland Comet I. First flight around world without landing, but refuelled in flight, by a USAF Boeing B-50 bomber
1954	First VTOL flight, the Rolls-Royce 'Flying Bedstead'
1968	First supersonic transport aircraft flew, the Soviet Union's Tupelev Tu-144
1976	World's first regular scheduled supersonic passenger service started by BAC/Aerospatiale Concorde
1979	Human-powered aircraft the Gossamer Albatross, designed by Paul MacCready and piloted by Bryan Allen, crossed the English Channel
1984	First flight of Grumman X-29A forward-swept wing demonstrator research aircraft
1986	First non-stop, unrefuelled, around-the-world flight by Dick Rutan and Jeana Yeager in the Rutan Voyager aircraft
1988	Human-powered aircraft the Daedalus, piloted by Kanellos Kanellopoulos, flew 74 miles from Crete to Greek island of Thíra (Santorini)

light is emitted. Although this is a two-stage process, the efficiency of a fluorescent lamp is much greater than that of comparable *incandescent lamps, since little energy is wasted as heat. Fluorescent tubes are widely used for office and industrial lighting. Recently, compact fluorescent bulbs have been introduced, which can be used in place of domestic light bulbs.

fluoridation, the treatment of a piped drinking-water supply with fluoride, usually in the form of hydrofluorosilic acid. Fluoridation reduces the incidence of dental caries, particularly in young people. The usual UK dosage is 1.0 mg/l, but the World Health Organization and European Community standards vary according to water temperature.

fluorine (symbol F, at. no. 9, r.a.m. 19.00), a pale yellow gas of low density, the most reactive of the halogen family of elements, which also includes *chlorine, *bromine, and *iodine. It is the most reactive element, an extremely powerful oxidizing agent (see *oxidation and reduction), and ignites most organic materials on contact. Fluorine is produced electrolytically, and its extreme reactivity requires the use of fluorine-resistant materials in constructing manufacturing plant. Fluorine is used in the refining of *aluminium and in separating isotopes of uranium (see *nuclear fuels). Since the 1920s, there has been a growth in the production of organic fluorine compounds. The use of some of these materials (*chloro-fluorocarbons) as refrigerants, propellants, and in expanded foam plastics has declined with concern about pollution, but *fluorocarbons and fluorinated polymers still have a wide range of specialist applications. Fluorine is also used for the *fluoridation of drinking water.

fluorocarbon, a *hydrocarbon in which some or all of the hydrogen atoms are replaced by *fluorine. Fluorocarbons are unreactive, stable, and non-flammable. The most useful is tetrafluoroethene. As reactions between fluorine and hydrocarbons are difficult to control, tetrafluoroethene is produced industrially by the reaction of less powerful fluoridating agents (such as antimony trifluoride) with chloroform. It can be polymerized to produce *PTFE. (See also *chloro-fluorocarbons.)

fluoroscopy *radiology.

flux, a material that is added to metallic ores during *smelting to remove impurities in the form of a light, low-melting-point, fluid slag. The term also describes materials that are used to clean the surfaces of metals before joining them by *soldering or *brazing.

fly-by-wire system, an *avionics system in which the control surfaces of an aeroplane are activated by electrical signals, or by light pulses transmitted through *optical fibres (fly-by-light systems). Such systems reduce weight, provide more control options, and can be closely integrated with flight computers. This has allowed the development of CCVs (control-configured vehicles): aircraft that are inherently unstable in which a computer continually feeds corrections to the control systems to keep the craft in stable flight. *Fighter aircraft that are designed on such principles, like the General Dynamics F-16, are extremely agile and responsive. In commercial airliners fly-by-wire systems are used to maximize efficiency: on-board computers are programmed to keep the aircraft in optimal trim at all times, and to prevent accidental stalling or overspeeding.

flying, history of. Although such aeronautical devices as the *arrow, the *kite, and the *boomerang have been known since very early times, human flight was not realized until the 18th century. Research developed along two paths: lighter-than-air *balloons and *airships, and heavier-than-air *gliders and *aeroplanes. Balloon flight was pioneered in France by the *Montgolfier brothers and the physicist J. A. C. Charles. After making several models, the Montgolfiers built a hot-air balloon that made the first ever human-carrying flight in 1783. Charles, on hearing of the Montgolfiers' experiments, independently developed a hydrogen-filled balloon, which flew on 1 December of the same year. Heavier-than-air flight was first extensively studied by *Cayley, who researched many aspects of the theory of flight. The glider flights which he and others such as *Lilienthal carried out in the second half of the 19th century contributed much to the knowledge of heavier-than-air flight.

By the mid-19th century the main stumbling-block to powered flights was the lack of a suitable engine. With the advent of the *internal-combustion engine in the late 1800s, developments occurred rapidly. By 1900 practical airships were being built in Germany by von *Zeppelin, while the USA became the crucible for the development of heavier-than-air flight. Extensive experimental work by Samuel Langley (1834–1906) and Octave Chanute (1832–1910) provided the groundwork for the achievements of the *Wright brothers, who made the first sustained, powered human flight in an aeroplane in 1903. Their aeroplane, 'Flyer 1', was the result of three years of intensive research. Over the next six years the Wright 'Flyers' inspired many aeroplane designers and builders in the USA and Europe. In the USA Glenn Curtiss designed many prize-winning aircraft and provided the first *seaplanes to the US Navy. In Europe progress was initially slow, but between 1906 and 1914 France and Germany in particular developed strong aviation industries.

World War I was a major period of development for military aviation. At the start of the War aircraft were used mainly for reconnaissance, but by 1918 all the major combatants had large fleets of *fighter and *bomber aircraft with hugely improved performance. In the immediate post-war period few new aeroplanes were built due to the large military surpluses, and thousands of pilots trained during the war looked for new ways to use their skills. Sport flying became popular and competitions to fly higher or faster led to many innovations. The late 1920s and early 1930s saw a revolution in aeroplane design, the 'stick-and-wire' biplanes being replaced by streamlined monoplanes of all-metal construction. This design revolution was reflected in performance: the period from 1919 to 1930 saw the first transatlantic, trans-Pacific, and round-the-world flights, as well as large improvements in altitude and speed records. The period also saw the rise of commercial aviation. Airmail services were pioneered in the USA, and by 1936 both Europe and America had extensive *airline networks, using fleets of comfortable, purpose-built aircraft.

World War II provided another boost to aviation: huge numbers of military aircraft were produced, and there were innovations in design, materials, engines, and in the use of *radar. Research into *jet engines and *rocketry accelerated; by 1946 both the UK and Germany were producing jet fighter planes. After World War II jet aircraft gradually replaced propeller-driven aeroplanes in many contexts. *Supersonic flight was achieved in 1947, and produced radical changes in military and commercial aircraft design. Intensive military development, particularly in the USA and the Soviet Union in the 1950s and early 1960s, led to higher and faster aircraft, culminating in the X-15 experimental rocket planes, which reached heights of over 80 km (50 miles) and speeds in excess of *Mach 5. But in the 1960s the rapidly expanding space programmes and changes in military thinking shifted the emphasis in combat aircraft to low-level flying and electronic countermeasures. In the 1970s aircraft development was strongly affected by world-wide inflation and greatly increased fuel prices. Far fewer new projects reached production, while fuel economy, noise reduction, and pollution control became important design criteria. In the 1980s the major advances have been in the areas of *avionics and materials science. Avionic advances have led to the development of *fly-by-wire systems, and the change from conventional flight instruments to multi-function display monitors that present only the information required at any particular time. New materials used in aircraft include new *alloys and *composite materials such as *fibre-reinforced plastics.

flying boat, an aeroplane than can land on and take off from water, whose main body or hull supports it on the water. The first successful flying boat was 'The Flying Fish', built by Glenn Curtiss in the USA in 1912. In the 1930s the scarcity of aerodromes, particularly outside Europe and North America, led to the use of flying boats for intercontinental passenger travel. A typical example was the three-engined British Short Calcutta, carrying fifteen passengers at a cruising speed of 145 km/h (90 m.p.h.). During World War II this and other flying boats were adapted for military use, but by 1950 they had been largely replaced by land-based aircraft. (See also *seaplane.)

flying shuttle, a *shuttle invented by *Kay in 1733, which increased the output of the hand-loom and opened the way to power-loom weaving. Kay provided a smooth board immediately below the lower *warp threads to support the shuttle in its passage across the *loom; a box at each end of the board to receive the shuttle on its arrival and to act as guide on its departure; and a simple mechanism by which the shuttle was shunted from one box to the other as required.

flywheel, a heavy, rotating wheel designed to act as an energy store or to regulate machinery. To maximize the kinetic energy, the mass is often concentrated near the rim, with a thin or open-structured central section. In reciprocating machines such as *petrol or *steam-engines, flywheels smooth out power fluctuations by absorbing energy at each power stroke and releasing it between strokes. They are also used more generally for *energy storage. Urban buses have a type of regenerative brake, in which the energy is taken up by the flywheel as the vehicle slows down, and then used later to accelerate the bus.

FM (frequency modulation) *modulation.

f-number *aperture.

focal length *lenses and lens systems.

food additive, any of a group of chemicals added to food to alter and improve its desirable qualities. Chemical substances were added to food long before the advent of *food technology: salt, for example, has been used to preserve meat for over 2,000 years. However, the intensification of food production within Western populations has meant that food quality may deteriorate at any point during its production, dispersal, or storage, and food additives are used to improve keeping qualities and to enhance or restore the food's characteristics. Food colourings may be added to food to restore colour where it has been destroyed or altered by food processing; to ensure that there is no variation in the colour of different batches of food; or to give colour to otherwise colourless foods. More controversially, they can be used to mask the use of inferior ingredients in food, for example, red colouring to hide the use of bone or rusk in sausages. Flavourings are added to foodstuffs to alter their taste. They may be concentrated natural extracts or *essential oils, or they may be entirely synthetic. *Chocolate and vanilla are the most popular flavourings in *confectionery manufacture. *Sweeteners are an important group of flavourings used particularly in the production of *soft drinks and in confectionery. Anti-oxidants inhibit the onset of rancidity and stabilize oxidation. Emulsifiers and stabilizers prevent the coalescence of oil droplets and *food preservatives are added to inhibit spoilage. The table gives examples of the different types of food additives. In many countries some food additives are under government control, and only approved additives can be used in food. Additives must be of a certain purity, they must not adversely affect the nutritive value of the food, and they must be identified to the consumer. However, only about 10 per cent of all additives are controlled in this way, and consumer pressure has led to a recognizable movement away from artificial additives. Adventitious additives to food also concern the food scientist: for example, it has been found that cows treated with penicillin (an antibiotic) may produce milk from which it is not possible to make cheese, because the cheese-forming bacteria are unable to develop properly in the presence of penicillin. Other adventitious additives are potentially harmful: metal cans, for example, may contaminate canned food, although cans are now enamel-coated to help eliminate this particular problem.

food and nutrition. Food provides nutrients for maintenance of the body's tissues and for their growth and repair. Maintenance requires energy, which is supplied mainly by carbohydrates and *fats. Growth and repair especially require protein. In addition, the body needs minerals, such as iron and calcium, vitamins, and water.

Before the nutrients in the diet can be absorbed into the body, the larger food molecules must be broken down into smaller ones that can pass through the intestinal (gut) wall into the blood. This is the process of digestion. Aided by chewing and the churning of the gut, *enzymes in digestive juices break down large carbohydrate molecules into sugars, and proteins into amino acids. Fats are partly chemically digested, partly reduced to minute droplets (emulsified) by the bile salts. Vitamins, minerals, and water need no digestion as their molecules are already sufficiently small. Once inside the body the nutrients become the raw materials for metabolism, the body's chemical processes. Many hundreds of different chemical reactions occur within the body, each controlled by a specific enzyme. Catabolic reactions break down nutrients into simpler molecules. In respiration, for example, sugars and fats are broken down to carbon dioxide and water, with the aid of oxygen, in order to release energy. Anabolic reactions synthesize complex body materials from simple nutrients.

Our modern understanding of nutrition goes back to the mid-19th century, when chemists such as *Pasteur were laying the foundations of biochemistry. By the end of the century the main components of the diet had been characterized as carbohydrates, fats, proteins, water, and certain minerals. In the first decade of this century, *Hopkins demonstrated that these were not enough to maintain health and growth, and that certain chemicals were required in very small amounts. These came to be known as vitamins. Nutritionists have devoted much work since to attempts to define precise amounts of each foodstuff required in the daily diet. Because of individual variation, differences in nutrient availability between food sources, and interaction between nutrients, this has proved difficult, although broad principles have emerged. Other aspects of nutrition, such as the importance of roughage (indigestible material, mainly cellulose fibres), the dangers of excess animal fat (including cholesterol) and salt, and the undesirability of refined sugar, remain controversial. None the less, regulations in many countries today demand that nutritional information be given on food packaging. (See also *food technology.)

food preservation, any method applied to prevent or delay the deterioration of food. Early hunter-gatherers prepared dried meats such as pemmican, and used caves and other cool places for *refrigeration of food. Foods were preserved by *fermentation from early times, including milk and preserved *dairy products such as cheese and yoghurt. Fruits, vegetables, and meat were preserved by pickling, a process in which the food is salted to selectively control micro-organisms such as *bacteria, then fermented to stabilize the treated tissues. Preservation of fruit can also be achieved by concentrating to 56 per cent or more soluble solids, as in jams, marmalades, and jellies. The sugar added to these foods also acts as a preservative. Chemical food preservatives include anti-oxidants, which retard decay due

A selection of common food additives

†E number	Name	Typical uses
Colours (E100–180)		
E101	Riboflavin	Sauces, processed cheese
E102	Tartrazine	Soft drinks, salad cream, marzipan
E150	Caramel	Gravy browning, beer, soft drinks, sauces
E160a	Alpha, beta, and gamma carotene	Soft drinks, margarines, ice cream
E162	Beetroot red (betanine)	Ice cream, liquorice, jams
E175	Gold	Cake decorations
—	Paprika	Canned vegetables
—	Tumeric	Soups, sauces
Preservatives (E200–297)		
E200	Sorbic acid	Processed cheese, soft drinks, fruit yoghurt
E201, 202	Sodium, potassium sorbitate	Frozen pizzas, cakes, biscuits
E220–7	Benzoates	Beer, jam, soft drinks, salad cream, fruit pie fillings
E252	Potassium nitrate	Cured meats, including bacon and ham; some cheeses
E253	Sodium propionate	Bread, flour, cakes, puddings
Antioxidants (E300–321)		
E300	L-ascorbic acid	Fruit drinks, jams, beer, wine, sausages: used to improve flour and bread dough
E310	Propyl gallate	Vegetable oils, chewing gum
E320	Butylated hydroxyonisole (BHA)	Beef stock cubes, fruit pies, sweets
E322	Lecithin	Low-fat spreads: emulsifier in chocolates
Emulsifiers (E322–495)		
E406	Agar	Ice cream, flavoured yoghurts, meringues
E410	Locust bean gum	Salad cream, packet soups, confectionery, canned vegetables
E440a	Pectin	Jams, puddings, ice cream
E470	Sodium and other salts of fatty acids	Cake mixes
E471	Mono- and diglycerides of fatty acids	Frozen desserts
Sweeteners		
—	Saccharin	Soft drinks, processed food, canned vegetables
E420	Sorbitol	Diabetic jams, soft-scoop ice cream, sausages, some toothpastes
—	Aspartame	Soft drinks, yoghurts, dessert mixes
Miscellaneous additives		
E508	Potassium chloride	Salt substitute, gelling agent
E545	Ammonium polyphosphates	Emulsifiers, texturizers
E621	Monosodium glutamate (MSG)	Flavour enhancer in savoury foods, soups, sauces etc. May cause allergic reaction in some people

†E numbers: numbers introduced by the European Commission to provide identification and approval for approximately 300 food additives.

Sun-drying of fish in Kerala, India. Sun-drying is a common method of **food preservation** where the climate is suitable.

to oxidation, and preservatives such as sodium benzoate, which slow down microbial growth. Other preservation methods include *canning, *freeze-drying, and *irradiation. (See also *food technology and table in *food additive.)

food processors and mixers, electrical appliances for the preparation of food. Mixers date from the 1920s and consist of a variety of detachable motor-driven tools that can beat, blend, knead, or whisk foodstuffs in an open bowl. Modern mixers are fitted with variable-speed electric motors and can be either hand-held or mounted on a stand with an integral bowl. The domestic food processor was invented in 1971 by Pierre Verdon of France and has an enclosed bowl with a flat blade rotating at the base. This blade can perform all the operations of a food mixer and has extra attachments such as perforated discs that can grate, chop, and slice. Liquidizers contain a small multi-bladed knife that rotates at high speed, reducing soft foodstuffs to a pulp or liquid, depending on the original fluid content.

food technology, the application of scientific knowledge to the preparation, preservation, and storage of food. Food technology can slow or halt the natural degradation processes of certain foodstuffs and thus make foods available out of season. The drying or preservation of fruit, the making of *dairy products from milk, and the drying, salting, or smoking of fish are all practices which may be found in use in many cultures world-wide. The palatability or nutritional qualities of many raw food materials can be enhanced by selective processing. For example, *cereals may be crushed by *milling to produce flour, a process which removes or breaks down the indigestible outer husk of the cereal seeds. The flour can be made more palatable by making it into bread or pasta. Some varieties of cassava, one of the most important food plants in the tropics, have a high content of very toxic, cyanide-containing compounds, and must undergo prolonged and controlled *fermentation before being eaten.

The progressive intensification of *agriculture since the 18th century has led to a corresponding intensification of the way in which the food is subsequently handled. In recent years the market has seen new processing and packaging technologies, allowing an increase in production of, and demand for, 'convenience foods': ready-prepared or easily prepared meals, and foods with an increased shelf life. Traditional methods of *food preservation—techniques such as curing, salting and smoking of meat, and pickling or drying of fruit and vegetables—have been supplemented by newer practices such as *canning and *freeze-drying. More recently, advances in technology have led to the extensive use of chemical preservatives, although growing consumer awareness has led the food industry to limit the use of such *food additives.

Modern food processing technology has also allowed the production of 'new' foods. *Extrusion, for instance, is a process whereby food is compressed to form a semi-solid mass, and then forced through a small aperture so as to increase the variety of texture, shape, and colour obtainable from a basic food ingredient. By extrusion cooking of defatted soya flour, a highly fibrous textured vegetable protein (TVP) is produced. TVP is not only more palatable than soya beans, but is also more digestible. With extrusion techniques it is now possible to produce very good meat analogues from mycoprotein (protein obtained from *fungi) and vegetable proteins.

footwear manufacture, the making of boots and shoes. Most footwear manufacture is carried out either in large batches, or by continuous *mass production methods. The first step involves cutting out the pieces of leather (or other appropriate material) to form the 'upper' of the boot or shoe with sharp-edged dies; for small batches, templates and a sharp knife may be used. The assembly of the shoe begins with joining the pieces that form the upper, using a *sewing-machine. The insole is attached to the upper with the aid of a wood or iron last the exact size of the foot. Upper and insole are secured by sewing, stapling, *riveting, or with *adhesives. The upper is stretched, manually or automatically, so that it mates properly with the insole. Finally, the sole and heel are attached. Traditionally this involves either sewing or nailing, but a more recent method is to use adhesives, which permit assembly to be done in a single moulding operation.

forage crop, a crop grown for animal consumption. The main forage crops are root vegetables—turnip, mangel, swede, and fodder beet—and such crops as kale, which are grown for their green tops. Maize may also be grown to be cut green and converted into *silage for winter feeding. All forage crops, whether fed direct or harvested, stored, and fed later, are palatable and either high-yielding or fast-growing. Some, like rape, are used as 'catch' crops, which are sown after harvest and grow quickly to provide autumn feed. (See also *arable farming.)

forage harvester, an *agricultural machine designed to harvest grass or other green crops used in the making of *silage. Early machines used a rotary flail to cut the crop close to the ground. The speed of the blades was such that the cut fibres were blown through a chute into a collecting trailer. A similar principle is used in modern equipment, though the crop is usually pre-cut and wilted, and the force of the pick-up blades forces the crop through knives set to ensure a uniform length of fibre.

force, the effort which, applied to a stationary free body, causes motion. Newton's second law of motion states that force is equal to mass×*acceleration ($F = ma$). Since mass is in kilograms and acceleration is in metres per second squared, the units of force are kg m/s^2 (newtons, N). When a force is exerted over a given distance, work is done; work (or *energy) equals force×distance. It is measured in Nm or joules (J). A force continually applied at a certain speed gives rate of working, power, measured in J/s or watts (W).

Ford, Henry (1863–1947), US pioneer of the motor-car industry and the first to perceive its possibilities as a form of mass transport. Born on a Michigan farm, at 15 he left to work as a machinist's apprentice in Detroit. Later he became chief engineer for the Edison Company. While in Detroit he built his first experimental car (1894). In 1899, with backers, he formed the Detroit Automobile Company, and in 1903 established his own Ford Motor Company. Five years later he built the first Model T ('a motor car for the great multitude'), and by 1913 had developed highly efficient *assembly-line techniques that resulted in an eightfold reduction in the production time for a car chassis (see *mass production). By 1923, Ford had built many overseas plants and accounted for more than half of the US motor industry. In 1927 the Model T was replaced by the Model A, and in 1932 Ford introduced the V-8 engine. In 1936 Ford established the philanthropic Ford Foundation, concerned with the welfare of poorer countries, the arts, and resources management. Today Ford is a huge multinational corporation.

fore-and-aft rig, a *rig in which most of the sails are aligned with the long axis of the vessel. The early history of the fore-and-aft rig is unclear, but certainly by Roman times the spritsail (a square sail supported by a spar running diagonally through it) and the *lateen rig were in common use in the Mediterranean. A third development was the gaff sail, supported at its lower edge by a boom and at its upper edge by a shorter spar, the gaff. The first known examples of this rig were on Dutch craft in the 16th century. Local developments from the gaff rig introduced a variety of sailing vessels with fore-and-aft rig, such as *cutters, *schooners, and *ketches. Further innovations were not seen until the 20th century, when the Bermuda rig was introduced from the West Indies for use on sailing *yachts. Since the 1950s the Bermuda rig has been further developed on aerodynamic principles. (See *sailing, principles of, and *sailing ships and boats for illustrations.)

Henry **Ford**, with his son Edsel, at the wheel of one of his motor cars.

forensic medicine, the branch of medicine whose purpose is to provide evidence to be used in civil or criminal law cases. Before 1800 medical advice in legal matters was sought only sporadically. In the present century, forensic medicine, using the pathologist's techniques of post-mortem and laboratory examination, has become firmly established. Additional procedures are designed to maximize information regarding unnatural causes of injury or death, such as assessing the time of death, determining the age and cause of an injury, and identifying bodies, for example from dental evidence. Highly sophisticated laboratory techniques such as *DNA fingerprinting play an increasing role in forensic medicine.

forestry, the science and practice of managing forests. The management of trees as a commercial commodity is a branch of forestry termed silviculture. Forests, both coniferous (softwood) and broad-leaved (hardwood) are a source of many valuable products. Apart from timber and fuel, forests provide rubber, dyes, gums, syrups, and pharmaceuticals. Forests world-wide have a buffering effect on local climate and protect soils from erosion. Despite their importance, forests have generally been exploited rather than managed. The enormous consumption of *wood for the paper industry, construction, and explosives causes the deforestation of hundreds of square kilometres of land every week. The aim of forestry is to reverse this trend and manage forests as renewable resources. Good management involves controlling the type, arrangement, and density of trees and protecting them from pests, diseases, and fire. Cutting trees at the peak of their growth and replanting with carefully chosen stock allows natural forest to remain perpetually productive. Forestry has largely been applied to the coniferous forests of northern latitudes. Tropical forests have been cleared to make way for plantation crops, widely plundered of valuable hardwoods like teak and ebony, and further depleted by local demands for fuel and agricultural land. The safeguarding of tropical forests lies in the development of 'agroforestry', where the growing of trees and raising of crops and livestock are combined. Agroforestry was a traditional form of subsistence agriculture and is now being applied in plantations of trees which can be profitably farmed, such as rubber. An important element of forestry is the planting of trees in areas previously unforested. This has occurred in Israel, New Zealand, southern Africa, and increasingly on marginal lands in Europe.

forging, a method of shaping metal and increasing its strength by hammering and pressing. Originally practised by the *blacksmith, it has become mechanized and de-

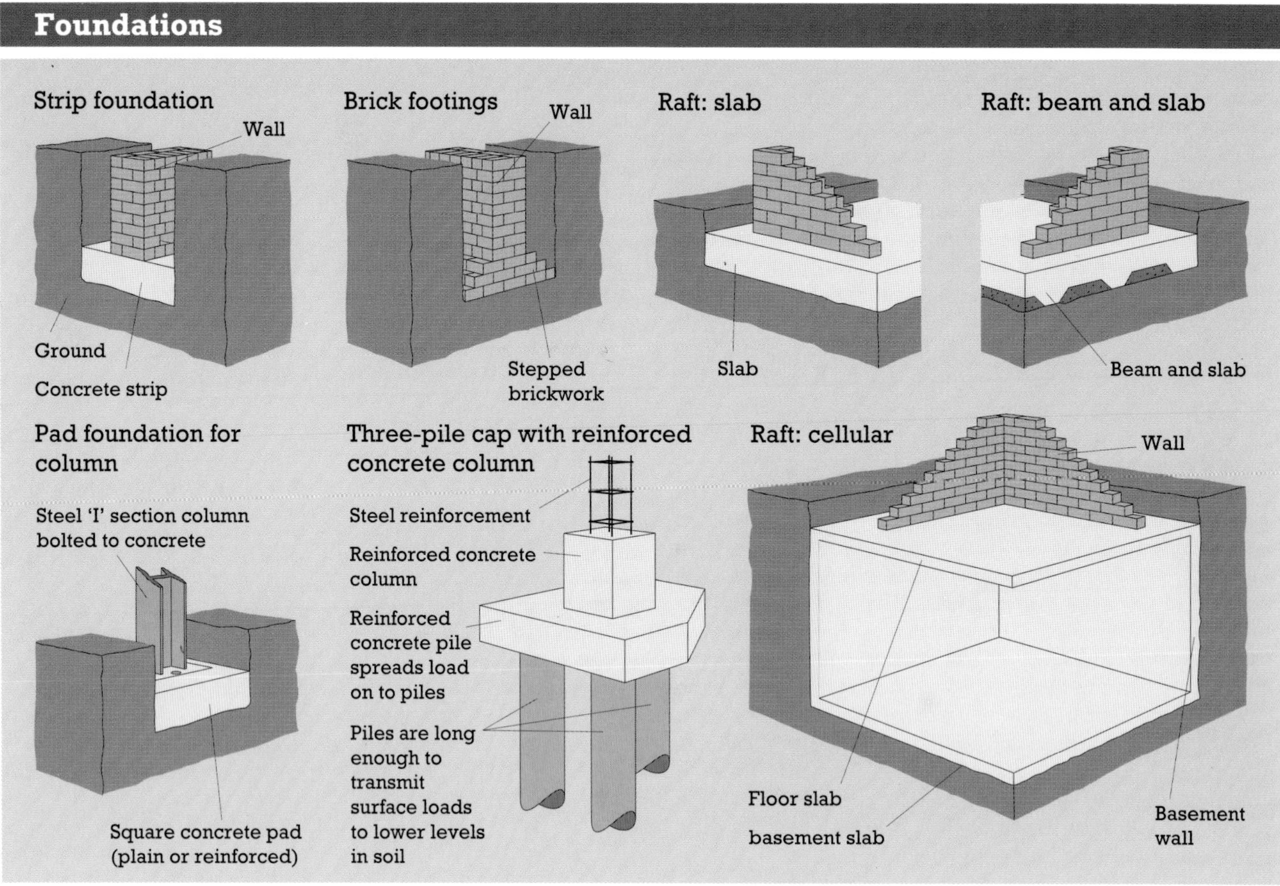

veloped into a major manufacturing process, particularly in the *iron and steel industry. In most forging operations an upper die (a block of hardened material) is forced against a heated workpiece on a stationary lower die. In drop-forging, a hammer is simply raised and then allowed to fall under gravity on to the workpiece. Sometimes the hammering is power assisted, usually at a slow rate with high-force blows. Higher-speed work with lighter blows is also possible, using a mechanical helve-hammer, which is raised by a revolving *cam, and allowed to fall under gravity. In some forging, the blank can be hammered from both sides simultaneously: impact forging uses dies that converge horizontally, while counterblow forging has dies approaching each other vertically. In such machinery the dies absorb each other's energy, and the equipment does not need heavy foundations. Some forging techniques use pressing, with forces ranging from a few hundred to many thousands of tonnes. Roll forging employs matched rotating rolls that have impressions sunk into their surfaces. The metal blank is run between them and emerges with a shape determined by the roll profile.

formic acid *methanoic acid.

formwork, the temporary works erected to mould *concrete to the shape required in a particular structure. The panels in contact with the concrete (shuttering) are held in place by supports known as falsework. Inexpensive plywood and timber are adequate if the formwork will only be used a few times. Steel and glass fibre give a very smooth finish to the concrete, but the higher cost is normally justified only if they can be used many times. Formwork must remain in place until the concrete is self-supporting, perhaps a month for a floor slab or beam.

FORTRAN *computer language.

fossil fuel, any member of the class of carbon-based fuel resources that includes *coal, *petroleum, and *natural gas. All fossil fuels, whether solid, liquid, or gas, are the result of organic material being covered by successive layers of sediment over the course of millions of years. As the sediment solidifies into rock, the organic material decomposes under the influence of great pressure and high temperature. Fossil fuels are essentially finite, or non-renewable, and are currently the world's primary *energy resources. The burning of fossil fuels for energy is a major source of *air pollution, contributing in particular to *acid rain and the *greenhouse effect.

foundations, the lowest load-bearing part of a building, usually below ground level, through which the loads of a structure are distributed on to the ground. The quality of the ground and the kind of structure determine the type of foundation used. Spread foundations are broad and shallow and, where firm ground exists near the surface, are the simplest to build. Otherwise, where solid material lies beneath unsuitable ground, the loads are transferred through the poor surface material to considerable depths using *piling or a *caisson. In the past, foundations for brickwork consisted of large stones, timber beams, or simply a thicker base, or footing (see figure). Wide walls were built on the ground without special foundations. Nowadays, for load-bearing walls, the spread foundation is a continuous concrete strip that is wider than the wall. For a column or pier, the spread foundation is a rectangular pad of concrete. In the 19th and early 20th centuries, before the adoption of *reinforced concrete, steel columns were often supported on layers of steel joists (grillage). Where poor ground requires the foundation to be of about the same area as the building, a raft is used. A small raft may be a reinforced concrete slab; a larger raft may be a slab stiffened with beams. For buildings with basements, the lower storeys may be built as a stiff box.

foundry *casting.

Fourdrinier machine, a machine for continuous *paper manufacture invented by the Frenchman Nicholas Robert in 1799 and patented in the UK during the early 1800s by Henry and Sealy Fourdrinier. *Donkin greatly improved the design between 1803 and 1851. Pulped cellulose fibre mixed with water, *size, and appropriate filling material is spread as a liquid across a moving wire-mesh screen, under which are rows of suction boxes. The wire screen is agitated sideways to intermingle the cellulose fibres as the water is sucked away. The web of damp paper so produced is then passed through pressing rolls, heated in drying cylinders, and finally calendered to the required finish. (For illustration, see paper manufacture.)

Fourneyron, Benoît (1802–67), French inventor of the outward-flowing *water turbine. After training as a mining engineer, he worked in an ironworks at Le Creusot, where engines were required to drive machinery. He developed a new design for a water turbine in which, unlike a traditional water-wheel, the water flowed outwards through a vertical rotor. Fourneyron eventually built a 3.75-kW (50-horsepower) unit. His turbines were used at Niagara Falls, Canada, for the world's first major *hydroelectric plant.

four-wheel drive *motor car.

Fox Talbot, William Henry *Talbot, William Henry Fox.

fractional distillation, a distillation process designed to separate mixtures of liquids whose boiling-points are close together. Fractional distillation is the primary method of separating products in *petroleum refining. An industrial fractionating column typically consists of a series of fractionating trays (as many as 100 in a superfractionator), each of which is effectively a separate distillation step (see figure). Material is introduced part-way up the column: rising vapours become progressively richer in the more volatile components as they gradually cool, while liquids that boil above the entry temperature descend the column, becoming progressively richer in less volatile material. At the top of the column any remaining vapour is condensed, and a proportion of this condensate (the reflux) is passed back down the column. Vapours rising up the column bubble through the reflux liquid on successive trays. When the column reaches equilibrium each tray stays at a constant temperature, and contains mainly liquid boiling at just above that temperature. This counterflow process greatly improves the separation of the liquid mixture into different boiling-point fractions, and is characteristic of fractional distillation.

frame (building), an engineering structure in which the roof, floors, and other loads are supported by a framework of vertical posts or columns and horizontal beams. In the box-frame, a traditional method of construction using timber framing, the walls were supported at either end by two main posts, between which were intermediate vertical members (studs) and short horizontal timbers (noggings). Brick-

Fractional distillation (petroleum)

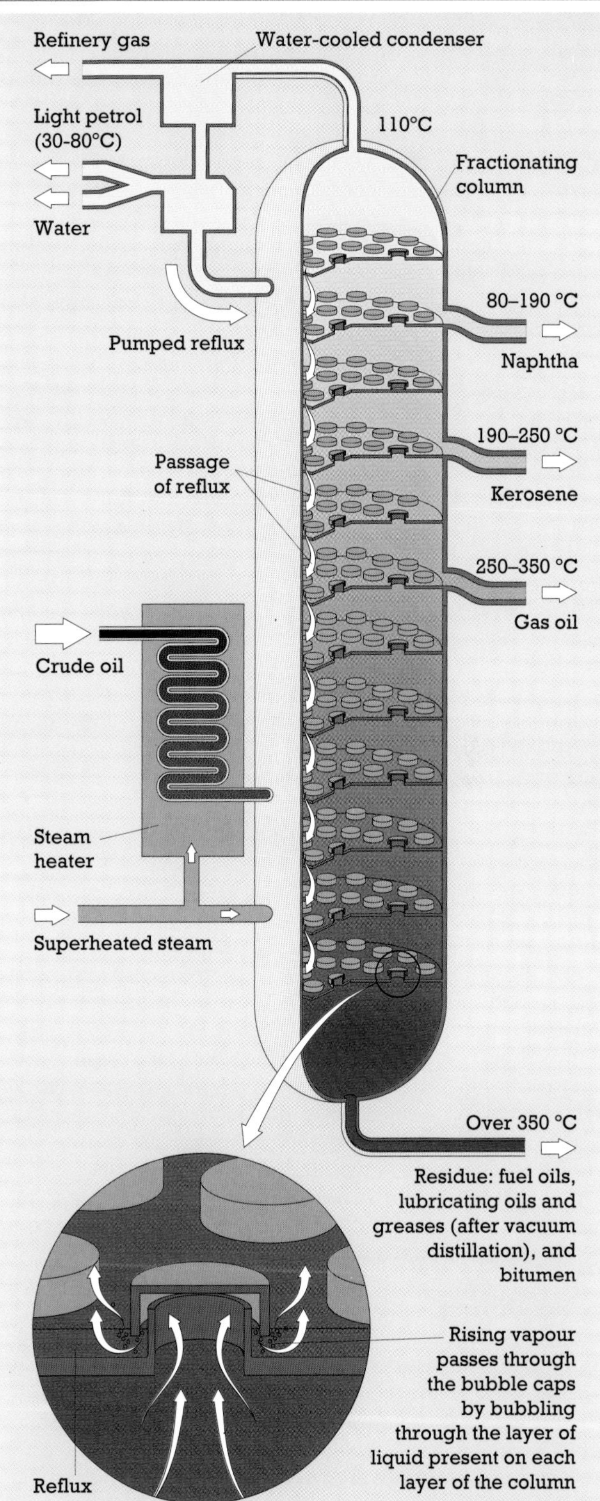

The crude oil is heated in a furnace and enters part-way up the fractionating column. As the vapour passes up the column it gradually cools; different fractions of the oil condense at different levels and are tapped off. The refinery gas collected at the top may be distilled at a low temperature (-20 °C) to separate the gaseous components. The residue at the bottom of the column may be vacuum distilled to obtain lubricating oils.

work or *wattle and daub commonly filled the spaces between the timbers, and the roof rested on the walls. Later, concealed timber walls became common, in which the outer surface was finished with *tiles or *lath and plaster. Modern timber-frame construction is used mainly for domestic housing. Prefabricated, storey-height panels are assembled on-site: the joists of the upper-storey floor rest on the ground-storey panels, while the roof is supported on the upper-storey panels. (In a balloon frame, the vertical studs span two storeys in a single length.) The outer surface of the *house is often a brick or other facing tied to the timber frame, while the interior walls are formed by covering the frame with plasterboard. For large, single-storey buildings *portal frames or *space frames are often used. For *skyscrapers and other multi-storey buildings, columns and beams of steel or concrete form a load-bearing skeleton frame, and the outer surface is formed by a *curtain wall. Within the building, loads are concentrated on to columns of small cross-section, which obstruct the interior much less than load-bearing walls. In some reinforced or *pre-stressed concrete structures there are no horizontal beams, and floors are supported directly on columns.

Franklin, Benjamin (1706–90), American statesman and scientist. Self-taught, he had his first success in journalism and publishing, later devoting himself to the struggle for American independence. He invented the Franklin stove in about 1744 (see *cookers and stoves). From 1746, he took an active interest in the then little understood phenomenon of electricity and gave it a unity and scientific basis. Franklin's famous experiments with a kite (1752) led to the development of the *lightning conductor. He also invented the bifocal *spectacles.

Frasch process, an industrial method employed in Louisiana and Texas for obtaining *sulphur buried beneath layers of quicksand, which prevent conventional mining. It was devised in the 1880s by the German-born US chemist Herman Frasch. Three concentric pipes are sunk to the level of the sulphur deposits. Superheated water, at a temperature of 170 °C and a pressure of 7,000 g/cm^3 (100 pounds per square inch), is pumped down the outer pipe and melts the sulphur. Compressed air is pumped down the central pipe and forms an emulsion with the sulphur which, because it is less dense than water, readily flows up the third pipe. The emulsified sulphur solidifies on cooling and is almost completely pure (99.5–99.9 per cent).

freeze-drying, a method of drying foodstuffs in which the water content is removed by freezing and then heating the material in a high vacuum. Ice crystals that form in the food during freezing are converted straight to vapour without passing through a liquid phase (sublimed). Freeze-drying provides a method of long-term storage without undue effect on flavour. The removal of water inhibits micro-organism growth, but the physical structure of the food is retained. Instant coffee is one of a wide range of freeze-dried products. (See also *food technology.)

freezer *deep-freeze, *refrigerator.

frequency, the number of complete *waves or cycles repeated by a vibrating system in one second. The *unit is the hertz (Hz). Frequency is inversely proportional to the *wavelength of wave motions such as sound and electromagnetic radiation. Waves of different frequency can be added together by *modulation to give a composite wave of complex frequency.

freshwater fishing, the catching of fish and invertebrate animals from freshwater habitats in lakes, ponds, rivers, and streams. One-third of the freshwater catch world-wide is carp and tilapia caught in China and India. Other important species are salmon, bream, carp, and sturgeon. Invertebrates are caught by *traps or by dredging; fish by means of a baited hook and line or with small *nets. In large lakes, lines and nets may be towed behind boats. Pollution by industries and agricultural chemicals has adversely affected freshwater fishing, turning the attention of commercial interests to *aquaculture.

Fresnel lens, a converging lens made up of a series of concentric rings, each being an element of a simple lens. These rings are assembled on a flat surface to make a lens of short focal length that is much thinner and lighter than the equivalent simple lens. Fresnel lenses are used in lighthouses, spotlights, and car headlights, applications in which conventional large-diameter *lenses would be too thick and heavy.

Freyssinet, (Marie-) Eugène (-Léon) (1879–1962), French civil engineer who in 1928 developed *pre-stressed concrete. The innovation was not initially successful, but in 1938 Freyssinet developed a practical tool for applying tension to steel, and this led to the world-wide adoption of pre-stressed concrete. Freyssinet designed and built many pre-stressed concrete structures, for example the bridge across the River Marne at Esbly, France, completed in 1949.

friction, the force opposing the movement of one surface over another. The usual definition of friction relates to sliding friction, but a wheel, ball, or roller has rolling friction, and friction also occurs in fluids (see *fluid mechanics). Study of the behaviour of sliding surfaces is known as tribology. All forms of friction imply loss of energy, which appears as heat. In wheeled vehicles, the sources of rolling friction are between the wheel and the axle and between the wheel and the ground. Low-friction bearings at the wheel hub minimize the former, while the latter is reduced by the use of either steel wheels on a steel rail, or pneumatic tyres on a smooth surface. In all rotating machinery, friction is reduced by using appropriate bearings and lubrication.

frigate, a type of medium-sized warship. The term has been in use since at least the 16th century, but the 'true' frigates were developed by the French in the 1730s and 1740s. These were three-masted, *square-rigged ships with a single, continuous gun-deck and a continuous, unarmed lower deck, a quarterdeck, and a forecastle. They were initially armed with between twenty-eight and thirty-two medium-sized guns. Later, frigates grew larger and their armament increased; this trend continued with the introduction of steam. From 1880 the word frigate largely dropped out of use, but towards the end of World War II it was revived for a type of escort ship. After the War frigates became the main medium-sized vessels in most navies. Modern frigates are standard surface warships, very often optimized for anti-submarine work.

Frontinus, Sextus Julius (AD 35–104), Roman soldier and water engineer. After a distinguished military career and a brief governorship of Britain (AD 74–8), Frontinus was put in charge of the water-supply of Rome (AD 95), with a labour force of 700. He took a keen interest in water engineering, and in his new capacity wrote *On the Waters of the City of Rome*, a comprehensive treatise of great historical interest dealing with all aspects of urban water supply.

fruit cultivation, the planting and tending of crops for their edible fruit. Horticulturally, a distinction is made between tropical and temperate fruits, with *citrus fruits falling somewhere in between. In each group are fruit borne on trees, on shrubs, or on low-growing herbs. In fruit cultivation, individual plants of high productivity and superior fruit are multiplied vegetatively (that is, without change in genetic composition) from root cuttings on to which shoots have been *grafted. Fruit cultivation is costly to initiate and maintain. Crops may take years to establish before becoming productive, and the continuous monoculture exacerbates problems of pests and diseases. Pruning and harvesting operations are labour-intensive, although new technology such as the vine-cropping spacing bar is increasingly being adopted. Most fruits are perishable at maturity. Preservation by drying and *canning is often possible. Although *refrigerated storage has expanded the range of fresh fruit available, many types remain virtually unknown beyond their area of cultivation.

fuel additive, a substance added in small proportions to fuels to modify their properties and make their use more effective. One of the best known additives is *lead tetraethyl, which makes *petrol burn more evenly and prevents *knock in petrol engines. Concern over toxic lead emissions from cars led many governments to discourage the use of lead additives during the 1980s. Other additives generally used in petrol include anti-oxidants, to prevent gumming up of petrol fuel lines, anti-rust agents to protect petrol tanks, and detergents to keep the insides of engines clean. Other fuel additives include amyl nitrate, added to *diesel oil to make it ignite readily under pressure, and additives to prevent diesel oil from foaming, or from freezing in winter.

fuel cell, an electrochemical cell or *battery that produces an electric current from chemical reactants continuously supplied to its *electrodes from an external source. This arrangement differs from ordinary cells, which cease to function when their original reactants are exhausted. Two reactants are consumed in a fuel cell: one must be oxidizing and take in electrons, and the other must be reducing and liberate electrons (see *oxidation and reduction). The usual oxidant is oxygen, and the reductant fuels have, to date, included hydrogen, hydrocarbons, and alcohols. Fuel-cell technology is still under active investigation. Unlike electrical *generators, fuel cells contain no moving parts and are silent and efficient in operation. Their waste products—generally water and carbon dioxide—are relatively harmless, and the cells require little maintenance. They are therefore used in space vehicles and in remote areas where independent but reliable sources of electricity are required. Fuel cells still have only specialist applications because they are expensive to manufacture and use rare or exotic materials. For optimum efficiency and size, high internal pressures and temperatures (up to 1,000 °C) are required. Fuel cells offer a possible future method of motor-car propulsion.

fuel injection *carburettor.

fuel-oil, a heavy oil burnt in *boilers to provide heat for homes, factories, ships, or power generation. The main components of fuel-oil are high-molecular-weight, involatile residues from various *petroleum refining processes, mixed with lighter refining products to produce the correct physical characteristics for the type of burner. Low viscosity is important for small domestic boilers. The melting-point, or pouring-point of the oil may also be important. Many fuel-oils melt in the range 2–20 °C, and may need warming before use.

Fuller, R(ichard) Buckminster (1895–1983), US engineer, architect, philosopher, and writer. He was a brilliant inventor who believed that technology should be used to solve social problems and benefit humanity. His inventions include an electric car and the factory-assembled Dymaxion (*dy*namic plus *max*imum efficiency) House, but he is probably best known for his *geodesic domes. These lightweight structures enable large spaces to be enclosed with great efficiency—in line with Fuller's ideals of using the world's resources to maximum purpose with the least waste.

fulling (milling), a finishing process applied to *woollen and worsted fabrics. The object of the process is to convert a soft cloth (woven or knitted) into a firmer one. Originally, this was achieved by treading the material underfoot in water. Later, it was done with power-driven wooden hammers known as fulling stocks. Today rollers repeatedly force the material, soaking in soapy water, through compressing devices. The process has much in common with felt-making.

Fulton, Robert (1765–1815), US engineer and pioneer of steam propulsion. A failed artist, in 1796 he went to Britain to seek his fortune and became associated with the Duke of Bridgewater's canal projects; this led him to explore the possibility of steam-powered dredgers. Whilst in France (1797–1806), he put to the French government (and later to the British government) proposals for a submarine and torpedoes, but practical trials proved unsuccessful. Returning to the USA he built his own *steamships and had a much publicized succcess with his *Clermont* paddle-steamer (1808).

fungicide, any *pesticide that kills fungi. Fungicides based on the broadly toxic elements copper, mercury, and sulphur were amongst the earliest *agrochemicals: copper sulphate and mercury chloride were used in the 18th century, and lime sulphur was used to treat mildew from 1802 onwards. These compounds have now been largely superseded by synthetic systemic compounds which enter the plant via the roots or shoots and are then transported to all other tissues. Diseases such as rusts, mildews, and blights spread rapidly once established. Fungicides are thus routinely applied to growing and stored crops as a preventive measure, generally as foliar sprays or seed dressings. Disease forecasting aids the farmer in determining when to spray for early protection.

fungus, a eukaryotic, non-photosynthetic organism that obtains nutrients by absorption of organic compounds from its surroundings, and reproduces with the formation of spores. A eukaryote is an organism consisting of a cell or cells in which the genetic material is contained within a distinct nucleus. Fungi include destructive plant pests such as mildews and rusts; they are also important soil organisms, and contribute to the decay of food, fabrics, and timber. Yeast is a type of fungus essential for *bread-making, *wine-making, and *brewing, while some species of mould are used in the making of blue cheeses. Mould is also an important ingredient of tempeh, a food based on soya beans.

Such fungi as mushrooms, truffles, and black fungus are grown or collected for food. Mushrooms are a good source of fibre, are low in fat, and contain more protein per unit weight than almost any other vegetable.

funicular railway, a railway in which a cable is used to move a vehicle running on rails up and down a steep slope. In most systems two vehicles, running on separate lines, are joined by the haulage cable and as one descends the other ascends, so minimizing the power required. Early funiculars used water balance, steam, or hydraulic power, but most have now been rebuilt to use electrical power.

fur-farming, the farming of animals such as rabbits, foxes, polecats, mink, and chinchillas for their pelts. Fur-farming developed as the hunting of wild species failed to provide the volume of skins necessary to supply the fur industry. The animals are fed a diet of poultry, fish, or offal. Pelts are dressed (a process like *tanning), which preserves the skin and ensures that hairs remain firmly attached. Sometimes the longer guard hairs are plucked or trimmed; the pelt may also be dyed. Many skins are required to make a garment—between twenty-two and thirty minks for a jacket, up to seventy-seven musquash for a full-length coat. Seal cubs, though not strictly farmed, are culled for their fine fur. In recent years, changing public attitudes and the development of synthetic furs of good quality have led to a decline in the number of furs made from animal skins.

One of the electromagnetic field coils used in the tokamak **fusion** reactor at the Joint European Torus Laboratory in Culham, UK. The magnetic field of these coils acts to contain the extremely hot plasma within the central chamber of the tokamak.

furnace *blast-furnace, *boiler, *fluidized-bed furnace, *solar furnace.

fuse, a simple safety device for preventing excessive or damaging electric current flow. The fuse consists of a short piece of bare wire with a low melting-point, suspended between two contacts by which it is connected into an electrical circuit. On overload, the current rapidly heats the wire; the wire quickly melts, breaking the circuit and cutting off the current. Fuses are specified according to the maximum current that they will carry before melting. Unlike a *circuit-breaker, fuses are not reusable and must be replaced after being overloaded.

A fuse is also a device used to ignite a *shell, *mine, or other explosive device. Waxed paper fuses were used on Chinese *fireworks in the 10th century, while in Arab countries slow matches of twine impregnated with saltpetre were used at about the same period to ignite fire-pots. In 17th-century Europe timed fuses, comprising hollow beechwood cylinders filled with alcohol and gunpowder, were used in artillery shells. The firing of the shell's propellant charge lit the fuse, and when it had burnt to its end, it ignited the contents. An impact fuse in the shell's nose was developed in the late 19th century; this consisted of a percussion charge that ignites on striking the target, thus detonating the shell's explosive. Recently, more sophisticated timing mechanisms and devices, such as those that respond to *radar, or to barometric pressure, have been incorporated into fuses.

fusion, nuclear, a nuclear reaction in which two or more light atomic nuclei combine to form a heavier atomic nucleus, with a concomitant release of very large amounts of energy. In the fusion of, for example, two hydrogen nuclei to form a helium nucleus, there is some loss of mass, and this mass is completely converted to energy (see *nuclear energy). The loss of mass resulting from the fusion of light elements tends to be greater than that resulting from the nuclear *fission of heavy elements, and therefore fusion generates more energy than fission. Most of the world's energy comes ultimately from fusion reactions taking place in the Sun, in which hydrogen nuclei are fused at extremely high temperatures (10 million °C) to form helium. An enormous amount of money and effort has been invested world-wide in fusion research, because of its potential as a limitless source of energy. The first result of this research was the manufacture of the hydrogen bomb (see *nuclear weapon) in 1952. Since then progress has been slow. Research has been along two main lines. In the first, a plasma (a totally ionized gas) of deuterium and tritium is raised to a temperature of about 100 million degrees in a toroidal (ring-shaped) reactor called a tokamak. The plasma is prevented from melting the reactor vessel by containment within a powerful magnetic field. A second line of research is laser fusion, in which a small pellet of deuterium and tritium is imploded by concentration of the energy of several powerful lasers on it. Until the early 1990s, neither method had yielded more energy from fusion than had been put into the system. However, in 1991 scientists at the Joint European Torus project in Culham, Oxfordshire, UK, took a large step forwards. They fused deuterium and tritium in a plasma, producing about 1 million watts of energy, sustained for around two minutes. This was considerably nearer 'ignition point', which would produce a self-sustaining fusion reaction.

G

Gabor, Dennis (1900–79), Hungarian-born British scientist who invented *holography (1947), a means of creating a image in three-dimensional space. Early holograms were poor in quality, but the possibilities of holography were enormously increased with the advent of the *laser in 1960. Gabor was awarded the Nobel Prize for Physics in 1971.

gain, electrical, the numerical value of amplification of a given electrical input that an electronic component or circuit provides. Thus a gain of ×35 means that the signal output from the circuit is five times larger than the input. Gain is often measured in *decibels.

Galileo Galilei (1564–1642), Italian mathematician, astronomer, physicist, and a founder of modern science. He formulated the law of uniform acceleration for falling bodies and, about 1602, discovered the constancy of time of a pendulum's swing, subsequently of great practical importance in regulating mechanical *clocks. In 1609 he improved the primitive *telescope for astronomical purposes. He was arraigned for heresy (1633) by the Roman Catholic Church for stating that the earth and other planets move around the sun. His great *Dialogue Concerning Two New Sciences* (1638) contained the basis of the classical mechanics later developed by, among others, the Dutch physicist Christiaan Huygens (1629–95) and the English physicist and mathematician Isaac Newton (1642–1727).

galleon, a type of ship developed from the carrack, probably originating in Spain in the 16th century (see *sailing ships and boats). It was slimmer than the carrack, and decked in a series of steps at each end, but particularly at the stern. Galleons formed a part of the Spanish Armada of 1588, but in general the galleon was used as a combination of trading ship and warship. 'Plate fleets' of Spanish and Portuguese galleons brought large quantities of gold and silver from the Americas to Europe during the 16th and early 17th centuries. Spain continued to use galleons until the late 17th century.

galley, a *warship used principally in the Mediterranean from the 2nd millennium BC. The galley's major weapon was originally a ram on the water-line, used to hole enemy ships or to smash their oars. It was propelled by oars in battle, and carried sails for use in favourable winds. The success of the galley as a warship was due to its great speed and manœuvrability. This type of galley reached its furthest development in ancient Greece. The best-known type of Greek galley was the trireme, with three banks (rows) of oars. Galleys of various types continued to be important war vessels in the Mediterranean throughout the Roman period and the Middle Ages. In the later period, archers and boarding parties became more important than the ram, and eventually forward-firing guns were used. Byzantium, Genoa, Venice, and other medieval sea powers also built large, elaborate galleys for trading, which by the 13th century were travelling to England and north-west Africa. Galleys continued to be of military importance until the 16th century, and were used as convict ships until the 18th century.

gallium (symbol Ga, at. no. 31, r.a.m. 69.72), a silvery-white metallic element that melts in the hand. Its major commercial application is in combination with *arsenic or *phosphorus as a dopant in *semiconductor devices. It is also used in light-emitting diodes and phosphors.

galvanizing, the process of covering a metal, usually iron, with a layer of *zinc to protect it from corrosion. Grease is removed from the surface with hot sodium hydroxide solution; any oxide layer is removed by 'pickling' in dilute sulphuric acid. The coating may be applied by dipping the iron into molten zinc. A layer of zinc–iron alloy forms on the surface; a further layer of zinc adheres to this and solidifies to produce a protective layer. Alternatively, the zinc may be applied by *electroplating, giving a layer of uniform thickness. (Compare *sherardizing.)

galvanometer, a type of *ammeter used to measure extremely small electric currents. The commonest type consists of a fine coil of wire wound on a cylinder and suspended between the poles of a permanent magnet by a phosphor-bronze wire. When current passes through the coil, it interacts with the magnetic field of the magnet (see *electromagnetic induction), producing a twisting force (torque) on the coil. The coil rotates an amount proportional to the amount of current passing through it: the angle of rotation is measured either by a pointer mounted on the coil, or by the angle through which a mirror attached to the coil deflects a beam of light.

A replica of a Greek trireme undergoing sea trials at Poros, Greece, in 1988. The reconstruction demonstrated that it was possible for a **galley** to be propelled by three banks of oars, all of the same length.

gantry harvesting, a method of harvesting crops in which a large gantry is used to straddle areas of the crop. Harvesting units move along the length of the gantry, while the gantry itself moves the length of the field, reducing soil damage caused by heavy machinery. Gantry harvesting is also applied on a *greenhouse scale.

gas, one of the three states of matter, the other two being liquid and solid. The particles comprising a gas (see *atoms and molecules) move at high speeds and so have sufficient energy to overcome their mutual forces of attraction. This results in a gas having high fluidity and the ability to expand indefinitely unless constrained by a container. The relatively large distances between gas particles means that a gas is about one thousand times less dense than its corresponding liquid. A gas may be liquefied by applying a suitable combination of temperature and pressure (see *gas, liquefaction of). The pressure of a gas is proportional to the force exerted by the gas particles on the walls of its container during collision. (See also *natural gas, *town gas, *coal-gas, and individual gases.)

gas, liquefaction of. Gases can be liquefied by cooling, by applying pressure, or by a combination of both methods. Liquefaction allows a large volume of gas to be compressed into a small space. Above what is known as its critical temperature, a gas cannot be liquefied no matter how much pressure is applied. The further below the critical temperature the gas is, the less pressure is needed to liquefy it. Gases such as *oxygen, *hydrogen, and *nitrogen have critical temperatures well below ambient, and so must be both cooled and highly compressed to achieve liquefaction. The liquid gases are then stored in cylinders under pressure. Substances such as *ammonia and the *hydrocarbons propane and butane have critical temperatures well above ambient temperatures, and are thus easier to liquefy. Liquefied gases are used in many applications, for example, as coolants, as rocket fuel, for heating, for welding, in aqualungs, and so on. (See also *liquid petroleum gas, *liquefied natural gas.)

gas-cooled reactor *Magnox reactor, *advanced gas-cooled reactor.

gas-discharge lamp, a lamp in which light is produced by the application of a high voltage across a tube containing gas at low pressure. Normally gases are poor conductors, but at a sufficiently high voltage, gas molecules are ionized (become charged), and current is carried through the tube by the ions. Light is produced by collisions between the *ions; such collisions also cause further ionizations, which help to maintain the current even when the voltage across the tube is reduced. Gas-discharge lamps are used for luminous signs, the colour of the light emitted being dependent on the gas in the discharge pulse. The best-known example is neon, which gives an orange light.

gas-engine, an *internal-combustion engine using a gaseous fuel. This was the first successful form of internal-combustion engine, dating from about 1860, when *Lenoir's first engines appeared. Although now replaced for transport purposes by *petrol and *diesel engines, gas-engines are still used in many stationary applications. They can burn almost any type of flammable gas; most engines now use *natural gas (methane), but *liquid petroleum gases are used in some vehicles. The low cost of gas-engines makes them suitable for *combined heat and power generation.

gas grid, a system of pipes carrying gas and linking storage points with user pipe networks. A grid prevents local shortages through surges in demand, by removing dependence on a single source of supply. It also allows flexibility in locating sources of supply or storage facilities. Gas grids are generally constructed of pipelines of about 1 m (3 feet) diameter, set underground. Most countries with a gas grid developed the grid to take advantage of a regular supply of *natural gas. For example, the UK has a gas grid that was set up in the 1970s and 1980s to take advantage of natural gas from beneath the North Sea.

gas lighting, a method of *lighting based on the combustion of a gas, typically *coal-gas or *natural gas. The latter was first used for illumination in China in about the 2nd century AD, being conveyed from the ground through bamboo pipes. In 1784 Jean-Pierre Minkhelers used gas for lighting, and in 1799 *Lebon patented his 'thermolampe'. The British engineering firm Boulton and Watt manufactured the first commercial gas-lighting systems in 1806, but the real pioneer of the gas industry was *Winsor, who in 1812 established the National Light and Heat Company in the UK. The first street-lighting using coal-gas was installed in Westminster, London, in 1814. The original burners—in which the gas burned as a simple non-aerated jet—were smoky and had low luminosity. Aerated burners, introduced from about 1840, were a considerable improvement, but the situation was transformed by the advent of *Auer's gas-mantle in 1885. Today, gas lamps are mainly used where portable lighting is required. They commonly use a burner and are fuelled with *propane gas from an attached cylinder.

gasoline *petrol.

gastraphetes *crossbow.

gastroscope *endoscopy.

gas-turbine, a form of *engine in which a continuous stream of hot gases is directed against the blades of a *turbine, causing it to turn. In most cases the gas, usually air, is first compressed in a *compressor before passing into combustion chambers, where a portion of the gas is mixed with fuel and burned. The rest of the gas bypasses the combustion chamber and mixes with the hot gases emerging after combustion. This is then forced through nozzles to drive a turbine. Part of the power from this turbine is used to drive the compressor; the remaining power can be used in various ways, depending on the function of the engine: it may drive the propeller shaft of an aircraft or ship, the drive-shaft of a locomotive, or an electric generator. Alternatively, a turbine just big enough to drive the compressor can be used, and the remaining energy of the hot exhaust gases used to give a high-speed exhaust jet and hence a forward thrust; this is the *jet engine. Gas-turbines are used in electricity generation for standby and peak-load service, in portable power plants, and in *combined-cycle power generation. The high power-to-weight ratio of gas-turbines has led to their use in *aeroplanes, and also in *diesel locomotives and naval vessels. (See jet engine for illustration.)

gauge, railway, the distance between the inner faces of the rails of a railway track. For public railways the gauge now varies from 381 to 1,676 mm (15 inches to 5 feet, 6 inches), though the most common or standard gauge is 1,435 mm (4 feet, 8.5 inches). The Soviet gauge is 1,500 mm (5

Gear

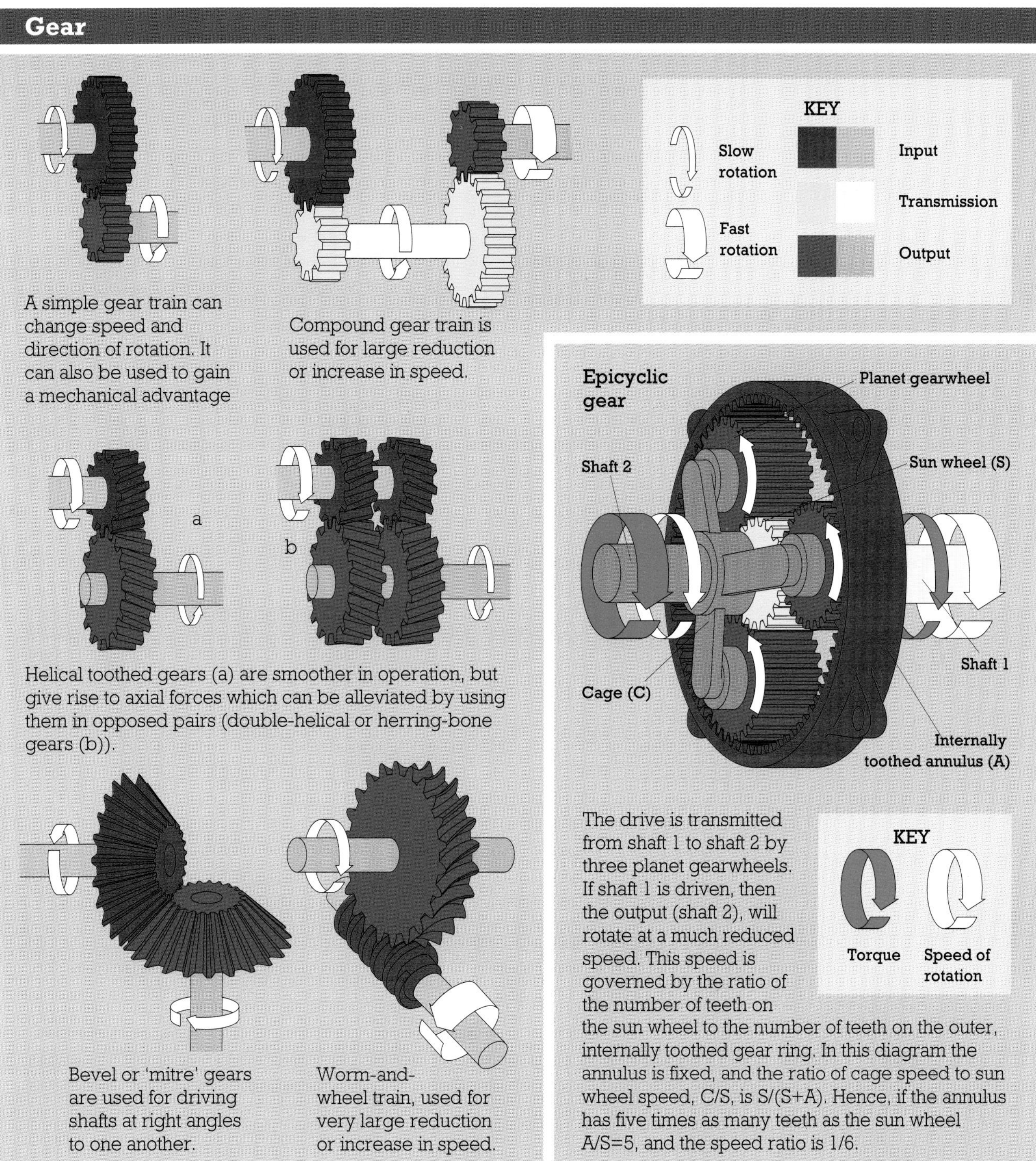

A simple gear train can change speed and direction of rotation. It can also be used to gain a mechanical advantage

Compound gear train is used for large reduction or increase in speed.

Helical toothed gears (a) are smoother in operation, but give rise to axial forces which can be alleviated by using them in opposed pairs (double-helical or herring-bone gears (b)).

Bevel or 'mitre' gears are used for driving shafts at right angles to one another.

Worm-and-wheel train, used for very large reduction or increase in speed.

The drive is transmitted from shaft 1 to shaft 2 by three planet gearwheels. If shaft 1 is driven, then the output (shaft 2), will rotate at a much reduced speed. This speed is governed by the ratio of the number of teeth on the sun wheel to the number of teeth on the outer, internally toothed gear ring. In this diagram the annulus is fixed, and the ratio of cage speed to sun wheel speed, C/S, is S/(S+A). Hence, if the annulus has five times as many teeth as the sun wheel A/S=5, and the speed ratio is 1/6.

feet). Today, most new railway lines are built to standard gauge. The loading gauge of a railway system defines the height and width of the vehicles that may run on it, determined by the clearance of structures such as bridges and tunnels along the line. The loading gauge in the UK is much less than that of mainland Europe.

gear, a toothed or grooved wheel or other shape that can be used to transmit mechanical power. The earliest gearwheels were made of wood, with wooden teeth; by the 1st century AD all the simple gear types were well known. By the 6th century AD they were used in *windmills, *water-wheels, and other mechanical devices. For more precise machines, smaller metal gears were evolved; a calendrical device from 87 BC used small bronze wheels, and miniature gears were later developed for *clocks and navigational instruments. In the early 19th century *machine-tools made it possible to stamp out gearwheels automatically: the clock trade was among the first to adopt this system. Today gears are most commonly cut by a gear-hobbing machine, using a type of milling machine. Although gears are mostly in rolling contact there is a degree of sliding, and lubrication is needed to reduce friction and wear. As well as transmitting rotary power, gears can be used to obtain a *mechanical advantage: if one gearwheel has twice as many teeth as the gear that drives it, it will travel half a turn for every full turn of the smaller wheel, but will exert twice the *torque (turning force). Conversely, gears can be used to obtain a speed increase: if a large wheel is used to drive a smaller one, the smaller wheel will turn faster (but with less torque). The wide range of applications in which gears are used has led to the development of many gear types (see figure).

Epicyclic gears are used to give a step-up or step-down gear ratio to shafts in line. They are used in hub-type *bicycle gears, and in some types of *automatic transmission. The epicyclic gear comprises three elements, the sun-wheel (S), the cage (C), and the planet gearwheel or annulus (A). Any one of these may be fixed, and the drive taken to or from the other two (see figure).

gearbox, strictly the casing of a gear train, an arrangement of *gears designed to transmit motion between two shafts, but in some applications, in particular in the *motor car, the term refers to both casing and gear train. A car needs a gearbox because *internal-combustion engines work efficiently and give high power only at high engine speeds, whereas the car needs to be able to travel at a wide range of road speeds. The gearbox solves this problem by keeping the engine speed fairly high and varying the road speed through the use of different gears. Generally motor cars have four or five gear ratios, although tractors and heavy goods vehicles may need up to fifteen gears, a range achieved by using two gearboxes in series. With a manual gearbox (see figure), the engine is disengaged from the drive during gear changing, and then progressively re-engaged, by means of the *clutch. (In vehicles with *automatic transmission this disengagement does not occur.) Synchromesh on all gears except reverse aids smooth changing from gear to gear. In the synchromesh system, a collar fixed to the transmission shaft, and rotating with it (see figure), is moved by a selector rod to engage with a cone on the front of the gear wheel to be engaged. Friction between the collar and the cone acts on the freely rotating gearwheel to smoothly bring its rotational speed up to that of the transmission shaft. When both gear and collar are rotating together, dog teeth on the gear engage with an outer toothed ring on the collar, locking the two together.

Geiger–Müller counter, an instrument for detecting and measuring nuclear *radiation, one of the first electrical devices to be used in radiation research, perfected by Hans Geiger and W. Müller at Kiel University, Germany, in 1925. It consists of an aluminium tube containing argon gas at low pressure, through which passes a wire *electrode. A potential difference of about 400 V is applied between the electrode and the tube wall. The end of the tube is sealed with a

Gearbox

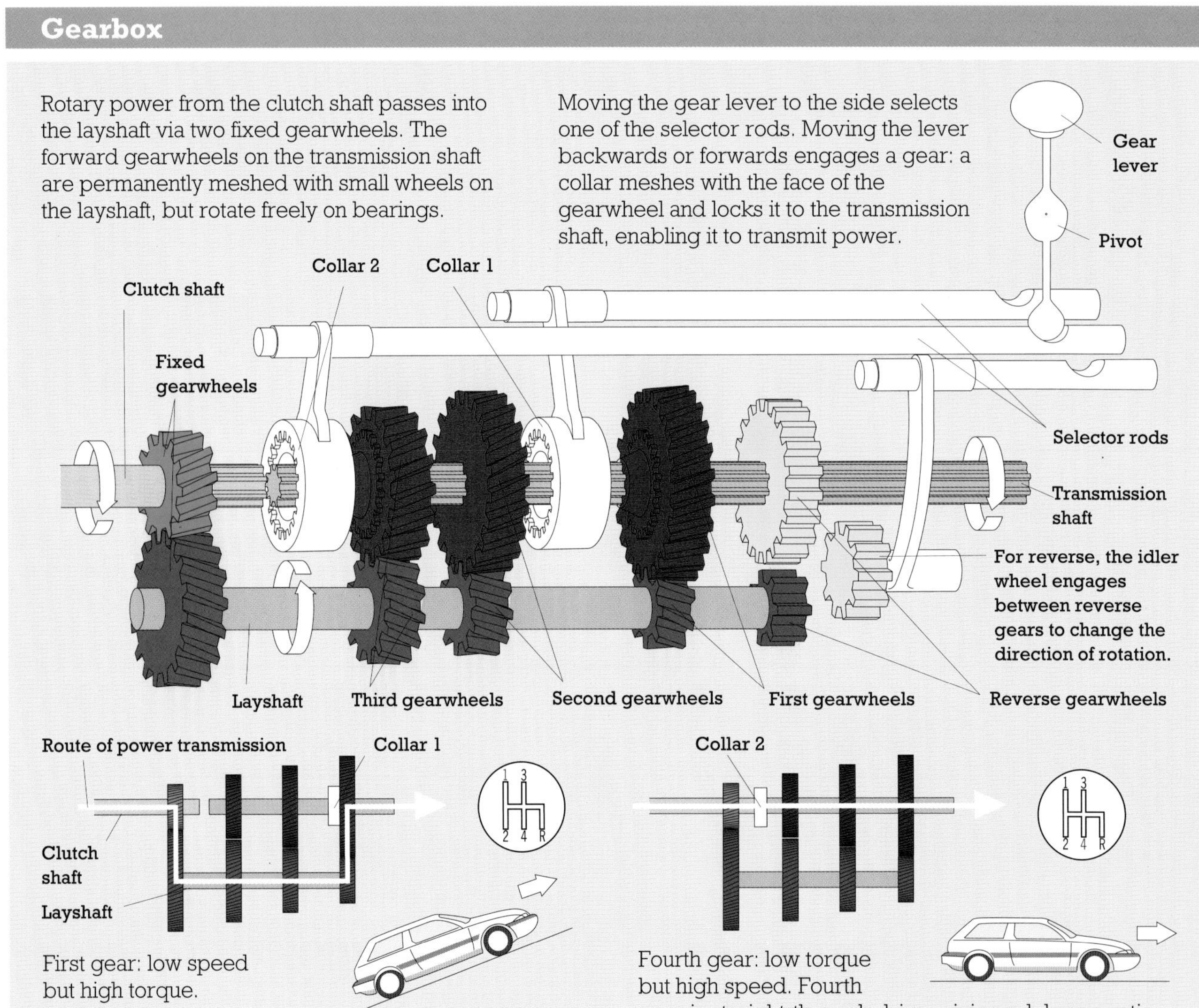

Rotary power from the clutch shaft passes into the layshaft via two fixed gearwheels. The forward gearwheels on the transmission shaft are permanently meshed with small wheels on the layshaft, but rotate freely on bearings.
Moving the gear lever to the side selects one of the selector rods. Moving the lever backwards or forwards engages a gear: a collar meshes with the face of the gearwheel and locks it to the transmission shaft, enabling it to transmit power.
Gear lever
Pivot
Collar 2
Collar 1
Clutch shaft
Fixed gearwheels
Selector rods
Transmission shaft
For reverse, the idler wheel engages between reverse gears to change the direction of rotation.
Layshaft
Third gearwheels
Second gearwheels
First gearwheels
Reverse gearwheels
Route of power transmission
Collar 1
Clutch shaft
Layshaft
First gear: low speed but high torque.
Collar 2
Fourth gear: low torque but high speed. Fourth gear is straight-through drive, giving a 1:1 gear ratio.

mica window thin enough to allow alpha-, beta-, and gamma-radiation to pass through. When a charged radiation particle enters the tube, the argon becomes ionized (charged), triggering an avalanche of *ions between the electrodes, and a pulse of current flows. Each pulse is recorded, and can be displayed as radioactive counts per second. The frequency of pulses is proportional to the radiation intensity.

gel, a dispersion of a finely divided solid in a liquid in which particles of the solid link up to form a network in which droplets of the liquid become trapped. Gelatine forms gels in this manner: droplets of water are trapped in the protein network that forms as the gel solidifies. Photographic *film consists of a layer of gelatine gel containing silver bromide particles, supported on a film of *cellulose acetate. Gelatine is an elastic gel, but other gels (for example, silica gel) may be rigid.

gelignite, a stable and *explosive jelly, which is both plastic and water-repellant, composed of 8 per cent gun-cotton (a form of *nitro-cellulose) and 92 per cent *nitro-glycerine. Discovered and produced by *Nobel in 1875, it is one of the most powerful and shattering explosives known. It is used for blasting rocks. Reducing the proportion of nitro-glycerine to gun-cotton produces a slower-burning explosive.

generator, electrical, a device for the conversion of mechanical, chemical, or other form of energy into electrical energy. The most common type of generator, for example a bicycle dynamo, relies on *electromagnetic induction to convert mechanical energy into electrical energy. Such a generator is essentially a reversed *electric motor, with a rotor carrying one or more coils surrounded by a magnetic field, typically supplied by a permanent magnet or *electromagnet. Mechanical energy (often from a *steam-turbine) is used to rotate the rotor, which induces an electric current in the rotor coil. In the case of a generator providing direct current, a mechanical switch or commutator switches the current every half-rotation so that it remains unidirectional. Large modern generators (alternators) in *power-stations provide alternating-current output for general distribution (see *electricity generation and supply). There are many other types of electric generator. Electrostatic generators like *Wimshurst machines, and on a larger scale *van de Graaff generators, are principally used for specialist applications that require very high voltages but only a low current, such as providing power for *particle accelerators. Other types of generator include *batteries, *fuel cells, and *solar cells. (See also *Siemens.)

genetic engineering, the deliberate modification of the genetic make-up (genome) of an organism by manipulation of its DNA. Genetic engineering techniques include cell fusion and the use of recombinant *DNA (rDNA). Since the late 1960s these techniques have held out the most exciting promise for *biotechnology.

Many efforts have been made to combine desirable properties of two species in one, for example, the wool of the sheep with the hardiness of the goat. The main barrier to this is the failure of fertilization—sperm of one species will not fuse with eggs of the other (although with closely related species there is some chance of breeding success). Recently, however, cells with the potential for growth into whole organisms have been fused together *in vitro*, with mixing of their genetic material. In some cases such organisms have developed into adult chimeras (mixtures of two species), but these are, as yet, of no commercial significance. Practical results of cell fusion are more likely where cells are to be grown in a culture rather than as whole organisms, and already the production of *monoclonal antibodies using such techniques has proved a success.

Whereas cell fusion is a somewhat imprecise 'shotgun' approach to creating genetic novelty, recombinant DNA (rDNA) techniques are capable of transferring specific genetic activity from one organism to another. If, for example, a gene for a property such as production of the hormone insulin is isolated from a human or animal cell and transferred to a swiftly replicating bacterium like *Escherichia coli*, insulin can be produced in large enough quantities to be commercially profitable (see *biotechnology). The success of such techniques relies on 'tools' supplied by micro-organisms: bacterial plasmids and *enzymes. Plasmids are small, circular pieces of DNA lying outside the main bacterial chromosome. The most important enzymes are restriction endonucleases, which cut DNA strands at specific points; reverse transcriptase, which makes a DNA strand from a strand of RNA; DNA ligase, which can be used to join strands of DNA together; and Taq polymerase, which can make a double-stranded DNA molecule from a single-stranded 'primer' molecule.

The first step in genetic manipulation is to isolate DNA strands known to contain the desired genetic activity or property. Several methods of isolating suitable DNA are shown in the figure. In order to obtain practical working quantities of the isolated DNA, many thousands of copies are made by a technique known as the polymerase chain reaction (PCR), in which the double-stranded DNA is split into two single-stranded primers, from which Taq polymerase forms two double-stranded copies. The two copies are then split to make four primers, and so on. Once sufficient quantities of DNA have been formed, the long chains are fragmented using restriction endonucleases. The next step is to combine these fragments with vectors (carriers), which will carry them into bacterial cells. The circular plasmids are opened up using an endonuclease, and the DNA fragments are 'spliced' on to the plasmid DNA using DNA ligase. The hybrid plasmids are now mixed with the host cells, and enter them to form tranformed cells. Only some of the transformed cells exhibit the desired gene activity (for example, production of insulin). In order to test for such activity, the transformed cells are separated and cultured (grown) individually. Cultures showing the desired activity can then be *cloned in a *bioreactor to obtain a commercial product.

Transformed bacterial cells can be produced relatively easily; it is more difficult to transform animal and plant cells. One technique for transforming plant cells involves the use of the bacterium *Agrobacterium tumefaciens*, which normally reproduces by transferring a piece of DNA from its plasmid to a host plant cell, thus causing the plant cell to start producing bacteria. This natural system can be manipulated to introduce genes for disease resistance, for example into crop plants. Other examples of successful transgenic organisms (organisms with genetically transformed cells) include sheep with human proteins in their milk, and plants with disease-resistant genes. Unlike transformed bacteria, few of these transgenic organisms are ready for commercial exploitation, but there are many possibilities for the near future.

In such a new field controversy inevitably abounds. Worries concerning release of genetically novel bacteria into the environment, or the possible manipulation of human embryos, have led to the setting up in the USA of the

Genetic engineering

Structure of DNA

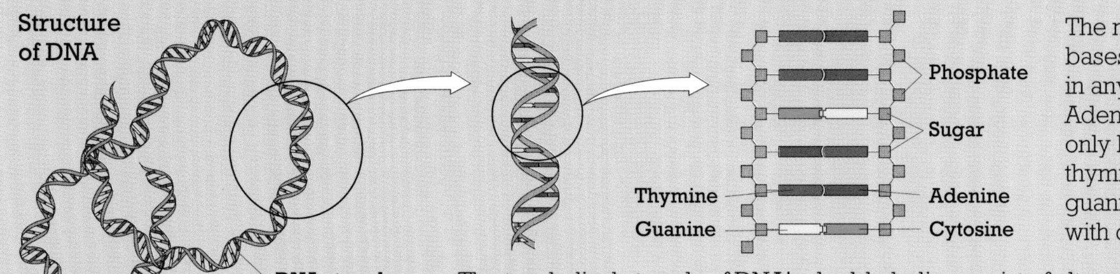

The nitrogenous bases can occur in any order. Adenine will only bind with thymine and guanine only with cytosine.

The two helical strands of DNA's double helix consist of alternate sugar and phosphate groups. Bound to each sugar is one of four nitrogenous bases.

Common sources of DNA used in genetic engineering

1 Extraction from cells

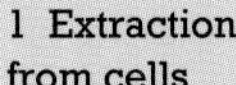

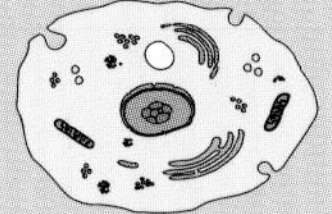

or

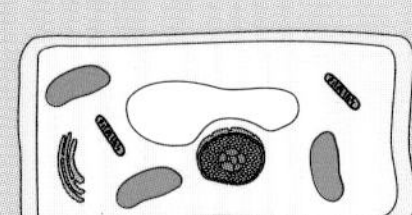

or

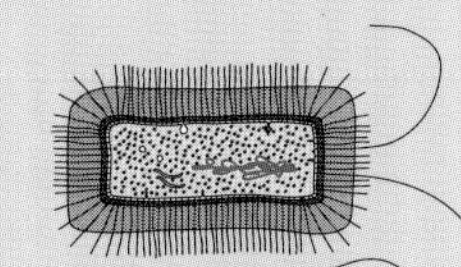

2 With reverse transcriptase present, mRNA is used as a template to produce a complementary DNA (cDNA) strand. Note that in mRNA thymine is replaced by the base uracil.

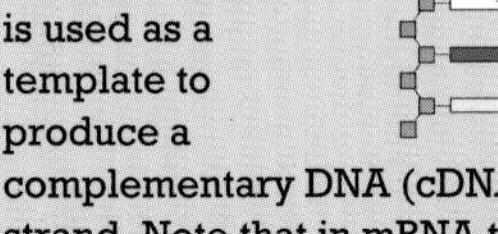

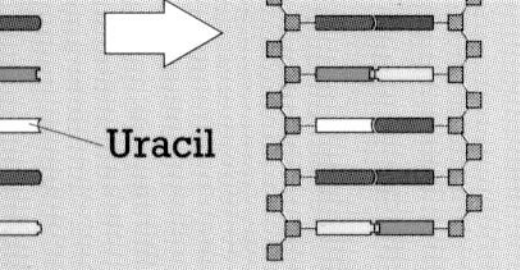

The RNA is destroyed using an alkaline treatment.

The cDNA is used as a template to form a complementary DNA strand.

3 Chemical synthesis from nucleotides

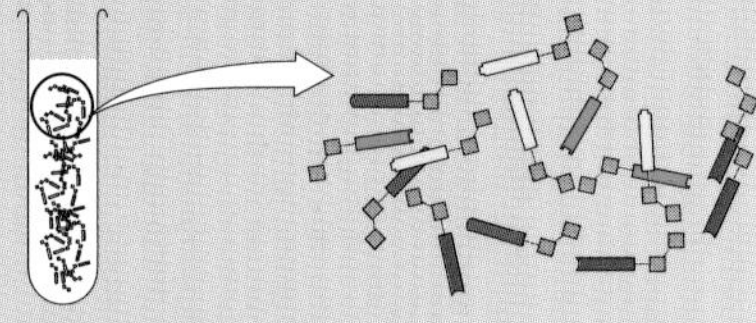

DNA is synthesized from nucleotides, without the use of materials obtained from the cell.

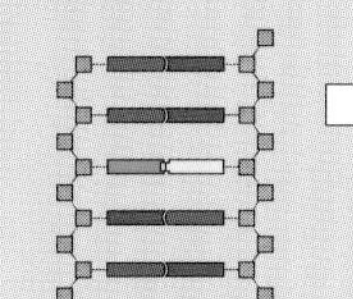

Suitable DNA strand or fragment

Inserting a DNA fragment into a bacterial plasmid

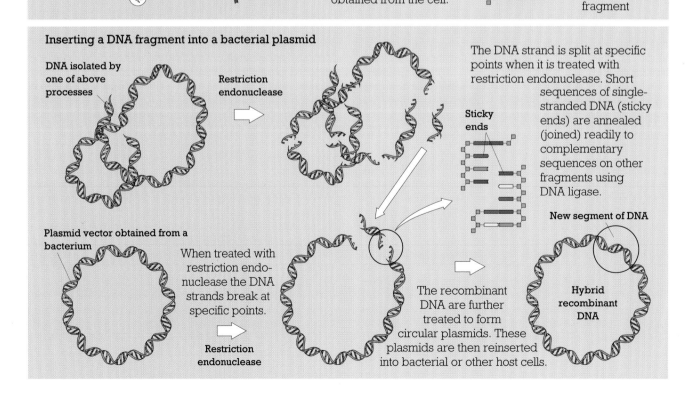

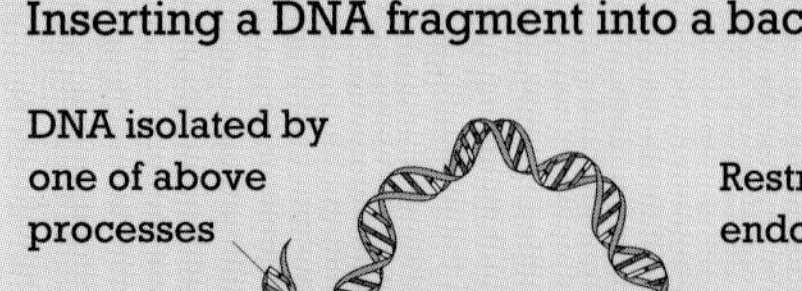

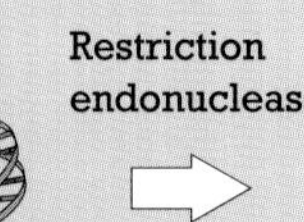

The DNA strand is split at specific points when it is treated with restriction endonuclease. Short sequences of single-stranded DNA (sticky ends) are annealed (joined) readily to complementary sequences on other fragments using DNA ligase.

Sticky ends

New segment of DNA

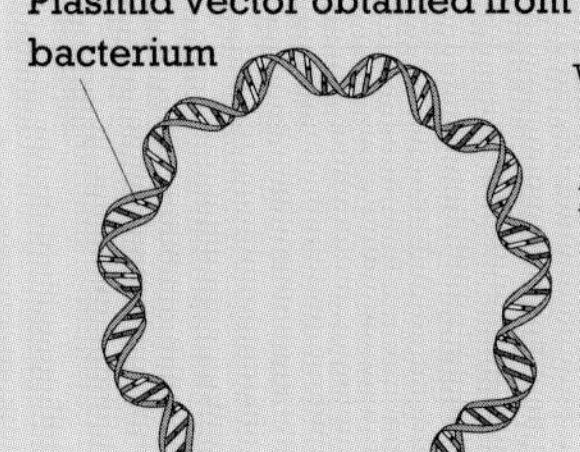

When treated with restriction endonuclease the DNA strands break at specific points.

Restriction endonuclease

The recombinant DNA are further treated to form circular plasmids. These plasmids are then reinserted into bacterial or other host cells.

Hybrid recombinant DNA

Genetic Manipulation Advisory Group (GMAG). Legislation governing genetic research has also been passed in several other countries.

genetic resources, the variety of genetic material (gene pool) contained within the world's animals and plants. The form of an organism (its phenotype) is determined by the genes it possesses (its genotype), and its environment. Wild populations of a given species are genetically heterogeneous and individuals within them thus show variation in their characteristics. A major effect of domestication is a reduction in this natural genetic variability. By selecting for agriculturally desirable traits in crops and livestock, humans have favoured the perpetuation of some gene combinations and excluded many others. Genes governing certain traits, such as resistance to pests or drought, may be lost completely. Genetic resources, particularly genes present in wild relatives of domestic types, provide a source of diverse genetic material for *plant and *animal breeding. Much effort is now devoted to the collection and preservation of the progenitors of agriculturally significant species.

geodesic dome, a three-dimensional load-bearing structure usually formed by a hemisphere, whose surface is divided into triangles by rods in compression (struts) lying on geodesics (a geodesic is the shortest line joining two points on a curved surface). The vertices of the triangles forming this lattice are known as nodes. The structure is made weatherproof by a lightweight covering supported on the lattice. The dome can also be formed with solid, rigid panels linked at the nodes. The idea was patented by *Fuller in 1954.

geostationary orbit *satellite, artificial.

geothermal energy, the heat energy of the Earth's interior. The Earth's temperature rises with increasing depth below the surface, mainly as a result of energy released in radioactive decay of *uranium. In most places the rise is less than 1 °C per 30 m (100 feet), but in some locations temperatures above 100 °C are reached within a few hundred metres. If water is present, geysers or hot springs may appear, natural energy sources that have been used to heat buildings for over 150 years. In more recent times boreholes have been drilled to tap sub-surface water, and more than a dozen countries now use this source for industry, agriculture, and domestic heating. The injection of water through deep shafts to extract the heat from dry rock is also under investigation. Nearly a century ago it was recognized that geothermal steam could be used to generate electric power. An industrial plant at Larderello in Italy, already using geothermal energy, was the site of the first commercial geothermal power-station, in 1913. This is still in operation, and similar stations have since been built elsewhere, raising the total world generating capacity to about 4,000 MW.

A **geothermal energy** plant in Svartsengi, Iceland. Springs, heated by volcanic activity in the earth's interior, provide steam to power turbines for electricity generation.

germanium (symbol Ge, at. no. 32, r.a.m. 72.59), a grey-white metallic element. Germanium purified by *zone refining is used to make transistors, rectifiers, and other *semiconductor devices. Germanium dioxide is used in the manufacture of specialized *optical glasses.

Gibbon, John Heynsham (1903–74), US heart surgeon. In 1953 Gibbon introduced the *heart–lung machine, which can take over the heart's role in circulating blood around the body. This enabled lengthy heart operations to be performed while the heart was stopped.

Giffard, Henri (1825–82), French aeronautical engineer. Initially a railway engineer, he became attracted to the design and construction of *airships. He built a propulsion unit, comprising a 2.25-kW (3-horsepower) *steam-engine driving a 3-m (10-foot) screw *propeller. In 1852, he propelled a semi-rigid airship with rudder steering at 8 km/h (5 m.p.h.) for a distance of 27 km (17 miles). He later built huge captive balloons for various international exhibitions.

gig mill, a machine for raising a *nap or pile on the surface of a cloth, in order to give the fabric a softer and warmer feel. The original gig mills had rotating rollers on which teasels (the dried, prickly heads of plants of the genus *Dipsacus*) were mounted. The nap was raised by the action of the moving teasels as the cloth is drawn over the rollers. Today, fine steel spikes embedded in a heavy base fabric are also used.

girder *structural engineering.

glass, a hard, brittle, amorphous (non-crystalline) *ceramic, usually comprising inorganic polymers of mixed oxides based around the silicon dioxide (SiO_2) unit. Glass is transparent to light, generally inert to chemical attack, and a very good electrical insulator. Other materials can also form glasses if cooled sufficiently rapidly from the liquid or gaseous phase to prevent the formation of an ordered crystalline structure. Glasses such as obsidian (see *flint) occur naturally. Commercial glasses are manufactured by fusing together sand (silica, SiO_2), *limestone, and soda (*sodium carbonate) at temperatures around 1,400–1,500 °C. On cooling, the melt becomes very viscous: at about 500 °C (known as the glass transition temperature) the melt solidifies to form soda glass.

The earliest glass objects are thought to have been made from *c.*2500 BC in both Egypt and Mesopotamia, with glass vessels appearing about 1,000 years later. A major turning point was the development of *glass-blowing in about 100 BC. From the 9th to the 14th centuries AD, extremely high-quality glassware was made in several Near Eastern centres, for example Raqqa in Damascus, and elsewhere in Syria. The 15th century saw the revitalization of European glass-making from two centres in Venice and Normandy, which laid the foundations of the modern glass industry. Glass has the property that above a certain temperature it behaves like a highly viscous liquid and can be easily shaped without breaking, allowing complex and beautiful shapes to be made. Glasses can be coloured by the addition of tiny amounts of metal oxides. The colours of the oxides bear no relation to the colours they produce in the glass: the oxides of nickel, cobalt, and copper are all black, yet they produce grey, deep blue, and blue-green glasses, respectively. Other additions to glass can change its physical properties. The inclusion of lead oxide increases the density and refractive index of glass and makes it much softer. It can then be cut with diamond tools to make cut glass and lead crystal. The addition of *borax to glass, pioneered by the Corning Glass Works in Corning, USA, produces glass with very low thermal expansion, which is used in cookware and laboratory equipment.

Silica-based glasses are of enormous importance in the modern world. Windows and light bulbs are their most obvious uses, while *optical glass is manufactured for lenses for spectacles, cameras, telescopes, and microscopes. Glass is also used for drinking vessels, containers, and cooking utensils. The brittleness of glass can be reduced by thermally treating the surface (*safety glass), or by making a *laminate of glass layered with plastic sheets. Glass can be drawn when molten into very thin *glass fibres, used in insulation, *composites, and in optical applications. A large amount of glass is produced as flat sheets: from the 18th century this was commonly done by rolling the melt (see *plate glass), but since the 1960s the *float glass process has become much more important.

glass-blowing, the art of shaping molten *glass by blowing air into it. The technique was invented in about 100 BC, probably in Syria. A mass of molten glass is gathered on to a narrow iron tube about 1 m (3 feet) long, and air is blown down the tube, forming a bubble of air within the glass. During the gradual hardening of the glass as it cools, it is possible to shape the bubble into a wide variety of forms. A balloon of glass can also be blown inside a mould, to make a predetermined shape.

glass ceramic, a ceramic manufactured by the controlled crystallization of a silica-containing glass. This allows the material to be shaped whilst in the form of a viscous melt and then crystallized to achieve the better mechanical properties of a crystalline ceramic. Glass ceramics of many different properties are possible. Those based on the lithium–alumino-silicate system have almost zero thermal expansion and are used to manufacture cookware and tops for electric cookers.

glass fibre (fibreglass, spun glass), thin filaments of glass used to make yarns and textiles, for insulation, in *fibre-reinforced plastics, in other *composites, and for *optical fibres. Mats of glass fibre were first produced in the 1930s from molten glass in both the USA and the UK. This form of glass fibre is mainly used for thermal insulation, and for air filters. Later, continuous glass fibres were melt-spun through spinnerets (see *spinning), in a similar way to *synthetic fibres. Glass-fibre yarns are used to make fire-resistant fabrics, electrical insulation materials, and glass-fibre-reinforced plastics. For optical-fibre use the glass must be very pure and of constant diameter. This is achieved by *vapour deposition of filaments using silica-containing gases. Extremely long fibres may be manufactured by this method.

glass-fibre-reinforced concrete, *concrete reinforced by combining it with short, randomly orientated fibres to make a material that has the same strength in all directions. Alkali-resistant *glass fibres are now widely used. They are dispersed uniformly throughout the concrete by adding them at mixing. The technique is also applied to glass-fibre-reinforced gypsum.

glass-reinforced plastic (GRP) *fibre-reinforced plastics.

glaze (ceramic), a glassy finish on *pottery and other traditional ceramics. Glazes serve two purposes: to impart an impervious layer to the surface of porous pottery ware; and to provide a decorative medium. The glaze is usually applied after the pot has been 'biscuit-fired' to harden it: the glazed pot is then fired a second time to a higher temperature, to harden the glaze. Salt glazing is a cheap finish for earthenware products: salt reacts with the constituents of the fired clay to produce a sodium-containing, low-melting-point glass. More usual pottery glazes are a mixture of metal oxides and silica. Lead used to be a common glazing oxide, but is of less importance now because of its toxicity. Glazes of many different colours are known and glazed porcelain has achieved a high level of artistic development.

glider, a fixed-wing *aeroplane that is unpowered whilst in flight. Gliders are launched either by being towed into the air behind an aircraft or motor vehicle, or from a winch or catapult, or using a small engine in the glider itself. The first successful glider was devised by *Cayley and flown across Brompton Dale in Yorkshire in 1853. *Lilienthal made over 2,000 glider flights between 1893 and his death in 1896, and the *Wright brothers did much aerodynamic research and gained valuable flying experience with gliders. Originally made of wood and fabric, modern gliders use *fibre-reinforced plastics and high-technology designs to produce a very efficient, lightweight aeroplane. By using thermals (rising currents of hot air) and warm fronts often found on the windward side of hills and mountain ridges, a glider can stay airborne for long periods and travel great distances. (See also *hang-glider.)

glue *adhesive.

glycerol (propan-1,2,3-triol, glycerine, $CH_2OH{\cdot}CHOH{\cdot}CH_2OH$), a clear, colourless, viscous, sweet-tasting liquid belonging to the *alcohol group. It is obtained as a by-product of the production of *soap and is synthesized industrially from propene and sugar. It is used domestically as an ingredient of soft icing, and industrially as a sweetener and in the manufacture of paints, cosmetics, and explosives.

Goddard, Robert Hutchings (1882–1945), US pioneer of the *rocket motor. He developed rockets primarily to carry meteorological instruments high in the atmosphere. Perceiving that success lay with liquid fuels, in 1926 he launched the first liquid-fuelled rocket, using a mixture of petrol and liquid oxygen. Among his subsequent major successes were the first smokeless-powder rocket and the first practical automatic steering device for rockets.

gold (symbol Au, at. no. 79, at. wt. 196.97), a soft yellow metal. It is extremely unreactive and so is found free in nature. For centuries gold was obtained by panning, but this has been largely replaced by *hydraulic mining and deep *mining. Gold is extracted from the deposit by treatment with cyanide and displacement with zinc. It is further purified by *electrolysis or treatment with nitric and sulphuric acids. Gold is the most ductile and malleable of metals; a piece weighing 1 g (0.035 ounces) can be drawn into a wire more than 2.5 km (1.5 miles) in length. Pure gold is too soft to be used in jewellery and coinage and for such purposes it is alloyed with other metals (commonly copper, palladium, nickel, or zinc). Gold is a good conductor and is widely used in electronics.

goniometer, any instrument for measuring angles. This includes the protractor, a transparent plastic semicircle or circle marked in degrees and used for measuring or setting out angles. More specifically, a goniometer is an instrument that measures the angle between the reflecting surfaces of a crystal or prism. Two rays of light from a collimator (a system of lenses and slits designed to create parallel light beams) are directed on to two adjacent surfaces of the crystal: the beams are reflected from the two faces, and the angle between the two reflected beams (twice the angle between the prism or crystal surfaces) is measured.

A goniometer is also a device sometimes used with radio or radar transmitters. It allows a signal to be transmitted in any direction, or the direction of an incoming signal to be determined, without the use of a physically rotating antenna.

goods wagon (US, freight car), a railway vehicle used for the transport of any of a wide range of merchandise, from bulk commodities such as coal and grain to specialist materials such as radioactive waste and chemicals. Early goods vehicles were based on single open wagons with a capacity of 5 tonnes. The development of steel rails enabled four-wheeled wagons to carry 12 tonnes and this became a common size for a wagon. Today, some specialist goods wagons can support loads of up to 100 tonnes; they are designed to carry materials in bulk and to speed transhipment by road or water. Coal, grain, bauxite and iron ore are carried in hopper wagons, which can be loaded and unloaded without the train stopping. Containerization has brought about specialist container-liner and 'piggyback' trains for articulated lorries operating between ports and specially equipped yards. Greater demand for refrigerated goods led to the development of insulated vans and, later, refrigeration wagons.

Goodyear, Charles (1800–60), US inventor of the *vulcanization process for rubber. As a young man in his father's hardware business, he became aware of the tendency of rubber goods to become tacky when warm, and brittle when cold. After some years of experimenting with additives to overcome the defect, he eventually achieved

The US pioneer of liquid-fuel rocket motors, Robert **Goddard**, during a demonstration at his laboratory in Worcester, Massachussetts, USA.

success in 1839, when he accidentally dropped some rubber blended with sulphur and white lead on to a hot stove. He was granted a patent in 1844, a year after *Macintosh and *Hancock in the UK had patented similar vulcanization processes.

gouge *chisels and gouges.

governor, a mechanism to control the speed of a machine. The centrifugal governor, originally evolved to control windmills, was adapted by *Watt for steam-engines and later other engine types. In this type of governor, weights attached to the engine shaft tend to move outwards as rotation speed increases; this movement raises a grooved collar, which in *steam-turbines and engines moves a lever controlling the steam supply. *Gas-engines use a hit-and-miss governor, which cuts off the gas supply for one or more strokes of the engine if its speed rises too greatly. In *petrol engines, *diesel engines, and *gas-turbines the governor controls the rate of fuel supply. For large installations the power of the governor has to be augmented by a *servo-mechanism.

grab, a device used with a *crane for lifting loose material such as coal, gravel, and ore. The common form consists of two half-buckets hinged at their upper end and suspended so that their lower ends are apart when lowering. When hoisted, the buckets close and scoop up material, which can then be transported and released where required. Some *dredgers use a grab to remove mud, silt, or gravel from the bottom of the sea or a river. A magnetic grab is a powerful *electromagnet, used for handling iron or steel scrap.

grader, a six-wheeled machine that accurately shapes surfaces (particularly for roads) after bulk excavation by an excavator, scraper, or bulldozer. It is also used to maintain unsurfaced roads. The grader is steered by the two front wheels, which are linked by a beam to the four-wheeled tractor unit. A steel blade (the mould board) is suspended from the beam and can be raised, lowered, and precisely angled. As the grader advances, the mould board shaves the ground surface or smoothes out loose material until the required camber is formed.

Graeco-Roman technology, technology of the ancient Greek and Roman civilizations. It is particularly relevant to modern Western technology, being its most immediate source. Although Greece and Rome made some original contributions, they derived much of their technology from other civilizations in the ancient world—particularly those of *Egypt and Mesopotamia, and the Indus Valley (see *Indian technology). The Romans excelled in practical civil and military engineering projects, such as *roads, *bridges, and *aqueducts. They made extensive use of the arch and the vault in *building, and developed the first hydraulic *cement. *Coal was first mined in Roman times, and the Romans were probably the first to use fire in mining to crack the rock face. The Greeks developed the *galley to its most advanced form, and invented such weapons as the *crossbow and the *ballista. They made *automata and toy *steam-engines, and Greek geographers mapped the known world. In medicine they used a range of metal *surgical instruments, and made the earliest *artificial limbs.

grafting, in surgery, the removal of tissue and its transplantation to a new site. Autografting (using the patient's own tissue) is generally successful provided that infection is avoided and adequate replacement tissue is found. Skin grafting, which was first achieved in 1817, is the major example of autografting and a mainstay of modern plastic surgery. Large skin grafts are used to treat extensive burns. Recently, small samples of patients' skin have successfully been grown in laboratory conditions to produce larger areas for grafting. Tissues used as autografts need not necessarily replace identical tissues: vein grafts, for example, may replace blocked sections of coronary arteries. Homografting (using donor tissue) can give rise to problems of incompatibility: that is, the body may reject the 'foreign' tissue. Since the late 1960s, tissue typing and immunosuppressant drugs have reduced these difficulties (see *transplant surgery). Certain blood disorders can be treated by bone-marrow transplantation from matched donors. Some homografting, notably of corneas, does not encounter rejection problems.

In horticulture, grafting is the practice of cutting a shoot from one plant and inserting it into a cut in another (the stock), from which it receives sap. It is undertaken to propagate plants quickly, or because a cutting on its own is not as vigorous as one grafted into existing root stock (this is particularly true for roses). Grafting is used extensively in *fruit cultivation to propagate selected plants. The genetic characteristics of the shoot, rather than those of the root stock, determine the character of the mature plant, but the root stock may have some influence, for example on tree shape in apple production.

grain storage, the storage of cereal seed for later use, or for sowing the following season. Grain dried to contain less than 14 per cent moisture will keep for several years. The drying is now usually done mechanically, by passing warm air through the grain. The grain is stored in *silos or large open sheds. Grain can be chemically treated to allow storage undried, but the treatment leaves the seed sterile and suitable only for feeding livestock. Undried grain for livestock can also be kept by storage in airtight silos.

Gramme, Zénobe-Théophile (1826–1901), Belgian electrical engineer who designed and built the first practical electric *generator. In 1870 he invented a continuous-current dynamo with a ring *armature, which produced much higher voltages than other dynamos of the time. The manufacture of the Gramme dynamo was developed by the Société des Machines Magnéto-electriques, which he founded with Hippolyte Fontaine in 1871. Designed to be driven by *steam-engines, these dynamos were immediately successful and were used for a variety of purposes, including factory lighting, *electroplating, and *lighthouses.

gramophone (phonograph, record player), an instrument that records or replays sounds using the vibration of a stylus in the groove of a cylinder or disc. In 1857 Léon Scott produced his phonautograph, which used a horn to direct sound on to a parchment diaphragm. A bristle attached to the diaphragm recorded the vibrations as a scratch on a rotating blackened cylinder. Thomas Edison's phonograph of 1877 could both record and replay. The sound was recorded by the varying amount of indentation a needle made in a tin-foil cylinder, and was reproduced by another needle following the inscribed pattern. Gramophone was the trademark of Emil Berliner's instrument of 1894, which was the first to use a flat disc instead of a cylinder; by 1915 the *record had virtually replaced the cylinder. The advent of electrical *sound recording in the 1920s led to develop-

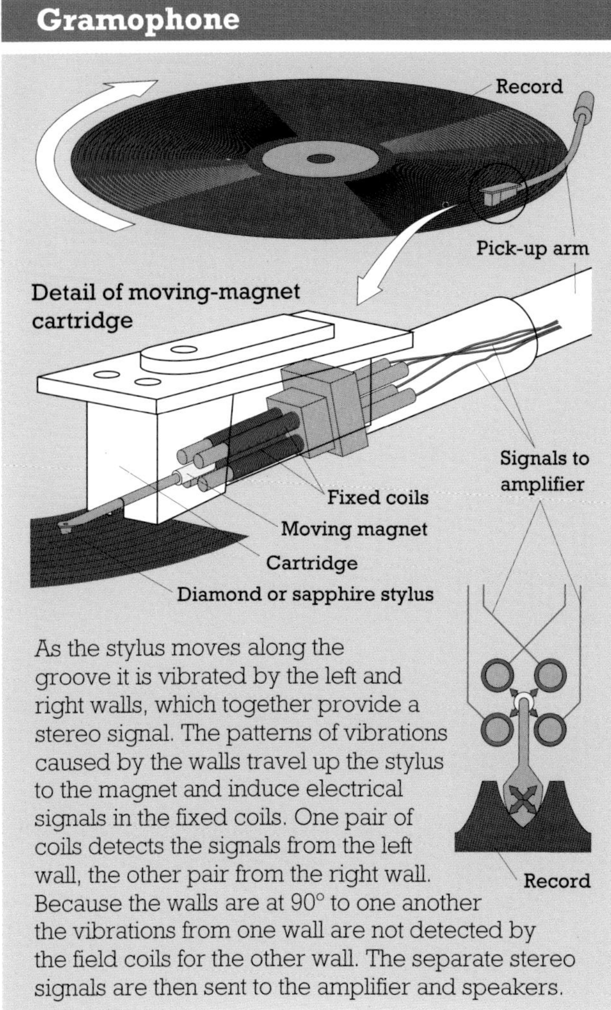

As the stylus moves along the groove it is vibrated by the left and right walls, which together provide a stereo signal. The patterns of vibrations caused by the walls travel up the stylus to the magnet and induce electrical signals in the fixed coils. One pair of coils detects the signals from the left wall, the other pair from the right wall. Because the walls are at 90° to one another the vibrations from one wall are not detected by the field coils for the other wall. The separate stereo signals are then sent to the amplifier and speakers.

ment of the electric gramophone, in which a pick-up passed electrical signals to an amplifier, and the amplified signal drove electrical loudspeakers (see figure). About this time competition from radio broadcasts led to a demand for longer playing times. Automatic record changers were introduced on many gramophones, but the problem was not effectively solved until the introduction of the long-playing record after World War II. *Stereophonic records became commercially available in 1958, and the improved sound quality led to the production of *high-fidelity sound systems.

Grand Canal, China (Da Yunhe), the world's longest *canal, extending 1,700 km (1,100 miles). Parts of the 1,000-km (620-mile) southern section were built as early as the 4th century BC, but this whole section was rebuilt between AD 607 and 610, serving to transport grain from the lower Jinsha Jiang (Yangtze) River to the cities of Kaifeng and Luoyang. The northern section of the canal, from Huainan to Beijing, was built between 1280 and 1293, by the engineers Li Yue and Lu Chi. The section crossing the Shandong foothills, completed in 1283, was the earliest example of a 'summit level' canal (one which crosses a watershed). Since its completion, the canal has been periodically enlarged and rebuilt, and some sections are today used by vessels of up to 2,000 tonnes.

graphic image manipulation (printing), the control and adjustment of variables in the printing process, at a stage prior to committing the image to production. Traditionally the information to be reproduced was derived from a number of original sources, such as typesetting, designs, artists' drawings, and photographs. All of these had to be manually processed, modified, planned, and superimposed in order to produce an image or series of images suitable for reproduction. Current technology enables such varied information to be fed into a computerized system, where it may be stored, analysed, and retrieved at will. Text and graphic images may be displayed either individually or in multiples on a video screen. Techniques that may be employed include superimposition, merging, rotating, enlarging or reducing, image distortion, text running around pictures, sharpening or softening, colour editing, and retouching. The most important uses of the technique are for *electronic page make-up and *digital proofing.

graphics (computer), the use of computers to process and display visual information. Computer graphics are used for a wide range of tasks, from the presentation of numerical information as simple graphs to the generation of complex images of near-photographic quality. Early digital computers were used to produce graphics, but they were initially severely limited by the available *output devices and the amount of computer power needed to process pictorial information. Advances in technology throughout the 1970s and 1980s reduced the cost and improved the performance of graphics hardware. Most computers now have visual display units and printers that can produce graphics as well as text. The rapid advances in hardware have been accompanied by the development of software to support many new applications, such as *desk-top publishing, *computer-aided design, *image processing, computer animation, and molecular modelling. The availability of graphic visual displays for personal computers and *workstations has led to the development of graphic user *interfaces. A number of manufacturers are developing so-called multi-media systems based on very high capacity *compact discs, which can store images, sound, and even moving pictures, as well as conventional *data.

graphite, a form of the element *carbon. It occurs naturally, but can also be synthesized from petroleum or coke.

An example of the use of computer **graphics** to visualize a complex mathematical expression, in this case the three-dimensional waves of chemical change produced in an excitable medium (for example the nerve net of the cerebral cortex).

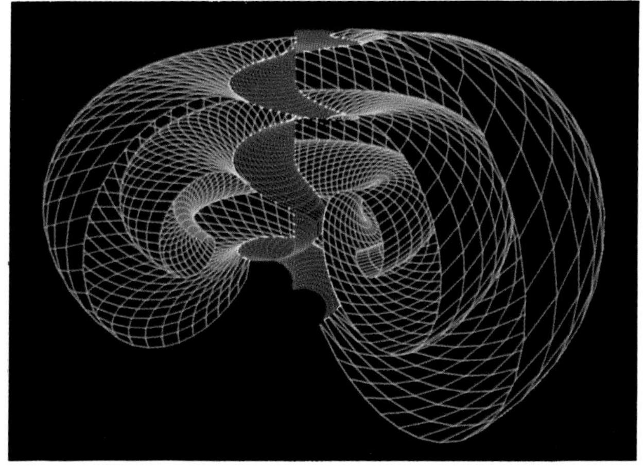

A section of the **Great Wall of China** near the Badaling Mountains, which was rebuilt in the 14th and 15th centuries. The wall is approximately 7.5 m (25 feet) high and 4 m (13 feet) wide, constructed of earth with a stone facing.

Graphite has a laminar crystal structure, consisting of layers or sheets of strongly bonded carbon atoms that slide very easily over one another. The first use of graphite was for the manufacture of pencil 'leads' in the 17th century, but it now has many other applications. Graphite is a good solid lubricant. It also conducts electricity like a metal, and is used in sliding electrical contacts in motors. It is also used as a moderator in some *nuclear reactors.

grass crop. Grasses are a group of small plants with green blades that form the basic food of cattle, sheep, and other grazing animals. Annual growth patterns produce very high volumes of grass in the spring, much of which is cut and conserved for winter feed. Later growth is slower, and is susceptible to temperature and moisture changes. In temperate climates, winter growth is minimal. Livestock are grazed directly, or fed conserved material together with high-protein feeds. The process of conserving grass involves drying it in the sun to form hay, or packing it into airtight pits, where anaerobic fermentation creates the more digestible *silage. Grass may be in permanent pasture, usually because the nature of the land precludes cultivation, or it may be sown as a short-term crop of three or four years, producing much greater volumes for conserving and grazing.

gravure printing, an *intaglio printing process, in which the printing image is made up of a series of very small cells etched into the surface of a metal cylinder. When printing, the cylinder is flooded with liquid ink, and the surface is then scraped clean with a 'doctor blade'. This leaves ink only in the image areas, which are recessed into the cylinder. To transfer the image, paper is rolled against the cylinder under heavy pressure, and absorbs ink from the recessed cells. Gravure cylinders are expensive to produce, but the gravure process gives a high-quality product and can accommodate very long print runs. It is now used mainly for popular illustrated magazines. (See *printing for illustration.)

'Great Britain', SS, the most important of I. K. *Brunel's three ship designs. The *Great Britain* was a large iron *steamship driven by a screw *propeller, designed as a transatlantic liner. It was the first large, screw-driven iron ship to be built, and it embodied many other constructional innovations, such as a double bottom to the hull, and bulkheads dividing the ship into watertight compartments.

Great Exhibition, a major international trade exhibition held in London in 1851 under the sponsorship of Prince Albert. It was housed in the vast Crystal Palace, designed by

Joseph Paxton (1801–65), which was made entirely of glass and iron, except for the flooring and joists. The exhibition, which lasted 23 weeks, attracted 17,000 exhibitors and more than 6 million visitors. The profits were invested, and are still being used to promote education and science today. Outwardly, the Exhibition presented the UK in an unassailable position as the world's greatest manufacturing nation, although in reality British industry was already in decline and being overtaken by Europe and the USA.

Great Wall of China, a fortification built across northern China as a protection against the nomadic tribes of Mongolia and Manchuria. The emperor Shi Huangdi (259–210 BC) ordered the existing frontier walls of northern provinces to be joined to form the Great Wall, extending 2,250 km (1,400 miles) from the Gulf of Liaodong to southern Mongolia. During the Han dynasty (202 BC–AD 220) the wall was extended west to Yumen, and subsequent dynasties reconstructed or added to the wall. Most of the wall standing today was constructed during the Ming dynasty (1368–1644).

Greek fire, a combustible composition set alight on contact with water. It was invented around AD 673 by Kallinikos, a Syrian architect in Byzantine service. Its main ingredients were probably naphtha and quicklime, which started burning on contact with water. It was first used against Arab ships besieging Constantinople in AD 674–6.

greenhouse, a building of glass or clear plastic supported by a light framework of wood or metal, used to grow plants more quickly than would be possible out of doors, or to grow plants that would not normally flourish in the local climate. Greenhouses provide the maximum possible light to an enclosed area, and tend to trap and retain heat. In most cases the temperature and humidity levels are artificially controlled. (See also *hydroponics.)

greenhouse effect, global warming caused by the water vapour and various gases, especially carbon dioxide in the atmosphere, reflecting long-wave radiation emitted from the Earth back on to the planet. The concentration of carbon dioxide in the atmosphere has increased significantly since the *Industrial Revolution, due to the massive use of *fossil fuels. This, coupled with vast deforestation, is reducing the planet's ability to maintain the carbon dioxide balance, which could result in long term changes in weather patterns, melting of the polar ice caps, and a rise in sea-level.

green revolution, an agricultural programme of the 1960s and 1970s, funded by private charities and governments of the industrialized nations, that attempted to solve the problems of Third World hunger by a package of measures to improve crop yields. The package comprised high-yielding varieties of cereal crops combined with mechanization, increased use of *fertilizers to increase yields, *pesticides to combat disease, and water for irrigation. Large increases in crop yields have been achieved in some countries, for example India and the Philippines. However, there has been much criticism of the programme, as it has tended to benefit the large landowner at the expense of smaller farmers. Large monocultures also make the crops much more vulnerable to disease, and in the tropics heavy rainfall may wash away newly cultivated soil, drastically reducing soil fertility. An increase in the amount of land used for cash-crops for export has meant that the programme has actually done very little to combat malnutrition.

grenade, an explosive weapon, used by special troops (grenadiers), from the 17th century to the 19th century. Modern grenades date from early in World War I. All hand grenades operate in a similar way, whether they are fragmentation, smoke, blast, incendiary, or gas grenades. A safety pin is pulled and the grenade is thrown, releasing a striker-lever that sets off a timed fuse. The fuse ignites, detonating the explosive filler; the grenade explodes, breaking up the case. Rifle grenades use the energy of a bullet leaving the muzzle of a rifle to propel an explosive grenade.

grid, electricity *electricity generation and supply.

Griess, Johann Peter (1829–88), German organic chemist who made important contributions to the dyestuffs industry. He worked in London with the German chemist A. W. von Hofmann before joining Allsopp's Brewery at Burton-on-Trent, UK. There, he pursued his own research interests and discovered the *azo dyes, perhaps the most important single discovery in dyestuffs chemistry. He later (1884) patented the first direct cotton *dyes, which required no mordant (fixing agent).

grinding machine, a *machine-tool introduced in the 1860s for grinding steel or other hard materials accurately and to a high standard of finish. A grinding wheel made of *abrasive particles is rotated at a high surface speed and moved slowly against the workpiece (for illustration see machine-tools). For cylindrical grinding the workpiece is rotated slowly on its axis; for (flat) surface grinding the wheel is moved slowly across the workpiece. Grinding machines for making *gears and screw-threads have special wheel-forms and both wheel and workpiece are moved to give the desired shape. Glass *lenses are ground by a quite different process.

ground-guidance system, any system developed as an alternative to the concept of a coned and flanged steel wheel running on steel rails. Following experiments in the 1930s, the Paris Métro adopted pneumatic-tyred rolling stock for running on concrete track outside the normal track. Guidance on the special surfaces was provided by horizontally mounted pneumatic-tyred wheels at each corner of the *bogie; these press against guide rails mounted outside the running lines. Normal, flanged wheels mounted inside the rubber wheels are retained to carry the load in the event of a puncture. Similar systems have been adopted at Lille (France), Montreal (Canada), Mexico City, and elsewhere. More recent experiments have involved lifting the vehicle clear of the track, either with a cushion of air (as in the hover-train) or by use of magnetic fields (the maglev). The first hover-train was developed in the UK and achieved a speed of 200 km/h (125 m.p.h.) before the project was abandoned. With a magnetic levitation system (maglev) the principles of the *linear motor are used in conjunction with a special track to provide a lifting force as well as traction. At present a small, low-speed system operates in the UK at Birmingham Airport, and in Germany and Japan, where experiments continue, test vehicles have reached speeds of about 500 km/h (310 m.p.h.).

ground station, an installation that controls and tracks artificial *satellites and spacecraft from Earth. The simplest ground stations are satellite dishes designed to receive television signals. Larger dishes send and receive the radio signals that control spacecraft; computers process the

The Japanese MLU 001 maglev vehicle, a form of **ground guidance system** being developed as an alternative to conventional railway track.

information received. Unless a satellite or spacecraft is in geostationary orbit (in which the satellite remains over the same point on the Earth's surface), a ring of ground stations round the Earth is needed to maintain continuous contact. The Soviet Union and China, lacking access to suitable island sites, use ships as ground stations. Working satellites and spacecraft are tracked by their radio signals; the many 'dead' satellites and pieces of space debris are tracked optically and by *radar.

guidance system *guided missile, *warning and detection system.

guided missile, a *missile, though not usually a *torpedo, that is powered for part or all of its flight and is guided or steered to its target. It has a control mechanism, which changes the flight path when instructed by the weapon's guidance system. Most missiles change direction using aerodynamic forces, like an aeroplane; others have small thrusters to do the job, or a swivelling rocket nozzle. Long-range *ballistic missiles and *cruise missiles launched against fixed targets are guided by *inertial navigation systems. Shorter-range missiles directed against moving targets may be steered by an operator, sending signals by radio or along wires (command line-of-sight guidance); for targets that are outside the operator's line of sight the missile may incorporate a television camera. Some missiles carry detectors that lock on to radiation emitted from the target, so that, after launching, they require no intervention by an operator. These are known as 'fire-and-forget' missiles. Those using infra-red guidance home in on heat sources, such as engines, while radar-homing missiles lock on to the target's *radar or electromagnetic radiation signals. Guidance systems may be active, semi-active, or passive. A missile with semi-active radar guidance is equipped with a radar receiver, but needs the target to be continuously 'illuminated' by radar transmissions from an external source, such as an aircraft or a ship, so that it can home in on the reflections of these signals from the target. The system will work within a range of about 100 km (60 miles), but the transmitted signal may expose the source to detection and enemy counter-attack. With active radar homing, the missile itself contains both a radar receiver and a transmitter for illuminating the target. Passive homing entails no preliminary illumination of the target; an infra-red (heat-seeking) missile, for example, simply identifies the heat source and homes in on it. Generally, passive homing is used for short-range missiles, semi-active radar homing for medium-range missiles, and active radar homing for long-range missiles. There are many variants of homing systems, some using laser beams or *electromagnetic radiation of higher frequency than radio waves.

gum, an *adhesive substance obtained from plants. Gum exudes as a sticky secretion from the bark of certain trees. Gum arabic is a widely used water-soluble adhesive, and gum tragacanth is used as a binding and coating agent in pill manufacture and as an emulsifier (see *food additive) in processed foods.

gun *artillery, *firearm, *pistol, *rifle.

gun-cotton *nitro-cellulose.

gunpowder, an *explosive consisting typically of a mixture of 75 per cent potassium nitrate, 13 per cent *charcoal, and 12 per cent *sulphur. The constituents are first ground separately, then mixed, moistened with water, and ground together. The mass is then pressed into grains of the desired size and dried. The potassium nitrate provides the *oxygen for the rapid combustion of the sulphur and charcoal and the almost instantaneous production of a large volume of hot gas. In addition to gas, several solid substances are produced, and these, together with any unburned sulphur and charcoal, constitute the smoke that results from the explosion. Gunpowder was known to the Chinese, and possibly to the Arabs, by the 10th century; its use in European warfare dated from the 14th century until about 1904. It has now been replaced by other explosives and is rarely used.

gun-sight, a device to help aim when using a *firearm. Foresights and backsights for *rifles became common in the 19th century. The foresight is usually a vertical blade, while the backsight is V-shaped with a sliding scale to adjust its height according to the estimated distance of the target. To aim, the tip of the foresight and the V of the backsight are aligned with the target. Artillery uses a telescopic or stereo-

A US soldier using an M-16 rifle. The **gun-sight** can be seen clearly. The foresight is a fixed post, protected by a guard. The rearsight is incorporated as part of the carrying handle.

Gyroscope

A three-frame gyroscope consists of a spinning flywheel encircled by three gimbals. Each gimbal pivots, allowing rotation of the flywheel in one plane. As there are three gimbals, each with their rotational axes at 90° to one another, the flywheel can rotate in any orientation in space.

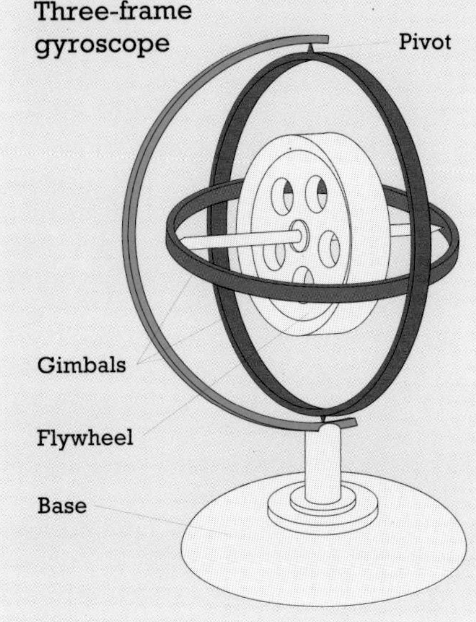

A gyroscope demonstrates the fact that a spinning body will resist changes in the orientation of its spin axis. When the flywheel is spun fast enough, the base can be moved in any direction or plane and the flywheel will continue to spin in the same orientation in space.

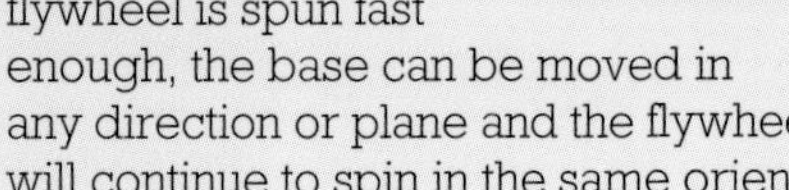

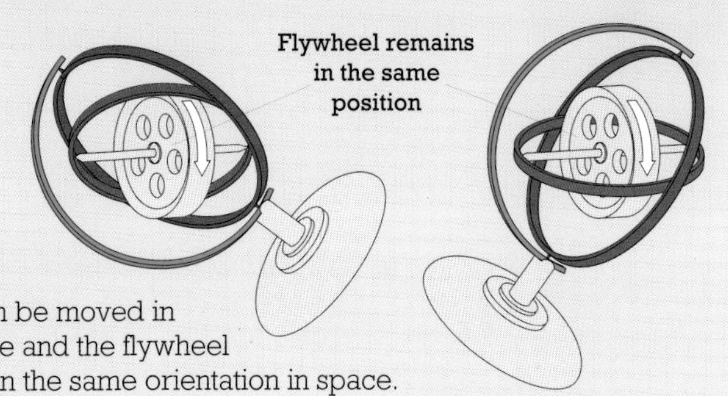

Precession

If a force is applied to the spin axis of a gyroscope as if to turn the axis, the gyroscope does not turn, but tilts. This is called precession.

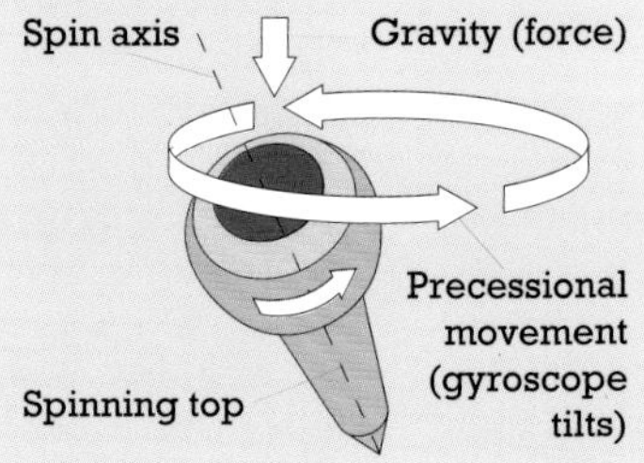

One end of the axle of a spinning gyroscope is tied to a length of string and held up. This applies force to the axis of spin as if to tilt that axis, resulting in the axis turning in azimuth (it rotates around the piece of string).

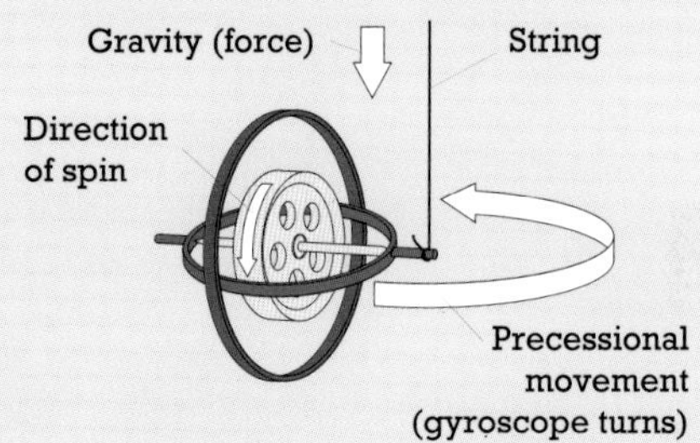

scopic sight on the gun-carriage and marked with a reticle. Tank gun-sights often have infra-red devices for night use.

Gutenberg, Johannes (*c.*1397–1468), German pioneer of printing with movable type. From 1430 he spent time in Strasburg experimenting with metal type. By 1448 he was printing from movable type in his native Mainz, a metal-working area with plenty of craft workers able to cast the type and build the presses. Although printing was known in China from the 11th century, Gutenberg's invention included new features such as metal matrices for moulding the type, and a press akin to a wine press. However, Gutenberg lost possession of all his printing equipment and gave up his work to date on his famed Bible after a legal dispute with his partner Johann Fust.

gynaecology *obstetrics and gynaecology.

gypsum, hydrated calcium sulphate, $CaSO_4{\cdot}2H_2O$. Gypsum occurs naturally as mineral deposits; its fine-textured form is known as alabaster. On heating, gypsum gives the hemihydrate $(CaSO_4)_2{\cdot}H_2O$, which can be ground to a fine powder to form plaster of Paris. Plaster of Paris sets solid when mixed with water, and the setting results in a slight increase in volume, so the plaster fits into any mould. It is the main constituent of plaster for the interiors of buildings. Gypsum is also used in the manufacture of *Portland cement, blackboard chalk, *plate-glass, terracotta, *pottery, and orthopaedic and dental plasters.

gyro-compass (gyroscopic compass), a compass that relies on the properties of a *gyroscope for its action. It was invented independently (*c.*1908) by two men, Hermann Anschutz-Kaempfe in Germany and *Sperry in the USA, after a principle first demonstrated by the French physicist J.-B.-L. Foucault in 1852. In a gyro-compass, a gyroscope is aligned on a north–south axis, and maintains this alignment as the ship or aircraft carrying it changes direction through gyroscopic inertia. The gyro-compass is unaffected by the metal components of a vehicle, and points to true rather than magnetic north. A 'master' compass can be used to operate several repeater compasses, and can provide information to an *automatic pilot or helmsman. The gyro-compass has replaced the *magnetic compass for *navigation in most ships, and is standard equipment in virtually all aircraft.

gyromagnetic compass *magnetic compass.

gyroscope, a small, accurately made *flywheel mounted in gimbals (see figure). If the flywheel is spun at high speed, it will maintain its spin axis in space no matter how the frame is tilted. A second property of gyroscopes is known as precession. If a force is applied to the axis of the spinning gyroscope, the rotor axle moves, not directly away from the force, but at right angles to it. The gyroscope was named and first accurately described by the French physicist J.-B.-L Foucault in 1852. Its ability to maintain a fixed direction (gyroscopic inertia) has led to its widespread use as a direction indicator in the *gyro-compass. Gyroscopes are also used in *inertial navigation, automatic pilots and helmsmen, ship *stabilizers, rate-of-turn indicators, *artificial horizons in aircraft and other vehicles, stabilized bomb and *gun-sights, and stabilized platforms for guns and radar.

Haber, Fritz (1868–1934), German chemist. In the early 1900s, he was Professor of Chemistry at Karlsruhe and subsequently (in 1911) became Director of the Kaiser-Wilhelm Institute in Berlin. His fame rests largely on his development of the *Haber–Bosch process for fixing atmospheric nitrogen (1909), which formed the basis of the nitrogenous *fertilizer industry and led to vastly improved yields of many crops. Haber was also responsible for introducing poison gases for *chemical warfare in World War I. Haber was awarded the Nobel Prize for Chemistry in 1918.

Haber–Bosch process, a method for producing *ammonia from the elements *nitrogen and *hydrogen. Hydrogen is produced by the reaction of *natural gas with steam in the presence of a nickel *catalyst. (Carbon monoxide is also formed, but it is converted to carbon dioxide and then removed by absorption.) Air is introduced, and the oxygen in the air is removed by reaction with some of the hydrogen to form water. The remaining mixture of hydrogen and nitrogen is then passed over an iron catalyst at a high pressure (150–300 bar) and moderately high temperature (350–450 °C) to form ammonia. Any unreacted nitrogen and hydrogen are recycled. The ammonia is liquefied and removed for storage. The process represents the most viable way of 'fixing' atmospheric nitrogen and is therefore essential for nitrogenous fertilizer production.

hackling machine (heckling machine), a machine for the automatic combing-out and separating of flax, jute, and other bast fibres (flexible, fibrous barks and similar materials). The machine has much in common with the *carding machine (used for wool and cotton), but, because bast fibres are so much longer and stronger, the hackling machine is bigger and more rugged. In modern hackling machines the fibres are combed, separated, and aligned by drawing the material slowly between heavy steel spikes attached to two continuous leather belts moving in opposition to each other.

haematology, the study of the blood and its disorders. Blood consists of a liquid plasma, a solution of salts and proteins in water; and a solid phase consisting of red cells (erythrocytes), white cells (leucocytes), and platelets, structures involved in blood coagulation. A low concentration of haemoglobin (the protein responsible for the transport of oxygen to the tissues), or the production of defective haemoglobin, is known as anaemia. It is commonly associated with abnormal numbers and sizes of erythrocytes in the blood. The most common cause is a deficiency of one of three compounds needed for haemoglobin synthesis—iron, folic acid, or vitamin B_{12}. Diagnosis of anaemia can usually be made on the basis of *microscopic examination of a sample of blood or bone marrow. Leucocytes are responsible for the immune response (see *immunology). Deficiencies or abnormalities result in a defective defence reaction and usually are associated with an increased susceptibility to infection. An increase in white cell numbers (detectable using microscopy) commonly results from the presence in the body of invading *bacteria, but inappropriate and excessive multiplication of white cells is characteristic of *cancers of the white-cell system (leukaemias and lymphomas). Most blood cells and platelets are produced in the bone marrow, and diseases or disorders of the bone marrow may result in anaemia, immunodeficiency, a failure in the blood coagulation system, or all three. Bone-marrow *transplants may help to correct an immunodeficiency caused by bone marrow disease.

haemodialysis, the removal of waste products that accumulate in the blood in cases of kidney failure. In the artificial kidney (dialyser), blood diverted from the patient's circulation flows over one side of a selectively permeable membrane (one that allows the passage of some particles but not others) before being returned to the body. On the other side of the membrane, a specially prepared fluid (the dialysate) circulates, into which waste products pass by diffusion (the movement of particles from a region of high concentration to one of low concentration). Since its introduction in the 1940s, haemodialysis has become widespread for patients waiting for donor kidneys. Smaller, portable dialysis units can be used in the home. From 1960 increasingly sophisticated arteriovenous shunts, which provide semi-permanent connections to the patient's circulation, have facilitated haemodialysis and made it safer.

hafnium *zirconium.

half-tone process, a process in which tonal variations in photographs and other continuous-tone originals are converted into patterns of dots, in order to allow reproduction by printing. Traditionally done in a camera or contact frame, the process interposes a finely ruled screen between the original and the reproduction, dividing the image into dots that differ in size according to the density of the tones in the original. The screen gradation—normally 12–21 dots per cm^2 (80–133 dots per square inch)—is varied to suit the quality of paper on which the image will be printed. Screening is now more often achieved by *electronic scanning. In colour printing, the first stage is colour separation, in which an *electronic scanner or a camera using blue, green, and red filters, separates out the primary *colour elements of yellow, magenta, and cyan present in the original, plus a black element. These separations are then screened to produce dotted images for each colour. The resultant film images are transferred to separate printing plates, and the original is re-created by printing the four colour elements on the same sheet. The dotted images are aligned so that the colours do not print on top of each other but very close together. The eye combines the colours in each area to re-create the original shades.

Hall, Charles Martin (1863–1914), US chemist who, in 1886, independently of *Héroult, invented the electrolytic process for the manufacture of *aluminium. Aluminium was expensive to produce and available only in small quantities. In 1885 Hall discovered a process that paved the way for the widespread use of aluminium and its alloys. This involved passing an electric current through an electrolyte composed of a solution of alumina (aluminium oxide) in molten cryolite (sodium–aluminium fluoride). In 1889 Hall formed a company to produce aluminium commercially.

hammer, a hand tool with a heavy metal head perpendicular to the haft (handle), designed to deliver short, sharp blows. Its development followed the same line of evolution as the *axe and the adze: indeed, the hammer-head often serves a dual purpose, for example, as hammer and axe. Since Roman times, claw-headed hammers have been used for extracting nails. There is a vast range of hammers available. There are specialized hammers for cobbling, splitting slate, use in geology, and so on. The hammers used for woodworking are quite light in weight, so that they can be held in one hand. For heavier work, such as driving posts into the ground or forging iron, two-handed sledgehammers are necessary. The mallet is closely related to the hammer, the main difference being that mallet heads are made of wood, rubber, or rolled rawhide, to give a more diffuse blow. (See *tools, history of for illustration.)

Hancock, Thomas (1786–1865), British pioneer of the rubber industry. His first venture was a patent (1826) for the use of *rubber for elasticizing clothing. His major invention was the rubber 'masticator': he found that in trying to shred rubber to make it more manageable, he obtained a homogeneous mass of solid rubber, which he could then mould to shape. He also modified the properties of rubber by blending it with other ingredients, and in 1843 he took out the first British patent for *vulcanization with sulphur, marginally anticipating a similar application from *Goodyear.

hand weapon, an armament in which the energy from human muscles, swinging, pulling, thrusting, or throwing, provides the lethal action. Examples include knives or daggers, *swords, *spears, *bows, *boomerangs, and *bolas. Most hand weapons have a sharp point to puncture flesh, or an edge for cutting. Others, such as the mace (a club with a spiked metal head), are intended to smash armour and bones. Two-handed axes and swords, because of their weight, usually combine the effects of cutting and smashing. One class of hand weapons—the pole arms—were developed from *spears. The halberd (a combined spear and battleaxe), bill (a hook-bladed weapon), and glaive or lance are all European examples. Broadly, they work on the same principle as the hand-operated tin-opener: a spike or the long edge of an axe is used to rip open armour, while the point stabs the victim. The Japanese *naginata* has a blade similar to a Japanese sword and is used to slash the opponent.

hang-glider, a lightweight type of *glider, usually manœuvred by shifting of the pilot's body weight. Often the pilot is suspended beneath the flexible or rigid wing. Hang-gliders can have a monoplane or biplane configuration. Hang-gliding as a sport began in California in the late 1960s, and came to Europe in around 1973. It has since grown in popularity with the introduction of lightweight materials.

harbour *ports and harbours.

hardboard *manufactured board.

hard disk (Winchester disk), a device capable of storing large quantities of information (usually more than ten million *bytes) for long periods in a computer system. Unlike a *floppy disk, a hard disk is made of rigid aluminium covered by a magnetic layer. The disk spins continuously and is sealed within the disk drive. Data is read from or written to the disk by the magnetic heads of the disk drive.

hardware (computer), the general term for the physical parts of a computer system, including the *central processing unit, *memory, *bus, and *clock, as well as *peripherals such as *printers, disk and tape drives, keyboards, and *visual display units. Hardware cannot function usefully without *software.

Hargreaves, James (*c.*1720–78), British engineer who played a major role in mechanizing the cotton industry. While a hand-loom weaver in Blackburn, Lancashire, he invented (*c.*1760) a *carding machine that doubled the speed of the carding process, but his major invention was the spinning-jenny (1764), a hand-driven *spinning-machine that could spin a number of threads at once.

harness and saddlery, a harness is the equipment worn by a *draught animal when drawing a *cart or wagon, a *carriage, or a *sledge; saddlery refers to the equipment worn by a horse or other animal while being ridden. The earliest type of harness was used in Mesopotamia *c.*3000 BC. It consisted of a yoke fitted over the necks of two draught animals, and fastened to a single pole attached to the vehicle. War chariots of about the same period were steered by reins from a ring in the animal's nose, but by the 2nd millennium BC the snaffle-bit (two linked pieces of bone or metal in the animal's mouth) had appeared. By this time, wagons and *chariots were in use in China, where the horse harness underwent a number of improvements. The yoke was replaced by a padded collar, which did not restrict the horse's windpipe as do the straps securing a yoke. The collar reached Europe in about AD 800: by the 12th century it was well padded, and sat on the shoulder and breast rather than riding up the neck. It has changed little in essence since this period (see figure). In many countries the ox or bullock

Harness and saddlery

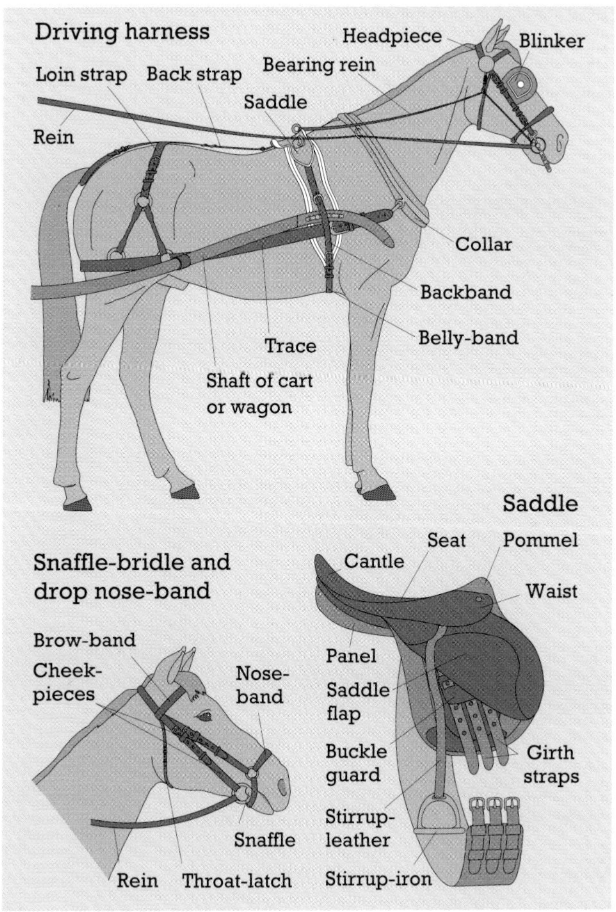

remains the major draught animal: here the harness used is of the yoke type.

As with most items of saddlery, the saddle originated in the Asian steppes: Scythian horsemen were using saddles by the 4th century BC. The saddle underwent considerable development in medieval Europe, particularly in France. Modern saddles are broadly of two types, the Western or Moorish saddle, which has a high pommel and deep seat for cattle-roping, and the English saddle, a lighter, flatter saddle developed for sport and recreation.

harpoon, a spear-like missile with barbed head and rope attached, used for catching whales and other sea creatures. Skin divers use hand-held harpoon guns operated by stretched rubber cords or compressed air. *Whaling harpoons, 2 m (6.5 feet) long, have explosive heads and weigh around 55 kg (120 pounds). They are fired from guns, and are accurate up to 25 m (80 feet).

harquebus *firearm.

Harrison, John (1693–1776), British horologist. In 1726, he invented the grid-iron pendulum, which increased the accuracy of clocks by automatically compensating for changes in pendulum length caused by temperature variations. To meet the urgent need to measure local time at sea, which is essential for determining longitude, Harrison designed a spring-driven marine *chronometer, regulated by a compensating balance wheel.

harrow, a type of *cultivator used to break up soil clods to produce a suitable seed-bed, or to break up the root systems of weeds such as couch grass. Some harrows have solid spikes, known as tines. These may be fixed or sprung, and more recently power-operated machines have been designed that perform several operations at one pass. Chain-link harrows are used to tear out the matt of dead grass, allowing air into the soil and encouraging the regrowth of fresh shoots. (See *agricultural machinery for illustration.)

haymaking, the process by which fresh grass, or a grass–legume mixture, is made into a high-volume feed with a low moisture content, suitable for storage. Grass for hay is cut later than for *silage, after the seed has set. Traditionally it was turned using forks, exposing it to drying by the wind and sun. Modern *agricultural machinery lightly crushes the stem to speed water loss. When dry, the hay used to be tightly compressed into stacks or carried to barns for storage. Modern *balers make high-density bales, reducing labour requirements at harvest time. Hay quality is judged by its colour, smell, and the absence of dust or fungus.

hearing aid, an electrical or electronic device designed to make sounds audible to those with hearing problems. It comprises three elements: a microphone, an amplifier, and an earphone or vibrator. Its predecessors were the acoustic ear-trumpet and the speaking-tube. The earliest electrical hearing aids (*c*.1898) used batteries and carbon transducers similar to those then found in *telephone receivers. The development of the miniaturized *thermionic valve made portable electronic hearing aids possible. Modern hearing aids use integrated circuits and miniaturized batteries: they can be worn behind the ear, or even fit inside it.

heart disease and treatment *cardiology and cardiac surgery.

heart–lung machine, the apparatus that replaces the functions of the heart and lungs during major cardiac surgery. Its use allows the heart to be stopped, making intricate heart surgery possible. It was first used by *Gibbon in 1953. To replace heart action, the patient's blood circulation is diverted through tubing to a peristaltic *pump, specially designed to avoid damaging the blood. Lung function is usually replaced by passing blood and oxygen over opposite sides of a selectively permeable membrane to remove carbon dioxide from the blood and to absorb oxygen.

heat and temperature. Heat is a form of *energy, while temperature is a definable and measurable indicator of hotness and coldness as perceived by the senses or measured by a *thermometer. Temperature is related to the energy of the particles (*atoms or molecules) that make up solids, liquids, and gases. The greater their speed, the greater their energy, and the higher the temperature of the body concerned. The SI *unit of energy is the joule (J). Other units of energy applied to heat are the calorie (cal: 1 cal = 4 J) and the British Thermal Unit (BTU: 1 BTU = 1,055 J). Temperature is most commonly measured in degrees Celsius (°C: see *temperature measurement).

Heat energy flows spontaneously from a body at high temperature to one at a lower temperature until the two are at equal temperatures. If the two bodies are in direct contact, then heat flow is by conduction. Rapidly moving particles in the hotter body collide with slower-moving particles in the colder body at the interface between the two. Heat transfer can occur by convection if the two bodies are separated by a fluid medium which can act as an intermediary. Most domestic *heating appliances warm their surroundings by means of rising convection currents of heated air. A third method of heat transfer is by radiation. All bodies emit radiant heat energy, which is a form of *electromagnetic radiation. Incandescent bodies (see *incandescent lamp) emit visible light, while infra-red radiation is emitted at lower temperatures. Radiant energy (the primary means by which the Earth receives energy from the Sun) can be absorbed by another body, when it changes back from radiation to thermal energy. When a substance melts or boils, it can gain heat energy without a corresponding change in temperature, because the energy added to the substance is being used to overcome the forces of attraction between the particles (changing its state). Conversely, when a substance condenses or freezes, the change in state is accompanied by a loss of heat energy without a corresponding drop in temperature.

All other forms of energy readily convert into heat. Resistance losses in electrical *circuits change electrical energy into heat energy. Frictional losses change mechanical energy into heat energy. Light and sound energy are partially converted to heat as they are imperfectly reflected from surfaces. Heat can be converted into other forms of energy by machines and other devices. Electrical energy can be directly generated from heat by *thermoelectric devices. Heat *engines (for example, steam- or petrol engines) use a working fluid, such as water or air, which is heated and expands, the expansion being harnessed to do useful work. The thermal *efficiency of such engines is low: they convert less than a third of the energy in the fuel into useful mechanical energy.

heat engine *engine.

heat exchanger, a system for transferring heat energy between two fluids. The aim is to achieve good thermal contact while maintaining physical separation. A common system allows one fluid to pass over pipes through which the other flows, for example in a motor-car radiator. An alternative is a slowly rotating drum of honeycombed metal. Each section absorbs heat as hot gas passes through it, and transfers this to a cool gas half a revolution later. Such 'heat wheels' are increasingly being employed for regenerative warming of the air entering a building, using heat from the departing stale air.

heating, domestic, the use of various forms of energy to maintain the temperature inside a dwelling above that of the surroundings. The earliest domestic heating was an open fire burning wood in the living area, with a vent in the roof for smoke to escape through. Smoke problems were avoided in the Roman *hypocaust system by the use of an external furnace. From the 14th century, integral fireplaces were built which had central chimneys radiating heat throughout the dwelling and carrying the smoke outside. Enclosed stoves (see *cookers and stoves) were introduced in the 17th century. The design of domestic-heating appliances improved steadily, based on the use of hot flue gases to draw fresh air through a fire supported on a grate. Wood continued to be the chief fuel, although peat and *coal were used where available. Urban development and the *Industrial Revolution saw a change of fuel to coal and coke. Small room-heaters burning coal-gas were widely used in the 1880s. *Central heating systems were developed for large houses, hotels, offices, and factories, with a central boiler piping hot water or steam to radiators to warm the air in each room. Alternatively, a furnace provided hot air through ducts. In the 1860s, the expanding petroleum industry introduced liquid hydrocarbon fuels such as paraffin and fuel-oil. The combustion of these is easier to control than that of solid fuels. Modern domestic heating is frequently provided by central heating boilers fired by *natural gas, oil, or smokeless fuel. *District-heating systems, *geothermal sources, and *solar panels can also provide hot water for heating, but only the latter is widely used for domestic purposes. Electric *storage heaters are an alternative to central heating systems, as are free-standing fan-heaters and portable stoves fuelled with paraffin or liquefied petroleum gas. Other free-standing space heaters which use electricity include incandescent-element fires. Some *air-conditioning systems include the option of heating the incoming air. Domestic heating should always be complemented by thermal *insulation.

heat-pump, a machine that transfers heat from a cooler to a warmer environment. The cooling units of *refrigerators and *air-conditioning units are heat-pumps in the technical sense, but in common usage the term is usually restricted to systems whose purpose is to provide space heating. To heat a building, the pump extracts heat energy from the surroundings and delivers it to the interior. Another type of heat-pump is the Peltier pump, in which an electric current through the junction of two dissimilar metals causes cooling at one junction and heating at the other. Peltier pumps are used commercially to cool sensitive electronic components such as solid-state lasers. (See also *thermoelectric device.)

heat treatment *annealing, *quenching, *tempering.

heavy chemical *chemical industry.

heavy goods vehicle *lorry.

heavy water, water in which the hydrogen atoms are replaced by a heavier *isotope, deuterium. The most common form of the hydrogen nucleus consists of a single proton: in deuterium the nucleus contains a proton and a neutron. In normal 'light' water, less than one molecule in 7,000 contains deuterium. Heavy water is used as both coolant and moderator in the *CANDU reactor. For CANDU reactor use, heavy water is extracted from light water by *fractional distillation.

heddle (heald) *loom.

helicopter, an aircraft that derives both lift and control from one or more sets of rotors (rotating *aerofoils), driven by piston or jet engines about a vertical or near-vertical axis. In a helicopter the rotor blades act as a series of wings, which generate lift through circular rather than forward motion. Each rotor blade is also hinged (an arrangement first developed for the *autogyro) so that it can move up and down independently of the others; without such hinging, small movements of the blades as they rotate would tend to destabilize the aircraft and make control difficult. The pitch of each rotor blade (the angle at which it meets the air-stream) can also be varied. At take-off all the blades are pitched steeply, to give maximum lift. For forward flight the pitch control is adjusted so that the pitch of each blade increases as it moves to the rear of its sweep. This has the effect of lifting the whole aircraft forwards, giving a forward component to the rotor's thrust in addition to the lift. The circular motion of the helicopter rotor generates an opposite, reactive force on the rest of the vehicle, tending to spin it in the opposite direction. This tendency is overcome either by using two opposite-rotating rotors, or by the use of a small tail rotor or jet generating a thrust in the opposite direction (this tail rotor can also be used to steer the aircraft). A string-pulled helicopter model is illustrated in a Flemish manuscript of *c.*1325, and *Leonardo da Vinci drew and described a helicopter-like aircraft in the 15th century. Paul Cornu flew the first free-flight, piloted helicopter in 1907 to a height of 30 cm (1 foot) and was airborne for about 20 seconds, but the craft was not really practicable. The Focke-Achgelis Fw61 (1936) was the first twin-rotor helicopter to fly; the first really practical helicopter was the single-rotor *Sikorsky VS-300 (1940). The Vietnam War (1962) saw the development of the helicopter as a heavily armed, ground-attack gunship. Helicopters also played a major role in the Gulf War (1991). Despite their slow speed and very high fuel consumption, helicopters are invaluable to the military, ambulance, and rescue services, and also to the police, due to their manœvrability. They are especially useful over difficult terrain, where no landing strip may be available.

helium (symbol He, at. no. 2, r.a.m. 4.0), an odourless, colourless gas of very low density, first discovered by *spectroscopy of sunlight. It is completely inert and, being lighter than air, is used to inflate large balloons and airships where its non-flammable nature makes it a safer alternative to *hydrogen. It is used as an inert medium to protect high-purity metals during heat treatment, and in breathing mixtures used in *deep-sea diving. Helium has the lowest boiling-point (−268.6 °C) of any gas, and liquid helium is an important coolant for *superconducting systems and other low-temperature applications. Helium is obtained from natural gas by lowering the temperature until all other components liquefy.

hemp *fibre, textile (table).

herbal medicine, a system of alternative medicine using plants and plant extracts to prevent and cure disease by stimulating the body's own powers of healing. Until quite recently, many drugs were based on plant extracts (with some animal and mineral products), but the *pharmaceutical industry has isolated the active components of some plant extracts and now synthesizes them by industrial chemical techniques. Herbal medicine is a reversion to the use of pure plant extracts, on the principle that humans should exist in harmony with their environment, and that local plants are likely to be able to cure many ailments: for example, asthma is said to be responsive to local honeys on the grounds that they will lead to desensitization to local pollens that can cause asthma.

herbicide, a *pesticide toxic to plants, used to kill weeds or other unwanted vegetation. Herbicides may be non-specific *agrochemicals, killing all plants: examples of such 'total' herbicides are sodium chlorate and paraquat. Alternatively they may be more selective, for example killing only broad-leaved plants. These herbicides are effective when growing cereals or other thin-leaved crops. Herbicides are usually used in a liquid form, and sprayed on to the crops. Although designed to be selectively toxic to plants, some herbicides also have limited toxicity in humans, and must be used with great care. Concern about the harmful effects of persistent chemicals has led to the development of products that break down when they enter the soil. In contrast, pre-emergent herbicides are designed to persist in the soil, and kill weeds at their most vulnerable stage, as they germinate.

Hero(n) of Alexandria (1st century AD), Greek mathematician and mechanical inventor. His surviving works include the *Metrica*, a treatise on plane and solid geometry; *On the Dioptra*, describing a surveying instrument resembling a *theodolite; the *Mechanics*, discussing levers and the concept of centre of gravity and the parallelogram of velocities; *Catoptrics*, discussing the reflection of light; and *Engines of War* and *Pneumatics*, which owed much to *Ctesibius and Philo of Byzantium. This last describes a variety of mechanical devices, including a simple *steam-turbine, a water-organ, a pump, a siphon, and various *automata in human or animal shape.

Héroult, Paul-Louis-Toussaint (1863–1914), French chemist who invented the *electric-arc furnace and (independently of *Hall) an electrolytic process for manufacturing aluminium. After a year at the Paris School of Mines, he began experimenting with the production of aluminium by *electrolysis of alumina (aluminium oxide) dissolved in fused salts. He patented his process in 1886, but was involved in some fifteen years of litigation with Hall, whose process was basically very similar. Héroult's process was first worked in 1887 at Neuhausen, using *hydroelectricity from the famous falls on the Rhine.

Hertz, Heinrich Rudolf (1857–94), German physicist and pioneer of radio communication. He sought evidence of the British physicist James Clerk Maxwell's theory that light is only a part of a whole spectrum of *electromagnetic radiation. In 1887–8, he designed a spark transmitter, in which a spark generated by a high-voltage source induced a spark in an unconnected circuit at a distance from the source. Hertz postulated that the transfer of the spark was caused by

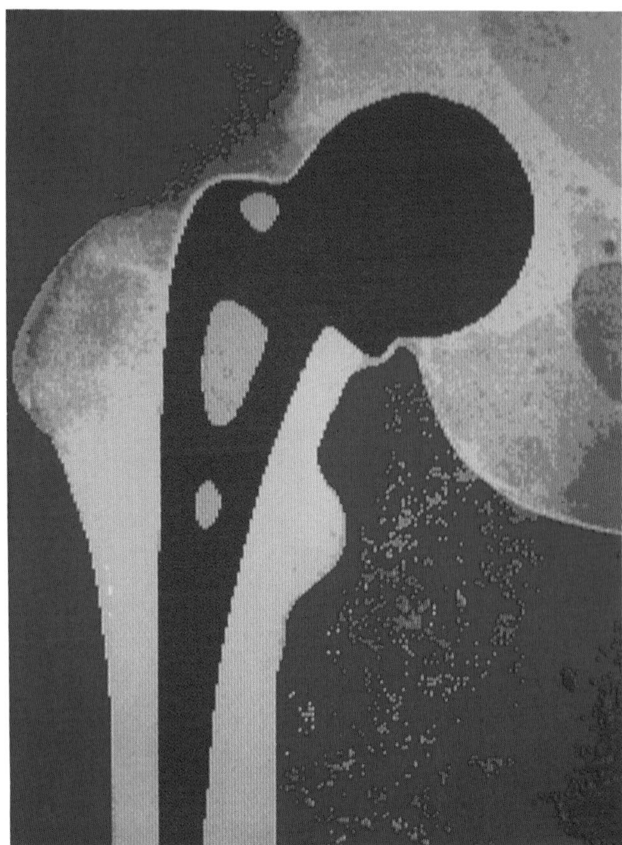

A false-colour X-ray of the pelvic area in a patient with an artificial **hip replacement**. The femur and pelvis appear yellow, while the implant, which forms the ball of the ball-and-socket joint of the hip, is coloured red.

a form of electromagnetic radiation (*radio waves in this case). He later showed that radio waves travel at the speed of light and can be reflected and refracted.

high-fidelity system, an electronic device capable of producing sound, particularly music, virtually indistinguishable from the original recording. The expression 'hi-fi', when introduced in 1950, was used to describe sound systems with 'above average' quality. Technological improvements over the years have meant hi-fi definitions have needed constant updating. Good hi-fi systems aim to reproduce sound with the minimum of distortion over a wide range of frequencies, and with a broad dynamic range and low levels of background noise. Human hearing has a frequency range of about 20–20,000 Hz, and the maximum range of sound intensity required is around 90 *decibels (dB). Most *gramophone, *tape, and *radio reproduction falls short of these ranges, with a frequency range of around 14,000 Hz and a dynamic range of about 70 dB. However, the digital sound recording and reproduction of *compact discs produces virtually distortion-free sound reproduction between 4 and 20,000 Hz, with a dynamic range of around 90 dB.

high-speed train, a train developed to travel at speeds in excess of 200 km/h (125 m.p.h.). Such trains fall into two main categories. First, there are those trains designed to operate on completely new railways at speeds of 260 km/h (160 m.p.h.) or more, such as the Japanese *shinkansen* ('bullet') trains and the French *train à grande vitesse* (TGV). Second are new trains for operation on existing railways. These include the British high-speed train (HST or InterCity 125) and the French and Canadian turbo-trains, powered by *gas-turbines. Higher speeds may be attained with acceptable passenger comfort by tilting the train by up to 9 degrees on curves. Passive-tilting trains (which tilt on a pendulum principle) have successfully operated for a number of years in Spain, while active-tilting trains are now operating in Italy, and being developed in Sweden.

hinge, a form of movable joint, as distinct from the fixings used to give a rigid structure. The modern conventional hinge, in which a metal pin passes through an odd number (usually five) of pierced knuckles, first appeared in pre-Christian times. Other forms of hinges have been devised for special purposes: strap hinges are often used for heavy doors; rising hinges serve to lift doors as they open—for example, to clear the pile of a carpet. The hinges on farm gates commonly consist of rings on the gate resting on hooks on the posts, so that they can easily be removed.

hip replacement, the surgical removal of the upper end of the femur (thigh bone) and its replacement by a *prosthesis of steel, plastic, or other material. The operation is performed either because the joint surfaces have worn out (osteo-arthritis) or because the bone has fractured. Fractures are more common in older women who suffer from weakened bones (osteoporosis). If the fracture tears the blood vessels to the bone, it will not heal normally and a replacement operation is necessary. If the blood vessels are not damaged, then instead of replacement, the bone may be 'pinned' with steel wires or screws to hold it steady during the healing period.

hoe, a long-handled implement with a thin metal blade, used to cut weed plants at ground level (see *agricultural machinery for illustration). Before the advent of *herbicides it was a major tool of weed control, and was used to thin out crops once seedlings had become established. Horse-drawn hoes were developed in the 18th century, and were among the first *agricultural machines to gain widespread acceptance. The development of machine hoes for use with tractors followed the same design, using a frame to support adjustable tines. Hoeing remains a necessary part of *organic farming.

Hoe, Richard March (1812–86), US pioneer of high-speed *printing. In 1827 he entered his father's printing works, where he soon began to build presses. Recognizing that substantially higher speeds were impossible with traditional flat-bed machines, he turned to rotary presses. In 1846 he introduced one with type set on a central cylinder: this was first employed by the *Philadelphia Public Ledger*. By 1857 *The Times* in London was using a Hoe press capable of 20,000 impressions an hour. After 1871, his company began to develop the web-press (using a continuous web of paper rather than sheets).

Hollerith, Herman (1860–1929), US inventor of tabulating machines. A mining engineer by training, he joined the US Census Bureau in 1880 to assist in the analysis of that year's census. The task was completed only just before the 1890 census, and this led Hollerith to develop a punched-card system of information storage, retrieval, and analysis, based on the system of cards used to control the *Jacquard loom. In 1896 he established the Tabulating Machine Company—a parent of IBM (1924)—which developed a variety of mechanical calculators and introduced the keyboard principle in 1901.

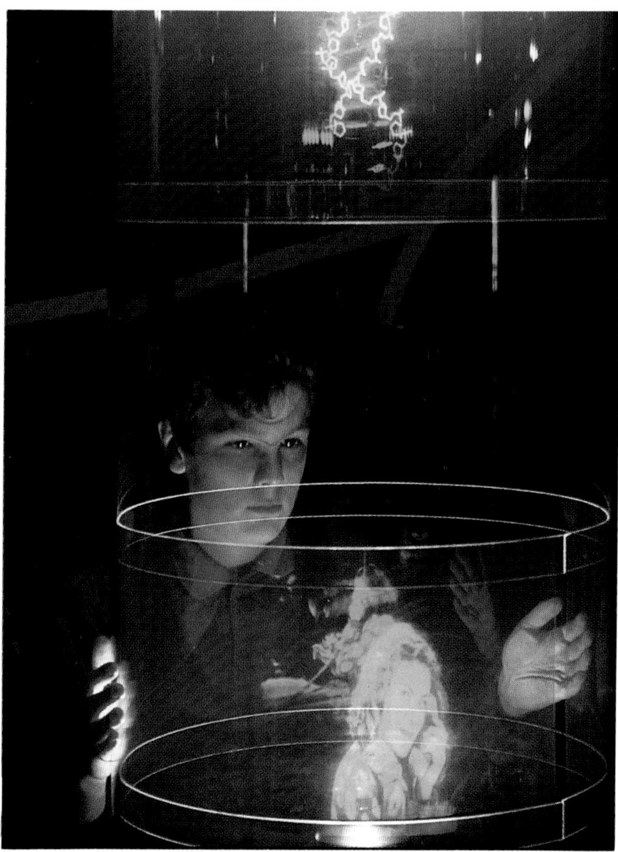

Circular **holograms** at the Museum of La Villette, Paris.

holography, the production and recording of holograms, three-dimensional images formed by the interference of (usually *laser) light beams from a coherent light source. Holography was first proposed by *Gabor in 1947, but only became practicable when the laser was invented in 1960. For recording, laser light is split into two beams, one being reflected from an object, and the other being used as a reference beam. The two beams are then recombined. The light from a laser is coherent, which means that the light *waves are all in step. After the light has been reflected from an object, this is no longer the case. As a result, some of the reflected waves tend to cancel the waves in the unaltered reference beam, while others reinforce each other. This produces an interference pattern of dark and bright areas which, when recorded on a photographic plate, is called a hologram. The reflected beam can be reconstructed from the hologram by illuminating it with a laser beam. This produces a three-dimensional image of the original object. A different view is seen when the hologram is looked at from different angles, just as if it were a real object. Some holograms, like those placed on credit cards to prevent fraud, can be seen with ordinary white light. Holograms can also be made with other coherent electromagnetic radiation, for example sound or radio waves.

homoeopathy, a system of alternative medicine, first described by the German physician Samuel Hahnemann (1755–1843). Hahnemann observed that quinine (an antimalarial drug) taken by healthy patients produced symptoms similar to those of malaria, and proposed that any compound that produced symptoms similar to those of an illness could cure the illness. This is now known as 'proving', and is the basis of modern homoeopathic practice; compounds are taken in very small doses and the symptoms they produce are noted. A medicine (the simillimum) whose symptomatology in the proving stage is exactly similar to that of the patient will be curative. Homoeopathy requires the practitioner to treat the patient as a whole, rather than treating a specific symptom. It also advocates the 'minimum dose', the aim being simply to stimulate the body's own power of healing. Remedies are therefore often given in very dilute solutions: the most potent remedies are so dilute that there is a negligible probability of even one molecule of active constituent being present.

Honda Kotaro (1870–1954), Japanese inventor of new magnetic alloys. He graduated in physics from Tokyo Imperial University, thereafter devoting himself to research on ferromagnetism. During World War I he developed and patented Kotaro steel (KS), which displayed an exceptional ability to retain magnetism, and later (1933) an improved new KS steel (NKS), which at the time was the world's most powerful permanent magnetic alloy.

Hopkins, Sir Frederick Gowland (1861–1947), pioneer British biochemist, remembered particularly for work leading to the discovery of vitamins. After research on natural pigments and proteins and the physiology of muscle contraction, he directed his attention to the relationship between growth and diet, and by 1906 he had identified 'accessory food factors' (vitamins) as being essential for health. He was unable, however, to isolate any of these substances. Later, he sought vitamins among the sulphur-containing proteins. In 1929 he shared the Nobel Prize for Physiology and Medicine with Christiaan Eijkman. (See also *vitamin treatment.)

Frederick Gowland **Hopkins**, who first established the existence of vitamins.

hormone, a chemical that is secreted by a group of cells, known as endocrine glands, in one part of the body, and then carried in the blood to exert an effect on some other tissue, the target organ. Insulin, for example, is produced in the pancreas and causes liver and muscle cells to take up excess glucose from the blood. In general, hormones control body functions over longer periods than the nervous system and also direct growth and development. A number of medical conditions result from hormone deficiency, such as some types of infertility, dwarfism, and diabetes. Such conditions may be corrected by supplying the patient with the hormone, orally or by injection. Hormones extracted from animals are expensive and can lead to immunological problems: for example, the body may recognize the hormone as a 'foreign substance' and produce antibodies to it, causing sickness. *Biotechnology therefore aims to insert human genes coding for specific hormones into micro-organisms, which will then synthesize the hormone relatively cheaply. Human insulin and growth hormone are already made in this way. In addition to correcting deficiencies, hormone treatment is used to increase weight in humans or animals (anabolic *steroids) and the hormones oestrogen and progesterone are the active ingredients of *contraceptive pills. Synthetic mimics of insect hormones (*pheromones) may soon be used as pollution-free pesticides. (See also *plant hormones.)

horn, a hard permanent outgrowth on the head of cattle, sheep, deer, and other (especially hoofed) mammals. It contains no bone, but is protected by a hard outer layer of keratin. Horn is now largely a waste product of animal husbandry, as are hooves, which are made of the same tissue. When boiled, it produces a sticky substance which is used as a glue, while dried and ground horn continues to be used as fertilizer. The keratin layer becomes plastic when warmed, and in the past was shaped to form a number of domestic products. Spectacle frames were originally made from horn, as were drinking cups and handles for cutlery.

horsepower *unit.

horseshoe, a flat U-shaped protective plate, usually made of metal, which is burnt into the rim of the hoof of a horse or other hoofed animal and then nailed to it. It protects the hoof from the abrasive surface of a road or track and allows the horse to have a better grip on the ground. Horseshoes were probably first used by migratory Eurasian tribes, perhaps as early as 300 BC. The Romans had horseshoes in the 1st century BC, but the nailed iron horseshoe was a European invention, from around AD 500. Recently plastic horseshoes that can be glued to the hoof have been introduced.

horticulture, the intensive cultivation of *vegetable crops and soft fruits for human consumption, or for ornamental or recreational purposes. The most intensive production is carried out in *greenhouses, where vegetables, tropical plants, and seedlings are grown. Other horticultural methods include *row cultivation, and also beginning seedlings in the greenhouse or seed-bed and then transplanting them, thus allowing early harvesting.

hot isostatic pressing (HIP) *ceramic.

House

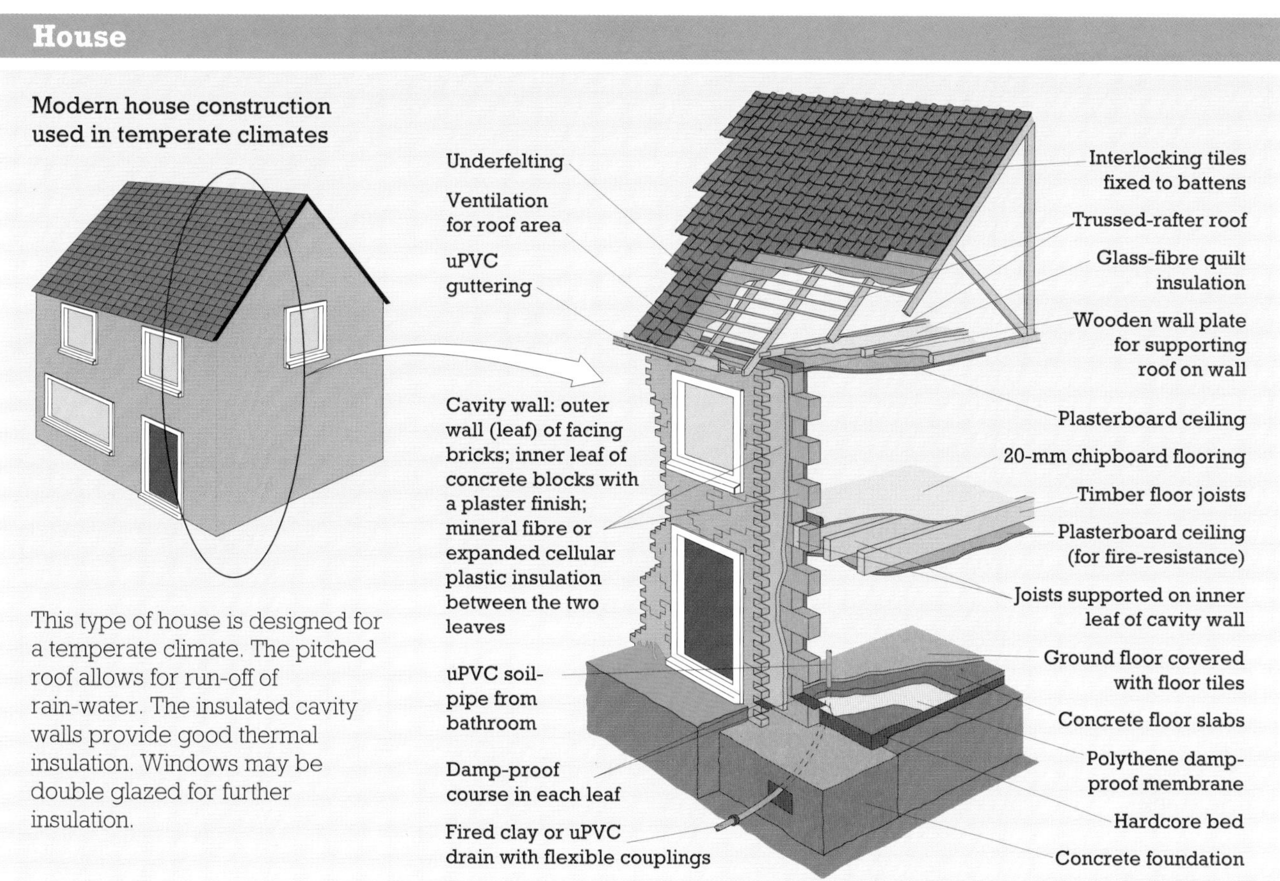

This type of house is designed for a temperate climate. The pitched roof allows for run-off of rain-water. The insulated cavity walls provide good thermal insulation. Windows may be double glazed for further insulation.

Houdry, Eugène (1892–1962), French-born US chemical engineer who developed a catalytic *cracking process for petroleum. In the 1920s the heavier oils in petroleum were 'cracked' to lighter, more valuable petrol fractions using high-pressure, high-temperature processes. Houdry invested much of his personal fortune in developing a much cheaper catalytic process, operating at lower temperatures and pressures, which was achieved in 1937.

house, a building for human shelter and habitation. Houses are designed to protect the occupants from extremes of climate and to provide comfortable, practical living spaces. Most societies have a traditional house-building technology that is appropriate for the local climate and social structure. Such technology is often simple, and generally uses locally available materials. In the West, building has largely become a specialization, and house building involves increasingly complex technologies. The figure shows constructional details of a house for a temperate climate, where good thermal insulation is needed in winter. Insulated *cavity walls are supported from *concrete spread *foundations, while the ground floor is often a concrete slab laid on hardcore (hard material used to fill soft ground), covered by a decorative finish. The floor must include a *damp-proof course (usually a polythene sheet laid below the slab), and often also insulating material. Upper floors are usually wooden, laid on joists supported by both internal and external walls. The pitched *roof is built with trussed rafters, covered with interlocking tiles. A mineral-fibre insulation quilt over the upper-storey ceiling reduces heat losses through the roof. Between 1975 and 1977 research in the USA and Scandinavia led to the development of 'super-insulated' houses, incorporating extra thermal *insulation in the walls, windows, and roof; complete sealing against draughts; and mechanical ventilation, with heat exchangers to warm incoming air. Such houses use only about one-tenth the annual heat energy of a conventional house. Houses embodying similar principles are also being built in mainland Europe.

hovercraft, a vessel designed to float on a cushion of compressed air between the hovercraft itself and the surface over which it is travelling. The idea was first researched by the British engineer John Thorneycroft, who tested several models in the 1870s and in 1877 filed a patent. However, the solution to the problems of designing and building such a vehicle were not solved until the 1950s, when *Cockerell designed the first practical hovercraft, the SRN-1, launched in 1959. Like later vessels of the same type, it used a *gas-turbine engine to power a large aircraft *propeller, which drew air into a space under the craft. The air-cushion was contained by a rubber skirt, and forward motion was achieved by a second propeller. The hovercraft's amphibious ability has led to its successful use as a ferry, assault craft, and survey vessel. Another type of hovercraft has been developed, with rigid side-walls to contain the air cushion: it can be used only on water, but has the advantage that it can use conventional screw propulsion. Both types of hovercraft are still in a relatively early stage of development.

hover-train *ground-guidance system.

Howe, Elias (1819–67), US inventor of a *sewing-machine. He gained mechanical experience (1835–7) as an apprentice in a textile machinery works and then to a watchmaker in Boston. Allegedly inspired by a random suggestion, he

An SR.N4 **hovercraft**, used since 1969 on ferry services across the English Channel. The largest vessels can carry up to 424 passengers and 55 cars.

applied himself to the invention of a sewing-machine, and by 1845 he had built a lockstitch machine working at 250 stitches a minute. Finding no interest in the USA, he sold the UK patent rights to William Thomas of London in 1846.

howitzer, *artillery capable of firing at an elevation of over 45 degrees. Development may have commenced as early as 1325, and the name 'howitzer' was first used around 1650. Howitzers were introduced in an attempt to combine the mobility of *cannon with the plunging fire of *mortars. They were so successful that they virtually replaced heavy mortars on the battlefield. Most artillery in modern armies employ combination gun-howitzers.

hull-and-core structure *skyscraper.

human-powered flight, flight by a heavier-than-air machine propelled entirely by human power. Stories and myths of human flight have existed since earliest times, the best known being perhaps the ancient Greek myth of Daedalus, who designed wings attached by wax for himself and his son Icarus, and flew north to Greece from Crete. The achievement of powered flight in 1903 brought human-powered flight into the realms of possibility rather than fantasy, but despite many attempts progress was slow. In 1959 a large prize was offered through the Royal Aeronautical Society of Great Britain for the first human-powered aircraft to fly 1 mile (1.6 km) over a designated course. Despite many attempts this prize was not won until 1977, when the British designer Paul MacCready's aircraft Gossamer Condor flew the designated course. Two years later another MacCready aircraft, the Gossamer Albatross, was piloted by Bryan Allen across the English Channel, a distance of over 32 km (20 miles). In 1988 an aircraft designed and built by a team based at the Massachusetts Institute of Technology (Daedalus 88) was flown by Kanellos Kanellopoulos 119 km (74 miles) from Crete to the Greek island of Thíra (Santorini), thus achieving in reality Daedalus' mythical flight.

Huntsman, Benjamin (1704–76), British inventor of the crucible process for making steel (see *iron and steel industry). After apprenticeship to a clock-maker, in about 1740 he set up his own business in Doncaster to make clocks, locks, roasting-jacks, and other small mechanisms. Dissatisfied with the steel available, he set out to improve it, moving to the steel-making area of Sheffield. There, he designed a coke-fired furnace (*c.*1745) that could melt steel in small crucibles, separating out impurities to leave a high-quality steel. Huntsman initially had to sell his steel in France, as the Sheffield cutlers rejected it as being too hard. However, the superiority of imported French cutlery forced them to accept Huntsman's steel.

Hussey, Obed (1792–1860), US inventor of a mechanical *reaper. He devoted his life to the inventing of machines for light engineering and agriculture, but his most successful invention was the grain-reaping machine that he patented in 1833. It embodied a saw-toothed cutter working with two guard bars. He began manufacture in Cincinnati, but encountered a rival in *McCormick, who had patented his own reaper in 1834. Bitter competition developed between them, but Hussey's refusal to adapt his machine in light of other new inventions resulted in McCormick's firm emerging as leader of the US market.

Hyatt, John Wesley (1837–1920), versatile US inventor and pioneer of the plastics industry. His inventions included a water-purification system, a sugar-cane mill, a machine for straightening steel rods, a multi-stitch sewing-machine, and a widely used roller bearing. In the 1860s he became interested in finding a substitute for the ivory used to make billiard balls. With his brother Isaac he developed *celluloid, a blend of *nitro-cellulose and camphor, for which he took out a patent in 1870.

hydrant, a valve on a water main that allows water to be drawn for *fire-fighting. Hydrants are spaced to give good coverage in urban areas. An 80-mm (3-inch) diameter hydrant can deliver directly at mains pressure a supply adequate for fires in low-rise buildings. For high-rise buildings, mains pressure is augmented by fire-fighting pumps.

hydraulic mining, a surface *mining technique in which mineral deposits are removed by a large jet of water under high pressure. It requires an enormous supply of water together with a means of recovering the ore from the rock–water slurry produced. In the hydraulic mining of *gold, the gold settles behind baffles, while the lighter waste matter is washed away. In hydraulic *coal-mining, the water simply breaks coal fragments from the seam and washes them to a collecting point. Debris disposal is a problem, and hydraulic mining has been criticized for its effect on the environment. It is used only where less drastic techniques cannot be employed. Hydraulic mining coupled with suction removal is also used for the mining of mineral deposits on the sea-bed.

hydraulic power, a method of power transmission using a fluid, usually water or oil, to transmit power from a *pump to a hydraulic motor or a *hydraulic ram. (Hydraulics is the study and use of fluids for engineering purposes.) Since liquids are almost incompressible, large pressures can be used to exert very great force by means of a hydraulic ram. In 1795 *Bramah invented the hydraulic press using this principle, and in 1802 went on to propose hydraulic power transmission, using a pump and motor. During the 19th century hydraulic power was widely adopted in ports and cities, using water in an extensive pipe distribution system, with central steam-driven pumping stations and hydraulic accumulators. The latter were tall, vertical rams carrying a large dead weight which could move up and down to accommodate fluctuating loads. The chief uses of hydraulic power were for cranes, dock gates, swing-bridges, and lifts: Tower Bridge in London is hydraulically operated. Oil later replaced water as the working fluid, being a better lubricant for pumps, motors, and rams, and avoiding *corrosion and freezing. A range of hydraulic pumps is available which can achieve pressures of more than 300 bar. Hydraulic motors are generally similar to pumps. A typical hydraulic circuit consists of supply tank, filter, pump and relief valve, control-valve, motor or ram, and oil cooler—the last is needed because energy losses in any component appear as heat, which must be removed. A major application is in farm *tractors for controlling the plough or other implement. Hydraulic power is also used in earth-moving equipment. Many *machine-tools, especially presses, are hydraulically operated, as are winches, steering gear, and other items aboard ships. Many large aircraft rely on hydraulic operation of main control surfaces, landing gear, and brakes. Motor-car *braking systems are usually hydraulic.

hydraulic ram, the piston–cylinder combination used to operate a press, a jack, or part of a machine such as the jib of a *crane or an agricultural implement (see *hydraulic power). The term is also applied to a type of water pump, a simple and reliable device that is used in rural areas and in Third World countries for domestic or farm water supply from a stream.

hydrocarbon, a member of a large group of *organic chemicals, containing only the elements *hydrogen and *carbon. They are major constituents of crude petroleum and *natural gas, from which certain fractions are extracted for use as fuel and as raw materials for the *chemical industry. In hydrocarbon molecules, carbon atoms form chains, which may be straight, branched, or joined head-to-tail to form rings. Hydrocarbon molecules containing only single bonds between carbon atoms (alkanes) are said to be saturated; those with double (alkenes) or triple bonds (alkynes) are unsaturated. Hydrocarbons that contain the *benzene ring in their structure are called aromatic; those without such a ring are called aliphatic. The wide range of structural features in hydrocarbon molecules gives rise to a vast number of different compounds, many of which are important in manufacturing plastics, textiles, and drugs.

hydrochloric acid (HCl), an aqueous solution of the strong corrosive acid, hydrogen chloride. Hydrogen chloride gas was made originally from the reaction of *sulphuric acid with sodium chloride (*salt), but it is now obtained as a by-product of reactions between *chlorine and *hydrocarbons. Hydrochloric acid is used widely in the chemical industry to manufacture metal chlorides, dyes, adhesives, and glucose. Large quantities are used to remove oxide coatings from iron or steel that is to be galvanized, tin-plated, or enamelled.

hydroelectricity, the generation of electric power using the energy of flowing water. Hydroelectric systems range from small local generators producing a few hundred watts to major *power-stations producing more than 1,000 MW (1GW). The earliest hydroelectric plant was commissioned in 1880 on a private estate (Cragside) in Northumberland, UK, and the first installation in the USA followed within two years. The mid-1890s saw outputs reach 5 MW, and the first Niagara Falls power-station began operation. Capacities rose to 100 MW in the 1920s, 1 GW two decades later, and now reach tens of gigawatts. Total production also continued to grow, and in the late 1980s hydroelectricity accounted for nearly a fifth of the world's electric power. The main features of any hydroelectric installation have remained essentially the same for 100 years (see figure overleaf). They are the *generators and the *turbines which drive them, and a *dam, or barrage, which stores water to allow a degree of independence from fluctuations in the natural supply. The head (the vertical distance through which the water falls) determines the speed and pressure of the water at the turbines, and the power output depends upon this and on the volume of water delivered per second. These two factors also largely govern the design of the installation. A power-station on a slowly flowing river or a tidal estuary requires a water control system and turbines suitable for large volumes of water at a relatively low head. In mountainous regions, where the head is much greater, the water is usually fed through tunnels, shafts, and pipes (the penstocks) and reaches the turbines as a fast-flowing stream, often at high pressure. (See also *pumped storage.)

hydrofluoric acid (HF), an extremely corrosive acid, a solution of hydrogen fluoride in water. It reacts with glass (it is used for etching glass) and is stored in either wax or plastic bottles. Anhydrous liquid hydrofluoric acid is widely used as a *catalyst in the *petrochemicals industry and as a reagent for producing fluorine-containing compounds.

hydrofoil, a light craft designed to travel largely above rather than along the water surface. Below the hull are foils (specially shaped surfaces akin to *aerofoils) mounted on struts. Sails or engines provide power, and as the craft gains speed the foils rise, lifting the hull out of the water. Hydrofoil research began in 1891, and on Lake Maggiore (Italy) in 1906 a hydrofoil designed by Enrico Forlanini achieved a speed of 38 *knots. Further development was slow because of the difficulties of obtaining adequate stability, control, and power. In 1956 the first commercial hydrofoil went into operation. There are two basic types of hydrofoil. In the first, surface-piercing foils support the vessel completely out of the water, with the foils travelling along the surface. In the

Hydroelectricity

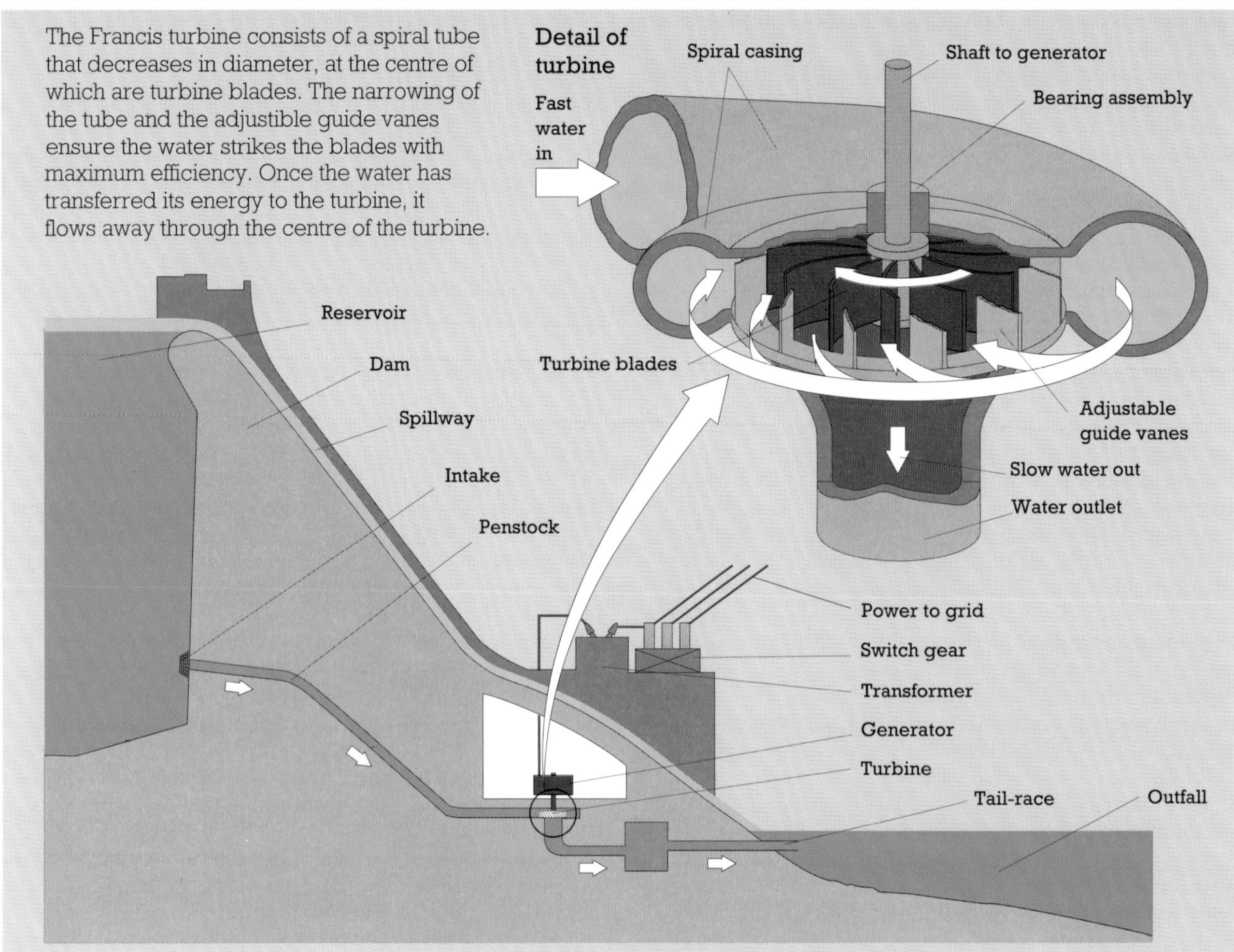
The Francis turbine consists of a spiral tube that decreases in diameter, at the centre of which are turbine blades. The narrowing of the tube and the adjustible guide vanes ensure the water strikes the blades with maximum efficiency. Once the water has transferred its energy to the turbine, it flows away through the centre of the turbine.
Detail of turbine
Fast water in
Spiral casing
Shaft to generator
Bearing assembly
Turbine blades
Adjustable guide vanes
Slow water out
Water outlet
Reservoir
Dam
Spillway
Intake
Penstock
Power to grid
Switch gear
Transformer
Generator
Turbine
Tail-race
Outfall

second type the foils remain partially submerged, improving stability and control but reducing speeds.

hydrogen (symbol H, at. no. 1, r.a.m. 1.01), a colourless, odourless gas that burns readily in air. Hydrogen is produced industrially as a by-product of the *Castner–Kellner cell, and by the reaction of *natural gas with steam at high temperatures and pressures in the presence of a nickel *catalyst. Its main uses are in the production of ammonia by the *Haber–Bosch process and in hydrogenation reactions with unsaturated *hydrocarbons (see *hydrotreatment). Small quantities of hydrogen are used in meteorological balloons and for high-temperature welding and cutting. Liquid hydrogen is used as a fuel for *rocket motors. Hydrogen is in many ways the ideal fuel, providing large amounts of energy when burned, with water vapour as the only combustion product. There has been much interest in the idea of a hydrogen energy 'economy', in which hydrogen produced from water (most probably by *electrolysis) is used for heating, powering vehicles, and so on. However, this can at best be regarded as an option for the mid-21st century.

hydrogen bomb *nuclear weapon.

hydrogen peroxide (H_2O_2), a colourless, viscous liquid usually produced as an aqueous solution. It is a powerful oxidizing agent (see *oxidation and reduction) and is used industrially as a *bleach and in rocket propellants to provide a source of *oxygen. Domestically it is used as a sterilizing agent, bleach, and disinfectant.

hydrology, the study of water and its effects on land areas. The hydrological cycle is the continuous process of evaporation of sea-water; movement of water vapour in air masses over the land; precipitation as rain or snow; and return to the sea in stream flow or to the atmosphere by evaporation or transpiration by plants. Estimating the relative proportions of precipitation, evaporation, transpiration, infiltration, and surface run-off in a particular locality is fundamental to *water resources management. Hydrology is also concerned with changes in the quality of water as it moves through the hydrological cycle, and land erosion due to surface water flow.

hydrometer, an instrument used to measure the specific gravity (density) of a liquid. It consists of a large glass float with a long calibrated stem. The hydrometer is weighted so that it floats vertically with the stem partially immersed. The depth of immersion depends on the specific gravity of the liquid: the greater the specific gravity, the less liquid is displaced by the hydrometer, and the less it is immersed. To avoid an unduly long stem, hydrometers usually cover only a limited range. Optical and electrical systems can be linked with a hydrometer if continuous recordings are required.

hydroponics, the process of growing plants on a sterile inert material such as sand, gravel, or liquid, without soil but continuously provided with nutrients in solution. In this way it is possible to control the balance of inorganic nutrients such as potassium, sulphur, magnesium, and nitrogen, supplied to the plant, and to provide the correct mixture for a particular stage of plant growth. Crops are planted in 1-m (3-foot) wide beds with movable shades to control sunlight. Hydroponics has a particular application for the production of crops such as green peppers and aubergines in *greenhouses, but has also been applied on a much larger scale, particularly in desert regions such as Kuwait, where water supply and soil are very poor.

hydrotreatment, a process used in *petroleum refining, involving chemical treatment of a petroleum product with hydrogen gas. In hydrotreatment, hydrogen is used in combination with catalysts to remove impurities such as oxygen, nitrogen, and sulphur from petroleum fractions. A related process is hydrocracking, a form of catalytic *cracking. Certain types of *reforming are also carried out in the presence of hydrogen.

hygrometer *meteorological instruments.

hypersonic flight, flight at speeds much greater than *Mach 1, at which speeds a thin layer of highly turbulent, extremely hot air is formed around the forward portion of the vehicle. Fully hypersonic flow can usually be said to occur at Mach numbers greater than about 8, but the term is usually used for flight speeds of Mach 5 or greater. Many rockets reach hypersonic speeds, and the projected US and German *spaceplanes are designed for hypersonic flight.

hypertext, a generic term for computer systems used to store, retrieve, and view multidimensional documents. Hypertext systems are more flexible than conventional *databases. Links may be made between parts of a hypertext document so that it can be read in a non-standard order, when pursuing a particular topic. Viewed text may be selected by using a *mouse or keyboard, and displayed in a *window. The first practical hypertext systems were developed in the 1980s, and are particularly suited to multimedia applications.

hypnotic *psychotropic drug.

hypocaust, a Roman heating system in which hot air from a furnace circulates inside a hollow floor. *Vitruvius wrote that the base of the hypocaust be sloped 'in such a way that if a ball is thrown in, it must return to the furnace room'. Off this base, 60-cm (2-feet) high brick pillars support large tiles on which the decorative floor is laid. Hollow tiles often line the walls above, forming flues with outlets at high level and increasing the area emitting heat.

hypodermic syringe, an instrument designed principally to administer drugs beneath the skin. It consists of a piston running in a tube that terminates in a (usually detachable) hollow needle. Hypodermic injection was first employed by the Irishman Francis Rynd in 1845, but it is only in this century that it has become an indispensable tool for injecting drugs or other substances and for withdrawing body fluids (most often blood) for analysis. The earlier glass or metal syringes required *sterilization, but modern plastic syringes come in sterile packages and are used once only.

ice-breaker, any ship built or adapted to break ice. Typically, an ice-breaker is a large ship with extremely powerful engines and a specially strengthened and shaped hull, used to open a passage through pack-ice in high northern or southern latitudes. Where ice is particularly thick, the engines force the bows to ride up over the ice face, and the weight of the ship breaks the ice. *Hovercraft have also proved effective in breaking ice by this method. Some ice-breakers also have a special propeller under the stern which helps to break the ice. Major ports and harbours that become frozen in winter (for example St Petersburg, formerly Leningrad) use ice-breakers to clear a passage in and out. They are also used to keep open longer routes such as the Northern Sea Route, from the Arctic Ocean to the Pacific north of the Soviet Union and Soviet Siberia. Very large *nuclear-powered ships have been built as ice-breakers in the Soviet Union, capable of clearing a channel 30.5 m (100 feet) wide through pack-ice 2.5 m (8 feet) thick.

iconoscope, the earliest electronically scanning *television camera, patented by *Zworykin in 1923. The iconoscope focused an image of the scene being filmed on to a mica plate coated with a mosaic of minute caesium–silver droplets (the signal plate). These droplets became positively charged when exposed to light, the amount of charge being proportional to the light intensity. An electron beam scanning the plate then discharged each droplet of the mosaic in turn. The discharge of each droplet induced a pulse of current in a cable attached to the signal plate, the size of the pulse being proportional to the amount of charge on the droplet, and hence to the light intensity. Thus the visual image was converted into a series of electric impulses in the signal plate, which passed into the cable and were transmitted. (See *television camera for illustration.)

identikit, a composite picture of a person's face, often someone wanted by the police, made up from eye-witness descriptions. Descriptions from different sources often emphasize different features, such as shape of ears and nose, level of hair-line, regularity of teeth, and so on. The police identikit uses all these separate features to reconstruct a likeness. Identikit features may be drawn by an artist, or photographs of facial features (photofit pictures) may be used.

ignition system, a means of initiating combustion, either for a steady flame, as in an oil or gas burner, or of the fuel–air mixture in a *petrol engine. A common method of gas ignition is by means of a *piezo-electric crystal; when struck a sharp blow a voltage is produced in the crystal, which can be used to make a spark. In oil burners a continuous spark is produced by an induction *coil, a form of high-voltage transformer. An induction coil is also at the heart of a petrol-engine ignition system. The primary winding of the coil is supplied with a current from the battery through a contact in the distributor. This circuit is broken at exactly the right time by a *cam-operated contact-breaker. The sudden stoppage of current causes a very high voltage, about 25,000 V, to be induced in the secondary winding of the induction coil. This voltage is passed to a *spark-plug by the rotating arm of the distributor, which connects each cylinder in turn to the supply. More recent ignition systems use an electronic switch instead of the mechanical contact-breaker.

Ikeda Kikunae (1864–1936), Japanese food technologist. He developed an interest in the chemical identity of substances that give foods—especially the Japanese seaweed dish *kombu*—their distinctive flavours, and discovered that the tang of *kombu* was due to the sodium salt of glutamic acid, a constituent of proteins. He patented his discovery (1908), and after retiring in 1923 devoted himself to developing its manufacture. Today, monosodium glutamate is one of the most widely used food *additives.

Ilyushin, Sergey Vladimirovich (1894–1977), Soviet aircraft designer. He qualified as a pilot in 1917, and as an engineer in 1926, and rose to the rank of lieutenant-general in the Red Army. He designed the series of military and civilian aircraft which bear his name, including the DB-3 twin-engined *bombers deployed against Finland in 1939–40. He designed jet bombers with I. Yakovlev, and after 1950 also designed jet airliners. His main Soviet rival was *Tupolev.

image intensifier, an electronic instrument that increases the brightness of an image too dim to be seen with the naked eye. The original image is focused on to the screen of a photo-cathode. This device emits electrons in proportion to the light falling on the screen, thus forming an image with electrons. The image is focused on to one or more amplifying elements, each increasing the electron intensity typically fifty times. Finally, a fluorescent screen converts the electrons back to visible light, reproducing the original image, which is now bright enough to see. Image intensifiers are used for night vision with cameras or military equipment, and in astronomy.

image processing, techniques used by computer systems to extract useful information from an image, or two-dimensional representation of a real-world scene. Image processing is related to *pattern recognition and *artificial intelligence and is often used, in some form, in *robotics. It is also widely used on images from, for example, *Earth resources satellites. In most real-world scenes or other images there is an enormous amount of information, much of it extraneous. The task of the image processing system is to select only those features which are important for interpretation of the image. Such features include boundaries, contours, points, and regions of high contrast or specific texture.

immersion heater, an electric heater fitted inside a water tank forming part of a domestic hot-water system. It consists of an electrical heating element surrounded by insulating material and sheathed in a thin metal casing. The element usually has a power of 3 kW and is controlled by a *thermostat.

immobilized cell technology, the technique of immobilizing cells by absorbing them on to glass or plastic beads or some other solid support. (*Enzymes can also be immobilized in this way.) Large tonnages of high-fructose syrups and of aspartic and malic acids are produced by *fermentation of immobilized bacteria in a *bioreactor. Immobilized mammalian cells are used to produce vaccines (see *immunization), enzymes, *hormones, and other substances. Immobilized cells remain productive for longer than cells in a conventional culture, and they are easier to separate from the fermentation products.

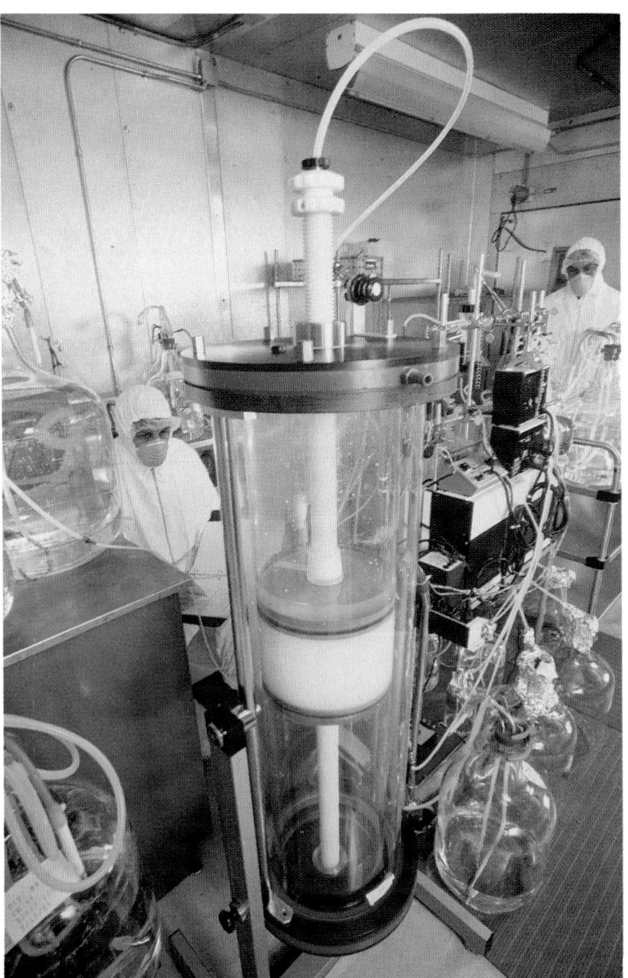

Apparatus used for the production of a vaccine for **immunization** against hepatitis B. Genes coding for the vaccine are inserted into yeast cells, which undergo fermentation in a bioreactor to produce the vaccine. The vaccine is then separated from the yeast and other products in a chromatography column (*foreground*).

immunization, the practice of inducing immunity (especially to infection) in a person or animal. This is usually achieved by vaccination, in which a vaccine (a preparation containing antigens) is used to stimulate the production of antibodies (see *immunology). The vaccine is usually administered by injection, and generally contains either live but attenuated organisms (reduced in virulence), or dead organisms which retain their ability to stimulate antibody production. The earliest form of immunization was variolation, a type of inoculation against smallpox in which part of a scab from a smallpox sufferer was introduced into a scratch on the recipient's skin. The practice, developed in about the 5th century AD in India, was potentially very dangerous, since it involved the live smallpox virus, but it greatly reduced overall mortality from the disease. Variolation was not known in Europe until 1721, when Mary Montagu, the wife of the British ambassador to the Ottoman Empire, introduced it from Turkey. In 1796 *Jenner successfully protected an 8-year-old boy from smallpox by inoculating him with the related but much less dangerous cowpox virus. In 1885 *Pasteur adopted Jenner's principles to find a vaccine against rabies. Vaccines have subsequently been produced for other diseases and non-infectious agents, including diphtheria (by the German immunologist Emil von Behring in 1889) and snake venom (by *Ehrlich in 1889). In 1890 von Behring and *Kitasato first showed that immunity was due to antibodies that appeared in the blood a few days after immunization.

immunology, the scientific study of immunity, the ability of an organism to resist infection by means of the immune system. The immune system has two main parts: white blood cells, and antibodies circulating in the bloodstream. Antibodies are proteins produced by beta-lymphocytes (a type of white blood cell) in response to exposure to antigens (*anti*body *gen*erators). Antigens are substances foreign to the body, for example toxins. Antibodies are dormant until they attach to the specific antigens against which they are effective. They then become activated, and may directly destroy the antigen or 'label' it so that a white blood cell can engulf and destroy it. After the body has been exposed to an antigen, a later exposure causes antibodies to be produced more quickly and in larger amounts than on the first occasion. This can produce immunity to a harmful antigen such as a virus, since it is eliminated before it has time to act. Thus, artificially exposing a person to a safe dose of antigen as the first exposure (active *immunization) will protect him or her from its effects in the future. Antibodies produced by one person can, through a transfusion of serum, give temporary immunity to another person (passive immunity). It is also possible to diagnose certain diseases by mixing known antibodies with serum from a suspected case and observing the reaction: an example is the Wasserman test for syphilis. By combining molecules of dye with antibodies, microscope slides of tissues containing certain antigens (for example, liver infected with a virus) can be selectively stained with colour. Immunosuppressant drugs such as *steroids deliberately suppress immune reactions: they are used to prevent the rejection of transplants in *transplant surgery. When the immune system is deficient or suppressed, the person is at serious risk from infections such as pneumonia and septicaemia. The drugs given are corticosteroids (see *steroids and steroid treatment), which reduce the number of beta-lymphocytes; cytotoxic drugs are also used. In addition to possibly harmful side-effects from the drugs, immunosuppression carries the risk that the patient becomes highly susceptible to infection by micro-organisms, especially viruses. Immunosuppression is also used to treat auto-immune diseases: rheumatoid arthritis, for example, is treated with *steroids.

impedance, the total opposition to current flow in an electrical *circuit, measured in ohms (Ω). In a direct-current circuit the impedance is equivalent to the resistance, but in an alternating-current circuit it is the ratio of the alternating voltage to alternating current, and is composed of the combined resistance, inductive *reactance (inductance), and capacitive reactance (capacitance).

Imperial College of Science and Technology, a school of London University, founded in 1907 to give specialized instruction in science, with an emphasis on its application to industry. It is a federation of three earlier institutions, the Royal College of Science, the Royal School of Mines, and the City and Guilds College, which have preserved their respective identities within the College framework. In 1953 Imperial College was chosen as the leading UK institution to provide more university-trained scientists and engineers.

Glass bulbs for **incandescent lamps** being manufactured. The 'pearl' light bulbs are made of satin glass: the dull, matt finish is achieved by immersing the glass in hydrofluoric acid.

imperial unit *unit.

incandescent lamp, a source of illumination consisting of a glass bulb filled with an inert gas at low pressure, and containing a finely wound metal filament (usually tungsten, but osmium and *tantalum are also used). When current is passed through the filament, it heats up, attaining temperatures of up to 2,500 °C, and emits intense visible light. The modern light bulb is a direct descendant of the lamps devised independently by *Swan in the UK in 1878, and by *Edison in the USA in 1879. The early lamps had a filament made of carbon; it was not until 1908 that *Coolidge devised a workable tungsten filament. The incandescent lamp is a convenient source of light, but has relatively poor efficiency: only about 10 per cent of the energy supplied is converted into visible light. More efficient *fluorescent light bulbs are now available as replacements for domestic incandescent bulbs.

inclined plane, a flat surface sloping at an angle to the horizontal: examples are wedges and ramps. The inclined plane was one of the earliest mechanical devices. Wheeled or sliding loads can be raised by pulling or pushing them up ramps, and they are thought to have been used extensively in the building of such structures as *pyramids. Wedges are used to split logs and quarry stone, to retain axe- and hammer-heads, and to fasten timbers together. Opposed wedges of equal taper, known as folding wedges, are used to exert a force between parallel surfaces.

incubator, a transparent container, the internal environment of which is controlled to keep temperature and humidity at constant and pre-set levels, used to maintain premature babies in a controlled environment, protected from infection. Incubators are also used for hatching eggs, and to grow bacteria.

Indian technology, technology derived from the ancient civilizations of the Indian subcontinent. Although far less closely studied, the Harappan civilization, which flourished in the Indus Valley (in modern Pakistan) around 4,000 years ago, ranks with those of Egypt, Mesopotamia, and China. The ancient town of Mohenjo-Daro covered 85 ha (210 acres), and had an advanced town-planning scheme. In historic times Indian science and technology has made important contributions to Western civilization. Wootz steel (a type of crucible steel made in southern India) was prized by the Romans. The great 8-m (26-foot) iron pillar at Delhi (5th century AD) testifies to the skill of early Indian metalworkers. Early Hindu surgeons such as *Suśruta performed advanced eye operations and practised lithotomy (surgical removal of a stone from the urinary tract) and plastic *surgery. Variolation (see *immunization) was used for protection against smallpox from at least the 5th century AD. Indian philosophers were skilled in astronomy and mathematics—especially algebra and geometry—and their decimal notation found its way to the West via the Arab world.

induction *electromagnetic induction.

induction motor *electric motor.

inductor, a component in an electric or electronic *circuit that possesses inductance. Inductance is a constant relating the current flowing in a circuit to the magnetic flux (amount of magnetism) produced by the current flow; the unit of inductance is the henry (H). *Coils are the commonest inductors: their inductance is increased if they have an iron core. The most important property of inductors is that they oppose the passage of high-frequency signals, but offer little or no opposition to low-frequency and direct-current signals (in contrast to *capacitors). Inductors are important components of filters (see *filter circuits), *tuners, *transformers, and *ignition systems.

inductor compass (flux-gate compass), a *magnetic compass in which the magnetized needle and compass card are replaced by a bar of easily saturated magnetic material—a material which easily gains and loses its magnetism. The magnetic flux through such a material is maximal when it is oriented in the magnetic north–south direction. The difference between this maximal flux and the actual flux value at any orientation can be converted electronically into a compass reading. An induction compass has no moving parts, and several read-outs can be run from one compass.

industrial archaeology, the systematic study of industrial artefacts. It concerns itself with archaeological remains

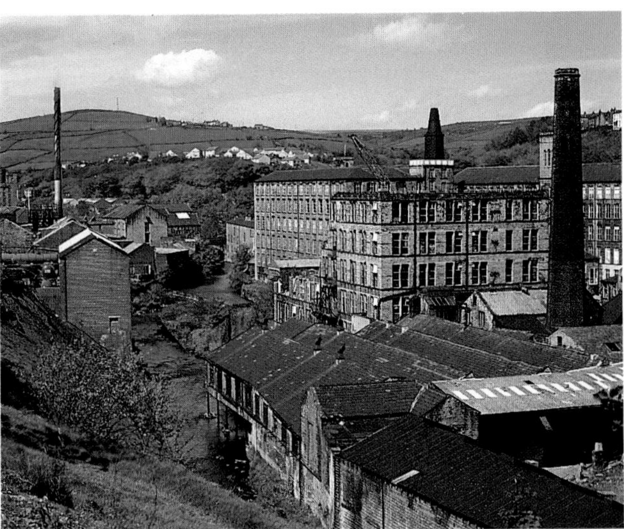

Nineteenth-century woollen mills at Slaithwaite, near Huddersfield, UK. Such buildings are now being preserved as examples of **industrial archaeology**.

of all ages—such as the copper mines of Tharsis in Spain and the water-mill at Barbegal, in France, both dating from Roman times—but particularly with commercial enterprises since the *Industrial Revolution of the 18th and 19th centuries. Although machinery and transport systems are its major areas of interest, it also draws on information from archival material, such as account and order books.

Industrial Revolution, the term used to describe the process of change from an agrarian, craft-based economy to an urban, industrial one based on large-scale mechanized manufacturing processes. The change began first in Britain around 1750, and lasted until 1830. Similar changes followed in other European countries, in the USA, and in Japan during the 19th century, while in the 20th century Eastern Europe, China, India, and South-East Asia have undergone a similar industrialization process. The technological changes involved in the Industrial Revolution began with improved agricultural techniques, which freed workers from the land and made it possible to provide food for a large non-agricultural population. New techniques of metal production, new uses for iron, steel, and other raw materials, and new power sources (initially steam but later also the *internal-combustion engine and electrical power) led to the rise of modern industrial methods and the *mass production of manufactured goods. Mechanization of manufacturing processes began in the textile industry, creating a demand both for machines and for tools for their manufacture in other industries. Work was organized into large factories, in which there was increased specialization and division of labour. Improved transport became necessary, and was provided initially by expansion of the *canal system, and later by the development of *railways and of *roads. The increased application of science to industry, and the modern definition of technology as the practical application of scientific knowledge, date from the period of the Industrial Revolution in Britain.

inertial navigation, a system of *gyroscopes and *accelerometers, mounted on an extremely stable platform and linked to a *computer that continuously monitors a vehicle's position and heading. The gyroscopes maintain the alignment of the platform horizontally, vertically, and in a north–south direction. Changes in the relationship of the vehicle to this stable platform are monitored to provide precise information about the vehicle's orientation, while velocity data is obtained from the accelerometers, which measure the vehicle's acceleration in the horizontal and (if necessary) vertical planes. The orientation and speed information is used by the computer to calculate the vehicle's position. Inertial navigation was first developed in 1942 by von *Braun for the V2 rocket: it is now used in submarines, ships, aircraft, spacecraft, and *guided missiles.

inflatable boat, a small craft obtaining its buoyancy from air contained in sealed tubes of waterproof material. The inflatable was suited to many World War II roles, for example commando attacks and life-saving operations, being a safe boat with good carrying capacity on the water, which could be deflated and folded into a compact portable item on shore. Subsequently, improvements in the technical properties of synthetic *rubberized fabric have led to widespread use of inflatables, usually with outboard motors, as *ships' boats, inshore *lifeboats, for exploration, as platforms for divers, and for recreation.

in-flight refuelling, the refuelling of an aircraft in flight to extend its range. A cone-shaped device (drogue) fitted to the end of a delivery hose is lowered from a tanker aircraft. The aircraft requiring fuel is fitted with an extended refuelling intake pipe (probe). Its pilot flies the aircraft up to the tanker aircraft until its probe engages into the drogue. Fuel is then transferred into his tanks and, when full, the drogue is released. In-flight refuelling is much used for *military aircraft, particularly *fighters and *helicopters.

information retrieval, the use of *computers to access information stored electronically. Digital computers were originally developed to perform calculations and process *data. Early systems were slow and had limited storage capacity, but with advances in technology, especially the development of fast, high-capacity magnetic disks, computers began to be used to store as well as process data. For many applications there are significant advantages over traditional paper-based storage. A computer, running suitable retrieval *software, can search vast quantities of data and recover information very rapidly. For example, many *databases containing medical, financial, or legal information are available on-line (directly under the control of the central processor) via computer *networks or *modems over telephone lines. With the continuing reduction in the cost of storage, and particularly the development of *compact discs, information retrieval is likely to become an increasingly important use for computers.

information technology (IT), the umbrella term used to describe the practical applications of *computer systems. The term has become prevalent with the increasing use of computers such as *word processors for office systems, but it also embraces the more traditional areas of *data processing and *information retrieval. Key factors in the recent rapid spread of microelectronics and information technology (often known simply as 'new technology') have been the drastic reduction in electronic hardware costs during the 1970s and 1980s; the so-called 'convergence' of *computing and *telecommunications (sometimes denoted by the term telematics); and the emergence of various formal standards and informal agreements within the IT industry.

The mass production of *microprocessors and other electronic components at low unit cost has made it possible to incorporate digital electronics into a wide range of products for commerce, industry, and the home. New technology has made an enormous impact on the design and performance of consumer goods, for example, cameras, video and hi-fi equipment, and personal computers. In offices and business, new technology was introduced for text processing, using dedicated (special-purpose) word processors. Now, however, it is usual to find general-purpose small computers and *workstations being exploited for a much wider range of office applications using special-purpose *application software such as financial planning packages, management support software, information storage and retrieval applications, *desk-top publishing, and so on. *Expert systems using *artificial intelligence techniques to aid decision-making can also be run on suitable personal computers.

The combination of computing with private and public telecommunication networks has been particularly significant in banking and retailing. *Bar codes on products can be read automatically at check-outs, and the information used both to print a customer's receipt and to reorder necessary stocks. *Electronic funds transfer using an 'intelligent' cash register or *point-of-sale terminal can then complete the cycle of electronic information flow by automatically debiting the customer's bank or credit-card account by the appropriate amount. Sales records held by the store's central computer can be used to develop overall retailing strategies; records of the purchasing patterns of particular customers can be exploited for direct marketing of goods or services.

The IT revolution has been just as great in the manufacturing and processing industries. An early application was the *numerical control of machine-tools, in which digital electronics were used to control lathes and other equipment. Now it has become common for a wide range of industrial equipment (sensors, control systems, robots, and so on) to incorporate microelectronics and to be interconnected (*networked) so that information can be gathered, communicated, and processed in order to optimize the activity. *Artificial intelligence, in which computer programs mimic certain aspects of human behaviour, is beginning to play a role in areas such as process control, as well as in *mechatronic products combining aspects of electronic, mechanical, and software engineering. Again, the convergence of telecommunications and computing has been a vital factor, allowing the computer to become fully integrated into the manufacturing or other processes (see *computer-integrated manufacturing), thus transcending individual applications such as *computer-aided design.

The introduction of new technology into areas which have not traditionally used computers has had a great influence on working practices. Some traditional tasks—or even whole categories of tasks—have disappeared completely and new ones have appeared. In some sectors (*printing in the UK, for example), adoption of new technology has led to serious industrial conflict.

Once it became commonplace for information retrieval and data processing to be carried out by digital computers in business and industrial settings, it was also natural for such information to be transmitted digitally using a range of new services; telecommunications has therefore become an essential part of many working environments. Small computers are often linked by means of local area networks within an office or company, so that expensive resources such as laser printers or databases can be shared; a further advantage of such networking is that in-house communication can then include *electronic mail, computer conferencing, or even voice messaging, as well as the traditional telephone and memo. Digital telecommunication links extend such facilities to the outside world, providing electronic communication between widely dispersed organizations or individuals, as well as access to external databases or information services. It is even becoming possible for certain employees to work partially or entirely from home, communicating with colleagues via a computer and *modem. There has yet to be a breakthrough in telematic services in the home. Information is already available electronically through *teletex services such as Ceefax and Oracle as well as call-up *videotex such as Prestel, but the market has often proved more limited than was originally envisaged. In the future, the combination of telecommunication services (including television), home computer, and new storage media such as videodisc and CD-ROM (see *compact disc) is likely to form the core of domestic entertainment and educational applications of IT.

All the above applications of new technology are based upon a *computer architecture which has remained virtually unchanged since the early days of the digital computer. Alternative structures such as *neural networks are currently arousing much interest, particularly for their potential in artificial-intelligence applications, while *parallel computing offers possibilities for faster processing. In the immediate future, however, further exploitation of new technology is more likely to result from a continuing expansion of telecommunications services and economies of scale in the provision of hardware than from radical changes to computer design.

information theory, the mathematical theory of communication that deals with the coding and transmission of information. Developed by the US engineer Claude Shannon in the 1940s, information theory is of central importance in analysing the requirements and limitations of *computer and *telecommunications systems. It offers a means of determining the quantity and speed of information transmission and uses statistical concepts, such as probability, to assess the extra information (redundancy) needed to compensate for distortion and losses that may occur during transmission. Information theory describes the capacity of a *channel, such as a telephone line, to transmit information reliably using error detection and correction techniques.

infra-red photography *photography.

ink, a *pigment mixed with a liquid or semi-liquid vehicle, used for writing or printing. Inks were first used in China *c.*2000 BC. Most early inks were a mixture of carbon, oil, and gum. Writing inks today are formulated for the *pens they serve—free-flowing water-based inks for fountain pens, and thicker, more concentrated mixtures for ball-points. In the 15th century varnish was introduced into printing ink, heralding the development of the many inks used today for *letterpress, *lithography, *gravure, and other processes. Apart from the differing pigments, vehicles, resins, and varnishes that they use, printing inks are now largely distinguished by their drying methods. Lithography and letterpress inks dry by penetration and oxidation; flexographic and gravure inks by evaporation; and newspaper inks mostly by absorption. Many of the web (continuous-paper) and some of the sheet-fed printing processes use hot air, infra-red, or ultraviolet radiation to force-dry the ink.

ink-jet printing, a form of computer-controlled printing developed during the 1970s. Ink is ejected under pressure from a fine nozzle as a series of tiny droplets. These droplets cross a small gap between the nozzle and the printing medium, and are precisely steered in flight so as to form the desired image on the printing surface. The positioning of the droplets on the print surface is controlled by a computer, which works from an electronic record of the image to be printed. Various methods of controlling the ink droplets in the air are used, and printers may have one ink-jet to scan the whole image, or an array of ink-jets, making much greater print speeds possible. Ink-jet printers are used in applications such as customized letters, where the information varies from one copy to the next.

inoculation *immunization.

input device (computing), a *peripheral which allows information from an external source to be fed into a computer system. The standard input device for most modern computer systems is a keyboard, similar to a typewriter's but with additional keys which provide a larger range of characters and control functions. Many computers are also equipped with a *mouse. Before the advent of *interactive systems, computers used punched card or paper-tape readers as their standard input devices. Many different input devices are available for more specialist applications. Scanners, digitizers, or even video cameras are used for *graphics systems. Point-of-sale terminals may have *bar-code readers. *Optical character recognition systems are used in banking, to read codes printed on cheques, or in *desk-top publishing systems to convert printed documents into *ASCII codes so that they can be stored and processed digitally.

insecticide, a *pesticide designed to kill insects. The term embraces both natural and chemical agents directed against insects, mites, nematodes, and molluscs. The earliest insecticides, pyrethrum, derris, and nicotine, were extracted from plants. Pyrethrum, obtained from flowers of the genus *Chrysanthemum*, is particularly effective and synthetic analogues have been produced. A major advance was the introduction of chlorinated *hydrocarbon (organochlorine) insecticides, such as *DDT. Persistent, and active against most pests, organochlorines found widespread use in the UK and USA during the 1950s and 1960s. Concerns over their safety have led to most of them being restricted or banned in the West. Today, the most important insecticides are the organophosphates and carbamates. They vary widely in individual persistence, toxicity, and selectivity, and can be formulated as liquid sprays and dips, dusts, granules, or pellets. Insecticides are used most heavily on cotton crops. Over-use of some compounds rapidly led to the extinction of some species of insects and to other species becoming resistant to their effects.

instrumentation, devices used for measurement and observation. In some contexts, the unaided human senses can be used for measurement and observation, for example skilled craftsmen can shape materials by eye, and metalworkers can judge the quality of their material during smelting by changes in colour. However, much of the progress in the fields of science and technology has relied on the development of instrumentation. Instruments may serve one or more of three functions. They may extend the range or scope of the human senses (for example, the *telescope or

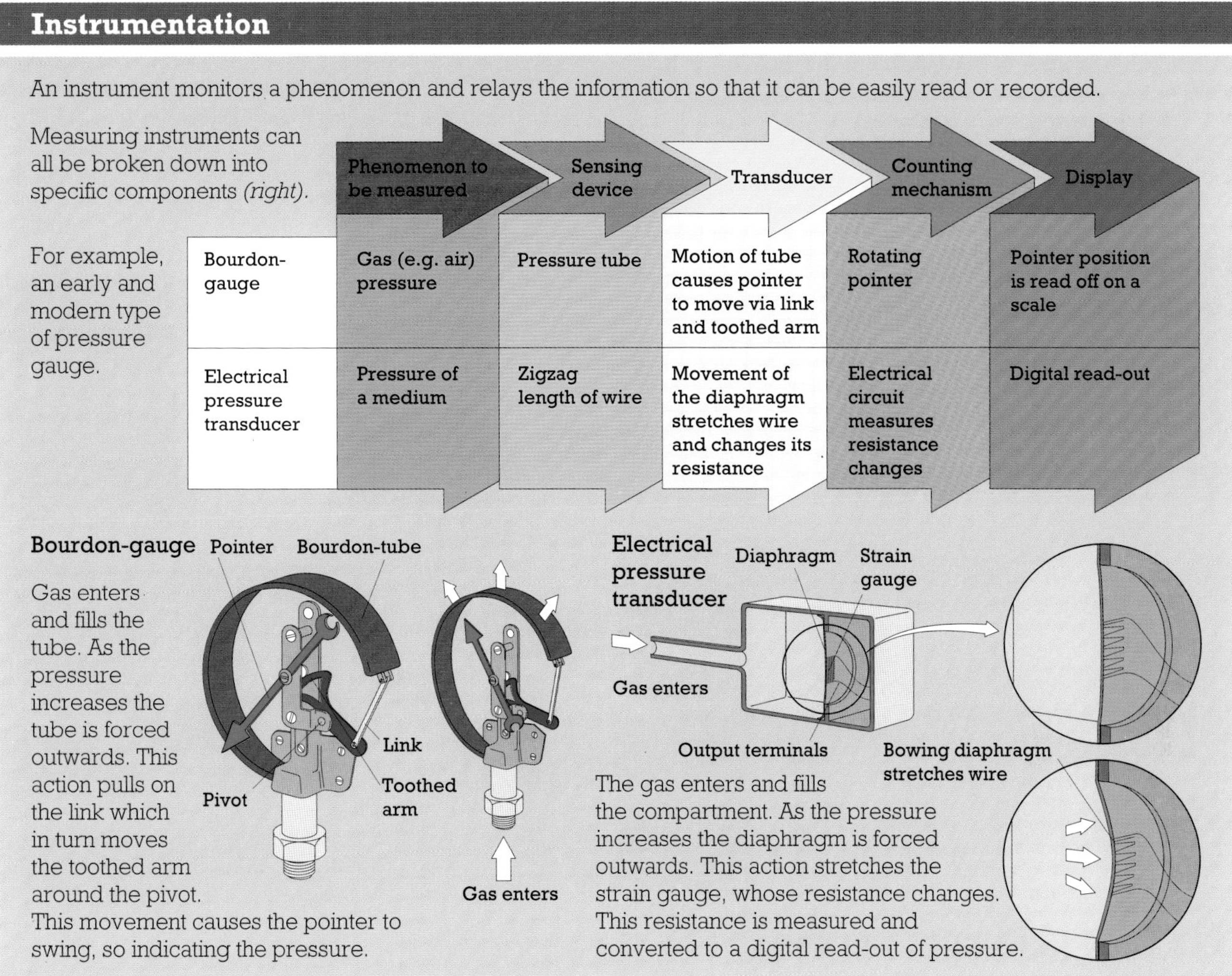

the *microphone); precisely quantify parameters that unaided can only be estimated (as in *length measurement, or in instruments for measuring wind-speed and direction); or allow the measurement of phenomena undetected by human senses (for example, *radio waves, magnetic flux, or *nuclear radiation).

Instrumentation
An instrument monitors a phenomenon and relays the information so that it can be easily read or recorded.
Measuring instruments can all be broken down into specific components (right).
Phenomenon to be measured
Sensing device
Transducer
Counting mechanism
Display
For example, an early and modern type of pressure gauge.
Bourdon-gauge
Gas (e.g. air) pressure
Pressure tube
Motion of tube causes pointer to move via link and toothed arm
Rotating pointer
Pointer position is read off on a scale
Electrical pressure transducer
Pressure of a medium
Zigzag length of wire
Movement of the diaphragm stretches wire and changes its resistance
Electrical circuit measures resistance changes
Digital read-out
Bourdon-gauge
Pointer
Bourdon-tube
Gas enters and fills the tube. As the pressure increases the tube is forced outwards. This action pulls on the link which in turn moves the toothed arm around the pivot. This movement causes the pointer to swing, so indicating the pressure.
Link
Toothed arm
Pivot
Gas enters
Electrical pressure transducer
Diaphragm
Strain gauge
Gas enters
Output terminals
Bowing diaphragm stretches wire
The gas enters and fills the compartment. As the pressure increases the diaphragm is forced outwards. This action stretches the strain gauge, whose resistance changes. This resistance is measured and converted to a digital read-out of pressure.

Astronomy, navigation, weighing, and surveying were early fields where precision instruments were developed. The commercial and fiscal importance of weighing led to the very early development of remarkably accurate balances and other *weighing machines. Early surveying instruments included measuring rods or chains, plumb-lines, and devices to indicate a level. The *armillary sphere and later the *astrolabe were early sighting instruments used for astronomical observation, probably among the most elaborate instruments of their time. Simpler navigational sighting instruments were the *cross-staff and the astrolabe, later superseded by sophisticated optical instruments like the *sextant. However, from around the 13th century in Europe, and a century earlier in China, the most important navigational instrument was the *magnetic compass.

The *Industrial Revolution of the 18th and 19th centuries saw the development of a whole new range of instruments, and the establishment of new standards of precision. The screw *micrometer, first developed in 1638, was greatly improved by mechanical engineers during the 19th century. Precision in measurement paved the way for the widespread adoption of *mass production, since parts could be made accurately enough to be interchangeable. The 19th century also saw the development of the *electricity industry, with the consequent need for electrical instruments such as the *galvanometer for measurement of current or voltage and the Wheatstone bridge for resistance measurement. A third important area of advance in the 19th century was in the field of analysis. Improvements in the *microscope, and the invention of analytical tools such as the *spectroscope and the *polarimeter, opened up new areas of investigation.

During the 20th century large numbers of instruments have been developed, many of them to serve the needs of the production and process industries. Instruments have become more precise and faster in their response, and automated continuous monitoring is important for many applications. New instruments were required early in the century for the new field of *radio communications, and for the pursuit of laboratory research. Increasingly, instruments operate electrically or electronically; the central component in such instruments is often a transducer, a device for converting one form of energy into another. In electrical instruments the transducer converts the energy of the variable being measured into an electrical signal (see figure). The field of chemical and physical analysis was transformed by the introduction of new instrumentation after World War II. Before this time such analysis was usually a slow process requiring fairly large samples of the material to be analysed. With the development of such instruments as the spectrophotometer (see *spectroscopy), the *mass spectrometer, and the gas *chromatograph, it became possible to perform rapid, accurate analyses on a very small sample of material.

Since the 1950s, many developments in the fields of electronics, telecommunications, and computing have affected instrumentation. The miniaturization possible with *integrated circuits has meant that many instruments or *sensors have become much smaller and more compact; new transducers, based on semiconductors, are also very small, and can in some cases be included in the integrated circuitry (see, for example, *photocell). *Telemetry (the transmission of instrument output to a distant location) is now widely used in the fields of meteorology, space exploration, and biomedical research. Computers can easily store, process, and display information received from several measuring instruments, and programs can be developed to display the information in different ways, and to correlate or combine data from different instruments. In certain applications (such as in *automatic pilots) the information supplied by the instruments is used to actuate control systems.

instrument landing system *automatic landing.

insulation, thermal, a process or material which inhibits the passage of *heat. The best possible insulator is a vacuum, in which neither conduction nor convection can occur. The *vacuum flask makes use of this, the insulation being further improved by silvered surfaces, which minimize radiation. Perfectly still air would also be a good insulator, but convection currents which circulate near any hot or cold surface serve to transmit heat. Foam insulating materials consist mainly of pockets of air small enough to inhibit these convection effects. The insulating quality of a building compon-

Integrated circuit

A microchip is made mostly of p–type silicon which is produced as a cylinder. It is sliced into wafers and on each wafer, hundreds of copies of the same microchip are formed. The wafer is then cut into individual chips.

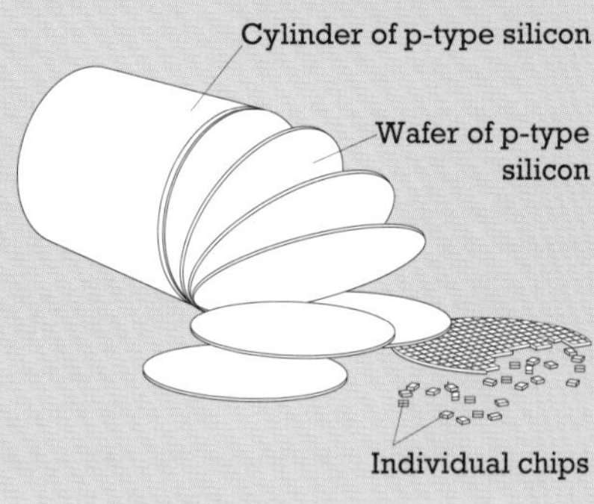

Detail of microchip

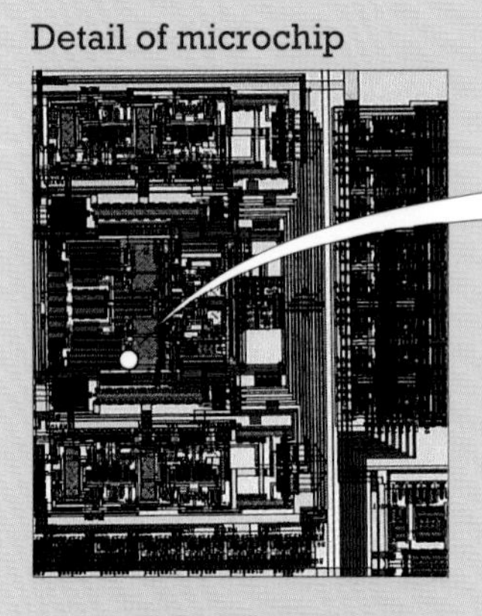

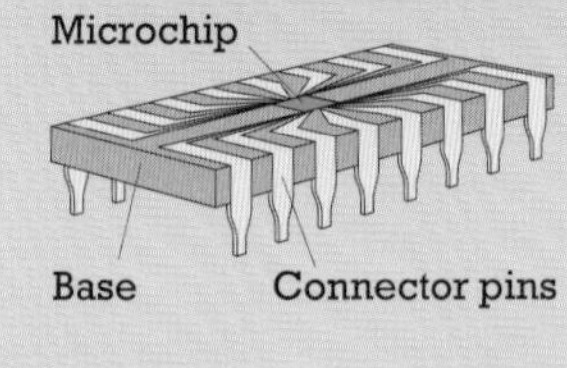

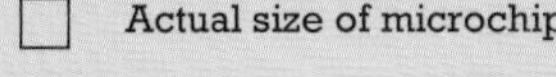
Actual size of microchip

Transistor

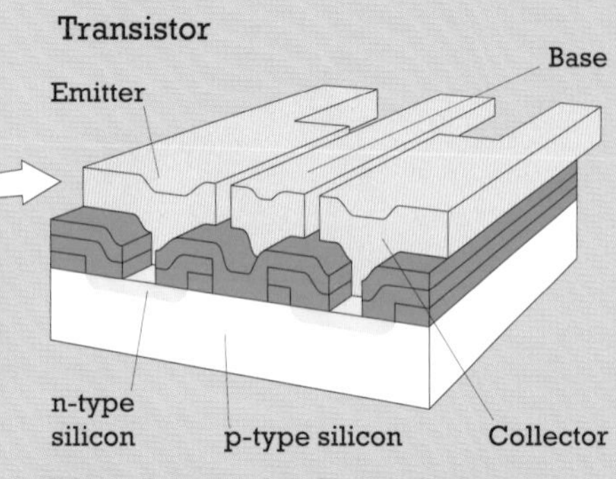

Many thousands of components may be present on one tiny microchip. This vastly enlarged view of a transistor is only one small portion of a chip.

The chip is dwarfed by the base and pins required to fit it into a computer's circuit board.

Manufacture of a microchip

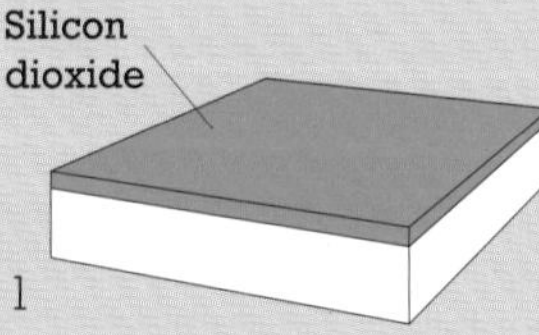

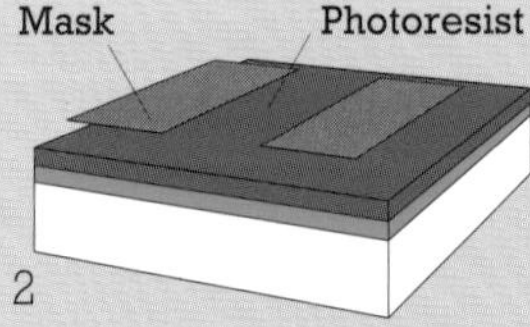

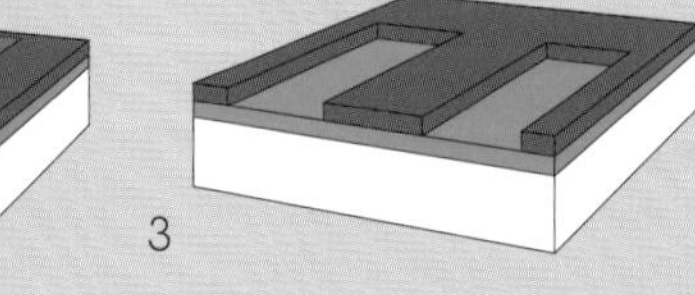

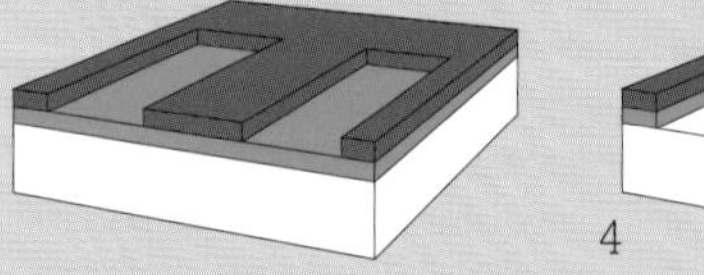

By heating the p-type silicon an insulating layer of silicon dioxide is formed on its surface.

A photoresistant layer is applied to the surface, and a light-opaque mask is placed on top of it (2). The chip is then exposed to ultraviolet light. This hardens the unmasked areas of photoresist; the masked areas remain soft. The soft areas of photoresist are washed away by solvent, exposing areas of the silicon dioxide beneath (3). The exposed areas of silicon dioxide are then washed away with hydrofluoric acid (4).

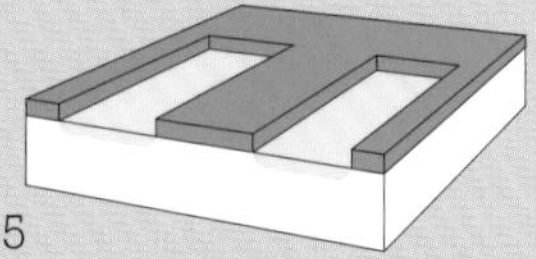

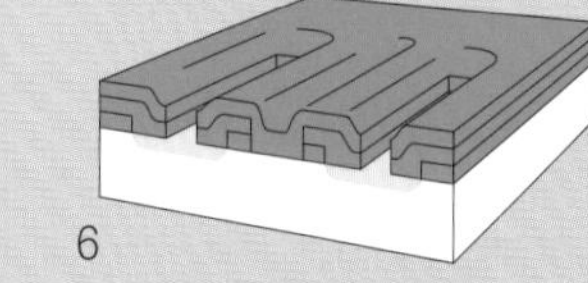

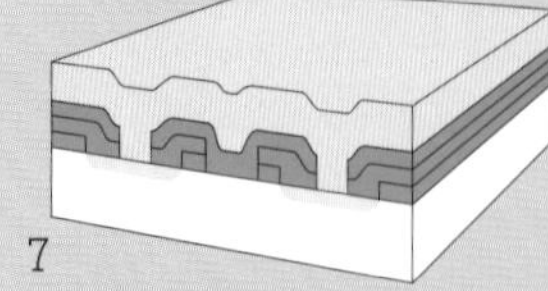

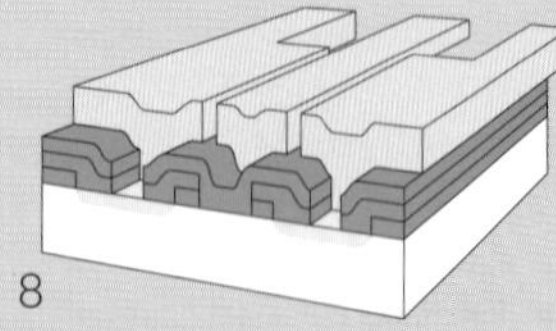

The photoresist is removed, exposing areas of p-type silicon which are converted to n-type (5), a process known as doping. Stages 2–4 are then repeated producing a multi-layered structure of silicon dioxide (6).

A layer of vaporized aluminium is deposited over the chip.

The aluminium is masked and etched to produce the components' connections.

ent is characterized by its U-value: the heat flow (in watts) through each square metre when there is a 1 °C difference between interior and exterior temperatures. U-values can be as high as 5 for a single pane of glass, or as little as 0.5 for a well-insulated outer wall.

insulator, electrical, a material that does not conduct *electricity, or does so only very weakly. Common electrical insulators include dry air, glass, porcelain, mica, some oils, most plastics, and rubbers. The *atoms and molecules of insulators, unlike conductors, have no free *electrons, so normal current conduction is impossible. However, if high enough voltages are applied across the insulator it will conduct, sometimes destructively. This is called 'breakdown'. Electrical insulators are used to cover or separate electrical conductors so that current and charge do not leak away from the desired path. The applications of insulators are very wide. Porcelain or glass insulators are used to support overhead power lines, rubber and plastics to cover conventional *cables, and silicon dioxide films are usually used to provide electrical insulation and a dielectric material for *capacitor construction in *integrated circuits.

insulin *hormone.

intaglio printing, a printing process in which the image is *engraved, scratched, or *etched into the surface of the printing plate. The plate is then coated with printing ink and the surface rubbed clean, leaving ink in the grooves. High pressure transfers the ink from the plate to paper. *Flexography and *gravure are also intaglio processes.

integrated circuit (IC), a single chip of silicon or other suitable semiconductor carrying a complete electronic circuit, manufactured as one unit. Each chip contains *transistors, *diodes, *resistors, and *capacitors as the main building blocks of the electronic circuit. The principles of semiconductor integrated circuits were first put forward in the late 1950s by Geoffrey Dummer working in the UK and Jack Kilby in the USA. The first practical circuits were made in the USA by Texas Instruments in 1959. The integrated circuit underpins all microelectronics technology. The manufacture of an integrated circuit is a complex process, which may embody fifty or more separate stages. Silicon chips are made from specially grown, extremely pure, tubular silicon crystals up to 1 m (3.3 feet) long and 15 cm (6 inches) in diameter. The crystals are first sliced into wafers or circular discs. Individual, identical chips are made simultaneously on each wafer in a series of optical and chemical processes (see figure). These processes introduce specific impurities into defined areas of the chip, forming *semiconductor devices. The devices are connected electrically by deposits of aluminium, and the wafer is then broken into separate chips, which are individually encapsulated. Integrated circuits can serve many functions. *Microprocessor chips carry out arithmetical operations and can control other circuits. The latest dynamic random-access *memory chips (DRAMs) can store up to 4 million *bits of data. Other chips may carry computer programs, and applications-specific circuits are tailored to the requirements of a particular device.

intensive-care unit (ICU), a specialist hospital ward dedicated to the (usually short-term) monitoring, treatment, and nursing of life-threatening conditions. A unit may be devoted to the care of patients with respiratory failure (see *respirator) or renal failure (see *haemodialysis). Other spe-

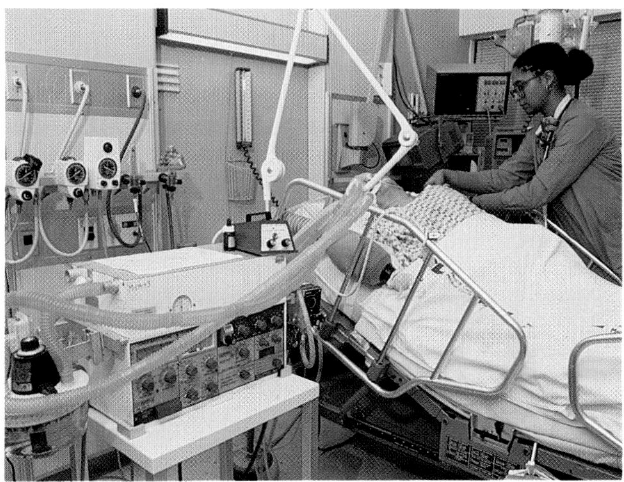

A nurse attending a patient on a respirator in an **intensive-care unit**.

cialist ICUs deal with people having severe burns, or premature babies, or patients who have had cardiac surgery or a heart attack. Some patients admitted to ICUs require immediate support of the function of one or more vital organs, using drugs or machines; for other patients, constant monitoring may be sufficient. ICUs are expensive to run because of the equipment and staffing levels needed, and their availability is limited. Not all patients who might benefit from treatment can be admitted. In some cases of coma, intensive-care can sustain life functions when there is little prospect of the patient's recovering consciousness. Such instances led in the late 1960s to the description of the state of 'brain death', which provided a criterion for deciding whether to switch off life-support machinery.

interactive system, a *computer system which responds to instructions from the user as they are given. The system responds fast enough to allow transactions to be completed almost continuously. The success or failure of each transaction is immediately obvious from the way in which the computer responds. The instructions are input via a device such as a *mouse or keyboard.

interceptor aircraft *fighter aircraft.

intercontinental ballistic missile (ICBM) *ballistic missile.

intercropping, the practice of growing one crop between rows of another. The technique is used both by conventional and by *organic farmers: the by-products of one crop can provide nutrients, shade, or support to the other and can encourage insects that eat the pests of the neighbouring crop. Intercropping also ensures that the earth is never left totally bare and exposed to erosion by wind or rainfall.

interface (computing), the boundary or channel between different components of a *computer system through which information is transferred. The main components of a computer system—the *central processing unit, *memory, and *disk store—are normally interfaced via an internal *bus, which allows extremely rapid transfer of data between them. A *peripheral, such as a *printer or *terminal, is usually connected to a computer system via either *parallel or *serial interfaces. A number of interface standards exist describing such features as the physical layout of connectors, the values of electrical signals, and the way in which signals are interpreted. Some interfaces contain circuitry to translate between the otherwise incompatible signals of the components being connected. By analogy, the way in which a human user interacts with a computer system is frequently called the user interface or the human–computer interface (HCI). The term graphic user interface is often applied to the use of *graphics to provide an interactive and user-friendly interface between computer and user. Phrases such as menu interface, window interface, or mouse interface are often used to describe specific characteristics of the user interface to computer systems or an *applications program.

interference, spurious signals which disturb the signal in any communication system. Interference may arise from *electromagnetic induction affecting radio and television reception. The source of the transmission may be automobile engines, machines, even refrigerators and personal computers, or interference picked up from the mains. Electronic equipment containing tracking or wiring that acts as a primitive antenna system will often receive or generate interference. Filtering and enclosing sensitive equipment in a shielded housing (*earthing) often eliminates most interference, while use of *optical fibres, which possess no metallic tracking, greatly reduces the problem. (See also *wave.)

interferometer, an instrument in which interference between two beams of light (or other type of *wave) from a common source is used to make precise measurements of length or displacement. In astronomy, interferometers are used to measure the sizes of stars: they can also be used to plot the positions of radio stars, by comparing the phases of radio signals from a star as received by two precisely spaced antennae. In space exploration, interferometers are used in space vehicle guidance and tracking systems. Acoustic interferometers are used to measure the velocity and absorption of sound waves. Interferometers using *laser light can make short linear measurements with an accuracy of better than 0.5 μm (2×10^{-5} inches). (See also *length measurement.)

interferon, a protein discovered by *Isaacs in 1957, produced by cells when they are attacked by viruses. Interferons inhibit the growth of the virus and are an important first stage in the development of immunity, before the appearance of antibodies (see *immunology). Because they are present only in minute amounts, however, it is difficult to obtain them pure and in quantities sufficient for clinical purposes. It has been suggested that interferons would be useful in treating diseases such as herpes and hepatitis, but trials have yielded very disappointing results. Interferons may protect patients having undergone immunosuppression from dangerous viral infections. They inhibit the growth of some tumours and offer a promising form of *cancer treatment.

intermediate technology *appropriate technology.

internal-combustion engine, a heat-engine in which the fuel is burnt within the *engine itself so that the working fluid is a hot gas, produced by combustion of air and fuel. Thus it is distinguished from an external combustion system such as a *steam-engine, where fuel is burnt in a *boiler to provide steam as the working fluid. The flow of hot gas may be continuous, as in a *gas-turbine, or intermittent, as in a *reciprocating engine or a *rotary engine. Uses of reciprocating piston engines are widespread; on land they are used for purposes such as electricity generation, for pumping, and for combined heat and power (CHP) production, in which otherwise wasted heat is used for heating purposes. At sea, *diesel engines are almost universal except in outboard motors, where *petrol engines are used, and in naval vessels, which use gas-turbines. In the air the petrol engine dominated until the advent of the jet engine, and piston engines are still used in small aircraft. By far the largest use of internal-combustion engines is in land vehicles: diesel engines in lorries, coaches, tractors, and locomotives, and petrol engines in motor cycles and motor cars.

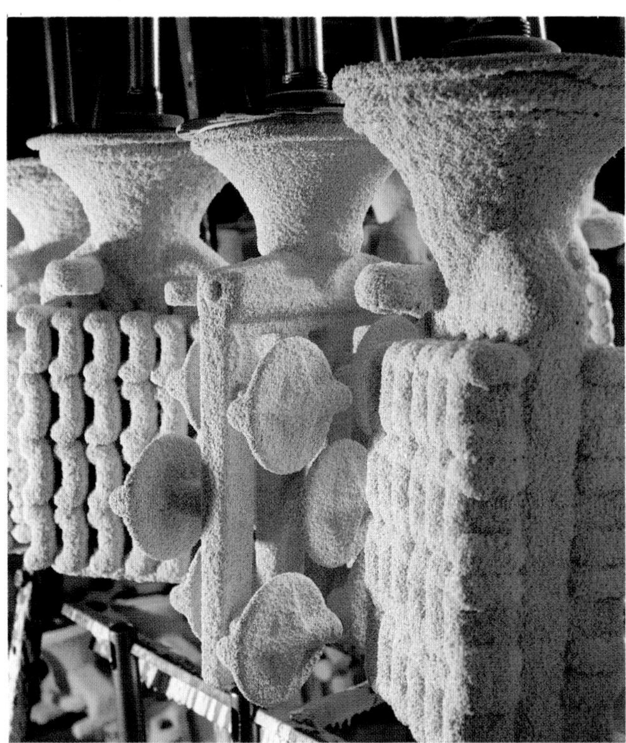

Rows of ceramic moulds being used for **investment casting**. The ceramic cast is made by coating a wax pattern with liquid ceramic, and then drying it in air and ammonia.

International Atomic Energy Agency (IAEA), an international agency of the United Nations Organization, founded in 1957 and located in Vienna, to promote the peaceful uses of atomic energy for the purposes of improving world health and prosperity. The IAEA maintains a number of laboratories, including the International Centre for Theoretical Physics (Trieste, Italy) and the International Laboratory of Marine Radioactivity (Monaco), and has a specialist division—run jointly with the Food and Agriculture Organization—concerned with the uses of *radioactive isotopes in food and agricultural production.

International Telecommunication Union (ITU), an organization founded in Paris in 1865 as the International Telegraph Union; it became a specialized agency of the United Nations in 1947. Its role is to promote and co-ordinate *telegraph, *telephone, and *radio services worldwide, including space telecommunications. It is responsible for allocating and registering radio-frequency *wavebands.

interpreter (computing), a piece of software that translates a computer program directly into a series of computer actions. Programs written in a high-level language such as BASIC are translated and executed a line at a time. Interpreters are better for interactive programming, but the resulting programs run more slowly than if a *compiler were used.

intra-uterine device (IUD) *contraception.

invar, an alloy of iron containing 36 per cent nickel with small amounts of carbon, manganese, and silicon. It has a negligible coefficient of thermal expansion: that is, it does not expand or contract on heating or cooling. It is used for measuring tapes and pendulum rods, and in precision instruments and *thermostats.

investment casting ('lost-wax' or *cire perdue* process), an ancient process for *casting small, three-dimensional complex metal objects such as jewellery or small industrial parts. A gelatine mould is made from a metal original, and is filled with wax or plastic. The wax form is then coated with a heat-resistant clay or cement to form a second mould. This mould is baked, hardening the clay but melting the wax, which is poured away to leave a void that reflects the shape and surface detail of the original item. Molten metal can then be poured into the mould. On cooling, the metal solidifies and the cast item is released by breaking the mould.

'in vitro' fertilization (IVF, 'test-tube' baby technique), a technique for helping infertile couples to conceive, in

Iron and steel industry (steel-making)

Steelmaking involves the removal of excess carbon from the iron produced by a blast furnace.

Bessemer converter

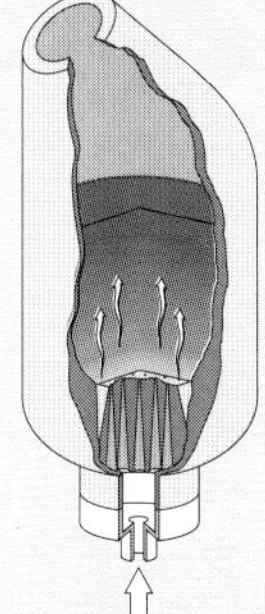

Molten iron straight from the blast furnace is poured into the converter. Air blown through the bottom of the converter passes through the iron, removing excess carbon, manganese, and silicon. After 12 minutes the converter is discharged.

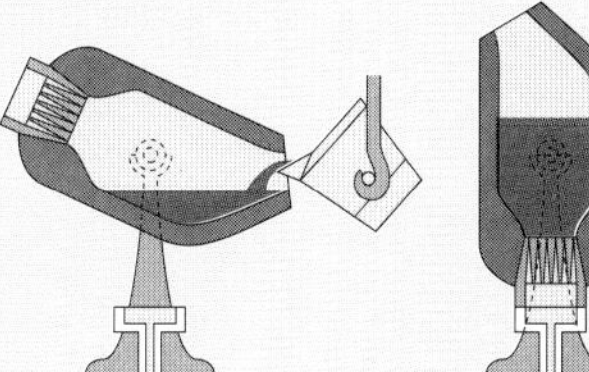

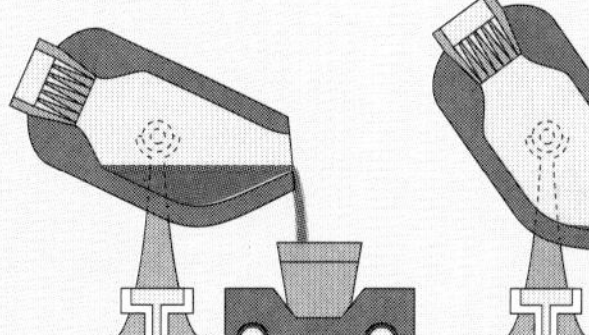

Siemens–Martin process

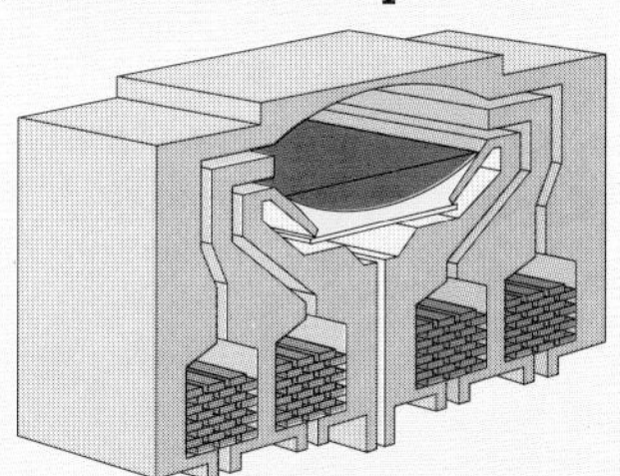

A fuel and air mixture is burned above the scrap and pig-iron. Air enters from one side of the furnace and hot gases leave by the other side through brickwork which absorbs much of the heat. When the air-flow is reversed this heat returns to the furnace.

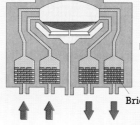

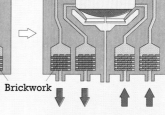

Brickwork
Air enters
Cooled gases leave
Cooled gases leave
Air enters

Electric-arc process

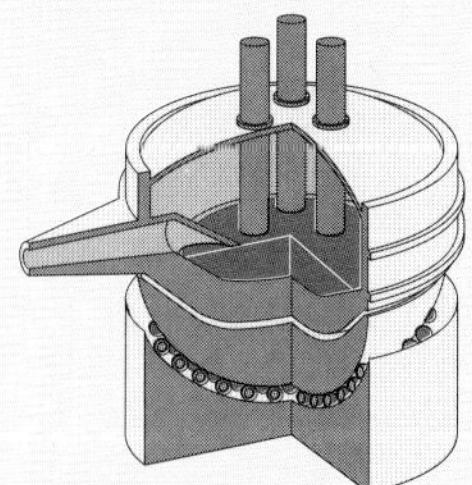

Three graphite electrodes carry a large electric current into the furnace. An electric arc passes between the electrodes and the charge (scrap and pig-iron), providing the heat for the process.

During meltdown
Electric arc
Pig-iron
Scrap iron

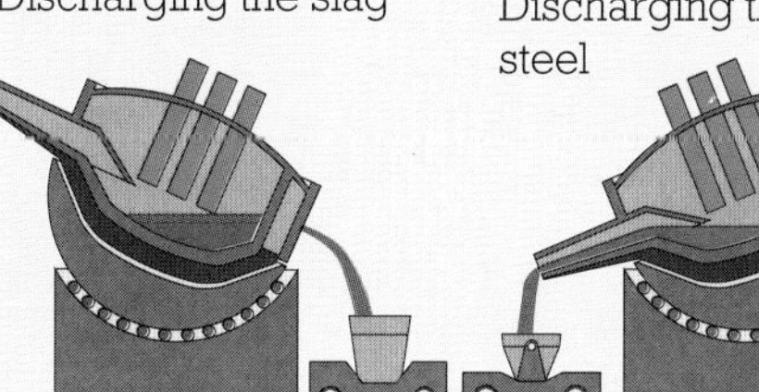

Basic oxygen process

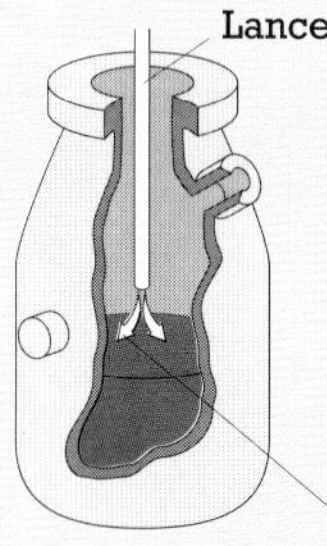

The lance delivers pure oxygen to the surface of the molten iron. The oxygen burns away the excess carbon, producing steel. This burning carbon provides enough heat to keep the iron molten.

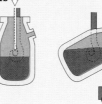

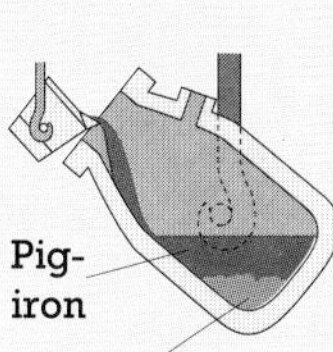

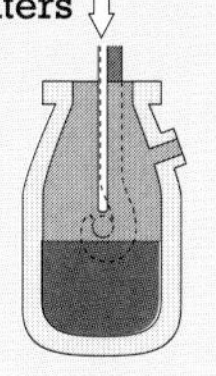

Discharging the steel

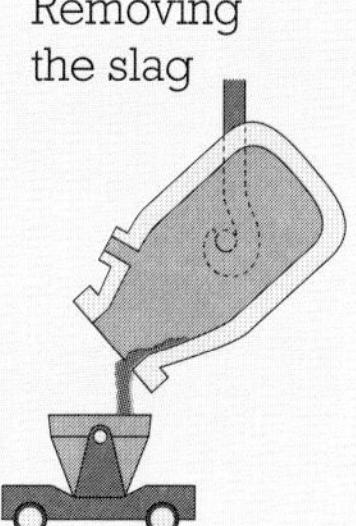

which a woman is induced to produce eggs (ovulate) by *hormone treatment. The eggs are then removed and fertilized in the laboratory (*in vitro*) by her partner's sperm. The resulting early embryos are checked for normal development before being placed in the woman's uterus to continue growing until birth. The technique is also used in animals, to produce a large number of offspring from the eggs of one female. The embryos are placed in the uteri of other, surrogate mothers, suitably treated with hormones to maintain the pregnancy. Unless the patients are chosen very carefully, the success rate of *in vitro* fertilization in humans is very low. IVF in animals, however, is widely used with success.

iodine (symbol I, at. no. 53, r.a.m. 126.90), a black, crystalline solid element that sublimes (changes directly from solid to gas when heated) to form a purple vapour. It is essential in the human diet. It is obtained mainly from a mineral found in Chile called caliche, but can also be extracted from seaweed. It is used in quartz-halogen lamps, to make photographic materials, and as an antiseptic. Iodine is concentrated in the body in the thyroid gland: a *radioactive isotope of iodine is used in medicine to check for abnormal activity of the thyroid (see *nuclear medicine).

ion, an *atom or molecule that has gained or lost one or more electrons, and therefore has either a positive or a negative charge. Solids such as *salts are made up of positive and negative ions held together by electrostatic forces: in solution in water such ionic solids dissociate into their constituent ions. Ions may be produced in a gas by the action of high-energy *electromagnetic radiation, or by an electron beam. The *Geiger–Müller counter, the *mass spectrometer, and other devices make use of this latter property for their operation. Ions in solution or in a gas can act as conductors of electricity, as in an electric cell or *battery.

ion-exchange resin, an insoluble polymer in the form of small granules that is used to remove *ions from solutions. In water softeners, the resin contains active sites that exchange their sodium ions (which do not cause hardness) for magnesium and calcium ions (ions in the water that cause hardness). When the active sites become spent, the resin can be regenerated by treatment with sodium chloride (*salt) solution.

ion implantation, the insertion of atoms of controlled impurities just below the surface of a pure substance by the use of highly energetic *ion beams. The material to be implanted (usually phosphorus, boron, or arsenic) is ionized and the ions accelerated to high energies by a special *particle accelerator. On reaching a surface they penetrate a little way before coming to rest within the material. The technique is used to 'dope' *semiconductor devices (insert controlled amounts of impurity into a pure semiconductor in order to obtain particular electrical characteristics). It is also used to produce hard, wear-resistant surface layers.

ionizer, an electrical appliance for increasing the concentration of free positive oxygen and nitrogen *ions in the atmosphere of a room. This is reputed to impart a feeling of well-being to those in the room. Ionizers are either free-standing units or an integral part of an *air-conditioning system. A positive potential difference of several kV is applied to a number of pointed electrodes. A fan passes air over these electrodes, which ionize the atmospheric oxygen and nitrogen molecules. The electrodes also clean the air by attracting charged pollutant particles.

iridium (symbol Ir, at. no. 77, r.a.m. 192.22), a hard, unreactive element, one of the *platinum metals. It is found free in nature, usually associated with other platinum metals and mixed with gold, silver, copper, nickel, or iron. Mixed with platinum, it produces very hard alloys used for the tips of fountain-pen nibs, surgical tools, and chemical equipment.

iron (symbol Fe, at. no. 26, r.a.m. 55.85), a silvery-grey ferromagnetic metal. The main ores are haematite (Fe_2O_3), and magnetite (Fe_3O_4). Iron is made by heating iron oxide, the ore's main constituent, with carbon (from *coke). The carbon reacts with oxygen to form carbon dioxide, releasing the iron. In the *blast-furnace carbon is provided in the form of *coke. The resulting pig-iron is brittle and contains 3–4 per cent carbon and other impurities. Cast iron is made from pig-iron by re-melting and cooling. It is especially useful in *casting. Wrought iron is produced from pig-iron by *puddling. It has less than 0.2 per cent carbon, is malleable and ductile, and was used for making chains, anchors, bolts, and ornamental frameworks until it was superseded by mild *steel. Iron oxide (Fe_2O_3) is a red powder used as a paint pigment. Iron sulphate ($FeSO_4{\cdot}7H_2O$) is employed as a weed-killer and wood preservative and in the manufacture of inks, dyes, and pigments. Pharmaceuticals containing iron are important for treating anaemia. (See also *iron and steel industry.)

An iron is also an appliance for removing creases from *textiles using heat and pressure. Simple flat-irons were in common use by the 17th century and consisted of an elongated triangular plate of cast iron fitted with a handle. These were heated on a fire or stove; later, they were internally heated by charcoal and then by coal, gas or paraffin. Modern irons are heated electrically and are maintained at the appropriate temperature by a *thermostat. Some types also produce steam from an internal water reservoir to facilitate the removal of creases. Other types of iron are cordless and rechargeable. Some industrial irons have a rotary motion.

iron and steel industry, the industry that extracts *iron from its ore and produces iron and *steel. Iron and its derivative steel are the most widely used metals: most tools and machinery are made from one or the other. Iron was originally made from its ore in small-scale smelting operations, using charcoal as the source of carbon. The introduction of the *blast-furnace to England at the beginning of the 16th century enabled pig-iron to be produced continuously. The use of coke as the reducing agent was pioneered by *Darby at the beginning of the 18th century. *Puddling, the process of producing wrought iron, was invented by *Cort in 1783. In 1828 the British engineer James Neilson used pre-heated air to improve the efficiency of the furnaces.

To convert pig-iron into *steel, it is necessary to reduce its carbon content to between about 0.1 and 1 per cent, depending on the type of steel being made. Steel was made on a small scale from early times, and *Huntsman's crucible process could make steel in batches of 100 kg (220 pounds). However, until the mid-19th century there was no large-scale steel-making process. In the 1850s *Bessemer in the UK and *Kelly in the USA developed furnaces for the conversion of large tonnages of pig-iron into structural steel (see figure on page 185). However, the Bessemer converter was not very successful initially and, despite being improved by

The **Iron Bridge** spanning the River Severn at Coalbrookdale, Shropshire, UK. The main structural units of the bridge are 20 m (66 feet) long.

Sidney Thomas in 1878 so that it could use pig-iron with a high phosphorus content, it still met commercial resistance. At about the same time, Charles *Siemens in association with the brothers Émile and Pierre Martin developed the *open-hearth process for the conversion of pig-iron to steel. In 1879 the disastrous collapse of the Tay Bridge in Scotland undermined confidence in wrought and cast iron for structural purposes and there was renewed interest in both the Bessemer and open-hearth processes, resulting in their becoming the major means of producing steel. With the increasing availability of electricity in the 20th century, the *electric-arc furnace was developed for the production of high-grade alloy steels. In the 1950s the Linz–Donawitz (LD) process was developed in Austria. Sometimes called the basic oxygen process or oxygen-lance process, it is used to convert pig-iron from the blast-furnace into usable steel. A jet of pure oxygen is blown into a molten mixture of pig-iron and scrap steel, converting the non-metallic impurities to oxides, which either escape as gases or form a slag floating on the surface. Four hundred tonnes of molten iron can be converted to steel in about 12 minutes. The process thus combines the low capital cost of the Bessemer process with the high-quality product of the open-hearth process, and is now the major means of steel production in many countries.

Once produced, liquid steel can be converted into a variety of forms required by manufacturing industry. It may be cast into one of three types of ingot. 'Killed' steel contains no dissolved oxygen, so that the ingot solidifies without releasing gas. The resulting ingot is non-porous and is used where high strength and resistance to impact are needed or where *welding is required. A 'rimming' steel contains dissolved oxygen that reacts with carbon in the steel to form carbon monoxide gas, which is released at the interface during solidification. This gives a skin (rim) on the ingot which is almost free of carbon and impurities; this steel is rolled and used in products such as car bodies, where surface quality is important. 'Semi-killed' steel is only partially deoxidized before solidification; it is used in some structural applications. Ingots can be rolled, hammered, pressed, or drawn to produce the required shapes. Alternatively, the liquid steel may be cast continuously: as the steel solidifies it is trapped between rolls and handled as a solid bar.

Steel is particularly useful as a structural material because it is strong and stiff, is easy to obtain from ores that are widely available, and is readily shaped through *forging, rolling, and *extrusion. However, it has the major disadvantage that it corrodes easily; although there are special (and expensive) *stainless steels that resist corrosion, these are not used for general structural purposes. Steel can be protected by painting, *electroplating, *galvanizing, or by cathodic protection (see *corrosion). A large range of steels with widely differing properties can be made by alloying steel with different metals. Exceptional degrees of strength, stiffness, toughness, hardness, and magnetism can be obtained.

Iron Bridge (Coalbrookdale Iron Bridge), the world's first all-iron bridge, built in 1779 across the River Severn in Shropshire, UK. It was designed by the British ironmaster Abraham Darby III (grandson of *Darby), and erected by him in only three months. The bridge sections, weighing up to 6 tonnes, were cast in Darby's Coalbrookdale ironworks. The sections were connected together by mortise-and-tenon joints to form five semicircular ribs, which together formed a single arched span of 30 m (100 feet) supporting a roadway 7 m (24 feet) wide. (See the photograph on page 187.)

ironclad, a large warship built of iron or steel, or with iron (or steel) plates covering the existing wooden hull to protect it from explosive shell-fire. The first true ironclad was the French wooden *frigate *Gloire* (1859), which had iron plates covering its hull to below the water-line; the second, built entirely of iron with an internal wooden backing, was the British *battleship *Warrior*, launched in 1860. The name remained in use for iron or steel warships until the 1880s, when it began to be dropped in favour of battleship.

iron lung *respirator.

irradiation (food), a method of *food preservation in which harmful micro-organisms are destroyed by controlled doses of radiation. High doses of radiation kill all organisms in food, but also produce an unpleasant taste. Lower doses kill most micro-organisms, but do not markedly affect food flavour. At present few countries allow food to be irradiated, and those that do impose very strict controls. There are fears that changes caused by irradiation, such as the production of highly reactive substances known as free radicals, may be harmful. Another problem with irradiation is that though the micro-organisms themselves are killed, any toxins that they may have produced remain in the food.

irrigation, supply of water to land to grow crops or to increase crop yields. The amount of water used or lost to the atmosphere by crops, minus the annual rainfall, determines the quantity of irrigation water needed. In traditional irrigation systems, water is spread over the ground surface. Efficiency is between 40 and 75 per cent, and such systems are relatively inexpensive to build and maintain. Sprinkler and trickle-feed systems are generally between 60 and 80 per cent efficient, but have high capital and maintenance costs; they are suited to high-value crops. In 'basin' irrigation—commonly used in paddy-fields for growing rice—the ground is levelled and a low bund (embankment) retains the irrigation water. 'Furrow' and 'border' methods, with sloping ground for drainage, suit crops that cannot tolerate waterlogging. All irrigation water contains some salts in solution; an increase in salinity can cause a reduction in soil fertility if the water applied is insufficient to leach the salts from around the plant roots. (See also *agriculture.)

Isaacs, Alick (1921–67), British virologist and discoverer of *interferon. At Sheffield University, he began the research on influenza which became his main preoccupation. He then spent two years in Australia before returning to the UK to work at the National Institute for Medical Research. His research into the known phenomenon that one *virus can suppress the growth of an unrelated virus within the same cell led to the discovery of interferon in 1957 and revealed the existence of a hitherto unsuspected natural defence mechanism against viruses.

isotope, one of two or more forms of an element having the same number of protons in their nucleus, but different numbers of neutrons (see *atoms and molecules). Isotopes have the same chemical properties, but show slight differences in physical properties, and may differ markedly in their nuclear properties (for example, radioactivity). Many elements have more than one isotope, and heavier elements may have as many as twelve. Separation of the isotopes of uranium is important in the manufacture of *nuclear fuels.

IVF **in vitro* fertilization.

J

Jacquard, a mechanism invented in 1801 by Joseph-Marie Jacquard (1754–1834), for automating the weaving of patterned fabrics. The lifting of the *warp threads, carried out by assistants on earlier draw *looms, was placed under the control of the weaver. A system of perforated cards controlled the rise and fall of the warp threads to produce the desired pattern; the system was operated with a treadle. Punched-card control systems derived from the Jacquard were later used in a number of early computers, including *Babbage's analytical engine (1832), *Hollerith's punched-card machines (1887), and an early modern computer (the ASCC in 1944). In modern weaving machines, punched-card Jacquards have largely been replaced by Jacquard mechanisms controlled by *microprocessors.

Jenner, Edward (1749–1823), British physician who pioneered vaccination. After training under the surgeon John Hunter in London, Jenner set up in 1773 as a medical practitioner in Berkeley, Gloucestershire. Aware of a local tradition that those who had had cowpox were immune to smallpox, he showed experimentally that this belief had a factual basis. He published his results in 1798; this led to the widespread use of cowpox for vaccination against smallpox. By 1800 some 100,000 people had been immunized, and a dramatic decrease in the death-rate from smallpox resulted.

jet engine, term used to describe the *gas-turbine engines used in aircraft, in which the thrust is generated by a jet of exhaust gas discharged from a nozzle at the rear of the engine. Jet engines were developed concurrently in the UK and in Germany. *Whittle's centrifugal flow turbojet was patented in 1930 and first tested later in the same year. The first jet aeroplane to fly was the German Heinkel He. 178 in 1939, powered by an engine designed by von *Ohain. In a turbojet, air is taken into the engine and compressed, then mixed with fuel and burnt. The combustion gases then pass through a turbine, the power from which drives the *compressor, after which the remaining energy in the gas is converted to kinetic energy in the exhaust cone and propelling nozzle, and ejected as a high-velocity jet (see figure). The configuration of the propelling nozzle is critical for maximum efficiency at a given speed. Turbojets are most efficient at high speeds: for speeds below 800 km/h (500 m.p.h.) a more efficient type of engine is the turboprop. This works on the same principle as the turbojet, but most of the

Jet engine

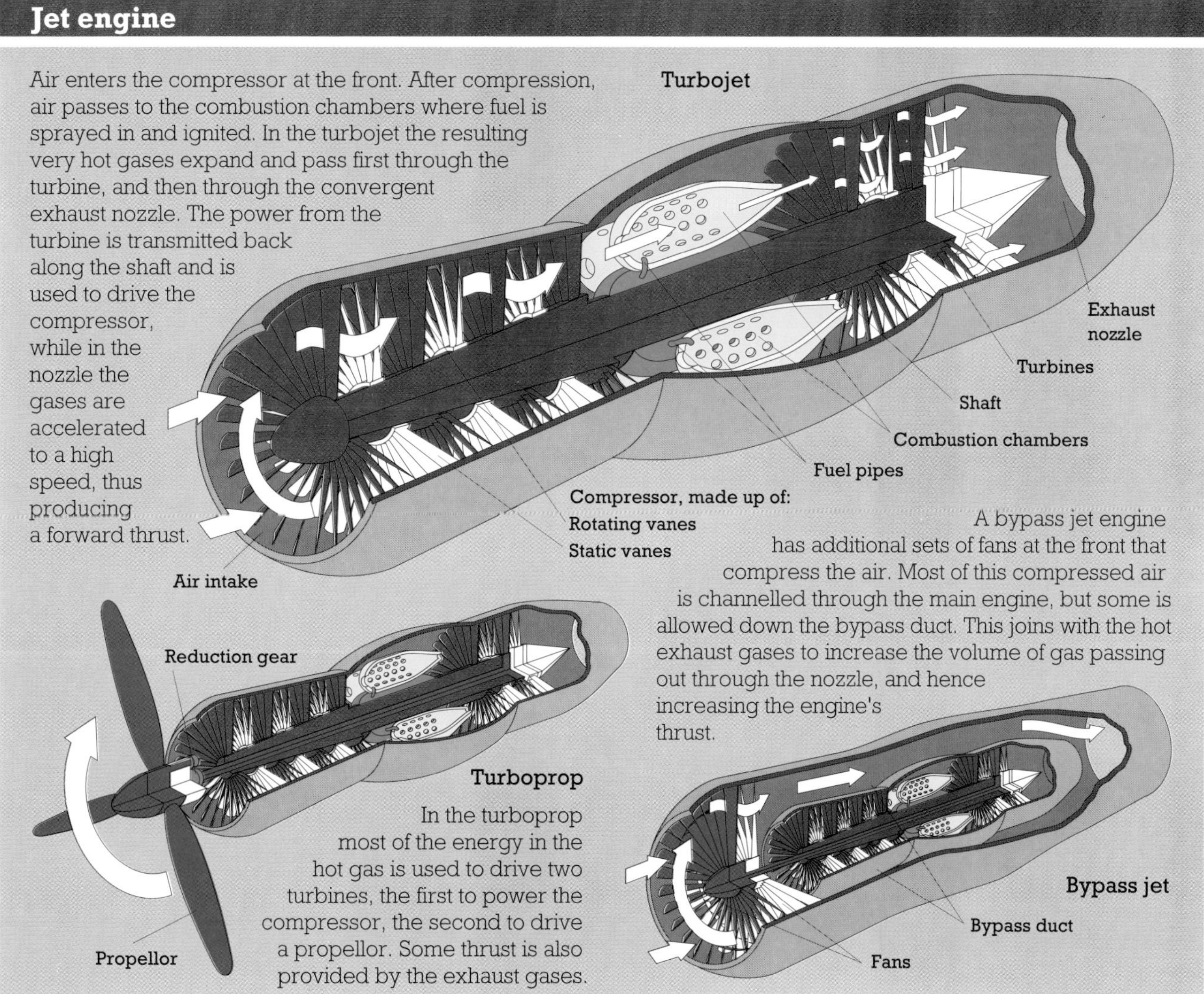

Air enters the compressor at the front. After compression, air passes to the combustion chambers where fuel is sprayed in and ignited. In the turbojet the resulting very hot gases expand and pass first through the turbine, and then through the convergent exhaust nozzle. The power from the turbine is transmitted back along the shaft and is used to drive the compressor, while in the nozzle the gases are accelerated to a high speed, thus producing a forward thrust.

A bypass jet engine has additional sets of fans at the front that compress the air. Most of this compressed air is channelled through the main engine, but some is allowed down the bypass duct. This joins with the hot exhaust gases to increase the volume of gas passing out through the nozzle, and hence increasing the engine's thrust.

In the turboprop most of the energy in the hot gas is used to drive two turbines, the first to power the compressor, the second to drive a propellor. Some thrust is also provided by the exhaust gases.

energy of the combustion gases drives the turbine, which is used to power a propeller as well as the compressor. A small amount of forward thrust is also obtained from the exhaust gases. A major use of turboprop engines is in *helicopters. In the bypass jet engine two air compressors, one low-pressure and one high-pressure, are used. After passage through the first, low-pressure compressor, part of the air intake bypasses the combustion chamber and turbine. The combination of this cold air jet and the hot exhaust jet gives a much larger mass of air and therefore increased thrust, without an increase in fuel consumption. This principle is taken even further in the turbofan engine, which incorporates a large fan to accelerate still more air outside the engine proper, as well as using the bypass principle. Current research priorities include the reduction of polluting emissions from jet engines, and the development of *ceramic engine components, which are lighter and can work at higher temperatures than metals. (See also *ram-jet.)

joinery *carpentry and joinery.

joint, woodworking *woodworking joint.

joule *energy, *unit.

jumbo jet *wide-bodied aircraft.

junk, a flat-bottomed, high-sterned sailing vessel, common to seas in the Far East and used especially by the Chinese. Junks developed in China from about 1500 BC. Over seventy different types are now found, though all junks have essentially similar characteristics. The hull is strong and rigid, with a wide, flat stern, a square, sloping bow, and a deep rudder that can be raised or lowered to act also as a *centreboard. From at least the 10th century AD, the junk's hull was divided by *bulkheads into watertight compartments, a practice not adopted in the West until the 19th century. The sails consist of a series of narrow panels of cloth or matting, stiffened with horizontal battens, each panel having its own sheets (ropes). They can be hauled round to allow the boat to sail somewhat into the wind, and are easily adjusted. Junks during the Middle Ages made regular trading trips as far as India, while in the 15th century fleets of large junks sailed as far as Madagascar.

jute *fibre, textile (table).

Kay, John (1704–*c.*1764), British inventor of textile-weaving machinery. As a young man, he set up as a clock-maker in Lancashire, the centre of the cotton-weaving industry, and assisted *Arkwright. His interest in mechanical devices led him to invent the *flying shuttle (1733), which greatly increased the speed of weaving and the width of the woven cloth. His machinery was attacked by angry weavers who feared unemployment, and he retired to France in 1741, introducing his shuttle there.

keel, in a wooden ship, the principal timber running the length of the base of the hull, and serving as its spine; in a steel ship the keel is the lowest continuous line of plates, extending the whole length, to which are attached the stem, stern-post, and frames. The keel may extend downwards into the water, to reduce sideways drift: this kind of keel probably appeared first in the 6th century AD. Wooden ships often have a 'false keel', for protecting the true keel or further reducing sideways movement. In large steel ships two additional keels, known as bilge or docking keels, are fitted along each side of the hull where it narrows and turns underneath: these support the ship in *dry dock. Some small modern yachts are fitted with twin bilge keels instead of a single central keel. To increase speed under sail, designers shorten and deepen keels, leaving a central fin rather than a full-length keel. To make such fin keels as efficient as possible, wings may be fitted to the base of the fin, or the keel itself may be curved outwards so that it is thicker towards its base.

Kelly, William (1811–88), US pioneer of the *iron and steel industry. He began experiments at his ironworks in Kentucky in 1847, and discovered that an air blast could be used to burn the carbon out of molten iron, reducing fuel costs and converting iron into steel. Between 1851 and 1856 he secretly built converters that used this technique, and in 1856 applied for a patent. Although *Bessemer had already acquired a US patent for a similar 'air-boiling' process for steel, Kelly succeeded in gaining his patent in 1857, on the grounds of prior discovery. He was bankrupted, and the first steel made in the USA under his patent (1864) used a Bessemer converter.

kermes *dyes and dyeing.

kerosene *paraffin.

ketch, a two-masted *sailing ship with a mizen (rear) mast and sail considerably smaller than the mainmast and sail. The original 'catches' were small coastal traders (though the name may imply a type of fishing boat) in the 17th century. These early ketches may not have been ketch-rigged, the name possibly referring to a type of hull or the vessel's use.

kidney machine *haemodialysis.

kiln, an oven for drying or roasting items, particularly clay products, but also grains, wood, and limestone. Kilns used to fire ceramics and pottery often need to reach very high temperatures: such kilns are lined with special bricks or other *refractory materials. Kilns can be of two types: those in which the materials in the kiln come in contact with the furnace flames (as, for example, in *lime kilns), and those in which the kiln chamber is heated indirectly (for example, pottery kilns). In the ceramics industry, batch kilns are being replaced by tunnel and other continuous kilns. In tunnel-kilns, the objects to be fired travel through a long kiln which is cool near the entrance and exit, but becomes hotter towards the centre.

Kipping, Frederic Stanley (1863–1949), British pioneer of the chemistry of silicon. In 1897 he was appointed Professor of Chemistry at University College, Nottingham. His research ranged widely, and his work laid the foundation for the development of *silicone polymers, with applications ranging from heavy greases to mobile fluids and synthetic rubber.

Kitasato Shibasaburo (1852–1931), Japanese physician and bacteriologist. From 1885 to 1891 he worked in the bacteriologist Robert Koch's laboratory in Germany, and, together with Emil von Behring, developed an anti-toxin for *immunization against diphtheria. On returning to Japan, he founded an institute for the study of infectious diseases, and in 1894 discovered the infectious agent of bubonic plague.

kite, a non-powered, heavier-than-air aircraft anchored to or towed from the ground and sustained in flight by the wind. Kites come in a variety of forms and materials, often with a tail for stability. More than one control line can be fitted to manœuvre the kite in flight. The Chinese have used kites since 1000 BC, and kites had reached Europe by the 13th century. Kites have had many uses, including military observation, signalling, fishing, and sport.

klystron *thermionic valve.

knitting, a method of making fabric by forming interlocking *yarn (especially *wool) loops. The advantage it has over weaving is that it can be done by working directly from one simple ball or bobbin of yarn. Knitting by forming loops around pins mounted on a board was practised in the Middle East in biblical times; the method using two hand-held needles came much later. Simple knitted fabrics have high flexibility and conformability, and a cellular construction which, by trapping air in the fabric, gives thermal insulation. These attributes have led to the widespread use of knitting for the manufacture of stockings and cold-weather clothing. Hand knitting involves laying a single thread of yarn to and fro across the width of the fabric (*weft knitting). Knitting machines may also form stitches in this way, or they may form loops simultaneously on threads running along the length of the fabric (*warp knitting). Warp knitting is more productive, but weft knitting is more versatile. Both types of machine are widely used commercially.

A knitting machine has one or two closely packed rows of needles (similar to crochet hooks), one needle for each stitch in the width of the fabric. Yarn is laid in the needle hooks as they are sequentially withdrawn, forming new stitches and shedding the old. For hosiery manufacture the needles are mounted not in a straight line, but in a closed circle, to produce fabrics which are tubular. The first knitting machine was the stocking frame, invented by a British clergyman, William Lee, in 1589. Rotary-driven machines were introduced in 1769, and the first warp knitting machine was patented in 1775. In the early 19th century over-production caused stagnation, but from the mid-1800s innovations and inventions were again encouraged. With the introduction of *nylon and other synthetic fibres in the 1930s and 1940s, warp knitting machines increased in importance. Successive improvements have led to the modern versatile, high-speed domestic and commercial machines.

Illustration from *The Costume of Yorkshire* (1814), by George Walker, showing a family in Wensleydale, UK, **knitting** socks and stockings from local wool. Hooks on the belt were used to hold the wool and one needle, allowing knitting to continue while standing or walking.

knives and edge tools, tools which have a cutting action. They can be divided into those in which the cutting is effected by a chopping action (for example, *chisels), and those in which the blade is drawn along the material to be cut, as in the scythe and sickle. Some tools, such as billhooks, combine elements of these actions with a slashing action, as do shears and scissors. Half-moon knives, used by modern cooks and by cobblers in ancient Greece, cut by a rocking action. Modern mincing machines have continuously rotating blades. The simplest and most versatile of all edge tools is the knife. Appearing in flint form in Stone Age cultures, the knife had a wide back so that it could be held in the hand; it also served as a scraper. When knives were later made successively in bronze, iron, and steel, a tang (pointed end) was formed to fit into a wooden handle. Over the years a variety of patterns have evolved to meet specialized needs. These include hook-ended and half-moon knives to cut leather and linoleum; pocket knives in which the blade folds into the handle; potato peelers with a guide to limit the depth of cut; and knives with heavy triangular blades to cut baled hay. Another specialized form of knife is the razor. Knives and sickles are used for harvesting in many countries: in Sri Lanka, for example, coconuts are harvested using knives on long poles, and split using a bayonet-type blade. Knife blades become blunt after prolonged use and sharpeners are a necessary complement. Steel (often used for cooks' knives), oil-impregnated whetstone, or *silicon carbide, are commonly employed for this purpose. Very fine blades, such as razors, are honed on leather.

knock (pinking), a term describing the characteristic noise in *internal-combustion engines when uncontrolled combustion occurs. In petrol engines this may happen when the 'end gas', the last part of the mixture to burn, becomes overheated and undergoes spontaneous combustion: shock waves strike the cylinder head and walls. In *diesel engines knock occurs because of delay in the onset of ignition. The *compression ratio and *octane number of the *petrol or other fuel are the chief factors in determining the onset of knock. *Fuel additives such as *lead tetraethyl are used to prevent knock from occurring.

knot, the unit of speed measurement at sea. One knot is one international nautical mile (1,852 m; 6,076 feet) per hour. The term originated from the early methods of speed measurement in ships, in which a *log tied to a knotted rope was thrown over the stern, and the number of knots paid out within a fixed time period gave an estimate of the ship's speed.

knowledge engineering *expert system.

Kolle, Wilhelm (1868–1935), German bacteriologist. He worked under the pioneer German bacteriologist Robert Koch in the Institute for Infectious Diseases, Berlin. He had a lifelong interest in the treatment of bacterial diseases by vaccines and chemotherapy. With August Pfeifer, in 1896 he used killed cultures against typhoid, and he introduced Asiatic cholera vaccine. He also did research on rinderpest in cattle. With the German bacteriologist August von Wassermann, noted for his diagnosis of syphilis (1906), he edited the multi-volume *Manual of Pathogenic Micro-organisms*.

Koller, Carl (1857–1944), Austrian-born US ophthalmologist and pioneer of local *anaesthesia. He became a close friend of Sigmund Freud, who in 1884 became intensely interested in the possibility of using cocaine to cure morphine addiction. Koller noticed that cocaine had a numbing effect on the tongue and, after experimenting with animals, introduced it as a local anaesthetic in ophthalmology. It was also quickly adopted for nose and throat surgery and for dentistry.

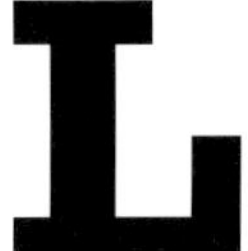

L

laboratories and laboratory equipment, places designed for scientific research and development, teaching, or the manufacture of drugs or chemicals. The various *instruments used in the laboratory are concerned with extending the human senses and with quantifying observed phenomena. Compound light *microscopes magnify the image seen by the unaided eye hundreds of times, while *electron microscopes have magnifications of many thousands of times. Electronic *weighing machines weigh accurately to 0.001 g (3.5×10^{-5} ounces), and have an instant digital read-out: the data can be logged automatically into the memory of a computer. Electronic timing using quartz crystal or atomic *clocks allows measurements to millionths of a second to be made. *Spectroscopy can measure and record the *electromagnetic radiation absorbed or emitted by materials over a wide range of wavelengths. A variety of instruments for *temperature measurement allow accurate measurements from near absolute zero (−273 °C) to several thousand degrees centigrade.

Simple solid-fuel furnaces or liquid-burning lamps were all that was available to apply heat in the laboratory until the

A technician wearing plastic protective glasses: this is a routine safety precaution when using **laboratory equipment.**

mid-19th century, when the *Bunsen burner was introduced. Similar burners are still used for small-scale heating, but today electric heating mantles, hot-plates, and immersion heaters are used for most purposes. The availability of thermostats in the early 20th century has resulted in reliable electric ovens. Materials that are toxic or noxious are usually handled in fume cupboards. These were introduced during the 19th century. Special safety techniques are available for use with pathogens or extremely toxic substances. With more recent developments in radiochemistry, remote-handling apparatus has had to be developed. 'Clean rooms' used for biological or electronic work are kept at a pressure slightly above or below atmospheric, and entry or exit is through an *airlock. Materials that are sensitive to air are studied in apparatus that is either evacuated or filled with an inert gas (usually *nitrogen). The complex systems of glassware for such studies were developed during the early part of the 20th century. Stainless-steel apparatus for exploring reactions under high pressure was developed at around the same time. Special sterile environments and equipment are used for cultures in *biotechnology. Mechanization in the first half of the 20th century has eased many standard laboratory procedures. Automatic stirrers, shakers, and collectors are now standard, and in medical laboratories automatic machines carry out a range of tests on, for example, small samples of blood and urine. (See also *chromatography.)

lace-making, needlework producing lace, an intricate, open textile *fabric, especially of cotton or silk. Whereas weaving and *knitting produce fabrics with rectangular cells, lace-making can produce polygonal cells, thus making possible the creation of an enormous variety of fabrics. Lace is almost exclusively ornamental, and much is still made by hand, by weaving thread in patterns. At the end of the 18th century machines for making lace began to appear, and several complex types were developed in the early 19th century. Most modern lace is made on machines of the type developed by John Levers (*c.*1820), based on an earlier machine by John Heathcoat. Many lace-like fabrics are made on a large scale, using warp *knitting machines.

lacquer *varnish.

Laënnec, René-Théophile-Hyacinthe (1781–1826), French inventor of the *stethoscope. A professor at the Charité hospital and the Collège de France, in Paris, he observed in 1816 two children with their ears close to the ends of a long stick, listening to the transmitted sound when they tapped it. This inspired his invention of the stethoscope, initially a wooden tube 30 cm (1 foot) long, for listening to sounds within the body, especially the heart and lungs.

laminate, a *composite in which thin layers of one or more materials are bonded together. Laminates of more than one material have properties intermediate between those of the materials they are made from. Materials that are anisotropic (whose physical properties vary with direction) can be laminated to produce a more homogeneous material. Plywood is an example of this type of laminate: it is made from thin sheets (veneers) of wood, each oriented differently from those either side, bonded together with resins. Plywood is dimensionally stable, of uniform strength, and can be made in large panels; it can also be made in curved shapes for boat hulls and furniture. Laminated wood is similar to plywood, but the grains of the different veneers all run in the same direction. It is used in columns, arches, boat keels, and helicopter rotor blades. Laminates can also be made from sheets of asbestos, cloth, and paper impregnated with thermosetting resins. They are much stronger than the resins themselves, and are used when insulation and strength are required together. Such materials are, however, increasingly being replaced by improved plastics, which are cheaper to manufacture. Laminated glass uses metal wires or plastic sheet in conjunction with glass to make a transparent material that cracks but does not fragment on impact. A further important laminate is used in power transformer cores, where the iron in the core is laminated to minimize eddy currents.

lamp *incandescent lamp, *lighting, *oil lamp.

Lanby buoy, a large automatic navigational *buoy introduced in the latter part of the 20th century, as a cheaper substitute for a *lightship. The buoy is circular, and fitted with a lattice mast carrying a characteristic light with a visibility of about 25 km (15 miles) in clear weather, a fog signal, and a *radar beacon. The buoy is designed to operate for six months without attention, and its performance and position are monitored from a shore station.

land drainage, the removal of water from the land in regions of high rainfall to improve agricultural yield or to prevent destruction of playing surfaces in sports fields. Pipes, typically of perforated *PVC permeable concrete, or fired clay, are laid 75–150 cm (30–60 inches) below the surface and between 5 and 45 m (16–150 feet) apart in a grid or fan layout. The pipes drain to a collector, and thence to the main channel, normally an open ditch ultimately connecting with a river. In heavy soils, drains made with a *mole plough are preferred, though they need renewing more frequently.

landing craft, a flat-bottomed vessel, usually of box-section, designed to lift assault troops and vehicles from ships at sea and land them ashore. There is an opening ramp at the bow, propellers usually set into the stern for protection when taking the ground, and efficient arrangements for streaming and retrieving anchors when approaching the beach. Since the Suez War (1956), helicopters have also been used in a landing craft role, and more recently *hovercraft and *hydrofoils.

land reclamation, the improvement of land for agriculture, building, or other purposes. Arid land requires *irrigation. For example, the Imperial Valley Project in California, USA, has reclaimed a virtual desert for intensive agricultural production. Irrigation water is distributed by a *canal system from a reservoir in the lower Colorado River and is also pumped from natural underground reservoirs (aquifers). *Coastal defences protect land reclaimed from the sea. The IJsselmeer (Zuider Zee) in The Netherlands, originally flooded by very high storm tides in about 1300, was closed by embankments (dikes), the first built between 1927 and 1933. Since then, the reclaimed land has been continually drained and desalinated. Since the 1960s the south-west and south-east coasts of Singapore have been the site of large land reclamation projects. Bogs and swamps are usually drained by a network of open ditches and channels sloping towards a river. The river banks may need to be raised to prevent flooding of the reclaimed area. Land derelict from mining or industry may need stabilizing; for example, loose ground can be compacted, holes filled in, and any noxious residues treated. Poisonous substances can either be

A yellow **laser** beam surrounds the steel casing of an 'atom trap' at A.T. & T. Bell Laboratories in Holmdel, New Jersey, USA. The device confines the atoms of a gas at temperatures close to absolute zero (−273 °C) in a 'bottle' made from a single laser beam.

removed (though their transport may be hazardous) or left in place and isolated by an impenetrable casing. Methane and other gases generated in landfill sites can be vented to prevent their migration or build-up in the ground.

Landsat *Earth resources satellite.

Landsteiner, Karl (1868–1943), Austrian-born US immunologist and pathologist. His most important research was on human blood grouping: in 1900, he discovered that one person's blood serum may agglutinate the red cells of another's, and from this discovery formulated (1909) the basic ABO blood group system, which, with many sub-groups, is still used today. This paved the way for large-scale blood transfusion, previously hazardous because of possible blood incompatibility. He was awarded the Nobel Prize for Physiology and Medicine in 1930.

Langmuir, Irving (1881–1957), US chemist responsible for many important industrial inventions. He joined the research laboratories of General Electric at Schenectady in 1909, where he spent the rest of his working life. While studying phenomena in high vacuum, he showed that the blackening of *incandescent light bulbs was due to evaporation of metal from the filament and that this blackening could be reduced by replacing the vacuum with an inert gas. Efficiency could be further improved by replacing the straight filament with a fine helix. He also developed the mercury vapour lamp and the atomic-hydrogen welding torch, the latter capable of temperatures of up to 3,000 °C. Many of the phenomena that interested him took place on surfaces, and he was awarded the Nobel Prize for Chemistry in 1932 for his work on mono-molecular layers.

laryngoscope *endoscopy.

laser (*l*ight *a*mplification by *s*timulated *e*mission of *r*adiation), an instrument producing an intense, parallel beam of light, or ultraviolet or infra-red radiation. (A related instrument is the *maser.) Laser light is monochromatic and coherent—the light *waves are in phase, with the crests and troughs coinciding. Before a laser can operate, it must be 'pumped': an energy source is used to excite the *atoms in the lasing material, so that most of them are in a high-energy state. Spontaneous emission of light from one atom in the excited material then produces a chain reaction, whereby the light emitted from one atom excites emission of light of the same wavelength and phase from others. The ends of the lasing material are mirrored, one mirror being half-silvered: light is reflected between these mirrors, stimulating more emission, until the beam becomes bright enough to pass through the half-silvered mirror. The first laser, built by *Maiman in 1960, produced pulses of red light from a ruby rod using light from a flash tube as the energy source. By 1963 lasers had been made from liquids, gases, and *semiconductors, giving continuous or pulsed beams of many different wavelengths. Liquid dye lasers can be tuned to give a range of wavelengths. Gas lasers (such as the low-power, red helium–neon laser and the high-power, infra-red carbon dioxide laser) use electrical discharge for energy. The tiny but durable and efficient semiconductor or diode lasers also use electrical energy, producing red or infra-red beams. They are used in *optical-fibre communication systems, and for recording and playing compact discs. Laser light can be focused to a very tiny spot, concentrating its energy so that it can be used for cutting and welding in industry and in medical surgery. Other uses include alignment and *length measurement, weapons-guidance systems (see *laser weapon), reading supermarket *bar codes, and *holography. Lasers are also used in printing (see *laser engraving, *laser printing), and in nuclear *fusion research.

laser engraving, the *engraving of plates for printing using a *laser. Laser-engraved plates and cylinders for relief printing are produced by means of computerized scanning equipment, in which a laser beam examines the artwork as it revolves on a 'copy' cylinder. The scanner relays *digitized information to the central computer, which analyses the information and initiates the cutting of the image. This is performed by a second laser located above an 'engraving' cylinder, rotating in synchronization with the copy cylinder. The fastest method of producing printing surfaces, it is a direct copy-to-cylinder system, without intermediate stages. The initial capital investment may be higher than for moulded rubber plates or *photopolymers, but in addition to speed, computer control has the advantage that it allows a great deal of flexibility of image reproduction. Repetitive designs or images can be 'stepped and repeated' from a single master; continuous designs can be seamlessly joined; and the profile of individual lines and dots cut to provide the strongest support for the image. Rubber is the preferred image medium as it is easily vaporized by the laser and can receive and release ink readily. For economy, plate 'patches' may be mounted on the cylinder so that only those parts containing the image will be engraved.

laser printing, printing using a minute, digitally controlled beam of *laser light directed by an optical system towards a rotating drum. The drum is coated with a photoconductive material, which becomes electrically charged on exposure to light. Areas of the photoconductive layer exposed to the laser become selectively attractive to tiny particles of powder, supplied from a toner cartridge. As the drum turns, the powder image is electrostatically transferred to the paper stock and fused to the paper by heat (see *photocopier). Resolution is usually at least 120 dots/cm (300 per inch), sufficient for most *desk-top publishing work.

laser weapon, a targeting, ranging, or attacking device that employs high-energy *laser beams. Laser weapons normally consist of a power source and a projector. In range-finders, with which all modern tanks are equipped, a laser is used to calculate the distance to the target. The beam from the targeting device is detected by sensors in a missile or artillery *shell, which then homes in on the target designated. Similar devices are used by aircraft to drop laser-guided bombs. Laser beams can also be used to 'blind' enemy tanks by directing them at the delicate range-finding optical equipment or even into the crew's eyes. High-energy laser beams of the order of hundreds or thousands of kW could melt through the armour of enemy tanks, or easily puncture any thinner metal. However, the large power requirements at present preclude such weapons from effective use. (See also *Strategic Defense Initiative.)

lateen rig, a form of *fore-and-aft rig, used mainly in Arabian and Mediterranean waters. A triangular sail is set on a long yard attached to a short forward-raked mast, the upper corner or peak of the sail being checked by braces (see *sailing ships and boats for illustration). The lateen rig was used on the mizen (rear) mast in early three-masted sailing ships.

lath and plaster, a traditional *plaster surface in which the laths (thin wooden strips) are nailed across floor joists (for a ceiling) or across studs (for a wall). The first coat of plaster is then applied over the laths and is pushed into the gaps between them, forming a 'key' for further coats of plaster.

lathe, the earliest and still the most important *machine-tool. Its major function is to produce items of circular cross-section by spinning the workpiece on its axis and cutting its surface with a sharp stationary tool: the tool may be moved sideways to produce a cylindrical object and moved towards the workpiece to control the depth of cut (see illustration in machine-tool). The earliest lathes had fixed conical 'centres' between which the workpiece was supported. A cord was wrapped round the workpiece and held taut by a bow: by reciprocating this bow the workpiece rotated to and fro. A chisel supported by a tool rest was used for cutting. Lathes had spread from the Middle East to the Mediterranean and India by the second millennium BC. A development was the pole lathe, in which the cord was attached at its upper end to a springy pole and at its lower end to a foot treadle, so freeing both hands to hold the tool. In the *Industrial Revolution, lathes were power-driven (an electric motor is now commonly used), which allowed continuous rotation of the workpiece at a variety of speeds. In the early 19th century, all-metal lathes were developed in which the cutting tool was held in a slide rest, the movement of which could be accurately controlled by two screws at right angles to each other. Lathes of this kind could be used to machine-cut screw-threads. A further development in the later 19th century was the turret lathe, in which several cutting tools could be clamped in a rotatable turret, allowing them to be rapidly and successively brought to bear on a workpiece. The modern lathe is driven by means of a headstock supporting a hollow spindle on accurate *bearings and carrying either a 'chuck' or a faceplate, to which the workpiece is clamped. The movement of the tool, both along the lathe bed and at right angles to it, can be accurately controlled, so enabling a part to be 'turned' (machined) to close tolerances. Modern lathes are often under *numerical control.

latitude and longitude, a conceptual grid of lines covering the Earth's surface and used on *maps and charts to enable positions to be accurately specified (see *navigation for illustration). Latitude lines (parallels) run around the Earth parallel to the equator (latitude 0°); a latitude is expressed as the angle between the plane of the equator and a vertical to the Earth's surface at the latitude being measured. Longitude lines (meridians) run from North to South Poles; a longitude is expressed as the angle east or west of the meridian running through Greenwich, UK (longitude 0°). Celestial observations are used to measure latitude, for example, the altitude of the Sun at its highest point in the sky can be used to calculate latitude provided that the date, and hence the declination ('celestial latitude') of the Sun is known. Longitude is most easily calculated by comparing local time with that at a known reference latitude using a *chronometer: if the Earth's rotational speed is known, this time difference can be converted into a longitude.

laughing gas *anaesthesia.

launch site, a site from which *missiles or *rockets are launched. Each site has a launch platform with fuelling facilities, a building for assembly and testing, and facilities to control and track the vehicle immediately after launch. Launch sites are usually away from populated areas, so that used rocket stages can fall to Earth safely. Sites near the equator allow geostationary orbit (an orbit in which the satellite remains in the same position relative to the Earth's surface) to be reached with the minimum of power. The USA has two major launch sites: Kennedy Space Center in Florida, for manned space-flights and some satellite launches, and Vandenburg Air Force Base in south-west California, for launches into orbit over the poles. The Soviet Union also has two major launch sites: Plesetsk, in Arkhangelsk province, for military launches, and Tyuratam in Kazakhstan for manned and scientific launches. China, Europe, India, and Japan each have launch sites for their satellite *launch vehicles; there are many other sites around the world for missile or smaller rocket launches.

launch vehicle, a vehicle used to send an artificial *satellite or spacecraft into space. Enormous power is needed to accelerate a spacecraft sufficiently to reach Earth orbit or to escape Earth's gravity completely. Such power requires large *rocket motors, whose fuel constitutes most of the weight of the vehicle at launch. When the fuel is exhausted these large motors are useless weight, and so vehicles have several 'stages' which separate and fall away when their fuel is used up. Extra power is often supplied by booster rockets strapped to the first stage. Conventional rockets can only be used once; to reduce costs partly reusable launch vehicles like the *space shuttle have been developed. The Soviet Union now has three basic launch vehicles: *Soyuz* and *Proton* rockets that launch satellites, *space probes, and spacecraft, and a larger version of *Proton* that launches *space stations. The new *Energiya* rocket, which launches the Soviet Union's space shuttle *Buran*, is the most powerful since America's *Saturn V*, which launched the **Apollo* flights in 1969–72. The USA's main launch vehicle is now the Space Shuttle; conventional rockets (*Delta*, *Atlas-Centaur*, and *Titan*) are also used for satellite launches. The *Ariane* launch vehicle (see figure) is built by a consortium of eleven member countries to launch artificial satellites commercially, while China, India, and Japan also have their own satellite launch vehicles.

Launch vehicle (Ariane)

Empty third stage falls back to earth and burns up on re-entry.
Payload delivered into orbit 210 km (130 miles) up.
Third stage travels at a speed of 35,400 km/h (22,000 m.p.h.).
Second stage separates at 140 km (87 miles) up. Speed is 17,200 km/h (10,700 m.p.h.).
First stage separates at 51 km (32 miles) up. Speed is 6,730 km/h (4,180 m.p.h.).
Third stage
Second stage
First stage
Payload
Electronic control equipment bay
Liquid oxygen and liquid hydrogen tanks
Third stage engine
Oxidizer tank (nitrogen tetroxide)
Fuel tank
Second stage engine
Oxidizer tank (nitrogen tetroxide)
Fuel tank
Stabilizing fins
Size of person

Laval, Carl Gustaf Patrik de (1845–1913), Swedish inventor. An engineer by profession, his interests ranged from aerodynamics to metallurgy and his diaries record several thousand inventions. Laval is probably best known for his high-speed centrifugal cream-separator (1878), adopted by large dairies throughout the world. He also experimented with *steam-turbine designs (1882–93).

Lawes, Sir John Bennet (1814–99), British agricultural scientist. After early academic failure, from 1834 he devoted himself to the management of his family estate at Rothamsted, Hertfordshire, UK. There, with the help of J. H. Gilbert, he established the principles of scientific agriculture, showing a particular interest in the use of synthetic *fertilizers. In 1843 he established the first factory to make artificial fertilizer. In parallel, he conducted careful field trials at Rothamsted to determine the mineral requirements of a number of field crops. In 1889 he established a trust to ensure that Rothamsted continued as an internationally famous *agricultural research station.

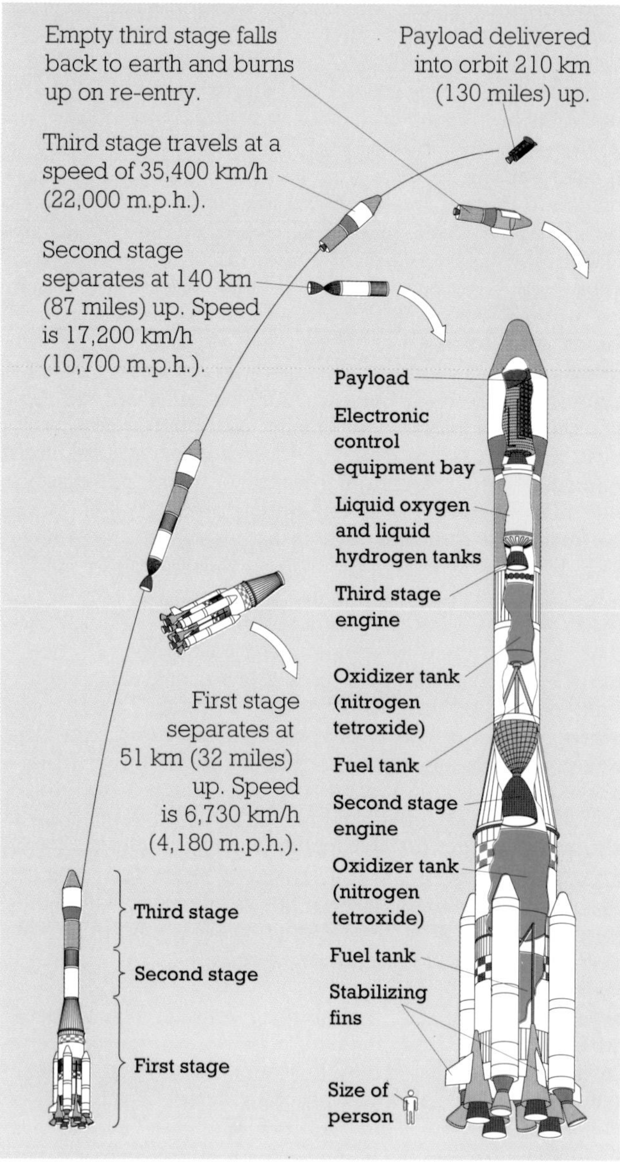

lawn-mower, a machine used to cut grass close to the ground and to a uniform length, in order to create a lawn. The original design of 1830, by the British inventor Edwin Budding, used a revolving cylinder blade slicing the grass against a fixed horizontal blade. The first machines were pushed by hand. Larger machines were pulled by flat-shod horses, and later powered by steam or petrol engines. More recently, electric motors have been applied. Some modern designs make use of a horizontal spinning disc with blades attached at its circumference.

Lawrence, Ernest Orlando (1901–58), US physicist and inventor of the cyclotron (see *particle accelerator). From 1929 he sought to find a means of accelerating light *ions (charged atoms) to the high energies at which nuclear reactions might occur. Linear accelerators with the necessary path-length were impracticable, and with M. S. Livingston he devised the cyclotron, in which protons are accelerated along a compact spiral path between two electrodes. He was awarded the Nobel Prize for Physics in 1939, and in 1961 an artificial element was named lawrencium in his honour.

LD process *iron and steel industry.

lead (symbol Pb, at. no. 82, r.a.m. 207.2), a soft, dense metallic element having little tensile strength. The principal ore is lead sulphide (PbS), commonly called galena. Lead oxide is obtained by roasting the ore, which is then reduced to lead by heating in a *blast-furnace with coke and scrap iron. It can be further refined by *electrolysis. Lead can be easily worked, has a low melting-point, and is resistant to corrosion. Lead itself, and all soluble lead salts, are poisonous. Lead is used in storage batteries and ammunition and is a major component of pewter and electrical and soft solders. It is used to protect roofs and cables, and as a shielding material against nuclear radiation. Lead carbonate and lead chromate are used as paint pigments, and paints containing *red lead oxide are effective rust inhibitors. In some petrol, *lead tetraethyl acts as an 'anti-*knock' agent.

lead chamber process, the first industrial method for the manufacture of *sulphuric acid, developed originally by the British physician and inventor John Roebuck in 1746 but refined and improved over the next hundred years. Sulphur dioxide, obtained by burning *sulphur or roasting sulphide ores, was converted to sulphuric acid by reaction with gaseous *nitric acid and oxides of nitrogen in a lead-lined reaction vessel (hence the name). This method of production has been largely superseded by the *contact process.

lead-line, a lead weight attached to a line, usually marked in fathoms but sometimes in metres, and used to measure the depth of a body of water. The lead-line has been known since antiquity and has remained basically unchanged for over 2,000 years. The lead weight, known as the sounding-lead, is sometimes hollowed at the base and filled with tallow to indicate the nature of the sea-bed by the substances adhering. Modern depth recording is carried out with *echo-sounders, and the lead-line is now used only in some small boats and yachts.

lead tetraethyl, a liquid compound added to petrol to increase its *octane number and thus reduce engine *knock, caused by premature combustion of the fuel. The anti-knock properties of lead tetraethyl were discovered in 1921 through empirical investigations made by *Midgley. However, lead compounds from car exhausts cause *air pollution and are a health hazard, and during the last decades of the 20th century lead-free compounds have begun to supersede lead tetraethyl as anti-knock additives.

leather, the skin of an animal preserved and made flexible by chemical and physical processes known as *tanning. It is water-repellent, strong, flexible, and very long-lasting if kept well. Leather can be used for a wide range of applications, depending on the animal from which it comes, and the way in which it is cured. Examples include footwear, clothing, upholstery, *harness and saddlery, musical instruments such as drums, and industrial equipment such as buffing wheels and machine belts. In the past, leather was even more widely used: examples of such applications include shields and armour, buckets, bottles and other containers, boats, vellum as a writing material, and leather panelling. Today, leather is an important by-product of domestic *livestock farming. Woven, knitted, and *nonwoven fabrics coated with synthetic finishes (leather cloths) are today widely used as cheap, resistant substitutes for leather.

Leblanc, Nicolas (1742–1806), French industrial chemist. In 1783, Leblanc was awarded a prize (offered since 1775 by the Academy of Sciences) for discovering a process for making *sodium carbonate from non-vegetable sources. Based on *salt, the process was widely worked for more than a century, though Leblanc profited little from it. He never received the prize, and both the works and his process were confiscated.

Lebon, Philippe (1767–1804), French pioneer of *gas lighting and heating. Brought up in a charcoal-burning area, he was familiar with the emission of flammable gas when wood is strongly heated. With the chemist A. F. Fourcroy, he experimented with making gas from sawdust. To publicize his process (patented in 1799), he exhibited in Paris in 1801 two gas-burning *thermolampes*—one for lighting and one for heating. He also experimented with a *gas-engine.

Leclanché, Georges (1839–82), French chemist and a pioneer of the electric *battery. While working as a railway engineer, he spent much time in developing the electric cell which bears his name. It consisted of a zinc *anode and a carbon *cathode immersed in a solution of ammonium chloride, with a mixture of powdered manganese dioxide and carbon surrounding the cathode. In 1867 Leclanché resigned from his post to devote himself to improving the cell. It was soon widely adopted wherever small intermittent currents were required (for example in telegraphy), and was later developed into the universally familiar dry battery.

Drawings made by Antoni van **Leeuwenhoek** to accompany a letter sent to the Royal Society (1698) describing his observations of insect eyes and optic nerves, made through a simple microscope.

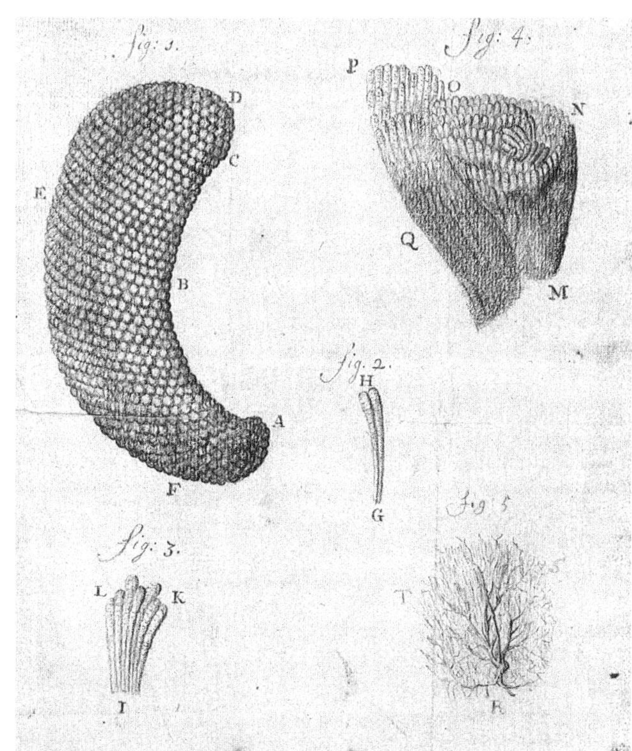

Lenses and lens systems

Effects of converging and diverging lenses on light rays parallel to the principal axis.

Principal axis
Converging lens
Principal focus (F)
F'
P
Incoming light rays
Focal length (f)

Parallel rays of light are brought to a focus on the far side of a converging lens.

Concave (diverging) lens
Principle focus (F)
F
P
F'
Focal length
Optical axis

Parallel rays leave a diverging lens as if they had come from a focal point on the near side of it.

1 Images formed by a converging lens

a. Object beyond 2F'

Object
2F'
Focal point (F')
P
Principal focus (F)
Image

The image is real, inverted and smaller than the object – as in a camera lens system. At 2F' the image is the same size as the object.

b. Object between 2F' and F'

The image is real, inverted and larger than the object – as in the image formed by the lens system of a projector.

Object
F'
P
F
Image

c. Object between F' and P

Image
Object
F'
P
F

The image is virtual, upright and magnified. This is the principle of a magnifying glass

2 Images formed by a diverging lens

The image formed is always upright, virtual and closer to the lens than the object.

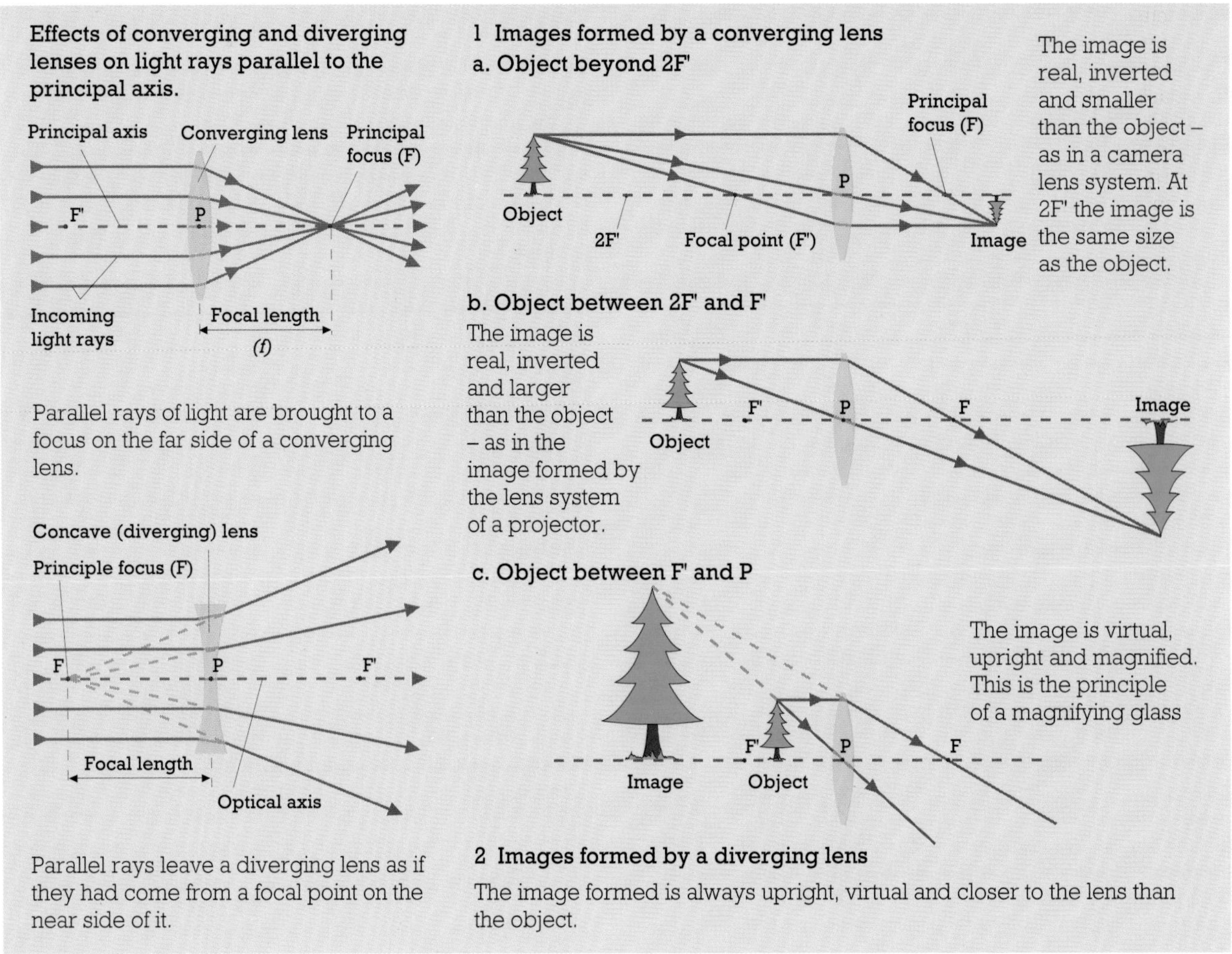

Leeuwenhoek, Antoni van (1632–1723), Dutch pioneer of microscopy. His livelihood was his draper's business in Delft, but his true interest was in making and using *microscopes, of which he constructed several hundred. These were, in fact, no more than very powerful biconvex magnifying glasses held close to the eye, with magnifications ranging from × 50 to × 300. His observations, which he described in letters (1673–1723) to the Royal Society, London, ranged from insects to bacteria. He was the first to accurately observe blood corpuscles and bacteria, and he pioneered the examination of opaque objects by cutting thin sections with a razor.

Leibniz, Gottfried Wilhelm *calculator, *computer, history of.

length measurement. The choice of which method to use for measuring a certain length depends on its magnitude, and the accuracy required. For relatively short lengths, where great accuracy is not required, a graduated scale or tape suffices. For longer lengths, for example in road surveying, the *odometer can be used. To measure short lengths with precision, a *micrometer, or a graduated calliper incorporating a *vernier scale, is used. By the end of the 18th century, precision instruments of this kind made for surveying or for calibrating weights and measures were capable of accuracies of around 2 μm (8×10^{-5} inch). Today, high-precision methods of length measurement generally depend in some way upon optical devices. These methods range from microscopes travelling along a graduated beam to instruments that measure the time of travel of a *radar pulse, or of a *laser beam. In such optical methods length is not measured directly, but is calculated from time measurements, or derived by comparison of the phase of the measurement beam of radiation with that of a reference beam.

Lenoir, Jean-Joseph Étienne (1822–1900), Belgian pioneer of *gas-engines. A self-taught engineer, with wide-ranging interests, he built his first gas-engine in 1860. Over a period of five years, he made several hundred engines of around 1.5 kW (2 horsepower), which were popular within small-scale industry. Later, however, the superior four-stroke engine introduced by *Otto in 1876 offered severe competition to Lenoir's gas-engine.

lenses and lens systems. A lens is a piece of glass or other transparent material with one or both sides curved to refract (bend) rays of light, especially in optical instruments. Devices for focusing other types of *electromagnetic radiation may also be called lenses. Single lenses are used in magnifying glasses and in *spectacles. Lens systems contain more than one lens: they are used in instruments such as *cameras, *microscopes, and *telescopes. A lens always has at least one regular, curved surface, usually a section of the surface of a large sphere. Various lens shapes are possible, but they can be broadly classified as either converging or diverging, according to how they bend light. In the case of beams of light parallel to the lens's principal axis (see figure), a converging lens focuses the light approximately to a single point, the principal focus or focal point of the lens. In a diverging lens parallel light rays are spread, so that they appear to come from a focal point on the other side of the lens. The thickness and curvature of a lens determine its focal length, while the diameter of the lens determines its light-gathering power. When a lens refracts diverging light rays from an object or light source, a real or apparent focus is produced at a different location, at which a visual image is formed. This image may be real (detectable on a screen or on photographic paper) or virtual (visible upon looking through the lens). Converging lenses may form real or virtual images, while diverging lenses always form virtual images. A single lens with spherical surfaces will not produce a sharp image of a large object or scene unless the diameter of the lens is made very small. Blurring and distortion effects called aberrations are present even in a lens with perfectly shaped spherical surfaces. Chromatic aberrations may also occur, due to light of different colours being differently refracted (see *achromatic lens). Aberrations can be reduced by combining several lenses together along a common axis according to a pre-calculated design; also precisely calculated non-spherical surfaces can be used to minimize aberrations.

Lenses with spherical surfaces (concave or convex) can be shaped to roughly the required curvature and thickness by machine grinding using a correctly shaped tool and abrasive, or by a diamond-edged cutting tool adjusted for the correct curvature. Fine grinding or smoothing is achieved using accurate tools for each surface and a succession of increasingly fine abrasives. This finishes the shaping process. Several lenses can be mounted together for grinding and polishing. The surfaces are polished with a tool covered with pitch or wax, moulded to the correct shape, and grooved to hold the wet polishing material. The edges of the lens are then ground to centre it and to give it the correct diameter, and anti-reflective or other coatings are applied. Non-spherical surfaces can be moulded or cut by a blade, and plastic lenses are often shaped by moulding, in order to give a high polish. New gradient index lenses are made from a glass with graded composition, with a refractive index ranging through the lens. These lenses can be manufactured to avoid optical aberrations present in many spherical lenses much more cheaply than can aspherical conventional lenses.

lens, photographic, any *lens or lens system for a *camera. Various types of photographic lenses are primarily, but not exclusively, designed as interchangeable lenses for single-lens reflex cameras. The standard camera lens gives an image that resembles the eye's normal vision as closely as possible. Wide-angle lenses have a relatively short focal length, and record a wide angle of view. Extremely wide-angle (fish-eye) lenses give a field of view of over 100 degrees, but they produce a distorted image. Telephoto lenses have a relatively long focal length: they act like a telescope to enlarge distant objects, the degree of magnification being directly related to the focal length of the lens. In zoom lenses, the focal length can be continuously altered so as to produce differing degrees of magnification, allowing the photographer to 'zoom' in on the subject. A wide variety of zoom lenses is available, covering a range of focal lengths.

Leonardo da Vinci (1452–1519), Italian painter, architect, and civil and military engineer, a genius whose invention and breadth of imagination have not been equalled. During his career he was artist and technical adviser to the Duke of Milan, military engineer to Cesare Borgia, and painter and architect to King Francis I of France. The surviving 5,000 pages of Leonardo's notebooks contain research into anatomy, mechanics, hydraulics, and a wide range of other sciences. The notebooks also detail many civil and military engineering schemes, plus designs for an enormous variety of mechanical devices—a helicopter, a bicycle, a screw-cutting machine, furnaces, breech-loading cannon, rifled firearms, coinage machines, and a double-swivelling crane. Some of these machines were many years ahead of their time, and were never made, but some designs were of major importance: mitred canal *lock-gates, for example, are still used today, and his half-gear mechanism for converting rotary to reciprocal (back-and-forth) motion was widely used throughout the 16th century.

Lesseps, Ferdinand-Marie, vicomte de (1805–94), French civil engineer. In 1849, he sought to further a long-cherished scheme to build a *canal across the isthmus of Suez. This became feasible when his friend Muhammad Sa'id became Khedive (Viceroy of Egypt) in 1854; work began in 1859 and the canal was completed in 1869. In 1881 Lesseps began work on the Panama Canal, but in 1892–3 the management was charged with breach of trust by the French government.

letterpress printing, the original method of relief *printing, whereby paper is pressed into contact with previously inked raised metal type and illustration blocks. The Chinese were printing from wooden type by the 11th century, while *Gutenberg was the first to use metal type, in 1448. This method progressed from hand-operated presses, through specialized flat-bed printing presses, where the type passes mechanically under inking rollers and paper carried on an impression cylinder, to rotary presses using curved printing plates. Speeds have increased dramatically during the last two centuries, and with better paper and machine controls, quality has also improved. Recently, however, letterpress printing has been largely superseded by *offset lithography. (See printing for illustration.)

lever, a simple device used to move a large load by means of a small *force, or to move a small load through a large distance. It is of very ancient origin; the mathematical basis of the lever was understood by the 4th century BC. The figure overleaf shows three possible arrangements of load, pivot (or fulcrum), and operating effort in a lever. In the first-order levers the fulcrum is between load and effort; if the distance from fulcrum to force is five times that from fulcrum to load there is a *mechanical advantage of 5:1—five times as much force is exerted at the load. However, the total work (force × distance) done by the effort is the same as that done by the load, since the load moves only one-fifth the distance of the effort. In second-order levers the load is between fulcrum and effort; the same principle of mechanical advantage applies. In third-order levers the operating force is between fulcrum and load. Here the mechanical advantage is less than one, but the load moves a greater distance than the operating force.

Libby, Willard Frank (1908–80), US chemist who developed the *radio-carbon dating technique for determining the age of organic matter. A graduate of the University of California, he taught there until 1945, when he moved to the University of Chicago. From 1941 to 1945 he also worked on the *Manhattan Project, helping to develop a method of separating uranium isotopes for the building of an atomic bomb. In 1947 he and a group of his students developed the technique of radio-carbon dating. He was awarded the Nobel Prize for Chemistry in 1960.

lie detector *polygraph.

lifeboat, any water craft specially built for rescue purposes. Relatively simple lifeboats are carried by ships for use in case of accident: many vessels now also carry inflatable life-rafts for this purpose. Shore-based lifeboats are generally larger, and are designed to stay afloat in extreme conditions. Several 'insubmergible' boat designs were produced in the 18th century in Britain and France, but it was not until the wreck of the ship *Adventure* in British waters in 1789 that public attention was drawn to the need for lifeboats. A competition for the best lifeboat design was won by the boatbuilder Henry Greathead. His boat, the *Original*, remained in service for many years, and was the prototype of many other lifeboats. In 1824 the UK became the first country to organize a national lifeboat service, shortly followed by Denmark and other countries. Modern lifeboats are sturdy, self-righting craft, manœuvrable in severe seas. They vary in size from 5-m (15-foot) inflatables to vessels of 17 m (55 feet) or more, capable of taking on board as many as 150 people.

life-jacket, a buoyancy aid worn like a waistcoat to keep the body safely afloat and prevent drowning. Formerly, kapok or cork provided the buoyancy, but by World War II inflatable life-jackets were being used by aircrew. These have since become more widely used, many having carbon dioxide gas injected under pressure from a small cylinder

Lever

The effort required to move a load with a lever can be calculated using the principle of moments, where load × distance from fulcrum = effort × distance from fulcrum. In the examples below, x = distance from fulcrum, y = force applied or moved, and z = distance moved by load or effort.

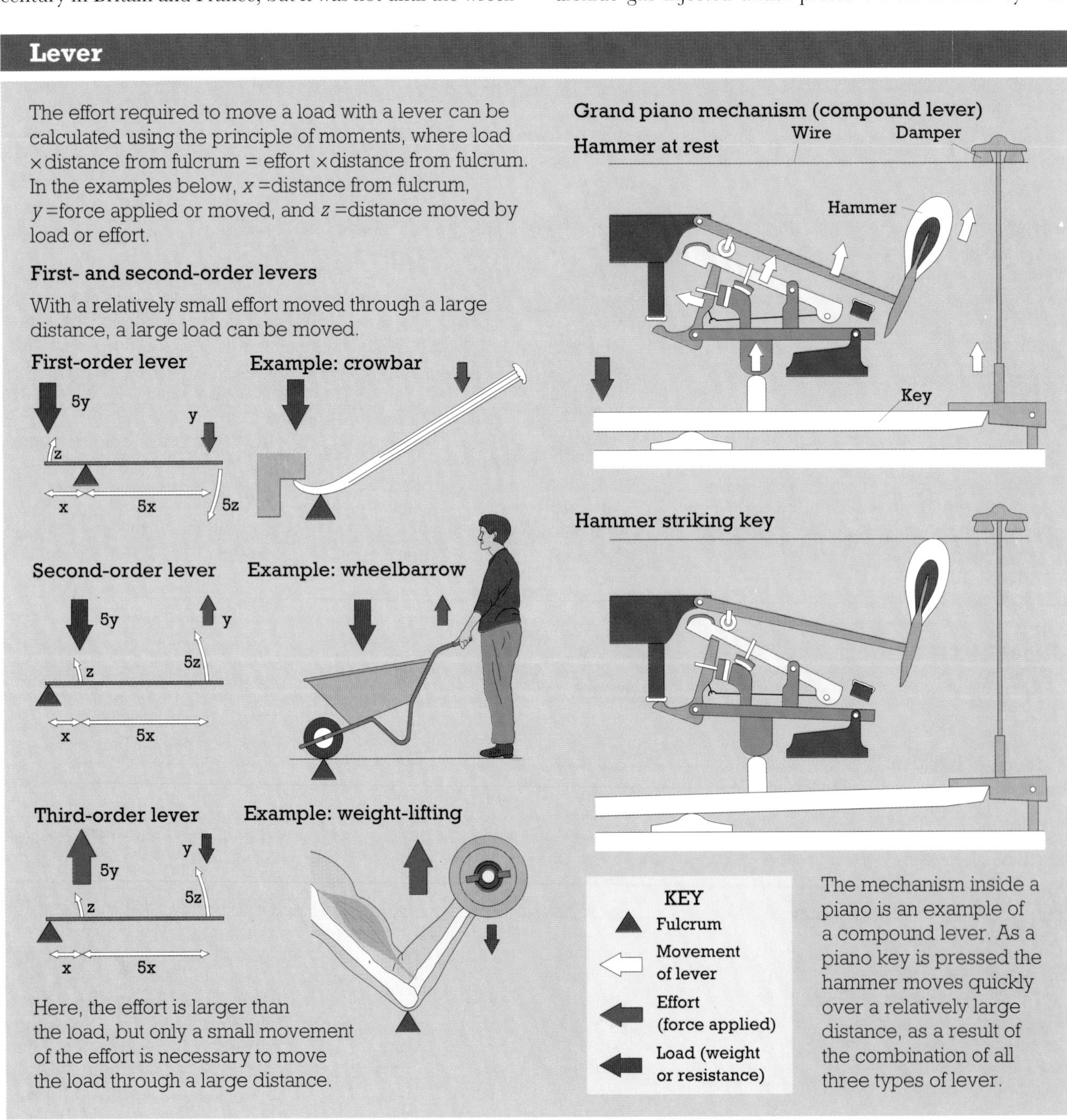

Here, the effort is larger than the load, but only a small movement of the effort is necessary to move the load through a large distance.

The mechanism inside a piano is an example of a compound lever. As a piano key is pressed the hammer moves quickly over a relatively large distance, as a result of the combination of all three types of lever.

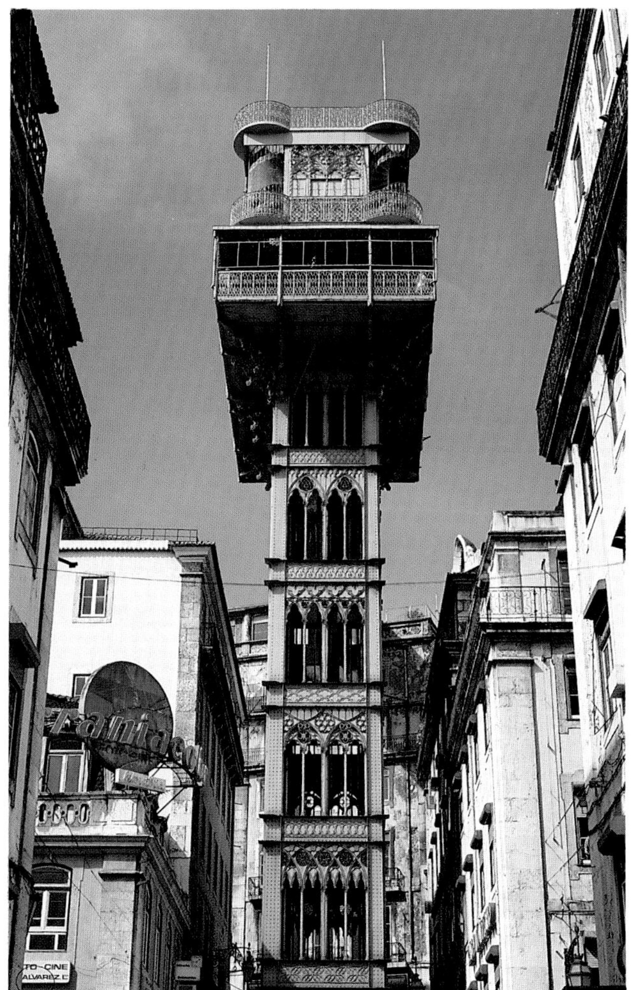

The Santa Justa **lift** in Lisbon, Portugal. It was designed by the French engineer Gustave Eiffel.

attached to the jacket. Life-jackets worn by divers contain air rather than carbon dioxide, the air providing a reserve for breathing. Life-jackets may also carry a light and a smoke signal to aid rescue.

life-support machine *heart lung machine, *respirator, *intensive-care unit.

lift (US, elevator), an enclosed platform (car) that transports goods or passengers in a vertical passage (shaft). In the electric lift, wire ropes run over a pulley support the car at one end and a counterweight at the other. The mechanism is driven by an electric motor at the shaft top. The load to be raised is thus the difference in weight between the car and the counterweight. A hydraulic lift is supported from below by a vertical ram extending beneath the lift shaft, and the car is raised by pumping oil into the ram. In 1990, the first lifts driven by *linear motors were installed in Japan. The motor is incorporated into the lift counterweight. Modern automatic lifts are directed by microprocessors to answer calls in physical rather than chronological sequence. Doors will open only when the car is properly aligned with the floor. Door-edge sensors detect obstructions, stopping the lift until they are cleared. In skyscrapers, a combination of local and express lifts is used. The 110-storey World Trade Center in New York is divided into three zones: twenty-four local lifts carry passengers within each zone, while eleven express lifts carry passengers directly from street level to the upper zones.

light bulb *incandescent lamp.

light-emitting diode (LED), a solid-state source of illumination, essentially a semiconductor *diode that emits light when it conducts. LEDs are used in electronics principally as indicators, since they do not generally provide enough power for usable illumination; they are also used in optical transmitters in *optical fibre systems. Common applications include displays for calculators and digital watches, and numerical read-outs of all kinds. In these instances, they are usually arranged as groups of *seven-segment displays. However, for much battery-powered portable equipment, LEDs consume too much power, and have been superseded in these instances by *liquid crystal displays.

lighter *barge.

lighthouse, a tower or other structure containing a beacon light to warn or guide ships at sea. A lighthouse at Sigeum (now Sigeon in Turkey) is mentioned in the writings of the Greek poet Lesches of Mytilene as early as 660 BC, and the Pharos of Alexandria, built in the reign of Ptolemy II (283–247 BC), was one of the Seven Wonders of the World. During the 1st and 2nd centuries AD lighthouses were also erected by the Romans. The first lighthouse built at sea was at Cardouan in the Gironde estuary on the Bay of Biscay, in about AD 800. In the mid-18th century *Smeaton greatly improved lighthouse design by building the Eddystone lighthouse off the Plymouth coast (UK) with dovetailed stone blocks for added strength against the waves. Most lighthouses are now built using steel and concrete. Until the 19th century lighthouses were lit by wood, oil, or coal. The light signal was dramatically improved by the use of *lenses (especially the *Fresnel lens) and reflectors to concentrate the beam. Later, beacons were rotated using motors. In the early 20th century acetylene gas lamps, and later electricity, were used instead of oil lamps. Individual lighthouses display characteristic patterns of light—fixed, flashing, fixed and flashing, or occulting (with short dark intervals)—that allow them to be identified. Light signals are often supplemented by sound produced by horns, sirens or radio and radar beacons that are detectable by navigators. Until recently, lighthouses were crewed, but increasingly they are changing to automatic operation. In conditions where lighthouses cannot operate, *lightships or *Lanby buoys are used.

lighting, the production of illumination by artificial means. All forms of lighting used up to 100 years ago depended on the combustion of either solid or liquid fuels. Mesopotamian *oil lamps date from 8000 BC, and *candles were first used in ancient Egypt. In the Middle Ages, pedestrians carried a flambeau—a torch of twisted fibres coated with a flammable material. The next major advance was the *Argand lamp, with a tubular wick and glass chimney, which gave a brighter, steadier light. Oil lamps were improved steadily until the beginning of the 20th century. The paraffin lamp was extensively used in rural districts.

*Gas lighting was in common use in urban areas by the mid-19th century in houses, factories, and for street-lighting. Around 1870 the *incandescent electric lamp was invented independently by *Swan and *Edison, heralding the beginning of the modern lighting era. The *electricity generation

A **lighthouse** in the north reef of the Great Barrier Reef, Australia. Like many other modern lighthouses, although originally tended by lighthouse keepers, it is now fully automatic in operation.

and supply industry initially arose to supply power for electric lighting. The development of tungsten filaments in the early 1900s was an important advance, allowing lamps to run at a higher temperature and therefore emit more and whiter light for the same electrical input. The neon light was developed during the late 19th century, and was used for decoration and advertising. Other *gas-discharge lamps using mercury and sodium were used for street-lighting; xenon discharge tubes are used in lighthouses. In the 1930s the *fluorescent lamp was developed; this is very efficient for lighting interiors. More recent developments include microscopic filament lamps, enabling surgeons to examine the internal cavities of a patient's body (*endoscopy).

light meter *exposure meter.

lightning conductor, a pointed metal rod projecting above a building to provide an easy path for a lightning strike to discharge to earth, without causing structural damage. The point of the rod ionizes the surrounding air, making it more conductive so that it attracts lightning. Several lightning conductors may be fixed to the highest parts of a structure and connected to a thick metal tape running down the structure and into the ground. The principle was discovered by *Franklin in the late 18th century.

lightship, a dumb vessel (one without motive power) moored over a shoal or bank, serving the same purpose as a *lighthouse. The warning light is mounted on a mast amidships, and the ship carries special markings for recognition by day. The lightship is also fitted with acoustic fog and submarine signalling equipment, and with a *radar beacon. Lightships were first used in the late 18th century. Normally each ship carries a crew of three or four men, but increasingly they are changing to automatic operation. (See also *Lanby buoy.)

lignite *coal.

Lilienthal, Otto (1848–96), German pioneer of aeronautics. In about 1880, after a close study of bird flight, he began to experiment with gliders. This stimulated popular interest in gliding as a sport, and he himself made more than 2,000 flights. In 1895 he built a biplane incorporating a small motor to flap the wings, but a mechanical defect led to a fatal crash the following year.

lime (quicklime, calcium oxide, CaO), a white, caustic, alkaline solid, obtained by roasting limestone (calcium carbonate) to drive off carbon as carbon dioxide. Lime reacts vigorously with water to form slaked lime (calcium hydroxide). Lime and slaked lime are used in building for *mortars, *plasters, and *cement, and in agriculture to neutralize acid soils. Lime is a major raw material for the chemical industry, and in the *iron and steel industry it is used to form slag. It is also used as a refactory, and as a dehydrating agent.

limestone, a non-combustible, sedimentary rock consisting mainly of calcium carbonate ($CaCO_3$) in the form of calcite. It is obtained by quarrying and used extensively for a wide range of purposes. In the construction industry, it is used as a structural material in building and sculpture, and as road ballast. It is subject to attack by acid, and high levels of industrial pollution cause rapid and obvious corrosion. It is one of the raw materials used to make *cement. On heating, it decomposes to produce *lime and carbon dioxide gas. It is used to remove sulphur from coal and sulphur dioxide from industrial waste gases. It is also used to remove silicon-based impurities in the *blast-furnace production of iron.

Linde, Carl Paul Gottfried von (1842–1934), German engineer, an early innovator of *refrigeration. In 1879 he designed the first domestic refrigerator, which he manufactured until 1892. In 1895 he designed a plant for the large-scale liquefaction of air, some seven years before *Claude. He later (1901) developed a process for obtaining oxygen from liquid air, which led to the development of many industrial processes utilizing oxygen.

linear motor, a type of induction *electric motor, providing straight-line movement rather than rotation, principally designed for high-speed railway systems and other traction applications (see *ground-guidance systems). In high-speed railway systems, one conductor is attached to the track and the other mounted on the vehicle base. Electric power for energizing the conductors is provided on board the train, or from a track-based supply. Coils on the vehicle generate a magnetic field in which the poles move along the length of the vehicle. The field induces electric currents in the track, which itself generates a magnetic field. The two fields interact, moving the vehicle along the track. The vehicle and track do not make significant contact, ensuring high speeds and comfort. However, because the technology is radically different from established traction systems, linear motors have not yet found widespread use in transportation. Other proven applications include high-speed conveyor systems, and electrostatic *pumps.

linen, a textile material made from the cellulose bast (stem) fibres of the flax plant (*Linum usitatissimum*). Typical stems are about 1 m (40 inches) long and have about 1,000 bast fibres running along their length. In addition to the fibres, the stems consist of woody and pectin-like material. To conserve the length of the fibres, the plants are harvested by pulling them out of the ground, complete with roots. The stems are then exposed to weather or water, and to bacteria, in order to disintegrate the woody material and much of the pectin, a process known as 'retting'. The stems are then 'scutched'—they are broken down mechanically to separate the fibres. For the finest *yarns, the separated fibres are drawn through a trough of warm water. They are then spun into yarn for making linen fabrics. Heavier yarns are spun dry and used for *canvases.

liner, a ship employed on a scheduled trans-ocean route carrying passengers, although some liners also carry cargo. Most of the *steamship companies operating such services began as mail-carriers, the government subsidies providing the economic base for future expansion. The introduction of the marine steam-engine in the early 19th century, its growing reliability as it developed, and the use of iron and steel as shipbuilding materials all contributed to the development and growth of early liner services. The extensive emigrations of Europeans to the USA during the 19th century led to a rapid expansion of liner services. By World War I liners of over 30,000 tonnes and capable of carrying more than 2,000 passengers were in operation to accommodate the demand for travel world-wide. In the years between the two World Wars demand doubled, with liners of up to 83,000 tonnes carrying passengers in luxury at speeds of about 30 *knots. After World War II air travel began to compete seriously with the ocean liner. By 1957 more passengers were travelling by air than by sea. Most of the large liners became obsolete, but a few continue to operate as cruise ships, alongside new liners specifically built for cruising.

linoleum, a durable floor-covering material. First made *c.*1860, linoleum consists of a layer of a cork-like material, typically about 3 mm (0.12 inch) thick, backed by a textile *fabric. The cork-like material (consisting of finely ground cork bound together by natural resins and oxidized linseed oil) is extruded as a uniform sheet and is pressed into *adhesive contact with the base fabric (usually woven jute). Linoleum has now been almost completely displaced by cheaper synthetic materials.

Linotype, the trade name of a *typesetting machine for metal type invented by *Mergenthaler in 1884. An integral keyboard first selects and assembles the letter matrices and word spaces needed in each line. After expanding the spaces to achieve consistent line length ('justification'), the matrices then pass to a *type metal casting box to cast each line of type as a solid 'slug'. Such machines were universally adopted by newspaper and other printers needing fast, economic typesetting. The name is now German-owned and is synonymous with a range of modern phototypesetting equipment.

linseed oil *drying oil.

lipid *fats and oils.

liquefied natural gas, *natural gas which has had its *liquid petroleum gas fraction removed, and has then been cooled and pressurized to make it liquefy. At normal pressure, natural gas (largely *methane) liquefies at about −160 °C. Until the 1960s, this low temperature made it impractical to produce and move large quantities of liquefied natural gas, although liquefaction reduces volume by a factor of 600. Since then, specialist tankers have sailed with liquefied gas cargoes to areas or countries where pipeline gas delivery would be impractical. Liquefied gas is also used as an underground storage medium.

A poster advertising travel on the 83,000-tonne SS *Normandie* during the years between World Wars I and II, the heyday of the luxury **liner**.

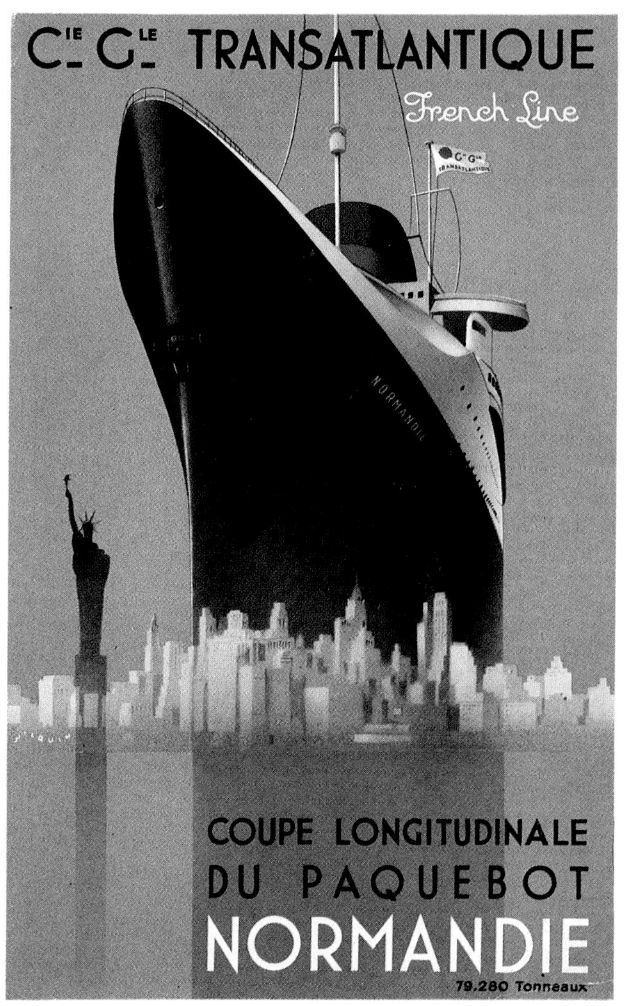

liquid crystal display (LCD), a type of display that has replaced the *light-emitting diode in *watches, *calculators, and other portable, battery-operated applications. It consists of two polarizing filters, each of which allows passage of light waves in one plane. Below the filters is a mirror, and between them is a liquid crystal, a complex chemical whose molecules rearrange their crystal structure when an electric voltage is applied. When no voltage is present, the crystal rotates the light through 90 degrees. This allows the light to pass through both polarizing filters, and reflect back from the mirror, giving the display a light appearance. When a voltage is applied to any portion of the display, the liquid crystal in that portion rearranges, and light passes through it unrotated. The light cannot now pass through the second polarizing filter and the display appears black. Digits thus appear in black on a light background. LCDs are most commonly in the form of *seven-segment displays, but also appear in many other forms, including complete screens and lap-top portable computers. The power consumption of an LCD is negligible.

liquid-crystal polymer, a class of polymers with a wide range of physical and electro-optical properties, characterized by a liquid-crystal structure. Some polymers have a regular, crystalline arrangement of their molecules, while others are amorphous, like glass. In liquid-crystal polymers, the molecules are all oriented similarly, but their relative positions remain random. The first such materials to be developed were the aramid fibres (see *nylon), which are stronger than steel and find a wide range of structural applications in *fibre-reinforced plastics. Other liquid-crystal polymers have unique electro-optical properties: liquid-crystal side-chain polymers, for example, can be made transparent by the application of an electric field, and opaque by the action of a laser. Such materials are being developed for use on erasable *compact discs, and for *holographic plates that do not need to be photographically developed.

liquidizer *food processors and mixers.

liquid petroleum gas (LPG), a mixture of gases obtained from petroleum or *natural gas, and stored as a liquid. The gases are kept in liquid form either by dissolving them in solvent oils or by storage in pressurized containers. The two main LPG gases are *propane (C_3H_8) and *butane (C_4H_{10}), which are either extracted from natural gas or produced in *petroleum refining. LPG will stay liquid at much lower pressures than unprocessed natural gas, and is therefore easier and safer to store and transport. It is used in pressurized bottles as a fuel in caravans, boats, and homes without piped gas supply. LPG is also a viable alternative to petrol for powering vehicles. (See also *liquefied natural gas.)

Lister, Joseph, Baron (1827–1912), British surgeon who established antiseptic medicine. After qualifying in medicine, he went to Edinburgh University to gain experience under James Syme, the leading Scottish surgeon, whom he succeeded as Professor at Edinburgh in 1869. The work of *Pasteur convinced Lister that the very high numbers of post-operative deaths due to sepsis (infection) were caused by micro-organisms, rather than the entry of air into the wounds, as was generally believed. This led him to adopt carbolic acid (*phenol) dressings for wounds and, later, antiseptic sprays to sterilize the air in operating theatres. The results proved revolutionary and his methods were soon widely adopted.

lithium (symbol Li, at. no. 3, r.a.m. 6.94), a soft, silvery, highly reactive metallic element obtained by the *electrolysis of a fused mixture of potassium and lithium chlorides. Soft metals become harder when alloyed with lithium. Lithium salts of fatty acids are widely used in *lubricating oils as thickeners, and lithium carbonate is used as a treatment for manic depression. Lithium is also used in the manufacture of tritium, an important component of thermonuclear weapons.

Animals used in livestock farming

Animal	Origin and domestication	Common breeds/uses
Cattle, sheep, pigs		
Cattle	Eastern European or Middle East	Ayrshire, Friesian, Jersey (dairy); Braham, Boran, Hereford, Limousin (beef); Charolais, Holstein (dual-purpose). Leather and manure also obtained
Sheep	Middle East	Cheviot, Herdwick, Border Leicester, Merino, Southdown, Suffolk. Farmed for wool, meat, milk, sheepskin, and manure
Pigs	Many parts of world	Large White, Pietran, Berkshire, Duroc, Gloucester Old Spot. Farmed for pork, bacon, and leather
Other animals		
Alpaca	South America	Wool, meat
Camel	Middle East and Central Asia	Draught and pack work, riding, milk, meat, wool, dung (fuel)
Donkey	Middle East	Draught and pack work, riding, breeding mules
Duck	Various	Eggs, meat, feathers, down
Elephant	Indian subcontinent	Draught and pack, meat, ivory
Goose	Northern temperate regions	Eggs, meat, guarding and defence
Goat	Middle East	Milk, meat, skin, wool (angora goat)
Hen	Indian subcontinent	Eggs, meat
Horse	Caucasus	Draught and pack work, riding, milk, meat, manure
Llama	South America	Pack work, milk, meat
Reindeer	Northern Europe	Draught and pack, riding, milk, meat, hair, leather
Water buffalo	Southern China/South East Asia	Draught work
Yak	Himalayas	Pack work, riding

Lock

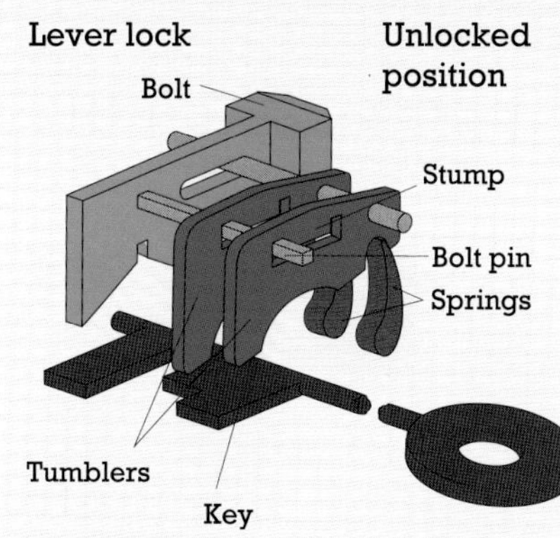

The springs hold down the tumblers preventing the bolt from moving.

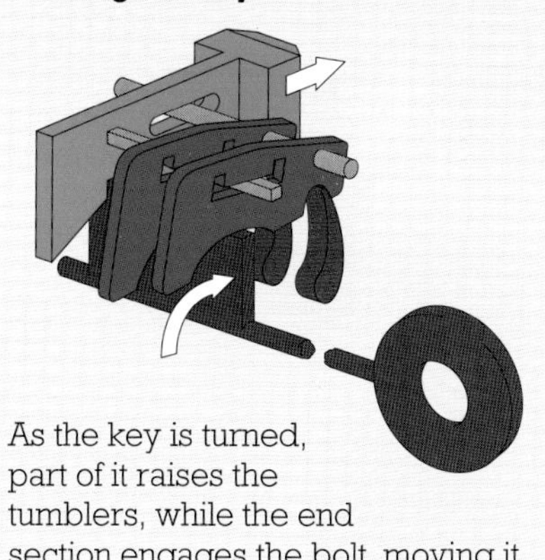

As the key is turned, part of it raises the tumblers, while the end section engages the bolt, moving it outwards and thus locking the door.

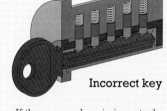

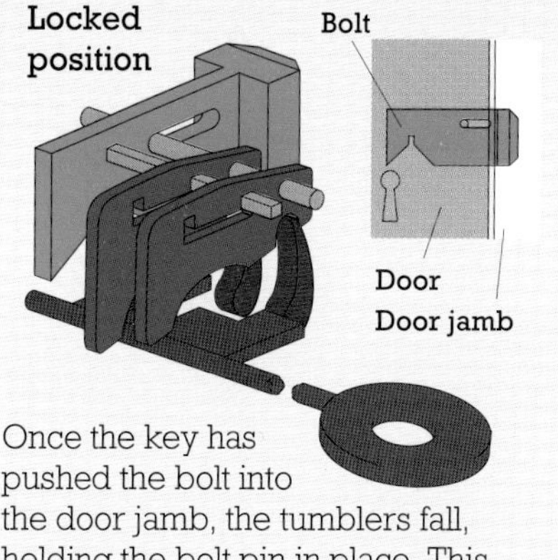

Once the key has pushed the bolt into the door jamb, the tumblers fall, holding the bolt pin in place. This prevents the door being opened until the key is used again.

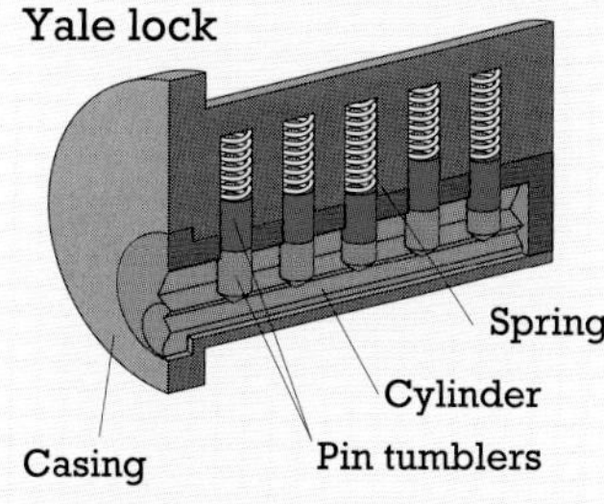

Drilled across the cylinder and casing are five holes, each containing two pin tumblers held down by a spring. Inserting a key pushes the pin tumblers up.

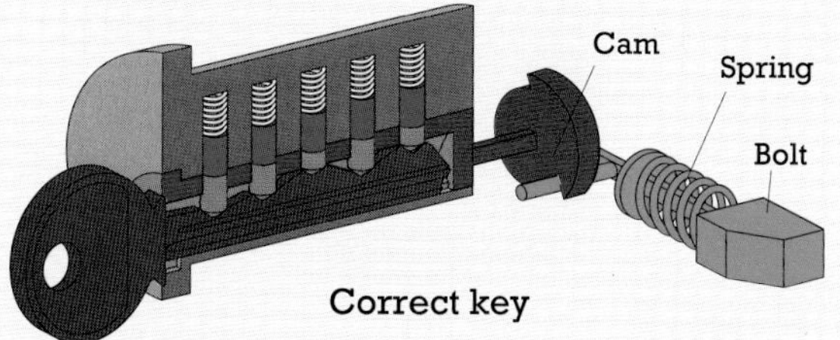

The pin tumblers in each hole are of different lengths. When the correct key is inserted, the junctions of the upper and lower pin tumblers align with the junction between the casing and the cylinder. The key is now able to turn, drawing the bolt back.

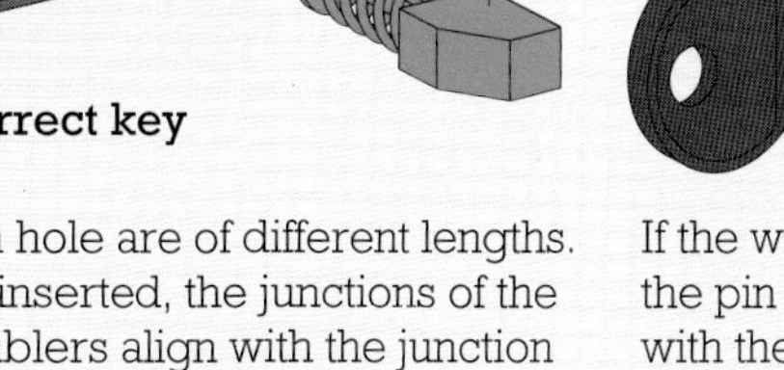

If the wrong key is inserted, the pin tumblers fail to align with the junction between the cylinder and casing. As a result, the pin tumblers prevent any rotation of the cylinder.

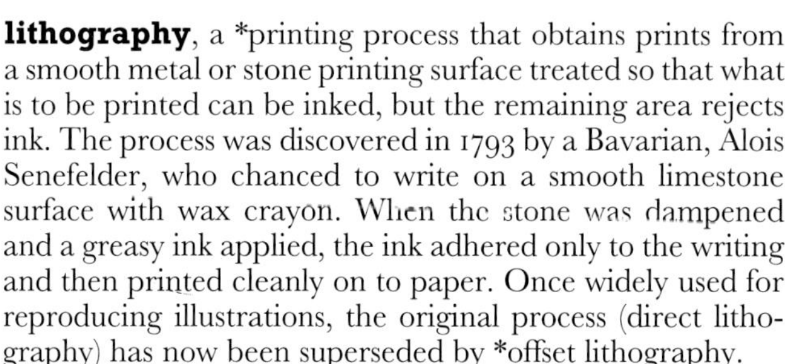

lithography, a *printing process that obtains prints from a smooth metal or stone printing surface treated so that what is to be printed can be inked, but the remaining area rejects ink. The process was discovered in 1793 by a Bavarian, Alois Senefelder, who chanced to write on a smooth limestone surface with wax crayon. When the stone was dampened and a greasy ink applied, the ink adhered only to the writing and then printed cleanly on to paper. Once widely used for reproducing illustrations, the original process (direct lithography) has now been superseded by *offset lithography.

lithotripsy, the crushing of abnormal stone-like deposits within the bladder, using an instrument (a lithotrite) introduced into the urethra. After the operation was first successfully performed in 1824 by the French surgeon Jean Civiale, many types of lithotrite were developed, most employing a screw action to crush the stone. As anaesthesia and asepsis made abdominal surgery safer, lithotripsy was performed less frequently. The invention of the lithotripter in 1973 has made it possible to fragment some stones of the renal system, and of the gall bladder, using high-powered *ultrasound.

litter, a vehicle containing a couch upon which a person can be carried, with a framework incorporating long horizontal shafts by which it can be lifted and carried on men's shoulders or by pack animals. Litters continued to be used by the rich after the introduction of wheeled vehicles, because of their greater comfort. In Europe in the 17th century, *carriages and coaches replaced the litter for long journeys, but in towns an enclosed variant of the litter, the sedan chair, continued in use to the end of the 18th century.

livestock farming, the raising of animals on a farm. Dairy and beef *cattle, *sheep, *poultry, and *pigs are raised for meat, milk, eggs, and wool (see table on page 204). Horses are bred for recreation or sport, and animals such as mink and ermine are bred in *fur-farms. Bovine and equine species are also raised as *draught animals. Ruminant (cud-chewing) animals such as sheep, cattle, and goats are important for their ability to convert pasture, roughage, and non-protein nitrogen sources such as urea into meat, milk, and wool. Over 60 per cent of farmland world-wide is used for pasture. With the exception of *organic farming, modern livestock farming practices are highly intensive. *Animal breeding is controlled to select animals for a particular function. Pigs and poultry are often raised on *factory farms, where food intake, temperature, light, and other conditions are tailored to maximize conversion of food into the desired product. A more scientific understanding of the nutritional requirements of animals has made it possible to develop *feedstuffs that provide a balanced and palatable diet throughout the year. Overall, these methods have led to

A **lock** on the Welland Canal, Canada, the section of the St Lawrence Seaway that links Lake Erie with Lake Ontario. Each of the eight locks on the canal can accommodate ships up to 70 m (230 feet) in length.

increases in production, and in some cases to the creation of large surpluses at a local or regional level.

local area network (LAN) (computing) *network.

lock, a device for securing a door, lid, or item of movable property against unauthorized entry or removal. In its usual form it consists of a sliding bolt on the door or other moving part, which can be made to engage or disengage with the fixed part only by means of a removable key. Sophisticated locks have been made from a very early period; an early Egyptian lock used movable pins similar in principle to the Yale cylinder lock. The most common type of lock uses a number of lever tumblers (see figure on the previous page), each of which has to be raised to the right level to allow the bolt to slide. This can be achieved only by use of the correct key, which has corresponding wards filed to the right height. In addition, the sides of the tongue of the key are sometimes grooved to correspond with grooves cut in the slotted part of the keyhole. The pin tumbler lock was invented in the USA by Linus Yale Junior in 1848; this type is common for the doors of houses and cars. It can be copied easily by a simple machine, although the key blank must be grooved lengthwise to match the lock. More secure is the mortise lock, which requires a key to engage and disengage the bolt. A variant is the key-in-knob lock, popular in hotels. For highest security, as required for a *safe, additional devices are used, such as a time-lock, the use of two different keys, an elaborate combination lock, or electrical operation. Locks operated by electronic key cards, which send a signal to the lock mechanism, are becoming common.

A lock is also an enclosed part of a *canal in which the water level can be changed by using gates. It allows boats to transfer between sections (reaches) of the canal with different water levels. In navigating upstream, for example, a boat enters the lock from the lower reach. A gate closes behind it and water is allowed to flow into the lock from the upper reach until the level in the lock is raised to that in the upper reach. The gate to the upper reach can then be opened.

locomotive *fireless locomotive, *railways, history of, *steam locomotive, *electric locomotive, *diesel locomotive.

log, an instrument used to measure the speed of a vessel through water. The name derives from the early practice of throwing a log tied to a knotted line over the ship's stern, and measuring the distance (in *knots) travelled away from the log in a fixed time period. This was recorded in the log-book. Modern measurement methods include recording the speed of rotation of an impeller attached to the keel of a vessel; measuring the current generated by the flow of seawater over an electromagnetic probe; and the use of Doppler *sonar.

logic gate (computing), one of the fundamental electronic circuits from which a digital *computer is built. Originally constructed from individual components (first *thermionic valves then *transistors), they are now made as *integrated circuits (ICs). A very complex IC, such as a *microprocessor, may contain many thousands of logic gates. Each gate has one or more inputs and a single output, the value of which is determined by the states (voltage levels) of the inputs (see figure). As they are digital devices, both inputs and outputs can assume only one of two states, representing 0 or 1.

Other than the three basic logic gates shown in the figure, NAND, NOR, XOR, and XNOR gates are also important in digital electronics. In a NAND gate, the output is 0 only when all inputs are 1; otherwise the output is 1. NAND gates alone can realize any other logic operation and are easy to implement with transistors. In a NOR gate, the output is 1

Logic gate

Logic gates are electronic decision-making circuits containing transistors and other electronic components. These switch outputs 'on' (logic value 1), or 'off' (logic value 0) in accordance with a 'truth table' which describes how the gate responds to all possible on/off inputs.

AND gate

The AND gate has two or more inputs and one output. It only gives an on output when both inputs are on.

A	B	C
0	0	0
0	1	0
1	0	0
1	1	1

OR gate

The OR gate has two or more inputs and one output. It gives an on output when either one or both inputs are on.

A	B	C
0	0	0
0	1	1
1	0	1
1	1	1

NOT gate

The NOT gate has one input and one output. It gives an off output when the input is on, and an on output when the input is off.

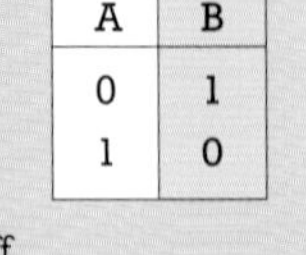

A	B
0	1
1	0

Example

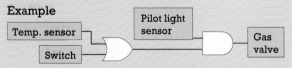

The gas valve will be switched on only when the pilot light sensor is on AND when either the room is cold OR the manual switch is turned on.

Long-wall mining

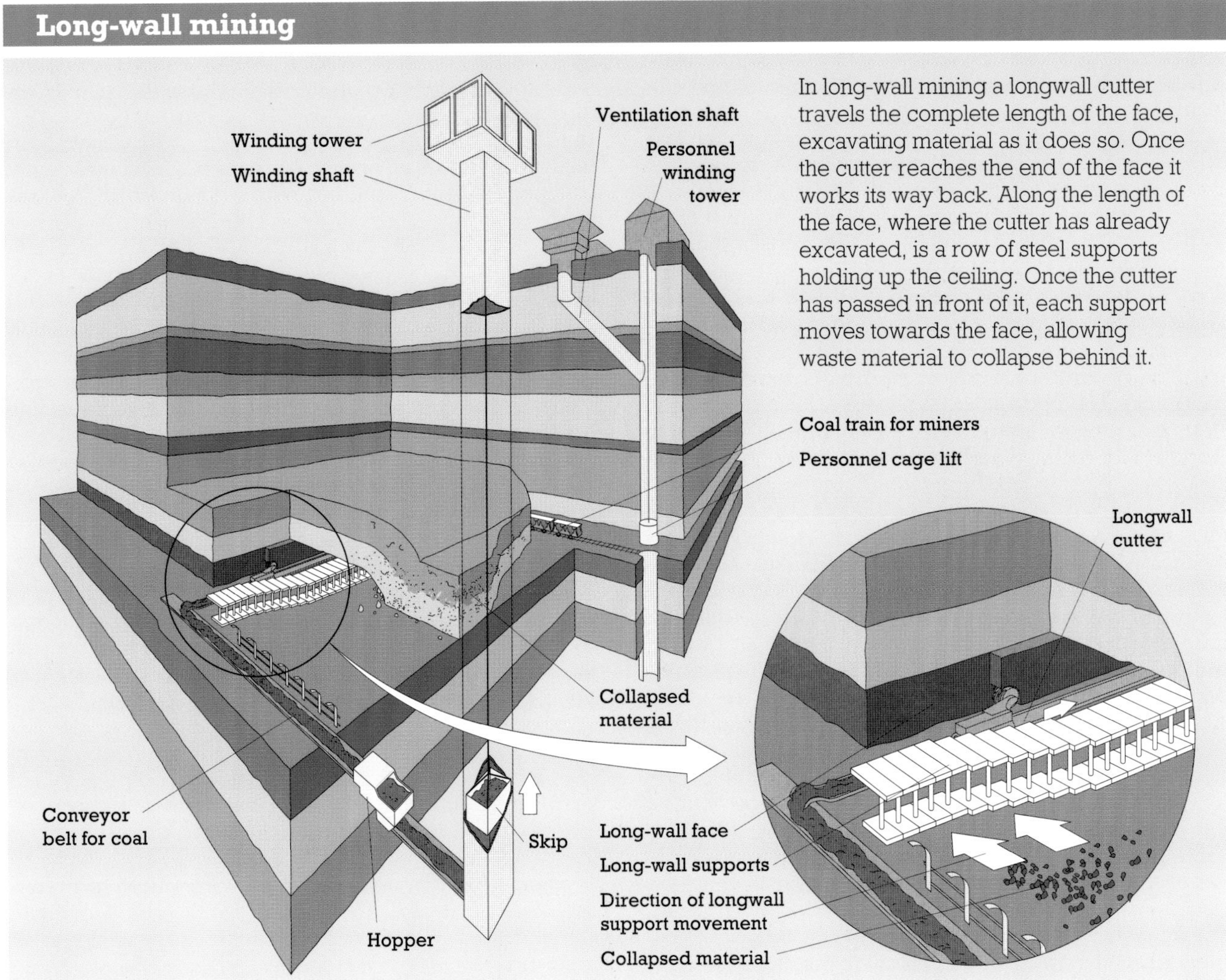
Winding tower
Winding shaft
Ventilation shaft
Personnel winding tower
In long-wall mining a longwall cutter travels the complete length of the face, excavating material as it does so. Once the cutter reaches the end of the face it works its way back. Along the length of the face, where the cutter has already excavated, is a row of steel supports holding up the ceiling. Once the cutter has passed in front of it, each support moves towards the face, allowing waste material to collapse behind it.
Coal train for miners
Personnel cage lift
Longwall cutter
Collapsed material
Conveyor belt for coal
Skip
Hopper
Long-wall face
Long-wall supports
Direction of longwall support movement
Collapsed material

only if all the inputs are 0; otherwise the output is 0. XOR (exclusive-OR) gates have their output as 1 only when any one of the inputs is 1 and all others are 0. XNOR is 0 when one input is 1 and the others are 0. Boolean algebra, invented by the British mathematician George Boole in 1857, allows calculations to be made about systems which have only two allowed states. It can be used to prove that combinations of logic gates, known as logic circuits, will perform their intended function.

longitude *latitude and longitude.

long-line fishing, a commercial method of *fishing using a line fitted with many hooks. Bottom long-lines are used to catch demersal (bottom-dwelling) fish such as cod, haddock, hake, halibut, and sea bream. They consist of a heavy, weighted line, about 90 m (300 feet) long, with short side-lines to which baited hooks are attached at intervals. Drifting long-lines are used for large fish, in particular tuna and albacore. They consist of about 400 sections, each of which is up to 400 m (1,300 feet) long. The whole assembly is supported by floats and can carry as many as 2,500 baited hooks. Long-lines (some using automated systems) are set and retrieved from one vessel in the duration of a day.

long-wall mining, a system of mining of deposits, especially *coal, in which the whole seam is removed, leaving no pillars. It developed from a system where a working face or wall, often several hundred metres long, was advanced in a continuous line by up to 100 people, with several roadways being formed concurrently. The space created by the removal of material was partially or completely filled with stone and debris. This method has generally been superseded by total caving of the space, using *coal-cutters and hydraulic *pit-props. Access roadways are formed 50–350 m (160–1,150 feet) apart at the ends of the long-wall face. The most productive underground mines now employ the retreat long-wall method (see figure), where roadways are formed prior to the extraction of material, and the coal face moves back towards the mine entrance. Highly mechanized long-wall mines can produce 20,000 tonnes per day.

long wave (low frequency) *waveband.

loom, an apparatus for weaving *yarn or thread into *fabric. Most woven cloth consists of lengthways threads (*warp) and crossways threads (*weft). A loom interweaves these threads by passing the weft thread to and fro across the width of the cloth, under and over the warp threads. The pattern of the interweaving of warp and weft threads determines the *weave of the finished fabric. A simple loom has two light heddle shafts—bars carrying fine wire loops through which the warp threads pass. When one heddle shaft is raised and the other lowered, alternate warp threads are separated to form a clear passage or 'shed' through the width of the fabric, through which the weft passes (see figure). The traditional way of passing weft through the shed is with a *shuttle, which unwinds the yarn as it crosses the loom.

Weaving is thought to have developed around 5000 BC; the earliest looms were frameless or ground-looms, in which the warp was stretched between two bars pegged to the ground, or between a peg and a belt around the waist of the weaver. In later ground-looms, still widely used in southern Asia and the Near East, the weaver sits on the ground with his or her legs in a pit, and operates the heddle bars via cords attached to the big toes. This leaves both hands free to pass the weft. Other early looms had vertical frames, with the warp either stretched between two bars or weighted at its lower end. The horizontal hand-loom, which appeared in Europe around the 13th century AD and probably earlier in Asia, largely replaced earlier looms in many countries. It comprised a rigid wooden horizontal frame, supporting a roll of warp yarn at one end, and the roll on to which the finished cloth was wound at the other. A superstructure integral with the frame supported heddles harnessed to treadles below the loom, worked by the weaver's feet (see figure). In most hand-looms, a batten or reed was suspended from the superstructure, with which each successive shot of weft was 'beaten-up' (pushed firmly into place against its predecessor).

From the mid-18th century most hand-looms had *flying shuttles, which substantially speeded their operation. Pattern weaving in fabrics was limited by the number of heddles that could be operated on one loom (about twenty-four on the most elaborate looms). For more complex designs, a draw-loom was used. A draw-loom is equipped to raise individual warp threads independently, thereby making it possible to weave fabrics with complex integral patterns. Draw-looms were hand-operated until the early 19th century, when the *Jacquard mechanism was introduced, in which the rise and fall of the warp was controlled by a system of punched cards. In the 17th century, bar-looms or Dutch loom-engines were built that were capable of automatically weaving ribbons or laces with warps only a few inches wide.

The first true power-driven loom is said to have been made in 1785 by *Cartwright. Cartwright's machine was not commercially successful, but others developed the power-loom for various applications, such as weaving of worsted yarn, cotton weaving, linen weaving, and *carpet manufacture. In the UK, the power-loom largely replaced the hand-loom in the mid- to late 19th century. In Europe and elsewhere, mechanization of weaving came somewhat later. Modern industrial looms are generally shuttleless, using a method of weft insertion other than a shuttle. The first commercially successful shuttleless loom was the Sulzer weaving machine, introduced in about 1950. In it the weft was inserted in measured lengths from one side of the loom only. Each length of weft was drawn through the shed by a small projectile, which gripped the leading edge of the weft length as it was shot across the loom by a spring-gun. Other looms use single or double 'rapiers' with grippers at their tips. These pick up the leading end of the weft, take it through the shed, and are then withdrawn to permit shedding. Jet looms use a jet of water, or more commonly air, to propel the weft threads through the shed. Modern air-jet weaving machines can insert up to 1,500 wefts per minute.

Loran (*lo*ng *ra*nge *n*avigation), a long-range *radio aid to navigation, developed in the USA from the British World War II navigation aid, GEE. The original system (Loran-A) was used extensively in Europe and North Africa in 1944 for night-bombing operations, but it has been largely replaced by Loran-C, developed in the 1950s. A Loran-C 'chain' consists of a master radio-transmitting station with two, three, or four secondary stations disposed around it at a distance of 1,100–1,800 km (600–1,000 nautical miles; see *knot). A ship

Loom

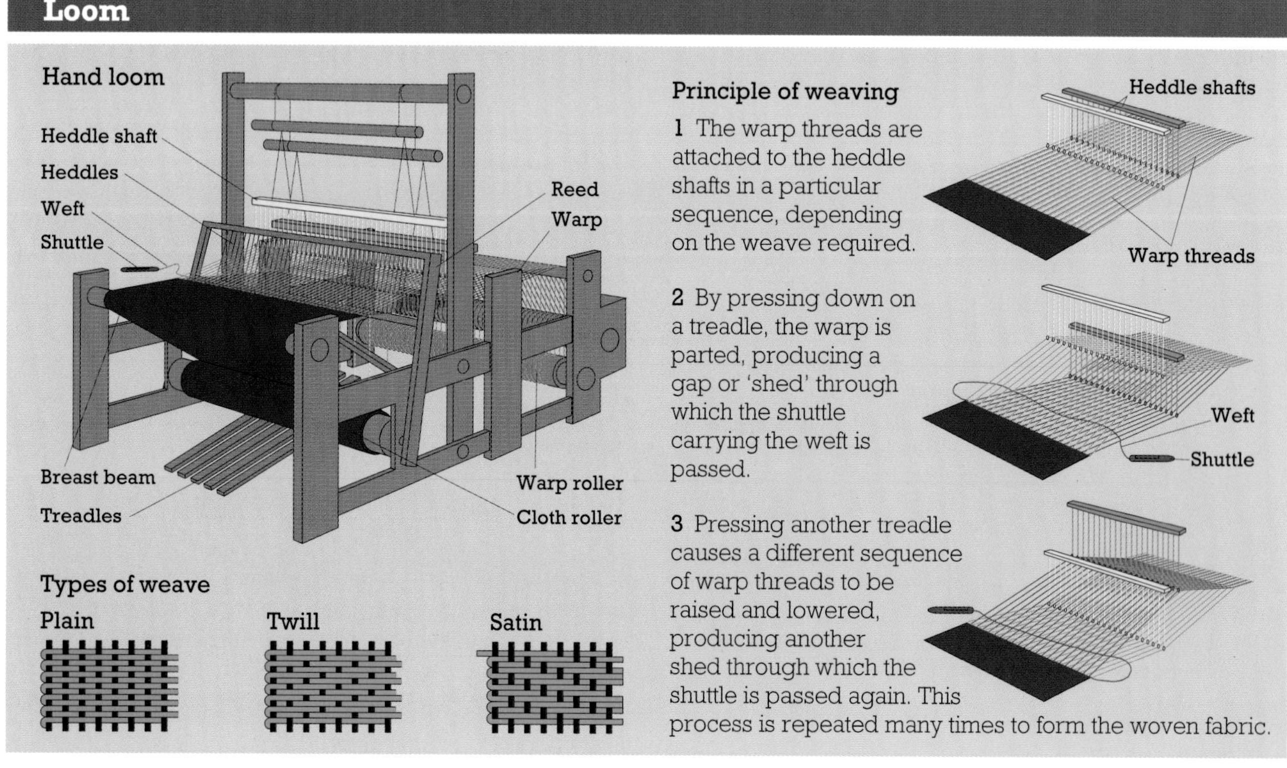

Hand loom
Heddle shaft
Heddles
Weft
Shuttle
Reed
Warp
Breast beam
Treadles
Warp roller
Cloth roller
Types of weave
Plain
Twill
Satin
Principle of weaving
1 The warp threads are attached to the heddle shafts in a particular sequence, depending on the weave required.
Heddle shafts
Warp threads
2 By pressing down on a treadle, the warp is parted, producing a gap or 'shed' through which the shuttle carrying the weft is passed.
Weft
Shuttle
3 Pressing another treadle causes a different sequence of warp threads to be raised and lowered, producing another shed through which the shuttle is passed again. This process is repeated many times to form the woven fabric.

A daguerrotype of Ada, Countess of **Lovelace** in 1850, when she was 35 years old.

or aircraft finds its position using this system by measuring differences in the phase and time of arrival of radio-wave pulses from master and secondary transmitters (for illustration see *navigation). Loran-C has an accuracy of about 500 m (1,640 feet) up to 2,000 km (1,080 nautical miles) from the master station. Loran-C covers the North Atlantic and North Pacific oceans, including the South China Sea, the Gulf of Mexico, the Norwegian Sea, the Mediterranean, and the waters around Saudi Arabia.

lorry (heavy goods vehicle, US, truck), a motor vehicle designed for the transport of heavy goods by road. The first lorry was a 3-kW (4-horsepower), belt-driven vehicle produced in 1896 by *Daimler. Lorries were being built in the USA by 1898, and other countries soon had their own designs. By World War I lorries were in widespread use; by World War II the use of motor lorries had largely replaced horse-drawn transport in developed countries. Lorries were initially limited to use over short distances, with the *railways dominating the long-haul market. More recently, the introduction of container transport (see *container ship) and efficient business organization have led to increased use of lorries for long-distance haulage. Modern lorries may be either straight (rigid) or articulated; in the latter, one or more trailers are connected to the power unit by standardized couplings. *Suspension systems have been improved so that delicate, high-value goods can be carried, and performance has been increased by the use of superchargers and *air-brakes. Many specialized lorries have been evolved, for example, refrigerated vehicles for the bulk distribution of foods, extremely powerful dumper trucks for transporting loose material, and tankers for carrying liquids.

lost-wax process *investment casting.

loudspeaker, a device for converting electrical audio signals into sound; loudspeakers perform the reverse function to *microphones. Common applications of loudspeakers are in *sound recording and reproduction equipment, in *telephone receivers, and in *radio and *television receivers. Most loudspeakers are of the moving-coil type. This comprises a coil, which is free to move backwards and forwards short distances within the field of a permanent magnet. Attached to one end of the coil is a stiff paper or plastic cone. When an electrical signal is applied to the coil, the coil is pushed backwards and forwards due to the interaction between the magnetic field and the signal (see *electromagnetic induction). The rapid oscillations of the coil are reproduced in the cone, producing sound waves.

Lovelace, Augusta Ada King, Countess of (1815–52), British mathematician and active collaborator with *Babbage, the pioneer of mechanical computing. Lovelace, the daughter of Lord Byron, met Babbage in 1833; she began to assist in the development of the *analytical engine and published notes on the work. She was one of the first to recognize the potential of computers and has been called the first computer programmer. The programming language Ada is named after her.

low-ground-pressure vehicle, an all-terrain vehicle (ATV) designed to be able to move on all surfaces. Such vehicles originated in Canada around 1960. Typically they consist of sturdy watertight hulls with as many as eight driven wheels fitted with wide, soft, low-pressure tyres that

The Croco, a Swiss all-terrain **low-ground-pressure vehicle** designed for a variety of military and civil uses. The Croco weighs only 500 kg (1,100 pounds) and is fully amphibious: its large, low-pressure tyres have a tread designed to remain unclogged in the muddiest conditions.

obviate the need for conventional springing and suspension. The large-volume tyres also make these vehicles amphibious, the spinning tyres providing 'paddle-wheel' propulsion when used on water.

lubricating oil, any of a group of oils used to reduce friction in engines, and to protect metal against wear and corrosion. Originally, tallow and caster oil were used. Modern lubricating oils are produced in *petroleum refining by *vacuum distillation of the involatile residue (the atmospheric residue) from the *fractional distillation of petroleum. The most important group of lubricating oils are those for internal-combustion engines, which are graded according to their viscosity at −18 °C, according to the system of the Society of Automotive Engineers (SAE) in the USA. SAE numbers generally range from about 5 to 50. Multigrade car oils have a second grading indicating the relative viscosity at 99 °C. Gear oils have sulphur additives, developed to prevent actual contact between metal surfaces, and to reduce corrosion, promote stability at high temperatures, and control viscosity. Greases are lubricating oils thickened by substances such as soaps, lithium, carbon, or polyethylene.

lumbar puncture, introduction into the spinal canal, normally between the third and fourth lumbar vertebrae, of a hollow needle, either for removal of cerebrospinal fluid (CSF), or for administration of a drug or a radio-opaque contrast medium for *radiology. Measurement of CSF pressure and analysis of CSF composition are techniques used in the diagnosis of several different conditions. Drugs may be administered via lumbar puncture for *anaesthesia, or to access the central nervous system directly, rather than via the bloodstream.

Lumière, Auguste Marie Louis Nicholas (1862–1954), and **Louis Jean** (1864–1948), French pioneers of *cinematography and colour *photography. The Lumière brothers were born into the photographic industry: their father manufactured roll film and photographic paper at Lyon. In 1895 they constructed the first effective *cine-camera and projector, and in the same year gave the first public cinema performance to a paying audience, in Paris. The projector incorporated the modern technique of a claw mechanism engaging with perforated film. In 1904, they patented the autochrome process for colour films, and launched it on the open market in 1907. It was the first direct colour process to be commercially successful.

luminous paint, paint that glows in the dark. It contains phosphor, a material that absorbs short-wavelength light and re-emits it as transient light of a longer wavelength after the energy source has been withdrawn (examples are zinc sulphide and calcium sulphide). Luminous paints that glowed indefinitely, containing small amounts of *radium salts, were used extensively for the hands and numbers on watch faces, but the dangers of the radioactive radium salts led to their withdrawal (see *occupational disease).

lunar module **Apollo* programme.

lunar roving vehicle (Moon buggy) **Apollo* programme.

lyddite *explosive.

McAdam, John Loudon (1756–1836), British *road engineer, of Scottish extraction. After making a fortune in commerce in the USA, he returned to Scotland in 1783 to finance experiments designed to improve the construction of roads. In 1798 he moved to Cornwall, UK, to continue his experiments under government auspices. Unlike his contemporary *Telford, who believed in massive construction, he established that relatively light roads could bear heavy traffic provided that they were well drained, impervious to water, and laid on a well-compacted subsoil. In this, he had much in common with *Trésaguet. He also stressed the importance of systematic road maintenance.

McCormick, Cyrus Hall (1809–84), US agricultural engineer. His father was a manufacturer of agricultural implements, but failed in his attempt to construct a mechanical *reaper. McCormick took up the challenge and had a prototype model at work in 1831. Hearing of the rival machine of *Hussey in 1834, he patented his design, involving a knife and cutter-bar. This led to serious rivalry with Hussey and competition from at least thirty US manufacturers, but McCormick eventually emerged as market leader.

Mace gas *tear-gas.

machine code, the *binary code used to represent the instructions that a *computer executes. It represents the lowest possible level at which a computer can be programmed. Any *program written in a high-level *computer language or *assembly language must be translated into machine code before it can be executed.

machine-gun, a *firearm that shoots a number of rounds of ammunition in rapid succession. Experimental multiple-fire weapons were made from as early as 1350, but the earliest practical weapons were the US Gatling gun (1862) and the French mitrailleuse (1870), both multi-barrelled guns fired by means of a hand crank. The first successful automatic machine-gun was developed by *Maxim in 1884. It used the energy of the recoil as a bullet was fired to push back the bolt, eject the spent cartridge, and load the next round of ammunition. Other machine-guns were gas-operated, utilizing the pressure of gas from the barrel to reload. The calibre of machine-guns was originally that of rifle ammunition, but heavier-calibre weapons were later developed. Light gas-operated machine-guns have become the most common kind in modern armies. (See also *sub-machine gun.)

machine-tool, a machine used in a wide variety of engineering applications to shape metals and other materials. Most machine-tools are now electrically driven, but animal, wind, water, steam, and gas-engine power have been used, and the first *lathes were driven manually. Machine-tools are faster and more accurate than equivalent hand *tools: they were an important element in the development of *mass-production processes, as they allowed individual parts and shapes to be identically reproduced in large numbers so as to be interchangeable. All machine-tools have facilities for holding both the workpiece and the tool, and for accurately controlling movement of the tool relative to the workpiece. Most machining operations generate large amounts of heat, and use cutting fluids (usually oils) for cooling and lubrication. A selection of the many different types of machine-tool are listed in the table overleaf, and some machining processes are illustrated in the figure. Machine-tools work materials by a variety of means. A majority are purely mechanical, but other machining methods have been developed. They include chemical machining, in which material is etched away chemically, and electrolytic machining, in which an electrolyte and an electric current are used to accelerate the process of metal removal. Spark erosion is used to machine very hard materials to any shape by means of a continuous high-voltage spark between an electrode and a workpiece, both of which are immersed in oil. Other machining methods include drilling using *ultrasound, and cutting by means of a *laser beam. New methods of control of machine-tools revolutionized manufacturing processes in the 1980s. *Numerical control of machine-tools has made automatic production of extremely intricate shapes possible. *Transfer machines can be used to link together several machine-tools in sequence, and *flexible manufacturing systems have made it possible for complete systems of machine-tools to be used flexibly for the manufacture of a range of products.

machine translation, a branch of *artificial intelligence concerned with the use of computers to translate between natural human languages such as English and French. An all-purpose translation machine that can retain the subtleties and nuances of meaning between languages is far beyond current computing capabilities. However, there are simpler machines that provide limited translation facilities. Examples are METEO, an English–French translation system used in Montreal, Canada, since 1977 to translate public weather forecasts; and SYSTRAN, a system developed in the USA, initially for Russian–English translation, and now used by the US Air Force, NASA, and (since 1976) the European Commission.

Mach number, the speed of an object expressed as a ratio relative to the speed of sound: thus Mach 1 is the speed of sound itself. It is named after the Austrian physicist Ernst Mach (1838–1916). The speed of sound varies with density and temperature. Thus Mach 1 is 1,240 km/h (770 m.p.h.) in air at sea-level and 20 °C, but decreases at higher altitudes and lower temperatures.

Macintosh, Charles (1766–1843), British industrial chemist, of Scottish extraction, best known for his method of waterproofing clothing. In 1785 he set up as a dyer and manufacturer of sal ammoniac (ammonium chloride); twelve years later he founded the first Scottish *alum works. In 1823 he patented a process for waterproofing fabric by treating it with *rubber dissolved in naphtha. Later, he went into partnership in Manchester, UK, with *Hancock, inventor of a rubber *vulcanizing process. Waterproof coats were soon so popular that they became universally known as 'mackintoshes' (*sic*).

Macleod, John James Rickard *Banting, Sir Frederick Grant.

madder *dyes and dyeing.

Machine-tool

Centre lathe

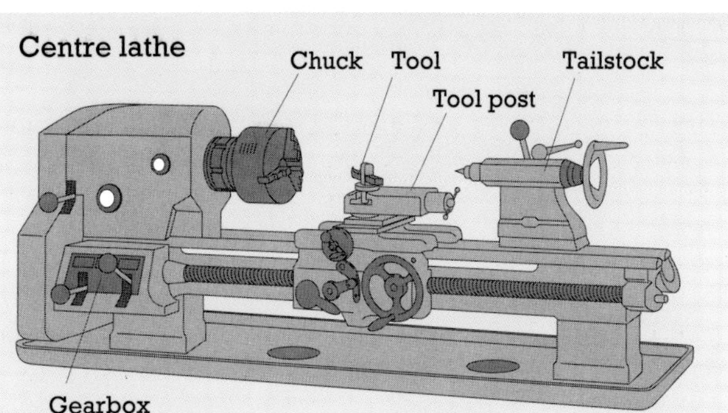

The lathe is used for holding and rotating material so that it can be worked on by cutting tools. The material is either held in the chuck or held between the chuck and tailstock while tools, held in the tool post, shape it.

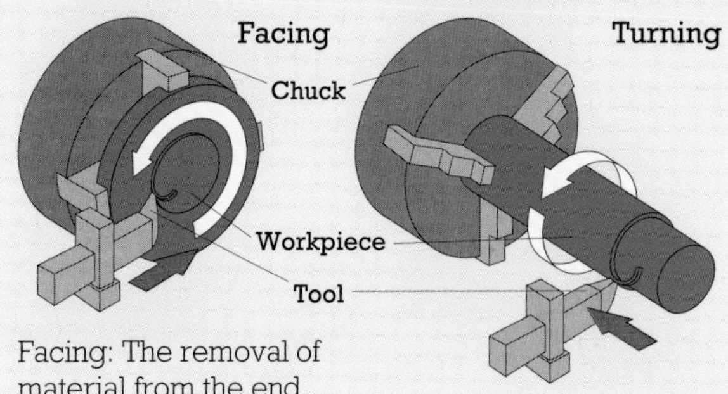

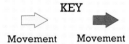

Facing: The removal of material from the end face of the workpiece.

Turning: The removal of material from the length of the workpiece.

KEY

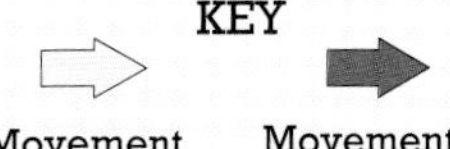

Movement of workpiece — Movement of tool

Some operations are carried out on specialist machines. On many of these the tool stays in one place while the workpiece moves.

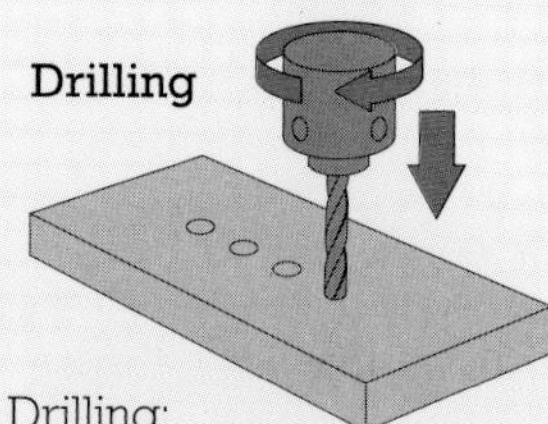

Drilling: The production of circular holes in the material.

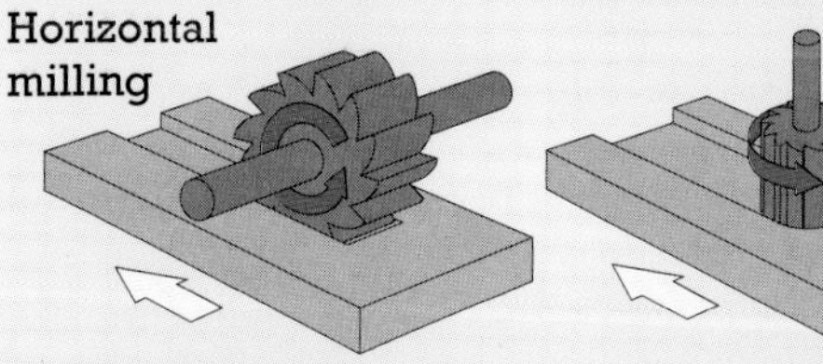

Milling: The shaping of the material by a variety of sharp-edged cutters.

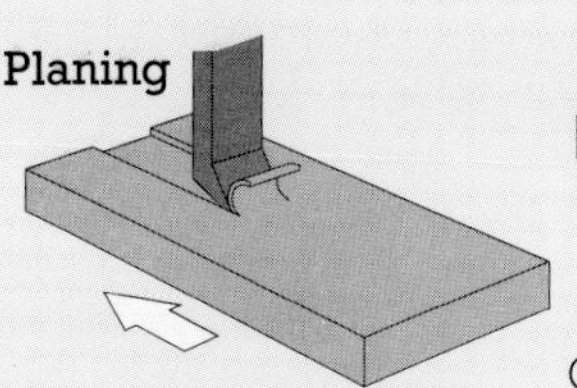

Planing: The removal of thin shavings of material.

Grinding: The removal of a thin layer of material by an abrasive wheel.

Important machine-tools

Tool	Uses	Method of action
Basic machine-tools		
Lathe	Variety of turning, facing, and drilling operations; cutting screw threads	Cutting tool held against horizontally rotating workpiece
Boring machine	Enlarging and finishing cored or drilled holes. Boring and turning operations on pieces too long or large for lathe	Workpiece mounted on horizontal rotating table that rotates about vertical axis
Drilling machine	Cutting holes, boring, countersinking, tapping internal threads	Helical drill or other tool rotates as it is fed into workpiece
Grinding machine	Removes small chips from workpiece: most accurate of basic machining processes	Workpiece moved against rotating abrasive wheel or belt
Milling machine	Cuts grooves and other shapes in surface of material	Rotating, multiple-point cutting tool removes material as workpiece fed against it
Power saws	Cutting through materials	Rotating or reciprocating toothed blade, band, or disc, which cuts as workpiece fed against it
Shaping machine	Machines flat surfaces, grooves, T-slots, and angular surfaces	Workpiece feeds against cutting tool, which reciprocates back and forth, cutting on forward stroke
Planing machine	As shapers, but can machine longer workpieces	Work-table traverses under cutting tool or tools, which may be fixed or rotating
Modified or special-purpose tools		
Turret lathe	Can combine variety of turning, boring, drilling, reaming, and thread-cutting operations	Multiple-sided turrets can hold variety of cutting and boring tools
Broaching machine	Cuts precisely shaped holes or external grooves	Multi-toothed, wedge-shaped, reciprocating tool feeds into workpiece
Lapping machine	Fine finishing and polishing operations	Abrasive plates or abrasive-impregnated cloth rubbed against workpiece
Honing machine	Removing small amounts of material from ground or machined surfaces	Abrasive sticks or stones rotate slowly with an oscillating motion against workpiece
Gear-cutting machine	Cutting gears	Several different types: most common method is gear generation, in which a specially ground cutting tool, in the shape of a worm gear, is used

maglev *ground-guidance system.

magnesium (symbol Mg, at. no. 12, r.a.m. 24.31), a reactive, silvery-white metal which is malleable and ductile at high temperatures. Magnesium metal is produced by *electrolysis of fused (melted) chlorides, largely obtained from sea-water. Magnesium is used extensively as a component of lightweight, strong alloys in the *die casting or *extrusion of articles such as luggage frames, ladders, pistons, crankcases, car and motor-cycle wheels, airframes, and propellers. It is also used in flash-bulbs and flares, as it gives a bright white light when it reacts with oxygen.

magnet, a device that possesses magnetism, producing a magnetic field external to itself. Natural magnets (lodestones) of magnetic iron oxide have been known for many centuries. A simple bar magnet has two poles, north and south, around each of which there is a magnetic field. Magnets can be permanent magnets, or *electromagnets (temporary magnets), and the materials used for each type of magnet differ. A ferromagnetic material (one that can be magnetized) can be made into a magnet by placing it in the centre of an electric coil or solenoid and passing a large current through the coil. If the material is magnetically 'hard', it will retain its magnetism once the current has been switched off. Permanent magnets are made from such hard materials as steel, nickel, and cobalt. Such magnetic alloys are used in electrical equipment and electronic devices. Magnetically 'soft' materials retain little or no magnetism once the current has been removed: they are used in electromagnets, *transformers, and other applications. (See also *electricity and magnetism.)

magnetic alloy, an *alloy designed to have magnetic properties better than those of pure iron. Alloys designed for very soft magnetic characteristics (to be magnetized and demagnetized very easily) include iron–silicon alloys used in transformer cores, and metallic glasses of iron and boron. There are also alloys developed for their hard magnetic properties (ability to retain magnetism), for example alloys of aluminium, nickel, and iron (Alcomax), and of aluminium, nickel, cobalt, iron, and copper (Alnico). Newer alloys include *rare earth elements.

magnetic compass, an instrument comprising a magnetized needle pivoted so that it can always point to magnetic north, used, often in conjunction with a *map or chart, for direction-finding. The origins of the compass are obscure: it is thought that it may have been in use in China as early as the 5th century AD. However, there is no evidence of a compass being used at sea until the 11th century in China, and the 12th century in Europe. The earliest compasses consisted of a magnetized needle floating on a bowl of water. Later, the needle was attached to a card marked with the cardinal directions and balanced on a pivot. By the 16th century the compass was mounted on gimbals (self-aligning bearings) that kept it level at sea. The use of iron in shipbuilding caused compasses to deviate from true reading because of the magnetic effects of the ship's ironwork. This problem was overcome by mounting the compass on a stand or binnacle containing pieces of unmagnetized iron and small magnets to neutralize the ship's magnetic influence. In the 19th century, liquid compasses were introduced, in which the compass card and needle are immersed in fluid to reduce friction and damp down oscillations due to the ship's motion. With the development of aviation in the 20th century, compasses that could be used in aircraft became necessary. One answer to the problem was the gyro-magnetic compass, in which the inertia of a *gyroscope was used to keep the compass card level as the aircraft banked or dived. However, it was not until the introduction of the *gyrocompass that the problems of direction-finding in aircraft were satisfactorily solved. (See also *inductor compass.)

magnetic ore separation, a technique for isolating magnetic *ores from non-magnetic materials such as earth, clay, sand, rocks, and non-magnetic ores, by dropping the crushed ore on to a travelling belt passing over a magnetic roller. For example, it is possible to separate tinstone (SnO_2) from wolfram ($FeWO_4$) by this method. As the ores have very similar densities, separation by other means is difficult.

magnetic resonance imaging (MRI), the application of nuclear magnetic resonance (NMR) techniques to obtain images of cross-sections through the human body. The technique involves passing low-frequency radiation through the soft tissues of the body in the presence of a strong magnetic field, and scanning the temporary magnetic realignment this produces in the nuclei of certain elements (for example, hydrogen, fluorine, and phosphorus). This gives valuable information about the structure of the substance. By varying the field strength across the part of the body under study, it is possible to locate and obtain information about specific molecules within that part. MRI can produce cross-sectional images in all three planes, like *computerized axial tomography (CAT); unlike CAT, however, an MR scanner produces a clear image of soft tissue even if it is obscured by bone, and it produces images with greater contrast. It can be used to visualize brain tumours and the lesions of the brain characteristic to multiple sclerosis or Alzheimer's disease. Imaging using other elements such as phosphorus, rather than hydrogen, allows the visualization of physiological processes and provides a non-invasive alternative to *nuclear medicine. NMR itself is used as an analytical tool in chemistry to provide information about the molecular structure of various solids and liquids.

Magnetic resonance imaging being used to examine a patient's brain. The screen in the foreground shows a profile section through the brain.

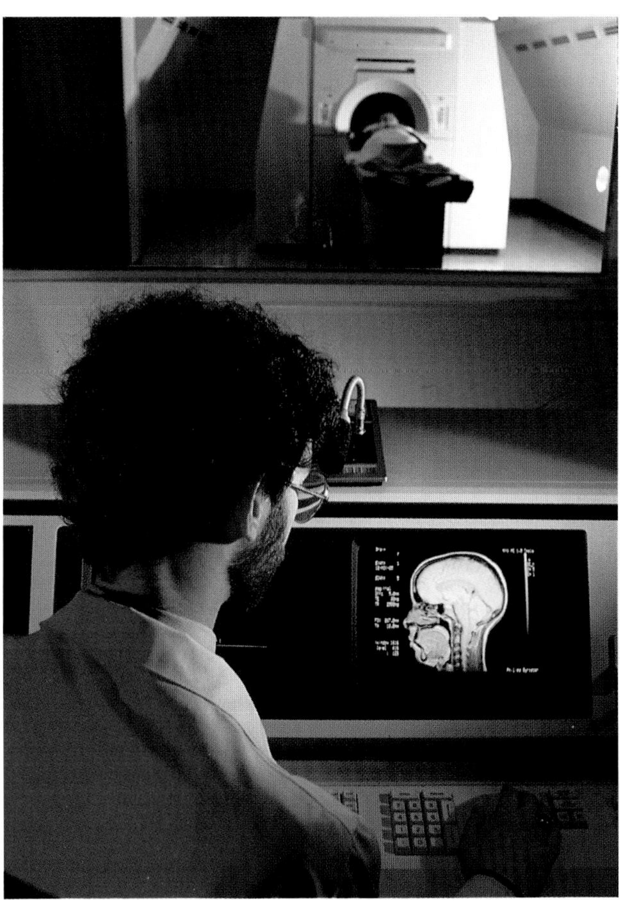

magnetic tape, a plastic strip coated or impregnated with magnetic particles, which can record and play back audio or video signals or store information. The earliest *tape recorders used steel wire or ribbon; plastic tape coated with iron oxide particles was first used in the German magnetophon tape recorder of 1935. Modern magnetic tape is coated with iron oxide, chromium dioxide, or pure iron particles: the latter gives the highest-quality sound. Professional recording studios use multi-track tapes on open reels, and *sound recordings are now usually *digitized. Compact cassettes, introduced by Philips in 1964, dominate the domestic market. Open reels of magnetic tape are used as a storage medium on larger computers and *video recorders, while some microcomputers use tape cartridges for back-up storage. Domestic video recorders use videotape cassettes.

magnetohydrodynamic generator (MHD), a system for the generation of electric power using the effect of a magnetic field acting on a stream of electrically charged particles. Magnetohydrodynamic (MHD) effects are related to the fact that a beam of charged particles experiences a sideways force if it travels through a magnetic field. The observation that this will cause a voltage to develop across the beam is known as the Hall effect (discovered 1879). Its practical application as a power source is more recent, however. The intention is to use hot combustion gases for the direct production of power, by electrically charging them and passing them through a strong magnet. Several decades of MHD research in the Soviet Union and the USA have led to output powers of 50,000 kW, and it is claimed that the *efficiency of fossil-fuel and nuclear *power-stations could be increased to perhaps 60 per cent by combining MHD with *steam-turbines.

magnetron *thermionic valve.

Magnox reactor (*magn*esium *ox*ide), a type of thermal *nuclear reactor developed in the UK, which uses carbon dioxide gas as a coolant, and graphite as a moderator (see nuclear *fission). Magnox reactors were the first to be used for commercial nuclear power generation, the first, at *Calder Hall, being opened in 1956. The fuel used in Magnox reactors is uranium metal, encased in a cladding of magnesium alloy. In the mid-1960s the *advanced gas-cooled reactor was designed as an improvement on the Magnox.

Maillart, Robert (1872–1940), Swiss civil engineer, one of the first to fully exploit the potential of *reinforced concrete. Maillart used it in buildings to eliminate beams as separate units in floor construction. He also employed it in the design of a number of graceful bridges in the Swiss Alps, including the bridge over the River Inn at Zuoz (1901), and the 90-m

(295-foot) Salginotobel bridge near Schiers (completed in 1930).

Maiman, Theodore Harold (1927–), US engineer who in 1960 built the first working laser, which produced pulses of very intense monochromatic light. This was a major achievement, although a number of earlier workers—notably C. H. Townes and A. L. Schawlow in the USA, and N. G. Basov and A. M. Prokhorov in the Soviet Union—had explored the theoretical background to the amplification of microwaves. In 1961, A. Javan, of Bell Telephone, USA, improved on Maiman's design by inventing a laser capable of continuous emission. In 1962 Maiman set up his own laser-manufacturing business.

mainframe computer, a large *computer system which can be accessed by many users simultaneously. Mainframes are the most powerful computer systems commonly available. They are characterized by a very wide data *bus (usually 64 *bits) and high-speed operation, usually several tens of millions of instructions per second (MIPS). Mainframes have traditionally been the dominant computer configuration, but advancing microelectronics technology has created super-*minicomputers and *workstations, which are preferable for some applications. A *supercomputer is a special type of mainframe for highly advanced tasks.

mammography, an imaging technique for the diagnosis and screening of breast *cancer. Mammography initially used specially sensitive X-ray film and intensifying screens (see *radiology) developed for soft tissues. Since the 1970s, xeroradiography, which produces images by means of a reusable light-sensitive receptor similar to those found in *photocopiers has been used.

manganese (symbol Mn, at. no. 25, r.a.m. 54.94), a hard, brittle metal obtained from its main ore, pyrolusite (MnO_2), by reduction with carbon in an *electric-arc furnace. Manganese is added to metals to improve their hardness and toughness. Manganese steel containing up to 13 per cent manganese is used for railway lines, the jaws of rock crushers and other items subject to very heavy wear.

Manhattan Project, the code name for the secret project to develop the atomic bomb (see *nuclear weapons) in the USA during World War II. When it became apparent in the late 1930s that it was feasible to build such a bomb and that German scientists were working on the technology, the project received high priority. The task of designing and assembling the bomb at Los Alamos, New Mexico, was directed by *Oppenheimer, who had the collaboration of the University of Chicago, where *Fermi built the first *atomic pile. Also involved were Columbia University, New York; the Berkeley Radiation Laboratory, University of California; and scientists from the UK. *Uranium-235 was produced at Oak Ridge, Tennessee, and *plutonium-239 at an atomic plant at Hanford, Washington state. The project culminated in the successful explosion of the first atomic bomb at Alamogordo, New Mexico, on 16 July 1945.

man-made fibre *rayon, *synthetic fibre.

manned space programme, any programme involving the sending of astronauts (Soviet, cosmonauts) on *spaceflights. Manned spacecraft must carry air, water, and food sufficient to keep astronauts alive. Their walls must maintain air pressure against the vacuum of space, and protect against micrometeorites and the heat of re-entry into the Earth's atmosphere. These extra requirements necessitate more equipment, and thus heavier spacecraft and more powerful *launch vehicles, than for unmanned programmes. The first man in space was Yury Gagarin (Soviet Union), on 12 April 1961. His *Vostok* and the US *Mercury* spacecraft could each barely accommodate one person, but the larger *Gemini* and *Soyuz* spacecraft that replaced them allowed several astronauts to stay in space for longer, developing techniques for living and working under weightless conditions, and for manœuvring and docking with other spacecraft. The US **Apollo* programme included a series of manned Moon missions; after use with the *Skylab* *space station and in the **Apollo–Soyuz* project, *Apollo* was replaced by the *Space Shuttle. The *Soyuz* spacecraft has continued, with regular improvements, as a ferry craft to the *Salyut* and *Mir* space stations.

Mannesmann, Max (*fl.* 1886–91) and **Reinhard** (1856–1922), German ironmasters. The Mannesmann brothers were *steel manufacturers at Remscheid. In about 1860, Reinhard conceived a method for making seamless *tubes by drawing a hot metal rod between two mutually inclined power-driven rollers. This novel process was first operated by the Landore Siemens Steel Company in Wales in 1887: the largest machine could pierce steel billets up to 25 cm (10 inches) in diameter. In 1891, Max Mannesmann was granted a patent for the hot-*forging of steel tube.

manometer, a U-shaped tube, generally containing mercury, used as a pressure gauge for gases and liquids. One end is connected to the fluid under pressure and the other end is left open to the atmosphere. The level of the mercury rises or falls in relation to the pressure difference between the fluid and the atmosphere. A Pitot tube can also be used as a manometer. It is an open-ended, right-angled tube used to measure the speed or flow of a fluid by measuring the pressure of the fluid flow.

manufactured board, a sheet material made by compacting and bonding chips or fibres of wood or other material. The strength of some manufactured boards allows them to be used for structural purposes, while others are confined to use as insulating or decorative linings. Wood chips are bonded with resin *adhesives to form chipboard, widely substituted for natural wood in floor-boarding. Wood fibres are bonded to form low-density fibreboard with good thermal insulation, or high-density hardboard used as a substitute for plywood. Fire and moisture resistance is higher in *cement- and gypsum-bonded boards; mineral fibre reinforcement is added to improve strength and impact resistance.

maps and charts, diagrammatic representations of all or part of the Earth on a plane surface. A map is usually of a land area, a chart of a sea area. The earliest maps of which we have knowledge were made by the Babylonians on clay tablets, dating from around 2300 BC. The ancient Greeks drew maps of the known world and speculated on its form: around the 3rd century BC Greek geographers agreed that the Earth was spherical; at this time the Greek astronomer and geographer Eratosthenes estimated its circumference to be around 46,000 km (29,000 miles), not far from modern values of around 40,000 km (24,800 miles). Chinese map-making from the 3rd century BC was based on the use of a reference grid of parallel lines running N–S and E–W, and on-the-spot surveys. These maps were remarkably accurate, but Chinese world maps remained poor until the introduction of Western cartography in the 17th century. Probably the greatest figure of early geography was *Ptolemy, whose *Guide to Geography* included a world map that was revived in Europe in the early 15th century. Medieval European geographers believed that the known world of Europe, Asia, and Africa covered only one-quarter of the Earth's surface. In their *mappa mundi* (world maps) they often drew only this portion of the Earth, and the locations of features upon it were not mathematically related to their true positions on the globe. In the Arab world, however, classical astronomy and cartography continued to be studied. Islamic geographers drew world maps, based on new tables of latitude and longitude, in which the habitable world extended well south of the equator, and the Indian Ocean was open towards the Far East. In the 13th and 14th centuries, the travels of Europeans across Asia, and the introduction of sea-charts based on *magnetic compass directions improved the detail of world maps. In the 15th and 16th centuries the translations of Greek and Arabic geographical works introduced European cartographers to the concept of map *projection, while the discoveries of such explorers as Christopher Columbus led to a more accurate view of the globe. The best-known cartographer of the period was *Mercator, whose method for *projection of the globe on to a flat surface enabled navigators to plot bearings as straight lines. In the 18th century a more scientific approach to map-making began to predominate, and many European countries began systematic national topographic surveys. Others followed suit, but some parts of the world remained largely unmapped until World War II, when vast areas were mapped using information from aerial photographs.

Modern maps can be classified as either topographical, showing the physical and natural features of an area, or thematic, based on topographical maps but showing some sort of statistical data (for example, population) in map form. Navigational charts for air or sea use show selected topological features, but also such information as the location of *radio navigation beacons, lights and buoys, and water depths and prevailing currents. Until the advent of aerial photography, land *surveying provided most of the basic topological information for maps. However, modern map-making relies much more on aerial surveying techniques using *stereo photography, and information obtained from *Earth resources satellites using remote sensing techniques such as infra-red photography. Topographical information from photographs and land surveys is now usually *digitized in some way and fed into a computer. This provides a flexible database from which many different kinds of map can be drawn.

Marconi, Guglielmo (1874–1937), Italian pioneer of *radio communication. In 1894 he began to experiment with techniques for wireless communication after reading about the experiment on electric waves carried out by *Hertz. Within a year, he had transmitted and received signals over a distance of more than 2 km (1.2 miles). Unable to gain support in Italy, he came to London, and in 1896 took out a UK patent and demonstrated his invention to the British Post Office. By 1899 he had sent messages to France, and in 1901 he bridged the Atlantic. He patented a magnetic detector of electrical signals in 1902, and a horizontal directional *antenna in 1905. From 1916 Marconi devoted his attention to exploring the possibilities of short-wave radio transmission and to the considerable business interests that had grown up around his invention. He shared the Nobel Prize for Physics in 1909 with *Braun, who invented a coupled wireless transmitter and receiver.

margarine, a butter-like spread made from a mixture of animal and/or vegetable *fats and oils with aqueous milk products, plus such additives as salt, emulsifiers, and flavouring. Margarine was first developed in the late 1860s by the Frenchman H. Mège-Mouriès; the manufacturing process was later simplified in the USA. Animal fats were originally most commonly used in margarines, but there has been a trend towards the use of vegetable oils, often hardened by hydrogenation with a *catalyst. In recent years, high-cholesterol foods such as *butter have come to be seen as something of a health risk, and this has led manufacturers to develop margarines high in polyunsaturated fatty acids.

marine engine *diesel engine, *steamship, *steam-turbine.

marine resource management, an activity designed to aid recovery of depleted fish stocks and maximize their yields, and to prevent depletion of stocks newly subjected to exploitation. Most countries that border on the sea have laws to protect and conserve the fishing resources that lie within 320 km (200 miles) of their coasts. The laws may reduce the fishing effort or delay the age at which fish are first captured. Effort can be reduced by limiting the number of local and foreign vessels fishing, by restricting fishing time, by imposing closed seasons, or by closing areas. The commonest method is by the imposition of an annual catch limit or total allowable catch (TAC). Increasing age at first capture can be achieved by imposing a minimum landing size. Undersized individuals of crustaceans such as lobsters, and molluscs such as scallops, survive on being returned to the sea after capture. Fish generally cannot survive, so selective nets such as trawls have an appropriate legal mesh size to prevent the capture of undersized fish. The species which may be caught are also specified.

marshalling yard, a large, ordered layout of tracks on which wagons are marshalled into trains for appropriate destinations. These yards were developed to handle wagon-load traffic, where each wagon in a freight train contained a different load and was intended for a different destination. Individual wagons are disconnected as they are pushed over a hump. They roll down on to the track containing the train for their next destination. The points are automatically set from information received from the vehicle, and the rate of roll is controlled by magnetic retarders acting on the wheels. The advent of 'block' trains, operating as a complete train from loading to unloading, has reduced the need for marshalling yards.

maser (*m*icrowave *a*mplification by *s*timulation *e*mission of *r*adiation), a source of intense, coherent (in-phase) radiation of a single frequency in the microwave area of the *electromagnetic spectrum (see *waves). Masers are used as *oscillators, and as microwave *amplifiers. They operate by 'pumping' or exciting the *electrons of a solid or gas to higher energy levels, by means of an input of energy. The electrons are then allowed to return to their unexcited state, and in doing so they emit energy in the form of electromagnetic radiation of a single frequency. A *laser works on similar principles to a maser, but emits energy in the form of visible light.

Aerial view of a **marshalling yard** in Ontario, Canada.

masonry, stone, the craft of dressing and assembling stone for walls and other building structures. Limestones are most widely used because they combine adequate weather resistance with relative ease of working. A 'banker mason' in a quarry or yard shapes the stones very accurately to produce high-quality work (ashlar). The exposed faces of the stone may be smooth- or rough-hewn; hard stones (granites, quartzites, and marbles) may be polished. Nowadays simple rectangular stones are sawn by computerized frame saws: linear mouldings can also be machined, and pieces such as columns and balusters are turned on a lathe. Stone is now often applied only as a wall facing—perhaps 10 cm (4 inches) thick for limestones or sandstones and 2–2.5 cm (0.75–1 inch) thick for polished granites and marbles. The stones are bedded and jointed in mortar and are linked by non-corrodible metal ties (bronze or stainless steel) that also tie them to the backing wall. In *cavity walls, the outer leaf may be wholly of stone. Stones for arches and *vaults are supported on a wooden framework (centring); this is removed when all the stones are in place and the arch is self-supporting. Artificial stone—a form of high-quality *pre-cast concrete made with stone dust and pigments—may also be used.

Massachusetts Institute of Technology (MIT), a privately controlled US university with an emphasis on science and technology. It was founded in 1861 as part of a move to meet a growing demand for engineers in US industry. Its priorities are basic research in computing, engineering, the social and physical sciences, and management. It offers state-of-the-art research facilities to students from undergraduate level upwards.

mass production, the manufacture of a product or part in large quantities at comparatively low unit cost. Important factors in the early development of mass production included the development in the early 19th century of highly accurate *machine-tools by means of which components could be produced with such precision as to allow complete interchangeability of parts; the use of *time-and-motion studies from the end of the 19th century onwards to analyse and improve efficiency; the consequent detailed division of labour in mass-production operations; the introduction of the *assembly line; and the automatic transfer of parts between processing stations. Such developments led to many-fold reductions in the time taken to perform certain operations and hence to corresponding decreases in cost. Until recently, the high degree of mechanization and *automation involved in mass production required the standardization of both the product and the raw materials used in its manufacture. However, the development of *flexible manufacturing systems for product monitoring and control has led to improved flexibility. The development of mass-production methods for high-quality items, in particular electronic devices, has led to a shift in emphasis from quality control, in which sub-standard or damaged products are rejected at the end of the production process, to quality assurance, in which the whole production process is designed to ensure that the products are of a high standard.

mass spectrometer, an analytical instrument for determining the structure of complex molecules (see *atoms and molecules) or the isotopic content (see *isotope) of elements. A small sample of the material under investigation is introduced into an evacuated area, where it is vaporized and ionized (charged). The positively charged ions are then accelerated by an electrical field, and separated by mass, most commonly by means of a magnetic field, which causes each ion to follow a curved path. The amount each ion is deflected by the magnetic field depends upon its mass. The separated ions are then detected either by a collector (which converts the ion impacts into electrical currents that are either recorded or stored in a computer) or on a photo-

Mass production of Ford cars in River Rouge, Michigan, USA, in 1929. The plant could produce one Ford Model T car every three minutes.

graphic plate. Complex molecules are fragmented by the ionization process, and the pattern of ion fragments produced gives information about their structure. Mass spectroscopy used in combination with gas *chromatography (GC–MS) is a very efficient tool for the separation and analysis of the components of a mixture, and the process can be automated. GC–MS is used extensively in *forensic science.

match *fire-making device.

matchlock *firearm.

Mauchly, John William (1907–80), US research engineer and computing pioneer. While on the staff of the University of Pennsylvania, he and J. Presper Eckert developed (1946) for the US Army Ordnance Department what was probably the first general-purpose electronic computer (see *computer, history of). Called ENIAC (Electronic Numerical Integrator And Calculator), it was a vast machine, consuming 100 kW of electric power and containing 18,000 electronic valves. Their successful UNIVAC computer (1951) was the first commercial computer, and introduced *magnetic tape for programming.

Maudslay, Henry (1771–1831), British mechanical engineer and inventor. After making machine-tools for *Bramah, he set up his own business in 1798 and constructed for M. I. *Brunel the machinery he required for mass-producing pulley-blocks, paralleling *Whitney's experiments with *mass production in the USA. In 1807 he patented a table engine, a much needed compact power unit, and made many improvements to the *machine-tools of his day, his most important invention perhaps being the metal *lathe. He also made the first screw-cutting lathe to be widely adopted in the engineering industry. Maudslay also trained some of the best engineers of his day, among them *Nasmyth and *Whitworth.

Maxim, Sir Hiram Stevens (1840–1916), versatile US-born British engineer and inventor of the Maxim *machine-gun. A keen inventor from early days, he obtained his first patent in 1866. In London in 1889, he produced the first fully automatic, water-cooled gun, firing ten shots per second from a 250-round cartridge belt. This was adopted as a standard weapon by the British Army (1889) and Navy (1892) and subsequently by many countries throughout the world. He also developed a type of smokeless powder (*see nitro-cellulose), cordite, to improve the gun's efficiency.

Max Planck Society for the Promotion of Sciences, a German national organization for scientific research. Founded in 1911 as the Kaiser Wilhelm Society, it quickly established a high reputation, attracting scientists of great ability. It declined under the Nazi regime, but was reconstituted after World War II. As a change of title was politically desirable, it was renamed after the physicist Max Planck, who had been its Director from 1930 to 1937. It now has fifty-three autonomous laboratories covering the arts, the physical sciences, biology, and medicine.

Maybach, Wilhelm *Daimler, Gottlieb.

meat and meat products, the flesh of animals used for food. Only a limited number of domesticated animals are used in meat production: these are generally cattle, sheep, pigs, horses, goats, poultry, and rabbits. After killing at the *abbatoir, the meat must be properly hung for several days to tenderize it, and may be marinaded for greater tenderness and flavour. Generally the saddle, fillets, and loins provide the best cuts, followed by the shoulder, ribs (for chops), neck, and breast. Lean and fat meat are minced together for sausages and traditionally encased in the small intestine. Black pudding is made from pig's blood, and brawn from the head, ears, and trotters. Faggots are made from offal, and pâté from a pounded mixture of livers. The preservation of meat includes salting, pickling, freezing, drying, or *canning. Hams and bacons may be salted and then sweet-cured for flavour.

mechanical advantage, the ratio of the force exerted by a mechanism to the force put in. The simplest example is the *lever, where the ratio of forces is equal to the ratio of the lengths of the lever arms. Another example is a rope-and-pulley arrangement; if the rope passes up and down twice between upper and lower *pulleys, then the mechanical advantage is four to one. According to the law of conservation of energy, the total *energy put into a system cannot be greater than the energy got out. Thus, for a mechanical advantage of 4:1 the input force has to move through a distance at least four times that moved by the load.

mechanical engineering, that branch of engineering which deals with machines and mechanized processes. In particular, mechanical engineering is concerned with power production, transmission, and utilization. Thus it includes *machine-tools, *engines, transport of all kinds, *cranes, *lifts, *locks, *pumps, *servo-mechanisms, and *robotics. Originally mechanical engineering was regarded as a branch of civil engineering, that is, non-military engineering. With the development of locomotives for *railways and *steam-engines for industrial and marine uses, mechanical engineering came to be recognized as a separate discipline. The British Institution of Mechanical Engineers was founded in 1847, followed soon afterwards by similar societies in other countries.

mechanization *automation.

mechatronics, a term coined by the Japanese to describe an interdisciplinary engineering area combining features of electronic, mechanical, and software engineering. Mechatronics is often concerned with the design, manufacture, and operation of machines capable of some sort of 'intelligent' behaviour—that is, behaviour involving programmed operation, self-regulation, communication, and so on. Mechatronics therefore also involves aspects of *artificial intelligence, *instrumentation, *ergonomics, and *control-system design. Examples of mechatronic products or systems include many consumer electronic products, for example, video and audio equipment; automatic cameras incorporating digital electronics and precision mechanical engineering; *robots for automated manufacturing systems; and automatically guided vehicles.

medical technology, the application of medical and allied sciences for the treatment or prevention of disease. The term medical technology is very broad, including not only the recent introduction of *lasers and *ultrasound, but also such devices and techniques as *acupuncture, cupping glasses, *surgical instruments, obstetric forceps, *stethoscopes, *ophthalmoscopes, the clinical *thermometer, and the *sphygmomanometer, all of which were invented before

Brief chronology of medical technology, 1700–1990

1713–16	Introduction of smallpox inoculation in Britain
1730	General adoption of obstetric forceps, invented in the early 1600s by the Chamberlen family but kept secret
1796–98	Introduction of smallpox vaccination by Edward Jenner
1819	Stethoscope invented by French physician Théophile Laennec
1835	Medical statistics introduced by Pierre-Charles-Alexandre Louis, allowing effectiveness of techniques to be tested mathematically
1847–8	Introduction of ether and chloroform as anaesthetic agents
1851	The German physiologist Herman von Helmholtz invented the ophthalmoscope
1855	Introduction of laryngoscopy
1860s	Introduction of clinical thermometry
1865–85	Introduction of antisepsis and asepsis, first in operative surgery and then obstetrics
1870s	Beginning of blood counts and thus haematology
1870s	Introduction of bacteriology, principally through work of Louis Pasteur and the German bacteriologist Robert Koch
1895	Discovery of X-rays by German physicist Wilhelm Röntgen
1896	Introduction of clinical sphygmomanometry
1898	Discovery of radium by physicists Marie and Pierre Curie and beginnings of radiotherapy
1901	Concept of electrocardiography introduced by Einthoven
1929	Invention of electroencephalography
1950	Radioactive isotopes and scanners first used for diagnostic purposes
1950s	Heart–lung machine makes open-heart surgery possible
1950s–60s	First organ transplants: the cornea, kidney, liver, heart, and bone-marrow
1960	The successful design of an artificial hip joint led to the rapid growth of medical engineering in orthopaedic surgery
1960s–70s	Ultrasound initially used in obstetrics. Aminocentesis introduced for detection of fetal abnormalities
1970s	Cardiac pacemakers introduced. Synthetic eye lenses developed. Fibre-optics introduced. First use of computerized tomography (CAT) scanners
1980s	Genetic engineering. *In vitro* fertilization developed. Nuclear magnetic resonance imaging first used

the 20th century. The term also covers the techniques used by doctors when they examine patients. One might even argue that sanitary engineering is a branch of medical technology: in the late 19th and early 20th centuries, clean water and efficient sewage disposal did more to improve general health in the developed world than the whole of clinical medicine. This entry deals only with techniques based on instruments or apparatus; drugs are dealt with in the entry on *pharmacology.

Historically, there were two kinds of medical technology: the diagnostic and the therapeutic. In *surgery and *obstetrics, technology consisted of the continual invention of new techniques requiring new instruments. These were usually designed by doctors and made at first by blacksmiths and later by instrument-makers. In medicine, almost all technology was diagnostic, using stethoscopes and ophthalmoscopes. Until the mid-19th century, however, medical technology was a small, specialized world. Thereafter it expanded rapidly with the introduction of *anaesthesia, bacteriology (the study of *bacteria), *haematology, biochemistry, the invention of *antisepsis and *asepsis, and *radiology. All of these disciplines grew so fast that they created a new world in which doctors depended to an increasing extent on specialized techniques and technicians.

Where the doctors in 1800 were solely dependent on their own senses, aided occasionally by instruments of their own design, their successors at the beginning of the 20th century were using additional information from laboratories and X-ray departments. Since 1900, and especially since 1950, there has been an enormous growth in laboratory medicine and in biomedical engineering (see *bioengineering). Many examples exist, not only of new and better apparatus for biochemical, haematological, and bacteriological analyses, but also of *ultrasound, *optical fibres, *computerized axial tomography, *magnetic resonance imaging, and so on.

Medical technology has improved rapidly in some areas, but not in others. Today the chances of surviving a surgical operation, childbirth, infectious diseases, and major injuries are very good indeed, although the cost of medical provision in such areas is so expensive that there are crises in the cost of medical care in many countries. However, techniques for treating sprained ankles, bad backs, influenza, colds, coronary heart disease, and strokes have improved little since the 19th century. The very successes of medical technology have produced unrealistic expectations of being treated successfully. There is also a perception that technological advance in specific areas has led to a neglect of the patient seen as a whole, and this has encouraged the development of holistic, unorthodox, and alternative medicines.

medicine *drug.

medium wave (medium frequency) *waveband.

megalithic structure, a prehistoric monument built of very large stones. It may range from single standing stones (menhirs) and grave chambers (dolmens) to large and complex arrays such as the circles at *Stonehenge and Avebury in the UK, and the stone avenues at Carnac (France), all built in a series of stages between *c.*3000 and 1800 BC. Some structures, such as those oriented to the summer solstice, clearly had a ritualistic or religious function; many show an advanced understanding of some aspects of astronomy. The movement, handling and dressing of these large stones (the largest recorded weighs an estimated 100 tonnes), and their sometimes precise orientation, indicate that those responsible had considerable skill in mechanics, mathematics, and the organization of labour.

Meitner, Lise (1878–1968), Austrian-born Swedish physicist. A professor (1926–33) at the University of Berlin, she left Germany in 1938, and moved first to Sweden, then in 1960 to the UK. In 1938 Meitner's colleague in Germany, Otto Hahn, repeated *Fermi's famous experiment in which he bombarded uranium with neutrons. Meitner was the first to interpret the results of this experiment as the *fission of the uranium nucleus.

memory (computer), the part of a *computer system that is used to store *data temporarily or permanently. There are many types of computer memory, each with a specific application. Most types of computer memory are made from *semiconductors. For very high-speed operations associated with the *central processing unit (CPU), real (primary) memory is used. This includes read-only memory (ROM) and random access memory (RAM). Information is stored permanently in a ROM and cannot normally be altered once programmed, but various types of erasable programmable ROM (EPROM) are now quite common. Computers use ROM-based information for some essential tasks such as *bootstrapping. The *operating system and some small programs may also be stored in ROM. RAMs are used for short-term storage of information and programs, including instructions, data, and partial results, and are intimately associated with the high-speed operation of the CPU. Virtual (secondary) memory is not directly addressable by the CPU, but is used to store much larger amounts of data, although this is only accessible at relatively low speeds compared with the operation of the computer. It usually resides on disk units such as *hard and *floppy disks. Large programs can be run on computers using a relatively small amount of real memory, by continually exchanging information between real memory and a hard disk (containing the virtual memory) so that only those parts of the program currently in use take up space in real memory. Cache memory is a small but very fast memory interposed between a computer and its main memory. The computer first checks whether data is in the cache before going to the (relatively slow) main memory. In operation, the CPU controls the read and write operations of memory and the transfer of data between real and virtual memories. A new erasable computer memory chip made partly from a *ceramic, and known as a ferroelectric random-access memory (FRAM) is under development. It retains data when its power source is switched off, and could eventually replace ROM and RAM.

memory metal, an *alloy that changes from one crystalline state to another as a result of a change in temperature or mechanical stress. If such an alloy is heated, then cooled and deformed plastically, it will return to its original undeformed shape on re-heating, almost as if it had 'remembered' its original shape. Memory metals have a range of applications, as compressible joints; in orthodontic braces; in orthopaedic devices such as bone implants; and in many mechanical devices, for example circuit-breakers and relays, thermostatic valves, and so on.

menu (computing), a list of *program or function options which is presented to the user by a *computer on a *visual display unit. The user selects the desired option by keyboard or *mouse. Menu-based software is used extensively in *interactive systems because of its convenience and ease of use.

Mercator, Gerardus (Gerhard Kremer) (1512–94), Flemish cartographer best known for his map *projection on which lines of longitude and latitude are straight lines, which allows navigators to plot courses as straight lines. Mercator obtained a master's degree from the University of Leuven, Belgium in 1532, and later studied and worked with the mathematician Gemma Frisius and an engraver and goldsmith, Gaspar à Myrica. The three men collaborated on the construction of globes, maps, and astronomical instruments. In 1537 Mercator began a series of printed maps that established him as the greatest cartographer of the century, culminating in 1569 with the world map on what became known as the Mercator projection. He later published a series of maps which he called his *Atlas*, the first known use of the term for a collection of maps.

merchant ship, any civilian working vessel, usually excluding fishing vessels, yachts, and naval auxiliaries. Wooden Egyptian merchant boats carrying a square sail plus a few oars are known to have been trading on the Nile from around 3000 BC. In the eastern Mediterranean, the merchant 'roundship' was evolved: this had a short, rounded hull and used sails as its main method of propulsion. Similar boats continued to be used throughout the Greek and Roman period, although the Romans built some much larger vessels that could carry up to 1,200 tonnes of cargo for importing grain from Egypt. From at least the 5th century BC, Chinese merchants were trading in the Red Sea, in multi-masted 'sand ships' and *junks.

In the Middle Ages and until the mid-17th century, the same ships were used as both merchant ships and *warships, since it was often necessary to defend cargoes against marauders. An example of this type of vessel was the East Indiaman, used by European traders to India and South-East Asia. Later, there was increasing differentiation between cargo-carrying vessels and warships. The early 19th century saw the appearance of the *clipper, one of the few merchant ships to be built for speed rather than carrying capacity. The earliest merchant *steamships were passenger vessels, but by the 1880s most merchant ships were steam-powered. The first oil *tankers and *bulk carriers appeared between the 1870s and 1890s. From the early 1900s there was a slow increase in the number of motor ships using internal-combustion engines as opposed to steam-power. Since the 1950s, changes in cargo handling have revolutionized merchant shipping. Roll-on, roll-off (ro-ro) ships and *container ships have taken over most ordinary cargo tasks, while bulk and liquid carriers have increased in size and numbers. Some passenger *liners have survived as cruise ships, while smaller merchant ships such as *cable-ships, *dredgers, and *tugs remain important.

mercury (symbol Hg, at. no. 80, r.a.m. 200.59), a highly toxic silver-white liquid metal, the only metal element that is liquid at room temperature. The main ore, cinnabar (MgS), is reduced to mercury by roasting in air, and purified by distillation. Mercury is used extensively in *thermometers and *barometers, batteries, vacuum pumps, mercury vapour lamps, dental fillings, liquid seals, and for electrical contacts. Its compounds find limited use in the manufacture of explosives, paint, pharmaceuticals, and agricultural chemicals.

Mergenthaler, Ottmar (1854–99), German-born US engineer who invented the *Linotype machine. To avoid military service, he emigrated to the USA in 1868 and established himself as an instrument-maker. With James Clephane, he made two unsuccessful attempts to devise a mechanized *typesetting system. In 1883 Clephane commissioned him to make a third attempt, and he conceived the idea of casting molten *type metal on type bars. This was successful, and he patented the idea in 1884 as the Linotype (line-of-type) machine.

meso-American technology, the technology of civilizations existing in the Americas before the European discovery of the continent in the 16th century. The Maya civilization of southern Central America developed an urban civilization from about 300 BC, with cities of up to 40,000 people and well-developed systems of *irrigation and *terraced agriculture. The prinicpal buildings were flat-topped *pyramids on which temples were built; these and other major buildings were usually of stone, covered with plaster and stucco and then painted. Many houses had underground cisterns for drinking water. In western South America the Incan empire reached its peak between 1476 and 1525. It had few large settlements but well-developed systems of agriculture, irrigation, and *road communication. There was no written language, but knotted strings

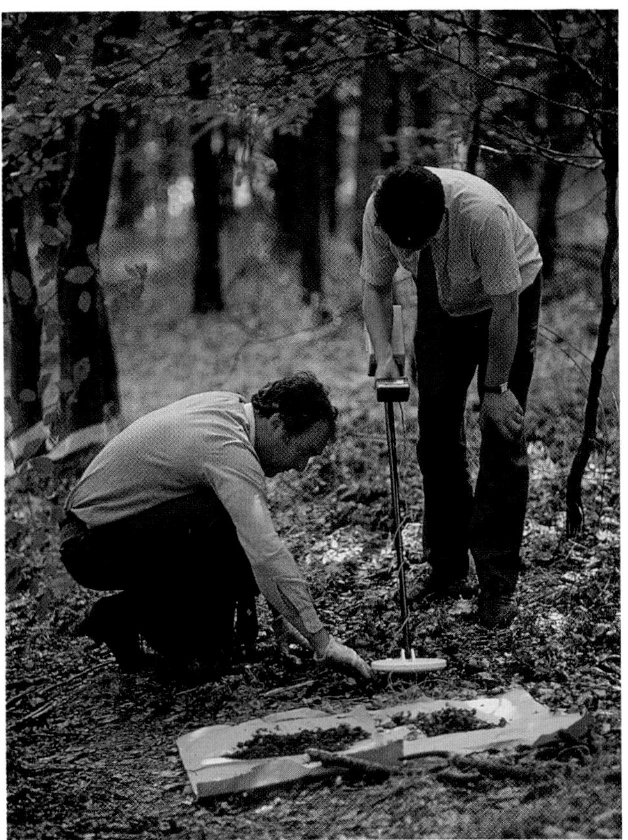

A **metal detector** being used by forensic scientists to locate spent bullets.

(*quipu*) were used for numerical records. The Aztecs of Central America (13th–16th centuries) developed extremely large urban communities (up to 250,000 people), and a complex system of agriculture and commerce. The main city, Tenochtitlan (now Mexico City) was built on reclaimed swampland, and the Aztecs built dykes, canals, pipes, and aqueducts to carry water for drinking and for irrigation.

Mesopotamian technology *Egyptian and Mesopotamian technology.

Messerschmitt, Willy (1898–1978), German designer and manufacturer of aircraft. He entered the industry during World War I and designed his first aeroplane in 1916. In 1923 he established the Messerschmitt Aircraft Company. When Germany rearmed, following the rise of Hitler, he supplied the Luftwaffe (German air force) with a succession of stressed-skin fighters and fighter-bombers, notably the Me.109 (of which 33,000 were built). After World War II, he was associated with the revived civil airline Lufthansa and also became involved in motor-car manufacture.

metal detector, an instrument for detecting hidden metal objects, developed during World War II to detect landmines. One type of metal detector has two tuned circuits, one carried in the head of the device. The presence of metal near the tuned circuit in the head changes its oscillating frequency. The difference between this fequency and the frequency in the other, reference, circuit creates a signal which can be heard through headphones or registered on a meter. Today metal detectors have many applications: in the food industry, they are routinely used to test for metal contamination; archaeologists use them to survey their digs; and builders use them to detect hidden pipes or wiring.

metal fatigue, the weakening and eventual failure of metals, resulting from the repeated application of loads far smaller than those required to cause failure in a single loading (stress cycle). In most metals the larger the number of stress cycles, the lower the stress level needed to cause failure. For such metals an endurance limit is quoted. However, for other metals, such as steel and titanium alloys, there is a definite stress level (the fatigue limit) below which fatigue failure will never occur. It has been estimated that 90 per cent of all mechanical failures are caused by fatigue. Parts of machines and engines that are subject to vibration are particularly susceptible. Fatigue failures often occur in a catastrophic manner, with no gross distortion preceding collapse. The size and location of the cracks formed in a structure by the fatigue process often make their detection during routine inspection almost impossible.

metallic glass, an amorphous (non-crystalline) form of *metal created by very rapid cooling of liquid metal, discovered by the US materials scientist Pol Duwez in about 1960. Metallic glasses will crystallize on re-heating. They are hard and extremely strong, but have little ductility. Some alloys have special magnetic properties which, combined with their great wear resistance, make them useful in the record/playback heads of *video recorders. Normally produced as thin sheets, metallic glass objects of any shape can be made by *powder metallurgy techniques.

metals and metalworking. Metals are a large class of elements with characteristic properties which are a consequence of their electronic structure. The study of the production and properties of metals is known as metallurgy. The separation of the *atoms is small, so most metals are dense. A proportion of the *electrons are free to move within the material and are not associated with any particular atom, making metals good conductors of heat and electricity. The atoms are in regular arrangements that can slide over each other without becoming detached, which is why metals are malleable (capable of being hammered and bent without fracture) and ductile (capable of being drawn into wire). Within these broad categories metals vary greatly in their properties. For example, lead is soft and can be shaped by hand, while iron can only be worked by hammering at red heat: gold and platinum are almost inert, while potassium ignites on contact with water.

The regular arrangement of atoms in metals gives them a crystalline structure not easily seen on the surfaces of polished metals, comprising a patchwork of irregular crystals called grains. The size, shape, orientation, and composition of these grains have a significant effect on the properties of the metal. In general, a metal with fine grains will be harder and stronger than one with coarse grains. The early workers of metal developed, by trial and error, techniques that modified the grain structure to produce desirable properties. Heat treatment such as *quenching, *tempering, or *annealing controls the nature of the grains in the metal. Adding even small amounts of other metals (less than 1 per cent in some cases) to a pure metal (*alloying) can have a significant effect on its grain structure and hence its properties. The variety of properties that can now be obtained is quite remarkable, with combinations of lightness, strength, and stiffness unimaginable 100 years ago.

The rate at which metals have become available since

they were first discovered is largely a consequence of their chemistry. The more chemically reactive a metal, the more difficult it is to extract from its *ores. Gold and silver are amongst the least reactive and occur naturally as the free metal. Copper, tin, and lead are easily extracted at relatively low temperatures, while significantly higher temperatures are required for *iron.

The most important metal is iron and its alloy, *steel. Originally a precious metal in the Near East because of its rarity, iron was well known to the Romans, who used it for weapons and for a variety of fixings, including nails. Iron proved superior in strength, hardness, and stiffness to *bronze, although its *corrosion resistance is poor. During the Middle Ages, iron-based alloys became the main materials worked by armourers and *blacksmiths, who exercised their skills to make a variety of arms and armour, agricultural implements and cooking utensils, as well as rivets, nails, wheel-rims, horseshoes and hinges. In the 18th century, zinc was isolated from its ores as a pure metal for the first time and this led to the development and use of a wider range of brasses. Improvements in production methods in the 19th century made good-quality iron and steel available in much larger quantities. This development aided the *Industrial Revolution, providing the materials needed to construct manufacturing machines. It also gave rise to the *iron and steel industry and to the use of these materials on a massive scale.

The plasma-arc torch produces a high-velocity jet of an extremely hot, ionized gas (a plasma) at temperatures up to 28,000 °C. This cuts through **metal** by melting and displacing material. Heavy-duty torches can cut through up to 15 cm (6 inches) of stainless steel.

Early in the 19th century the discovery that metals could be prepared by *electrolysis increased the range of available metals and provided a powerful technique for purifying metals obtained by other methods. In the 20th century the use of electrolysis and advances in extraction techniques made *aluminium available at reasonable cost. This metal and its alloys, with their combination of lightness, strength, and electrical conductivity, now rank second only to steel in importance.

The ways of working a metal are dependent on its properties. Many metals can be melted and cast in moulds, but special conditions are required for metals that react with air. *Powder metallurgy allows complex shapes to be formed without melting. All metals can be formed by drawing, rolling, hammering, and *extrusion, but some require hot-working. Metals are subject to *metal fatigue, and to creep, the slow increase in length under stress causing deformation and eventually failure. Both effects are taken into account by engineers when designing, for example, aeroplanes, gas-turbines, and pressure vessels for high-temperature chemical processes. Metals can be shaped and finished by removing waste material, using *machine-tools such as the lathe, milling machine, shaper, and grinder. (See also *cermet, *composite, *metallic glass.)

meteorological instrument, an instrument for studying the Earth's atmosphere, especially weather-forming processes, and used in weather forecasting. Until the advent of scientific instruments in the 17th century, the prediction of weather was necessarily subjective, based on such observations as cloud formation, changes in wind direction, the presence of seabirds inland, and so on. In modern meteorology, three parameters are of particular significance: pressure, temperature, and wind-speed. These are measured by the *barometer, the *thermometer, and the *anemometer, respectively. An important variation of the simple thermometer is the maximum–minimum thermometer, which records both maximum and minimum temperatures over a given period of time. Auxiliary instruments include hygrometers to measure humidity; precipitation gauges to measure falls of rain and snow; and gauges to measure the daily hours of sunshine. Simple hygrometers depend on the contraction and expansion of a natural fibre (for example, a human hair) with changes in humidity. Electrical instruments are more accurate, and depend on the changes in resistance of an electrical element (a hygristor) corresponding to changes in ambient humidity. The rain gauge, which is usually used for 24-hour readings, consists of a funnel leading into a vertical graduated collecting vessel. Weather is determined not only by conditions on the surface of the Earth but also by those high in the atmosphere. In the 18th century kites were used for upper-air measurements. They were replaced by manned and free balloons in the 19th century, but systematic recording has only been possible during the second half of the 20th century. This has involved high-altitude sounding balloons (see *radiosonde), aircraft, rockets, and *meteorological satellites, using *telemetry to relay observations quickly to ground stations. Perhaps the most significant new meteorological tool is the *computer. Extremely fast computers with large amounts of memory are needed to digest the vast amounts of observational data collected and formulate it into a forecast sufficiently quickly to be of use. Computer 'models' of the atmosphere can also be used to make longer-term, more speculative predictions of climate change.

meteorological satellite, an artificial *satellite that orbits the Earth collecting information on the atmosphere and weather. The satellites carry *radiometers, which measure light and infra-red radiation from the clouds and from land and sea surfaces. These data, processed to produce visual images, give information on cloud heights and temperatures, land and sea surface temperatures, wind-speeds, and humidity. The satellites also collect information from remote automatic weather stations, such as buoys at sea, weather balloons, and aircraft, and relay it to *ground stations. An example is the European Space Agency's *Meteosat*, one of a ring of five meteorological satellites in geostationary orbit which together maintain a continuous weather watch for almost the whole world. *Meteosat* produces an image for Europe, Africa, and the Middle East every 30 minutes.

methane (CH_4), the simplest *hydrocarbon. It is the chief constituent of *natural gas and is formed by the decomposition of plant and animal matter. It is familiar as marsh gas (from the decomposition of organic matter under water) and in coal mines as fire-damp (marsh-gas), where, because it forms an explosive mixture with air, it constitutes a major fire hazard. It is the major component of natural gas and an important starting material for the manufacture of organic solvents, ammonia, methanol, and other chemicals.

methanoic acid (formic acid, HCOOH), a colourless liquid with a pungent aroma, made by the action of sulphuric acid on sodium formate (NaCOOH), which is itself made from carbon monoxide and sodium hydroxide. Methanoic acid is used as a reducing agent (see *oxidation and reduction) in the textile and leather industries, and has miscellaneous uses, including as a coagulant in making latex rubber, and as a *food preservative.

methanol (methyl alcohol, CH_3OH), the simplest *alcohol, a clear colourless liquid, sometimes known as wood spirit because it was first produced by destructive distillation of wood. Today it is produced by the reaction of carbon oxides with hydrogen. Methanol is very toxic, causing blindness and death. It is used for *antifreeze, as a solvent, and for the manufacture of methanal (formaldehyde) and other important industrial chemicals.

methylated spirits, a mixture of distilled (ethyl) alcohol to which up to 10 per cent *methanol has been added, making it unfit to drink. Traces of pyridine, to give an unpleasant taste, and a purple dye are often also added. Methylated spirits are used commercially as a fuel and as a solvent.

metric unit *unit.

microcomputer, a complete computer based around a *microprocessor. Primary *memory, input and output interfaces, and a *clock are added to the microprocessor to make a microcomputer. Personal computers, *word processors, video games, and most *workstations are microcomputers. For relatively simple computing needs, such as in domestic products and toys, the complete microcomputer can often be implemented on a single *integrated circuit.

microelectronics *electronics, *information technology.

microfiche, a sheet of photographic film on which a large number of pages of text are stored by photographically reducing an image of the text. Low-density microfilming was first used in the 1920s for copying bank cheques, but the popularity of the process accelerated in the 1960s as a means of storage in libraries and for business records. High-density microfiche can now store 3,000 pages on one 105 × 148-mm (4 × 6-inch) sheet of high-resolution, fine-grain film. The reader must have a viewing device with high magnification and resolution, and a rapid-scan facility.

microlight (US, ultralight aircraft), in its most basic form a *hang-glider powered by an engine. The official definition of this very lightweight, simple type of aeroplane is a one- or two-seat aeroplane whose empty weight does not exceed 150 kg (330 pounds), with a wing area in square metres of not less than $W/10$, where W is the weight in kilograms (for example, a wing area of at least 10 m^2 for a weight of 100 kg). Many variants of this type of aeroplane, first seen in the pioneer designs before World War I, have been built since about 1970, when microlight flying became a popular sport.

micrometer, an instrument for accurately measuring very small distances or objects. The commonest type is that in which the distance is measured by the rotation of a fine-pitched screw. The outer casing of the instrument is graduated so that fractions of a single rotation can be easily determined. This type of micrometer consists of a G-shaped clamp with a fixed anvil, against which the object is held by a graduated screw. The screw is tightened until the gap between it and the object is just closed. With fine adjustment, such a gauge is accurate to around 2.5 μm (10^{-4} inches). In *microscopes and *telescopes, a rack-and-pinion or micrometer screw mechanism can be used in conjunction with a graduated scale to measure the size of objects seen through the instrument.

microphone, a device that converts sound energy into electrical energy. Microphones have many uses, for example, in *telephones, *tape recorders, *hearing aids and in *radio and *television broadcasting. In all microphones, sound waves are translated into mechanical vibrations in a thin, flexible diaphragm. These vibrations are then converted by various methods into an electrical signal. In a condenser microphone the diaphragm acts as one plate of a capacitor, and vibrations produce changes in a voltage maintained across the capacitor plates. Condenser microphones are expensive and require an external power supply, but give a high-quality sound signal and are used in laboratory and studio recording applications. In the dynamic microphone a small movable *coil, in the field of a permanent magnet, is attached to the diaphragm. When the diaphragm vibrates, the coil moves in the magnetic field, producing a varying electrical signal in the coil (see *electromagnetic induction). Dynamic microphones are robust and relatively inexpensive, and are used in a wide variety of applications. In ribbon microphones a thin, corrugated metal ribbon is suspended in a magnetic field: vibration of the ribbon in the magnetic field generates a changing voltage. Ribbon microphones detect sound in a bidirectional pattern: this characteristic is useful in applications such as radio and television interviews, where it cuts out much extraneous sound.

microprocessor, one of a small number of *integrated circuits that implements all the functions of the *central processing unit of a computer. When combined with memory, a clock, and interfaces, a microprocessor functions as a *microcomputer. The earliest microprocessor was the Intel 4004, developed in 1972. This was a 4-*bit processor, but in the last eighteen years 8-, 16- and even 32-bit processors have been developed. Microprocessors are small and cheap enough that they have been incorporated into a very wide range of products. Thirty-two-bit processors are used in small, very powerful desk-top computers, but the largest market is in 4-bit microprocessors, which are extensively used in domestic products such as washing-machines, video recorders, and televisions.

microscope. An optical microscope is an instrument that uses a *lens or combination of lenses to magnify very small structures, for example *cells. Other microscopes are analogous in function but employ radiation other than visible light. A magnifying glass is a simple microscope, but the compound microscope gives higher magnification. It was probably invented in about 1590 by a Dutch spectacle-maker, Zacharias Janssen, although others working at the same time have also been cited as the inventor. The object to be magnified is placed on the 'stage' and the objective lens forms an inverted image inside the microscope tube. The eyepiece lens gives an enlarged, inverted image of the first image, thus reproducing the original object (see figure). Generally light passes through the specimen into the microscope. Specimens thin enough to transmit light, usually mounted on glass slides and protected by thin glass cover slips, are often colourless, so stains are used to reveal structures. Polarized light is used to study crystals, and ultramicroscopy, in which liquid suspensions are illuminated from the side, shows particle movement as flashes against a dark background. Stereoscopic microscopes, often used in surgery, have one microscope for each eye, arranged so that the specimen is viewed from slightly different angles, giving a three-dimensional picture. Oil-immersion objective lenses increase resolving power (ability to distinguish detail) at high magnifications by using a drop of special oil between the objective lens and the cover slip. Light microscopes have an inherent upper magnification limit of about ×2,000, but *electron microscopes can magnify over 1 million times. Other types of microscope have more recently been developed for specialist and research applications. Proton microscopes use a tightly focused beam of high-energy protons to scan a specimen. They can be used on thicker specimens than electron microscopes, and can provide information on the chemical composition of the sample. In X-ray microscopy, concentrated *X-ray sources scan a sample to produce images of the crystalline structure of materials. In emission microscopy, electrical fields or high temperatures are used to stimulate the sample to emit subatomic particles: such microscopes can show reactions at solid surfaces, such as *corrosion and *vapour deposition. Acoustic microscopy uses high-frequency *ultrasound in place of visible light: sound waves reflected from the sample vary in intensity depending on how much acoustic energy has been absorbed by that portion of the sample. Acoustic microscopy is used in biological research, and for detecting faults in *integrated circuits. A very recent development for studying surfaces is the scanning tunnelling microscope (STM). This measures the separation distance between a fine-point detector and the surface of the sample, using a phenomenon known as tunnelling, by which electrons transfer between the sample surface and the detector, causing a minute current flow. The STM can resolve images down to below atomic dimensions.

Microscope

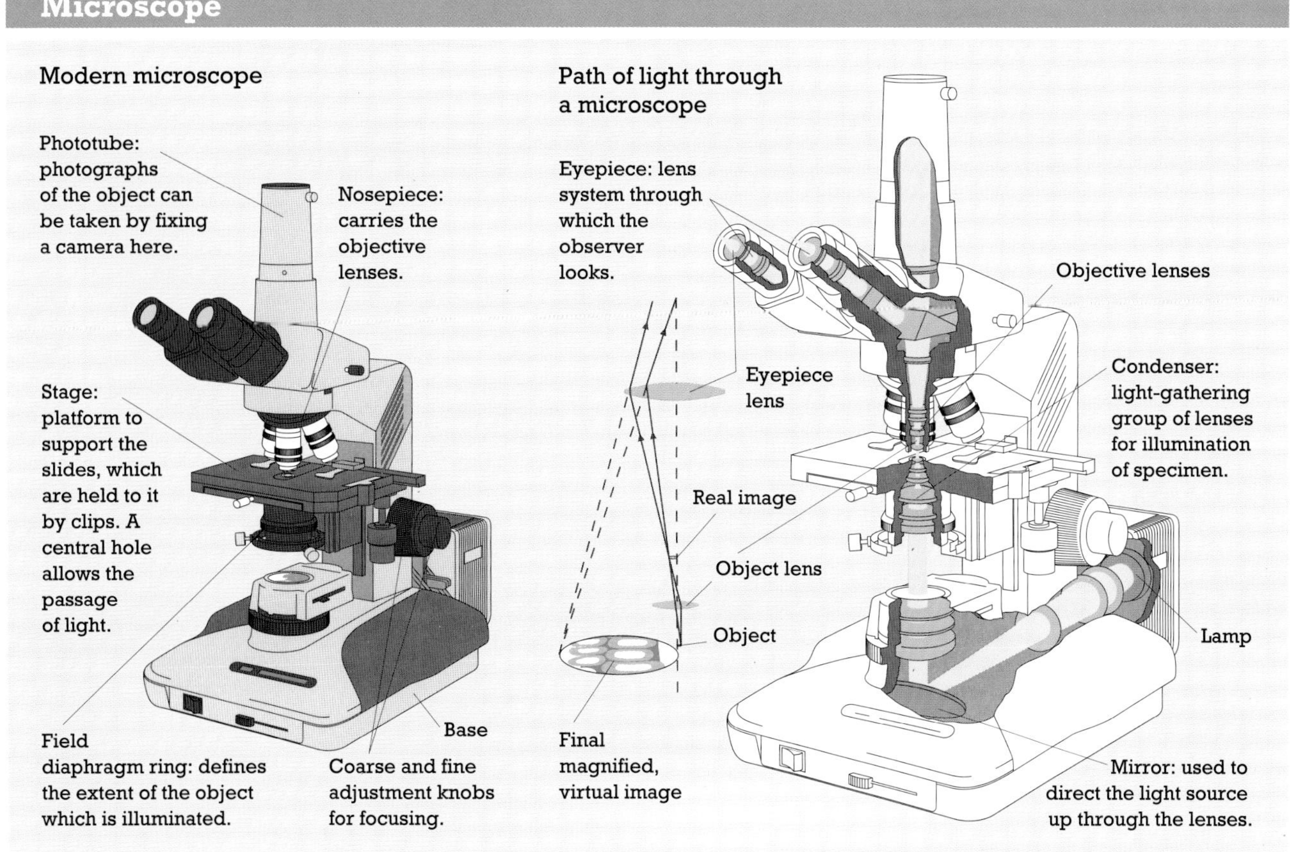
Modern microscope
Phototube: photographs of the object can be taken by fixing a camera here.
Nosepiece: carries the objective lenses.
Stage: platform to support the slides, which are held to it by clips. A central hole allows the passage of light.
Base
Field diaphragm ring: defines the extent of the object which is illuminated.
Coarse and fine adjustment knobs for focusing.
Path of light through a microscope
Eyepiece: lens system through which the observer looks.
Eyepiece lens
Real image
Object lens
Object
Final magnified, virtual image
Objective lenses
Condenser: light-gathering group of lenses for illumination of specimen.
Lamp
Mirror: used to direct the light source up through the lenses.

microsurgery, intricate surgery performed using *microscopes, enabling the tissue to be operated on with miniaturized *surgical instruments. Microsurgery has only become possible in recent years. It relies on the surgeon's ability to connect together the ends of very small arteries, veins, nerves, or muscles in order to preserve nutrition to tissues, which may otherwise die. It is used in a variety of surgical specialities, for example to reattach severed limbs, in brain surgery, and in ear and eye surgery.

microtome, an instrument for cutting very thin sections of material for examination under a *microscope. In its simplest form, it consists of a hollow metal cylinder, in which the material for examination is placed, containing a piston that can be pushed up a measured amount by turning a screw. As the material is extruded, sections are cut with a razor. For routine use this process can be mechanized. Soft material can be made firmer by embedding in wax or by freezing. In the ultramicrotome, a glass or diamond blade is used and delicate extrusion is effected by thermal expansion of a rod.

microwave cooker, an appliance that cooks food by *electromagnetic radiation in the microwave region, of *wavelength 1–300 mm (0.04–12 inches). Microwave cookers for the catering trade were first sold in the USA around 1953, but domestic microwaves did not achieve widespread popularity until about 1980. Microwaves are generated by a magnetron, a type of *thermionic valve first developed for use in *radar. A rotating blade scatters the microwaves into the small box-shaped oven. Water molecules in the food become excited by the radiation, generating heat throughout the food. Food cooks much more quickly in a microwave than in a conventional oven. However, microwave heating alone does not brown or crisp food on the outside, and microwaves cook some foods unevenly.

Midgley, Thomas, Jr. (1889–1944), US engineer and chemist. While at Dayton Engineering Laboratories Company in Ohio, he studied the problem of *knock in *petrol engines, and discovered that *lead tetraethyl is an effective anti-knock additive (1921). He also introduced the concept of *octane rating for petrol. In the 1930s, while working for the Du Pont Company, he developed Freons (*chlorofluorocarbons) as refrigerants and fire-extinguishing agents. By the 1980s both lead tetraethyl and Freons had been condemned as dangerous atmospheric pollutants.

military aircraft. Aircraft have been used for military purposes since very early in their history. The French formed the first *balloon corps in history in 1793, and first used free balloons for military reconnaissance at the battle of Fleures, France, in 1794. With the development of the navigable *airship from the balloon, true military aviation began. Airships were used extensively in World War I, when the German Zeppelins proved invaluable for long-range reconnaissance flights and night-time bombing raids. Experiments with the use of guns and bombs in aeroplanes were made from 1910 onwards, and by the end of World War I purpose-built *fighter and *bomber aircraft had been developed, with performance capabilities far beyond those of aircraft flying in 1914. Twin-engined flying boats were being used for long reconnaissance flights over water, and the first flights had already been made from the deck of a moving ship.

By the start of World War II most European and American aircraft were all-metal monoplanes (see *flying, history

The Northrop B-2A advanced-technology Stealth Bomber. The B-2A and several other new **military aircraft** have low-observable characteristics, aimed at minimizing their radar profiles.

of). Supercharged engines, closed cockpits, and oxygen masks meant that fighter aircraft could operate effectively at heights of 4,500–6,300 m (15,000–20,000 feet), while bombers reached heights of 9,000 m (30,000 feet). Fighter armament improved as the War progressed, and bomb weights rose from 225–550 kg (500–1,000 pounds) to around 10,000 kg (22,000 pounds). The widespread adoption of *radar, for detection and guidance of aircraft from the ground and for use on board aircraft, led to improvements in air defence, night flying, and bombing accuracy. The first *jet aircraft flew towards the end of World War II. Soon afterwards the intercontinental *ballistic missile was developed, and by the mid-1960s had largely replaced the long-range bomber as the major nuclear deterrent. At around the same time, *military satellites took over many of the aeroplane's roles in reconnaissance and information-gathering. In the 1950s and early 1960s ever-faster military jets were tested, but by the mid-1960s military aviation had begun to change. Strategies were evolved to avoid radar detection, such as low, terrain-following flights and electronic or other means of jamming or confusing enemy radar. More recently the USA has put much research effort into 'stealth' aircraft, designed to have low radar visibility and made of radar-absorbing materials. Developments in *avionics in the 1970s and 1980s provided aircraft that could automatically fly at very low altitudes, and weapons and navigation systems that would automatically locate and attack targets. Fighters and bombers have been replaced by strike aircraft, which attack targets deep in enemy territory, interceptors designed to shoot down enemy aircraft, and close air-support aircraft with the role of supporting ground troops. Aircraft are designed to carry a variety of different weapons so as to be able to fulfil multiple roles, while further flexibility is found in *VTOL or *STOL aircraft, which can operate from sites other than conventional airstrips. *Helicopters have become increasingly important as manœuvrability and flexibility take precedence over speed.

military engineering, a discipline primarily concerned with the design and construction of military installations, but also including the building of temporary bridges and other tasks. Defensive earthworks were already well developed by the 2nd millennium BC, as exemplified by the sophisticated fortresses of Tiryns (in Greece) and Troy (in modern Turkey). The development of *siege warfare led not only to stronger walls but to greater obstacles to access. The advent of gunpowder in the 14th century rendered virtually all existing fortresses obsolete and they had to be redesigned, with particular attention to the incorporation of bastions for cannon and to the geometry of defensive lines of fire to avoid 'blind' spots in which the enemy could lurk. For the attack, geometry was applied to the planning of trench systems by which fortresses could be approached without exposing troops to fire. The work of de *Vauban in the 17th century was widely influential in this respect. The destruction of fortifications by mining the foundations became an important new task for military engineers (sappers). In the 20th century permanent fortifications have largely become obsolete, but the building of temporary entrenchments and other defences is still a vital part of military engineering. Other areas of responsibility include the erection of temporary bridges; the repair of bomb-damaged roads and runways; provision of temporary fuel lines; laying barbed wire; excavating bomb-proof shelters; and moving all kinds of heavy equipment. Much of the work for which military engineers are now responsible is carried out by civilian contractors.

military satellite, any artificial *satellite orbiting the earth that is used for military purposes. More than 2,000 have been launched to date, mainly by the USA and the Soviet Union. They include *communications satellites, *meteorological satellites, and *navigation satellites, some of these being shared by civilian users. Spy satellites (called 'ferrets') listen in to enemy radio communications and track military movements by radio signals or *radar. Surveillance satellites photograph military installations or battle areas: originally photographic film was used for this purpose, as it gave great detail, but it had to be returned to earth for processing. Modern surveillance satellites transmit to Earth images detailed enough to distinguish between military and civilian personnel and between real vegetation and camouflage. Early-warning satellites can detect missile launches and nuclear explosions, and progress has been made towards developing 'killer' satellites, which will be able to destroy enemy military satellites, either by exploding near them or by using *laser weapons to destroy them or disable their instruments.

military technology. Military technology and *military engineering have been important factors in warfare since prehistoric times. The archaeological evidence from excavated skeletons indicates that the earliest weapons were those used in hunting—clubs, *axes, knives, and *spears. Rock paintings show the *bow and arrow to be at least 30,000 years old; it is technologically significant as the first device in which energy is stored slowly and released quickly. From the 13th century BC the power of the bow was increased by using composite materials, but the major advance was the introduction of mechanical devices to draw the bow, as in the *crossbow (see figure overleaf). From these bows, more powerful siege weapons were developed, such as the *catapult and the onager, a huge sling deriving its power from torsion.

The earliest weapons were of stone or wood; the arrival of bronze in the 4th millennium BC, and of iron around 2,000 years later, made weapons more deadly. No less revolutionary was the introduction in about 2500 BC of the horse-drawn *chariot. Cavalry appeared soon afterwards, their mobility being much improved by the invention of the stirrup. Improved weaponry led to increasingly sophisticated *body armour and shields, the culmination of this trend being the armour of medieval European knights. At a very early date recourse was made to temporary or permanent fortifications strong enough to resist the most powerful weapons of the day. These in turn engendered a range of weapons for *siege warfare, such as assault towers and battering-rams.

Incendiary devices were used in war from an early date. The best known was the *Greek fire of the 7th century AD, revived in the 20th century as *napalm. It was from such incendiary mixtures that the Chinese derived *gunpowder, first used for *bombs in the 13th century but developed soon afterwards as a propellant. It was first used in the West early in the 14th century, originally for heavy cannon and subsequently in hand-held *firearms. Gunpowder revolutionized war in western Europe. It reigned supreme for some 500 years, until displaced in the late 19th century by other *explosives. The 20th century saw the introduction of both the *submarine and the aeroplane (see *military aircraft). The *aircraft carrier united naval and air forces. The escape from the surface was accentuated by the development of *ballistic missiles ascending high into the stratosphere, and *military satellites in orbit. Two other major military developments in the 20th century were the *tank and the *self-propelled gun. However, the single most important military development of the 20th century was that of *nuclear weapons. Although only two bombs have ever been exploded in war, their effect on military strategy has been enormous.

milk *dairy product.

milking machine, a machine used in *dairy farming to extract and collect milk. Milking machines are usually employed for cows, but ewes and goats may also be machine-milked. The machine applies an intermittent suction to the animal's teat, and the animal responds by releasing milk, which is drawn away by the suction to a central area, where it is cooled to reduce bacterial action. Milking machines considerably increase the speed with which animals can be handled.

milling (cereal), the grinding of cereal grain to produce the coarse meal or finer flour for the production of a range of basic foodstuffs. The way in which the seed is ground, the size of particle produced, and the degree of sifting undertaken will determine the type of flour or meal produced. Most cereals are milled dry, but maize is often milled by wet processes. Wheat-grain may be crushed between grinding stones to produce a coarse, wholemeal flour, or it may be milled by steel cylinders, followed by air purification and

Military technology

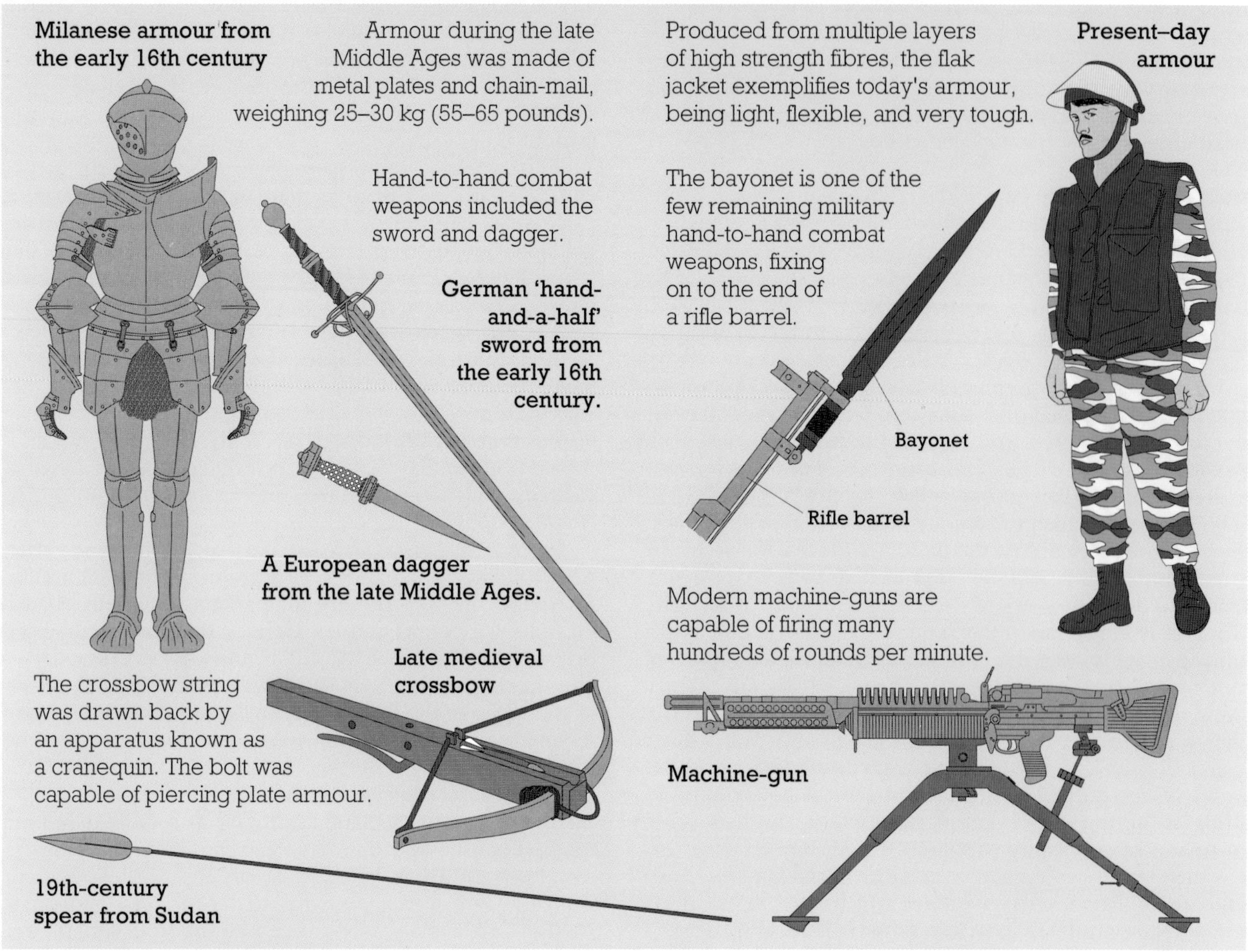

Milanese armour from the early 16th century
Armour during the late Middle Ages was made of metal plates and chain-mail, weighing 25–30 kg (55–65 pounds).
Produced from multiple layers of high strength fibres, the flak jacket exemplifies today's armour, being light, flexible, and very tough.
Present–day armour
Hand-to-hand combat weapons included the sword and dagger.
German 'hand-and-a-half' sword from the early 16th century.
The bayonet is one of the few remaining military hand-to-hand combat weapons, fixing on to the end of a rifle barrel.
Bayonet
Rifle barrel
A European dagger from the late Middle Ages.
Modern machine-guns are capable of firing many hundreds of rounds per minute.
Late medieval crossbow
The crossbow string was drawn back by an apparatus known as a cranequin. The bolt was capable of piercing plate armour.
Machine-gun
19th-century spear from Sudan

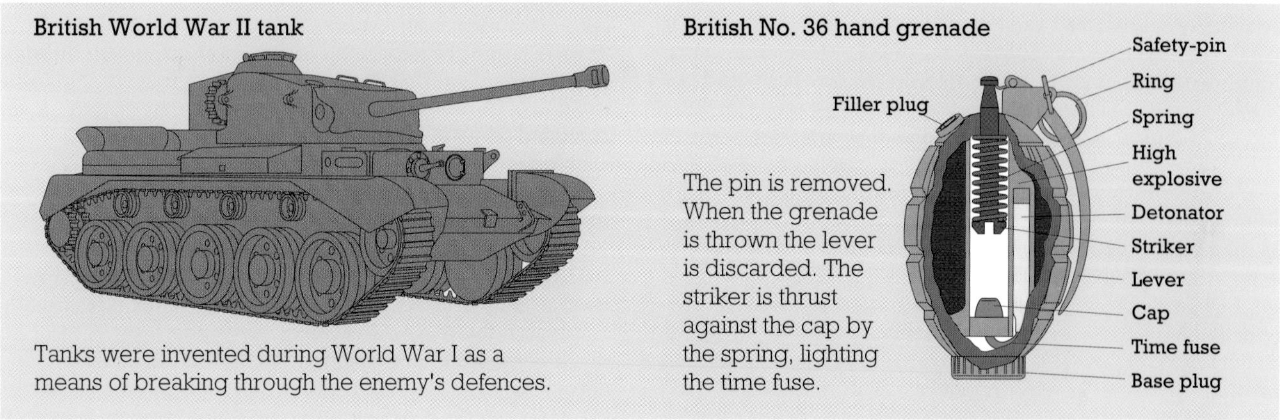

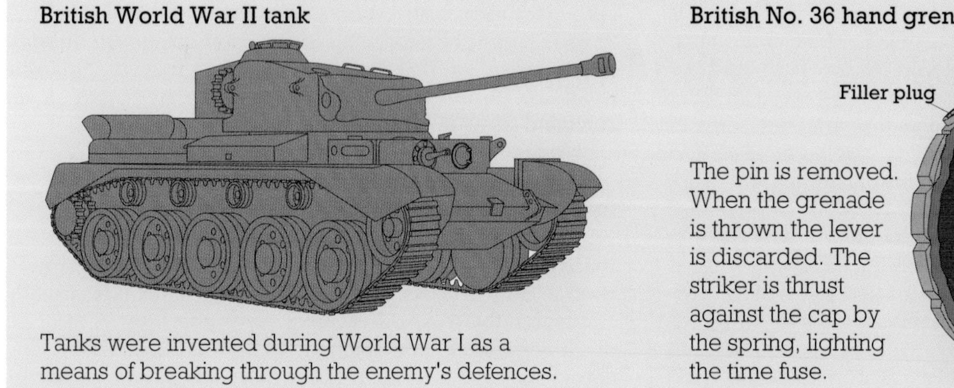

British World War II tank
Tanks were invented during World War I as a means of breaking through the enemy's defences.
British No. 36 hand grenade
Filler plug
Safety-pin
Ring
Spring
High explosive
Detonator
Striker
Lever
Cap
Time fuse
Base plug
The pin is removed. When the grenade is thrown the lever is discarded. The striker is thrust against the cap by the spring, lighting the time fuse.

numerous sievings, to make white flour. Some cereals (for example, rice) are not milled but may be polished to remove the bran and germ.

milling machine *machine-tool.

mine (mineral extraction) *mining.

mine, an explosive device placed in water or buried underground, that is designed to destroy ships, vehicles, and personnel. Naval mines were first employed in the late 18th century. Originally called torpedoes, they were little more than barrels filled with gunpowder with enough air for buoyancy. Moored mines, fired on contact or by a chemical *fuse, were used by the Russians in the Baltic during the Crimean War (1854–6). Some late 19th-century mines were triggered by an electric current transmitted from shore through a cable. More recent naval mines are triggered by the magnetic field of a passing ship, the effect of a ship on the local water pressure, or the sound waves from a ship's engines or propellers. Some mines combine two of these mechanisms. Limpet mines are fixed by divers on to the hulls of ships and detonated by a timed fuse. Land-mines were developed between the two World Wars. At first they had metal cases, but the use of *mine-detectors led to alternative casings of plastic or wood. Land-mines are fitted with a fuse that is triggered by pressure. They are placed in position by hand or scattered by packing them into artillery *shells.

Underground tunnels or galleries filled with explosives and dug beneath enemy trenches or fortifications are also called mines.

mine-detector, a device for locating *mines. The simplest form of detection is a soldier with a knife. The soldier goes forward on hands and knees, carefully probing the ground ahead until a mine is located. More advanced is the use of a *metal detector. At sea, *minesweepers are used for mine detection and clearance, and on land the *flail tank is used.

mine-layer, a ship purpose-built or adapted to lay *mines. The mines are stowed on or below deck on rails, and are laid through stern doors, usually at precisely calculated positions. Some submarines have been adapted to lay mines, and other ship types can also temporarily be fitted as mine-layers. Ground mines, laid on the sea-bed in shallow water, are usually laid by aircraft.

miner's friend, the name given to the earliest form of steam pump, invented by Thomas Savery in 1698. As its name implies, it was designed to pump water from mines, but it was also used to supply water to towns. The pump had two chambers, each with inlet and discharge valves. Steam filled one chamber and was then condensed by cold water flowing over the outside of the chamber, so reducing the chamber pressure and drawing in water. Steam under pressure was then used to deliver the water to a higher level while the second chamber was filling. The performance was very limited, both as regards the height to which water could be pumped and the extravagant use of steam. Newcomen's *beam-engine was much more efficient, but a modern version of Savery's pump, the pulsometer, has found applications as a vacuum pump because of its simplicity and robustness.

A **milking machine** in use in Dorset, UK. Metal suction tubes are attached to the cow's teats, down which the milk is rhythmically squeezed.

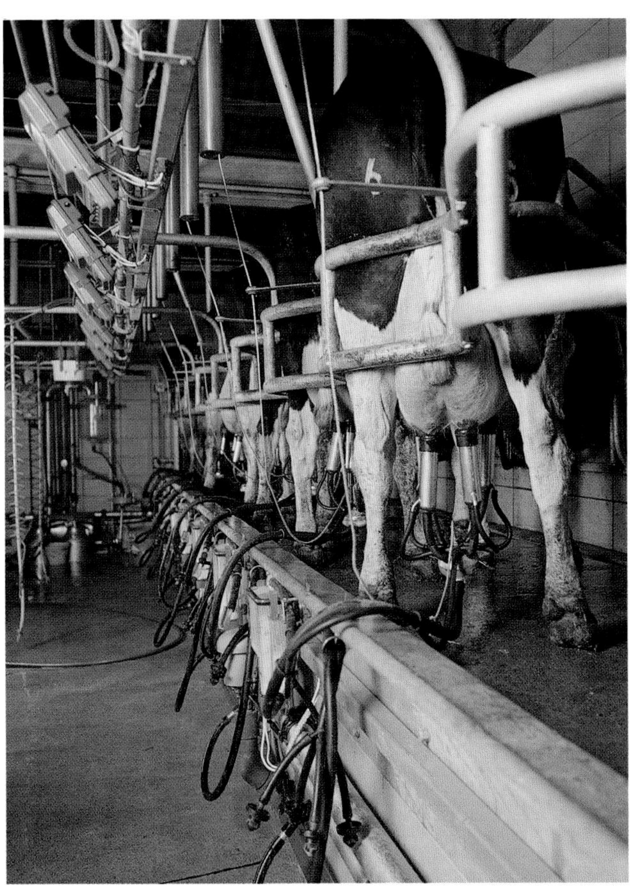

minesweeper (mine-hunter, mine counter-measures vessel), a vessel designed or modified to sweep or explode *mines laid at sea. Early minesweepers were adapted *ships' boats; later, during World War I, pairs of *trawlers towing an underwater sweep of serrated wire between them were used to cut mines' mooring ropes. A development from this was the Oropesa sweep, a serrated sweep towed by a single trawler, the sweep being kept taut and at a certain depth by a device known as a 'kite and otter'. The development of magnetic, pressure-sensitive and acoustic mines has required new minesweeper designs. Wooden or glass-reinforced plastic hulls are necessary to avoid detection by magnetic mines, which can be detonated by an LL sweep. This consists of two electric cables that generate an electric charge in the water between them, exploding any magnetic mines present. Acoustic mines are destroyed by simulated propeller noise, while pressure mines can be located by *sonar and detonated by a remote-controlled *submersible.

minicomputer, the general term for a *computer that is intermediate in performance between a *mainframe computer and a *microcomputer. The minicomputer first appeared in the mid-1960s to meet a demand from scientists and engineers who wanted computing power for specific applications but did not require a mainframe. The machines generally incorporated 16-*bit and then, later, 32-bit data *bus architecture. In the 1970s minicomputers spread into business applications, but the development of sophisticated microcomputers has eroded the traditional minicomputer market.

minimum tillage, a labour-saving technique for the sowing of seed directly into the stubble of previous crops. In practice some work may be needed to destroy existing weed growth: 'total' *herbicides are used to kill all vegetation in an area, then the ground is lightly cultivated and sown. Minimum tillage is advocated by those who feel that the intensive mechanical activity of modern *arable farming damages soil structure and causes unnecessary water losses. It is also used to enable early sowing.

mining, excavation for the removal of *ores and minerals from the Earth's crust. One of the earliest mined materials was *flint: evidence of flint mining at Grimes Grave, Norfolk, UK, dates back to 2400 BC. Tools such as antler picks and ox shoulder-blade shovels have been found on such sites, and the structure of the mines indicates the use of simple hoisting devices. Mining techniques chronicled by *Agricola in his book *De Re Metallica* ('On Metals') (1556) are recognizable today. Picks, hammers, and shovels were used for loosening and moving the mineral; ventilation and pumping systems were installed to keep air pure and to avoid flooding; and cart-like trucks linked to pulley systems carried minerals along the tunnels. The Romans used fire to crack rock faces, but during the Middle Ages the advent of *gunpowder as a blasting agent aided the initial loosening of material. Gunpowder was replaced by *dynamite in the mid-19th century; today *explosives based on ammonium nitrate are also used. Drills to aid the loosening of minerals were first used in the early 1800s, and compressed-air piston drills were commonplace by the end of the century. Modern *coal-cutters and other mining equipment simultaneously cut material from the face and load it on to a conveyor.

*Prospecting for mineral deposits is now a highly technical operation requiring extensive knowledge of earth sciences and the use of a wide range of techniques. Such surveys must take into account the nature of the rocks surrounding the ore deposit, as they will affect the overall economics of the operation. If the located deposit lies near the surface, *open-cast mining or *hydraulic mining might be appropriate. For deeper deposits a vertical shaft may be sunk, with horizontal *tunnels running off into the mineral (deep mining); a horizontal tunnel running into the deposit may be dug into the side of a hill or mountain (*adit mining or *drift mining); or an inclined shaft may be sunk parallel to the deposit, with horizontal tunnels connected to the mineral vein at intervals. Large rotary drills plus blasting are used for tunnelling, in conjunction with systems for hauling and hoisting the debris to the surface. Some excavated sections will need no reinforcement, but sometimes both ceilings and walls need support. In *bord-and-pillar mining the mine is constructed so that unmined material supports the roof. In *long-wall mining the seam is excavated along a face up to 350 m (1,150 feet) in length.

A variety of methods exist for preventing tunnel collapse. Traditionally, timber frames were assembled within tunnels, and wooden ceilings and walls could be attached to these if necessary. More recently, steel arches, hydraulic jacks, and embedded steel rods have been introduced (see *pit-prop). In addition, rapid-setting concrete can be sprayed into faults and fissures to reinforce ceilings. Mined material is usually removed by trains of steel boxes drawn along tracks by electric locomotives. In large mines, these trains are often fed from the cutting face by conveyor belts. For mines with a deep vertical shaft, powerful lifting or winding gear is required. A ventilation system to remove harmful gases is essential; large *air-conditioning units are used. It is also necessary to have an electric lighting system throughout the mine. (See also *coal-mining.)

Mir *space station.

mirror, a smooth surface that reflects light, forming images. A plane (flat) mirror forms a full-sized, reversed image that appears to be as far behind the mirror as the object is in front. Concave curved mirrors give upright enlarged images of close objects or inverted images of far objects. They are used as reflectors for searchlights and headlights (condensing the beam), and to collect light in astronomical telescopes. Convex curved mirrors produce smaller upright images with a wide field of view and are used as rear-view driving mirrors. The earliest mirrors were made from highly polished metal and some still are today. However, most mirrors are made by depositing a very thin layer of aluminium (formerly silver) on glass in a vacuum, followed by a protective layer. Ordinary mirrors are coated on the back, while precision ones for scientific use have coatings on the front, to avoid confusion of the image by a faint reflection from the uncoated front surface of the glass. Half-silvered mirrors have thinner coatings that let some light through, reflecting the rest.

MIRV *multiple independently targetable re-entry vehicle.

missile, an object, normally a weapon, that is thrown or projected at a target. In modern usage of the term, missiles are self-propelled, flying, explosive weapons, usually powered by a *rocket motor. Many missiles are simply aimed at the target and fired; others, *guided missiles, are steered on to the target during flight, either automatically or under remote control by an operator. Some guided missiles can pursue a target even when it is taking evasive action.

The earliest missiles were sticks or stones aimed by primitive humans at a prey or an enemy. These developed into hand-powered projectiles such as spears, to which devices using mechanical propulsion, such as the slingshot, bow and arrow, and ballista, were later added. The ancestor of today's missile first appeared some 1,000 years ago in China, when *gunpowder was introduced to boost the flight of arrows, and used in self-propelled rocket weapons, similar to the modern firework rocket. The war rocket was further developed in the early 19th century by William Congreve in the UK. These rockets, which were unguided and inaccurate, were mass-bombardment weapons. Indeed, the unguided, solid-fuelled rocket is still widely used as a weapon today. Guided missiles were possible only after the development of *radio and *electronics. Early prototypes, which were, in fact, pilotless radio-controlled model aircraft, appeared in the 1920s and 1930s. The first truly guided missiles were used operationally during World War II, when Germany bombarded London and other Allied cities with the V2 rocket, a *ballistic missile, and the V1 pulse jet, a primitive *cruise missile. Other types, including air-to-surface and surface-to-air missiles, were also being developed in Germany before the War ended. Subsequently, the USA, the Soviet Union, France, the UK, and many other countries began research on this type of weapon. Today, guided missiles are standard military equipment throughout the world.

Modern-day missiles are classified according to their use (see table). Air-to-air missiles (AAMs) are fired from an aeroplane or a helicopter at an airborne target. They are usually guided missiles employing active or semi-active radar homing. Infra-red (heat-seeking) missiles of the 'fire-and-forget' type—that is, once launched, they receive no further guidance—are effective in good conditions at ranges of up to 20 km (12 miles), but cannot so easily find their targets at low altitudes through dust, smoke, haze, or fog. They are now being developed for very short-range use in dog-fights. A missile launched from an aircraft to attack a target on the ground or at sea is called an air-to-surface missile (ASM). Some unguided ASMs are employed in mass bombardment of a local target. Many others, however, use sophisticated guidance technologies, including television, infra-red radiation, laser-illumination, and active or semi-active radar homing. Some ASMs are tactical (short-range) weapons, directed against targets such as ships, tanks, and bridges; they include unpowered, so-called 'smart' bombs, which are controlled by vanes and glide to their targets. Long-range ASMs, including the air-launched cruise missile, are part of the strategic weapons arsenal. Normally armed with nuclear *warheads, they are an extension of the ICBM (intercontinental ballistic missile) deterrence strategy. Surface-to-air

Technicians in a laboratory in Oak Ridge, Tennessee, USA, testing the accuracy of the surfaces of several metal **mirrors** using a laser interferometer.

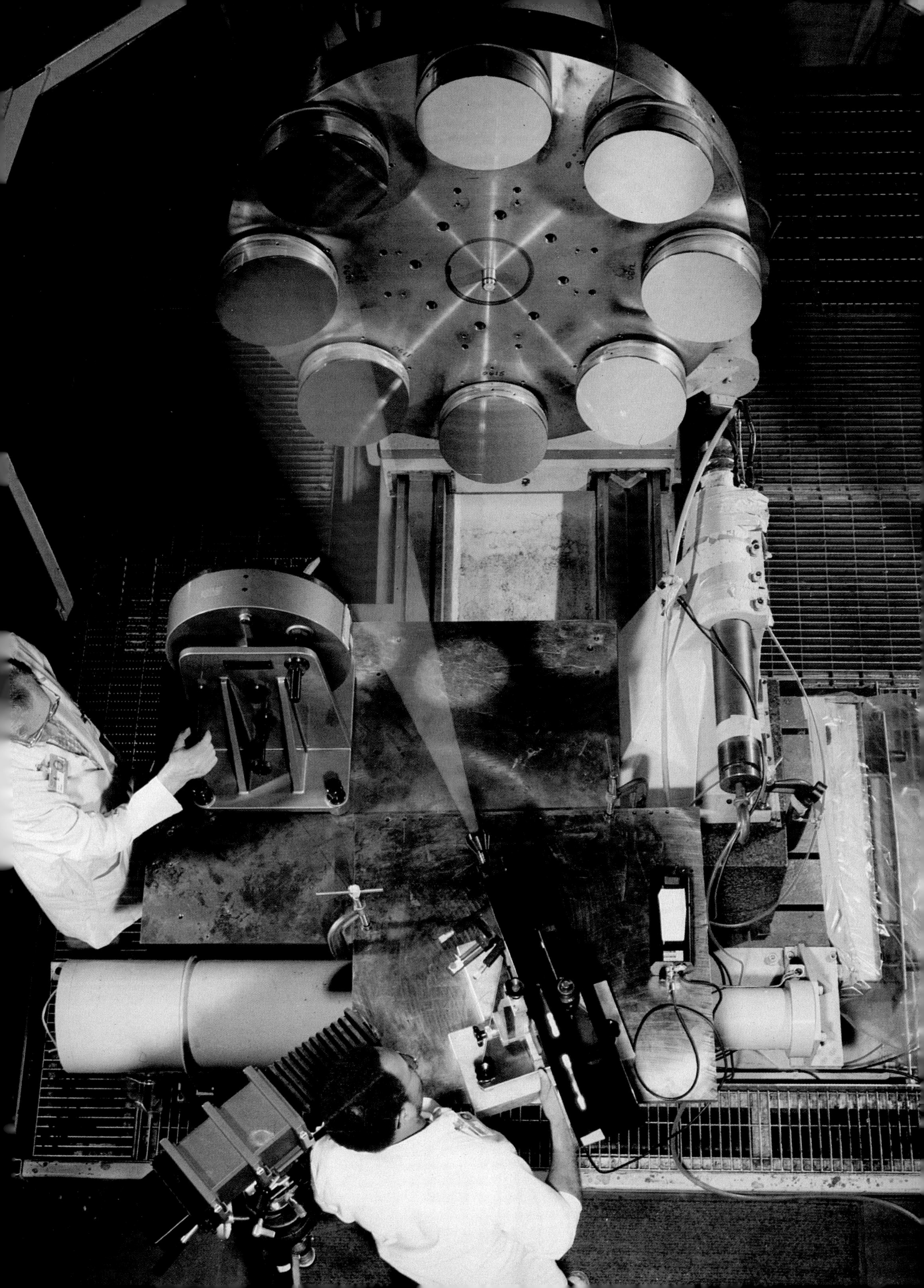

A selection of missiles currently in service around the world

Entered service	Missile	Range km (miles)	Country	Comments
Air-to-air missiles (AAM)				
1956	Sidewinder	18 (11)	USA	Basic infra-red homing missile, used throughout the world
1956	Sparrow	50 (31)	USA	Semi-active radar homing missile
1970	Phoenix	>200 (124)	USA	Semi-active radar homing missile
1975	Skyflash	50 (31)	USA	Semi-active radar homing missile
1976	AA-7-Apex	40 (25)	Soviet Union	Infra-red or semi-active radar homing missile
—	AA-9	100 (62)	Soviet Union	Under development
—	ASRAAM	15 (9)	UK/Germany	Infra-red homing missile under development for NATO
Air-to-surface missiles (ASM)				
1968	Maverick	40 (25)	USA	Tactical missiles using various guidance systems
1977	AS-6-Kingfisher	560 (348)	Soviet Union	Nuclear missile using inertial guidance and terminal semi-active radar homing
1977	AS-8	10 (6)	Soviet Union	Fire-and-forget missile
1982	ALCM	2,500 (1,550)	USA	Cruise missile with nuclear capability
1984	HARM	19 (12)	USA	High-speed anti-radar missile
1987	ALARM	N/A	UK	Anti-radar missile using passive radar homing
Surface-to-air missiles (SAM)				
1969	ABM-1B-Galosh	320 (200)	Soviet Union	Only anti-ballistic missile in service
1969	Standard	120 (75)	USA	Ship-to-air missile with semi-active radar homing
*c.*1970	SA-7-Grail	10 (6)	Soviet Union	Man-portable anti-aircraft missile with infra-red homing
1975	Blowpipe	3 (2)	UK	Man-portable, optical line-of-sight missile
1978	SA-10	64 (41)	Soviet Union	Medium- and high-altitude area defence missile. Semi-active radar homing
1979	Seawolf	6 (4)	UK	The only anti-missile system in use in any navy. Common line-of-sight, radar-guided homing
1983	Patriot	60 (37)	USA	Medium- and high-altitude defence missile, with semi-active radar homing
1984	Stinger	5 (3)	USA	Man-portable infra-red homing missile
Anti-tank (surface-to-surface or air-to-surface) missiles				
1965	Milan	2 (1)	France/Germany	Man-portable, wire-guided missile with infra-red tracker
1969	Swingfire	4 (2)	USA	Wire-guided, vehicle-mounted missile
1977	HOT	4 (2)	France/Germany	Ground- or air-launched missile with optical remote guidance
1979	AT-4	2 (1)	Soviet Union	Man-portable or vehicle-mounted missile
1983	AT-6-Spiral	5 (3)	Soviet Union	Laser-guided missile, air-launched from helicopters or close-support aircraft
Surface-to-surface missiles (SSMs)				
1960	Polaris	4,600 (2,860)	USA	First NATO submarine-launched ballistic missile, still used by UK
1962	Minuteman	13,000 (8,080)	USA	Three-stage, solid-fuel ICBM. Main element of USA's land-based nuclear forces
1971	SSBS	3,300 (2,050)	France	Ballistic missile
1972	Lance	120 (75)	USA	Battlefield missile
1972	Pershing	1,800 (1,120)	USA	Tactical battlefield ballistic missile with nuclear capability
1974	SS-18	12,000 (7,500)	Soviet Union	Largest missile in service, and one of most accurate Soviet ICBMs
1976	SS-21	120 (75)	Soviet Union	Vehicle-mounted tactical missile
1977	Tomahawk	3,700 (2,300)	USA	Tactical ground-, ship-, or submarine-launched cruise missile
1979	Trident	7,400 (4,600)	USA	Submarine-launched ballistic missile
1980	SS-19	10,000 (6,200)	Soviet Union	First successful Soviet solid-fuel, submarine-launched ballistic missile
1986	Peacemaker	10,000 (6,200)	USA	Solid-fuel ICBM
Late 1980s	SSC-X-4	3,000 (1,860)	Soviet Union	Ground-based cruise missile similar to Tomahawk
Ship-to-ship missiles				
1972	Exocet	70 (43)	France	Medium-range missile with inertial guidance plus terminal active radar homing
1976	Harpoon	90 (56)	USA	Over-the-horizon, anti-ship missile using terminal active radar homing
1980	SS-N-19	400 (250)	Soviet Union	Anti-ship and tactical missile
Early 1980s	SS-N-9	280 (175)	Soviet Union	Over-the-horizon anti-ship missile

A vertical-launch Seawolf ship-borne surface-to-air **missile**, designed to intercept anti-ship missiles at speeds of up to Mach 2. The Seawolf is fired through a frangible door.

missiles (SAMs) are launched from the ground or a ship against enemy aircraft or enemy missiles. They often use infra-red or semi-active radar homing as well as command line-of-sight guidance, in which a human operator steers the missile on to the target. Ship-to-air missiles are particularly important because ships are very vulnerable as targets. The SAMs with the longest range can cover 100 km (60 miles); some very short-range missiles are portable, battlefield weapons. The ABM (*anti-ballistic missile) also belongs to the SAM class. Surface-to-surface missiles (SSMs) include strategic land-based ICBMs; submarine-launched ballistic missiles; battlefield and anti-tank missiles; tactical cruise missiles; and ship-to-ship missiles launched from one ship against another. Ship-to-ship missiles are often modified ASMs, homing on to optical, infra-red, or radio-wave signals emitted by the target ship. They are difficult to detect, approaching at just above sea-level. Most SSMs are guided missiles, with the exception of some battlefield weapons.

modem (*mod*ulator–*dem*odulator), a computer *peripheral used to provide *telecommunications links for computer data. The modem generally converts digital electrical signals into tones which can be transmitted along a telephone line. At the other end of the line, a similar modem operating in reverse converts the frequencies back into digital electrical signals. Modems work to internationally agreed standards, the most important characteristic being the rate at which the data is transmitted, which is measured in bits per second. (See also *baud.)

modulation, the superimposition of an electrical information signal on to a *radio or other carrier wave, allowing the information to be transmitted over long distances. The signal is modulated before transmission, then at the receiver the carrier wave is removed to regain the information signal (demodulation). The simplest form of modulation is turning the carrier wave on and off in accordance with some sort of code, as in *telegraphy. For transmission of audio and visual signals, other forms of modulation are needed. In amplitude modulation (AM), the information signal is used to modify the amplitude of the carrier wave. Frequency modulation (FM) works on a similar principle, but the frequency of the carrier wave is modified rather than its amplitude (see illustration in *radio). FM transmission is less susceptible to noise than AM, but it requires a greater *bandwidth, available only in the VHF or UHF wavebands. *Pulse-code modulated, digital signals are used in telegraphy, *telephony, and increasingly in other applications. They are amenable to *multiplexing, and are less affected by interference.

mohair, a textile fibre obtained from the angora goat. The fineness and lustre of the fibre combines the richness of *silk with the warmth of *wool, making mohair a luxury material in great demand. Since the early 19th century, the supply from Turkey has been insufficient to meet demand, leading to cross-breeding and the introduction of the angora goat in Australia, South America, and other parts of the world.

molecular distillation, a special form of *distillation, conducted under extremely high vacuum, in which the condensing apparatus is located so close to the boiling liquid that the molecules condense without colliding with each other. This makes the process extremely efficient. Industrial applications include the separation of vitamins; the separation of mono-, di-, and triglyceride *fats, and the distillation of paraffin wax for coating milk cartons.

molecule *atoms and molecules.

mole plough, a specialist plough used for drainage, invented by John Fowler (UK) in the 1850s. It comprises a solid metal cylinder, drawn horizontally through the soil to produce a hollow drainage tube. The technique may be improved by pulling a string of pipes into the tube, creating a more permanent channel.

Angora goats, from which **mohair** fibre is obtained. Wild strains of Angora goat have an outer coat of coarse guard hairs, but in domestic breeds this has been largely eliminated by selective breeding.

Molotov cocktail (petrol bomb), a simple anti-tank or anti-personnel projectile. A glass bottle is filled with flammable liquid, and an oily rag is tied to the neck. Before throwing the weapon, the oily rag is set alight so that, when the bottle breaks, the liquid is ignited. The device is named after the Soviet foreign minister Vyacheslav Molotov, who during World War II ordered the production of these weapons.

molybdenum (symbol Mo, at. no. 42, r.a.m. 95.94), a grey metal of high melting-point obtained from its main *ore, molybdenite (MoS_2), by roasting and reducing the oxide with hydrogen. It is alloyed with other metals to increase their high-temperature strength: it is used in electric lamps as a support for tungsten filaments, while molybdenum steels are used for high-speed *lathe tools.

moment of force *torque.

momentum, the quantity which measures the tendency of a moving body to continue in motion. It is measured by the product of mass and velocity, hence it has both magnitude and direction. Angular momentum is the tendency of a rotating body to continue to turn.

Mond, Ludwig (1839–1909), German-born British industrial chemist. He moved to the UK in 1862, and patented a process for recovering *sulphur from the waste produced in the *Leblanc *sodium carbonate process. In 1873, he went into partnership with J. T. Brunner (UK) to work on the much improved soda-manufacturing process perfected by *Solvay in Belgium. He also developed a new process for refining *nickel and devised a gas battery.

Monel metal *alloy.

monoclonal antibodies, antibodies (see *immunology) derived from a single antibody-producing cell, or produced artificially by a single *clone and consisting of identical antibody molecules. Antibodies resulting from *immunization are a complex mixture, impossible to separate. Monoclonal antibodies are produced by injecting a mouse or rabbit with a specific antigen. After some weeks, antibody-producing cells from its spleen are extracted and fused with myeloma (cancer) cells, producing hybrid cells which can thrive in culture and will produce antibodies indefinitely. From the many different hybrid cells formed, a cell producing the required antibody is identified; it is then cultured separately, providing a source of identical antibody molecules. Because monoclonal antibodies are specific to one particular antigen, they can be used in *pharmaceutics as analytical reagents to detect the presence or absence of peptides, hormones, and proteins. They are also used in medicine as diagnostic reagents, for example, for screening blood for infections, such as a particular virus.

monoplane *aeroplane.

Monotype, the trade name of an automated *typesetting system for metal type, invented in the USA by Tolbert Lanston in 1887 and developed during the 1890s by the Lanston Monotype Corporation (USA). Keyboards produce coded paper tape to control casting machines which cast each letter and space sequentially in *type metal from individual matrices (moulds). The system was universally adopted for quality typesetting. Hot-metal typesetting has now been superseded, and the Monotype Corporation today makes filmsetting equipment.

Montgolfier, Joseph-Michel (1740–1810) and **Jacques-Etienne** (1745–99), French pioneers of lighter-than-air flight. In 1783 the two brothers launched a series of hot-air *balloons, ranging from small models to large ones capable of carrying animals The balloons consisted of linen bags inflated with hot air. In 1783 a Montgolfier balloon made a 2-km (7.5-mile) flight, rising to over 1,000 m (3,300 feet). This was the first free-balloon flight to human passengers. The brothers' experiments were ended by the outbreak of the French Revolution in 1789.

mordant, a substance used to improve the fastness of natural *dyes. The material is treated with the mordant before dyeing, and the resultant colour is much less likely to fade or be washed out. The term 'mordant' is based on an old French word meaning 'to bite', so called because the mordant 'bit' into the dye and prevented its escape. The most commonly used mordant is *alum. The colour of some dyes (for example, madder) can be changed by the use of different mordants.

morphine *analgesic, *psychotropic drug, *pharmacology (table).

Morse, Samuel Finley Breese (1791–1872), US pioneer of *telegraphy. In 1832, while on a return journey from Europe, he was prompted by a conversation to consider the possibility of an electric telegraph. By 1837, he had developed a practicable system, but found he had been anticipated by *Wheatstone and *Cooke in the UK. Eventually the US Government commissioned him to build an experimental telegraphic line from Washington to Baltimore, completed in 1844. He simplified the telegraph receiver to a pen which made dots and dashes on paper, a system that became known as the *Morse code.

Morse code, the representation of letters and numbers by different combinations of dots and dashes. Devised by *Morse in the late 1830s, it was used for electric *telegraphy. The code can be transmitted audibly, the dots and dashes being represented by short and long bursts of sound respectively; visually, by short and long flashes of light; or by printed dots and dashes on a paper tape. In the telegraph, a switch in an electrical circuit was used for sound or visual messages, a brief closing being used for a dot, three times longer for a dash or for interletter spacing, five times longer for interword spacing.

mortar, a mixture of binder, *aggregate, and water which forms a cohesive paste for bedding *bricks and stone and for finishing walls and ceilings. Normally, lime and cement are used as binders, with fine sand as the aggregate; sometimes chemicals are added to improve properties. In primitive technology, mud, dung, and straw mixtures are widely used.

A military mortar is an artillery piece that fires projectiles in a high, arching trajectory. The earliest mortars were very heavy guns and were used mainly in sieges. The modern mortar can be carried by two people. It consists of a smooth-bore barrel with a base plate; a bipod stand is attached about halfway up the barrel. A *bomb is dropped into the barrel and slides down until it strikes a fixed firing pin, which ignites propellant *cartridges on the bomb. The subsequent explosion hurls the bomb out towards the target. Because of their lightness, mobility, and ease of camouflage, mortars have taken over the role of light artillery in much of modern warfare. Their high angle of fire also enables mortars to reach targets inaccessible to other supporting weapons.

Morton, William Thomas Green (1819–68), US pioneer of *anaesthesia. In 1844 he set up in practice in Boston as a dentist in partnership with Horace Wells, who was interested in the anaesthetic properties of nitrous oxide. He was also in touch with Charles Jackson, who was using ether as a local anaesthetic for pain relief when filling teeth. This led Morton to use ether as a general anaesthetic in dental surgery (1846). The same year, ether anaesthesia was used for general surgery, and it was soon widely adopted. Morton became involved in protracted controversy and litigation with Wells, Jackson, and others over claims of priority.

motor, electric *electric motor.

motor car (US, automobile), a vehicle driven by an engine for *road transport of passengers and luggage. In its typical modern form (see figure) it consists of four pneumatically tyred *wheels supporting a strong body by means of a *suspension system. The *steering system generally controls the front wheels only to determine direction, while all four wheels are acted on by a *braking system. Cars may be front-wheel drive (FWD), rear-wheel drive (RWD), or four-wheel drive (4WD), the wheels being driven from the *engine through a transmission system consisting of *clutch, *gearbox, a *differential gear, and drive-shafts. The body is designed with a strong central section to contain the passengers safely and to provide rigid attachment points for the suspension system, engine, and bumpers. At the front and rear of the body are crumple zones designed to absorb energy during severe impact and so to protect the passengers by reducing their rate of deceleration. Other safety features include the provision of seat-belts, attached to strong-points at the sides and floor, and may include anti-burst door locks, a reinforcing beam across the middle of the door to resist side impact, a padded steering wheel on a collapsible column, and head restraints to prevent whiplash injury to the neck if the car is struck from behind. *Safety glass is used in all windows, either toughened, which shatters to small rounded crystals when broken; or *laminated, which has a central layer of tough plastic to retain fragments.

The car's engine, usually a *petrol engine, is normally placed at the front under the bonnet and may drive either the rear wheels or, increasingly, the front wheels. In 4WD cars the drive system acts on all four wheels, which gives increased traction and better power distribution. If the front wheels are driven, the engine is usually installed transversely instead of longitudinally. An advantage of this layout is the saving in space lengthwise, so that four passengers and their luggage can be accommodated in a shorter overall length.

Motor car

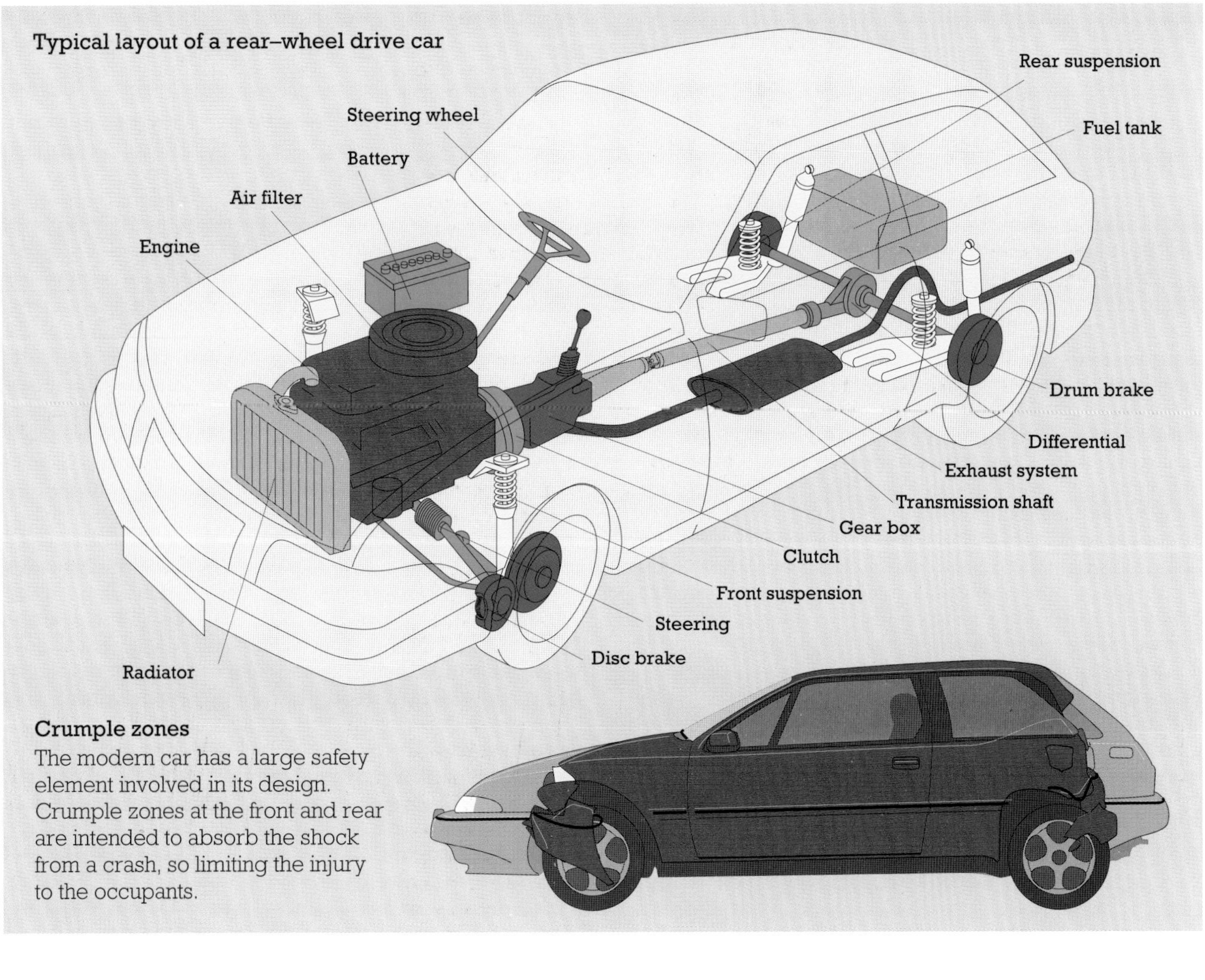

Crumple zones

The modern car has a large safety element involved in its design. Crumple zones at the front and rear are intended to absorb the shock from a crash, so limiting the injury to the occupants.

Some cars, notably the original Volkswagen 'Beetle' and the Citroën 2CV, have their engine at the rear, but this can lead to problems of stability. With a front engine and rear-wheel drive, a two-piece propeller shaft connects the engine–gearbox unit to the rear axle differential through *universal joints at either end. With front-wheel drive the differential is contained within the engine–gearbox unit and constant velocity (CV) joints are used for final drive to the wheels.

The controls and instruments of a motor car are designed for maximum convenience and safety. The most important controls are the steering wheel and the three pedals—accelerator, brake, and (for manual transmission cars) clutch. The gear lever and handbrake are usually central between the front seats, and the remaining controls—direction indicators, lights, horn, windscreen wipers and washer—are on 'stalks' close to the steering wheel. Instruments and other switches are grouped on the instrument panel. Under the bonnet, apart from the engine itself, are the radiator with its header (overflow) tank, the heater, screen washer, brake-fluid reservoirs, and the battery. In RWD cars the petrol tank is at the rear, not too close to the rear bumper in case of a rear-end collision, while in FWD cars it is located centrally, below the floor. The boot is generally at the rear, forming the rear crumple zone; the spare wheel is usually stored under the floor of the boot. The electrical system is complex; apart from the *ignition system it includes the *starter motor, the comprehensive lighting system, and auxiliary systems such as the horn, windscreen wipers, heater, and (increasingly) electronic instrument panel displays.

motor car, history of. As with the aeroplane, the idea of self-propelled *road transport was current for many years before the technology for a practicable vehicle became available. *Leonardo da Vinci, for example, considered the idea of a self-propelled vehicle, and wind-powered carriages using sails or kites were built in the 17th century. The vehicle generally recognized as the first motor car was in fact a *steam-powered vehicle, built by *Cugnot in 1769. Over the next 100 years this idea was developed, particularly in the UK, but steam-powered vehicles never achieved widespread acceptance. The development of vehicles with internal-combustion engines can be attributed to two men, *Benz and *Daimler, working independently in Germany. Vehicles using an internal-combustion engine had previously been built, but none had been developed commercially. Benz began to sell his car in 1887, and Daimler in 1889. In France in 1891, Panhard-Levassor built the first vehicle to adopt what was to become the most common layout: four *wheels, a front *engine, *gearbox, foot-operated *clutch, and rear-wheel drive. Early improvements to the motor car included the float-type *carburettor, designed by Daimler's partner Wilhelm Maybach in 1892; the steering wheel (1894); the propeller-shaft transmission (1895); and the *universal joint (1899). Developments were rapid in most of Europe and in the USA, but in the UK until 1896 progress was stifled by restrictive laws, by which no motor vehicle was allowed to travel on a highway except in the charge of at least three people, one of whom had to precede on foot with a red flag. In the early days of the car both steam and *electric vehicles provided competition to the petrol engine, and electric vehicles remained popular until 1912, particularly in the USA, when the electric *ignition tipped the balance in favour of the petrol engine.

In 1901 the Oldsmobile Company in the USA began manufacture of their Curved Dash Runabout using *mass-production techniques. These techniques were further developed by *Ford for his Model T, introduced in 1908. Ford used mass production and standardization to achieve economies of scale, and thus brought the car within the price range of ordinary people. Similar economy cars, such as the Fiat 500 (Italy) and the 'Baby' Austin (UK), appeared in Europe after World War I, and by the early 1920s the car was no longer a plaything but a practical means of transport.

The 1930s was the era of the 'classic car': cars at the top end of the market that combined engineering excellence with style and sumptuous elegance. Rolls-Royce, Hispano-Suiza, and Bugatti exploited the luxury car market, while firms such as Citroën, Volkswagen, and Fiat mass-produced small cars. The original Volkswagen 'Beetle', designed by Ferdinand Porsche in 1937, continues in limited production in Brazil. After World War II much technical progress made in the aircraft industry was applied to motor-car manufacture. Lightweight, chassis-less car bodies and curved windscreens were adopted, and the designer became as influential as the engineer.

From the 1950s onwards, car manufacturers increasingly thought in terms of an international rather than a national market. One stimulus for this trend was the demand in the USA from ex-servicemen for European cars, particularly sports and luxury cars. In the 1960s the Japanese car industry began its rise to its present position as the world's largest car manufacturer. Car safety became an increasingly important aspect of design, and *aerodynamic principles began to be applied to body design. The world-wide fuel crisis in the 1970s saw a shift in emphasis towards fuel economy, particularly in the USA, and public concern about the environmental pollution caused by cars has led to the introduction of *catalytic converters and unleaded petrol in many countries. The major changes in the car industry in the 1980s were in terms of electronics: the increasing use of robots for car assembly, and the use of *microprocessors to control such systems as the fuel supply to the engine.

A British Holden **motor cycle** from around 1900. The engine has been cut away to show its structure. Interesting features include the simple direct drive from the cylinders, and the front-wheel pedals, used to assist the engine on uphill slopes.

motor cycle, generally a two-wheeled, motor-driven vehicle, although some may have three wheels. A Michaux velocipede (see *bicycle) was fitted with a steam-engine in 1868; this was perhaps the first motor cycle. Early motor cycles were adaptations of bicycles or tricycles: tricycles and even quadricycles were initially popular, but in 1901 several practical two-wheeled, *petrol-engined designs appeared which established the classic layout of the motor cycle.

During World War I motor cycles were used for dispatch-carrying and as mobile machine-gun platforms. Many technical improvements were made during this war and in the postwar period motor cycles enjoyed a boom. After World War II new developments included the smaller moped and motor scooter, and the motor-cycle industry continued to grow. British and European models predominated until the 1960s, when Japan began to dominate world production, which it has continued to do into the 1990s. Modern motor cycles incorporate many features of the *motor car, such as electronic ignition, shaft drive, water-cooled engines, and disc brakes. The traditional spoked wheels have been largely replaced by ones of cast *magnesium alloy, which are stronger, cheaper to make, and require less maintenance.

motor-drive (photography), a device attached to a *camera that automatically releases the *shutter and advances the *film after each exposure. Contacts on the base of the camera are connected to an external motor, which is coupled to the camera's shutter and film-transport mechanisms. Rapid shooting rates of five frames a second or more are possible using a motor-drive.

motorway *road.

mould (metalworking) *casting.

moulding, a technique used to obtain complex three-dimensional forms from a malleable material by the application of pressure or heat. Moulding processes are used for many *plastics, *glass, *bricks, and other materials. In vacuum forming, a thin sheet of heated, softened material is sucked down over a shaped mould and takes on the surface contours of that mould. On cooling, the plastic sets into this shape and can then be removed. This process is used extensively to produce shell-shaped objects. Blow moulding (for illustration, see plastics) uses a heated tube of material, sealed at one end, which is surrounded by a shaped mould of cylindrical cross-section. The tube is inflated so that it fits the contours of the mould. Large numbers of glass and plastic objects are produced in this way. Injection moulding requires softened material to be injected into a cavity that is exactly the shape of the desired object. It is used to produce a variety of articles, from nylon gearwheels to polypropylene washing-up bowls.

mouse (computer), a small device which can be moved with one hand over a flat surface: movements of the mouse are communicated to a computer and cause corresponding movements of a cursor on the screen of a *visual display unit. The mouse can be used for drawing, or for selecting options from a *menu.

mowing-machine, an *agricultural machine used to cut grass for *hay or *silage. The earliest machines were reciprocating blade types developed in the 1850s. During the 1950s rotating flail machines were developed, particularly for use in forage harvesters. Disc mowers with blades at the disc circumference can cope with the thick crops grown in modern farming. (See also *lawn-mower.)

MS-DOS *operating system.

mud building, a building with walls built of earth. Mud buildings are found in hot, dry climates world-wide: the thick, dense walls absorb the sun's heat and radiate it at night. In *pisé de terre* techniques, shuttering (see *formwork) fixed along the wall is filled with soil, and the soil is rammed in in 150–200-mm (6–8-inch) layers. Clay soils do not compact easily and are commonly used to make adobe—sun-dried bricks bedded in a mud mortar. *Cob may also be used. Wet mud is sometimes applied to a lightweight wall to form a windproof outer skin, as in *wattle and daub.

mule *spinning machine.

multiple independently targetable re-entry vehicle (MIRV), a package of several *warheads, each aimed at a separate target, launched by a single *ballistic missile. MIRVs are mounted on a 'bus', which releases each warhead (or re-entry vehicle) in space, with the correct speed and direction. To confuse and overwhelm the enemy's defences, decoy warheads are often mixed with genuine ones, and metallic chaff (radar-reflective particles) is released to blind the radars. The warheads can be guided on to their individual targets with an accuracy of about 100 m (330 feet). Large ballistic missiles like the Soviet Union's SS-18 can carry up to ten re-entry nuclear warheads, each with the explosive power of 50 kilotonnes of TNT.

multiple-unit train, a passenger train consisting of two or more connected carriages, with one or more self-powered vehicles and with driving cabs at each end. Power for such trains is usually electric or diesel. Multiple units are very flexible and are used on commuter services, cross-country routes, and branch lines. Newer trains have carriages made of aluminium alloy with double-glazing, air-conditioning, and catering services.

multiplexing, a method of sending several messages simultaneously along the same *channel, used mainly in telephony and telegraphy. In frequency-division multiplexing (FDM), suggested by the US inventor Elisha Gray in 1890 and first used during the 1920s, signals of different frequency, each carrying a different message, travel down the cable simultaneously. Complex *filters then separate the messages at the receiver. In 1875 the French engineer J.-M.-E. Baudot suggested time-division multiplexing (TDM), in which high-speed samples of several message sources are interleaved. Used with *pulse code modulation, this system allows many hundreds of telephone channels to use a single *optical fibre or *communication satellite link.

Mushet, Robert Forester (1811–91), British pioneer of alloy *steels. The son of an ironmaster in the Forest of Dean, he founded the Forest Steelworks, using his father's process for improving pig-*iron by adding iron oxide to increase the yield. He developed a number of tough alloy steels containing *tungsten, *chromium, *manganese, and *titanium for use in the machine-tool industry. In 1865 he founded the Titanic Steel Company and three years later invented self-hardening steel for tools, perhaps his greatest achievement.

musket *firearm.

mustard gas, a *chemical warfare agent, dichloroethyl sulphide [$(ClCH_2CH_2)_2S$], first used by the German Army at Ypres (Belgium) in 1917. It is a colourless oily liquid whose vapour causes painful blistering of the skin and swelling around the eyes, and strips away the mucous membrane of the bronchial tubes. The effects take time to appear, and in severe cases lingering death may take four or five weeks.

nail, a small, sharp metal spike, with a broadened head, usually driven in with a hammer and used to join things together. Nails were used from the 3rd millennium BC in Mesopotamia. Until the 18th century, when nail-making machines were introduced, all nails were handmade. Nails all end in a point, but vary widely in length, cross-section, and size of head, from tiny panel pins to nails 30 cm (12 inches) long for securing timber. They can be round, oval, or rectangular in section. Flat-headed nails are the most common. Lost-head nails taper and can be punched fully into the wood; screw-nails twist as they are hammered in.

napalm (*na*phthalene *palm*itate), a thickening agent made from vegetable oils and acids and aluminium; also the term for a mixture used in incendiary bombs, comprising thickening agent and *petrol. Napalm was developed in 1942 at the request of the US Army. It is mixed with a flammable jelly which, when ignited, becomes a viscous liquid. It is used in *flame-throwers, or as an incendiary weapon, when it is usually dropped from aircraft in canisters.

naphtha *petroleum refining.

nap shearer, a device for trimming the nap of raised cloth. After a nap or pile has been raised by a *gig mill, the surface of the cloth appears untidy. To remedy this, the nap is trimmed to a uniform height by shearing. For centuries, shearing was done with hand-held pairs of shears. Today, a mechanical multi-bladed rotary cutter shears the nap fibres against an adjustable fixed blade—similar in action to a lawn-mower.

narcotic, a drug that induces drowsiness, stupor, or insensibility. The term is used particularly for derivatives of opium (such as morphine), but also includes synthesized compounds. Narcotics are powerful *analgesics, used in medicine. They cause a state of euphoria in the recipient, and readily lead to dependence. A narcotic in the legal sense is any addictive drug subject to illegal use.

narrowboat *canal barge.

Nasmyth, James (1808–90), British mechanical engineer of Scottish extraction, best known for his invention of the *steam-hammer. Born in Edinburgh, he was apprenticed for two years to *Maudslay in London before returning to Edinburgh to work as a manufacturing engineer. In 1834 he moved to Manchester, where he built his Bridgewater Foundry, manufacturing a variety of *machine-tools. His steam-hammer was originally designed in 1839 for *forging the giant paddle-wheel shafts of the **Great Britain* (subsequently changed to screw propulsion) and was so precise that it could be set to crack an egg without smashing it. This invention greatly increased the possible size of forgings. From 1839, Nasmyth began to manufacture steam locomotives and high-pressure steam-engines.

National Academy of Sciences (NAS), a US institution founded in 1863, under Congressional charter, as a non-governmental organization to advance science and its applications, and to advise the government on scientific matters. In 1916 it created the National Research Council to effect a wider representation of scientists and engineers in its affairs. The NAS is currently divided into some twenty sections, covering the principal physical and biological sciences, as well as social, economic, and political sciences. In 1964 a parallel National Academy of Engineering was created under its charter.

National Physical Laboratory, a UK government research centre founded in 1900 to undertake work useful to industry as a whole and to standardize *units. It is comparable with the *Max Planck Society for the Promotion of Sciences in Germany and the National Institute of Standards and Technology in the USA. The laboratory has a research staff of around 200 and comprises six divisions, handling electrical science; materials applications; mechanical and optical metrology; numerical analysis and computer science; quantum metrology; and radiation science and acoustics. The Laboratory also undertakes appropriate contract research for industry. It houses the British Calibration Service, the National Testing Laboratory Accreditation Scheme, and the National Corrosion Service.

Natta, Giulio (1903–79), Italian industrial chemist. While Director of the Milan Institute of Industrial Chemistry, he initiated a programme for the production of synthetic *rubber. As consultant to the firm Montecatini, he advised them to purchase the rights for commercial development of *Ziegler's low-pressure process for making *polythene, from which he developed *polypropylene as an analogous new plastic. He also devised processes for polymerizing styrene and butene. He shared the Nobel Prize for Chemistry with Ziegler in 1963.

natural gas, a *fossil fuel found trapped in the earth, often in association with *petroleum. Natural gas was probably first noticed in prehistoric times, burning in association with petroleum seepage. In Szechuan province, China, natural gas was encountered during the Han dynasty (202 BC–AD 220) while drilling for salt. From the 2nd century AD it was extracted for *gas lighting, and as a fuel for evaporation of brine. During the 19th century, natural gas was found in association with petroleum, but, except in the USA, storage and transport difficulties prevented it from competing widely with *coal-gas, which could be cheaply produced close to most market areas. In many oilfields, natural gas was a waste product that had to be burnt on site for safe disposal. It is only since World War II that use of natural gas has grown rapidly around the world, because of the development of *pipeline transport and underground storage. Also important was the discovery and development of large new natural gas fields, such as those in the North Sea, the eastern Soviet Union, Canada, and Algeria. Natural gas is now the world's second most important fuel, after petroleum.

Natural gas is obtained by the same basic methods as petroleum (see *petroleum, exploration and recovery). Some wells produce natural gas alone; others produce petroleum as well as natural gas. Liquid petroleum generally contains much dissolved natural gas, which separates as the petroleum reaches the surface, and can be removed in a separator at the oil well. Gas is moved from the well by pipeline to a cleaning and processing plant and on to a *gas grid or storage facility. Small-scale storage may be in spherical or cylindrical tanks, and large-scale storage is underground.

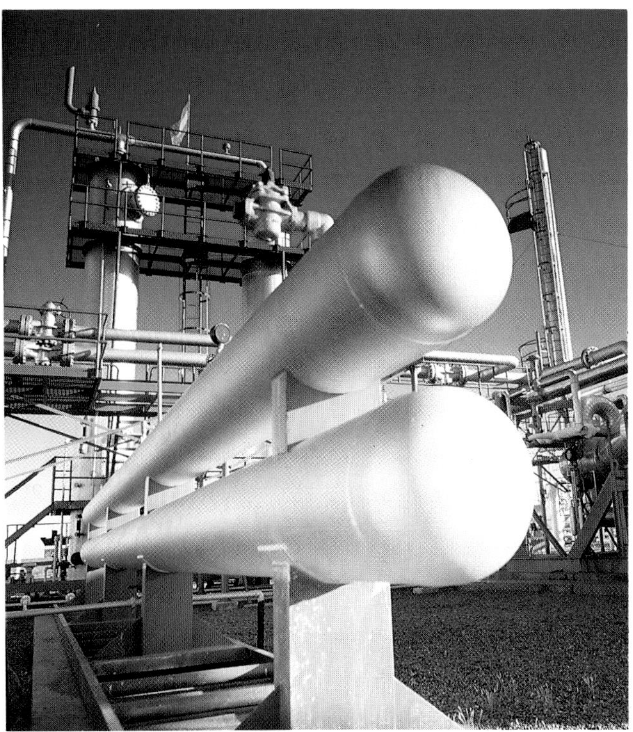

A plant for the distribution of **natural gas** near Buenos Aires in Argentina.

Disused oilfields are one type of underground storage, though some facilities are drilled especially for storage between layers of impermeable rock. Since the 1960s there has been increasing success in storage and transport by tanker of *liquefied natural gas.

Natural gas consists mainly of *methane and ethane, and generally occurs with smaller proportions of *propane and *butane. 'Wet' natural gas has a significant proportion of the latter two gases, plus some heavier *hydrocarbons, which may cause uneven burning and gumming up of pipes. 'Drying' of the gas is achieved by compression and cooling to condense out heavier hydrocarbons, or by dissolving them in an oil solvent. This process produces *liquid petroleum gas (LPG). Other components of natural gas which may have to be removed, and may be present in sufficient quantity to be commercially useful, are carbon dioxide and helium. Nitrogen may dilute the gas, but is seldom a problem. Sulphur compounds, such as hydrogen disulphide, must be cleaned out of gas for use in homes or in the chemical industry. In addition to its importance as a heating fuel in homes and industry, natural gas is widely used in *electricity generation and many specialist burning and heating applications. It is important as a feedstock in producing hydrogen, *plastics, and *petrochemicals. The main advantages of natural gas as a fuel are its economy and easy conversion into other forms of energy.

nautical mile *knot.

naval architecture, the science of designing ships and other floating structures. Early shipwrights made little use of plans and calculations, although small-scale models were sometimes made of larger vessels. From the late 17th century, attempts were made to apply scientific principles to ship design, with the French taking the lead. By the 19th century, the shipwright was being transformed into the naval architect. A major contribution to ship design was made in the UK by William Froude (1810–79), who developed the practice of testing ship models in testing tanks, and laid the foundations of hydrodynamics (see *fluid mechanics). Modern naval architecture involves extensive preliminary calculation of stresses on various hull parts, of power requirements for a particular design, and of optimum hull shape and dimensions. Initial plans are generated on computer (see *computer-aided design), from which a large-scale model of the hull is made. This is then used for tank tests. After any changes resulting from these tests, full construction plans are generated, and used to guide the *shipbuilding process.

navigation, the planning and directing of a vehicle or person along a set course or route, avoiding collision. For much of history navigation has been a skill used predominantly at sea, but in the 20th century air and space navigation have become important. Navigational aids are also sometimes used on land. Early navigation was concerned almost exclusively with course-finding: most early seafarers followed coastlines, and avoided the open sea. The Phoenicians and the Polynesians were among the earliest ancient peoples to use celestial bodies to navigate, to a limited extent, out of sight of land. There was a gradual development of instruments which made navigation at sea progressively more accurate. These were the *magnetic compass for direction finding; the *astrolabe, *cross-staff, and *sextant for celestial navigation; the ship's *log for speed measurement; the *lead line for depth measurement, and the *chronometer for the determination of *longitude.

Since the advent of aviation in the early 20th century, other devices such as the *gyro-compass, *radar, *sonar, *inertial navigation, *navigational satellites, and *radio aids to navigation (see figure) have made it possible to monitor a vehicle's position continuously. The increasing density of air and sea traffic has made continuous monitoring essential in order to avoid collisions: most civilian aircraft, for example, must now follow strict flight plans that specify course, speed, and cruising heights. Many navigational functions have been automated, with on-board computers monitoring position and course. In some cases (see *automatic pilot) the computer may use this information to automatically control the vehicle.

Navigation of a plotted course involves the integration of many pieces of information. Accurate plotting of the course on reliable *maps or charts will give course directions for the journey. Course direction and speed are monitored throughout the journey, and together with information on wind-speeds or water currents, such information can be used to find an estimated position. Positions based on course and speed measurements alone are known as dead reckoning: such estimates can accumulate errors if uncorrected. Usually, estimated or dead reckoning positions are checked periodically against measurements of *latitude and longitude. Traditionally, latitude was calculated from the altitude (angle above the horizon) of the Sun or another celestial body, and longitude from the accurate comparison of local time with the time on the 0 degree longitudinal meridian (Greenwich Mean Time). Other methods now available include the detection of radio signals from stations of known location to give an accurate position; the use of *inertial navigation systems; or the detection of positional signals from a *navigational satellite. Other navigational aids at sea are *buoys and *lighthouses or *lightships marking hazards

Navigation

Latitude and longitude

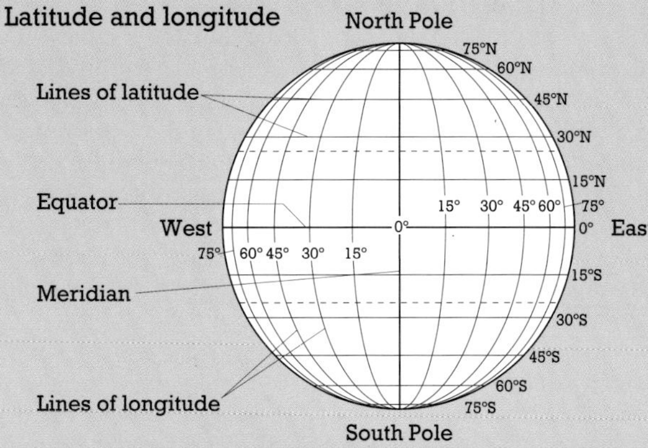

Navigational position is frequently expressed in latitude and longitude. Positions obtained during navigation are measured against the latitude and longitude scales of the chart.

Latitude is the angle between the plane of the equator and a vertical to the Earth's surface at the position, measured from 0° to 90° north or south of the equator. Longitude is the angle between the meridian of Greenwich and the meridian through the position measured from 0° to 180° east or west of Greenwich.

Celestial sphere

The celestial sphere is a conceptual model that gives an explanation of the positions and motions of heavenly bodies which can be seen with the naked eye from the Earth's surface.

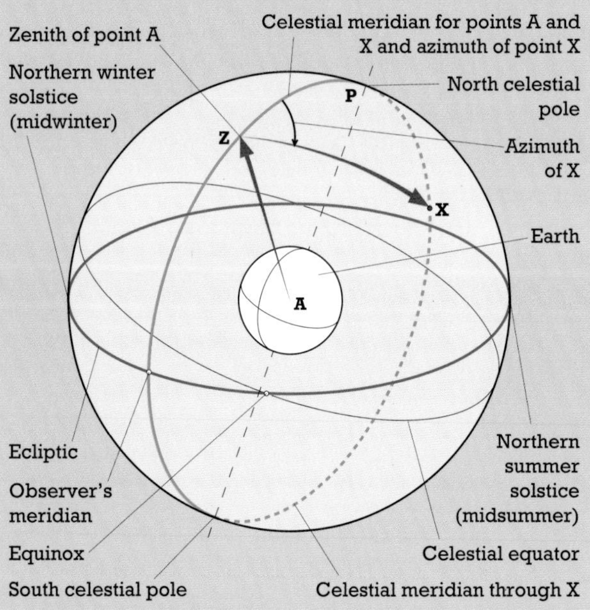

The ecliptic is the path of the Sun across the heavens during the year. The zenith is the point of the heavens directly above the observer. The azimuth (bearing) of a heavenly body X is the angle PZX. It is measured east or west from the observer's meridian from 0° to 180°, and named N or S from the elevated pole. For example the azimuth of X from Z is approximately N 70° E.

Velocity triangle

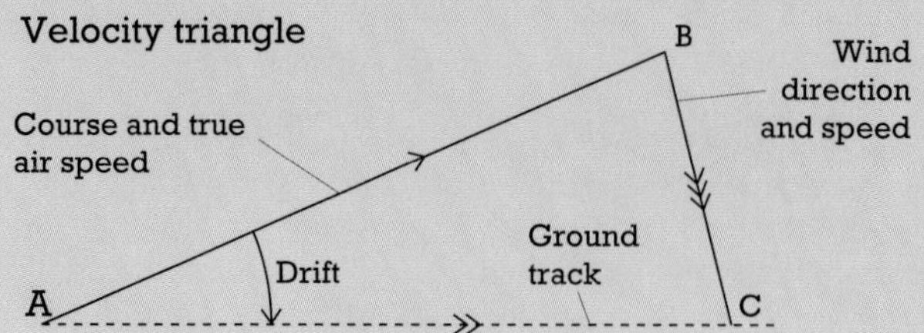

A plane flying in windy conditions will be blown by the wind. To find the true course and velocity of the plane in relation to the ground, the velocity triangle is used. The first vector drawn is the course and magnitude of the flight, the length of the line representing the distance the plane would fly in one hour. From the end of this is drawn a vector in the direction of the wind. The length of this represents the wind speed. The resultant line AC represents the course and speed in relation to the ground.

Hyperbolic navigation system

A radio aid to navigation in which co-ordinated radio transmissions from two transmitters, A and B, interact to produce a fixed pattern of curved (hyperbolic) interference lines.

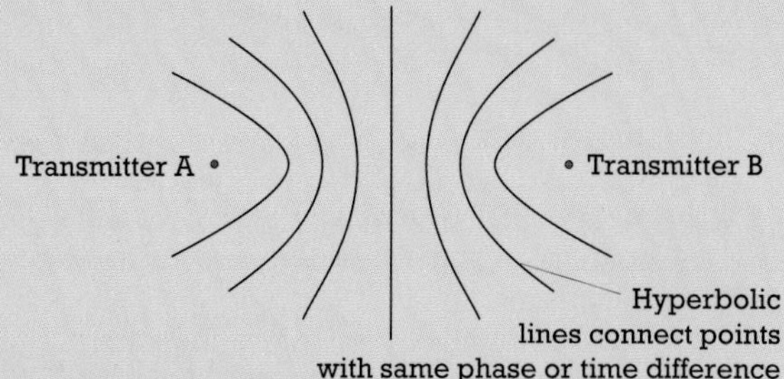

Finding a position

With three co-ordinated transmitters, A, B, and C, two intersecting hyperbolic patterns are formed; one by A and B, the other by A and C. By measuring the time or phase difference between transmissions from A and B, a position line MN may be obtained, joining all points with that phase or time difference. Similarly, a second position line QR may be obtained from the phase or time difference between transmissions from A and C. Position P, from which the measurements were made, lies at the intersection of MN and QR.

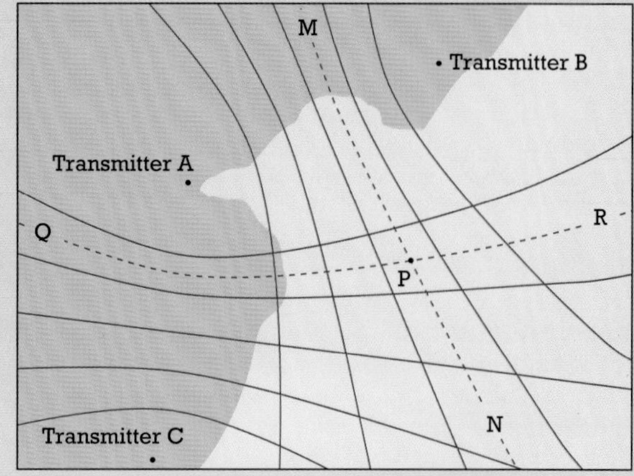

and navigational channels; and *echo-sounding equipment, used for depth measurement. In air navigation *altimeters for height measurement are also important. On commercial journeys, which often run to a timetable, timekeeping is an important additional factor to be taken into account.

navigation light, a light carried by a ship or an aircraft showing its presence, type, and orientation. Strict international rules govern the fitting and use of navigation lights. Particular lights are prescribed for specific situations. For example, power-driven boats over 50 m (164 feet) in length must display, when under way, two white mast-head lights (not visible astern), one white stern light (not visible ahead), and red port and green starboard sidelights.

navigation satellite, a *radio aid to navigation using artificial *satellites orbiting the Earth. Such satellites are used by ships, aircraft, missiles, or land vehicles (especially military vehicles) to find their position, height, and speed. The first practical system in operation was developed by the US Navy and known as Transit. It became available for commercial use in 1967. A more sophisticated US system, the Navstar Global Positioning System (GPS), will be fully operational in the mid-1990s. The GPS satellites carry atomic *clocks and daily transmit their position and time to *ground stations. The Soviet Union has its own system, and there are also commercial systems that operate using existing *communications satellites. The Transit system uses four to six operational satellites in circular polar orbits about 1,100 km (690 miles) above the Earth. The satellite works on a *Doppler shift principle, and can give a receiver's position accurate to around 200 m (660 feet) at approximately 90-minute intervals (the time taken for a single orbit). The GPS has eighteen satellites in uniformly spaced geostationary orbits above the Earth. It can give continuous positions accurate to about 20 m (70 feet), heights accurate to about 30 m (100 feet), and speeds accurate to about 0.1 m/s (0.3 feet per second). Commercial navigational receivers that use signals from GPS are now being used to make small navigational devices (about the size of a playing card) accurate to within 100 m (330 feet). Navigation systems for boats, aircraft, and cars are currently available.

needle, a tool used to stitch fabric or leather together with thread. The modern steel sewing needle differs little from its bone predecessor. Until the invention of the *sewing-machine, it provided the only means of stitching fabric together. There are three principal sorts of needle. The common sewing needle has a point at one end and an eye through which the thread is passed at the other. Sewing-machine needles have both point and eye at one end; the other end is attached to the reciprocating element of the sewing-machine. *Knitting-machine needles have eyes which can be opened and closed in such a way that, whilst carrying a loop of thread, a needle can pick up a running thread in the eye, draw the thread through the existing loop to form a new loop, and at the same time shed the old loop.

negative (photography) *developing and printing.

neon (symbol Ne, at. no. 10, r.a.m. 20.18), an inert gaseous element found in minute proportions in the Earth's atmosphere. It is obtained by the *fractional distillation of liquid air. Neon is used in *gas-discharge lamps, where it gives a bright orange-red glow, in gas *lasers, and as a cryogenic (very-low-temperature) refrigerant.

nerve gas, a *chemical warfare agent that attacks the nervous system. The first nerve gas, discovered by the German scientist Gerhard Schracher in 1936, was tabun. Sarin

Net, fishing

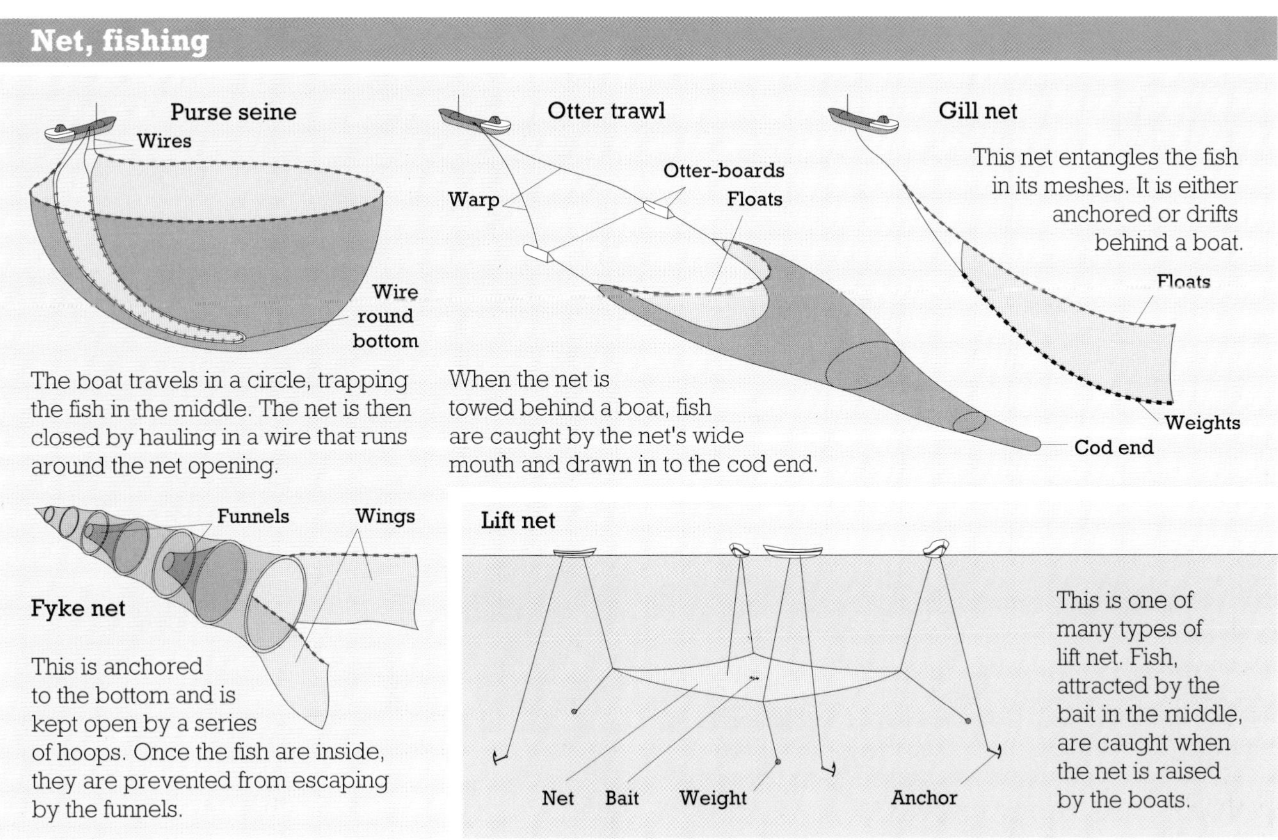

Purse seine
Wires
Wire round bottom
The boat travels in a circle, trapping the fish in the middle. The net is then closed by hauling in a wire that runs around the net opening.
Otter trawl
Otter-boards
Warp
Floats
When the net is towed behind a boat, fish are caught by the net's wide mouth and drawn in to the cod end.
Cod end
Gill net
This net entangles the fish in its meshes. It is either anchored or drifts behind a boat.
Floats
Weights
Funnels
Wings
Fyke net
This is anchored to the bottom and is kept open by a series of hoops. Once the fish are inside, they are prevented from escaping by the funnels.
Lift net
This is one of many types of lift net. Fish, attracted by the bait in the middle, are caught when the net is raised by the boats.
Net
Bait
Weight
Anchor

and soman were similar agents developed in Germany during World War II. These three agents plus VX, which was discovered by British researchers in the mid-1950s, are the main families of nerve gas stockpiled today. They are all organophosphorous compounds, and inhibit the body's breakdown of acetylcholine, a compound that chemically transmits impulses between nerve fibres. Hence, neural commands, including commands to the lungs, cannot be transmitted, inducing respiratory failure. Nerve gases are absorbed through the skin, killing the victim in minutes.

nervous system *neurology and neurosurgery.

net, fishing, an open-mesh structure made from natural or synthetic fibres, used to catch fish. Most modern nets are machine-made of rot-proof materials. Of the many different types of net used, seine-nets and trawl-nets are the most important commercially (see figure on the previous page). Seine-nets have very long wings and towing lines to surround the catch: they are used in both freshwater and saltwater fishing. Trawl-nets are funnel-shaped, with a wide mouth—up to 40 m (130 feet) in diameter—and a narrow, closed end. The mouth of the trawl is kept open either by a large horizontal beam (beam trawl) or, more commonly, by two large boards or plates (otter-boards) attached to each side of the net. A third type of net is the gill net, which catches fish by entangling them or trapping them in its meshes. Other important net types include dredges, which rake the sea-bed for shellfish; lift nets, which catch the fish from below; and falling gear, nets or baskets cast from above. Some types of *trap, for example the fyke net, are also made from nets.

network (computing), the connecting together of separate computer systems so that they can exchange *data, and sometimes *programs. The points at which individual systems are connected to the network are known as nodes. There are two main classes of computer network: broad area (wide area) networks and local area networks (LANs). As the name implies, the nodes of a broad area network may be widely dispersed geographically; in fact the largest networks may extend world-wide. Typically, broad area networks utilize *telecommunication channels to provide the connections between computers. Local area networks usually link computers or *workstations on the same site via coaxial cables or *optical fibres. LANs are often used to share expensive *peripherals such as *laser printers, or to share a central *disk store, known as a file server. Both types of network usually provide *electronic mail facilities to enable users to pass messages to each other.

Neumann, John von (1903–57), Hungarian-born, German–US mathematician and pioneer in computing. He became a professor at Princeton University, USA, from 1931, making important contributions to quantum physics, logic, and meteorology. He also helped develop the US hydrogen bomb after World War II. His book on game theory, published in 1944, subsequently had a significant impact on economic theory. In 1946 he proposed some of the central concepts of later computer development, particularly the advantages of the binary system for computer operation, and the 'stored program', in which the computer retains in its memory the instructions for its operation. In 1952 a team led by von Neumann at Princeton built the first computer in which information was processed a 'word' at a time rather than serially.

neural network, a densely interconnected network of simple *computer processing units (neurons) imitating some qualities of the biological nervous system. Unlike traditional computers, neural networks share out the computation simultaneously between many processors (*parallel processing), enormously increasing their collective power. Consequently, neural networks are well-suited to the computationally intensive tasks of *artificial intelligence, for example automatic *speech recognition and *image processing. The behaviour of a neural network is determined by the strength of its interconnections (synapses); large numbers of synapses help the network to recognize patterns in the presence of noise, and enable it to keep working after some of its synapses have been removed. (See also *analog computer.)

neurology and neurosurgery, the study and treatment of disorders of the nervous system. Diseases of the nervous system can result from disorders of conduction of an impulse along a nerve, or of chemical transmission of impulses between nerves by substances known as neurotransmitters. The EEG (*electroencephalograph) is used to measure indirectly activity within the central nervous system. Because it records from surface electrodes, it cannot localize activity within a particular nerve cell, but it can provide an indication of the type of activity over an area of the brain. One of the most common diseases affecting conduction of the nerve

A demonstration photograph, using a dead brain, to show the use of an argon laser in **neurosurgery**. Such lasers are more precise than a needle or scalpel, and generate enough heat to cauterize blood vessels as they cut.

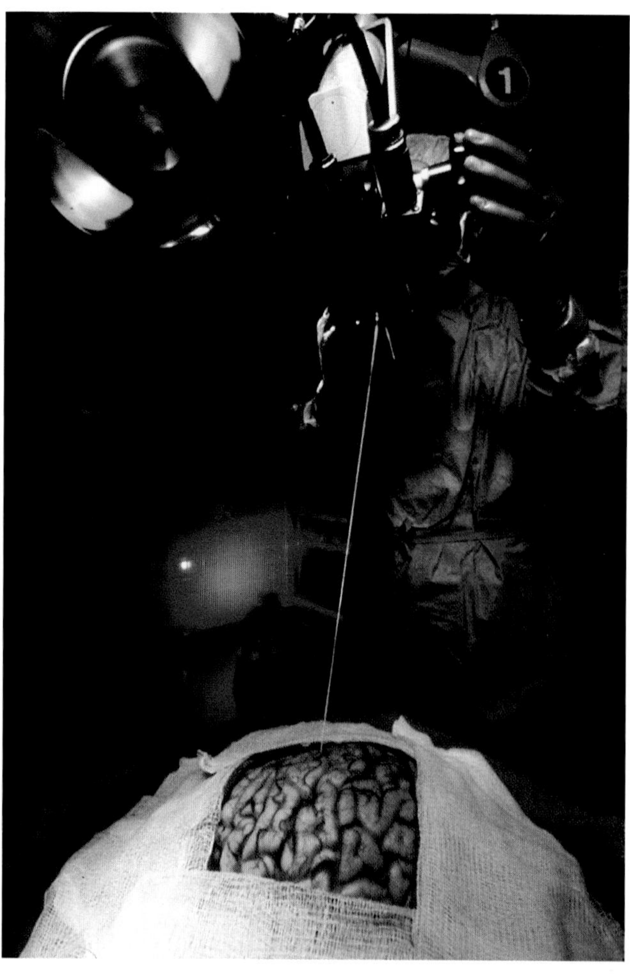

impulse is multiple sclerosis. This is caused by defects in the insulating fatty sheath around some nerves, resulting in slow conduction along these fibres, causing poor muscular co-ordination. The conduction defect can be measured by recording electrical activity in the brain (by EEG) in response to flashes of light. The delay between stimulus and response is greater in multiple sclerosis, because of the greater conduction time. Chemical neurotransmitter abnormalities are responsible for many neurological disorders. For example, a shortage of the transmitter dopamine produces the symptoms of Parkinson's disease, and many scientists think that schizophrenia also has a biochemical basis. Investigation of these disorders has proved difficult, but it has recently become possible to develop weakly radioactive markers (see *nuclear medicine), which can be attached either to neurotransmitters themselves or to antibodies that are targeted at receptors for the transmitter substances. This should allow us to study neurotransmitter function in living brains. Some neurological disorders result from tumours within the central nervous system. Localization of such growths has recently been made much easier by the development of new and better imaging techniques such as *positron emission tomography and *magnetic resonance imaging.

neutron *atoms and molecules, *nuclear energy.

neutron bomb *nuclear weapon.

Newcomen, Thomas (1663–1729), British engineer who invented the first *steam-engine. He was interested in the problem of pumping water from local metal mines. Newcomen set himself to design a steam-powered *pump, to replace the horse-powered bucket-chains in use at that time. The first known engine was erected in 1712 at Dudley Castle, Worcestershire, to extract water from a coal-mine. Newcomen's *beam-engine, as it was known, was clumsy and inefficient, but coal was a cheap fuel and the engine could be erected and maintained by local artisans. It was soon adopted for other purposes, such as working the bellows of blast-furnaces and to power trip-hammers for crushing ore.

new technology *information technology, *computer, history of.

nickel (symbol Ni, at. no. 28, r.a.m. 58.71), a silvery-white, ferromagnetic metal. It is hard, malleable, ductile, and resistant to corrosion, so is widely used to plate objects made from steel and copper. It is also the constituent of many important *alloys, such as *stainless steel, *nimonics, Monel metal, permalloy, nickel silver, nichrome, and *invar. Finely divided nickel is an important industrial *catalyst. A principal ore is pentlandite, which contains nickel sulphide. To obtain pure nickel, the nickel sulphide is first separated by *ore flotation, then roasted to form nickel oxide. This can then form nickel either by aqueous *electrolysis, or by the carbonyl process. In the latter, the oxide is reduced by hydrogen, then converted to nickel carbonyl using carbon monoxide. Finally, it is decomposed at around 200 °C to pure nickel.

nickel silver *alloy.

Niepce, Joseph Nicéphore (1765–1833), French inventor of the first effective photographic process (see *photography). He pursued a variety of scientific interests on his estate at St Loup-de-Varennes. In 1816 he recorded the view from his workshop window on paper sensitized with silver chloride. The image was negative, however, and he tried unsuccessfully to produce a positive from it. In 1826 he coated pewter plates with bitumen of Judaea, an asphalt that hardens and becomes insoluble in water when exposed to light. Areas on which bright light fell became hardened, while those corresponding to shadows could be dissolved in water. Exposure times were long (about 8 hours), but a distinct and permanent picture was achieved. In 1829 *Daguerre persuaded Niepce to enter into a partnership to develop the photographic process, but Niepce died before the process was perfected.

nimonic (US, superalloy), a proprietary name for various nickel-based alloys that have excellent resistance to oxidation and creep at high temperatures, where steel has little strength. Developed during the 1940s for gas-turbine engines, they were originally based on nickel with 20 per cent chromium and small amounts of other elements. Modern nimonics are much more complex and may contain large amounts of cobalt, rhenium, tantalum, molybdenum, or iron, and smaller quantities of aluminium and titanium.

niobium (previously columbium: symbol Nb, at. no. 41, r.a.m. 92.91), a dense silvery-grey metal, occurring naturally in the ores columbite and pyrochlore. Perhaps its most important use is in *superconducting magnets, the windings being made from alloys of niobium and tin or niobium and titanium, containing about 75 per cent niobium. Small amounts of niobium are added to *stainless steel to form stable carbides, enabling the steel to be welded.

Nipkow disc, a disc containing an array of small holes that spiral inwards towards the centre. Invented by the German engineer Paul Nipkow in 1884, it formed the basis of a mechanical scanning process in early *television cameras. As the disc is rotated, each hole traces out a line across the image, and the amount of light passing through the aperture varies in proportion to the brightness of that part of the image.

nitrate, any salt containing the nitrate group (NO_3), especially sodium, potassium, calcium, and ammonium salts. They find their main use in artificial inorganic *fertilizers, providing food crops with the *nitrogen they need to form proteins. Another important use of nitrates is in *explosives, nearly all of which contain ammonium nitrate or organic nitro-compounds.

nitric acid (HNO_3), an unstable, colourless liquid that fumes in moist air: in aqueous solution it is both a strong *acid and a powerful oxidizing agent (see *oxidation and reduction). Nitric acid is made industrially by the two-stage oxidation of *ammonia to nitrogen dioxide, which is then absorbed in water to form nitric acid. It is used in the manufacture of explosives, dyes, drugs, plastics, and fertilizers.

nitro-cellulose (cellulose nitrate), a highly flammable compound formed when cellulose materials (usually waste cotton fibres and wood-pulp) are treated with concentrated *nitric acid. The extent of the reaction between the cotton and acid can be varied to give a range of compounds, from the highly explosive gun-cotton to the flammable collodion cotton or pyroxilin. The explosive properties of nitro-cellulose were first discovered by the French chemist T.-J. Pelouze in 1838 and were explored by *Schönbein: by the 1880s it was being used as a high *explosive. Nitro-cellulose is unstable, and can decompose explosively. To counteract this tendency, the French chemist P.-M.-E. Vieille added stabilizing chemicals to produce a safe firearm propellant (1884), the first of the smokeless powders. These are now used world-wide as propellants in bullet cartridges and other ammunition. Some smokeless powders (for example, cordite) also contain *nitro-glycerine. Collodion cotton and other less reactive forms of nitro-cellulose are used chiefly in lacquers. They also form the basis of one of the earliest plastics, *celluloid.

nitrogen (symbol N, at. no. 7, r.a.m. 14.01), a tasteless, odourless, colourless gaseous element, forming around 78 per cent of the Earth's atmosphere. It is manufactured commercially by *fractional distillation of liquid air. Liquid nitrogen (boiling-point −195.8 °C) is used to cool foodstuffs before *freeze-drying, as a refrigerant, and in cryogenic (low-temperature) research. Nitrogen is quite inert, and the gas is used in the chemical industry to exclude *oxygen or moisture and as a diluent. It is also used as a neutral filter in electric light bulbs. Large quantities are used to produce ammonia by the *Haber–Bosch process.

nitro-glycerine, a powerful explosive, sometimes known as blasting oil, formed when a mixture of concentrated *nitric and *sulphuric acids acts upon *glycerol. It was invented by the Italian chemist Ascanio Sobrero in 1846. Nitro-glycerine is a colourless, oily liquid with a sweet, burning taste, which is extremely sensitive to detonation by shock. Its great sensitivity makes it hazardous both to manufacture and to handle. Great precautions have to be taken to avoid detonation. It is used in the manufacture of the more easily handled explosives *dynamite and *gelignite; it is also used medically to ease the pain of angina.

Nobel, Alfred (1833–96), Swedish industrialist and philanthropist, founder of the Nobel Prizes. Born in Stockholm, Sweden, he was brought up and educated in St Petersburg, the capital of imperial Russia. In 1850–2, he travelled widely in Europe and the USA, becoming fluent in five languages and acquiring a good knowledge of chemistry, engineering, and foreign business methods. Nobel became interested in the highly explosive *nitro-glycerine. In its raw state nitro-glycerine proved unmanageably dangerous, and Nobel, with his father, investigated methods of making it safe. In 1867 he patented the invention of *dynamite, in which the nitro-glycerine is made less reactive by mixing it with kieselguhr, a siliceous mineral. Nobel's blasting gelatine, in which collodion cotton (see *nitro-cellulose) was used to gelatinize the nitro-glycerine, followed in 1875. The last of his major inventions was ballistite, a smokeless propellant for *firearms (1887). On his death, Nobel left the greater part of his vast fortune to support the prestigious international Nobel prizes, first awarded in 1901.

nonwoven fabric, generally a *fabric made directly from fibre rather than from *yarn. *Felt is a nonwoven material of great antiquity, and there are several other types of more recent origin. Stitched web, a fabric widely used for domestic drapes and garment interlinings, consists of a layer of random fibres bound together by stitching. There are several fabrics in use which are made from cellulose pulp, and are essentially paper, yet feel like textiles. Some of these fabrics are disposable, but others are fairly durable and will withstand a number of launderings. Spun-bonded nonwovens are made from thermoplastic *synthetic fibres. The fibres are assembled as a randomly oriented layer and are then fused at their crossing points by rapid heating. Fusing conditions can be controlled to give the required flexibility or rigidity, and the resulting fabrics are both cheap and extremely durable.

Novosibirsk State University, a Soviet university located in a new 'science city' in Siberia. Although it is situated far from the capital, academic standards are high because of strong links with the Siberian Division of the *Academy of Sciences of the USSR. The university was established in 1959 as part of a policy of locating scientific institutions in deprived areas. It was the creation of M. A. Lavrentev, a distinguished scientist who was able to attract colleagues of high calibre. It became a model for other science cities, including Pushkhino (biology) and Dubna (nuclear) near Moscow, Troitsk (chemistry) in the Urals, and *Tsukuba in Japan.

nozzle, a small spout or mouthpiece used to convert pressure or heat energy in a fluid into kinetic energy in the form of a high-speed jet or spray. For a liquid, or for a gas at pressure differences low enough to regard the gas as incompressible, the nozzle is simply a convergent passage. For a gas at higher pressure, the shape of the nozzle is at first convergent to the throat, where a speed of flow equal to the speed of sound is attained; thereafter a divergent passage accelerates the flow to supersonic speeds. Nozzles have many applications: for example, in *turbines they are used to direct fluid on to the rotors. They are essential in jet engines for increasing the speed of the ejected fluid.

nuclear energy, energy derived from nuclear *fission or *fusion. In nuclear fission, the nucleus of a heavy *atom is split into two pieces of comparable size; in fusion, two or more relatively light nuclei combine to form a heavier one. Both these processes involve the release of very large amounts of energy. The energy of nuclear reactions has been harnessed for both peaceful and military purposes (see *nuclear power, *nuclear weapons). Controlled nuclear fusion, however, has yet to be achieved. Experiments investigating radioactivity and atomic structure in the late 19th and early 20th centuries led to the idea of a small, dense nucleus at the centre of the atom, and the detection of the neutron as a component of this nucleus. An experiment by Otto Hahn and Fritz Strassman in 1938 involved the bombardment of uranium with neutrons. They discussed the results of their experiments with *Meitner, who put forward the theory that they had split the uranium atom into two pieces. Her calculations showed that the total mass of the fission fragments was slightly less than the mass of the uranium that they came from: the mass difference had been converted to energy. Einstein had predicted that mass could be converted into energy in his equation $E=mc^2$ (E is energy, m is mass, and c is a constant, the velocity of light). Even though the mass loss in this fission reaction was tiny, the amount of energy released was great, because the value of c^2 is extremely large (about $9\times10^{16}\text{m}^2/\text{s}^2$). The discovery of fission led to a flurry of activity by scientists to unlock the energy of the atom. *Fermi's *atomic pile demonstrated the self-sustaining *chain reaction in which neutrons released by the fission of uranium atoms could be used to split more uranium atoms. It provided the basis for the design of nuclear

Storage of metal drums containing waste **nuclear fuel** near Oak Ridge, Tennessee, USA.

reactors, and the peaceful use of nuclear power. It also became apparent that an uncontrolled chain reaction could be used in an atomic bomb. The *Manhattan Project was set up to build such a device, and in July 1945 the first atomic bomb was successfully demonstrated. Further research after World War II showed that fusion of atomic nuclei could release even more energy. A vast programme of research led to the development of the *hydrogen bomb in 1952.

nuclear fuel, a material used to fuel a *nuclear reactor. In the thermal reactors used for nuclear-power generation the fuel is some form of *uranium: this may be either uranium metal or uranium dioxide. For some reactor types the fuel is enriched (see below) to increase the proportion of fissionable uranium-235 (U-235). *Fast breeder reactors use a fuel that is either a mixture of uranium dioxide and *plutonium dioxide, or an artificial *isotope of uranium, U-233, made from the element thorium. In the enrichment process, uranium is first converted to uranium hexafluoride ('hex'), which is a gas at temperatures above 57 °C. In gaseous form it is allowed to diffuse (more from a region of high concentration to one of low concentration) through a porous barrier: on average the lighter U-235 molecules diffuse more quickly than the heavier U-238 molecules. In order to achieve adequate enrichment, thousands of such diffusion barriers are used. An alternative enrichment process uses a high-speed centrifuge: in this case the lighter gas accumulates in the centre of the centrifuge. For use in a nuclear reactor, uranium-based fuel is formed into fuel elements, in which the fuel is encased in a mechanically strong, radiation-resistant cladding of aluminium, magnesium, or stainless steel to protect it from damage. A fuel element will be used in a nuclear reactor until it is unreactive or (more commonly) has become badly damaged by radiation or heat. It is then removed from the reactor core and may be reprocessed—any uranium or plutonium in the fuel element is separated out to be used again. Reprocessing poses major, long-term safety problems because the fuel wastes remaining after extraction of uranium and plutonium remain dangerously radioactive for up to 700 years. These wastes must be stored in such a way that they do not contaminate the ground or water supplies during this period. No truly adequate solution to this storage problem has yet been found.

nuclear magnetic resonance (NMR) *magnetic resonance imaging.

nuclear medicine, the use of injected radioactive substances to diagnose disease, particularly cancer. *Radioactive isotopes (radioisotopes) with short half-lives can produce images or other diagnostic records of parts of the body when used in conjunction with a detector. The radioisotopes 'label' substances metabolized in ordinary physiological functions. For example, in thyroid scans, abnormal functioning can be diagnosed by injecting radioactive iodine into the blood system and mapping its distribution in body tissues. In the gamma camera, a common type of detector, gamma-rays emitted by injected isotopes produce tiny scintillations of light in large sodium iodide crystals held above the organ being investigated. Magnified and converted into electrical signals, these scintillations can be analysed by a computer and displayed as sophisticated images. Recent applications include cardiac imaging—in which radioactive drugs are used to highlight loss of function in diseased hearts—and *positron emission tomography.

nuclear power, power, usually electricity, generated using a *nuclear reactor. The principles of the nuclear re-

Timechart of developments in nuclear power

1942	An atomic pile, the world's first nuclear reactor, demonstrated by Fermi at Chicago University, USA
1947	Experimental heavy-water reactor commissioned at Chalk River, Canada: forerunner of commercial CANDU reactors
1951	First electricity generated by nuclear power in experimental breeder reactor, Idaho Falls, USA
1953	First experimental PWR reactor tested: later (1954) installed in US nuclear submarine *Nautilus*
1955	First nuclear power station (100 MW), at Obninsk in the Soviet Union, began operation
1956	First commercially operating nuclear power station opened at Calder Hall, UK
1957	Prototype 60-MW PWR nuclear power station built at Shippingport, USA
1959	First experimental fast breeder reactor, at Dounreay, Scotland, UK, reaches designed output of 14 MW
1961	First commercial PWR nuclear power station (575 MW), at Yankee Rowe, USA, began operation
1962	Demonstration advanced gas-cooled reactor built at Windscale (now Sellafield), UK
1966	Nuclear fuel reprocessing plant opened at Windscale (now Sellafield), UK
1967	Prototype 208-MW CANDU nuclear power station built at Douglas Point, Canada
1974	Prototype fast breeder nuclear power station began operation at Dounreay, Scotland, UK
1976	First commercial advanced gas-cooled nuclear power station, Hinckley Point B, UK, began operation
1979	Accident at Three-Mile Island nuclear power station in Pennsylvania, USA, caused partial meltdown of the reactor core and release of a small amount of radioactive material
1986	Explosion at Chernobyl nuclear power station near Kiev in the Soviet Union killed thirty-one people outright and released a cloud of radioactive material

Nuclear reactor

A nuclear reactor's energy is generated by nuclear fission (the splitting of a heavy atom into two fast-moving lighter fragments).

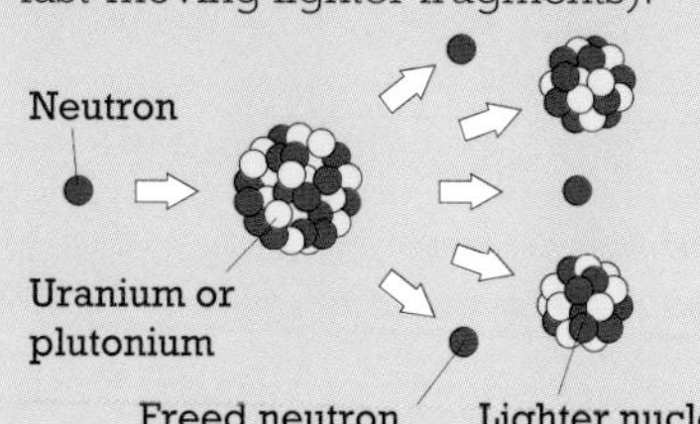

The released neutrons collide with more atoms which again split. A chain reaction is sustained.

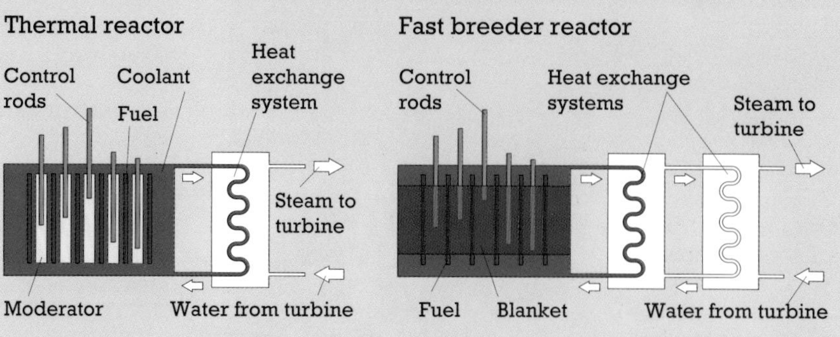

Thermal reactors utilize slow-moving neutrons. They contain a moderator which slows down the neutrons to the optimum speed, enabling further fission to take place. Fast breeder reactors have no moderator; the fast-moving neutrons are less effective, but the reactor fuel is enriched with fissionable material so that the chain reaction can be sustained.

Examples of thermal reactors

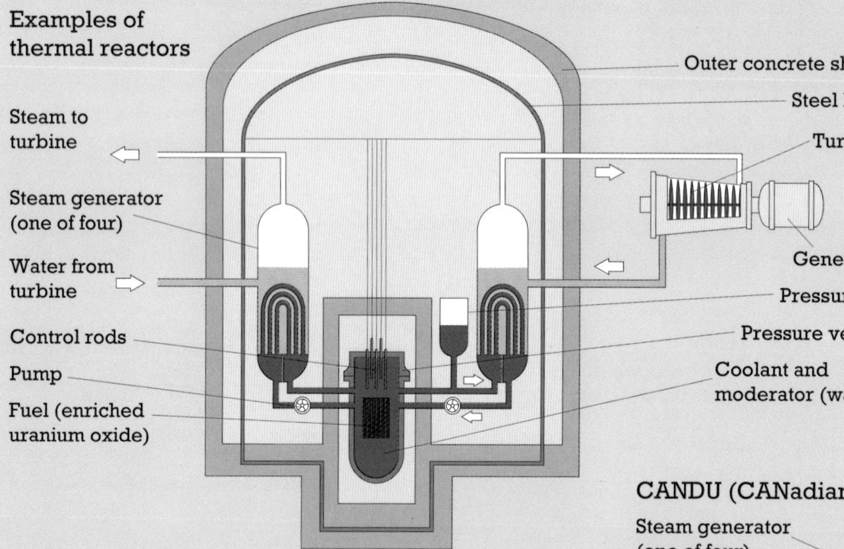

Pressurized water reactor (PWR)

The water in the reactor acts as both moderator and coolant, and is pressurized to 150 bar to prevent it from boiling. In the steam generators, heat from the pressurized water is passed to a separate water circuit at atmospheric pressure. The steam thus formed drives the turbines.

Advanced gas-cooled reactor (AGR)

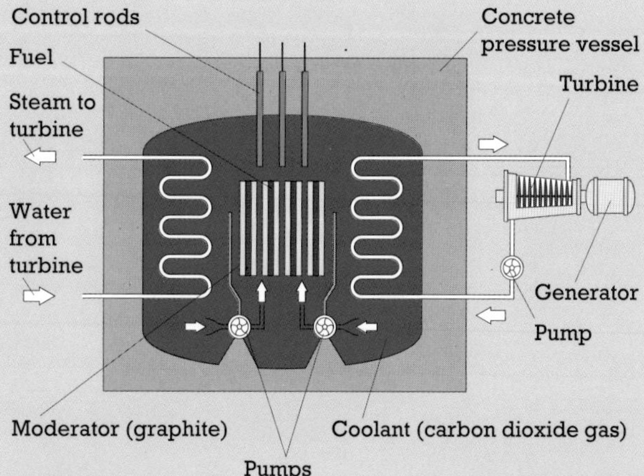

The coolant is carbon dioxide, which gives up its heat to water at atmospheric pressure flowing through a heat-exchange system. The resultant steam is pumped to the turbine.

CANDU (CANadian Deuterium Uranium) reactor

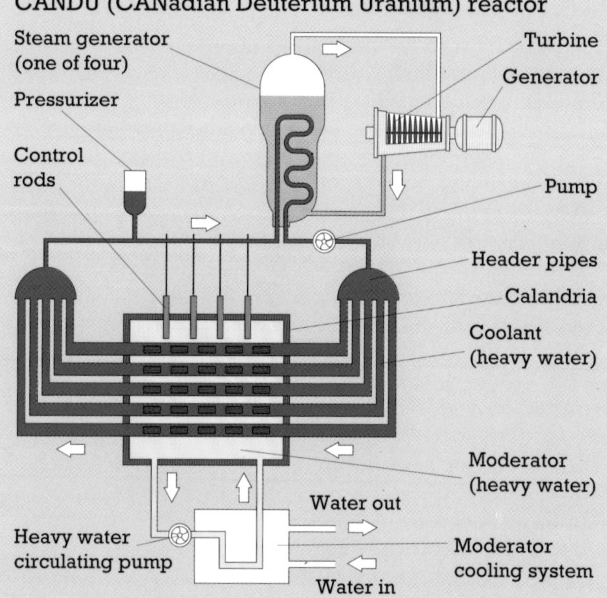

The reactor core (calandria) contains hundreds of channels holding the fuel, over which coolant at 90 bar pressure is pumped. Heavy water is used as both coolant and moderator, but the two are kept separate.

actor were first demonstrated in the *atomic pile built in 1942 by *Fermi. Until the end of World War II further development of nuclear power was almost exclusively military, but after the War several countries, notably the USA, the UK, Canada, France, and the Soviet Union, began research into the use of nuclear energy for power generation. Details of the historical development of nuclear power for electricity generation are given in the table. By 1989 there were over 400 nuclear power-stations operating worldwide, generating over 300 GW of electrical power per annum, about 7 per cent of total world consumption (see *energy resources). The USA and France were the largest producers, with France generating nearly 75 per cent of its total electricity requirements from nuclear power.

The future of the use of nuclear power for electricity generation is extremely difficult to predict. The fast breeder reactor and nuclear *fusion offer the possibility of virtually unlimited power if the technological problems can be overcome. Arguments against the further development of nuclear power centre on four main points: the fear of future nuclear catastrophes such as the breakdown at *Three Mile Island and the major accident at *Chernobyl; the tremendous storage and safety problems for future generations posed by the highly radioactive wastes from *nuclear fuel reprocessing; the fact that the *plutonium generated in particular by fast breeder reactors is a raw material of *nuclear weapons; and the problem that without reprocessing—one of the most controversial aspects of nuclear power, due to the large amounts of radioactive waste it produces—there is unlikely to be enough uranium in the world to fuel conventional reactors into the long-term future.

nuclear-powered ship, a sea-going vessel powered by a *nuclear reactor. It was the brainchild of Hyman Rickover of the US Navy, who was responsible for the construction of *Nautilus*, the world's first nuclear-powered *submarine, launched in 1954. A heavily shielded reactor generates heat to produce steam for turbo-electric propulsion. The advantages of nuclear propulsion lie in almost unlimited endurance without refuelling and the ability to generate steam without using oxygen—ideal for a submarine, which does not then need to surface to recharge batteries and thereby risk detection. As well as in submarines, nuclear propulsion is also used in *warships: both the cost of installation and the reluctance of many ports to admit ships carrying a nuclear installation inhibit its use in *merchant ships. A few large Soviet *ice-breakers are also fitted with nuclear propulsion.

nuclear reactor, an assemblage of materials designed to sustain controlled nuclear *fission (the splitting of the nucleus of a heavy atom into two lighter fragments). The fuel for most reactors is some form of *uranium, the only natural material that can sustain nuclear fission. Nuclear reactors generate large quantities of heat, beta- and gamma-*radiation, and large numbers of neutrons. Research reactors are used to test the effect of neutron bombardment on materials, and some reactors generate *plutonium for the manufacture of *nuclear weapons, but the most common use of reactors is for generation of power, in particular electricity (see *nuclear power). Reactors fall broadly into two categories: thermal reactors and fast breeder reactors (see figure). In thermal reactors, rods of nuclear fuel are embedded in a moderator, a material which slows down neutrons emitted in the fission process. Slow neutrons are more effective in producing fission, so the moderator sustains the nuclear *chain reaction. The best moderating material is deuterium, an *isotope of hydrogen (see *heavy water), but normal ('light') water and graphite are also used. In *fast breeder reactors, no moderating material is used, but the uranium fuel is enriched: the proportion of fissionable material in the fuel is increased, so that the chain reaction can be sustained even with high-energy, fast neutrons. Control of the chain reaction in both types of reactor is usually by means of control rods, made of a material such as cadmium or boron, with a high neutron absorption (although some reactors are controlled by insertion or withdrawal of the fuel rods). With the control rods completely inserted into the reactor core, neutrons are absorbed before they can produce fission, and the chain reaction is stopped. As the rods are removed, the reactivity of the core increases. Removal of heat from the reactor core is important both in controlling the chain reaction and for obtaining power from the reactor. The heat absorbed by the coolant is used to generate steam, which in turn drives turbine-powered generators. The material used must be a suitable coolant in terms of temperature range and heat-transfer properties, and must also have low neutron absorbency so as not to affect the chain reaction. The whole reactor must be shielded to prevent the escape of radiation, and elaborate safety systems are incorporated into the reactor design to prevent any escape of fission products or coolants. The PIUS (Process Inherent Ultimate Safety) reactor, a design proposed by the Swedish firm ASEA-ATOM, avoids problems of human error and mechanical breakdown by immersing the whole reactor in a huge pool of water containing borate, an efficient neutron absorber. Any problems in the cooling system of the reactor allows the borated water to flood the reactor core, causing power to fall, without the intervention of an operator or any electromechanical device. Despite the elaborate safety arrangements, nuclear breakdowns and accidents have occurred, most notably at *Three Mile Island and *Chernobyl. The figure shows the components of several different reactor types. (See also individual reactor types.)

nuclear weapon, an explosive device that owes its destructive power to the energy released by nuclear *fission or *fusion. These devices include the atomic bomb, the hydrogen bomb, and the neutron bomb. The power, or yield, of nuclear weapons is expressed as the weight of the explosive *TNT that would be required to produce an equivalent explosive power. (Thus, a 20-kilotonne bomb would have the same effect as 20,000 tonnes of TNT.) A typical nuclear explosion releases about half its energy as shock and blast, a third as heat, and the rest as *radiation. Almost all immediate casualties would be caused by blast, heat, or flying debris. Long-term radiation casualties would depend on the amount of *fall-out. A *nuclear winter might result from a large-scale nuclear war.

Nuclear weapons were developed in the USA during World War II under the code name *Manhattan Project. The first device, an atomic bomb, was exploded in New Mexico in July 1945. The following month, the USA dropped two atomic bombs, code-named Little Boy (a uranium bomb) and Fatman (a plutonium bomb), on the Japanese cities Hiroshima and Nagasaki, killing over 100,000 people outright. These are the only instances of nuclear weapons having been used against an enemy. The Soviet Union exploded its first atomic bomb in 1949, and the UK followed in October 1952. The next month, the USA tested the world's first hydrogen bomb, developed by *Teller and his associates, which had an explosive power of 10.4 megatonnes, more than 1,000 times greater than Little Boy's.

Broadly, modern nuclear weapons fall into three categories: strategic weapons, with a range of 5,500 km (3,400 miles) or more; intermediate or theatre weapons, with ranges of 1,000–5,500 km (620–3,400 miles); and short-range weapons, with an effective range of up to 1,000 km (620 miles). Aircraft provided the only delivery system for nuclear weapons until the late 1950s, when the *ballistic missile first entered service. Today's strategic nuclear weapons arsenals include both land-based and submarine-launched ballistic missiles as well as weapons delivered by long-range bombers. Supplementing these are land- and sea-based medium-range *cruise missiles. Tactical and battlefield nuclear *warheads are normally carried on short-range missiles, but can now be made small enough to be fired, like artillery shells, from guns.

Atomic bombs (also called fission bombs) utilize the fission of uranium-235 or plutonium-239, whose production requires complex technologies. If enough fissionable material is present for a 'critical mass', a self-sustaining *chain reaction occurs in which the neutrons that are shed during fission can induce further fission in other nuclei, releasing energy in ever-increasing amounts to produce a nuclear explosion (see figure). Hydrogen bombs rely on the fusion of two heavy *isotopes of hydrogen—either two molecules of deuterium or deuterium with tritium—to form helium atoms. Temperatures of about 10^7 °C are needed to sustain a fusion reaction, and these can be achieved by using an atomic bomb as a trigger. Hydrogen bombs, which are also known as thermonuclear or fusion bombs, are basically of three types: fusion-boosted bombs, in which fusion can be used to increase the yield of a fission bomb by as much as ten times (so that it can also be appreciably lighter in weight than a normal fission bomb); and double-stage (fission–fusion) or triple-stage (fission–fusion–fission) bombs, which are much more powerful and complex in design.

A special type of fission–fusion bomb is the 'neutron bomb'. An enhanced-radiation weapon, in which most of the yield is released as high-energy neutrons, it has an effective range wider than that of a conventional nuclear bomb of similar yield and is designed to kill or disable people by radiation, rather than destroy the surroundings by shock or blast. It was developed by the USA in the 1970s as a tactical weapon, primarily to penetrate the armoured vehicles of Warsaw Pact forces in Europe in the event of a conventional strike by the Soviet Union.

nuclear winter, the possible global cooling that might follow a nuclear war in which large numbers of *nuclear weapons were exploded. Extensive fires would produce thick smoke, blocking out sunlight and resulting in severe climatic changes, in particular much lower temperatures. These effects, caused by smoke particles reaching the stratosphere, would be catastrophic to animal and plant life and would last for several years.

nucleus, atomic *atoms and molecules.

numerical control (NC), a method of automatic control of a *machine-tool. Originally, numerical control involved the use of punched cards or punched tape; instructions were contained in the position of the holes, which were sensed by mechanical, pneumatic, or optical means. This principle dates back to the *Jacquard loom of 1801 and to the paper rolls used in pianolas. More recently *microprocessor con-

Nuclear weapon

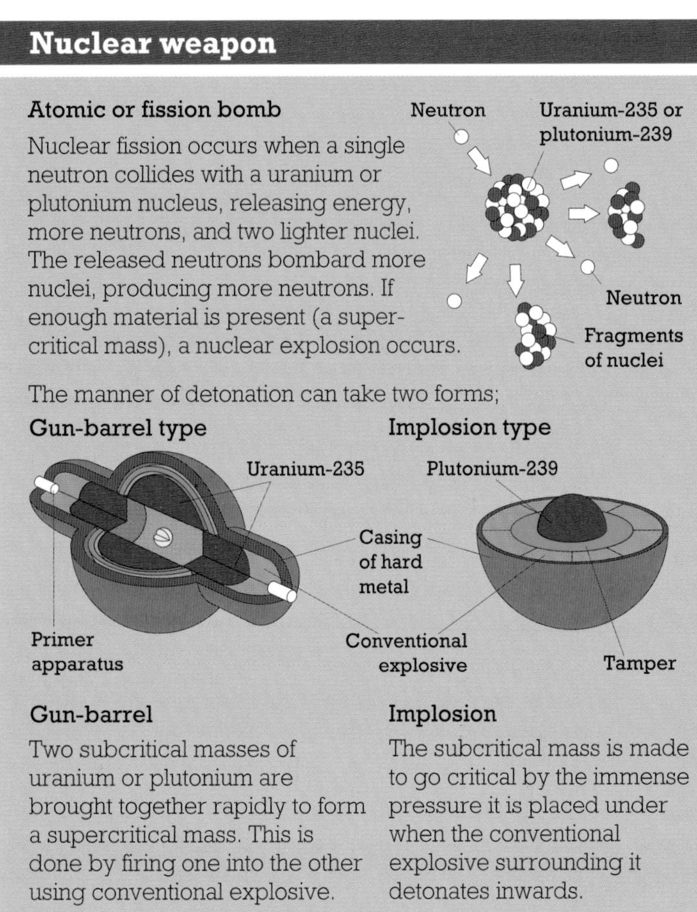

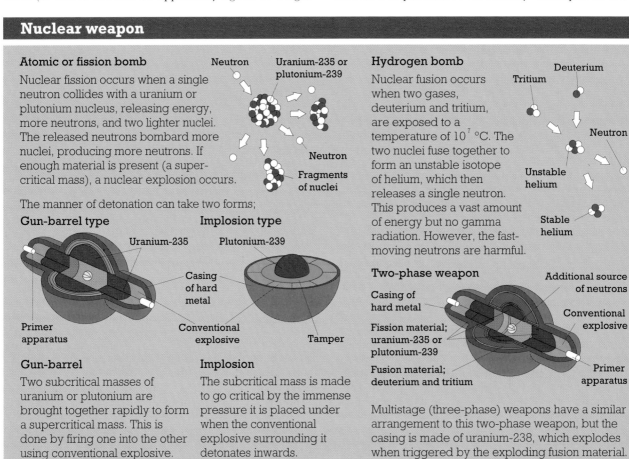

Atomic or fission bomb

Nuclear fission occurs when a single neutron collides with a uranium or plutonium nucleus, releasing energy, more neutrons, and two lighter nuclei. The released neutrons bombard more nuclei, producing more neutrons. If enough material is present (a supercritical mass), a nuclear explosion occurs.

The manner of detonation can take two forms;

Gun-barrel type **Implosion type**

Gun-barrel

Two subcritical masses of uranium or plutonium are brought together rapidly to form a supercritical mass. This is done by firing one into the other using conventional explosive.

Implosion

The subcritical mass is made to go critical by the immense pressure it is placed under when the conventional explosive surrounding it detonates inwards.

Hydrogen bomb

Nuclear fusion occurs when two gases, deuterium and tritium, are exposed to a temperature of 10^7 °C. The two nuclei fuse together to form an unstable isotope of helium, which then releases a single neutron. This produces a vast amount of energy but no gamma radiation. However, the fast-moving neutrons are harmful.

Deuterium
Tritium
Neutron
Unstable helium
Stable helium

Two-phase weapon

Casing of hard metal
Fission material; uranium-235 or plutonium-239
Fusion material; deuterium and tritium
Additional source of neutrons
Conventional explosive
Primer apparatus

Multistage (three-phase) weapons have a similar arrangement to this two-phase weapon, but the casing is made of uranium-238, which explodes when triggered by the exploding fusion material.

A 1951 UK advertisement for Kayser stockings. The most popular early application of **nylon** as a textile fibre was in the manufacture of stockings and tights for women.

trol of machine-tools (computer numerical control or CNC) has been developed. This allows the most intricate shapes to be produced automatically. Sophisticated methods of driving and controlling the various machine movements are required, using *servo-mechanisms and sensors for tool position, speed, and acceleration.

nutrition *food and nutrition.

nuts and bolts, metal fastening devices, consisting of a small, pierced metal block with an internal screw-thread (nut) into which screws a length of the metal pin with a complementary thread and a head at one end (bolt). Both nut and bolt head are usually shaped so that they can be turned by a spanner. Nuts and bolts were first used in Europe in about the middle of the 16th century. Screw-cutting lathes for mass production appeared in about 1800, and are particularly identified with *Maudslay. Today, bolts are made for a wide variety of purposes, from watch-making to bridge-building. They are particularly important in mechanical and structural engineering, both for the attachment of fixtures and for connecting together structural components. An important development in this context is the high-strength friction bolt, which is used to join two components with a high clamping force, so that friction between the contact faces prevents slip. In the building of bridges and other structures, friction bolts are now widely used instead of *riveting or *welding, as they are simple to assemble, economical, and reliable.

nylon, a synthetic *plastic, one of a class of polymers known as polyamides. Nylon was developed by *Carothers in America during the 1930s. It was first manufactured as a fibre, by extrusion of the molten polymer through a spinneret (see *spinning). As a textile fibre it is used in several ways. Where the appearance of silk is wanted, or great strength is needed (as in *rope), groups of filaments, or even single filaments may be used as continuous-filament yarns for weaving, knitting, and sewing. For other uses, continuous-filament yarns are textured (see *yarn texturing) or crimped to give both bulk and extensibility. Alternatively, filaments may be extruded as 'tow', consisting of up to 500,000 filaments. After stretching, the tow is cut or broken into short lengths and (alone or in blends with natural fibres) is spun into yarn on cotton, wool, or flax systems of spinning. Nylon is now also manufactured as sheeting, coatings, and in moulded form, and has a number of industrial applications, for example, for wire insulation, gearwheels, bearings, and reinforcement in tyres. A class of plastics related to nylon are the aramids. These are *liquid crystal polymers based on polyamides that form extremely strong fibres, used principally in *fibre-reinforced plastics and other *composites. Aramids were discovered by a research team at the Du Pont Company, USA, in the late 1960s: the best known example is Kevlar.

Oberth, Hermann Julius *Braun, Werner Maximilian von.

observatory, usually a place where astronomical observations and measurements are made, though some observatories study the weather or the Earth's structure. Even before the *telescope was invented, astronomical observatories had instruments to measure the positions of the Sun, the Moon, stars, and planets in the sky. The main instruments in most modern observatories are large optical telescopes housed in protective domed buildings, or *radio telescopes. The light collected by such telescopes is recorded by *cameras, image detectors using *charge-coupled devices, or other instruments, and analysed to retrieve the information it carries from distant astronomical objects. The best observatory sites are far from city lights, in climates with little cloud cover, and as high as possible above atmospheric turbulence. Such sites allow the study of infra-red radiation, which is absorbed in the lower atmosphere. Observatories studying radiation blocked by the atmosphere, like X-rays, must be operated in space on satellites or space stations.

obsidian *flint.

obstetrics and gynaecology, the branches of medicine concerned, respectively, with childbirth and the diseases of women. Before 1700 childbirth was a social occasion attended by a midwife and a group of female assistants. Surgeons were called only in an emergency. Obstetric forceps began to be widely used in the 1730s, predominantly by male practitioners. Thereafter obstetrics developed rapidly and became an accepted part of medical practice. Gynaecology emerged as a speciality during the mid- to late-19th century, and eventually it became a new speciality, as signalled by the establishment of the Royal College of Obstetricians and Gynaecologists in London in 1929. Thereafter obstetrics gradually moved away from home deliveries and general practice and became dominated by hospital specialists.

Technology in the modern sense came late to obstetrics and gynaecology, but recent advances have been considerable, although in obstetrics increased intervention and management have provoked some opposition. Relatively recent advances in obstetrics include epidural analgesia (an injection of local anaesthetic around the spinal cord); *ultrasound for antenatal imaging of the foetus; techniques such as *amniocentesis for the detection of foetal abnormalities; and *_in vitro_ fertilization techniques in the management of some forms of infertility. Pregnancy testing can now be done at home on a urine sample, and during labour the foetal heartbeat and the frequency of labour contractions can be continuously monitored in graphic form by the technique of cardiotachography.

In gynaecology, laparoscopy (see *endoscopy) is already established as a technique for diagnosis and sterilization; it is now being extended to include surgery of the uterus, in which it may replace, at least in some cases, the standard techniques of hysterectomy. Other techniques include *cervical screening for the detection of the pre-cancerous state, and examination of the neck of the womb and upper vagina with a colposcope (a type of endoscope). The colposcope can also be used to treat cervical cancer by cauterizing cancerous tissue using laser light.

The Jaipur Royal Observatory, Rajasthan, India, an open-air **observatory** built in the 18th century. It is one of only two naked-eye observatories still intact; the other is at Delhi.

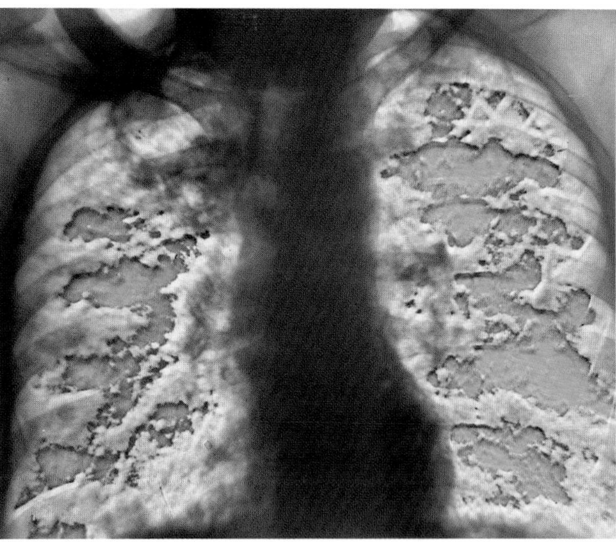

A chest X-ray of a patient with silicosis, a lung disease caused by inhaling silica dust. Silicosis is an **occupational disease** contracted in such jobs as stone-quarrying and boiler-scaling.

occupational disease, any disease closely identified with a specific occupation. In the first century AD Pliny described the incidence of mercury poisoning among mercury miners, but the generally acknowledged founder of occupational medicine is the Italian physician Bernardino Ramazzini (1633–1714). In his _Diseases of Workers_ (1700), which was translated into several languages, he described fifty-four occupational diseases associated with miners, masons, painters, blacksmiths, and others. New technologies brought new hazards. In the 1830s 'phossy jaw' was identified among workers using toxic yellow phosphorus in match factories. The Polish-born French chemist Marie Curie (1867–1934) and her daughter Irène Joliot-Curie (1896–1956) died from the effects of working with highly radioactive substances, and in 1916–23 in the USA many employees of a New Jersey factory were killed by diseases contracted through painting the dials of watches with *luminous paint. Probably the largest class of occupational diseases are lung complaints such as silicosis and asbestosis, caused by inhalation of dust particles of various kinds. Today, many countries have strict legislation requiring employers to protect workers from known hazards. However, risks are not always recognized or acknowledged until victims appear in statistically significant numbers.

octane number, a measure of the efficiency with which a specific grade of *petrol performs in a *petrol engine. It is the percentage by volume of iso-octane in an iso-octane and heptane mixture that produces the same amount of engine *knock as the petrol under test, as measured in the same test engine. Regular grade petrol has an octane number of about 90, supergrade about 95.

odometer, an instrument for measuring large distances, for example in surveying roads. It consists of a large wheel (whose exact circumference is known) attached to a handle, so that it can be pushed or pulled along the distance to be measured. The number of revolutions of the wheel are registered on a meter and thus the distance travelled can be calculated. The milometer incorporated in the *speedometer of a motor car is a type of odometer.

off-road vehicle, a wheeled vehicle for off-road use. The earliest was the jeep, a versatile four-wheel-drive US military vehicle used extensively in World War II. Off-road vehicles usually have four-wheel drive, high ground clearance, and additional low gears for difficult terrain. They may be used for many agricultural and forestry purposes, and for maintenance of power lines. They are also used for other commercial and military purposes, and for leisure activities. (See also *low-ground-pressure vehicle.)

offset lithography (offset litho), the most widely used variant of *lithography, whereby the greasy image is first 'offset' from an alternately inked and dampened plate cylinder on to a rubber-covered blanket cylinder. The image is then transferred under pressure on to the paper conveyed on an impression cylinder. This offset process enables relatively rough surfaces to carry fine printing, while the all-rotary action permits high printing speeds. Offset litho is almost universally used for work up to the highest quality on a range of machines. These may print on individual sheets, or may use a large roll (web) of paper. Web offset printing machines are extremely fast, and are particularly suitable for large print runs (for example, national newspapers). For publication work, printing units are placed on either side of the paper web, so that both sides are printed simultaneously. Colour *printing may use a succession of machines; alternatively a number of blanket cylinders, each for a different colour, may be grouped around a common impression cylinder. (For illustration see printing.)

Rockwell web **offset lithography** printing presses in operation at West Ferry Printers Ltd., UK, where several national newspapers are printed.

Ohain, Hans Pabst von (1911–), German engineer and pioneer of jet propulsion. He studied at Göttingen University under the physicist Ludwig Prandtl, considered the father of aerodynamics. In 1936 von Ohain joined the Heinkel aircraft company, where he developed a design he had already made for a *jet engine. By 1939 a working engine had been built, and was installed in the Heinkel He. 178, the world's first jet aircraft.

ohm *impedance, *reactance, *resistor, *unit.

oil, crude *petroleum.

oil gasification, the process of producing fuel-gas from heavy oils, sometimes used to supplement *natural gas supplies during peak demand periods. The main method of gasifying oil involves spraying fuel-oil on to very hot bricks. This can be done in a cyclic process in which the bricks are first heated using burning oil, then oil and steam are sprayed on and react to produce gas. A continuous process can be achieved by spraying the oil on to the bricks while admitting controlled amounts of air. Part of the oil burns, providing energy to convert the rest to gaseous *hydrocarbons.

oil lamp, a lamp that produces light by the combustion of oil. Prehistoric oil lamps consisted of a flat stone with a hollow full of animal oil which burned at a moss wick. By 500–400 BC, clay, copper, and bronze oil lamps had come into general use. These burned vegetable oil at a vegetable-fibre wick. Lamps using mineral oil were introduced in about AD 50, and in 1490 *Leonardo da Vinci designed a light with a glass chimney, though this was not widely adopted. A great advance was made in 1784 when Aimé Argand of Switzerland patented the *Argand lamp, which burned more brightly and steadily. In 1885 highly efficient pressure lamps were introduced, which burned vaporized *paraffin oil to heat a gas-mantle to incandescence.

oils, animal and vegetable *fats and oils.

oilskin, a fabric impermeable to water, consisting of a cotton or silk woven fabric covered with a thin layer of polymerized linseed oil. It has long been used for rainwear and for protecting objects from water damage. Synthetic plastic film has now largely displaced traditional oilskin.

Omega, a very long-range *radio aid to navigation, developed in the USA from about 1954 and first used in about

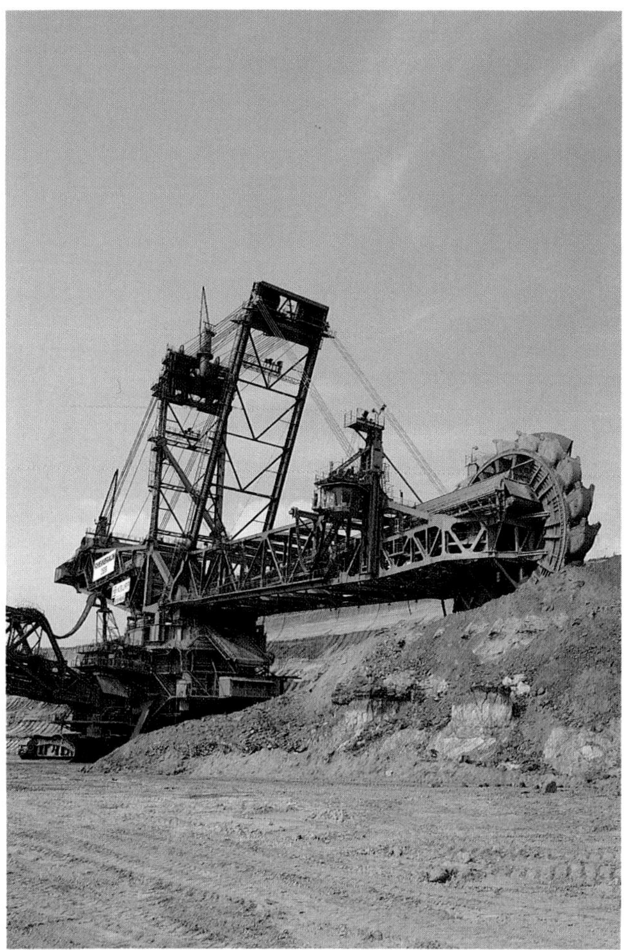

A bucket-wheel excavator in use at an **open-cast mine** near Cologne, Germany. Each bucket on the wheel is large enough to hold a small car. The excavator is so large that it must be constructed on-site, a process that can take up to 20 months.

1968. It is a phase difference hyperbolic system that operates at very low *frequency, thus achieving world-wide coverage. There are eight transmitting stations, located in Norway, Liberia, Hawaii, USA, Réunion, Argentina, Australia, and Japan. The system has an accuracy of about 4 km (2.2 nautical miles; see *knot) by day and 7.5 km (4 nautical miles) by night, in areas declared operational by the US coastguard. However, solar activity can affect accuracy considerably.

open-cast mining, the *mining of ores from the earth without tunnelling. This requires a large ore deposit on or very near the surface which can be broken up by *explosives. The resulting debris is then removed by a variety of heavy excavating equipment, such as mobile power shovels and *drag-lines, or continuous bucket-and-wheel *excavators feeding conveyor belts. The ore is then transported directly to processing plants.

open-hearth furnace (Siemens–Martin furnace), a furnace used for making steel from a mixture of scrap-iron and pig-iron, for *glass-making, and in several other industrial processes. (For illustration see *iron and steel industry.) The iron or other material is placed in a shallow hearth, and heated by a mixture of fuel-gas and air burnt above it. Waste gases leaving the furnace give up much of their heat to the incoming fuel-gas and air in a heat regenerator. As a result, the temperature of the flame in the hearth reaches about 1,650 °C. The open-hearth furnace was first developed by C. W. *Siemens, and steel production using a mixture of scrap- and pig-iron was developed by Pierre-Emile Martin in 1864.

operating system, the software that manages the resources of a computer system, independent of the use to which the computer is put. In addition to controlling the operation of *hardware, the operating system also manages the transmission of data to and from *memory, the disk drives, and *peripherals such as keyboards, displays, and *printers. Widely used operating systems include MS-DOS (MicroSoft Disk Operating System) and UNIX (used on systems ranging from personal computers to super computers). OS/2 is an operating system intended to be the successor to MS-DOS.

operating theatre, a room specifically designed and equipped for *surgery. The routine incorporation of operating theatres into hospitals is a relatively recent development. Their original purpose was to allow spectators a clear view (hence the term 'theatre'), and 19th-century designs with tiered seating resemble older anatomical dissection theatres. Throughout the 19th century, operations were often conducted in the patient's home to avoid the risk of infection in the hospital. The introduction of aseptic operating techniques (see *asepsis) revolutionized theatre design. Complex sterilization procedures were adopted for the surgeon's hands and instruments, the surgeon wore sterile outer garments and rubber gloves, and sterile drapes surrounded the operation site. Today, technologies that are indispensable to the modern theatre include mechanized operating tables; powerful, shadow-free operating lights; electrical cautery (destruction of tissue and control of bleeding by application of a heated instrument); suction apparatus to clear blood from the operating site; and anaesthetic machines, often with gases piped from a central supply. Instruments such as the *electrocardiogram and the *electroencephalogram are used to monitor body functions, and apparatus such as the *respirator is used to maintain essential body processes during surgery.

operational research (operations research, OR), the application of mathematical, scientific, and engineering techniques to model and improve the operation of complex systems involving people, machines, and information. OR thus has much in common with *systems engineering. Operational research emerged in the UK during World War II as an interdisciplinary attempt to solve wartime logistical problems. Since then it has been applied to many planning and scheduling problems in industrial, commercial, and public sectors—often using the mathematical technique known as linear programming. Typical OR problems might include the control of traffic flow within a city; and *optimization of industrial production and distribution.

ophthalmic surgery, the branch of *surgery concerned with the eyes. The ancient practice of couching cataracts (displacing a damaged lens downwards into the eye) was widespread until the 18th century. However, the treatment of eye disease was not accepted into mainstream medicine until the 19th century, when specialist hospitals were founded. The invention of the *ophthalmoscope in 1851 aided diagnosis, while local anaesthetics (particularly cocaine after 1884) and asepsis made more complex operations possible. Thereafter, forms of cataract, squint, glaucoma (raised pressure within the eye), and retinal disorder all gradually became amenable to surgery. Technological developments such as the operating microscope, titanium instruments for microsurgery, and, in the last decade, artificial (polymethyl methacrylate) lens implants have greatly improved results. Knifeless techniques including *diathermy, cryosurgery (localized freezing and hence destruction of unwanted tissues), and, since 1962, *lasers have also played an important role.

ophthalmoscope, an instrument for viewing the internal structures of the eye. Looking through the pupil, the specialist can see the retina and is able to diagnose eye disorders and some general conditions such as diabetes and high blood pressure. The modern ophthalmoscope was invented by the German physicist and physiologist Hermann von Helmholtz in 1851, and was the first type of instrument to allow direct visualization of the interior of a living organ.

Oppenheimer, (Julius) Robert (1904–67), US physicist. He was appointed in 1942 as Director of the *Manhattan Project, based at Los Alamos, New Mexico, which in 1945 made the first atomic bomb. In 1953, at the height of the witch-hunting campaign led by the US Senator Joseph McCarthy, Oppenheimer was excluded from sensitive research on the grounds that he had Communist sympathies, but subsequently (1963) he was unreservedly rehabilitated.

optical character recognition (OCR), a technique for providing computers with input data directly from text or other symbols printed on paper, obviating the need for keying in the information. OCR systems generally use *photocells or a modified television camera to scan the text. The signal is then fed to the computer. In most systems the computer identifies each character by matching it with stored characters, but advanced systems use *artificial intelligence techniques to improve accuracy. Some typefaces are specially designed to be read by computer, and are often used on financial documents such as cheque-books.

optical disc *compact disc.

optical fibre, a thin transparent fibre of glass or plastic that allows the transmission of light. Light can be retained within the fibre if the core is covered with a material (cladding) of a lower refractive index: the core–cladding boundary acts as a mirror, reflecting the light continuously back into the core. This principle of total internal reflection was demonstrated by the British physicist John Tyndall in 1854; the technique was first used in the 1920s, when acrylic rods, with air as the cladding, were used to illuminate aircraft instrument panels and medical instruments. Rods were subsequently replaced by fibres to enable light to be guided around corners, a feature particularly useful medically for the visual investigation of internal body cavities by *endoscopy. In 1953 it was discovered that a solid cladding, such as low-refractive index glass, reduced light loss through the sides of the core. This sheathed structure had the ability to transmit light over huge distances with little loss, and made telecommunication by light possible. A light source, usually a *laser, can be *modulated, and can carry a large number of channels each of enormous *bandwidth (due to its very high frequency), and can be *multiplexed. An additional advantage is that optical-fibre transmission is not vulnerable to electrical *interference, a problem associated with conventional electrical cable and radio. Major rewiring of the UK telephone system with optical fibres began in 1982, and there are now several trans-oceanic optical-fibre cables.

optical glass, *glass used to make *lenses, *prisms, and optical equipment. It has very few imperfections (such as unmelted particles, bubbles, or uneven chemical structure) to affect the passage of light. Removal of impurities which cause absorption allows the transmission of up to 99 per cent of the range of visible light. There are many types of optical glass, including different crown and flint glasses and special barium and lanthanum glasses. The most important properties of an optical glass are its refractive index (the degree to which it bends light) and its dispersion (the extent to which it differentially refracts light of different wavelengths or colours).

optimization, the process of obtaining a 'best' or optimal solution to a problem under given constraints. Optimization

Using **optical fibres**, light from a laser can be bent to follow convoluted pathways, as illustrated in this demonstration photograph.

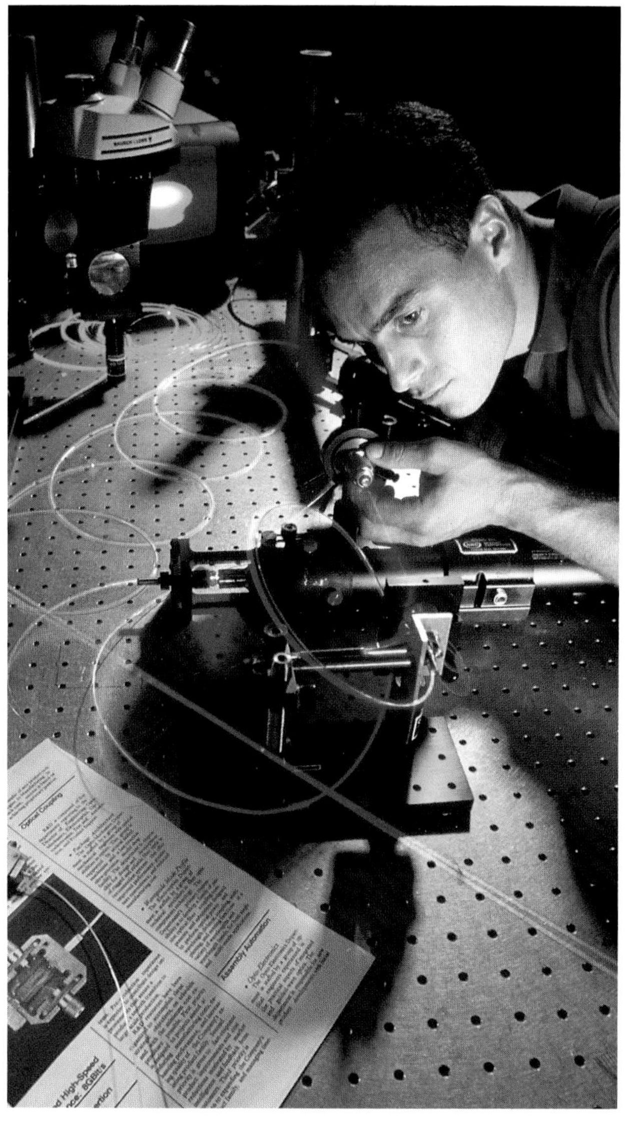

Common classes of organic chemical and their uses

Type	Definition	Formula	Applications
Alkanes	Compounds of carbon and hydrogen in which all the carbon atoms are saturated, i.e. no multiple carbon–carbon bonds	C_nH_{2n+2}, e.g. C_2H_6, ethane; C_4H_{10} butane	Fuels. Methane (CH_4) is in natural gas, and petroleum contains a mixture of alkane hydrocarbons. Refrigerants and solvents are alkanes
Alkenes	Compounds of carbon and hydrogen containing one or more carbon–carbon double bonds	C_nH_{2n}, e.g. C_2H_4, ethene, $H_2C{=}CH_2$	Used to make plastics, e.g. polythene and polypropylene. Oxidized to ketones, aldehydes, and carboxylic acids, and diols as chemical feedstocks. Used in Diels–Alder reaction
Alkynes	Compounds of carbon and hydrogen containing one or more carbon–carbon triple bonds	C_nH_{2n}, e.g. C_2H_2, ethyne, $HC{\equiv}CH$	Used to make polyacetylene conducting polymers. These are beginning to appear as constituents of field effect transistors. Ethyne also used industrially to make vinyl chloride for PVC, ethanal, and ethanoic acid. Ethyne previously used in welding (oxy-acetylene blowtorch), but has been supplanted by propane and butane.Liquid ethyne is explosive. Ethyne used in Reppe synthesis
Haloalkanes or alkyl halides	Compounds of carbon, hydrogen, and one or more halogen atoms	$C_nH_{2n+1}X$, e.g. CH_3CH_2I, iodoethane	Used as solvents and as basic chemical feedstocks for many compounds used by chemical industry.
Alcohols	Compounds of carbon, hydrogen, and one or more oxygen atoms to which is attached a hydrogen atom	e.g. CH_3CH_2OH, ethanol	Used as solvents, fuels, in alcoholic beverages, antifreeze, chemical feedstocks and reagents, surface-active agents, plasticizers
Ethers	Compounds of carbon, hydrogen, and one or more oxygen atoms which are bonded to two carbon atoms	e.g. $CH_3CH_2{\cdot}O{\cdot}CH_2CH_3$, diethyl ether, and oxirane, $H_2C{-}CH_2$ (with O bridging), an epoxide. Also cyclic polyethers called 'crown' ethers	Used mainly as solvents. Diethyl ether has been used as an anaesthetic. Other ethers are still used as such, e.g. methyl propyl ether and ethyl vinyl ether. Epoxides (or oxiranes) are used to make polymers, resins, alcohols and eliols. Cyclic polyethers are used as phase-transfer catalysts
Aldehydes	Organic compounds containing a carbonyl ($>C{=}O$) group, to which is attached an alkyl (or aryl) group and one hydrogen atom	e.g. $CH_3{-}C({=}O){-}H$, ethanal	Used as reagents, preservatives, for industrial synthesis, as sedatives, and in the manufacture of ethanol and polymers. Used in the Wittig reaction to make alkenes
Ketones	Organic compounds containing a carbonyl group to which are attached two alkyl (or aryl) groups	e.g. $CH_3{-}C({=}O){-}CH_3$ propanone	Used as solvents, e.g. propanone. More complex ketones used in processing nuclear fuels. Also used in the Wittig reaction
Carboxylic acids	Organic compounds containing a carbonyl group to which are attached a hydroxyl group (so making a carboxylic group, $-C({=}O){-}OH$), and an alkyl group	e.g. $CH_3{-}C({=}O){-}OH$ ethanoic acid	Weak acids used as solvents and reagents in organic synthesis. Adipic acid used in manufacture of nylon. Ethanoic acid used to make cellulose acetate plastics
Esters	Organic derivatives of carboxylic acids formed by the replacement of the hydroxyl hydrogen atoms by aryl groups	e.g. $CH_3{-}C({=}O){-}O{\cdot}C_2H_5$ ethyl elthanoate	Used in food flavourings (e.g. pear drops) and solvents. Cellulose esters used as photographic film. Aspirin, an analgesic, is an ester
Amines	Organic derivatives of ammonia (NH_3) in which one, two, or three of the hydrogen atoms are replaced by alkyl or aryl groups	e.g. $(C_2H_5)_3N$, triethylamine	Organic bases, solvents, reagents. Nylon is an amine derivative
Aromatic compounds	Otherwise known as arenes. They are all cyclic compounds related to benzene	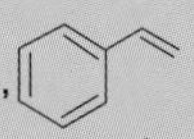 e.g. benzene, (C_6H_6) 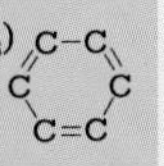 [ring structure], styrene, [structure] and toluene, [structure with CH_3] 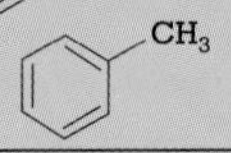	Solvents. The benzene ring is present in a vast number of industrially and commercially important chemical compounds
Heterocyclic compounds	Organic compounds of carbon, hydrogen, and another element or elements in which all the atoms are joined in a ring. If double bonds are present, the compound may demonstrate aromatic properties (like benzene) to a greater or lesser extent	Common examples are: pyridine (C_5H_5N) 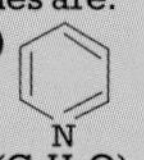 [structure, N], tetrahydrofuran (C_4H_8O), 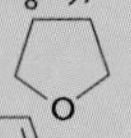 [structure, O] thiophen (C_4H_4S), 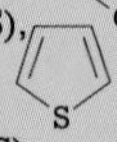 [structure, S] thiazole (C_3H_3NS), 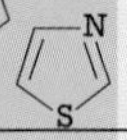 [structure, N, S]	Pyridine is an organic base and a solvent. Tetrahydrofuran is an organic solvent. In general, heterocyclic compounds have a wide variety of applications as pharmaceuticals, insecticides, and pesticides
Amino acids	Organic compounds containing both a carboxylic acid group ($-CO_2H$) and an amino group ($-NH_2$)	e.g. alanine, $NH_2{-}CH(CH_3){-}COOH$	Over 100 amino acids have been isolated from natural sources. Twenty are essential for protein formation. Their prime uses are as food additives (e.g. monosodium glutamate) and supplements

is an important part of *operational research and *systems engineering, in which a practical problem is modelled mathematically and the predictions of the model are used to suggest an optimal solution. In any optimization process, a parameter is chosen which satisfactorily measures the performance of a system; minimization (or maximization as appropriate) of this parameter then leads to the optimal strategy. For example, the *control system for positioning a space station might be optimized so as to minimize fuel consumption.

orbit *satellite, artificial, *space-flight, principles of.

ore, extraction and processing. Ores are naturally occurring mineral aggregates from which *metals or their compounds may be extracted. They normally contain large amounts of a non-metallic impurity called gangue. After *prospecting, followed by *mining or quarrying, the ore is usually pulverized by crushing and grinding. The lighter particles of gangue can then simply be washed away, leaving the denser metal-bearing particles behind. If the metal-bearing particles are magnetic, they can be extracted from the non-magnetic component by *magnetic ore separation. *Ore flotation is particularly useful for extracting sulphides of lead, zinc, and copper. Once concentrated, the ores are often treated chemically to convert them into substances from which the metal may be extracted more readily. Ores containing moisture or water chemically combined in hydrates or hydroxides, or ores containing metallic carbonates, are heated to expel water and other volatile matter and to decompose the carbonates to form the metal oxide. This process is known as calcination. Most sulphide ores are heated in air to change the sulphides to oxides and to expel sulphur as sulphur dioxide. This treatment is known as roasting. After this preparation the ore is subjected to *smelting. Some metals are produced as a by-product of refining another. For example, copper sulphide contains precious metals that can be released from the smelted copper by *electrolysis.

ore flotation, a process for removing metal *ore from unwanted material (gangue), such as earth, clay, sand, and rocks, before *smelting (purification). Finely crushed ore is agitated in water containing chemicals that form a surface froth. Particles of metal ore stick to this froth, while unwanted materials sink to the bottom of the water. Careful control of the acidity and concentration of the mixture is required for maximum effectiveness.

organic chemical, a compound of *carbon, usually also containing hydrogen: organic chemicals may also contain other elements such as oxygen, nitrogen, chlorine, and fluorine. The structures and important functional groups of the molecules of some industrially important hydrocarbons are shown in the table. The introduction of elements other than carbon or hydrogen builds new functional groups into the structures of organic molecules, thereby creating new properties. For example, ethane (a hydrocarbon) is a gas at room temperature. The addition of an oxygen atom into an ethane molecule produces *ethanol, a low-boiling-point liquid. The addition of two oxygen atoms into an ethane molecule and the removal of two hydrogen atoms produces ethanoic (acetic) acid, the main constituent of vinegar. The introduction of four chlorine atoms into an ethane molecule results in a substance (tetrachloroethane) that can be used for dry-cleaning.

organic farming, a method of farming that aims to operate within the natural ecosystem, without using artificial *fertilizers, *pesticides, or other *agrochemicals. Many different strategies are adopted to combat pests. Growing crops and grazing livestock in a balanced *rotation prevents pest and parasite build-up. Hedgerows, mixed plant breaks (strips of grass, herbs, and wild flowers within fields), and companion planting (mixing certain non-crop plants with the main crop) all encourage predators that feed on pests. Mixed cropping (for example, oats with clover) hinders weeds, and disease-resistant plant strains are used wherever possible. Planting can also be timed to avoid the period during which weeds and pests are most active. Manure and *compost are used to fertilize the soil, along with added nutrients such as rock phosphate, seaweed, and other natural fertilizers. Some of these materials release nutrients only after further breakdown in the soil: this prevents leaching of soil nutrients and promotes soil health. In contrast to *factory farming, animals are allowed to mature without growth hormones and are stocked at low levels. This reduces stress on the animals, thus improving their disease resistance. Deep-rooting herbal mixes sown in grazing areas provide mineral-rich pasture for livestock and help maintain a good soil structure. Organic farming is labour-intensive and produces lower crop yields, but in the West many consumers are willing to pay a premium on organic produce to cover the extra costs.

orthodontics *dentistry.

orthopaedics, the surgical treatment of disorders of bones and joints. Since prehistoric times broken bones have been 'set' using splints. Orthopaedics as a speciality began in 1741, when the French surgeon Nicolas André suggested that the skeletal deformities of adults started in childhood, and embarked on a study of how to treat them. The discovery of *X-rays in 1895 had an almost immediate impact on orthopaedic medicine, allowing orthopaedic surgeons to diagnose accurately fractures and other conditions of the skeletal system. Today *antibiotics and *immunization have almost eradicated diseases such as tuberculosis and poliomyelitis, which caused many of the deformities described by André. Artificial hips (see *hip replacement) and other joints (such as knee, shoulder, and elbow) are widely used to replace those worn out by osteo-arthritis and other diseases. A valuable tool for examining joints internally and performing small operations is the *optical fibre arthroscope.

oscillator, a circuit that converts direct-current power into a periodic, alternating-current wave-form of constant frequency. These wave-forms can include sine waves, square waves, and saw-tooth waves, which have several different applications. A simple low-frequency, square-wave oscillator circuit, for example, could be used to flash a light on and off. At radio frequencies, sine-wave oscillators provide 'carrier' signals on which radio and television images may be transmitted during broadcasting (see *modulation). *Microwave ovens incorporate a *magnetron (a type of *thermionic valve) as a microwave oscillator. All oscillators incorporate a *transistor, thermionic valve, or similar device, plus a resonant circuit that determines the oscillation frequency.

oscilloscope, an instrument which can provide a visual display of the electrical *signals passing through a circuit on a *cathode-ray tube screen. Oscilloscopes are used in the design and testing of electronic circuits, and are especially useful for the display of high-frequency alternating-current signals, which conventional meters cannot follow. The signals are used to deflect the electron beam of the cathode-ray tube, and the beam traces a continuous wave-form on the screen. Typical oscilloscopes can monitor signal *frequencies in the range from 10 to 100 million Hz. They may be equipped with storage facilities to capture very high-speed or short-lived electronic events.

otorhinolaryngology, the study of the diseases of the ear, nose, and throat. It was not until the 19th century, when the British physician Joseph Toynbee (1815–66) analysed over 2,000 post-mortems, that causes of deafness were identified with any certainty. The need for surgery in otorhinolaryngology has been much reduced by the use of *antibiotics, but it is still needed to treat the many diseases that arise from infections and require the removal of tonsils and the drainage of sinuses. Examination and diagnosis have been greatly advanced by the introduction of small, hand-held *otoscopes, and electronic *audiometers for analysing hearing loss. Technological advances and the development of *microsurgery have made it possible to repair the fine structures of the middle ear and to produce *hearing aids and cochlear implants.

otoscope (auriscope), an instrument using reflected light to examine the eardrum and parts of the ear external to it. Invented in 1860 by the German physician Anton von Tröltsch, it is now employed routinely to diagnose infection of the middle ear chamber (interior to the eardrum) and certain chronic conditions leading to deafness.

Otto, Nikolaus August (1832–91), German engineer who developed the four-stroke *petrol engine. Despite a lack of technical training, he became interested in the *gas-engine developed by *Lenoir and built a small model in 1861. Three years later he went into partnership with the industrialist Eugen Langen to manufacture an improved version. He opened a bigger factory at Deutz, near Cologne, in 1869, with *Daimler as his chief assistant. In 1876, he began to sell his famous four-stroke engine, the 'silent Otto'. His patent was invalidated in 1886, but by this time he had sold more than 30,000 engines.

output device (computing), a *peripheral that communicates information from a computer system to users. The most common output devices are *printers and *visual display units: they can provide both text and *graphics data output. Graphics printers are commonly used, for example, in *computer-aided design and to present business statistics in pictorial form on paper. Output devices are controlled by interfaces that communicate with the host computer. *Interfaces to *electromechanical devices under computer control are often required in *robotics, and speech synthesizers present output in a way that simulates a human voice.

overshot wheel *water-wheel.

oxidation and reduction, ways of describing two important classes of chemical reaction. Literally, oxidation means the addition of *oxygen, and reactions in which materials combine with oxygen are oxidations. Combustion is an oxidation process, involving the rapid, high-temperature oxidation of fuels. This definition has been extended to include reactions where atoms in the reacting materials can be shown to lose electrons. Reduction is the opposite of oxidation, that is, reactions in which oxygen is removed. This definition has likewise been extended to include reactions where atoms in the reacting materials can be shown to gain electrons. Although oxidation and reduction are often described as separate processes, in fact in any oxidation–reduction reaction both processes occur simultaneously, since if one reactant is oxidized, another must be reduced to achieve this.

oxygen (symbol O, at. no. 8, r.a.m. 15.994), a colourless, tasteless, odourless gas and the most abundant and widely distributed element on Earth. Oxygen is needed to support combustion processes (see *oxidation and reduction), and it is an essential element in the chemical reactions by which most living organisms generate energy. It usually occurs as the oxygen molecule O_2, but it can also exist as O_3, or ozone. The *ozone layer in the stratosphere plays an important role in shielding the Earth from harmful ultraviolet radiation. Pure oxygen is obtained commercially by *fractional distillation of liquid air. Oxygen is used in steel-making, in conjunction with acetylene (*ethyne), for cutting and welding metals, and in hospitals and high-altitude flying to aid respiration. Liquid oxygen is one component of rocket fuel.

ozone depletion, the thinning, or in places complete loss, of the ozone layer, a zone in the upper atmosphere (between 10 and 50 km, 6–30 miles, above the earth). In this layer, the gas ozone (triatomic *oxygen, O_3) is formed by the action of ultraviolet radiation on the oxygen in the atmosphere. Ozone absorbs *electromagnetic radiation in the ultraviolet region, and thus prevents high levels of ultraviolet radiation, which can be harmful to plant and animal life, from reaching the earth's surface. Depletion of the ozone layer first became a matter for concern in 1985, when a hole was observed in the ozone layer over Antarctica by a UK research team led by Joseph Farman. The major cause was found to be *chloro-fluorocarbons (CFCs) in the upper atmosphere. In 1987 over fifty governments signed the Montreal Protocol, agreeing to halve CFC emissions by the year 2000. The countries of the European Community agreed in 1990 to phase out CFC production altogether by the year 2000, but scientists and environmentalists argue that a total ban is needed now to prevent irreparable damage.

P

pacemaker, a device used to correct an abnormal or irregular heart rate. Implantable pacemakers date from the 1960s. They comprise a pulse generator, inserted under the skin of the shoulder or abdomen, which delivers minute, regular electrical impulses via a connecting wire to an electrode touching the heart. These impulses stimulate the heart muscle to contract, thus regularizing the heartbeat. Technical advances have progressively decreased the size of pacemakers and increased their life to ten years or more. A *microprocessor senses when the pacemaker needs to operate, and can be adjusted by an external programmer (similar to a small computer), transmitting radio-frequency signals.

packaging technology. Packaging has three main functions: to protect goods from damage, to ease handling, and to promote sales. The nature of the goods determines which of these functions is the most important. Cardboard is the most widely used packaging material, because it is light, inexpensive, and easy to print on and store. Plastics made using *moulding and *extrusion techniques are used for a wide range of packaging, such as trays, bags, bottles, boxes, and transparent films. Plastic containers are particularly useful for liquids and perishable foodstuffs. Stiff, thin-film plastic is combined with a card backing in 'bubble packs' for small items like drawing-pins. Flexible plastic films are increasingly being combined with card in the production of small cartons for drinks. Other packing materials include wood (used in crates and packing cases), metal (tins), glass (bottles), and some textiles (for example, jute for sacks). The increasing use of plastics for packaged goods creates problems of disposal, as plastic does not degrade and is difficult to *recycle.

pack animal *draught and pack animals.

A patient with a heart **pacemaker** implanted beneath the skin of the chest.

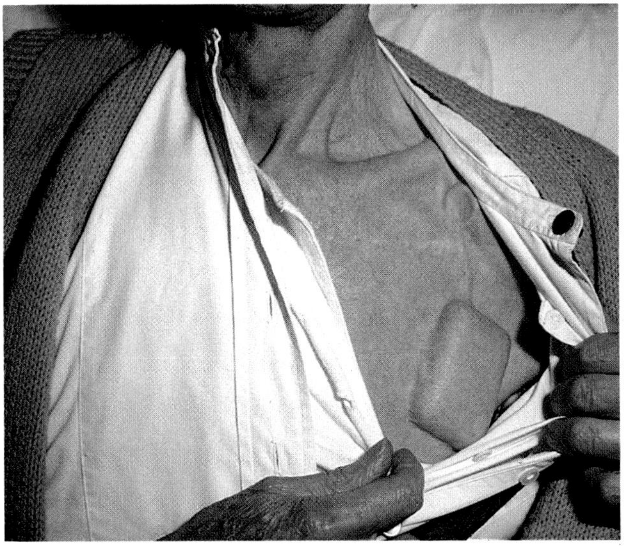

paddle-wheel, a wheel carrying a series of paddles or flat blades, used as a means of ship propulsion. Hand-operated paddle-wheels were first used in Chinese *warships from at least the 12th century AD, and possibly earlier. In Europe, paddle-wheels were first used in the Middle Ages on floating water-mills. Towards the end of the 18th century, paddle-wheels were adopted by the early *steamships. In the 1840s the screw *propeller largely replaced the paddle-wheel. Although paddle-wheels were unsuited to the open sea, they were efficient in calm water, with good manœuvrability both ahead and astern, and were more suited than the propeller to shallow, weed-infested waters. They were used in harbour tugs until well into the 20th century, and are still used on some river ferries and excursion steamers.

paging system, a system in which a *radio transmitter and a small personal receiver are used to alert an individual or deliver a short message. Each receiver is identified by a code, and responds only to messages bearing that receiver's code. In the simplest systems the receiver emits a 'beep' when the individual is being signalled; other receivers can transmit a simple written or spoken message. Transmitters may be low-power units covering a single building, or cover a whole city or country. Most operate in the VHF or UHF *wavebands.

paint, an opaque, fluid suspension that is spread in thin films over surfaces to decorate and protect them. It may be applied with a brush, a roller, a pad, or by spraying. Paint consists of a liquid (the vehicle) in which a coloured *pigment is suspended. When applied to a surface, the vehicle dries to form a tough film that binds the pigment. Paint may be applied to a variety of surfaces, including wood, metal, stone, paper, cloth, and leather. Paints have been used for representational and decorative purposes for thousands of years, but it was not until the 18th century that buildings were painted for protection. This came about through the increased availability of both vehicles and pigments. Such materials were sold separately until the 19th century, when ready-mixed paints became available. Early paints generally consisted of linseed oil (see *drying oil) as the vehicle, plus a metal oxide powder as the pigment. Modern paints are more complex. The vehicles contain synthetic resins, of which a variety are now available. By manipulating the molecular structure of the resin the manufacturers can control the viscosity (and hence ease of brushing) of a vehicle, the toughness, hardness, and flexibility of the coating, and its adherence properties. The development of water-soluble vehicles gave rise to *emulsion paints. Modern paints also contain extenders—salts such as calcium and barium sulphate, which have little covering power but are used to supplement expensive pigments and to improve the brushability of the paint and the mechanical strength of the dried film. Large quantities of extenders are used in architectural and maintenance finishes, particularly on interior walls, where protection is not as critical as uniform coverage. New solvent-free paints currently under development contain no hydrocarbons, which cause *air pollution. Instead a free-flowing binder such as Vernonia oil is used.

Palais de la Découverte, a French national museum founded in Paris in 1937 to popularize science. Its departments cover chemistry, physics, biology, medicine, earth sciences, and the history of science; it also has a planetarium. It is one of the world's leading museums, comparable with the *Science Museum and the *Smithsonian Institution.

palladium (symbol Pd, at. no. 46, r.a.m. 106.42), a ductile and malleable white *platinum metal. The element occurs in association with other platinum metals. Its main use is as an industrial *catalyst, particularly in reactions involving hydrogen. It is also used in some electrical components.

Panama Canal, the ship *canal joining the Atlantic and Pacific oceans across the isthmus of Panama. Various canals had been proposed since the 1550s, and one was begun by *Lesseps in 1882, but abandoned through bankruptcy. The present canal was built by the US government between 1906 and 1914. It is 64 km (40 miles) long and can carry ships of up to 80,000 tonnes.

panning *ore, extraction and processing.

paper, a material manufactured in thin sheets from wood-pulp, rags, or other fibrous substances. *Paper manufacture now largely uses cellulose fibre obtained from the cell walls of plants, mainly softwood trees. Taking its name from *papyrus, true paper was invented by the Chinese in about AD 105. Paper was initially imported into Europe from the Middle East, but in the mid-13th century paper-making reached Spain and Italy and thence spread to the rest of Europe. The major use of paper is as a medium for writing, drawing or printing. It is also widely used for packaging, especially as *cardboard, and some *nonwoven fabrics are essentially paper.

Photographic paper is paper coated with an emulsion of silver salts which, when correctly exposed to light and chemically processed, produces a photographic image. Most modern photographic paper has a coating of plastic resin on both sides to prevent chemicals from being absorbed by the paper and to speed up the processing, washing, and drying. The silver halide emulsion is covered by a gelatine layer, which protects the emulsion from damage during handling. The chemical constituency of the emulsion can be varied to produce paper of different 'grades'. The term grade refers to the degree of contrast a paper will give and is a crucial factor in controlling the appearance of the final photograph.

paper manufacture, the conversion of suitable fibres into rolls and sheets of *paper. Early European paper was hand-made by dipping a tray with a mesh base into a vat of pulped rag fibres and shaking it sideways to intermingle the fibres and drain away the water. The wet sheets were then pressed on to woollen felt and hung up to dry. Such paper was thick and rough; subsequently, mechanical milling shortened the fibre length to give thinner, smoother products, which were further improved by *sizing and glazing. The nature and quality of a paper depends greatly on the length of the fibres in it, and on additives in the pulp. In 1673, a variable beating machine was developed in The Netherlands that greatly enhanced the control of pulp manufacture. The *Fourdrinier machine (see figure) for continuous paper manufacture was first developed in 1799 in

Paper manufacture

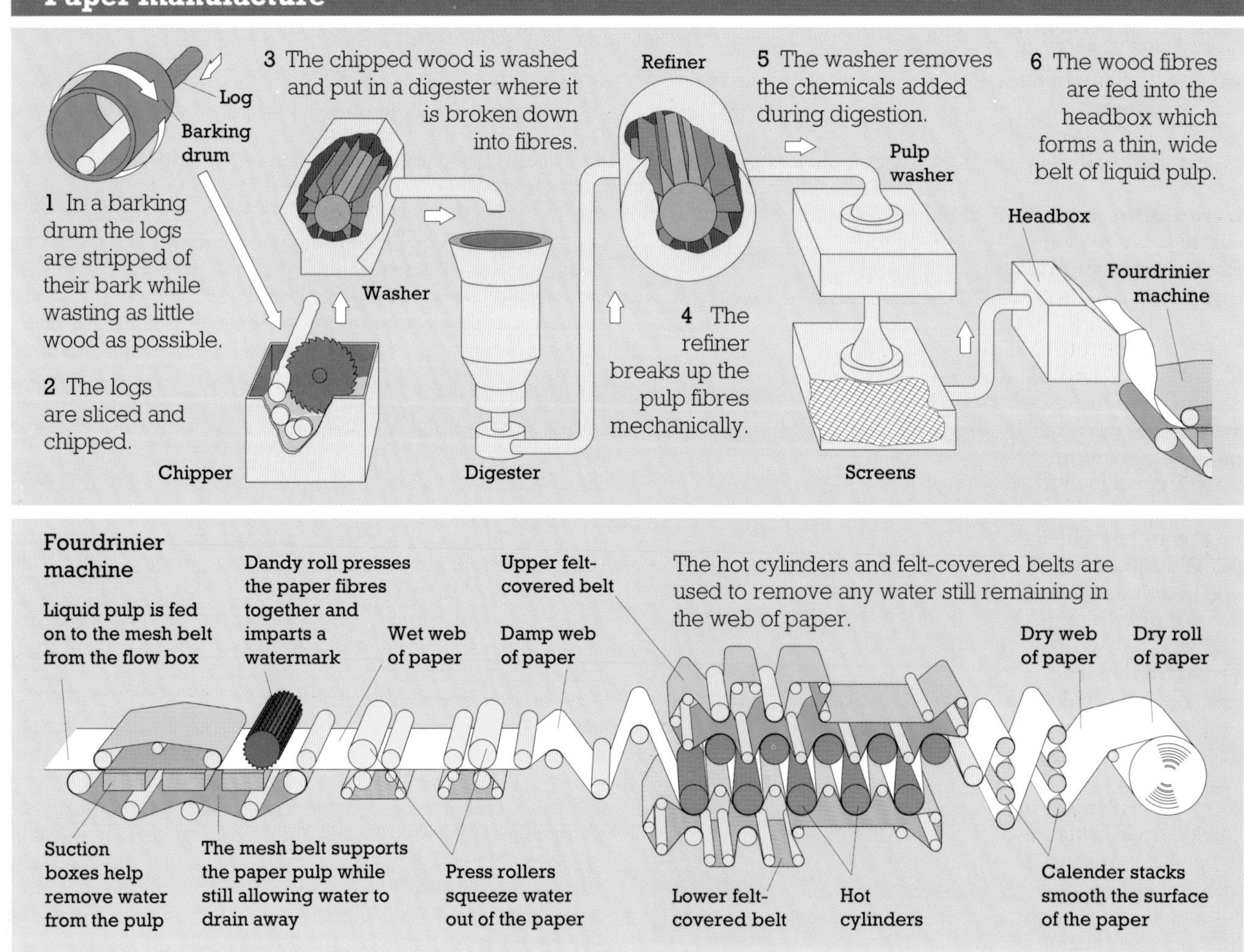
Log
Barking drum
1 In a barking drum the logs are stripped of their bark while wasting as little wood as possible.
2 The logs are sliced and chipped.
Chipper
3 The chipped wood is washed and put in a digester where it is broken down into fibres.
Washer
Digester
Refiner
4 The refiner breaks up the pulp fibres mechanically.
5 The washer removes the chemicals added during digestion.
Pulp washer
Screens
6 The wood fibres are fed into the headbox which forms a thin, wide belt of liquid pulp.
Headbox
Fourdrinier machine
Fourdrinier machine
Liquid pulp is fed on to the mesh belt from the flow box
Dandy roll presses the paper fibres together and imparts a watermark
Wet web of paper
Upper felt-covered belt
Damp web of paper
The hot cylinders and felt-covered belts are used to remove any water still remaining in the web of paper.
Dry web of paper
Dry roll of paper
Suction boxes help remove water from the pulp
The mesh belt supports the paper pulp while still allowing water to drain away
Press rollers squeeze water out of the paper
Lower felt-covered belt
Hot cylinders
Calender stacks smooth the surface of the paper

France. Wood-pulp for making paper varies in its manufacture according to how the fibre is extracted, but a general method involves cooking woodchips with chemicals in a digester, then passing the pulp through a disc refiner, which mechanically separates the fibres. The resulting pulp is washed (and sometimes bleached), screened for impurities, and then beaten (refined) again with additives to give the paper the required properties. The pulp is then about 98 per cent water, yet it forms a continuous web of paper on the wire of the paper-making machine. The paper web is dried and then calendered, a process in which it passes between a series of heated, polished metal rollers, which impart a smooth finish to the paper.

papyrus, a writing material prepared in ancient Egypt from the pithy stem of the aquatic plant *Cyperus papyrus*, from which paper takes its name. Fresh stalks of the grass gathered from the River Nile were teased out with a needle to give strands of damp fibre. These strands were laid out in two crossed layers on a moistened board and compacted in a press, their juice and the added moisture bonding them together. After drying, the sheets so formed would accept writing in ink. Sheets could be joined by overlapping and meshing the ends together to form continuous scrolls.

Paracelsus (Philippus Aureolus Theophrastus Bombast von Hohenheim) (1493–1541), Swiss-born German founder of medicinal chemistry. He learnt chemistry in the workshop of the alchemist Sigismund Fugger in Austria, and gained experience of medicine during extensive travel, becoming City Physician at the University of Basel, Switzerland, in 1527. He pioneered the use of pure chemicals, rather than indeterminate mixtures, in the treatment of disease, devised a treatment for syphilis, and anticipated the modern practice of homeopathy.

paracetamol *analgesic.

parachute, a rectangular or umbrella-shaped apparatus that allows a person or load attached to it to descend slowly from a height, especially from a *balloon or *aeroplane. The first human parachute descent was made in 1797, when Jacques Garnerin parachuted from a balloon over Paris. Folding parachutes were first used in America in 1880, and towards the end of World War I aviators first used parachutes to escape from their aeroplanes. Early parachutes were made of canvas, and later silk. Modern parachutes comprise many separate panels of nylon, so that tears are confined to a small area. Until recently parachutes were umbrella-shaped, but parafoils (air-filled *aerofoils) are now common. In addition to their use as safety devices, parachutes are used for sport, for aerial drops of supplies and equipment, and as braking devices (drogues) for landing aircraft or other vehicles.

paraffin (US, kerosene), a mixture of liquid hydrocarbons, now obtained chiefly from petroleum, but in the past also obtained from coal, shale, and wood. In the early years of *petroleum refining during the latter half of the 19th century, paraffin represented the most important petroleum fraction, because of its use in lamps. With the introduction of electric lighting at the end of the 19th century, demand dropped sharply and its use was confined largely to paraffin heaters. However, as the main constituent of *aviation fuel for jet engines, it has shown a marked resurgence during the latter half of the 20th century.

A **parachute** display team 'stack', in which open parachutes are linked one above the other. This stack of twenty-four is the world record, set in 1988.

paraffin wax, a mixture of high-molecular-weight *hydrocarbons (straight-chain alkanes) obtained from *petroleum refining. About 90 per cent of the wax used commercially is recovered from petroleum. It is used to make polishes, wax crayons, and candle wax (a mixture of paraffin wax with alcohols and acids); in the moulding of sculptured bronzes; and for waterproofing wood and paper products.

parallel connection *circuits, electrical and electronic.

parallel processing, an advanced form of computing in which many operations happen simultaneously, thus speeding up programs. There is a physical limit to the speed of any computing circuit, and the only way to extend performance beyond this limit is to use parallel processing. *Supercomputers use parallel arithmetic units for fast numerical computations. New forms of computers use multiple *microprocessors (currently tens, or hundreds of them) all working on the same task. Other forms use tens of thousands of simple 1-*bit processors to achieve the same end, and *neural networks are also inherently parallel. With multiple processors, the task can still be completed even with the failure of some computers (fault-tolerant computing). Parallel processing is widely used in *artificial intelligence applications. (See also *serial processing, *transputer.)

Charles **Parsons**' ship *Turbinia* at speed, 1894. *Turbinia* was the first ship to be powered by steam-turbines.

paraquat *herbicide.

parchment, an animal skin, especially that of a goat, sheep, or calf, prepared so as to take writing or painting; it is also known as vellum. Rough skins were used up to the 2nd century BC when, at Pergamum (now Bergama in Turkey), smooth skins were prepared by repeated scrapings, first with a blunt iron tool and then with a sharpened scraper. Today, parchment is a general term for smooth, thick, high-grade paper made to resemble parchment.

Parsons, Sir Charles Algernon (1854–1931), Irish engineer, inventor of the compound *steam-turbine. He entered the engineering industry in 1877, later joining a firm that aimed to exploit the *incandescent lamp. He realized that this would be possible only if the electricity supply industry expanded rapidly, and that expansion would be greatly facilitated by the availability of a high-speed *steam-engine to drive electrical *generators. This led him to explore the possibilities of a steam-turbine. Parsons patented and built his first turbine in 1884, a 7.5-kW (10-horsepower) engine working at 18,000 r.p.m. He later improved this by adding a condenser to utilize low-pressure steam, which was formerly wasted, and by using superheated steam. Parsons designed a high-speed, direct-current *generator to work with the turbine, and in 1900 he built two 1,000-kW turbo-alternators for a power-station at Elberfeld in Germany. He also developed the use of turbines for marine propulsion, in his famous ship the *Turbinia*.

particle accelerator, a machine used in nuclear physics research to accelerate charged, subatomic particles such as protons and electrons (see *atoms and molecules). These are used to bombard and fragment atomic nuclei, providing information about the structure of matter. The higher the energy of bombardment, the more effective the fragmentation. They are also used commercially to generate high-energy X-rays and gamma rays for industrial and medical radiography, and for *radiotherapy. Accelerator energies are typically measured in millions of electron-volts (MeV). The earliest successful experiments using artificially accelerated particles were made in 1932 by the British physicists J. D. Cockcroft and E. T. S. Walton. To obtain the high accelerating voltages needed, they designed a voltage multiplier; other accelerators of that time used *van der Graaff generators. In linear accelerators, electrons are accelerated down a long pipe by a succession of electrodes. However, for higher energies, infeasibly long accelerators would be required. To overcome this problem, *Lawrence in 1930 devised the cyclotron, which used a special magnetic field combined with a rapidly oscillating voltage to accelerate the particles along a spiral path inside a toroidal chamber. Because the particles are accelerated many times in a cyclotron, energies of around 40 MeV can be achieved. Another development was the betatron, an electron accelerator that used an alternating magnetic field. After World War II the synchrotron was developed: this could accelerate electrons and protons to energies of several thousand MeV. A further advance in 1956 was the development of storage rings, in which high-energy particles of opposite charge are collided to produce the highest reaction energies currently obtainable.

particle detector (position-sensitive detector), any scientific instrument used to detect subatomic particles (see *atoms and molecules). The passage of subatomic particles through a gas causes localized heating and ionization of the gas atoms. It is these two properties which can be tracked by particle detectors. In traditional particle detectors, first used extensively in the 1920s, the tiny signals from a particle are amplified into a visible track, from which measurements can be made. The now outdated cloud chamber contains a super-saturated vapour, in which subatomic particles leave a trail of droplets. A bubble chamber uses a superheated liquid as the detection medium, which is unstable enough to boil along the path made by a subatomic particle, leaving a trail of bubbles. A spark chamber consists of a series of closely spaced, parallel metal plates, each at a high voltage. Subatomic particles ionize air molecules behind them, causing a visible spark to pass briefly between the plates. The more modern multi-wire chamber produces electrical sig-

Aerial photograph of the super proton accelerator (SPS) and the large electron–proton storage ring (LEP), two **particle accelerators** operated by the European Laboratory for Particle Physics (CERN).

nals that can be recorded directly by a computer. It consists of an array of fine, closely spaced wires, each at a high positive potential, in a chamber filled with argon gas. Ionization of the argon by the passage of a particle releases a few electrons, which are attracted towards the positively charged sense-wires. As the electrons draw close to a sense-wire, they gain energy, and cause further ionization of the argon gas. This creates an avalanche effect in which many electrons are released, enough to cause a detectable electrical signal at the sense-wire. The pattern of signals is recorded by a computer, which can reconstruct the paths of the particles. The most popular particle detector today is the drift chamber, a development of the multi-wire chamber that has fewer wires, and consequently less readout electronics. Multi-wire chambers can also be made sensitive to X-rays and to gamma rays if different gases are used in the chamber. This has led to the development of multi-wire chambers as detectors in *positron emission tomography.

PASCAL *computer language.

Pascal, Blaise (1623–62), French mathematician, scientist, and theologian. He was a precocious student; at 16, he wrote a treatise on conic sections so brilliant that the French mathematician René Descartes doubted his authorship. To assist his father, an exchequer official, in 1642 he constructed a mechanical calculator, the first true calculating machine to be built. He also conducted and described many experiments in hydrostatics and on the nature of a vacuum, and invented the hydraulic press.

Pasteur, Louis (1822–95), French bacteriologist. While Professor of Chemistry at Lille University, he became interested in the local beet-sugar industry (see *sugar processing) and problems arising from unwanted *fermentations. These he rightly ascribed to infection by micro-organisms present in the air, finally demolishing the old belief in spontaneous generation. His research suggested that micro-organisms might be the cause of many diseases, and greatly influenced *Lister in his work on *antisepsis. In 1865 Pasteur identified and devised a preventive for *pébrine* (silkworm disease), which was afflicting the French silk industry. In 1870 he devised the *pasteurization process for destroying *bacteria in milk and developed vaccines (see *immunization) against chicken cholera and anthrax (1881). He also developed immunization against rabies (1885), by inoculation with attenuated virus. Acknowledged as France's greatest scientist, in 1888 he became director of the Institut Pasteur, specially created for him in Paris.

pasteurization, a method of *food preservation, particularly for *dairy products, in which the product is heated to and maintained at a certain temperature (for example 72 °C for milk) for a specific time, before being quickly cooled. The process (named after *Pasteur) reduces the bacterial content and activity within a product without unduly affecting its taste or appearance. In wine treated this way the yeast responsible for souring will be destroyed, but not the yeast necessary for *fermentation. Pasteurization of milk destroys any tuberculosis bacteria present and improves the milk's storage life, but some bacteria remain. The vitamin C content of milk is slightly reduced by pasteurization.

patent, a government authority to an individual or organization conferring, in particular, the sole right to make or sell an invention for a set period of time, commonly 14 years in the UK. Patents were first granted in Italy in the 14th century and thence spread to Britain and other European countries. In Elizabethan Britain they were granted in respect of existing processes introduced from abroad, provided that it was in the national interest. Not until the 18th century did the concept of 'intellectual property' and originality begin to emerge. The foundation of the British Patent Office, and the regulation of patents by statute, dates from 1852.

pattern recognition, a branch of *artificial intelligence concerned with devising ways in which computer systems may identify, interpret, and classify scenes and objects presented to them. Although pattern recognition is usually concerned with visual information processed using *image processing techniques, it can also be used to interpret other complex information. Pattern recognition is becoming increasingly important in *robotics, where it is used, for example, to identify the component parts of a unit in various orientations when they are being assembled by a robot system. Pattern recognition is usually achieved by comparing the visual images with so-called template forms previously stored in memory; these techniques are used in, for example, *optical character recognition machines that can read typewritten pages. Another method is to classify the objects depicted in the image by statistically analysing simple shapes or gross dimensions.

peat, vegetable matter decomposed in water and partly carbonized, used when dried as a domestic fuel, for power generation, or in horticulture. Peat is a precursor of lignite and the higher-ranking *coals, being formed less than 1 million years ago.

pedometer, a small instrument for measuring the distance travelled by a pedestrian. It works by advancing the recording needle a fixed amount at the impact of each footfall. It must be set according to the stride of the user, but its accuracy is low as a person's stride length can vary greatly.

PEEK (polyether etherketone) *composite.

Pelton wheel *water-wheel.

pen, a drawing or writing implement for use with a liquid *ink, originally consisting of a shaft with a sharpened quill or, usually, metal nib. The ancient Egyptians made the earliest pens, sharpened reeds for writing with ink on papyrus. In Europe, the *penna* or quill pen, made from large bird feathers, was developed in the 5th century. The thick end of the feather was cut into a V-shape and slit upwards from the tip for flexibility, a design that remains essentially the same in modern gold and steel nibs. Improvements were made to quill pens, but in the early 19th century flexible steel nibs were developed, which revolutionized writing. John Mitchell, of Birmingham, UK, produced the first machine-made steel nibs in 1828. Fountain pens with ink reservoirs were in use before the end of the quill pen era, but the first practical, self-filling fountain pen (produced by Lewis Waterman in the USA) was not made until 1884. Ball-point pens, with a rolling ball in place of a nib, were first patented by the Hungarian Lazlo Biro in 1938. Since the 1960s two other types of pen have come into use: the rollerball (an adaptation of the ball-point), and the fibre-tipped pen.

pendulum, a weight suspended from a fixed point and able to swing freely under the influence of gravity. In about

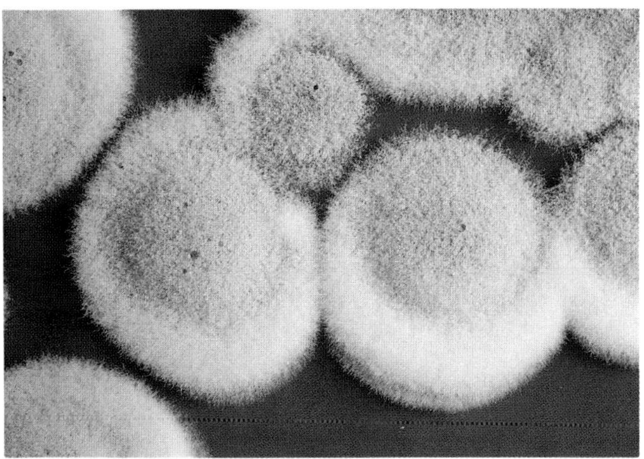

A culture of the mould *Penicillium notatum*, from which the antibiotic **penicillin** is produced. Penicillin was the first antibiotic to be used therapeutically, during World War II.

1602, *Galileo discovered that, for small amplitudes, the time of swing of a pendulum is dependent only on its length and not on its amplitude. He realized that this had great possibilities for the measurement of time, and pendulums began to be used for astronomical observations. In 1657, Christiaan Huygens patented an invention using a pendulum to regulate the mechanism of a *clock. Pendulum clocks remained the most accurate timekeeping devices until the introduction of the quartz clock in 1929.

penicillin, any of various *antibiotics produced naturally by moulds of the genus *Penicillium*, or synthetically, and able to prevent the growth of certain disease-causing bacteria. In 1928 *Fleming isolated the first penicillin, from the mould *Penicillium notatum*. In 1939 *Florey and *Chain at Oxford, UK, began an investigation of penicillin as part of a wider study of antibiotic action. They showed that it had unique properties: minimal toxicity to animal tissues and an antibacterial activity far greater than that of other drugs, for example the *sulphonamides, then in use. Penicillin first became available in 1941, and it was used to treat military casualties during World War II. Penicillins are still widely used in certain situations, for example, in the treatment of some forms of meningitis. However, not all bacteria are sensitive to the drug, and even those that are may develop permanent resistance, though this has been countered to some extent by the use of chemically altered varieties such as methicillin. Some patients suffer side-effects from penicillin, which are occasionally severe, and this prompted the development of new antibiotics such as the cephalosporins.

penstock, originally a sluice controlling the flow of water from a pond or 'pen' to the *water-wheel of a mill. Later the term came to mean the channel leading to the sluice, and now commonly refers to the pipe carrying water to the turbines in a *hydroelectric power-station.

perfume, a fragrant liquid for giving a pleasant smell, especially to the body. Perfumes have been known and used for thousands of years. Until recently, they comprised only natural materials, but advances in natural product chemistry have made it possible to synthesize the active ingredients. Perfumes are usually *alcoholic solutions of substances that have an attractive smell. On application, body heat causes the alcohol to evaporate quickly, leaving the fragrant substances on the skin to evaporate gradually over several hours. A fine perfume may contain more than a hundred ingredients. Fragrant *essential oils are important components of most perfumes. Certain fragrant animal secretions, now often made synthetically, can be used to prevent the more volatile ingredients of a perfume from evaporating too rapidly. Examples are ambergris and *spermaceti from the sperm whale, civet from the civet cat, and musk from the musk deer. Perfumes used to scent *cosmetics are specially formulated so that they do not become unstable in the product or cause it to discolour.

peripheral (computing), a device that is connected to a computer system but is not part of the *central processing unit or associated *memory. Common peripherals include *output devices such as *printers and plotter units, disk drives, *input devices such as keyboards attached to *visual display units, and *modems. Peripherals usually require hardware and software *interfaces to function under control of the computer's *operating system. The interface circuits ensure that information is transferred from the central processing unit in the correct way, and that input data is correctly received.

periscope, an optical instrument that deflects light, allowing the user to see over obstacles, round corners, or into inaccessible places. Their main use is in tanks and submarines. The simplest periscope uses two parallel mirrors or prisms to reflect light through two right angles, displacing the beam by the distance separating the reflectors. Lenses arranged as a telescope can be included to magnify the scene. Submarine periscopes obtain a wide field of view using a series of lenses inside a tube of rectangular section, with telescope arrangements at the top and bottom.

Perkin, Sir William Henry (1838–1907), British inventor of the first synthetic dye, mauveine. While a student of the great German chemist A. W. von Hoffmann at the Royal College of Chemistry, London, he attempted, unsuccessfully, to make quinine artificially. In the course of these experiments he obtained an intensely mauve solution which proved to be an excellent *dye. In 1856 he began to manufacture the dye, mauveine, at Greenford near London. In 1868 the German chemists Carl Graebe and Carl Liebermann synthesized alizarin, the active component of madder. Perkin developed a cheaper process, and became licensed to make the dye in the UK.

permalloy *alloy.

perpetual motion, the motion of a hypothetical machine which, once set in motion, would run for ever unless subject to an external force or to wear. Such a machine is contrary to the basic laws of thermodynamics. This, however, has not deterred ingenious inventors, and in the 19th century the US Patent Office refused patents for perpetual motion machines unless accompanied by models, some of which are now exhibited in the *Smithsonian Institution. The British Patent Office banned such patents in 1949.

Perronet, Jean-Rodolphe (1708–94), French civil engineer. After training as a military engineer, he became director in 1747 of the newly established École des Ponts et Chaussées, the national training centre for engineers and surveyors. In 1763 he also became director of the Corps National Interministériel des Ponts et Chaussées, with responsibility for France's roads and bridges. He designed eleven major bridges, including the Neuilly and Concorde bridges over the Seine. They were notable for the flatness of their arches and the thinness of their piers, establishing a new architectural style.

personal computer *microcomputer.

Perspex *polymethyl methacrylate.

pesticide, a natural or synthetic *agrochemical used to kill organisms that are harmful to cultivated plants or to animals. *Herbicides are used to kill weeds, *insecticides act against insect pests, and *fungicides are anti-fungal agents. Pesticides are designed as far as possible to be effective against a specific pest in a particular context, to avoid unwanted toxic effects in other organisms. However, many pesticides are toxic to humans in large doses, or after long-term exposure. Until recently it was the practice to spray with pesticides only when a specific pest was evident. However, with modern chemicals it is possible to provide protection before symptoms are apparent: seeds may be coated with an anti-fungal agent, the crop itself may be sprayed against fungal threat, or fields may be sprayed to kill off weeds that would compete with a crop. New pesticides are always needed, because resistant pest strains often develop after a particular agent has been used for a number of years. In some countries, certain pesticides have been banned because of their toxic effects or their persistence in the food chain. Methods of *biological pest control are also being developed, either to reduce or to replace pesticide use.

pestle and mortar, an apparatus for breaking up by hand solid lumps of material and reducing them to fine powder. The mortar, bowl-shaped and thick-walled, holds the material; it is made from porcelain, glass, or agate. The pestle, made from similar materials, is club shaped, sometimes with a wooden handle, and is pounded against the material in the mortar.

PET (polyethene terephthalate) *plastic.

Petri dish, a shallow, circular glass or clear plastic dish about 10 cm (4 inches) across, with a loose-fitting lid, named after J. Petri (1852–1921). A standard piece of laboratory equipment, it is easily sterilized and is used mainly in pharmaceutical testing, to contain bacteria or fungi growing on a nutrient medium.

petrochemical, any of the enormous range of chemicals produced from petroleum by further processing after *petroleum refining or extraction from *natural gas. Fuels, lubricating and specialist oils, tars, and natural gas go direct from a refinery for end use. Everything else from a refinery, and the products made from these raw materials (see table), is a petrochemical. The first petrochemical was probably *carbon-black, made from natural gas in the 1850s. For most of the next hundred years, *coal-tar was the main raw material for making organic chemicals and plastics. Convenience and economy started a change to petrochemicals in the 1920s, and since World War II coal has been almost entirely supplanted by petroleum products. For example, more than 80 per cent of synthetic fibres and fabrics come from petroleum. Natural gas is still the main source of carbon-black, and *methane from natural gas is used to make *methanol and methyl chloride (chiefly used in the manufacture of *silicone).

Alkenes (see *organic chemicals table) are a product of *cracking processes, some of which are run specifically to produce alkenes for the chemical industry. *Ethene is the main product of thermal cracking, and propylene and butenes are co-products of thermal cracking and catalytic cracking. Alkenes, and particularly ethene, are important source materials in the petrochemical industry. They are used in making chemical products such as detergents, ethylene glycol (see *antifreeze), plastics such as polythene and polystyrene, paints, synthetic fibres, synthetic rubber, and *lead tetraethyl.

Aromatic compounds (chemicals containing one or more

Some important petrochemicals

Major petrochemical intermediate	Source	Downstream products
Ethene	Cracking of ethane, propane, naphtha, or gas oil	Polythene, vinyl chloride, ethylene oxide and ethylene glycol, styrene, vinyl acetate, acetaldehyde, ethanol
Propene	Co-product in manufacture of ethene by cracking of propane, naphtha, or gas oil. Co-product in manufacture of petrol by catalytic cracking	Polypropylene, isopropyl alcohol and acetone, propylene oxide, butyl alcohols, acrylonitrile, acrylic acid, and acrylates
Butenes	As for propene	Butan-2-ol, methyl ethyl ketone, butyl rubber, methyl *t*-butyl ether
Butadiene	Co-product in manufacture of ethene by cracking of naphtha or gas oil. Dehydrogenation of butenes and butanes	Synthetic rubbers, nylon intermediates
Benzene	Catalytic reforming of naphtha. Co-product in manufacture of ethene by cracking of naphtha or gas oil	Styrene, cyclohexane and nylon intermediates, phenol, aniline, maleic anhydride, alkylbenzenesulphonate detergents
Toluene	As for benzene	Tolylene di-isocyanate (for polyurethanes), benzoic acid, trinitrotoluene (TNT)
o-Xylene	As for benzene	Phthalic anhydride (used to make plasticizers and insect repellants)
p-Xylene	As for benzene	Terephthalic acid, dimethyl terephthalate (used in manufacture of polyesters and alkyd resins)
Methanol	Synthesis from carbon monoxide–hydrogen mixture produced by steam-reforming of methane or naphtha	Formaldehyde, acetic acid, chloromethanes, methylamines, methyl *t*-butyl ether
Ammonia	Synthesis from nitrogen (from air) and hydrogen produced by steam-reforming of methane or naphtha	Fertilizers, nitric acid, organic chemicals

*benzene rings) are extracted from some light petroleum refining fractions or formed from heavier fractions by catalytic *reforming. The most important feedstocks are benzene, toluene, and xylenes. Benzene is particularly significant in making dyestuffs, detergents, plastics, synthetic rubber, and synthetic fibres such as nylon. Toluene is important in making TNT, and xylenes are used in making plastics, surface coatings, and synthetic fabrics. More complex synthesis from aromatics produces thousands of specialist chemicals such as agricultural chemicals, pharmaceuticals, and chemicals used in industrial processes. Some inorganic chemicals are also produced from petroleum, in particular *ammonia, which is synthesized from hydrogen produced by steam reforming. *Sulphur is removed from many petroleum products, providing a source of elemental sulphur and sulphuric acid.

petrol (US, gasoline), a volatile oil which readily produces an explosive mixture with air, the fuel used in most *internal-combustion engines. Until about the end of the 19th century, petrol was regarded as a dangerous waste product of the process of producing paraffin from oil. With the development of petrol vehicles, petrol became important, and there have been continual changes in *petroleum refining to increase the proportion of crude petroleum which can be converted to high-grade petrol. Petrol is graded according to its anti-knock quality—its evenness of burning inside an engine (see *knock). Anti-knock quality is indicated by petrol's *octane number. Most petrol is a blend of about twenty-five *hydrocarbons, and the blend is constantly checked and varied in manufacture to maintain the correct octane number. Adding *lead tetraethyl improves the octane number, but causes lead pollution from car exhausts. Its use is, therefore, being increasingly discouraged. Unleaded petrol does not have that problem, but, like all petrol, still causes emissions of toxins such as carbon monoxide and hydrocarbons. *Catalytic converters and other devices have been used to reduce such emissions.

petrol engine, an *internal-combustion engine fuelled by petrol in which combustion is initiated by a spark-plug (spark *ignition). Petrol engines have a wide variety of applications, but the most important is as the power unit for the *motor car (see figure). At the centre of the engine are a number of cylinders, each containing a piston. There may be from two to twelve cylinders in a car engine, but most commonly there are four. The motion of the piston is achieved by the four-stroke cycle shown. One or two inlet valves on the cylinder head admit the fuel–air mixture from the *carburettor, while an exhaust valve or valves releases the exhaust gases after combustion. The action of these valves is controlled by the camshaft, which is driven by a belt, chain, or gears from the *crankshaft at half the crankshaft speed. Most modern engines use overhead valves (OHV) and many have one or two overhead camshafts (OHC). Each cylinder also has a spark-plug for ignition of the fuel–air mixture. Because useful work is done on only the third stroke of the four-stroke cycle, a *flywheel is needed on the crankshaft to maintain rotation and smooth out speed fluctuations. In a four-cylinder engine, the power strokes of the pistons are staggered so that on each stroke one of the cylinders is supplying power to the crankshaft. Besides converting the reciprocating motion of the pistons into rotary motion and driving the car's wheels via the transmission system, the crankshaft provides power for other systems. The oil pump is driven from the crankshaft via the camshaft, and provides constant lubrication of the engine's moving parts. The fan, part of the engine's *cooling system, is sometimes powered from the crankshaft. Power for the alternator, which generates electricity for the *ignition, for charging the battery, and for other electrical systems, is supplied via the camshaft.

Some smaller engines, for example marine outboard and small *motor-cycle engines, use a simpler two-stroke cycle. Instead of valves, the two-stroke engine uses inlet and exhaust ports in the sides of the cylinder, which are covered and uncovered at appropriate points in the engine cycle. Two-stroke engines have advantages of lightness and

Petrol engine

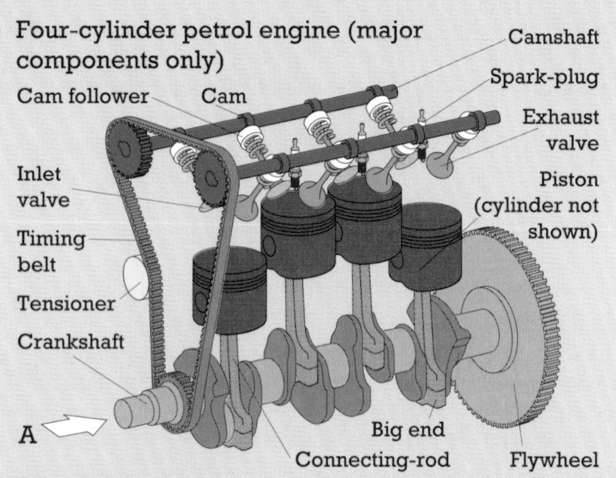

Four-stroke cycle

The sequence of diagrams below shows the actions of one cylinder from intake of fuel to expulsion of the exhaust gases. It is viewed from direction (A) in the above diagram.

1. Induction

The inlet valve opens. As the piston moves down, a petrol–air mixture is drawn into the cylinder.

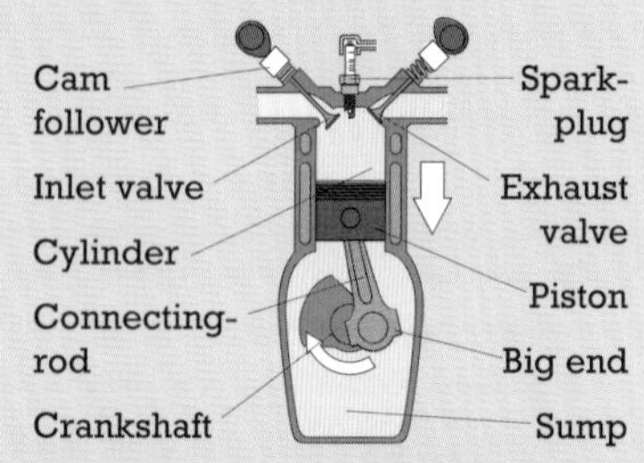

2. Compression **3. Power** **4. Exhaust**

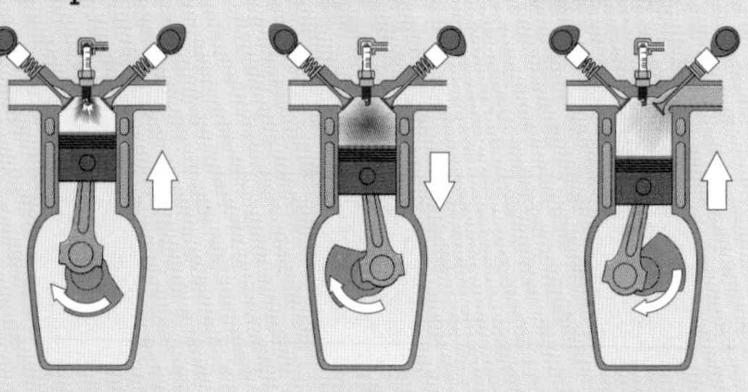

2 The inlet valve closes. The rising piston compresses the fuel–air mixture.

3 As the piston reaches its highest point, the spark-plug ignites the fuel. The burning mixture expands, pushing the piston down.

4 Towards the end of the downstroke the exhaust valve opens. When the piston rises again the waste gases are expelled. The valve then closes.

smoothness, but they are less *efficient, and the exhaust is more polluted. Under optimum conditions, modern four-stroke engines can achieve thermal efficiencies of around 30 per cent, but in town driving, the average efficiency is below 10 per cent, while overall efficiency is around 18 per cent. A good *diesel engine can reach a peak efficiency of 40 per cent, and under light loading is more efficient than a petrol engine. (See also *Wankel engine.)

petroleum, a complex mixture, consisting mainly of *hydrocarbon gases and oils, formed in the upper strata of the earth by the fossilization of vegetable matter over a period of millions of years. It is generally found trapped between layers of impervious rock, usually in the spaces in a layer of porous rock or sand. About 5,000 years ago *bitumen, a form of petroleum occurring at the earth's surface, was being collected at Hit in the Euphrates Valley, Iraq. Its uses included cementing bricks, lining water courses, building roads, and sealing joints between timbers of boats. In China in about 200 BC, petroleum was encountered in digging salt wells; within a few hundred years the petroleum was being used, and piped *natural gas found application both for lighting and as a fuel. In the middle of the 19th century, the need for lighting fuel (mainly paraffin, but natural gas in some areas) led to the development of the petroleum industry. Since about 1900 the growth of motor transport has caused the industry to grow very rapidly. Today, petroleum provides a large proportion of the world's energy for transport, and is the leading source of energy for all other purposes. In the last fifty years, petroleum has also become the source of thousands of *petrochemicals.

Some petroleum occurs at the earth's surface as *shale oil in tar lakes or sands, which can be exploited directly, as in the Athabasca tar sands in Canada. But most is recovered from traps deep underground (see *petroleum, exploration and recovery). Petroleum occurs in all continents, but the consistency and content produced by oil wells vary considerably. Almost all crude oils are liquid, but in some oilfields the oil is so viscous that considerable heat and pressure are needed to make it flow to the surface. Some natural gas is dissolved in the oil; generally, the deeper the oil trap, the higher the proportion of dissolved gas. The gas may form bubbles as the pressure drops in the petroleum moving upwards. From deep wells, the volume of gas can be more than 90 per cent of the fluid reaching the surface. By weight, between 94 and 98 per cent of petroleum is either carbon or hydrogen. Lighter grades contain more aromatic compounds (compounds containing one or more *benzene rings) and fewer impurities. *Petroleum refining of such grades is less costly, and can produce a higher proportion of petrol. Heavier grades of crude petroleum may contain as much as 5 per cent sulphur, which must be removed in refining as it causes corrosion and pollution problems if present in burning fuels. Sodium chloride occurs in all crudes, and if its proportion approaches 1 per cent, it must be removed. The nature of the crude, and market conditions, determine the balance of processes used in petroleum refining.

Petroleum's wide occurrence in fluid form makes it economical to extract, process, and use. But world reserves are running out, and there are few places left for new exploration and recovery. Many pollution problems are associated with the extraction, refining, and use of petroleum, and widespread demand has led to its becoming in effect an international currency, with many associated political problems. Technological improvements are reducing the problems associated with petroleum, but if petroleum consumption continues at current rates, the known recoverable petroleum reserves will be exhausted within the next few decades, and alternative energy sources will have to be found.

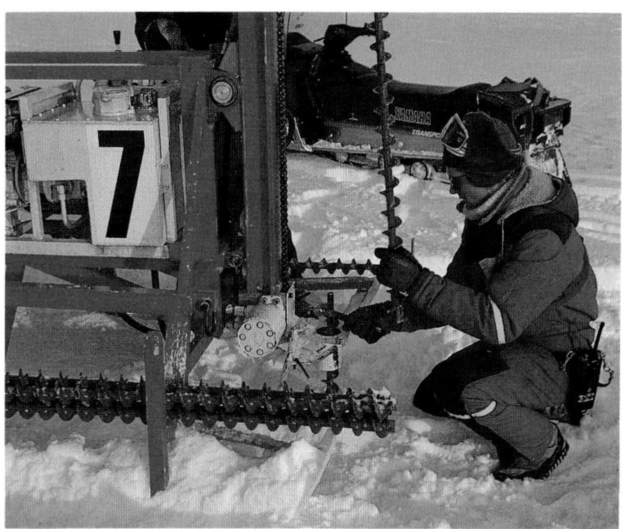

A drilling rig being used in **petroleum exploration** on the island of Spitsbergen in the Arctic Ocean. Explosive charges placed in holes drilled at regular intervals are detonated to generate shock waves, which reflect from the rock strata below and provide data on the underlying geological formations.

petroleum, exploration and recovery, the process of finding and extracting petroleum from reservoirs ('traps') in underground rock. Petroleum seeping out at the earth's surface was first extracted as a fuel in prehistoric times, but systematic exploration and recovery dates from 1859, when a well was drilled at Oil Creek in Pennsylvania, USA, near a site of surface seepage.

Exploration for oil is still not an exact science, and predicts only the likelihood, not the certainty, of traps. Few reservoirs give obvious surface signs such as seepage of oil or natural gas. Sometimes surface formations indicate folds or faults below, which might be traps. Exploration for potential traps now generally starts with aerial or satellite surveying using devices such as gravity meters or magnetometers. Variations in gravitational or magnetic fields indicate underground rock features. Likely trap locations are selected for follow-up with seismography. In this technique, shock waves are generated at the surface using explosives, and measurement of the behaviour of these waves in the earth provides information on the underlying rock formations. The next stage is to select sites for test drilling. A *drilling rig is used to bore a hole through possible oil-bearing locations. Information is collected at each stage of drilling, and the depth of productive rock formations is measured: this process is known as well logging. A production test may follow, when liquid and gas from any possible trap layer is brought to the surface and analysed. If the test shows that production will be economic, the well is completed by lining it with concrete. At each productive layer, the concrete is pierced with explosive, and the hole linked to the surface with a narrow pipe called a production string.

The method of recovering the oil depends on the pressure in the trap. Often, well production starts with enough natural pressure to bring up the oil. As the oil stock declines,

Petroleum refining

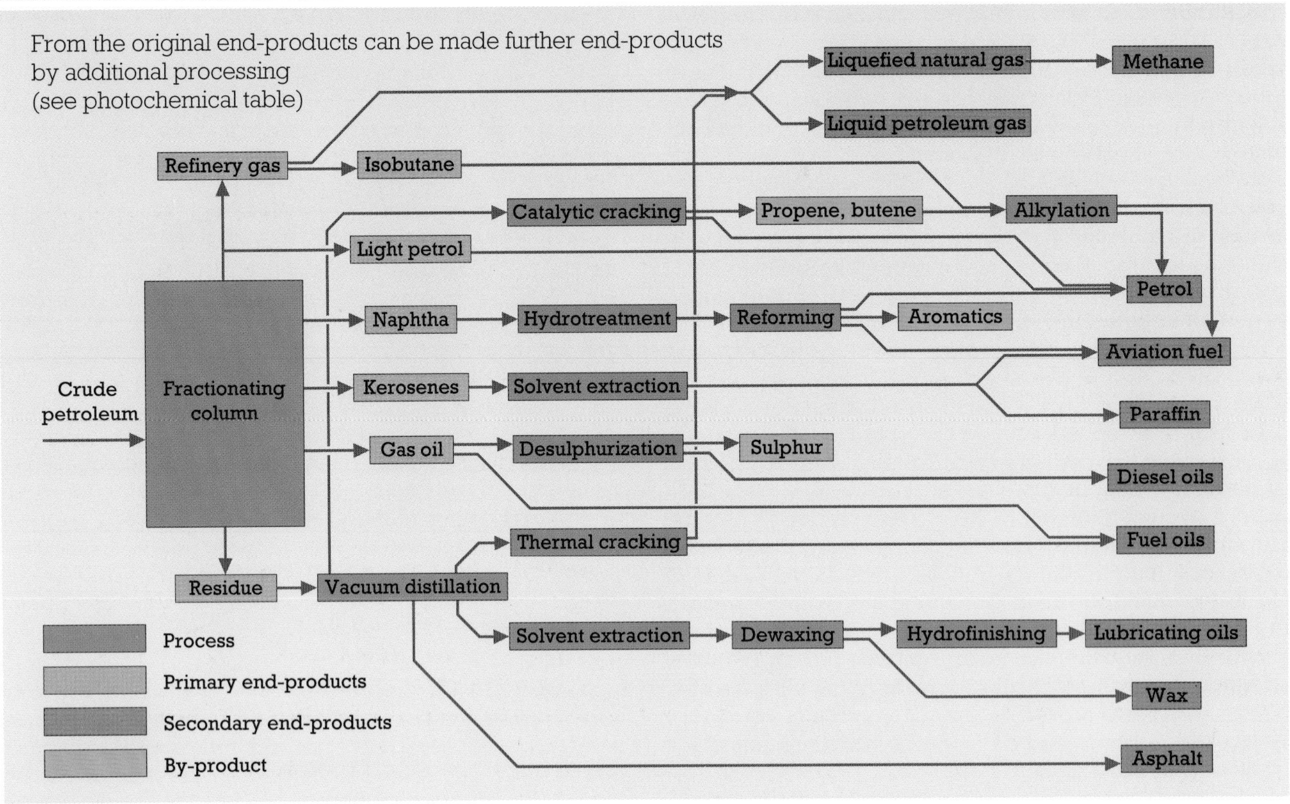

From the original end-products can be made further end-products by additional processing (see photochemical table)

Refinery gas
Liquefied natural gas
Methane
Liquid petroleum gas
Isobutane
Catalytic cracking
Propene, butene
Alkylation
Light petrol
Petrol
Crude petroleum
Fractionating column
Naphtha
Hydrotreatment
Reforming
Aromatics
Aviation fuel
Kerosenes
Solvent extraction
Paraffin
Gas oil
Desulphurization
Sulphur
Diesel oils
Thermal cracking
Fuel oils
Residue
Vacuum distillation
Solvent extraction
Dewaxing
Hydrofinishing
Lubricating oils
Wax
Asphalt

Process
Primary end-products
Secondary end-products
By-product

pressure drops, and artificial methods of lifting it may be needed. Various kinds of pump may be used, or gas lift may be possible. This involves forcing natural gas bubbles to rise up the well, drawing the petroleum up by their buoyancy like the air-powered water circulator in an aquarium. The amount of oil produced by a well can be increased by injecting gas or water to increase reservoir pressure. In declining oilfields, water or steam is pumped down into some wells to drive oil up other wells nearby. Oil produced by a well is separated from *natural gas in a pressurized separator. Water and solids are then removed, and the oil is piped to a local storage tank, usually a large closed cylinder standing on the ground. It may be shipped from the tank by *pipeline, by *barge on inland waters, or by ocean-going oil *tankers.

petroleum jelly *petroleum refining.

petroleum refining, the processes used to produce fuels, chemicals, and gas by treatment of *petroleum. Petroleum has been known and used for thousands of years, but systematic separation of its components has only been carried out for just over a century. Initially, petroleum was refined almost entirely to produce fuels. Since World War II the use of refinery products as a source of *petrochemicals has become more important, but over 90 per cent of crude petroleum is still used for fuel.

The key to petroleum refining is the initial separation of *hydrocarbons into various groups of similar compounds. The groups are distinguished by their boiling-points, and they are separated by *fractional distillation (see the figure in that entry). A group of hydrocarbons with similar boiling-points is called a fraction. Each fraction has a distinct treatment within the refinery. Fractions for which there is little demand may be converted to other fractions by later refinery processes (see figure). Refinery gas is the petroleum fraction with the lowest boiling-point, and does not condense in a fractional distillation column. Propane and butane may be extracted from refinery gas to make *liquefied petroleum gas. The residual gas, containing mainly hydrogen, methane, and ethane, is used as a fuel to operate the refinery. The most economically important product of petroleum refining is the range of fractions called *petrol, which boils at 30–140 °C. Light petrol condenses at boiling-points of 30–80 °C, right at the top of the fractionation column. It is used to make fuel for *motor cars and other *petrol-engined vehicles. Next down the column, at boiling-points of 80–190 °C, naphthas are drawn off. They may be used in blending fuels. Individual naphthas are separated and used to make solvents, and as a raw material in producing many organic chemicals. Much of the naphtha fraction is *reformed for use in petrol. The fraction next below the naphthas in the fractionation column condenses at boiling-points of 190–250 °C. This fraction contains the kerosenes, which include *paraffin, traditionally burnt with a wick for heating and lighting. This fraction is now more important for making *aviation fuel for jet aircraft. The final group of fractions condensing in the column is *diesel oil, or gas oil, with boiling-points in the range 250–350 °C. Their main use is in *diesel engines. Heavier oil which does not evaporate in the initial fractional distillation passes through the bottom of the column. In some refineries these residues pass on to another stage of *vacuum distillation. Products separated this way include *lubricating oils and petroleum jelly (used as a grease, or as a base for making ointments).

Separating individual compounds from the various fractions and residues is done by several methods. Solvent extraction, for example, is another way of extracting lubricating oil from residues. Further solvent treatment can eliminate undesirable contaminants from lubricating oil or kerosenes. Some substances are removed or separated by crystallization, in which the heavier fractions are cooled until waxes crystallize, and other semi-solids solidify. The solid particles are then filtered out. Preparing fractions or products for final use involves many complicated processes. Impurities, of which the most important are sulphur compounds, are generally removed by *hydrotreatment. In blending, different fractions are mixed to achieve specific properties. For example, fuel-oils for domestic and industrial heating are a blend of heavy residue oils with lighter fractions which reduce their viscosity. Oils to be burnt in engines generally need *fuel additives blended in to improve their performance and safety. Chemical treatment of fractions to change them into other fractions or into feedstocks for petrochemicals is a large and growing part of refinery work. These processes include *cracking, in which heavier hydrocarbons in residues are broken down into lighter fractions, particularly petrol. In hydrotreatment, unsaturated hydrocarbons may be saturated with hydrogen. To make slightly heavier hydrocarbons, or to turn straight-chain molecules into ring molecules, a reforming process is used. This produces more petrol, and many aromatic hydrocarbons for use in the chemical industry to make explosives, synthetic rubbers, food preservatives, and many other specialist chemicals. Other building-up processes include polymerization, in which identical molecules combine, and alkylation, in which hydrocarbon groups or chains are added to molecules.

Storage facilities are a vital part of the work of a refinery, which may have hundreds of tanks, generally above ground and about 30 m (100 feet) in diameter. A huge network of pipes connects the tanks with various processes, so that a tank may be used for storing intermediate fractions, separate compounds, or finished product awaiting transport to users or chemical factories. Large tanks hold the crude oil delivered to the refinery, with each tank used for oil from a particular source. Switching between crude tanks enables selection of the crude to give the properties best suited to the refinery's current workload. Transport of crude to the refinery is by *pipeline or by oil *tanker (most refineries are near the sea). Transport of finished products is generally by pipeline, road, or rail.

pewter, an *alloy of tin known since the 3rd and 4th centuries AD. Originally consisting of four parts tin to one part lead, pewter was widely used until the 18th century to produce plates and drinking vessels. Modern pewter contains no lead: it is roughly 92 per cent tin with 5 per cent antimony and 3 per cent copper. It has a white lustre, is resistant to corrosion, and is now used mainly for decorative drinking vessels.

pharmaceutical industry, the industry concerned with the manufacture, preparation, and marketing of *drugs. Until the 20th century, the industry was concerned almost entirely with the extraction of drugs from raw materials and their preparation in suitable form. Since 1940 improvements in chemical techniques and advances in *pharmacology have allowed new drugs to be screened for useful biological effects. More recently, it has been possible to design and synthesize new drugs using *X-ray analysis and computer *graphics and modelling, and research in these fields is now the most important activity. Growth has been remarkable, and the number of drugs available has increased equally dramatically: about 80 per cent of the drugs now in use were unknown thirty years ago. A new drug must undergo rigorous testing in animals, and later also in humans, before being put on the market, and the time taken from the start of research to clinical use may well be as long as ten years. A drug has three names: chemical, describing its structure; generic or approved, by which it is normally known; and proprietary, a name given to it by the company that produces it. Thus, *para*-acetoaminophenol is the chemical name of an *analgesic; its approved name is paracetamol or acetaminophen; and a common proprietary formulation is known as Panadol. Another of the industry's activities is the formulation of medicines: special preparations to ensure that the drug will reach the patient's tissues at the desired time and in the right concentration.

pharmaceutics, the science of preparing and dispensing medicines. *Drugs are designed by pharmaceutical chemists, who test them on animals and investigate their mode of action. They are manufactured and distributed by the *pharmaceutical industry, and dispensed by pharmacists, who sell them as medicines. (See also *pharmacology.)

pharmacology, the study of the actions of *drugs on the body. Until the 20th century most pharmacological knowledge was derived from a few observations by physicians on the effects of drugs given to their patients. Now, however, experimental work on animals has enabled scientists to classify drugs by their actions, to describe relationships between the structure of a drug and the actions it exerts, and even to predict (if not always with confidence) the effects that a newly synthesized drug will have. More recently, computers have been used to display the conformation of substances before they are synthesized and to model their probable biological properties. These pharmacological advances, together with modern chemical techniques, have led to an immense expansion of the *pharmaceutical industry and to a huge increase in the number of drugs available for the treatment of disease. Each new drug is tested thoroughly on animals and then, since humans do not always react like other animals, on both sick and healthy volunteers. Even with such rigorous testing, a drug may subsequently prove unacceptable. The sedative thalidomide, for example, introduced in 1958, was withdrawn in 1961. It was found to cause major birth defects if administered early in pregnancy. The clinical pharmacologists performing these tests look not only for curative properties but also for possible harmful actions. They study the effects on blood levels of administering the drug by different routes. Only after exhaustive tests is the new drug passed for use in therapy. Drugs may be classified by the physiological systems they affect, for example, the urinary system or the central nervous system, and within these systems according to the main effects they have, such as *diuretics and *tranquillizers. Some drugs—*antibiotics, for instance—are described in more general terms or, like antimalarials, according to the diseases for which they are used (see table). The scheme is not always satisfactory, since drugs may affect more than one system and be used to treat more than one disease.

Sometimes a drug can be described more specifically and in a more useful way. There is evidence that many drugs exert their effects by combining with a receptor, situated usually on the surface of a cell but sometimes in the nucleus or surrounding cytoplasm. The combination of a molecule of drug with a receptor causes a reaction. This may be simple, like the contraction of a muscle, or more complex and gradual, like the effect of a hormone. Drugs that stimu-

Different classes of drug and their uses

Class of drug	Examples of drugs	Uses
Gastro-intestinal system		
Antactid	Alkalis (magnesium trisilicate)	Hyperacidity
Ulcer-healing	Ranitidine	Gastric and duodenal ulcer
Laxative	Salts (magnesium sulphate), purgatives (phenolphthalein)	Constipation
Lubricant	Liquid paraffin	Constipation
Antidiarrhoeal	Codeine	Diarrhoea
Cardiovascular system		
Antidysrhythmic	Beta-blockers (propranolol)	Disordered cardiac rhythm
Anti-anginal	Nitrites (glyceryl trinitrate)	Angina
Antihypertensive	Methyldopa, beta-blockers	High blood pressure
Anticoagulant	Heparin, warfarin	Cardiac surgery, thrombosis
Diuretic	Frusemide	Oedema
Used for migrane	Ergotamine	Migraine
Central nervous system		
Analgesic (narcotic)	Morphine	Severe pain
Analgesic (non-narcotic)	Aspirin, paracetamol	Mild pain
Hypnotic	Benzodiazepines (nitrazepam)	Sleeplessness
Tranquillizer (major)	Phenothiazines (chlorpromazine)	Schizophrenia, mania
Tranquillizer (minor)	Benzodiazepines (diazepam)	Anxiety
Antidepressant	Tricyclics (imipramine), mono-amine oxidase inhibitors	Depression
Anti-emetic	Antihistamines (cyclizine)	Motion sickness, vertigo
Anticonvulsant	Phenytoin, barbiturates, benzodiazepines	Epilepsy
Used for Parkinsonism	Levodopa (L-dopa)	Parkinson's disease
Musculo-skeletal system		
Anti-inflammatory	Ibuprofen; aspirin; corticosteroids	Arthritis
Used for gout	Allopurinol	Gout
Endocrine system		
Thyroid	Thyroxine	Myxodema
Antithyroid	Cartimazole	Graves Disease
Hypoglycaemic	Insulin, chlorpropamide	Diabetes
Genito-urinary system		
Uterine stimulant	Oxytocin, ergometrine	Childbirth
Respiratory system		
Cough suppressant	Codeine	Dry cough
Bronchodilator	Salbutamol	Asthma
Anti-allergy	Cromoglycate	Asthma, allergies
Antihistamine	Diphenhydramine	Hay fever, allergies
Blood system		
Iron	Ferrous sulphate	Iron-deficiency anaemia
Vitamin B12	Hydroxocobalamine	Pernicious anaemia
Eye		
Mydriatic	Atropine	Iritis, examination of the eye
Meiotic	Pilocarpine	Glaucoma
Infections		
Antibiotic	Benzylpenicillin, ampicillin, oxytetracycline, streptomycin	Bacterial infections
Antifungal	Griseofulvin	Fungal infections of skin
Antituberculous	Ethambutol, rifampicin	Tuberculosis
Antimalarial	Chloroquine, proguanil	Malaria
Antiviral	Acyclovir	Herpes

late receptors, and therefore produce an action, are called agonists. Other drugs combine with the receptors without stimulating them, thus preventing the agonists from having an effect. They are called antagonists and are usually similar chemically to the agonists. Both types are used in medicine. For instance, the heart and blood vessels possess numerous receptors with different functions and different sensitivities, known by Greek letters, and all these can be acted on by both agonists and antagonists. Alpha receptors cause arteries to constrict. If an agonist is given, the blood pressure will rise; if an alpha antagonist is given, it will fall. Beta receptors are important in the heart, and if they are stimulated the heart rate will rise; if a *beta-blocker is given it will fall. Drugs acting on receptors are either identical with, or chemically related to, substances that occur naturally in the body. Receptors to them would seem to have evolved as part of a physiological system. Many drugs do not act through receptors. *Anaesthetics, for instance, affect the composition of the nerve–cell membrane, making it unable to generate or conduct impulses. Drugs used in *chemotherapy interfere with the metabolism of micro-organisms in amounts too low to harm the host, a property known as selective toxicity.

phenol (carbolic acid, C_6H_5OH), a colourless, low-melting-point, organic, crystalline substance with a characteristic 'disinfectant' smell. It is poisonous and can cause blistering of the skin. Dilute phenol solutions were used as disinfectants and for cauterization in 19th-century hospitals; modern antiseptics (for example, trichlorophenol, TCP) are phenol derivatives. Carbolic soap for household cleaning contains phenol. Phenol can be extracted from *coal-tar, but is now more commonly synthesized from *benzene. Commercially it is used in the manufacture of dyes, drugs, photographic developers, explosives, and thermosetting plastics.

phenol-formaldehyde resin, a thermosetting *plastic produced by the polymerization of phenol (C_6H_5OH) and methanal (formaldehyde, HCHO). In alkaline conditions the reaction produces a viscous resin that forms a hard, intractable material on heating. In acid conditions a type of resin called novolak is produced. This can be ground to a fine powder and dissolved in solvents for use as a varnish, or mixed with fillers and binders and moulded under pressure, whereupon additional polymerization takes place, producing an insoluble, infusible material. The first phenol-formaldehyde resin to be produced commercially was *bakelite.

pheromone, an airborne, *hormone-like chemical that functions as a sexual attractant, especially in insect species. Pheromones are effective in minute concentrations: those of some female moths may attract males from up to 12 km (7.5 miles) away. Use is now being made of pheromones in pest control: they are used to attract male insects, which are then killed. Because they are highly specific, pheromones lack the damaging side-effects of *insecticides. Examples of their successful use include the control of cotton boll-weevil (*Anthonomus grandis*) in Pakistan, and the cotton leafworm alabama (*Alabama argillacea*) in Peru.

pH meter, an instrument for measuring the acidity or alkalinity of an aqueous solution (see *acids and bases). pH is an inverse measure on a logarithmic scale of the hydrogen ion concentration of a solution: the more hydrogen ions a solution contains, the more acid it is, and the lower the pH. A neutral solution has a pH of 7, acids have pH values of less than 7, and alkalis have values greater than 7. In a pH meter, hydrogen ion concentration is measured electrically: the solution whose pH is being measured forms part of an electrochemical cell (see *battery) containing a standard or reference electrode of known pH, with which the pH of the unknown solution is compared.

phonograph *gramophone.

phosgene, a gaseous *chemical warfare agent that attacks the respiratory system, first used by the German Army in 1915. When inhaled, phosgene corrodes the lungs, making lesions in the membrane and causing fluid congestion. Death is by asphyxiation.

phosphate (PO_4^{3-}) any natural or synthetic salt of *phosphoric acid. Synthetic phosphates are used chiefly as *fertilizers, to supply the essential element *phosphorus in the form of superphosphate and triple phosphate. They are also used in *washing powders, water softeners, baking powder, and processed foods and drinks. Phosphates occur naturally in guano (sea-bird droppings), and in rocks (phosphorite) found in northern Africa, Peru, and Chile.

phosphor, a synthetic fluorescent or phosphorescent substance that converts the energy of incident electrons into light. Phosphors have many uses, the most important being in *cathode-ray tubes, especially in *television receivers to display the picture. The green and blue phosphors in a colour television screen are zinc sulphide activated by copper (green) or silver (blue). The red phosphor is a compound of *rare-earth elements.

phosphoric acid (orthophosphoric acid, H_3PO_4), a colourless, crystalline solid, usually encountered as a syrupy concentrated solution. It is manufactured industrially by treating phosphate rock with dilute *sulphuric acid, filtering, and concentrating the filtrate by evaporation. Its main uses are in the manufacture of *phosphates and for rust-proofing *steel before painting.

phosphorus (symbol P, at. no. 15, r.a.m. 30.97), a chemically reactive, non-metallic element that exists in two main forms—white and red. White phosphorus is a white, waxy, phosphorescent, highly toxic, low-melting-point solid. It was used in Victorian times in the manufacture of matches. Red phosphorus, a dark red powdery solid, is stable in air and non-toxic: it has replaced white phosphorus in match manufacture. It is obtained industrially by heating calcium phosphate with sand and coke in an electric furnace. Large quantities of phosphorus are converted into acids and *phosphates for use in fertilizers and for making fireworks and smoke bombs. Smaller quantities are used in manufacturing alloys that are used, for example, in integrated circuits.

photocell, a *transducer that converts light into electrical energy. The term originally referred to a photoelectric cell, in which light of a suitable wavelength falling on the cell results in the emission of electrons, and, in the presence of a small driving voltage, the flow of electric current. Such a cell can be used to measure light intensity. A photocell is now more commonly a photoconductive cell, which exhibits high electrical resistance in the dark, but becomes conductive when illuminated. Photodiodes and photovoltaic cells may also be called photocells. A photodiode produces a significant current when illuminated, while a photovoltaic cell (see *solar cell) generates a potential difference or voltage on exposure to light. Photocells are often used to detect the passage of an object: most commonly, the photocell is illuminated by a thin beam of light, and passage of an object between the light and the photocell produces an interruption in the photocurrent. Such devices are frequently used as automatic door-opening *sensors, intruder alarms, automatic exposure meters, and to control machinery in factories for safety purposes.

photochromic lens, a glass lens that darkens when exposed to sunlight and clears again when light levels fall. The glass contains minute crystals of silver halide, so small that the glass is normally transparent. The blue and ultraviolet light in sunlight turns parts of the crystals into silver, which absorbs light and darkens the glass, just as photographic film darkens when exposed. However, unlike photographic film, the silver reverts to silver halide when the ultraviolet light levels fall, making the glass transparent again. Photochromic lenses are used in sunglasses, and are especially convenient for *spectacle wearers.

photocopier, a device for making a duplicate or duplicates (photocopies) of documentary material, generally using xerography, a photoelectric process involving the action of light on a specially prepared surface. In this process, a drum or belt of photoconductive material such as *selenium is electrostatically charged with negative *ions, and then exposed to light reflected from the image to be copied. White areas of the image reflect strongly, and in these areas the charge on the belt is neutralized. Black areas of the image reflect little light, and here the belt remains charged. The belt or drum is then dusted with positively charged toner particles that are attracted to the negatively charged image areas and create a duplicate of the original image on the belt. This toner image is then transferred to a sheet of paper, and fixed with heat. Most photocopiers are designed to reproduce only black-and-white images, but colour photocopiers—which scan the document with red, green, and blue filters—are becoming increasingly common. It is also possible to insert a screen into the photocopier to mimic the *half-tone process for images with intermediate tones.

photoelectric cell *photocell.

photoengraving *process engraving.

photography, the recording of a permanent image by the action of light, or other *electromagnetic radiation, upon a sensitive medium. The earliest photographic images were made in 1826 by *Niepce, but his process was very crude, requiring an eight-hour exposure to obtain a picture. More practical processes were developed by *Daguerre and *Talbot, and were widely used throughout the 1840s. In 1851 the British inventor Frederick Archer published details of a process which was to supersede both the daguerreotype and Talbot's calotype. Archer's process used an emulsion containing silver salts on a layer of collodion (nitro-cellulose in a mixture of alcohol and ether). It became known as the wet-collodion process, because the plates had to be exposed and developed before the light-sensitive coating dried. In 1871 the British doctor and amateur photographer Richard Maddox published details of a dry-plate process, in which gelatine was substituted for collodion. Modern photography essentially uses this dry-plate process, though there have been many improvements and refinements since 1871. The sensitivity of photographic emulsions has steadily increased, allowing shorter exposure times. Transparent roll film, first introduced by *Eastman in 1889, has replaced glass plates.

A picture of a fox taken at night, using infra-red **photography**.

*Dufay and the *Lumière brothers almost simultaneously introduced colour photography in 1907–8. Modern colour films based on multiple layers of emulsion date from the introduction of Kodachrome film in 1935.

The basic photographic process has changed little since the late 19th century, although photographic *emulsions have been greatly improved, and the *camera has undergone radical changes. The image is focused on to the film through a *lens system and an *aperture. After exposure to light the film is developed in a series of chemical processes to obtain a negative image, from which positive photographic prints are then made by exposing light-sensitive paper through the negative (see *developing and printing). In a reversal system, the film from the camera is processed to produce a positive slide rather than a negative image.

Photography has a wide range of applications in journalism, advertising, fashion, art, architecture, and many other areas. In scientific and technical research it has made a direct contribution to work in many disciplines, and many specialist forms of photography have been developed. Aerial photography uses large-format, 12.5- or 24-cm (5- or 9.5-inch) film to achieve maximum clarity and resolution of fine detail. In aerial *surveying, photographs are taken in a precisely determined, overlapping pattern: stereographic pairs of photographs are used to enable height measurements to be made. Similar techniques are used in photography from artificial *satellites. In astronomical cameras, photographic plates are attached to high-powered telescopes that rotate to keep the stars in the sky stationary with respect to the camera. In both satellites and astronomical contexts, *charge-coupled devices are increasingly used in place of photographic film. High-speed photography allows the recording of very rapidly changing events, such as explosions, movement of high-speed machines, or dynamic fractures of materials. Exposure times of less than 1 μs are achieved using special electronic flash units, and up to 1 billion images per second can be obtained using an image converter. In this device, light falling on a photo-cathode causes electrons to be emitted. The electrons are accelerated and focused on a *phosphor screen, producing light images that can be recorded by a conventional camera. At the other extreme, time-lapse photography—in which exposures are made automatically at intervals of hours or even days—is used to record events involving a very slow rate of change. Photomicrography (at magnifications above $\times 20$) and photography in conjunction with electron microscopy (at magnifications up to $\times 10^6$) are invaluable in applications such as biotechnology, or for quality assurance of miniature electronic components. In contrast, microphotography involves the photographic reproduction of an extremely small image of a much larger object. Applications of microphotography include the production of microfilm or *microfiche, and the miniaturization of complex electronic *integrated circuits. Photographic materials sensitive to other regions of the *electromagnetic spectrum have specialist uses. Ultraviolet radiation is used in medical and forensic photography, and both ultraviolet and infra-red photography are used in aerial and satellite imaging. Infra-red or heat-sensitive film is also used in *thermography. *Radiology, which is applied in industry and medicine, uses film sensitive to X-rays or gamma radiation, both of which can pass through optically opaque objects.

photogravure *gravure printing.

photometer *spectroscopy.

The trans-Alaskan oil **pipeline**, about 1,000 km (620 miles) from the oilfields in Prudhoe Bay, Alaska.

photomultiplier, a device for detecting extremely low light levels. The photomultiplier is a type of *electron tube with a cathode (negative electrode) that emits electrons when light falls on it. Electrons emitted from the cathode are accelerated towards the first of a series of anodes (positive *electrodes) called dynodes. The dynode is made from a material that emits several electrons in response to each electron received from the cathode. Each subsequent dynode multiplies the number of electrons emitted. This 'avalanche effect' results in a measurable electrical current being produced from an initially very small light input, with an amplification of up to 1 million times typically being provided. Photomultipliers are used in very sensitive optical detectors, for example, by astronomers to measure the intensity of light from stars.

photopolymer, a light-sensitive material that can be used to produce a printing plate by exposure to a photographic positive or negative image. Exposure to light initiates a photochemical change in the material, enabling non-image areas to be washed away and leaving the image areas ready for printing. (See also *platemaking.)

phototypesetting *typesetting.

picric acid *TNT.

pier *structural engineering.

piezo-electric effect, an effect shown by certain materials, which generate an electrical output when placed under mechanical stress. Applying an electrical voltage to these materials will often cause them to mechanically deform predictably. Piezo-electric materials are used in quartz *watches and *clocks, and in many *sensors and *transducers, such as *microphones and *gramophone styluses.

pig farming, the rearing of pigs to produce pork and bacon for human consumption: for pork they are slaughtered at 70–90 kg (155–200 pounds) and for bacon at 80–100 kg (175–220 pounds). Among large animals, pigs offer the most *meat in relation to their volume. They may be factory-farmed or raised free-range: traditional pig breeds remain highly prized for the quality of their meat. Sows have a gestation period of about 114 days, and litters average ten piglets. They can therefore produce twenty piglets or more each year, from the age of twelve months. Because of this high reproductive rate, selective *animal breeding has been highly successful in pig production.

pig-iron *iron.

pigment, a substance that imparts colour to another substance or mixture, a basic ingredient of *paints, *inks, *dyes, and *cosmetics. With the exception of some naturally occurring organic pigments, such as chlorophyll, which dissolve in organic *solvents, most pigments are insoluble in water and organic solvents. Examples of pigments include metal oxides such as iron oxide (red-brown), naturally occurring earths that are easily ground into fine powders (for example, sienna and ochres), metal powders such as aluminium dust (silvery), metal salts such as lead chromate (chrome yellow), amorphous carbon (black), and insoluble dyes such as Prussian blue.

pile-driver, a machine that hammers posts (piles) deep into the ground for *piling. The pile is held vertically or at the required angle by a lattice mast. Guided by the mast, a winch raises a steel drop-hammer, and allows it to fall on the pile top, which is protected from excessive impact by a resilient helmet. Auger or percussion bore rigs are used for bored rather than hammered piles.

piling, a deep *foundation formed either by driving a preformed steel, concrete, or timber post (pile) into the ground, or by excavating a circular hole in which a reinforced concrete pile (bored pile) is formed *in situ*. Piles are used to transfer the load of a building to a point where the soil resistance is sufficient to withstand the downward force of the structure. Driven (displacement) piles can be rapidly hammered into the ground by a *pile-driver, a steel drop-hammer, supported above the pile by a lattice mast, that is successively raised and dropped on the pile top. Bored piles 2.5 m (8 feet) in diameter and 60 m (200 feet) deep can carry loads of up to 3,000 tonnes each. In some sandy soils piles can be installed by vibration, which is faster and quieter than using a pile-driver. A steel or reinforced concrete wall of interlocking sheet piling can be used to carry horizontal loads, as in a retaining wall or coffer *dam. Piles can also be installed for *underpinning existing foundations by jacking against an existing structure.

pincer *pliers, tongs, and pincers.

pinchbeck *brass.

pipeline, a long pipe used particularly for conveying *petroleum products, water, or *natural gas. A pipeline is used wherever it is cheaper than alternative transport, particularly for moving oil from oilfields far inland, or to dramatically reduce the shipping distance to a regular market. Pipelines from oilfields either lead to a terminal where tankers are loaded, or to a refinery. Many large pipelines are in thinly populated regions such as Alaska and the Arabian peninsula. Such pipelines are generally above ground, and have pipes of about 1 m (3 feet) in diameter, with two or three pipes running in parallel. Pumping stations at intervals keep liquid moving through the pipelines. Natural gas is particularly well suited to pipeline transport, partly because of the high cost of liquefying it for alternative methods of movement. Linked pipelines carrying natural gas form a *gas grid. Solids are sometimes transported through pipelines in the form of a slurry.

pipette, a graduated glass tube for delivering accurate quantities of a liquid. It is a standard piece of laboratory equipment. The liquid was originally sucked up by mouth, but rubber bulbs with control valves are now used. Automatic or 'Oxford' pipettes draw up liquid by a plunger mechanism into a disposable tip: depression of the plunger dispenses a fixed quantity of liquid.

pistol, a *firearm small enough to be fired with one hand. The earliest pistols (16th century) were wheel-locks (see *firearm) and were used primarily by cavalry, who found the two-handed musket too unwieldy while riding a horse. Flintlocks replaced the wheel-locks at the end of the 17th century. In the early 19th century percussion ignition was introduced, as for other firearms. Towards mid-century several inventors, among them *Colt, developed repeating pistols incorporating a revolving cylinder with five or more chambers, each of which could be loaded with a percussion cap and a round of ammunition. The revolver placed a new firing chamber at the base of the barrel after each shot, and could fire several rounds in succession before reloading. At the beginning of the 20th century, automatic pistols were developed, using a blow-back system of operation. A slide, pushed back by surplus propellant gases after the bullet has left the barrel, forces open the breech to eject the spent *cartridge. A spring at the base of the magazine forces the next round into the breech. (See firearm for illustration.)

pit-prop, a strong device for supporting the roof in an underground mine. Props have evolved from wooden posts, fixed in position with wedges, through steel girders, to rock- or roof-bolts that pin strata together. For long-wall faces (see *coal-mining), wooden supports have been replaced by steel legs, hydraulic props, and latterly by 'powered supports'—steel frames held open by up to six hydraulic props, together capable of resisting forces of several hundred tonnes. The powered supports provide an integrated canopy throughout the face, protecting both coal-miners and the production equipment.

pivot *lever.

plane, a tool with an adjustable *chisel blade set obliquely in a wooden or iron body, used for shaving wood. Planes were a normal part of the Roman carpenter's tool-box. There are two basic kinds of plane: bench planes, which reduce the overall thickness of wood or shave off strips of wood to smooth a surface; and rebate planes, which cut recesses, grooves, and mouldings. Both types of plane have a blade that can be removed for sharpening. For large-scale repetitive work, planing machines are used. An allied tool is the spokeshave, which shaves curved items. It differs from the plane in that it cuts as it is drawn towards the worker, rather than during an outward motion. (For illustration see *tools, history of.)

plantation farming, the farming of large areas of cash-crops that generally require more than a single season to establish themselves, but are then productive for a number of years. Cash-crops are those grown for sale (usually for export) rather than for local food supply. The term plantation farming is generally applied to tropical crops, though modern forestry practice is typical of plantation farming. Examples of plantation crops are sugar-cane, *rubber, *beverage crops, sisal, and oil-palm. Many such crops were originally associated with colonial settlement in the tropics. Planting is generally from seedlings, which are sown in long rows of equally spaced plants. Harvest is traditionally labour-intensive, though mechanization has been developed for some crops. Some additional processes are often needed at the point of harvest.

plant breeding, the genetic adjustment of plants for the benefit of commercial production. It has been widely applied in the improvement of major economic crops, and has greatly increased cultivation on poorer soils and in harsh climates. The basis of plant breeding is the creation and selection of novel genetic types. This may be achieved by a variety of breeding methods, differentially used for particular crops. Simple self-pollination of a selected *cultivar often reveals progeny with improved characteristics. In other cases advances depend on the controlled hybridization (crossing) of two different cultivars to create new genetic combinations. Hybridization of related domestic and wild species is often the starting-point for the introduction of disease resistance. *Genetic engineering may eventually allow genetic traits to be transferred across natural breeding barriers.

plant hormone a substance that, like an animal *hormone, is produced in one part of the organism and acts on distant target cells. Auxins have many functions in the plant, including growth promotion by cell elongation, flower initiation, sex determination, and fruit growth. Auxins are used in agriculture and horticulture on a large scale, for example, to encourage fruit growth and prevent fruit drop in orchards, to grow tomatoes without pollination, and to prevent sprouting in stored potatoes. Modifications (analogues) of natural auxins are used as selective weedkillers (*herbicides). A second group of hormones, the gibberellins, promote a number of effects including bolting (elongation of plant stems), breaking of seed dormancy, and fruit set. Commercially they are used to promote early fruiting in strawberries, to improve clusters in grapes, and to control the malting process in brewing. A third hormone is ethylene, which promotes fruit ripening and may become useful as a defoliant to aid mechanical harvesting.

plant propagation, the natural process by which desirable plant stocks are bred from the parent stock. Many annual crops, including *cereals, are propagated almost entirely from seed. The method is cheap and reliable, and numerous offspring are obtained from a single parent. Other crops are propagated vegetatively, the method employed varying with species. *Root-crops naturally propagate themselves via underground organs, and in some yam cultivars the capacity for seed production has disappeared completely. Cocoa and tea are propagated from leaf cuttings, bananas from suckers, mango and *citrus crops by *grafting. In nutmeg, where fruit is borne solely on female trees, vegetative propagation eliminates the production of male trees, which have no commercial value. Vegetative propagation allows *cloning of high-yielding individuals of a species. An increasing range of commercial crops is propagated by plant tissue culture (the maintenance of plant tissue fragments after removal from the plant).

plasmapheresis, a process in which blood is removed from the body and centrifuged to separate the blood cells from the plasma (the aqueous medium in which the cells are suspended): the cells are then resuspended in a synthetic plasma, and reintroduced into the body. The process is useful for removing unwanted chemicals or proteins from a patient's blood, for example, unwanted antibodies in an auto-immune disease (see *immunology). It is also used to obtain large amounts of plasma rich in immunoglobulins and blood-grouping reagents.

plaster, a soft, pliable mixture applied to surfaces such as walls, which hardens to give a smooth, easily cleaned finish. In this century, *gypsum has largely replaced *lime as a plaster for interior work; other constituents include sand, *Portland cement, and hair. Plaster surfaces can be decorated by incising patterns in the wet plaster or by fixing precast mouldings of fibrous plaster (reinforced gypsum). Plasterboard—a replacement for *lath and plaster—has a gypsum core strengthened with paper facings. Plasterboards are also produced with cellular plastic backings, giving improved thermal insulation.

plastic, any of a group of non-metallic, synthetic, carbon-based materials that can be *moulded, shaped, or extruded into flexible sheets, films, or fibres (see figure). Plastics are synthetic *polymers, long-chain molecules synthesized by joining together large numbers of identical small molecules (monomers). In co-polymers, more than one species of monomer is used. The nature of the monomer from which it is made gives a plastic its characteristic properties. Most plastics are synthesized from organic chemicals originally derived from *petrochemicals, or from *natural gas or *coal. (See also *silicones.) Plastics can be classified into several broad types. Thermoplastics soften on heating, then harden again when cooled: typical examples are *polystyrene, *acrylic fibres, and PET (polyethene terephthalate), a transparent polymer used for soft-drinks bottles. Thermoplastic molecules are also coiled, and because of this they are flexible and easily stretched. They are also viscoelastic, that is, they flow (creep) under stress. Examples are *polythene, polystyrene, and *PVC. Thermosetting plastics do not soften on gentle heating, and with strong heating they decompose. They have a higher density than thermoplastics, are less flexible, more difficult to stretch, and less subject to creep. Examples of thermosetting plastics include *urea-formaldehyde and *epoxy resins, most *polyesters, and phenolic polymers such as *phenol-formaldehyde resin. *Elastomers are similar to thermoplastics, but have sufficient cross-linking between molecules to prevent stretching and creep. Some common plastics are listed in the table.

The plastics industry began in 1870, when *Hyatt patented *celluloid, for use in the manufacture of billiard balls. The first mouldable industrial plastic was *bakelite, and similar plastic resins were soon developed for use in *paints and *varnishes. *Laminated plastics quickly followed bakelite, and in 1912 PVC was first produced from the vinyl chloride monomer. In the 1920s, increased understanding of the theoretical background of polymerization led to the industrial development of processes long known in the laboratory. Styrene was used in 1925 as the basis of a process for producing synthetic rubber, and *polymethyl methacrylate, first synthesized in the laboratory in 1880, came into indus-

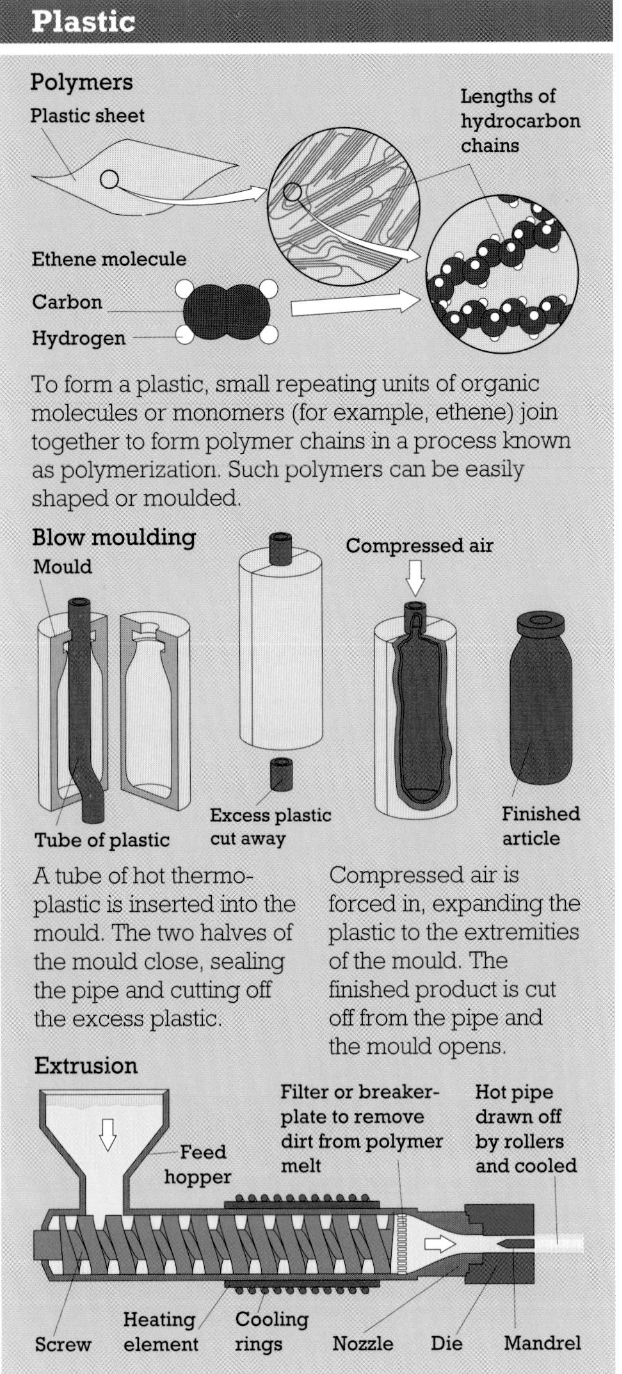
Plastic
Polymers
Plastic sheet
Lengths of hydrocarbon chains
Ethene molecule
Carbon
Hydrogen
To form a plastic, small repeating units of organic molecules or monomers (for example, ethene) join together to form polymer chains in a process known as polymerization. Such polymers can be easily shaped or moulded.
Blow moulding
Mould
Compressed air
Tube of plastic
Excess plastic cut away
Finished article
A tube of hot thermoplastic is inserted into the mould. The two halves of the mould close, sealing the pipe and cutting off the excess plastic.
Compressed air is forced in, expanding the plastic to the extremities of the mould. The finished product is cut off from the pipe and the mould opens.
Extrusion
Feed hopper
Filter or breaker-plate to remove dirt from polymer melt
Hot pipe drawn off by rollers and cooled
Screw
Heating element
Cooling rings
Nozzle
Die
Mandrel

trial production in 1927. In the 1930s thermoplastics became important *moulding materials, as a result of the introduction of vacuum-forming machines utilizing *cellulose acetate, and, later, automatic blow-moulding machines. Plastics were also spun to make *synthetic fibres for use in *textiles. *Nylon and polythene were first produced in the 1930s. Development of thermoplastics continued with the production of polycarbonate plastics in 1956, and polysulphone plastics in the 1960s. Of the thermosetting plastics, the urea-formaldehyde resins were introduced commercially in the 1930s, the alkyd polyesters in 1941, epoxy resins in 1943, and allyl plastics in 1955.

plastic bullet, a *bullet made of rigid plastic, designed for practice firing or to disperse crowds without causing fatal injuries (although they can be fatal at close range). Bullets for riot control are large calibre (37 mm), and are fired from adapted *rifles or purpose-built weapons, using small *cartridges of propellant to restrict the bullet's flight velocity.

plastic explosive, a putty-like *explosive capable of being moulded by hand, used by the military for demolition. Plastic explosives differ from other explosives of similar power in remaining usable over a wider temperature range (from −57 °C to 77 °C). They contain about 80 per cent RDX (a high-energy, non-toxic nitramine explosive) combined with a mixture of oils, waxes, and plasticizers. One type, 'Semtex' (named after Semt, Czechoslovakia, its place of manufacture), is favoured by terrorists for its malleability and odourlessness.

plasticizer, a chemical agent added to plastics or ceramics to make them softer, more flexible, and easier to process. Plasticizers are chemically and thermally stable and therefore do not undergo reaction during processing.

plate girder, an I-section beam made from flat steel plates and usually of greater depth than a girder of standard rolled sections. Plate girders occur commonly in *bridges, buildings, and structures that span large open spaces. The web (the central portion of the girder) is formed from full-depth plates connected end to end. The top and bottom flanges are also plates and can be built up to different thicknesses along their length, depending on the loads to be supported. To avoid buckling failure, the web is stiffened by vertical strips running between the projecting flanges.

plate-glass, clear *glass produced in thick sheets. In the 18th century, plate-glass was prepared by pouring molten glass on to a casting table and then quickly rolling it flat with a manually operated iron roller. This operation had to be completed in less than one minute and the resulting glass sheet was then put into an *annealing oven, where it was left for about ten days before being ground and polished. The process was mechanized during the 19th and early 20th centuries, but has now been superseded by the *float glass process.

platemaking (printing), the creation of a 'plate', a surface carrying an image in a form suitable for *printing. Letterpress printing and flexography use relief plates, in which the printing image is raised above the surface of the rest of the plate. In the past such plates were made from moulds (see *stereotype). Today, relief plates are most commonly made from *photopolymers, which are exposed to the image and undergo light-induced changes that harden the image areas and allow non-image areas to be washed away. For *offset lithography, flat plates are made on sensitized paper, plastic, or metal by transferring the printing image to their surface, either electrostatically or photographically. Depending on the material, the images are then fixed or slightly etched on to the plate, so as to take ink. Plates for *gravure printing are usually made either by *etching or by *laser engraving.

platinum (symbol Pt, at. no. 78, r.a.m. 195.99), a soft, white, unreactive metal. It gives its name to a group of metals with similar properties. Platinum occurs as the free element, in association with other platinum metals, in the form of fine black grains in alluvial deposits of heavy sands. Platinum and its alloys are used in the manufacture of many types of equipment for handling corrosive liquids and gases, such as reaction vessels, tubing, valves, and laboratory ware. It is also used as a *catalyst, for electrical contacts, in *thermocouples, and in jewellery.

pliers, tongs, and pincers, tools with two hinged arms and serrated jaws, used for gripping. They are used, for instance, in work with very small items, when the fingers may be too clumsy, or in working metals, when the heat generated may make the item too hot to hold. They all operate on similar principles. Differences in design reflect differences in their function. Long-nose pliers, for example, are used when access to the work is very limited. Many pliers incorporate a pair of wire-cutting blades, and for electrical work the handles are insulated. Pincers are used particularly for extracting nails and have rounded jaws so that strong leverage can be exerted by the handles. Tongs are often used to pick things up, so as to avoid touching them directly. If the task to be performed requires the use of both hands, the workpiece can first be secured in a *vice. (For illustration see *tools, history of.)

Plimsoll line, a mark painted on the sides of *merchant ships to show the maximum depth to which a ship may be loaded. It allows variations according to season and location. Named after the politician Samuel Plimsoll (1824–98), a merchant and shipping reformer, it was made compulsory in the UK in 1875. An internationally agreed loading line was adopted by fifty-four countries in 1930, and revised in 1968.

plough, an implement with a cutting blade fixed in a frame, which is drawn through the soil in order to till it. The earliest evidence of the use of ploughs derives from the Near East in about 6000 or 7000 BC. The first ploughs were human-powered, but *draught animals, particularly oxen, were soon harnessed for this purpose. The wooden point of the early plough was later protected by a metal cap called a share. Roman ploughs were fitted with shares. Iron ploughs were in use in China from about the 4th century BC. Important additions to the plough were made in Europe in the late 10th century AD. Wheeled ploughs were used with a coulter, a vertically attached metal knife that made a cut in the soil, and a mould-board, which turned the soil. The inversion of the soil was an extremely important innovation, since this buried weeds and previous crop residues. In 1730 the Rotherham plough was patented in England: it had a strong triangular frame which left less area in contact with the soil, making it easier to pull. This remained the basic design for horse ploughs, and although the support frame was altered for *tractor use, the part working in the soil has remained virtually unchanged. With the increased power available from tractors, and improvements in metals, larger ploughs have become possible, although the trend toward *minimum tillage has meant that ploughs are used less fre-

Some important plastics and their derivation

Polymer name	†Chemical derivation	Common uses
Thermosetting plastics		
Polyurethanes (PU)	Ethylene glycol+adipic acid (from benzene)+di-isocyanate (from ethyne)	Moulded PU used for window frames; foamed PU used as insulation material
Nylon	From intermediates such as caprolactam, derived from benzene	Important textile fibre; coating for some metal items; gearwheels. Nylon film or extrusions used for vacuum packing of foods
Polycarbonates (PC)	Made from phenol derivatives and phosgene (synthesized from ethyne)	Rigid transparent covers for record players etc.; rear and side windows in cars. Metallized PC used for compact discs
Phenol-formaldehyde resin	Phenol+formaldehyde (from methanol)	Cavity-wall insulation; used in some varnishes
Polyethene terephthalate (PET)	Ethylene glycol+terephthalic acid (from *p*-xylene)	Major use is for carbonated drinks bottles
Urea-formaldehyde resin	Urea (from ammonia)+formaldehyde (from methanol)	Used as an adhesive, and in permanent-press fabrics
Melamine-formaldehyde	Melamine (derived from limestone) + formaldehyde (from methanol)	Used in kitchenware and for work surfaces
Thermoplastics		
Polystyrene (PS)	Styrene (from benzene)	High impact PS used for casings of radios and cassette players; expanded PS has many packaging and insulation uses; injection-moulded PS used for water tanks
Polymethyl methacrylate	Methanol+acetone (from propene)+hydrocyanic acid (from ammonia)	Used as a replacement for glass in many applications
ABS plastics	Acrylonitrile (from propene and ammonia)+butadiene+styrene (from benzene)	Used for housings of computers and other durable goods; bathroom and kitchen fittings; film wrap for food
Polythene	Ethene	High-density form used for containers such as buckets and bottles; low-density form used for shopping and rubbish bags
Polyvinyl acetate	Vinyl acetate (from ethene and acetic acid)	Adhesives; coatings on drinks cartons
Polyvinyl chloride (PVC)	Vinyl chloride (from ethyne and hydrochloric acid)	Cable and wire insulation, protective clothing; unplasticized PVC used for bottles, electrical fittings, guttering, and piping. Injection-moulded PVC used for records
Polypropylene (PP)	Propene (propylene)	Pipework, kitchen and bathroom fittings, and for food wrappings; PP fibre used for carpets
Polytetrafluoroethene (PTFE)	Chloroform (trichloromethane) combined with hydrofluoric acid to make tetrafluoroethene monomer	High-temperature electrical insulator. Low-friction coating on cookware, skis, bearings, gaskets, etc.

†See petrochemicals table for derivation of starting materials from petroleum.

quently than they once were. (See *agricultural machinery for illustration.)

plumbing, the system or apparatus of water and gas supply within a building, including *central heating and sanitary equipment. The incoming *water supply is usually piped directly to individual appliances. Copper pipes with soldered or solderless joints have generally replaced lead piping, while for *drains and for underground piping *PVC and polythene (which resist corrosion) are widely used. After its use, water is discharged into a drain through pipework sized to suit the expected flow. At each appliance, a water seal, such as the water in the U-bend of a lavatory, isolates drain odours.

The term plumbing also applies to impervious metal coverings used on flat *roofs. Such coverings (usually lead) are laid in sheets ('bays') of about 250 × 60 cm (8 × 2 feet), with lap (overlapping) joints at the edges to allow for expansion or contraction.

plumb-line, a string or wire with a lead or other heavy weight (the plumb-bob) attached to the lower end. The line is hung clear of a wall or column in order to check whether the structure is vertical.

plutonium (symbol Pu, at. no. 94), an artificial, fissionable element (see nuclear *fission) created in nuclear reactors when an atom of uranium-238 absorbs a neutron to form Pu-239. (A second isotope, Pu-238, can be formed from neptunium). *Fast breeder reactors create large amounts of plutonium during operation: this may be used to further fuel the reactor, or it may be used to make *nuclear weapons.

A dentist using a **pneumatic** dental drill to remove decayed material from a tooth prior to filling.

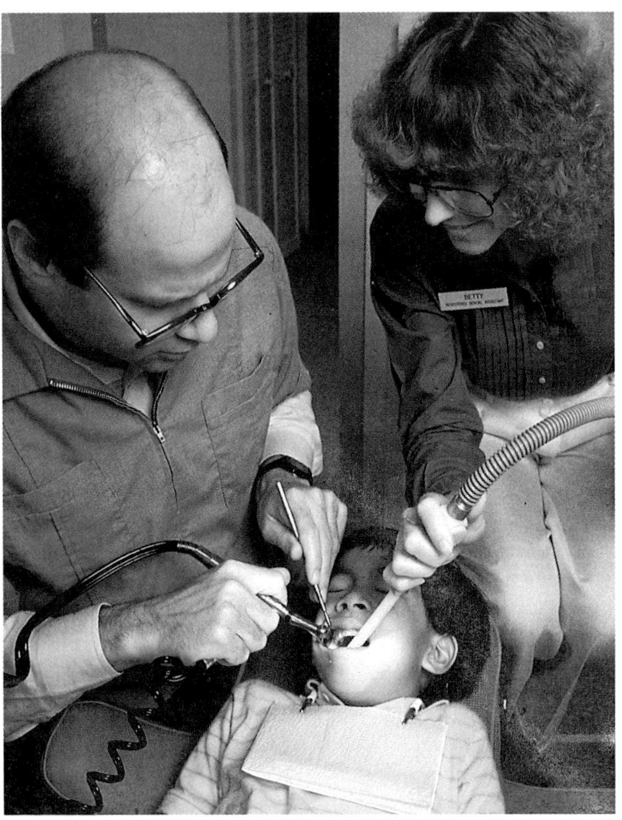

plywood *laminate, *manufactured board.

pneumatic device. Pneumatics is a branch of mechanical engineering concerned with the mechanical properties of gases, particularly air. There are two classes of pneumatic devices: air *compressors (power-driven machines for compressing air to a higher pressure) and pneumatic tools, which are operated by the force of compressed air. Pneumatic power is flexible, economic, has few moving parts, and is without the hazards of sparks or electric shocks. Air motors do not become hot when overloaded. Actions are controlled by the manipulation of valves, with relief valves acting to protect the system. It is easy to connect one device to another, using flexible pipe. Pneumatic tools act either with a rotary mechanism—in which compressed air enters the housing, pushes on the vanes of a turbine, and rotates a central shaft—or with a reciprocating-piston action. In the latter, compressed air enters a cylinder, expands, and forces the piston to move. Examples of pneumatic devices include railway brakes, rock drills, and portable tools such as shears, grinders, and chipping hammers. Pneumatic tubes were used in the 19th and early 20th centuries to send messages or small objects short distances. Modern air-driven *dental drills operate using air turbines, with bearings of compressed air which separate the working parts; air bearings are also used in some *centrifuges. (See also *air-brake.)

point-of-sale terminal (POS terminal), the modern cash register, a computer-based unit able to calculate and record retail financial transactions. Each transaction at the terminal is recorded for auditing at the end of the day's trading, and can supply information to central computers for stock control and forecasting. Some POS terminals automatically supply change. To minimize keyboard use, they may also use optical *bar code readers to record the prices of the goods being sold. (See also *electronic funds transfer.)

polarimeter, an apparatus to study and measure the way polarized light (light in which the light *waves vibrate in only one plane) is affected by substances. Polarized light is passed through a solution of the substance, and any rotation of the plane of polarization is detected by examining the light in the emergent beam. Polarimeters are used in the qualitative and quantitative analysis of some organic chemicals, particularly sugars.

polarography, the measurement of low concentrations of dissolved substances. Polarography uses an apparatus in which the current flowing through a solution between two electrodes—a reference *anode kept at constant potential, and a dropping mercury *cathode—is measured at different voltages. The constituents of the solution can be analysed from the resulting current–voltage curve.

Polaroid Land camera, an 'instant' camera producing processed photographs in seconds or minutes, developed by the US inventor Edwin Land in 1947. It works like a normal camera, but the film pack includes printing paper and processing chemicals. The exposed film is pulled between two rollers while in contact with the paper. The rollers break a pod containing chemicals, spreading them between the film and paper. The chemicals develop a negative on the film and a positive print on the paper. With peel-apart instant films the negative is peeled from the photograph and usually discarded. More popular for amateur use are film packs in which the negative, print, and processing chemicals are per-

A false-colour photograph of Ferrybridge coal-fired power-station in Yorkshire, UK. It highlights the atmospheric **pollution** caused by such plants, in particular the release of sulphur dioxide.

manently sealed inside a plastic envelope. After exposure, a motor ejects the envelope from the camera, and a coloured picture appears in it within a few minutes. Instant 35-mm transparencies are now also available.

polish, a material for producing a shine on a surface. Soft polishes are mixtures of waxes and oils that can be spread over a wood or leather surface and buffed to give a high lustre. The waxy nature of the polish also gives water-repellant properties, and polishing leather keeps the material supple. Metal polishes comprise suspensions of fine abrasive powders which, on being buffed on to the surface of an already smooth metal, remove any traces of corrosion and leave the metal shiny.

pollution, contamination of any kind, but especially of the environment. Pollution can be classified according to whether it affects the air, water, or land, but other classifications are also possible, for example, chemical, physical or thermal pollution. Types of pollution include excessive noise (for example, from an airport or motorway), which is localized and has few long-term effects; local, long-term pollutants such as smelting slag; pollution that has global effects, such as radioactive *fall-out; and *pesticides, such as DDT, that enter the food chain through micro-organisms and are progressively concentrated. Other large-scale pollutants may effect climatic changes or damage trees and other plant life. Most commonly pollution can be attributed to specific chemical substances. For example, sulphur compounds from fossil fuels cause *acid rain; carbon dioxide emissions from car exhausts and other sources are responsible for the *greenhouse effect; and such compounds as the *chloro-fluorocarbons used as aerosol propellants are depleting the stratospheric *ozone layer that protects the earth from excessive ultraviolet radiation. Pollution can arise through failure adequately to control normal processes, as when untreated sewage is discharged into the sea, or excessive nitrate fertilizers are leached from the soil into water supplies; or it may be caused by some major disaster, such as at the *Chernobyl nuclear power-station in the Soviet Union or the *Bhopal chemical works in India. (See also *air pollution, *water pollution.)

polyamide fibre *nylon.

polycarbonate, any of a class of thermoplastic *polymers in which the monomer units are linked through carbonate groups. Polycarbonates have a unique combination of strength, stiffness, toughness, high softening temperature and processability. Their only drawback is their susceptibility to attack by organic solvents. Applications include safety helmets, street-lighting, protective windows, and electrical terminals.

polyester fibre, a synthetic *polymer fibre made by the same melt-spinning process as *nylon fibres. *Whinfield discovered the polyester fibre Terylene in 1941, some six years after *Carothers discovered nylon. The two fibres have much in common: both are strong and durable, and both are used in large amounts world-wide to make clothing, either alone or in blends with natural fibres.

polygraph, a machine for detecting and recording physiological activity, such as pulse rate and blood pressure, popularly known as a 'lie detector'. The polygraph is attributed to British physiologist James Mackenzie, who built the first apparatus in 1892. It is used in police work and in recruitment for high-security jobs. The theoretical basis is that lying evokes an emotional response which is reflected in physiological changes. Its evidential value is doubtful, however, as it is necessarily subjective in the case of both questioner and suspect.

polymer, a compound composed of very large molecules, formed from a chain of repeating simple chemical sub-units (monomers). Natural organic polymers include proteins, DNA, and latexes such as rubber; while diamond, graphite, and quartz are examples of inorganic natural polymers. Synthetic polymers include inorganic compounds such as glass and concrete, but the great majority are *plastics. Most plastics are polymers of small organic (carbon-based) chemicals derived from *petroleum, *coal, or *natural gas. The polymer is formed from monomers under the influence of heat, pressure, or the action of a *catalyst. The exact nature of the polymer produced depends on the nature of the monomer (or monomers) and the conditions of polymerization. Two classes of polymers are usually recognized. In condensation polymers (for example, *polyurethane), the joining together of the monomers involves the elimination of a small molecule, commonly water. In the second, addition polymers, the monomers join together without elimination of a small molecule; examples are *polythene and *polystyrene. Co-polymers are made by the combination of two or more different monomers in the same polymer chain. The properties of a co-polymer can be varied by altering the relative amounts of the different monomers. The ABS (acrylonitrile–butadiene–styrene) family of plastics are co-polymers: uses include telephone and computer body shells and piping.

polymethyl methacrylate, a *plastic composed of *polymers of methyl methacrylate. It is sold in the UK under the brand name of Perspex. Polymethyl methacrylate is transparent, and is lighter and more impact-resistant than glass. It is used as a replacement for glass in many applications, for example aircraft domes, optical instruments, roofing, and lighting fixtures.

polypropylene, a tough, lightweight, rigid *plastic made by the polymerization of high-purity propene (propylene) gas in the presence of an organometallic *catalyst at relatively low temperatures and pressures. It is widely used for domestic containers and appliances because it is cheap, and will withstand hot water, detergents, and harsh treatment. Other typical applications include some automotive parts, pipes, rope, nets, and carpets and other heavy-duty textile products. (See also *Natta.)

polystyrene, a thermoplastic (see *plastic) produced by the polymerization of styrene ($C_6H_5-CH=CH_2$, vinyl benzene). The electrical insulating properties of polystyrene are outstandingly good and it is relatively unaffected by water. Typical applications include light fixtures, toys, bottles, lenses, capacitor dielectrics, medical syringes, and light-duty industrial components. Extruded sheets of polystyrene are widely used for packaging, envelope windows, and photographic film. Its resistance to impact can be improved by the addition of *rubber modifiers. Polystyrene can be readily foamed; the resulting expanded polystyrene is used extensively for packaging.

polytetrafluoroethene *PTFE.

polythene (polyethene, polyethylene), a *plastic made from *ethene, one of the most important thermoplastic polymers in terms of the quantity used. It was first developed in the 1930s in the UK, by the polymerization of ethene at a pressure of 2,000 bar, at 200 °C. This produced a highly branched, low-density polythene (LDPE). An unbranched, relatively high-density form (HDPE) was synthesized in the 1950s using a complex catalyst. Polythene is a white waxy solid with very low density, reasonable strength and toughness, but low stiffness. It is easily moulded and has a wide range of uses in containers, packaging, pipes, coatings, and insulation.

polyunsaturated fatty acid *fats and oils.

polyurethane, any of a family of thermosetting *plastic resins produced by reacting compounds containing an isocyanate group ($-N=C=O$) with organic compounds containing hydroxyl ($-OH$) groups. Polyurethanes are made in many forms, ranging from flexible and rigid foams to rigid solids and highly abrasion-resistant products. They can be shaped by *extrusion or *moulding. The flexible foams are used for upholstery. Rigid urethane foams are excellent heat insulators: they are used to insulate the low-temperature fuel in rocket motors, and most domestic refrigerators. As coating resins and varnishes, the urethanes provide an exceptional degree of toughness and hardness, plus flexibility and chemical resistance. Polyurethane elastomers are useful synthetic *rubbers. Other typical products include gearwheels, shock mounts, pulleys, industrial lorry tyres, drive belts, and synthetic leather.

polyvinyl chloride *PVC.

pontoon bridge *bridge.

porcelain, a *ceramic made from china clay (kaolin) and feldspar (china-stone), closely related to *pottery but fired at a much higher temperature to produce a fine, hard, translucent, white material. Porcelain was first developed in China during the 13th century, where a combination of easily accessible raw materials and superior *kiln design resulted in the ceramic industry being many hundreds of years in advance of the West. It is produced by mixing feldspar and kaolin and firing at 1,450 °C. The high temperatures are needed because only a small amount of low-melting-point glass is present in the clay (see ceramics). This process produces a very hard and brittle porcelain known as hard paste. In Europe a soft-paste porcelain, fired at 1,200 °C, was produced in an effort to duplicate Chinese porcelain. This material was not a true porcelain, being much less hard and fine. The first true European porcelains were developed by *Böttger in Germany during the 18th century, but large-scale porcelain manufacture did not begin in the West until new deposits of kaolin were found, such as those in Cornwall, UK. The first major western development was the discovery of bone china by the British potter Josiah Spode in about 1800. Spode added calcined bone to hard paste mixes to produce a hybrid porcelain, still widely used in the UK. Decorated porcelain is an important commercial product, but porcelain is also a useful engineering ceramic, with properties similar to *alumina, that is used in many electrical insulating applications.

portal frame, a structure in which, typically, two columns are rigidly connected at the top to either end of a beam. The rigid connection ensures combined action between the members and allows large spaces to be spanned. Steel portal frames with rigid joints between columns and inclined rafters are widely used for large, single-storey structures.

Portland cement, the most widely used hydraulic *cement. Named from a supposed resemblance to natural Portland stone, it was developed by Joseph Aspdin of Wakefield, UK, and patented in 1824. It is made by *sintering together chalk or limestone and clay in a rotary kiln. The resulting ash is then finely ground with *gypsum.

ports and harbours. A harbour is a shelter for ships; a port is a harbour (or harbours) together with the facilities that serve it and have grown up around it. Some locations around the world's coastlines provide natural harbours, while others have been adapted artificially to meet a need for port facilities in a particular location. The basic structure involved in such harbours is the *breakwater or jetty. Recent archaeological investigations have shown that quite sophisticated harbours were built in the eastern Mediterranean from the 2nd millennium BC. The main concerns of early harbour builders were to protect the relatively fragile ships from storm damage, and from military attack. Facilities included breakwaters designed to suit local conditions, inner fortified harbours, and special 'galley sheds' for warships, in which *galleys and their gear could be stored out of the water. As trading by sea continued to develop and merchant

Container ships unloading at Rotterdam, The Netherlands. Rotterdam has been a major **port** since 1340, when a canal was first dug between the town and the North Sea. It has successfully adapted its facilities to meet the demands of containerization.

ships grew in size, port facilities for handling cargoes grew up. Animal- or human-powered cranes were common in Roman ports, and well-built wooden wharves that allowed ships to lie alongside have recently been discovered as features of Saxon London and Viking Dublin. *Dry docks probably originated in the tidal waters of northern Europe. By the 17th century, such northern naval ports as Copenhagen (Denmark), Portsmouth (UK), and Toulon (France) had naval dockyards that were the largest economic organizations in the world at that time, containing all the works, stores, and services necessary to build and maintain a large navy.

Traditionally, merchant ships had unloaded into lighters (*barges) while at anchor or on a mud berth, or directly on to wharves along the banks of rivers. In the 18th century, closed basins that were entered by locks provided huge docks independent of the tide that could hold many ships. Such basins were first built at Liverpool and London in the UK, and later also in other places. In the 19th century, steam-powered *dredgers were used to deepen harbours and prevent silting. Steam (then later *hydraulic and *electrical power) also powered mechanical *cranes and cargo-handling equipment. Growth in world trade brought a steady increase in the size of ships. Consequently, some ports fell into disuse because they could not expand sufficiently; others required extensive and continual dredging to provide deep enough water within the harbour. Port facilities grew in size and sophistication to accommodate the expanding trade, with ports relying increasingly on rail links rather than inland waterways for distribution of the cargo.

Ports specializing in particular cargoes began to appear in the 20th century, each with its own specific requirements. Oil and other bulk terminals, for example, need naturally sheltered anchorages with deep water. Since the 1950s there has been a revolution in cargo handling that has had a profound effect on many ports. The *container ship and the use of roll-on, roll-off (ro-ro) ferries have demanded a complete change in port facilities. Some old dock systems, such as London's, have disappeared; other harbours, such as Rotterdam in The Netherlands, have adapted to the new circumstances. Many new ports have appeared and flourished, for example, Tema in Ghana, an entirely artificial deep-water harbour first opened in 1962. In the West, road vehicles have taken over from rail for the transportation of goods to and from ports.

positron emission tomography (PET), a technique of *nuclear medicine used to monitor physiological and biochemical change within the body. A substance 'labelled' with a *radioactive isotope having a short half-life is administered to the patient and its distribution is traced. The substance is chosen for its capacity to be metabolized in the part of the body under examination; for example, labelled fluoro-deoxyglucose can make visible glucose metabolism in the brain. PET was developed in the 1970s and, like *computerized axial tomography, it relies on a computer to produce the final image. It is capable of providing information on cerebral palsy and the metabolism of brain tumours (see *neurology and neurosurgery). Until recently, application of the technique was limited because large *particle accelerators were required to produce the isotopes. However, with the development of specialized miniature particle accelerators, the technique may become more widespread. Another new development is the application of multi-wire *particle detectors to improve the sensitivity of PET. This has led to the use of PET in other areas, such as to study the dynamics of *fluidized beds, and oil-flow in jet engines.

postal system technology, mechanical and electronic aids used by postal systems world-wide to facilitate mail delivery. Since the 1950s many postal systems have been researching and developing ways to handle mail automatically. A mechanical segregator can separate letters, which can be sorted semi-automatically, from parcels and other items that must be hand-sorted. A letter facer can then cancel the stamp and separate letters sent at different postal rates. Further sorting is at present generally semi-automatic, depending on manual coding on the basis of postal codes. But systems that can read elements of the address using *optical character recognition, or that use a spoken code, are now in limited operation. Advances in computer and message transmission technology have led to *fax services in many countries, and several countries have introduced a tele-impression service, whereby bulk correspondence is electronically transmitted to regional post offices for printing, enveloping, and delivery.

post-mill *windmill.

potassium (symbol K, at. no. 19, r.a.m. 39.10), an *alkali metal element, similar in properties to *sodium, obtained either by the electrolysis of molten potassium chloride or by the reaction of metallic sodium with molten potassium chloride. It is produced on a small scale only, offering few advantages over the much cheaper sodium. Compounds of potassium are important as fertilizers, in the production of soft soaps, in the manufacture of *gunpowder and photographic chemicals, and in extracting *gold and *silver from their ores.

potential difference (p.d.) *electricity and magnetism.

potentiometer, a variable *resistor for electric circuits, similar to a *rheostat. The potentiometer is also used for the accurate measurement of an unknown electrical potential or voltage: the unknown voltage is connected in a circuit with a source of known voltage, and the two voltages are balanced using the potentiometer. The unknown voltage can then be calculated from the known voltage and the potentiometer setting.

potter's wheel, a horizontally revolving disc used for the production of deep, circular clay vessels such as bowls and pots. A lump of wet clay is placed on the centre of the wheel and hand-worked by gouging and squeezing as the wheel turns. Early wheels were powered by the potter's foot, but electric motor-driven wheels are now common.

pottery, objects made from clay and hardened (fired) by heating. Pottery was one of the earliest technologies to be developed, because the raw material, clay, was widely available and easily shaped. The earliest pottery was sun-dried, but wood-burning *kilns were soon developed. Earthenware is the oldest and simplest type of pottery. Stoneware, made

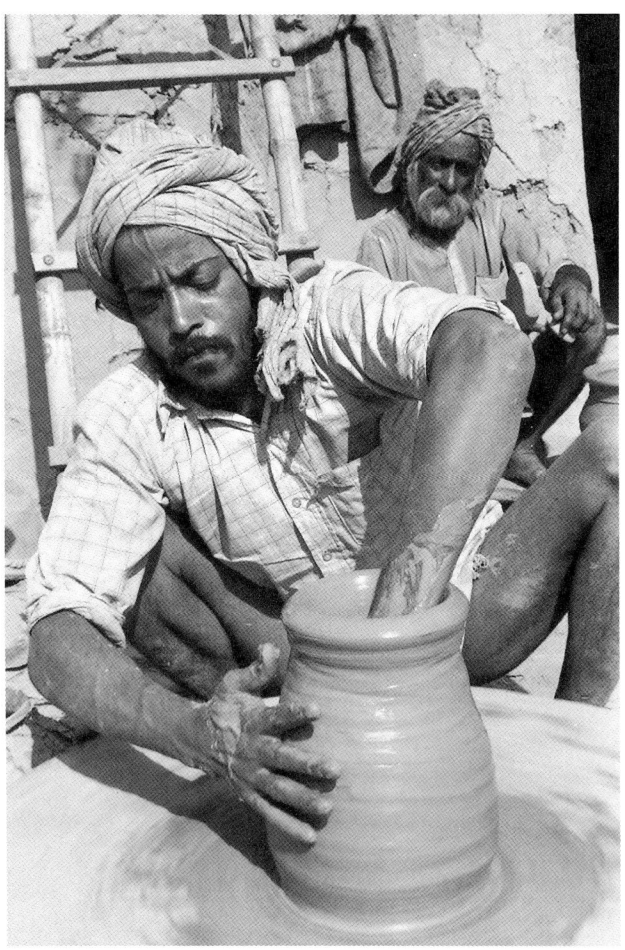

A **potter's wheel** in use in Jandali village, Punjab, India. In this example the heavy wheel (used for its high inertia) is rotated by hand. More common is a lighter platform for the clay, mounted above a heavy kickstone, powered by the potter's foot.

by firing the pot at a temperature high enough to vitrify the outer surface, is harder and more durable, while *porcelain is equally hard but finer and translucent. The surface of a pot can be coated with a glaze before baking or firing to make it water-impermeable. Coloured glazes, based on metallic compounds, were used on pots from a very early date: examples exist from the 4th millennium BC. Another early development was the *potter's wheel, which is first known from Mesopotamia in about 3000 BC. The most sophisticated early pottery culture came from China. The Chinese developed high-temperature pottery at an early stage, producing stoneware from as early as the 10th century BC. They also developed lead *glazes during the Han dynasty (202 BC–AD 220), and by the 13th century were producing porcelain. Classical Greek pottery was of a very high quality, and the Islamic cultures of the Middle East made some important technical innovations. The technique of tin-glazing was introduced to Italy from the Middle East; tin-glazes were used on much of the best European pottery from the 15th to the 18th century (for example, Dutch Delftware). In the early 19th century *Wedgwood introduced *assembly-line techniques for pottery manufacture, which were later widely adopted. A more technological approach to pottery manufacture developed in the 19th century, and in the 20th century a clearer understanding of the materials and processes involved led to the establishment of pottery as an important branch of the *ceramics industry.

poultry farming, the farming of fowl for meat and eggs. Poultry farming began with the domestication of Indian jungle-fowl, ancestor of the modern hen, in about 3200 BC. Both egg and meat production used free-range geese, turkeys, ducks, and hens until the late 19th century, when poultry farms were first established. Broiler production, the keeping of chickens and turkeys in a controlled environment under artificial daylight to maximize production, originated in the USA. Intensive egg and meat production followed, with specialist birds bred for each purpose and controlled by hormone-enriched feeds. Vertical integration led to the control of all aspects of production by one company, from the hatching of chicks in *incubators to the production of feed. Animal welfare groups have highlighted the keeping of chickens in battery cages as one of the most cruel forms of *factory farming, with a high disease level.

powder metallurgy, the fabrication of objects from powdered metal by compressing the powder into the desired shape and then heating (*sintering) to a temperature below the melting-point of the metal. The powder particles weld to form a solid. For small components this is often more economical than *casting, which involves machining and scrap loss, and, in the case of metals with high melting-points, there is a considerable saving of energy. This process also permits the manufacture of porous components and the production of an 'alloy' from mutually insoluble materials.

power *energy.

power-station, a place where electric power is produced. *Electricity generation accounts for about a quarter of world *energy consumption, with coal providing over half the input and smaller contributions from *hydroelectricity, petroleum, nuclear power, and gas. In almost all present systems, the conversion to electric power is by means of a turbo-generator: a rotating *generator driven by a *turbine.

Intensive **poultry farming**.

Power-station (thermal)

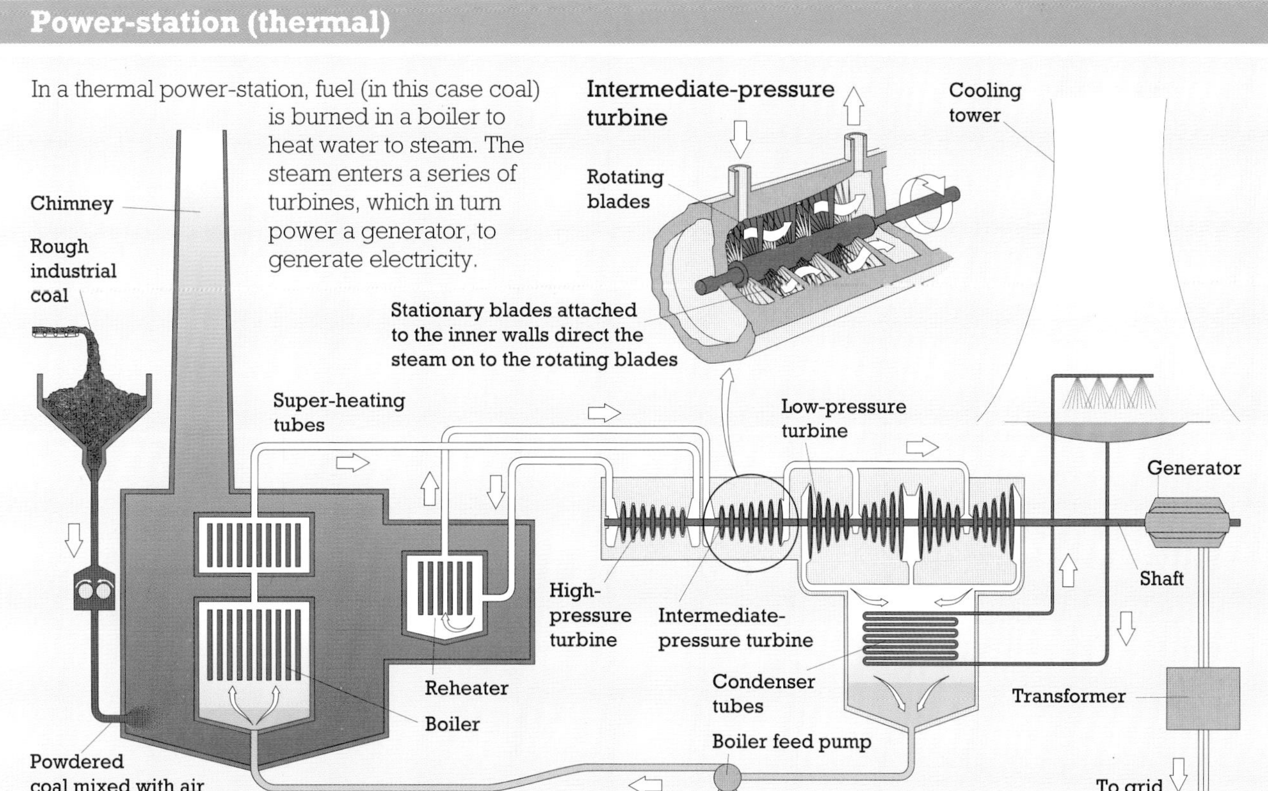

(Exceptions such as *solar cells make only a very small contribution.) In *hydroelectric or *tidal energy plants the driving power comes from flowing water, in *gas-turbines from hot combustion gases, and in all other types from superheated steam, which is produced either by burning fossil fuels (see figure) or in a *nuclear reactor. *Combined-cycle power-stations use both gas and steam-turbines, while the waste heat from some power-stations is used for space-heating (see *combined heat and power). The earliest generator to be driven by a coal-fired steam-engine was operated in 1844 (for electroplating), but it was only in the 1880s that power-stations in the modern sense began to appear. The first public station offering electricity for sale to private consumers (Holborn Station, in London) was commissioned in 1882. The turn of the century saw the first megawatt (million-watt) systems, with *steam-turbines replacing the older engines. *Boilers became more efficient with the introduction of pulverized coal (1919) and improved *heat exchangers. Output reached 100 MW in the 1930s and over 1,000 MW from a single turbo-generator by 1970. The electricity produced per tonne of coal rose from 200 kWh to over 2,000 kWh. Nevertheless, even the best modern plant can achieve only 30–40 per cent *efficiency. Other emissions also cause concern. Electrostatic precipitators remove much of the fine ash from flue gases, but the high cost and technical problems have limited the introduction of desulphurization to remove acid gases (see *acid rain). *Fluidized-bed combustion is able to reduce both these emissions, but not the carbon dioxide, a necessary by-product of fossil fuel burning that is a major contributor to the *greenhouse effect.

power tool, power-driven hand tool for shaping wood and metal. Heavy drills powered by compressed air were introduced in the 1860s during the building of the Mont Cenis tunnel through the Alps between France and Italy, and they are still widely used in civil engineering. Electric drills appeared in Germany in about 1895, but became commonplace only after World War II, when the availability of small, cheap, reliable electric motors made them very popular with amateur builders and decorators. As a result, a variety of accessories were developed to enable the drill to be converted to a jig-saw, circular saw, sander, grinder, and so on. Gradually, however, these rather awkward adaptations gave way to individual hand tools incorporating their own electric motors. Today, the manufacture of electric hand tools is a major industry world-wide, with products ranging from hedge trimmers to hair clippers, from *chain-saws to hammer drills. For the huge amateur market the tools are mostly of comparatively low power, in the range 500–1000W. They usually take their electricity from mains supply, but the use of rechargeable batteries is on the increase. These not only avoid the inconvenience of a trailing cable but can be used where there is no mains supply.

pre-cast concrete, the process of making a *concrete product or component prior to fixing it in its final location. The alternative is to cast the concrete in its permanent position. Pipes, masonry blocks, kerbs, paving slabs, posts, floor planks, bridge beams, and similar components are usually manufactured in a pre-casting factory. Large wall-panels, stair flights, and *system buildings may be made on the construction site itself. Decorative finishes are often produced; exposed *aggregate (with decorative aggregates and coloured *cement) and profiled surfaces improve the appearance of normal concrete.

pre-Columbian technology *meso-American technology.

prefabrication, the process of wholly or partially making a structure (or component of a structure) in a location different from its final position. For example, roof trusses can be prefabricated by cutting and making the joints of the members in a workshop. They are then transported to the site, assembled at ground level, and hoisted by crane into their final position. In *system building, whole buildings are prefabricated. Prefabrication techniques originated in the late 18th century. Early examples of prefabricated iron constructions include the Coalbrookdale *Iron Bridge and the Crystal Palace, UK.

pregnancy test, a urine test to detect the presence of the hormone chorionic gonadotrophin, which is produced during pregnancy. Until the end of the 19th century diagnosis of pregnancy most often relied on the woman's account of her condition. For the next fifty years or so the use of X-rays was popular, but this method became less common after a 1956 study revealed its dangers to the foetus. The first hormone test, published in 1928, involved injecting samples of the woman's urine into immature female laboratory mice. Pregnancy was diagnosed if the animals' reproductive organs became fully developed. Modern home pregnancy tests use *monoclonal antibodies to detect the same hormone.

prehistoric technology, technological developments occurring before written history. Although a somewhat artificial concept, in that it presupposes that technology advances uniformly world-wide, prehistoric technology generally includes the skills that were practised before the rise of the earliest civilizations in the Middle East and the appearance of cuneiform writing (about the middle of the 4th millennium BC). This is roughly coincidental with the first known use of *copper and *bronze, so the working of these metals can be recognized as a prehistoric technology. *Iron did not come into use until about 1200 BC; however, many different cultures in Europe used iron long before they had

A Solutrean 'laurel-leaf' flint spearhead. Such implements were made in the Upper Palaeolithic era (*c.*19,000–15,000 BC), and have been found at sites across central and western Europe. Flint weapons and tools are among the most common examples of **prehistoric technology**.

any mastery of written language. Before the availability of metals, the main building materials were wood and stone. Stone was also used for axes and other *tools, flint being skilfully worked to give a cutting edge to knives and arrow heads. *Leather from the hides of slaughtered animals was plentiful, and provided material not only for clothing but also for screens to give protection from the weather and for making buckets and other containers. *Basket-work and weaving (see *loom) originally used fibres collected in the wild, and date from around 5000 BC. The most important feature of prehistoric development was the transition from a hunter-gatherer culture to a settled way of life associated with the beginnings of *agriculture, in about 9000 BC. The earliest permanent settlement for which much detailed information has come to light is Jericho, Jordan, where the original walled city dates from about 8000 BC.

pressure-cooker, a sealed pan that cooks food rapidly at elevated temperatures by the generation of steam pressure. At higher pressures, the temperatures at which liquids boil increase, thus allowing food to be cooked faster. The pressure-cooker was introduced in 1679 by the French physicist Denis Papin. Modern pressure cookers consist of a large metal saucepan and removable lid sealed together with a rubber gasket. Water boils in the bottom of the pan, and the steam is trapped. The internal pressure rises, elevating the boiling temperature of the water to around 130 °C. A steady pressure is maintained by a safety-valve that allows excess steam to escape.

pressure gauge, an instrument for measuring the pressure of a liquid or gas. There are several kinds of pressure gauge. Mechanical devices include the aneroid *barometer, and the Bourdon gauge, in which the distortion of a curved tube provides a measure of pressure (see *instrumentation for illustration). Other pressure gauges balance the pressure to be determined against the pressure of a column of liquid (usually mercury). Devices for measuring very low pressures include the Pirani gauge, which measures the thermal conductivity of a gas (this increases with pressure), and the Penning gauge, which measures the electrical conductivity of an ionized gas.

pressurized-water reactor (PWR), the type of *nuclear reactor most commonly used for *nuclear power generation. PWR reactors use normal water under high pressure, as opposed to *heavy water, both as a reactor coolant and as a moderator (see nuclear *fission). The reactor core and the water are contained within a cylindrical pressure vessel: after being heated in the reactor core the water passes to a heat exchanger, where its heat is passed to a secondary coolant. The boiling-water reactor (BWR) is similar to the PWR, but the circulating water is allowed to boil, and is used to power steam-turbines directly rather than using a secondary coolant. One major problem with PWR and BWR reactors is that if the primary coolant water loses pressure then it evaporates into steam, which has much poorer coolant properties. The reactor then overheats, as in the breakdown of the nuclear power-station on *Three Mile Island. (See nuclear reactor for illustration.)

pre-stressed concrete, *concrete in which a stress has been induced prior to its incorporation into a structure. It was first developed by *Freyssinet in 1928. Normally, a compressive stress is induced in the tension zone of a beam. When subjected to working load, the net stress to be carried by the concrete will be the difference between the pre-stress and the working-load stress. In pre-tensioned, pre-stressed concrete, steel wires are tightened between the ends of a pre-casting mould. After placing, the concrete binds to the wires and prevents them from returning to their original length when the mould is removed, thus inducing compression in the concrete. In post-tensioned pre-stressed concrete, ducts are cast in the member. When the concrete has matured, high-tensile steel wires, rods, or cables are threaded through the ducts, tightened by hydraulic jacks, and anchored at each end, again inducing compression.

prime mover, an original natural or mechanical source of motive power, rather than a machine that only transmits power or transforms it into another form. Thus any form of heat *engine is a prime mover because it generates mechanical power from a source of heat. An electric motor is not a prime mover because it merely converts electric power generated elsewhere into mechanical power output.

printed circuit (printed circuit board, PCB), an assembly of electronic components on a sheet of material (usually fibreglass), in which the interconnections between components are made by copper-based tracks integral with the board. These tracks are formed by coating the board with copper, then photographically depositing a protective coating over the track areas. The board is then *etched to remove the unprotected copper. Components are attached by soldering them to the copper tracks at specified positions. In most contexts printed circuits now contain *integrated circuits instead of individual components.

printer (computer), an *output device for providing printed text and sometimes graphics from a computer. Four main types of printer are in common use. Dot-matrix printers form each character by using combinations of inked needles which are impacted on to the paper under computer control; *ink-jet printers use tiny nozzles to spray ink on to the paper. Daisy-wheel printers are sophisticated developments of conventional typewriters, while *laser printers resemble photocopiers in operation. Dot-matrix printers are inexpensive and can operate fairly rapidly, but lack the quality of daisy-wheel machines. Laser printers provide high speed and quality, but are at present relatively expensive.

printing, the process of reproducing copies of text, pictures, or designs on to a suitable material such as paper, board, plastic, or metal, usually by pressing an inked image against the material being printed. Early civilizations in the Far East developed the first known forms of printing. In the 8th century the Chinese produced a million copies of Buddhist texts using *wood-blocks, and there is evidence of printing from separate wooden type in China and Korea from the 11th century. In the West, monks used wood-blocks in the late 14th century to print pictures of the saints. However, *Gutenberg in Germany initiated the real development of European printing through his invention of a *typesetting mould for casting individual metal letters.

This new craft of printing spread rapidly across Europe. During the next three centuries, artists, type-founders, artisans, and printers all contributed to advances in the design and quality of printing. New and elegant typefaces were designed, the use of illustration and ornamentation increased, and copper was used for fine engravings. Various non-relief printing processes such as *lithography and *gravure were also developed. Improvements were made to

Printing

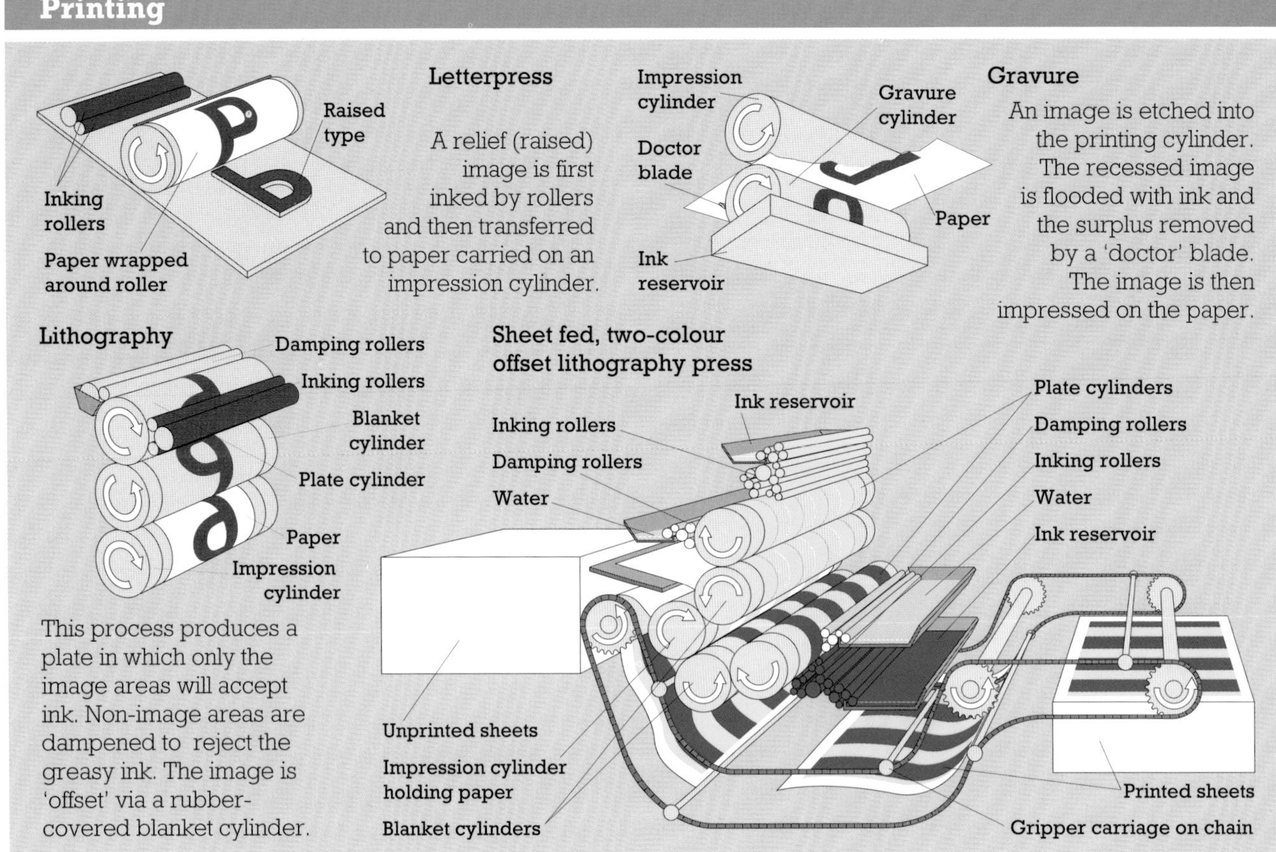
Letterpress
Raised type
Inking rollers
Paper wrapped around roller
A relief (raised) image is first inked by rollers and then transferred to paper carried on an impression cylinder.
Impression cylinder
Gravure cylinder
Doctor blade
Paper
Ink reservoir
Gravure
An image is etched into the printing cylinder. The recessed image is flooded with ink and the surplus removed by a 'doctor' blade. The image is then impressed on the paper.
Lithography
Damping rollers
Inking rollers
Blanket cylinder
Plate cylinder
Paper
Impression cylinder
This process produces a plate in which only the image areas will accept ink. Non-image areas are dampened to reject the greasy ink. The image is 'offset' via a rubber-covered blanket cylinder.
Sheet fed, two-colour offset lithography press
Ink reservoir
Inking rollers
Damping rollers
Water
Plate cylinders
Damping rollers
Inking rollers
Water
Ink reservoir
Unprinted sheets
Impression cylinder holding paper
Blanket cylinders
Printed sheets
Gripper carriage on chain

the basic screw press, including a lever action instead of the screw, and metal construction in place of wood. However, output remained relatively low because of the need to redistribute type before setting it again, the slowness of hand presses, and the need to damp paper before printing on it. The 19th century brought a surge of mechanical inventiveness, which included the development of the platen press, in which a plate presses the paper against the type; the flat-bed cylinder press, in which an inked frame carrying the metal type (known as a forme) moves beneath a cylinder carrying the paper; and the rotary press, using curved printing plates that rotate against paper that is sheet-fed (individual sheets) or reel-fed (continuous sheet). Later in the century, advances were made in the technologies of *typesetting, with the development of *Linotype and *Monotype, of *stereotyping, and of illustration. The principles of *half-tones, *offset lithography, *colour printing, and photography for *platemaking were also laid down during this period, so that by the beginning of the 20th century most of the basic forms of *letterpress, lithographic, and *intaglio printing had been established. Between the two World Wars print engineering was much improved, and photographic methods grew in importance, while modern electronics have made a major impact since 1950.

The three most common printing processes are shown in the figure. The development and use of letterpress printing reached its peak during the first half of the century, but its use has subsequently declined. Gravure and offset printing grew more slowly, but are now highly developed and have set new standards, especially for illustrated work. In these processes, text and pictures do not have to be converted to relief metal images; plates for printing (see platemaking) can be created photographically from camera-ready type and pictures. Thus, while many printing firms themselves still typeset and reproduce pictures, these processes have become increasingly independent of printing. Modern typesetting and *electronic scanning can rapidly provide *digitized forms of image that can be stored on computer, manipulated, transmitted by satellite, and reproduced on film or paper world-wide. Platemaking and printing machines, many of them computer-controlled, can produce quality work at speeds of up to 10,000 sheets per hour, or between 20,000 and 60,000 impressions (copies) per hour on reel-fed presses (see offset lithography). Bookbinding and print finishing have also become increasingly automated to keep pace with the increase in print speeds. Many forms of printing have become specialized for the products that they generate, for example, newspapers, books, banknotes, mail-order material, computer stationery, wallpaper, *textile printing, cartons, or metal containers.

printing (photography) *developing and printing.

prism, a transparent, geometric body, usually triangular in section, having refracting surfaces at acute angles to each other. A simple triangular-section prism can be used to spread light into a spectrum of colours; this was demonstrated by the English scientist Isaac Newton (1642–1727). Other prisms are used to deflect a light path or to invert an image, as in *binoculars, a *periscope, or a *camera viewfinder.

procedure (subroutine), a fundamentally important tool for writing complex computer programs. It is a program which has a well-defined *interface and accomplishes a well-defined task. The procedure can be used, perhaps many times, within a higher-level program. To use, or 'call' a procedure, the programmer needs to understand only the interface of the procedure, not the complexities of its internal details. Writing programs like this is often called structured, or modular, programming. The study of all methods to improve the writability, reliability, and usability of programs is called software engineering.

process engraving, any of various methods of reproducing line or *half-tone printing blocks. Normally, this involves transferring a photographic image to a metal surface, chemically etching away the non-printing areas, and finally mounting the result on a wood or type-metal base. It is mostly used for letterpress illustrations, photogravure cylinders, and bookbinders' blocking stamps. (See also *laser engraving.)

processor *central processing unit, *microprocessor.

progeny testing, a method used to select prospective males for use in *animal breeding. This is done by measuring the meat or milk production of some of the male's offspring (progeny), under normal field conditions in a commercial herd. Males whose progeny show desirable characteristics are selected for breeding using such techniques as *artificial insemination.

program, a set of coded instructions (the *software) to control the operation of a *computer or other machine. For example, utility programs perform tasks usually related to the *operating system. Since the *central processing unit only processes *machine code, programs written in a high-level computer language or assembly language must be translated into machine code before execution. The figure shows a simple program, written in BASIC, to calculate the square root of a number. The program is a sequence of statements which are executed in order. In BASIC each line is numbered. Lines 10–30 are REMarks that help make the program intelligible to users. They have no effect on the execution of the program. Line 40 PRINTs a message on the *visual display unit and line 50 causes the program to wait for the user to INPUT a number from the keyboard. This is stored as a variable named *X*. Variables are stored in *memory and may change their value during the course of the program. Line 60 tests IF the value stored in *X* is less than or equal to zero. If it is THEN the program GOes back TO line 40 and repeats the request for input. If not it goes on to execute line 70, which PRINTs a message and the values of *X* and its square root on the screen. The value of the root is calculated by the function SQR(*X*). Most languages have a number of built-in functions and also allow programmers to define their own. Line 80 causes the program to END. (See also *algorithm.)

programming language *computer language

projection, map, any method used to map the curved surface of the Earth on to a plane surface with the minimum of distortion. Simple graphical projections can be made by fitting a plane surface around a sphere in a variety of ways, for example, as a cylinder or a cone. If the detail on the sphere is now projected on to the plane surface, the points at which it touches the sphere are mapped without distortion, while elsewhere there is some distortion of scale, bearing, shape, or area. Most projections used in *map- and chart-making use mathematical methods based on simple graphical projections but with their formulae adjusted in some way. For example, in some projections there is no distortion of the true shape of the land (orthomorphic projections), while in others the relative areas of the different land masses remain consistent (equal area projection). Orthomorphic projections are essential for *surveying and *navigation, because angles around any point on the map or chart are correctly represented. In navigation this is essential for the

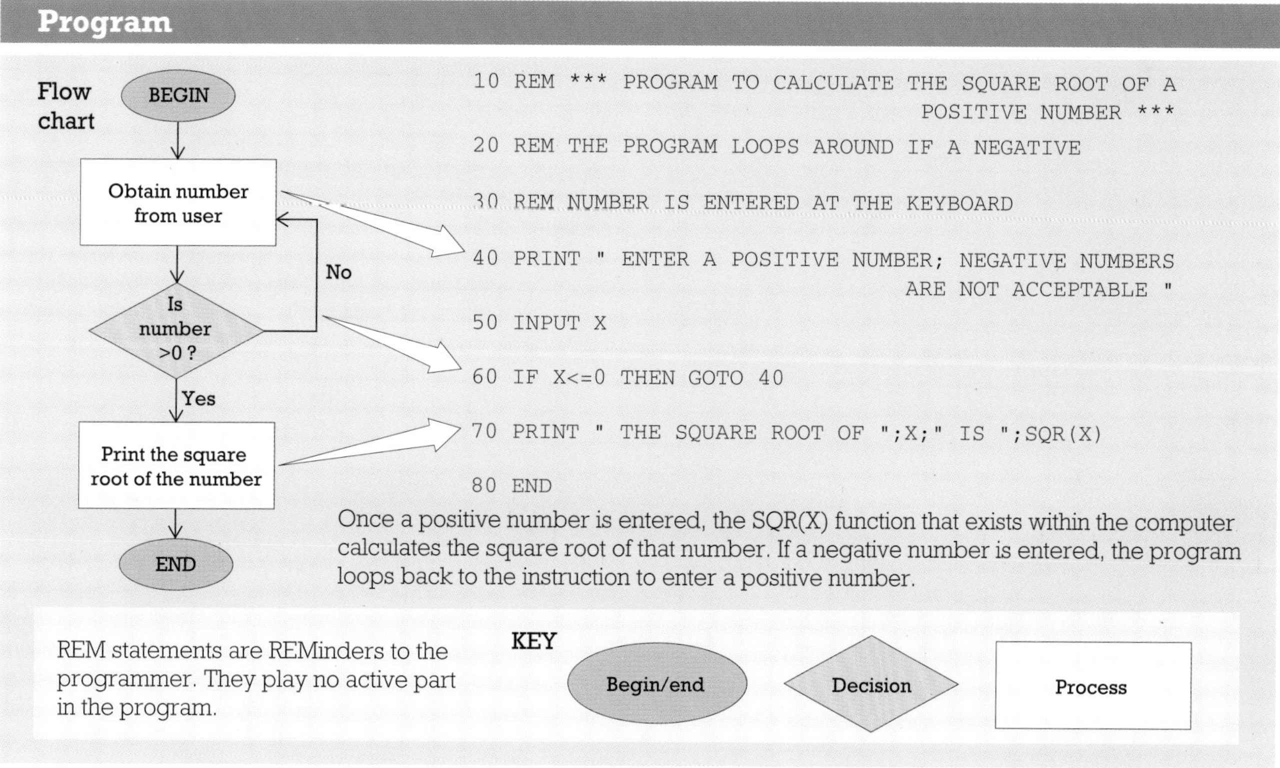
Program
Flow chart
BEGIN
Obtain number from user
Is number >0 ?
No
Yes
Print the square root of the number
END
10 REM *** PROGRAM TO CALCULATE THE SQUARE ROOT OF A POSITIVE NUMBER ***
20 REM THE PROGRAM LOOPS AROUND IF A NEGATIVE
30 REM NUMBER IS ENTERED AT THE KEYBOARD
40 PRINT " ENTER A POSITIVE NUMBER; NEGATIVE NUMBERS ARE NOT ACCEPTABLE "
50 INPUT X
60 IF X<=0 THEN GOTO 40
70 PRINT " THE SQUARE ROOT OF ";X;" IS ";SQR(X)
80 END
Once a positive number is entered, the SQR(X) function that exists within the computer calculates the square root of that number. If a negative number is entered, the program loops back to the instruction to enter a positive number.
REM statements are REMinders to the programmer. They play no active part in the program.
KEY
Begin/end
Decision
Process

Projection, map

This diagram shows how the globe can be projected on to a plane surface. At the line or point where the plane surface touches the globe (the standard parallel) there is no distortion of scale or shape.

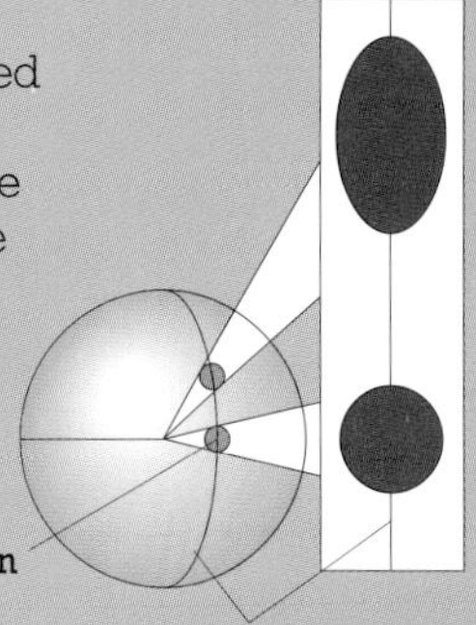

Peters projection

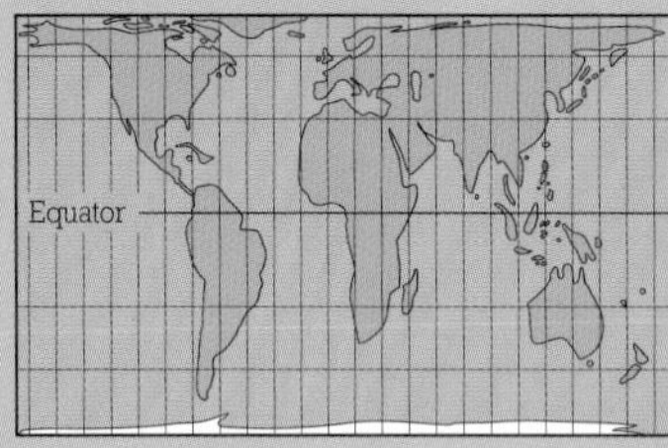

A mathematically derived projection showing the relative sizes of the land masses. It shows the size of the poor South compared to the rich North.

Modified conical

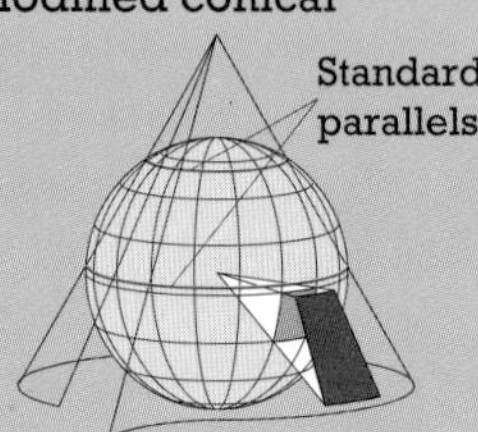

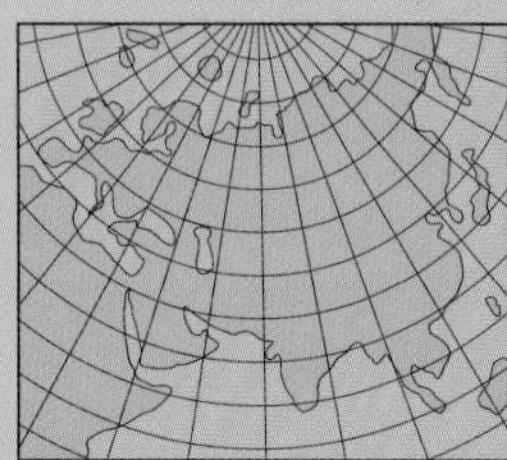

A conical projection, but with two standard parallels. Widely used in atlases for mapping small countries.

Mercator

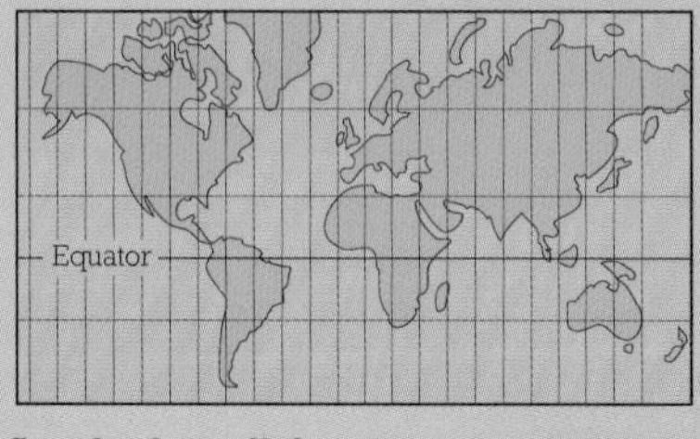

Based on a cylindrical projection with the equator as the standard parallel. Widely used for navigational charts, but has large scale distortions at high latitudes.

Transverse Mercator

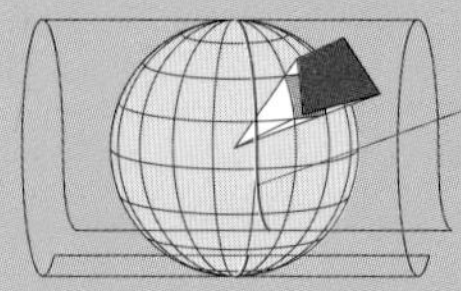

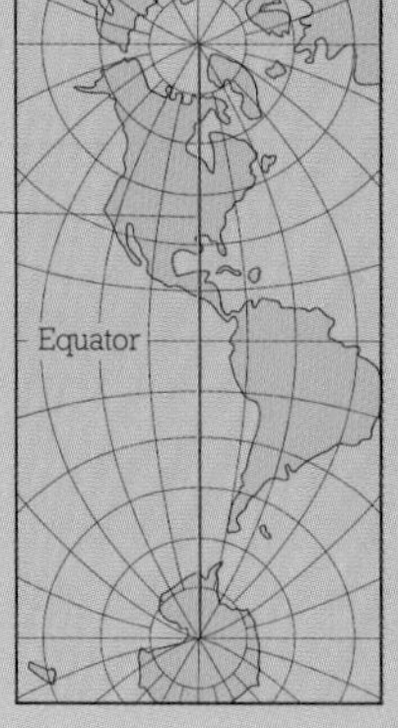

Based on a cylindrical projection at a chosen standard longitude. Widely used for sea-navigation charts. Can be used to map the poles.

plotting of bearings, while in surveying it is necessary for accurately plotting details of a triangulation.

projector (photography), a device for shining an enlarged image (still or moving) on to a screen. All projectors work on the same basic principle. A light source is used to illuminate an image which is held accurately in position, while a lens focuses an enlarged version of this image on to a screen. Most modern still projectors are designed to be used with transparencies (slides) made on 35-mm *film. To create the illusion of movement, cine-projectors have to show a rapid succession of images at a regular speed, keeping each image steady on the screen for an instant. An intermittent claw mechanism and a rotating shutter are used to achieve this, as in a *cine-camera.

propane ($CH_3CH_2CH_3$), a *hydrocarbon obtained from natural gas or from *petroleum refining. It is readily liquefied by compression and cooling, and in pressurized containers it constitutes an important industrial and domestic fuel (see *liquid petroleum gas). In particular, it is being increasingly used for welding torches and as a cheaper alternative to petrol in specially adapted automobile engines.

propanone (acetone, $CH_3 \cdot CO \cdot CH_3$), a colourless, low-boiling-point, highly flammable liquid with a characteristic pungent odour. It was originally made by distilling wood, but is now produced commercially by fermentation of corn or molasses, or by controlled oxidation of *hydrocarbons. It is widely used as a solvent for *nitro-cellulose, *ethyne (acetylene), and varnishes; as a remover of paint, varnish, and fingernail polish; and in the manufacture of drugs.

propellant *explosive, *rocket motor.

propeller, a power-driven rotating hub fitted with helical blades that propels an aeroplane or ship by its rotation. The *aerofoil section and overall shape of each propeller blade acts to accelerate a stream of air or water through the propeller disc, thus providing thrust. Experiments with screw propulsion for ships were made in the 18th century, but it was not until 1836 that patents on practical screw propellers were taken out, by Francis Pettit Smith in the UK, and by *Ericsson in the USA. Early ship's propellers were two-bladed, but multi-bladed designs soon evolved to improve efficiency. Earlier designs were fixed pitch, that is, the propeller blades met the water at a fixed angle. Fixed-pitch propellers are optimally efficient when the ship is travelling at one particular speed: variable-pitch propellers have therefore been evolved, in which the blade angle adopts optimally to the changing speed of the vessel. More recently several other forms of propeller have come into use, for example, the cycloidal or Schneider propeller, used on some tugs and large ferries, which is vertically mounted and requires no rudder.

Aeroplane propellers are larger than marine screw-propellers, since air is a much less dense medium, and much larger volumes must be accelerated to obtain adequate thrust. Propellers are more efficient than *jet engines at speeds below about 800 km/h (500 m.p.h.). For most propeller-driven aircraft today, variable-pitch propellers are used. Contra-rotating propellers are used with some more powerful engines: in these, two propellers rotate in opposite directions on the same axis, counteracting the twisting force induced by a single propeller.

prospecting, exploration in search of mineral deposits. Prospecting techniques can be broadly divided into two categories: direct and indirect. The former includes study of existing geological maps and guides to *ores, supplemented by surface examination in the field, which may involve exploratory probes by drilling or trenching. If a potentially workable vein outcrops at the surface, an estimate must be made of how far it extends; it may, for example, end abruptly in a major fault, plunging too deep to be followed. Samples of ore must be analysed to see whether working the vein is economically worthwhile. Indirect techniques include looking for surface signs of underlying ore, such as rock staining or a distinctive pattern of vegetation. For example, outcrops of the enormous copper–cobalt deposits of Zaïre and Zambia support a characteristic flora of metal-tolerant plants. Modern methods include magnetic surveys on the ground and from the air; seismic probes (see *petroleum, exploration, and recovery); analysis of gas that has seeped up through the overlay; and observation from *Earth resources satellites in space. Certain elements, notably uranium and thorium, can be located by their radioactivity using a Geiger–Müller counter. (See also *mining, *quarrying.)

prosthesis, an artificial replacement for part of the body, which may be functional, structural, or both. Some prostheses, such as cardiac *pacemakers or *hip replacements, are surgically implanted. Others are worn, such as *hearing aids, dentures, or *artificial limbs.

protocol (computing), a set of rules determining the formats by which information may be exchanged between different computer systems. Protocols for data communication are set by international bodies such as the International Standardization Organization (ISO) and the International Telegraphy and Telephone Consultative Committee (CCITT), a branch of the *International Telecommunication Union.

protractor *goniometer.

psychotropic drug, any member of a large group of substances used in the treatment of psychological disorders. They are classified according to the conditions for which they are given, and each class is further divided according to the chemical nature of the drug. Major *tranquillizers, such as phenothiazines, may be given for severe psychotic disorders such as schizophrenia and mania; they are sometimes called neuroleptics. Minor tranquillizers, of which the most popular are the benzodiazepines, are effective in anxiety states. Antidepressants are used to relieve severe depression and are classified according to their chemical structure (for example, tricyclic antidepressants) or their biochemical actions (for example, monoamine oxidase inhibitors). The mode of action of psychotropic drugs may give information about the nature of the disease in which they are effective. For example, antidepressants are known to increase the concentration of certain chemical transmitters at the ends of nerves in the brain. This fact has led to the hypothesis that depression is caused by an abnormally low concentration of such transmitters. Many such hypotheses depend on an over-simplified view of an exceedingly complicated subject, and have not stood the test of time. Nevertheless, the discovery and marketing of psychotropic drugs has been an important branch of pharmaceutics over the last twenty years. Psychotropic drugs are sometimes used in conditions other than mental disease: for example, the neuroleptic chlorpromazine is effective in stopping severe vomiting, and the benzodiazepines may be used to treat some forms of epilepsy. (See also *pharmacology table.)

PTFE (polytetrafluoroethene), a thermoplastic *polymer made from the monomer tetrafluoroethene ($CF_2=CF_2$). It has a very high resistance to attack by chemicals, stability at high temperatures, and a very low coefficient of friction. It is used for its low-friction properties as a coating on cooking equipment, gaskets, skis, chemical apparatus, and laboratory ware, and on handling equipment for food and drugs. It is also used in high-temperature cable and wire insulation.

Ptolemy (Claudius Ptolemaeus) (*fl.* AD 127–145), Alexandrian Greek mathematician, astronomer, and geographer. Ptolemy's major astronomical work was the *Almagest*, which synthesized much of the work of Greek astronomers; as a mathematician he performed important work in geometry, and published five books on optics. His geographical work consisted of eight books entitled the *Guide to Geography*; the maps in these volumes include a world map that formed the basis of European maps in the 15th century.

puddling process, a method (now obsolete) of making wrought *iron by melting down pig-iron in the presence of iron oxide. Silicon, sulphur, and other impurities are removed as slag. On raising the temperature, carbon reacts with the iron oxide and the carbon monoxide gas evolved causes 'boiling' of the melt. As the puddling process reaches completion, the iron melt becomes stiff and pasty, and is removed from the furnace in large lumps. These are hammered to squeeze out some of the slag, then rolled.

pulley, a wheel mounted on an axle and used with a rope or belt. Pulleys can be used to obtain a *mechanical advantage, or to change the rotational speed of a shaft. When used in a pulley-block it is known as a sheave, and such blocks were much used in the running rigging of sailing ships. Later, rope belts and pulleys were used as a means of power transmission, particularly in textile mills, where an engine with a large flywheel drove a horizontal shaft on each floor of the mill. Flat leather belts were commonly used with pulleys to connect each machine to this shaft. By having a free-wheeling pulley adjacent to the drive pulley and a means of moving the belt sideways, each machine could be started or stopped. Speed increase or decrease could be obtained by using pulleys of differing diameter. For a more compact drive 'vee' pulleys and belts are used (see *belt and chain drive). Jockey pulleys are small idling pulleys used to tighten a belt or to change its direction.

pulse code modulation (PCM), a method of *digitalization and *modulation of an information signal. The information signal is sampled frequently and the instantaneous value is coded in digital form. Each coded sample is then transmitted as a group of pulses of light (in optical fibres), electricity (in copper cables), or radio waves (for free-space transmission). A PCM system was patented in the UK in 1926 by P. M. Rainey. However, the innovation was ignored, and in 1937 A. H. Reeves independently proposed the idea. PCM lends itself to *multiplexing, and is used extensively in *telephony. A similar technique is used in digital audio searching on tape or *compact disc.

pump, a machine used to transport, raise, or compress fluids. The earliest pumps were used to lift water from wells:

Pump

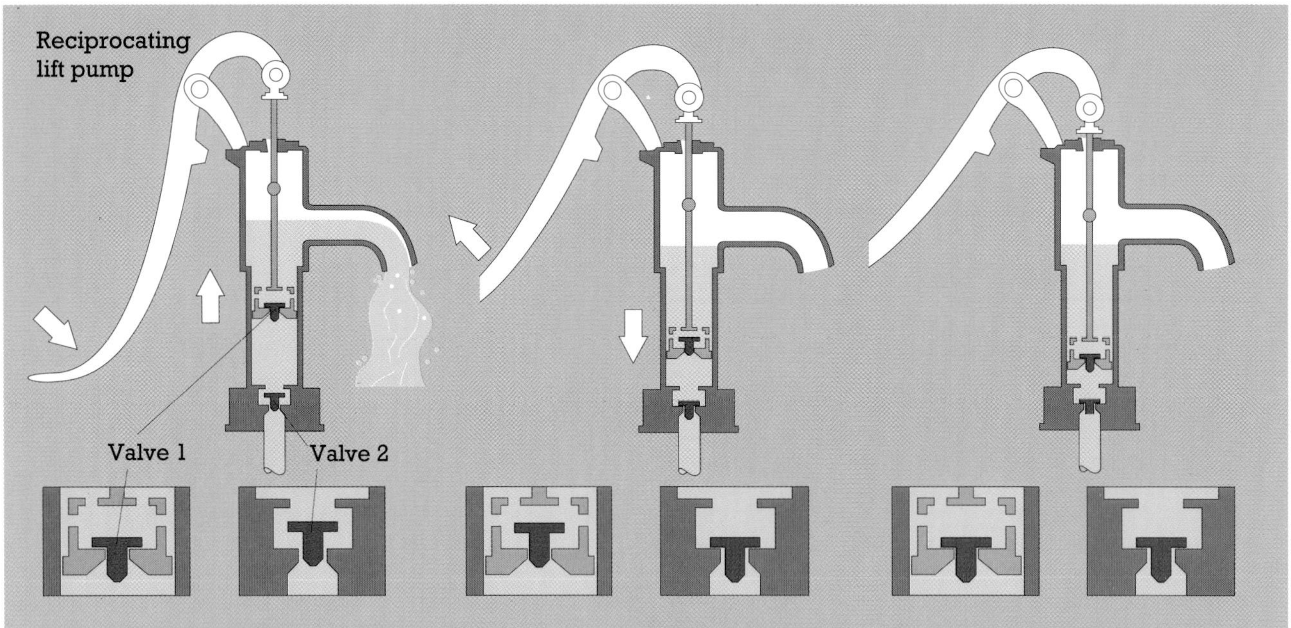

Reciprocating lift pump

As the piston is raised, valve 1 is closed by the weight of liquid above it, while suction opens valve 2 to let in more liquid from below.

Having delivered some liquid, the piston is lowered. Valve 1 opens to allow water through. Valve 2 is pushed down, preventing loss of liquid back down the supply pipe.

The pump is now ready to lift another column of liquid.

Reciprocating diaphragm pump

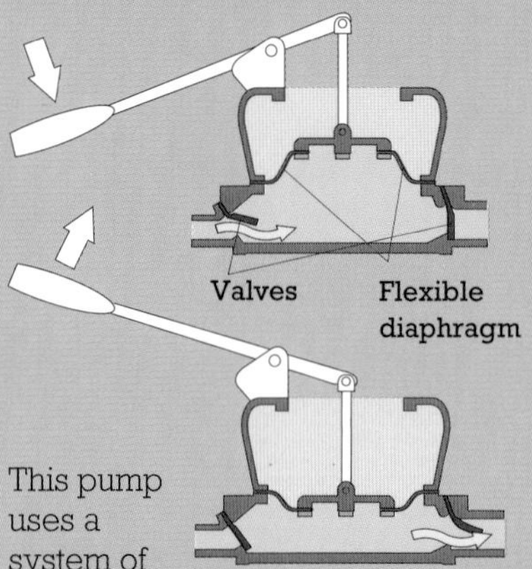

This pump uses a system of two pressure-operated diaphragm valves, like the lift pump.

Gear pump

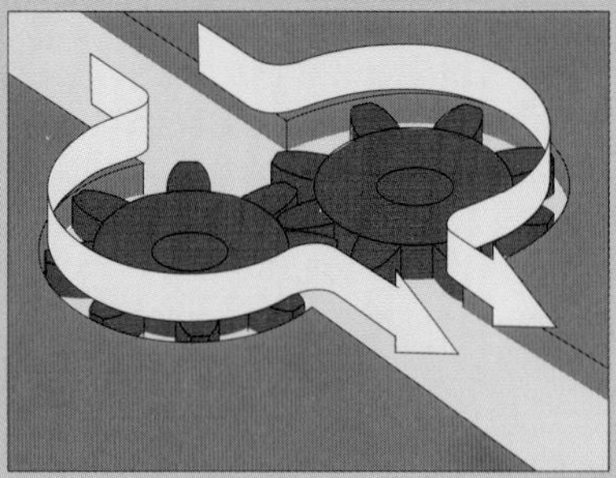

This pump has no valves. Liquid moves between the gear teeth and the casing; back-flow is prevented by meshing of the teeth.

Centrifugal pump

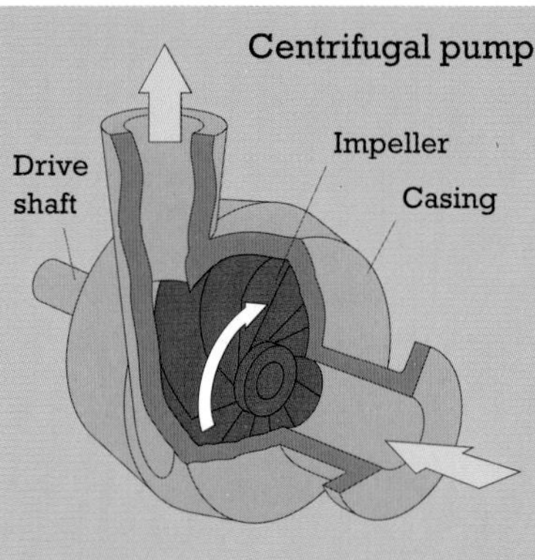

The fluid enters the pump, and the rotating impeller creates a vortex in the fluid, giving a greater pressure at the outer edge than at the centre. Fluid is continuously pumped without the use of valves.

a type of reciprocating lift pump (see figure) was known in Egypt from the 2nd century BC; other early devices for pumping water were *water-wheels and the *Archimedean screw. During the Middle Ages reciprocating pumps were reinvented for pumping water from mines, and in the 19th century many different types of rotary pump were developed. In the 20th century there has been a proliferation of pump types for a wide range of uses, including mine drainage, water supply, sewage pumping, pumping oil through pipelines, hydraulic power, pumping lubricants or coolants, and fire-fighting. The many pump types can be broadly classified as positive displacement, in which fluid by a rotor is displaced either mechanically or by another fluid; kinetic (rotodynamic), in which motion is imparted to the fluid; or electromagnetic, in which electromagnetic force is used to move or compress the fluid. Most pumps are of the positive displacement or kinetic variety.

pumped storage, a method of *energy storage using electric power to pump water from a lower reservoir to an upper one. The stored water can then be released to generate *hydroelectric power. Pumped storage is not in itself a source of energy, but it increases the efficiency with which other sources are used. Demand for electricity fluctuates continuously, but *power-stations, particularly *nuclear-power plants, run most economically with a steady output. Storing the surplus during times of low demand for use when demand rises can therefore improve the overall efficiency of the network.

punched-card machine *computer, history of.

putty, a stiff paste of linseed oil mixed with whiting (ground chalk), used for fixing panes of glass. An airtight seal is achieved between the glass and the surrounding frame whilst the putty is still plastic; the oil then slowly oxidizes on exposure to air, hardening the putty. Putty is also used as a filler for woodwork.

PVC (polyvinyl chloride), a thermoplastic *polymer made from vinyl chloride (C_2H_3Cl), itself derived from *ethene. PVC is a colourless solid with outstanding resistance to water, alcohols, and concentrated acids and alkalis. It is obtainable as granules, solutions, lattices, and pastes. When compounded with *plasticizers, it yields a flexible material more durable than *rubber. It is widely used for cable and wire insulation, in chemical plants, and in the manufacture of protective garments. Blow *moulding of unplasticized PVC (uPVC) produces clear, tough bottles which do not affect the flavour of their contents. uPVC is also used for *drains and other types of *tube or pipe.

PVD (physical vapour deposition) *vapour deposition.

PWR *pressurized-water reactor.

pyramid, a monumental structure, often built as a royal tomb and usually made of stone, with a square base and sloping sides meeting centrally at an apex. Pyramids are of two main types: the step pyramid, exemplified by that of Zoser at Saqqara, Egypt, (*c.*2800 BC), and the true pyramids, introduced at Giza, Egypt, *c.*2500 BC, and continuing until *c.*1640 BC. Stepped pyramids known as ziggurats survive from the 3rd millennium BC in Mesopotamia. Stepped-pyramid structures were also built as bases for temples by the Mayan, Aztec, and Toltec civilizations of Central America (AD *c.*250–1520). True pyramids, such as the Great Pyramid of Cheops at Giza, were built of enormous blocks of stone, the largest weighing more than 200 tonnes. Using abundant slave labour and wooden sleds, these could be transported to the site with little difficulty, probably using a large stone causeway. To construct the lower tiers, the blocks could have been lifted on ramps, but how the higher levels were built is less certain. Certainly, the Egyptians, though they knew the wheel, were not familiar with the pulley. It is probable that the pre-shaped blocks were finally manœuvred into position by floating them on a layer of liquid mortar.

pyrethrum *insecticide.

pyrometer *temperature measurement.

quadrant, probably the earliest astronomical instrument to be used at sea, consisting of a flat plate in the shape of a quarter-circle, with a plumb-line suspended from the apex. It was used in the 15th century to measure the altitude (height above the horizon) of a celestial body, usually the pole star. The English quadrant or back-staff, first described in 1595, was a more complex instrument that measured the altitude of the Sun by the shadow the quadrant cast. The back-staff was more accurate than previous instruments, and had the advantage that the observer had his back to the Sun. It generally superseded the old quadrant, the *astrolabe, and the *cross-staff in the 17th century.

quality assurance, quality control *mass production.

quarrying, the extraction of granite, limestone, slate, or other stone from an open working. The process of obtaining coal and metallic ore from surface workings is known as *open-cast mining. There are two distinct types of quarrying. One involves the preparation of blocks of specific size and shape (dimension-stone quarrying) for building, paving, memorial stones, and so on. The second is the production of crushed and broken stone, for road-making and other civil engineering purposes, and for use in some chemical and metallurgical processes. For dimension-stone a first requirement is suitable deposits of uniform colour and texture. Explosives can be used only sparingly because of their shattering effect, and much of the stone is cut out with mechanical saws. Drilling-and-broaching is a method in which a row of holes is drilled close together; the solid areas between the holes are then broken down, using a broaching tool, to complete the cut. In quarrying for crushed stone, explosives are freely used and thousands of cubic metres may be thrown down in one firing. Large blocks are broken down with smaller charges or by having a heavy steel ball dropped on them. The stone is then taken away to be crushed and graded.

quartz clock, quartz watch *clocks and time measurement, *watch.

quenching, a heat treatment in which metal at a high temperature is rapidly cooled by immersion in water or oil. This may maintain the properties associated with the crystal structure present at the high temperature or cause a transformation different from that which occurs on slow cooling. Quenching *steel produces a hard, brittle structure known as martensite.

racing car, a *motor car adapted or specially designed for racing. Car manufacturers often maintain racing teams as a test-bed for new ideas and innovations. Examples include the use of new materials such as *fibre-reinforced plastics and new types of *ceramic in car bodies and materials; and the development of electronic systems controlling the engine (for example, electronic *ignition). Monocoque construction—in which the car body is made as one unit, with the chassis integral with the body—was first applied to racing cars. Current racing-car features, such as electronic automatic transmission, may be developed for future mass-produced vehicles.

rack-and-pinion railway, a railway that uses toothed gears to ensure that locomotives do not slip when working on inclines with gradients greater than 1 in 20. A driver pinion (geared wheel) in the locomotive meshes with a rack (or racks) attached to the sleepers or rails of the running line. Rack-and-pinion railways are used in mountainous areas for both passenger and large-scale freight operations.

radar (*ra*dio *d*etection *a*nd *r*anging), a device for remotely determining the direction, range, or presence of objects using *radio waves. It is used in *air-traffic control, for navigation by ships, aircraft, and some *missiles, and in *warning and detection systems. It provides a means of detecting objects over quite long distances or when visibility is poor. The principle of radar was first discovered in 1904 by the Austrian Karl Hülsmeier. In 1935 R. M. Page in the USA constructed a radar device that was used to determine the positions of aircraft. A comprehensive radar system, then called radio direction finding (RDF), was developed independently in the UK from 1935 by *Watson-Watt and others. The invention in 1939 of the magnetron, a *thermionic valve capable of producing pulsed radio waves of very high (microwave) frequencies, made radar a practical proposition, and it played a decisive role in World War II. From 1945 radar became commercially available.

Radar measures the distance of an object from a radar transmitter by timing the interval between the transmission of a pulse of radio waves and the reception of the echo of the pulse from the object. The distance can be calculated from the time interval because the speed of the radio waves (the speed of light) is known. The pulses of radio waves are usually directed in a narrow beam from the transmitting *antenna, enabling the bearing of the object to be determined. Usually, the radar antenna rotates continuously, so that the radar beam is scanned through 360 degrees. The positions of objects detected by the radar are normally displayed on a plan position indicator (PPI), in which the radar transmitter is at the centre of the screen, and the objects detected appear as bright spots or areas of light. The position of the object on the screen corresponds to its position in space. Another form of radar is secondary radar, in which the reception of a radar pulse at the target object triggers another pulse from a transmitter carried by the target (usually a ship or aeroplane). Secondary radar can be used over a longer range than normal radar, and information about the target object can be obtained from the triggered pulse. (See also *Doppler effect.)

Gornegrat railway in Zermat, Switzerland, an example of a **rack-and-pinion railway**. The toothed rack, visible down the centre of the track, engages with a cog on the locomotive, providing tractive power on steep slopes.

radiation, nuclear, energetic particles, or energy, emitted by *radioactive isotopes, or during nuclear *fission or *fusion. Radioactive *isotopes decay in specific ways by emitting certain particles, or quanta of energy. The three most common ways are by alpha-, beta-, and gamma-radiation. Alpha-radiation, for example from *uranium, is the emission of positively charged alpha particles (two neutrons plus two protons), like the nucleus of a helium atom. Alpha-radiation has a range of a few centimetres in air, and can be deflected by electric or magnetic fields. Beta-radiation is the emission of beta particles, electrons moving at high speed. Beta-radiation has a range in air of many centimetres and is strongly deflected by an electric or magnetic field. Gamma-radiation consists of photons (high-frequency *electromagnetic radiation with no mass or charge), and is not deflected in an electric or magnetic field. It has a range of many centimetres even in lead. Gamma-radiation can accompany both alpha- and beta-radiation and is more harmful to life than other forms, being able to pass through body tissues and cause *cancers. Radiation can be detected by several devices, including the *Geiger–Müller counter and subatomic *particle detectors.

radiator *cooling system, *central heating.

radio, communication by the transmission of information via *electromagnetic radiation in the *frequency range 3 kHz to 40,000 MHz, *wavelength range 1 cm to more than 1 km (0.4 inch to 0.6 mile). The radio-frequency spectrum is arbitrarily divided into a number of *wavebands, from very low frequencies (long wavelengths) to ultra-high and microwave frequencies (short wavelengths). Sections of the spectrum have been allocated by international agreement to use for telegraph, telephonic speech, and radio and televi-

Radio

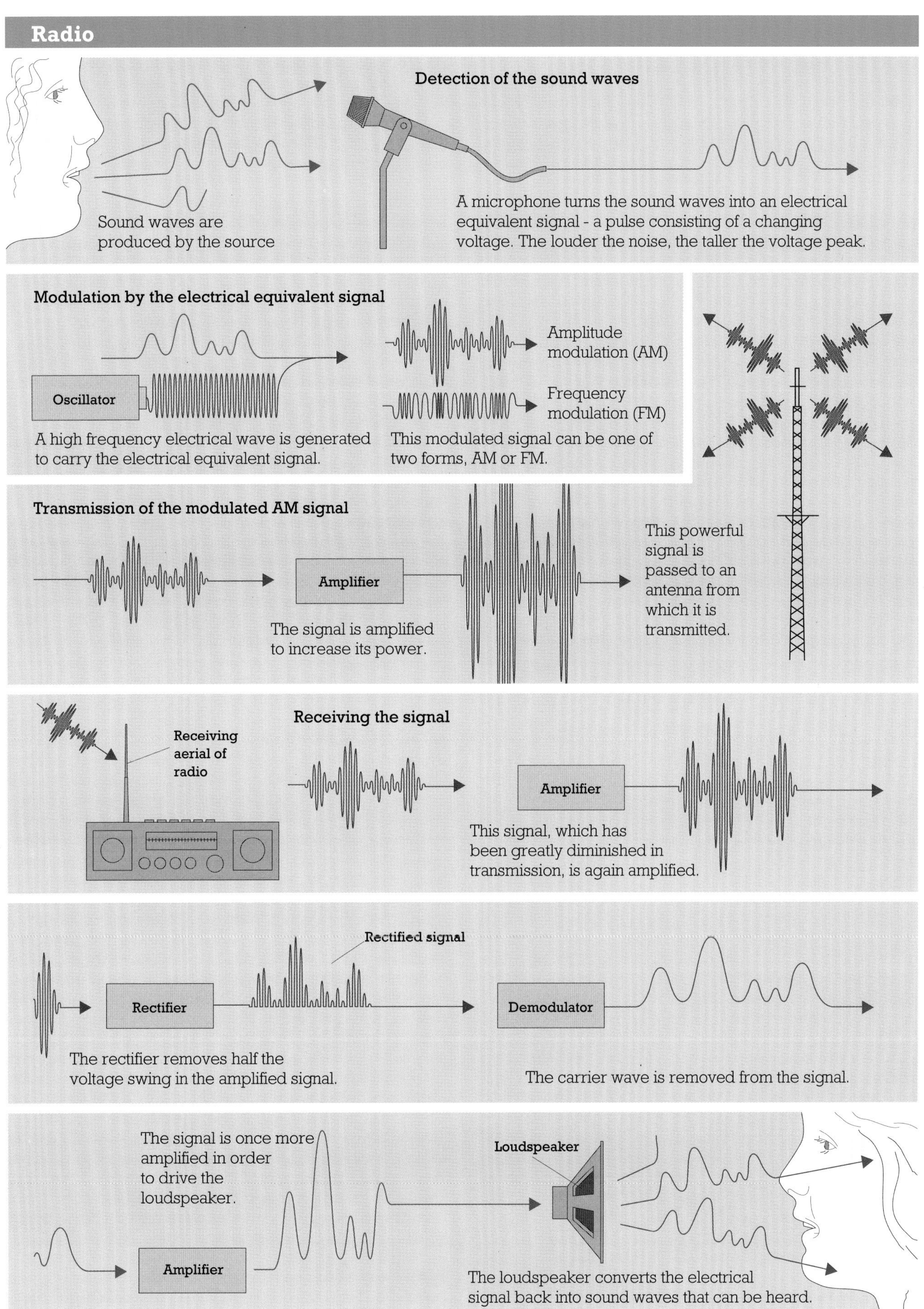
Detection of the sound waves
Sound waves are produced by the source
A microphone turns the sound waves into an electrical equivalent signal - a pulse consisting of a changing voltage. The louder the noise, the taller the voltage peak.
Modulation by the electrical equivalent signal
Oscillator
Amplitude modulation (AM)
Frequency modulation (FM)
A high frequency electrical wave is generated to carry the electrical equivalent signal.
This modulated signal can be one of two forms, AM or FM.
Transmission of the modulated AM signal
Amplifier
The signal is amplified to increase its power.
This powerful signal is passed to an antenna from which it is transmitted.
Receiving aerial of radio
Receiving the signal
Amplifier
This signal, which has been greatly diminished in transmission, is again amplified.
Rectified signal
Rectifier
Demodulator
The rectifier removes half the voltage swing in the amplified signal.
The carrier wave is removed from the signal.
The signal is once more amplified in order to drive the loudspeaker.
Loudspeaker
Amplifier
The loudspeaker converts the electrical signal back into sound waves that can be heard.

sion broadcasting. In order to be transmitted, the information in a radio signal is used to *modulate a radio-frequency wave. The modulated radio signal is then amplified, and a transmitting *antenna projects as much as possible of the radio-frequency energy into space. The signals are picked up by a *radio receiver tuned in to the wavelength of the transmission (see figure). In 1864 the British physicist James Clerk Maxwell predicted the existence of electromagnetic radiation and its ability to travel through space at the speed of light. *Hertz confirmed Maxwell's theories experimentally in 1888, but it was *Marconi who developed these discoveries with regard to communications. In 1896 he transmitted a radio signal from Penarth to Weston-super-Mare, UK; in 1901 he transmitted the letter 's' in Morse code across the Atlantic from Poldhu in Cornwall, UK, to St Johns, Newfoundland, Canada, using a large antenna supported by two 60-m (200-foot) towers. Marconi's broadcasts were *telegraphic signals rather than sound transmissions. Early in the 20th century *Fessenden developed amplitude modulation, which made it possible to transmit sound by radio. In 1906 he made a music transmission that was picked up by several wireless operators and was claimed as the first radio broadcast. These innovations led to the development of simple crystal *radio receivers after World War I. By 1921 regular programmes were being transmitted from eight stations in the USA; the BBC was transmitting in the UK by 1923, and by 1925 there were 600 radio stations world-wide. Since the 1920s radio has changed enormously due to research work in Europe, the USA, and Asia. The introduction of *transistors and *integrated circuits revolutionized receiver design. As the number of radio-frequency users has increased, higher radio-frequencies have been exploited. Wavebands in the microwave range are increasingly being used for national communications using transmission masts, and for international communications using *satellites.

radioactive isotope (radioisotope), an unstable chemical *isotope that decays to a lighter element with the emission of *radiation. Very few naturally occurring elements are radioactive (examples are *uranium and *radium), but radioactive isotopes of many common elements occur naturally in minute quantities. Other radioactive materials have been produced artificially, for example through nuclear *fission: examples are *plutonium, strontium-90, and caesium-137. Radioactive decay occurs because the nuclei of such elements are unstable. The rate of this decay can vary enormously: the half-life (the time taken for half of a given mass of the material to decay) of a radioactive isotope may vary from over a billion (10^9) years to a tiny fraction of a second. Radioactive elements have a variety of uses. Uranium and plutonium are *nuclear fuels and provide materials for *nuclear weapons. The rate of decay of radioactive isotopes such as carbon-14 can be used as a *dating system to estimate the age of rocks, fossils, and other artefacts. Small quantities of radioactive material can be used to 'tag' a compound, so that its presence can be detected remotely using a radiation detector. Such tagging is used in many applications, for example in *nuclear medicine. Radioactive materials are also used to treat some *cancers and as power sources for small *thermionic and *thermoelectric generators used in space *satellites and other applications.

radioactive waste disposal *nuclear fuel.

radio aid to navigation, a term used to describe any of the large range of navigational instruments and systems that rely on *radio waves for their operation. Such aids include radio *altimeters, and *automatic landing systems that help a pilot approach and land at an airport in poor visibility. However, most important are the large range of radio devices that enable a vehicle to fix its position. One type of positional device is the hyperbolic navigation system. In this a group of co-ordinated radio transmitters in different locations transmit synchronized radio pulses, from which, with suitable receiving equipment, a vehicle can calculate its position (for illustration see *navigation). The position may be plotted using a specially gridded map or chart, or calculated by a computer in the receiver. Other radio navigation aids include VOR (VHF Omni-Range) and DME (Distance Measuring Equipment), two short-range systems used mainly by aircraft, which provide readings of distance and bearing from a particular radio beacon. (See also *navigational satellite.)

radio-carbon dating, a method of dating organic materials, based on the decay of the *radioactive isotope carbon-14 to nitrogen-14. This method of dating was invented by *Libby in 1947. Living material contains the carbon *isotopes carbon-14 (C-14) and carbon-12 (C-12) in equilibrium with the same isotopes in the atmosphere. When an organism dies, however, it no longer takes in carbon dioxide from the atmosphere and the C-14 begins to decay to nitrogen-14, at a known rate. By measuring the C-14 : C-12 ratio in an organic artefact, its age (up to a limit of about 40,000 years) can be determined. However, there are some problems in interpretation. For example, the atmospheric C-14 : C-12 ratio has not stayed absolutely constant over the last 40,000 years. To compensate for this, radio-carbon dates have been calibrated by comparison with other *dating systems, notably dendrochronology (the study of the annual rings of trees).

radio-frequency heating, a method of heating materials using an alternating electric current. The heat is generated in the material itself—as distinct from other methods of heating, which rely on an external heat source. Radio-frequency energy of up to 40 kW of power can be generated by *transistor-based *oscillators. The two radio-frequency heating techniques in use are dielectric heating (frequency range 100 kHz–10 MHz) and eddy current or induction heating (5–3,000 MHz). Dielectric heating is used with electrically non-conducting materials that are sandwiched between two metal electrodes connected to the generator. The molecules of the material move in step with the radio-frequency field, and heat is produced uniformly throughout the material. Applications include the domestic *microwave cooker, medical *diathermy, the welding of some thermoplastics, and the rapid curing of glues. Induction heating is used with conducting materials that are surrounded by a coil connected to the generator. The coil constitutes the primary winding of a *transformer and the material the secondary. Currents induced in the material generate heat on its surface only. Applications include brazing and heat-treatment of alloys prior to *quenching. Radio-frequency heating allows precise and rapid heating, but only of suitable materials. Unshielded radio-frequency heating equipment causes interference to radio communications and can be a health hazard.

radioimmunoassay, a type of biochemical assay using antibodies 'tagged' with a *radioactive isotope to measure how much chemical or protein is present in a blood sample or other specimen. The antibodies will attach very specifically to one type of molecule (for example, a hormone such as thyroxine). The amount of combined hormone–antibody complex can then be determined from the quantity of radioactivity in a sample. Using very sensitive instruments, this technique enables minute amounts of material to be measured very accurately.

radiology (medicine), the application of radiation for diagnostic or therapeutic purposes. (Separate but related specialities include *radiotherapy and *nuclear medicine.) Doctors used *X-rays within months of their discovery in 1895 to detect broken bones. In the following decades, medical practitioners accumulated knowledge of the X-ray appearances of normal structures. By 1948, radiology was a recognized medical speciality, such that only radiologists, who were medically qualified, reported on X-ray films, even though highly qualified radiographers were (and still are) responsible for taking most of the X-ray pictures. X-rays have also been used to screen symptomless people for disease, most notably in the anti-tuberculosis campaigns of the 1940s and 1950s. Some parts of the body do not show clearly on an X-ray, however, and so techniques have been developed for injecting such parts with non-toxic, radio-opaque substances (contrast media). For example, barium suphate is commonly given orally to reveal the upper or lower gut.

Essentially, radiography involves placing a patient between an X-ray tube and a chemically coated X-ray-sensitive film. Until the 1960s it was common to make a fluoroscopic examination to reveal the movement as well as the structure of the organ. This entailed using a glass viewing screen coated with chemicals to convert the X-rays into visible light. Today, this technique has been largely superseded by the image intensifier, which simultaneously displays the X-ray image on a television screen. X-rays can be converted to and recorded in digital form, to allow compact storage. Moreover, electronic data can be manipulated to enhance the image, so that, for example, the dose of contrast medium needed for some types of examination may be reduced. Minimizing patient dosage and protecting operators from exposure have been important concerns of conventional radiology since the hazards of radiation were appreciated early this century. Radiology now incorporates sophisticated techniques such as *computerized axial tomography, as well as some imaging methods that do not use ionizing radiation, such as *ultrasound and *magnetic resonance imaging.

radiometer, any instrument to detect and measure the energy of *electromagnetic radiation. One of the earliest examples was the Crookes radiometer. In this, very lightweight vanes are attached to a vertical axis, in a globe evacuated to low pressure. Alternate faces of the vanes are coloured black. The absorption of radiation by the black surfaces causes a slight rise in temperature, warming the air in contact with them, and causing the vanes to rotate. Another type of radiometer is the bolometer. This is a sensitive device for measuring microwave or infra-red energy, which it detects as changes (caused by an increase in temperature) in the electrical resistance of a fine strip of metal such as platinum or semiconductor, for example an oxide of manganese or nickel.

radio receiver, a device that detects *modulated *radio signals and converts them into sound. The earliest receiver was the simple 1920s crystal set. In this, a *tuner selected the appropriate channel from the variety picked up by the *antenna. A *rectifier changed the radio-frequency wave from alternating current into pulses of direct current. These pulses of current were then fed to headphones, which operated in a similar way to the speaker in a *telephone receiver. Such a crude system was deficient in strength and quality. In 1904 J. A. *Fleming discovered that an electrode operating inside the evacuated envelope of a heated filament lamp would pass a current in only one direction. Fleming's diode, as he called it, was the earliest *thermionic valve. It could be used to detect radio-frequency waves, but the possibilities of this discovery were not immediately explored. Then in 1906 *De Forest produced a modification of Fleming's diode that gave a large voltage at the output for a small voltage change at the input. De Forest called his invention the audion: it was a major breakthrough because it made it possible to amplify the radio signal, enabling much weaker signals to be detected. The diode and audion revolutionized radio receiver design. *Shockley's invention in 1948 of the semiconductor *diode and the *transistor, replaced valves and heralded radio miniaturization. Modern radio receivers operate on the superheterodyne principle. In such receivers, the rectified radio signal is mixed with a signal from an oscillator inside the radio, to give an intermediate signal. The frequency of this intermediate signal is the same whatever frequency the radio is tuned to. The amplifiers and other components of the receiver operate on this intermediate frequency: they are thus much simpler and more efficient than if they had to cope with a whole range of frequencies.

radiosonde, a small package of meteorological instruments, carried through the atmosphere by a balloon or other

The dish of the Mark 1A **radio telescope** at Jodrell Bank, near Manchester, UK. The dish, which measures 76m (250 feet) in diameter, pivots around its supporting axis, and can be rotated through 360° on a circular track, enabling it to cover any part of the sky.

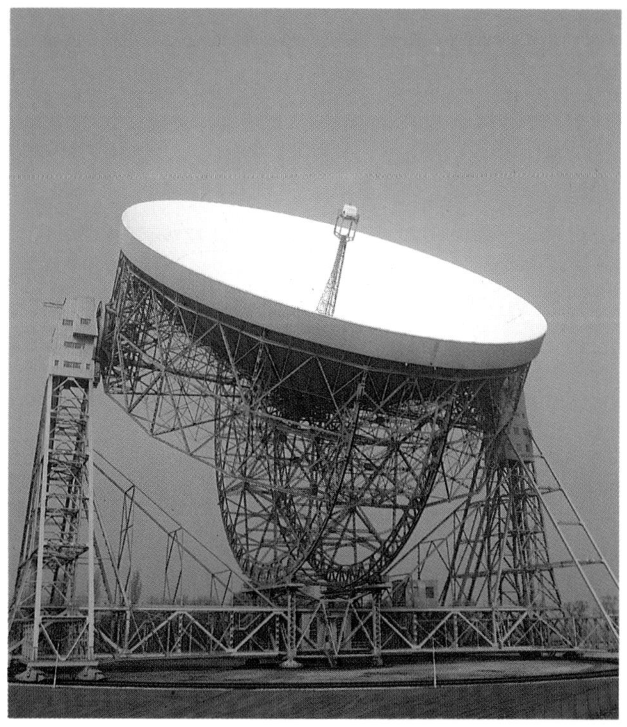

vehicle, that makes automatic radio transmissions of meteorological measurements at various heights to a ground monitoring station. Some types of radiosonde also carry a radar target: this allows the ground station to track the balloon's course, from which information on wind-speed and direction can be gathered.

radio-telephone, a *telephone receiver that transmits and receives messages via *radio waves. Initially used for international and marine communication after *Marconi's demonstration in 1901, it is now used additionally on a local basis for *cellular telephones, *paging systems, and in the cordless telephone.

radio telescope, a directional *antenna system that can collect and analyse faint radio signals from space. Celestial bodies such as hot, bright stars or certain giant galaxies emit radiation in the radio-frequency range that can be detected on Earth, and such emissions provide information additional to that available from an optical *telescope. A radio telescope comprises a steerable, parabolically curved dish that focuses radio waves on to a receiving antenna at the centre. Larger dishes are more sensitive than smaller ones, although increased sensitivity can also be achieved by combining information from an array of smaller dishes or of *dipoles. (See also *observatory.)

radiotherapy (radiation therapy), the use of ionizing electromagnetic radiation such as X-rays and gamma-rays for the treatment of disease, particularly *cancer. Before the late 1920s radium in hollow needles was often inserted into tumours, but since then controlled irradiation from a distance of a metre or more (teletherapy) has been the favoured approach, bombarding the cancerous cells with radiation. X-ray tubes have been superseded first by *radioactive isotopes such as radium and cobalt-60, and later by *particle accelerators. Radiotherapy is more effective in localized forms of *cancer but less so in others, where therapy with cytotoxic drugs is sometimes more suitable. In some cases radiotherapy is combined with surgery or cytotoxic-drug therapy. The critical factor in all radiotherapy is dosage, since normal tissues are also sensitive to radiation. Tumour sites can now be accurately identified using techniques such as *computerized axial tomography, and modern apparatus can deliver a precise, localized dose of radiation. Adverse effects are also reduced by the use of multiple, lower-intensity dosages.

radium, a radioactive element (symbol Ra., at. no. 88, r.a.m. 226.03) discovered by the physicists Marie and Pierre Curie in 1898. Radium decays slowly to the naturally occurring radioactive gas radon. Its chief ore is pitchblende. The discovery of radium led to numerous crucial experiments on radioactivity, paving the way for the rapid advances in atomic physics in the 20th century. Until the 1920s radium was used in *radiotherapy.

raft, a flat, floating platform of timber or other materials (for example, reeds, pots, or inflated animal bladders) for conveying people or objects. Rafts were one of the earliest forms of water transport. In South America, balsa-wood rafts served for coastal trading and later for fishing, and among the Pacific islands similar rafts were used for inter-island trade. Rafts made of papyrus reeds were used from an early date on inland lakes and rivers in Africa and in South America. Today, in many areas where logging is an important activity, lumber is lashed together into rafts and floated downriver to the coast.

rail-bus, a simple form of passenger railway vehicle. In the UK it comprises essentially two passenger-carrying vehicle bodies joined back-to-back and mounted on a four-wheel underframe, housing the engine, transmission, and running gear. The simple design results in considerable weight-saving compared with conventional vehicles. Rail-buses of a similar basic design are used throughout the world on branch lines; they may be operated together in *multiple-unit trains.

railway carriage, a passenger-carrying railway vehicle. The earliest railways were constructed to carry freight, but provided a very basic adaptation of their wagons for ordinary passengers. Wealthy passengers travelled in their own horse carriage placed on a flat wagon. Later, railway companies built carriage bodies on to freight-wagon underframes. As speeds and journey distances increased in the 1860s, improved accommodation was built with gas lighting, steam heating, and continuous brakes. In Europe passengers were confined to compartments, while in the USA the use of open carriages with a centre gangway allowed passengers to move around. In 1859 in the USA, George Pullman began to introduce dining cars, sleeping cars, and vestibule connections between carriages. From the 1890s such facilities began to be available to all travellers, not just the very wealthy, and corridors were introduced for compartment carriages. In the 1920s and 1930s trains carried cinemas, bars, and observation cars to attract more passengers. Air-conditioning was also introduced on some trains in the USA, but did not become widespread elsewhere until the introduction of electric and diesel–electric traction.

railway construction. The construction of large railway networks to carry goods and passengers, which began in the 19th century, stimulated tremendous engineering developments, first in the UK and later in Europe, the USA and Canada, imperial Russia, and other countries. Early rail-

Laying railway track on the 3,200-km (2,000-mile) Baikal–Amur railway, which crosses the Soviet Union by a more southerly route than the trans-Siberian railway. One of the largest **railway construction** projects ever undertaken, the line was officially completed in 1984, but much of the track is now disused.

ways followed routes similar to those of the canals, along river valleys and contour lines, avoiding steep gradients wherever possible through the use of cuttings, *tunnels, embankments, and *viaducts. This was necessary largely because of the poor quality of early *railway track, which could not carry heavy locomotives and therefore limited the available power. With track improvements in the second half of the 19th century, the weight and power of trains grew rapidly. This growth led to important advances in *bridge design, as large numbers of very long bridges capable of sustaining heavy loads were required. In the UK, Robert *Stephenson's *box-girder bridge over the Menai Straits (1857) was a unique solution; a decade later the first steel bridge was built by *Eads in the USA.

As the need to traverse mountainous areas grew, so did the feats of engineering. In Cornwall, UK, after crossing the River Tamar on I. K. *Brunel's Royal Albert Bridge (completed 1859), the railway line stayed at a high level, crossing the deep inlets on high trestle bridges. This technique was later used to great effect in the USA. In central France, gorges were spanned by spectacular bridges such as that built by *Eiffel at Garabit in 1881, some 122 m (400 feet) above the river. In the Alps, the 20-km (12-mile) tunnel at Simplon was built 2,100 m (7,000 feet) beneath the mountain, and encountered major difficulties: it took eight years to complete (1898–1906). Another major construction was the trans-Siberian Railway (begun in 1891 and finally finished in 1915), stretching 9,311 km (5,786 miles) between Moscow and Vladivostok. A more recent engineering feat is the Chengdu to Kunming line in China, whose 653 bridges and 427 tunnels represent 60 per cent of its total length. For modern high-speed trains, tracks are designed with minimum curves, but gradient is less of a concern as modern locomotives are much more powerful.

railways, history of. The advent of railways brought together the technology of the *steam-engine, developed in the early 18th century, and horse- or human-powered *wagon-ways used in mining. *Trevithick was the first to build a *steam locomotive to run on such wagon-ways (1804); other early steam-locomotive pioneers, also British, were John Blenkinsop (1783–1831), William Hedley (1779–1843), and George *Stephenson. Early locomotives were handicapped by the weakness of the available *railway track: it was not until technical advances were made in track construction that the railway became truly practical.

In 1830 the Liverpool and Manchester Railway opened in the UK, the first public railway to handle both passengers and freight using mechanical traction for all traffic. The selection of the locomotive to be used on the line was made in a series of trials at Rainhill, Lancashire, in 1829: the *Rocket*, designed by George *Stephenson, was the outright winner. The opening of the Liverpool to Manchester line was followed by a period of rapid expansion and development of railways throughout the world. By 1847, 250,000 navvies were employed in *railway construction in the UK, and in the USA between 1850 and 1860 nearly 34,000 km (21,100 miles) of railway were constructed. By the end of the century railway networks covered Europe, the USA, Canada, and parts of imperial Russia. Railways climbed high into the Alps, the Andes, and the foothills of the Himalayas, spanned wide estuaries such as the Forth near Edinburgh in Scotland, and tunnelled beneath hills. In Canada, the need for railways to link new industrial centres across frozen wastes prompted the invention of the rotary snow plough by J. W. Elliot in 1869. The first *electric locomotive was demon-

Timechart of railway development	
1738	Iron rails first used for wagonways, Whitehaven Colliery, UK
1804	Richard Trevithick successfully demonstrated steam locomotive on Pen-y-Darren tramway in South Wales
1813	William Hedley's *Puffing Billy* and other engines worked on Wylam tramway, near Newcastle, UK
1825	Opening of Stockton and Darlington Railway, UK, with G. Stephenson's *Locomotion*. First public railway to use steam from outset
1828	First public railway in France, St Etiénne to Andiézieux
1829	Rainhill locomotive trials, for Liverpool to Manchester Railway (UK), won by R. and G. Stephenson's *Rocket*
1830	Liverpool to Manchester Railway opened in the UK—first public passenger main-line railway
1847	250,000 navvies at work building railways in the UK
1863	First part of London Underground opened, Bishop's Road (Paddington) to Farringdon Street
1864	Pullman sleeping car introduced in USA
1879	E. W. Siemens demonstrated first electric locomotive in Berlin
1890	City and South London underground railway opened with electric-powered vehicles. Construction begins on trans-Siberian railway. First locomotive testing station opened by Professor Goss at Purdue University, Indiana, USA
1903	Speed of 210 km/h (130 m.p.h.) achieved with electric locomotive near Berlin
1932	Rebuild of *Nord Pacific* locomotive achieved all-time record for power to weight for a steam locomotive
1920–39	Experimental high-pressure and turbine locomotives built in Europe, USA, and Canada. Introduction of first automatic train control (ATC) systems in UK
1935	Introduction of streamlined, high-speed, steam-hauled trains in UK and USA
1938	British A4 class streamlined Pacific *Mallard* captured steam locomotive world speed record of 203 km/h (127 m.p.h.)
1963	Main-line steam locomotive production ceased in Western Europe. First hover-train operated at 161 km/h (100 m.p.h.) in UK
1965	New Tokkaido Line opened in Japan, electric *shinkansen* trains operating at 210 km/h (130 m.p.h.)
1966	Electrification of trans-Siberian railway started, Soviet Union
1968	First fully automatic train control, on Victoria Line in UK
1981	French introduced *train à grande vitesse* (TGV) running from Paris to Lyon at speeds of 260 km/h (160 m.p.h.)
1982	Maglev shuttle began operation at Birmingham International Airport, UK
1983	China completed the line from Chengdu to Kunming, with 427 tunnels and 650 bridges
1984	South African Railways adopted overhead electrification. Official completion of 3,200-km (2,000-mile) Baikal–Amur Railway across the Soviet Union
1988	Last steam locomotive built at Datong, China
1990	Modified unit of latest version of SNCF *l'Atlantique* TGV set world speed record for locomotives of 515 km/h (320 m.p.h.)

strated at an exhibition in Berlin in 1879. Electric traction was commercially applied first on suburban and metropolitan lines, but was quickly adopted for *underground railways. One of the earliest users of electric locomotives on main-line routes was Italy, where a line was opened in 1902.

The period before World War I was a time of consolidation, with comfortable, heavy trains running at average speeds of over 95 km/h (60 m.p.h.) throughout Europe and North America, and freight trains of 1,000–2,000 tonnes carrying goods and raw materials to urban and manufacturing centres. Between the Wars many railway companies grouped together as national railway systems or large geographical concerns. Road and air transport began to challenge railways, and many experiments were undertaken to find better forms of motive power and rolling stock. In the late 1930s the steam locomotive reached its zenith, but electric locomotives were already in widespread use in Europe and Scandinavia, and main-line *diesel locomotives were coming into service in the USA.

Following World War II there was a period of reconstruction: new steam locomotives were introduced in the UK and mainland Europe, and new diesels were also under test. Steam locomotive production ended in the USA in the 1950s, and in Europe in the 1960s, and, as the competition from roads increased, there were major cutbacks in the rail network. In Japan in 1964, the high-speed *shinkansen* or 'bullet' trains began operation, running on specially developed track at speeds of up to 210 km/h (130 m.p.h.). At around the same period experiments began using *ground guidance-systems other than conventional track.

In the last quarter of the 20th century, railway construction world-wide has started to grow again, though in developed countries few new lines are being built. In Europe, notably in France and more recently Germany, other *high-speed trains have been developed following the success of the Japanese *shinkansen*, and tilting rolling stock have been introduced on a few lines. There has also been a considerable investment in commuter trains and light railway rapid-transit systems to ease congestion on roads and in response to increasing concern about air pollution from car exhaust. A new development in Jakarta, Indonesia, is the Aeromovel, a light, engineless train powered by compressed air blown through a duct below the track. New underground railways have been built in some of the newer large cities (for example, the Metro in Mexico City), while in China the railway network is growing at a rate of some 1,000 km (600 miles) per year.

railway signal system, a network of signals that ensures the safe and efficient passage of trains around a rail network. Until the 1830s 'policemen' controlled the passage of trains between stations, using flags and lights, and trains were run on a time-interval basis. As the railways became more complex, the point levers directing trains from one track to another were grouped together, and the police flags and lights were replaced by mechanical semaphores operated from one signal-box. In 1852 a system of mechanical interlocks was introduced, ensuring safe operation of the signalling equipment. However, it was not until the general introduction of the electric telegraph in the 1850s and the division of the railways into 'blocks' with only one train in each block that a fundamentally safe system was in place. Despite changes in technology that have replaced semaphores by coloured lights and mechanical interlocks by electronic computers, the basic principles of the system remain. On many lines the passage of the train automatically resets the signals to stop, only to be changed by the *track circuits that monitor the train's passage. Junctions are controlled manually or by a computer fed with the train running order.

railway track, the support and guidance system on which railway vehicles run. Early *wagon-ways and tramways used a variety of materials and patterns for the track, all of which were too fragile for use by *steam locomotives. It was only with the development in 1815–20 of wrought-iron rails that locomotives with sufficient weight to attain the required adhesion could be carried without breaking the rails. A further great improvement was achieved with the introduction of rolled-steel rails in the 1860s. Stone rail-support blocks gave way to timber cross-ties or 'sleepers', laid on to a levelled bed of stone ballast with the rail pinned directly to them or (in the UK) held in cast-iron 'chairs'. Rails were bolted together with 'fish-plates', leaving a small gap between the rail ends to allow for thermal expansion. Modern track uses a considerable depth of ballast, concrete or wooden sleepers, and a deep, flat-bottomed steel rail that allows use of long sections of continuously welded track, whose fastening prevents any distortion due to thermal expansion. In areas where there is dense traffic and rails must be replaced often, older style rails and cast-iron chairs are still used.

rain gauge *meteorological instrument.

rake, a long-handled implement with a head, set at right angles to the handle, containing a row of teeth or tines. It is used to smooth earth, or with a wider head to rake hay or gather straw or leaves. The principle has been applied to larger machinery, particularly for gathering or turning hay. (See *agricultural machinery for illustration.)

RAM *memory (computer).

ram-jet, a *jet engine with no compressor, in which air is drawn in and compressed by the forward motion of the engine. It has no moving parts, and is essentially a shaped duct, consisting of an intake section which acts as a compressor by slowing down the entering air, a combustion chamber where fuel is added and burnt, and a *nozzle section in which the stream of hot gas is accelerated to give a high-speed exhaust jet. The jet provides propulsive thrust in a manner similar to that of a rocket. The ram-jet is only efficient at high speed, so has found limited application.

Ramsden, Jesse (1735–1800), British instrument-maker. In 1762, after an apprenticeship with a maker of mathematical instruments in London, he set up his own business, particularly for the manufacture of optical instruments. He invented a number of machines to facilitate his work, including a dividing-engine for circular and linear scales and two screw-cutting *lathes. He also made improvements to the *theodolite, the *barometer, the *micrometer, and the *sextant. The precision and quality of his products earned him a European reputation.

Rance barrage, a dam across the Rance River, France, between Dinard and St Malo in Brittany, housing the world's only large *tidal power-station. The average tidal range is more than 8 m (26 feet), and half a billion tonnes of water can flow through the barrage during a spring tide. The plant, commissioned in 1966, has a maximum output of

240,000 kW from twenty-four turbo-generators. The use of doubly reversible *turbines, generating or pumping in both flow directions, increases the flexibility of the plant by allowing it to act as a *pumped storage system.

rare earths, oxides of the group of elements known as the lanthanides. Rare-earth metals have properties similar to *aluminium. The lanthanides (about one-sixth of the known elements) are scarce, expensive, and produced only in small quantities. A mixture of yttrium (not a lanthanide, but found in association with rare earths) and europium oxides is used to make a brilliant red *phosphor for colour-television screens, and other rare-earth phosphors are used in mercury arc lamps to give an intense white light. Other applications are in gas mantles, as additives to steels and superalloys, and as components in nuclear energy plants, solar energy devices, magnetic alloys, and electronic devices.

rasp *files and rasps.

ratchet and pawl, a mechanical device that allows movement of a wheel or linear member in one direction only. It consists of a saw-toothed wheel in which the teeth are shaped to engage with the point of a hinged arm, the pawl (see figure). This allows forward movement but not reverse, unless the pawl is lifted. Common uses are in hand-operated winches, in the escapement of a mechanical *clock, and in the free-wheel mechanism of a *bicycle rear sprocket. Silent free-wheels have been designed which use the wedging action of rollers instead of a pawl.

Ratchet and pawl

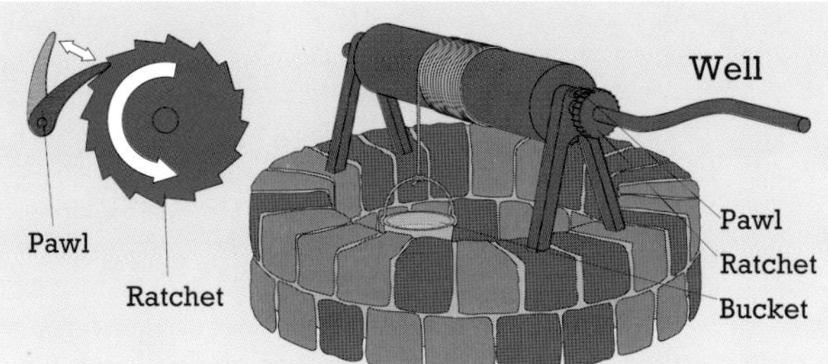

When raising the bucket from the well, the toothed ratchet rotates anticlockwise and the pawl slides over the teeth. Clockwise rotation of the ratchet, which would let the bucket drop down the well, is prevented by the pawl, which catches in the ratchet's teeth. The pawl can be pulled back to allow the bucket to be lowered.

Bicycle: power applied

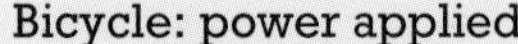

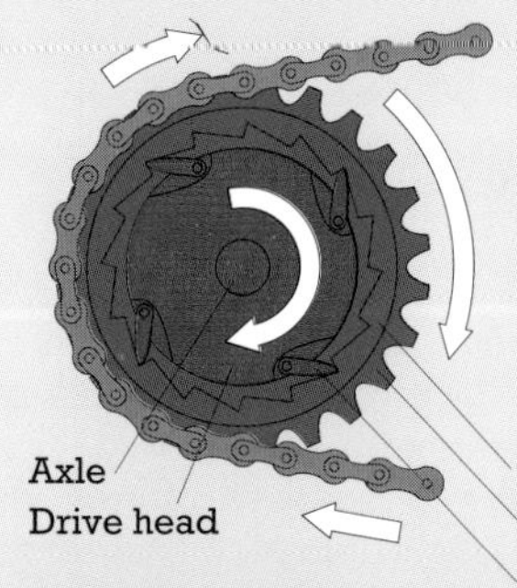

Power from the pedals is supplied via the chain and sprocket to the free-wheel body on the rear wheel, which rotates. This causes the pawls to be caught in the notches of the ratchet, transferring power to the wheel's axle and making it rotate.

Free-wheel body
Sprocket
Pawl

Free-wheeling

During free-wheeling, no power is supplied via the sprocket, but the axle continues to rotate. The pawls skip over the notches, allowing the free-wheel body and sprocket to remain stationary.

rayon, the first successful manufactured fibre, made from *cellulose patented by *Cross in 1892. There are two main categories of rayon: viscose and acetate. Both are made from natural cellulose, usually wood-pulp or cotton linters (very short fibres), and both are made into filaments by extrusion through spinnerets (see *nylon). Unlike the synthetic polymer materials nylon and Terylene, cellulose cannot be extruded in the molten state. Instead, it is dissolved in caustic soda (*sodium hydroxide) for making viscose and in *propanone when making acetate rayon, extruded as a solution (wet *spinning) and subsequently coagulated. The wet-spinning process for viscose rayon was patented in 1892 by *Cross and Bevan. As with synthetics, rayon fibres are made in varying degrees of fineness and are used both as short or staple fibre (alone or in blends) and as long, continuous filament yarn. Rayon is still produced in significant quantities, in spite of the success of the many newer synthetic fibres.

reactance, the opposition, measured in ohms (Ω), of a reactor (a *capacitor or an *inductor) to alternating current. Unlike resistance (see *resistor), reactance varies with the frequency of the alternating current; the reactance of an inductor increases with increasing frequency, while that of a capacitor decreases.

real time (computing), the computer analysis of events as they happen rather than data stored for later processing. Real-time computing is extremely important in the automatic control of, for example, vehicles or machinery, where decisions need to be executed as soon as possible after an event has occurred.

reamer, a hand tool for finishing drilled holes. It consists of a cylindrical or slightly tapering steel shank with spiral or longitudinal cutting edges. Reamers normally come in sets of different sizes, but adjustable ones are also available. The reamer may be turned in a hole by a wooden handle or by a brace.

reaper, a machine which harvests corn. There is evidence for the existence of a reaping machine in northern France during the Roman period. Mechanical reapers were first invented in the 19th century; Patrick Bell (1799–1869) built one in 1826 in Scotland which was imitated locally, but *McCormick's machine (1851) from the USA became the standard design from which later developments were made. Modern reapers cut the grain with reciprocating (back-and-forth) blades, and also have a device for binding the sheaves.

receiver *radio receiver, *telephone receiver, *television receiver.

reciprocating engine, any engine in which a sliding piston is constrained to move to and fro, usually transmitting power via a crankshaft and connecting-rod. The earliest *steam-engines were reciprocating *beam-engines, later replaced by crankshaft engines. *Gas-engines, *petrol engines, *Stirling engines and *diesel engines are almost all reciprocating engines, although some, for example the Wankel engine, have a *rotary action.

recombinant DNA *genetic engineering.

reconnaissance aircraft, a type of aeroplane used, particularly in the military context, to make a preliminary survey of a region, to locate an enemy, or to ascertain strategic features. The aeroplane might be high-flying, such as the US Lockheed SR-71 Blackbird, or it may be an unmanned or remotely piloted vehicle (RPV). Such aircraft are usually fitted with infra-red or other recording cameras. Reconnaissance aircraft are light, for endurance, and fast to avoid enemy attack. In the late 1960s much high-altitude reconnaissance work shifted to *military satellites.

record, a thin plastic disc on which sound is recorded as a horizontally undulating pattern on the inside of a continuous groove which spirals inwards from the outer part of the disc. The first record was produced by Emil Berliner in 1887, for his *gramophone. Large-scale reproduction was developed in 1894. Berliner also pioneered the use of electroforming techniques for the large-scale reproduction of records. In this process the master disc is first made electrically conductive and then plated with either nickel or copper, making a negative mould. After separation from the master the negative can be used directly in a plastic-moulding press. For commercial quantities of records, positive copies of the master, called stampers, are used to make many negative moulds, so that thousands of records can be made. Early records were made of shellac (a varnish made from tree resin), or vulcanite (vulcanized rubber), but vinyl plastics are now used, which are lighter, more resilient, and have better moulding characteristics. From the 1960s the record began to be replaced by the audio-cassette and in the 1980s by the *compact disc.

record player *gramophone.

rectifier, a device that passes current in one direction only, offering a low resistance to signals of one polarity, but a very high resistance to signals of the opposite polarity. The commonest rectifiers are solid-state and thermionic *diodes. They are used in power supplies as the first stage of converting alternating-current signals into direct-current signals; the second stage typically being a *smoothing circuit. Rectifiers are also used to detect radio and television signals. (See *circuits, electrical and electronic for illustration.)

recycling, the processing of waste so that it can be recovered and reused. Historically, recycling has been done mainly for economic reasons, but recently its value in reducing the depletion of natural resources has been emphasized. Metals such as scrap steel are returned to the steel mill for reprocessing, though problems are faced when different metals are intimately associated, for example, steel and tin in tin plate. Much *paper and *glass is recycled, the latter exceeding 3 million tonnes every year in Europe alone. Road materials such as asphalt and concrete can be planed off the road, heated, mixed, and relaid. Thermoplastics can quite easily be recycled if the waste is a fairly pure sample of one plastic, but recycling of mixed plastics gives poor results. One answer to this problem is the use of compatibilizers, molecules that are added to a mixture of molten plastics and bind them together at a molecular level, to make plastic 'alloys'. Some manufacturers of engineering plastics for the motor car and aerospace industry design plastic products that are easier to recycle.

Crushed car bodies in a breaker's yard in Toronto, Canada. The bodies are shredded, then the steel is separated magnetically from the other materials. The scrap steel can be **recycled** by mixing with pig-iron in a steel furnace.

red lead (Pb_3O_4), a scarlet crystalline powder, an oxide of *lead, used in making storage batteries, paints, ceramic products, and flint glass. It is formed by heating yellow lead oxide in air at 400–500 °C. Red-lead paint provides particularly effective rust protection for ironwork.

reduction (chemistry) *oxidation and reduction.

reforming process, a method of rearranging the structure of *hydrocarbons to alter their properties, used in particular in *petroleum refining to form petrol with a high *octane number. Thermal reforming was first carried out in the 1930s, by heating the vapour of naphtha paraffins under pressure. In this process a small proportion of the naphtha is cracked to smaller-sized molecules, or forms products heavier than petrol, but about 80 per cent becomes petrol. Straight-chain *hydrocarbons form aromatics (molecules containing one or more *benzene rings) and lose some hydrogen. Since the 1950s, a platinum catalyst has generally been used in reforming, making lower processing pressures possible. The reactions are carried out in the presence of hydrogen, to inhibit the formation of coke, which deposits on, and deactivates, the catalyst. The increasing restrictions on the use of *lead tetraethyl since the 1980s have increased the importance of reforming processes to produce high-octane, unleaded petrol.

refractory, a substance that can withstand very high temperatures. Refractories are used to line *kilns, *blast-furnaces, incinerators, and other high-temperature environments. They must be unreactive at high temperatures and have good load-bearing properties. Oxides of the minerals magnesite and dolomite are important refractories used in steel furnaces and cement kilns. Other widely used refractories are *silicon carbide and oxides of *aluminium and *zirconium.

refrigeration, a method of preservation in which foods and other perishable products are kept at low temperatures to slow down or stop deterioration processes. Storage of foods in cool places or on ice is an ancient food-preservation method, but mechanical refrigeration was not developed until the mid-19th century. The earliest mechanical refrigeration plant was installed in a brewery in Bendigo, Australia, by the British-born engineer John Harrison. The most important use of early refrigeration was in the shipment of chilled or frozen meat from the Americas and Australia to Europe: the first successful trip from Australia (1880) used ammonia as the refrigerant, and this became standard until the 1930s, when *chloro-fluorocarbons were introduced. From the 1850s simple iceboxes were used as domestic refrigerators, but the first successful mechanical domestic refrigerator was manufactured by von *Linde from 1879. Electrical refrigerators were introduced in the early 1920s, initially in the USA. Mechanical refrigerators operate by the successive evaporation and condensation of a liquid refrigerant. The refrigerant evaporates within the refrigerator, a process that requires heat, and therefore cools the surrounding air. It is then pumped out of the refrigerator and condensed under pressure, giving up its heat to the atmosphere via metal cooling fins. (See also *deep-freeze.)

register (computing) *central processing unit.

reinforced concrete, *concrete, developed in the 1880s, that is strengthened by combining it with a second constituent. Reinforcement is necessary where the material is likely to be under tension, as concrete itself does not have good tensile strength. Most commonly the reinforcement is in the form of steel bars, but chopped polypropylene, steel-wire fibres, bamboo, and *glass fibres are also used. Concrete members used as simple beams (supported at the two ends) or as floors are reinforced in the lower part, where bending under load causes tension. Concrete columns require vertical reinforcing bars because bending stresses are produced when loads on the column do not act at its exact centre. Steel-reinforcement bars do not suffer from *corrosion because the alkaline environment of the concrete provides protection. (See also *pre-stressed concrete.)

relay, an electromechanical device used to switch one or more signals under the control of other signals. A typical relay consists of an *electromagnet which, when energized, is able to open or close other contacts. Relays have largely been superseded by solid-state switches such as *transistors, but they are still used for switching high-voltage signals.

A relay is also a signal booster circuit that amplifies weak signals in international telecommunication circuits to make them audible (see *telephony). Undersea telecommunications cables and television broadcast networks are fitted with relays at regular intervals.

reliability, the probability that a component, device, or system will perform satisfactorily under given circumstances. Reliability is affected by design, maintenance, operating conditions, and many other factors. A number of measures of reliability are commonly used: the reliability function is the probability that a given device or system will survive in operation for a certain period of time; the failure probability is the probability that the device or system will fail in a certain time period. Failure rate is defined as the number of failures per unit time, divided by the number of components exposed to failure. Typically, the failure rate will decline with time for a comparatively short first period of operation or early life, when weak or substandard elements fail ('infant mortality'). This is followed by a period of fairly constant failure rate over the useful life of the device or system. Finally, failure rate will increase steadily with time during the wear-out or old-age period. Other useful measures are the mean time to failure (MTTF) and, for devices which can be repaired, the mean time between failures (MTBF). In series reliability, a system will fail if any individual component fails; in parallel reliability all components have to fail for the system to fail. Parallel reliability is an example of redundancy, which can be designed into systems to improve reliability. Redundancy is particularly important in safety-critical systems, such as nuclear installations or air traffic control systems, where incorrect functioning might pose a severe risk to human safety.

Rennie, John (1761–1821), British civil engineer of Scottish extraction. He was commissioned by *Watt to build the Albion Mill in London (1784), the first building to have a *frame made entirely of cast iron. Rennie built or improved the harbours at Holyhead, Hull, and Wick. His other major enterprises included Waterloo Bridge in London (1810–17), and London Bridge designed in about 1821, and erected by his son in 1824–31. He designed the London and East India dock, and the great breakwater at Plymouth (1811–48).

repeater, an electronic device placed at strategic positions along a long *telephone or other telecommunication line to pick up a weakened signal and re-transmit an identical amplified signal, thereby improving the *signal-to-noise ratio. Initially designed for telegraphic cables in the late 1840s, repeaters have been used for radio, telephone, optical fibre, and other cable links.

Reppe synthesis, a family of processes, named after their discoverer the German chemist J. W. Reppe in which *ethyne is reacted at high pressure and in the presence of a *catalyst with methanal (acetaldehyde) or other reactants. These reactions, developed in the early 20th century, are of particular importance in the synthesis of high polymers and other *organic chemicals.

reprocessing, nuclear *nuclear fuel.

reservoir, a water-storage system. An impounding reservoir provides bulk water storage by damming a river valley. After treatment, the stored water is fed directly into the water-supply system. A regulating reservoir stores water for subsequent release into a river in times of low natural flow in order to safeguard the availability of water at a downstream water-supply intake.

resistor, an electrical device that opposes electrical current flow. Resistors employed in electronics are usually constructed from carbon or metal films. The resistance of a resistor, measured in ohms (Ω), is usually depicted on its body as a series of coloured rings. The values of resistance may vary from 10 Ω to 10 MΩ or higher. Resistors are used in electrical and electronic *circuits as a means of controlling the current flow through the circuit, or a part of it. If a circuit component can tolerate only a small amount of current, a large resistance may be used to keep the current value low.

respirator, a device providing artificial respiration by mechanical means, used in the treatment of respiratory disease and paralysis, and in *anaesthesia. The 'iron lung', which was extensively used in the poliomyelitis epidemics of the 1930s and 1950s, consisted of a sealed box enclosing the whole patient except for the head. The rhythmic removal of air from the box forces the patient to take in air through the nose or mouth (negative-pressure ventilation). In positive-pressure ventilation, air is forced into the lungs, usually through a close-fitting tube in the trachea. Over time, respirators have been made smaller; they have become recognized as essential both to modern anaesthetic techniques and to the *intensive-care unit. Modern devices use sophisticated electronics to monitor the patient's own breathing efforts and can vary the depth, rate, and pattern of respiration.

retaining wall, a wall built to hold back earth. Usually vertical, or nearly so, it is subject to earth pressure exerted over its full height. Retaining walls may be used in cuttings, embankments, or as basement walls. Masonry walls resist overturning or sliding by means of their dead weight and consequently tend to be thick. Slender *reinforced concrete walls are designed to form a vertical cantilever secured in a large base. Walls of interlocking steel sheets may be cantilevered from the ground or anchored back into the supported face to resist overturning.

revolver *pistol.

rhenium (symbol Re, at. no. 75, r.a.m. 186.2), a silvery-white, very hard metallic element that resists wear and corrosion. Uses include alloy steels, fountain-pen nib points, high-temperature *thermocouples, electrical components, and as a catalyst.

rheostat, a variable *resistor. Rheostats are generally used in higher-power circuits. The commonest form consists of a large bare-wire *coil, along which a movable terminal can slide. As the terminal is moved, a smaller or larger portion of the coil is incorporated into the circuit, and the resistance in the circuit is thus increased or decreased.

rhodium (symbol Rh, at. no. 45, r.a.m. 102.91), a silvery, unreactive *platinum metal. The element occurs in association with other platinum metals and is used mainly as an alloying addition to strengthen platinum or palladium. It is also used in making searchlight reflectors, in electroplating, *thermocouples, and as an industrial catalyst.

rice cultivation, generally the wetland farming of rice, the swamp grass *Oryza sativa*. By weight, rice is the world's second most important crop (after wheat), and its labour-intensive cultivation has been practised for centuries, especially in Asia. The primary requirement for cultivation is a dependable water supply, as most rice is grown partially submerged. On hills, slopes are *terraced to retain water. Seedlings raised in nursery plots are transplanted into flooded, fertilized paddy-fields to complete development. Rice is cut before the crop is fully ripe, threshed, and polished to remove the grain husk. Additionally, however, much rice is grown like other *cereals as a dryland crop.

rickshaw, a form of light, two-wheeled, passenger-carrying cart invented in the 1880s and used as a taxi in the Far East. The rickshaw is pulled by a man running along between the shafts, holding one shaft in each hand. It has now been widely superseded by the pedal-powered tricycle rickshaw and the three- or four-wheeled motor-powered auto-rickshaw, but rickshaws are still in use in some areas.

rifle, a *firearm with a gun barrel that has rifling (internal grooves that impart spin to the *bullet) for greater accuracy. The term is nowadays commonly applied to the foot-soldier's personal weapon. The first rifles (late 18th century) were identical to the muzzle-loading flintlock *muskets of their day except for their longer, rifled barrels. The improvement in accuracy was such that, by the middle of the 19th century, the armies of most European nations equipped their soldiers with rifled muskets. At about the same time, a percussion cap replaced the *flintlock, and breech-loading rifles were developed. Different methods of operation were employed, but the commonest type was the bolt-action rifle. A sliding bolt is pulled back from the base of the barrel, and the *bullet and *cartridge are inserted, and moved forward as the bolt is closed. A firing pin inside the bolt pushes into the base of the cartridge when the trigger is pulled, striking a percussion cap to begin the firing procedure. Automatic rifles harness some of the propellant gases produced in firing to drive back the bolt immediately after a round has been fired. The spent cartridge is ejected, and a new round is automatically inserted. In early semi-automatic rifles the trigger was pulled for each round. Today's fully automatic weapons merely require the trigger to be kept pulled; they will then fire continuously until the magazine is emptied.

rig, the arrangement of masts and sails carried by a sailing vessel. Most *sailing ships can be broadly classified as either having a *square-rig or a *fore-and-aft rig. Some specific types of ship are characterized by their rig, for example, the *barque, the *brig, and the *schooner. The rigging comprises all the ropes and wires used in sailing vessels to support and control the sails. Standing rigging supports masts, yards (spars from which sails are hung), and the bowsprits (the spar projecting from the bow); running rigging is used to hoist, lower, and trim yards and sails. Until the invention of flexible wire rope in the 19th century, much of the rigging in ships was of special four-stranded rope. Later, wire rope was used for shrouds (ropes supporting the mast or topmast), stays (supporting masts or spars), and lifts in standing rigging, and natural or synthetic rope for running rigging.

ring mains *wiring, electrical.

Riquet de Bonrepos, Baron Pierre-Paul (1604–80), French civil servant and engineer, constructor of the greatest civil engineering project of its time, the Languedoc canal (also called the Canal du Midi) in southern France. The 240-km (150-mile) canal linked the rivers Aude and Garonne, thus providing continuous navigation from the Atlantic to the Mediterranean. In 1661 Riquet was a tax official when, with the assistance of engineer François Andreossy, he proposed a scheme for building the canal. His project was backed by the French finance minister, Jean-Baptiste Colbert. Work began in 1667 and was completed in 1681; Riquet died in 1680, seven months before the canal opened.

RISC (Reduced Instruction Set Computing), a computing technique, developed in the early 1980s, in which only the most frequently used instructions are incorporated into the computer's *central processing unit, the rest being moved to the *software. This means that the computer is able to work much faster and can use a larger date 'word' (see *binary code) than a conventional computer. RISC microprocessor chips developed in 1991 can work at speeds of 50 million instructions per second (mips): powerful personal computers using conventional computing have speeds of only 5 mips.

river navigation, a river that has been modified to permit easy passage by boats. The water flow is slowed by constructing *weirs across the river; this maintains adequate depth for navigation and facilitates upstream journeys. Artificial cuts (short *canals with *locks) allow boats to pass the weirs. In many cases, journeys are also shortened by cuts across large bends. The wash from boats can erode the natural banks of the river and protective walls have to be built and maintained. River navigations are linked by canals to provide a waterway network.

riveting, a method of joining metals together, used since the Bronze Age. A metal dowel (rivet) with a head at one end is pushed through holes drilled in the two pieces to be joined, and the other end of the dowel (the tail) is then hammered flat (usually after heating) so that it cannot be withdrawn. Riveting was widely used in the 19th century in large iron structures such as bridges and ships, and has largely been replaced by *welding. However, riveting is still used for aluminium panelling for aircraft bodies. On aircraft wings, where only one side of the panel is accessible, rivets have explosive charges in the tail, to set the rivet.

A riveter at work on a New York skyscraper early this century. From the late 19th century until at least the 1920s, **riveting** was essential to all steel construction. It was gradually superseded by welding and the use of friction bolts.

road, a way, often with a prepared surface, by which people, animals, or vehicles may travel between places. A street is a road through a built-up area. The first road-builders were probably the Mesopotamians, and the earliest long-distance route was probably the 3,000-km (1,865-mile) Royal Road from Susa to Smyrna, which is thought to have been in use as early as 3500 BC. China had a fully developed road system by the end of the Shang dynasty (11th century BC); bridges were built across rivers and mountains were traversed by stone-paved stairways. By the 4th century BC the Mauryan civilization in India had also developed an extensive road network. In Europe the pre-Roman roadways were mostly tracks worn by the feet of people and animals, or by the wheels of wagons. The first important European road-makers were the Romans. They originally built roads to speed troop movements. Their road design is shown in the figure on page 300; on minor roads, a gravel or broken stone layer replaced the flagstones. Streets were laid with large polygonal blocks. By AD 200 the road networks of the Roman, Mauryan, and Chinese empires provided trade routes from most of Europe to India and the Far East. Between the 3rd and the 18th centuries there was a road-building decline throughout Europe, the Middle East, and Asia. In contrast, in South America this period saw the development of the Inca road system, which by the time of the arrival of the Spaniards in the early 16th century served an area of some 2 million km^2 (750,000 square miles), populated by around 10 million people. Particularly impressive were the roads running through the Andes, which included galleries cut through solid rock and extremely high retaining walls, built to support the road surface.

The modern road-building era began in 1747 with the establishment of the École Nationale des Ponts et Chaussées in Paris to train engineers. *Trésaguet improved the École's methods of construction, which were based upon Roman techniques, using about half the quantity of material. Before the Revolution (1789), France led the world with a network of 40,000 km (25,000 miles) of paved roads, extended later by Napoleon. In the UK *Telford built roads with a more level subsurface formation and thinner surface. *McAdam, Telford's contemporary, dispensed with the foundation of large stones, which was expensive. He emphasized the need to keep the natural formation dry by covering it with an impervious surface with good drainage. His road surface, known as water-bound macadam, was almost universally used until the invention of the wide inflatable tyre, which tended to disrupt the surface. The origin of modern Tarmac(adam) dates from the 1830s, when tar was first used in Nottinghamshire, UK, to bind the surface stones. In France, from 1832 onwards, powdered rock, asphalt, and bitumen

Road

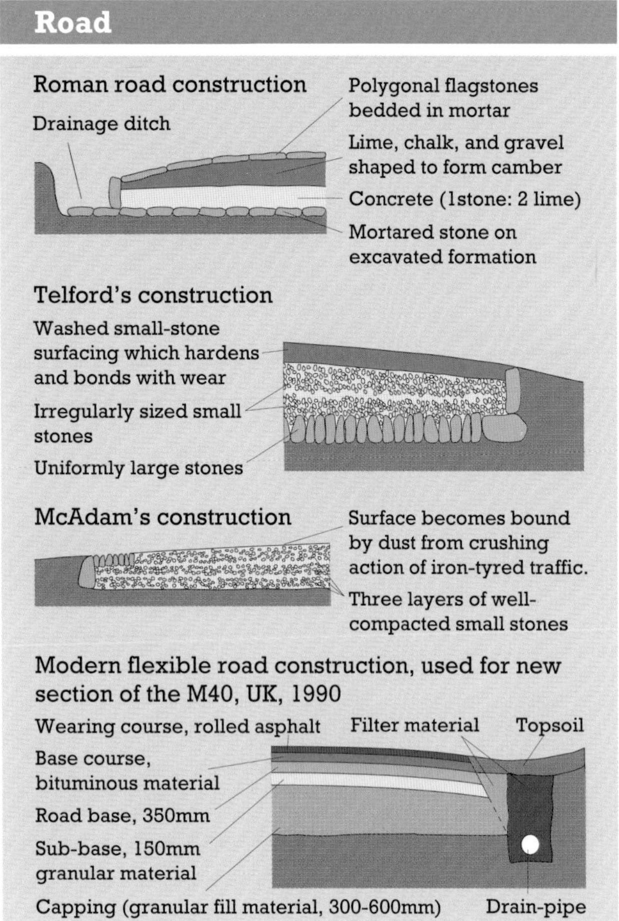

mixtures were used for roads.

During the 19th century, busy urban streets were paved with hard-wearing stone blocks (often of granite) on a broken stone foundation. *Concrete was first used for roads in the 1850s in Austria. By the 1920s, highways designed specifically for heavy and fast traffic were being built in the USA, and as three-lane, limited-access autostradas in Italy. The most advanced modern road system of its time was the German autobahn network built in the 1930s. In the UK during the same period main roads, sometimes with dual carriageways, were built, but it was not until the late 1950s that the building of the motorway network began. Motorways are dual-carriageway roads with gradual bends and gradients, designed for fast-moving traffic. Junctions are designed as roundabouts, and to avoid interrupting traffic flow, vehicles enter the motorway by means of acceleration lanes. (The final section of the figure shows the construction used for the M40 to the north of Oxford, UK.) A feature of post-war urban road development, especially in Japan, has been the double-or even triple-decked expressways over existing streets. Road building is now eased by the use of the *bulldozer, *scraper, *grader, and *road roller. Slip-form pavers, machines that can rapidly lay concrete on to a prepared base, are used in the building of concrete roads.

road roller, a heavy diesel-engined (formerly steam-engined) machine with a smooth steel roller for compressing the surface, or any of the intermediate layers, of a road or paved area. The traditional machine relies simply on its own weight, while a sheep's-foot roller has projections on its surface that concentrate the roller's weight on to a smaller area, thus increasing the compression. Machines with vibrating rollers are frequently used.

road sign *traffic control.

road transport, methods for moving people and goods along roads or tracks. Early peoples were nomadic, and techniques for carrying loads evolved very early in human history. Probably one of the earliest load-carrying inventions was the travois, a V-shaped wooden frame with the apex resting on the back of a pack animal and the other end dragging on the ground. The load was carried on a frame slung between the poles. From this developed the *sledge, which was in common use in many parts of the world by 5000 BC. The use of *draught and pack animals for load-carrying and pulling is also thought to have evolved around this time: the first animal used in this way was the ass, which by 3000 BC was in use on long-distance trade routes in north-east Africa, the Mediterranean, and the Near and Far East. The application of the *wheel to vehicles in about 3000 BC marked a major step forward in land transport. Four-wheeled *carts and wagons were the earliest wheeled vehicles, but lighter, two-wheeled *chariots were quickly evolved. By about 1500 BC wheeled vehicles had spread as far as China in the east and Scandinavia in the north. The Chinese improved animal *harness and saddlery, and also developed the first extensive *road network. The Romans used two- and four-wheeled vehicles for transporting goods; they also had four-wheeled passenger vehicles. The pivoted front *axle was a feature of their four-wheeled wagons, an invention they probably copied from the Scandinavians.

During the Middle Ages, the horse became the main form of personal transport in western Europe—wagons were too uncomfortable for long journeys, and roads were very poor. In eastern Europe, however, wagons were developed in which the body was suspended from posts attached to the axles, and this idea spread west in the later Middle Ages. New methods of harnessing and animal training led to the horse replacing the ox and mule for transporting goods as well as people. In the late 15th century lighter, more comfortable coaches were developed for the very rich in Hungary, and during the 16th century these were adopted in other parts of Europe. The majority of people continued to ride in wagons or on horseback, or walk.

By the 17th century there was a clear division between the *carts and wagons used for goods transport and agriculture, and the lighter, suspended *carriages and coaches for passenger use. In the early 19th century the introduction of the macadamized road and the development of elliptical springs for coach *suspension greatly improved the quality of road travel. Travel and trade became more widespread, and omnibuses, cabs, and coaches for public transport became available. Although in the second half of the 19th century *canals and later *railways took over much long-distance passenger and goods traffic, horse-drawn transport remained important within cities and for servicing the railway networks. Some experiments were being made with *steam-powered vehicles, but the supremacy of the horse for road transport was not seriously challenged until the advent of the *motor car. Mass production methods for cars were not widely applied until after World War I, but since that time the use of cars, *buses, and coaches for passenger transport has increased enormously, while *lorries and tankers have become increasingly dominant for goods transport.

Road travel remains the most flexible and versatile land transport system, but increasing awareness of the *pollution and environmental problems caused by the internal-combustion engine, in particular its major contribution to the *greenhouse effect, has led to curbs on motor-vehicle emissions in some countries, and a search for alternative power sources. The economic and environmental problems of traffic congestion and *traffic control and of the massive expansion of road systems is also a matter for concern.

robotics, the science and technology of machines designed to function in place of a human being, especially to carry out tasks automatically. The term robot (from the Czech *robota*, 'compulsory service') was coined by the playwright Karel Čapek in 1920. Practical robotics was first formulated by the British inventor C. W. Kenward in 1957, and subsequently exploited in the USA for industrial automation to handle parts for die casting, injection moulding, and metal-cutting machines. A robot which could manipulate a tool (for painting) was first used in Norway in 1966, and in the USA, robots were developed for spot-welding on assembly lines. Since then, there has been a continual evolution towards robots of greater precision, such as the Japanese *s*elective *c*ompliance *a*ssembly *r*obot *a*rm (SCARA).

A modern robot has a mechanical manipulator (usually an arm) and *sensors, controlled by a computer. Early hydraulically powered robots have given way to direct-drive machines using electric motors. The main goal of robot research in *artificial intelligence is to enable robots to sense and move intelligently around their environment.

rocket motor, a motor that propels a vehicle forward by expelling combustion gases from nozzles at the rear. It differs from a *jet engine in that it carries its own oxidizer, allowing the motor to operate in the absence of an air supply. Rocket motors have been extensively applied in *spaceflight, where their great power and ability to work in a vacuum are essential, but they can also be used to power *missiles, aeroplanes, and cars. The forward force acting on a rocket (its thrust) is produced because the combustion of fuel within the rocket exerts a great pressure on the walls of the combustion chamber, except where the gases escape at the rear. The resulting unbalanced force on the front wall of the chamber propels the rocket forward. The magnitude of the thrust depends on the mass and velocity of the expelled gases. Rocket motors may use solid or liquid fuel. Solid fuels contain an oxidizer intimately mixed with the fuel. The motors consist of a casing and the fuel, with an igniter to begin combustion and a central cavity to ensure even and complete burning. Liquid fuel motors are more complex, as the fuel and oxidizer are stored separately and then mixed in the combustion chamber, but they are more controllable than solid fuel motors. Liquefied oxygen and hydrogen are the most common liquid fuels. (See also *launch vehicle, *rocketry, history of.)

rocketry, history of. The earliest use of rockets was in China, where war rockets propelled by black powder (*gunpowder) were used as incendiary devices, probably by AD 1300. Their use in war and as *fireworks spread quickly to the Middle East and Europe, reaching Italy in the 14th century and France in the 15th century. Having seen rockets in India, the English artillery expert William Congreve (1772–1828) developed a more powerful rocket with a range of 2,750 m (9,030 feet), which was first used against France in 1806. Rockets were also used peacefully to fire lifelines and as distress signals. All these rockets were powered by gunpowder, but at the end of the 19th century a Russian schoolteacher, Konstantin Tsiolkovsky, proposed the use of liquid rocket fuels and pointed out that rockets could be used to power spacecraft. In the USA, in 1926, *Goddard launched the first liquid-fuelled rocket; meanwhile, in Germany and the Soviet Union, experimenters worked on solid-fuelled *rocket motors for cars and aeroplanes as well as on liquid-fuelled rockets. In the 1930s rocket research in Germany was supported by the military authorities. Here, von *Braun led a team that built rocket weapons, culminating in the V2 rocket (1942), the first *ballistic missile. Subsequent liquid-fuelled rockets were developed from the V2. As the cold war intensified, efforts were directed towards building rocket-powered *missiles to carry nuclear warheads; modified ballistic missiles launched both the Soviet *Sputnik 1*, the world's first artificial satellite (1957), and *Explorer 1*, the USA's first satellite (1958). These satellite launches initiated the space race between the Soviet Union and the USA, each trying to build more powerful rockets to send people and machines into space. Von Braun, by now leading the team in the USA, built the giant *Saturn V* rocket that took the *Apollo programme to the Moon in 1969; from 1971 the Soviet Union's rockets launched *space stations, equipped for prolonged occupation, into Earth orbit. Economy has now dictated the development of reusable rocket-powered spacecraft like the *Space Shuttle.

rolling bearing, a type of *bearing for a rotating shaft in which *friction is reduced by the rolling action of a ring of hardened steel balls, cylinders, or cones running in grooves. Ball-bearings (the name for both the bearing and the individual balls) found an early use in *bicycles. They are noisier than plain bearings and are unsuitable for use at very high speeds. Roller bearings are a type of rolling bearing that use cylinders or cones instead of balls. Such bearings can carry heavy loads; sometimes the cylinders are tapered to resist axial (sideways) loads, for example, in motor-car and locomotive wheels. (For illustration see *bearing.)

rolling mill, an industrial facility, performed hot or cold, in which metal slabs (ingots) are formed into sheet or shapes for use in manufacturing and construction. The metal is passed between pairs of rollers revolving at the same speed but in opposite directions. The distance between the rollers is adjustable and is set slightly less than the thickness of the metal, so that it emerges thinner and longer. Hot rolling is used to break up the cast structure of the ingot. Cold rolling is often used as a finishing processs, to improve mechanical properties, or to create a special size, a bright surface, or a thinner gauge than can be achieved with hot rolling.

rolling stock *brake van, *goods wagon, *railway carriage.

roll-on, roll-off ship (ro-ro ship) *car ferry.

ROM *memory (computer).

Roman technology *Graeco-Roman technology.

roof, the upper covering of a *house or other building. Pitched roofs are desirable in wetter climates to ensure effective drainage; the slope varies with the covering material. In small buildings, the external walls support inclined wooden rafters, which meet at the ridge. Ceiling joists tie the external walls together and prevent the thrust at the rafter feet from pushing the wall outwards. In larger roofs, the

A continuous-plate **rolling mill** for steel at Lackenby Works in Teeside, UK. The red-hot steel is passed through six successive pairs of rollers: as well as forming the cast steel into plates, the process improves its toughness and ductility.

rafters are also supported by a purlin (horizontal beam), which transfers roof load to a cross-wall or to a truss (see *structural engineering). At the ends, the roof may rest upon a triangular gable or the roof slope may be continued around to form a 'hipped end'. The *tiles or slates are supported on battens spanning between the rafters; wooden boarding or a bituminous underfelting is fixed over the rafters to exclude wind and snow. Flat roofs (usually built with a slight slope for drainage) are finished with an impervious covering of metal (*plumbing) or of bituminous or plastic materials. All of these require continuous support, such as a *reinforced concrete slab, a *vault, ridged metal sheeting, or wood boarding and joists as in a floor. Problems arise from the degradation of some of these coverings by ultraviolet radiation. (For illustration see *house.)

root-crop, a plant grown for its high-yielding underground roots, tubers, or bulbs. Root-crops are rich in carbohydrate and highly digestible; they are grown for human consumption, sugar extraction, and stock feeding. The world's main root-crops are staple foods: potato in temperate regions, sweet potato and yam, taro, and cassava in tropical areas. Root-crops consumed as fresh vegetables, such as carrots and the onion group, are prized for their flavour more than for their dietary contribution. *Sugar-beet production is important in Europe and the area of beet sown has markedly increased in recent years. The pulp left after sugar extraction provides feed for livestock, as do other root-crops: fodder beet, mangels, and turnips. These *forage crops may be lifted and stored or grazed directly. Root-crops require minimal care after planting, but their handling, preservation, and transportation are problematical.

rope, heavy cord made by twisting strands of wire or fibre together. Ropes were first made over 10,000 years ago using vines or leather. The Egyptians had strong leather or papyrus ropes about 3500 BC. From that time, rope was used for the *rigging of *sailing ships and for anchor cables. Most of it was made from strong natural fibres which have low extensibility, such as hemp, sisal, and flax. Ropes are still used for a great variety of purposes, but increasingly natural fibres are being replaced by even stronger continuous-filament synthetic yarns such as *nylon, *polyester, and polypropylene. Most ropes consist of three (or sometimes four) strands twisted ('laid') together. The strands are made from many spun yarns, which are twisted together lightly in one direction; the strands are then brought together and twisted in the opposite direction. This ensures that the rope has little tendency to untwist, either when relaxed or when under load. Three or more ropes laid together make a cable-laid rope or hawser. Ropes that will be subjected to much handling are often braided rather than simply twisted together. Although most rope is now produced on rope-making machines, some is still made in rope-walks, where the strands are laid on the ground and then twisted manually. Ropes used for climbing have a core of synthetic filaments with little or no twist, surrounded by a smooth, tubular, braided sheath which has a high resistance to abrasion. Such ropes have some elasticity, to absorb the sudden, heavy load of a fall.

rotary engine, an *internal-combustion engine that generates rotary motion directly, rather than converting reciprocating motion through a crankshaft. The most successful example to date has been the Wankel engine, developed by the German engineer Felix Wankel in 1959. Instead of a piston the engine has a three-lobed rotor, which rotates within an oval casing containing inlet and exhaust ports for fuel. As the rotor revolves, the three spaces between the rotor and the casing execute a four-stroke cycle similar to that of a normal *petrol engine. The engine has found only limited application due to difficulties in obtaining a seal between the rotor and the outer casing. A new rotary engine design, the Rotorcam, uses conventional cylinders and pistons arranged radially outwards from a central axis. The engine, developed by the US inventor Jerome Murray, is more efficient, can run on a variety of fuels, and requires fewer gears than a conventional engine.

rotation of crops, the growing of different crops successively, in a predetermined order, used for several purposes. It may be arranged so that the nutrient requirements of one crop differ from those of the one preceding it. It may put back into the soil a nutrient such as nitrogen, as for example with pulses (leguminous plants such as lentils, beans, and peas). The rotation may be designed to reduce the risk of a build-up of diseases specific to one crop. *Root-crops may be used to smother the weeds that have grown between plants of the previous crop. Rotation may be used to give land a fallow period, or to optimally use the land by growing an early sown crop after one that is harvested early.

row cultivation, the growing of crops in rows to facilitate the cultivation, spraying, weeding, and harvesting needed for optimum yields. Modern *seed drills have made highly ordered sowing possible. The tramline method of cereal planting is a form of row cultivation. This allows tractor-mounted equipment to enter a crop without damage to it.

Royal Greenwich Observatory, a UK observatory founded in 1675, with John Flamsteed as first Astronomer Royal. Its original role was practical, 'to perfect the art of navigation', particularly by devising a means of determining longitude at sea. In 1767 the Observatory began publication of the annual *Nautical Almanac*, a compendium of navigational information, which still continues to this day. In the same year, *Harrison's marine chronometer solved the problem of longitude, provided that the instrument was accurately set at the start of a voyage. From 1833 the Observatory provided a visible time-signal each day at noon: a 'six-pip' radio signal was introduced in 1924. Greenwich Mean Time (GMT)—now almost universally used for scientific and navigational purposes—became the UK's legal time in 1880. The Observatory now occupies new buildings in Cambridge, and manages three telescopes at a new international observatory in the Canary Islands.

Royal Institution, a body founded in London in 1799 by the Anglo-American Benjamin Thompson, 'to teach the application of science to the common purposes of life'. In effect, the Royal Institution has devoted itself primarily to scientific research, and to the presentation of science to non-scientific audiences. The change of emphasis resulted from the work of *Davy (from 1801) and *Faraday (from 1813) at the Institution. They were followed in the 19th century by men of equal distinction, including John Tyndall, famous for research on heat; James Dewar, inventor of the *vacuum flask; and John Strutt (Lord Rayleigh), discoverer of *argon. In the 20th century W. H. Bragg and his son W. L. Bragg, who conducted early research into *X-ray crystallography, succeeded one another as directors.

Royal Society (of London for Improving Natural Knowledge), one of the world's oldest and most prestigious scientific societies. It was founded in 1660 as a fellowship of some forty natural philosophers meeting in London, and received its first Royal Charter from Charles II in 1662. It is an independent, self-governing institution for promoting the natural sciences, including mathematics and applied sciences such as engineering and medicine. It operates both nationally and internationally, by encouraging the exchange of scientific ideas through meetings and publications; making grants and research appointments; collaborating with national academies overseas; providing independent advice to the UK government and others; representing the interests of the UK scientific community; and supporting research on the history of science. The Fellowship now numbers around 1,100, including about 100 Foreign Members.

Royal Society for the Encouragement of Arts, Manufactures, and Commerce, (the Society of Arts), a UK institution conceived by William Shipley (a friend of *Franklin), and founded in 1754. It received a Royal Charter in 1908. The Society originally encouraged industry by offering premiums for new inventions, especially in agriculture. Today the Society encourages innovation through lecture programmes, fellowships, and award schemes.

rubber (natural), a natural *elastomer obtained from latex, the sap of the rubber tree (*Hevea brasiliensis*). Rubber trees are grown by *plantation farming methods: Malaysia and Indonesia are leading rubber producers. A short diagonal incision is made into the bark of the rubber tree to allow the latex to run out into a collecting cup. The latex is treated so that the rubber coagulates and settles into thin sheets. These can then be separated from the residual liquid. Alternatively the latex can be processed in a *centrifuge to yield a concentrate. The natural rubber is very soft, inelastic, and perishes rapidly on contact with air. Working the rubber between rollers, masticating it, and treating it with sulphur (*vulcanization), generates a material with greater elasticity and resilience than any other solid. Rubber deteriorates in the presence of direct sunlight because of its reaction with oxygen. The introduction of *carbon black slows down this process, but it still deteriorates slowly, especially in the presence of oil or grease. Rubber is thermoplastic (becomes flexible on heating), and can be shaped by *extrusion and *moulding. It is used extensively in the production of tyres and also in combination with fabrics to produce *waterproof cloth for use in raincoats and groundsheets. Vulcanization with excess sulphur produces a rigid plastic called ebonite. Foam rubber, made by frothing latex and vulcanizing it, is used as padding in upholstery and other applications. Liquid latex is used extensively in the manufacture of flexible masks for puppets and in special effects for the cinema.

rubber (synthetic), a range of compounds manufactured to reproduce the properties of natural *rubber. The first synthetic rubber was a *polymer of dimethyl butadiene (C_4H_6)

manufactured in Germany during World War I. This methyl rubber was very inferior to natural rubber. Interest in synthetic rubbers was revived in Germany in 1926, and between 1930 and 1935 several good synthetic rubbers were developed. During World War II, Asian sources of natural rubber were cut off and the USA developed a huge synthetic rubber industry virtually overnight. After the War production was taken up in other countries. Many different synthetic rubbers are now in use, the most widespread being rubber produced by polymerization of butadiene with styrene (the monomer from which *polystyrene is made). For many purposes this rubber can directly replace natural rubber, and it has better resistance to ageing, cracking, and abrasion than the natural product. However, it has poor strength and resilience, and in some applications (notably tyre treads) it is mixed with natural rubber. Another synthetic rubber is butyl rubber, which is exceptionally impermeable to gases and is used for inner tubes and the inner linings of tubeless tyres. Other examples of synthetic rubbers include polychloroprene (neoprene), used in the cable and wire industry, and oil-resistant nitrile rubbers, for gaskets and for the ink-spreading rollers on printing machines. Some forms of *silicones, *polyurethane, and *PTFE are also used as synthetic rubbers. Synthetic rubbers, like natural rubber, are compounded with carbon black and other additives such as colouring agents, plasticizers, softeners, and vulcanizing agents, to change or improve their qualities.

rubberized fabric, textile laminated with *rubber. Early waterproof garments were made from sheet rubber bonded to cloth, and although effective, were heavy and clumsy to wear. Light garments proofed with rubber were introduced in 1824, when *Macintosh developed a fabric composed of two layers of fine cotton cloth cemented together with a thin layer of rubber dissolved in naphtha. Later, *vulcanization made it practicable to make ultra-light, single-layer, rubberized fabric. Many products, including pneumatic *tyres, driving belts, conveyor belts, and inflatable dinghies, are made from specialized forms of rubberized fabric.

rudder (marine), a movable plate fitted to the rear part of a hull and used to control its direction. When the rudder is turned, the pressure of water on one side of it becomes greater than that on the other, imparting a sideways thrust to the vessel's stern. Rudders fitted permanently on the centre-line of the vessel were first used in the Chinese *junk. They did not appear in Europe until the 13th century, before which time a *steering-oar or side rudder was used. Small rudders are usually pivoted from the stern-post of the vessel, and controlled by a tiller attached to the head of the rudder. In larger vessels the rudder is controlled by the ship's wheel, movement of the wheel being transmitted mechanically or electrically to the rudder itself. Balanced rudders are pivoted at their centre rather than at one edge: this arrangement has the advantage of needing less force to turn. Active rudders incorporate a small propeller into the rudder. Other devices to improve a ship's manœuvrability include new rudder shapes, cycloidal *propellers, and thrusters at the bow of a vessel. (See *flight, principles of, for the aircraft rudder.)

ruthenium (symbol Ru, at. no. 44, r.a.m. 101.07), a white *platinum metal. Ruthenium occurs in association with other platinum metals as fine black grains in alluvial deposits. It is harder than other platinum metals and is used in electrical alloys and jewellery. Ruthenium red compound is used to stain silk, and animal tissue in biological research.

S

saccharin *sweetener, artificial.

saddlery *harness and saddlery.

safe, a strong, lockable container for valuables designed to be proof against theft, fire, and collapse of a building. The first effective safes were designed by Thomas Milner (1846) and Samuel Chatwood (1860). The body of a safe is usually of thick, high-strength steel. The door hinges are strong and protected, with several strong bolts controlled by the *lock. Small safes are firmly fixed against removal; a common method is to build the safe into a wall or the floor and to conceal its presence. Larger safes may be walk-in, and often have time locks that allow access only at specific times.

safety-belt, a restraining strap or harness used to secure a person against injury that might result from sudden deceleration or violent motion, as in an aeroplane or car accident. Early lap safety-belts allowed the upper body and head to be catapulted forward. The most common design today is the three-point inertia-reel belt. This allows free movement in normal travelling, but any sudden deceleration activates a *ratchet and pawl mechanism, which locks the safety-belt strap and restrains the wearer. Up to 50 per cent of injuries can be prevented by safety-belt use.

safety-critical system *reliability.

safety-glass, *glass that has been toughened by rapid cooling of the surface after *annealing. This produces a skin which is in compression, while the glass beneath is held in tension. When safety-glass breaks, the release of internal stresses causes it to shatter into many small rounded pieces, which are not dangerous. Laminated safety glass has a central layer of tough plastic to retain fragments when broken.

safety-valve, a device invented by the French physicist Denis Papin in 1679 to guard against excessive pressure in a *boiler or pipe system. Boiler explosions were common until safety-valves were required by law. Early valves were operated by a weighted lever, but these could be wilfully overweighted, so a spring-loaded valve was developed. This could be locked to prevent unauthorized adjustment. The *valve itself is usually of the poppet type, mushroom-shaped, similar to those used in internal-combustion engines. It is designed to lift suddenly when a critical pressure is reached and to close sharply when the pressure lowers.

sail, a piece or assemblage of material, extended on *rigging, to catch the wind and provide the propulsive force in *sailing ships and boats. The number and shape of the sails vary according to the type and *rig of the vessel. For centuries canvas was the most common cloth from which sails were made, although other materials such as leather and matting were also used. Canvas is still the cloth used in *square-rigged ships, but today most small *fore-and-aft rigged sailing vessels and *yachts use synthetic fibres such as polyester and nylon, which are less prone to stretching. In modern fore-and-aft sails the leech (trailing edge) of the sail

Sailing, principles of

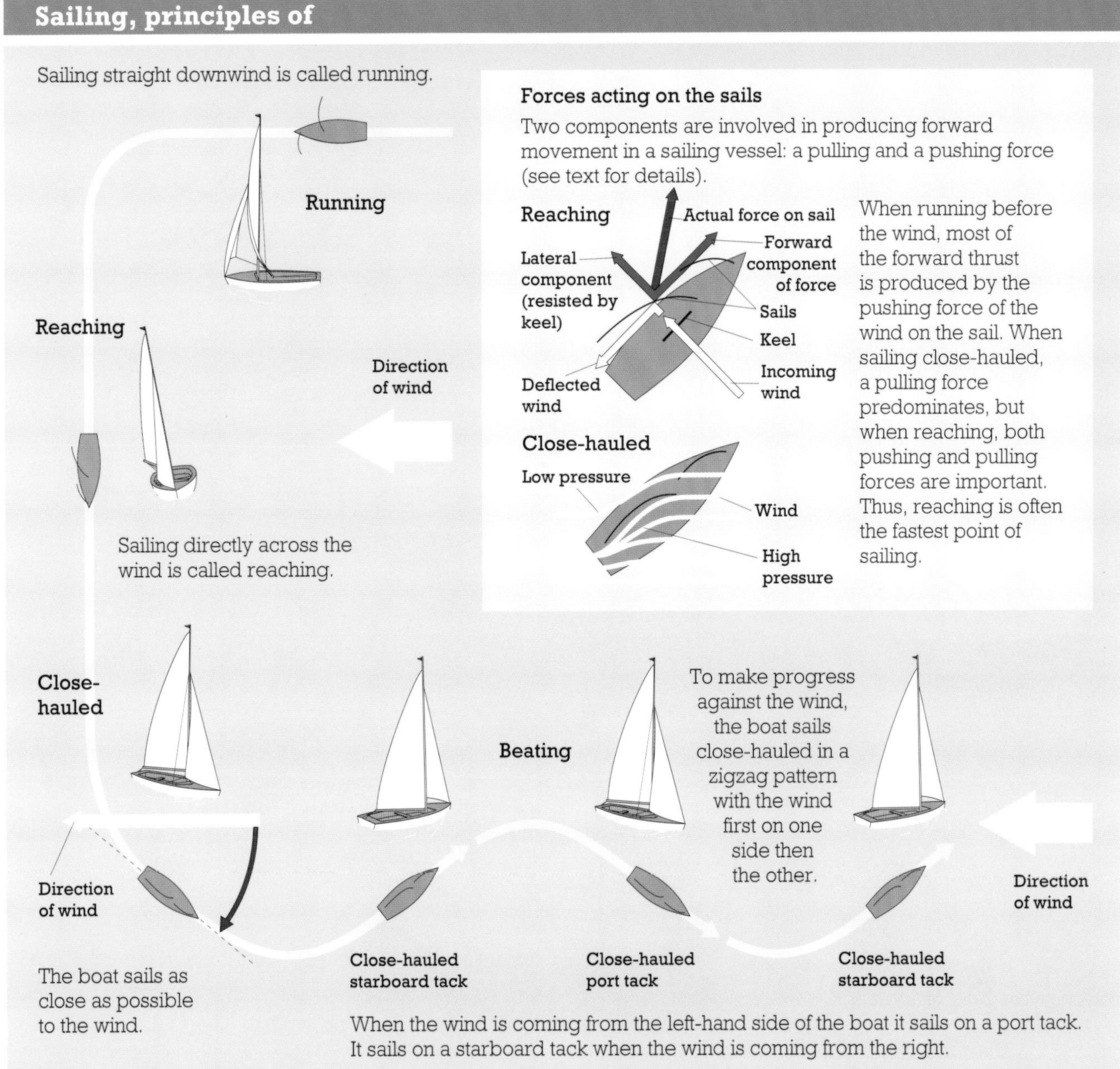

Sailing straight downwind is called running.
Running
Reaching
Direction of wind
Sailing directly across the wind is called reaching.
Forces acting on the sails
Two components are involved in producing forward movement in a sailing vessel: a pulling and a pushing force (see text for details).
Reaching
Actual force on sail
Forward component of force
Lateral component (resisted by keel)
Sails
Keel
Incoming wind
Deflected wind
When running before the wind, most of the forward thrust is produced by the pushing force of the wind on the sail. When sailing close-hauled, a pulling force predominates, but when reaching, both pushing and pulling forces are important. Thus, reaching is often the fastest point of sailing.
Close-hauled
Low pressure
Wind
High pressure
Close-hauled
Beating
To make progress against the wind, the boat sails close-hauled in a zigzag pattern with the wind first on one side then the other.
Direction of wind
Direction of wind
The boat sails as close as possible to the wind.
Close-hauled starboard tack
Close-hauled port tack
Close-hauled starboard tack
When the wind is coming from the left-hand side of the boat it sails on a port tack. It sails on a starboard tack when the wind is coming from the right.

is shaped to produce an aerodynamic curve, to take full advantage of the wind acting on its surface. (See *sailing, principles of, and *sailing ships and boats for illustrations.)

sailing, principles of. Over the centuries sailing ships have used many different arrangements of sails to make maximum use of the wind as a power source. Like aeroplane wings, sails are aerodynamically designed to obtain lift from the wind as well as push. When sailing downwind (running), the wind pushes into the sails to provide the driving force for the boat. When sailing across the wind (reaching), the force on the boat has two components, a lateral (sideways) one and a forward or driving force (see figure). In a sailing yacht or dinghy, the lateral force on the boat is resisted by the *keel or *centreboard, while the forward component drives the boat forward. In addition, wind-flow across the front surface of the sail produces a pulling force, so the boat is both pushed and pulled. When sailing close-hauled (as nearly into the wind as possible), the air encounters the sail, and because of the sail's shape, changes direction to flow across its surface. This phenomenon is known as attached flow: the air is held to the surface of the sail by the lower pressure on the leeward side of the sail (the side away from the wind). The force that pulls the wind on to the surface of the sail also pulls the sail into the wind stream: this force is known as lift, and it is this pulling force that enables the boat to sail close to the wind (as close as 39 degrees to the wind in some modern Bermuda-rig *yachts). Even the most efficient sailing boats cannot travel directly into the wind; in order to reach an upwind destination, a boat must travel on a zigzag course, with the wind first on one side, then on the other. This type of sailing is known as beating. Changing direction so that the wind is on the other side of the boat is called tacking or coming about. There are an infinite variety of routes to an upwind direction—you can tack once or many times—but if the wind is steady, the distance travelled on each route is the same.

sailing ships and boats, water-going vessels using sails as a means of propulsion. Ships with a single square sail were

Sailing ships and boats

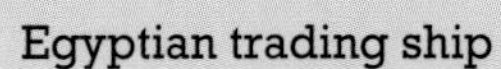

Egyptian trading ship

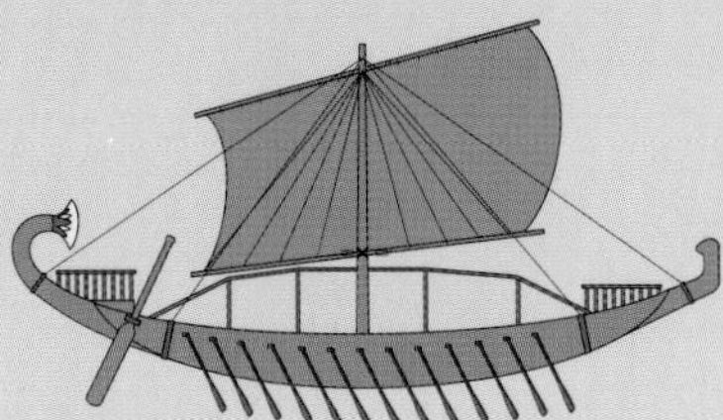

This ship was developed about 1500 BC and carried about thirty rowers.

Greek trireme

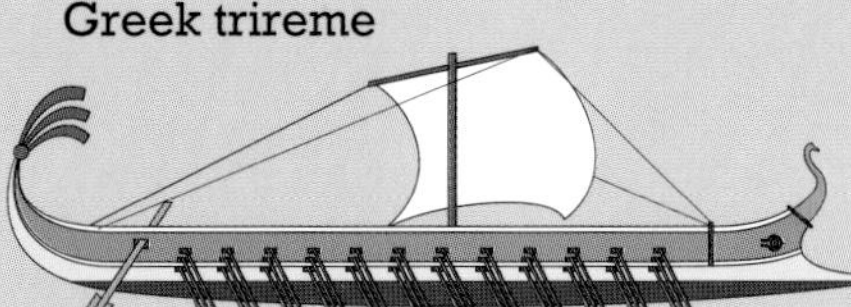

This warship had three banks of oars as well as the sail. It dates from the 5th century BC.

Chinese junk

The distinctive and effective junk has existed in many different forms since the 5th century BC.

Lateen-rigged boat

A 'fore-and-aft' rig, in which the sail is carried in line with the keel. It was introduced around the 3rd century AD.

Viking longship

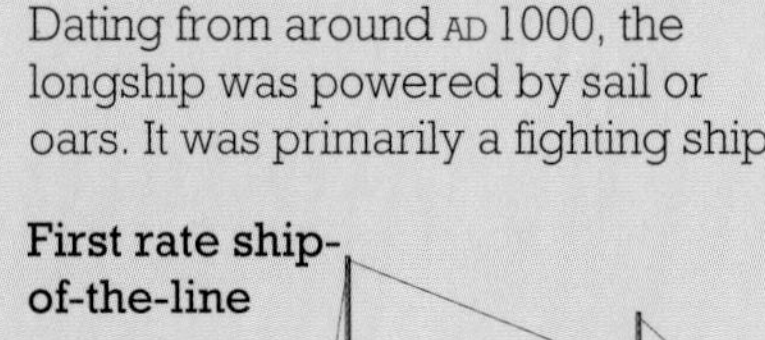

Dating from around AD 1000, the longship was powered by sail or oars. It was primarily a fighting ship.

Portuguese caravel

Dating from the mid-15th century, many of the great voyages of discovery were made in caravels.

Galleon

The galleon originated in Spain in the 16th century and was an armed trading ship.

First rate ship-of-the-line

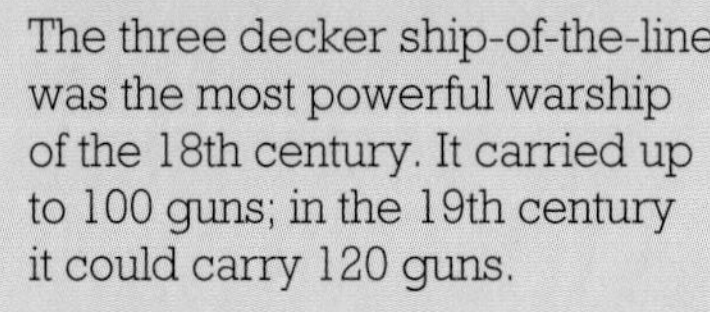

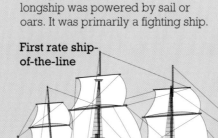

The three decker ship-of-the-line was the most powerful warship of the 18th century. It carried up to 100 guns; in the 19th century it could carry 120 guns.

Barque

Very large four- and five-masted barques traded in grain and nitrate to South America in the late 19th and early 20th centuries.

Thames barge

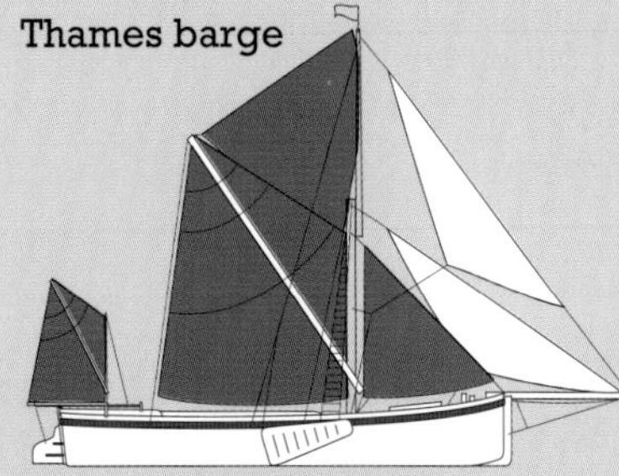

Developed during the 18th and 19th centuries, this barge was used extensively on the south-east coast of England for distributing cargo.

Gaff-rigged ketch

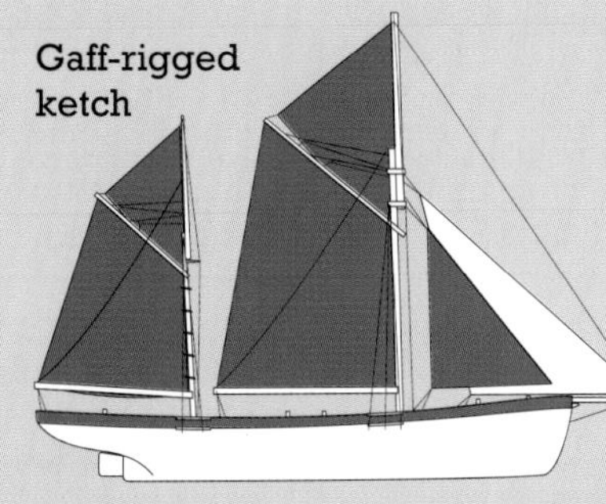

This rig was widely used for fishing boats and sea-going traders because of its easy handling.

Bermuda sloop

The Bermuda rig developed from the gaff rig, and is the most common rig on modern sailing craft.

built in Egypt some 5,500 years ago: the earliest vessels were made of papyrus reeds. The sail acted as a supplement to crews of oarsmen, and *steering-oars over the stern guided the boat. This combination of oars and sail predominated in the Mediterranean and northern Europe for several thousand years. In other parts of the Mediterranean, wooden ships were being built by about 2000 BC. They were nearly all narrow to facilitate rowing, and this design continued to be important in the development of *warships. In the eastern Mediterranean, broader, shorter *merchant ships were developed in which the sail was the main method of propulsion. During Greek and Roman times the long ships for war and the round ships for trade continued to improve: the Greeks perfected a form of the oared *galley (the trireme), while the Romans built larger merchant ships, some carrying a small mast and sail forward of the mainmast. From around the 6th century the *lateen rig largely replaced the square sail in the Mediterranean until the late Middle Ages.

In China and South-East Asia, sailing vessels developed along different lines. The Chinese *junk, a large, flat-bottomed vessel with a rudder placed on the centre-line, had sails that could be hauled about, to allow the ship to sail into the wind. In the 15th century junks were larger, stronger, and more seaworthy than any European ships of the period.

Medieval shipbuilders in the Mediterranean developed the 'frame-first' method of construction (see *shipbuilding). Ships with two or three decks, and often with two masts were built, usually with a lateen rig. The new constructional techniques were not adopted in northern Europe until the 15th century. However, northern ships such as the cog were perhaps the earliest European vessels to employ a rudder. The cog was initially a single-masted, *square-rigged merchant ship with raised 'castles' at the fore and stern for defence, and was used throughout northern Europe from the 13th to the 15th century. In square-rigged ships the sails are set square to the mast. In the Mediterranean, some of these characteristics were copied in the carrack, a large three-masted merchant ship that first appeared in the 16th century. A later development from the carrack was the *galleon. During the 15th century the three-masted, square-rigged ship evolved out of a merging of the shipbuilding technologies of the Mediterranean and the north. This type became the basic pattern for ships for the next 300 years (see the ship of the line in the figure). A further development, just after the start of the 16th century, was the mounting of *cannon that fired through the ship's sides.

From the 17th to the 19th century the form of the sailing ship was gradually diversified and refined. Economical, load-carrying merchant ships were developed, many later becoming specialized by trade or cargo (for example, East Indiamen trading to the East Indies, or colliers carrying coal). The number of sails carried gradually expanded, with each mast carrying four, six, or even eight sails on the mast. Studding sails were rigged outboard of the major sails for use

Satellite, artificial

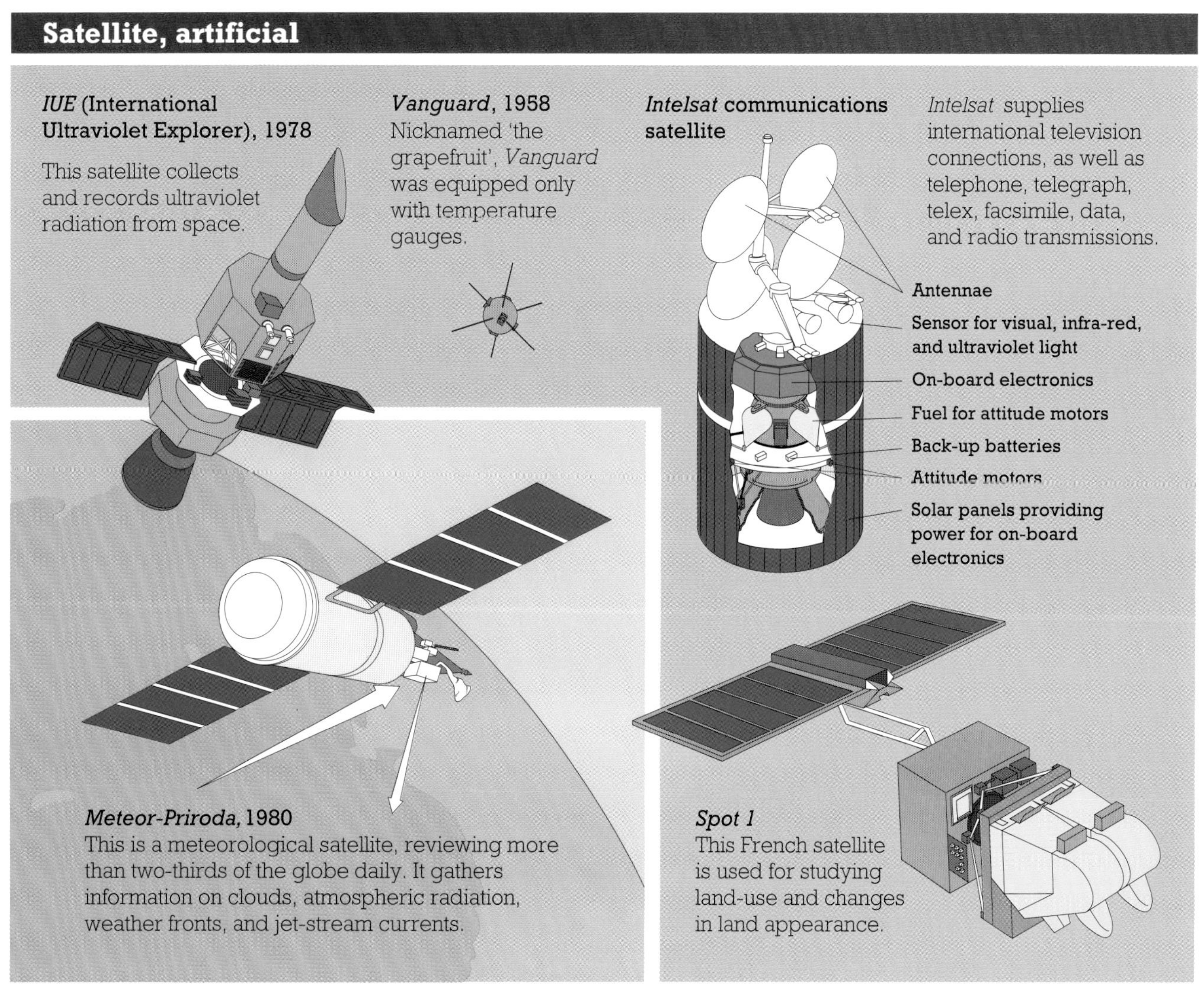
IUE (International Ultraviolet Explorer), 1978
This satellite collects and records ultraviolet radiation from space.
Vanguard, 1958
Nicknamed 'the grapefruit', *Vanguard* was equipped only with temperature gauges.
Intelsat communications satellite
Intelsat supplies international television connections, as well as telephone, telegraph, telex, facsimile, data, and radio transmissions.
Antennae
Sensor for visual, infra-red, and ultraviolet light
On-board electronics
Fuel for attitude motors
Back-up batteries
Attitude motors
Solar panels providing power for on-board electronics
Meteor-Priroda, 1980
This is a meteorological satellite, reviewing more than two-thirds of the globe daily. It gathers information on clouds, atmospheric radiation, weather fronts, and jet-stream currents.
Spot 1
This French satellite is used for studying land-use and changes in land appearance.

in light winds, and triangular jibs and other fore-and-aft sails hoisted on lines extending from the masts to the deck (see barque in the figure). During the 18th century the *fore-and-aft rig, long used in smaller boats, became increasingly important in ships (for example, in *schooners). By the late 18th century two-masted ships such as the *brig were becoming more important. From the mid-19th century, *steamships offered serious competition to sail and by 1880 had all but made sailing ships obsolete. Ironically, during this period sailing ships reached a peak of reliability and efficiency; longer, streamlined iron and steel hulls offered less resistance to the water, and the use of steam-powered winches greatly reduced crew numbers. Sailing as a sport increased in popularity early in the 20th century, with the use of fore-and-aft rigged *yachts and smaller *dinghies. Interest in new forms of sail propulsion for commercial purposes continues to this day: the oil crisis of the 1970s prompted experiments on *tankers and long-distance carriers with rigid sails, to supplement their power and save fuel. (See also specific ship types.)

salt, a white, crystalline solid that is soluble in water; more generally a compound formed by neutralization of an acid by a base (see *acids, bases, and salts). Common salt (sodium chloride, NaCl) is an essential constituent of human diet and is used domestically to flavour food. It can be extracted from sea-water by solar evaporation in salt pans, but the major source is underground rock-salt deposits derived from ancient seas. These can be mined using high explosives to break up the rock: crushed rock-salt for de-icing roads in winter (by lowering the freezing-point of water) is obtained in this way. Salt for use in the chemical industry is obtained by pumping water down into rock-salt deposits. The salt dissolves and is carried to the surface in solution (brine), while insoluble impurities remain underground. Sodium chloride is used as a starting material for the production of *sodium hydroxide, *sodium carbonate (soda), *chlorine, and *hydrochloric acid.

saltpetre (nitre) *nitrates, *gunpowder.

Salyut *space station.

sand blasting, a process in which the surface of a material is bombarded with sand or mineral grit in an air or water jet. It is done to clean the surface, for example in preparation for painting. A very fine dust is produced, and so breathing apparatus and protective clothing are necessary.

sanitation *sewage treatment and sewerage, *water supply and treatment.

satellite, artificial, usually an unmanned spacecraft orbiting the Earth, although the term can refer to any spacecraft orbiting a larger object in space. The first artificial satellite to be placed in Earth orbit was the Soviet **Sputnik* in 1957. The USA's first satellite, *Explorer 1*, flew in February 1958; it carried instruments that revealed the presence of radiation belts around the earth. Since then over 5,000 satellites have been launched, several hundred of which are currently operational. They include *meteorological satellites, *scientific and *Earth resources satellites, *military satellites, *communications satellites, and *navigation satellites (see figure on the previous page). The orbit of a satellite may be elliptical or circular, and its height above the Earth's surface and angle to the equator vary depending on its purpose. Most *communications satellites have a geostationary orbit, an equatorial orbit at a height of 35,800 km (22,300 miles). At this height a satellite orbits once every 24 hours, so that its position relative to the Earth's surface remains constant. Thus *ground stations can receive signals 24 hours a day. Satellites that study the Earth use a polar orbit, circling over the poles in a north–south track. Because the Earth is rotating beneath their orbit, such satellites can observe almost the whole Earth over a period of hours or days. Many satellites must maintain a fixed orientation in space; often this is achieved by sensors that register the position of the Earth's horizon. Power for the equipment aboard a satellite is usually provided by *solar panels and back-up batteries, though some satellites have small nuclear reactors. Information from a satellite's instruments is relayed to ground stations by a microwave radio link. Satellites also transmit radio signals that allow them to be tracked from Earth.

satellite dish, a dish-shaped *antenna sending and receiving radio signals to and from satellites. The dish collects and focuses the signals on to a receiver; they are then amplified and converted for use. Major *ground station dishes are usually around 30 m (100 feet) in diameter, while domestic *television dishes can be as little as 30 cm (12 inches) across.

Saturn rocket **Apollo* programme, *launch vehicle.

Savery, Thomas *miner's friend.

saw, a tool with a toothed blade used for cutting materials such as wood, stone, and metal by a reciprocating (forward and backward) or rotary action. Bronze Age saws differ little in appearance from simple hand-saws made today. However, modern Western saws cut on the push stroke, but the early saws and those used in modern Japan cut on the pull stroke. Over the years many different designs have been developed, but broadly these fall into three categories: hand-saws, back saws, and saws for cutting curves. The size of the teeth and their number per unit length depend on the work to be done. The teeth are 'set', that is, they are bent slightly outward, alternately to left and right, from the plane of the blade. Hand-saws are used for cutting timber: rip-saws cut with the grain, cross-cut saws against it. Back saws are mainly for cutting joints, and have a blade with a stiffening spine of brass or iron. In bow-saws, used for cutting curves, the thin blade is kept under tension. Today, many types of saw are available as *power tools. Some, such as jig-saws, mimic the movement of the hand tool; others, such as circular saws and band saws depend on continuous rotary action. (For illustration see *tools, history of.)

scaffolding, a temporary framework erected to provide access for construction or repair work. Upright and horizontal members are spaced 1.5–2 m (5–7 feet) apart and are stabilized by diagonals and by tying back to the structure. The boarded working platform is supported by short cross-members resting on the horizontals or on the wall of the structure. Where readily available, fir poles are used for scaffolding, with rope or wire lashings to join the members where they cross. Bamboo scaffolding is still in general use in China and much of the Far East. Otherwise steel or

A merchant ship being built in dry dock in Ancona, Italy. Work on the hull is facilitated by an elaborate system of **scaffolding**.

aluminium alloy tubes are used and are connected with friction-grip couplings.

Schawlow, Arthur Leonard *Maiman, Theodore Harold.

Schönbein, Christian Friedrich (1799–1868), German chemist who explored the properties of *nitro-cellulose. In 1845–6, while Professor of Chemistry at Basel University, Switzerland, he developed both the highly explosive gun-cotton, and also cellulose nitrate, a much less reactive substance that can be moulded and shaped. Schönbein patented these in the UK in 1846. Manufacturing plants for gun-cotton were set up in several countries, but a series of explosions led to the discontinuing of manufacture in all countries except Austria. Cellulose acetate was later developed by *Hyatt as celluloid.

schooner, a *fore-and-aft rigged sailing vessel whose foremast is the same length as, or shorter than, the mainmast, which is situated towards the rear. The sail conformation is more efficient for sailing across the wind than towards it; schooners were developed during the 18th century on the eastern seaboard of the USA, where the prevailing wind is across the coast rather than along it. In the late 19th and early 20th centuries schooner design culminated in two forms. Grand Banks schooners were fast, two-masted vessels used for fishing on the Newfoundland Grand Banks, similar designs now being used as *yachts; larger schooners, some with as many as seven masts, were built as bulk carriers.

Schott, Otto (1851–1935), German *glass manufacturer. In the 1870s his family business was experimenting with new kinds of glass, including ones containing *lithium. This interest brought him in touch with *Abbe and *Zeiss, makers of high-quality optical instruments, who were seeking glasses of unusual refractivity to make *achromatic lenses. In 1884 Schott persuaded them to join him in forming the Jena glassworks of Schott and Son, which made the glass for Zeiss instruments. Within two years a range of totally new glasses was being offered commercially. Other glasses were also developed, resistant to thermal and mechanical shock.

Science Museum, a UK museum instituted in 1853 as the National Museum of Science and Industry. It now houses one of the world's great collections relating to the history of science and technology, comparable with those of the Deutsches Museum, the *Palais de la Découverte, and the *Smithsonian Institution. Until 1909 it was associated with London's Victoria and Albert Museum, dedicated to fine and applied art. Its main collections are at South Kensington in London, along with the Science Museum Library, which specializes in the history of science and technology. It also includes the Wellcome Museum of the History of Medicine, the National Railway Museum in York, and the National Museum of Photography, Film, and Television in Bradford.

scientific satellite, artificial *satellite used for studying the Earth and the space around it, and for collecting light and other radiation from the Sun and distant astronomical objects. Instruments on the satellite detect gamma rays, X-rays, and ultraviolet or infra-red radiation, relaying data to *ground stations for processing. Much of this radiation is prevented from reaching the surface of the Earth by our atmosphere: satellite monitoring of it helps astronomers to study such phenomena as pulsars, quasars, and black holes, and has added enormously to our understanding of the universe. The Hubble space telescope (1990) is a US instrument detecting light and ultraviolet and infra-red radiation. It was originally designed to detect from Earth orbit objects that are seven times further away than can be detected by *telescopes on the ground, which are restricted by blurring effects of the atmosphere. A fault in the main mirror and unforeseen vibrations in the telescope's solar panels have greatly reduced its actual resolution; possible solutions are being considered to improve the telescope's performance.

scissors, a hand tool used for cutting, with two crossed, pivoted blades that cut by a shearing action. The earliest scissors, from the Bronze Age, had two overlapping blades joined by a C-spring, so that when the pressure of the cutting stroke was relaxed the blades automatically separated. Modern sheep shears work with the same action, and garden secateurs operate on a similar principle, except that the spring is a coil of steel. Modern scissors are made of steel; they were not widely used until the 16th century.

scrambler, an electronic device that ensures the security of transmitted speech, data, and video information. Speech scramblers either split the frequency spectrum into groups and interchange them, or digitally code the sound, and as for data scramblers, add a fixed pre-arranged code. Video scramblers modify the synchronization signal at the start of each television line.

scraper, an earth-moving machine with a large-capacity, open-fronted bowl in which excavated material is carried. As the scraper advances, it cuts a layer of soil, which is pushed up into the bowl by the machine's motion. The soil is ejected by tilting the bowl or by pushing it out with a ram. The area cut by the scraper can then be levelled by a *grader. Scrapers towed by track-laying tractors are efficient on poor-quality ground and over short distances. Faster, self-propelled scrapers carry material more economically over longer distances.

screen printing, a printing process in which the image is formed using a *stencil on a fine mesh screen (originally silk), through which ink is forced by a squeegee on to the paper or substrate underneath. Screen-printing (adapted from the ancient technique of stencilling) was first used in the 19th century for transferring patterns on to pottery and textiles. Modern screen-printing is very versatile, utilizing photo-mechanical stencils on screens of manufactured fibre and stainless steel in both flat and rotary machinery. It is particularly used for advertising material, posters, packaging, plastic containers, clothing, and other difficult printing surfaces.

screw, a device for turning rotary motion into linear motion, thereby achieving a mechanical advantage. Wooden (or occasionally metal) screws were used in olive presses in ancient Greece. A medieval development was the screw-jack, used to lift heavy weights. *Leonardo da Vinci first described the use of long lead screws to control mechanical devices, for example, in moving the cutting tool on a lathe. By the 17th century fine screws were used to adjust scientific instruments. Screw-based devices are widely used in engineering today, for example, in the *micrometer. Screws are also metal fixing devices which appeared in the 16th century, but their use was limited until screw-cutting machines were developed in the mid-18th century. The long-bladed

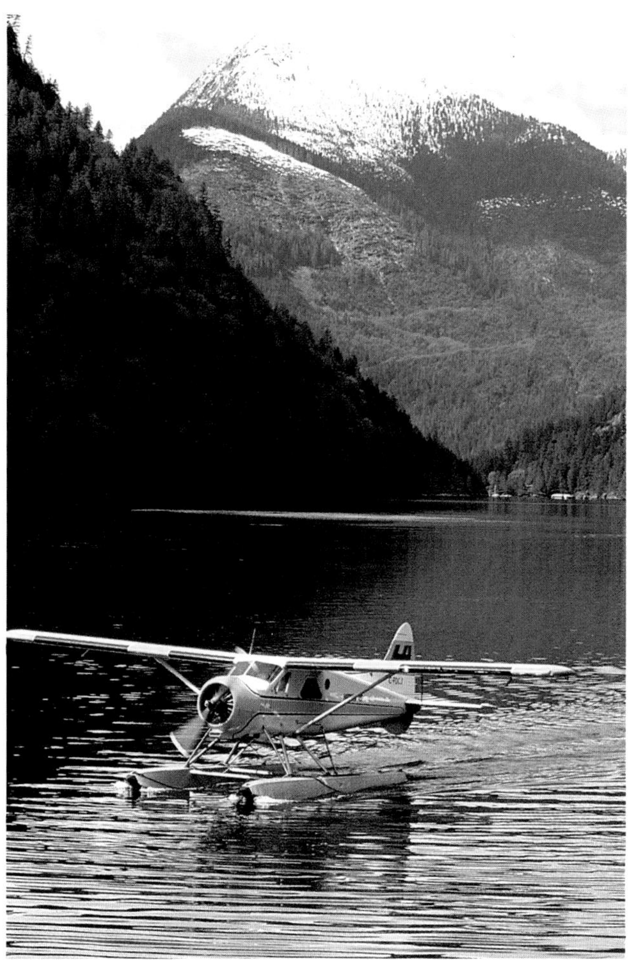

A **seaplane** taking off from a Canadian lake. In mountainous terrain such as this, a lake may offer the only suitable runway for an aircraft.

*screwdriver appeared at about the same time. Screws are classified according to gauge (diameter) and length.

screwdriver, a tool for turning *screws in order to secure or release them. Originally, all screws were made with a transverse slot in the head, into which the flat blade of the screwdriver fitted. Recently, however, the cross-head variant has become popular: this has a cross-shaped depression in the head of the screw and a screwdriver of corresponding design to turn it. The cross-head screw gives a more positive engagement, especially when a power tool is being used. Many hand-held screwdrivers are fitted with a ratchet device so that continuous turning by hand is unnecessary. (See *tools, history of, for illustration.)

scythe, a large, long-handled tool with a slightly curved blade set at right angles to the handle, used primarily for cutting grass and cereal crops. The earliest harvesting tool was the sickle, a one-handed, short-handled tool with a sharp, semicircular, serrated blade. From Roman times onwards, this was gradually superseded by the scythe, which is a powerful two-handed implement and cuts a much bigger swathe. The blade is about 1 m (3.3 feet) long, used in a sweeping motion about 15 cm (6 inches) from the ground. (See *agricultural machinery for illustration.)

SDI *Strategic Defense Initiative.

seaplane, an aeroplane that can land and take off from water; it differs from a *flying boat in that it has a conventional fuselage supported by floats rather than a floating hull. The first seaplane was designed by the Frenchman Alphonse Penaud (1876) but never built. Another Frenchman, Henri Fabre, made the first seaplane flight at Martigues, France (1910), but it was the US aircraft designer Glenn Curtiss who flew the first practical craft at San Diego, USA, and carried the first passenger, both in 1911. By the 1920s and 1930s many countries were building seaplanes for both civil and military use. Today they are used in Canada and other areas where lakes abound; in the winter the floats are often replaced by skis.

searchlight, a powerful incandescent electric light with a concentrated beam that can be turned in any direction. Searchlights were introduced in World War I, but were especially effective in World War II against bombers flying at night, temporarily blinding the bomb-aimer with their brightness or illuminating the sky for anti-aircraft guns. Searchlights are used in naval battles to light up target ships, and in land warfare to create artificial moonlight by bouncing beams off low clouds.

seat-belt *safety-belt.

sedan chair *litter.

sedative *pharmacology (table), *psychotropic drug.

sedimentation tank *sewage treatment and sewerage, *water supply and treatment.

seed dressing, the application of a *fungicide or *pesticide to seeds to protect them from damage. Chemicals may be applied to prevent attack by fungus during storage or to repel birds at the time that seeds are most susceptible, just after sowing and whilst the first shoots are developing.

seed drill, a machine that plants seeds in rows at a set depth, and a predetermined distance apart. Some drills place fertilizer in the same operation. An adjustable mechanism inside a hopper controls the flow of seeds through one or more chutes, which pass down into the soil. A simple manual drill was first used in Sumeria in the 3rd millennium BC, but drills were not used in Europe until the 16th century AD. Mechanical drills were not common until the late 19th century. Specialized forms of seed drill include direct drills, which sow into uncultivated land, and machines for planting potatoes. (See also *Tull.)

Seguin, Marc (1786–1875), French civil and mechanical engineer. A nephew of the *Montgolfier brothers, he was self-taught. From 1824, he built a number of *suspension bridges using cables of parallel wires rather than chains, working with the Swiss engineer Henri Dufour and later his own brother, Camille. The first bridge was built over the Rhône south of Tain. Another major achievement was his invention, independently of George *Stephenson, of the multi-tubular *boiler for *steam locomotives.

seismograph, an instrument for detecting and measuring movement of the ground before and after earthquakes or explosions. In AD 132 an elaborate instrument, about 2 m (6.5 feet) high, was constructed by *Zhang Heng in China. This utilized a heavy pendulum, which swung in response to the shock of an earthquake. Most modern instruments also incorporate some sort of pendulum, but they additionally involve an electromagnetic recording device. In a strain seismograph, two firmly anchored piers are connected by a fused-quartz tube containing a transducer, a device which measures the strain on the tube due to earth movement. The newest high-precision seismometers have at their centre a leaf spring with a weight attached at one end. An electronic force detector senses any motion of the weight. Until 1935, the magnitude of an earthquake was assessed subjectively in terms of its observed effects. In 1935 C. F. Richter introduced a quantitative scale related to the logarithm of the maximum amplitude of the shock waves recorded, allowing for the distance from the epicentre.

selenium (symbol Se, at. no. 34, r.a.m. 78.96), an element that occurs in several forms (allotropes), including a metallic form. It is usually found in small amounts associated with sulphur. Selenium is used to colour glass red, in colour glazes and enamels for ceramics, in *photocopiers, and in the electronics industry for *photocells and alternating-current *rectifiers.

self-propelled gun, an *artillery piece mounted on a military vehicle (commonly one with *caterpillar tracks) to give it mobility. The first self-propelled guns were introduced by the French Army during World War I. During World War II their use became widespread as a way to keep artillery moving at battle pace. Many vehicles had open-topped compartments into which a gun, usually a *howitzer, was fitted. Since 1945, a turreted mounting has become standard.

semaphore, a coded means of visual communication using different positions of two movable arms to represent different letters of the alphabet. Semaphore was originally transmitted by a relay of machines erected on towers on hills; the system was invented by *Chappe in 1794 for the French Army. The most common form of semaphore involves the sender holding a flag in each hand. *Railway signal systems have also used a type of semaphore.

A cutaway model of a **seismograph** made by Zhang Heng (AD 78–139) showing the mechanism whereby movement of an internal pendulum causes a ball to be released from the mouth of one of the dragons.

semiconductor device, a solid-state device such as a *transistor or a *diode that is made from a semiconductor material such as *silicon, *germanium, or gallium arsenide. When in an extremely pure state, semiconductor materials like silicon are electrical insulators, and do not conduct electricity. However, semiconductor devices are 'doped' by adding small amounts of specific impurities such as phosphorus, arsenic, or boron, using a process known as *ion implantation. Doping with different elements can produce either n-type semiconductors, in which the impurity provides additional electrons that can act as negative current carriers; or p-type materials, in which the impurity reduces the number of electrons and current is carried by positively charged 'holes' in the crystal lattice.

The simplest semiconductor device is the diode, in which there is one p–n junction between a region of p-type semiconductor and a region of n-type material. Variants of this basic junction are employed in all other semiconductor devices. A *transistor (see figure) has three differently doped regions and two junctions (p–n–p or n–p–n), while a thyristor has three junctions. However, once switched on, the device will continue to pass current even when the gate circuit is broken. Semiconductor devices made from gallium arsenide (GaAs) can work at higher frequencies than silicon-based devices, and they can both detect and emit light. Such devices are currently used in high-frequency microwave circuits, and are likely to become important in optoelectronics for *optical fibre communications. New organic *polymers developed recently have semiconducting properties suitable for the manufacture of electronic devices. (See also *circuits, electrical and electronic, *integrated circuit.)

sensor, any device that detects, records, or measures a physical property, such as temperature, sound, light, or radio waves. The definition includes a very wide and disparate variety of devices, ranging from *mass spectrometers to *smoke detectors and burglar alarms. Many sensors detect some form of electromagnetic radiation or other form of *wave: examples include the *photocell for detecting light, the *microphone for sound, and the *Geiger–Müller counter for nuclear radiation. They are usually also *transducers, converting the incoming energy into an electrical signal. Sensors are often associated with some sort of *servo-mechanism, which can operate a control system on the basis of the information from the sensor. For example, in many tracking systems, information from a sensor about the position and movement of the target object feeds back to a servo-mechanism that controls the movement of the sensor to track the object. Sensors operating in remote or inaccessible locations make use of *telemetry to relay information. Examples include the *radiosonde and *meteorological satellites, which transmit meteorological information from the upper atmosphere to ground stations.

septic tank, a small-scale *sewage treatment installation for a single building or small group of houses. Waste water passes through underground chambers, where the solids settle and are decomposed by anaerobic bacteria. The resulting effluent is further treated, normally by subsoil *irrigation. The tank requires desludging every year. A cesspit is a watertight underground chamber for storing sewage, which needs emptying more frequently than a septic tank.

serial processing, a term used to describe *computer architecture in which operations take place sequentially

Semiconductor device

Diode

A diode allows current to flow in only one direction. It consists of n- (negative) and p- (positive) type silicon.

N-type silicon is doped with phosphorous so that it has an excess of negative electrons for conducting. P-type silicon is doped with boron so that it has a lack of electrons. It uses the resulting positive holes for conducting.

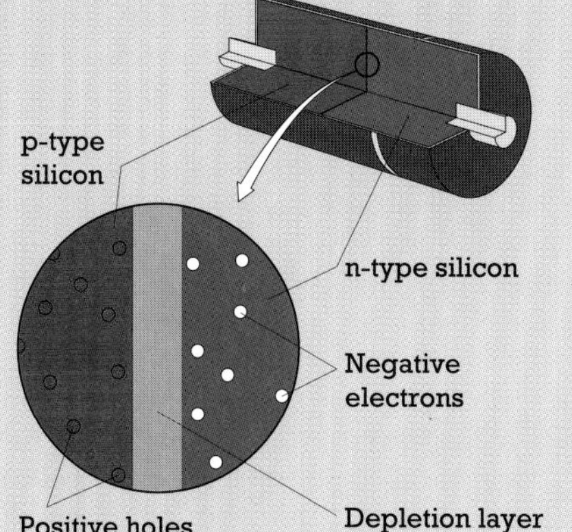

At the diode's p–n junction, neighbouring positive holes and negative electrons are attracted to each other and combine to form uncharged molecules. This causes a depletion layer which is a barrier to conduction.

Forward biased

Large electron flow

No depletion layer

+ve -ve

When connected to an electrical circuit with a forward bias, the holes move towards the negative terminal and the electrons move towards the positive terminal. The depletion layer disappears, the battery can push electrons through the diode, and thus a current flows.

KEY

Conventional current flow

Actual electron flow

Reverse biased

Increased depletion layer

-ve +ve

When the diode is reversed biased, the movement of the holes and electrons tends to widen the depletion layer. There is very high resistance to electron flow through the diode.

Transistor

Detail of traditional transistor

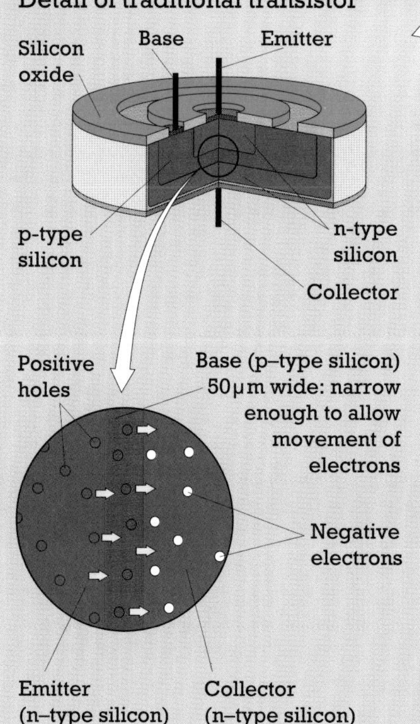

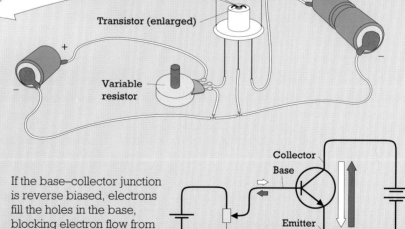

Transistor (enlarged)

Variable resistor

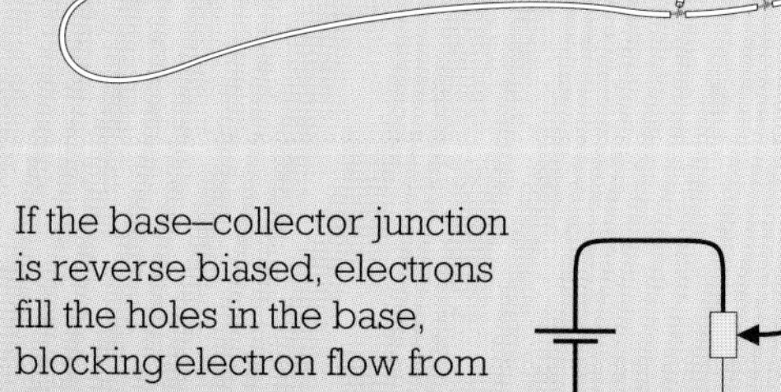

If the base–collector junction is reverse biased, electrons fill the holes in the base, blocking electron flow from the power supply, and no current flows.

Collector

Base

Emitter

If a small p.d. is applied across the base–emitter junction, it becomes forward biased. Electrons leave the base, creating holes. The power supply forces electrons to move from the emitter to the base and then to the collector. A small current in the input signal causes a current fifty to one hundred times larger, but exactly in step, to flow in the output circuit.

rather than simultaneously. Conventional digital computers are based on a single *central processing unit which executes a series of instructions sequentially. They are sometimes termed serial processors to distinguish them from *parallel processors, which use multiple processing units to perform a number of operations simultaneously. Similarly, a serial *interface transmits information as a sequence of signals along a single path, in contrast to a parallel interface, which can transfer one or more *bytes of information simultaneously along several conductors.

series connection *circuits, electrical and electronic.

servo-mechanism, the means of powered automatic control of a larger system; this involves amplification of low-power command signals (mechanical, electrical, hydraulic, or other) so that they can control the motion of heavy equipment. An example of a servo-mechanism is the power steering used on some motor vehicles. The term is also used loosely as a general synonym for feedback *control systems—particularly those designed to force the controlled variable to change with time in a controlled way, rather than simply remain constant in the presence of disturbances. Typically the position (and often also velocity and acceleration) of the device being controlled is measured by a *sensor and fed back to a controller, usually as an electrical signal. The controller then generates the control action needed to correct any error via an actuator (power source) such as a servo-motor. Applications of servo systems include satellite-tracking systems, and the control (in three dimensions) of the position and velocity of a moving robot arm.

settlement (engineering), subsidence of a structure, usually due to the gradual compression of the supporting ground. Small uniform settlements do not normally cause problems, but differential settlement, where one part of a *foundation settles by a greater amount than another, causes strain and possibly damage to the supported structure.

seven-segment display, a way of displaying a number by illuminating seven bar-shaped segments in different combinations. The segments are usually *light-emitting diodes or *liquid crystals that can be switched on or off. Some alphabetic characters can also be represented. Such displays are frequently used in electronic *calculators and digital watches.

Seveso, a village near Milan in Italy, the site in 1976 of a major industrial accident at a Swiss-owned chemical plant, resulting in a large cloud of weed-killer being released into the atmosphere. The most toxic substance in the emission was *dioxin. As the seriousness of the accident was realized, strong measures were taken to limit the damage and spread of the pollution. The village of Seveso and 30 km^2 (12 square miles) around were evacuated and turned into a no-go area, which still exists today. Livestock and crops were destroyed. Pregnant women exposed to the emissions were allowed to undergo abortions, because the toxins involved are known to cause foetal defects.

sewage (waste water), all the liquid discharged into the sewer from a household, including human waste and the water used for washing and food preparation. In the UK each person produces on average 180 litres of sewage daily. Sewage may also include surface or *storm water from pavements and roads, which may be disposed through a separate system. Waste water from industrial processes is now commonly treated separately from sewage. Such wastes include toxic materials from chemical and pharmaceutical manufacture, heat from power-stations, and waste matter from food-processing plants. Agriculture also produces large quantities of wastes—for example, silage water, animal wastes, pesticides, and fertilizers—that can cause *water pollution or affect water quality (see *water resources management).

sewage treatment and sewerage. Sewerage is the system of pipes (sewers) through which *sewage is conveyed to the treatment plant to prevent *water pollution. Sewers are made to be self-cleansing, and are laid to assist sewage-flow by gravity, though pumping is sometimes necessary. Manholes provide access for inspection and maintenance. In a combined sewage-treatment system, both sewage and *storm water are carried to the plant; in separate systems, untreated storm water is discharged directly to the nearest watercourse. Sewage treatment is divided into a series of stages. Preliminary treatment involves the removal of gross solids—oil, grease, and grit—and the separation of storm water. In primary treatment the sewage passes slowly through sedimentation tanks, where larger particles sink to the bottom as a sludge. Chemicals may be added to encourage smaller particles to coagulate. Sewage discharged into the sea may receive only preliminary and perhaps primary treatment, but most discharges into inland waters also undergo secondary (biological) treatment. In this, dissolved and *colloidal organic material are oxidized by micro-organisms such as *bacteria. The bacteria may be layered on percolating filters over which the sewage flows, or mixed with the sewage by a vigorous aeration device (the activated sludge process). Where the receiving watercourse is used for domestic supply, or is very susceptible to pollution, it undergoes tertiary treatment (polishing), involving the removal of residual organic matter, suspended solids, pathogens, nutrients such as nitrogen and phosphorus, and toxic metals. Separated sludge is dewatered by filtration, compaction, drying, or withdrawal of water using a vacuum. The sludge is then stabilized, and disposed of in landfill, farmland, or by incineration. New, stricter controls on sewage treatment being introduced in both Europe and the USA have led to research into new treatment methods. Promising developments include the use of reed-beds to detoxify sewage, peat or lignite to absorb pathogenic bacteria and other materials, bacteria immobilized in a solid medium such as carbon powder, and ultrafiltration membranes (see *filtration) fine enough to remove viruses.

sewing-machine, a machine for *stitching together *leather, *textiles, and other materials. From about the middle of the 18th century, there was growing interest in creating sewing-machines. Several were used commercially, but none was entirely satisfactory. Between 1830 and 1840, a new stitch which could be formed by a relatively simple mechanical process was devised independently by several different inventors. Known as the lockstitch, it is used by most sewing-machines today (see figure). *Howe of Massachusetts, USA, constructed a lockstitch machine and patented it in 1846, but it was *Singer, also of Massachusetts, who five years later produced the first practicable domestic sewing-machine. Most domestic and industrial lockstitch sewing-machines today are direct descendants of Singer's machine and use the same mechanism of stitch formation. Machines are now generally powered by electricity rather

Sewing-machine

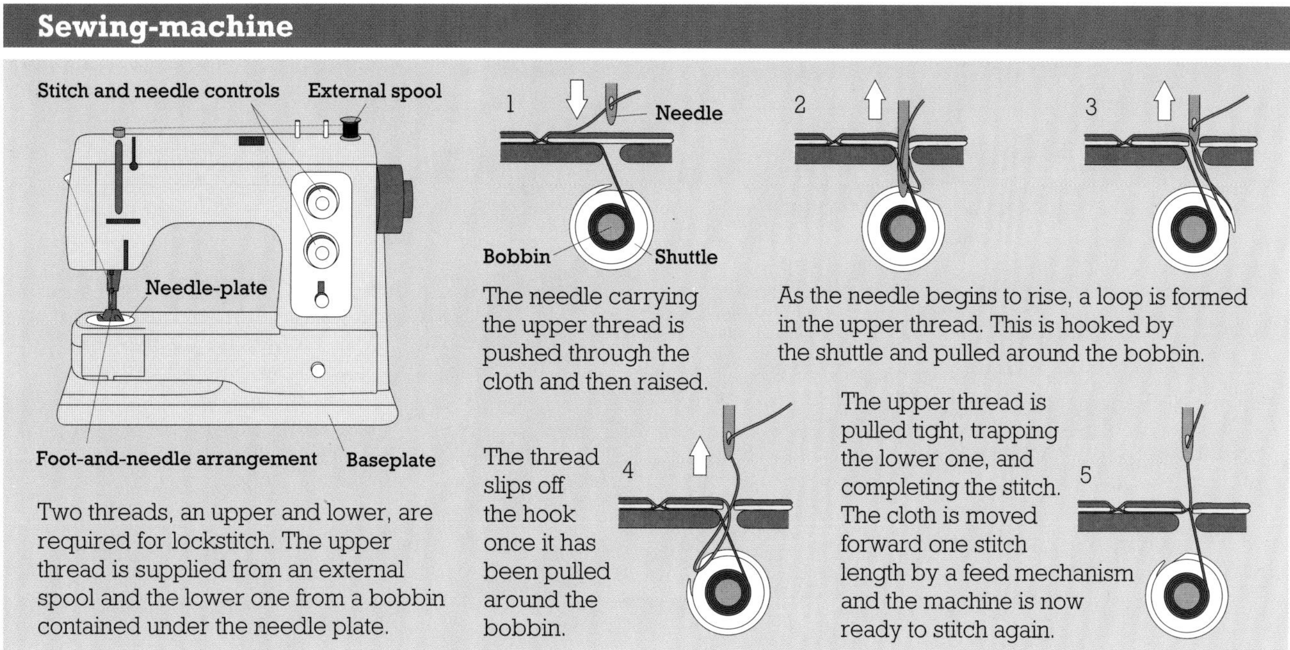

Two threads, an upper and lower, are required for lockstitch. The upper thread is supplied from an external spool and the lower one from a bobbin contained under the needle plate.

The needle carrying the upper thread is pushed through the cloth and then raised.

As the needle begins to rise, a loop is formed in the upper thread. This is hooked by the shuttle and pulled around the bobbin.

The thread slips off the hook once it has been pulled around the bobbin.

The upper thread is pulled tight, trapping the lower one, and completing the stitch. The cloth is moved forward one stitch length by a feed mechanism and the machine is now ready to stitch again.

than by hand or treadle. Other machines can make single-thread or two-thread chain-stitches, which are used where an extendable seam is required (as in knitted fabrics). More complex machines can carry out overlocking, machine embroidery, button sewing, and buttonhole making. (See also *needle.)

sextant, a light, portable instrument with a graduated arc of 60 degrees used for measuring the angular distance between two objects, most commonly the altitude (angle above the horizon) of a celestial body. It is the most recent of a succession of navigational instruments designed for this purpose. Its immediate predecessor was the reflecting quadrant, developed independently by Thomas Godfrey in the USA (1730) and John Hadley in Britain (1731). The sextant was developed from the quadrant (which measured altitudes up to 90 degrees) in 1757. In the sextant, the observer looks through a small telescope at the horizon (or a small spirit bubble if the horizon is obscured). A mirror on a movable arm above the telescope is adjusted to reflect the light from the Sun or other body on to a half-silvered mirror and back into the telescope, so that the observer seems to see the body sitting on the horizon. The angle of the sextant arm at this correct adjustment is half the altitude of the celestial body.

shaduf, an ancient Middle Eastern water-lifting device, still widely used in many countries. It comprises a beam pivoted in the fork of a vertically fixed branch. At one end the beam carries a bucket on a rope, and at the other a counterweight just heavier than the filled bucket. The operator pulls the beam down to fill the bucket, which is then raised by the counterweight.

shale oil, oil obtained by the application of heat to certain oil-bearing sedimentary rocks (oil-shales). Unlike crude *petroleum, shale oil is not accumulated in a reservoir but is distributed throughout pores in the rock. Heat (generally in the form of steam) is required to make the oil flow in a recoverable stream. The bulk of the world's petroleum reserves exist in the form of shale oil, the world's largest known deposits being the Athabasca tar sands, along the Athabasca River in Alberta, Canada. The *bitumen in the sands has been used as a petroleum source since the 1960s, but the high cost of recovery has in general limited the exploitation of shale-oil.

shears, a hand tool similar to large *scissors, used since Roman times, mainly for agricultural purposes such as cutting grass and trimming hedges. Many shears incorporate a small notch for cutting twigs that are too tough for the blades. Hand shears for clipping sheep consist of two blades connected by a C-spring: for large numbers of sheep, electric or motor-driven shears are now used. The cutting bar, in which a series of blades on a movable bar act against others on a fixed bar, is a mechanized type of shear used in hedge-trimmers and some *mowing-machines.

sheep farming, the husbandry of sheep to produce meat, wool, and milk. There are around 200 sheep breeds worldwide: examples are the various Merino and Rambouillet breeds, noted for their fine fleece; mutton breeds like the Leicester, Hampshire, and Romney sheep; and meat-and-wool breeds such as the US Targhee and Montadale. Most commercial sheep represent two- or three-breed crosses. Sheep are ruminants, utilizing pasture and roughage for nutrition; their agility and hardiness allow them to be grazed in upland areas unsuitable for cattle. The main emphasis of sheep breeding since the 18th century has been on meat production, at the cost of those breeds producing the finest wool. (See also *livestock farming, *animal breeding.)

Sheffield plate, copper coated with a thick layer of silver, first produced in Sheffield, *c.*1742, made by laying a silver strip on a clean copper bar, heating, and rolling the bar to the required thickness. The layers of silver that adhere to the copper are much thicker than in the case of *electroplating, which superseded this process from the mid-19th century.

shell, *artillery ammunition filled with explosive. Early shells were cannon-balls hollowed out and filled with gunpowder. They were used in sieges, against infantry occupying civilian houses, and against cavalry. At the end of the

17th century, accurate pocket watches that could measure minutes and seconds made timed *fuses practicable. Placed within the shell, the fuses permitted it to be exploded over the target. Following the Crimean War (1854–6), a new kind of shell was developed for rifled breech-loading guns. It was essentially a cylinder with a rounded nose, similar to a modern shell. The shaped nose provided greater accuracy. Steel became the standard material for shells in the 20th century. During World Wars I and II many types of specialist shells were developed. They included illumination, smoke, anti-aircraft, armour-piercing, anti-tank, naval, and gas shells (see *chemical warfare).

A building shell is a thin, curved structure, commonly used to cover large areas, which requires no internal support by virtue of its shape. The shell is subjected to direct compression from its own weight and external loads. Examples are the *vault, which has a single axis of curvature (like a semi-cylinder), and the dome, which is doubly curved. The saddle-shaped hyperbolic paraboloid is now widely used for shells, because its shape can be formed by parallel straight lines. This simplifies *formwork where a *reinforced concrete shell is being built.

shellfish farming, the branch of aquaculture concerned with cultivating crustaceans and molluscs, mostly in sea-water. Farming supplements shellfish fishing, rather than replacing it. World-wide production of crustaceans, mainly shrimps, now exceeds half a million tonnes per year. Crustaceans are carnivores, and food needs to be provided for them, but their high market price means that farming is still profitable. Farmed molluscs, such as mussels, oysters, and clams, are generally herbivores. They feed on naturally occurring phytoplankton and need no additional feeding. Being sessile or semi-sessile, they are easy to harvest. More than 4 million tonnes of molluscs are produced per year.

sherardizing, a process for protecting iron and steel from *corrosion by coating with zinc. It was named after the British chemist Sherard Cowper-Coles (1867–1936). The object to be coated is heated in a sealed container with zinc powder at a temperature between 350 and 450 °C. The coating consists largely of a zinc–iron alloy which is thin enough not to interfere with any pattern or design on the original article. (Compare *galvanizing.)

shield excavator (tunnelling shield), a machine used when excavating a *tunnel in soft ground to provide temporary support at the face. Invented by M. I. *Brunel, the shield is a short, rigid cylinder of the same profile as the tunnel and has platforms from which the face is excavated. As the shield cuts the face, the tunnel is lined with concrete segments. The shield then advances by pushing against the completed lining behind it. A closed shield, which excludes water by the presence of compressed air, is used when excavating in waterlogged ground.

shifting cultivation, the practice of cutting small clearings in virgin forest, burning the wood to create ash for fertilizer, and then using the land for *arable farming. When the soil is exhausted, a new plot of land is sought and cleared: if left long enough, the original plot will return to forest. The system is used particularly in tropical areas, where forest regeneration is swift, but it can only be sustained if the population is sufficiently small to allow a reasonable time for the land to recover before being brought into productive use a second time.

ship, most commonly any large seagoing vessel, although the term ship can also refer to a type of *rig, 'ship rig', describing the arrangement of sails on three- or four-masted ships of the 16th and 17th centuries, which were *square-rigged on all but the rearmost (mizen) mast. The earliest seagoing vessels were probably used about 60,000 years ago by the earliest colonizers of Australia. Their craft were probably *canoes or *rafts, propelled by paddles. Later, oars and then sails were developed. With the advent of sail power, *sailing ships became the predominant form of power at sea, and remained so until the mid-19th century. *Steamships were developed throughout the 19th century, and in the 20th century motor ships were introduced, generally powered by *diesel engines. Until the 19th century most ships were built of wood, but in 1839 the development of techniques of using *magnetic compasses in iron-hulled ships made seagoing iron ships possible. The use of iron, and later steel, for *shipbuilding led to changes in hull design and growth in ship size.

Modern ships are usually built of steel, though glass-fibre-reinforced plastic, concrete, and wood are also used. The most common method of propulsion is by a diesel engine through a screw *propeller. Since the early 19th century, but particularly in the late 20th century, ships have grown in size. A ship's size is measured in several ways. *Merchant ships are usually referred to in terms of gross or net tonnage, a measurement of their capacity rather than their weight. Displacement tonnage, measured by the amount of water the ship displaces, is the chief size-measurement method for *warships. (See also specific ship types.)

shipbuilding. The earliest evidence of shipbuilding techniques comes from ancient Egypt, where wooden *ships were built 'shell first', the outer planking being joined edge to edge by wooden dowels or wedges (later copper pins) and then strengthened with an inner skeleton of lateral ribs. This basic method of construction was used in the Mediterranean until about the 6th century AD. Shipbuilding seems to have developed independently in north-west Europe. Ships were still built shell first, but the skin was made up of overlapping planks nailed together, a form known as clinker or lapstrake construction (see figure). Ships continued to be clinker-built in northern Europe until the 15th century. By the 10th century, shipbuilders in the Mediterranean had evolved a method of construction whereby the shape of the ship was defined by a skeleton frame, to which was fixed an outer shell of planks fastened edge to edge. *Caulking helped to keep the integral strength of the shell as well as stopping leaks. This 'skeleton-first' method of building, with the planks meeting flush at the seams, gave a smoother, more streamlined hull, and was more suited to the construction of larger vessels. It became the standard method of shipbuilding in Europe and America from the 16th century onwards.

From the 16th to the 19th centuries development in shipbuilding techniques was slow, as the essentially practical and empirical skills of the shipwright gradually evolved into the more scientific methods of *naval architecture. Constructional methods improved in detail but remained basically the same: the use of timber as a building material set upper limits to the size and rigidity of hulls, even with the use of iron framing in the structure. The introduction of iron hulls and steam-power in the mid-19th century brought widespread changes. Initially, traditional shipbuilding methods were, as far as possible, simply transferred from wood to iron, but techniques adapted for the new material were soon introduced, notably by I. K. *Brunel in his ships

Shipbuilding

Wooden-hull construction

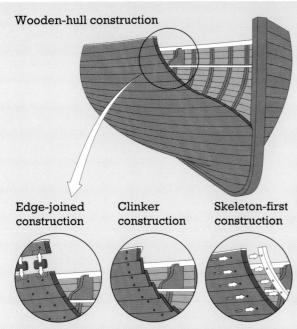

Edge-joined construction

Clinker construction

Skeleton-first construction

In early types of vessels, the planking or shell was built first and the ribs were inserted last. Later this was reversed, with the planking being constructed around the ribs.

Modern ship construction

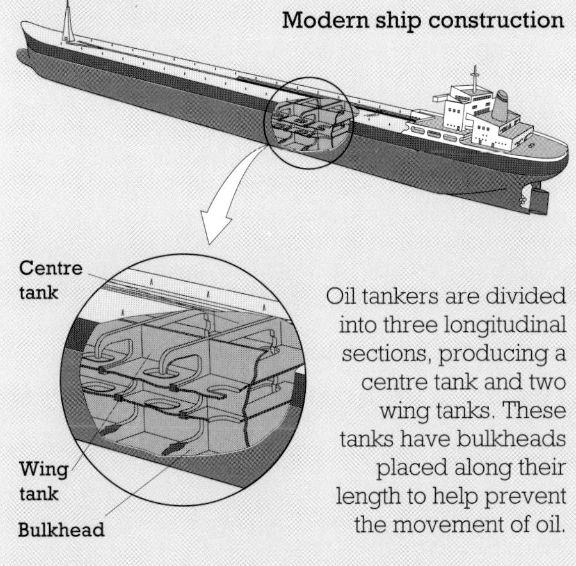

Oil tankers are divided into three longitudinal sections, producing a centre tank and two wing tanks. These tanks have bulkheads placed along their length to help prevent the movement of oil.

Lines plan

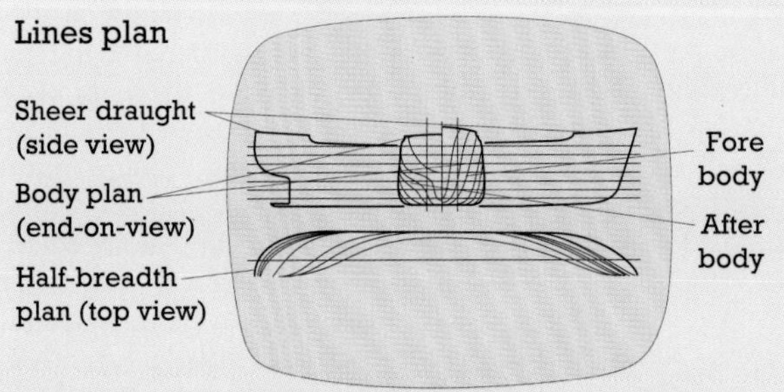

A simplified lines plan for a medium-sized cargo vessel. The different contours show the outlines of successive sections through the ship's hull.

the *Great Britain* and *Great Eastern*. Shipbuilding became an industry, requiring much more permanent machinery and equipment than in the days of wood, and ships became progressively larger and more complicated as the 19th century drew to a close.

In the 20th century, building techniques adapted to the use of steel have put the emphasis on longitudinal rather than lateral strengthening of hulls. Hull construction using riveted steel plates has given way to welding methods. Increased use of prefabrication means that work at the actual launch site consists of assembly of a few large sections rather than building of the whole hull *in situ*. Design and manufacturing processes are largely computerized, with the constructional plans for the ship being recorded on computer disk and used directly to operate cutting machines in the shipyard (see *computer-aided manufacture). Materials such as *fibre-reinforced plastics and *concrete are now used for some ships' hulls. (See also *sailing ships and boats, *steamship.)

ship of the line, a large warship capable of fighting in the line of battle. From about the mid-17th century, naval engagements were fought between opposing battle lines at ranges of 100 m (330 feet) or less. Only ships of a certain size and fire-power could be used in this type of warfare: these were the ships of the line. They varied in size from vessels with three decks and a hundred or more guns, to two-deckers with a minimum of fifty (later seventy) guns. They were classified, in diminishing order of power, as first- to fourth-rate ships. When steam-powered iron ships began to replace wood and sail power, ships of the line became known as battleships.

ship's boat, a small boat carried in davits (small cranes for hoisting or lowering boats) on the upper deck of a ship, or towed behind it. Such boats are used for life-saving, communicating with the shore and other ships, and many other purposes. From the 17th to the 19th centuries many different kinds of boat were carried on sailing ships. These included longboats, launches, jolly boats, pinnaces, gigs, barges, *dinghies, skiffs, and whalers. Towards the end of the 19th century, larger ships' boats began to be fitted with steam-engines (and later, internal-combustion engines) rather than sails and oars. Of the many types in use today, the most important is the *lifeboat.

ship-to-ship missile *missile.

shock absorber, the device in the *suspension system of a vehicle whose function is to damp out oscillation; 'damper' being the correct term for a shock absorber. The *spring is the means of absorbing shocks due to the wheel passing over an irregularity, but without dampers the result would be uncomfortable oscillation. Originally dampers were solid, of a friction type, which gave poor dynamic control and wore badly. Hydraulic dampers are now used, which consist of a piston sliding inside a cylinder filled with oil, the flow of which is controlled by spring-loaded valves. In this way a resistance to motion in either direction is provided. (See also *buffers.)

Shockley, William Bradford (1910–89), US solid-state physicist who invented the *transistor. After World War II, while at Bell Telephone Laboratories, Shockley organized a group with John Bardeen and Walter Brattain to research into the physics of solids. By June 1948, they had developed the point-contact transistor, a *semiconductor device fulfilling the same purpose as the *thermionic valve but on a much smaller scale. This eventually made possible the miniaturization of a wide range of electronic devices, especially radio and television equipment and computers. However, the original point-contact transistor had restricted applicability, was noisy, and could not control high power inputs. This led Shockley to develop the more generally useful junction transistor, for which he, Bardeen, and Brattain shared the Nobel Prize for Physics in 1956.

Sholes, Christopher Latham (1819–90), US printer and inventor of the modern *typewriter. From 1867 he directed most of his attention to the possibility of a mechanical writing machine. The concept was not new, but Sholes's typebar machine was the first to achieve technical success. He patented it in 1868, but failed to achieve backing for manufacture and marketing. He sold his rights to the Remington Arms Company in 1875.

shorthand (US, stenography), any system for rapid writing, usually used for the transcription of spoken language. The first known form of shorthand was developed by the Roman Marcus Tullius Tiro in about 63 BC. The earliest modern shorthand was published in 1588 by the English clergyman Timothy Bright. Most early shorthand systems were orthographic, following normal spelling, but in the 18th century phonetic systems began to appear. In 1837 the Englishman Isaac Pitman published a phonetic shorthand system which is still widely used in the UK. In the USA, the shorthand system developed in 1888 by the Irish-born US inventor John Gregg is most common. Twentieth-century shorthand systems have tended to use normal alphabetic characters: they are easy to learn and to transcribe, but they are slower than other systems. Stenotypy is a typed shorthand using a limited keyboard, used widely in the USA for recording court proceedings.

short wave (high frequency) *waveband.

shotgun, a smooth-bore *firearm that shoots clusters of pellets, which fly out of the muzzle in a diverging pattern. Shotguns are one- or two-barrelled, shoulder weapons with a short range—up to about 45 m (150 feet). Repeating shotguns were developed in the 1880s. Some incorporate a pump slide that opens the breech to discharge the *cartridge and then reloads from the magazine; others have a lever which is pushed away from the stock. US soldiers in World War I found repeating shotguns very effective in attacks on trenches. Today, the shotgun is used by many police forces, and for shooting small targets such as birds. The sawn-off shotgun, which is a notorious criminal weapon, has the choke at the end of the barrel removed, allowing the shot to spread more quickly. This makes the weapon more effective at close range.

shovel *digging tools.

shrapnel, specialized anti-personnel *shells. Shrapnel was developed by the British lieutenant Henry Shrapnel, in 1784. The shells incorporated lead balls as well as the regular gunpowder filling. The *fuse was timed to explode the shell over enemy troops, scattering the lead into their ranks. High-explosive shells largely replaced shrapnel after World War II. The term shrapnel is now more commonly used to describe the fragments of exploding bombs or shells.

shrink-resistant fabric, a woven *fabric that does not shrink appreciably when laundered. There are several shrink-resist processes. These do not prevent true shrinkage of the textile, but compress the fabric lengthways and temporarily fix this compression using heat. When such garments are laundered, the compression is released at the same time as the natural shrinkage of the fabric occurs.

shutter (photography), a device in a *camera that controls the length of time during which light is able to reach the *film. Shutter speed and *aperture together control the amount of exposure to light that the film receives. Modern shutters are of two main types: focal-plane and leaf. The focal-plane shutter forms an integral part of the camera and is positioned at the focal plane (immediately in front of the film). When the shutter is activated, two blinds move across the film, the width of the gap between them determining the shutter speed. Leaf shutters consist of a number of thin, overlapping metal blades which open to form a diaphragm of a particular aperture, and then close after exposure.

shuttering *formwork.

shuttle, a tool used in weaving, which lays a thread of weft yarn between the warp threads when these have been separated by the heddles (see *loom). The traditional wooden shuttle is boat-shaped and contains a small package or 'pirn' of yarn, which runs out through an eye as the shuttle passes across the loom between the separated warp threads. A small metal shuttle is used to pass the lower thread through a loop in the upper thread of a lockstitch *sewing-machine. (See also *flying shuttle.)

sialon, a family of ceramic alloys, mixtures of *silicon nitride (Si_3N_4) and *alumina (Al_2O_3). Sialons have very similar mechanical properties to silicon nitride, but have greater creep resistance and resistance to oxidation. Sialon was originally synthesized in 1970 at Newcastle University, UK, by a group led by K. Jack. Major applications are for wear-resistant, high-temperature parts such as cutting tools and *extrusion dies. It has potential applications in turbochargers and gas-turbines.

sick building syndrome *air conditioning.

sickle *scythe.

siege warfare, military operations aimed at the capture of a fort or walled town. A besieging force tries to make a breach in the defences and then launch an assault through the breach. Alternatively, the besiegers might use scaling ladders, a ramp, or a siege tower to climb the wall. In ancient and medieval times *catapults and battering rams made of iron-tipped timber beams were used to breach walls. From the 1420s heavy *cannon replaced the catapults and rams. Another technique was to dig 'mines' (underground tunnels) beneath the walls to weaken their foundations and cause them to collapse. With the development of the longer ranges of gunpowder *artillery from 1680 onwards, the besiegers were forced to keep at a distance from the walls, and to dig a network of entrenchments giving cover to assault troops and guns. From around 1860, powerful breech-loading rifled artillery was developed. Together with the use of *bomber aircraft from World War I onwards, such weapons rendered traditional fortifications obsolete. (See also *military engineering.)

Siemens, Ernst Werner von (1816–92) and **Sir Charles William** (Karl Wilhelm von) (1823–83), German pioneers in electrical engineering and the iron and steel industry. While an army officer, Ernst carried out chemical experiments that led to the invention of an *electroplating process. Thereafter he specialized in the electrical field, in particular in *telegraphy, and he was associated with many major telegraph systems in Germany and Russia. In 1847, with Johann Halske, a mechanic, he founded the Siemens and Halske firm of electrical manufacturers which laid cables across the Mediterranean and from Europe to India. In 1866 he described the principle of the self-exciting dynamo, a *generator in which the electromagnet providing the magnetic field is powered by electricity from the generator itself. Charles Siemens, younger brother of Ernst, studied engineering, then in 1843 moved to the UK where he sold his brother Ernst's electroplating process. The following year he settled in London, working as an inventor. In 1861 he and his younger brother Frederick patented an *open-hearth furnace for use in glass-making, and later in steel production. From the 1850s Charles Siemens was also involved in his brother Ernst's telegraphy business: in 1875 his independent London firm laid the first transatlantic telegraph cable.

Siemens–Martin furnace *open-hearth process.

signal, electrical, a variable electrical current or voltage, used to carry information in an electronic circuit or system. The changing electrical current generated by a *microphone is an example of an electrical signal carrying sound information.

signal processing, a computing application in which analog signals from devices such as television cameras, microphones, temperature and other sensors undergo *digitization using an analog-to-digital converter (ADC) circuit. The digital form is processed by special-purpose signal-processing computers to filter or rearrange the signal. It may then be converted back to analog form by a digital-to-analog converter (DAC). Extensive digital signal processing is used in audio compact discs and in television special effects, in which moving images are folded, wrapped, or re-coloured in real-time.

Igor **Sikorsky** piloting his Vought-Sikorsky VS-300 helicopter, in April 1941. The helicopter was airborne for over an hour, the first time any helicopter had made a sustained flight.

signal-to-noise ratio, a measure of the power of an electrical signal relative to the accompanying unwanted electrical noise, expressed in decibels (dB). The higher the signal-to-noise ratio, the better the sound quality. To operate satisfactorily systems require an acceptable minimum value for the ratio; for telephones the ratio is 40 dB, for television it is 50 dB.

Sikorsky, Igor Ivan (1889–1972), Russian-born US aeronautical engineer and aviator. In 1909 he designed and built his first aircraft, an unsuccessful *helicopter. He then went on to design and construct the first successful four-engined aircraft (1913). In 1919 he moved to the USA, where he established the Sikorsky Aero Engineering Corporation. In the 1930s he built some of the early *airliners for Pan American World Airways. In 1939 he built the first satisfactory *helicopter, the VS-300, which he piloted himself. From 1941 to 1945 three variants of this were developed for the US Government, some 400 aircraft in all. Later, he designed other military and civil helicopters.

silage, an animal *feedstuff produced when any fodder crop, but predominantly grass, is cut green, pressed, and preserved by its own partial *fermentation in an airtight *silo or storage pit. If sealed, the silage partially ferments to a slightly sour mixture, after which the contents remain stable. More recently, chemicals have been added to aid the ensiling process. Large *balers are used to bale fresh-cut grass, which when sealed into a plastic bag makes high-grade silage without the need for expensive storage facilities. The advantages of silage-making over haymaking are that it is much less labour intensive and, as it is not dependent on dry weather, the crop may be harvested at the best time in its growing cycle.

silencer (US, muffler), a device for reducing the noise emitted by a gun or an engine. Airborne engine noise results from the sudden release of a pulse of gas; this noise can be reduced by means of an expansion chamber in the *exhaust system. Further reduction in noise transmitted along a pipe can be achieved by use of a perforated wall surrounded by sound-absorbent material. In a vehicle exhaust system, baffles within the silencer body dissipate sound waves by multiple reflection. At the outlet from a gun or a jet engine *nozzle the use of corrugations increases the surface area of the air-stream and so reduces its sharp shearing action, the source of noise.

silicon (symbol Si, at. no. 14, r.a.m. 28.09), a high-melting-point, grey-black solid, the second most abundant element in the Earth's crust. Silicon is formed by the reduction of silicon dioxide (silica). It is used in the production of *steel, *copper, and *bronze, and is incorporated in some acid-resistant steels. It is also an essential component in *semiconductor devices. Silica (silicon oxide) is used to make glass and crystals for quartz watches. *Silicon carbide (carborundum) is also used extensively.

silicon carbide (carborundum, SiC), a very common *abrasive material, manufactured by fusing a mixture of carbon and sand or silica (SiO_2) in an electric furnace. It is almost as hard as diamond, and is used in fine powder form as a high-melting-point, wear-resistant *ceramic used for *refractory materials and abrasive tools. Silicon-carbide fibres are made for use in *composites, and silicon-carbide films can be formed by *vapour deposition as wear-resistant coatings.

silicon chip *integrated circuit.

silicone, any of a family of *polymers in which the central backbone or chain is made up of silicon and oxygen atoms. (*Plastics and natural organic polymers have a central backbone of carbon atoms.) Silicones are water-repellent, resistant to heat and are used in applications where this property offsets their greater cost. Examples include greases for lubrication, rubber-like sheeting for gaskets, and thermosetting, insulating varnishes for coating and laminating.

silicon nitride (Si_3N_4), a very hard, stiff, and light *ceramic, which retains its properties up to very high temperatures. It is of particular importance in mechanical engineering because of its creep resistance. It is made by the reaction of silicon with nitrogen gas at high temperatures, or by *vapour deposition reactions between ammonia (NH_3) and chlorosilanes (for example, $SiCl_4$).

silk, a natural fibre from the cocoon of the silkworm. After soaking the cocoons in hot water to soften the glutinous matter, the 1–3 km (0.6–1.9 miles) of twin silk filaments which constitute each cocoon are unwound (reeled) and dried in skein form. Silk thread to be used as *warp in weaving is known as tram. It is made by combining the twin filaments from several skeins by drawing them through warm water and then through a small metal orifice which both removes adherent impurities and compacts the thread. It is then further compacted on throwing machines, which are used for twisting continuous filaments. Silk thread to be used as *weft is known as organzine. It is processed in a similar way to tram except that it is twisted only lightly and in the opposite direction. Silk damaged during reeling is unsuitable for throwing, and is made into *yarn by cutting it into lengths and *spinning it in the same way as cotton, linen, and wool. Before this can be done, all the natural gums must be removed from the silk by *fermentation treatment or by boiling in an aqueous soap solution.

silo, a pit or circular tower for the storage of *silage or grain. Silos can be made from wire mesh lined with plastic, but are most commonly tall, metal-skinned towers with a non-corrosive fused-glass or porcelain lining. The tower is filled from the top, and emptied from the bottom. Inside the sealed chamber bacterial *fermentation of the stored grain takes place until the concentration of fermentation products becomes too high for it to continue. Carbon dioxide gas evolved during fermentation prevents oxidative decay of the silage or grain.

silver (symbol Ag, at. no. 47, r.a.m. 107.87), a white, lustrous, metallic element. It is the best conductor of heat and electricity and is very malleable and ductile. Silver can be extracted from ores before smelting, by treating with cyanide and then displacing with zinc, or by amalgamating with mercury followed by distillation. A considerable amount of silver is used in making coins, jewellery, silverware, and ornaments. To be hard-wearing, silver is alloyed with copper. Copper and brass objects are coated in silver

The bottle held by the technician contains a cell culture for use in the production of **single-cell protein**. The bottles are rotated on rollers in their racks, causing cell-cultures to be formed in sheets on their inner sides.

by *electroplating. Large amounts of silver halide are used in photographic *film.

Simpson, Sir James Young (1811–70), British pioneer of *anaesthesia. He studied medicine in Edinburgh and was appointed Professor of Midwifery (1840) and later (1847) Physician to the Queen in Scotland. In 1846 *Morton introduced ether anaesthesia in the USA, but this was not ideal and other agents were sought. Simpson, like J. P. M. Flourens in France, experimented with *choloroform and in 1847 began to use it for obstetrics. This brought him into conflict with the Calvinists, opposed to any form of anaesthesia in childbirth, but the technique was widely adopted after 1853, when Queen Victoria accepted it during the birth of Prince Leopold.

simulation (mathematical), the computation of the (usually dynamic) behaviour of a device or system based on an appropriate mathematical model (see *dynamic modelling). Typical applications of simulation might be to analyse the behaviour of an existing system, to evaluate possible designs of a new system before construction, or to train users or operators of a system without them needing access to the often expensive or dangerous system itself (for example, in a *flight simulator). In continuous simulation, the continuous behaviour with time of the system under consideration is mirrored or 'simulated' by the continuous behaviour of the simulator. This technique is used in *analog computers. In discrete simulation, the values of simulated variables are calculated numerically at certain instants of time only (the sampling instants). Provided that the sampling instants are sufficiently closely spaced, the discrete model will be an accurate reflection of the continuous behaviour of the system, and the computed discrete values can be used for dynamic simulation. Hybrid simulation combines both discrete and continuous techniques.

Singer, Isaac Merrit (1811–75), US inventor of the domestic *sewing-machine. He patented various machines for rock-drilling and shaping wood and metal. Engaged to repair a *sewing-machine, he quickly devised an improved version, which he patented in 1851. He began manufacture, but found himself in conflict with an earlier inventor, *Howe, to whom he had eventually to pay royalties. Nevertheless, it was Singer's machine, improved in a number of patents up to 1863, which came into general use world-wide.

single-cell protein (SCP), dried cells of algae, bacteria, yeasts or fungi that are rich in protein. Such cells could provide foodstuffs cheaply from such raw materials as oil, methane, molasses, or sewage. *Fermentation of micro-organisms and substrate in a *bioreactor can give high yields of SCP, which requires little processing apart from drying. Production of SCP animal feeds is competitive with other sources, but so far economic production of SCP for human consumption has not been achieved.

sintering, the welding together of powdered particles of a substance or mixture by heating to a temperature below the melting-point of the components. The particles stick together and form a sinter. The process is used in *powder metallurgy and also as a treatment for iron ore in which a mixture of fine ore and high-grade coal (or coke) powder is sintered for use in a *blast-furnace. The porous glass used in laboratory filtering equipment is made by sintering small glass granules.

sinusoidal wave *wave.

siphon, a U-shaped pipe with one longer leg. Inverted, it is used to convey a liquid from a container to a lower level. The slight difference in atmospheric pressure between the liquid's surface and the (lower) outlet causes the flow. In *aqueducts, siphons often convey water over high ground, or underneath rivers.

sisal *fibre, textile (table).

SI units (*Système International d'Unités*), a system of *units proposed in 1960 as a rational and coherent replacement for the older CGS (centimetre, gram, second) system, which has since been widely adopted throughout most of the world. The SI system defines seven basic units: the metre (m), the basic unit of length; the second (s), the unit of time; the kilogram (kg), mass; the ampere (A), electric current; the kelvin (K), temperature; the candela (cd), a measure of luminous intensity; and the mole (mol), which measures the amount of matter. All other units of measurement are defined with reference to these seven: for example, the definition of the newton (the SI unit of force) is the force required to impart an acceleration of 1 m/s to a mass of 1 kg (see table in units entry for definitions of the basic and derived units). Definitions of the seven basic units have in some cases changed since 1960, in order to achieve the highest degree of precision, accuracy, and reproducibility necessary for modern scientific research. The metre was initially defined as one ten-millionth of the distance between the equator and the North Pole. However, this definition was changed in 1970 to the length of a certain number of wavelengths of an electron transition within the krypton atom, as this could be measured with greater accuracy and reproducibility. In 1983 the metre was redefined as the distance travelled by light in a vacuum in 1/299,792,458 of a second.

size, a gelatinous solution used in glazing paper, stiffening textiles, and so on. Traditionally, size was a paste to which a lubricant was added, but modern sizes include other film-forming substances, such as drying oils. Paper is commonly sized with *alum to reduce porosity. *Warp yarns are sized preparatory to weaving, to minimize damage during their passage through the loom. This size is usually removed in textile finishing.

skates. Ice skates consist of a pair of boots, each with a vertically mounted blade, usually of metal, allowing the wearer to travel on ice. Such skates owe their origin to Scandinavian bone 'runners', bound to the foot by thongs. Skating is still used as a means of transport in countries such as The Netherlands, using the canal network, which freezes in winter. Elsewhere skating is now mainly for recreational purposes; sports such as speed skating, figure skating, and ice dancing are represented in the Winter Olympic Games. Roller-skates have metal frames with four small wheels fitted to the soles of boots so that the wearer can travel over a hard surface.

The headquarters of the Hong Kong–Shanghai National Banking Corporation under construction in Hong Kong. The picture shows the hull-and-core building technique used in constructing **skyscrapers**.

skis, a pair of long, narrow runners, generally pointed and turned up at the front, fastened under the feet for travelling over snow. Skis are at least 4,000 years old; a rock carving in northern Norway from 2000 BC clearly shows a man skiing. Until recently the most common material for skis was wood, but they are now made from various kinds of synthetic material. Skis are still used as a practical means of cross-country winter transport both by civilians and the armed forces, and downhill skiing is a popular winter sport. However, the powered snow-mobile is becoming more widespread in use for transport purposes.

Skylab *space station.

skyscraper, a very tall building with many storeys. Buildings with many more than five storeys were built from 1882 in Chicago, and soon afterwards in New York, following the development of a safe passenger *lift. The Home Insurance Building (1883) built in Chicago by William Jenney, was the earliest to use a *frame rather than load-bearing walls. By the end of the 19th century there were about fifty steel-framed skyscrapers in Chicago and New York, up to 118 m (386 feet) high, most with thin, masonry, non-load-bearing external walls. Skyscrapers steadily increased in height up to the 381-m (1,250-feet) high Empire State Building (New York, 1931), their structures remaining as steel skeleton frames with masonry walls. Modern skyscrapers such as the World Trade Center, New York, have steel and concrete hull-and-core structures. The central core—a reinforced concrete tower—contains lift shafts, staircases, and vertical ducts. From this core, the concrete and steel composite floors span on to a steel perimeter structure; a lightweight aluminium and glass *curtain wall encloses the building. This type of construction is the most efficient so far designed against wind forces. It is used in the tallest skyscraper in the world, the 109-storey Sears-Roebuck Tower in Chicago, built in 1974, which is 443 m (1,454 feet) high.

sledge, a vehicle, usually on runners, that can travel over snow, marsh, clay, or grass, used for transporting people or loads. As early as 5000 BC the Egyptians and Assyrians used sledges to transport materials for pyramids and other constructions; some of the earliest known *roads were built to enhance the sledge's capabilities. The advent of the wheel and *axle, however, ended its use for all but snow transport. Sledges may be pulled by reindeer, horses, or dogs, propelled by sails, or pushed or pulled by one or more people; motorized sledges are now widely used in polar regions.

slide-rule, a hand-held device for rapid mathematical calculation of multiplications or divisions, now largely superseded by the electronic *calculator. The first known slide-rule was made by Robert Bissaker (England) in 1654. The slide-rule consists of an accurately machined ruler, usually engraved with a number of logarithmic scales, together with a sliding central strip. Calculations are made by moving the strips and the result is indicated on the ruler's scale. Adding logarithms is equivalent to multiplying. Hence a simple relative shift of the sliding scales corresponds to multiplication. Some slide-rules have a helical scale to obtain extra length within manageable dimensions.

sling, an early missile weapon for hurling stones or rounded metal shot. Commonly it comprised a thong of leather or similar flexible material with a pocket at the centre. One end of the thong was tied to the hand or wrist. The shot was placed in the pocket, and the other end of the thong grasped by the user. It was then whirled around the head to build up momentum and loosed to release the shot towards the target. Heavier shot could be thrown from a sling mounted on a pole.

sloop, in modern usage, a *yacht carrying a mainsail and a single foresail or jib. Historically, the term sloop has been applied to other ship types. In the late 17th century a sloop was a single-masted merchant vessel, similar in rig to the modern sloop. In the early 18th century the term was also applied to the largest British warships that were not *ships of the line. The term sloop continued to be used for steam-powered vessels when they replaced sailing ships. During World War I, sloops became specialized escort vessels, but by World War II these types of warships were known as frigates, and sloop acquired its modern meaning.

sluice, a gated arrangement controlling the flow of water in a channel. The simplest type slides vertically, changing the size of the aperture through which the water can flow. In a radial sluice the gate height may be automatically adjusted by a float that rises or falls as water levels change.

Smeaton, John (1724–92), British civil engineer. Smeaton began as a successful maker of navigational and astronomical instruments, but increasingly became involved in engineering on a larger scale. He made many improvements to the design of water-mills and windmills, the *diving-bell, and of steam-engines. He rediscovered hydraulic *cement, unknown since Roman times, and designed large atmospheric pumping engines. In 1771 he founded the Society of Engineers. Smeaton rebuilt the Eddystone Lighthouse (1775–9), and built the Forth and Clyde Canal, Ramsgate harbour, and many bridges.

smelting, the process by which an ore concentrate is fused (melted) at high temperatures to extract a matte or impure metal. Usually a *flux is added to remove impurities as a slag. In the smelting of iron ore, *coke is added to the blast-furnace to reduce the oxide to iron metal.

Smithsonian Institution, a US museum, one of the world's greatest for science and technology, comparable with the Deutsches Museum, the *Palais de la Découverte, and the *Science Museum (UK). Its foundation was made possible by a large legacy bequeathed to the USA by an English scientist, James Smithson (who died in 1829), for the purpose of founding an 'establishment for the increase and diffusion of knowledge among men' in Washington. However, because of legal wrangles the Institution did not come into existence until 1846. Originally its aims were threefold: to promote research, to maintain a library, and to serve as a museum. The library was transferred to the Library of Congress in 1866, and the research activities diminished in 1878, leaving the Institution largely as a museum.

smoke detector, a device to give warning of a fire by detecting the presence of smoke. Smoke detectors were first used in situations where a fire might be expected to produce particularly dense smoke, as in paint warehouses or aircraft baggage compartments, but they are now more common, and are often found in private houses. The device is a sensitive *photocell. When the intensity of light falling on the cell is diminished by smoke, an alarm sounds. In principle, smoke detectors have the advantage over thermal devices of

The **Smithsonian Institution** building on the Mall, Washington, DC, USA. The building was designed by Thomas Renwick and completed in 1855.

giving warning before a dangerous temperature rise occurs, though in practice the alarms are sometimes difficult to maintain in good working order.

smokeless fuel, a solid mineral fuel that, when burned, produces combustion products containing less than a specified amount of particulate matter. An authorized smokeless fuel is one approved by statute for use in smoke-control areas. These fuels can be naturally occurring (such as anthracite *coal) or manufactured (such as *coke or smokeless briquettes). Naturally smoky bituminous coals can be rendered smokeless by low-temperature carbonization at 425–450 °C, followed by *briquetting of the resulting carbonized coal.

smokeless powder *nitro-cellulose.

smoothing circuit, an electronic circuit, usually a part of a power supply, that removes undesirable 'ripple' from a *rectified alternating-current signal to give a direct-current voltage. The simplest smoothing circuit is a very large-value electrolytic *capacitor, which acts to store charge and maintain a nearly constant output voltage.

snorkel, a breathing-tube used by divers enabling them to remain under water for long periods. A snorkel is also a tube which can be used on some submarines to supply air to the diesel engines and to expel exhaust smoke. It can only be used if the submarine is submerged no deeper than periscope depth. A snorkel has a flap valve at the top to prevent the entry of sea-water in rough weather, and is hinged at the bottom to lie along the submarine's casing when surfaced. A Dutch invention, it was used by German submarines towards the end of World War II, after which it was adopted by other navies.

soap, a cleaning agent, comprised of sodium or potassium salts of fatty acids, made by treating *fats and oils with *alkali. Soap was used as a medicine as early as 2300 BC, but it was not manufactured as a cleansing agent until the 2nd century AD. It was made by boiling animal fat (tallow) with wood ash: the alkali provided by the wood ash reacted with the animal fat to produce soap. This is still the basis of present-day manufacture. A mixture of fat or oil and *sodium hydroxide solution is heated by steam in huge soap pans until all the fat has been broken down. The soap is separated from the mixture by the addition of concentrated sodium chloride solution ('salting out'). The crude soap floats on the surface of the mixture. The liquid underneath is called 'lye', and is a solution of *glycerol (from the fat), sodium hydroxide, and salt. The glycerol is valuable and is recovered. The soap is further treated or 'fitted' with sodium hydroxide solution, sodium chloride solution, or water to bring it to the desired smooth consistency. The resulting molten soap is then pumped off and left to solidify. Perfume and colouring are added to make the soap more appealing. Soap made from animal fat (sheep and cattle) must be used with hot water because it is only slightly soluble in cold water. Soap made from vegetable oils (coconut and palm-kernel) can be used in cold or warm water. The cleaning action is identical to that of *detergents, but soaps are less effective in hard water. Metallic soaps (salts of calcium, magnesium, lithium, copper, and zinc) are used in greases and lubricating oils.

Sobrero, Ascanio *nitro-glycerine.

sodium (symbol Na, at. no. 11, r.a.m. 22.99), a soft, silvery metal, the sixth most abundant element in the Earth's crust. It is manufactured by the electrolysis of a molten sodium chloride (*salt)—calcium chloride mixture in a Downs cell, which is designed to keep the products of the electrolysis apart and so prevent the re-formation of sodium chloride. Sodium metal reacts with oxygen and extremely violently with water, and must therefore be stored under liquid paraffin. Wire made from sodium metal is used to dry hydrocarbon *solvents in chemical laboratories. Sodium is also used in the production of the metals titanium and zirconium, and to make sodium peroxide (a powerful bleach) and sodium cyanide (used in metal extraction and electroplating), neither of which can be made directly from sodium chloride. It is used in sodium lamps for motorways because its yellow light penetrates fog and mist well. Another important use of sodium is as a coolant in fast breeder *nuclear reactors. A large proportion of sodium manufactured is used to make the fuel additive *lead tetraethyl, although this application is becoming less important with the increased use of unleaded petrol. Other important sodium compounds are *sodium carbonate and *sodium hydroxide.

sodium carbonate (soda, Na_2CO_3), a white solid, alkaline in solution, which is widely distributed in nature, especially in Lake Magadi, Kenya. It is found in mineral waters. It is used extensively in the chemical industry in the manufacture of glass, caustic soda (*sodium hydroxide), soap, paper, cleansers, and water softeners; it is also used in *petroleum refining and textile manufacture. It is produced by the Solvay process, based on the reaction of sodium chloride (*salt) with ammonium hydrogen carbonate, or by the action of carbon dioxide on sodium hydroxide solution. Soda should not be confused with cooking soda (sodium bicarbonate).

sodium hydroxide (caustic soda, NaOH), a white, translucent, hygroscopic solid, which forms a strongly alkaline solution in water. The solution attacks glass slowly and reacts with carbon dioxide from the air to form *sodium carbonate. Industrially, it is produced from *salt in very large quantities by the *Castner–Kellner process. Sodium hydroxide is an important starting material for the manufacture of other chemicals; it is also used in the production of rayon and other textiles, paper and pulp, aluminium, petrochemicals, soaps, and detergents. It is a standard laboratory reagent. (See also *acids, bases, and salts.)

soft drink, a non-alcoholic drink, usually carbonated and containing sweetening agents, edible acids, and natural or artificial flavouring. The first soft drinks were tonic waters, developed in the mid-19th century as substitutes for natural mineral waters. By the late 19th century sweetened drinks had been developed: Coca-Cola was first made in 1886. Soft drinks are made from a wide variety of ingredients. In Egypt, carob or locust bean extract is used, while in Brazil a soft drink is made from maté (a tea-like *beverage crop). In commercial soft-drink manufacture, water is treated and filtered to remove micro-organisms and some minerals. Carbon dioxide is then added to give the water effervescence and taste and to stop spoilage. A concentrated sugar syrup containing flavourings, edible acids, colour, and sometimes preservatives is then mixed with the water, and the drink is put into bottles or cans. Non-carbonated soft drinks are *pasteurized to improve their shelf life.

software, a general term for computer *programs, and sometimes also *data, as opposed to *hardware, the physical components of a computer system. All working computer systems comprise both hardware and software, the hardware performing tasks and operations under the control of a sequence of instructions provided by the software. The term software is often used as a synonym for program, particularly when it is applied to a whole class of programs as in system software, which make up the operating system of a computer.

software engineering *computer, *information technology, *mechatronics.

soil mechanics, the science of the engineering properties of soils as opposed to rocks. When designing foundations, the engineer assesses the bearing capacity of the soil and the likely *settlement of the structure. Earthwork projects such as the construction of embankments and cuttings and the assessment of soil pressures on *retaining walls all rely on soil mechanics. For tunnel-building and excavation works, predictions of earth pressures and water flow are required for the design of supports and water-control techniques.

solar cell (photovoltaic cell), a device for producing electric power directly from light. It consists of two layers of *semiconductor material, the upper layer being sufficiently thin for light to penetrate to the boundary, where electrons are released and allow a current to flow. Selenium photovoltaic cells were first introduced in the 1920s and the present silicon devices in the 1950s. Their relatively high cost, and low power output have limited their use to low-power applications (light meters, pocket calculators, and so on), and situations where other sources are not available (lightships, spacecraft, remote houses, or defence installations). New materials such as *gallium arsenide may, however, prove cheaper and more efficient.

solar furnace, an arrangement for achieving very high temperatures by focusing solar radiation. A parabolic mirror concentrates the radiation on the central focus. To track the Sun, an array of tiltable flat mirrors is often used, reflecting the sunlight into the parabola. Solar furnaces have achieved temperatures of over 3,000 °C.

solar panel, a flat or concave panel designed to collect solar energy to provide heat; alternatively, a sheet of *solar cells. Solar heating panels are a development of a simple hot-water system consisting of a black hosepipe coiled on the roof and connected to the water supply. The modern panel absorbs solar radiation through a black surface in close contact with pipework, through which a fluid circulates (usually water, less commonly another liquid or air). A sheet of glass in front of the panel and insulating material surrounding it reduce heat losses. New transparent insulation materials (TIMs), made from honeycombed polymers or porous gels of silicon dioxide, can greatly reduce heat losses and improve the efficiency of thermal solar panels.

solar power, power derived from solar energy. The total radiation reaching the Earth from the Sun is equivalent to about 20,000 times the world's current rate of energy consumption and the intensity at the Earth's surface can reach one kilowatt per square metre. Solar energy originates in nuclear *fusion in the Sun's interior and travels through space as *electromagnetic radiation. It is the ultimate source of nearly all the world's *energy resources, and 'passive' solar heating is a major factor in maintaining temperatures in buildings. However, solar energy appears in estimates of energy consumption only when harnessed in some way, for example, in *solar cells, *solar furnaces, and solar-powered vehicles such as cars and aeroplanes. Research in solar power has tended to focus on the generation of electricity from solar radiation. However, new research into the direct use of the thermal energy of the Sun seems very promising. Developments in transparent insulation materials (TIMs), which transmit light but also provide good heat insulation, could be used to cut heating costs for buildings by a large amount, and also to heat water. (See also *solar panel.)

solar sail *space-flight, principles of.

soldering, a method, practised since antiquity, of joining metals together using a layer of *alloy, which is applied

The Odeillo-Font-Tomeau solar power-station in the eastern Pyrenees, France. The huge parabolic reflector tracks the sun's course across the sky, concentrating solar energy on to a **solar furnace** at its focus. Temperatures within the furnace can reach 3,800 °C and the system can generate up to 1,000 kW of power.

when molten and then solidifies on cooling. The surfaces of the two metals to be joined are placed next to each other, heated with a gas torch or soldering iron, and cleaned by adding a *flux. When both pieces are sufficiently hot the solder is introduced at the join. Plumbing work uses soft solder, an alloy of tin and lead with a low melting-point. Solder for electrical work also has a low melting-point and contains an integral flux; it is applied as rapidly as possible to avoid damaging heat-sensitive components. Hard solders consist of various alloys of copper, nickel, zinc, bismuth, and silver, with melting-points around 600 °C. They provide stronger joints than soft solders, but not as strong as *brazing or *welding. Soldered joints are water- and gas-tight, yet also conduct electricity.

solenoid, a cylindrical coil of wire that acts as a magnet when carrying an electric current. Solenoids are usually coils that provide some form of mechanical movement when activated, for example, in bells, valves, *relays, and many other *electromechanical devices. Solenoids commonly contain a solid core to concentrate magnetic flux, and include a nearby movable iron component, or armature, which moves when the coil is electrified under the action of the magnetic field.

solid-state device, an electronic component or device that uses the electronic properties of solids, usually semiconductors, to replace those of valves. Such devices have no moving parts, depending on the movement of charge carriers within the solids for their operation.

Solvay, Ernest (1838–1922), Belgian industrial chemist. In 1861 he developed a process for the manufacture of *sodium carbonate (soda) to replace the *Leblanc process. Subsequently he made great improvements to the process, establishing several manufacturing plants world-wide.

solvent (industrial), a liquid that can dissolve another substance to form a solution. Polar solvents generally dissolve materials composed of *ions, while non-polar solvents will generally dissolve materials composed of uncharged molecules. Water is the most common polar solvent and among its many solvent uses is the extraction of *salt. Liquid *hydrocarbons are non-polar solvents used extensively in the petrochemical and polymer industries as well as for degreasing and cleaning purposes. Chlorinated hydrocarbons are good non-polar solvents, but their use may be a health risk. *Alcohols, esters, and ketones are non-polar solvents used extensively in industry.

sonar (*so*und *na*vigation and *r*anging), a method used to find the position, speed, or nature of an object at sea using sound. It was initially developed for use by warships in detecting submarines during World War II, and was originally known as ASDIC (from Allied Submarine Detection Investigation Committee). Active sonar works in a similar way to *radar, transmitting a pulse of sound and measuring the time taken for the echo to return from the object. The use of a narrow transmission beam enables the object's bearing to be calculated. Furthermore, changes in the frequency of the returning echo can be measured, and give some indication of the object's speed and direction, using the *Doppler principle. An *echo-sounder is a specialized type of active sonar used for depth measurement. Passive sonar operates by using a listening device to determine the direction of an underwater sound. The sound may give clues as to the nature of the object, for example, a ship's engine or the call of a whale. In warfare, passive sonar has the advantage of not betraying the presence of the listener.

A sixteen-track, tapeless digital audio system in use in Superdyne **sound-recording** studios, New York. Tapeless systems store the sound on computer optical discs: editing is faster, and non-destructive and therefore easily modified.

sound, longitudinal pressure *waves that travel through elastic media (gases, liquids, or solids). Sound waves are caused by a source vibrating to and fro and causing successive compressions and rarefactions in the medium; hence sound cannot travel in a vacuum. Sound travels faster through liquids than through gases, and even faster through solids. Its speed also varies in proportion to temperature (sound travels faster through a hot medium than through a cold one) and pressure (at an altitude of 10,000 m, 32,800 feet, the speed of sound is about 13 per cent slower than at sea-level). Sound is detectable by the human ear at *frequencies between 20 and 20,000 Hz. Below this range are subsonic sounds; above it is the *ultrasound range. The conversion of sound waves into electrical impulses, and vice versa, is the basis of most *sound reproduction and recording equipment, and of sound transmission by *radio or *telephony. (See also *acoustics, architectural, *sonar, *echo-sounding.)

sound barrier *supersonic flight.

sounding lead *lead-line.

sound recording and reproduction. Sound recording techniques involve the transcription of audible air vibrations on to a storage medium such as *magnetic tape; sound reproduction reverses the process, converting the stored information back to sound. Sound can be stored on mechanical (*records), magnetic (tape), or optical (film sound-track, *compact disc) media; associated equipment includes *amplifiers, *loudspeakers, and *microphones. The earliest sound-recording device was the mechanical *gramophone. Early gramophones were entirely acoustic—electrical recording methods were not introduced until the 1920s. Optical sound reproduction was first used for film soundtracks in 1923, using a process developed by *De Forest. Early sound recordings were made with an acoustical horn, which concentrated sound on to a diaphragm connected to a cutting stylus. The stylus cut a groove—the variations of which corresponded to the vibrations of the diaphragm—in a wax master record. In 1924 an all-electric recording system was perfected by H. C. Harrison of the Western Electric Company, USA, in which *microphones were used to collect the sound, and the resulting signal was amplified electrically before driving an electrical disc-cutting head. However, recording still had major limitations, notably the time limit of 4.5 minutes imposed by the 78 r.p.m. record. The situation was improved by the introduction of the long-playing record, but the real breakthrough did not come until 1949, when *tape recorders were first used to make a master recording, from which discs could be cut later. Recordings of virtually any length could now be made, and the ease with which magnetic tape could be edited meant that restarts or retakes became possible. The advent of multi-track tapes meant that each instrument or sound could be recorded on its own track, and the relative levels of each track could be balanced electrically after recording. Many other innovations in recording have followed since the introduction of magnetic tape. Digital recording techniques (see *digitization) can produce recordings of extremely high fidelity, and provide more flexibility than analog techniques. For example, a poor recording can be digitally remastered and surface noise can be removed from between the desired sounds. Monophonic recordings can be split into two tracks to give a *stereophonic effect using digital techniques. A further innovation is tapeless recording, in which the sound is digitally encoded on *compact discs. With tapeless recording any part of the disc can be accessed accurately and almost instantly, and new techniques, such as speeding up or slowing down a piece of music without affecting the note pitches, become possible.

Soyuz *manned space programme.

space-flight, principles of, the theoretical and practical aspects of *manned space programmes or robot travel beyond the Earth's atmosphere. The atmosphere extends to a height of 320 km (200 miles): for a spacecraft to travel beyond this and achieve an orbit (a condition where the craft's forward momentum balances gravitational attraction, and it circles the Earth), it must attain a velocity of at least 7.8 km/s (4.9 miles per second). To escape the Earth's gravity altogether (for example, for interplanetary travel) its velocity must be at least 11.0 km/s (6.8 miles per second)—the escape velocity. The enormous power needed to accelerate a vehicle to such speeds is provided by rocket-powered *launch vehicles, which propel the craft close to its final velocity and are then jettisoned. *Satellites orbiting above 320 km (200 miles) will continue to do so indefinitely, since there is no air resistance; they can also be of any shape as streamlining is unnecessary. *Space probes and other spacecraft travelling beyond Earth orbit use rocket motors for propulsion, and jets of compressed gas are used to orient and manœuvre the craft. Ion or plasma engines, in which smaller amounts of matter are ejected at very high energy for longer periods, and solar sails, large, extremely thin sheets of reflective material driven by the pressure of light falling on their surface, are two alternatives to rocket power that are currently under research. Interplanetary travel requires sophisticated navigation and communications systems in order to maintain a course and relay data over the vast distances involved. Travel beyond the solar system is impracticable with current technology, as it would take thousands of years to reach the nearest star. Spacecraft that return to Earth must be able to re-enter the atmosphere without being burnt up by frictional forces. Re-entry at a shallow angle minimizes downward velocity, and vehicles carry a protective covering that is either burnt away slowly or dissipates the heat.

space frame, a three-dimensional structure, frequently used to build a large-span roof for a single-storey building, leaving the interior unobstructed by supporting columns. It is usually constructed from an upper and a lower grid of rods made of steel or aluminium alloy. The two grids are linked by inclined members forming pyramids between them, giving a stiff, lightweight structure on which the roof can be fixed. Commonly, a space frame is assembled at ground level and lifted by a team of cranes on to columns set in from each of the corners.

Spacelab *space shuttle.

space-plane, a one-stage vehicle capable of carrying a crew or cargo into space and landing back on Earth. The US *Space Shuttle and others under development, including the Soviet 'shuttle' and the European *Hermes*, are not real space-planes because they require rocket launchers. Preliminary design work on space-planes, with engines capable of both atmospheric flight and space-flight, has been carried out in the USA (the X-30), the UK (HOTOL), Germany (the Sänger space-plane), and Japan (HOPE). The German and Japanese designs are still conceptual, but development work on the US X-30 is under way.

space probe, an unmanned spacecraft visiting a planet, moon, or comet to gather information about the solar system. Space probes have sent back information from all the planets except Pluto. Probes have flown past Mercury, the outer planets, and Halley's comet, while the Moon, Venus, and Mars have been investigated by orbiting and landing probes and by *space robots. Fly-past probes can measure magnetic fields, radiation levels, surface and atmospheric temperatures and pressures. They have transmitted many thousands of images and much other data relating to the planets and their moons. Landing probes obtain more detailed information, including data on seismic activity. Probes orbiting Venus used radar to map the surface, which is permanently hidden by clouds; and the *Pioneer* and *Voyager* probes monitored the solar wind (gas from the sun's corona that blows out like a wind through the solar system).

space robot, an automatic or remote-controlled device that actively investigates surface conditions on other planets or moons. Three Soviet unmanned *Luna* spacecraft have collected moon rock samples and brought them back to Earth. Two US *Viking* landers on Mars in 1976 and two Soviet *Venera* landers on Venus in 1981 scooped up soil samples for automatic analysis in their spacecraft. *Viking* tested for signs of life on Mars, but gave inconclusive results. Two eight-wheeled, radio-controlled vehicles (called *Lunokhod*) explored the moon in 1970 and 1973. They sent back thousands of pictures as well as testing the planet surface and analysing the soil.

space shuttle, a partly reusable spacecraft to carry people and cargo into Earth orbit and then return. The US Space

Shuttle began flights in 1981, while the Soviet shuttle, *Buran* made its first flight in 1988 from the *Energiya* booster rocket. The European Space Agency is also developing a small shuttle, the *Hermes*. The US Space Shuttle comprises a main vehicle with three rocket motors (the orbiter), two solid-fuelled rocket boosters that are jettisoned two minutes after take-off and later recovered, and a non-recoverable external fuel tank. The orbiter can carry a payload of up to about 30 tonnes. On re-entry the orbiter is flown like a glider, and lands on a runway. The US Space Shuttle programme was suspended from January 1986 to September 1988, following the explosion of the US shuttle *Challenger*, which killed seven astronauts.

space station, an orbiting spacecraft containing accommodation for astronauts living and working in space. The first was the Soviet *Salyut 1*, 14 m (46 feet) in length, launched in 1971 and occupied for 23 days. The largest was the only US space station to date, *Skylab*, which was 27 m (89 feet) long. It was launched in 1973 and occupied by three crews before wandering from its orbit in 1978. The Soviet Union continued with five more successful *Salyut* stations and then the space station *Mir*. More docking ports allowed the unmanned *Progress* spacecraft to refuel and resupply the later *Salyut* space stations, extending endurance records to about a year. *Mir* has been expanded by the addition of extra modules: *Kvant 1*, an astrophysical laboratory; *Kvant 2*, with improved crew facilities; and *Kristall*, designed for producing semiconducting materials in space. Space stations open up new areas of study in astronomy and earth resources, and the weightless conditions facilitate processing of crystals, alloys, and pure drugs.

spacesuit, a sealed suit that enables an astronaut to survive in space. The inner layer of the suit is an inflatable bladder that maintains a constant pressure on the body: this is necessary because at low pressures the boiling-point of the blood is reduced, and it boils at normal body temperature. The many outer layers of tough material protect against radiation and micrometeorites, folds in these layers allowing for some restricted movement. Under the main suit, water in a network of tubes carries excess body heat to a backpack to be radiated into space. This backpack also has batteries for power, a radio transmitter and receiver, and a system supplying oxygen and removing carbon dioxide as the astronaut breathes.

spade *digging tools.

spanner (US, wrench), a tool for turning a nut on a bolt. Like *nuts and bolts, which it complements, the spanner first appeared in the 16th century. Its principle of operation is simple: a recess in the tool fits over the (normally) square or hexagonal nut, and leverage is applied to tighten or loosen it. There are many types of spanners; the simplest having a single open jaw, designed to fit a specific-sized nut, in a flat haft. Others may have a different-sized jaw (or ring) at each end. Small flat spanners that fit up to eight or ten different nuts have been designed for bicycles. In the adjustable spanner the jaws can be adjusted by a screw-thread. A mole wrench is adjustable and incorporates a locking device, so that it grips even if unsupported. Socket spanners are designed to enclose the nut completely, giving a firmer grip: a single handle can be fitted to a number of different-sized sockets. Usually the handle is equipped with a ratchet so that it only needs to be moved through a small arc. For precision engineering work the spanner handle may incorporate a torque-control mechanism.

spark chamber *particle detector.

spark-plug, a device for initiating combustion in a *petrol engine by means of a high-voltage spark between electrodes. The central electrode is held by a ceramic insulator, while one or more electrodes project towards it from the plug body, which is screwed into the cylinder head. The high voltage is supplied by the induction coil (see *ignition system).

spark transmitter *Hertz, Heinrich Rudolf.

spear, a sharply pointed weapon on a long shaft. In earliest times spears were used in hunting and were mostly thrown, but as techniques of warfare developed, the spear became primarily a thrusting weapon used by massed formations of closely ranked men. Spears were used in this way by the Sumerian army as early as 3000 BC. The spears of the ancient Greeks were 2–3 m (6–9 feet) long; longer spears, or pikes, about 4 m (13 feet) in length, were introduced in about 350 BC by the Macedonians. Spear-like lances were also carried by cavalry. In the 14th to 16th centuries in Europe more elaborate pole-axes and halberds (a spear combined with a battleaxe) were developed, for example with axe-heads for cleaving helmets. The military use of spears declined with the introduction of *firearms, but between the late 15th and late 17th centuries, firearm infantry used pikes as defence against cavalry charges before the invention of the bayonet. By the 18th century they were obsolete in more developed countries.

spectacles, a pair of *lenses in a frame, worn in front of the eyes to correct defective sight, or for protection. Spectacles first appeared in about AD 1300, but were little used until the mid-15th century, when the advent of printing and concomitant increase in literacy stimulated demand. By 1600 there was an optician in most European towns. Spectacle lenses are made from shatterproof plastic or glass; sometimes they are *photochromic or coated to reduce reflections or protect the eye from ultraviolet light. They curve away from the eye to ensure accurate correction over the whole lens. Concave lenses correct near sight, when the eye focuses light in front of the retina, and convex lenses correct far sight, where the eye's focus is behind the retina. A cylindrical lens can often correct astigmatism, caused by the front surface of the eye curving unevenly. Bifocal lenses have two areas, for distance vision at the top and near vision at the bottom. Protective spectacles include sunglasses, and safety goggles to protect the eyes from chemicals or flying particles. *Contact lenses can replace spectacles.

spectrometer, spectrophotometer *spectroscopy.

spectroscopy, the analysis of electromagnetic spectra, arrangements formed when light or other *electromagnetic radiation is separated into its constituent wavelengths. Spectroscopic techniques may be used to determine the structures of chemical compounds, to analyse mixtures of compounds, or to examine radiation from space. There are several types of spectroscopy. The simplest spectroscope splits incident visible light into spectral lines that can be observed by the human eye. In spectrochemical analysis, the substance under investigation is heated, so that it emits radi-

The US statesman, scientist, and inventor Benjamin Franklin wearing the bifocal **spectacles** he invented in 1775.

ation. Each component of the substance emits a characteristic radiation, and this can be used as a means of identification. The radiation is passed through a *diffraction grating or a *prism to separate it into its constituent wavelengths. Detectors are then used to observe or record details of the spectrum, and instruments can be used to measure the wavelengths and intensities of spectral lines. A permanent record of the results (a spectrograph) may be made to allow more detailed analysis. Comparison of the spectrum with the spectra of known, pure, substances allows the components to be identified and, with quantitative analysis, their relative proportions determined. This offers an extremely sensitive method of analysis of chemical substances, and automated spectroscopic procedures are now used routinely in laboratories around the world. The composition of stars can be investigated spectroscopically by taking spectra of the radiation they emit and comparing them with the spectra of known elements. Another type of spectroscopy is spectrophotometry, in which the luminous intensity of each colour or wavelength in a spectrum is measured. The radiation used may be in the visible region, but ultraviolet radiation is very useful for detecting colourless substances in solution and measuring their concentration, while infra-red spectrophotometry is used to study the molecular structures of organic compounds (see also *mass spectrometer).

speculum, an instrument used to open normally closed passages of a patient's body for examination purposes. The earliest type was the vaginal speculum, which originated in ancient Greece. It was only in the 19th century, however, with the development of disease theories based on localized pathology, that specula became widely used, mainly for diagnostic purposes. Today some are also used for surgical manœuvres.

speech recognition (computing), the ability of a computer system to recognize human speech. Speech recognition systems need considerable computing power and memory, and existing systems are generally restricted in the number of words or kinds of voice that they can recognize. Due to the huge amounts of processing required, such systems tend to be slow to respond. One objective of *artificial intelligence is to provide systems that can both recognize and respond to speech in general. This could, for example, provide a *word processor operated by verbal instructions.

speedometer, an instrument for measuring the speed of a vehicle. It consists of a pointer attached to an aluminium ring, which surrounds a permanent magnet. The magnet is connected to the propeller shaft or front axle of the vehicle, and rotates when the vehicle is in motion, the speed of its rotation being proportional to the vehicle's speed. As the magnet rotates, eddy currents are produced which produce a second magnetic field. The interaction of the two fields produces a torque (turning force) in the ring, and the pointer is swung over a graduated speed scale. The ring is attached to a restraining spring, so that it cannot turn a full circle. Speedometers usually include *odometers to indicate the mileage travelled.

spermaceti, a crystalline wax found in the forehead of sperm whales and also obtained from other whales, dolphins, and porpoises. It is used in medicinal preparations and in the manufacture of candles, confectionery, and *perfumes, but widespread concern for the survival of the whale species has resulted in the decline of such uses. Ambergris is a similar substance produced in the intestines of sperm whales and found floating in the sea.

Sperry, Elmer Ambrose (1860–1930), US inventor and industrialist. In the course of his career he filed over 400 patents and founded eight companies. His interests ranged from coal-mining machinery to electric road vehicles, electric-arc lamps, and storage batteries. His greatest contribution, however, was the *gyro-compass. Although a similar gyro-compass was developed independently by Hermann Anschütz-Kaempfe in Germany, it is the Sperry design on which the modern instrument is based. Sperry also introduced a gyroscopic *stabilizer for ships (1913).

sphygmomanometer, an instrument for measuring arterial blood pressure. The most common type, which was devised by the Italian Scipione Riva-Rocci in 1896, consists of a rubber bag fastened round the upper arm and attached to a *manometer. The bag is inflated until the pulse at the elbow cannot be detected with a *stethoscope, giving the systolic pressure (the pressure produced by the heart in contraction). The diastolic pressure (when the heart is between contractions) is found by releasing pressure until the pulse is again audible. Recently, electronic devices for blood pressure measurement have been introduced.

spindle *spinning.

spinning, the process of making a *yarn or thread. This may involve the compaction and twisting of long polymer fibres, as for example, in *silk processing. Alternatively, it may be by the alignment and twisting together of short (staple) fibres, such as cotton or wool. The spinning of staple fibres into yarn is a very ancient craft: in India, for example, cotton was spun from at least 3000 BC. Essentially it consists of disentangling and aligning the fibres (carding), drawing them out to provide an assembly to give a yarn of the required thickness, and then inserting twist to form a coherent structure. Early manual methods included the use of hand-held teasel cards and the distaff and spindle. Teasel cards are flat wooden plates with dried, spiky teasel plant heads attached, or rows of wire spikes, used to card (comb) the fibres. The distaff is a cleft staff on which a carded sliver of wool, cotton, or other fibre is loosely wound; the spindle is a slender, cylindrical spinning implement that is set in motion by hand, then allowed to fall, drawing out and twisting the fibres from the distaff into yarn. The spindle and distaff were used in Europe until the Middle Ages, and are still widely used in Third World countries. The spinning-wheel (see *spinning machine) was invented in India and introduced into Europe in the 14th century. It was faster than hand-spinning, and gave a more uniform yarn.

In the late 18th century the *Industrial Revolution brought improved looms, which required more rapid yarn production. This promoted a spate of inventions relating to spinning: *Hargreaves's spinning-jenny, *Arkwright's water-frame, *Crompton's mule spinning frame, and efficient mechanical *carding machines to provide fibre for the spinning frames. By the beginning of the 19th century these developments had been combined into a low-cost, mechanized system for staple yarn manufacture that is essentially the same today. The modern spinning process typically consists of the following stages. Bales of tightly packed fibre are opened, then disentangled and aligned by carding. The assemblies of parallel fibres are then drawn out by successive pairs of rollers, each pair running faster than the last: this gives successively finer strands. (Wool is not drawn out in this way before twisting.) Finally, the fibres are twisted to give cohesion, compactness, and strength. In the modern industry, a few mule frames are still in use (in the mule, the drawing out of strands and their twisting take place alternately). However, most staple yarn is now spun on ring frames or open-end spinning machines.

Silk is produced by the silkworm, which extrudes a viscous liquid through two small orifices (spinnerets) on its lower lip. The liquid solidifies on contact with air to form a pair of solid, adhering, fine protein filaments. The silk is then processed to make it into yarn. Manufactured filaments are similarly extruded or 'spun' by pumping a long-chain polymer, in solution or in molten form, through the fine holes of a spinneret. In the 'wet spinning' of, for example, *rayon and some *acrylic fibres, the polymer is in aqueous solution and solidification is achieved by chemical reaction (coagulation). In 'dry spinning' (for example, of acetate fibre and other acrylics), the solvent is organic, and solidification is through evaporation of the solvent. In the 'melt spinning' of *nylon (polyamide) and other thermoplastics, solidification is by cooling of the molten polymer. After extrusion, the filaments are pulled away from the spinneret and stretched to orient the polymer molecules parallel to the fibre axis. On some modern machines, production of filament yarn may be up to 10 km (6 miles) of yarn per minute. The continuous filaments may then be used as they are, crimped to give them more bulk and texture, or broken into short lengths for use as staple fibres.

spinning-jenny *spinning machine.

spinning machine, a machine which twists prepared assemblies of short textile *fibres to form *yarn. The earliest form of spinning machine was the spinning-wheel. It was essentially the same as the distaff and spindle (see *spinning), except that the spindle was driven by a cord from a wheel, rather than being set spinning and then allowed to fall. The earliest spinning-wheels had no mechanism for winding the spun yarn, but in the 16th century the Saxony wheel was developed. This had an arm (the flyer) fixed to the spindle: yarn was wound on to a bobbin mounted loosely on the flyer, making continuous spinning possible. Saxony wheels were originally human-powered, but some later versions were water- or wind-powered. In the 1760s many attempts were made to combine the spinning capability of the Saxony wheel with a technique used for drawing out the textile fibres by running them through successive pairs of rollers, each pair running faster than the preceding one. *Arkwright's water-frame was the first commercially successful mill of this type. His water-powered machine was widely copied, and later a higher-speed version of it (the throstle) was developed. In 1767 *Hargreaves invented a multiple-wheeled spinning machine, the spinning-jenny. The jenny substantially simulated the actions of a spindle and distaff, and produced yarns of similar character. A natural development from the work of Hargreaves and Arkwright was the mule, a machine that combined the spinning action of the spinning-jenny with the fibre-controlling rollers of the water-frame. Invented by *Crompton in 1789, the mule was extremely successful, even though early versions were manually operated. The first automatic mule was patented by Richard Roberts of Manchester (UK) in 1830, and quickly dominated the industry.

Early in the 20th century the ring-frame spinning machine began to supplant the mule, due to its simplicity and higher productivity. The ring frame has many individual spinning elements, continuously rotating vertical spindles on to which the yarn being spun is wound. A tiny wire loop, allowed to move freely round a steel ring concentric with the spindle, guides the yarn on to the spindle and at the same time twists the fibre assembly to form yarn. Each frame carries 300 to 600 spindles driven at 8,000 to 16,000 r.p.m. Ring-spinning is being supplanted on economic grounds by open-end spinning. The most common open-end process has a small centrifuge as its basic spinning element. Fibre is carried in an air-stream and deposited on the inner surface of the centrifuge. From there, yarn is continually stripped, withdrawn axially through the hollow shaft of the centrifuge, and wound on to a large bobbin. Manufactured yarns are made on melt-spinning, wet-spinning, and dry-spinning machines, which extrude polymer filaments at rates of up to 10 km (6 miles) per minute (see spinning). New spinning frames of all types are now microprocessor controlled, with mechanized replacement of the fibre supply, robotic detection and mending of broken yarns, and automatic doffing (removal) of completed yarn packages.

spinning-wheel *spinning machine.

spirit-level, a kind of levelling instrument for determining a horizontal line or surface. A spirit-level comprises a slightly curved transparent tube with sealed ends partially filled with a liquid ('spirit'), thereby forming a bubble. The tube is set lengthwise into the long edge of a metal or wooden batten. When the bubble is centred in the tube, the surface on which the level is resting is horizontal.

spreadsheet, an *applications program for a computer that can rapidly perform arithmetical calculations on many values. Spreadsheets are widely used in business and accountancy for the generation of financial statements and business projections. The spreadsheet is divided into a set of rows and columns, the intersections of which form large numbers of 'cells'. A typical spreadsheet program may permit 2,048 rows and 256 columns. Numerical values and formulae are entered by the user in any cell and mathematical operations can be performed on the contents of the cells.

spring, a means of storing elastic energy in bending (leaf and spiral springs) or torsion (helical coil and tubular springs) of a metal or as compression of a gas. The earliest use was for clocks and watches, which used a spiral spring, and in the *suspension systems of carriages, which used steel leaf springs. Other spring types include rubber springs, which were an element in the 'hydrolastic' suspension of the Mini motor car, and springs that rely on the compression of air or some other gas for their resilience. Newer materials such as *carbon fibre have been used for springs.

sprinkler system, a self-activating device that sprinkles water on a fire after detecting a large rise in temperature. A sprinkler system is often combined with an alarm system and a *smoke detector. A prerequisite is a ready supply of water at sufficient pressure. Sprinklers are commonly triggered by plugs made of alloys, with a melting-point of around 70 °C. In very hot weather the interior of a building—for example, under a glass roof exposed to the sun—may produce such temperatures even in the absence of fire. Careful location of sprinklers is, therefore, very important.

Sputnik, a series of Soviet *satellites. *Sputnik 1* was the first artificial satellite to orbit the Earth, in October 1957. *Sputnik 2* carried the first animal into space, the dog Laika. The main purpose of *Sputniks 1* to *10* was to prepare for a *manned space flight. Subsequent *Sputniks* (*11* to *24*) were also designated by the name *Cosmos*.

sputtering *vapour deposition.

square-rig, the arrangement of a sail or sails in a vessel whereby the majority are set square to the mast. Evidence suggests that the square-rig is the oldest sail arrangement, having been used on Egyptian vessels from 5000 BC. It was also the rig of the European three-masted *sailing ships that voyaged to most parts of the world from the 15th to the 19th centuries.

stabilizer, a device used to minimize the rolling (side-to-side) motion of a ship at sea. One type is the fin stabilizer, a continuously adjusting fin projecting from the side of the vessel, which opposes and thus minimizes rolling. An on-board *gyroscope senses deviations of the ship from the vertical; these deviations are opposed by the action of the fins. Other types of stabilizer utilize the inertia of a specially shaped tank of fluid carried on board to oppose the ship's rolling action.

stacking system (aircraft), a system used by *air-traffic controllers at busy *airports whereby incoming aircraft fly a descending, flattened oval course while awaiting their turn to commence landing. There are usually several stacking points in an airport's vicinity, each situated above a radio beacon. The approaching aircraft turns when it reaches the beacon and flies a timed outward leg at a fixed height. Its inward leg back to the beacon is flown at a lower height, and it gradually descends until it can land.

stage-coach *carriages and coaches.

stainless steel, *steel, usually containing 18 per cent *chromium and 8 per cent *nickel, that is very resistant to corrosion and cannot be hardened by *quenching. It is used for cutlery, surgical instruments (but not scalpel blades, since it cannot take an edge), reaction vessels, and for many other purposes. The corrosion resistance is due to chromium, which forms a thin layer of chromium oxide on the surface and prevents rusting of the iron. It was commercially developed by *Brearley. There are many types of stainless steel, each with its own special properties: for example, some types can be *welded, while others have high strength and toughness.

starch, the main storage carbohydrate of plants, a complex polysaccharide made up of glucose sub-units. To obtain pure starch the plant crop must be mechanically ground to break open cell walls, the starch grains separated by filtration or flotation, and the grains disrupted by heating. Starch itself is used in pastes, for stiffening paper and fabrics, and as a filler in pills. It may be broken down (hydrolysed) by enzymes called amylases, to yield *sugars.

starter motor, a means of starting a vehicle engine using an electric motor to turn the engine's crankshaft. It was invented by the US electrical engineer Charles Kettering in 1912; before this time the crankshaft had to be turned manually using a starter handle. The use of an electric motor is possible because such motors can be greatly overloaded for short periods of time. Thus a relatively small motor can supply the high power needed to start an engine.

statistics *applied mathematics.

steam distillation, a process in which steam is passed into a mixture that is to be distilled. Direct external heating often causes local overheating and decomposition. This is avoided in steam *distillation because the steam condenses, giving up its latent heat of vaporization evenly throughout the mixture and eventually causing the mixture to boil and distillation to occur. An example of its use is in the purification of *essential oils.

steam-engine, the first effective heat *engine, in which steam from a *boiler is used to drive a piston in a cylinder (see figure). Although the ancient Greeks built small steam-powered models (see *steam-turbine), the first successful steam-engine was the *beam-engine, developed by *Newcomen in 1712 for pumping water out of mines. It was improved by *Smeaton and further developed by *Watt, who in 1769 introduced a condenser separate from the cylinder and made many other improvements. *Trevithick in Cornwall and *Evans in the USA developed high-pressure steam-engines that exhausted into the atmosphere rather than to a condenser. These could produce the same power and efficiency in a much smaller and lighter unit, thus making portable engines possible. The first *steam locomotive, developed by Trevithick, was built in 1804. *Steamships were first built in the late 18th and early 19th century; they continued to develop throughout the 19th century. Compound engines, in which steam is expanded in two stages, originated with the UK engineer Jonathan Hornblower in 1781 and were subsequently developed by several others. The *triple-expansion engine became standard for marine use, where fuel economy is important, in the late 1880s.

Steam-engine

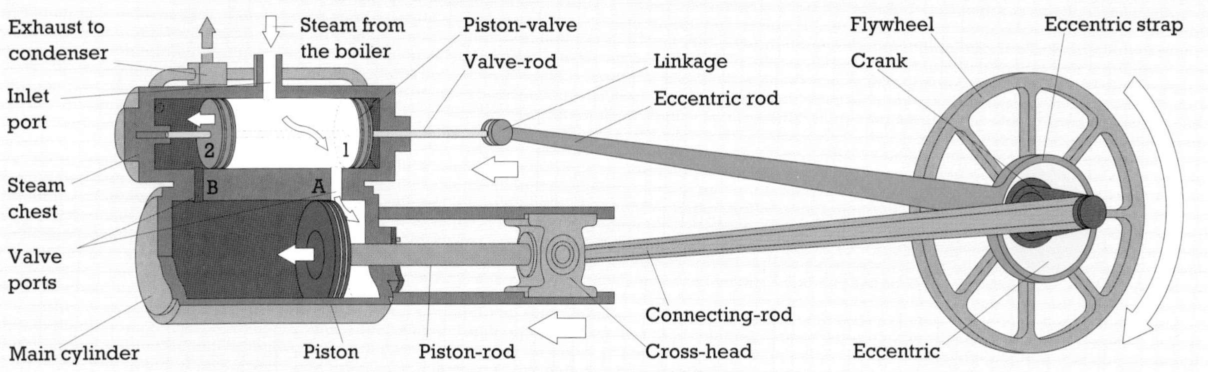

Steam enters the steam chest via the inlet port and then enters the main cylinder via valve port A. This produces pressure on the right-hand side of the cylinder piston, causing it to move to the left. The crank converts the reciprocating motion of the piston into the rotary motion of the flywheel, which rotates in a clockwise direction.

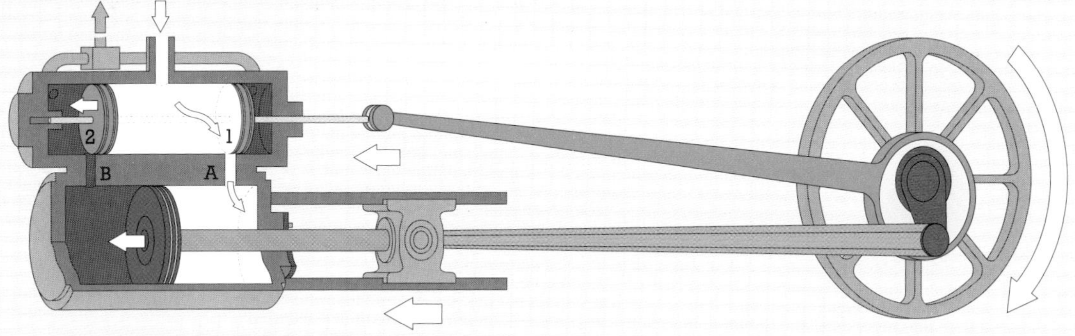

The eccentric rod is attached to a strap sliding round the eccentric. As the flywheel rotates, so does the eccentric, and the wide part of the eccentric pushes the eccentric rod, and hence the piston valve, to the left. At a critical point the inlet to the right-hand side of the piston (valve port A) is cut off by piston valve 1.

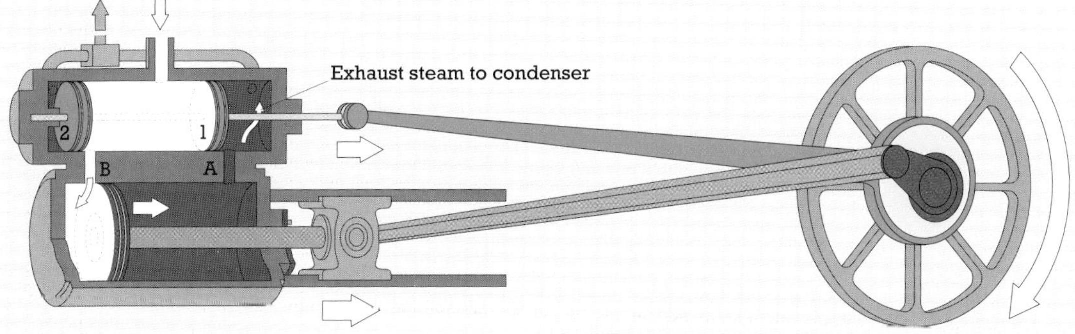

As valve port A is closed, valve port B is opened by the movement of piston valve 2. This allows steam to enter and produce pressure on the left-hand side of the cylinder piston causing it to move to the right. The flywheel keeps the crankshaft moving in a clockwise direction. The eccentric also rotates, pulling on the valve rod and sliding the piston valve across the valve ports ready to begin the cycle again.

Large steam-engines were used to drive workshops and mills, while an engine with a high rotational speed, needed for electricity generation, was designed by P. W. Willans. By 1900 the steam-engine was a versatile power unit with 200 years of design and constructional development behind it. But within a very few years its widespread use had largely given way to *steam-turbines, which could work at higher speeds, and the *internal-combustion engine, which was lighter and more efficient.

steam-hammer, a powerful machine-tool for large *forgings. It was the invention of *Nasmyth, who developed it in 1839 for the production of forgings for Brunel's steamship the **Great Britain*. It consists of a vertical steam cylinder supported by a massive frame spanning the anvil below. Steam can be applied to either side of a piston in the cylinder, and the forging tool is carried on the lower end of the piston rod. The tool is raised and then forced down at speed to strike the workpiece. Control is so precise that quite delicate blows can be struck if required.

steam locomotive, a railway locomotive powered by a *steam-engine. The first steam locomotive was built in 1804, by *Trevithick: his use of high-pressure steam set a precedent for all future steam locomotives. Between 1804 and the building of the locomotive the *Rocket* in 1829 by R.

Steam Locomotive

Steam locomotive (mid-20th century)

Fuel burnt in the firebox produces hot gases, which pass along steel tubes in the boiler and heat the circulating water to steam. The steam collects in the steam dome: it then passes into the superheater, and hence to the valve chest and the cylinder. Expansion of the superheated steam then moves the cylinder piston, and thus, via the connecting-rod, the wheels. Spent steam is exhausted through the chimney.

Water turning into steam
Superheated steam
Hot gases

Early steam locomotive

George Stephenson's *Locomotion*, used from 1825 for short hauls on the Stockton and Darlington railway.

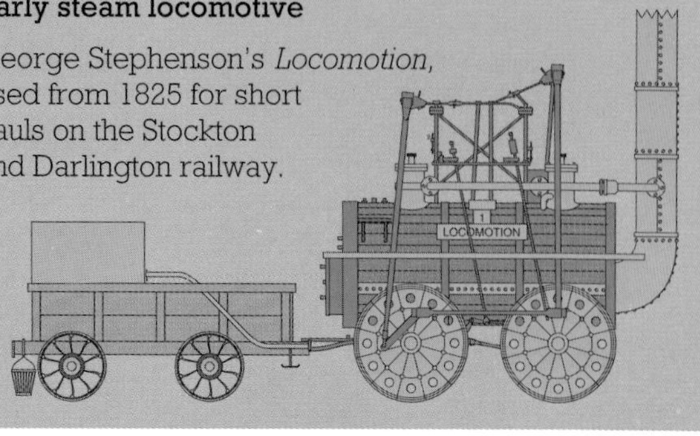

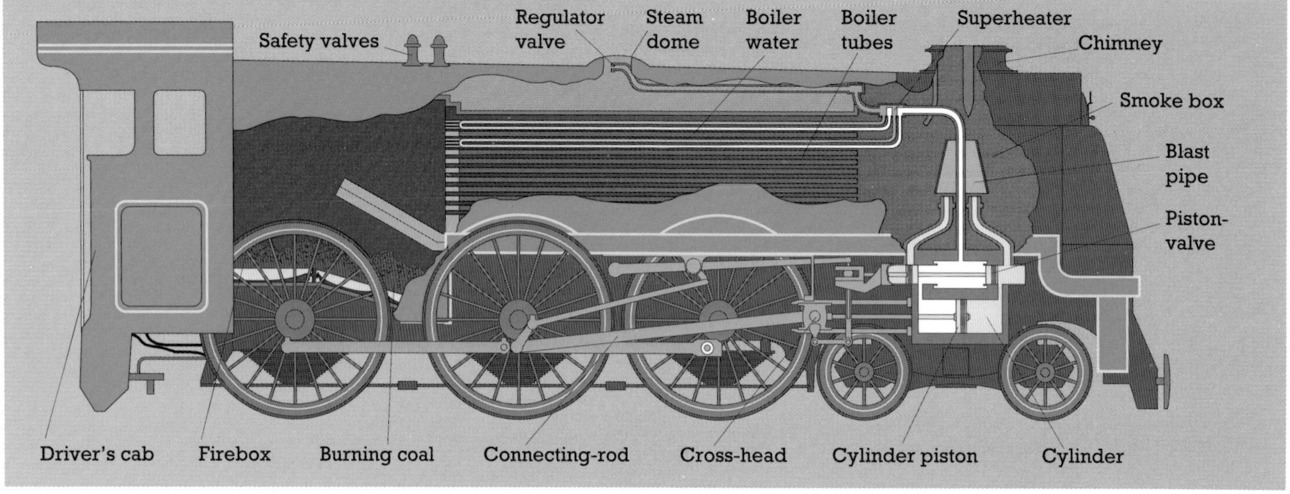

Safety valves
Regulator valve
Steam dome
Boiler water
Boiler tubes
Superheater
Chimney
Smoke box
Blast pipe
Piston-valve
Driver's cab
Firebox
Burning coal
Connecting-rod
Cross-head
Cylinder piston
Cylinder

*Stephenson, the basic layout for most subsequent steam locomotives was evolved. Hot gases from a water-jacketed fire-box pass into a *boiler made up of a large number of copper tubes; the gases heat water circulating around the tubes and turn it into steam. The steam passes into a pair of double-acting cylinders, which drive the powered wheels through connecting-rods. The spent steam is exhausted through a chimney to the atmosphere, the draught from the exhaust being used to draw the fire-box fire (see figure). Fuel (usually coal) and water are carried in a tender behind the locomotive (except on the *tank locomotive). Later improvements included superheating the steam, using three or four cylinders instead of two, and (in the compound steam locomotive) using the steam from the high-pressure cylinders to drive a set of low-pressure cylinders. Steam locomotives could achieve very high power for a given size, could exert a high tractive force when starting, and gave constant power output at high speeds. However, even the most advanced designs had a thermal *efficiency of only about 6 per cent. It was this low efficiency and the growing cost of the labour-intensive maintenance that led to the development of *diesel and *electric locomotives to replace them. Steam locomotives are still in use, notably in India, South Africa, and China, but virtually no new ones are being built.

steam-powered vehicle, a vehicle propelled by a *steam-engine. The first steam-powered vehicle was a three-wheeled tractor built by *Cugnot and designed to haul artillery. It was never put to use, but in the UK *Trevithick and others developed the *steam locomotive, and the manufacture of steam road vehicles became a small industry. Steam coaches ran regular short routes between 1831 and 1838, but steam carriages encountered strong opposition from many interests, and by 1840 the steam carriage era was over. In the 1850s *traction-engines were introduced and had a major effect on agricultural practices. Lighter, steam-powered cars were developed in the 1890s, and were particularly successful in the USA. In 1907 the US-built Stanley 'Wogglebug' took the world land speed record with a speed of 240 km/h (150 m.p.h.). Since the mid-1920s few steam cars have been built, but experimental vehicles are still occasionally produced.

steamroller *road roller.

steamship, a *ship powered by a *steam-engine. During the late 18th century numerous trials of steam-powered vessels were carried out in France, Britain, and the USA. The steamship *Charlotte Dundas* of 1802 was intended as a canal steamer, but was withdrawn after four days because of fears that its wash would erode the canal banks. The first commercially successful steamers were *Fulton's steamer *North River* (*Clermont*) in the USA (1807) and the British engineer Patrick Bell's *Comet* in Scotland (1812). By the mid-1820s *paddle-wheel steamers were carrying passengers on rivers and short sea runs in North America and Europe, and navies were beginning to use steam for smaller warships. The marine *propeller was developed in the late 1830s, and was widely adopted by navies in the 1840s. By then, steam was replacing sail for carrying passengers and mail on all but the longest oceanic routes. With the introduction of steam colliers in the 1850s, steam also began to take over in cargo-carrying. As steam-engines became more reliable and efficient, the use of steamships continued to grow. As a result of the introduction of the *triple-expansion engine at the end of the 1880s, steam tramp ships became the dominant general-purpose cargo carriers, and ships no longer carried sails for assistance and safety. The demonstration of the *steam-turbine by *Parsons in 1897 led to a change from the reciprocating steam-engine to turbine power. Many of the large *liners of the early 20th century used steam-turbines. In the early 20th century the marine *diesel engine made its appearance, and has steadily increased in importance, although steam-turbines are still used in some large ships.

steam-turbine, an *engine that uses the thermal energy of steam produced in a *boiler to drive a *turbine at high speed. Jets of steam from nozzles around the periphery of the turbine impinge on the turbine blades, causing them to turn: in effect steam-turbines work like *windmills, but using steam instead of wind power (see *power-station for illustration). Steam-turbines can work at high rotational speeds and generate high powers from a relatively small unit. Their major use is in *electricity generation; for a time they were also important marine engines. The concept of using steam jets to produce rotation was described by *Hero of Alexandria in the 1st century AD, and the use of steam jets to turn a wheel was proposed by Italian architect Giovanni Branca in 1629. The first practical steam-turbine was built by *Parsons in 1884. His design was a response to demands from the electricity industry for generators that could run at very high speeds. In his turbine, Parsons used steam expansion in a combination of both fixed and moving turbine blades, which was more efficient. Steam-turbines are now used in most power-stations. They have the advantage over *gas-turbines in that they can be built in much larger capacity units: power outputs from the largest turbines may exceed 1,000 MW. The steam that powers the turbines may be produced using either *fossil fuels or *nuclear power.

steel, the major industrial metal, primarily an alloy of *iron and *carbon, of immense importance in all developed countries. It is strong and stiff, but corrodes easily through rusting, although *stainless and other special steels resist *corrosion. The amount of carbon in a steel influences its properties considerably. Steels of low carbon content (mild steels) are quite ductile, and are used in the manufacture of sheet iron, wire, and pipes. Medium-carbon steels containing 0.2–0.4 per cent carbon are tougher and stronger and are used in railway tracks, structural steel, and boiler plates. Both mild and medium-carbon steels are suitable for *forging and *welding. High-carbon steels contain 0.4–1.5 per cent carbon, are hard and brittle, and are used in cutting tools, surgical instruments, razor blades, springs, and cutlery. Tool steel, also called silver steel, contains about 1 per cent carbon and is strengthened and toughened by *quenching and *tempering. The inclusion of other elements affects the properties of the steel. *Manganese gives extra strength and toughness, whereas 4 per cent silicon steel is used for transformer cores or electromagnets. The addition of *chromium gives extra strength and corrosion resistance. Heating in the presence of carbon- or nitrogen-rich materials is used to form a hard surface on steel (case-hardening). High-speed steels, which are extremely important in *machine-tools, contain chromium and *tungsten plus smaller amounts of *vanadium, *molybdenum, and other metals.

steering-oar, an oar used over the side of a vessel at the stern to direct its heading. Steering-oars were depicted in Egyptian bas-reliefs from as early as 3000 BC. The earliest types were simple oars, but on some ships they became more elaborate, being attached in a vertical position, with a tiller to control the oar's movement. Steering-oars continued in use in Europe and the Mediterranean until the 13th century, when the stern *rudder came into use.

steering system, the mechanism by which a road vehicle is steered. The simplest form of steering, used for centuries on horse-drawn vehicles, is a front axle pivoted at the centre, with a wheel at each end. When cornering at high speeds, however, this system is unstable. In 1818 a system was patented in which the front wheels were separately pivoted. In the Ackermann principle, named after Rudolph

Steering system

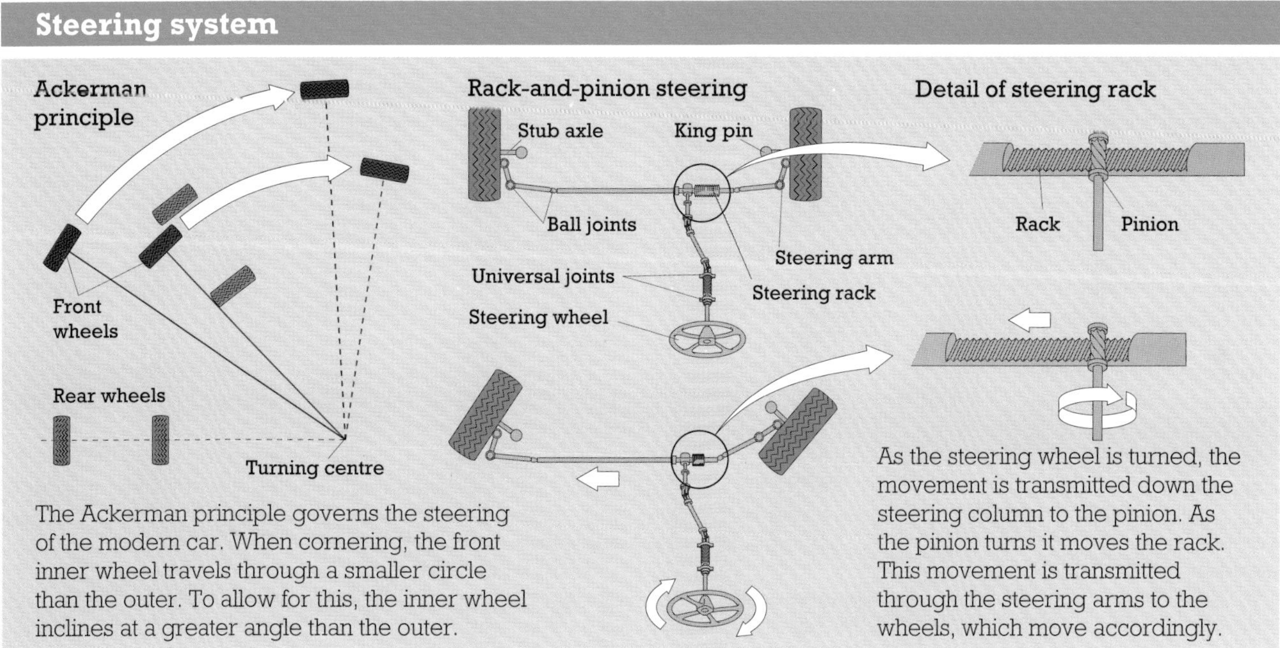

The Ackerman principle governs the steering of the modern car. When cornering, the front inner wheel travels through a smaller circle than the outer. To allow for this, the inner wheel inclines at a greater angle than the outer.

As the steering wheel is turned, the movement is transmitted down the steering column to the pinion. As the pinion turns it moves the rack. This movement is transmitted through the steering arms to the wheels, which move accordingly.

Ackerman, a London print-seller who first patented the concept, the inner wheel is inclined more than the outer, since it is rolling along a curve of smaller radius (see figure). The most common steering system is the rack and pinion, in which the turning of the steering wheel moves the rack from side to side. The axis around which the front wheels pivot is slightly in front of the area of wheel in contact with the road, so that the wheels have a tendency to maintain a straight path, like castors on furniture. Steering systems are designed to ensure that the driver obtains the correct amount of 'feel' when cornering, and that road shocks are not transmitted through the steering. Larger vehicles commonly use power steering, in which a hydraulic *servo-mechanism makes the steering wheel easier to turn.

stencil, a flat, thin sheet of plastic, metal, or card, into which a pattern or lettering is cut or etched. A stencil is used to produce a corresponding pattern (either by drawing the outline or by solid inking) on the surface beneath it by the application of ink or paint. Stencils are commonly used for lettering, drawings, and for *screen printing.

Stephenson, George (1781–1848) and **Robert** (1803–59), British railway engineers. George was the son of a colliery fireman, and became familiar with the *steam-engines used in mines for pumping and haulage. With this experience, he began to manufacture stationary steam-engines before turning to steam traction. In 1814 he built his first colliery *steam locomotive, and in 1825 constructed the first public railway between Stockton and Darlington, followed by the Manchester–Liverpool line in 1830. At his Newcastle upon Tyne works, he and his son Robert built the *Rocket* (1829) and many of the next generation of railway locomotives. In 1815, independently of *Davy, he invented a miner's safety lamp. Robert Stephenson worked as a mechanical engineer in his father's locomotive works at Newcastle until 1824, when he spent three years superintending mines in Colombia. He then returned to Newcastle and collaborated with his father in many railway ventures. He also became famous as a *bridge builder, constructing among others the Menai tubular-girder bridge in the UK, which was opened in 1850, and the Victoria Bridge over the St Lawrence River in Canada (1859).

stepper motor, a special *electric motor that can perform very accurate movements. Stepper motors are usually driven by a train of electrical pulses, each pulse advancing the motor one part of a revolution. Any desired rotation can be formulated by supplying the appropriate number of pulses. The use of a pulse-driven system makes it possible for computers to accurately and directly control movement. Applications include computer printers, which require careful side-to-side and up–down control of the printing head and carriage during operation.

stereophonic reproduction, a recording technique that attempts to re-create the spatial effect a listener would usually experience at a live performance (for example, the sounds of different instruments emanating from different regions in an orchestra). The first stereophonic demonstration involved relaying a live Paris Opera performance to the Paris Exposition in 1881. Stereophonic recording, first proposed in 1931 by *Blumlein, was achieved by recording the signals from two microphones at a live performance on the two sides of a record groove. Stereo *records were first marketed in 1958.

stereophotography, the making of stereoscopic photographs—a pair of photographs of a scene taken from slightly different viewpoints, which give a three-dimensional effect when seen through a viewer (a stereoscope). The photographs are shot simultaneously by a stereo-camera, which has two identical lens systems separated by several centimetres, mimicking the separation of the eyes. The stereoscope allows each eye to see only one of the two photographs: this gives the image an impression of depth. Stereophotography was first popular in the late 19th century; a major use today is in aerial surveys, where it allows height measurement from photographs.

stereotaxic surgery, surgery on an area of the brain located by precise three-dimensional measurements. It was first practised on humans in 1947. Small, accurate lesions are made at specific points, either mechanically or by the use of heat, cold, or an electrical current. The technique has been used, controversially, to treat psychiatric disorders, Parkinson's disease, and epilepsy, and to recover foreign bodies situated deep in the brain.

stereotype (printing), a *letterpress printing plate which is made from taking a thick paper mould of the original composed metal type and illustration blocks under pressure. Molten, lead-based metal that hardens quickly is poured into the mould to produce the plate. The back of the plate is then planed to a uniform thickness. To fit rotary presses, stereotypes are cast in a curve.

sterilization, the practice of making medical equipment free from microbiological contamination, and hence greatly reducing the incidence of infection in patients. Heat sterilization using boiling water, steam, or steam under pressure in autoclaves has replaced the earlier, chemical methods of *antisepsis. Other agents, including ethylene oxide and certain gas mixtures, are suitable for sterilizing more complex equipment. Disposable items such as dressings, needles, and *hypodermic syringes are supplied pre-packed and sterilized (sometimes by gamma irradiation) by the manufacturer. (See also *asepsis.)

Sterilization is also a surgical operation or any other process by which a person or animal is made sterile (rendered incapable of reproducing).

steroids and steroid treatment. Steroids are a large group of fat-soluble compounds, having a basic structure of seventeen carbon atoms arranged in four linked rings. Steroids are widely distributed in living organisms and include sex hormones, vitamin D, sterols such as cholesterol, and digitalis, present in the foxglove. Therapeutically, corticosteroids are used as immunosuppressants in the treatment of auto-immune diseases and in *transplant surgery. Applied to the eye or skin, they are relatively safe to use, since little is absorbed into the body. However, large doses taken orally over long periods can produce serious side-effects. These include a reduced ability of the body to repair injury and resist infection, and a loss of calcium from the bones. Anabolic steroids are derived from the male hormone, testosterone. They cause the deposition of protein in tissues, and were formerly given to aid convalescence. They are sometimes taken by athletes and weight-lifters for their muscle-building properties, but can cause serious damage to the liver. Large amounts may lead to bouts of aggressive behaviour, or even death. Steroids form the active ingredients of most oral *contraceptive pills.

stethoscope, a diagnostic instrument for listening to sounds inside the body (auscultation). Invented by *Läennec in 1816, it became accepted when the view was established that disease was localized in organs of the body, and was not due to an imbalance of bodily humours. Early monaural stethoscopes (for one ear) were wooden tubes about 30 cm (1 foot) long, but these were superseded by the binaural stethoscope from the 1890s. Stethoscopes are mostly used in the diagnosis of lung and heart conditions, but also in *obstetrics, and together with the *sphygmomanometer to measure blood pressure.

Stirling engine, an engine which depends for its power on the displacement of air or other gas inside an externally heated cylinder. It was patented by the British clergyman Robert Stirling in 1816. Constructional problems have limited its use, although it has recently aroused interest because it is quiet, extremely efficient, and can use a wide variety of fuels. In the usual form it consists of a hot and a cold cylinder, containing two enclosed, oscillating pistons phased about 90 degrees apart. The passage between the two cylinders contains a regenerator, a matrix of fine passages whose function is to act as a heat exchanger. Heat applied to the hot cylinder causes the gas to expand, doing work; the gas is cooled by the regenerator on its way to the cold cylinder, where it is compressed before being heated again on its way back to the hot cylinder. Recent improvements using compressed working fluids have led to the development of silent but costly engines.

stitch, a way of fastening thread between two *needle holes when sewing. The best stitch for strength and firmness is the saddle-stitch. This can be made manually using two *needles and two threads, but machines able to carry out saddle-stitching are complex and inconvenient. The basic lockstitch is almost as strong and, as it can be made on a *sewing-machine, it is the stitch most widely used for hemming and seaming woven fabrics. Where seam extensibility is desired, or just for decoration, the zigzag lockstitch is used. The single-thread chain-stitch unravels easily (as knitting does) and is used for temporary sewings. A more expensive and elaborate sewing-machine is needed to make the three-thread over-lockstitch used for hemming of lightweight fabrics, particularly *warp knits. It minimizes fraying and also gives flexibility when used for seaming.

Medical stitches (sutures) are threads used to close a wound or surgical incision until healing is complete. Catgut stitches and synthetic equivalents are broken down by the body over varying periods. Stitches of silk, cotton, polyester, nylon, polypropylene, and stainless steel are not broken down and either become embedded in the scar tissue or are removed. Wounds are closed either with a 'running' stitch or with 'interrupted' stitches, which are tied separately. Newer techniques include the use of specialized adhesive paper tapes, clips, stainless-steel staples, and 'micromechanical Velcro', which has tiny silicon dioxide arrowheads which pierce human tissue and hold wounds closed.

stocking frame *knitting machine.

STOL (Short Take-Off and Landing aircraft), aeroplanes capable of a short take-off and landing. This is usually achieved by the extension on landing and take-off of special slats and flaps on the wing (see *flight, principles of) to increase its lift at low speeds. STOL aircraft are particularly useful where the area of an *airport is limited, such as at London's Dockland Airport. Such an airport is called a Stolport. Examples of STOL aircraft include the De Havilland DHC-7 *airliner, and the Swedish Saab-37 Viggen air defence *fighter.

Stonehenge, a prehistoric *megalithic structure located on Salisbury Plain, UK. The site was used between about 3100 and 1100 BC. Although its purpose is not clearly known, the main axis of the structure is aligned on the summer solstice, and may have been astronomical or calendrical in function. Archaeological evidence suggests that it was built in three stages: the first, completed in about 2100 BC, consisted of a low bank and a ditch of earth. The second, a double ring of standing bluestones (pillars of igneous rock) may have originally formed part of a stone circle elsewhere, and was dismantled before it had been completed. The final stage was the present monument, built around 1800 BC. This consists of an inner horseshoe of five trilithons (each consisting of two upright stones of about 40 tonnes and a horizontal lintel), a central altar stone, and an outer ring of uprights (each weighing about 26 tonnes) joined by lintels, all made of a local stone known as sarsen.

stonework *masonry.

storage heater, a space-heating appliance that is charged with *heat which is subsequently emitted by convection in response to the temperature difference between the storage heater and the surrounding air. The heat store is made of a material of high thermal capacity, typically high-density bricks arranged in a stack. Electricity is the usual energy source, with the charging phase timed to take advantage of cheaper overnight supply charges. Highly insulated water heating or storage vessels are also sometimes called storage heaters.

storm-water drainage, *drains that carry the run-off from precipitation (rain, snow, and so on) and discharge it, usually to a watercourse. The underground pipework is sized in accordance with predictions for peak flows from storms. Where the *sewage treatment system is combined or partially separate, peak flows of storm sewage, exceeding the capacity of the treatment plant, may be discharged directly into a watercourse. However, modern practice is to provide temporary storage for the excess until it can be treated, since the run-off from roads and pavements may be polluted with organic matter, lead, and salt.

stove *cookers and stoves.

strain gauge, an instrument to measure the deformation of a material subjected to strain. It consists essentially of a fine zigzagged wire attached to a backing sheet which is fixed to the object being tested. The wire is incorporated in an electric circuit. If strain occurs, the wire is stretched, and its length increases, thus decreasing its diameter. This increases its electrical resistance, and the change in resistance can be equated to the mechanical movement of the material. As the resistance of a wire also depends on the ambient temperature, provision must be made to compensate for this in tests of long duration.

Strategic Defense Initiative (SDI, 'Star Wars'), a research and development programme intended to provide a multi-layer *anti-ballistic missile space defence system for the USA. It was initiated by President Reagan in 1983 and was based on the use of new weapons, including high-powered *laser weapons and particle beams fired from space platforms, to eliminate ballistic missiles, ideally early in flight before they have released their *warheads. However, the programme has now been scaled down and renamed GPALS (Global Protection Against Limited Strikes). This is based on deployment of approximately 1,000 small interceptor missiles in space, an equal number of ground-based anti-missile missiles in the USA, and mobile ground missiles in several other parts of the world. A new type of gun, the rail gun, which uses electromagnetic forces to propel a projectile or shell at extremely high velocities, is being developed as a further layer of defence.

streamlining, the shaping of an object so that it offers the least possible resistance to a flow of air, water, or other fluid. A non-streamlined object moving through a fluid creates eddies and turbulence, which cause drag on the object. The rounded, smooth shapes of many aeroplanes, motor vehicles, and boats are designed to produce a smooth, regular flow of fluid around them, thus minimizing drag and improving efficiency. Optimal streamlined shapes tend to be long ellipses tapering in the direction of flow, for example, an *aerofoil cross-section. At *supersonic speeds this optimal shape changes, and a sharper front end is required.

stroboscope, an instrument that intermittently illuminates a rotating or vibrating object so as to study its motion or determine its rotational or vibrational speed. It consists of a light that gives a rapid series of flashes of very short duration (typically one-millionth of a second). If the speed of the flashes is close to the speed of rotation or vibration of the object being studied, the object will appear to slow down and can be examined: adjusting the flash speed so that the object appears stationary will give its exact rotational or vibrational speed. The stroboscope is also used in high-speed photography to obtain very short exposures.

strontium (symbol Sr, at. no. 38, r.a.m. 87.62), a silvery-white, malleable and ductile metallic element. It is highly reactive and occurs in the ores celestite and strontianite. Strontium nitrate and strontium perchlorate are volatile, and colour flames a brilliant red; they are used in flares, *tracer bullets, and *fireworks. The *radioactive isotope Sr-90 is an important *fission product, and is considered to be one of the most dangerous components of nuclear *fall-out. This is because it can replace calcium in food, and becomes concentrated in the bones and teeth, causing radiation damage in surrounding tissues.

structural engineering, the design of engineering structures, particularly those with load-bearing subsidiary elements (members). These include *frames and structural supports for *buildings, *bridges, aircraft hangars, towers, *cranes, and storage and *conveyor systems. The structural engineer assesses the loads to be supported as well as the effects of wind, snow, ice, and earthquakes. To design the structure, the variations in temperature and humidity to which it will be subjected are predicted, then a form of structure is selected and analysed to determine its response to loadings. The dimensions of its members are calculated to ensure that it will have adequate strength. The most important of the members used in structures is the beam, a member designed to support loads that bend it. A cantilever is a beam that is securely fixed at one end and is unsupported at the other (see figure). The *box-girder and the *plate girder are examples of beams. An arch is a curved structure designed to bear heavy loads. Its shape is such that the load

Structural engineering

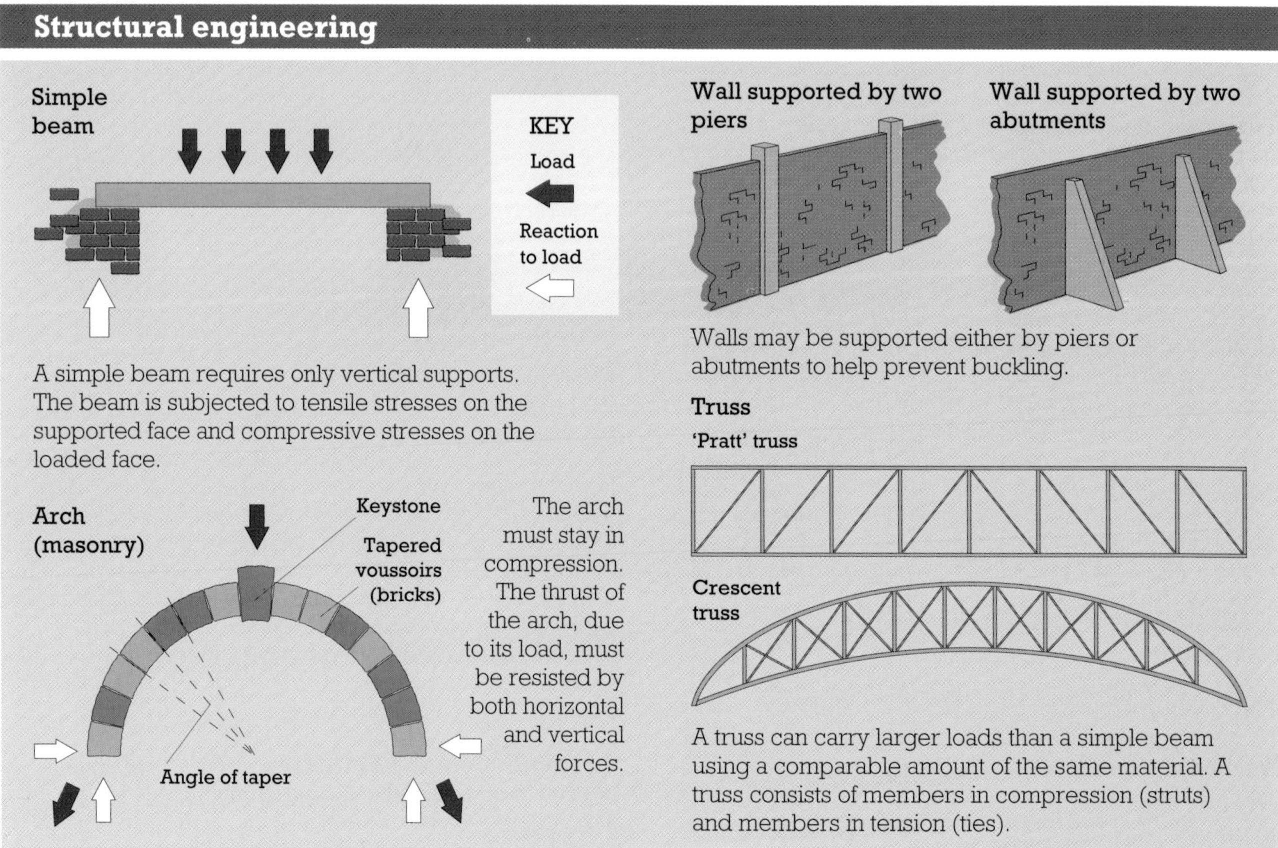

Simple beam
KEY
Load
Reaction to load
A simple beam requires only vertical supports. The beam is subjected to tensile stresses on the supported face and compressive stresses on the loaded face.
Arch (masonry)
Keystone
Tapered voussoirs (bricks)
Angle of taper
The arch must stay in compression. The thrust of the arch, due to its load, must be resisted by both horizontal and vertical forces.
Wall supported by two piers
Wall supported by two abutments
Walls may be supported either by piers or abutments to help prevent buckling.
Truss
'Pratt' truss
Crescent truss
A truss can carry larger loads than a simple beam using a comparable amount of the same material. A truss consists of members in compression (struts) and members in tension (ties).

causes outward thrusts at the supports (abutments). In rows of arches and *vaults, the thrusts between adjacent arches counterbalance. In structures such as the frame, columns and walls that support beams bearing heavy loads can fail by buckling sideways at stresses well below their material's compressive strength. A wall can be built to resist buckling if it is supported by a pier (a wide column designed to carry heavy loads) or a buttress (a thick supporting pier built at right angles to the wall). Floors can also support a wall against buckling. Bridges and roofs are commonly supported by a truss, a framework in which some of its members form the sides of triangles, giving it great stability. Lattices are more complex frameworks of interconnecting rods and are frequently used to provide lightweight support for roofs, as in the *space frame. A roof can also be built as a *tension structure, a *shell structure, or as a *geodesic dome.

sub-machine-gun, a small *machine-gun that does not require a rest from which to fire it. Sub-machine-guns commonly fire ammunition of the same calibre as that used by pistols. They operate on the blow-back system, in which the rear of the barrel is closed by a bolt that is held in place by a spring. On firing, the seal is maintained until the bullet leaves the barrel; what remains of the propellant force then pushes back the bolt, opening the breech and permitting the spent *cartridge to be ejected and a new round inserted.

submarine, a vessel, especially a warship, capable of operating under water and usually equipped with torpedoes, missiles, and a periscope. The essential requirements are an ability to lose and regain positive buoyancy; a means of underwater propulsion that does not use oxygen; and a hull sufficiently strong to withstand the pressure of water at depth. Over the centuries the idea of submerged navigation has attracted inventors: many designs are recorded between 1578 and 1801, of which only David Bushnell's USS *Turtle* (used during the American War of Independence, 1776–7) and *Fulton's *Nautilus* are noteworthy. Further experiments, particularly by French and US engineers, made some progress in the 19th century, and the introduction of the internal-combustion engine in the 1890s, coupled with sufficiently powerful electric motors and effective batteries, made the submarine a real possibility. The earliest practicable designs were French and US. They all had the same basic features: ballast tanks, which were flooded when diving and emptied when surfacing; electric motors for underwater propulsion, with steam or petrol (later diesel) engines to recharge the batteries and for surface propulsion; and usually an internal hull with a circular cross-section to withstand high pressures. The *torpedo provided submarines with an effective weapon, and they were soon adopted by many navies. During World Wars I and II submarines played an extremely important role. In 1954 nuclear-powered submarines were introduced; a nuclear power-plant provides heat to drive steam-turbines, which then generate electricity for propulsion and other power applications. Nuclear submarines can remain submerged almost indefinitely, travel at speeds of up to 30 *knots, operate at great depth, and fire intercontinental *ballistic missiles while submerged. (See also *inertial navigation system, *nuclear ship, *submersible.)

submersible, a *submarine operating under water for short periods. One of the most widely used types is the lock-out submersible. Its crew (normally two people) work at normal atmospheric pressure, but a separate, pressurized chamber, carries one or more divers (see *deep-sea and diving technology). Such craft are used for repair and inspection work, particularly on marine oil rigs. For work at great depths, submersibles with remotely controlled robot arms can be used. Increasingly, such submersibles are without a crew, and are remotely piloted from the surface. (See also *bathysphere.)

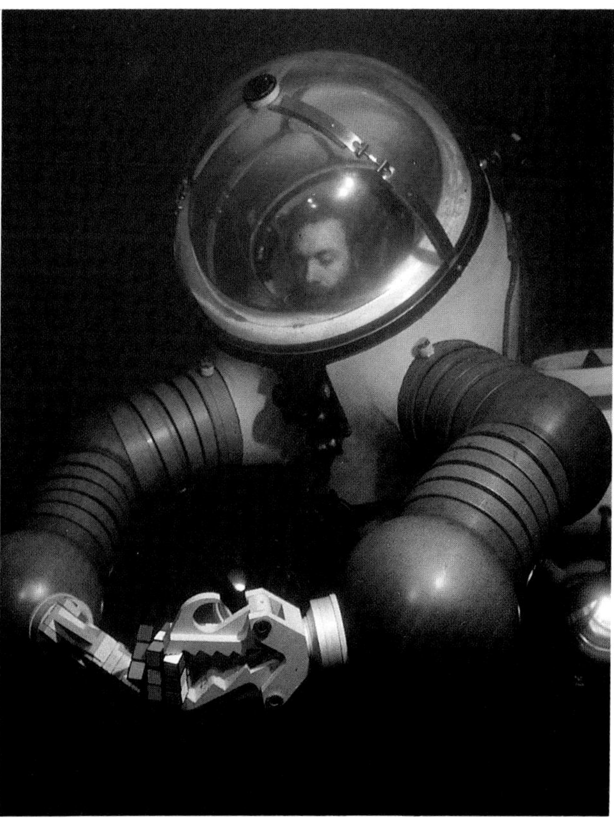

A single-person **submersible**, an armoured diving suit with remote-controlled robot arms for use in deep-water situations.

Suez Canal, a ship *canal joining the Mediterranean Sea and the Gulf of Suez, built to provide a sea route from Europe to Asia without having to sail round Africa. The present canal is 171 km (106 miles) long and was built by *Lesseps between 1859 and 1869. It has no locks, since the two sea-levels are virtually the same and the isthmus reaches a maximum height of only 11 m (36 feet) above sea-level. Twenty thousand labourers dug the initial excavation until water could be flooded in, and *dredgers were used to deepen and widen the channel. The canal has been further enlarged to accommodate tankers of up to 250,000 tonnes.

sugar, types of. Sugars are small carbohydrate molecules, commonly containing between three and twelve carbon atoms. Glucose and fructose are hexose (six-carbon) sugars that form the immediate energy source for most animals and plants, respectively. Other common sugars such as sucrose (table sugar), maltose (found in malt), and lactose (the sugar found in milk) are combinations of two hexose sugars. Sugars play a wide variety of roles in organisms: they are important constituents of DNA, and form part of some glycoproteins and lipids (*fats and oils). Simple sugars are also the building blocks for much larger carbohydrates such as *starch and cellulose.

A Cray X-MP/48 **supercomputer**, installed in 1988 at the European Laboratory for Particle Physics (CERN).

sugar processing, the production of crystalline sugar from cane or beet. Sugar is extracted from cane by rolling it to release the juices. Lime is added to clear the liquid, and gradual evaporation drives water from the juice. As the concentration of sugar increases, crystals form; these are separated from the waste molasses in a centrifuge. The process of extracting sugar from beet begins by slicing the root and heating it in water to which lime has been added. The resultant juice is then evaporated in a vacuum until the sugar crystallizes, the crystals being separated in a centrifuge. Waste sugar-beet fibres are used as fuel or in livestock feed; they also provide the raw material for fibreboard. Molasses can be used as the bonding agent in fibreboard, or may be used as a fertilizer or animal feed. Cane molasses is also used in the production of rum.

sulphonamide, any organic compound that is an amide of sulphuric acid, in particular a class of drugs that were the first of the modern chemotherapeutic agents. The sulphonamide prontosil was discovered by *Domagk in 1935, and was widely employed during World War II. The sulphonamides inhibit the growth of bacteria (bacteriostatic) rather than killing them (bactericidal), and organisms easily develop resistance to these drugs. Consequently, in most countries they have been superseded by *antibiotics.

sulphur (US, sulfur: symbol S, at. no. 16, r.a.m. 32.06), a yellow, crystalline, low-melting-point solid. Free sulphur occurs chiefly in volcanic deposits throughout the world, while sedimentary deposits are found in Texas and Louisiana, USA, and are extracted by the *Frasch process. The main use of sulphur is in the production of *sulphuric acid by the *contact process. It is also used in the *vulcanization of rubber, in the manufacture of *gunpowder, and to produce carbon disulphide, a valuable solvent. Sulphur dioxide is a toxic gas formed when sulphur burns in air, which is used to bleach straw and wool. It is a major cause of *air pollution and *acid rain. Hydrogen sulphide, an extremely toxic gas with a characteristic smell of bad eggs, is produced in large amounts at petroleum refineries. Pollution is reduced by controlled burning, in which one-third is burned to sulphur dioxide, which then reacts with the remaining two-thirds to produce water and sulphur.

sulphuric acid (H_2SO_4), a colourless, corrosive, oily liquid that dissolves in water with the evolution of a large amount of heat. Sulphuric acid is the most widely produced industrial chemical. It is used in the production of ammonium sulphate and soluble phosphate fertilizers; in petroleum refining to remove impurities from gasoline and paraffin; in the pickling of steel to clean its surface before galvanizing or plating; in the production of dyes, drugs, and disinfectants; and in the manufacture of textiles, paints, pigments, plastics, explosives, and lead storage batteries. The main method of production is the *contact process, but some is still manufactured by the *lead chamber process. Concentrated sulphuric acid is used in the laboratory as a drying agent for gases, and the dilute aqueous solution is a standard laboratory reagent.

sundial *clocks and time measurement.

supercharger, a compressor used to increase the amount of air admitted to an *internal-combustion engine cylinder during the admission stroke. It enables more fuel to be burnt, so increasing the power output. Originally superchargers were mechanically driven from the crankshaft, but now most are driven by a turbine utilizing the power of the exhaust gas. The combination of a directly coupled turbine and compressor is termed a turbo-charger, and is widely used in *diesel engines. It enables the engine to give more power for a given weight, reduces noise, allows a cheaper fuel to be used, and maintains power at the higher altitudes encountered in mountainous country. High-performance petrol-engined cars are also sometimes turbo-charged.

supercomputer, a computer of very high power which can execute instructions at an extremely high speed, typically greater than 40 million instructions per second (MIPS), using data *buses at least 64 *bits wide. Such computers are used for special tasks, for example, complex *simulation such as modelling weather patterns and ballistic behaviour. Employing very high-speed *integrated circuits, supercomputers are extremely costly to make, and present considerable engineering difficulties. A key problem is heat generated by the computer circuits; this necessitates sophisticated cooling systems on all supercomputers. As the limits of *semiconductor technology are reached, future supercomputers will rely increasingly on *parallel processing to deliver higher performance levels.

superconductivity, the phenomenon by which certain metals exhibit zero electrical resistance at temperatures close to absolute zero (−273°C). It was first discovered by the Dutch physicist Heika Kamerlingh Onnes in 1911. Superconductivity is important because it enables coils and *cables to be built that do not dissipate power. Very large electrical currents may be passed down such cables, making possible very efficient distribution of electrical power, for example, in a grid system. Superconductivity also makes possible the manufacture of extremely powerful but very small electromagnets, which could be used in medical instrumentation and electrical traction. Electronic circuits using superconductors can work one hundred times faster than conventional circuits. The high cost of the advanced cooling systems needed for superconductivity has meant that its applications are limited. However, in 1987 several research groups discovered a class of *electroceramics that exhibit superconductivity at much higher temperatures than previously known. When developed, these may make available the benefits of superconductivity on a large scale.

superheterodyne reception *radio receiver.

superplasticity, deformation in tension of several hundred per cent without failure. Superplastic alloys can be moulded at elevated temperatures and will undergo extensive deformation without cracking. The process is associated with metals of a very fine grain-size and is related to creep. It is of particular importance in *titanium alloys, when combined with diffusion bonding (a solid-state *welding technique). Using this combination, very complicated, large aerospace components, such as *jet engine fan-blades, have been manufactured from superplastic titanium alloys.

The airliner Concorde at take-off. The long, sharp nose and acutely swept-back delta wings are characteristic of aircraft designed for **supersonic flight**.

supersonic flight, the flight of an aircraft or missile at speeds greater than that of sound (*Mach 1). For many years aeroplanes had difficulty in achieving supersonic speeds even in a dive. This was because at around the speed of sound the air-flow around an aeroplane is compressed into a shock wave (often heard on the ground as a 'sonic boom'). Such shock waves cause excessive drag and create large stresses on the aircraft. The first aeroplane to achieve supersonic flight was a US rocket-engined Bell X-1, on 14 October 1947. Its design was modelled on that of a bullet, which was known to travel faster than sound. Modern supersonic

A polarized light micrograph of a pond skater (*Gerris locustris*) eating a scorpion fly (*Panorpa communis*). The scorpion fly is held by the **surface tension** of the water: the pond skater, however, has a water-repellent outer coating that allows it to walk on the 'skin' of the water.

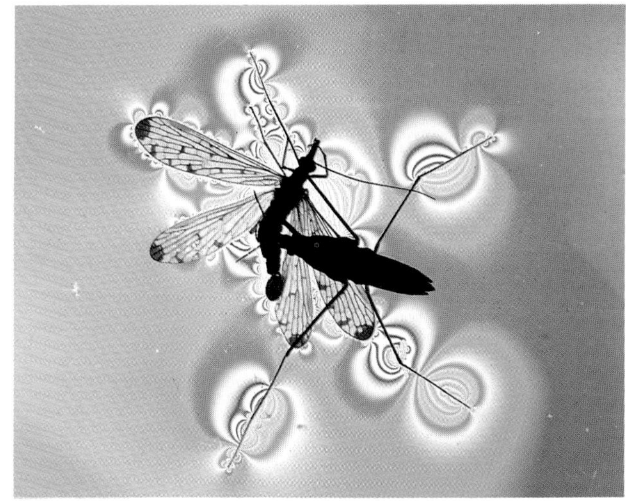

aircraft are designed with a sharply pointed nose and smaller, swept-back wings. At speeds above Mach 2, heating due to air friction becomes appreciable, and special materials must be used in aircraft construction (see also *hypersonic flight). Nearly all supersonic aircraft are military vehicles; the only exception being the supersonic airliner Concorde. Second-generation supersonic airliners are being developed by the UK and France, and in the USA.

surface tension, a property of liquids due to unbalanced forces of attraction between the constituent atoms or *molecules near the surface. It leads to the apparent presence of a surface film and to capillarity (the distortion of the surface of a liquid in contact with a solid). It affects how liquids interact with, and wet, solid surfaces, for example, drawing liquids into droplets. A surfactant is a substance that causes a change in the surface tension of a liquid. Often called 'wetting agents', surfactants usually lower the surface tension, allowing the liquid to interact with, and wet, solids. *Detergents are surfactants, enabling dirt particles to become detached from fabrics and suspended in water.

surface-to-air missile (SAM) *missile.

surface-to-surface missile (SSM) *missile.

surfactant *surface tension.

surgery, the physical repair of diseased or injured organs and tissues. Surgery has been practised since prehistory. Large numbers of Neolithic skulls show evidence of *trephining, and scrolls from ancient Egypt and China describe surgical instruments and the use of splints to set broken bones. Early Hindu medicine (see *Suśruta) included several complex surgical operations. However, as recently as 100 years ago surgery was a dangerous and unpleasant practice, since *anaesthetics were restricted to alcohol and opium, and fatal infections produced mortalities of over 90 per cent in some hospitals. Nevertheless, some early surgeons achieved notable results. The French monk Jean de Saint Côme (1703–81) reported cures in 90 per cent of over 1,000 operations to remove bladder stones. Recent surgical triumphs have only been made possible by modern anaesthetic practices. These have now advanced to the point where it is possible to keep a patient alive whilst such vital organs as the heart and lungs are removed (as in *transplant surgery). Other important developments include the use of intravenous fluids and *blood transfusions. Post-operational intravenous feeding helps patients to overcome the protein breakdown that occurs after surgery. Such feeding allows patients to survive more major operations than would otherwise be possible.

Many surgeons in the past noted the association between dirt and disease although many ignored it. However, it was not until the invention of the microscope that the cause of this 'poison' was identified as microbial infection. Thereafter *Lister and others began using chemicals to combat infection through *antisepsis and, later, *antibiotics that could treat such infections were discovered. Modern techniques rely heavily on new tools and devices such as the *optical fibre *endoscope to examine bowels, renal tracts, and joints. Laparoscopy (insertion of a rigid tube through the abdominal wall), when combined with endoscopy, can be used to perform minor operations without opening the abdomen. *Ultrasound is used to aid diagnosis, and has been used in gall-stone removal (see *lithotripsy). Finely focused *lasers are used, for example, in *neurology and neurosurgery, to cut and cauterize tissue. Other recent devices include *artificial joints, lens implants for the eye, and *pacemakers for the heart. *Robots designed to perform delicate surgery in the brain and throat are under development. (See also *microsurgery.)

surgical instrument, any instrument used in medical operations. The earliest types were presumably flint tools for the *trephining of the skull. Metal instruments, including knives, probes, and the *speculum, were known to the ancient Greeks. Early Hindu surgeons used a variety of knives, forceps, scissors, needles, hooks and later the catheter. The instruments were largely of steel. In 18th-century Europe, specialist surgical-instrument makers produced sophisticated instruments such as the lithotrite (see *lithotripsy). All-metal instruments superseded designs using wooden handles when the techniques of *antisepsis and *asepsis were adopted in surgery. Nickel plating was introduced in the late 19th century, followed by stainless steel in the 1930s. Modern surgical operations commonly use tens or even hundreds of instruments. New materials, such as titanium, provide lightweight precision instruments for use with, for example, the operating microscope in *ophthalmic surgery. Increasingly, instruments such as scalpel blades and needles are disposable, and items such as *hypodermic syringes and speculae are made of plastic.

surveying, the determination of position, form, and boundaries of an area of land by measuring distances and angles. Conventionally, a topographic survey is one used to produce *maps covering large areas at scales smaller than about 1 : 10,000. A cadastral survey, at a scale of perhaps 1 : 500, is used for engineering and building projects and shows accurately the extent and measurement of every plot of land. In such a survey, the horizontal features of the land are surveyed by triangulation (see figure). Details on the land, such as irregular boundaries and buildings, are measured as perpendiculars (offsets) from the principal lines. A *theodolite focused on a calibrated staff can be used to measure relative heights, while electronic devices employing *lasers or infrared emitters give accurate, long-distance *length measurement. Another important technique for mapping is the use of aerial *stereophotography, using photographs taken by optical or infra-red cameras in aircraft or satellites. To measure contours, the heights and locations of several easily recognizable features of the land must be known in advance.

Su Song (1020–1101), Chinese astronomer and imperial minister. He is famous for his hydro-mechanical clock (built in 1088), which was used to rotate an *armillary sphere. This consisted of metal rings to represent the equator and the tropics, and served (prior to the *telescope) to determine the positions of the stars and the planets. Such accurate records of the clock survive that a replica was built in the 1950s and is now exhibited in the Museum of Chinese History in Beijing.

suspended structure, usually, a multi-storey building in which floors are suspended by supporting their edges with steel bars (hangers). These can be stressed to full tensile strength and are slender compared with conventional columns in compression. Each hanger can be fixed to a roof-level truss, which forms a cantilever across the top of a central concrete core. Suspended structures are used for modest multi-storey buildings but not for *skyscrapers.

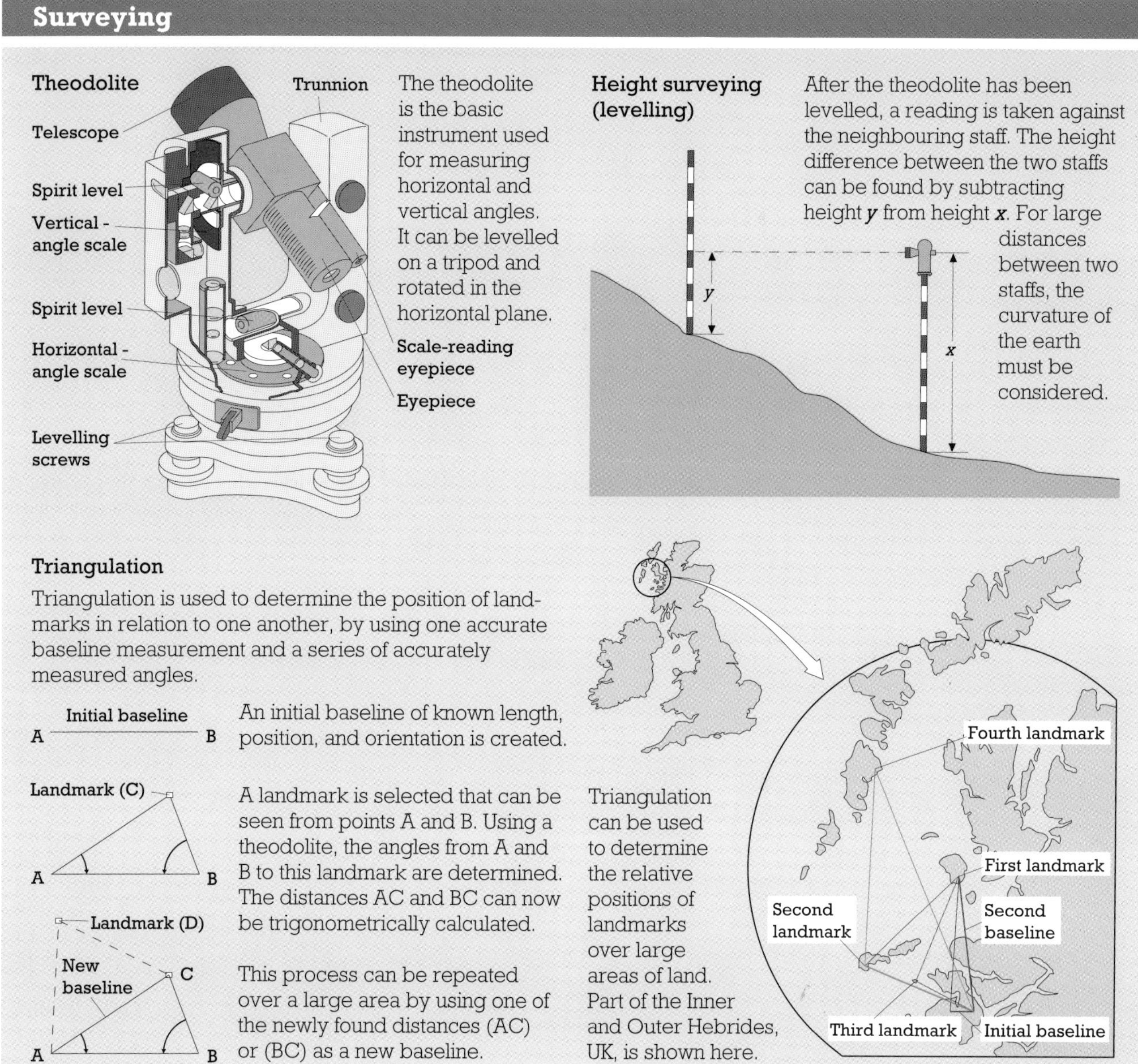

Surveying
Theodolite
Telescope
Trunnion
Spirit level
Vertical-angle scale
Spirit level
Horizontal-angle scale
Levelling screws
Scale-reading eyepiece
Eyepiece
The theodolite is the basic instrument used for measuring horizontal and vertical angles. It can be levelled on a tripod and rotated in the horizontal plane.
Height surveying (levelling)
After the theodolite has been levelled, a reading is taken against the neighbouring staff. The height difference between the two staffs can be found by subtracting height y from height x. For large distances between two staffs, the curvature of the earth must be considered.
y
x
Triangulation
Triangulation is used to determine the position of landmarks in relation to one another, by using one accurate baseline measurement and a series of accurately measured angles.
Initial baseline
A
B
An initial baseline of known length, position, and orientation is created.
Landmark (C)
A
B
A landmark is selected that can be seen from points A and B. Using a theodolite, the angles from A and B to this landmark are determined. The distances AC and BC can now be trigonometrically calculated.
Landmark (D)
New baseline
C
A
B
This process can be repeated over a large area by using one of the newly found distances (AC) or (BC) as a new baseline.
Triangulation can be used to determine the relative positions of landmarks over large areas of land. Part of the Inner and Outer Hebrides, UK, is shown here.
Fourth landmark
First landmark
Second landmark
Second baseline
Third landmark
Initial baseline

suspension bridge, a bridge suspended by vertical rods (hangers) from cables supported by towers on each bank. The cables are anchored to the bank behind the towers and loads are distributed evenly among the hangers by a stiffening girder beneath the roadway (deck). A related bridge type is the cable-stayed bridge, in which spans are supported on either side of a high tower by cables fanning out from the tower to points along the deck. (For illustrations of both bridge types, see *bridge.) Although early bridges used rope or iron chains, most modern bridges use wire for the suspension cables. Twisted-wire cables were probably first used by *Seguin, but the US engineer John Roebling (1806–69), in his Niagara Bridge (1842), pioneered the use of bundles of parallel-stranded wire, spun *in situ* and then compacted into ropes. Deck instability in wind caused the spectacular failure of the Tacoma Narrows Bridge, Washington, USA, in 1940. The Severn Bridge in the UK (see table overleaf) was the first suspension bridge to use *box-girders of aerofoil cross-section for the deck. This minimizes turbulence and uplift in high winds. The deck hangers are inclined rather than vertical, to damp down wind-induced oscillations.

suspension system, the means whereby the wheels of a land vehicle sustain the vehicle's body in such a way that the irregularities of track or road are not transmitted. Road vehicles had no suspension until the development of systems for use on horse-drawn *carriages, in which the carriage body was suspended by leather braces from curved wooden or iron members. In about 1804, elliptical *springs were developed for coaches, and early 'horseless carriages' used a similar arrangement. Most modern *motor-car suspension systems use helically coiled steel springs, which are designed with the required amount of flexibility for a particular load. Springs with linear characteristics (where the flexion of the spring is proportional to the load on it) allow an excessive amount of movement when heavily loaded. For this reason springs which flex less as the load on them is increased are commonly used. Usually a *shock absorber is contained within the spring, the combined unit being known as a McPherson strut. Railway wagons and *lorries formerly used heavy-duty leaf springs for suspension, but springs that use compressed air are now becoming usual on these vehicles.

Important suspension bridges

Name	Location	Date	Main span m (feet)	Remarks
Lan Jin	Yunnan, China	*c.*65	76 (250)	Iron chains with a timber deck
Menai	Menai Strait, Wales, UK	1826	177 (580)	Chains with wrought iron links; rebuilt 1940
Fribourg	Sarine Valley, France	1834	265 (870)	Iron wire cables
Wheeling	Ohio River, W. Virginia, USA	1849	308 (1,010)	First long-span wire cable bridge in USA
Brooklyn	East River, New York, USA	1883	486 (1,596)	
George Washington	Hudson River, New York, USA	1931	1,067 (3,500)	Major leap forward in distance spanned
Golden Gate	San Francisco, California, USA	1937	1,280 (4,200)	
Mackinac	Michigan, USA	1957	1,158 (3,800)	Two side-spans of 549 m (1,800 feet) make this longest continually suspended bridge in world
Severn	River Severn, near Bristol, UK	1966	988 (3,240)	Major design advances, including box deck of aerofoil section
Atatürk	Bosphorus, Istanbul, Turkey	1973	1,074 (3,524)	Used design features developed for Severn Bridge
Humber	River Humber, Kingston-upon-Hull, UK	1979	1,410 (4,626)	Main span currently longest in world
Akashi–Kaiko	Akashi Straits, Japan	Projected completion 1998	1,780 (5,840)	Double-decked road and rail bridge, open-truss design

Suśruta (2nd century AD), Indian physician, thought to have been a surgeon, to whom is attributed the *Suśruta-samhitā*, an important early medical treatise (*samhitā* means a collection of texts or verses). Although Suśruta is judged to have written the treatise in the 2nd century AD, many of the techniques described are much older. The treatise is of particular importance for its description of surgical techniques, in which ancient Hindu medicine excelled. Of particular note are operations for removing stones from the bladder, and plastic surgery of the nose (rhinoplasty). The *Suśruta-samhitā* and a second important treatise, the *Charaka-samhitā*, were translated into Arabic in about AD 800, and through Arabic translations influenced European medicine until the 17th century.

Swan, Sir Joseph Wilson (1828–1914), British chemist, inventor of the light bulb. In 1848 he first became interested in the possibility (suggested by J. W. Starr in 1845) of making a lamp which was based on an electrically heated filament glowing in an evacuated glass bulb (see *incandescent lamp). However, it was not until 1878 that he was able to demonstrate a satisfactory light bulb, which incorporated a carbon filament. He proceeded to manufacture the light bulb, but came into conflict with *Edison over patents. The conflict was eventually resolved, and a joint company was formed in 1883. Swan also invented a dry photographic plate (1871), foreshadowing the development of photographic film.

sweetener, artificial, any substance other than a *sugar that is capable of producing a sweet taste. One of the most widely used artificial sweeteners is saccharin, discovered by the US chemists Ira Remsen and Constantine Fahlberg in 1879, and found to be 500 to 600 times sweeter than sugar. It was considered to be inert and therefore harmless, but some research suggests that it may have toxic properties when fed in large doses to rats. In recent years a more popular alternative has been found, aspartame. This is the product of two naturally occurring amino acids, phenylalanine and aspartic acid. In the UK only twelve sweeteners are permitted as *food additives and strict regulations govern their addition to foods such as fruit drinks, preserves, ice-creams, and slimmers' products.

swing bridge, a bridge that is supported at its centre by a pier, on which it can be rotated. The bridge, usually a steel truss cantilever, is used to cross waterways at a low clearance height while permitting tall shipping occasionally to pass through. Its clear channel for shipping is slightly less than half the bridge length. The *Suez Canal is crossed at Al-Firdān by a twin swing bridge spanning 168 m (552 feet) between piers.

swing-wing aeroplane (variable geometry aeroplane), an aeroplane that has its wings pivoted so that the angle of sweep can be altered in flight. It can thus take off and land at slower speeds (and hence on shorter runways) than otherwise similar aircraft, with the wings extended out from the fuselage. In flight, the wings can be swung back at a sharper angle for efficient *supersonic flight. Examples include the General Dynamics F-111 and Panavia Tornado *fighter-bombers. The device should not be confused with the folding wings on some naval aircraft, which aid storage aboard ship.

switch, an on–off means of controlling the operation of an electric circuit. Switches are usually *electromechanical devices in which the action of pushing a lever makes, or breaks, a pair of contacts connected to the electric circuit. Various types of switch are available depending on the application. These include toggle and rocker switches, microswitches (miniature switches designed to be actuated by a mechanical force), *relays, and push-buttons. The latter provide a pulse-type output, because they quickly return to their initial state when released. Electronic switches usually embody a semiconductor device such as a *transistor, and have no mechanical actuation. Rather, as in a relay operation, one electronic signal is used to control another. Electronic switches have the advantages of a very high operation speed (10 million to 100 million times faster than other switches), high reliability, and low cost. However, they cannot be used for high-power applications. Digital *computers depend on the operation of millions of electronic switches. The term 'switch' is also used to denote the complex digital electronic equipment in a *telephone exchange that switches a call from any incoming channel to any outgoing one.

switch gear, the general arrangement of *switches, *circuit-breakers, *transformers, *fuses, and associated equipment used in the generation and transmission of electrical power. Considerations of the working voltage and current requirements primarily determine switch gear arrangement. Adequate spacing of conductors and insulation is needed to ensure that short circuiting does not take place, and conductors must be large enough to ensure appropriate current-carrying capacity without overload. Switch gear should be sited as closely as possible to the heaviest electrical load in the circuit, to avoid expensive cabling.

sword, a *hand weapon with a metal blade and a handle (hilt) with a handguard. The history of the sword began in the Bronze Age when the discovery of bronze-casting made possible the production of a weapon heavier and longer than the flint knife. The blade of a sword can be designed to cut, to thrust, or to do both, and it may be given a single or a double edge. Many different kinds of swords have been made: the sabre, the Indian *tulwar*, and the Japanese *katana* are all examples of cutting swords; the rapier and the Turkish *kilj* are thrusting swords; the Roman *gladius* and most swords of medieval Europe were cut-and-thrust weapons. The sword has been regarded by civilizations around the globe as the symbol of the professional warrior; of all hand weapons, it has remained the longest in use. Swords of modified design are used in the sport of fencing, in which opponents wear protective clothing and face masks.

synchromesh *gearbox.

synchronous motor *electric motor.

synchrotron *particle accelerator.

synthesizer, an integrated system for the production of electronic sounds in real time. The earliest synthesizer was a research instrument built by the US electrical engineer Harry F. Olson and first demonstrated in 1955. Commercial synthesizers first came on the market in 1964. These instruments used continuously varying voltages to manipulate electronically generated sound waves, and were capable of producing an enormous range of sounds. In 1970 the first digital synthesizers appeared: these combined the flexibility of a voltage-controlled synthesizer with the control of a computerized music studio. Modern instruments offer a wide range of facilities, and can be used for composition, recording, or live performance.

synthetic fibre, a fibre made from synthetic materials. In contrast to *rayons and other manufactured fibres derived from naturally occurring *polymers, synthetic fibres are polymeric molecules, usually *plastics, manufactured from simpler chemical materials (often *petrochemicals). The fibres are 'spun' by *extrusion of liquid polymer through the fine holes of a spinneret (see *spinning). Synthetic fibres may be used directly as continuous filaments, but more often they are cut or broken into shorter (staple) fibres, which can be spun into *yarn either alone, or in blends with such natural fibres as cotton or wool.

There are many synthetic fibre types, but the *polyesters, *acrylic fibres, and the polyamides or *nylons are the most widely used. They are used principally in *textiles, but nylon and polyester fibres also have industrial applications, where strength and durability are required. Other important synthetics are spun fibres of *polythene and *polypropylene. These are used in large quantities for carpets and other floor-coverings, for rot-resistant sacking, for *nets, cord, and *rope. Since problems with dyeing these materials have been overcome, they have also increasingly been used for woven and knitted fabrics. Polyurethane and other synthetic, rubber-like fibres are used in the making of elastic, and for manufacturing stretch fabrics such as Lycra. Other synthetic fibres are used structurally: aramids (see *nylon) and *carbon fibres are used in the manufacture of light, strong *composite materials. (See also *yarn texturing.)

synthetic fuel, any liquid fuel made from coal for use either in *internal-combustion engines and other combustion systems or as a feedstock in the *chemical industry. There are essentially two routes to the production of synthetic fuels. In the synthesis route, the coal structure is completely destroyed to produce a gas mixture which, in its passage over a catalyst, is synthesized to gasoline, diesel fuel, and methanol. The Fischer–Tropsch process (invented in 1925), which operates this route, is the only coal liquefaction process in commercial operation. In the liquid solvent extraction (LSE) route, crushed coal is heated with a coal-derived solvent and is then reacted with hydrogen to give a liquid product rich in aromatics (*hydrocarbons containing a *benzene ring) and suitable for *reforming to valuable fuels at low cost and with available refinery techniques. The LSE process is more efficient and cheaper than the synthesis process, although these advantages are offset by the latter's ability to use cheap, high-ash coal. The future demand for gasoline, diesel, and aviation fuels could be met in part by using coal-derived liquid fuels as the refinery feedstock.

system building, a labour-saving building method in which structural assemblies far larger than could easily be made on site are prefabricated in factories. For low- and high-rise residential buildings, large floor units and storey-height wall panels are built at the factory in *pre-cast concrete. The units are then transported to the site and assembled on a conventional *foundation by a tower *crane. For lightweight buildings, storey-height timber *frames are

Temporary yurts (traditional central-Asian dwellings) **system-built** from modern materials and erected for homeless victims of the 1988 earthquake in the Soviet republic of Armyanskaya, SSR (Armenia).

used; units can be linked horizontally or vertically to a limited height. Problems with system-built housing include inadequate structural connections between units, as exemplified by the partial collapse in 1968 of the Ronan Point flats in London after a small gas explosion. Rain penetration at ineffective joints causes dampness, often exacerbated by severe condensation where the wall–floor junction interrupts thermal insulation.

system identification *dynamic modelling.

systems analysis, the investigation, analysis, design, implementation, and evaluation of an information system, usually with the aim of computerizing some human activity. The main functions of systems analysis may be broken down as follows. First, the problem to be solved (for example, the computerization of a business's accounting system) must be accurately defined. The existing system is then investigated to understand how it works, using techniques such as *flow charting and decision tables (tables that indicate actions to be taken under various conditions, the decision being the selection between alternatives). Next, the results of the investigation are analysed and used as the basis for the design of a new system, making optimum use of the available computer hardware, software, and staffing resources. The new system is then implemented and evaluated, and those people concerned with using and running it are taught how to operate and maintain it efficiently.

systems engineering, the design of complex systems with many interacting elements so as to optimize performance in some agreed way. Systems engineering grew out of *operational research, a discipline developed in the UK during World War II in an attempt to solve wartime logistical problems. The invention of the digital computer was a key influence on the development of systems engineering as an interdisciplinary area, since rapidly evolving *information technology not only increased the complexity of engineered systems many times, but also provided the tools with which to analyse, design, and control such complex systems. Application areas of systems engineering vary widely, including the core technological fields of *automation, *control systems, and *mechatronics, but also public services, large commercial organizations, and ecological management and conservation. In systems engineering, the problem to be solved is first formulated in as precise a manner as possible by specifying system goals, performance measures, and important variables. Next, the problem is broken down, the important sub-systems and their interrelationships (interfaces) being identified. The individual sub-systems are then modelled and designed, followed by design of the complete system. Finally, the sub-systems and then the complete system are implemented and tested. Each individual stage may itself involve the repeated validation, testing, and possible modification of the various earlier stages. Provided the problem has been appropriately identified, specified, and partitioned, the modelling and design of individual system elements will often be carried out by specialist engineers, together with experts in *reliability and risk assessment, mathematical modelling, computer *simulation, and so on. An important task of the systems engineer as 'technical generalist' is to ensure that the eventual integration of the work of such specialist individuals or teams results in an overall system conforming to specification.

T

Takamine Jokichi (1854–1922), Japanese industrial chemist. In 1887 he left government service to establish a factory making superphosphate fertilizer. He later developed a process for making the starch-digesting enzyme diastase, which was adopted in 1894 by the pharmaceutical manufacturer Parke, Davis and Company (USA). In 1901 he was the first to isolate a pure hormone, adrenalin.

Talbot, William Henry Fox (1800–77), British inventor of the calotype, the basis of modern photographic processes. In 1835, he took a paper negative photograph of his home, Lacock Abbey. Later he made the negative transparent, which allowed many positive prints to be made from one negative. In 1841 Talbot found that, using a paper sensitized with silver iodide and bromide, a latent negative was formed, which could be developed later using the arsenic salt of gallic acid (3,4,5-tribenzoic acid). The latent image system made much shorter exposure times possible. Talbot's *The Pencil of Nature* (1846) was the first book to be illustrated with photographs.

tank, a heavy, enclosed, armoured fighting vehicle that moves on *caterpillar tracks. Tanks were developed concurrently in the UK and France in 1915 and 1916, as a possible method of breaking through the German trenches. They were first used in action in 1916 during the Battle of the River Somme (France). By 1918 the design included a central turret on top of the chassis, which replaced the frontal or side gun-mountings of most early tanks. The tank's tactical role largely changed from *artillery support for infantry to the defeat of other tanks. Tanks are driven by internal-combustion engines, and have all-round armour, with the thickest plating at the front of the hull. Today they are usu-

An early calotype by Fox **Talbot**. Talbot's calotype process was the first to involve a film negative, from which many positive prints could be made.

The *Esso Europa*, a German oil **tanker** built in 1969.

ally armed with a large-calibre *anti-tank gun (105–120 mm, 4.1–4.7 inches) carried in a turret. Some tanks can also fire missiles, and most carry two or three *machine-guns. They have a crew of four or five and constitute the main ground offensive weapon in modern armies.

tanker, a ship designed to carry bulk liquid cargoes, especially petroleum, at sea. The tanker hull is almost completely taken up by several large tanks, separated by narrow transverse compartments as a safety measure. The earliest tankers were built in the late 19th century. Until 1956 their size, around 30,000 tonnes, was dictated by the limitations of the *Suez Canal. Closure of the canal due to local wars in 1956 and 1967, coupled with huge increases in the demand for oil stimulated by world-wide growth in the use of motorized transport, led to vastly bigger tankers of 400,000–500,000 tonnes. Tankers are also designed and built for the transport of liquefied gas and, on a smaller scale, of wine.

tank locomotive, a *steam locomotive in which all the required coal and water is carried on the main frame rather than in a separate tender. The coal is stored in a small bunker at the rear behind the cab, while the water is stored in tanks over, under, or alongside the boiler. Tank locomotives were designed so that they could readily be driven either forwards or backwards. They were particularly suitable for shunting duties or for operations where turning facilities were limited.

tanning, the process by which animal hides are made into leather. The tanning process displaces water from the interstices of the hide's protein fibres, and binds the fibres together. The oldest tanning method, still widely used, is vegetable tanning, in which the hide is soaked in a tannin-rich extract from the bark and roots of plants or trees. In mineral tanning, the hide is soaked in a solution of mineral salts, usually of chromium. This process is much faster than vegetable tanning and is used particularly for light leathers. Oil tanning uses fish or other oils or fats. Synthetic tanning agents are also widely used. After the leather has been tanned, it is dried, dyed, lubricated with oils and greases, and then dried again. Final finishing involves stretching and softening the leather, and coating the surface to resist abrasion and cracking.

tantalum (symbol Ta, at. no. 73, r.a.m. 180.95), a dense, blue-grey metallic element. It occurs in the ore tantalite. Tantalum alloys are used for dental and surgical instruments and for spinnerets for *synthetic fibre production. It is added to *steels to prevent weld-decay and improves the performance of *nickel alloys in gas-turbines. *Sintered tantalum is used for electrolytic *capacitors. Tantalum forms an extremely hard carbide, which is used as an abrasive and in cutting tools for machining steel.

tap (US, faucet), a device for controlling liquid flow from a pipe. The water passes upwards through the *valve seating—a horizontal opening within the body of the tap—to discharge from the mouth into a basin or other receptacle. The opening is closed by screwing down a circular disc faced with a soft washer, which is compressed against the valve seating. The valve stem is sealed against the body of the tap by a gland, which prevents water escaping upwards when the tap is closed.

A tap is also a hard steel hand-tool used for cutting internal screw-threads. A tap of appropriate size, with pre-cut threads, is thrust into the hole to be threaded and then turned with a tap wrench. Bolts and other external threads are cut with a similar tool, the die or die stock.

tapeless recording *sound recording and reproduction.

tape recorder, a machine that records and replays sound on *magnetic tape. During recording the sound is converted by a microphone into an oscillating electrical signal, which when passed through the coils of an electromagnet produces an equivalent magnetic field. As it passes the electromagnet (the recording head), the magnetic tape becomes magnetized in a pattern reflecting the sound being recorded. On replay the magnetic pattern on the tape induces in a second electromagnet (the replay head) an electrical signal which, after amplification, drives a loudspeaker. The Danish engineer Valdemar Poulsen invented the earliest tape recorder in 1898, which recorded sound on a wire. Subsequent developments have included plastic tape in 1935, stereophonic recording in 1958, and *Dolby systems to reduce surface hiss from cassettes in 1966.

tear-gas, any of a group of gases that affect the mucous membranes of the eyes, causing irritation and copious watering. Tear-gases are usually organic halogen compounds, the most widely used being Mace gas (alpha-chloroacetophenone) and CS gas (1-*ortho*-chlorophenyl-2,2-dicyanoethene). Tear-gases are designed principally as riot-control agents, and are used in this role by police forces in many countries.

Technicolor *cinematography.

technology. Technology can be defined as the study of the mechanical arts and applied sciences, but the term has changed its meaning over the years and is still to some extent fluid. Many fundamental technologies—the *smelting and working of metals, *spinning and weaving of textiles, and the firing of clay, for example—were empirically developed at the dawn of civilization, long before any concept of science existed. (See *prehistoric technology.) With the advent in about 3000 BC of the first major civilizations in *Egypt and Mesopotamia (and a little later in *India and *China), many new technologies were developed—*irrigation systems, *road networks and wheeled vehicles, a pictographic form of writing, and new *building techniques. Other civilizations subsequently became important technological centres, notably those of *Greece and Rome, the *Arab empire of the 7th to 10th centuries, and the Mayan, Aztec, and Toltec civilizations of *meso-America. In the mid-16th century the focus of technological change shifted to Europe, with the beginning of the Scientific Revolution. This was both an intellectual revolution and a practical one, questioning established dogma, reinterpreting old ideas, and seeking to advance knowledge of the natural world by observation and by experiment. Initially the new ideas and techniques engendered official persecution, but by the mid-17th century the tide of opinion had changed, as indicated by the formation under royal patronage of the *Académie des Sciences in France and the *Royal Society in Britain.

By the late 17th century, technology essentially meant engineering, as is indicated by the title of a British book by T. Phillips, published in 1706: *Technology: A Description of Arts, Especially the Mechanical.* Half a century later, however, *Diderot's monumental twenty-eight volume *Encyclopédie* (1751–72) encompassed not only the mechanical but also what he called the liberal arts, including glass-making, agriculture, brewing, and soap-boiling. In the UK in 1866, the teacher and author Charles Tomlinson published his three-volume *Cyclopaedia of Useful Arts, Mechanical and Chemical, Manufactures, Mining, and Engineering*, which, by including the old empirical processes as well as those that had arisen through the application of scientific knowledge, approached the modern concept of technology.

During the 19th century science began to create many new technologies, such as the electric *telegraph, the *telephone, *electricity generation and supply, and *photography. The trend continued into the 20th century with the introduction of many goods and services made possible only because of further advances in science. These have included *radio and *television, *sound recording and reproduction, *synthetic fibres, a wide range of pharmaceutical products, *nuclear power, and perhaps most important of all, the development of the *computer and *information technology. Since the 1970s *pollution, depletion of *energy resources, and other adverse effects of technology have caused increasing public concern. This has led to the growth of alternative technologies, with an emphasis on renewable energy sources such as *solar and *wind power, the *recycling of raw materials, and the conservation of energy.

Outside the West, only the most basic technology is available to hundreds of millions of people. *Tropical agriculture remains resistant to the application of science, and medical technology has made only limited impact in the Third World: according to a recent estimate by the World Health Organization, four-fifths of the world's population still have no regular access to health services of any kind. For people still locked into subsistence agriculture, the convergence of technology and applied science, which the Western world takes for granted, is largely irrelevant. Moreover, attempts to introduce Western technology have in many cases produced little improvement and often created an economic reliance on Western products that has sapped the wealth of Third World countries. More recently, Western aid has sought to develop *appropriate technologies, using local materials and techniques, in partnership with the indigenous peoples.

Teflon *PTFE.

telecommunications, the communication of information (usually audio, visual, or computer data) over a distance, transmitted by various means. Early techniques included signal fires and *semaphore; modern systems include *telephony, *telex, *radio, and *television. Over short distances electrical telegraph or telephone signals can be transmitted via two-wire telephone lines without additional processing. For longer distances, various techniques of *modulation and/or coding at the transmitter, followed by *demodulation or decoding at the receiver, are employed to match the transmitted signal to the properties of the telecommunications channel. Transmission may be to a single receiver or it may be *broadcast to many individual receivers; it may be direct or *switched through a complex *network. Until recently most telecommunications systems were analog in nature, but now the message signal commonly undergoes *digitization at the transmitter, using *pulse code modulation or similar techniques: it is then decoded into usable form (sound, print, video, and so on) at the receiver. The widespread digitization of telecommunications signals has begun a trend in many countries towards the combination of hitherto separate systems into a single Integrated Services Digital Network (ISDN). It has also resulted in the convergence of computing and telecommunications (see *information technology). Because of the complexity of modern telecommunications systems, standardization bodies such as the *International Telecommunications Union (ITU), and the International Organization for Standardization (ISO) have taken on great importance, particularly in the design of 'open' systems which can be easily interconnected. (See also *communications satellite, *optical fibre.)

telegraphy, the transmission of information by coded electrical impulses, transmitted and received manually or by machine. Telegraph channels require only a narrow frequency *bandwidth, and can be *multiplexed to allow many transmissions along one line, so telegraphy is a cheap and efficient communications medium. The earliest electrical telegraph was built in 1774 by Georges Lesage in Geneva, but it was a complicated arrangement requiring a wire for each letter of the alphabet. In the mid-19th century equipment designed by *Morse in the USA transmitted information along a single wire, using the *Morse code: a similar electric telegraph was developed by *Cooke in the UK. Initially, skilled operators were needed to code and send messages, but subsequently telegraphic transmission and reception became mechanized (see *teleprinter). Submarine *cables provided the first transatlantic telecommunications link in 1866, but most telegraph signals today are carried by telephone lines or radio waves. *Fax and *telex are the most common modern telegraphic systems.

telemetry, the rapid transmission of readings from an instrument or instruments to a location remote from the site of measurement. Telemetry has many applications: it may be used because the measurement site is physically remote, as in space exploration or meteorology; because the site is dangerous or lethal to humans, for example, the interior of a nuclear reactor; or because a site is in some way inaccessible, for example, at the bottom of a borehole through rock, or within the body. Occasionally fluid transmission or some other mechanical linkage may be used for data transmission, but usually the data travels either as electrical signals in a wire or as *radio signals through space. Three stages are involved in telemetry. At the measurement site, the output from the instrument is converted by a *transducer into an electrical or radio signal. The signal is then transmitted to a receiving station. Finally, at the receiving station the data signal is interpreted and displayed in some way, and may also be recorded for future reference.

telephone exchange (US, telephone office), a common connecting point for the telephone lines through which calls to and from receivers in a particular area are routed. The earliest exchange (1878) handled twenty-one lines, but by the mid-1880s exchanges could handle hundreds or thousands of subscribers. The first automatic telephone exchange was invented by a US undertaker, Almon Strowger, and became operational in 1897. In the 1920s and 1930s such automatic electromechanical switchboards were introduced in Europe and North America. These switchboards could monitor thousands of telephone lines, determine which required service, provide a dialling tone, remember a telephone number as it was dialled and then set up appropriate connections, monitor the call while in progress, and break the connection at the end of the call. Electromechanical exchanges have now largely been replaced by electronic switchboards, which serve similar functions but are smaller, faster, more reliable, more flexible, and cheaper. Newer connection systems integrate subscribers not only to telephones but also to numerous other facilities and databases.

telephone receiver, an instrument used in *telephony to convert sound waves into a corresponding electrical signal for transmission, and to receive incoming electrical signals and convert them back to sound, thus allowing two-way communication between a pair of receivers. *Bell demonstrated the first practical telephone receiver in 1876. It used the same device for both transmission and reception of sound, but soon afterwards the carbon microphone, patented by *Edison in 1878, was added. Early receivers were basically similar to those used today. Sound entering the mouthpiece is converted into the mechanical vibration of a thin diaphragm, which is pressed against an assembly of carbon granules. The electrical resistance of the granules fluctuates as they are vibrated by the diaphragm, causing changes in strength of an electrical current through the granules. The receiving apparatus consists of a steel diaphragm adjacent to an electromagnet. Incoming electrical signals cause fluctuations in the attraction of the magnet for the diaphragm, causing it to vibrate and produce sound. In modern receivers, signals are *digitized before transmission, to reduce the effects of noise and distortion. (See also *cellular telephone.)

telephony, the transmission of speech via an electrical signal between one *telephone receiver and another, the signal being transmitted either along a *cable or by *radio or *optical-fibre transmission. *Bell patented the first telephone receiver and transmitter in the UK and the USA during 1876 and demonstrated it in Philadelphia. Transmission between receivers was electrical, along wires, the signal being an exact copy of the sound wave. Telephony quickly developed into a sophisticated communications system over fairly short distances; by 1887 there were over 100,000 telephone subscribers world-wide. Further development took place more slowly. Hard-drawn copper wire soon replaced steel for telephone wires, being a better conductor of electricity. Underground and submarine cables were introduced in cities and for crossing water. Interference between two or more adjacent lines was reduced by using an all-metal (two-wire) circuit instead of one in which the earth was used as a conducting path. *Inductors at regular intervals along a telephone line were found to reduce distortion over long distances, and later *repeaters, which boosted or amplified the telephone signal, were introduced. Transatlantic telephone transmission relied on high-frequency *radio transmission until 1956, because submarine cable links were not sufficiently reliable. *Communications satellite links using microwaves are now used for many international calls. Optical-fibre cables are a recent introduction; they give virtually noise-free transmission. Another recent development has been the *digitization of telephone signals. Digital signals can be *multiplexed easily, and *pulse code modulation offers a way of transmitting the digital signals with minimal noise or distortion. In addition, such a signal can be strengthened and reshaped *en route*, and digital signals are in an appropriate form for computer processing. Telephone circuits now also carry *telex, *fax, and *television signals in a form that can be fed directly into appropriate receivers. Additionally, they are used to enable computers to communicate over large distances. As a consequence, telephone systems have become an integral part of modern telecommunications. (See also *cellular telephone, *paging system, *radio telephone.)

teleprinter (US, teletypewriter), a device that transmits messages entered through its keyboard and prints the messages at the receiver. Invented in the 1900s as the printing *telegraph, the first teleprinter exchange was not available until the 1930s. Originally, relays converted the message into electric signals; subsequent developments concentrated on various methods of displaying the message prior to transmission, enabling operators to check for errors and perhaps store the message. Such methods included punched tape, printing on gummed tape for telegrams, magnetic tape, or more recently computer disks and *visual display units.

telescope, an instrument used to view magnified images of very distant objects. Optical telescopes collect and focus light to produce images of distant objects. *Radio telescopes use arrays of *antennae or concave metal dishes to collect radio waves from objects in space. Optical telescopes were probably first manufactured in about 1608 by the Dutch spectacle-maker Hans Lippershey, though their invention pre-dates this. They soon became astronomy's most important instrument, and now also form part of binoculars, gunsights, and periscopes. Reflecting telescopes use concave

Television camera

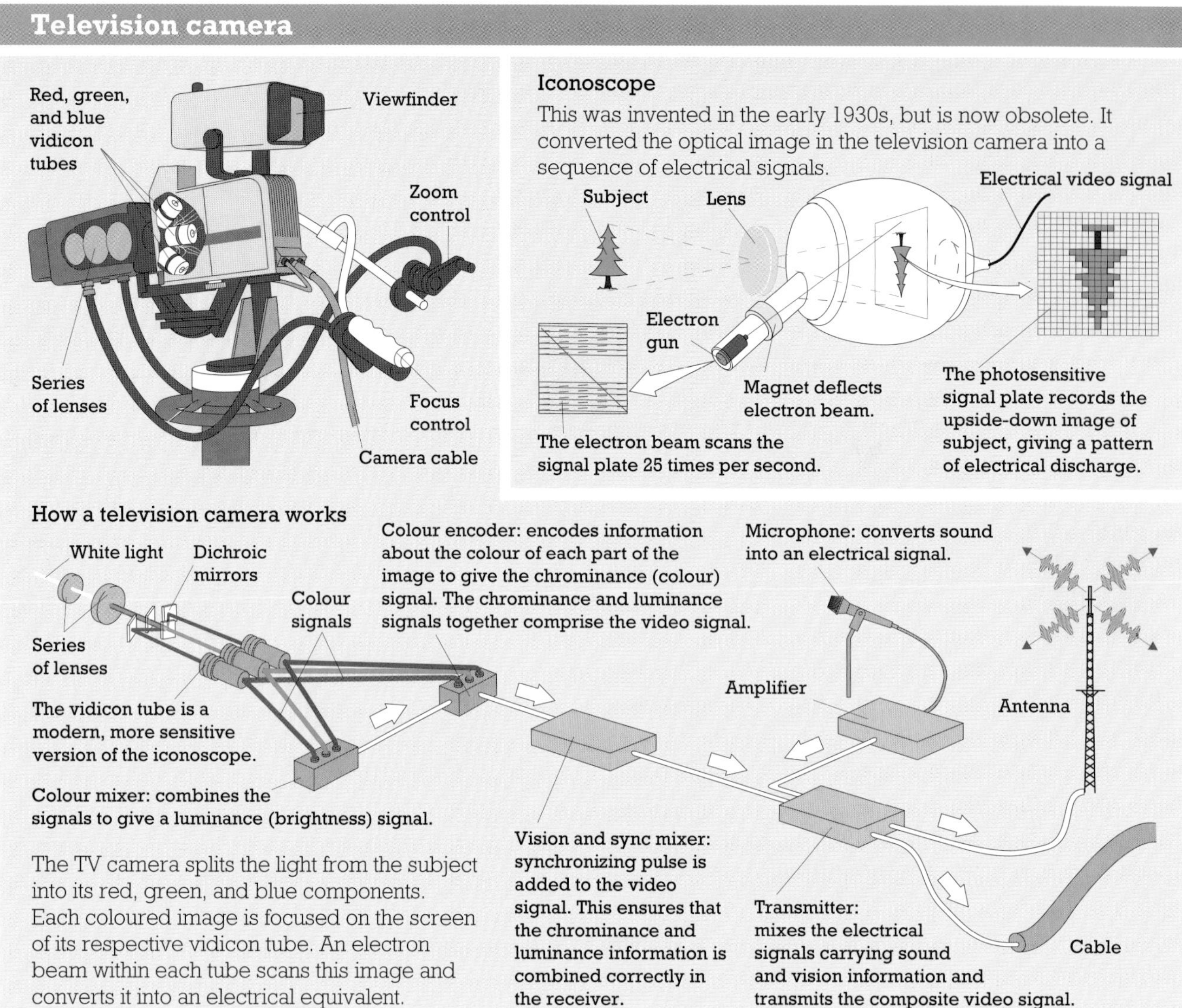

Red, green, and blue vidicon tubes
Viewfinder
Zoom control
Series of lenses
Focus control
Camera cable
Iconoscope
This was invented in the early 1930s, but is now obsolete. It converted the optical image in the television camera into a sequence of electrical signals.
Subject
Lens
Electrical video signal
Electron gun
Magnet deflects electron beam.
The photosensitive signal plate records the upside-down image of subject, giving a pattern of electrical discharge.
The electron beam scans the signal plate 25 times per second.
How a television camera works
White light
Dichroic mirrors
Colour signals
Series of lenses
Colour encoder: encodes information about the colour of each part of the image to give the chrominance (colour) signal. The chrominance and luminance signals together comprise the video signal.
Microphone: converts sound into an electrical signal.
Amplifier
Antenna
The vidicon tube is a modern, more sensitive version of the iconoscope.
Colour mixer: combines the signals to give a luminance (brightness) signal.
The TV camera splits the light from the subject into its red, green, and blue components. Each coloured image is focused on the screen of its respective vidicon tube. An electron beam within each tube scans this image and converts it into an electrical equivalent.
Vision and sync mixer: synchronizing pulse is added to the video signal. This ensures that the chrominance and luminance information is combined correctly in the receiver.
Transmitter: mixes the electrical signals carrying sound and vision information and transmits the composite video signal.
Cable

mirrors, and refracting telescopes use convex *lenses to collect light from distant objects, focusing it to form an inverted, real image. This image acts as a close object for the eyepiece lens, which forms a magnified but inverted virtual image of it. In astronomy a photographic plate, or more recently a *charge-coupled device, often replaces the eyepiece. Telescopes for non-astronomical uses have extra lens systems (prisms in binoculars) to give an upright image. In astronomical telescopes light collection is as important as magnification. Large mirrors are used (up to 6 m, 20 feet, in diameter) to collect as much light as possible from faint objects. Mirrors are easier to make and support than large lenses and cause fewer distortions. They are mounted so that they can be driven to follow the movement of the stars across the sky. Astronomers are now developing telescope mirrors with adaptive optics, which can change shape to compensate for distortions of images cuased by the Earth's atmosphere. (See also *observatory.)

teletext, a television-based information system. Teletext is a *videotex service, transmitting information in the unused area (usually the top four lines) of a normal television signal. By using a special decoder attached to the television set, this information becomes visible on the entire screen as pages of text and graphics.

television, a system for converting visual images (and accompanying sound) into an electrical signal that can be transmitted, either through an electrical cable or on a radio *waveband, to receivers that reproduce the images on a screen. Transmission of all the visual and sound information of a moving scene through one electrical circuit or radio beam requires considerable processing; all the visual information in a scene cannot be transmitted simultaneously. Instead, the *television camera electronically scans the scene and divides it into 300,000 or more elements, for each of which an electrical impulse, proportional to the amount of light in that area of the scene, is emitted. In order to depict rapid motion smoothly, twenty-five of these scans must be made each second; motion is simulated by a rapid succession of still scenes, as in a cine-camera. A television system must thus transmit more than four million electrical impulses per second in order to give a detailed, moving image on the television screen. For transmission, the television signal is *modulated: a very large *bandwidth is needed to transmit all the information from a moving picture. The transmitted signal is picked up by the household television *antenna and reassembled in the *television receiver, which reconstructs the images so quickly that the eye is unaware that they have been assembled sequentially.

The conversion of pictures into electrical impulses first

became a possibility in 1873, when Willoughby Smith noted that the electrical resistance of selenium changed in proportion to the amount of light falling on it. A mechanical means of scanning a scene (the *Nipkow disc) was developed in 1884, and in 1926 *Baird used this mechanical system to demonstrate the first electrical transmission of moving pictures. Baird's demonstration stimulated research in the USA, the UK, the Soviet Union, and Germany. Already in 1923 *Zwyorkin had patented the *iconoscope, an electronic scanning television camera that provided the basis for the modern camera. By 1935 Germany had a regular broadcasting service, though the picture quality was poor. In the UK, the BBC began broadcasting in 1927, using Baird's mechanical system: in 1937 they began the world's first high-quality public television broadcasting service, using an electronic system developed by *Blumlein. In 1938 Baird developed a photo-mechanical colour television system, but colour broadcasts did not become viable until 1953, when a standardized electronic system compatible with existing black-and-white receivers was developed in the USA. This system, known as the NSTC system, is currently used in the USA and Japan. Elsewhere two other systems—SECAM (used in France and the Soviet Union) and PAL (used by most of Europe)—have been developed. More recent developments in television technology include the growth of *cable television; the introduction of *stereo sound; and satellite television, in which microwave transmissions are broadcast via *communications satellites either directly to domestic satellite dishes, or to *ground stations for relay via cable. The increased *bandwidth of satellite and cable systems has led to tens of television channels often being available to viewers. New developments include high-definition television (HDTV) broadcasting, in which the television images are made up of over 1,000 scanning lines instead of the current 525 or 625, and the transmission of television pictures as digital rather than analog signals. Japanese analog HDTV (Hi-Vision) television receivers were first sold in 1990. (See also *video recorder, *videotex.)

television camera, a device that converts the light from moving visual images into a series of electrical signals, which can be reconstructed by an appropriate *television receiver. The modern camera works on similar principles to the *iconoscope, although it is much more sensitive to light and produces a more detailed image (see figure). In order to make a colour television signal compatible with either black-and-white or colour receivers, it has to be split into two components, one is a high-resolution signal containing information on the brightness of the various parts of the image, the other, less detailed, containing the colour information.

television receiver, an apparatus for receiving *television signals, either from an antenna or an electrical cable, and converting the video and sound information into a picture on a screen, with accompanying sound. In a black-and-white receiver the phosphor-coated screen of a *cathode-ray tube is scanned by an electron beam. The scanning pattern is a series of parallel, near-horizontal lines that start at the top left-hand corner of the screen. Where the beam strikes the screen the phosphor glows for a moment, the intensity of the glow being proportional to the strength of the electron beam. The electron beam is controlled by information from the television signal, which regulates the strength of the electron beam as it scans, thus causing changes in light intensity on the screen corresponding to those in the original image. In a colour television receiver each portion of the screen contains microscopic dots of red, green, and blue *phosphor. The receiver carries

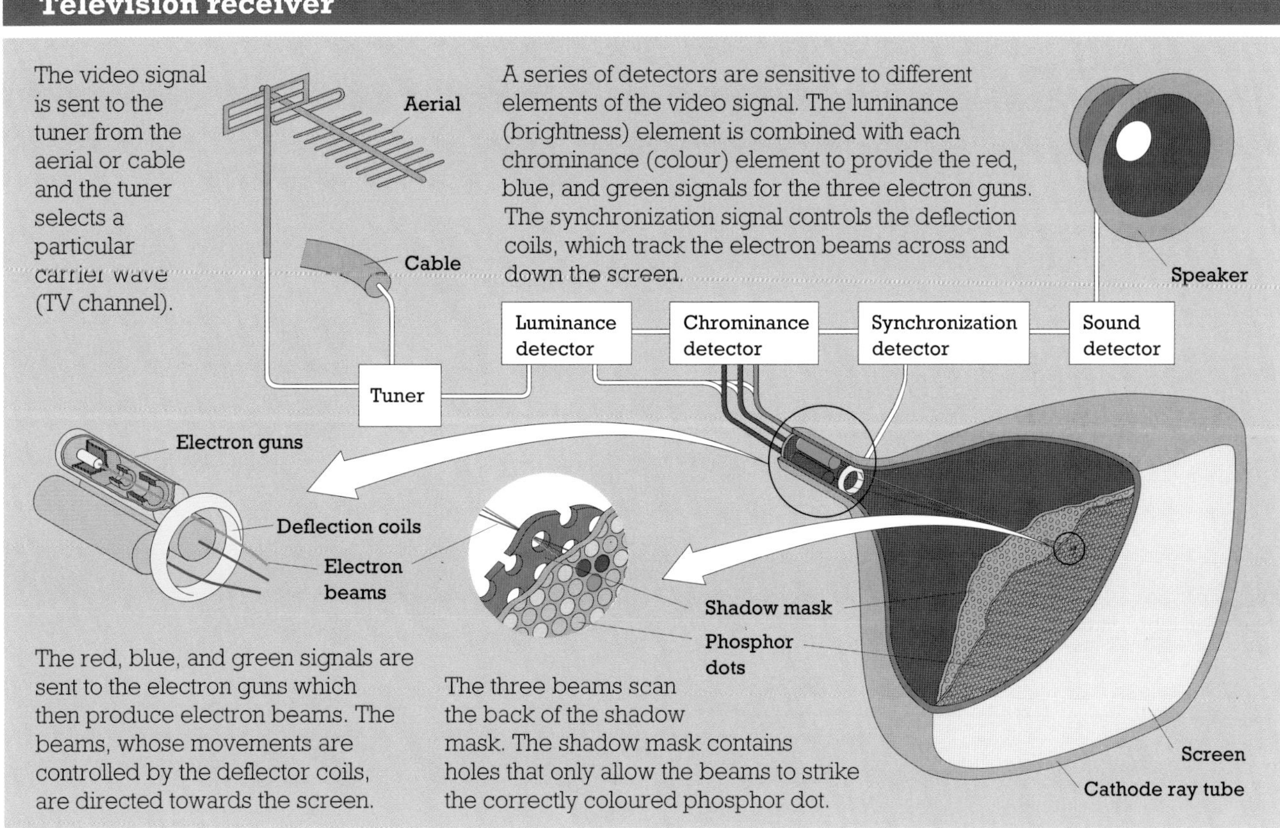
Television receiver
The video signal is sent to the tuner from the aerial or cable and the tuner selects a particular carrier wave (TV channel).
Aerial
Cable
A series of detectors are sensitive to different elements of the video signal. The luminance (brightness) element is combined with each chrominance (colour) element to provide the red, blue, and green signals for the three electron guns. The synchronization signal controls the deflection coils, which track the electron beams across and down the screen.
Speaker
Luminance detector
Chrominance detector
Synchronization detector
Sound detector
Tuner
Electron guns
Deflection coils
Electron beams
Shadow mask
Phosphor dots
The red, blue, and green signals are sent to the electron guns which then produce electron beams. The beams, whose movements are controlled by the deflector coils, are directed towards the screen.
The three beams scan the back of the shadow mask. The shadow mask contains holes that only allow the beams to strike the correctly coloured phosphor dot.
Screen
Cathode ray tube

a separate electron beam for each phosphor. Thus three separate primary *colour images are formed on the screen simultaneously, but because the dots that form each image are so small and uniformly distributed, the eye combines the three images to produce a full-colour picture (see figure). In early television receivers the screen was formed of only thirty lines, with only ten screen scans per second, resulting in a flickering, jerky motion. In most modern receivers the picture is formed of either 525 or 625 lines. Recently small *liquid crystal receivers, which do not require a tube and can therefore be much slimmer, have been developed, and research is continuing into replacing the single, large *cathode-ray tube (CRT) with thousands of very small CRTs, which are more compact and require less power.

telex, an international communications network designed on a similar basis to the *telephone network, to carry *telegraphic messages between *teleprinters. For simple messages telex has the advantage over *fax that one telex message can be transmitted to several receivers simultaneously. In 1985 an improved telex system was launched, which can use any public communications network, and is faster and cheaper.

Telford, Thomas (1757–1834), British civil engineer of Scottish extraction. In 1793, he was appointed engineer for the Ellesmere *Canal project, which included the construction of two great aqueducts. In 1804 he was engaged to build the Caledonian Canal (completed 1847); he also built the Göta Canal in Sweden. He was a great builder of *roads, building 1,500 km (930 miles) of roads in the Scottish Highlands and reconstructing the London–Holyhead highway, including the Menai suspension bridge (1826).

Teller, Edward (1908–), Hungarian-born US physicist who helped develop the hydrogen bomb. In 1941 he was briefly transferred from the George Washington University, USA, to work on the atomic bomb project, under *Oppenheimer. From 1949 to 1952 he was assistant director of the Los Alamos Scientific Laboratory and played a leading role in the development of the hydrogen bomb (see *nuclear weapon), first detonated in 1952. He helped to develop further US nuclear capability until 1960, when he returned to academic life.

tellurium (symbol Te, at. no. 52, r.a.m. 127.60), a brittle, silvery-white solid element, intermediate in properties between a non-metal and a metal. The chief use of tellurium is in the *vulcanization of rubber. It is also used to colour glass, to increase the hardness of lead in battery plates, and to improve the machinability of stainless steel.

Telstar *communications satellite.

temperature measurement For much of human history ideas about temperature have been subjective: it was recognized that objects could be relatively hot or cold, but absolute temperature values could not be attributed. In the 2nd century AD the Greek physician Galen attempted to quantify temperature on a scale of eight degrees, relative to the temperature of an equal mixture of ice and boiling water. *Galileo in 1592 developed a thermoscope, an air-filled bulb with an open-ended stem which was inverted over a container of water. The level of water in the stem varied with the ambient temperature, but it was also affected by air pressure. Variation due to pressure changes was eliminated in about 1644 by Ferdinand II of Tuscany, who sealed the neck of the flask. Ferdinand also established a society in Florence whose members conducted extensive thermometric experiments, and whose workmen became skilled at making accurate thermometers. In the early 18th century G. D. Fahrenheit, a Dutch instrument-maker, perfected the mercury *thermometer. His Fahrenheit temperature scale found widespread use, but has now been largely replaced by

Temperature measurement

Maximum–minimum thermometer

Alcohol

Steel markers

Air

Minimum temperature scale

Mercury

Maximum temperature scale

At high temperatures, the alcohol in the bulb above the minimum scale expands, pushing the mercury around the tube and up the maximum scale. As a result, the air above the maximum scale is compressed. At low temperatures the alcohol contracts, allowing the air to push the mercury around the tube and up the minimum scale. The steel markers which record the high and low temperatures are held in position by weak springs and are reset by a magnet.

Bimetallic thermometer

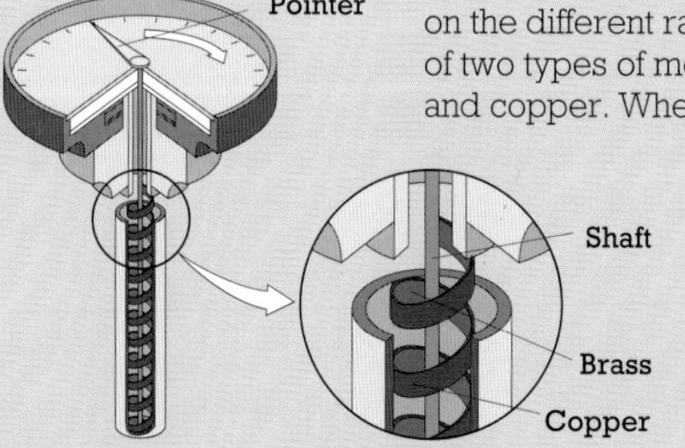

The bimetallic thermometer relies on the different rates of expansion of two types of metal, usually brass and copper. When heated, brass on the inside of the spiral expands more than the copper, and the spiral unwinds a little, moving the pointer around the scale.

Thermocouple

If two wires of different metals are joined at both ends, and the junctions between them are at different temperatures, then a potential (i.e. a voltage) is set up between them. Providing one junction is at a known temperature, the unknown temperature can be found using the millivoltmeter.

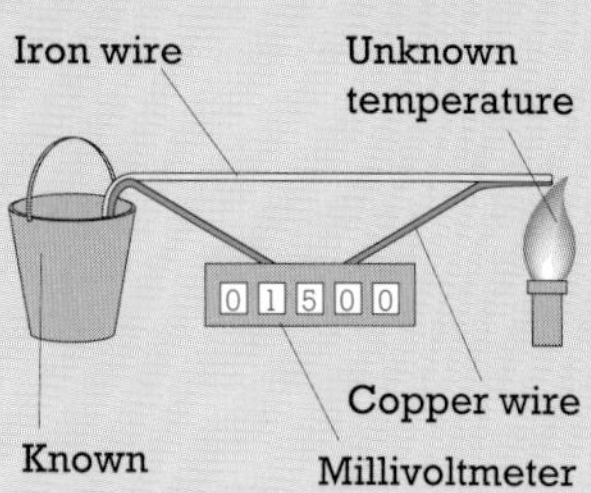

Textile fabrics

Fabric type	Description	Examples
Woven	A textile structure of interlaced warp (lengthwise) and weft (crosswise) yarns, normally at right angles to each other (see weave)	Plain weave (cambric, calico, poplin), twill, herringbone, hopsack, satin, honeycomb, crêpe, and terry. Axminster and Wilton are woven carpet structures
Knitted		
Warp-knitted	Intermeshed loops of yarn in which the yarns run substantially along the length of the fabric	Main groups are raschel, tricot, and crochet. Examples include raschel lace, queenscord, and velour (pile fabric)
Weft-knitted	Intermeshed loops of yarn in which the yarns run substantially across the fabric	Main groups are single and double jersey, and purl. Examples include plain knit (jersey), lacoste, fleece (pile fabric), rib, interlock, and piqué
Lace	Fine, open-structured fabric, made by looping, plaiting, or twisting yarns around each other	Plain net or bebbinet, Leavers lace
Tufted	Pile fabric made by inserting tufts of yarn into an existing base fabric. (This base may be woven or nonwoven.)	Tufted carpet, tufted furnishing fabrics
Nonwoven	Textile structure made substantially from fibre, rather than yarn. Techniques include adhesive bonding, needling, fluid-jet entaglement, thermal bonding, and stitch-bonding	Nonwoven interlinings, floor coverings, filter fabrics, geotextiles

the Celsius (centigrade) scale devised by the Swedish astronomer Anders Celsius in 1742. In Celsius's original scale, 0 °C was the boiling-point of water at a standard pressure, and 100 °C the freezing-point, the reverse of the modern Celsius scale. In 1848 the British physicist William Thomson (Lord Kelvin) proposed a temperature scale based on thermodynamic theory, which provides a fundamental standard with which other scales can be compared. The kelvin (K) was adopted in 1960 as the international *unit of temperature. Since the 19th century other physical properties that vary with temperature, such as electrical resistance and the thermoelectric effect (see *thermocouple), have been used for temperature measurement. Many modern thermometers are designed for specific applications and temperature ranges (see figure). Cryogenic (low-temperature) thermometers include types made from doped *semiconductors, used for ranges from 0.2 to 20 K (−272.8 to −253 °C). Thermistors—small beads or cylinders of semiconductors or complex metal oxides—can measure temperatures ranging from 4 to 600 K (−269 to −327 °C). For high temperatures, radiation thermometers such as the optical pyrometer are used: these need not touch the material being monitored, and can measure temperatures up to 1,800 K (1,527 °C). (See also *thermography.)

tempering, a heat treatment applied to steel and certain alloys. Fully hardened steel, made by *quenching from a high temperature, is too hard for many applications and is also brittle. Tempering, which involves re-heating to an intermediate temperature and cooling slowly, reduces this hardness. Tempering temperatures depend on the composition of the steel, but are frequently between 100 and 650 °C; higher temperatures give a softer, tougher product. The temperature reached can be judged by the colour of the oxide film produced on the surface of the metal, though this also depends on alloy composition.

Tennant, Charles (1768–1838), British chemical industrialist of Scottish extraction who invented bleaching powder. His apprenticeship to a weaver made him familiar with the method of *bleaching cotton by exposure to sunlight. He investigated faster bleaching methods using chemicals, and in 1799 took out a patent for a process to manufacture bleaching powder from chlorine and slaked lime (calcium hydroxide). This was an immediate success.

tension structure, a structure in which loads are carried by members in tension rather than compression. It is often a *suspended structure. In cable roofs, for example, the roof surface is carried by steel cables suspended from a high-level perimeter beam. Durable polymer woven fabrics can form tent-like buildings or stadium roofs when supported by guy cables over masts. Fabrics in tension also occur in air-supported buildings; a convex tent-like profile is produced by maintaining an internal air pressure slightly above that of the exterior. Entry is through a simple *airlock.

terminal (computing), the generic name for a *peripheral used to communicate with a computer. Terminals are frequently *visual display units and can be either 'dumb', consisting simply of a keyboard and display or *printer, or 'intelligent' *workstations, with significant storage and processing power.

terrace cultivation, a method of growing crops on steep hillsides by creating a series of narrow steps or terraces following the contours of the hillside. The method is labour-intensive, but it reduces soil erosion and water loss, maximizes the use of arable land, and better retains fertilizer to give substantially higher yields. Terrace cultivation has been practised for many centuries in China, Japan, the Philippines, around the Mediterranean, in parts of Africa, and in the South American Andes. More recently, terracing techniques have been applied in new areas such as Mexico, Australia, and parts of the USA.

Tesla, Nikola (1856–1943), Croatian-born US electrical engineer and versatile inventor. He worked as an engineer in Budapest before emigrating to the USA in 1884. For a short time he worked with *Edison on direct-current electric *generators and motors. He then transferred to *Westinghouse and concentrated on alternating-current devices, resulting in a bitter struggle with Edison over the future of the electricity industry. He developed the first alternating-current induction motor in 1888, and the Tesla coil (1891), which is widely used in radio and television sets. He ultimately became a recluse and died in poverty.

test-tube, a clear glass tube most commonly around 15 cm (6 inches) long and 1–2 cm (0.4–0.8 inches) wide, open at one end, with a rim to facilitate pouring. It is the most common

piece of chemical *laboratory equipment and is used for many routine processes, especially simple observation and small-scale testing, including gentle heating.

test-tube baby **in vitro* fertilization.

tetracycline *antibiotic.

textile. The term textile has sometimes been restricted to mean a woven fabric, but strictly it includes all types of natural and manufactured *fibres, filaments, *yarns and *fabrics together with a wide variety of products made from fibres or fibre-based materials (see table on page 351). The earliest textile fibres were based on quite coarse materials such as grasses, reeds, and rushes. They were used in prehistoric times to make screens, *basket-work, fishing *nets, matting, and *ropes. Later, techniques for using finer natural materials such as flax, jute, and animal hair were developed. From the third millennium BC other fibres, notably *cotton, *wool, and *silk, were increasingly exploited. Towards the end of the 19th century, the first significant manufactured fibres were produced: these were the *rayons, regenerated from natural cellulose. From the 1930s onwards *synthetic fibres based on polymeric materials were developed. These included *nylons, *polyesters *acrylics, and polyolefins.

Textile fibres are converted into yarn by *spinning. Fibres of different types may be spun together to form blends, for example, polyester and cotton, or wool and nylon. Yarns are then used to make fabrics by such processes as weaving on a *loom, *knitting, or *felting. *Textile-finishing processes are then often applied, to give the fabric particular properties. Some of these processes (for example, dyeing) may be used on raw fibres, yarns or complete articles. The variety of textile products is almost endless. In the developed countries, roughly half of the total weight of textiles is used for clothing. About 10 per cent is used for furnishings and household goods, while an increasing quantity of textile fibre is used in industrial, transport, sporting, and medical applications. In industry, textiles are used in conveyors, tyres, hoses, belts, containers, tarpaulins, temporary buildings, filters for liquids and gases, papermakers' wires and felts, and electrical and thermal insulation materials. In *civil engineering, textiles are used in some buildings, especially as roofing materials; geotextiles are used for earth stabilization and drainage in dams and dikes, for filtration, and for separation of aggregates such as silt from other materials in road building. High-performance fibres such as *carbon fibre and aramid fibres (variants of nylon) are used as reinforcement in *composites to form light, strong materials of high modulus (resistance to stretching). Such composites were developed for the aerospace industry, but are now used in many applications, such as tennis rackets and bicycle parts. Other sporting applications of textiles include 'breathable' garments, sails for boats, wings for hang-gliders, and artificial turf. In medicine, a variety of textiles are used for absorbing liquids in swabs and other sanitary products; for slings, bandages and other dressings; for sutures and stitches; and for prostheses, and artificial ligaments and tendons.

textile-finishing processes, ways in which fabrics are made more serviceable or attractive. Finishing processes fall into two categories—wet and dry. Wet processes include scouring, *bleaching, *fulling, and *dyeing. Scouring rids the textile material of fatty and oily substances, vegetable and mineral contaminants, and impurities resulting from *sizing. It is carried out in hot alkaline solutions for cellulosics such as cotton and in gentler solutions for wool and silk. A preliminary breakdown of the size can be achieved with *enzymes. Bleaching is used to produce finished white goods or as a preliminary treatment before *dyeing. Cotton and linen goods are commonly bleached with sodium hypochlorite, wool and silk with hydrogen peroxide. Crease-resistant treatments are now often applied to textiles: the earliest (1927) used formaldehyde to treat cotton, but treatments for most other textiles have since been developed. Dry textile-finishing processes include printing, calendering, and compressing. *Textile printing utilizes colour pastes, which are thermally fixed to the fabric after application. In calendering, cotton and linen cloths are treated with heavy rollers to produce a hard, smooth, and lustrous surface. With other cloths, the *nap is raised and sheared to produce a soft surface. Lengthways compression of cloth produces *shrink-resistant fabrics.

Terrace cultivation of rice in Bali.

textile printing, a process by which coloured designs are reproduced on textile *fabrics. In *wood-block printing, which has long been practised in the East, the pattern is carved in relief on a hardwood block. The printer spreads coloured paste on the raised pattern and then presses the block firmly on to the cloth. It is a labour-intensive process, used in the West for the printing of exclusive designs. The roller-printing machine (1875), in which the pattern is engraved on metal rollers, greatly reduced the printing costs for long runs of one design. *Screen printing is now the most common textile printing method. It is versatile, cheap, and gives a high standard of definition. In transfer printing, used especially for cotton T-shirts, a design is first printed on paper, then transferred to a fabric under conditions of high temperature and pressure.

texturized vegetable protein (TVP) *food technology.

thalidomide *pharmacology.

thallium (symbol Tl, at. no. 81, r.a.m. 204.37), a soft, white, malleable metallic element with a bluish tinge. It occurs in the minerals crookesite and lorandite and is found associated with the sulphides of heavy metals. Thallium compounds are used to make optical glass of high refractive index. The metal and its salts are poisonous and are used as pesticides.

theodolite, an optical *surveying instrument used for measuring angles in the horizontal or vertical plane. A *telescope with internal cross-hairs for sighting the target pivots up and down within a frame (trunnion); the trunnion and telescope can also be rotated horizontally. The theodolite is mounted on a *tripod. A spirit-level on the instrument is used for levelling it. Angles are read off circular scales to an accuracy of fractions of a degree. The theodolite is used for triangulation (see *surveying) in road- and tunnel-making, and other civil engineering work.

thermionic converter, a device containing no moving parts that generates electrical energy directly from heat energy by the thermionic emission of electrons. Electrons emitted from a *cathode that has been heated to about 1,800

°C flow either through a vacuum or through the vapour of a metal to a cooled anode collector. The cathode–anode gap must be small and is typically 0.025 mm (0.001 inch); long-term changes in this gap lead to deterioration of these devices. The heat energy may be derived from any convenient source—chemical, nuclear, or solar. Lightweight units, with a mass one-hundredth that of a standard thermoelectric generator, have been designed for use in space. They are powered by the decay of *radioactive isotopes and generate more than 5 kW of power with 15 per cent efficiency.

thermionic valve, a type of *electron tube used in electronic circuits to achieve amplification and switching. Thermionic emission was first noted by *Edison in 1883, when he modified an ordinary light bulb by introducing an extra conductor close to the filament. An electric current flowed through the vacuum between the filament (the *cathode) and the conductor (the *anode). This current resulted from free electrons emitted by the heated filament. *Fleming and *De Forest followed up Edison's finding, and invented the thermionic diode and triode. The diode can pass current in one direction but not in the other (rectification). If a positive voltage is applied to the anode, electrons produced at the cathode will be attracted to the anode, and current will flow. If, however, the voltage is reversed, electrons will be repelled from the anode by its negative charge, and no current will flow. The properties of a diode can be modified by the addition of extra electrodes (grids) between the anode and cathode. The triode, the pentode, and other valves formed in this way can be used as *amplifiers. For most applications, valves have been replaced by *semiconductor devices, which are smaller, cheaper, more reliable, and use less power. However, specialized valves such as the *cathode-ray tube, klystron, and magnetron are still used for specific applications.

The first **thermionic valve**, the diode invented by John Fleming in 1904.

thermite *welding.

thermocouple, a thermoelectric device used mainly for measuring temperatures, especially high temperatures, remotely. If wires made of two different metals are joined at their ends, and the two junctions are kept at different temperatures, an electric potential is generated and a current proportional to the temperature difference will flow in the circuit. This is the thermoelectric effect, which can be used to measure temperature differences using a millivoltmeter. One junction is placed at the point where the temperature is to be measured, and the other is maintained at some fixed reference temperature, usually that of melting ice (0 °C). Although nearly all pairs of metals show the thermoelectric effect, only a few are used in practical instruments. For accurate measurement up to 1,700 °C, a junction of pure *platinum with platinum–rhodium *alloy is used; a cheaper junction of chrome and aluminium alloys can be used up to 1,300 °C. For lower temperatures, thermocouples using iron and constantan (up to 700 °C) or copper and constantan (up to 400 °C) are in common use. (For illustration see *temperature measurement.)

thermoelectric device, any system which makes use of thermoelectric effects. The effects, first observed in the 19th century, are twofold. If an electric current flows in a circuit consisting of different metals, it is observed that some junctions become cooler and others warmer (the Peltier effect). Conversely, if the junctions are heated or cooled, a voltage is generated. This second effect (the Seebeck effect) has been used for over a century in *thermocouples. More recently, the much greater output obtained with semiconducting materials has led to the development of thermoelectric power supplies. Although not economic for general use, these have the advantage of having no moving parts and have found application in spacecraft and heart pacemakers, the heat input in both cases coming from an encapsulated *radioactive source. The reverse effect, thermoelectric cooling, has a number of technological applications where a compact device without moving parts is required.

thermography, the production, by electronic or photographic means, of diagnostic images showing the different heat levels of an object. In medicine, thermography can be used to detect 'hot spots' caused, for example, by cancer of the breast, but results have proved unreliable. Its use for assessment of rheumatic conditions has been much more successful.

thermometer, liquid-in-glass, an instrument for *temperature measurement, dependent on the thermal expansion of a liquid in a tube. Depending on the temperature range to be measured, a variety of liquids is used. Alcohol and pentane (coloured to make them visible) are used for very low temperatures, but the commonest liquid is mercury. The principle and design of the thermometer are both simple. The liquid is contained in a bulb at the end of an evacuated glass capillary tube, into which it extends. When the temperature rises, the liquid in the bulb expands, and is forced further up the tube, the rise being proportional to the temperature increase. By recording the position of the liquid

A **thermograph** of a domestic house, showing heat distribution over the exterior. Warm areas appear in white or orange, colder areas in green.

at certain fixed points—notably the melting-point of ice (0 °C) and the boiling-point of water (100 °C)—a graduated scale can be calibrated so that ambient temperatures can be measured. The scale may be etched on the glass stem or fixed behind it. For accurate work, the thermometer is usually calibrated against a standard instrument at fixed temperatures. (For illustration see *temperature measurement.)

thermonuclear bomb *nuclear weapon.

thermoplastic *plastic.

thermosetting plastic *plastic.

Thermos flask *vacuum flask.

thermostat, a device that maintains a system at a pre-set constant temperature. Modern thermostats are of two main types: on–off and gradual-action thermostats. The former, introduced at the beginning of the 20th century, usually incorporates a *bimetallic strip, which bends as the temperature changes, and can be used to open or close electrical contacts or valves to maintain a predetermined temperature. A typical gradual-action thermostat is used in the 'regulo' thermostat for gas cookers, introduced in the UK in 1923. In this, a rod of invar alloy (with a very small coefficient of thermal expansion) is welded to a brass tube located within the oven. The brass expands with heat, causing the invar rod to move and control a valve regulating the supply of gas to the burners. Thermostats are used in many control applications, including central heating systems, electric irons, refrigerators, greenhouses, and washing-machines.

Thomson, Elihu (1853–1937), British-born US electrical engineer and inventor. Thomson registered some 700 patents, including a successful alternating-current motor, high-frequency generators and transformers, and a method of electrical welding. He was also the first to suggest the use of helium gas to prevent the 'bends' in *deep-sea diving.

thorium (symbol Th, at. no. 90, r.a.m. 232.04), a soft, ductile, *radioactive metal closely related to *uranium. Thorium is alloyed with magnesium to improve its performance at high temperatures. Thorium oxide (ThO_2) is an important catalyst, and is added to some creep-resistant alloys. Although one of its isotopes (thorium-232) can undergo *fission, thorium is not currently used as a nuclear fuel.

Three-Mile Island, an island in the Susquehanna River in Pennsylvania, USA, the site of a potential nuclear disaster in March 1979. The problem began with the breakdown of one of the pumps that circulated water through the steam generators connected to the *pressurized-water reactor of the nuclear-power station on the island. Emergency lines then failed to supply extra coolant water, and a pressure relief valve stuck open, leading to a loss of water coolant from around the reactor core. The core reached a temperature of over 2,000 °C, and underwent partial melt-down. Although many people in the area were evacuated, an official investigation found the levels of radiation in the vicinity (in milk, for example) to be little changed. However, the reactor was damaged beyond repair, and the incident showed that despite elaborate safety precautions, a nuclear accident could still occur.

threshing machine, a power-driven agricultural machine for separating the grain from the straw or husk. An early form was invented in 1768 by the British millwright Andrew Meikle, and was generally accepted in the UK and the Americas by the 1840s. It comprised a rapidly revolving cylindrical drum, close to which was a concave curved screen of the same circumference. Closing the gap between the drum and the screen increased the pressure on the plant material between them, forcing the grain clear of its protective layers. The grain and the lighter chaff then passed through fan-generated air blasts to separate the two, a process originally carried out by *winnowing machines. Today threshing is carried out by *combine harvesters, using essentially the same method.

throstle *spinning machine.

thyristor *semiconductor device.

tidal energy, the energy carried by the regular tidal movement of the sea. Tidal energy could in principle supply a significant amount of the world's energy needs, but economic factors limit its use to coastlines where the tidal range is particularly great. Of the many methods proposed for extracting tidal energy, only one has been widely used, whether for ancient *tide-mills or modern *power-stations. The rising water enters an enclosed basin through *sluices in a dam or barrage; the sluices are then closed, the sea-level outside falls and the captured water flows out, driving *water-wheels or *water turbines. The tidal cycle of about twelve and a half hours and the fortnightly cycle of maximum and minimum range (springs and neaps) pose a problem in maintaining a regular power supply, and have led to ideas for more complex systems—with several basins for instance, or using *pumped storage. The *Rance barrage and two smaller schemes in the Soviet Union and China are the only existing operational tidal power installations.

tide-mill, a water-mill deriving its power from tidal flow. Tide-mills were in use from early classical times until the mid-20th century, mainly for grinding flour, but also for driving industrial machinery and as pumping stations, usually on tidal rivers. Tide-mills under London Bridge pumped water from the River Thames for over three centuries. Some mills used only the natural flow of water, but most incorporated a dam with sluices. Broad undershot *water-wheels suited to the wide streams and low heads of tidal waters were commonly used.

tile, a thin slab of *ceramic material, generally rigid, applied to the surface of a roof, wall, or floor. Tiles serve to protect, decorate, or to improve the acoustic, chemical resistance, or hygiene properties. One of the most common uses for tiles is roofing. When laying roof tiles, a jointing system ensures that rain and snow are excluded. Mediterranean channel tiles (S-shaped in section), and more modern interlocking tiles, provide a light roof covering of only a single thickness of material. Plain tiles, which (like slates) have butt-joints at the side and overlap at the head, make a heavier roof covering, with two thicknesses of tile to prevent rain penetration.

timber-frame construction *frame (building).

time-and-motion study, the detailed analysis of the individual elements of a task or process with the aim of reducing the effort and time involved in carrying it out. The approach is generally attributed to Frederick W. Taylor, who during the 1880s studied shovelling of raw materials and the machining of metals in a Philadelphia steel plant. In the following decades time-and-motion studies made a significant contribution to the development of *mass production by standardizing working procedures and allowing efficiency and productivity to be improved and monitored.

time-scale, a system used for measuring the passage of time. Three major systems are currently in use: rotational time, dynamic time, and atomic time. Rotational time is based on a fundamental unit of a day, the time taken for the Earth to complete one full revolution around the Sun. Current international scales of rotational time are based on the mean solar day, actually calculated from accurate astronomical observations of stars. Dynamic time is derived from mathematical descriptions of the motion of the Moon and the planets: it is independent of variations in the Earth's rotation. The first dynamic time-scale was Ephemeris Time, first proposed in 1896; in 1960, a modified version of it became the basis for the definition of the *SI second. Atomic time is based on extremely regular oscillations that occur within *atoms and form the basis of atomic clocks. In 1967 the SI second was redefined in terms of atomic time, and atomic clocks are now used as international time standards.

tin (symbol Sn, at. no. 50, r.a.m. 118.69), a soft, silvery-white metallic element. The major *ore is cassiterite, SnO_2, which after some initial purification is reduced by *smelting with carbon to form the metal. Tin is refined by re-heating just to melting-point in a furnace with an inclined hearth; the purer tin flows down the slope, leaving impurities in the dross. It can be further purified by *electrolysis. At temperatures below 13.2 °C, pure white tin slowly changes its structure into that of grey tin, and breaks down to a powder. The presence of impurities in commercial tin normally prevents this from happening. The main use of tin is in the production of tin plate. Tin plate is used in the manufacture of a wide variety of cans and utensils, although many of these are now made from aluminium or from *polymer-based products. Most tin plate is now produced by electroplating, which requires less tin than the original process of dipping the sheet in molten metal, and gives a better coating. Tin is also used in the production of various alloys, such as solder, *bronze, and *type metal. Tin compounds are used in the manufacture of opaque glasses and enamels, and as *mordants in

Tomography

When X-rays pass through the body, the various organs and bones cast shadows that are recorded on film. Shadows of structures lying at different levels in the scan overlap one another, making it hard to see any detail. In the original technique of tomography *(below)*, the X-ray tube and the film move in a linear manner to give a sharp image in one plane of the body.

A computerized axial tomography (CAT) scanner

In a CAT scanner the X-ray tube and the receiver are located opposite each other. They rotate rapidly in unison as the patient's body is slid through the scanner. The receiver records the X-ray data as electrical impulses. These are fed to a computer, which processes the information to give images of a series of body sections.

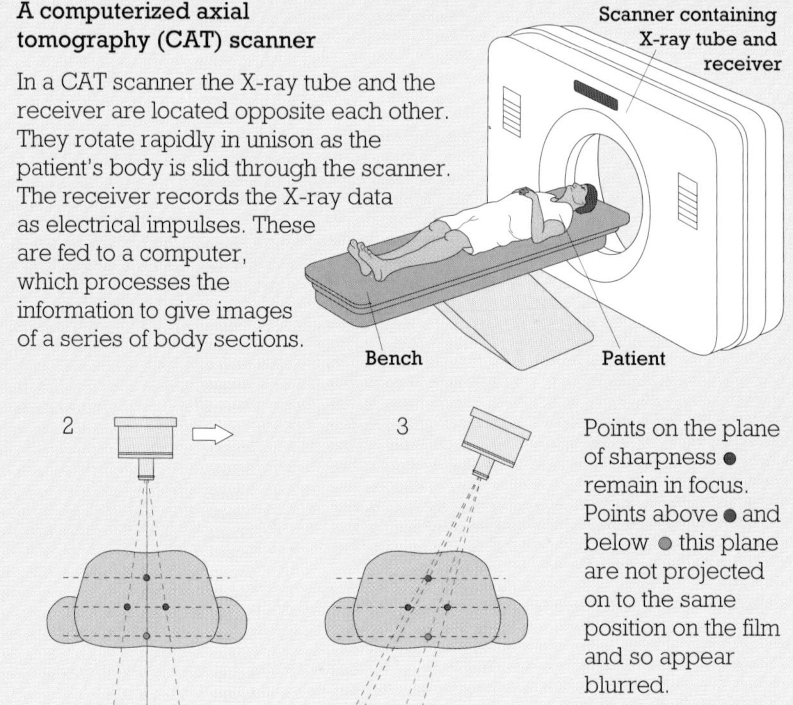

Principle of tomographic scanning

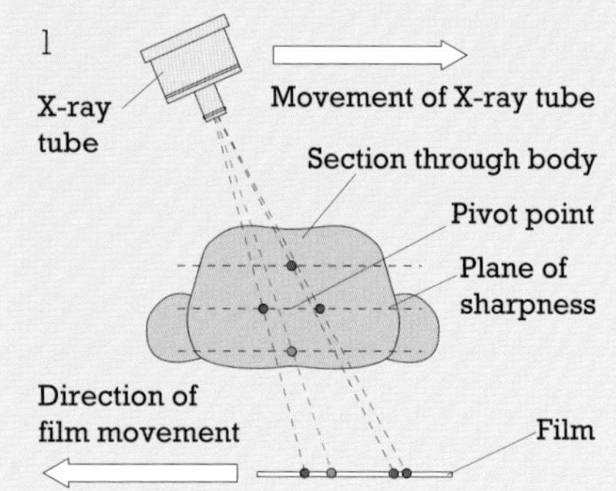

Points on the plane of sharpness ● remain in focus. Points above ● and below ● this plane are not projected on to the same position on the film and so appear blurred.

dyeing. Tin fluoride (SnF_2) is the additive in fluoride toothpastes.

tinder-box *fire-making device.

titanium (symbol Ti, at. no. 22, r.a.m. 47.88), a very strong, light metallic element. It has a high melting-point and is resistant to corrosion. The principal ores are ilmenite ($FeTiO_3$) and rutile (TiO_2). Titanium alloys are used extensively in aerospace technology and other applications requiring lightness and high strength. Titanium is also used for *hip replacements as it is not attacked by body fluids. Titanium dioxide is a white solid used as a pigment in *paint, and as a filler in paper, soap, and rubber. Titanium nitride is used to form a hard coating on *steel cutting tools.

TNT (2,4,6-trinitrotoluene), an important high *explosive, discovered by J. Wilbrand in 1863. It is a yellow, crystalline solid with a low melting-point. TNT has low shock sensitivity and even burns without exploding. This makes it easy and safe to handle and cast. However, once detonated, it explodes violently. It is manufactured by treating toluene (obtained from petroleum) with a mixture of concentrated nitric and sulphuric acids.

tobacco processing, the harvesting, curing, and conditioning of the leaves of the tobacco plant. Tobacco plants may be harvested whole, or individual leaves may be picked as they mature. The leaves are then air-, fire-, or flue-cured. In air-curing the leaves are mechanically ventilated at an even temperature for one to two months. In fire-curing, wood fires are lit in a curing barn to impart a characteristic flavour to the tobacco (the process takes between three and four weeks). Flue-curing involves hanging leaves for two to six days in a small, tightly built barn heated by pipes or flues. After curing, the leaves must be held for a time in humid conditions before they can be further processed. Cured leaves may be used for smoking tobacco or snuff, or processed to extract nicotine, which is used as an *insecticide, though its toxicity is a severe disadvantage.

tokamak *fusion, nuclear.

tomography (body-section radiography), in diagnostic *radiology, a technique that produces a sharp image of a layer within the body while deliberately blurring structures at other depths. In the original device (1921), the effect was achieved by mounting the X-ray tube and a photographic plate at opposite ends of a lever, thus showing the body structures in one plane (see figure). In *computerized axial tomography, *positron emission tomography, and certain applications of *ultrasound, a similar effect is created by electronic and software techniques rather than by photomechanical means.

tongs *pliers, tongs, and pincers.

tools, history of. The earliest Stone Age settlements yield abundant evidence of six basic hand tools—the *adze, auger, *axe, *knife, *hammer, and *chisel (see figure on page 358)—and of products made with these tools. They were followed by the *saw, which appeared early in the Bronze Age. Primitive forms of *drill were also introduced at about this time. These simple tools sufficed to build the ships that sailed the Mediterranean in pre-Christian times, to erect the pyramids, and to produce the fine examples of craftsmanship recovered from Egyptian tombs. Roman artisans used essentially the same tools, with the important addition of the *plane. There were no further major developments for a thousand years, until the invention in medieval times of the brace, the tenon saw, and the spokeshave. The familiar modern hand drill, of all-metal construction with bevel gears, is a 19th-century development. In the 18th and 19th centuries, *machine-tools gradually gained in importance over hand tools.

Within each class of tool, there are many differences in design, and even in Stone Age times there were considerable local variations. Indeed, it is possible for archaeologists to deduce the main trade routes of the ancient world from studies of unearthed axe-heads. Most modern hand tools closely resemble those from earlier centuries, but differ in two respects. First, the relatively recent availability of high-grade alloy *steels has made possible sharper and longer-lived cutting edges. Second, the introduction of small, reliable electric motors has resulted in the development of a major new set of light *power tools.

torpedo, a cigar-shaped, self-propelled underwater missile used by warships and *submarines that explodes on impact with a ship; also a similar device dropped from an aircraft. In 1867 Robert Whitehead, a British engineer, developed the Whitehead locomotive torpedo, which carried an explosive warhead and was powered by compressed air. Early torpedoes were too slow and unreliable to be effective weapons, but extensive development work gradually improved their performance. By the start of World War I torpedoes propelled by an engine burning an air, water vapour, and oil mixture could reach speeds of 44 *knots over a range of about 3.5 km (2.2 miles). They were held at the required depth by a hydrostatic valve, and directed by a preset, *gyroscopically controlled *rudder. Between 1936 and 1940 Japan produced the Long Lance torpedo, driven by liquid oxygen, and at about the same time acoustic homing torpedoes were developed. Today's torpedoes all possess passive or active homing mechanisms or are remotely guided (see *guided missile), while miniaturization has brought lightweight torpedoes fired from aircraft for use as anti-submarine weapons.

torpedo-boat, a type of small warship developed during the 1870s and designed to discharge *torpedoes from above-water tubes. The first effective torpedo-boat was Britain's HMS *Lightning*, modified in 1879 for torpedo discharge. Other navies developed similar vessels, and by the 1890s they were so successful that a new type of small warship, the torpedo-boat *destroyer, was evolved to counter their threat. During World War I a smaller type of fast torpedo-boat with *internal-combustion engines was produced. This vessel was developed during World War II into a significant and successful high-speed weapon. Similar boats in use today are generally classed as fast patrol boats.

torque (moment of force), the tendency of a force to rotate a body to which it is applied. Torque is specified with regard to a specific axis of rotation and is an important quantity in the measurement of the power of an *engine or other rotating body, since the power is measured as torque multiplied by angular *velocity (speed of rotation). It can be measured using a *dynamometer.

touchstone, black, fine-grained siliceous stone used for *assaying gold and silver. The gold or silver is rubbed on the

Tools, history of

Chopper
(c. 2,000,000 BC)

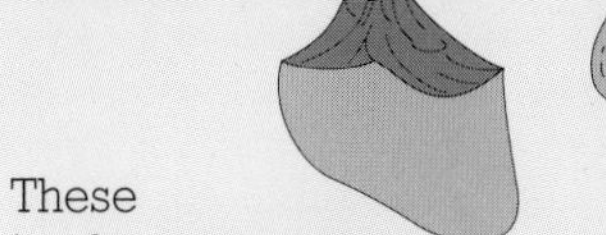

These implements were general-purpose tools used for chopping and hacking.

Neolithic hammer
(c. 7000 BC)

Modern hammer

Today's hammer has evolved from Neolithic times. The hammer-head, a grooved stone, was held in a handle formed by a branch.

Adze

Axe

This adze and axe also date from the Neolithic age. The adze's head was made by a stone inserted into an antler, which was then fitted into a stick. The axe had a sharp, polished, stone head.

Roman chisel

Chisels date back to the Stone Age when they were made from flint. Roman chisels were similar to the ones used today.

Frame saw

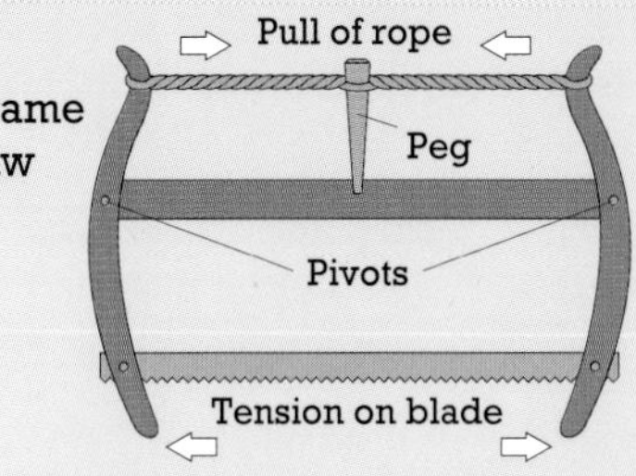

The frame saw was introduced by the Romans. Its blade is held taut by twisted rope, which is prevented from unwinding by the peg.

Roman plane

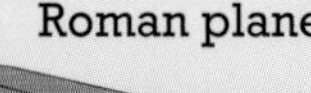

The plane dates from Roman times. The iron blade was held in place by being wedged against a bar across the opening.

Modern file

Files made of bronze existed in Egypt as early as 1500 BC. Nowadays there is a great variety of steel files used mainly on cast iron and soft metals.

Tenon saw

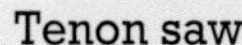

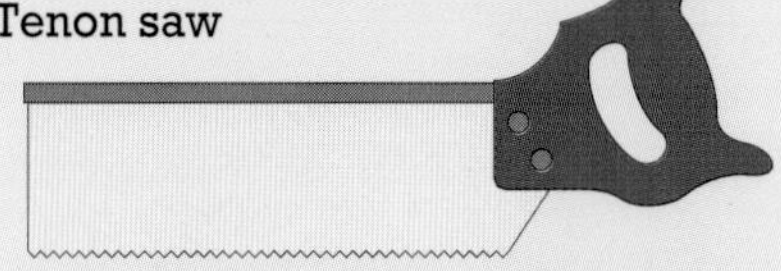

The tenon saw has a blade length of 25–30 cm (10 –12 inches). It is the largest of the back saws, which have a strengthening strip of metal on the top edge of the blade.

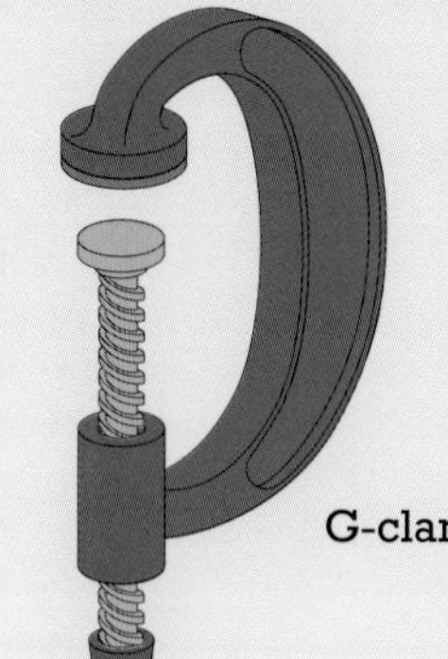

G-clamp

Developed during the 16th century, the clamp is used for securing the workpiece while it is being worked on.

Blacksmith's vice

The screw-threaded vice originated during the 16th century. Prior to this it was tightened using a nut and bolt.

Wrench
(c. 16th century)

The earliest wrenches were made of cast iron. Each fitted a specific-sized nut.

Screwdriver

Screwdrivers only became common once screws were mass produced during the mid-19th century. They are available in many shapes and sizes.

Spokeshave

Originating from Holland around the mid-18th century, the spokeshave was primarily a wheelwright's tool.

Pliers

Pliers are used to hold objects firmly, enabling them to be worked on more easily. They were developed from the larger tongs used by blacksmiths.

New technologies call for new tools. Wire strippers were introduced after the advent of electricity.

Wire strippers

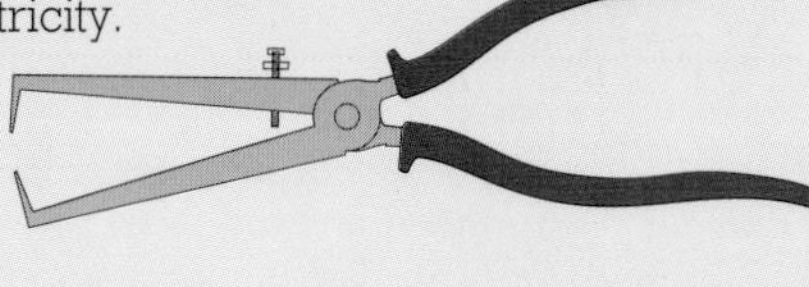

Tractor

The power take-off (PTO) is an auxiliary source of power that is driven from the engine via the gearbox. A shaft, extending to the rear of the tractor, drives any machinery that is attached. The hydraulic lifting apparatus enables implements on the back of the tractor to be raised and lowered.

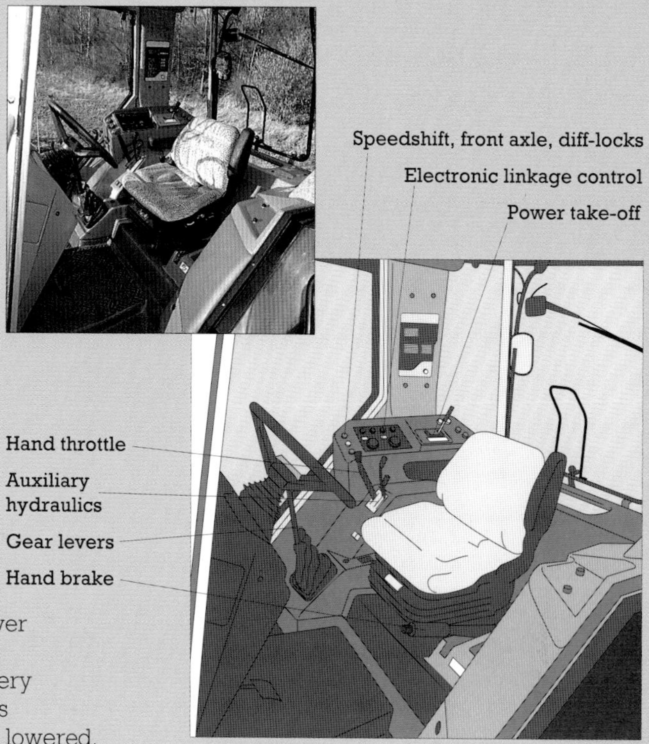

stone to produce streaks, which are compared with streaks made by metals of known purity. The comparison is made easier by treating the streaks with nitric acid, which dissolves impurities and leaves streaks of metal only. The method is not reliable for silver, but is still used today for assaying gold.

town gas, a flammable, manufactured gas for domestic and commercial use, made originally from coal and comprising a mixture of methane, hydrogen, and carbon. It dates from experiments with *coal-gas by the British steam-engineer William Murdock at the end of the 18th century, and gasworks were a common sight all over Western Europe for over 150 years, providing gas for heating and lighting. Town gas is made by the thermal decomposition of coal in a closed retort; the process also produces large quantities of residual carbon called gas coke, which can also be used as a fuel. In the 1960s this process began to be displaced by the production of gas from oil-based feedstocks, which, in turn, has been displaced in some countries by *natural gas.

Townshend, Charles, Viscount (1674–1738), British politician and agriculturist. After a distinguished political career, he retired in 1730 to Norfolk to improve his family estate. He introduced the turnip, then only a garden crop, as winter fodder, earning the nickname Turnip Townshend. This was the basis of the Norfolk four-course system (see *agriculture); it enabled farmers to keep many more cattle alive during the winter, and avoided the need to keep one field in three fallow every year.

track circuit, an electrical circuit passing along the running rails (suitably insulated) to detect the presence of a train on a section of railway track. When a train occupies the track circuit, it short circuits the track current through its wheels and axles. This causes a detector to operate in the signal-box, indicating the position of the train. Although susceptible to bad weather and rusty or dirty rails, the track circuit is an important part of *railway signal systems. For this reason, all trains carry bonding straps, which can be clipped across the rails in the event of a derailment or similar emergency, to confirm the presence of the train.

tracked vehicle *caterpillar track.

traction-engine, a mobile *steam-powered vehicle used for haulage, for agricultural purposes, or as a mobile power source. The earliest portable steam-engines were not self-powered but were pulled by teams of horses. Self-propelled engines first were built in 1834 by Walter Hancock (UK) and in 1842 by J. R. and A. Ransome, but they gained little popularity. It was not until the 1850s, when engines by Charles Burrel and by Thomas Aveling appeared, that the traction-engine gained acceptance. By the late 19th century, traction-engines were in use on many farms, but by World War I they were being replaced by *tractors. Some traction-engines continued to be used for heavy road haulage until World War II.

tractor, a motor vehicle used to haul *agricultural machinery and for general farm work. Modern tractors (see figure) derive from steam-powered *traction-engines. The first petrol-engined tractor was made in 1892 in the USA, and by World War II tractors were well established. Modern tractors use either two- or four-wheel drive, and have caterpillar tracks or large, rubber-tyred wheels for good traction and weight distribution. A major feature is the power take-off, which can be either an extension of the tractor's transmission system or an independent drive. This can power a wide range of agricultural machines, which are carried or towed behind the tractor. Hydraulically powered, rear-mounted arms on the tractor are used to raise and lower such implements as harrows and ploughs, controlling the depth to which they penetrate the soil. A tractor can also be used to pull a *mole plough for drainage, to operate a hedge-cutter for trimming hedged boundaries, or for short-haul transportation using a trailer.

traffic control. Traffic congestion is not a new problem: wheeled traffic was banned from Rome during the day in the 1st century AD, and around 1500 *Leonardo da Vinci proposed separating pedestrian and wheeled traffic on to different levels, to overcome congestion problems. Modern traffic control has five overlapping objectives: the reduction of accidents; the more efficient use of available road capacity; the priority treatment of particular vehicle types (for example, emergency vehicles); the reduction of the adverse environmental effects of road traffic; and the control of the amount of road traffic. Traffic-control measures aimed at improving road safety include the design of junctions to minimize vehicle conflicts; the provision of a variety of types of pedestrian crossing; the control of parking so that pedestrians and sight-lines are not obscured by parked cars; and the provision of safety barriers. The application of traffic management measures to reduce accidents has been very successful, with the number of accidents falling despite major growth in traffic. Traffic-control measures aimed primarily at increasing the capacity of existing street networks are generally referred to as traffic management and include the channelling of traffic, the introduction of one-way and gyratory (roundabout) systems, the improved design of junctions, and the use of *traffic-lights.

Traffic-control measures may be designed to give priority to certain types of vehicle. Bus lanes and bus-only streets are typical of this approach in the UK, while elsewhere, certain lanes are allocated for vehicles carrying several passengers. The adverse effects of traffic on the environment, especially in residential areas and shopping streets, have led to the development of environmental management or 'traffic-calming' techniques. These include the pedestrianization of some streets, the widening of pavements, the use of special paving, and the introduction of speed humps or width restrictions to slow down traffic. Until recently, the major measure used to limit the amount of traffic in urban areas was the control of parking. In a few cities, however, permit systems have now been introduced to control the amount of traffic entering central areas. Another proposed measure is electronic road pricing, whereby vehicle owners are charged for the amount of road space used.

A motorway junction in Berlin. The many slip roads and flyovers allow **traffic** to approach from any direction and join either carriageway at speed.

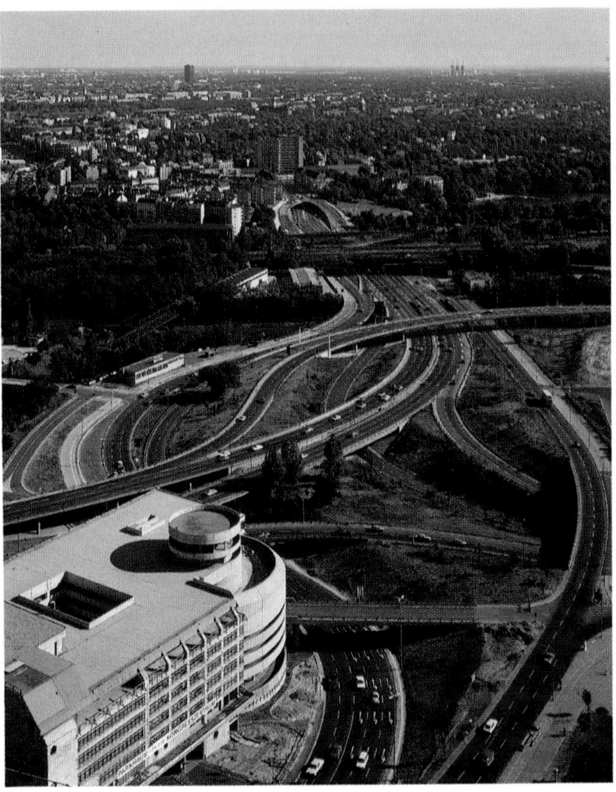

traffic-light, a set of three coloured lights, often red, amber, and green, that control the flow of traffic at intersections on main roads. First used in the USA in 1914, they are now employed universally to alleviate congestion at junctions where vehicles enter or leave side roads, or at intersections where two main roads cross. At complex junctions microprocessors co-ordinate the phasing of lights to optimize traffic flow. In conurbations, computerized *traffic control systems monitor and regulate the traffic-lights over whole districts. Such control may be either to a series of fixed plans introducing different signal timings at different times of the day or week, or to a continuously varying signal timing plan designed by the computer in the light of continuously monitored traffic conditions, measured by traffic detectors under the road.

tram (US, streetcar), a passenger vehicle that operates on rails laid along public roads. Originally horse- or steam-hauled, trams now operate electrically, usually by means of overhead wires or a third rail buried beneath the track. They often work in multiple units of two to four cars, all of which may be powered. As the European cities in which most trams operate have grown larger, tramlines have been built leading off the public roads into the suburbs. This avoids congestion and allows the trams to reach speeds approaching those of commuter trains. Trams are frequently allowed to run through pedestrianized areas because they are quiet and non-polluting. In the USA, the famous San Francisco streetcars are cable-hauled. (See also *trolleybus.)

tramway *wagon-way.

tranquillizer, a drug having a calming effect. Tranquillizers calm and relax patients with less sedative and hypnotic actions than other drugs. 'Major' tranquillizers (for example, chlorpromazine) are used to treat severe psychotic disorders such as mania and schizophrenia. 'Minor' tranquillizers are effective against anxiety and insomnia, and have largely superseded *barbiturates; an example is diazepam, the best-known formulation of which is Valium. Minor tranquillizers are less liable to produce dependence than barbiturates, and overdoses are far less dangerous. (See also *pharmacology, *psychotropic drug.)

transducer, any device that converts one form of energy into another. Generally, transducers are *sensors, providing an electrical output in response to some physical variable such as pressure, temperature, humidity, acidity, sound intensity, light intensity, or chemical constitution. However, some transducers, for example, *relays and *loudspeakers, function as actuators, providing a defined physical output for some defined electrical input. Transducers are selected for their function, dynamic range (the maximum response they can give), linearity (how faithfully the output follows the input), resolution (the smallest input that will create an output), and accuracy. Transducer technology is a rapidly developing field, and an increasing number of transducers can be made at very low cost in a highly compact form. Some transducers can now be fabricated directly on to a silicon chip as part of an *integrated circuit.

transfer machine, a *machine-tool linking together other machine-tools in such a way that a succession of machining operations can be carried out automatically. Transfer machines allow complex components to be machined in one automatic process. The workpiece is transferred from one machining operation to another by, for example, a rotary indexing table or linear indexing device, which can position it precisely. Transfer machines are important elements of *flexible manufacturing systems.

transformer, an electrical device that can provide a low-voltage supply from a high-voltage, alternating-current (a.c.) power source (step-down), or a high-voltage supply from a low-voltage a.c. source (step-up). It comprises two interacting coils, the primary and secondary coils, wound on a core of magnetically 'soft' iron (see *magnet). Alternating current supplied to the primary coil induces a current in the secondary coil (see *electromagnetic induction). The ratio of primary and secondary voltages is determined by the number of turns on each coil: for example, if the secondary carries twice the number of turns of the primary, it will supply double the voltage. Transformers have many applications. For example, in mains *electricity supply, a.c. power is transmitted at high voltage, and transformers are used to step this high voltage down to mains domestic voltage. Radio, television, and computer circuits usually require further step-down transformers that are incorporated in the equipment.

transgenic organism *genetic engineering.

transistor, a three-terminal, solid-state *semiconductor device used in electronic *circuits to provide amplification or as a high-speed *switch. Transistors were first developed in 1948 by *Shockley and colleagues. They may be used individually, or as part of an *integrated circuit. There are two principal types of transistor, the bipolar transistor and the field-effect transistor (FET). The bipolar transistor consists of a sandwich of three regions of doped semiconductor, the emitter, the base, and the collector. The emitter and collector are connected into a circuit carrying a large current, while the base and emitter form a circuit that can carry a much smaller current in the reverse direction (see semiconductor device for illustration). No current can flow in the emitter–collector circuit if the base–emitter circuit is off. However, a small current flow in the base circuit 'turns on' the transistor and allows a much larger current (fifty to a hundred times greater) to flow in the emitter–collector circuit. Bipolar transistors can operate at very high speeds, and for this reason are used in radio circuits. They are also used in *amplifiers. FETs can be of several types. A common type comprises a channel of n-type material through some p-type material. The channel can act as a conducting path for electrons, the input being known as the source, and the output as the drain. A third electrical connection, the gate, is made to the p-type material between the source and the drain. A small voltage applied to the gate acts to 'squeeze' electrons in the n-type material into a narrower channel, thus making it harder for current to flow between the source and drain. Varying the voltage on the gate therefore controls current flow along the n-type channel. Field-effect transistors can be made much smaller than bipolar transistors, and they are therefore used in random-access computer *memory and other circuits with a high density of components.

transmission, mechanical *belt drive and chain drive, *clutch, *differential, *gearbox, *hydraulic power.

transmitter *radio, *television.

transplant surgery, the practice of replacing diseased organs or tissues with healthy ones taken from another part of the patient's body (such as skin *grafts), or from another person (for example, heart transplants). Normally, transplanted organs taken from another person are treated by the body as a foreign tissue and are destroyed by the patient's immune system (see *immunology). This rejection tendency is much reduced if the donor and recipient are of a similar tissue type, and by using special drugs to suppress the immune response, it is possible to prevent rejection altogether. Sometimes a patient's immune system can be made inactive by radiation treatment, as in bone-marrow transplant operations. Heart transplants require, in addition to drugs, a *heart–lung machine to keep the recipient alive during the operation.

transponder, a radio receiver and transmitter that transmits in response to predetermined signals. In *communications satellites, transponders receive information signals from Earth carried on one microwave frequency, and transmit them back after amplification on another, lower microwave frequency.

transporter bridge, a bridge that carries vehicles and passengers in a container across a waterway. It consists of tall steel towers on each bank supporting a high-level *girder, usually of lattice construction. A trolley runs on tracks on the girder and the container is suspended by cables. In effect, the bridge is an aerial ferry. Notable examples are at Newport and Middlesbrough in the UK; and at Rochefort in Charente-Maritime, France.

transputer, a chip that incorporates all the functions of a microprocessor, including *memory. Transputers have in-built communications links so that they can easily be linked to similar processors to form *parallel processing systems. Transputers can divide up tasks between several identical processors, enabling them to handle large amounts of data very quickly. Conventional serial *computers carry out tasks serially using one very fast processor. The transputer was built in 1978 by Inmos in the UK. The programming language designed for the transputer is occam, a *computer language based upon the concept of parallel execution. It can provide automatic communication and co-ordination between concurrent processes. Arrays of transputers are used to run applications where a significant increase in speed over conventional computers is required.

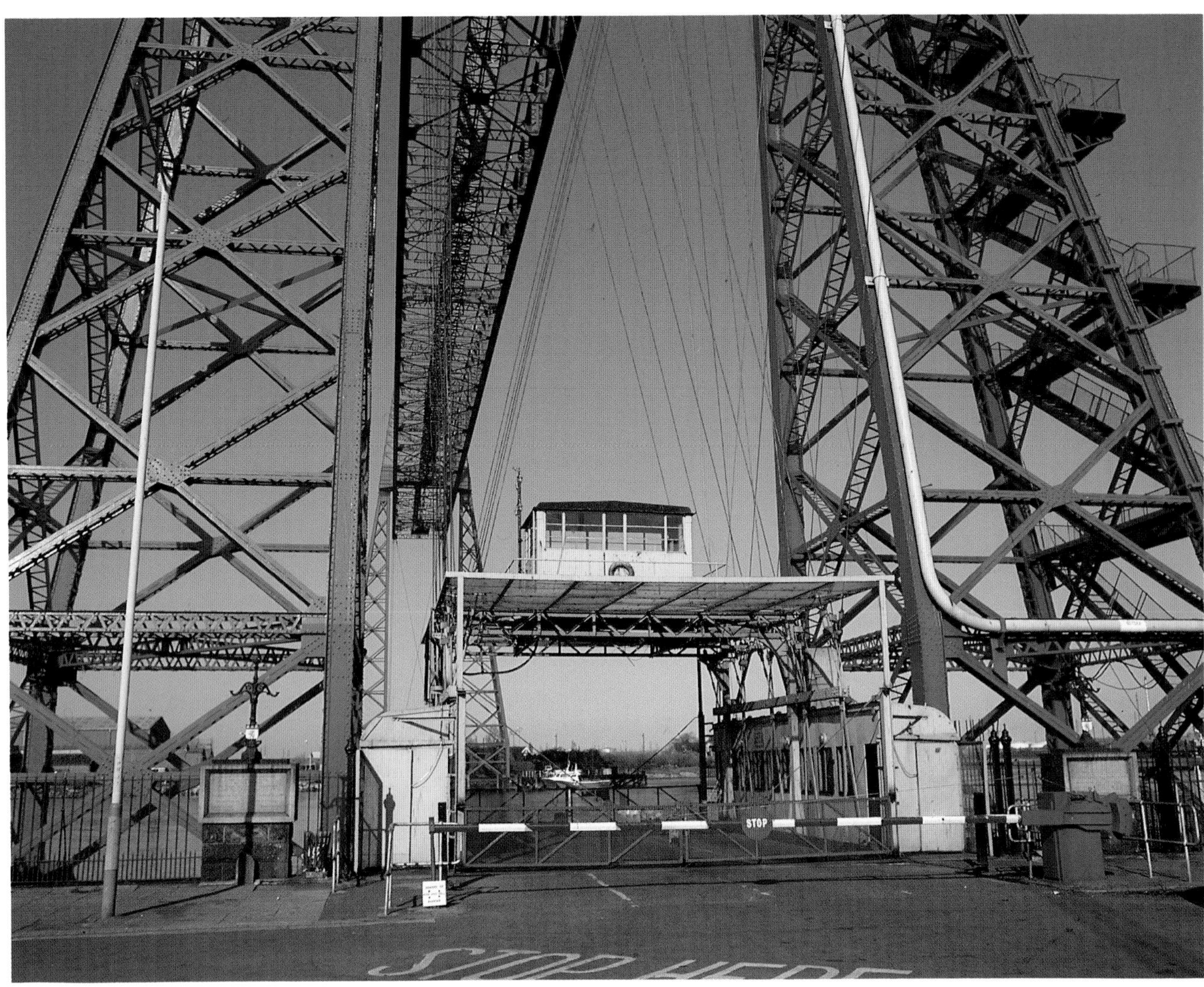

A **transporter bridge** across the River Tees at Middlesborough, UK. The yellow transporter unit is suspended by steel cables from a trolley running on rails 68 m (220 feet) above the river.

traps, fishing, passive and stationary devices for catching fish, crustaceans, and molluscs in salt-water and *freshwater fisheries. Most traps depend on the living or migratory habits of the animals sought. The most primitive trap is a simple hiding-place from which the animal has no time to escape as the trap is hauled in, for example, the clay octopus pot. Crab and lobster pots are made from netting, cane, or plastic, with restricted funnel-shaped entrances that give easy access to the bait inside but deny an exit. Fish are caught in bag-shaped fyke nets, which are long and tapered and held open by a series of hoops. Pound nets have walls that guide fish past a series of baffles towards the catching area. These net-traps catch migrating fish such as herring along shore-lines, and salmon and eels in rivers. (For illustration see *net, fishing.)

travelator *escalator.

trawler, a commercial fishing vessel that tows a trawl-*net. About a third of the world's annual fish harvest is taken by trawlers, most of which are now stern-trawlers, operating the trawl-net over the rear of the boat. They have powerful engines for towing the net and machinery for hauling the net and catch on board. A small wet-fish trawler may be only 10 m (30 feet) long, with a crew of three or four. The catch is cooled with ice in the hold. Factory or processing trawlers are 45 m (150 feet) or more in length and carry fish processing, packing, and freezing equipment. Most trawlers operate in waters less than 200 m (650 feet) deep, catching fish and shellfish that live on or near the sea-bed. However, some trawlers work in waters up to 1,000 m (3,300 feet) deep, using *sonar and other sensors to locate concentrations of fish.

treadmill (tread-wheel), a large wheel driven by movement of the weight of a person or animal. Tread-wheels were in use more than 2,000 years ago in the Middle East. The early form was a cross-braced hollow wooden wheel inside which people or animals could walk, with wooden slats acting as footholds. One use was as an irrigation pump, with the shaft driving another wheel carrying buckets around its rim. The treadmill as a penal device was introduced into prisons in the UK in the early 19th century and remained in use for nearly 100 years. The treads were on the outside of the wheel, compelling the operator to move continually to each step in turn.

trephining (trepanning), the surgical removal of a small section of the cranium. The remains of skulls from prehistoric times indicate that successful trephining was performed using flint tools at least 12,000 years ago. It is thought that the procedure had both medical and ritual significance.

Today surgeons occasionally trephine to allow access to the brain, either to implant electrodes measuring electrical activity, or to perform surgery. The most common procedure is the draining of an expanding blood clot (subdural haematoma), which would otherwise produce pressure on the brain and cause death.

Trésaguet, Pierre-Marie-Jérôme (1716–96), French civil engineer. He was one of the great *road builders who, along with *Telford and *McAdam in Britain, rebuilt and enlarged the European road system in the 18th and 19th centuries. He built hard-wearing durable roads that were less thick than those of his contemporaries, thereby reducing both the labour and the quantity of material required and making great savings in cost (see *road for illustration). His method, using layers of broken stone, also made it possible to reduce the camber substantially without affecting drainage, and was soon widely adopted in central Europe and Sweden. He also recognized the long-term economy of systematic road maintenance.

Trevithick, Richard (1771–1833), British steam-engine pioneer. His first acquaintance with *steam-engines was at the age of four, when his father, a mine manager, installed a *Newcomen engine at his mine in Cornwall. Later, he recognized the need to improve the efficiency of steam-engines and, when *Watt's basic patent expired in 1800, he built a double-acting steam-engine that used high-pressure steam. Over the next four years he built fifty such engines. Concurrently, he built a number of steam *locomotives, including the first steam railway locomotive, used to supply the Pendarren ironworks in South Wales (1804). He thus established the basic principles of railway traction, in particular refuting the belief that friction between an iron wheel and an iron rail would be insufficient for traction.

tricycle, a vehicle with three wheels, normally two on an axle at the back and one at the front, driven by pedals like a *bicycle. The first successful tricycle was the Coventry Lever tricycle, patented by the Englishman James Starley in 1876. By the 1880s large numbers of tricyles were being built, but the invention of the safety bicycle (1884), combined with the greater weight and expense of tricycles, led to their decline by the end of the 19th century. Smaller numbers of tricycles continue to be made, and are used especially for commercial purposes: the tricycle *rickshaw, for example, is used extensively in parts of southern Asia.

Trident *missile (table).

triode *De Forest, *thermionic valve.

trip-hammer (tilt-hammer), an early *machine-tool used for *forging. It was frequently driven by a *water-wheel carrying on its axle short bars acting as *cams. These pushed down one end of the pivoted arm carrying the hammer-head at its other end, so raising the head. When the other end tripped off the cam arm the head fell under gravity, so striking a blow on a die held above the workpiece on the anvil. Similar devices were used for ore-crushing and for *fulling cloth by beating.

triple-expansion engine, a form of *steam-engine, patented in France in 1871 by Benjamin Normand, which in the late 19th century became the standard marine engine. In the triple-expansion engine, the expansion of steam from the high *boiler pressure to the low condenser pressure was accomplished in three stages, thereby greatly improving efficiency. A small high-pressure cylinder exhausted to a larger intermediate cylinder, and thence to one or often two low-pressure cylinders in parallel. These cylinders all shared a common crankshaft.

tripod, a three-legged support for an instrument, such as a *camera or a *theodolite. In photography, tripods are used to prevent camera movement during long exposures—normally regarded as being anything longer than 0.017 s (that is, 1/60 s). They are available in a range of sizes and with a variety of tripod heads, offering different possible adjustments.

trireme *galley.

trolleybus, an electric bus running on wheels on the road, but obtaining its power from overhead cables, like a *tram. The first trolleybus service began in Germany in 1901, and trolleybuses are still operated in Moscow and a few other cities. Trolleybuses are quiet, pollution-free, and have rapid acceleration, but they lack the flexibility of the motor bus, having to follow the overhead cables. The high costs of electricity supply and cable maintenance make the trolleybus expensive to operate. Nevertheless, there is currently a revival of interest in their use.

tropical agriculture, the practice of farming in tropical regions, largely in Third World countries. Broadly, tropical agriculture can be divided into subsistence farming, and the growing of cash-crops, although in some areas herding is the

Passengers boarding a London **trolleybus**, 1948.

only form of farming. Examples of cash-crops exclusive to tropical areas are palm oil, cocoa, sugar, fibre-producing crops such as jute and *cotton, and *beverage crops such as tea and coffee. Most of these crops are grown by *plantation farming methods. Subsistence farming usually employs mixed farming methods: integration of livestock and crops, *intercropping, and agroforestry (where the growing of trees and raising of crops and livestock are combined). The small size of holdings, farm tenancy structures, and the lack of support industries all inhibit specialization. Yields are low and unreliable, due to poor soils, the high cost of fertilizers, labour shortages, and a climate typified by high temperatures and often unreliable rainfall. New crop varieties selected as part of the *green revolution have increased yields in parts of Asia, but have not been as widely adopted as had been hoped. Developments in livestock farming have been minimal, and attempts to introduce mechanization have met with problems of unsuitable climate and terrain, lack of skilled labour, and scarcity of spare parts.

truck *lorry.

truss *structural engineering.

Tsukuba Science City, a Japanese complex for advanced scientific and technological research and education, established in 1961. The first institutions were completed in 1966, and the new Tsukuba University, with 6,500 undergraduate and 2,000 postgraduate students, opened in 1980. The Science City's 30,000-ha (74,000-acre) site houses some fifty national research and educational institutions, and a large number of private firms closely connected with government research are established on an adjacent industrial park.

tubes and pipes, hollow cylinders of metal, plastic, earthenware, or other material, used to conduct fluids. They can be manufactured in metal from either sheets or solid bars. In welded tubing, a strip of steel or other metal is rolled up so that opposite edges meet, ready for *welding. The tube may then be drawn through a *die to reduce the wall thickness at the weld and introduce some *work-hardening. Large-diameter pipes are produced in presses that bend long plates into a U-shape and then into an O. The seam is welded by either gas or arc methods. High-pressure, thick-walled seamless tubing is produced by the *Mannesmann method, in which a red-hot steel rod is forced over a cylindrical shaft (mandrel) between two rolls or in a rotary forge. The rough tube is re-heated and the inner and outer surfaces smoothed by further use of mandrels and rolls. The tube is then drawn to size through a die with a floating mandrel. The finest tubes are smaller than fine sewing needles. Seamless tubes of softer materials, such as aluminium and *PVC, are produced by *extrusion through a die. (See also *cathode-ray tube, *electron tube.)

tube-railway *underground railway.

tug, a small, powerful vessel used in harbours and elsewhere for aiding large vessels to move in confined spaces, for towing at sea, for fire-fighting, and for salvage and rescue, particularly after groundings or engine failure. Towing was an obvious use for the early *steamships, and tugs evolved in the USA and Scotland during the second decade of the 19th century. There are several types of tug. Harbour tugs are usually around 250 tonnes and develop a power of up to 1,900 kW; ocean-going tugs are much larger (2,000 tonnes) and may develop over 11,200 kW. With the immense amount of power available from modern engines, there is the real risk of turning a tug over unless the pull is kept accurately over the stem or stern. For this reason tugs are usually designed with a wide beam and a pronounced incurving of the vessel's sides.

The British agriculturalist Jethro **Tull**. From a painting owned by the Royal Society for Agriculture.

Tull, Jethro (1674–1741), British agricultural engineer. He originally studied law, but soon abandoned this in favour of farming, improving his knowledge of current practice by extensive travel in Europe. In 1701 he conceived the idea of a mechanical seed-drill, based on an Italian version of a Chinese invention. He advocated aeration of the soil to improve fertility and the sowing of crops in rows to facilitate hoeing.

tumble-drier, an electrical appliance for drying damp washing by agitation in a stream of heated air. A tumble-drier consists of a perforated metal drum rotating inside an external case. Air is drawn by a fan into the casing and is then heated. The heated air passes into the drum and through the tumbling washing. Humid air then leaves the drum through a fluff filter at its rear, some designs exhausting to outside the building. Tumble-driers that form an integral part of an automatic *washing-machine condense the water vapour internally.

tuner, an electronic circuit which selects a particular frequency with high specificity, ignoring all others. As such, it is a special type of *filter. Tuners are used universally in broadcasting, where they allow separate stations to be selected in *radio and *television receivers. Tuning action takes place by means of a tuned circuit that enables frequency discrimination to take place. This frequency is a property of the *inductor and (more usually) *capacitor values that go to make up the circuit, and may be varied as these values are altered.

tungsten (wolfram: symbol W, at. no. 74, r.a.m. 183.85), one of the heaviest, hardest, and stiffest metallic elements. The main ores of tungsten are wolframite and scheelite, and the extraction process is complex. Tungsten has the highest melting-point (3,370 °C) of all metals and is used for filaments in electric lamps and contact points on *spark-plugs. Tungsten *steel retains its hardness even at red heat, making it useful in the production of cutting tools for high-speed machinery. Tungsten carbide is an extremely hard substance. It is used as an *abrasive and for the tips of industrial masonry bits.

tunnel, an underground passage for use by road or railway vehicles, or in *mining, or for water supply or sewage. The table gives details of some important tunnels. Tunnels in hard rock are generally self-supporting and are advanced by a cycle of operations: drilling, blasting, mucking out, and fixing temporary supports if required. Where the rock is faulted, potentially loose areas are bolted back into sound material. If a smooth profile is required, a permanent concrete lining is built in sections. In soft ground, where the tunnel cannot fully support itself, the permanent lining is usually fixed as the tunnel is excavated. In the 19th and early 20th centuries, brickwork linings were employed for this purpose, but they took a long time to construct, except in sewers of small cross-section. Their use has been superseded by the *prefabrication of linings, where successive rings are built from cast *iron or, more commonly nowadays, *precast concrete segments. Tunnels in soft ground are usually excavated with a tunnel boring machine (TBM), which was developed from the *shield excavator. A TBM excavates by toothed rotary cutters at the front of the shield. TBMs can also be designed for excavating soft rocks, instead of using the conventional blasting method. Water-filled fissures can be permanently sealed by *cementation or, temporarily, by freezing with injected liquid nitrogen, to allow work to progress. Shallow tunnels may be built by the cut-and-cover method, used particularly in urban streets. A section of road is temporarily closed and excavated, perhaps after the construction of diaphragm walls to support adjacent structures. When that section of the tunnel has been built, the excavation is covered over and work proceeds to the next section. For tunnels under shallow water the immersed tube technique is widely used. The tunnel structure is prefabricated in short lengths in a dry dock or on a slipway, and each section is sealed at its ends, making it buoyant. It is then towed out and sunk into a trench dredged in the sea- or river-bed, where it is jointed by divers to the previous section, sealed, and covered over.

Tupolev, Andrey Nikolayevich (1888–1972), Soviet aeronautical engineer. He was a pupil of Nikolay Zhukovsky, the father of Soviet aviation. He was responsible for more than 100 military and civilian aircraft, from the all-wood single-seater ANT-1 (1922) to the supersonic Tu-22 bomber (1961). Tupolev also designed *gliders, hydroplanes, and *torpedo-boats. His main rival was *Ilyushin.

turbine, a machine that converts the energy stored in a fluid into mechanical energy. It comprises a rotor with one

Important tunnels

Name/location	Length between portals	Date	Other details
Halab (Aleppo), Syria	12 km (7.5 miles)	before *c.*700 BC	Water conduit supplying city of Halab, built by King Sennacherib of Assyria
Samos, Greece	1 km (0.6 miles)	687 BC	Part of a water conduit driven through a mountain from two sides. Out of line by 5 m (16 feet) at meeting point
Lake Fucinus, near Rome	5.6 km (3.5 miles)	AD 41–51	Built to drain the lake. Driven from shafts up to 120 m (400 feet) deep
Malpas, near Béziers, France	157 m (515 feet)	1679–81	Tunnel on the Canal du Midi, the first in which rock was blasted out using explosives
Noirieu, France	12 km (7.5 miles)	1822	One of three tunnels on the St Quentin Canal, with a combined tunnel length of 18.6 km (11.5 miles)
Wapping to Rotherhithe, London, UK	366 m (1,201 feet)	1825–42	First major underwater tunnel. Driven using M. Brunel's tunnelling shield
Mont Cenis, Fréjus, France–Italy	12.8 km (7.8 miles)	1857–71	First tunnel under the Alps. First use of compressed-air drills (from 1860)
Simplon 1 and Simplon 2	19.8 km (12.3 miles)	1898–1906, 1912–21	Twin single-line railway tunnels, the world's deepest (2,135 m, 7,005 feet). Simplon 1 encountered enormous geological problems in tunneling
New York to Delaware water tunnel, USA	168.9 km (105 miles)	1944	Water supply tunnel for New York City. Longest tunnel in world
Bay Area Rapid Transit (BART) system, San Francisco, USA	10 km (6.2 miles) underwater	Opened in stages from 1972	Longest immersed-tube tunnel
Seikan, between islands of Honshu and Hokkaido, Japan	53.8 km (33.5 miles)	1971–81	High-speed, double-track rail tunnel, longest in the world
St Gotthard, Switzerland	16.3 km (10.1 miles)	Completed 1980	Longest Alpine road tunnel
Channel Tunnel, Strait of Dover	50.4 km (33.3 miles)	Projected completion date 1993	Longest underwater rail (or road) tunnel

or more rows of shaped blades: fluid is directed on to the blades, causing them to move and thus rotate the rotor. *Water-wheels and *windmills are simple turbines that have been used for many centuries; more recent developments include *water turbines, used in hydroelectricity generation, and *gas and *steam turbines, which are used as power sources in a variety of applications. Small, high-speed turbines are used in pneumatic tools such as *dental drills, and in gas-liquefaction plants expansion turbines are used to remove energy from hot gases, thus cooling them.

turbocharger *supercharger.

turbofan, turbojet, turboprop *jet engine.

Turing, Alan Mathison (1912–54), British computer scientist. In 1937 he published a seminal paper, 'On Computable Numbers', which was in effect a mathematical analysis of how a universal computer should work (see *computer, history of). During World War II, he worked for British Intelligence, and devised (1943) the Colossus deciphering machine, which broke the codes devised by the German coding machine Enigma. Afterwards he joined the National Physical Laboratory, London, where he worked on the earliest British electronic computers, and in 1948 moved to Manchester University, to direct the building of a computer with a memory larger than that of any previous machine.

turpentine, a strong-smelling, naturally occurring oil obtained by *steam distillation of the resin exuded by coniferous trees. Conifers are 'milked' for turpentine like rubber trees are milked for latex. Turpentine is used as a solvent and as a base for *paints and *varnishes.

twill weave *weaves.

two-stroke engine *petrol engine.

type-casting *letterpress printing, *Linotype, *Monotype.

type metal, an alloy (usually 74 per cent lead, 10 per cent tin, and 16 per cent antimony) used for casting type for *letterpress printing. The casting was done originally by hand, later in specialized type-casting machines. The alloy mix may vary according to the flow properties needed by the casting system and the hardness of type required.

typesetting, assembling metal or photographic forms of letters into words to a pre-arranged format. The process began in Europe in about 1450 when *Gutenberg cut matrices and developed a mould for the metal casting of individual letters that could be hand-assembled. Until the mid-1800s, all typesetting was done by hand, with the compositor (typesetter) picking letters from sectioned trays or cases, assembling them into lines in a composing stick, and then storing the lines on shallow, tray-like 'galleys' for correcting and page make-up (the arrangement of areas of type and illustrations into pages for printing). The 19th century saw the development of mechanical typesetting systems which greatly speeded up the process. *Monotype produced lines of individual letters, while *Linotype set words in solid lines. Pages of metal type may be used directly for printing, or they may provide a mould for *platemaking. After World War II, phototypesetting developed, at first using mechanical typesetters that exposed letters on to film through negative letter images. Then, to increase the speed of letter selection, rotating discs carrying the negatives and working in conjunction with timed flashes of light were introduced; later developments included other forms of image projection. Recently, *computers have been used to capture original text on *disk, store digital letter founts (different styles of letter), or control a *laser beam to set the type required on to film or paper at very high speed. Page make-up may involve pasting up individual pages of text and illustration by hand: alternatively *electronic page make-up may be used. Printing plates are made photographically from the completed pages (camera-ready copy).

typewriter, a desk-top machine with keys for producing print-like characters one at a time on paper inserted round a roller. A skilled operator can type sixty to ninety-five words per minute. Workable typewriting machines first appeared in the early 1800s, but enjoyed little commercial success until the Remington Arms Company (USA) marketed in 1874 a design bought from *Sholes. Most Western typewriters have forty-six character keys representing the Roman alphabet, numerals 0 to 9, punctuation marks, and other symbols. Shift keys allow for two different characters on each key, thus producing a total of ninety-two characters plus an inter-word space. When the keys are pressed, typeheads strike through an inked ribbon to print impressions of the characters on to paper behind, which is fed in round a rubber roller or platen. Most non-Western alphabets can be accommodated on a similar keyboard, but Chinese and Arabic require a different system altogether. In the Chinese typewriter there is only one key, and the typing mechanism is set above a movable tray containing up to 3,000 characters. Mechanical typewriters have largely given way to electrical and electronic models, with a spinning 'golf-ball' or 'daisy-wheel' typehead. In many contexts the typewriter has now been replaced by the *word processor.

tyre, a rubber covering, usually inflated, fitted to the outer rim of a *wheel to protect it from excessive wear, and to give a cushioned ride. The tread (that part of the tyre in contact with the road surface) may carry a pattern of grooves or projections to improve traction or road-holding. Before the development of tyres, metal rims protected wheels; later, solid rubber tyres in a metal channel were used, the first being made by the British inventor Thomas Hancock in 1846 for light horse-drawn vehicles and *bicycles. Solid rubber tyres are still used on some *tractors and *lorries. Pneumatic tyres were first patented in 1845 by the British engineer Robert Thomson; they were first produced commercially in 1888 by *Dunlop. However, the pneumatic tyre was not generally adopted until the invention of the dished wheel-rim, patented in 1890 by the British engineer C. K. Welch. By 1916 pneumatic tyres were standard on most passenger vehicles and lorries. Modern motor-car tyres are generally tubeless and radially built, comprising *rubberized fabric with steel reinforcement.

Tyrian purple *dyes and dyeing.

UHF *waveband.

ultracentrifuge *centrifuge.

ultrasound, vibrations in the *frequency range 20 KHz to 1,000 MHz. The effects of such high-frequency vibration on gases, liquids, and solids are diverse and have led to a number of industrial, biological, and medical applications since the 1940s. In gases, small droplets (aerosols) can be made to coagulate by ultrasound. In liquids, ultrasound can cause cavitation (the formation of small bubbles) and this effect can be used in cleaning metal surfaces. Emulsification, the fine dispersion of one liquid in a different liquid, is another use. The ability to focus a high-frequency beam of ultrasonic radiation and to pick up reflected vibrations enables ultrasonics to be used as a sensitive detector of foreign particles in liquids and gases and of any flaws in a solid. This last property is the basis of the important field of non-destructive testing (NDT), much used in industry. Ultrasonic vibration of a drill bit of any cross-section can allow holes to be bored more readily in hard materials. Ultrasound has recently been used to start or control chemical reactions, for example, to make *polymers. In medicine, echo-reflection ultrasonography, introduced in the late 1940s, is a diagnostic technique in which sound waves are transmitted into the body and bounce back from the internal tissues. The reflected sound waves can be detected and displayed as a moving image on a cathode-ray tube. The technique is used widely in physiotherapy, in *obstetrics to examine the foetus, and also in *cardiology and cardiac surgery to study heart function. In Doppler ultrasonography, for studying the flow of blood in vessels, the operator listens to audible versions of the reflected ultrasound beam in order to investigate, for example, damaged heart valves or impaired circulation to the limbs. Some organs are difficult to image because ultrasound is absorbed by bone and gas. Ultrasound can also visualize gallstones and has been used to fragment stones without the need for surgery (see *lithotripsy).

Ultrasound imaging being used in a US hospital to view a male foetus in the womb. The screen on the left shows the baby's foot, the central screen his folded arm and fist.

umbrella, a light portable screen, usually circular, mounted on a vertical handle, used to shield a person from sun or rain. Umbrellas were used as symbols of rank in China in the 11th century BC; they were not common in Europe until the 16th century, when they were used as sunshades. Waterproof umbrellas of leather or oiled fabric were first made in Paris in the 1730s; later (1874) sprung-steel frames were introduced, allowing the umbrella to be furled. Modern collapsible umbrellas have a light steel frame with a woven cover of synthetic material. Some may be collapsed or erected using a compressed spring released by a catch.

underground railway (US, subway; France, Métro; colloq., tube), a railway system carrying passengers in tunnels beneath the streets of a city. The first underground was opened in London in 1863, and ran from Paddington to Farringdon. It was built by the cut-and-cover method (see *tunnel). The line used coal-burning *steam locomotives, and was successful despite the sulphurous fumes. The first 'tube' railway, dug at a greater depth using a *shield excavator, was the City and South London line, which opened in 1890 and used *electric locomotives. The first line in mainland Europe was opened in Budapest in 1896, the Paris Métro was begun in 1898, and a subway line was constructed in Boston, USA, between 1895 and 1897. Other systems have subsequently been built in major cities around the world. Among the grandest of them is the underground railway in Moscow, begun in 1932, which now handles as many as 6.5 million passengers a day. Lines using fully *automatic train control have been developed for some undergrounds: the first was the Victoria Line in the London tube system. The Paris Métro, and other systems modelled on it, have introduced trains running on concrete track instead of rails, an example of a *ground-guidance system. New and extended underground railways, such as the BART (Bay Area Rapid Transit) system in San Francisco, USA, help ease problems of urban transportation.

underpinning, the process of increasing the depth or width of existing *foundations. This may be needed because the existing foundation has failed, or because planned alterations to a structure will increase the load on a foundation beyond its capacity. It is also frequently used in redevelopment where excavations are close to and below a foundation. A new spread foundation is built in sections beneath the original foundation and joined to it. Where the underpinning needs to be deep, *piling may be used instead of a spread foundation.

undershot wheel, a *water-wheel driven by the pressure of water flowing against the blades below its shaft. Undershot wheels are particularly suited to locations where a large volume of water flows at a low head. They are not very efficient, extracting only about one-fifth of the energy of the water, but were widely used from early times in floating mills and *tide-mills. They included some of the largest known wooden wheels, as much as 10 m (30 feet) wide and up to 6 m (20 feet) in diameter. (See water-wheel for illustration.)

underwater exploration *deep-sea and diving technology.

Unicode *ASCII.

unit (weights and measures), the name of a quantity, such as second or metre, chosen as a standard for use in meas-

SI units and equivalents in common use

Quantity	Unit name (abbreviation)	Imperial equivalent	Definition or equivalent basic units
Basic SI units			
Length	metre (m)	1 foot = 0.3048 m (exactly)	One metre equals the distance travelled by light in a vacuum in 1/299,792,458 of a second
Mass	kilogram (kg)	1 pound = 0.4536 kg	One kilogram equals the weight of a substance equal to the weight of the International Prototype Kilogram, held at Sèvres in France
Time	second (s)	—	One second equals 9,192,631,770 periods of the radiation corresponding to the transition between the two hyperfine levels of the ground state of the caesium-133 atom
Electric current	ampere (A)	—	One ampere in each of two infinitely long parallel conductors of negligible cross-section 1 m apart in a vacuum will produce on each a force of 2×10^{-7} N/m
Thermodynamic	kelvin (K)	—	One kelvin is 1/273.16 of the thermodynamic temperature of the triple point of water
Luminous intensity	candela (cd)	—	The luminous intensity of a black-body radiator at the temperature of freezing plantinum at a pressure of 1 standard atmosphere viewed normal to the surface is 6×10^5 cd/m^2
Amount of substance	mole (mol)	—	One mole is the amount of a substance containing as many elementary units as there are carbon atoms in 0.012 kg of carbon-12. The elementary unit (atom, molecule, ion, etc.) must be specified
Derived SI units			
Acceleration	metre/second squared (m/s^2)	1 foot/s^2 = 0.3048 m/s^2 (exactly)	
Area	square metre (m^2)	1 square foot = 0.292 m^2	
Capacitance	farad (F)	—	A s/v (C/v) (ampere-seconds per volt or coulombs per volt)
Charge	coulomb (C)	—	A s (ampere-seconds)
Density	kilogram/cubic metre (kg/m^3)	1 pound/cubic foot = 16.02 kg/m^3	
Energy (including heat)	joule (J)	1 calorie = 4.1868 J (exactly)	N m (newton-metres)
Force	newton (N)	1 pound force = 4.45 N	kg m/s^2 (kilogram-metres per second squared)
Frequency	hertz (Hz)	—	1/s^{-1} (seconds $^{-1}$)
Inductance	henry (H)	—	V s/m^2 (volt-seconds per square metre)
Magnetic flux density	tesla (T)	—	V s (volt-seconds)
Power	watt (W)	1 horsepower = 746 W 1 foot-pound/s = 1.36 W	J/s (joules per second)
Pressure	pascal (Pa) bar (10^5 Pa)	1 millimetre of mercury = 133.3 Pa 1 standard atmosphere = 101,323 Pa	N/m^2 (newtons per square metre)
Resistance	ohm (Ω)		V/A (volts per ampere)
Velocity	metre/second (m/s)	1 kilometre/hour = 0.278 m/s 1 mile/hour = 0.447 m/s	
Voltage	volt (V)	—	J/s/A (W/A) (joules per second per ampere, or watts per ampere)
Volume	cubic metre (m^3)	1 litre (1 dm^3) = 0.001 m^3 1 pint = 0.5682 dm^3 1 cubic foot = 0.0283 dm^3	

urement or comparison. Units measuring the quantities of mass, distance, area, and volume have existed since early in human history; more recently temperature, pressure, electric current, and other physical quantities have become important. In the Middle East, the ancient Egyptians and Babylonians developed systems of weights and measures, and an independent system was evolved in China. Early units of linear measurement were often derived from body measurements: the Egyptian cubit, for example (derived *c.*3000 BC), was based on the distance from the elbow to the fingertip, and the Chinese used a unit measured from the pulse to the thumb. Later, more accurate standards were developed. The Egyptian royal cubit (524 mm, 20.62 inches) was standardized against a master cubit of black marble: from 221 BC the Chinese also had standardized measures, introduced by the first emperor, Shi Huangdi. Measurement accuracies of 0.05 per cent were achieved using this system, in the building of the Great Pyramid at Giza, Cairo. Ancient Greek units drew from both the Egyptian and Babylonian systems of weights and measures. The Romans based their units on those of the Greeks: both the Romans and the Greeks, for example, used the foot as a length measurement. Medieval Europe inherited the Roman system, but in time many regional variations arose, and other units were borrowed from Scandinavia and elsewhere. The great European trade fairs of the 12th and 13th centuries forced merchants from different countries to adopt the same units of measurement, but many variations remained: in England, for example, there were three different sizes of gallon, one for corn, one for wine, and one for ale. In the late 18th century the metric system was introduced in France, in the aftermath of the French Revolution. The system was designed to be rational and practical, with each unit being subdivided or multiplied decimally, and a system of prefixes for multiples and submultiples covering all units (see table). The metric system spread through Europe and to many other countries during the 19th century, and in the 20th century became the basis for the modern *SI unit system, now used internationally by the scientific community. In the UK and the USA a system of imperial units, rationalized from the European medieval system, continued to be used for most purposes except scientific work. The UK began a changeover to the metric system in 1965, but the USA still has no national legislation to introduce metric units.

UNIVAC (computer) *computer, history of.

universal joint, a mechanism to allow transmission of power between shafts inclined at an angle. The first type was invented by the British physicist Robert Hooke in 1676 for astronomical use, and consisted of a C-shaped member on the end of each shaft, connected by a cross-shaped member pivoted to the ends of each C. Such couplings are generally used in almost every class of machinery. In automobiles, they are used at either end of the transmission shaft of a front-engined, rear-wheel-drive vehicle. Hooke's joint is, however, unsuitable for front-wheel-drive vehicles, because fluctuations in speed at the wheels occur. In such situations constant-velocity (CV) joints are used. CV joints transmit unvarying angular displacement even when the angle between driving and driven shafts varies.

uranium (symbol U, at. no. 92, r.a.m. 238·03), a heavy, *radioactive, metallic element, the only natural material capable of sustaining *nuclear fission. Natural uranium contains several *isotopes: only one of these, uranium-235, undergoes fission under neutron bombardment. Only about one molecule in 140 of natural uranium is U-235. Uranium ore is mined in various parts of the world (the best sources are in Canada and Zaïre), and converted during purification to uranium dioxide (UO_2). (See also *nuclear fuel.)

urea-formaldehyde resin, a synthetic thermosetting *plastic derived from the reaction of urea (carbamide) with formaldehyde (methanal) or its *polymers. It resists solvents, heat, and scratches, and is dimensionally stable (does not change dimensions on heating or cooling). Its main advantage over phenol-formaldehyde resins such as *bakelite is that it has a light coloration. Originally used in decorative applications (buttons and tableware), it is now used chiefly in such electrical applications as domestic plugs and sockets.

Urey, Harold Clayton (1893–1981), US chemist who discovered *heavy water. Urey began research into the *isotopes of hydrogen in the 1920s, and in 1931 isolated the heavy isotope deuterium (D) by *fractional distillation. He then devised a large-scale process for obtaining heavy water (D_2O), a process that was later crucial to the development of the *CANDU nuclear reactor. During World War II a team under Urey worked on the *Manhattan Project, providing data necessary for the separation of uranium-235 from U-238 (see *nuclear fuel). After the War Urey was involved in the manufacture of a second hydrogen isotope, tritium, for the hydrogen bomb. His later research was concerned with theories on the origin of the different elements, and how the Earth and other planets were formed. Subsequent research broadly supported these ideas. Urey was awarded the Nobel Prize for Chemistry in 1934.

V1 rocket *cruise missile.

V2 rocket *ballistic missile.

vaccination *immunization.

vacuum cleaner, a portable electric appliance that cleans with the aid of suction. The first vacuum cleaner was an industrial device powered by a petrol engine, patented by Hubert Booth in the UK in 1901. Portable electric vacuum cleaners were developed in the USA, the first being marketed by William Hoover in 1908. Cylinder vacuum cleaners were first made in Stockholm, Sweden, in about 1913. A cylinder vacuum cleaner contains a motor-driven suction fan that creates a partial vacuum inside the machine. Air is drawn in through a flexible hose fitted with various hand tools used to loosen debris from the surface being cleaned. The debris is then filtered from the airstream by a fabric or disposable paper bag. An upright vacuum cleaner contains a cylindrical 'beater bar', fitted with small brushes to loosen the dirt, in addition to the vacuum action. Some vacuum cleaners are combinations of these two designs, and others employ detergent sprays for cleaning heavily soiled carpets.

The 'Wizard', an early mechanical **vacuum cleaner**, from about 1910.

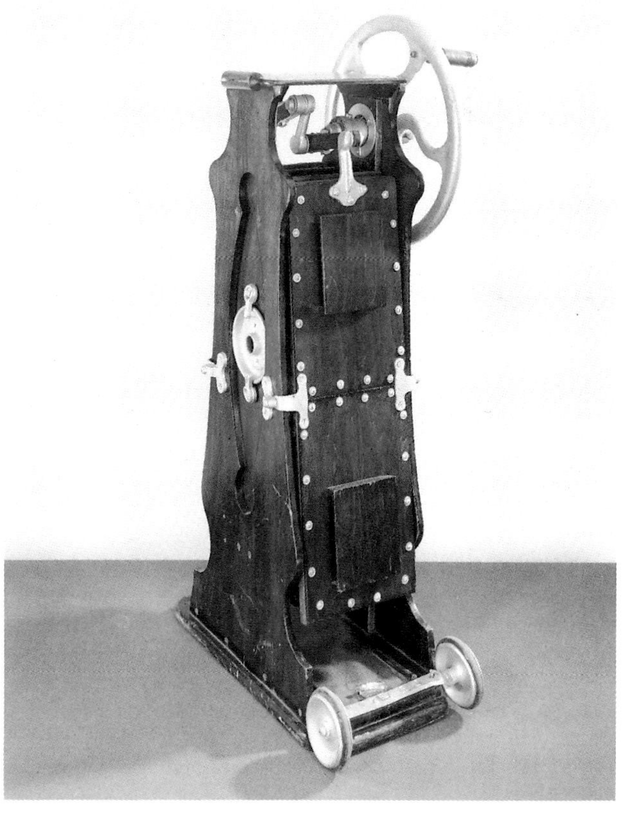

vacuum distillation, a *distillation process for materials that have very high boiling-points or are likely to decompose below their boiling-point. Air is evacuated from the apparatus with a vacuum pump, and the vacuum so formed causes the materials being heated to boil at a temperature lower than they would under normal atmospheric pressure. This enables distillation to take place at lower temperatures. One example of its use is in *petroleum refining.

vacuum flask, an insulated container which thermally isolates the contents from its surroundings. The space between the double walls of the flask contains a vacuum, in order to eliminate *heat transfer by convection. The walls are made from thin glass to limit heat conduction and are silvered to reduce radiant heat energy transfer. The vacuum flask was originally developed in the 1890s by James Dewar for storing liquefied gases at very low temperatures. The modern domestic Thermos flask is used to maintain the temperature of hot or iced drinks.

vacuum pump, a device for removing air from laboratory apparatus. The *pump may be required because the materials to be handled are air-sensitive or because a low pressure is needed—for example, in *vacuum distillation. A reliable vacuum can be obtained using a motor-driven oil pump. For very low pressures, the additional use of a mercury vacuum pump is required, in which a diffused jet of mercury vapour is injected at the inlet port and drives gas molecules towards the outlet. Another low-pressure pump is the turbo-molecular pump, basically a very high-speed *turbine. In a 'getter' pump, a film of some active substance such as titanium is deposited in the evacuation chamber and reacts chemically with any gas molecules present, thus removing them from the chamber.

valve (mechanical), a device for controlling the flow of liquids or gases in a pipe. Valves have several uses: to isolate part of a system, to regulate fluid pressure and flow, as relief or *safety-valves to guard against excess pressure build-up, or as non-return (one-way) valves to prevent back-flow. The range of valve types is extensive, and only a selection are discussed here. In a globe valve, a circular disc fits over a corresponding seating: an example of its use is in a *tap. Diaphragm pumps use a valve in which a flexible flap opens or closes, depending on flow direction. Butterfly-valves are circular pivoted discs that can be turned either edge-on to the fluid flow (open) or across the flow (closed). They are used in *carburettors, as is the tapered needle valve. Another type of valve used in engines is the poppet-valve, which in the four-stroke *petrol engine controls the entry and exit of fluids into and out of the cylinder. Other types of valve are electrical (*thermionic) valves and heart valves (see *cardiology and cardiac surgery.

vanadium (symbol V, at. no. 23, r.a.m. 50.94), a light, whitish metallic element. Small amounts of vanadium are added to *steel to improve its high-temperature strength. It is also added to copper alloys to increase strength and corrosion-resistance, especially in marine environments. Vanadium–aluminium alloys are used in airframe construction, and vanadium oxide (VO) is a good industrial catalyst.

van de Graaff generator, an electrostatic charge *generator, often used in a high-voltage *particle accelerator. The van de Graaff generator was invented by the US physicist Robert van de Graaff in 1931. It consists of a vertical, continuous, motorized belt, which is continually charged from an external source at one point by friction against a roller. The belt transfers the charge to a large, insulated, hollow metal dome, where a high voltage (up to millions of volts) is produced. Eventually, the accumulated potential can be fed to an electrode and used to accelerate particles.

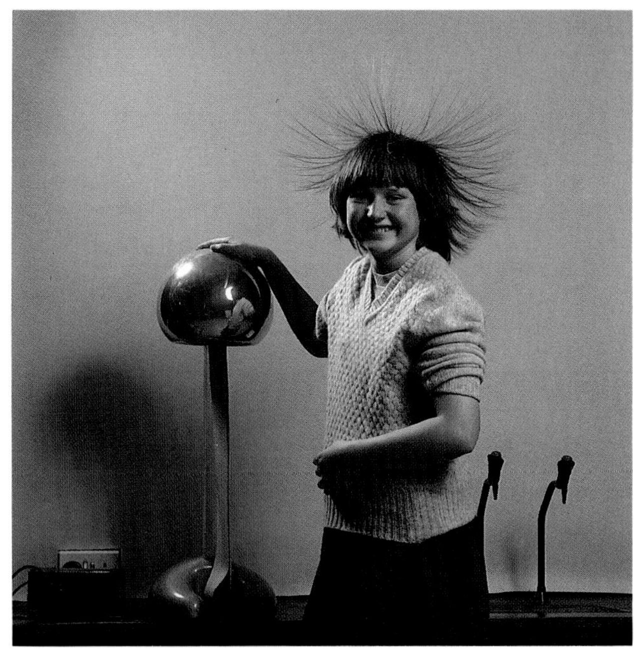

A **van de Graaff generator** for developing electrostatic charge. The charge on the generator induces a similar charge in the girl's hairs, which repel one another.

vapour deposition, a method of manufacturing materials, particularly in the form of thin films, by the deposition of gas or vapour atoms or molecules on a substrate. In chemical vapour deposition (CVD), the gas or vapour decomposes in a surface reaction to form a solid layer: decomposition is activated either by heat or by direct excitation using laser light. CVD is used to manufacture *semiconductor devices, wear-resistant ceramic films, *diamond films, and ceramic or *glass fibres. In physical vapour deposition (PVD) the vapour, produced by high-temperature evaporation of a solid or liquid in a vacuum, is condensed on to the substrate. PVD is used to manufacture semiconductor devices, and to evaporate thin layers of aluminium on to plastic food packaging films, or on to *polycarbonate discs in the manufacture of *compact discs. A vapour can also be produced at normal temperatures by the technique of sputtering. Sputtering is a physical process in which *ions extracted from an inert gas (for example, *argon) are accelerated and bombarded upon the solid target material (the *cathode) that is to be deposited. The target atoms are ejected (vaporized) by this bombardment and deposit on a substrate (the *anode). Sputtering is used mostly in the deposition of metals, which are difficult to deposit by other means.

varnishes and lacquers. A varnish is a transparent solution of a natural or synthetic resin (such as *polyurethane) or resinous gum in linseed or other *drying oil. Varnishes are applied to a material (usually wood) to provide a thin, transparent, and waterproof protective coating. They are also used in printing *inks. Lacquers are also film-forming substances (the most common are cellulose lacquers); however, they are dissolved in volatile solvents and dry entirely by evaporation, whereas the drying of varnishes involves *oxidation as well as evaporation. One use of lacquers is to coat the inside surfaces of tin cans.

Vauban, Sébastien Le Prestre de (1633–1707), French military engineer. Commissioned in the French Army as an engineer (1655), he compiled for the Minister of War an enormously influential treatise on siege warfare in 1669 (published in Leiden, 1740). Over the period 1672–8 he carried out nearly twenty successful sieges in the Low Countries, using a succession of parallel trenches to give advancing troops constant protection. He constructed many distinctive fortresses, based on geometrical principles of design to eliminate dead ground. He also developed the technique of indirect ricochet fire and the use of the bayonet (first used at Bayonne, 1650).

vault, a three-dimensional arched structure, curved transversely and sometimes lengthwise. Semi-cylindrical barrel vaults in *brick, stone, or *concrete were used to roof many Roman public buildings. In these vaults, loads are transmitted circumferentially to supporting walls, which were built massively to resist overturning forces. In the Gothic ribbed vault, columns are linked by a series of ribs, between which thin masonry membranes are built. The dome is a doubly curved vault. Modern barrel vaults, usually *reinforced concrete *shell structures, span longitudinally between supporting columns.

Vavilov, Nikolay Ivanovich (1887–1943), Soviet geneticist. He studied genetics and *plant breeding at the University of Cambridge and the John Innes Horticultural Institution, London. Returning to imperial Russia in 1914, he later became, under Lenin, Director of the Bureau of Applied Botany in Petrograd (now St Petersburg). With the aid of 400 Soviet research stations and a staff of 20,000, he embarked (1917–33) on a vast global venture to collect wild plants—ultimately in excess of 50,000 varieties—as the basis of a national plant-breeding programme to improve crop plants. He was discredited by political enemies (led by T. D. Lysenko), arrested in 1940, and sent to a concentration camp at Sanatov, where he died.

VDU *visual display unit.

vegetable cultivation, the production of a vast variety of plants, including many *greenhouse crops, for their edible vegetative parts. These can be roots, tubers, stems, leaves, buds, pods, or even petals. Many vegetables are of low calorific value, but provide dietary vitamins and minerals. Exceptions are *root-crops, and legumes, which provide the major source of protein in many diets. In the Third World, vegetable cultivation is often for subsistence or local consumption. Elsewhere it is a highly capitalized and intensive industry whose customers demand fresh produce of impeccable appearance. Commercial *horticulture relies on perfectly cultivated soil maintained at the correct level of moisture and fertility. Plants are optimally spaced for regular growth and shielded from damage by weather or pests. Traditionally, a variety of vegetables were grown in market gardens close to urban markets. Today the trend is towards larger enterprises in rural areas, specializing in one crop.

vellum *parchment.

velocity ratio, the ratio of the speeds of two points in a mechanism. The simplest example is a first-class *lever: a force at one end will move a load at the other in a velocity ratio equal to the ratio of the distances of force and load from the pivot.

venturi tube, an instrument used to measure the rate of fluid flow, or to draw in liquid from a reservoir. It consists of a tube with a short constriction in the middle designed to cause a drop in pressure in a fluid flowing through it. The rate of fluid flow is measured by attaching a pressure gauge to the constriction. A venturi tube is also used to draw petrol into the *carburettor of a *motor car.

vernier calliper, an instrument for making accurate measurements of objects using the vernier scale, introduced by the Frenchman Pierre Vernier in 1631. The vernier calliper is like a normal pair of measuring callipers, having two jaws between which the object to be measured is inserted, but it has a second scale, subdivided in a different way from the main scale. This is used to give accurate fractions of a single division on the main scale.

vertical take-off and landing aircraft *VTOL aircraft.

Very light, a flare fired from a hand-held pistol to serve as a signal or to provide temporary brilliant illumination, especially in warfare. It was named after its American inventor, E. W. Very (1847–1910). Pyrotechnically, it resembles a rocket and the colour of the light can be varied by including different metal salts in the charge.

veterinary medicine, the science dealing with the health and welfare of farm and domestic animals. Its practice includes both the treatment of sickness and injury, and preventive medicine. In the past, farmers were responsible for the diagnosis and treatment (mostly with herbal medicines) of animals on the farm. The increasing sophistication of drugs and surgical tools, together with the advent of the motor car, has made veterinary medicine very successful at saving animals' lives. Veterinary surgeons have also been concerned with animal welfare, including the design of buildings to achieve optimum comfort and productivity, as well as the development and administration of drugs and hormones. Sophisticated understanding of genetics, as well as the development of techniques such as *artificial insemination and embryo transplantation (see **in vitro* fertilization), have also increased the involvement of veterinary surgeons on the farm. Certain diseases such as tuberculosis and anthrax are transmitted between animals and humans, and the veterinary surgeon must control and isolate stocks bearing that disease. This generally involves regular blood sampling and testing for diseases such as tuberculosis in cattle, but is often carried out by officials of government ministries. Additionally, possibility of disease transfer in meat is monitored by strict controls, under the supervision of veterinary surgeons at the abattoir. In addition to its agricultural aspects, veterinary medicine also includes the treatment of domestic pets, and animals such as horses kept for sport, breeding, or leisure activities.

VHF *waveband.

viaduct, a bridge that crosses a valley in a continuous series of small linked arches. The earliest known examples of viaducts are Roman, for example the Ponte d'Augusto at Narni, near Rome. In the 19th century, brick or masonry viaducts were the normal means of maintaining the level of a railway across a valley in cases when an embankment would be too high or its base too wide. Viaducts are also used in the approaches to a large-span crossing of a waterway where the foundations for the piers would be difficult to build. In current practice, pre-stressed concrete beams supported on concrete piers are the most economical construction for a viaduct.

vice, a two-jawed bench tool used for holding objects securely while they are being worked. There are two main designs. In the older leg-vice, one jaw is fixed and the other is hinged: the opening is controlled by a screw. Its disadvantage is that the movable jaw moves through an arc of a circle, so that the jaws do not remain parallel as they are opened. In the parallel-jaw vice, the movable jaw is also screw-controlled, but slides through an opening in the fixed jaw. Vices commonly incorporate a quick-release device. (For illustration see *tools, history of.)

video camera, a camera for recording electronically encoded visual images. Video cameras for amateur use are designed to be used with *video recorders. These can be either separate portable units or, more commonly, videotape cassette recorders incorporated with the camera in devices known as camcorders. Video cameras are highly sophisticated, using the latest electronic technology to maximize ease of use. Recently, the still video camera was introduced, combining ordinary photography with electronic video technology. In both camcorders and still video cameras, the lens focuses images on to a *charged-coupled device (CCD). The image is then recorded either on to videotape, or (for a still camera) on to a magnetic disk or *compact disc, which acts as the 'film'. The videotape from a camcorder can be played back on a suitable *television receiver. Still video images can also be replayed on a television receiver using a computer, or printed out as a hard copy 'photograph' without the need for chemical processing.

videodisc *compact disc.

video recorder, a device that records on magnetic tape or *compact disc the audio and video signals that constitute a *television programme. In a videotape recorder, the picture is recorded in the same way as a *tape recorder records sound—as magnetic patterns on a tape—but the greater complexity of the video signal necessitates the use of a rotating recording head rather than a fixed one. The first video recorder was developed at the Ampex Corporation of America around 1956. It had four recording and playback heads mounted on a rotating drum, and recorded the video signal as vertical tracks across the tape. The Ampex system gave high-quality reproduction suitable for the television studio. Domestic video recorders did not appear until later,

Video recorder

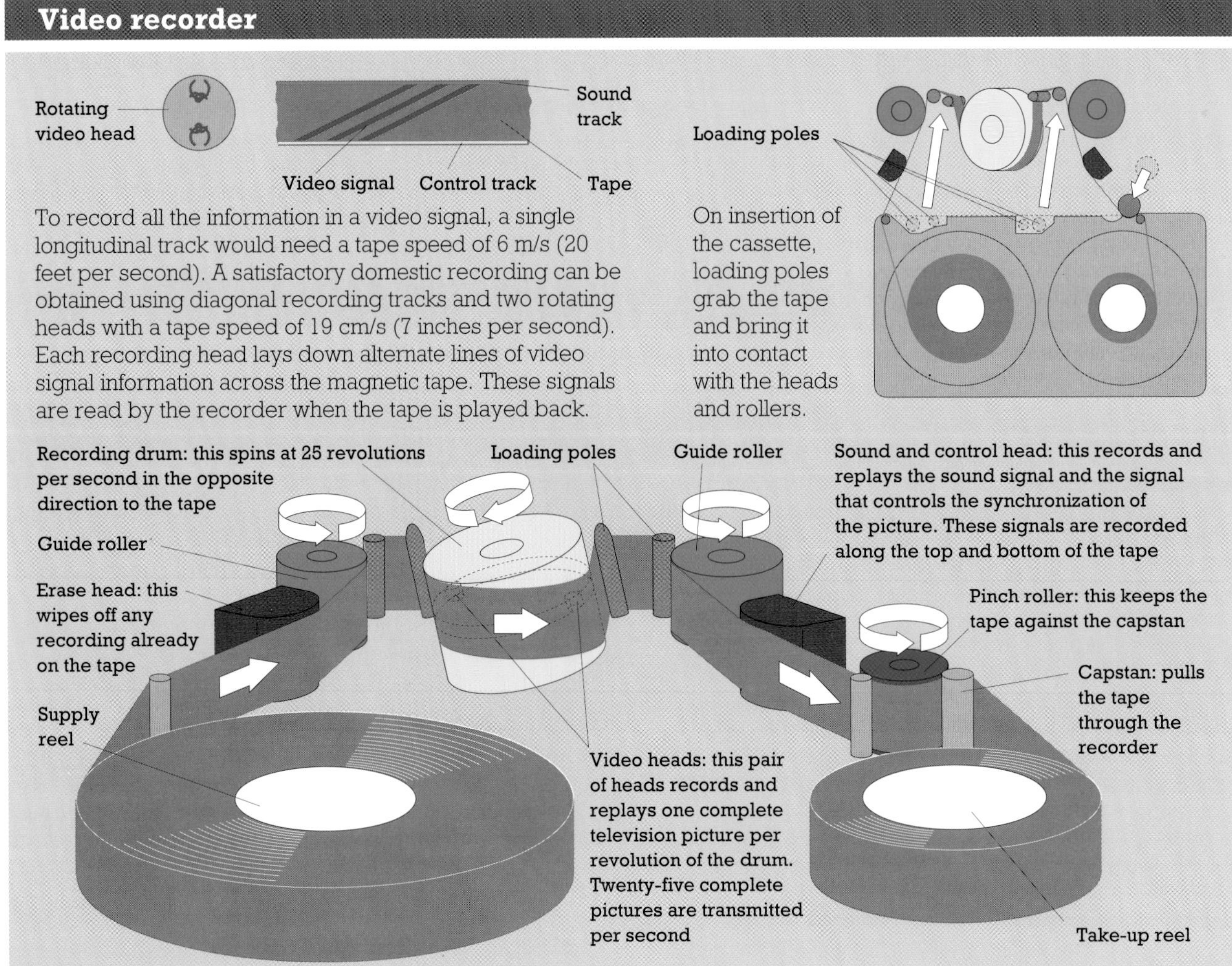

Rotating video head
Sound track
Video signal
Control track
Tape
To record all the information in a video signal, a single longitudinal track would need a tape speed of 6 m/s (20 feet per second). A satisfactory domestic recording can be obtained using diagonal recording tracks and two rotating heads with a tape speed of 19 cm/s (7 inches per second). Each recording head lays down alternate lines of video signal information across the magnetic tape. These signals are read by the recorder when the tape is played back.
Loading poles
On insertion of the cassette, loading poles grab the tape and bring it into contact with the heads and rollers.
Recording drum: this spins at 25 revolutions per second in the opposite direction to the tape
Loading poles
Guide roller
Sound and control head: this records and replays the sound signal and the signal that controls the synchronization of the picture. These signals are recorded along the top and bottom of the tape
Guide roller
Erase head: this wipes off any recording already on the tape
Pinch roller: this keeps the tape against the capstan
Capstan: pulls the tape through the recorder
Supply reel
Video heads: this pair of heads records and replays one complete television picture per revolution of the drum. Twenty-five complete pictures are transmitted per second
Take-up reel

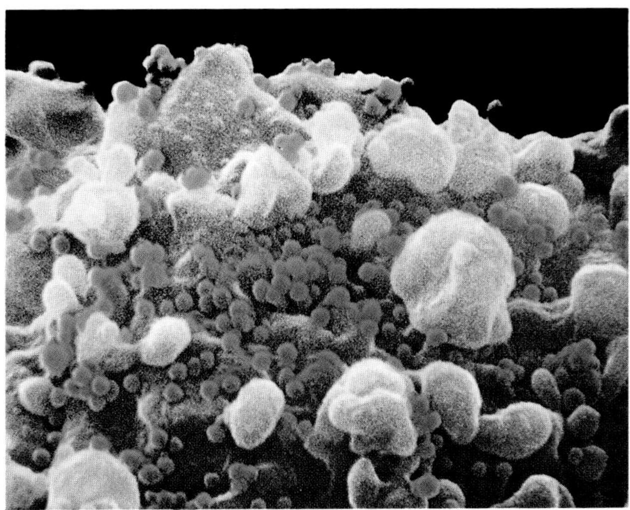

A false-colour scanning electron micrograph showing human T-lymphocyte cells infected with HIV (Human Immunodeficiency Virus), the **virus** that causes Aids. The green particles are viruses in the process of budding off from the host cell.

in the early 1970s. In the domestic VHS (Video Home System) system the rotating drum has only two recording heads, and the tape runs across the drum at an angle, producing a video signal recorded diagonally across the tape (see figure). The accompanying sound-track is synchronized with the pictures by a control signal; sound and control signals are recorded on narrow tracks at the edges of the tape.

videotex, the generic term for television-based information systems, using *computers holding extensive *databases. One format, called viewdata, is an *interactive system enabling the user to conduct a dialogue with a remote computer, using a *microcomputer, a *modem, and a telephone link. Viewdata is used in business and leisure, including home shopping and making travel and theatre reservations. Another format of videotex, *teletex, was developed in the UK in the 1970s and provides information as 'pages', selectable by the viewer, transmitted in unused areas of a standard television signal.

viewdata *videotex.

viewfinder *camera.

Viking ship, a Scandinavian vessel used for trade and warfare (AD *c.*850–1200). Viking warships were long, open, oared vessels, clinker-built (see *shipbuilding) and rowed by forty to eighty men. They had a short mast carrying a single square sail that could be braced to allow travel somewhat into the wind. The larger vessels had a part-deck fore and aft. Viking trading ships ('knorrs') were broader in beam and relied on sails much more than on oar power. The Vikings sailed in such vessels as far as Vinland (Newfoundland) to the west; northern Africa to the south; and the Black Sea to the east.

virus, a minute particle capable of infecting a living cell and directing it to make multiple copies of the virus's own components. The host cell may die as a result, as in chickenpox, measles, and influenza, or be persuaded to multiply uncontrolled, causing a *cancer. The smaller viruses consist of only a few protein molecules enveloping a core of *DNA or RNA. Larger viruses such as bacteriophages and HIV (human immunodeficiency virus, the cause of Aids) may comprise hundreds of protein molecules. *Enzymes from such viruses have provided key tools for *genetic engineering. Viruses are not destroyed by *antibiotics, so they can be controlled only by stimulating the immune system (see *immunology), by isolation or, outside the body, by antiseptics. *Interferon, a natural anti-viral agent produced by the body, has been isolated in small quantities, but it has as yet found few uses in combating viral disease.

visual display unit (VDU), a computer *output device that uses a *cathode-ray tube screen to display information from a computer. Commonly used as a *terminal, it is principally designed for text, but most modern types can also be used for *graphics of varying degrees of sophistication. It is an alternative to a computer *printer when a permanent record of the output information is not required. In graphics applications, a fast, high-resolution VDU can produce graphical output more quickly than a plotter. *Interactive systems and *microcomputers now frequently use VDUs.

vitamin treatment. Vitamins are compounds required by the body in very small amounts, which cannot be made in the body (or not in sufficient quantities) and so must be supplied in the diet. Lack of a vitamin results in a deficiency disease, for example, scurvy, which results from insufficient vitamin C. Defining the necessary amount of a vitamin is complicated by factors such as solubility, the presence of drugs and natural substances that destroy the vitamin (antivitamins), bacteria in the gut, infections, and interactions with other nutrients. Deficiency is therefore common, even in otherwise well-fed people, and vitamin treatment consists of supplying either the pure vitamin or a food source rich in that vitamin when deficiency symptoms are diagnosed. Excessive intake of vitamins not only does no good but may do harm. Pure vitamins may be extracted from natural sources, synthesized chemically, or produced by *fermentation technology.

vitrification, the formation of glass or a glass-like material, usually by heating. Vitrification is an important step in the *sintering of most commercial *ceramics. On heating, a small proportion of the ceramic material melts to form a highly viscous liquid, which draws the ceramic particles together during sintering. On cooling, the viscous phase transforms into a glass, which binds the ceramic together. *Glass-ceramics are characterized by a devitrification or crystallization, which occurs on cooling.

Vitruvius (Marcus Vitruvius Pollio) (1st century BC), Roman architect and engineer, remembered chiefly for his ten-volume *De Architectura*, written *c.*30 BC. Virtually nothing is known about his career, but he probably held some official position under Augustus. His book is the only one of its kind to survive from the Roman world. It covers the training of architects; choice of sites; building techniques and materials; the planning of public buildings, temples, and houses; the supply of water; and mechanical aids to building such as levers and pulleys. It was a powerful influence on the ideas of architects, including the Italian Andrea Palladio, until the Renaissance.

vocoder, a device that can break down speech and subsequently reconstruct it. It was originally designed in 1936 to

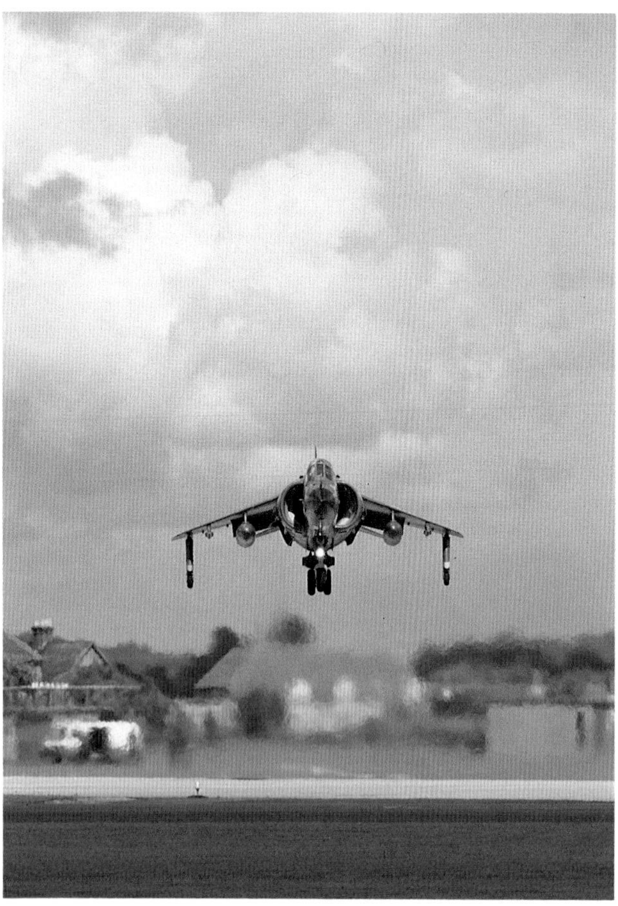

A Sea-Harrier, one of the many versions of the AV-8 or Harrier, made by British Aerospace in the UK and by McDonnell-Douglas in the USA. Since its introduction in 1966 it has been the most successful military **VTOL aircraft** in service.

reduce broadcasting *bandwidth by analysing speech into changes in pitch, and is now used for synthetic speech in, for example, vending machines and cars, working either from magnetic tape recordings or from memory stores of *digitized speech.

volt (V) *electricity and magnetism, *unit.

Volta, Alessandro Giuseppe Antonio Anastasio, Conte (1745–1827), Italian physicist, chiefly remembered for his invention in 1800 of the voltaic pile, an early form of *battery and the first reliable source of electrical current. Volta followed up the experiments of his friend Luigi Galvani (1737–98), who discovered current electricity but failed to interpret his results correctly. Volta found that if two dissimilar metals (such as copper and zinc) were dipped in an electrolyte (a solution able to conduct electricity) such as a salt solution, and the two metals were joined by an external wire, then an electric current flowed through the wire. His voltaic pile consisted of pairs of dissimilar metal discs, separated by salt-soaked cardboard strips and piled one on top of the other. Arranged in series connection, these produced a battery. Investigations by *Davy using the voltaic pile led to the discovery of several chemical elements. Volta's name is remembered in the electrical *unit the volt.

voltaic cell *battery.

voltaic pile *Volta, Alessandro (Giuseppe Antonio Anastasio), Conte.

voltmeter, a moving-coil or solid-state instrument that measures voltage potential in an electrical or electronic circuit. Voltmeters are two-terminal devices which, in contrast to *ammeters, have an extremely high internal resistance. This enables them to take very little current, allowing measurement of the voltage source without disturbing its value.

VTOL aircraft (Vertical Take-Off and Landing aircraft), an aeroplane capable of taking off and landing without a runway. While *helicopters can be considered as VTOL aircraft, the term is more usually applied to fixed-wing aeroplanes. Greater power is needed to raise an aeroplane vertically without the aerodynamic lift it obtains from its wings (see *flight, principles of). The first successful demonstration of VTOL was by the Rolls-Royce 'Flying Bedstead', on 3 August 1954. The most famous development of this principle is the British Aerospace Harrier jump-jet.

vulcanization, the reaction of crude rubber with *sulphur or other suitable agent under intense heat, producing extensive changes in the physical properties of the rubber. Vulcanization results in an increase in cross-linking between the *polymer molecules in the rubber, which make it more durable and adaptable. The changes in physical properties include decreased plastic flow, reduced surface tackiness, increased elasticity, much greater tensile strength, and considerably less solubility. Recently it has become possible to develop a version of *polythene which can be vulcanized, giving it increased resistance to deformation.

wagon *carts and wagons, *lorry, *goods wagon.

wagon-way (tramway), a grooved track or rails laid to provide guidance for wheeled vehicles travelling along it. Evidence for grooved stone wagon-ways can be found in Greece and in ancient Roman cities such as Pompeii. Wagon-ways were used in mines in Europe from the mid-16th century. By the end of the century they were also being built above ground, using either wagons with flanged wheels running on parallel wooden balks, or flangeless wheels on grooved stone blocks. The wagons were usually drawn by horses, although where the topography was suitable they were allowed to roll freely downhill under the control of a brakesman. Iron rails for the tracks were introduced at Whitehaven Colliery in Britain in 1738; cast-iron wheels also came into use around the same time.

Waksman, Selman Abraham (1888–1973), Russian-born US microbiologist. He emigrated to the USA in 1910. From 1938 he was a consultant to Merck, a leading chemical manufacturer, for whom he investigated the chemotherapeutic possibilities of *antibiotics. This led to Waksman and his associates discovering several interesting products, of which the most important was streptomycin (1944), which has anti-tubercular activity. He was awarded the Nobel Prize for Physiology and Medicine in 1952 with A. Schutz and E. Bugie.

Wankel engine *rotary engine.

war, technology of *military technology.

warhead, the destructive section of a *missile, *torpedo, or similar projectile. Normally mounted at the missile's head, it may be an explosive device or a chemical or biological weapon. A nuclear warhead is a missile-borne *nuclear weapon. It may be part of a *multiple independently targetable re-entry vehicle launched by a long-range *ballistic missile, but is often carried alone by shorter-range missiles.

warning and detection system, a system used by military forces to perceive an attack, and by civil users mainly for air and sea safety. Such systems include *radar, *radio, *sonar, aerial photography, and *image intensification. Military applications of these systems include air defence, aerial reconnaissance, *electronic warfare, anti-submarine defence, missile warning, mine countermeasures, and defence against attack by ground or sea forces. Civil authorities use such systems for *air-traffic control, monitoring sea lanes in busy areas, and search and rescue operations.

Radar is the main component of many warning and detection systems. It has many applications in both civil and military spheres. In air traffic control, radar can not only help keep aircraft apart in crowded air lanes but, using secondary radar (in which a radar pulse to an aircraft triggers a return signal from the aircraft), individual aircraft can be identified, and an aircraft in an emergency can use a special code to indicate distress. Military applications include land-based *early-warning systems, used to give long-range warning of missile attack. Airborne radar is carried in special aircraft (see *AWACS) to give warning of low-level air attack. Ground-based radar can warn of tank or infantry attack. Secondary radar is also used to distinguish friendly and hostile aircraft.

The receiving of radio signals using directional *antennae is used in many detection systems. In military circles it is known as electronic warfare. Radar is a specialized type of radio transmission, and can be detected in this way. The homing systems of active homing *guided missiles use radar transmissions, and a receiver tuned to such transmissions can give warning of the direction of attack. The same technique is used in search and rescue operations to find the bearings of ships or aircraft in distress. Radio waves do not travel far under water, so for detecting submerged objects sonar is used. Passive sonar gives warning of the presence of ships, submarines, or torpedoes, especially if they themselves are making sonar transmissions, while active sonar can also detect silent underwater objects such as mines. Photography, especially aerial photography or photo-imaging from reconnaissance satellites or aircraft, can give warning of troop movements, missile installations, or the positions of warships. Special photographic techniques such as infra-red *photography are also used, allowing photographs to be taken at night or through clouds. Infra-red detectors, and *image intensifiers, which can enhance a dark image to almost full daylight quality, are also used.

warp, the longitudinal threads in woven *fabrics. Warp threads are subject to high tension and frequent abrasion during weaving on a *loom. They are also highly stressed during *textile-finishing processes. For these reasons, *yarns to be used as warp are generally tightly twisted to give strength and are *sized to resist abrasion.

warship, a vessel specifically built or adapted for use in war. The first warships were probably canoes, used for raiding and piracy. The earliest types for which there is evidence were Egyptian warships that combined sail and oar propulsion. Their main weapons seem to have been carried by the crews. Around the 2nd millennium BC a new style of naval warfare was developed in the eastern Mediterranean, in which the ram was the major weapon. The oared *galley used in this style of fighting was developed further by the Greeks: these long, narrow ships, with large crews, contrasted strongly with the broad-beamed merchant ships of the time which carried only a handful of crew. The galley remained the standard Mediterranean warship until about the 6th century AD, when rams were abandoned and personal weapons again became important. However, the use of oared galleys, later armed with guns, continued in the Mediterranean into the 16th century and beyond. Byzantine galleys (dromonds) used a weapon that was a form of flame-thrower employing *Greek fire.

In northern Europe, the oared, rowing and sailing *Viking ship was gradually replaced by vessels with 'castles' in the bow and stern to provide platforms from which fire could be directed against enemy ships. During the 15th century the three-masted, square-rigged ship spread throughout Europe, and from about 1600 ships began to carry *cannon in their hulls. Techniques of warfare using sailing warships took some time to develop, and it was not until the Anglo-Dutch war of 1650 that the new methods became fully established, with the cannon as the ship's main weapon. Thereafter, warships were divided into *ships of the line and smaller scouting and auxiliary vessels. With the introduction

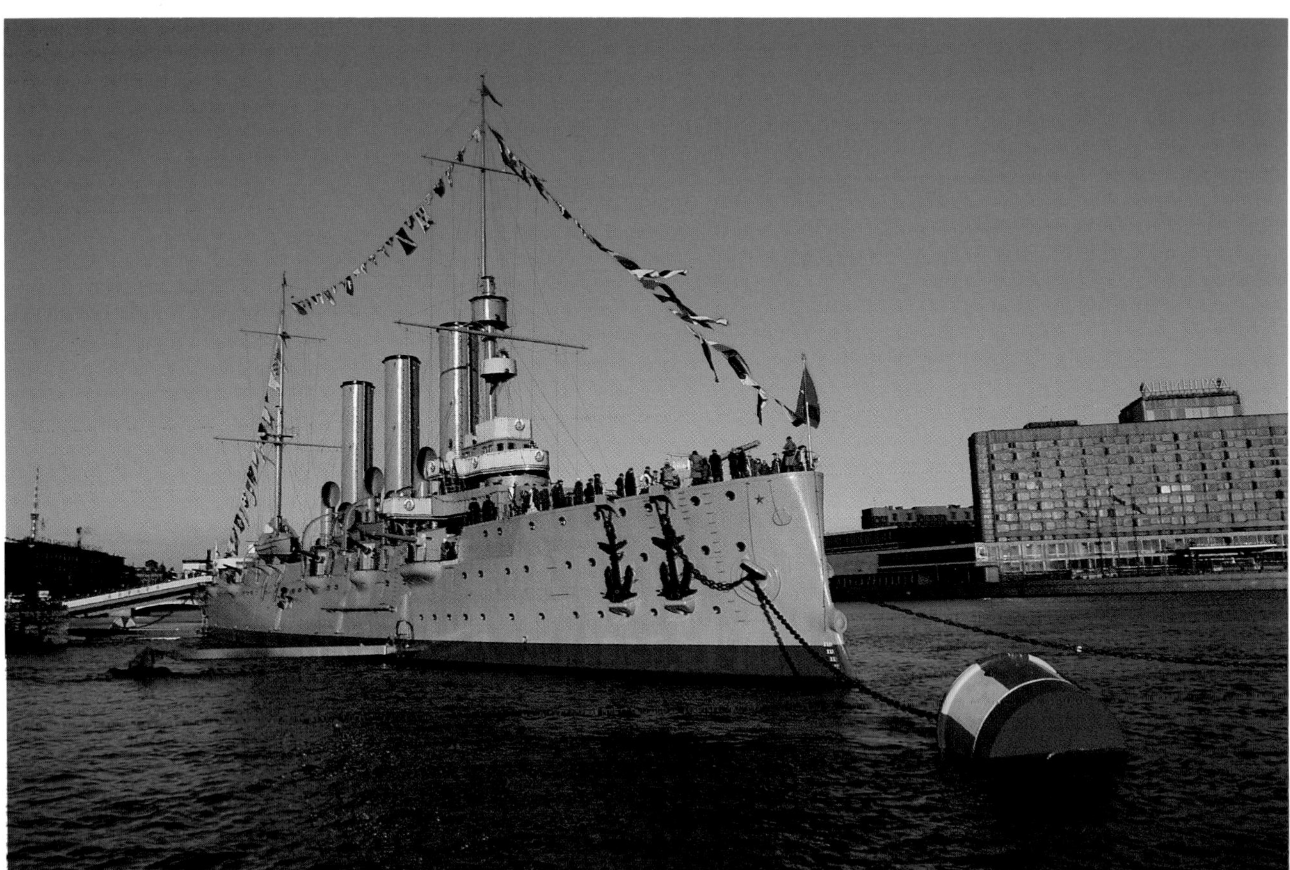

The Soviet **warship** *Aurora* at permanent anchorage on the River Neva in St Petersburg. *Aurora* fired the signal shot that began the Russian Revolution of October 1917. It is now preserved as a floating museum.

of steam propulsion and iron ships in the 19th century, armoured *ironclads and later *battleships replaced the largest wooden warships. Breech-loading guns superseded cannon, and development of the *torpedo led to the building of *torpedo-boats, as a counter to which the *destroyer was introduced. By 1900 the first practicable *submarines were being built, and during World War I the *aircraft carrier first appeared. After World War II a new type of naval warfare emerged, based on the use of aircraft, submarines, and *missiles. Important new ship types were guided-missile destroyers, anti-submarine frigates, and specialized amphibious *assault craft. Modern naval warfare is highly dependent on electronic equipment, *warning and detection systems being as important as the actual weaponry and its guidance systems. (See also specific ship types.)

washing-machine, a domestic appliance for the mechanical washing of clothes. Early machines from the 19th century were made of wood and were hand cranked; the washing was carried out in a tub by a reciprocating plunger or paddle. Later developments included drive by electric motor, internal water-heating, and an attached mangle. The 'twin-tub' washing machine introduced in the 1950s had a separate compartment containing a spin-drier. This is a perforated metal cylinder that spins on its axis at high speed, centrifugal force flinging the water out of the washing. The modern automatic washing-machine consists of a perforated steel drum which rotates inside a watertight case. The drum washes by slow rotation and also functions as a spin-drier. Various combinations of filling, heating, emptying, washing, rinsing, and spin-drying (called programs) are controlled by a time-switch or *microprocessor.

washing powder, a powdered *detergent for the domestic washing of clothes and household fabrics in water, either by hand or in a *washing-machine. The powder also contains other materials to improve the appearance of the washed fabric. These include *brightening agents, blueing ingredients (which make yellowing fabrics appear white), *phosphates (which help keep dislodged clay particles suspended in the water), *bleaches, and *perfumes. Some washing powders dissolve to give an alkaline solution and are good at removing grease. Some are neutral, allowing them to be used with delicate fibres or special fabric finishes. Recently, enzymes (bacterial proteases) have been incorporated into washing powders (the so-called 'biological' powders). These break down stains caused by proteins (wine, blood, chocolate) at low washing temperatures. Non-biological powders need higher temperatures to achieve the same effect, but biological powders can cause severe irritation to moist skin, eyes, and mucous membranes. Liquid or powder mixtures, of slightly different formulation, are sold for use in automatic washing-machines. These do not cause suds and therefore do not clog pumps.

waste management, the disposal or utilization of solid or semi-solid wastes. In most Western countries, economic and population growth has resulted in greatly increased amounts of waste. The most common methods of waste disposal in modern times have been sanitary landfill and incineration. Landfill disposal involves dumping and compacting waste in large pits on specially prepared sites. Landfill has been widely used because of its low cost, but the increasing scarcity of suitable sites has increased landfill costs in urban areas. Incineration of waste greatly reduces the volume of material to be disposed of, and the heat generated can be used in *district heating systems: disadvantages are capital and fuel costs, and the pollution caused by incinerator gases. The production of refuse-derived fuel (RDF), made by initial separation of combustible material followed by formation of pellets or *briquettes is a newer technique which is economic and energy-efficient. Up to 40 per cent of domestic waste (mainly metals, glass, and fibrous matrials for *paper manufacture) could be *recycled, although few schemes achieve this in practice. Organic waste can be made into compost, or fermented to produce ethanol or methane. Various processes can be used to produce gas, oil, steam, or electricity from wastes. Pilot waste management schemes have been set up that separate waste into several fractions, and process each by a different method.

watch, a portable instrument for measuring time, usually strapped to the wrist, carried in the pocket, or suspended from the neck. Although portable *clocks appeared in the 16th century, pocket or 'fob' watches only became practicable in the late 17th century, with the advent of the coiled spring drive and balance-spring regulator. Many watches incorporated a repeating mechanism, striking the hours and quarter-hours. Watches remained a luxury until 1868, when G. F. Rosskopf, in Switzerland, introduced cheap watches of simplified design. Wrist-watches appeared in the 1880s, originally in response to the demands of fashion. Self-winding watches, responding to movements of the wearer's wrist, appeared in the early 1920s. In the early 1960s electronic watches were introduced, and in 1969 the first quartz electronic watches were manufactured. In the quartz watch, an electronic circuit produces electrical oscillations of precise frequency, which are controlled by the vibrations of a quartz crystal with extreme accuracy. These oscillations are counted and used to advance the hands on a traditional watch face or a digital *liquid crystal display once every second. Digital watches often include other functions, such as day and date, stop-watch, and alarm.

water cannon, a device that shoots a high-pressure jet of water, used by police and paramilitary forces to disperse crowds without causing death or serious injury. Water cannon are mounted in box-shaped trucks. A tank of water, usually holding around 450 litres (100 gallons), takes up most of the space. The water is pumped through a tube, frequently mounted in a turret on top of the vehicle, which is aimed at the target. The water pressure is normally sufficient to knock a person over.

water-closet (WC, lavatory), a device for receiving solid or liquid human waste and passing it into a drain in a water-borne *sewage-treatment system. It was invented by the English courtier and writer John Harington in 1589. The waste is flushed out of the bowl into the drain by water, usually discharged around the bowl rim from a small cistern fixed above the pan and connected to it by a pipe. In some countries direct flushing from the mains water supply is allowed. The bowl outlet is shaped to form a water seal ('U-bend'); this retains a small depth of water which prevents odours rising from the drain and the entry of vermin. In more elaborate designs the outlet is shaped so that a *siphon is formed when flushing starts, giving more efficient removal of the waste. In areas where there is no sewage system, or where water is scarce, earth closet latrines are used.

water-frame *spinning machine.

watermark, a faint trade or recognition mark put into some paper during manufacture, visible when held against the light. During *paper manufacture, the raised watermark design is carried on a 'dandy' roller positioned over a suction box so that the paper incorporates the design required while it is still semi-liquid. The paper is thinner in the area of the watermark, allowing light to pass through.

water meter, a device that measures and records the volume of water consumed by a household. The object is to reduce consumption, particularly wastage from leaks, *taps, and overflowing storage tanks, by making the users pay for the quantity of water that they consume rather than charging them at a standard rate. In the UK and USA all commercial and some domestic properties are metered. Most European countries have a comprehensive metering system.

water-mill *water power.

water pollution, the fouling or contamination of *water resources. Population growth and higher living standards make greater demands on water resources than can be met by the natural *hydrological cycle. Consequently, the quality of surface and underground fresh water, and of seas and coastal waters, is increasingly impaired. A certain amount of water pollution can be assimilated by dilution or by organisms in the food web adjusting to changes in the water. Beyond that, however, pollution represents a real threat to water quality, health, and the environment. Toxic chemicals, such as the heavy metals cadmium and mercury, produced in some industrial and mining operations and discharged into rivers, lakes, or coastal waters, can kill living organisms and collect in the tissues of fish and shellfish, which then enter the human food chain. Other possibly harmful metal pollutants are aluminium, which is used in water treatment and has been linked with Alzheimer's disease, and lead, used for piping in some older houses and identified as a cause of brain damage in some children. Organic pollutants of fresh and salt water, such as inadequately treated sewage and animal waste, can threaten fish stocks by reducing the amount of dissolved oxygen available to them, while excessive use of agricultural fertilizers and the release of nitrogen may cause the spread of poisonous algae. Indeed, the nitrates and pesticides used in agriculture have been associated with cancers in humans. Thermal pollution, produced by water used for cooling in power-stations, also reduces oxygen solubility in rivers and lakes; and species diversity is further threatened when streams are choked by otherwise harmless inert solids, resulting from, for example, dredging or land drainage, or by urban rubbish. In Third World countries, water pollution from untreated sewage can contribute to the spread of cholera, typhoid, and malaria, as well as being responsible for water-borne, parasitic diseases such as schistosomiasis, which affects some 200 million people world-wide, and onchocerciasis (river blindness).

water power, the harnessed power of moving water. For 2,000 years water has been an important source of mechanical power. It remained the only significant source of stationary power in Europe until the introduction of windmills in the 12th century. Under the Romans there was widespread construction of water-mills, for example, the Barbegal water-mill, a 4th-century AD corn mill in southern France. It had a series of wheels, with a total power output of around 22 kW, and could grind one-third of a tonne of corn per hour. *Tide-mills and the floating mills (those floating in a river and worked by the current) were later employed on rivers such as the Danube and the Seine. With the developing technologies of the Middle Ages, the uses of water power extended from *water-wheels used in flour *milling, pumping, cloth manufacture, leather tanning, and the operation of sawmills and forges. The number of mills in England grew from the 5,000 listed in the 'Domesday Book' to a peak of 20,000 before the advent of the steam-engine. After a period of decline, *water turbines used in *hydroelectricity generation brought a revival, and the power extracted from water is now a thousand times the total from all the traditional mills during their supremacy. The later 20th century has also brought interest in the water power of the oceans, with revived plans for *tidal power-stations and research into the potential of *wave power.

waterproofing, a process applied primarily to textiles, to prevent water passing through a fabric, and also to prevent the fabric from absorbing water. Most waterproof fabrics are based on high-strength *synthetic fibres and heavy *polymer coatings. They are being increasingly used in industrial, military, domestic, and leisure applications. Many clothing fabrics are waterproofed by coating them with a thin layer of one of the rubber-like polymers. Because most of these are impermeable to air, perspiration condenses inside the garment. To overcome this difficulty, inherently waterproof but 'breathable' fabrics are tightly woven so that water cannot pass through, but air and water vapour can. These fabrics are usually treated with *silicones or natural waxes to provide water repellency. An alternative is to coat the fabric with a *polymeric finish which has micropores too small to allow the passage of water, but large enough to allow water vapour molecules to pass through. Such a fabric can be layered between outer and lining fabrics, giving a three-layered structure.

water purification *water supply and treatment.

water resources management, methods designed to ensure that adequate supplies of water of appropriate quality are maintained to meet demand. Water is a vital resource: demands on it include water for drinking; for domestic purposes (such as *sewage transport); for industrial processes; for *irrigation in agriculture; for fisheries; for hydroelectric power generation; for transportation in canals; and for recreation. Management involves an examination of the total *hydrological cycle: consumption, disposal, and subsequent recycling in rivers, lakes, and underground aquifers (porous rocks containing water). For instance, in countries such as the UK, where the areas of highest population are also the areas with lowest rainfall, water must be transported from high-rainfall areas to ensure that local needs are satisfied. To this end, upland reservoirs have been built, groundwater (in the earth or in rocks) and river supplies are exploited, and treated effluent is reused. In fact, about 70 per cent of the UK's drinking water is recycled. Generally, water management functions—land drainage, fisheries management, flood protection, the control of *water pollution—are the responsibility of specially appointed public or private water authorities. Standards of water quality are governed by national, and sometimes international, laws, defining the permissible water standards for different uses—bathing, drinking, livestock watering, and so on. In the arid environments of the Third World, where there may be little surface water, remote sensing using satellites can assist in finding new and more reliable aquifers. There, the primary task of water resources management is to ensure adequate supplies of drinking water.

water softening, treatment to alleviate hardness in water, caused principally by the presence of carbonates and sulphates of calcium and magnesium. These salts form scale in pipes and boilers when heated and make soap lather less effectively. In the lime–soda process, these salts are precipitated by reaction with lime or soda ash and then removed by sedimentation. In the base-exchange process (see *ion exchange resin), the magnesium and calcium ions are exchanged for sodium, which does not form scale. The water behaves as though it were soft, but in fact has the same quantity of dissolved solids. Formerly zeolites (sodium silicates) were used to achieve this exchange, but these have now been largely replaced by synthetic resins cross-linked to polystyrene beads.

water supply and treatment. Water is supplied by a network of pipes (see *plumbing), whose capacity must be

Water supply and treatment

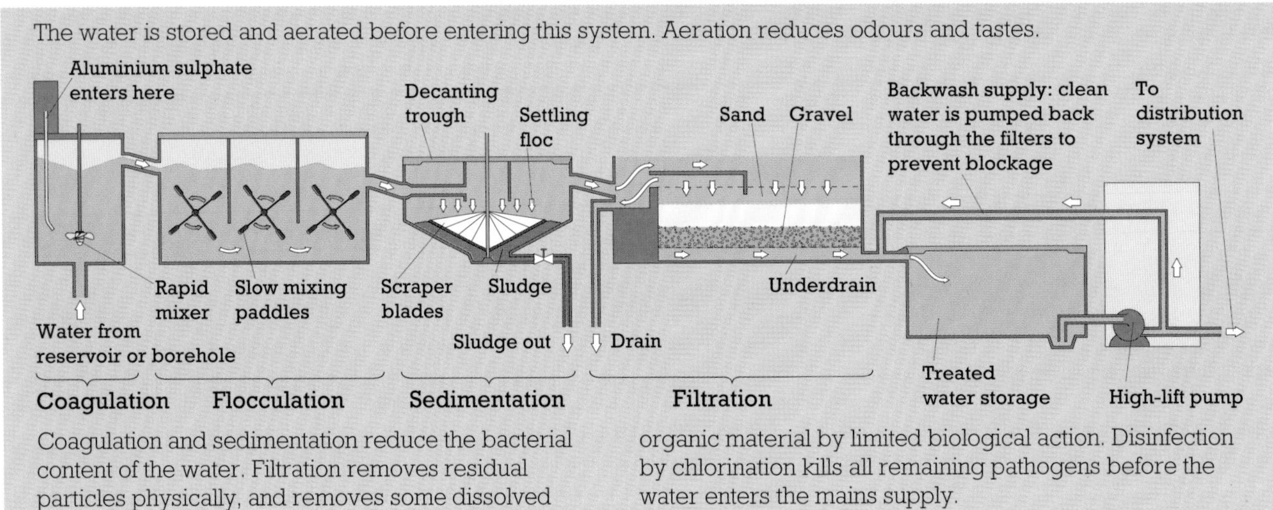

Coagulation and sedimentation reduce the bacterial content of the water. Filtration removes residual particles physically, and removes some dissolved organic material by limited biological action. Disinfection by chlorination kills all remaining pathogens before the water enters the mains supply.

able to meet domestic, industrial, and agricultural needs, while making a significant allowance for waste due to leaks. Average water consumption can range from about 740 litres per capita per day (l.c.d.) in urban USA, to as little as 1 l.c.d. in parts of Ethiopia or Somalia. Peak consumption may rise to as much as 350 per cent of the annual average. Water is supplied from both surface and subterranean sources. Upland reservoirs distant from towns require extensive *aqueducts; intakes from rivers or lakes usually have a local reservoir to provide adequate supply when water levels are low and to allow closure of the intake against any temporary pollution. Deep aquifers (water-carrying rocks) are tapped by *wells and often provide better-quality water. The first stage of water treatment is to store the raw water in a reservoir, where the combined action of sedimentation (settling of suspended materials due to gravity) and ultraviolet and visible light substantially eliminates bacteria. However, high-temperature areas in the water in summer can cause algal growth in nutrient-rich waters. To combat this, slow sand filtration has been used since the early 19th century; this relies on a combination of direct filtering and bacterial action within the upper layers of the sand bed. More modern fast filters use chemical treatments, particularly with aluminium sulphate, to coagulate suspended solids before they are removed in a clarifier (see figure). Water is commonly disinfected by chlorination, though this can cause an unpleasant taste when certain organic substances are present. After treatment, water is stored in a 'service reservoir', which is either an underground covered tank on high ground or, in flat country, a water tower. This stores a few days' supply and by its height provides pressure for local distribution. (See also *water resources management.)

Water-wheel

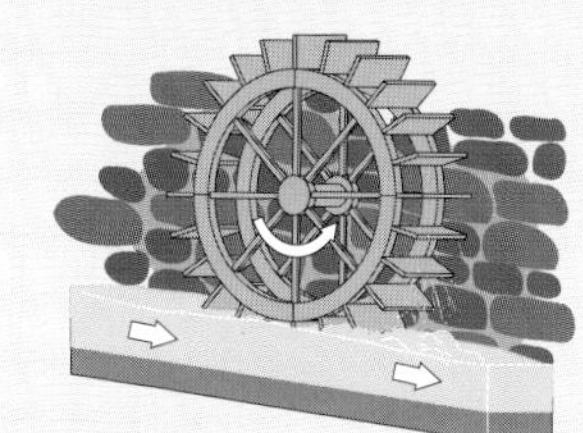

Undershot

Undershot water-wheels rely entirely on the force of moving water.

Overshot, breastshot, and backshot water-wheels all rely entirely on the weight of water, i.e. gravity, to produce their power.

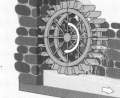

Overshot

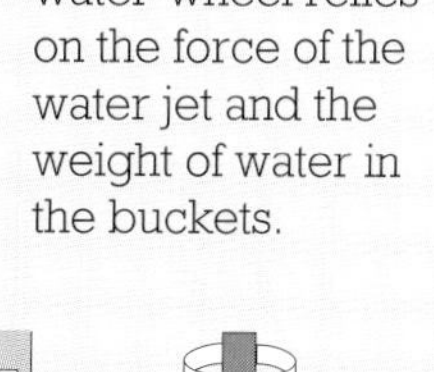

Pelton wheel

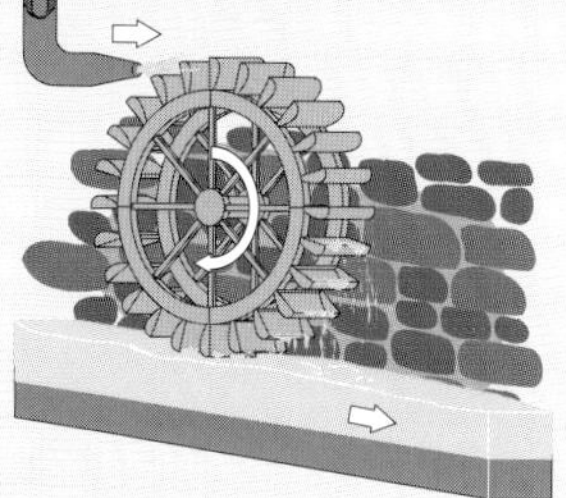

The Pelton water-wheel relies on the force of the water jet and the weight of water in the buckets.

Kaplan turbine

This turbine is positioned at the base of a large head of water. As gravity forces water past the blades, they are made to rotate, producing the power.

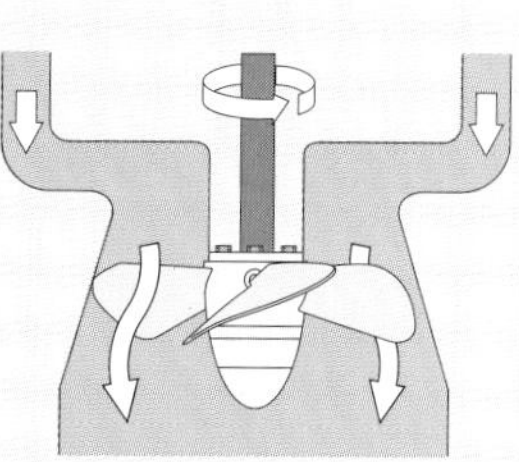

water turbine, a type of *water-wheel, which takes its name from the Latin word for a whirlwind. In early versions (*c.*1820), water entering a vertical central tube was expelled through curved horizontal pipes in the sides. In modern turbines the principle of a reaction force which causes rotation remains, but the arrangements for deflecting the water vary considerably. In the Francis turbine the water enters through a curved volute (shaped like a snail shell) and guide vanes direct it inwards on to concave vanes on the central rotor (for illustration see *hydroelectricity). After deflection it discharges along an axial outlet. Power and water speed are controlled by tilting the guide vanes, which means that the water enters under pressure. Machines where pressure contributes to the driving force are called reaction turbines, in contrast to impulse turbines such as the Pelton wheel, whose jets are at atmospheric pressure. The Pelton wheel was patented in the USA by L. A. Pelton (1880). It has spoon-shaped buckets into which jets of water are directed, and is used for *hydroelectricity installations with a water head of 250 m (800 feet) or more. Francis turbines are used for hydroelectricity generation at medium heads, producing up to 500 MW (million watts) at efficiencies that can exceed 90 per cent. For *tidal power and other low-head situations, the propeller or Kaplan turbine is more efficient, and this axial-flow machine has the additional advantage that its blades can be turned to allow operation in either flow direction. (See water-wheel for illustration.)

water-wheel, a wheel driven by the force of flowing water on blades or buckets around its rim. Water-wheels were in use in Asia Minor from at least the second century BC, and probably as early in China. *Vitruvius (1st century BC) describes an *undershot wheel (see figure) driving a millstone by means of right-angled gears, and a Chinese manuscript of AD 31 describes a horizontal wheel with its vertical shaft connected directly to the stone. A number of technological improvements came with the spread of *water power throughout Europe in Roman and medieval times. The more efficient overshot wheel was introduced, and tilted or curved blades were used instead of flat ones. Bearings, gears, and belt drives became more sophisticated. Wheel diameters reached 6 m (20 feet); but efficiencies remained low. Rotating at little more than 10 revolutions per minute, the wheels extracted less than two-thirds of the energy of the water and their power output rarely exceeded 10 kW. With the introduction of steam-power in the 18th century, development virtually ceased for over 100 years. Fresh impetus came with the advent of *hydroelectricity, but the demands of this new technology led within a few decades to the faster-running *water turbines and the final obsolescence in the West of the traditional wheel.

waterworks *water supply and treatment.

Watson-Watt, Sir Robert Alexander (1892–1973), British physicist of Scottish extraction, a pioneer of *radar. His interest in radio location stemmed from research with the British Meteorological Office to identify the position of thunderstorms as a service to aviators. In 1935 he put forward a plan for locating aircraft by detecting the echoes

Properties and uses of radio-frequency wavebands

Waveband	Frequency	Wavelength	Uses	Properties
Low frequency (long wave)	Less than 300 kHz	Greater than 1 km	AM radio broadcasts, ship-to-shore communications, navigation	Reflected by ionosphere: can follow curvature of earth
Medium frequency (medium wave)	300–3000 kHz (3 MHz)	100 m–1 km	AM radio, marine communications	Reflected by ionosphere: can follow curvature of earth
High frequency (short wave)	3–30 MHz	10–100 m	Intercontinental telephony, AM radio, marine and aeronautical communications, amateur radio	Reflected continuously between ionosphere and earth
Very high frequency (VHF)	30–300 MHz	1–10 m	FM radio, short-range communications (e.g. police, taxis)	Not reflected or diffracted: transmission requires masts
Ultra-high frequency (UHF)	300–3000 MHz (3 GHz)	100 cm–1 m	Television broadcasts, meteorological and space communications	Not reflected or diffracted: transmission requires masts
Microwave	3–30 GHz	10–100 cm	Satellite communications, telephony	Transmitters and receivers must be in line of sights: easily absorbed by buildings

from a pulsed radio signal. Many governments were working on this problem, but Watson-Watt's radar was conspicuously successful because it was a comprehensive system that could be operated in wartime by non-specialists.

watt *energy, *unit.

Watt, James (1736–1819), British engineer of Scottish extraction, best known for the improvements he made to the *steam-engine. Between 1767 and 1774 he was a successful canal surveyor. In 1764 he was asked to repair a *Newcomen engine and recognized its intrinsic inefficiency. Realizing that this could be much reduced if the cylinder were kept permanently hot instead of being cooled between strokes (as a result of the injection of condensing water), he introduced a separate condenser. He went into partnership with *Boulton in 1775, and they manufactured many such engines, to which they constantly made improvements. He coined the term horsepower; the watt, the *SI unit of power, is named after him.

wattle and daub, a traditional method of filling the spaces in the timber *frame of a building. Wooden rods were fitted into holes in the horizontal members; withies (tough, flexible branches) were then laced through these to form a wattle (lattice). Mud (daub) was then applied to seal the building against wind and rain.

waveband, a subdivision of the *radio region of the *electromagnetic radiation spectrum. Because today radio space is so crowded, particular sections of the radio-frequency spectrum are designated by the *International Telecommunication Union for specific uses (see table). Telecommunications systems that require a large *bandwidth, such as FM radio and television, use higher-frequency wavebands, which have a large frequency range. Historically, the first wavebands used were the low and medium frequencies. Radio waves of these frequencies can travel around the curvature of the Earth by reflection or refraction (bending) in the ionosphere, a layer of charged or ionized air 50–400 km (30–250 miles) above the Earth. The ionosphere has three layers, and the reflectivity of these layers to different radio frequencies varies with the time of day. Thus, for example, the lowest layer absorbs some shortwave frequencies during daylight hours. VHF, UHF, and microwave frequencies are not reflected by the ionosphere. Although such frequencies can thus only transmit over a limited range on the ground, the fact that they can pass through the ionosphere means that they can be used for *satellite communications.

waveguide, a hollow, conducting, metal tube or pipe used to direct very high-frequency electromagnetic radiation, and microwaves in particular. Waveguides are superior to conventional cables, which exhibit too high a loss at these frequencies. The microwaves are propagated along the inside of the waveguide, where they are continually reflected off the inside walls. The width and depth of the waveguide (which is often rectangular in cross-section) are carefully calculated so that one mode, or characteristic wave-form, of the microwave is selectively propagated.

wavelength, the distance between corresponding points on two successive *waves. The product of the wavelength and the *frequency gives the velocity of a wave. This relationship holds for transverse travelling waves such as *electromagnetic radiation, and longitudinal travelling waves such as sound, as well as for standing waves.

wave power, power extracted from the ocean waves, usually for the generation of electricity. In the open ocean,

The 'Clam', a small **wave-power** machine being tested on Loch Ness, Scotland, UK. It has flexible bags connected to an aluminium cylinder. Rising and falling waves force air from bag to bag, driving air turbines in ducting between the bags.

waves a few metres high carry several kilowatts of power for each metre of their width. The first proposal for extracting this power, in 1799, envisaged a huge lever pivoted on the shore and with one end on a pontoon. A century later, the first practical device used the oscillating water in a cliff-face borehole to compress air, which drove a small turbo-generator. This principle is used in the automatic buoys developed in Japan in the 1950s, generating the 100 W needed for a navigation light. In recent years other countries have also investigated systems based on oscillating water columns. Some devices have reached outputs of a few kilowatts, but none is yet economically and technically proven on a large scale. Other types of system studied in the late 1970s, mainly in the UK, included hinged rafts, compressible air-bags, and a chain of *cam-shaped rocking devices. While work continues on small-scale systems, it is unlikely that wave power could make a major contribution to world energy needs until well into the 21st century.

wave, a periodic or oscillating disturbance of particles or of space by which many forms of energy propagate away from their source. The energy released by a stone dropped into still water moves outwards as a series of concentric peaks and troughs. All wave motions through a medium are the result of individual particles oscillating about their own fixed point. This means that a travelling wave is the movement of an effect, rather than the bulk flow of the medium itself. A wave which oscillates regularly at a single fixed *frequency with a regular *wavelength is described as a sinusoidal wave (see figure). Waves in water are termed transverse waves because the displacement of the wave peaks and troughs is at right angles to the direction of travel. Sound waves travel as successive regions of compression and rarefaction of the air or other medium. They are termed longitudinal waves because the transmitting molecules oscillate back and forth in the same direction as the path of the wave's propagation (see figure).

Waves

Sinusoidal wave characteristics

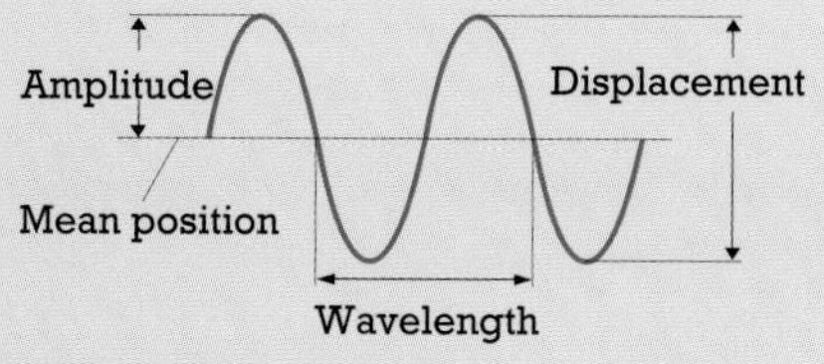

Amplitude
Displacement
Mean position
Wavelength

The amplitude of a wave is its maximum displacement from the mean position.

The frequency is the number of whole wavelengths passing a point in one second. The unit of frequency is the hertz (Hz).

Wavelength is the distance between successive, identical points of a wave.

Transverse waves

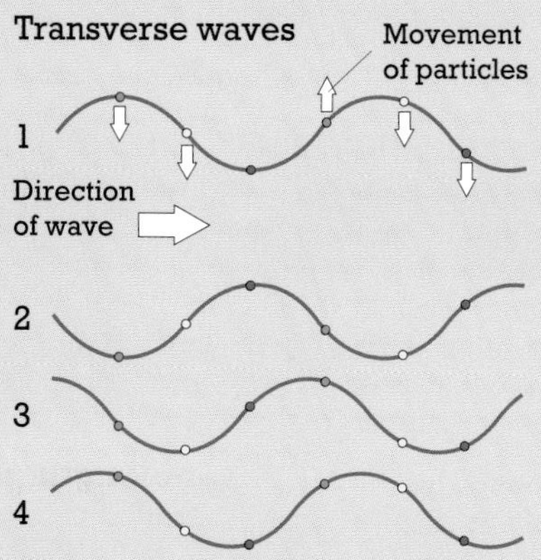

Movement of particles
1
Direction of wave
2
3
4

The movement of the particles is at right angles to the direction the wave is travelling.

Longitudinal waves (in a spring)

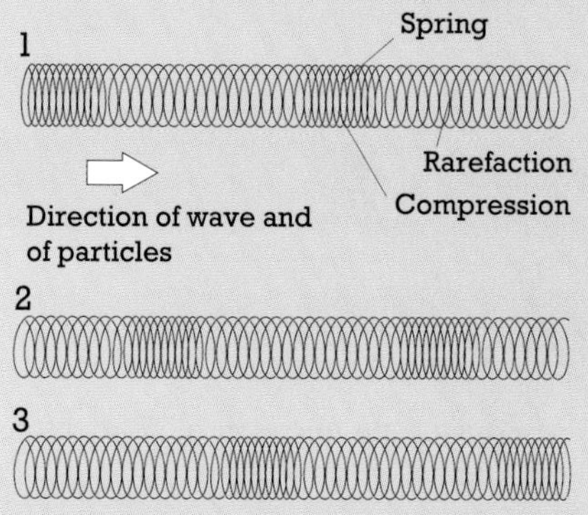

Spring
1
Rarefaction
Compression
Direction of wave and of particles
2
3

The movement of the vibration is in the same direction as that in which the wave is travelling.

Diffraction

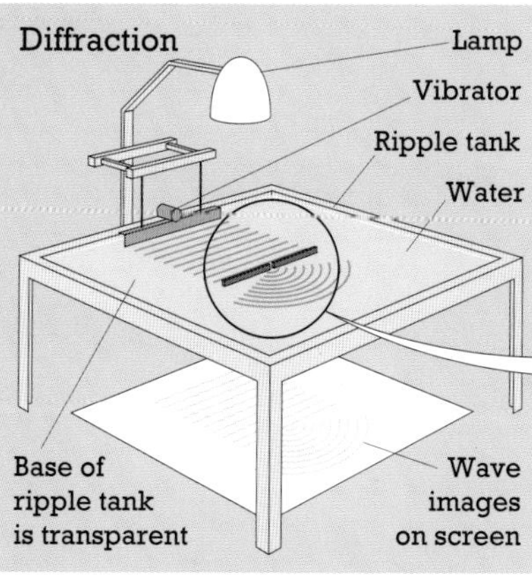

Lamp
Vibrator
Ripple tank
Water
Base of ripple tank is transparent
Wave images on screen

The properties of progressive waves can be studied in a ripple tank. A stroboscope can be used to apparently freeze the motion of the waves.

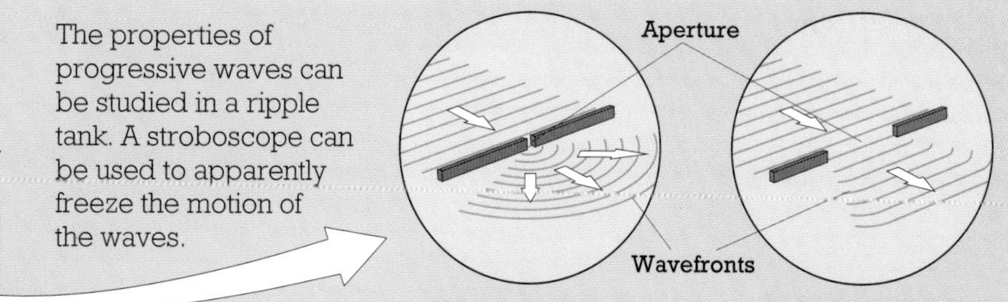

Aperture
Wavefronts

Diffraction is the changing shape of a wave caused when a wave meets an object or aperture.

If the aperture is similar in size to the wavelength then significant diffraction occurs.

If the aperture is larger than the wavelength then little diffraction occurs.

Electromagnetic waves

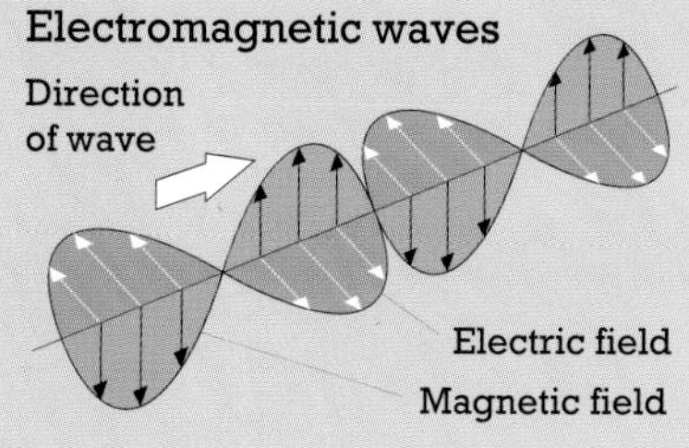

Direction of wave
Electric field
Magnetic field

Electromagnetic waves form the electromagnetic spectrum. They are transverse waves consisting of electric and magnetic fields at 90° to one another.

Stationary waves

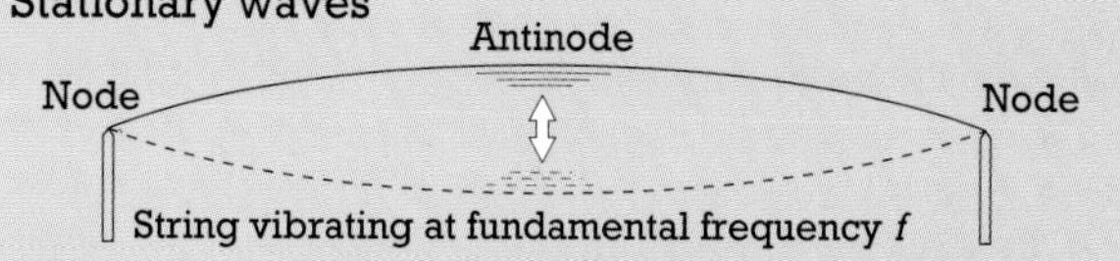

Antinode
Node
Node
String vibrating at fundamental frequency *f*

When a stretched string is plucked, waves are sent along it in both directions. The waves are reflected at the fixed ends, and as they pass through each other they combine to produce a stationary wave.

Light, *radio waves, and radiant *heat are examples of *electromagnetic radiation, and require no medium for propagation: they can travel through a vacuum. The wave-like nature of electromagnetic radiation is due to energy oscillating back and forth between a magnetic form and an electrical form as the wave travels. The magnetic and electrical fields are perpendicular to the direction of propagation, so this type of radiation is regarded as transverse wave motion.

Two or more waves can be superimposed upon each other to make a single composite wave. This composite results from the simple addition of the displacements of the component waves. The result of combining two waves of the same frequency depends on the phase relationship between the two. If the waves are in phase (oscillating in step with each other) then they will reinforce each other. If they are of the same amplitude but exactly out of phase, then they will cancel each other out. This type of interaction between waves is known as interference. Waves can be reflected when they meet an obstacle. *Sonar and *radar send out short pulses of waves, and detect waves reflected back from objects in the wave path. If reflected waves travel back over their original path, then the incident and the reflected waves will be superimposed on each other and a stationary pattern of standing waves will be set up. For example, a standing-wave pattern may be observed in a cup of tea when it is placed on a vibrating surface, such as a table on a moving train. The speed of a wave depends on the nature of the medium through which it is moving. If a wave moves from one medium to another, the change in speed results in a change in direction of travel. Thus when light passes from air into water it is refracted, or bent. Refraction and reflection of shock waves by rock strata allow seismological surveys to map underground formations, for example, in *petroleum exploration.

wax, any of a group of pliable carbon-based substances that generally melt between 35 °C and 95 °C and form hard, glossy films on polishing. Waxes share similar physical properties, but, depending on their origin, differ markedly in their chemical structures. They are allied to fats and oils and contain about thirty carbon atoms. *Beeswax and *spermaceti wax have animal origins, whereas small amounts of other specialized waxes are obtained from plants. *Paraffin wax accounts for about 90 per cent of the wax used in industry and is extracted from lubricating oil derived from crude petroleum. Large quantities are still used for *candle manufacture.

weapon *hand weapon, *firearm, *military technology.

weather-boarding *cladding.

weather satellite *meteorological satellite.

weave, the structure of *fabric produced by weaving (see *loom). The simplest and most common weave is the plain weave, which has a simple alternate over and under structure; such fabrics are often known as calico or tabby, and include muslins and *canvas. Poplin is a plain weave which has a fine and close warp and much thicker weft. To form a twill weave, sets of warp threads are raised sequentially for successive passages of weft, resulting in diagonal lines on the face of the cloth. To form a herringbone weave, the twill sequence is reversed after a given number of weft insertions. Denim is a twill fabric designed to have extra warp on the face of the fabric to enhance durability. Pile fabrics are woven in such a way that loops of warp or weft yarn form on the face of the fabric. The loops may subsequently be cut. Among such fabrics are velvets, corduroys, and terrys. (For illustration see *loom.)

weaving *loom.

web offset printing *offset lithography.

wedge *inclined plane.

Wedgwood, Josiah (1730–95), British industrial potter. He came from a family of Staffordshire potters and in 1759 set up his own factory. Apart from high-quality tableware (including Queen's ware) utilizing china clay from Cornwall, he made many finely designed and executed items in his famous Neoclassical-styled jasper-ware. He also invented a pyrometer (a type of thermometer) for measuring high temperatures, originally for use in *kilns.

weedkiller *herbicide.

weft, the lateral thread in woven cloth. In weaving on a *loom and in most *fabric construction it is protected by the warp, and so does not need great strength. *Yarn for weft is lightly twisted to reduce *spinning costs and to increase the bulk of yarn within the cloth.

A spring-balance **weighing machine** being used to weigh children at a health clinic in Bangladesh.

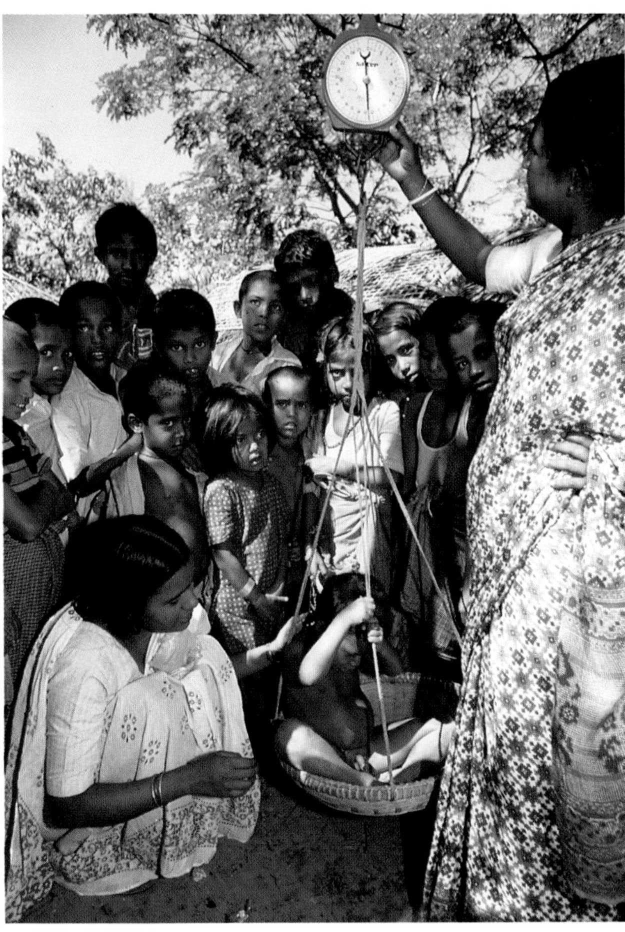

weighing machine, an instrument for measuring the weight of an object or substance. Methods of weighing have been relatively accurate since ancient times. The oldest known weighing machine is the equal-arm balance, used in Egypt from the 4th millennium BC, in which two pans are suspended one from each end of a centrally pivoted beam. The object to be weighed is placed in one pan, and balanced against a collection of standard weights in the other. Fine adjustment is effected by a light rider weight which can be moved along the beam. An adaptation of the equal-arm balance was the Roman steelyard, the arms of which were of unequal length. The object to be weighed was suspended from the short arm, and a rider on the graduated longer arm was adjusted until a balance was achieved. There was little further change in the balance until the 18th and 19th centuries, when the use of knife-edge suspension, and cases to exclude draughts and vibration, made accuracies of 10^{-3} g (3.5×10^{-5} ounces) possible. Improvements in the 20th century have increased weighing speeds, but not accuracy. Modern electronic balances measure the deformation of some mechanical element under stress, using a form of *strain gauge or *piezo-electric device. Other forms of weighing machine include the spring balance, which operates on the principle that the extension of a coiled spring is proportional to the force applied to it, and in the torsion balance, in which weights are measured by the amount of twist they induce in a metal wire or band. For weighing heavy loads, for example in weighbridges, *hydraulic or *pneumatic systems may be used. (See also *laboratories and laboratory equipment.)

weir, a wall or bank built across a river with a crest over which water flows. It is commonly used on a *river navigation to form a series of reaches of adequate depth linked by *locks. A weir may also be used for flood control, when it is often fitted with *sluices.

welding, a technique for joining metal parts without using low-melting-point fillers. It provides a stronger joint than either *soldering or *brazing. The earliest form of welding was forge welding, in which two pieces of red-hot iron were hammered together, a technique now used only by *blacksmiths. The modern pressure welding, in which the metal is deformed cold, is used widely for aluminium alloys. However, the most important method is arc welding, in which a continuous electric spark (arc) jumps from a metal rod to the join line where the two parts meet. The high temperature melts the end of the rod and material on either side of the join to form a welded joint. Gas welding uses an oxy-acetylene flame, and cold wire is added to the joint as a filler. Originally as important as arc welding, this method is now restricted to specialist sheet fabrication. In resistance welding, a high-current, low-voltage pulse of electricity is applied on opposite sides of the join line. The required heat is generated by the resistance across the joint. Welding on automated *robotic assembly lines is by this method. Cracked railway lines are welded with thermite. This is a mixture of aluminium powder and iron oxide that can be ignited to give a violent and spectacular reaction in which the iron oxide is reduced to iron, providing molten iron in a cheap and simple way. There are several specialized welding techniques using lasers, electron beams, and even friction (from rubbing the two parts together) as the heat source. Thermoplastics can be welded using lower-temperature variants of some of the above methods or by very specialized techniques involving *radio-frequency heating.

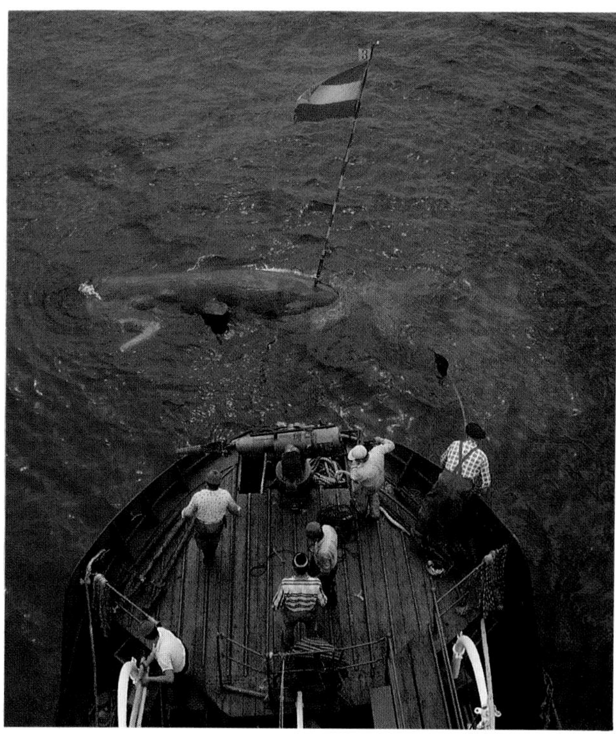

The whale flagged here was killed by a **whaling** ship. The flag identifies the catch for the factory ship following the smaller whalers.

well, a shaft sunk from ground-level to perhaps 50 m (170 feet) below to reach a water-bearing stratum (aquifer), usually a porous rock such as chalk, limestone, or sandstone. Having percolated slowly down from the surface, the water in a deep aquifer is usually of high quality. The upper part of the well is lined where it passes through water-bearing surface strata to prevent contamination by surface water or possibly polluted ground-water. A *pump is used to raise water to the surface. The pump motor may be located at the surface, or below ground in a dry chamber known as a pumping well. Alternatively, a submersible pump (an electrically driven centrifugal pump that can operate under water) may be used. The water reaches the surface in a rising main of large diameter to minimize friction losses. In an artesian well, underground water is confined under pressure, so that it rises up without being pumped. Such wells must be capped to prevent excessive water flow.

Welsbach, Carl Auer, Freiherr von *Auer, Carl, Freiherr von Welsbach.

Westinghouse, George (1846–1914), US engineer, industrialist, and inventor. He had no formal training in engineering, but by the end of his life he had lodged over 400 patents. The first major one, filed in 1869, was for an *air-brake, and he founded the Westinghouse Air Brake Company to manufacture it. This was the beginning of a vast industrial enterprise, the activities of which included making electrically controlled signals and points; the large-scale generation and distribution of alternating-current electricity in collaboration with *Tesla and in opposition to *Edison; and the transmission of natural gas by pipeline.

whaling, the pursuit and slaughter of whales. Whaling was first carried out in about 3000 BC in the far north. The

Nordic people of Europe were whaling by AD 900, and commercial whaling was established by the 12th century. In the early 19th century, whales were pursued by six-man rowing boats armed with hand harpoons and lances. Carcasses were dismembered alongside the mother ship and the blubber was rendered (melted down) in brick ovens. The resulting whale oil was used for lighting and lubrication and in the manufacture of varnish, linoleum, leather, and pharmaceuticals. Baleen (whalebone) was used for corsets, knife handles, umbrella ribs, and brushes. Whaling activity lessened in the 1850s due to dwindling stocks of suitable animals and to the replacement of whale oil and *spermaceti by petroleum products.

Modern whaling techniques were introduced in about 1870, when steam-powered whale catchers replaced the traditional rowing boats. A forward-mounted gun fired a heavy harpoon fitted with an explosive head. Power-driven winches could haul carcasses from depths where previously they would have been lost. Compressed air was injected into carcasses to keep them afloat. Increased demand for *soaps and *margarine in the early 20th century led to the development of self-contained factory fleets. A factory ship has a slipway at the stern for easy loading of the catch. Its power butchering machinery and pressure cookers can deal with a 100-tonne whale within one hour. The whaling industry declined in the 1960s, when no large concentrations of whales remained; alternatives to whale products were generally established. Since 1986 there has been an international moratorium on commercial whaling, although Japan, Norway, and Iceland continue to catch whales for research.

Wheatstone, Sir Charles (1802–75), British physicist and pioneer of electric *telegraphy. From 1834 he was Professor of Experimental Physics at King's College, London, where his research included work on the velocity of light. In 1837, with *Cooke, he patented an electric telegraph, and to exploit this interest commercially they became business partners. In 1843 he invented the Wheatstone bridge, a device for measuring electrical resistance. He also developed an interest in acoustics and binocular vision.

wheel, a circular revolving disc or frame used on a vehicle to reduce resistance to motion and for a variety of purposes in mechanisms and industry. Its earliest use was probably in the quern, consisting of two circular stones, for grinding cereals, and in the *potter's wheel. However, the most significant application of the wheel is for *road transport. It is thought likely that wheels for carts and chariots were derived about 6,000 years ago. The earliest evidence of a wheeled vehicle is an illustration of a cart from the Tigris–Euphrates valley, *c.*3000 BC. The earliest wheels were solid wood or made from three planks, but spoked wheels are known from around 2000 BC as far apart as Scandinavia, China, and Mesopotamia. On these early vehicles the wheels either turned on an *axle, or were rigidly fastened to an axle that revolved in a housing on the vehicle body. A major advance, due to the Chinese, was the dished wheel, which is slightly conical in section. This is stronger and stiffer, so the weight of the wheel can be reduced. The traditional construction of the wheel in medieval Europe was to make the hub or 'knave' of elm, to resist splitting, the spokes of oak, for strength, and the felloes (sections of the rim) of ash, for toughness. An iron tyre was shrunk on to give strength and resistance to wear. Lightweight wire-spoked wheels were devised by *Cayley in about 1808; they were developed for the *bicycle by James Starley in 1870. Originally the spokes ran radially out from the hub, but in 1874 Starley patented tangential spoking, in which spokes run diagonally from wheel to hub in a cross-over pattern, improving the wheel's strength. The invention of the steam locomotive led to the development of wrought-iron wheels. Motor vehicles now generally use pressed-steel or cast-aluminium wheels. Solid rubber *tyres were replaced in the 1890s by the pneumatic tyre. Another development first used on the bicycle was wheel *bearings. Wheels have numerous uses in addition to their role in land vehicles. These include spinning-wheels, *water-wheels for power production, *paddle-wheels for ship propulsion, steering wheels for ships or vehicles, *flywheels for maintaining an even motion, *pulley, *gear, and chain-wheels for power transmission, grinding-wheels, prayer-wheels (mechanical aids to prayer used by Tibetan Buddhists), and Ferris wheels (giant revolving wheels used in amusement parks).

wheelchair, a chair on wheels used as a conveyance by sick or physically disabled people. Since antiquity, wheels have occasionally been added to furniture for this purpose. The Bath-chair in the late 18th century was the first wheeled device to challenge the popularity of *litters and sedan-chairs for the transportation of the infirm. Improvements such as hand rims for self-propulsion, rubber tyres, and wire-spoked wheels were introduced at the end of the last century. Collapsible wheelchairs have been made since the 1930s. More recent developments include sophisticated battery-powered chairs, which are controlled by very small bodily movements, and ultra-lightweight chairs used in wheelchair sports.

wheel-lock *firearm.

Whinfield, John Rex (1901–66), British industrial chemist who discovered *polyester. The discovery of *nylon by *Carothers in 1935 convinced him that other classes of synthetic fibre were feasible, and in 1941, with J. T. Dickson, he discovered polyester fibre. After a long period of development, this fibre was marketed as Terylene by ICI (whose research staff Whinfield joined in 1947), except in the USA, where it appeared as Dacron, marketed by the Du Pont Company.

white lead, the common name for a type of lead carbonate, $Pb_3(OH)_2(CO_3)_2$. It is prepared commercially by the action of air, carbon dioxide, and ethanoic acid vapour on *lead. It is widely used as a *pigment in *paint, but has the disadvantages of both toxicity and blackening in the presence of hydrogen sulphide due to the formation of lead sulphide.

Whitney, Eli (1765–1825), US inventor and pioneer of *mass production. He invented and began to manufacture a machine to clean green-seed cotton, which enabled one person to do the work of fifty. The machine was patented in 1794, though his patent was widely infringed. In 1798 he obtained a government contract for manufacturing 10,000 muskets and developed such precise production methods that parts were interchangeable between muskets. This interchangeability of parts was a crucial step in the development of mass production.

Whittle, Sir Frank (1907–), British aeronautical engineer, pioneer of the *jet engine. Whittle joined the Royal Air Force as an apprentice in 1923. He soon turned his attention to *gas-turbines; he took out a patent for a jet engine as early as 1930. He formed the firm Power Jets Ltd. in 1935 to develop his ideas and by 1937 had a prototype jet engine running. However, the first British jet-propelled aircraft did not fly until May 1941, nine months after the German Heinkel He 178 jet, developed by von *Ohain.

Whitworth, Sir Joseph (1803–87), British engineer who won international acclaim as a machine-tool maker. After working as a mechanic, he joined *Maudslay in 1825 and had a rigorous training in the use of sophisticated machine-tools. In 1833 he opened his own business in Manchester, setting standards of precision never before attempted in tool-making. Aware of the need for standardization, he devised the British Standard Whitworth (BSW) thread for screws, which is still widely used in the USA. In the 1870s he extended his interests to armaments and shipbuilding.

wide-area network (WAN) *network.

wide-bodied aircraft, a modern commercial transport *airliner having a passenger cabin wide enough to allow three groups of seats, one central and the other two on either side of the aircraft, with two aisles between them. In practice this means that the cabin must be more than 4.7 m (15.5 feet) wide. The (US) Boeing 747 jumbo jet and the European Airbus A-320 are wide-bodied aircraft.

Wiener, Norbert (1894–1964), US mathematician and creator of *cybernetics. An infant prodigy, he graduated from Tufts College at the age of 14 and obtained his doctorate from Harvard at 18. Much of his early work was in pure mathematics, notably on harmonic analysis, but from 1940 he grew increasingly interested in computing machines and, in particular, in feedback control. This opened up a new discipline, cybernetics, concerned with the study of mechanical and human control mechanisms, and *artificial intelligence.

Wilkinson, John (1728–1808), British ironmaster. He inherited a small ironworks with his brother, and built up a substantial iron smelting and founding business of his own. He executed large government orders for artillery, and for this purpose devised an extremely accurate boring engine (patented 1775) to make the barrels of cannon and rifles. The machine was later adapted to bore the cylinders for *Boulton and *Watt's *steam-engine, and was an important factor in the engine's success. Wilkinson also designed the first cast-iron *barges (1787), and provided the castings used by Abraham Darby III in the Coalbrookdale *Iron Bridge.

Wimshurst machine, an early, manually operated electrostatic generator, invented by James Wimshurst in 1883. It consists of two wheels, under 30 cm (1 foot) in diameter, mounted on the same axis. These are made to rotate in opposite directions by turning a handle. The wheels are arranged to brush each other, and this action generates static electricity.

Winchester disk *hard disk.

winding gear, surface equipment to move people and material in a mine-shaft. There is evidence for windlasses having been used for this purpose as early as 1000 BC, but probably to raise heavy ore rather than to aid miners, who had to make do with ladders. *Agricola's *De Re Metallica* ('On Metals') (1556) illustrates the use of horse-powered whims (large capstans used for raising ore) and water-wheels as winding gear. In the 18th century the steam-engine provided a much greater power source, and was first used for winding gear in Cornwall, UK. Today, electric power is widely used.

A **windmill** used for domestic electricity generation in Göteborg, Sweden.

windmill, a structure designed to extract energy from the wind. Although windmills were used 2,500 years ago in India, the first detailed account is in a Persian manuscript of about AD 900, and windmills were common there by the 7th century. The ancient mills were of the vertical-axis type, with a curved wall to direct the wind, and the shaft connected directly to a millstone. European mills, developed in the 12th century from the design of Roman water-mills, adopted a horizontal shaft driving through right-angled gears. In the early post-mills, the entire body containing all the machinery was mounted on a vertical post and could be rotated manually into the wind by means of a slanting tail-pole. The sails, originally triangular jibs furled on wooden booms, were later stretched on rectangular frames and eventually, in northern Europe, replaced by wooden shutters. Fixed stone or wooden towers appeared in the 15th century, with sails mounted on a cap, which could be rotated. Automatic rotation was achieved with the fantail (1745), a set of vanes at right angles to the sails, geared to wheels on a circular track. From the 15th century the Dutch used windmills for land drainage, gearing the vertical shaft to a scoop wheel or *Archimedean screw. Other uses included flour-milling, oil-pressing, paper-pulping, and sawing timber, and by the 18th century tens of thousands of mills were operating throughout Europe and America, with power outputs as high as 50 kW. These large mills were gradually replaced by steam-power, but from the 1850s there were increasing numbers of small multi-bladed machines, producing about half a kilowatt of power to pump water. Over six million were built in the USA, an estimated 100,000 remaining in use today. Similar windmills are also used for water pumping in India, South Africa, Australia, and many other countries. The main development of the 20th century, however, has been the use of *wind power for electricity, with traditional windmills replaced by modern aerofoil machines.

window (computing), a rectangular area of a *visual display unit screen which can be sectioned off for a particular purpose. The term is particularly applied to *graphic user interfaces on *microcomputers or *workstations, which allow the results of different *programs or processes to be displayed simultaneously in different areas of the screen.

wind power, electric power generated by wind machines. It is estimated that wind generators could satisfy up to a fifth of the demand for electric power in many countries, but in 1990 the maximum was 1 per cent, in Denmark. The first wind generator was built in 1890, also in Denmark, starting a 30-year programme there which produced over 100 machines. In the years between the two World Wars cheap fuel everywhere gave little incentive for development of large-scale systems, but thousands of 1-kW machines were built for farms and remote communities. With a generator mounted behind the propeller, these no longer needed the vertical shaft and gearing of earlier machines. The 1940s saw new interest in generators in the 10- to 100-kW range, while the Putnam machine in Vermont, USA, 50 m (160 feet) in diameter, produced up to 1,250 kW for a few years. No larger machine was built until the period following the 1970s oil crises, which brought many two-bladed and three-bladed horizontal-axis turbines, with output from 10 to 3,000 kW. This period also saw the introduction of vertical-axis wind turbines. First proposed in 1931, these have the advantage of direct drive to a ground-level generator and an independence of wind direction. Their blades form either a bowed 'egg-beater' or a straight 'H' shape and, as in other modern machines, are thin *aerofoils.

wind-tunnel, an apparatus designed to produce a controlled air-stream, used for studying the *aerodynamics of *aeroplanes, *ships, buildings, and other shapes. It comprises a duct containing a scale or full-size model, connected to instruments that electrically measure the forces acting upon the model. Early tunnels were open-ended, with a small-bore test section in which the air was accelerated, but more recent designs use a closed circuit in which the temperature, pressure, and humidity of the air can be precisely controlled. Air-speeds in wind-tunnels vary from a few kilometres per hour up to *hypersonic speeds of 16,000 km/h (10,000 m.p.h.) or more. At hypersonic speeds the test air must be at extremely high temperatures in order to simulate flight conditions: such tunnels are operated in pulses of only a few milliseconds.

wine-making. Wine is an *alcoholic drink made from fermented grape or other fruit juice; wine-making is known to have been practised for over 5,000 years. Juice is extracted from grapes either by pressing them or by piling the grapes in a container with a false bottom and draining off the juice (free-run juice). For white wines, the juice and skins are then separated, and the juice may be settled or centrifuged to remove cloud. For red wines the skins, seeds, and juice are fermented together. The grape juice (must) is now fermented: the yeasts used in *fermentation may be those naturally present on the skins of the grapes, or a pure yeast culture that is added to the must. Temperature control during fermentation is essential for the production of wine with good colour and flavour. Fermentation usually ends after 10 to 30 days, when the sugar concentration in the must has fallen low. The wine is then 'racked' or drawn off to separate the lees (sedimentary material, including the majority of yeast cells) from the wine. It may be clarified at this stage (for example, with isinglass, a form of gelatine obtained from fish) to remove remaining suspended material. Wine is usually aged in oak or redwood casks: for red wines the ageing may be two to three years; but white wines need less time, and some are not casked at all. Before bottling, wines are often blended, and preservatives may be used to limit further microbial action. Better red wines improve from ageing in the bottle: some may mature for up to 20 years. In its wider sense, wine is a fermented liquor made from the juice of other fruits or from grain, flowers, or the sap of various trees.

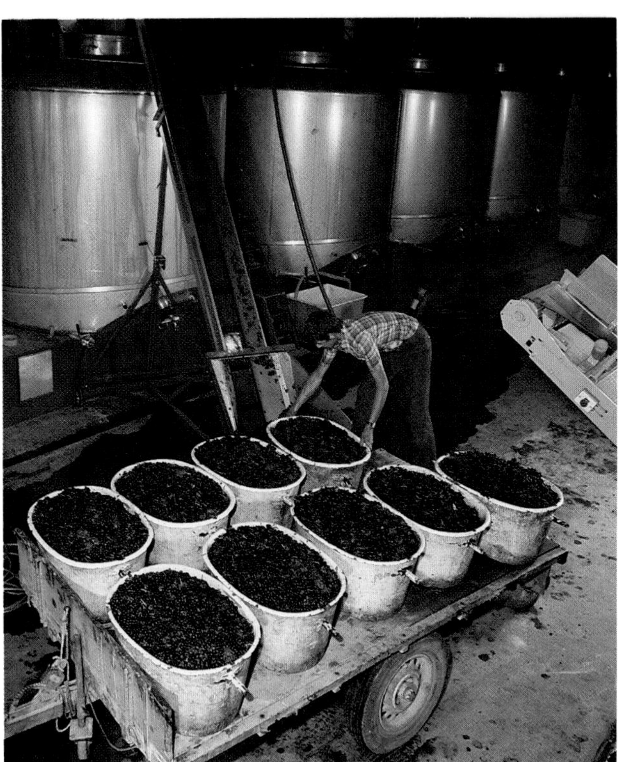

Grapes being loaded into large stainless-steel containers for fermentation during **wine-making** at the Château de Chaise vineyard in France.

winnowing, the separation of the husk or chaff of cereals from the grain. Originally, threshed corn was tossed into the air to separate the heavier grain from the lighter chaff, the wind carrying away the chaff. Winnowing machines using fans improved the speed and efficiency of this operation. Winnowing fans were incorporated into *threshing machines, and later into *combine harvesters.

Winsor (Winzer), Frederick Albert (1763–1830), German-born British pioneer of the coal-gas industry. Visiting Paris in 1802, he witnessed a demonstration of *gas lighting by *Lebon. Two years later, in London, he embarked on an intensive campaign to arouse public interest in gas lighting. This led to the foundation of the Gas Light and Coke Company in 1812, which grew to be the largest gas undertaking in the UK.

wire-drawing, the process by which metal wires are made. A pointed rod of a ductile metal is pulled through a circular hole, of smaller diameter than the rod, in a block of hardened material (the *die). The result is a wire, which is simply a more slender and flexible rod. By using dies with progressively smaller holes it is possible to produce wires of successively smaller diameter. Initially this process was carried out manually by a wire-drawer, using tongs to grip the rod and pull the wire through the die. The amount of reduction and length of wire depended on the strength and skill of the worker. The process was mechanized in the mid-19th century. The preparation of the rod prior to drawing is important. It is cleaned by either chemical or mechanical means and lubricated during the wire-drawing operation.

wireless *radio.

wiring, electrical, the interconnection of electrical components into *circuits using insulated conductors such as PVC-covered *cables. Connections must ensure an outward and return path for the current in order for the circuit to work. The mains wiring of domestic, commercial, and industrial premises usually consists of several circuits, each protected by a *fuse or *circuit-breaker. The circuits branch from the single mains supply cable at the consumer unit, or fuse-box. Domestic wiring in the UK consists of up to five circuits. Two 5-A circuits supply low current for lighting on upper and lower floors, a 15-A circuit supplies the water heater, and there is a 30-A circuit for an electric cooker; the fifth circuit is a 30-A ring main, in which live, neutral, and earth wires form a loop around the house, connecting in parallel all the mains sockets. The different current values of each circuit relate to the amount of power that can be drawn: since the supply voltage is fixed, appliances requiring high power draw more current than low-power appliances.

Withering, William (1741–99), British physician and botanist. The son of an apothecary, he qualified in medicine in Edinburgh and later set up a medical practice in Birmingham. In 1785, he published a treatise on the treatment of dropsy (oedema, or accumulation of water in the body tissues) with foxgloves, the active principle of which (digitalis) is still widely prescribed for certain forms of heart disease. He bought the digitalis remedy from a Shropshire woman (possibly a Mrs Hutton, a well-known herbalist of that period), and deduced that foxglove was the active ingredient in the herbal remedy.

woad *dyes and dyeing.

Wollaston, William Hyde (1766–1828), British metallurgist. In his scientific research he was attracted particularly by the relatively abundant, but very intractable metal *platinum, which had defeated all attempts to produce it in malleable form. He succeeded by developing a new technique of powder metallurgy (1804) in which grains of the metal were made to cohere by compression, heating, and forging. The product was very expensive but in considerable demand—from *sulphuric acid manufacturers and others—because of its high resistance to corrosion.

wood-block printing, printing from a relief image carved from a block of wood. Wooden blocks were first used for printing in the Far East in about the 8th century, and in Europe, by monks, in the 14th century. After the invention of metal type in the 15th century, the use of wood-blocks was principally for illustrations (woodcuts). They were the chief form of printed illustration in the 16th and 17th centuries, but later copper *engraving began to displace woodcuts. The development of fine wood engraving by the British engraver Thomas Bewick (1753–1828) extended the use of wood-blocks until the late 19th century, when the cheaper *process engraving prevailed. However, the process is still used by some illustrators, and for printing on textiles.

wood preservative, a solution of chemicals used to treat wood so that it is less prone to attack from micro-organisms and pests. The solution may be brushed on to the surface, or the wood may be totally immersed, allowing the active ingredients to soak in. Such materials are toxic to the life-forms that cause the damage, but their toxicity lessens with the passage of time; hence the need for retreatment. The preservative may also be harmful to humans and domestic animals, so care must be taken to prevent skin contact, particularly during application.

wood processing and utilization. Wood is the major commercial product of *forestry. Its high strength-to-weight ratio makes it an excellent *building material, while its grain pattern, resonance, and 'warmth' lead to its use in applications such as art objects, furniture, wood panelling, and musical instruments. Wood-pulp is the major ingredient in *paper manufacture, and a range of chemical products is derived from wood. The most important woods commercially are softwoods, which provide the bulk of wood for pulping and construction (see table). Much of this softwood comes from the belt of northern coniferous forest, or *taiga*, that extends through much of the northern latitudes. Hardwoods from broad-leaved trees, such as oak, ash, beech, teak, and mahogany, provide lumber with a wide variety of properties used for many purposes, but the slow growth rates of most broad-leaved trees make such wood expensive. A third type of wood is bamboo, grown extensively throughout Asia, which is one of the most versatile plants known, being used for construction, high-grade paper, as a foodstuff, and many other applications.

Wood is harvested by felling trees, usually with a *chainsaw: in managed forests, only a small proportion of trees are cut at one felling. Young trees are cut for poles and other light constructional material, but for most lumber mature trees are used. After felling, the trees must be delimbed and bucked (sawn transversely into logs) before transportation for further treatment, usually at a sawmill. At the sawmill, logs are converted into sawn boards of various sizes. The logs are sawn longitudinally in a series of parallel cuts; if required, they are turned through 90 degrees and sawn again to produce boards. Planks may be cross-cut to square the ends and remove defects. The boards are then seasoned by drying either under cover in the air, using low-temperature heating or fans to speed up the process, or in closed electric kilns, where conditions of temperature, humidity, and ventilation are controlled. The wood is usually also treated with preservative to prolong its life.

In addition to its use as boards or roundwood, wood is used to make *manufactured boards, plywood, and other types of *laminates. Wood is also the source of many chemical products. Examples include cellulose products such as *cellulose acetate, and *rayon, as well as *turpentine and pitch, and tannins often obtained from oak galls and tree barks used in leather *tanning and in making ink. Cellulose extracted from pine or spruce wood-pulp is treated with sulphuric and nitric acid to give various nitrates. Cellulose trinitrate (gun-cotton) is used in making explosives.

wood-pulp *paper manufacture, *wood processing and utilization.

woodworking joints, methods that are used to join together separate pieces of wood. Most wooden articles cannot be made from a single piece of timber, so joints have been evolved to overcome this problem. The choice of joint

Types of wood and their uses

Tree	Type	Uses
Alder	Hard	Bridge foundations, plywood, matches
Ash	Hard	Tool handles, baseball bats, tennis rackets
Beech	Hard	Furniture, parquet flooring, railway sleepers, cellulose
Cedar	Soft	Construction timber
Common maple	Hard	Turning, woodcarving
Cherry	Hard	Furniture
Douglas fir	Soft	Construction timber, railway sleepers. Bark used for tanning
Elm	Hard	Furniture, gun stocks, naves (hubs) of wooden wheels
Larch	Soft	Boat-buildings, light furniture, wall panelling
Lime	Soft	Pencils, woodcarving
Lombardy poplar	Soft	Plywood, cellulose
Norway spruce	Soft	Construction timber. Bark used for tanning
Oak	Hard	Furniture, parquet floors, barrels, boat building
Scots pine	Soft	Windows, doors, railway sleepers
Silver birch	Hard	Interior woodwork, wheels
Sycamore	Hard	Furniture, veneers, musical instruments
Teak	Hard	Furniture
Weeping willow	Soft	Cricket bats, wooden shoes, boats, cellulose. Young shoots used for baskets
White poplar	Soft	Cellulose, wood turning
Wild service tree	Hard	Rulers, gauges and other instrument components

in any circumstances will depend on factors such as the strength and appearance required. The simplest joint is the butt-joint, in which the two pieces of wood are put end to end and secured by nails, screws, or strong *adhesives. To join two pieces of timber of equal thickness transversely, cross-halving joints are used. Recesses as wide as the wood and equal to half the thickness are cut in both members, so that, when they are crossed, a perfectly even joint results. Diagonally cut scarf-joints are used to extend the length of timbers. One of the oldest joints is the mortise-and-tenon joint, which was used to secure the lintel stones in *megalithic structures. In this joint, a projection on one member slips into a socket on the other. The most elegant joint is the dovetail, whereby a series of wedge-shaped projections on one piece of wood fit into a similar number of recesses on the other piece.

wool, a fibre obtained from the domesticated sheep, used to make fabrics since antiquity. Before *yarn was spun, garments were made from woollen *felt. Wool is a protein fibre, similar to cotton in diameter but much longer. The length depends on the breed of sheep and on the part of its body from which the wool is taken. Long fibres are spun into worsted *yarn; shorter fibres are used for felting or for woollen yarns. All wool fibres are naturally wavy and, in addition, have an outer layer of very fine scales. These two features render the fibres mutually cohesive in a way which reduces the amount of twist needed in *spinning and makes true felting possible. At the same time, the crimp and scales are not wholly desirable because they give wool its propensity to shrink when washed. Wool is damaged by alkaline liquors, but is resistant to acids and can readily be dyed to good fast colours using acid *dyes. Recovered wool from discarded garments and tailors' clippings (shoddy) can be blended with virgin wool or other fibres. In modern textile production, wool is often blended with synthetic fibres such as *nylon, *polyester, or *acrylic to make clothes that are harder wearing.

wool-comber, a machine for removing unduly short fibres from raw wool. Before combing machines became available, combing was done manually, using two strong steel combs. With both combs heated, the comber would take a lock of oiled wool and work it to and fro from one comb to the other until all the unwanted short fibres had been removed. The first successful combing-machine was invented in 1827, and manual combing is now rare.

word processor (WP), a computer program or complete computer system designed to enable the user to manipulate text on screen and produce letters, documents, or other written material for printing. Text is entered using the keyboard, and displayed and edited under computer control. The edited document may then be stored on a *floppy disk or *hard disk for future use, or printed out on paper (hard copy). Using WP facilities, a block of text may, for example, be added, deleted, or moved from one location in a file (document) to another, or copied into a second file. After insertions or deletions, the text can be rearranged to re-form paragraphs, or as required, using the word-wrap facility. A document may be entirely reformatted by changing the margins, tabulation, justification, line spacing, number of lines per page, or highlighting. Some word processors also incorporate a spelling checker. Most are of wysiwyg ('what you see is what you get') design: that is, what appears on the computer screen (*visual display unit) is of identical format to the appearance of the document when printed on paper. Word processors also allow the frequent change or update of documents. Largely repetitive items may be quickly created and, with merge facilities, personalized letters, for example, are easily generated from a single basic form. For reproduction purposes word processors are capable of outputting print-quality images of an acceptable typographic standard, for both editing and printing purposes. This is more commonly the field of *desk-top publishing.

work-bench, a heavy, rigid table, first used in Neolithic times, on which wood or metal is worked. The precise design of a work-bench depends on individual taste and the nature of the work to be done. It must be of the correct height, usually about 85 cm (34 inches), and be strong enough to hold a vice. Normally, it is free of other fixtures in order to give a clear working surface, and there is usually a well to contain the small hand tools that are not immediately required. Since the 19th century, work-benches have had two vices: an end-vice and bench-stops, which hold the workpiece so that its long edges may be worked; and a woodworker's or metal-worker's vice for smaller work pieces. Modern portable work-benches have proved very popular.

work-hardening, the changes undergone by *metals as they are hammered, rolled, bent, or otherwise shaped when cold (cold working). The strength and hardness of the metal increases, but the ductility is reduced, making it more difficult for the metal to be worked and increasing the likelihood that it will fail before the desired form is reached. Work-hardening can be relieved by *annealing the metal at intervals while it is being worked. Many products are supplied in a partly work-hardened condition because the increased strength is desirable.

workstation, a powerful, desk-top computing system, generally with excellent graphics capability and a very fast processor, which is highly *interactive and usually forms part of a *network. Such systems are used in applications such as *desk-top publishing, *computer-aided design, and *artificial intelligence research. The basic equipment normally consists of a high-resolution *visual display unit, a keyboard, and a *mouse; other equipment may include magnetic storage devices or a *printer.

World Health Organization (WHO), a United Nations agency established in 1948 with the broad aim of attaining the highest level of health for all people, and supported by about 160 countries. WHO does not conduct its own research but promotes biomedical and health research in some 500 collaborating centres world-wide, arranging international medical conferences and the exchange and training of research workers. WHO compiles the *International Pharmacopœia*, monitors epidemics, evaluates new drugs, and advises on biological standards. It publishes quarterly an international journal of health development (*World Health Forum*) in Arabic, Chinese, English, French, Russian, and Spanish.

World Meteorological Organization (WMO), an international agency, established in 1951 and now supported by more than 150 countries, that promotes and co-ordinates meteorological observation world-wide. It also encourages research and training; standardizes observations and ensures their uniform publication; and furthers the application of meteorology to aviation, shipping, agriculture, and other human activities.

worsted *wool, *yarn.

wrench *spanner.

Wright, Orville (1871–1948) and **Wilbur** (1867–1912), US aviation pioneers, who made the first powered aircraft flight. The Wright brothers were mostly self-taught as engineers; they began by designing and building printing machinery, and later designed and manufactured bicycles. They became interested in aeronautics in 1896, when Wilbur read an account of the gliding experiments of *Lilienthal. Between 1899 and 1903 they undertook an extensive programme of research and development: it involved a period of serious theoretical study, experimentation with models and kites, exhaustive tests of full-sized gliders (both in a home-built wind-tunnel and in more than 1,000 open-air flights), and the design and building of an efficient propeller and a suitable engine. They made their first sustained, powered human flight, lasting 12 seconds, in 1903 at Kitty Hawk, North Carolina, USA. Their first practical aeroplane was the Flyer III (1905), which could stay airborne for over half an hour. Improved Wright machines appeared until 1911, but later, European designs became dominant.

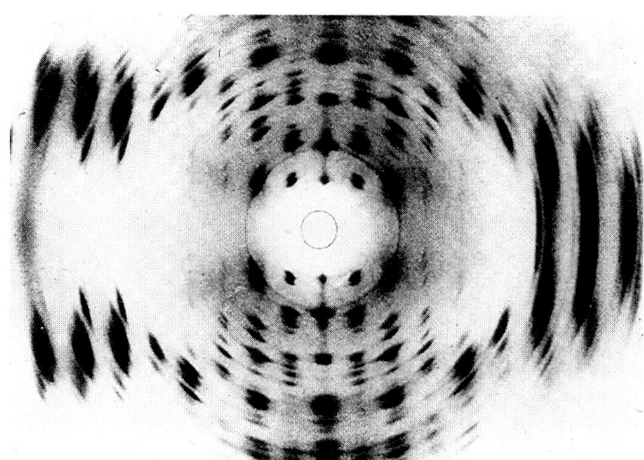

An image of the DNA molecule obtained by **X-ray crystallography**. The positions of the diffraction spots relate to the size and shape of the molecular 'bricks' from which the crystal is composed. The intensities of the spots relate to the detailed atomic structure within those bricks.

xerography *photocopier.

X-ray crystallography, a technique for determining the arrangement of *atoms within crystalline materials. A beam of X-rays is passed through a crystal, and the interference pattern caused by the interaction of the X-rays with the regular arrangement of atoms within the crystal is recorded on a photographic plate. The position and intensity of the spots in this pattern can be analysed to reveal the arrangement of the atoms in the crystal. At the start of the 20th century, this powerful technique was first used to discover the arrangement of atoms in simple ionic solids such as sodium chloride. The availability of computing power has enabled the technique to be applied to complex biological molecules and has revealed the structure of proteins and *DNA. It is now a standard procedure in research institutions throughout the world.

X-rays, *electromagnetic radiation of very high frequency discovered by the German physicist Wilhelm Röntgen in 1895. Typically, X-rays are produced in a vacuum tube by bombarding a target with high-energy electrons. They have found widespread use in diagnostic *radiology, *radiotherapy, X-ray *microscopy, non-destructive testing of materials (NDT), and the study of crystal structures by *X-ray crystallography.

yacht, originally a small fighting or dispatch vessel, which later developed into a vessel used by royalty and the rich, both for transport and for sport. The term has more recently been applied to any sail or power boat used for pleasure. An early English yacht was the *Mary* (100 tonnes), presented by the Dutch to Charles II in 1660 for his own use. Before World War I many yachts were large and crewed by paid hands, but many people subsequently began to find pleasure in handling their own craft for racing and occasional long voyages. Since the early 1950s the use of *fibre-reinforced plastic for hulls and synthetic fibres for sails and ropes has made yachts cheaper to build, and thus brought them to a much wider market.

Yagi, Hidetsugu (1886–1976), Japanese electrical engineer. He graduated in electrical engineering at Tokyo University in 1909, and in 1919 he was appointed professor at Tohoku Imperial University. He is remembered particularly for the VHF Yagi directional *antenna (patented in 1926), a simple directional antenna, often used for domestic radio and television receivers, which is more selective and less prone to interference than the basic *dipole antenna.

yarn (textile), *fibre prepared for use in weaving (see *loom), *knitting, and other processes. Textile yarns are of two basic types: those made from fibres of relatively short length (staple fibres), such as cotton, wool, or linen, and those made from long, effectively continuous filaments such as silk. *Synthetic fibres may be in either staple or filament form and are used in both types of yarn. Staple fibre is converted into yarns by first parallelizing the fibres by *carding or combing, then *spinning them together to form a compact, coherent, twisted structure. Fibres of different types may be used together to form blended yarns such as wool and acrylic or polyester and cotton. Continuous-filament materials may be directly converted into yarns by twisting, texturing (see *yarn texturing), or intermingling parallel filaments. There are a variety of yarn types within the two basic groups. Worsted yarns for making suits are spun from combed wool. Woollen yarns have a more open structure and are much used in knitwear. Yarns are often twisted together (doubled or folded) to give added strength and evenness, for example, in sewing threads. There are many fancy or novelty yarns made by twisting or intermingling yarns together. These may vary in colour along their length or may have snarls or other decorative features. Textured-filament yarns have fine crimps in their filaments to give enhanced bulk or stretch. Stretch yarns may also be made by wrapping or otherwise covering an elastomeric yarn of *rubber or *polyurethane with a staple or textured yarn. The fineness or coarseness of yarns is expressed as the length of yarn for a given weight or as weight of yarn for a given length. The most universal unit is the tex, defined as the weight in grams of one kilometre of yarn. Yarns used in women's stockings and tights may be finer than 1 tex, while yarns used in carpets are 500 tex or more. Industrial applications, such as reinforcements in tyres, drive-belts, and conveyors, often require very much heavier and stronger yarns.

yarn texturing, the processes by which synthetic continuous filament *yarns are made more voluminous and, in some cases, extendable. After extrusion and drawing, the filaments of *polymers such as *nylon, *polyester, and polypropylene are so straight and smooth that yarns made from them are silk-like in appearance and texture. In such a condition, they are no substitute for yarns made from naturally crimped fibres such as *wool and *cotton. To overcome this limitation, the filaments are crimped or otherwise deformed, to make them acceptable substitutes for natural-fibre yarns, and to confer on them desirable properties. In most texturing processes, advantage is taken of the thermoplastic properties of synthetic polymers to 'set' the mechanically formed crimps in the filaments. Texturing processes are sometimes carried out simultaneously with the drawing stage of synthetic yarn production. Such processes are known as draw-texturing. Typical uses include false-twist textured yarns for knitted fabrics; stretch stockings and tights; air-jet-textured yarns for suitings and automobile upholstery; and BCF (bulked continuous filament) yarns for tufted carpets.

yawl, a rig for a small sailing boat or *yacht in which the mizen (rear) mast, which is smaller than that of a *ketch, is stepped behind the rudder head. Boats with a yawl rig were often used as *ships' boats, and the rig was also common on *fishing vessels.

yoke *harness and saddlery.

Z

Zeiss, Carl (1816–88), German manufacturer of optical instruments. After qualifying in medicine, he began the manufacture of optical instruments, which he knew would be in increasing demand as science and medicine advanced. He spent seven years in the workshops of various European instrument-makers before establishing his own business in 1846 in Jena. There he took *Abbe into partnership and recruited *Schott, an established glass manufacturer. The firm of Carl Zeiss, Jena, quickly gained an international reputation for a wide range of instruments of superb quality: *microscopes, *telescopes, *binoculars, and *cameras.

zeolite *water softening.

Zeppelin, Ferdinand Adolf August Heinrich, Count von (1838–1917), German pioneer of the rigid airship. Commissioned in the German Army in 1858, he was impressed by the use of *balloons in the American Civil War in 1863 and during the siege of Paris (1870). He failed to persuade the German government to adopt them, and in 1890 began to experiment on his own. His first rigid airship, the LZ-1, made its maiden flight in July 1900. Six years and several models later, he achieved a 24-hour flight. He developed commercial airships for passengers and light freight, and during World War I nearly 100 airships were built for military use. Zeppelin airships were later used for commercial flights between Germany and North and South America.

Zhang Heng (AD 78–139), Chinese mathematician and astronomer. He invented the first *seismograph, consisting of a bronze dome in which was suspended a cylindrical weight. The outside of the dome was circled by eight dragon heads, each with a ball in its mouth. An earthquake caused the weight to swing, and the motion ejected a ball from the mouth of one of the dragons, supposedly the one nearest the direction from which the earthquake had originated. Zhang Heng is also credited with inventing a grid system for *maps.

Ziegler, Karl (1898–1973), German organic chemist. He was Director of the Kaiser Wilhelm (subsequently Max Planck) Institute for Coal Research at Mülheim from 1943 to 1969. There he researched in the fields of organic free radicals, organic compounds of aluminium and alkali metals, and polymerization. In the last of these he made a major technical advance with the invention of a low-temperature, low-pressure process for manufacturing *polythene, which revolutionized the plastics industry. *Natta later developed the process for the manufacture of *polypropylene, and shared with Ziegler the 1963 Nobel Prize for Chemistry.

ziggurat *building techniques, *pyramid.

zinc (symbol Zn, at. no. 30, r.a.m. 65.38), a soft, white metal that quickly tarnishes to a blue-grey appearance. The main *ore is the sulphide (ZnS), known as zinc blende. It is roasted to form the oxide and then reduced by *smelting with carbon, after which it is purified by distillation. Zinc is used widely in the manufacture of dry *batteries and in the production of alloys such as *brass. It is alloyed with *aluminium to give the aluminium properties suitable for *die casting. Zinc is also used for *galvanizing or *sherardizing iron. Zinc oxide is used as a white paint pigment that does not blacken in hydrogen sulphide, as a filler for automobile tyres and other rubber goods, and in medicinal ointments for skin irritations. Zinc chloride can serve as a *flux for soldering and as a wood preservative. Zinc sulphate is used in the production of the white paint pigment lithopone.

zip, a device for fastening together the edges of garments and other textile articles. Zips provide a rapid and more convenient way of fastening than buttons, hooks-and-eyes, straps, or toggles. The concept was patented in 1893 by Whitcombe Judson, an engineer from Chicago. The design for the modern zip was patented in 1913 by Gideon Sundbach (Sweden). The fastener consists of two tapes sewn on to the edges of the garment to be closed or opened. Each tape carries a row of fine teeth, which interlock when the zip is closed. The zip is opened or closed by the sliding of a simple clip mechanism. Zips were first used in the USA in 1917, and in the 1920s began to gain widespread acceptance in many applications. Early fasteners had metallic teeth riveted to the tapes, but teeth and slide mechanisms moulded from high-performance plastics are now often preferred.

zirconia (zirconium oxide, ZrO_2), an important *ceramic which can occur in a number of different crystal structures, stabilized by different alloying additions to form a solid solution. It can be much less brittle than conventional ceramics due to its property of changing its crystal structure when stressed (transformation toughening). This gives it properties that are valuable in engineering. Zirconia is an important artificial gemstone in single-crystal form. It is also an electrical conductor at high temperature: in this conducting form it is used as a sensor of oxygen concentration.

zirconium (symbol Zr, at. no. 40, r.a.m. 91.22), a silvery metal that occurs in the ores zircon (containing $ZrSiO_4$) and baddeleyite (containing *zirconia). Zirconium ores contain traces of the rare metal hafnium, which is highly neutron absorbent, and is used in *nuclear reactor control rods. Hafnium-free zirconium has low neutron absorbency and is used in cladding for *nuclear fuels. Zirconium is added to steel as a toughening agent. Zirconium dioxide is an excellent *refractory material. In a modified crystallographic form, zirconium is a substitute for *diamonds in jewellery.

zone refining, a method of purifying crystalline materials. A bar of the solid substance is moved progressively through a furnace in such a way that a small molten zone traverses its length. Impurities tend to remain in the molten zone and are moved along the bar. Repeating the operation many times causes the impurities to become concentrated in one end of the bar, which is then cut off. This technique is used to produce very pure *silicon and *germanium needed by the electronics industry for making *semiconductor devices.

Zworykin, Vladimir Kosma (1889–1982), Russian-born US physicist, a pioneer of modern television. Educated in St Petersburg and Paris, he emigrated to the USA in 1919. He was then already interested in the possibility of an electronic system of *television. He developed the *iconoscope, and patented it in 1923. In 1935 Zworykin, G. A. Morton, and L. Malter invented the *photomultiplier. His work paved the way for modern electronic television, displacing the photo-mechanical system of *Baird.

Acknowledgements

Photographs

Abbreviations: *t* = top; *b* = bottom.

Aviation Picture Library 4, 26, 38;

British Aerospace 231*t*;

British Steel 302;

Cambridge University: Dept. of Biochemistry, © Ramsey & Muspratt 170;

J. Allan Cash 43, 106;

CERN 117, 258*b*;

Bruce Coleman Ltd. 2, 206, 216*t*, 268;

Lesley Coleman 203;

Digital Audio Research Ltd. 325;

Mark Edwards 89, 90, 133, 142, 177, 278, 382;

Robert Estall 296;

Mary Evans Picture Library 5, 102, 112, 143, 216*b*;

Leslie Garland 362;

General Motors, Europe 116;

Robert Harding 44, 155, 201, 288, 339*t*, 352;

Michael Holford 54, 70, 280;

Holt Studios 15, 110, 227, 231*b*;

Libby Howells 31, 36;

Hulton-Deutsch 28, 49, 29, 157, 258*t*, 299, 319, 363, 364;

Hutchison Library 18*b*, 19, 95, 101, 248*b*, 321, 343;

Image Bank 39, 277, 311;

Intermediate Technology 18*t*;

Magnum Photos Ltd. 292;

Massey Ferguson 359;

Doris Langley Moore Collection 209*t*;

National Railway Museum 20;

Oxford University Press 370;

Pitt Rivers Museum 41*t*;

Planet Earth Pictures 202, 337;

Retrograph Archive 247;

Rex Features 113, 220, 257, 323;

Ann Ronan 41*b*, 191, 328;

Royal Institution 125;

Royal Society 197;

Science Museum 32, 77, 234, 312, 344, 354, 369;

Science Photo Library 7, 8, 12, 13, 21, 23, 37, 58, 63, 67, 73, 97, 111, 117, 119*t*, 119*b*, 148, 159, 168, 169, 176, 183, 184, 187, 194, 213, 221, 229, 237, 240, 243, 248*t*, 250, 255, 260, 263, 274, 275, 291, 320, 324, 338, 339*b*, 355, 367, 373, 380, 385, 389;

Frank Spooner Pictures 162*t*;

Ian Sumner 374;

TRH Pictures 98, 209*b*, 224;

Trireme Trust 149;

West Ferry Printers Ltd. 249;

Zefa Picture Library (UK) Ltd. 9, 10, 17, 30, 34, 56, 69, 71, 108, 160, 162*b*, 172, 178, 192, 251, 269, 279, 309, 345, 360, 376, 383, 386.

Picture researchers: Libby Howells, Catherine Blackie.

Illustrations

Russell Birkett, Information Design Unit: all line artwork;

Ladybird Books and Gerald Witcomb: 78, 103, 348;

Volvo AB, Sweden: 233;

Redrawn from *A History of Architecture* by Spiro Kostof, copyright ©1985 by Oxford University Press, Inc. Reprinted by permission: 50;

The Mitchell Beazley Illustrated Biographical Dictionary: Who Did What, 1974: 185;

AA Book of the Car, Reader's Digest © 1976 Drive Publications Ltd.: 45;

Gloucestershire Fire Service: 131;

Jean-Claude Corbeil and Michael Manser, *The Facts on File Visual Dictionary*, 1988: 22;

New Illustrated Science and Invention Encyclopedia, HS Struttman Inc., Westport, Connecticut, Marshall Cavendish, 1987: 45, 208, 211, 282, 341;

Inventions That Changed The World, Reader's Digest, 1982: 22;

David Macaulay, *The Way Things Work*, Dorling Kindersley, 1988: 152;

The New Illustrated Everyman's Encyclopedia, Octopus Books, 1986: 22, 185;

Atlas zur Baukunst, Volume 2, Deutscher Taschenbuch Verlag, Munich: 50;

Nikon: Optiphot 2 brochure: 223;

Singer, Holmyard, Hall, and Williams, *A History of Technology*: Volume 2, *The Mediterranean Civilizations and the Middle Ages*, 1956; and Volume 3, *From the Renaissance to the Industrial Revolution*, 1957, Oxford University Press: 50.

Tables

Textiles Terms and Definitions, 8th edition, The Textile Institute, 10 Blackfriars Street, Manchester: 351.